# DATE DUE

| | | | |
|---|---|---|---|
| FE--8 | | | |
| OC 26 '04 | | | |
| | | | |
| | | | |
| | | | |
| | | | |
| | | | |
| | | | |
| | | | |
| | | | |
| | | | |
| | | | |
| | | | |
| | | | |
| | | | |
| | | | |
| | | | |
| | | | |

DEMCO 38-296

# Introduction to Paralegalism

Perspectives, Problems, and Skills

*Fourth Edition*

# Introduction to Paralegalism

## Perspectives, Problems, and Skills
### *Fourth Edition*

**William P. Statsky**

West Publishing Company

ST. PAUL ■ NEW YORK ■ LOS ANGELES ■ SAN FRANCISCO

## MENT TO THE ENVIRONMENT

...lishing Company began recycling materials ...roduction of books. This began a tradition of efficient and responsible use of resources. Today, up to 95 percent of our legal books and 70 percent of our college texts are printed on recycled, acid-free stock. West also recycles nearly 22 million pounds of scrap paper annually—the equivalent of 181,717 trees. Since the 1960s, West has devised ways to capture and recycle waste inks, solvents, oils, and vapors created in the printing process. We also recycle plastics of all kinds, wood, glass, corrugated cardboard, and batteries, and have eliminated the use of styrofoam book packaging. We at West are proud of the longevity and the scope of our commitment to our environment.

Production, Prepress, Printing and Binding by West Publishing Company.

Production credits and photo credits follow index.

COPYRIGHT © 1974,
1982, 1986          By WEST PUBLISHING COMPANY
COPYRIGHT © 1992    By WEST PUBLISHING COMPANY
                    610 Opperman Drive
                    P.O. Box 64526
                    St. Paul, MN 55164-0526

99 98 97 96                    8 7 6 5 4

Library of Congress Cataloging-in-Publication Data

Statsky, William P.
    Introduction to paralegalism   perspectives, problems, and skills
/ William P. Statsky. — 4th ed.
        p.    cm.
    Includes bibliographical references and index.
    ISBN 0-314-92574-0 (hard)
    1. Legal assistants—United States.   I. Title.
KF320.L4S73   1992
340′.023′73—dc20

                                                    91-41708
                                        CIP

# Also by William P. Statsky

*Case Analysis and Fundamentals of Legal Writing,* 3d ed. St. Paul: West Publishing Company, 1989 (with J. Wernet)

*Essentials of Paralegalism.* St. Paul: West Publishing Company, 1988

*Family Law,* 3d ed. St. Paul: West Publishing Company, 1991

*Inmate Involvement in Prison Legal Services: Roles and Training Options for the Inmate as Paralegal.* American Bar Association, Commission on Correctional Facilities and Services, 1974

*Legal Desk Reference.* St. Paul: West Publishing Co., 1991 (with B. Hussey, M. Diamond & R. Nakamura)

*The Legal Paraprofessional as Advocate and Assistant: Roles, Training Concepts and Materials.* Center on Social Welfare Policy and Law, 1971 (with P. Lang)

*Legal Research and Writing: Some Starting Points,* 3d ed. St. Paul: West Publishing Company, 1986

*Legal Thesaurus/Dictionary: A Resource for the Writer and Computer Researcher.* St. Paul: West Publishing Company, 1985

*Legislative Analysis and Drafting,* 2d ed. St. Paul: West Publishing Company, 1984

*Paralegal Employment: Facts and Strategies for the 1990s.* St. Paul: West Publishing Company, 1988

*The Regulation of Paralegals: Ethics, Professional Responsibility, and Other Forms of Control.* St. Paul: West Publishing Company, 1988

*Torts: Personal Injury Litigation,* 2d ed. St. Paul: West Publishing Company, 1990

*Rights of the Imprisoned: Cases, Materials and Directions.* Indianapolis: Bobbs-Merrill Company, 1974 (with R. Singer)

*What Have Paralegals Done? A Dictionary of Functions.* National Paralegal Institute, 1973

■ For Patricia Farrell Statsky: A person whose ability and love
have sustained more than she knows

■ The pain and the excitement of paralegalism, and indeed of the law itself, are that the problem we are given will often be smaller than the problem we find.

# ■ Preface

This book provides an introduction to a still-developing career whose members may one day outnumber attorneys in the traditional and untraditional law office. The day has long passed when so many had to ask, "What's a paralegal?" Today the most likely question is, "What's the most effective way to use a paralegal?" Even the United States Supreme Court has taken note of the role of paralegals in encouraging the "cost-effective delivery of legal services." A great deal has happened since the publication of the first edition of this book in 1974. Yet the dominant themes of the field continue to be challenge, promise, and the opportunity to rethink the major assumptions that have characterized the practice of law.

## Changes in the Fourth Edition

In addition to updating the material in the book on employment, salaries, roles, ethics, certification, licensing, and other regulation issues, there are a number of large changes in the fourth edition:

- The ethics material has been extensively expanded, taken out of Chapter 4, and placed in a new Chapter 5 (Attorney Ethics and Paralegal Ethics).
- Chapter 6 (Introduction to the Legal System) has been rewritten. The major focus of the chapter is an overview of the judicial, executive, and legislative process. Most of the litigation material in the chapter has been moved to Chapter 10, the main litigation chapter.
- Chapter 7 (Introduction to Legal Analysis) has been expanded; it now includes new components of introductory legal analysis.
- There is a greater emphasis throughout the chapters on the recent experiences of paralegals on the job, e.g., more quotations from successful paralegals on the ingredients of their success, more quotations on what life is like working in a particular area of the law.
- A glossary has been added.
- Each chapter includes a chapter outline, chapter summary, and key terms.
- The How to Study Law chapter (the old chapter 5) has been moved to the front of the book.

## Teaching Aids and Supplements

The following teaching aids and supplements are available for use in conjunction with the fourth edition:

- *Study Guide and Workbook* (for student purchase) containing review questions and answers for all the chapters, short writing exercises, and other related material.

- *Instructor's Manual* covering each chapter of the book.
- *Transparency Masters* containing approximately fifty figures from the text that are easily used for overhead projection.
- *Test Bank,* prepared by Dorothy Moore (Fort Lauderdale College).
- *Westest Computerized Testing* which offers the complete Test Bank on disk.
- *PC WESTrain II,* a WESTLAW tutorial software package for students.
- *West's Legal Clerk* software, which provides further training in computerized legal research.
- *West's Legal Research Videotapes* covering the basics of legal research.
- *West's Law Finder* and *Sample Pages* covering the major research materials of West Publishing Company.

## Acknowledgments

It is difficult to name all the individuals who have provided guidance in the preparation of this book. Valuable suggestions for improvements in all or portions of the fourth edition were made by the reviewers: Joan Allen-Hart, University of San Diego; Therese Cannon, University of West Los Angeles; Jean Hellman, Loyola University; Jane Kaplan, New York City Technical College; Edie Koonce, Tulane University; Kathleen Mercer-Reed, University of Toledo; Dorothy Moore, Fort Lauderdale College; Virginia Noonan, Northern Essex Community College.

Since I began my association with West Publishing Company in the early 1970s, I have worked with some very talented people. Ken Ziegler's leadership has kept West's Paralegal Series in the forefront of paralegal education. Among his inspired decisions has been to install Elizabeth Hannan in the important position of acquisitions editor.

For the fourth edition, Laura Mickelson of WESTLAW provided invaluable help in the chapter on computers in the law. I also want to acknowledge Carrie Kish, the promotion manager, and Sandra Gangelhoff, the production editor for this edition.

Looking back over the years, there are a number of people who have played important roles in my initiation and growth as a student of paralegal education. I owe a great debt to: Jean and Edgar Cahn, founders of the Antioch School of Law and its Legal Technician Program; Susan Tubb, a forceful advocate of quality in paralegal education; Bill Fry, Director of the National Paralegal Institute and a valued colleague since our days together at Columbia Law School when it launched one of the first paralegal training programs in the country, the Program for Legal Service Assistants; Dan Oran, who helped me plan the first edition; Michael Manna, Holly Fox, Ed Schwartz, and Julie Clark-Molloy, more recent collaborators in the field; and finally, MaBel Juanita Hill, Willie Nolden, and Linda Saunders, some of my early students who taught me so much.

# ■ Contents

*Preface*

How to Study Law in the Classroom and On the Job    1
A. Classroom Learning    1
B. On-the-Job Learning: The Art of Being Supervised    15
Summary    19


# Part I   The Paralegal in the Legal System    21

. . . . . . . . . . . . . . . . . . . . . . . . . . . . . . . . . . . . . . . . . . .

## ■ 1   The Emergence and Development of a New Career in Law    23

A. Questions, Frustration, and Challenge    23
B. Major Players: The Big Five    24
C. Job Titles    26
D. Job Definitions    28
E. Salaries    34
F. Historical Perspective    36
G. Stages in the Development of Paralegalism    50
Chapter Summary    54

## ■ 2   Paralegal Employment    57

A. The Job Market    57
B. Where Paralegals Work    58
C. Paralegal Specialties: A Dictionary of Functions    100
D. Finding a Job: Employment Strategies    130
E. The Job Hunting Notebook    160
F. Your Second Job    170
Chapter Summary    174

## ■ 3   On the Job Realities: Assertiveness Training for Paralegals    175

A. The Ideal    175
B. The Big Three Employment Problems    178
C. Communication    180
D. Expectations    181
E. The Environment of a Law Office    182
F. Office Politics    183
G. Self-Assessment and Employer Evaluations    184
H. Characteristics of Some Attorneys    188
I. Assertive/Nonassertive/Aggressive Behavior    189
J. Keeping a Diary and a Career Development File    191
K. The "Swoose Syndrome"    194

L. Paralegal CLE    195
M. Responsibilities of Supervisors    196
N. Relationship with Secretaries    198
O. Sexual Harassment    199
P. Working with Systems    201
Q. Career Ladders    203
R. Your Next Job    204
S. Paralegal Associations and Networking    204
Chapter Summary    207

■ 4    The Regulation of Paralegals    209

A. Kinds of Regulation    209
B. Unauthorized and Authorized Practice of Law    210
C. Licensing of Paralegals    228
D. Bar Association Control of Paralegal Education    237
E. Should Paralegals Become Part of Bar Associations?    240
F. Self-Regulation by Paralegals: The Certification Debate    243
G. Fair Labor Standards Act    252
H. Tort Liability of Paralegals    255
I. Malpractice Insurance    257
Chapter Summary    260

■ 5    Attorney Ethics and Paralegal Ethics    263

A. The Ten Commandments of an Ethical Conservative    263
B. Enforcing Ethics    263
C. The Ethical Rules    267
D. Doing Research on an Ethical Issue    312
E. Ethical Codes of the Paralegal Associations    313
F. An Ethical Dilemma: Your Ethics or Your Job!    316
Chapter Summary    324

■ 6    Introduction to the Legal System    327

A. Basic Terminology    327
B. Judicial Systems    328
C. Administrative Agencies    334
D. The Legislative Process    337
Chapter Summary    340

Part II    The Skills of a Paralegal    343

. . . . . . . . . . . . . . . . . . . . . . . . . . . .

■ 7    Introduction to Legal Analysis    345

A. The Structure of Legal Analysis    345
B. The Element-Identification Skill    347
C. The Issue-Statement Skill    350
D. The Definitions Skill    351
E. Briefing Court Opinions    353
F. Applying Court Opinions    358
Chapter Summary    363

# ■ 8   Legal Interviewing   365

A. The Context of Interviewing in Litigation   365
B. The Format of an Intake Memo   366
C. Guides to the Formulation of Questions   368
D. What Does the Client Want?   376
E. Human Relations and Communications Skills   377
F. Analysis of a Legal Interview   382
Chapter Summary   399

# ■ 9   Investigation in a Law Office   401

A. The Nature and Context of Investigation   401
B. Fact Analysis: Organizing the Options   406
C. Distortions in Investigation   406
D. Sources of Evidence/Sources of Leads   409
E. Gaining Access to Records   410
F. Evaluating Testimonial and Physical Evidence   411
G. Interviewing Witnesses   411
H. Special Investigative Problems   416
I. Evidence and Investigation   421
J. Taking a Witness Statement   427
K. The Settlement Work-Up   428
Chapter Summary   432

# ■ 10   Litigation Assistantship   435

A. Overview of Litigation   435
B. Alternative Dispute Resolution   458
C. Litigation Assistantship: Pretrial Stage   459
D. Litigation Assistantship: Trial Stage   472
E. Litigation Assistantship: Appeal Stage   472
F. Litigation Assistantship: Enforcement Stage   473
Chapter Summary   473

# ■ 11   Legal Research   477

A. Strategy for Studying Legal Research   477
B. The Importance of Legal Research   479
C. Frustration and Legal Research   480
D. Flexibility in Legal Research   481
E. The Vocabulary of Legal Research: A Checklist   482
F. Finding Law Libraries   482
G. A Glossary of Law and Law Books   485
H. Authority in Research and Writing   517
I. Citation Form   524
J. Cite Checking   539
K. Components of a Law Book   541
L. The CARTWHEEL   544
M. The First Level of Legal Research: Background   549
N. Checklists for Using the Ten Major Search Resources   551
O. Finding Case Law   587
P. Reading and Finding Statutes   590

Q. Legislative History     596
R. Monitoring Proposed Legislation     599
S. Reading and Finding Constitutional Law     600
T. Finding Administrative Law     602
U. Finding Local Law     604
V. Finding Rules of Court     605
W. Finding International Law     606
X. The Third Level of Legal Research: Validation     606
Y. Annotated Bibliography     608
Chapter Summary     616

## ■ 12    Legal Writing     619

A. Kinds of Legal Writing     619
B. Memorandum of Law     620
C. Appellate Brief     627
D. Some Writing Guidelines     631
Chapter Summary     637

## ■ 13    Computer Literacy for Paralegals: An Introduction to the Use of Computers in a Law Office     639

A. Law Offices, Computers, and Paralegals     639
B. Survival Strategies     643
C. Terminology     643
D. Hardware     649
E. Software     651
F. The Real Investment: Time     680
Chapter Summary     683

## ■ 14    Introduction to Law Office Administration     685

A. The Practice of Law in the Private Sector     685
B. The Legal Administrator and the Legal Assistant Manager: Overview of Administration in a Large Law Firm     689
C. Expenses     693
D. Timekeeping     693
E. Billing     700
F. Administrative Reports     702
G. Procedures Manual: Mail, Copying, and Filing     707
H. Computer-Based Records Management System     712
Chapter Summary     717

## ■ 15    Informal and Formal Administrative Advocacy     719

A. The Nature of Advocacy     719
B. The Techniques of Informal Advocacy     721
C. Procedural Due Process     728
D. An Agency Problem     731
E. Preliminary Considerations     732
F. Hearsay, Opinions, and Relevance     737
G. Introduction to the Examination of Witnesses     738

H. Direct-Examination      739
I. Cross-Examination      741
J. Closing the Hearing and Preparing for an Appeal      744
Chapter Summary      745

Appendix A  Bibliography      747
Appendix B  Paralegal Associations and Related Organizations      765
Appendix C  Associations of Attorneys      773
Appendix D  Federal Government Organization Chart      779
Appendix E  Survey of Non-Lawyer Practice Before Federal
      Agencies      781
Appendix F  State Survey: Ethics Opinions and Related
      Materials      791
Appendix G  Paralegal Business Cards      811
Appendix H  Federal Job Information Centers      812
Appendix I  How to Start a Freelance Paralegal Business      815
Appendix J  "Legal Assistant Day" (Governors' Proclamations)      821
Appendix K  News Stories, War Stories, and Parting Shots      823
*Glossary*      *831*
*Index*      *851*
*Request Forms*      *879*

■ *The "expanded use of well-trained assistants, sometimes called 'paralegals,' has been an important development. Today there are ... double the number of ... schools for training paralegals [than the number of schools for training attorneys]. ... The advent of the paralegal enables law offices to perform high quality legal services at a lower cost. Possibly we have only scratched the surface of this development."*

Warren E. Burger, Chief Justice
of the United States Supreme Court, February 3, 1980

■ *"Paralegals are an absolutely essential component of quality legal services in the future."*

James Fellers, President,
American Bar Association, April 4, 1975

■ *"Employment is expected to continue to grow much faster than the average for all occupations through the year 2000."*

U.S. Department of Labor,
*Occupational Outlook Handbook*, 1988–89

# How to Study Law in the Classroom and on the Job

## ■ Chapter Outline

**Section A. Classroom Learning**
The Two Phases of Legal Education
Rules and Skills
Prior Experience in the Law
Goals and Context of Assignments
Study Plan
An Additional 50%
Distractions
Study Habits
Grammar, Spelling, and Composition
Study Groups
Research Skills
Definitions
Checklists
Note Taking
Memory Skills
Feedback
Ambiguity
Speed Reading

**Section B. On-the-Job Learning: The Art of Being Supervised**
"King's Clothes"
Repetition of Instructions
Instructions in Writing
Priority of Assignments
Priority of Tasks
Checklists
Manuals
Models
Independent Research
Secretaries and Other Paralegals
Feedback
Training Programs
Evaluations

## ■ Section A. Classroom Learning

Education does not come naturally to most of us. It is a struggle. This is all the more true for someone entering a totally new realm of training such as legal education. Much of the material will seem foreign and difficult. There is a danger of becoming overwhelmed by the vast quantity of laws and legal material that confronts you. How do you study law? How do you learn law? What is the proper perspective that a student of law should have about the educational process? These are our concerns in this introduction to the process of studying. In short, our theme is training to be trained—the art of effective learning.

The first step is to begin with a proper frame of mind. Too many students have false expectations of what legal education can accomplish. This substantially interferes with effective studying.

*1. Your legal education has two phases. Phase I begins now and ends when you complete this training program. Phase II begins when this*

1

*training program ends and is not completed until the last day of your employment as a paralegal.*

You have entered a career that will require you to be a perpetual student. The learning never ends. This is true not only because the boundary lines of law are vast, but also because the law is changing every day. No one knows all of the law. Phase I of your legal education is designed to provide you with the foundation that will enable you to become a good student in Phase II.

*2. Your legal education has two dimensions: the content of the law (the rules) and the practical techniques of using that content in a law office (the skills).*

*Rules.*    There are two basic kinds of law:

> Substantive Law: those nonprocedural rules that govern rights and duties; for example, the requirements for the sale of land;
>
> Procedural Law: those rules that govern the mechanics of resolving a dispute in court or in an administrative agency; for example, the number of days within which a party must respond to a claim stated in a complaint.

The law library contains millions of substantive and procedural rules written by courts (in volumes called reporters), by legislatures (in volumes called statutory codes), and by administrative agencies (in volumes called regulations or administrative codes).

A substantial portion of your time in school will involve a study of the substantive and procedural law of your state, and often of the federal government as well.

*Skills.*    By far the most important dimension of your legal education will be the skills of using rules. Without the skills, the content of the law is close to worthless. Examples of legal skills include:

- How to interview a client (see Chapter 8).
- How to investigate the facts of a case (see Chapter 9).
- How to draft a complaint, the document that initiates a lawsuit (see Chapter 10).
- How to digest or summarize documents in a case file (see Chapter 10).
- How to do legal research in a law library (see Chapter 11).

The overriding skill that, to one degree or another, is the basis for all others is the skill of legal analysis (see Chapter 7). There are some who make the mistake of concluding that legal analysis is within the exclusive domain of the attorney. Without an understanding of legal analysis, however, paralegals cannot understand the legal system and cannot intelligently carry out many of the more demanding tasks they are assigned.

*3. You must force yourself to suspend what you already know about the law in order to be able to absorb (a) that which is new and (b) that which conflicts with your prior knowledge and experience.*

Place yourself in the position of training students to drive a car. Your students undoubtedly already know something about driving. They have watched others drive and maybe have even had a lesson or two from friends. It would be ideal, however, if you could begin your instruction from point zero. There is a very real danger that the students have picked up bad habits from others. This will interfere with their capacity to *listen* to what you are saying. The danger is that they will block out those things you are saying that do not conform to previously learned habits and knowledge. If the habits or knowledge are defective, your job as a trainer is immensely more difficult.

The same is true in studying law. Everyone knows something about the law from government or civics courses as a teenager and from the various treatments of the law in the media. It may be that some of you have been involved in the law as a party or as a witness in court. Others may have worked, or currently work, in law offices. Will this prior knowledge and experience be a help or a hindrance to you in your future legal education? For some it will be a help. For most of us, however, there is a danger of interference.

This is particularly so with respect to the portrayal of the law on TV and in the movies. Those who grew up with TV's *Perry Mason* probably came to the conclusion that most legal problems are solved by dramatically tricking a hostile witness on the stand into finally telling the truth. Not so. The practice of law is not an endless series of confessions and concessions that are pried loose from opponents. Nor is the more modern TV program *L.A. Law* much more helpful. Every attorney does not spend all day engaged in the kind of case that makes front page news. Recently, a paralegal left her job as a paralegal with a solo practitioner in order to take another paralegal position with a firm that she thought was going to be like *L.A. Law*. Three months later, she begged her old boss to take her back. She had discovered that there was a great gap between reality and *L.A. Law*. While excitement and drama can be part of the practice of law, they are not everyday occurrences. What is dominant is painstaking and meticulous hard work. This reality is almost never portrayed in the media.

It is strongly recommended that you place yourself in the position of a stranger to the material you will be covering in your courses, regardless of your background and exposure to the field. Cautiously treat everything as a new experience. Temporarily suspend what you already know. Resist the urge to pat yourself on the back by saying, "I already knew that" or "I already know how to do that." For many students, such statements cause a relaxation. They do not work as hard once they have convinced themselves that there is nothing new to learn. No problem exists, of course, if these students are right. The danger, however, is that they are wrong or that they are only partially right. Students are not always the best judge of what they know and of what they can do. Do not become too comfortable. Adopt the following healthy attitude: "I've dealt with that before, but maybe I can learn something new about it." Every new teacher, every new supervisor, every new setting is an opportunity to add a dimension to your prior knowledge and experience. Be open to these opportunities. No two people practice law exactly the same way. Your own growth as a student and as a paralegal will depend in large part on your capacity to listen for, explore, and absorb this diversity.

## 4. *Be sure that you know the goals and context of every assignment.*

Throughout your education, you will be given a variety of assignments: class exercises, text readings, drafting tasks, field projects, research assignments, examinations, etc. You should ask yourself the following questions about each one:

■ What are the goals of this assignment? What am I supposed to learn from it?

- How does this assignment fit into what I have already learned? What is the context of the assignment?

Successfully undertaking the assignment depends in part on your understanding of its goals and how these goals relate to the overall context of the course. How do you identify goals and context?

- Carefully listen to and take notes on what your teachers tell the class about the assignment.
- Ask teachers questions about their expectations for assignments. Demonstrate a polite but probing interest.
- If the teacher has given a particular assignment before to other classes, ask former students. If they have had any papers returned to them by the teacher, try to read some of them to determine what comments/criticisms the teacher has made on them. These observations will be additional clues to what the teacher is after.
- Take note of what the authors of your texts have expressly or implicitly told you about the importance or purpose of certain tasks.
- Ask fellow classmates about their understanding of purpose and context.

In short, be preoccupied by these concerns. *Do not undertake assignments in isolation or in a vacuum.*

As we will see in greater detail later, this advice applies on the job as well as in school. A strong indication of one's commitment—an essential ingredient for progress and advancement—is a sincere interest in the broader picture. Avoid gaining a reputation as someone who simply wants to "get the job done and get out as quickly as possible." While speed is sometimes critical, speed is never a substitute for efficiency and professionalism. The latter are directly dependent on the extent of your involvement, interest, and enthusiasm in carrying out a task. Boredom and incompetence often feed on each other.

This is not to say that you must be wildly enthusiastic about everything you do. Sustaining such enthusiasm is unrealistic. At a minimum, you want to avoid undertaking tasks routinely—even routine tasks! One way to accomplish this goal is to have a constant eye on the broader picture. Why are you being asked to do something in a certain way? Has it always been done this way? Are there more efficient ways? After the pressure of the immediate need has passed, can you think about and eventually propose a more effective *system* of handling the task?

Of course, there is a danger of going to the opposite extreme. You cannot be so preoccupied with purpose, context, and systems that you fail to complete the immediate job before you. Timing is important. Often the office will have no tolerance for suggestions for improvement until immediate deadlines have passed. This simply means that you must always be operating at two levels. First, the *now* level. Mobilize all of your resources to complete the task as efficiently as possible under the present work environment. Second, the *systems* level. Keep your mind open and challenge your creativity to identify steps and procedures that might be taken in the future to achieve greater efficiency in accomplishing the task.

## 5. *Design a study plan.*

Make constant and current *lists* of everything that you must do. Divide the list into long-term projects (what is due next week or at the end of the semester) and short-term projects (what is due tomorrow). Have a plan for each day. Establish the following norm for yourself: every day you will focus in some way on *all* of your assignments. Every day you will review your long-term and short-term list. Priority, of course, will be given to the short-term tasks. Yet some time, however small, will also be devoted to the long-term tasks. At a minimum, this time can be used simply to remind yourself that these tasks are hanging over you and that you must make concrete commitments to devote substantial blocks of time to them in the immediate future. Make and renew these commitments every day. If possible, go beyond this. On a day that you will be mainly working on the short-term projects, try to set aside 5% of your time to the long-term projects, for instance, by doing some background reading or by preparing a very rough first draft of an outline. It is critical that you establish *momentum* toward the accomplishment of *all* your tasks. This is done by never letting anything sit on the back burner. Set yourself the goal of making at least *some* progress on everything every day. Without this goal, the momentum may be very difficult to sustain.

Once you have decided what tasks you will cover on a given study day, the next question is: In what *order* will you cover them? There are a number of ways in which you can classify the things that you must do—for example: (a) easy tasks that will require a relatively short time to complete, (b) complex tasks requiring more time, (c) tasks with time demands that will be unknown until you start them. At the beginning of your study time, spend a few seconds preparing an outline of the order in which you will cover the tasks that day and the approximate amount of time that you will set aside for each task. You may want to start with some of the easier tasks so that you can feel a sense of accomplishment relatively soon. Alternatively, you may want to devote early study time to the third kind of task listed above ("c") so that you can obtain a clearer idea of the scope and difficulty of such assignments. The important point is that you establish a *schedule*. It does not have to be written in stone. Quite the contrary. It is healthy that you have enough flexibility to revise your day's schedule in order to respond to unfolding realities as you study. Adaptation is not a sign of disorganization, but the total absence of an initial plan is.

### 6. *Add 50% to the time you initially think you will need to study a subject.*

You are kidding yourself if you have not set aside a *substantial* amount of time to study law outside the classroom. The conscientious study of law takes time—lots of it. It is true that some students must work and take care of family responsibilities. You cannot devote time that you do not have. Yet the reality is that limited study time leads to limited education.

Generally, people will find time for what they want to do. You may *wish* to do many things for which there will never be enough time. You will find the time, however, to do what you really *want* to do. Once you have decided that you want something badly enough, you will find the time to do it.

Most people waste tremendous amounts of time by worrying about all the things that they have to do and in taking rest periods from this worrying through socializing or other casual pursuits. How much *productive* time do you gain out of a single work hour? For most of us the answer is about twenty minutes. The rest of the hour is spent worrying, relaxing, repeating ourselves, socializing, etc. One answer to the problem of limited time availability is to increase the amount of *productive* time that you derive out of each work hour.

You may not be able to add any new hours to the clock, but you can add to your net productive time. How about moving up to thirty minutes an hour? Forty? You will be amazed at the time that you can "find" simply by making a conscious effort to remove some of the waste. When asked how a masterpiece was created, a great sculptor once responded: "You start with a block of stone and you cut away everything that is not art." In your study habits, start with a small block of time and work to cut away everything that is not productive.

There are no absolute rules on how much time you will need. It depends on the complexity of the subject matter you must master. It is probably accurate to say that most of us need to study more than we do—as a rule of thumb, about 50% more. You should be constantly on the alert for ways to increase the time you have available, or more accurately, to increase the productive time that you can make available.

Resolving time-management problems as a student will be good practice for you when you are confronted with similar (and more severe) time-management problems as a working paralegal. Many law offices operate at a hectic pace. One of the hallmarks of a professional is a pronounced reverence for deadlines and the clock in general. Time is money. An ability to find and handle time effectively can also be one of the preconditions for achieving justice in a particular case.

Soon you will be gaining a reputation among your fellow students, teachers, supervisors, and employers. One of the reputations that you should make a concerted effort to acquire is a reputation for hard work, punctuality, and conscientiousness about the time you devote to your work. In large measure, success follows from such a reputation. It is as important, if not more important, than raw ability or intelligence.

## 7. *Create your own study area free from distractions.*

It is essential that you find study areas that are quiet and free from distractions. Otherwise, concentration is obviously impossible. It may be that the worst places to study are at home or at the library, unless you can find a corner that is cut off from noise and people who want to talk. Do not make yourself too available. If you study in the corridor, at the first table at the entrance to the library, or at the kitchen table, you are inviting distraction. You need to be able to close yourself off for two to three hours at a time. It is important for you to interact with other people—but not while you are studying material that requires considerable concentration. You will be tempted to digress and to socialize. You are in the best position to know where these temptations are. You are also the most qualified person to know how to avoid the temptations.

## 8. *Conduct a self-assessment of your prior study habits and establish a program to reform the weaknesses.*

If you were to describe the way in which you study, would you be proud of the description? Here is a partial list of some of the main weaknesses of attitude or practice that students have in studying:

- The student has done well in the past with only minimal study effort. Why change now?
- No one else in the class appears to be studying very much. Why be different?
- The student learns best by listening in class. Hence instead of studying on one's own, why not wait until someone explains it in person?

- The student simply does not like to study; there are more important things to do in life.
- The student can't concentrate.
- The student studies with the radio on or with other distractions.
- The student gets bored easily. "I can't stay motivated for long."
- The student does not understand what he or she is supposed to study.
- The student skim reads.
- The student does not stop to look up strange words or phrases.
- The student studies only at exam time—crams for exams.
- The student does not study at a consistent pace. It's an hour here and there—no organized, regular study times.
- The student does not like to memorize.
- The student does not take notes on what he or she is reading.

What other interferences with effective studying can you think of? Or more important, which of the above items apply to you? How do you plead? In law, it is frequently said that you cannot solve a problem until you obtain the facts. What are the facts in the case of your study habits? Make your personal list of attitude problems, study patterns, or environmental interferences. Place these items in some order. Next, establish a plan for yourself. Which item on the list are you going to try to correct tonight? What will the plan be for this week? For next week? For the coming month? What specific steps will you take to try to change some bad habits? Do not, however, be too hard on yourself. Be determined but realistic. The more serious problems are obviously going to take more time to correct. Improvement will come if you are serious about improvement and regularly think about it. If one corrective method does not work, try another. If the fifth does not work, try a sixth. Discuss techniques of improvement with your fellow students and teachers. Prove to yourself that change is possible.

## 9. Conduct a self-assessment on grammar, spelling, and composition, and design a program to reform weaknesses.

The legal profession lives by the written word. Talking is important for some activities, but writing is crucial in almost every area of the practice of law. You cannot function in this environment without a grasp of the basics of spelling, grammar, and composition. A major complaint made by employers today is that paralegals are consistently violating these basics. The problem is very serious.

*Step One.*   You must take responsibility for your training in grammar, spelling, and composition. Do not wait for someone to teach you these basics. Do not wait until someone points out your weaknesses. You must make a personal commitment to train yourself. If there are English courses available to you, great. It is essential, however, that you understand that a weekly class will not be enough.

*Step Two.*   Raise your consciousness about the writing around you. Your training in writing cannot be compartmentalized. You must be constantly thinking about and worrying about writing. The concern should be a preoccupation. When you are reading a newspaper, for example, you should be conscious of the use of semicolons and paragraph structure in what you are reading. At least occasionally you should ask yourself why a certain punctuation mark was used by a writer. You are surrounded by writing. You read this writing for content. You must begin a conscious effort to focus on the structure of this writing as well.

*Step Three.*   Purchase several grammar books. Do not rely on only one grammar book. There are hundreds of texts on the market, and they each explain things differently, so you should consult more than one grammar book on difficult points. It must be admitted that some grammar books are poorly written! They are not always easy to use. They may give examples of grammar rules without clearly defining the rules. Or they may define the rules without giving clear examples of the application of the rules. A grammar book may be excellent for some areas of writing but weak for others. Hence, have more than one grammar book in your personal library.

You may have saved grammar books you used earlier in your education. In addition, go to second-hand bookstores. They often have a section on textbooks. Some of the best grammar books are old elementary texts that provide excellent overviews of the basics. Another way to cut down on the expense of purchase is to consider paperback texts. The characteristics to look for in making a purchase are:

- A comprehensive index.
- Clearly defined rules covering the basics.
- Numerous examples of the application of the rules.
- Exercises on the rules *with answers* so that you can check your own progress.

*Step Four.*   Use the grammar books almost as frequently as you would a dictionary. Have the books at your side every time you write. Force yourself to use these books regularly. The more often you use them now, the less you will need them later as you continue to improve. You will never be able to discard them entirely, however. You will need to consult them when doing any serious writing in the law. How often will you have to consult them? It depends on the extent of the weaknesses that you have and the frequency with which you begin consulting them now.

*Step Five.*   Improve your spelling. Use a dictionary often. Begin making a list of the words that you are spelling incorrectly. Work on these words. When you have the slightest doubt about the spelling of a word, check the dictionary. Again, the more often you take this approach now, the less often you will need to use the dictionary later.

*Step Six.*   Enroll in English and writing courses. Check offerings at local schools like adult education programs in the public schools or at colleges.

*Step Seven.*   Find out which law courses in your curriculum require the most writing from students. If possible, take these courses—no matter how painful you find writing to be. In fact, the more painful it is, the more you need to place yourself in an environment where writing is demanded of you on a regular basis.

*Step Eight.*   Simplify your writing. Cut down the length of your sentences. Minimize the use of semicolons that extend the length of sentences. Many people have the mistaken idea that legal writing must be "heavy," august, and flowery; this usually leads to verbosity. The best legal writing, no matter how technical, is evenly paced, clear, and concise.

*Step Nine.* Prepare a self-assessment of your weaknesses. Make a list of what you must correct. Then set a schedule for improvement. Set aside a small amount of time each day, say, ten minutes, during which you work on your writing weaknesses. Be consistent about this time. Do not wait for the weekend or for next semester when you will have more time. The reality is that you will probably never have substantially more time than you have now. The problem is not so much the absence of time as it is an unwillingness to dig into the task. Progress will be slow and you will be on your own. Hence, there is a danger that you will be constantly finding excuses to put it off.

## 10. *Consider forming a student study group, but be cautious.*

Students sometimes find it useful to form study groups. A healthy exchange with your colleagues can be very productive. One difficulty is finding students with whom you are compatible. Trial and error may be the only way to identify such students. A more serious concern is trying to define the purpose of the study group. It should not be used as a substitute for your own individual study. It would be inappropriate to divide a course into parts, with members of the group having responsibility for preparing notes on and teaching the assigned parts to the remainder of the group.

The group can be very valuable for mutual editing on writing assignments. Suppose, for example, that you are drafting complaints in a course. Photocopy a complaint that one member of the group drafts. The group then collectively comments upon and edits the complaint according to the standards discussed in class and in the materials of the course. Similarly, you could try to obtain copies of old exams in the course and collectively examine answers prepared by group members. Ask your teacher for fact situations that could be the basis of legal analysis memos (see Chapter 7) or other drafting assignments. Make up fact situations of your own. The student whose work is being scrutinized must be able to take constructive criticism. The criticism should be intense if it is to be worthwhile. Students should be asked to rewrite the draft after incorporating suggestions made. The rewrite should later be subjected to another round of mutual editing. Occasionally, you might want to consider asking your teacher to meet with your group in order to obtain further help in legal writing.

Do not hesitate to subject your writing to the scrutiny of your fellow students. You can learn a great deal from each other.

## 11. *Use your legal research skills to help you understand components of a course that are giving you difficulty.*

The law library is more than the place to go to find law that governs the facts of a client's case. A great deal of the material in the law library consists of explanations/summaries/overviews of the same law that you will be covering in your courses. You need to learn how to gain access to this material as soon as possible. In Chapter 11, a series of techniques is presented on doing background research through texts such as legal dictionaries, legal encyclopedias, treatises, annotations, etc. (p. 550). You should become acquainted with these kinds of law books. They will prove invaluable as outside reading to help resolve conceptual and practical difficulties you are having in class.

### 12. *Organize your learning through definitions or definitional questions.*

The most sophisticated question an attorney or paralegal can ask is: What does that word or phrase mean? What's the definition? To a very large extent, the practice of law is a probing for definitions of key words or phrases in the context of facts that have arisen. Can a five year old be liable for negligence? (What is *negligence?*) Can the government tax a church-run bingo game? (What is the *free exercise of religion?*) Can attorneys in a law firm strike and obtain the protection of the National Labor Relations Act? (What is a *covered* employee under the labor statute?) Can a person rape his or her spouse? (What is the definition of *rape?*) Can a citizen slander the president of the United States? (What is a *defamatory statement* and what are the definitions of the defenses to a slander action?) Etc.

For every course that you take, you will come across numerous technical words and phrases in class and in your readings. Begin compiling a list of these words and phrases for each class. Try to limit yourself to what you think are the major ones. When in doubt about whether to include something on your list, resolve the doubt by including it.

Then pursue definitions. Ask your teacher for definitions. Find definitions in your text and in the law library, for instance, in *Words and Phrases,* legal encyclopedias, treatises, annotations, legal periodical literature, statutory codes, etc. (See Chapter 11.)

For some words, you may have difficulty obtaining definitions. Do not give up your pursuit. Keep searching. Keep probing. Keep questioning. For some words, there may be more than one definition. Others may require definitions of the definitions.

Of course, you cannot master a course simply by knowing the definitions of all the key words and phrases involved. Yet these words and phrases are the *vocabulary* of the course and are the foundation and point of reference for learning the other aspects of the course. Begin with vocabulary.

Consider a system of three-by-five or two-by-three cards to help you learn the definitions. On one side of the card, place a single word or phrase. On the other side, write the definition with a brief page reference or citation to the source of the definition. Using the cards, test yourself periodically. If you are in a study group, ask other members to test you. Ask a relative to test you. Establish a plan of ongoing review.

### 13. *Translate important rules into checklists—developing your own practice manual.*

It is important that you learn how to write checklists that could be part of a manual. Every rule that you are told about or that you read about can be translated into a checklist. Checklist formulation should eventually become second nature to you. The sooner you start thinking in terms of dos, don'ts, models, etc., the better.

Suppose that you have before you the following statute of your state:

§1742. No marriage shall be solemnized without a license issued by the county clerk of any county of this state not more than thirty days prior to the date of the solemnization of the marriage.

One way to handle this statute is to create a checklist of questions that you would ask a client in order to determine whether the statute applies. (Breaking a statute down into its *elements* will assist you in identifying such questions, as you will see in Chapter 7.) Some of the questions would be:

1. Did you have a marriage license?
2. Where did you get the license? Did you obtain it from a county clerk in this state?
3. On what date did you obtain the license?
4. On what date did you go through the marriage ceremony (solemnization)? Were there more than thirty days between the date you obtained the license and the date of the ceremony?

These are the questions that must be asked as part of a large number of questions concerning the validity of a marriage. If you were creating a manual, the above questions in your checklist for section 1742 could go under the manual topic of "Marriage Formation" or "Marriage License." Whenever you have a class on this topic or whenever you analyze any law on this topic, you translate the lecture into checklists such as the brief one presented above.

To be sure, there are checklists written by others already in existence. They are found, for example, in manuals and practice books. Why create your own? First of all, your checklists are *not* intended as a substitute for those in manuals or practice books. You will undoubtedly make extensive use of the latter. You are encouraged to do so. Your checklists will supplement the others. More significantly, two of the best ways for you to learn how to use manuals are (a) to write checklists of your own and (b) to see the connection between the law (for example, a statute) and the guidelines and techniques within a checklist.

## 14. *Develop the skill of note taking.*

Note taking is essential in the law. You will regularly be told to "write it down" or "put it in a memo." Effective note taking is often a precondition to being able to do *any* kind of writing in the law.

First, take notes on what you are reading for class preparation and for research assignments. Do not rely exclusively on your memory. After reading hundreds of pages (or more), you will not be able to remember what you have read at the end of the semester, or even at the end of the day. Copy what you think are the essential portions of the materials you are reading. Be sure to include definitions of important words and phrases as indicated in guideline 12 above.

To be sure, note taking will add time to your studying. Yet you will discover that it was time well spent, particularly when you begin reviewing for an exam or writing your memorandum.

Second, take notes in class. You must develop the art of taking notes while simultaneously listening to what is being said. On the job, you may have to do this frequently. For example, when:

- Interviewing a client
- Interviewing a witness during field investigation
- Receiving instructions from a supervisor
- Talking with someone on the phone
- Taking notes during a deposition
- Taking notes from a witness giving testimony at trial

A good place to begin learning how to write and listen at the same time is during your classes.

Most students take poor class notes. This is due to a number of reasons:

- A student may write slowly.
- A student may not like to take notes; it's hard work.
- A student may not know if what is being said is important enough to be noted until after it is said—when it is too late because the lecture has gone on to something else.
- A student does not think it necessary to take notes on a discussion that the teacher is having with another student.
- A student takes notes only when he or she sees other students taking notes.
- Some teachers ramble.

A student who uses these excuses for not taking comprehensive notes in class will eventually be using similar excuses on the job when note taking is required for a case. This is unfortunate. You must overcome whatever resistances you have acquired to the admittedly difficult task of note taking. Otherwise you will pay the price in your schoolwork and on the job.

Common Abbreviations Used by Students in Litigation Classes

| π | plaintiff | lee | lessee | jdr | joinder |
|---|---|---|---|---|---|
| Δ | defendant | CN | contributory negligence | b/p | burden of proof |
| θ | third party | | | s/l | statute of limitations |
| c.l. | common law | CpN | comparative negligence | | |
| c/a | cause of action | | | s/f | statute of frauds |
| JV/π | jury verdict for plaintiff | rsb | reasonable | K | contract |
| | | A/R | assumption of risk | T | tort |
| R&R | reversed & remanded | cz | cause | IT | intentional tort |
| | | px cz | proximate cause | N | negligence |
| Dem | demurrer | ab dg | abnormally dangerous | SL | strict liability |
| $ | suppose | | | A&B | assault & battery |
| Q | question | inj | injunction | 4cb | foreseeable |
| O | owner | b.f.p. | bona fide purchaser | dfm | defamation |
| stat | statute | | | Dct | deceit |
| L | liable, liability | br/wrt | breach of warranty | lbl | libel |
| nj | injury | dft | defect | sld | slander |
| dmg | damages | dsn | design | impl | implied |
| dfs | defense | WD | wrongful death | impt | imputed |
| Tp | trespass | Svv | survival | jfc | justification |
| pvg | privilege | m- | mal-, mis- | std | standard |
| Tfz | tortfeasor | m-pr | malpractice | vln | violation |
| lz | license | m-rep | misrepresentation | pun | punitive |
| lzc | licensee | n- | non- | stfn | satisfaction |
| tpr | trespasser | [ | not, un- | rls | release |
| ktb | contribution | [4cf | unforeseeable | rem | remedy |
| lr | lessor | | | p.f. | prima facie |

**Source:** Prosser, Wade & Schwartz, *Cases and Materials on Torts*, p. 1263 (Foundation Press, 1976).

Of course, you do not want to write down everything, even if this were physically possible. You ought to make the assumption, however, that if it is important enough for someone to tell you something, it is important enough for you to make note of it.

If you do not know how to take shorthand, develop your own system of abbreviations. (See above figure.) Sometimes you will have to begin taking notes at the moment the person starts talking rather than wait until the end of what he or she is saying. Try different approaches to increasing the completeness of your notes.

If you are participating in class by talking with the teacher, it will obviously be difficult for you to take notes at the same time. After class, take a few moments to jot down some notes on what occurred during the discussion.

## 15. *Studying rules—the role of memory.*

Memory plays a significant role in the law. Applicants for the bar, for example, are not allowed to take notes into the exam room. An advocate in court or at an administrative hearing may be able to refer to notes, but the notes are of little value if the advocate does not have a solid grasp of the case. Most of the courses you will be taking have a memory component. This is true even for open-book exams, since you will not have time to go through all the material while responding to the questions.

Two mistakes are often made by students with respect to the role of memory:

- They think that memorizing things is beneath their dignity.
- They think that because they understand something, they know it sufficiently to be able to give it back in an examination.

Of course, you should not be memorizing what you do not understand. Rote memorization is close to worthless. Not so for important material that you comprehend. Yet you have not necessarily committed something to memory for later use, simply because you understand it.

Many systems for memorizing material can be effective:

- Reading it over and over
- Copying it
- Writing questions to yourself about it and trying to answer the questions
- Having other students ask you questions about it
- Making summaries or outlines of it
- Etc.

If you do not have a photographic mind, you must resort to such techniques. Try different systems. Ask fellow students for tips on how they make effective use of their memory.

You will have to find out from your teacher what material you will be expected to know for the course. You can also check with other students who have had this teacher in the past. It may not always be easy to find out how much a teacher expects you to know from memory. Teachers have been known to surprise students on examinations! Some teachers do not like to admit that they are asking their students to memorize a lot of material for their courses, yet they still give examinations that require a lot of memory preparation.

### 16. *Studying skills—the necessity of feedback.*

Memory obviously plays a less significant role in learning the skills of interviewing, investigation, legal analysis, drafting, coordinating, digesting, advocacy, and legal research. These skills have their own vocabulary that you must know, but it is your judgmental rather than your memory faculties that must be developed in order to become competent and excel in these skills.

They are developed primarily by *doing*—practice drills or exercises are essential. The learning comes from the feedback that you obtain while engaged in the skill exercises. What are the ways that a student obtains feedback?

- Evaluations on assignments and exams
- Role-playing exercises that are critiqued in class
- Comparisons between your work (particularly writing projects) with models provided by the teacher or that you find on your own in the library
- Critiques that you receive from fellow students in study groups

You must constantly be looking for feedback. Do not wait to be called on. Do not wait to see what feedback is planned for you at the end of the course. Take the initiative immediately. Seek conferences with your teachers. Find out who is available to read your writing or to observe your performance in any of the other skills. Set up your own role-playing sessions with your fellow students. Seek critiques of your rewrites even if rewriting was not required. Look for opportunities to critique other students on the various skills. Ask fellow students for permission to read their graded examinations so that you can compare their papers with your own. Create your own hypotheticals for analysis in study groups. (A *hypothetical* is simply a set of facts invented for the purpose of discussion and analysis.) Do additional reading on the skills. Become actively involved in your own skills development.

### 17. *Studying ambiguity—coping with unanswered questions.*

The study of law can be frustrating because there is so much uncertainty in the law. Legions of unanswered questions exist. Definitive answers to legal questions are not always easy to find, no matter how good your legal research techniques are. Every new fact situation presents the potential for a new law. Every law seems to have an exception. Furthermore, advocates frequently argue for exceptions to the exceptions. When terms are defined, the definitions often need definitions. A law office is not always an easy environment in which to work because of this reality.

The study of law is in large measure an examination of ambiguity that is identified, dissected, and manipulated.

The most effective way to handle frustration with this state of affairs is to be realistic about what the law is and isn't. Do not expect definitive answers to all legal questions. Search for as much clarity as you can, but do not be surprised if the conclusion of your search is further questions. A time-honored answer to many legal questions is: "It depends"! Become familiar with the following equation since you will see it used often:

If "X" is present, then the conclusion is "A," but if "Y" is so, then the conclusion is "B," but if "Z" is . . .

The practice of law may sometimes appear to be an endless puzzle. Studying law, therefore, must engage you in similar thinking processes. Again, look for precision and clarity, but do not expect the puzzle to disappear.

## 18. *The value of speed-reading courses in the study of law.*

In the study of law, a great deal of reading is required. Should you, therefore, take a speed-reading course? No, unless the course helps you *slow down* the speed of your reading! This advice may be quite distasteful to advocates (and salespersons) of speed-reading courses. The reality, however, is that statutes, regulations, and court opinions cannot be speed-read. They must be carefully picked apart and read word for word, almost as if you were translating from one language into another. If you are troubled by how long it takes you to read, do not despair. Do not worry about having to read material over and over again. Keep reading. Keep rereading. The pace of your reading will pick up as you gain experience. Never strive, however, to be able to fly through the material. Strive for comprehensiveness. Strive for understanding. For most of us, this will come through the slow process of note taking and rereading. It is sometimes argued that comprehension is increased through speed. Be careful of this argument. Reading law calls for careful thinking about what you read— and taking notes on these thoughts. There may be no harm in rapidly reading legal material for *the first time.* At your second, third, and fourth reading, however, speed is of little significance.

## ■ Section B. On-the-Job Learning: The Art of Being Supervised

A great deal of learning will occur when you are on the job. Some of it may come through formal in-house office training and by the study of office procedure manuals. Most of the learning, however, will come in day-to-day interaction with your supervisors as you are given assignments. The learning comes through *being* supervised. Being supervised is not always easy. It will take some effort on your part to maximize the learning potential of the experience. The following guidelines are designed to assist you in increasing this potential:

### *Don't play "king's clothes" with the instructions that you receive.*

Recall the story of the king's clothes. The king was naked, but everybody kept saying what a beautiful wardrobe he had on. As new people arrived, they saw that he had no clothes, but they heard everyone talking as if he were fully dressed. The new people did not want to appear stupid, so they too began admiring the king's wardrobe. When paralegals are receiving instructions on an assignment, they play king's clothes when the pretend that they understand all the instructions but in fact do not. They do not want to appear to be uninformed or unintelligent. They do not want to give the impression that they are unsure of themselves. For obvious reasons, this is a serious mistake.

Whenever you are given an assignment in a new area—that is, an assignment on something that you have not done before—there should be a great deal that you do not understand. This is particularly true during your first few months on the job, when everything is new! Do not pretend to be something you are not. Constantly ask questions about new things. Do not be reluctant to ask for explanations. Learn how to ask for help. *It will not be a sign of weakness.* Quite the contrary. People who take steps to make sure that they fully understand all their instructions will soon gain a reputation for responsibility and conscientiousness.

*Repeat the instructions to your supervisor before you leave
the room.*

Once your supervisor has told you what he or she wants you to do, do not leave the room in silence or with the general observation, "I'll get on that right away." Repeat the instructions back to the supervisor *as you understand them.* Make sure that you and your supervisor are on the same wavelength by explaining back what you think you were told to do. This will be an excellent opportunity for the supervisor to determine what you did or did not understand, and to provide you with clarifications where needed.

Supervisors will not always be sure of what they want you to do. By trying to obtain clarity on the instructions, you are providing them with the opportunity to think through what they want done. In the middle of the session with you, the supervisor may change his or her mind on what is to be done.

*Write your instructions down.*

Never go to your supervisor without pen and paper. Preferably, keep an instructions notebook, diary, or journal (p. 191) in which you record the following information:

- Notes on what you are asked to do
- The date you got the assignment
- The date by which the supervisor expects you to complete all or part of the assignment
- The date you actually complete the assignment
- Comments made by supervisors or others on what you submit

The notes will serve as your memory bank. Whenever any questions arise about what you were supposed to do, you have something concrete to refer to.

*Insist on a due date and on a statement of priorities.*

You need to know when an assignment is due. Ask for a due date *even if the supervisor tells you to "get to it when you can."* This phrase may mean "relatively soon" or "before the end of the month" to your supervisor, but not to you. If the supervisor says he or she does not know when it should be done, ask for an approximate due date. Tell the supervisor you want to place the assignment on your calendar so that it will not slip through the cracks because of all the other assignments.

Also ask what priority the assignment has. Where does it fit in with your other assignments? If you have more than enough to fill the day, you need to know what takes priority. If you do not ask for a priority listing, the supervisor will assume you are under no time pressures.

*If the instructions appear to be complicated, ask your supervisor to
separate and prioritize the tasks.*

As you receive instructions, you may sometimes feel overwhelmed by all that is being asked of you. Many supervisors do not give instructions in clear, logical patterns. They may talk in a rambling, stream-of-consciousness fashion. When confronted with this situation, simply say:

OK, but can you break that down for me a little more in terms of what you want me to do first? I think I will be able to do the entire assignment, but it would help if I approach it one step at a time. Where do you want me to start?

*As often as possible, write your instructions and what you do in the form of checklists.*

A methodical mind is one that views a project in "do-able" steps and that tackles one step at a time. You need to have a methodical mind in order to function in a busy law office. One of the best ways to develop such a mind is to think in terms of checklists. A checklist is simply a chronological sequencing of tasks that must be done in order to complete a project. Convert the instructions from your supervisor into checklists in the same manner as translating rules into checklists discussed earlier. In the process of actually carrying out instructions, you go through many steps—all of which could become part of a detailed checklist. The steps you went through to complete the task become a checklist of things to do in order to complete such a task in the future. To be sure, it can be time-consuming to draft checklists. Keep in mind, however, that:

- The checklists can be invaluable for other employees who are given similar assignments in the future.
- The checklists will be a benefit to you in organizing your own time and in assuring completeness.

You will not be able to draft checklists for everything that you do. Perhaps you will not be able to write more than one checklist a week. Perhaps you will have to use some of your own time to write checklists. Whatever time you can devote will be profitably spent so long as you are serious about writing and using the checklists. They may have to be rewritten or modified later. This should not deter you from the task, since most things that are worth doing require testing and reassessment.

Once you have a number of checklists, you have the makings of a how-to-do-it manual that you have written yourself.

*Find out what manuals and checklists already exist in your office.*

It does not make sense to reinvent the wheel. If manuals and checklists already exist in your office on the topic of your assignment, you should find and use them. The problem is that the how-to-do-it information is usually buried in the heads of the attorneys, paralegals, and secretaries of the office. No one has taken the time to write it all down (see Chapter 3). If this is *not* the case, you should find out where it is written down and try to adapt what you find to the assignment on which you are working.

*Ask for a model.*

One of the best ways to make sure you know what a supervisor wants is to ask whether he or she knows of any models that you could use as a guide for what you are being asked to do. Such models may be found in closed case files, manuals, form books, practice texts, etc. Care must be applied in using such material. Every new legal problem is potentially unique. What will work in one case may not work in another. A model is a guide, a starting point—and nothing more.

*Do some independent legal research on your own on the instructions you are given.*

Often you will be told what to do without being given more than a cursory explanation of why it needs to be done that way. But all the instructions you are given have some basis in the law. A complaint, for example, is served on an opposing party in a designated way because the law has imposed rules on how such service is to be made. You may be asked to serve a complaint in a certain way without being told what section of the state code (or of your court rules) *requires* it to be served in that way. It would be highly impractical to read all the law that is the foundation for an assigned task. It is not necessary to do so and you would not have time to do so.

What can you do, however, is to select certain instructions on certain assignments and do some background legal research to gain a greater appreciation for why the instructions were necessary. You will probably have to do such legal research on your own time unless the assignment you are given includes doing some legal research (see Chapter 11). Research can be time-consuming, but you will find it enormously educational. It can place a totally new perspective on the assignment and, indeed, on your entire job.

### Ask secretaries and other paralegals for help.

Secretaries and paralegals who have worked in the office for a long period of time can be very helpful to you if you approach them properly. Everybody wants to feel important. Everybody wants to be respected. When someone asks for something in a way that gives the impression he or she is *entitled* to what is being sought, difficulties usually result. Think of how you would like to be approached if you were in the position of the secretary or paralegal. What would turn you off? What would make you want to go out of your way to cooperate with and assist a new employee who needs your help? Your answers (and sensitivity) to questions such as these will go a long way toward enabling you to draw on the experience of others in the office.

### Obtain feedback on an assignment before the date it is due.

Unless the assignment you are given is a very simple one, do not wait until the date that it is due to communicate with your supervisor. If you are having trouble with the assignment, you will want to check with your supervisor as soon as possible and as often as necessary. It would be a mistake, however, to contact the supervisor only when trouble arises. Of course, you want to avoid wasting anyone's time, including your own. You should limit your contacts with a busy supervisor to essential matters. You could take the following approach with your supervisor:

> Everything seems to be going fine on the project you gave me. I expect to have it in to you on time. I'm wondering, however, if you could give me a few moments of your time. I want to bring you up to date on where I am so that you can let me know if I am on the right track.

Perhaps this contact could take place on the phone or during a brief office visit. Suppose that you have gone astray on the assignment without knowing it? It is obviously better to discover this before the date the assignment is due. The more communication you have with your supervisor, the more likely it is that you will catch such errors before a great deal of time is wasted.

### Ask to participate in office and community training programs.

Sometimes there are training sessions for attorneys conducted in the law firm. You should ask that you be included. Bar associations and paralegal associations often conduct all-day seminars on legal topics relevant to your work. Seek permission to attend them if they are held during work hours.

### Ask to be evaluated regularly.

For a number of reasons, evaluations are not given or are unhelpful when they are given:

- Evaluations can be time-consuming.
- Evaluators are reluctant to say anything negative, especially in writing.
- Most people do not like to be evaluated: it's too threatening to the ego.

Go out of your way to let your supervisor know that you want to be evaluated and that you can handle criticism. If you are defensive when you are criticized, you will find that the evaluations of your performance will go on behind your back! Such a work environment is obviously very unhealthy. Consider this approach that a paralegal might take with a supervisor:

> I want to know what you think of my work. I want to know where you think I need improvement. That's the only way I'm going to learn. I also want to know when I'm doing things correctly, but I'm mainly interested in your suggestions on what I can do to increase my skills.

If you take this approach *and mean it,* the chances are good that you will receive some very constructive criticism.

### One step at a time.

Perhaps the most important advice you can receive in studying law is to concentrate on what is immediately before you. One step at a time. What are your responsibilities in the next fifteen minutes? Block everything else out. Make *the now* as productive as you can. Your biggest enemy is worry about the future: worry about the exams ahead of you, worry about your family, worry about the state of the world, worry about finding employment, etc. Leave tomorrow alone! Worrying about it will only interfere with your ability to make the most of what you must do now. Your development in the law will come slowly, in stages. Map out these stages in very small time blocks—beginning with the time that is immediately ahead of you. If you must worry, limit your concern to how to make the next fifteen minutes a more valuable learning experience.

## ☐ Summary

Legal education is a lifelong endeavor; a competent paralegal never stops learning about the law and the skills of applying it. A number of important guidelines will help you become a good student in the classroom and on the job. Do not let the media blur your understanding of what the practice of law is actually like. To avoid studying in a vacuum, be sure that you know the goals of an assignment, and how it fits into the other assignments. Organize your day around a study plan. Since the time demands on you will probably be greater than you anticipated, it is important that you design a system of studying. Step one is to assess your own study habits, such as how you

*(Continued on next page)*

## ☐ Summary *(Continued)*

handle distractions or how you commit things to memory. Then promise yourself that you will do something about your weaknesses.

How many of the rules about the comma can you identify? Do you know when to use *that* rather than *which* in your sentences? How many of your paragraphs have topic sentences? On every page of your writing, are there zero spelling errors? You have entered a field where the written word is paramount. You must take personal responsibility—now—for the improvement of your grammar, spelling, and composition skills.

Use the law library to help you understand difficult areas of the law. But don't expect absolute clarity all the time. Seek out evaluations of your work. Become a skillful note taker. Get into the habit of looking for definitions and of translating rules into checklists.

These suggestions also apply once you are on the job. Don't pretend you understand what you don't. Repeat instructions back to your supervisor before you begin an assignment. Ask for due dates and priorities if you are given several things to do. Write down your instructions in your own notebook or journal. Find out if an assignment has been done by others in the past. If so, seek their help. Try to find a model and adapt it as needed. Ask for feedback before an assignment is due.

# I

# The Paralegal
# in the Legal System

## Contents

1 The Emergence and Development of a New Career
  in Law      23

2 Paralegal Employment      57

3 On the Job Realities: Assertiveness Training
  for Paralegals      175

4 The Regulation of Paralegals      209

5 Attorney Ethics and Paralegal Ethics      263

6 Introduction to Our Legal System      327

CHAPTER

# The Emergence and Development of a New Career in Law

## ■ Outline

**Section A. Questions, Frustration, and Challenge**

**Section B. Major Players: The Big Five**

**Section C. Job Titles**
 Employees of Attorneys
 Self-Employed Individuals Working for Attorneys
 Self-Employed Individuals Serving the Public

**Section D. Job Definitions**

**Section E. Salaries**

**Section F. Historical Perspective**
 The Pressure of Economics

 The Call for Efficiency and Delegation
 Promotion by the Bar Associations
 The Organization of Paralegals
 Restructuring of Professions and Occupations Generally
 Delivery of Legal Systems in Other Countries

**Section G. Stages in the Development of Paralegalism**
 The Era of Discovery
 The Era of Education
 The Era of Politics
 The Era of Management
 The Era of Credentialization

## ■ Section A. Questions, Frustration, and Challenge

Welcome to the field! You probably fall into one or more of the following categories:

- You have never worked in a law office and have many questions about the career of a paralegal.

- You are employed or were once employed in a law office and now want to upgrade your skills.

- You have not made up your mind about whether to become an attorney and see the paralegal career as a way to learn more about the legal profession.

As Chief Justice Burger points out in the quote at the beginning of this book, the paralegal career is still in a state of development. By definition, therefore, a number of important questions still exist. The task of the first part of this book is to address these questions:

- What is a paralegal?

- Where do paralegals work?

■

"Paralegals: a novelty
in the sixties, an asset
in the seventies, a
necessity in the
eighties."
Hon. Richard A. Powers III,
Magistrate, United States
District Court for the Eastern
District of Pennsylvania, 1986

■


■

"Our profession is still
growing and evolving.
Be part of this
evolution!"
Bobbi J. McFadden,
President, Cincinnati
Paralegal Association, 1991.

■

- What are the functions of a paralegal?
- How do I obtain a job?
- What is the difference between an attorney and a paralegal?
- What is the difference between a paralegal and the clerical staff of a law office?
- What problems do paralegals encounter on the job and how can these problems be resolved?
- How is the paralegal field regulated? Who does the regulating and for what purposes?
- What are the ethical guidelines that govern paralegal conduct?
- What is the future of the paralegal field?

Unfortunately *and* fortunately, definitive answers to these questions do not yet exist. As we shall see, considerable controversy surrounds many of them. It would be foolhardy for anyone to enter the field without having a comprehensive understanding of what the controversies are. According to Deanna Shimko-Herman, a paralegal in Milwaukee, "It is incumbent upon paralegals to be fully informed of the issues, and to operate from that informed base."[1] At times, however, the controversy seems to breed more confusion than constructive dialogue. This confusion can be frustrating to someone new to the field. From another point of view, however, this state of affairs presents you with the ultimate challenge of shaping your own answers to these questions. If Chief Justice Burger is correct that "we have only scratched the surface," the creative opportunities that exist for you are boundless. You will not simply be performing a job—you will be *helping to create a new profession*. This challenge would not exist if all the answers to the fundamental questions were already written in stone.

## ■ Section B. Major Players: The Big Five

During our examination of this challenge, we will meet many organizations. Five in particular have had a dramatic influence on the development of paralegalism. These five (not necessarily listed in order of influence) are as follows:

- National Federation of Paralegal Associations *(NFPA)*
- National Association of Legal Assistants *(NALA)*
- American Bar Association *(ABA)*
- Your state's bar association
- Your local paralegal association

While these organizations will be covered in some detail throughout the remaining chapters of the book, a brief word about each will be helpful at this point.

### National Federation of Paralegal Associations (NFPA)

NFPA is an association of local associations. There are local paralegal associations throughout the country. Over sixty of them have affiliated with

---

[1]Shimko-Herman, *Should Paralegals Be Regulated with Limited Licensing?*, 17 On Point 10 (National Capital Area Paralegal Ass'n, February 1991).

NFPA. (See Appendix B). From its national headquarters in Kansas City, Missouri, NFPA promotes paralegalism through education and political action.

## National Association of Legal Assistants (NALA)

NALA is primarily an association of individuals, although there are also a number of local paralegal associations that are affiliated with NALA. (See Appendix B.) From its national headquarters in Tulsa, Oklahoma, NALA is equally active in the educational and political arenas. One of the major differences between NALA and NFPA concerns the issue of certification. NALA has instituted a voluntary program of certifying paralegals through a series of examinations. For reasons we will explore in Chapter 4, NFPA strongly opposes this certification program.

## American Bar Association (ABA)

The ABA is a voluntary association of attorneys; no attorney must be a member. Yet it is a powerful entity because of its resources, prestige, and the large number of attorneys who have joined. The ABA has a Standing Committee on Legal Assistants that has had a significant impact on the growth of the field. Recently, paralegals have been allowed to become Associate Members of the ABA, a development not everyone initially welcomed.

## State Bar Association of Your State

Every state has at least one bar association that plays a major role in regulating attorneys under the supervision of the state's highest court. (See Appendix C.) Most of the state bar associations have taken formal positions (in guidelines or ethical opinions) on the use of paralegals by attorneys. A few have followed the lead of the ABA and have allowed paralegals to become associate members. Whenever a paralegal issue arises, you will inevitably hear people ask, "What has the bar said about the issue?"

## Your Local Paralegal Association

There are three main kinds of local paralegal associations: statewide, county or regionwide, and citywide.[2] In Appendix B, you will find a list of every local association in the country with an indication of whether it is affiliated with NFPA, affiliated with NALA, or unaffiliated. For a great many paralegals in the country, major career support and inspiration have come through active participation in their local paralegal association.

. . . . . . . . . . . . . . .

While these five organizations will dominate our discussion of paralegalism, we will also be referring to other important groups, such as *LAMA,* the Legal Assistants Management Association (an association of people who supervise other paralegals in large law offices); and *ALA,* the Association of Legal Administrators (an association of people who manage law offices).

---

[2]In addition, there are associations of paralegals connected with particular schools.

■ **ASSIGNMENT 1.1**

It is not too early in your education to make contact with paralegal associations. In the back of this book, after the index, you will find several forms: "Paralegal Associations: Local" and "Paralegal Associations: National." By filling out and mailing the forms now, you can begin this contact.

 Section C. Job Titles

For convenience, this book uses the job title *paralegal*. An equally common and synonymous term is *legal assistant*. Not everyone uses one of these titles. In fact, there is considerable diversity in the job titles that are used. There is also controversy (for example, a recent lawsuit was brought to prevent certain people from calling themselves paralegals or legal assistants); and confusion (for example, there are some licensed attorneys who work under the title of legal assistant, particularly in the government).

To begin sorting through the maze, we examine three categories of people: employees of attorneys (the dominant category), self-employed individuals who work for attorneys (a growing but much smaller category), and self-employed individuals who provide their services directly to the public without attorney supervision (the smallest but most controversial category). In none of these categories is there universal agreement on what job title should be used. Some titles (paralegal, legal technician) are used in more than one category, but not always on a consistent basis.

## 1. Employees of Attorneys

The vast majority (over 95%) are employees of attorneys. They may be called:

| | |
|---|---|
| paralegal | legal service assistant |
| legal assistant | paralegal specialist |
| certified legal assistant | junior legal assistant |
| senior legal assistant | legal technician |
| lawyer's assistant | legal paraprofessional |
| attorney assistant | case clerk |
| project assistant | legal assistant clerk |
| lay assistant | document clerk |
| lawyer's aide | depo summarizer |

The most commonly used titles are paralegal and legal assistant. As indicated, these titles are synonymous.[3] They are as interchangeable as the words lawyer and attorney.

---

[3]Someone once proposed that the word *paralegal* be used primarily as an adjective and the phrase *legal assistant* primarily as a noun. Under this proposal, a legal assistant would perform paralegal tasks. The proposal has never been considered seriously.

All of the titles listed thus far are generic in the sense that they do not tell you what area of law the person works in. Other employee job titles are more specific:

| | |
|---|---|
| litigation assistant | conflict-of-interest coordinator |
| corporate paralegal | family law paralegal |
| probate specialist | welfare paralegal |
| personal injury paralegal | international trade paralegal |
| real estate paralegal | worker's compensation paralegal |
| bankruptcy paralegal | claims negotiator |
| water law paralegal | |

Occasionally, when the office wants its paralegal to perform more than one job, *hybrid titles* are used. For example, an office might call an employee a *paralegal/investigator,* a *paralegal/librarian,* or a *paralegal/legal secretary.*

When a paralegal becomes part of management in an office with a large number of paralegals, titles reflecting this new status are often used—such as paralegal supervisor, legal assistant manager, or case manager.

## 2. Self-Employed Individuals Working for Attorneys

All of the above titles cover people who are employees of attorneys in one law office. A much smaller number are *independent contractors* who have formed their own businesses that provide services to attorneys from more than one office. (Independent contractors are self-employed persons who control the methods of performing tasks; the objectives or end products of the tasks are controlled by those who buy their services.) They move from office to office for relatively short-term projects and periods, or they work in their own office on projects mailed to them (or transmitted by "fax" machine or by modem) from different attorneys around town. Such self-employed individuals have different titles such as:

*freelance paralegal*

*independent paralegal*

*contract paralegal*

## 3. Self-Employed Individuals Serving the Public

Finally, there is a controversial category of people who do not work for (and who are not supervised by) attorneys. They sell their services directly to the public. Among the titles used by such practitioners are:

| | |
|---|---|
| legal technician | legal typist |
| limited practice officer | independent paralegal |
| certified closing officer | freelance paralegal |
| public paralegal | scrivener |
| forms practitioner | |

Bar associations have often tried to prosecute these individuals for unauthorized practice of law. Yet there is a movement, in the form of limited licensing, toward legitimizing some of their activities. We will examine this in Chapter 4.

. . . . . . . . . . . . . . .

Established paralegals are not always happy with the diversity of titles. For example, a number of paralegal associations object to anyone in the third category (self-employed individuals serving the public) using the word *paralegal* in his or her title. To avoid confusion in the mind of the public, such associations want to limit these words to those who work under the supervision of an attorney. They prefer the title *legal technician,* for example, to *independent paralegal.* One paralegal association refers to everyone in the third category as "nonparalegals"! For similar reasons, the National Association of Legal Assistants recently asked a court to prevent inmates from using the title of paralegal or legal assistant. They had completed a course in legal research to allow them to work on their own legal problems and those of fellow inmates.[4] Since they would not always be working under the supervision of attorneys, NALA wanted them to use a title other than paralegal or legal assistant.

There may come a time when a legislature or court will establish definitive titles for certain categories of individuals in this area. As the present time, however, official titles do not exist. There is no requirement, for example, that individuals be licensed by the state in order to work in any of the three categories listed above. Hence there are no rules on who can use titles such as paralegal or legal assistant. If a form of licensing is instituted, this may change. Again we will discuss this possibility in Chapter 4.

 ## Section D. Job Definitions

What comes to mind when people think of a paralegal? Perhaps the most common definition is: a nonattorney who helps an attorney. While essentially correct, there are problems with this definition—as we will see. In this book, the following definition is used:

> A paralegal is a person with legal skills who works under the supervision of an attorney or who is otherwise authorized to use those skills; this person performs tasks that do not require all the skills of an attorney and that most secretaries are not trained to perform.

Definitions have been formulated by the American Bar Association, the National Association of Legal Assistants, and the National Federation of Paralegal Associations. American Bar Association:

> A legal assistant is a person, qualified through education, training, or work experience, who is employed or retained by a lawyer, law office, governmental agency, or other entity in a capacity or function which involves the performance, under the ultimate direction and supervision of an attorney, of specifically delegated substantive legal work, which work, for the most part, requires a sufficient knowledge of legal concepts that, absent such assistant, the attorney would perform the task.

National Association of Legal Assistants:

> Legal Assistants [also known as paralegals] are a distinguishable group of persons who assist attorneys in the delivery of legal services. Through formal education, training, and experience, legal assistants have knowledge and expertise

---

[4]*Alan Gluth et al vs. Arizona Department of Corrections* (CB-84-1626 PHX CAM) (United States Court of Appeals for the Ninth Circuit). See 17 Facts & Findings 6 (NALA, Fall 1990).

regarding the legal system and substantive and procedural law which qualify them to do work of a legal nature under the supervision of an attorney.

National Federation of Paralegal Associations:

A paralegal/legal assistant is a person qualified through education, training, or work experience to perform substantive legal work that requires knowledge of legal concepts and is customarily, but not exclusively, performed by a lawyer. This person may be retained or employed by a lawyer, law office, governmental agency, or other entity, or may be authorized by administrative, statutory or court authority to perform this work.

---

### ■ ASSIGNMENT 1.2

Assume that John Jones is authorized by law to represent clients in social security hearings for a fee. He works alone in his own office. Is John a legal assistant or paralegal under the ABA definition? Under the NALA definition? Under the NFPA definition?

---

In Chapter 3, we will discuss the issue of career ladders within the paralegal field. Unless a law office employs a relatively large number of paralegals, career ladders usually do not exist. Yet career ladders are becoming increasingly common if there are three or more paralegals in the office. This requires more than one definition of a paralegal to reflect the different steps on the ladder—from the entry-level paralegal to the paralegal manager. In Figure 1.1 you will find an example of the definitions proposed by the Legal Assistant Management Association (LAMA), an organization of over 500 legal assistant managers. Of course, not all large offices use these titles or definitions, but their use is increasing.[5]

A number of points need to be made about the definition of a paralegal—or the absence of a definition about which everyone can agree:

### 1. To date, there is no official terminology imposed by law.

There are three ways that a person becomes a paralegal—by experience, by training, and by fiat.[6] See Figure 1.2. Twenty years ago, the first route was the most common way to become a paralegal. Today, the second route is the most common. While the third route still exists, those who enter the field this way are sometimes resented by paralegals who entered the field by experience or training.

Why do these three methods of becoming a paralegal exist? Primarily because there are no licensing or other laws on who can be a paralegal, at least at the present time. Consequently, there is nothing to prevent a law office from calling its messenger a paralegal! Bar associations, paralegal associations, and educators have attempted to formulate definitions, as we have seen, but nothing has emerged as universally acceptable. To some, this state of affairs is healthy since the absence of official terminology encourages diversity. To others, it is frustrating:

---

[5]For example, the legal assistant manager might be called a paralegal supervisor in some offices. For a more complete list, see Figure 2.2 in Chapter 2.

[6]Malone, *Let Your Staff Shine as "Paralegals,"* The Compleat Lawyer 4 (Winter 1990).

Unfortunately, some law firms seem to be using the phrases "legal assistant" and "paralegal" with alarming regularity without regard to the tasks being performed. And firms are hiring these people at a lower pay scale, thus lowering the salary of the average paralegal.[7]

## 2. *Definitions are often phrased in the negative.*

Some definitions do a better job of telling us what a paralegal is *not* than what one *is*. A paralegal is *not* an attorney, *not* a secretary, *not* a *law clerk* (someone studying to be an attorney), etc. This can be frustrating, as evidenced by the following statement of Karen Dodge, an Oregon paralegal: "I am, along with thousands of other legal assistants, more than a non-lawyer!" [8]

## 3. *Many definitions have four main components.*

- The paralegal is not an attorney.
- The paralegal has legal knowledge and skills.

**FIGURE 1.1**

Sample Job Descriptions of Paralegals in a Large Law Office Where a Career Ladder Exists

---

**Legal Assistant Clerk**

A person who, under the supervision of a legal assistant, performs clerical tasks such as document numbering, alphabetizing documents, labeling folders, filing, and any other project that does not require substantive knowledge of the transaction or litigation.

**Legal Assistant [also called a Paralegal]**

A person who assists an attorney in the practice of law. His or her duties can include factual research, document analysis, cite checking and shepardizing, drafting certificates and corporate transactional documentation, drafting pleadings, coordinating document productions, administering trusts and estates, assisting with pension plan administration, assisting with real estate transactions, and handling substantive functions in practice areas that do not require a law degree.

**Senior Legal Assistant**

An experienced legal assistant with the ability to supervise or train other legal assistants. He or she may have developed a specialty in a certain practice area.

**Supervising Legal Assistant**

Someone who spends about 50% of his or her time supervising other legal assistants, and about 50% on client cases as a legal assistant.

**Case Manager**

An experienced legal assistant who can coordinate or direct legal assistant activities on a major case or transaction.

**Legal Assistant Manager [also called Paralegal Administrator, Paralegal Coordinator, Director of Legal Assistant Services, and Supervisor]**

A person responsible for recruiting, interviewing, and hiring legal assistants. May also be responsible for training legal assistants, monitoring work assignments, and handling personnel and administrative matters that relate to legal assistants. May have budget responsibility for the legal assistant program, and play a role in salary and billing rate administration. The Legal Assistant Manager works few or no billable hours.

**Source:** Ernst & Young, *Legal Assistant Managers and Legal Assistants,* 388 (3rd ed. 1989), Legal Assistants Management Association.

---

[7]6 *Ka L'eo O* (Hawaii Ass'n of Legal Assistants, February 1983).
[8]Karen Dodge, Paragram (Oregon Legal Assistants Ass'n, September 1984).

| By experience: | A secretary, office clerk, or other member of the clerical staff starts to perform paralegal responsibilities. Eventually, he or she is given the title of paralegal. |
|---|---|
| By training: | A graduate of a paralegal training program who has never worked in a law office is hired as a paralegal. |
| By fiat: | An office hires an individual with the title of paralegal even though he or she has never had any law office experience or paralegal training. |

**FIGURE 1.2**

Three Ways to Become a Paralegal

- The paralegal works under the supervision of an attorney.
- The paralegal does not practice law.

### 4.  *There are problems with each of these four components.*

First, there *are* some attorneys who are classified as paralegals. There are attorneys working in America, for example, who are licensed in a foreign country. Some states consider such attorneys to be paralegals. The same may be true of attorneys working in one state but licensed to practice in another state. Occasionally a suspended or disbarred attorney will try to continue work in the law as a paralegal. Under certain circumstances, as we will see in Chapter 5, such work is ethical and legal. Finally, there is nothing to prevent an attorney from applying for and receiving a paralegal job. This is not uncommon in a tight market where there are many unemployed attorneys looking for work.

Second, we learn very little when we are told that a paralegal has legal knowledge and skills. So do attorneys, law clerks, legal secretaries, investigators, many real estate brokers, bankers, etc.

Third, not all paralegals work under the supervision of an attorney. As we will see later, many paralegals working for the government are not supervised by attorneys. There are also special laws that permit nonattorneys to engage in legal work independent of attorneys. To be sure, most paralegals work in private law offices under the supervision of an attorney. Yet there are some who are otherwise situated.

Fourth, it is inaccurate to say that paralegals cannot practice law. The more correct statement of the principle is that paralegals cannot engage in the *unauthorized* practice of law. The existence of rules on the *un*authorized practice of law governing paralegals presupposes the existence of an *authorized practice of law* by paralegals. It is true that the spectrum of authorized practice for paralegals is quite narrow—but it does exist. In our society, the practice of law is not the exclusive domain of the attorney. This will be explored in greater detail in Chapters 4 and 5.

### 5.  *The definitions that we have require further definitions.*

In law, the presence of a definition usually prompts a search for a definition of the definition! Paralegal definitions sometimes contain words and phrases such as *supervision, substantive legal work, practice of law, assistance,* etc. We must be concerned about what these words and phrases mean—they must be defined. These definitions will then probably require clarifications that are, in effect, further definitions. This phenomenon is not peculiar to paralegalism. The process of legal analysis itself calls for an extended series of definitions and subdefinitions, as we will demonstrate in Part II of this book.

Other disciplines face the same difficulty. In the medical profession, for example, a close counterpart to the paralegal is the *physician assistant*. The following is a proposed definition of this career:

> Physician assistant means an individual who is qualified by academic and clinical training to provide patient care services under the supervision and responsibility of a doctor of medicine or osteopathy.[9]

Among the major phrases in this definition that require further defining are: "qualified," "patient care services," and "supervision."

### 6. *A title and definition should serve three main functions.*

In the quest for an acceptable title and definition, there is a danger of losing sight of the reasons that should govern the search. A title and definition should:

- Convey enough information about the field to a prospective student.
- Convey enough information about the field to a prospective employer.
- Convey enough information about the field to the public, as prospective clients.

### 7. *Unanimity may be unnecessary, undesirable, and impossible to achieve.*

The above three purposes can arguably be served without ever achieving total agreement on terminology. We bang our heads against a stone wall when we insist on terminology that:

- Precisely and definitively distinguishes this career from that of other law office personnel.
- Includes everyone who should be included.
- Excludes everyone who should be excluded.

This is simply too much to ask because of the great diversity in the field. We do not yet know all the boundary lines. The wiser course at this stage of development is *not* to insist on trying to achieve unanimity.

### 8. *Terminology and credentialization.*

It does not seem to disturb anyone that we do not have a definitive definition of an attorney. An attorney is someone with a license to practice law. Attorneys are defined primarily by the *credential* that they hold. Any attempt to provide a descriptive definition poses substantial difficulties. There has been endless litigation, for example, on trying to define the *practice of law*. The same is true of terms such as *legal advice* and *professional judgment*. We will explore some of this controversy in Chapters 4 and 5. The point, however, is that a precise definition of an attorney (in terms of what an attorney does) is no more easy to identify than a precise definition of a paralegal. We should not ask of paralegalism that it achieve a level of definitional precision that the legal profession has never been able to achieve.

When a career is having difficulty defining itself, it sometimes tries to use credentialization as a way out of the difficulty. The paralegal career may also

---

[9]44 Federal Register 36,177 (No. 121, 6/21/79).

move in this direction. A paralegal may someday be defined primarily as someone with a license or a certificate to be a paralegal. If this happens, the debate on role will not end. Shifting the question from "What is a paralegal?" to "What credentials should a paralegal have?" will not stop the controversy.

## 9. Functional Definition

While many organizations and individuals are engaged in a theoretical debate over the definition of a paralegal, the marketplace may be forcing a practical definition on us. As we will see in a moment, there are several kinds of cases in which the winning party can force the losing party to pay the attorney fees *and the paralegal fees* of the winning party. (When this occurs, the paralegal fees, of course, go to the supervising attorney of the paralegal; they do not go directly to the paralegal.) But everything a paralegal does on a case does *not* qualify for an award of paralegal fees. Consequently, if attorneys want to increase the chance of obtaining an award of paralegal fees, they must make sure that the tasks of the paralegal fit within the criteria for such an award. The main criterion is that the paralegal is performing tasks that are not purely secretarial or clerical. This reality may lead to a practical or functional definition of a paralegal: a person who performs tasks that qualify for an award of paralegal fees.

---

### ■ ASSIGNMENT 1.3

In this assignment, we explore what the world thinks a paralegal or legal assistant is. So much will depend on what the public has heard about this field. It is not as well known as other new occupations such as *paramedic*. In many parts of the country, the word *paramedic* is printed in large bold print on ambulances racing throughout the city. This visibility has increased the public's understanding of what a paramedic is. Media attention is also important. Many paralegals were disappointed, for example, when a prime-time attorney soap opera, *L.A. Law,* failed to include a paralegal for a role in the law firm that was the center of this very popular television program. Some wrote to the program producer to protest this glaring omission, but to no avail. This does not mean, however, that any kind of media attention would be welcomed. Shelly Widoff, a paralegal consultant in Boston, has her fingers crossed: "I just hope we all don't cringe when the media get hold of us on a TV sitcom." [10] Recently, many paralegals not only cringed but also vigorously protested when *Quincy,* a medical television program, portrayed a paralegal as an arch villain. Thankfully this occurred in only one of its episodes!

Douglas Parker, a litigation paralegal, believes that the public has "as many different perceptions of our occupational status as there are craters on the moon."[11] To gauge whether this is true in your community, contact the following individuals in your area. Ask each of them the question: "What is a paralegal or legal assistant?"

(a) A neighbor or friend who does not work in a law office and who has probably never been in a law office.
(b) A neighbor or friend who does not work in a law office but who has hired an attorney at least once in his or her life.
(c) A legal secretary.
(d) An attorney who has never hired a paralegal.
(e) An attorney who has hired a paralegal.
(f) A working paralegal who is not now in school.

---

[10]S. Widoff, *On the Docket,* 4 Legal Assistant Today 10 (January/February 1987).
[11]Parker, *Legal Assistants: A Case of Uncertain Identity,* 7 Legal Professional 10 (September/October 1989).

(g) A high school student.
(h) A student in a law school studying to be an attorney.
(i) A police officer.
(j) A person who runs a small business.
(k) A local judge.
(l) A clerk in a local court.

Take careful notes on their answers to the question. Compare the answers.

- What common ideas or themes did you find in the definitions?
- What two definitions were the most different? List the differences.
- Do you think that your survey raises any problems about the perception of paralegals in your area? If so, what are these problems, and how can they be solved?

##  Section E. Salaries

How much do paralegals make? While some data is available to answer this question, there is no definitive answer because of the great variety of employment settings. According to a 1991 study of over 2,600 paralegals by the National Association of Legal Assistants, the national average annual salary of paralegals was $27,082, with an average annual bonus of $1,793.[12] A 1991 study of 587 paralegals reported that the national average annual salary was $27,772.[13] It is important to note that none of these are entry-level salaries; most of the paralegals surveyed had been on the job for one or more years.[14] The Legal Assistant Management Association conducted one of the most comprehensive surveys of paralegal salaries in 1989. Over 6,000 paralegal salaries were examined. The results are reported in Figures 1.3 and 1.4. Note that a paralegal's salary will tend to increase in direct proportion to his or her experience (Figure 1.3) and level of responsibility (Figure 1.4). A number of other generalizations can be made about salaries across the country:

- Paralegals who work in the law departments of corporations (banks, insurance companies, other businesses) tend to make more than those who work in private law firms. In a 1989 survey of just under a thousand corporate law departments, the average salary for a paralegal was $29,973. About 150 of them reported receiving an average bonus of $2,243 (Altman & Weil).
- Paralegals who work in large private law firms tend to make more than those who work in smaller private law firms.
- Paralegals who work in large metropolitan areas (over a million in population) tend to make more than those who work in rural areas.
- Paralegals who work for the government in civil service positions tend to make less than those who work for large private law firms or corporations.
- Paralegals who work in legal aid or legal service offices that are funded by government grants and charitable contributions tend to make less than all other paralegals.

[12]NALA, *The Legal Assistant Profession: National Utilization and Compensation Survey Report*, 35 (1991).
[13]Milano, *Salary Survey Results*, 8 Legal Assistant Today 27 (May/June 1991).
[14]One study of a relatively small number of law offices in Colorado showed that the average salary for entry-level paralegals was $17,900. Acree, *The CBA Economic Survey*, 20 The Colorado Lawyer 451 (March 1991).

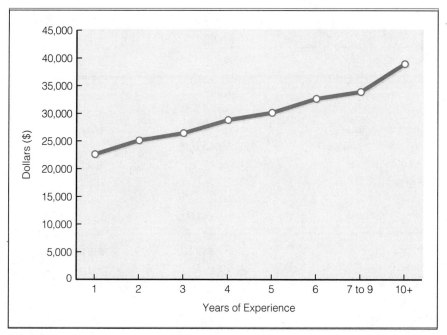

**FIGURE 1.3**

1989 Total Compensation (Median) by Years of Experience

**Source:** Ernst & Young, *Legal Assistant Managers and Legal Assistants,* ix (3rd ed. 1989).

| Position | NON-BONUS RECEIVERS | BONUS RECEIVERS | | |
|---|---|---|---|---|
| | Total Compensation* | Base Salary* | Bonus | Total Compensation** |
| Legal Assistant Manager | $37,180 | $43,112 | $4,131 | $47,243 |
| Supervising Legal Assistant | $37,847 | $39,819 | $3,050 | $42,868 |
| Senior Legal Assistant | $34,925 | $35,063 | $3,091 | $38,154 |
| Case Manager | $29,636 | $32,170 | $4,787 | $36,957 |
| Legal Assistant | $25,636 | $26,697 | $1,781 | $28,477 |
| Legal Assistant Clerk | $17,888 | $18,958 | $850 | $19,808 |

\*1989 base salary
\*\*1989 base salary plus 1988 bonus (does not include overtime where paid)

**Source:** Ernst & Young, *Legal Assistant Managers and Legal Assistants*, p. 16 (3rd ed. 1989).

**FIGURE 1.4**

1989 Average Compensation by Level of Responsibility

- Paralegals working for attorneys who understand the value of paralegals tend to make more than those working for attorneys who have a poor or weak understanding of what paralegals can do.
- Paralegals who work in an office where there is a career ladder for paralegals, plus periodic evaluations and salary reviews, tend to make more than those who work in offices without these options.
- Paralegals who are career-oriented tend to make more than those less interested in a long-term commitment to paralegal work.
- Salary projections to the year 2,000 are found in Figure 1.5.

**FIGURE 1.5**
Salary Projections
in the "Hot
Careers"

| JOB | CURRENT SALARY | PROJECTED SALARY |
|---|---|---|
| | 1989 | 2000 |
| Accountant | $26,000 | $41,600 |
| Computer Programmer | $30,600 | $48,960 |
| Dental Hygienist | $24,850 | $39,800 |
| Dentist | $75,300 | $120,480 |
| Electrical Engineer | $40,000 | $64,000 |
| Employment Interviewer | $16,000–$30,000 | $25,600–$48,000 |
| **Legal Assistant** | **$24,900** | **$39,840** |
| Management Consultant | $36,300–$44,000 | $58,100–$70,400 |
| Nurse | $26,800 | $42,900 |
| Nurse-Anesthetist | $34,000–$49,000 | $54,400–$78,400 |
| Photographer | $19,800–$40,500 | $31,700–$64,800 |
| Physical Therapist | $28,500–$60,000 | $45,600–$96,000 |
| Publicist | $29,000 | $46,400 |
| Real-Estate Agent | $20,550 | $32,880 |
| Real-Estate Broker | $39,800 | $63,700 |
| Retail Salesperson | $12,500–$16,800 | $20,000–$26,800 |
| Travel Agent | $18,200 | $29,120 |
| **Source:** Gates, *Hot Careers for the '90s,* Working Mother 68 (May 1989). | | |

There are a few paralegals in the country—*very few*—who command salaries of over $100,000. Lee Henderson, for example, is such a paralegal; she works for a large Dallas law firm. "Lee Henderson, a paralegal with 25 years' experience in the mortgage banking business, supervises a staff of 38. Her department manages closings for residential mortgage loans. She has also helped develop computer programs to assist other departments."[15] Again, such salaries, while possible, are rare.

In addition to the payment of bonuses, other fringe benefits must also be considered, e.g., vacation time, health insurance, parking facilities. A comprehensive list of such benefits will be presented in Chapter 2. (See Figure 2.12.)

One final point to keep in mind about salaries. Once a person has gained training *and experience* as a paralegal, there are possibilities of using this background to go into other positions that are law-related. For example, a corporate paralegal in a law firm might leave the firm to take a higher-paying position for a corporation as a securities analyst, or an estates paralegal at a law firm might leave for a more lucrative position as a trust administrator at a bank. A more extensive list of these law-related jobs will be given at the end of Chapter 2.

 Section F. Historical Perspective

In the late 1960s, most attorneys would draw a blank if you mentioned the words *paralegal* or *legal assistant.* According to Webster's *Ninth New Collegiate Dictionary,* the earliest recorded use of the word *paralegal* in English occurred in 1971. Today, the situation has changed radically. There are few offices that do not employ paralegals or that are not seriously thinking about

---

[15]Marcotte, *$100,000 a Year for Paralegals?,* 73 American Bar Association Journal 19 (October 1987).

hiring them. A recent survey reports that there is one paralegal for every four attorneys in law firms and one paralegal for every two attorneys in the law departments of corporations.[16] It has been estimated that the number of paralegals may eventually exceed the number of attorneys in the practice of law. The United States Bureau of Labor Statistics has projected that paralegals will constitute one of the fastest growing fields in the country, with a growth of over 75% between the years 1988 and 2000 (see Figure 1.6).

What has caused this dramatic change? The following factors have been instrumental in bringing paralegalism to its present state of prominence:

1. The pressure of economics.
2. The call for efficiency and delegation.
3. The promotion by bar associations.
4. The organization of paralegals.
5. The restructuring of professions and occupations generally.

## 1. The Pressure of Economics

Perhaps the greatest incentive to the development of paralegals has been arithmetic. Law firms simply add up what they earn without paralegals, add up

**FIGURE 1.6**
The Fastest Growing Occupations, 1988–2000

| OCCUPATION | EMPLOYMENT | | CHANGE IN EMPLOYMENT |
|---|---|---|---|
| | **1988** | Projected, **2000** | **1988–2000** |
| Paralegals | 83,000 | 145,000 | +75.3% |
| Medical assistants | 149,000 | 253,000 | +70.0% |
| Home health aides | 236,000 | 397,000 | +67.9% |
| Radiologic technologies and technicians | 132,000 | 218,000 | +66.0% |
| Data processing equipment repairers | 71,000 | 115,000 | +61.2% |
| Medical record technicians | 47,000 | 75,000 | +59.9% |
| Medical secretaries | 207,000 | 327,000 | +58.0% |
| Physical therapists | 68,000 | 107,000 | +57.0% |
| Surgical technologies | 35,000 | 55,000 | +56.4% |
| Operations research analysts | 55,000 | 85,000 | +55.4% |
| Securities and financial services sales workers | 200,000 | 309,000 | +54.8% |
| Travel agents | 142,000 | 219,000 | +54.1% |
| Computer systems analysts | 403,000 | 617,000 | +53.3% |
| Physical and corrective therapy assistants | 39,000 | 60,000 | +52.5% |
| Social welfare service aides | 91,000 | 138,000 | +51.5% |
| Occupational therapists | 33,000 | 48,000 | +48.8% |
| Computer programmers | 519,000 | 769,000 | +48.1% |
| Human services workers | 118,000 | 171,000 | +44.9% |
| Respiratory therapists | 56,000 | 79,000 | +41.3% |
| Correction officers and jailers | 186,000 | 262,000 | +40.8% |

**Source:** U.S. Department of Labor, Bureau of Labor Statistics, *Occupational Outlook Quarterly*, 6 (Spring 1990).

---

[16]Ernst & Young, *Legal Assistant Managers and Legal Assistants*, xi (3rd ed. 1989).

what they could earn with paralegals, compare the two figures, and conclude that the employment of paralegals is profitable. There "can be little doubt that the principal motivation prompting law firms to hire legal assistants is the economic benefit enjoyed by the firm." [17] The key to increased profits is *leveraging*. Leverage, often expressed as a ratio, is the ability to make a profit from the income-gathering work of others. The higher the ratio of paralegals to partners in the firm, the more profit to the partners (assuming everyone is generating income from billable time).[18]

In the best of all worlds, some of this increased profit will result in lower fees to the client. For example, Chief Justice Warren Burger feels that some attorneys charge "excessive fees for closing real-estate transactions for the purchase of a home. A greater part of that work can be handled by trained paralegals, and, in fact, many responsible law firms are doing just that to reduce costs for their clients." [19]

Figure 1.7 provides an example of the economic impact of using a paralegal. In the example, a client comes to a lawyer to form a corporation.[20] We will compare (a) the economics of an attorney and secretary working on the case, assuming a fee of $2,000, and (b) the economics of an attorney, secretary, *and* paralegal working on the same case, assuming a fee of $1,600. As you can see, with a paralegal added to the team, the firm's profit is increased almost 25% in spite of the lower fee, and the attorney has more billable time to spend elsewhere. Some studies have claimed an even higher profit increase because of the use of paralegals.

The example assumes that the attorney's fee is $200 per hour and that the attorney billed the client $40 per hour for the paralegal's time. According to a 1988 study of relatively large law firms, the billing rate that firms charged clients for paralegal work ranged from $41 to $60 an hour, and the average number of chargeable billable hours each paralegal reported in these firms was 1,350 per year.[21] A more recent study showed that the average paralegal fee allowed by the courts was $48.10 per hour.[22] (See also Figure 14.4 in Chapter 14.)

When a law firm bills clients for paralegal time, the paralegal becomes a *profit center* in the firm. In such cases, paralegals are not simply part of the cost of doing business reflected in the firm's *overhead;* [23] they generate revenue (and therefore, profit) for the firm. To calculate the amount of profit, the *rule of three* is often used as a general guideline. To be profitable, a paralegal must bill three times his or her salary. Of the total revenue brought in through paralegal bill-

---

[17]*The Expanding Role of Legal Assistants in New York State,* 7 (N.Y. State Bar Association, Subcommittee on Legal Assistants).

[18]The same, of course, is true of associates in the firm. The higher the ratio of associates to partners, the greater the profit to the partners.

[19]U.S. News & World Rep., Feb. 22, 1982 at 32.

[20]Adapted from Jespersen, *Paralegals: Help or Hindrance?* The Houston Lawyer 111, 114–16 (March/April 1977).

[21]Ernst & Young, *Legal Assistant Managers and Legal Assistants,* xii (3rd ed. 1989).

[22]Carla Teague, *Case Law Trends Affecting the Paralegal Profession,* 16 National Paralegal Reporter 18 (NFPA, Fall 1991). A 1991 survey of all members of NALA concluded that the average billing rate for NALA members was $55.00 per hour. NALA, *The Legal Assistant Profession,* see footnote 12 at p. 29.

[23]Overhead includes the cost of office space, furniture, equipment, and insurance, plus the cost of secretarial or other clerical staff whose time is usually not billed separately to clients.

| TASK: TO FORM A CORPORATION | | |
|---|---|---|

**a. Attorney and Secretary**

| | Time | |
|---|---|---|
| Function | Attorney | Secretary |
| 1. Interviewing | 1.0 | 0.0 |
| 2. Advising | 1.0 | 0.0 |
| 3. Gathering information | 1.0 | 0.0 |
| 4. Preparing papers | 2.0 | 4.0 |
| 5. Executing and filing papers | 1.0 | 1.0 |
| | 6.0 | 5.0 |

Assume that the attorney's hourly rate is $200 per hour. Assume that the overhead cost of maintaining a secretary is $20 per hour.

| | |
|---|---|
| Attorney (6 × $200) | $1,200 |
| Secretary (5 × $20) | 100 |
| Total cost | $1,300 |
| Fee | $2,000 |
| Less cost | 1,300 |
| Gross profit | $ 700 |

**b. Attorney, Secretary, *and* Paralegal**

| | Time | | |
|---|---|---|---|
| Function | Attorney | Paralegal | Secretary |
| 1. Interviewing | 0.5 | 0.5 | 0.0 |
| 2. Advising | 1.0 | 0.0 | 0.0 |
| 3. Gathering information | 0.0 | 1.0 | 0.0 |
| 4. Preparing papers | 0.5 | 1.5 | 4.0 |
| 5. Executing and filing papers | 0.5 | 0.5 | 1.0 |
| | 2.5 | 3.5 | 5.0 |

In addition, assume a paralegal hourly rate of $40 per hour.

| | |
|---|---|
| Attorney (2.5 × $200) | $500 |
| Paralegal (3.5 × $40) | 140 |
| Secretary (5 × $20) | 100 |
| Total cost | $740 |
| Fee | $1,600 |
| Less cost | 740 |
| Gross profit | $ 860 |

| COMPARISON |
|---|

Fee: a. Attorney and Secretary ................................................................. $2,000
    b. Attorney, Secretary, and Paralegal .............................................. $1,600
Saving to client ................................................................................. $400
Increased profitability to lawyer ($860 vs. $700) ........................................ $160

By using a paralegal on the case, the attorney's profit increases almost 25% over the profit realized without the paralegal. Furthermore, the attorney has 3.5 hours that are suddenly available to work on other cases, bringing in additional revenue of $700 (3.5 × the attorney's hourly rate of $200).

**FIGURE 1.7**

The Profitability of Using Paralegals

ing, one-third is allocated to salary, one-third to overhead, and one-third to profit. Phrased another way, when the gross revenue generated through paralegal billing equals three times the paralegal's salary, the firm has achieved its minimum profit expectations.

For example:

| | |
|---|---|
| Paralegal's salary: | $30,000 |
| Paralegal rate: | $35 per hour |

|  |  |
|---|---|
| Billings the firm hopes this paralegal will generate: | $90,000 |
| Rule-of-three allocation: | |
| —paralegal salary: | $30,000 |
| —overhead for this paralegal: | $30,000 |
| —profit to the law firm: | $30,000[24] |

---

### ■ ASSIGNMENT 1.4

(a) In the example just given, how many billable hours per year would this paralegal have to produce in order to generate $30,000 per year in profits for the firm? Is this number realistic? If not, what must be done?

(b) Assume that a paralegal seeks a salary of $25,000 a year and that the law firm would like to be able to pay this salary. Using the "rule of three," if this person is able to generate 1,400 billable hours per year, how much must this paralegal's time be billed at in order for the attorney and the paralegal to be happy?

---

Paralegals can be even more profitable to the firm in cases where clients pay a fixed fee or a contingency fee. A *fixed fee* (e.g., $20,000) is paid regardless of the number of hours it takes the firm to complete the case—and regardless of the outcome of the case. A *contingency fee* is usually a percentage (e.g., 33%) that is paid only if the client wins, regardless of the number of hours it takes the firm to complete the case. In most cases where a client pays a fixed fee or a contingency fee, there is no hourly billing. Greater use of paralegals on such cases can lead to greater profits. The "more the attorney uses legal assistant services as opposed to attorney services," the less cost is incurred, "thereby maintaining more of the fee as a profit." [25]

Not every law firm agrees, however, that hiring paralegals inevitably leads to greater profits for the firm. A number of factors complicate the attempt to determine the economic effect of hiring paralegals. For example:

■ At some firms, there is a relatively high turnover of paralegals. This means increased in-house training costs for newly hired paralegals and, therefore, higher overhead.

■ Many attorneys are looking for work, particularly recent law school graduates. Some are working part-time for law firms,[26] or are accepting comparatively low-paying *staff attorney*[27] positions at the firms. These attorneys have no hope of ever becoming partners in the firm—unlike the traditional associates at the firm. In fee-generating cases, some firms may be more likely to delegate work to a part-time attorney or to a staff attorney than to paralegals, since the firm can bill an attorney's time at a higher rate. This tendency is even greater if the salary of this attorney is not significantly different from the salary of the paralegals in the firm. When low-salaried attorneys are available, some firms are not as convinced that it's economical to hire paralegals.

---

[24]Adapted from State Bar of Texas, *Attorneys' Guide to Practicing with Legal Assistants*, VI(3) (1986).

[25]L. Hangley, "The Role of the Legal Assistant" in *The Team Approach to Practice Development*, 5 (Professional Education Systems, 1989).

[26]Part-time attorneys are sometimes called "contract attorneys" or "project attorneys."

[27]Also referred to as second-tier attorneys.

■ An experienced legal secretary can sometimes earn more than a new parale-gal. Where this is so, a firm might be tempted to assign some secretarial tasks to the paralegal. When this occurs, the profitability of paralegals may dimin-ish, since a firm cannot bill paralegal rates for secretarial tasks.

Yet such factors have not diminished the movement toward hiring increased numbers of paralegals. Furthermore, the cost-effectiveness of a paralegal should not be judged solely by the amount of revenue directly generated by his or her efforts. Paralegals often perform valuable but *nonbillable* tasks, such as recruit-ing new employees, managing other paralegals, updating and organizing plead-ings files, and doing most of the work on cases that the attorney would normally do for free (e.g., probating the estate of the attorney's brother-in-law). This, of course, enables attorneys to direct more of their efforts to fee-generating mat-ters. Furthermore, if a paralegal is not as profitable as an employer had hoped, the problem may be the lack of an effective strategy to incorporate paralegals into the office and to manage them effectively. "In fact, if the hiring, allocation and utilization of paralegals is not actively planned and managed by the law firm, productivity and profitability will not be improved." [28] We will examine this theme in greater depth later.

---

■ **ASSIGNMENT 1.5**

The following historical overview provides two theories to explain the develop-ment of paralegals. Why do you think the author feels that the "second has held the profession back"?

"Historically, the legal assistant's role evolved from efficient use of legal secretaries. There are two theories as to how this happened. One theory suggests that the attorney, seeing the benefit to his clients in providing increased services through the use of his legal secretary, provided his secretary with further education and training and she then per-formed substantive legal services. The other theory is that the attorney, looking for areas where he might bill his client for the secretary's service, determined that if he called his secretary a legal assistant, he could more easily charge for the secretarial services. Both of these approaches contributed to the evolution. While the first concept has elevated the paralegal profession, the second has held the profession back." [29]

---

Thus far the focus of our discussion has been law firm profit when the rev-enue generated by the law firm comes from the firm's own clients—through hourly fees, a fixed fee, or a contingent fee. Earlier we briefly mentioned another kind of case where the paralegal can play a significant role in the firm's profit picture. There are a number of special cases (for example, employment discrim-ination and antitrust violations), where *the losing side pays the attorney fees of the winning side.* Most courts agree that in addition to recovering attorney fees, the winning side can recover for its paralegal time spent in litigation. But in what amount? Two possibilities exist:

*(a) Prevailing Market Rate for Paralegals.*   This is the amount a law firm charges its clients for paralegal time, e.g., $50 an hour.

---

[28]A. Olson, *Law Firms, Paralegals and Profitability* 4 Journal of Paralegal Education and Practice 31, 32 (October 1987).

[29]L. Hangley, "The Role of the Legal Assistant" in *The Team Approach to Practice Development,* 3 (Professional Education Systems, 1989).

*(b) Actual Cost to the Law Firm.*  This is the amount that the law firm pays to keep its paralegal, e.g., $20 an hour, to cover the paralegal's salary, fringe benefits, and other overhead items related to the paralegal.

There can be a dramatic difference between market rate and actual cost, since the former includes the profit that the firm makes through the paralegal. When a losing party must may for the paralegal time of the winning party, how much is paid? Market rate or actual cost? Different states answer this question in different ways when the litigation involves a state matter.

For certain kinds of *federal* cases, however, the United States Supreme Court settled the question in the very important 1989 opinion of *Missouri v. Jenkins* when it ruled that the prevailing market rate was to be the standard of recovery. The relevant portions of this opinion are reprinted below.

The case involved a Kansas City suit in which a claim was made under § 1988 of the Civil Rights Act. The lower court awarded the winning party $40 an hour for paralegal time, which was the prevailing rate in Kansas City at the time. On appeal, the losing party argued that it should pay no more than $15 an hour, which represented the actual cost to the law firm of employing the paralegal. The United States Supreme Court did not accept this position.

Many consider this opinion to be a great victory for the paralegal movement. "Waves from the ripple effect" of the opinion "will wash the doorsteps

---

**Missouri v. Jenkins**

United States Supreme Court
491 U.S. 274,
109 S.Ct. 2463, 105 L.Ed.2d 229 (1989)

Justice BRENNAN delivered the opinion of the Court. . . . [T]o bill paralegal work at market rates . . . makes economic sense. By encouraging the use of lower-cost paralegals rather than attorneys wherever possible, permitting market-rate billing of paralegal hours "encourages cost-effective delivery of legal services and, by reducing the spiraling cost of civil rights litigation, furthers the policies underlying civil rights statutes." *Cameo Convalescent Center, Inc. v. Senn,* 738 F.2d 836, 846 (CA7 1984), cert. denied, 469 U.S. 1106, 105 S.Ct. 780, 83 L.Ed.2d 775 (1985).*

Such separate billing appears to be the practice in most communities today.** In the present case, Missouri concedes that "the local market typically bills separately for paralegal services," Transcript of Oral Argument 14, and the District Court found that the requested hourly rates of $35 for law clerks, $40 for paralegals, and $50 for recent law graduates were the prevailing rates for such services in the Kansas City area. . . . Under these circumstances, the court's decision to award separate compensation at these rates was fully in accord with § 1988. . . .

---

* It has frequently been recognized in the lower courts that paralegals are capable of carrying out many tasks, under the supervision of an attorney, that might otherwise be performed by a lawyer and billed at a higher rate. Such work might include, for example, factual investigation, including locating and interviewing witnesses; assistance with depositions, interrogatories, and document production; compilation of statistical and financial data; checking legal citations; and drafting correspondence. Much such work lies in a gray area of tasks that might appropriately be performed either by an attorney or a paralegal. To the extent that fee applicants under § 1988 are not permitted to bill for the work of paralegals at market rates, it would not be surprising to see a greater amount of such work performed by attorneys themselves, thus increasing the overall cost of litigation.

Of course, purely clerical or secretarial tasks should not be billed at a paralegal rate, regardless of who performs them. What the court in *Johnson v. Georgia Highway Express, Inc.,* 488 F.2d 714, 717 (CA5 1974), said in regard to the work of attorneys is applicable by analogy to paralegals: "It is appropriate to distinguish between legal work, in the strict sense, and investigation, clerical work, compilation of facts and statistics and other work which can often be accomplished by non-lawyers but which a lawyer may do because he has no other help available. Such non-legal work may command a lesser rate. Its dollar value is not enhanced just because a lawyer does it."

** *Amicus* National Association of Legal Assistants reports that 77 percent of 1,800 legal assistants responding to a survey of the association's membership stated that their law firms charged clients for paralegal work on an hourly billing basis. Brief for National Association of Legal Assistants as *Amicus Curiae* 11.

of virtually every law office which employs or which is contemplating utilizing legal assistants in its delivery of legal services." [30] The highest Court in the land not only acknowledged the value of paralegals, but also provided a clear demonstration of how profitable paralegals can be in these kinds of cases. Equally important is the admonition of the Court's footnote that "purely clerical or secretarial tasks [performed by a paralegal] should not be billed at a paralegal rate." If a law firm wants to recover paralegal fees at market rates from the opposing side, the firm must be able to show that it gave the paralegal substantial, nonsecretarial tasks to perform in the case. As we shall see later, a major complaint of some paralegals is that they are not delegated enough challenging tasks. *Missouri v. Jenkins* should help combat this problem. Attorneys will be more inclined to use paralegals properly when they see that their economic livelihood is enhanced by doing so.[31]

It must be noted, however, that some courts do *not* adopt the approach of the United States Supreme Court in *Missouri v. Jenkins*. This opinion involved the interpretation of the Civil Rights Act. If another court is interpreting a different statute, it might reach a different conclusion on how to handle paralegal time. There are a few courts that refuse to allow any separate compensation for paralegal time. In such courts, paralegal fees are simply not recoverable. Yet the trend is definitely in the direction of following the approach of *Missouri v. Jenkins*.

---

### ■ ASSIGNMENT 1.6

**(a)** Earlier in this chapter, you were given sample job descriptions of paralegals in a large law office: legal assistant clerk, legal assistant, senior legal assistant, supervising legal assistant, case manager, and legal assistant manager. (See Figure 1.1). Assume that the law firm of Smith & Smith is large enough to have employees under all of these categories and that employees within each of them work on a major case for which an award of paralegal fees can be made. How would a court make a determination of paralegal fees in this case?

**(b)** What has been the impact of *Missouri v. Jenkins* in your state?

---

## 2. The Call for Efficiency and Delegation

Attorneys are overtrained for a substantial portion of the tasks that they perform in a law office. This is one of the major reasons that traditional law offices are charged with inefficiency. Paralegals have been seen as a major step toward reform. The results have been quite satisfactory as evidenced by the following comments from attorneys who have hired paralegals:[32]

> A competent legal assistant for several years has been effectively doing 25% to 35% of the actual work that I have been doing for many years prior to that time.

---

[30]*The Paralegal Factor*, 9 The California Lawyer 47 (June 1989).

[31]There is another dimension to these fee-award cases that should be considered. Suppose that an attorney seeks an award of *attorney* fees to cover time spent on tasks that the attorney should have delegated to a paralegal. In such a case, a court might refuse to award the attorney his or her normal hourly fee. One court phrased the problem this way: "Routine tasks, if performed by senior partners in large firms, should not be billed at their usual rates. A Michelangelo should not charge Sistine Chapel rates for painting a farmer's barn." *Ursic v. Bethlehem Mines*, 719 F.2d 670, 677 (3rd Cir. 1983).

[32]Oregon State Bar, Legal Assistants Committee, *Legal Assistant Survey* (1977).

> The results of our 3 attorney—3 paralegal system have been excellent. Our office's efficiency has been improved and our clients are receiving better service.
>
> It has been our experience that clients now ask for the legal assistant. Client calls to the attorneys have been reduced an estimated 75%.

It has taken a *very* long time for attorneys to realize that something was wrong with the way they practiced law. The following historical perspective presents an overview of how attorneys came to this realization.[33]

During the American Colonial period, the general populace distrusted attorneys because many of them sided with King George III against the emerging independent nation. Some colonies tolerated the existence of attorneys, but established roadblocks to their practice. In 1641, for example, the Massachusetts Bay Colony prohibited freemen for hiring attorneys for a fee:

> "Every man that findeth himself unfit to plead his own cause in any court shall have libertie to employ any man against whom the court doth not except, to help him, Provided he gave him noe fee or reward for his pains." [34]

Furthermore, almost anyone could become an attorney without having to meet rigorous admission requirements.

Up until the nineteenth century, the attorney did not have assistants other than an occasional apprentice studying to be an attorney himself. The attorney basically worked alone. He carried "his office in his hat." [35] A very personal attachment and devotion to detail were considered to be part of the process of becoming an attorney and of operating a practice. In the early nineteenth century, George Wythe commented that:

> It is only by drudgery that the exactness, accuracy and closeness of thought so necessary for a good lawyer are engendered.[36]

The same theme came from Abraham Lincoln in his famous "Notes for a Law Lecture":

> If anyone . . . shall claim an exemption from the drudgery of the law, his case is a failure in advance.[37]

Attorneys would be somewhat reluctant to delegate such "drudgery" to someone working for them, according to this theory of legal education.

During this period, attorneys often placed a high premium on the personal relationship between attorney and client. As late as 1875, for example, Seward and his partners "would have none of the newfangled typewriters" because clients would "resent the lack of personal attention implied in typed letters." [38] The coming of the Industrial Revolution, however, brought the practice of law closer to industry and finance. Some law offices began to specialize. As attor-

---

[33]The research for part of the section on the historical background of paralegals was conducted by the author and subsequently used with his permission in the following article: Brickman, *Expansion of the Lawyering Process through a New Delivery System: The Emergence and State of Legal Paraprofessionalism* 71 Columbia Law Review 1153, 1169ff (1971).

[34]"Body of Liberties," cited in R. Warner, *Independent Paralegal's Handbook*, 8 (Nolo Press, 1986).

[35]Lee, *Large Law Offices*, 57 American Law Review 788 (1923).

[36]Lewis, ed., "George Wythe," in Great American Lawyers: A History of the Legal Profession in America, vol 1, 55 (1907).

[37]Nicolay & Hay, eds., "Notes for a Law Lecture," in Complete Works of Abraham Lincoln, 142 (1894). See also Frank, Lincoln as a Lawyer, 3 in (1961).

[38]Swaine, *The Cravath Firm and Its Predecessors: 1819–1947*, vol 1, 365, 449.

neys assumed new responsibilities, the concern for organization and efficiency grew. To be sure, large numbers of attorneys continued to carry their law offices "in their hats" and to provide an essentially one-to-one service. Many law offices in the 1850s, however, took a different direction.

Machines created new jobs. The typewriter introduced the typist. Librarians, investigators, bookkeepers, office managers, accountants, tax and fiduciary specialists, and research assistants soon found their way into the large law office. Although nonattorneys were primarily hired to undertake clerical or administrative responsibilities, they soon were delegated more challenging roles. As one study of a law firm noted with respect to several female employees who had been with the firm a number of years:

> In addition, these women were given considerable responsibility in connection with their positions as secretary or head bookkeeper. The head bookkeeper acted as assistant secretary to the partner-secretary of certain charitable corporations the firm represented. In this capacity, she recorded minutes of director's meetings, issued proxy statements, supervised the filing of tax returns for the organization and attended to other significant administrative matters.[39]

In this fashion, attorneys began delegating more and more nonclerical duties to their clerical staff. This was not always done in a planned manner. An employee might suddenly be performing dramatically new duties as emergencies arose on current cases and as new clients arrived in an already busy office. In such an environment, an attorney may not know what the employee is capable of doing until the employee does it. Despite its haphazard nature, the needs of the moment and *OJT* (on-the-job training) worked wonders for staff development.

By the 1960s, attorneys started to ask whether a new category of employee should be created. Instead of expanding the duties of a secretary, why not give the new duties to a new category of employee—the paralegal? A number of studies were conducted to determine how receptive attorneys would be to this idea on a broad scale. The results were very encouraging. The conclusion soon became inevitable that attorneys can delegate many tasks to paralegals without sacrificing quality of service. Today this theme has become a dominant principle of law office management. Most attorneys no longer ask, "Can I delegate?" Rather they ask, "Why *can't* this be delegated?" Or, "How can the delegation be effectively managed?" It is a given that substantial delegation is a necessity.

This is not to say, however, that all attorneys immediately endorse the paralegal concept with enthusiasm. Many are initially hesitant, as demonstrated by the following report on the hiring of legal assistants within the California Department of Health, Education, and Welfare (HEW):

> When the legal assistant program began in early 1977 in HEW, it was met with some skepticism, especially in offices in cities other than Sacramento. There was concern that the quality of the work might be diminished by legal assistants. However, team leaders and deputies are not only no longer skeptical, they are now enthusiastic supporters of the legal assistant program. The attorneys feel that the work product is at least as good, and more thorough, than that provided by attorneys, mainly because the legal assistants have developed an expertise in a narrow area of the law and the work is more stimulating to the legal assistants than it was to the attorneys.
>
> The legal assistants processed 152 cases in fiscal year 1977/78 and 175 cases in 1978/79. It was estimated that legal assistants are as efficient as attorneys in processing the preliminary phase of these cases. As a result, a legal

---

[39]Dodge, *Evolution of a City Law Office,* 1955 Wisconsin Law Review 180, 187.

assistant in this instance produces as many pleadings as a deputy attorney general would have produced in the same amount of time. For this reason the section has been able to provide a faster turnaround time for the client agencies.[40]

Proponents of greater use of paralegals in government argue that, in addition to efficiency, considerable savings can result from such use. For example, in order to save money and increase efficiency, a bill was introduced into the California Assembly:

"to require each state agency and department that employs attorneys to begin to utilize a combination of hiring practices and attrition which will result in a ratio of one paralegal . . . to every 5 attorneys employed by the state by January 1, 1990."[41]

Unfortunately, this bill was not enacted into law—largely because of opposition from government attorneys.

Another call for more cost-effective methods of practicing law by the government came from the Council for Citizens Against Government Waste (the "Grace Commission") which recommended that the United States Department of Justice increase the ratio of paralegals to attorneys in order to achieve a savings of $13.4 million over three years. Soon thereafter, legislation was proposed in Congress to establish an Office of Paralegal Coordination and Activities in the Department of Justice to work toward the increased use of paralegals in the department.[42] While this proposal was not passed by Congress, the effort is typical of the momentum toward paralegal use throughout the practice of law.

## 3.  The Promotion by Bar Associations

The bar associations assumed a large role in the development of paralegals. This has given great visibility to the field. In 1968, the House of Delegates of the American Bar Association established a Special Committee on Lay Assistants for Lawyers (subsequently renamed the Standing Committee on Legal Assistants), and resolved:

(1) That the legal profession recognize that there are many tasks in serving client's needs which can be performed by a trained, non-lawyer assistant working under the direction and supervision of a lawyer;

(2) That the profession encourage the training and employment of such assistants. . . .[43]

Most of the state bar associations now have committees that cover the area of paralegal utilization. As we will see in Chapter 5, some of these committees have established guidelines for the use of paralegals in a law office. The real impact on the growth of paralegalism, however, has come from those bar association committees that deal with legal economics and law office management. Such committees have sponsored numerous conferences for practicing attorneys. These conferences, plus articles in bar association journals, have extensively promoted paralegals.

---

[40]*Study of Paralegal Utilization in the California Attorney General's Office*, 23, Management Analysis Section. California Department of Justice, (December 1980).

[41]Assembly Bill No. 2729 (January 21, 1986).

[42]H.R. 5107, 99th Cong., 2d Sess.

[43]Proceedings of the House of Delegates of the American Bar Association, 54 American Bar Association Journal 1017, 1021 (1968).

## 4.  The Organization of Paralegals

Paralegals have been organizing. There are approximately 200 paralegal organizations throughout the country. (See list in Appendix B.) This has greatly helped raise everyone's consciousness about the potential of paralegalism. As indicated earlier, there are two major national associations, the National Federation of Paralegal Associations (NFPA) and the National Association of Legal Assistants (NALA). We will examine the work and the impact of these associations in the chapter on regulation. It is no longer true that attorneys are the sole organized voice speaking for paralegals and shaping the development of the field.

## 5.  The Restructuring of Professions and Occupations Generally

The creation of new careers within an established profession or occupation is not unique to the law.

### Doctors

There are approximately eleven paramedical personnel for every doctor in the United States. The hospital patient confronts a substantial number of non-doctor personnel: registered nurse, practical nurse, inhalation therapist, laboratory technician, occupational therapist, physical therapist, medical record librarian, medical technologist, cytotechnologist, radiologic technologist, radiation therapy technologist, nuclear medical technician, dietician, etc. It has been estimated that in the field of nursing alone, there are hundreds of different programs. The most recent stratification has been the licensing of the *physician assistant,* whose ranks were initially filled by many veterans who were medics or medical corpsmen while members of the armed services.

### Dentists

There are approximately 250 dental assistant training programs, 175 dental hygiene training programs, and 30 dental laboratory technician training programs. The demand for "dental auxiliary personnel" has been steadily increasing.

A more radical development is denturism. A *denturist* is a nondentist who produces and dispenses removable dentures directly to the public. As might be expected, denturists are vigorously opposed by organizations such as the American Dental Association.

### Teachers

Studies have shown that teachers spend from 20% to 70% of their time on nonteaching responsibilities. Teacher aides were initially created to relieve teachers of some of their clerical tasks so that they could spend more time on education. A growing number of aides, however, have been participating directly in the instructional process. It has been estimated that we may reach a ratio of one aide for every two teachers in the various departments of a large school.

### Architects

The American Institute of Architecture reports that the 30,000 American architects need 127,000 supportive personnel in areas such as drafting, estimation, information and data processing, and graphic arts. More than 250 architecture technician programs are currently offered at colleges and institutes.

### Law Enforcement

Auxiliary police, probation aides, and parole aides are becoming a standard part of law enforcement and correctional administration. In police science, for example, numerous programs have been developed to free the police officer from community relations responsibilities through the hiring of police aides so that the police officer can devote more energies to criminal work. The employment of ex-felons as probation and parole aides has been heralded as one of the most significant innovations in the field of corrections.

. . . . . . . . . . . . . .

The development of a new occupation is due to several different but related factors. One of these factors is *technological,* as we have seen. Just as there would be no such thing as an airline pilot without the development of the manned flight, there probably would never be the secretary in the modern sense without the development of the typewriter, telephone, etc.

Another basic factor is *economic.* As occupations become more and more complex (or more and more lucrative), the people who perform them begin to delegate their so-called routine tasks to other people who work for them. Nurses "paraprofessionalized" the field of medicine in this way. New specialists and subspecialists then emerged. Occupations not only "routinized down," but "specialized out." One example of the latter is the bank trust manager who is doing work that attorneys previously did. The ability of trust managers to specialize in one small area of the law allowed them to take away a share of the trust and estate market from attorneys. This was substantially due to economic forces; the generalist attorney simply could not compete with the services offered by this particular kind of banker. The public demand for the services of the latter is too acute for the legal profession to regain its full monopoly. The attorney, of course, saves face by agreeing to refrain from labeling the banker's activities "the practice of law." Underlying such a concession, however, are some elemental forces of economics.

The third major factor influencing the development of occupations is *social.* Society's insistence on universal education, for example, has led to the growth of a large civil-service teacher occupation. Urbanization has launched a variety of occupations, for example, social workers, criminologists, environmentalists, highway patrol officers, etc.

As occupations proliferate, competition among the occupations develops. This competition has led to some artificial results, the most prominent of which is a tendency to draw rigid jurisdictional lines among workers. Social workers are not psychologists; teachers are not social workers; attorneys are not accountants. We know, however, that such categorizations are misleading. Any one job often requires the individual to function within a variety of disciplines. Public school teachers, for example, would be quite surprised if told that they need have no skills in psychology, social work, or "police work" to perform in the urban classroom.

There is, however, security in the outward appearance of definitive boundary lines. Thirty years ago, researchers asked the following question at random: "Who are you?" Most often, they received a geographical answer ("I am a New Yorker"), then an ethnic answer ("I am a Canadian"), and finally an occupational answer ("I am a dentist"). The same question asked today produces an entirely different frequency of responses. An overwhelming majority of the respondents will base their answer on their occupation. We are what we *do*. Hence the increased tendency to insist on sharp career boundaries.

Within particular occupational categories, however, there is considerable turmoil over who should do what. As indicated, delegation within an occupation has created innumerable suboccupations or co-occupations. The best example of this is, again, the nurse. Doctors defined a series of functions that they were overtrained to perform. They then created the role of the nurse to undertake them. Nurses, in turn, defined a similar set of functions within their own sphere and delegated them to a new entity, the licensed practical nurse.

The legal profession is undergoing a comparable phenomenon. Typical of the progression in the law is the experience of the Paraprofessional Law Clinic at a state prison in Graterford, Pennsylvania. A group of inmates were authorized to set up a paralegal "law firm" to serve the needs of fellow inmates who need help processing their legal papers to challenge the validity of their incarceration. No attorneys are involved in the program, except for occasional outside attorneys who lend assistance to the paralegals on particular problems encountered in the firm's caseload. The most frustrating aspect of the program to the paralegals is its success. They have been able to win a large number of cases involving a miscalculation of sentence-time by prison administrators who have the responsibility of counting the day-to-day time owed by the inmates. Apparently the bureaucratic process of identifying the exact release date after deducting time served before trial, time earned for good behavior, etc., is complex. The prison staff often makes mistakes. During the first six months of the firm's existence, the paralegals claim to have had 15,924 days credited to the sentences of 103 inmates. Given the scope of the problem, the paralegals have been deluged with sentence computation cases; they have little time for anything else. While their success rate is a source of satisfaction to them, they are not happy with their caseload because they would prefer to work on cases that involve constitutional law, the so-called test cases. Their plan is to systematize computation cases and train other inmates to undertake them so that they can devote their energies to the more difficult cases. *In effect, these paralegals want to create a class of para-paralegals, or assistant paralegals, through delegation.* And so the process continues, leading potentially to an occupational structure of considerable stratification.

## Note on the Delivery of Legal Services in Other Countries

### England

The English legal profession has two main branches consisting of solicitors and barristers. The *solicitor* handles the day-to-day legal problems of the public with only limited rights to represent clients in certain lower courts. The bulk of litigation in the higher courts is provided by the *barrister*. When representation in such courts is needed, the solicitor arranges for the barrister to enter the case. Solicitors often employ one or more *Legal Executives,* who are the equivalent of the American paralegal. Legal Executives are delegated many responsibilities under the supervision of the solicitor. They undergo extensive training programs and take rigorous examinations at the Institute of Legal Executives. Once qualified, the Legal Executive obtains Fellowship in the Institute and is entitled to use the letters "F.Inst.L.Ex." after his or her name.

### Canada

The Institute of Law Clerks of Ontario defines a *law clerk* as "a trained professional doing independent legal work, which may include managerial duties, under the direction and guidance of a lawyer and whose function is to relieve a lawyer of routine legal and administrative matters and assist him in the more complex ones." The title of legal assistant is more common outside Ontario. The number of legal assistants throughout Canada is estimated to be 4,000. One of the important organizations of legal assistants is the Canadian Association of Legal Assistants.

### Japan

Attorneys are not the only providers of legal services in Japan. A separate category of workers called judicial scriveners has special authority to assist the public in preparation of legal documents such as contracts and deeds. The granting of this authority is conditioned on the successful completion of an examination.

### Cuba

In Cuba, legal assistants work with attorneys in law offices or collectives called *bufetes*. The assistants draft legal documents, interview clients, conduct legal research, file papers in court, negotiate for trial dates, etc.

### Russia

Attorneys-at-law in Russia are organized in lawyers' colleges. Membership in the colleges is granted to three kinds of individuals: first, graduates from university law schools; second, individuals with legal training of six months or more, with experience in judicial work, or at least one year as a judge, governmental attorney, investigator, or legal counsel; and third, persons without legal training but with at least three years' experience. Also, there are nonlawyer notaries who prepare contracts and wills for the public.

### Finland

In Finland, only members of the Finnish Bar Association can use the title of advocate. Advocates, however, do not enjoy an exclusive right of audience in the courts. Litigants can plead their own case or retain a representative who does not have to be an advocate.

### Germany

In Germany, as in many European countries, the *notary* has a major role in legal matters. As a skilled impartial advisor, the notary (who is not necessarily an attorney) oversees the contents of documents to insure that legal transactions will withstand court challenges. Notaries often advise parties on the legal implications of commercial affairs.

## ▮ Section G. Stages in the Development of Paralegalism

Paralegalism became a self-conscious movement in the late 1960s. The following stages, or eras, of development summarize the progress of the field since

| I. | 1967–1971 | The era of **discovery** |
| II. | 1972–1976 | The era of **education** |
| III. | 1977–1981 | The era of **politics** |
| IV. | 1982–1986 | The era of **management** |
| V. | 1987 and on | The era of **credentialization** |

**FIGURE 1.8**

Paralegal Development

then. A single theme characterizes each era, but there is overlap. The five themes have been discussed throughout the history of paralegalism. Yet, one theme dominates in each era.

## 1.  The Era of Discovery

During this time, we were finding out what paralegals are and can do. It was a time of discovery. Attorneys experimented with new roles for nonattorneys in the delivery of legal services. Surveys and studies were undertaken. The results were reported at national conferences and within the literature. Since the results were impressive, the news spread quickly. Attorneys were told that there was a new way to practice law. The discovery of paralegals generated considerable enthusiasm, debate, and controversy. There is little doubt that paralegals are now a fixture in the vast majority of settings where law is practiced. The one possible exception is in some rural areas of the country where it is taking a little longer for attorneys to integrate paralegals into the practice of law. To this extent, the discovery of paralegals is still going on.

This is not to say that most attorneys hire paralegals or use them effectively. The expansion and development of paralegalism has by no means reached its peak. The point, however, is that the day has long passed when it was common within the legal profession to ask, "What's a paralegal?"

## 2.  The Era of Education

In the early 1970s, there was an explosion in the creation of paralegal training programs. The American Bar Association introduced a controversial plan to approve paralegal schools, as we will see in Chapter 4. Texts for paralegals began to emerge from the law publishers. At times, it appeared that few schools were *not* considering the creation of a paralegal program. Today the growth in programs has leveled off; new programs are not as common as they were in the early 1970s.

A more recent development in the field has been the creation of programs for *continuing* education for employed paralegals. Almost every newsletter of paralegal associations throughout the country announces an upcoming seminar on substantive law topics (such as securities fraud or condominium conversions), or on paralegalism issues (such as overtime compensation or networking). These seminars may last several days or part of an afternoon in conjunction with the association's regularly scheduled monthly or annual meeting.

## 3.  The Era of Politics

Politics, of course, has always been part of paralegal history. For example, during the era of education, paralegals began to organize into local and national associations to protect their own interests as well as to pursue their professional development. Between 1977 and 1981, however, a period of intense political debate began both among paralegals and between paralegals and attorneys. While the debate continues today, it is no longer the dominant theme, as it was in those years. For example,

■ The lines were sharply drawn between the National Federation of Paralegal Associations and the National Association of Legal Assistants on the issue of whether the certification of paralegals was premature.

■ There were intensive lobbying drives by paralegal associations to slow down regulatory efforts of some bar associations, and to insure that paralegals would be close participants with attorneys in this regulation. Strategies were planned within most paralegal associations on how to combat problems common to paralegals.

■ New local paralegal associations were formed with the active encouragement of the older associations. Considerable debate existed within some of these new associations over whether to affiliate with the National Federation of Paralegal Associations, with the National Association of Legal Assistants, or to remain unaffiliated.

## 4. The Era of Management

Earlier in this chapter, factors such as economics and efficiency were listed as major reasons for the rapid expansion of paralegal use. While this enthusiasm has not died down, it became clear that the field needed a period of consolidation. Many law offices hired proportionately large numbers of paralegals within a short time. They were encouraged to expand by the promotional literature of the bar associations and by the increased income that the employment of the first paralegal generated. Some studies, however, have shown that a law office's increase in income tends to level off when larger numbers of paralegals are hired.[44]

Furthermore, not all offices are equipped to deal with the administrative problems that are found in an office with diverse personnel. Attorneys, for example, "who endorse the paralegal concept and hire recent graduates are often those whose workload is already too heavy. They have little time to provide individualized on-the-job training. The result is that paralegals feel frustrated with their lack of adequate preparation, and employers are disillusioned with their new employees."[45]

Attorneys are not trained as managers, yet management skills are fundamental to the effective use of paralegals. Hiring law office managers has helped, as has development of the relatively new career of legal administrator, but they have not eliminated the need for attorneys to educate themselves in the principles of management and systemization.

The mentality of the attorney is to work alone. Attorneys are trained to view each case as unique—every case can eventually be fought to the Supreme Court. This mentality and approach do not always encourage the attorney to delegate responsibility effectively. It certainly does not necessarily prepare the attorney to run an office in a businesslike and efficient manner. The skills required to have a law declared unconstitutional are radically different from the skills required to manage people. Unfortunately, paralegals can be one of the victims of this defect in attorney training. It is not enough that paralegals are

[44]Bower, *Can Paralegals Be Profitable?* Michigan Bar Journal 173 (March 1980).
[45]American Bar Association, *NFPA/NALA Focus: Two Perspectives,* 3 Legal Assistant Update 90 (1983).

competent; they must also be *used* competently. Paralegals must be challenged and be secure in their relationship with attorneys and with other law office personnel. This is easier said than done, as we will see in Chapter 3 on employment dynamics.

There are, however, visible signs of change. Greater attention is given by many law schools to the problems of law office administration. The bar associations are also intensifying their efforts in this direction. Slowly, attorneys have come to the realization that the incorporation of paralegals into an office requires careful planning and an understanding of human nature. Management assistance is becoming available. There is now a vast body of experience on which to draw.

An important sign that change is on the way is the relatively recent creation of a new position in the larger law office—the legal assistant manager or paralegal administrator. Many firms with four or more paralegals have added a paralegal administrator to oversee the recruitment, training, assignment, and management of the office paralegals. The paralegal administrator (see Figure 2.2 in Chapter 2 for the different titles used for this position) often reports to an individual with broader management responsibility in the office, such as a legal administrator, office manager, managing partner, or chairperson of the management committee. Almost always, the paralegal administrator is someone with several years of experience as a paralegal who is intrigued by the invitation to move into management. Depending on the size of the office, some still perform paralegal duties on client cases in addition to their management duties. The number of paralegal administrators is growing every day. As indicated earlier, they recently formed a national organization—the Legal Assistant Management Association (LAMA).

Attorneys now realize that they need this kind of specialized help to incorporate paralegals into the practice of law. In the old days, many attorneys had the mistaken notion that they could immediately make a lot of money simply by hiring paralegals. Thankfully, we are moving out of this era.

## 5.  The Era of Credentialization

The dust has not yet settled from all the controversies surrounding paralegalism. By the early 1980s none of the credentialing issues had been settled. Most people agreed that it was premature to launch extensive programs of licensing or certification. While some efforts in this direction were taken, as we will see in Chapter 4, the consensus was that more time was needed to sort out all the factors involved in a program of credentialization.

It is anticipated, however, that this will change. Momentum is building toward developing some form of official credentialization, such as limited licensing. According to Kay Field, former president of the National Association of Legal Assistants:

> Those of us who have worked hard to become qualified legal assistants resent the law firm who hires a high school girl to do the filing, [and] calls her a legal assistant, . . . We all agree that there needs to be some specific standards, but unfortunately we cannot all agree first of all who is to prepare them, secondly how stringent they will be, and lastly, who will enforce them. I say to you, however, that these matters must be addressed by us before they are done for us.[46]

---

[46]K. Field, *Legal Assistants: Where Do We Go from Here?* 10 Facts and Findings 17, 18 (National Association of Legal Assistants, May/June 1984).

President Field and her organization do not advocate licensing, but they do advocate action before it is too late. Intense debate rages among paralegals over the issue of credentialization, which we will examine in Chapter 4. There is a very real danger that while paralegals continue to fight among themselves over the issue, attorneys and legislatures might suddenly step in to impose a scheme of regulation and control that will satisfy no one. Unless paralegals resolve the issue, it will be resolved for them. How could this happen? One possible scenario is as follows: The legislature imposes a license requirement after widespread publicity is given to an incident of negligence committed by an untrained and unqualified paralegal. To prevent such precipitate action by the legislature, it is critical that paralegals collectively decide what they want and how it should be achieved. The next four chapters are designed to provide you with the data you need to participate in this still-emerging aspect of paralegalism.

## ☐ Chapter Summary

A *paralegal* is a person with legal skills who works under the supervision of an attorney or who is otherwise authorized to use those skills; this person performs tasks that do not require all the skills of an attorney and that most secretaries are not trained to perform. It is an exciting time to become a paralegal, even though many questions about the field remain to be resolved. There are three main categories of paralegals: those who are employed by attorneys (the largest), self-employed people working for attorneys, and self-employed people providing their services directly to the public. Within these categories, there is great diversity over the titles that are used. Nor is there universal agreement over the definition of a paralegal, or of the different kinds of paralegals. This diversity and lack of agreement are primarily caused by the fact that at present there are no licensing requirements to be a paralegal. People continue to enter the field by one of three routes: experience, training, or fiat. They do not enter through the vehicle of a unifying licensing system.

Paralegal salaries are influenced by a number of factors: experience, level of responsibility, kind of employer, geographic area, the employer's understanding of the paralegal's role, and the extent to which the paralegal is committed to the field as a career.

Bar associations and paralegal associations have promoted the value of paralegals extensively. The economic impact they have had on the practice of law is the major reason paralegals have flourished and grown so rapidly. In a properly leveraged firm, paralegals can be a "profit center" without any sacrifice in the quality of the service delivered by the firm. In most states, attorneys can charge their clients paralegal fees in addition to traditional attorney fees. Furthermore, under *Missouri v. Jenkins,* there are some cases in which a firm can obtain an award of paralegal fees at market rates from losing parties in litigation. Also, a paralegal can help attorneys redirect some of their energies from nonbillable to billable tasks. A firm operates more efficiently and profitably when it consistently and systematically delegates tasks to competent people with lower billing rates, so that other people with higher billing rates will be available to perform tasks at higher rates. This is not to say, however, that paralegals are always profitable to a firm. Proper use and supervision of paralegals are key components of profitability.

Since the late 1960s, paralegalism has gone through a number of stages. During the era of discovery, people were finding out what paralegals were capable of. This knowledge encouraged hundreds of institutions throughout the country to open paralegal schools during the era of education. The era of politics gave us a proliferation of paralegal associations at the national and local levels to address the emerging issues of this new field. In the era of management, greater attention was given to the ingredients of a successful paralegal-attorney relationship. Recognizing that attorneys have never been famous for their management skills, specialists emerged—for example, legal assistant managers—to help attorneys better integrate paralegals into an office. Today we are in the era of credentialization, during which we are likely to see limited licensing or other forms of official regulation.

# Key Terms

NFPA
NALA
ABA
bar association
LAMA
ALA
paralegal
legal assistant
hybrid titles
independent contractor
freelance paralegal
independent paralegal
contract paralegal
nonparalegal
legal assistant clerk

senior legal assistant
supervising legal assistant
case manager
legal assistant manager
law clerk (America)
authorized practice of law
physician assistant
credentialization
paralegal fees
leveraging
delegation
apprentice
OJT
Standing Committee on Legal
   Assistants
denturist
solicitor

barrister
legal executive
law clerk (Ontario)
notary
profit center
overhead
rule of three
fixed fee
contingency fee
staff attorney
contract attorney
project attorney
associate
nonbillable tasks
fee generating
market rate
*Missouri v. Jenkins*

2

# Paralegal Employment

## ■ Chapter Outline

**Section A. The Job Market**
**Section B. Where Paralegals Work**
Traditional Private Law Firms
Untraditional Private Law Firms
Government
Legal Service/Legal Aid Offices (Civil)
Law Departments of Corporations
Special Interest Groups or
   Associations
Criminal Law Offices
Freelance Paralegals

Service Companies/Consulting Firms
  Related Fields
**Section C. Paralegal Specialties: A**
  **Dictionary of Functions**
**Section D. Finding A Job:**
  **Employment Strategies**
**Section E. The Job Hunting**
  **Notebook**
**Section F. Your Second Job**

## ■ Section A. The Job Market

For many paralegals seeking their first job, these are difficult times. Even many attorneys are having a hard time obtaining their first job. Most employers are inundated with job applications. According to one expert, for every $10,000 in salary you hope to earn as a paralegal, you will need to set aside one month of search time. "So if you want $25,000 per year, your search should take about two and one-half months. But do not be disappointed if it takes longer." [1]

Competition for paralegal jobs is likely to come from several sources:

- Other recent graduates from paralegal training programs
- Secretaries and clerks now working in law offices who want to be promoted into paralegal positions
- Paralegals with a year or more of experience who are seeking a job change
- People with no legal training or experience who walk into an office "cold" seeking a job
- People with no legal training or experience but who have connections (a friend of an important client, a relative of a partner)
- Frustrated attorneys applying for paralegal jobs!

---

[1]Wagner, *Tips & Traps for the New Paralegal*, 8 Legal Assistant Today 78 (March/April 1991).

**FIGURE 2.1**

Where Do
Paralegals Work
and in What
Percentages?

---

I. Traditional private law firms
   A. Small firm—1–10 lawyers (26%)
   B. Medium firm—11–50 lawyers (15%)
   C. Large firm—over 50 lawyers (30%)

II. Untraditional private law firms (3%)

III. Government
   A. Federal government (4%)
   B. State government (2%)
   C. Local government (1%)

IV. Legal Service/Legal Aid Offices (Civil Law) (3%)

V. Law departments of corporations, banks, insurance companies, and other
businesses (8%)

VI. Special interest groups or associations (1%)

VII. Criminal law offices
   A. Prosecutor (1%)
   B. Defense (1%)

VIII. Freelance or independent paralegals (1%)

IX. Service companies/consulting firms (1%)

X. Related fields (3%)
   A. Law librarian
   B. Paralegal teacher
   C. Paralegal supervisor/office administrator
   D. Miscellaneous

---

Fortunately, the last category is relatively small, but such attorneys exist.[2] Recently, for example, a paralegal job announcement drew more than 100 responses from paralegals, plus "four from attorneys."[3]

In this environment, the two keys to success are *information* about the employment scene and *techniques* to market yourself. With these objectives in mind, we turn now to the following themes:

- Places where paralegals work
- Paralegal specialties
- Effective job-finding strategies
- Alternative career options

 Section B. Where Paralegals Work

There are ten major locations where paralegals work. They are summarized in Figure 2.1, along with the approximate percentage of paralegals working in each location.

---

[2]There are even some unemployed attorneys who are angry at bar associations for promoting the hiring of paralegals. "In the current market, a young attorney might well work for the same salary as a paralegal." After all, "bar associations represent lawyers, not paralegals. It must be pointed out that paralegals steal jobs from lawyers recently admitted to the bar." Anonymous, *Buddy, Can You Spare a Job,* 46 The Shingle 25 (Philadelphia Bar Ass'n, Fall 1983).

[3]Zavalney, *The Price of Success,* 6 Texas Lawyer 10 (January 21, 1991).

## 1. Traditional Private Law Firms

Most paralegals today work for *private law firms*. While the need for paralegals may be just as great in the other categories, it is the traditional private law firms that have been doing most of the hiring. A "private" law firm is simply one that generates its income primarily from the fees of individual clients.

There are a number of characteristics of paralegals working for traditional private law firms, particularly the larger ones:

- They are among the highest paid paralegals.
- They tend to experience more law office management and personnel problems than other paralegals.
- They tend to specialize more and hence have less variety in their work assignments.
- They have been the most politically active paralegals in forming associations and in dealing with the bar associations.
- They are predominantly women.

Figure 2.2 presents a survey of the employment of paralegals in many of the largest law firms in the country.

## 2. Untraditional Private Law Firms

Since the mid-1970s a new kind of private law firm (sometimes called a *legal clinic*) has come into existence. It also receives its income from fees, but it differs from the traditional law firm in a number of respects:

- It tends to charge lower fees.
- It tends to serve the middle class.
- It has branch offices that are storefront in character (as opposed to a single downtown office in a plush suite on the 11th floor).
- It tends to have a higher proportion of paralegals (there are more paralegals per attorney than in the traditional private law firm).
- It is more likely to advertise and to use such devices as credit-card payment.

Such law firms have been controversial in the past. The traditional bar generally does not like these firms. The charge is that they are not dignified enough for the professional image that the bar wishes to project. In fact, during the early days, the bar went to court to try to force such firms out of existence. The bar lost, particularly over the issue of whether attorneys were allowed to advertise, as we will see in Chapter 5.

The number of untraditional law firms is relatively small, but they are growing. The fear of losing business has caused many small traditional firms to begin imitating some of the characteristics of the more aggressive new breed.

## 3. Government

The civil service departments of federal, state, and local governments have established standards and classifications for many different kinds of government paralegals. These paralegals work in four main areas of government:

- In the office of the chief government attorney, e.g., attorney general, corporation counsel

**FIGURE 2.2**   Employment in Selected Large Law Firms*

Generally, a law firm is more likely to hire paralegals if it has hired them in the past, if it has a paralegal manager, and if it has many attorneys in the firm. This table tries to provide as much of this information as possible for selected—not all—large law firms in the country. Many law firms have branch offices. When you find two numbers separated by a slash, for example, 94/70, the first number is the total number in all offices of the firm (including headquarters), and the second number is the number in the city listed.

| Number of Attorneys | Title of Paralegal Manager | Number of Paralegals |
|---|---|---|
| **Alabama** | | |
| *Birmingham* | | |
| Balch & Bingham (66) | | 19 |
| Bradley, Arant, Rose (97) | | 23 |
| Burr & Forman (67) | | 12 |
| Sirote & Permutt (94/70) | | 32 |
| **Alaska** | | |
| *Anchorage* | | |
| Guess & Rudd (28) | | 6 |
| Perkins Coie (336/19) | | 85/5 |
| **Arizona** | | |
| *Phoenix* | | |
| Beus, Gilbert & Morrill (38) | | 15 |
| Brown & Bain (125/79) | Paralegal Coordinator | 48/24 |
| Bryan, Cave, McPheeters (367/20) | | 76/8 |
| Fennemore Craig (131/100) | | 15 |
| Jennings, Strouss & Salmon (106) | | 17 |
| Lewis & Roca (135/124) | Associate & Paralegal Coordinator | 38 |
| Mariscal, Weeks & McIntyre (33) | | 8 |
| Meyer, Hendricks, Victor (56) | | 18 |
| O'Connor, Cavanagh, Anderson (129/123) | Legal Administrator | 24 |
| Snell & Wilmer (238/171) | Paralegal Administrator | 50/39 |
| Squire, Sanders & Dempsey (430/29) | | 80/7 |
| Streich, Lang, Weeks (140/125) | | 50/37 |
| **California** | | |
| *Century City* | | |
| Irell & Manella (204/140) | Director of Legal Assistants | 41 |
| O'Melveny & Myers (560/64) | | 105/7 |
| *Costa Mesa* | | |
| Latham & Watkins (54) | Administrative Paralegal | 13 |
| Paul, Hastings, Janofsky (43) | | 9 |
| Rutan & Tucker (106) | | 11 |

Continued

**FIGURE 2.2**   Employment in Selected Large Law Firms*—*Continued*

| Number of Attorneys | Title of Paralegal Manager | Number of Paralegals |
|---|---|---|
| **California** | | |
| **Los Angeles** | | |
| Adams, Duque & Hazeltine (89) | | 20 |
| Alschuler, Grossman & Pines (41) | Paralegal Coordinator | 7 |
| Baker & Hostetler (503/85) | | 78/24 |
| Baker & McKenzie (1580/70) | Paralegal Coordinator | 11 |
| Bottum & Feliton | Paralegal Manager | |
| Bryan, Cave, McPheeters (367/38) | Administrator | 76/19 |
| Buchalter, Nemer, Fields (179/124) | Paralegal Coordinator; General Litigation Paralegal Supervisor | 55 |
| Cox, Castle & Nicholson (95) | | 11 |
| Dewey, Ballantine (394/39) | Senior Paralegal | 81/8 |
| Fadem, Berger & Norton | Paralegal Supervisor | |
| Finnegan, Henderson, Farabow | Director, Legal Assistant Services | |
| Frandzel & Share | Litigation Manager | |
| Gendel, Raskoff, Shapiro (49) | Paralegal Director | 9 |
| Gibson, Dunn & Crutcher (725/202) | | 145/60 |
| Graham & James (385/104) | | 83/19 |
| Hufstedler, Miller, Kaus | Paralegal Coordinator | 10 |
| Iwasaki, Thomas & Sheffield | Paralegal Coordinator | |
| Jones, Day, Reavis (1259/123) | Litigation Group/Administrative Assistant | 21 |
| Kindel & Anderson | | 11 |
| Latham & Watkins (570/257) | Senior Legal Assistant | 115/45 |
| Lewis, D'Amato, Brisbois (197/104) | | 33/25 |
| Loeb & Loeb (189/89) | Paralegal Administrator | 26 |
| Lyon & Lyon (50) | Paralegal & Data Processing Manager | 14 |
| Manatt, Phelps, Rothenberg (105) | | 15 |
| McCutchen, Black, Verleger (95) | | 15 |
| McKenna, Conner & Cuneo (197/43) | Paralegal Coordinator | 12 |
| Milbank, Tweed, Hadley (504/81) | | 12 |
| Mitchell, Silberberg & Knupp (155/153) | | 22 |
| Morgan, Lewis & Bockius (672/125) | | 113/21 |
| Morrison & Foerster (588/118) | | 210/15 |
| Munger, Tolles & Olson (83) | | 35 |
| Musick, Peeler & Garrett (117) | | 20 |
| O'Melveny & Myers (560/270) | Supervisor of Litigation Paralegal Services | 136/80 |
| Paul, Hastings, Janofsky (388/150) | Legal Assistant Administrator | 55/31 |
| Pillsbury, Madison, Sutro (625/46) | | 162/50 |
| Pretty, Schroeder, Brueggemann | Paralegal Supervisor | |

Continued

**FIGURE 2.2**   Employment in Selected Large Law Firms*—*Continued*

| Number of Attorneys | Title of Paralegal Manager | Number of Paralegals |
|---|---|---|
| **California** | | |
| *Los Angeles* | | |
| Rosen & Winston | Paralegal Coordinator | |
| Sheppard, Mullin, Richter (249/146) | | 21/18 |
| Sidley & Austin (707/93) | Legal Assistant Coordinator | 25 |
| Skadden, Arps, Slate (1133/132) | Administrative Supervisor | 77 |
| Tuttle & Taylor (61) | | 16 |
| Wyman, Bautzer, Kuchel (131/118) | Legal Assistant Manager | 22 |
| *Newport Beach* | | |
| Gibson, Dunn & Crutcher (725/93) | | 165/15 |
| O'Melveny & Myers (533/52) | | 136/10 |
| *Oakland* | | |
| Crosby, Heafey, Roach (192/225) | | 37 |
| Donahue, Gallagher, Thomas | Paralegal Administrator | |
| King, Shapiro, Mittleman | Legal Assistant Coordinator | |
| Lempres & Wulfsberg | Legal Assistant Coordinator | |
| *Palo Alto* | | |
| Brown & Bain (125/33) | | 48/20 |
| Cooley, Godward, Castro (174/64) | Legal Assistant Manager | 20 |
| Brobeck, Phleger & Harrison (414/53) | | 136/12 |
| Fenwick & West | | 30 |
| Ware & Freidenrich (89) | | 14 |
| Wilson, Sonsini, Goodrich (214) | Legal Assistant Coordinator | 63 |
| *Riverside* | | |
| Best, Best & Krieger (114/74) | | 27 |
| *Sacramento* | | |
| Kronick, Moskovitz, Tiedemann (60) | | 12 |
| Downey, Brand, Seymour (63) | | 10 |
| *San Diego* | | |
| Baker & McKensie (1580/27) | Paralegal Manager | 16 |
| Gray, Cary, Ames (183/170) | Paralegal Coordinator | 28 |
| Jennings, Engstrand & Henrickson (57) | | 13 |
| Latham & Watkins (570/64) | | 174/16 |
| Luce, Forward, Hamilton (146/134) | | 22 |
| Schall, Boudreau & Gore | Legal Assistant Supervisor | |
| Seltzer, Caplan, Wilkins (53) | Paralegal Administrator | 24 |
| Solomon, Ward, Seidenwurm | Paralegal Coordinator | |
| Stutz, Gallagher & Artiano | Paralegal Coordinator | |

Continued

**FIGURE 2.2**   Employment in Selected Large Law Firms*—*Continued*

| Number of Attorneys | Title of Paralegal Manager | Number of Paralegals |
|---|---|---|
| **California** | | |
| *San Francisco* | | |
| Brobeck, Phleger & Harrison (414/224) | Legal Assistant Manager | 136/62 |
| Bronson, Bronson & McKinnon (169/115) | Legal Assistant Administrator | 64/25 |
| Cooley, Godward, Castro (174/93) | Legal Assistant Administrator | 36 |
| Farella, Braun & Martel (75) | Director, Human Resources & Legal Support; Litigation Coordinator | 39 |
| Graham & James (385/133) | | 83/36 |
| Handcock, Rothert & Bunshof (53) | | 43 |
| Heller, Ehrman, White (355/193) | Legal Assistant Coordinator | 143/55 |
| Howard, Rice, Nemerovski (100) | Legal Assistant Administrator(s) | 41 |
| Jackson, Tufts, Cole (52) | | 24 |
| Jeffer, Mangels, Butler (90/74) | Legal Assistant Coordinator | 15 |
| Landels, Ripley & Diamond (82) | Legal Assistant Manager | 21 |
| Long & Levit | Legal Assistant Manager | 26 |
| McCutchen, Doyle, Brown (274/198) | Paralegal Manager | 59/52 |
| Morrison & Foerster (588/245) | Legal Assistant Coordinator | 175/125 |
| Orrick, Herrington (258/167) | Legal Assistant Manager | 62/34 |
| Pettit & Martin (249/148) | Legal Assistant Manager | 37/20 |
| Pillsbury, Madison, Sutro (625/321) | Director, Legal Assistant & Computer Litigation Support Departments | 116/58 |
| Sedgwick, Detert, Moran (167/92) | | 39 |
| Shartsis, Friese & Ginsburg (32) | Legal Assistant Supervisor | 15 |
| Thelen, Marrin, Johnson (361/168) | Legal Assistant Manager | 86/62 |
| *San Jose* | | |
| Gibson, Dunn & Crutcher (738/19) | | 165/15 |
| Hopkins & Carley (44) | | 11 |
| Pillsbury, Madison, Sutro (625/44) | Information Resources Coordinator | 162/14 |
| *Santa Monica* | | |
| Haight, Brown & Bonesteel (150/140) | Paralegal Training & Development Coordinator | 44/41 |
| **Colorado** | | |
| *Denver* | | |
| Coghill & Goodspeed | Paralegal Manager | |
| Davis, Graham & Stubbs (189/155) | Paralegal Coordinator | 35/30 |
| Gorsuch, Kirgis, Campbell (63) | Legal Assistant Coordinator | 19 |
| Hall & Evans (101) | | 43 |
| Holland & Hart (229/144) | Legal Assistant Coordinator | 37/22 |

Continued

**FIGURE 2.2**    Employment in Selected Large Law Firms*—*Continued*

| Number of Attorneys | Title of Paralegal Manager | Number of Paralegals |
|---|---|---|
| **Colorado** | | |
| *Denver* | | |
| Holme, Roberts & Owen (199/139) | | 54/40 |
| Hopper, Kanouff, Smith | Legal Assistant/Manager | |
| Kirkland & Ellis (425/45) | Legal Assistant Supervisor | 13 |
| Rothgerber, Appel, Powers | | 15 |
| Sherman & Howard (171/124) | Litigation Paralegal Supervisor | 30/23 |
| Tilly & Graves | Senior Legal Assistant | |
| **Connecticut** | | |
| *Hartford* | | |
| Cummings & Lockwood (159/28) | | 13 |
| Day, Berry & Howard (220/151) | Legal Assistant Supervisor | 50/39 |
| Murtha, Cullina, Richter (92) | | 16 |
| Robinson & Cole (141/120) | | 29 |
| Schatz & Schatz (75) | | 11 |
| Shipman & Goodwin (80) | | 23 |
| Tyler, Cooper & Alcorn (84) | | 14 |
| Updike, Kelly & Spellacy | Manager, Litigation Paralegals | 12 |
| *Stamford* | | |
| Cummings & Lockwood (159/100) | | 25/13 |
| Kelly, Drye & Warren (409/30) | | 47/10 |
| *Waterbury* | | |
| Carmody & Torrance (37) | | 12 |
| Gager & Henry (34) | | 12 |
| **Delaware** | | |
| *Wilmington* | | |
| Bayard, Handelman & Murdoc (28) | | 12 |
| Elzufor, Austin & Drexler | Paralegal Supervisor | |
| Morris, James, Hitchens (38) | | 16 |
| Morris, Nichols, Arscht (47) | | 14 |
| Potter, Anderson & Corroon (51) | | 9 |
| Prickett, Jones, Elliott (44) | | 11 |
| Richards, Layton & Finger (76) | Paralegal Administrator | 14 |
| Young, Conaway, Stargatt (42) | Paralegal Supervisor | 14 |
| **District of Columbia** | | |
| Akin, Gump, Strauss (485/233) | Legal Assistant Staff Manager | 68 |
| Anderson, Kill, Orlick (28) | | 16 |
| Arent, Fox, Kintner (251/218) | Legal Assistant Administrator | 40 |
| Arnold & Porter (341/294) | Coordinator, Legal Assistant Programs | 96 |

Continued

**FIGURE 2.2**   Employment in Selected Large Law Firms*—*Continued*

| Number of Attorneys | Title of Paralegal Manager | Number of Paralegals |
|---|---|---|
| **District of Columbia** | | |
| Baker & Hostetler (503/96) | Paralegal Coordinator | 78/15 |
| Beverage & Diamond (59) | | 16 |
| Brownstein, Zeidman & Schomer (69) | | 26 |
| Bryan, Cave, McPheeters (367/49) | | 76/13 |
| Cadwalader, Wickersham & Taft (295/62) | Coordinator of Legal Assistants | 11 |
| Covington & Burling (282/273) | | 76 |
| Crowell & Moring (182) | Coordinator, Legal Assistants | 45 |
| Davis, Polk & Wardwell (433/36) | Legal Assistant Coordinator | 123/20 |
| Dewey, Ballantine (394/66) | | 81/24 |
| Dickstein, Shapiro & Morin (160/135) | | 58/32 |
| Dow, Lohnes & Albertson (224/166) | Transaction Coordinator; Manager of Information Services | 47/31 |
| Dunnells, Duvall, Bennett (65) | Paralegal Coordinator | 12 |
| Finnegan, Henderson, Farabow (103) | Director, Legal Assistant Services | 30 |
| Fried, Frank, Harris (397/126) | | 143/34 |
| Fulbright & Jaworski (685/72) | | 160/14 |
| Gibson, Dunn & Crutcher (725/101) | | 165/20 |
| Heron, Burchette, Ruckert | | 28 |
| Hogan & Hartson (334/289) | Legal Assistant Administrator | 43/35 |
| Howrey & Simon (174) | Legal Assistant Administrator | 61 |
| Hunton & Williams (471/63) | | 146/16 |
| Jones, Day, Reavis (1259/123) | Litigation Group/Administrative Assistant | 221/46 |
| Kaplan, Russin & Vecchi (138) | | 19 |
| Keller & Heckman (43) | | 14 |
| Kirkland & Ellis (425/81) | Legal Assistant Supervisor | 110/26 |
| Kirkpatrick & Lockhart (315/84) | | 72/17 |
| Melrod, Redman & Gartlan (66) | Paralegal Coordinator | 13 |
| McDermott, Will & Emery (520/71) | Paralegal Coordinator | |
| McKenna, Conner & Cuneo (197/122) | Paralegal Coordinator | 36/28 |
| Morgan, Lewis & Bockius (672/169) | Personnel Administrator | 130/25 |
| Newman & Holtzinger (69) | Senior Paralegal | 22 |
| Patton, Boggs & Blow (173/143) | | 23/13 |
| Piper & Marbury (269/71) | Legal Assistant Administrator | 10 |
| Powell, Goldstein, Frazer (241/44) | Legal Assistant Coordinator | |
| Reed, Smith, Shaw (387/105) | | 85/18 |
| Shaw, Pittman, Potts (248/231) | Director of Legal Assistants | 52/46 |
| Sidley & Austin (707/124) | Legal Assistant Administrator | 27 |
| Skadden, Arps, Slate (1133/164) | Paralegal Supervisor | |
| Squire, Sanders & Dempsey (430/82) | | 80/14 |
| Steptoe & Johnson (232/220) | Director of Practice Support | 42 |
| Sutherland, Asbill & Brennan (244/134) | Chairman, Legal Assistant Committee | 51/32 |

Continued

**FIGURE 2.2**   Employment in Selected Large Law Firms*—*Continued*

| Number of Attorneys | Title of Paralegal Manager | Number of Paralegals |
|---|---|---|
| **District of Columbia** | | |
| Swidler & Berlin (86) | Paralegal Coordinator | 45 |
| Venable, Baetjer & Howard (295/67) | | 42/15 |
| Weil, Gotshal & Manges (552/46) | Paralegal Coordinator | 13 |
| Wiley, Rein & Fielding (105) | Legal Assistant Administrator | 21 |
| Williams & Connolly (126) | | 20 |
| Willkie, Farr & Gallagher (350/46) | Legal Assistant Supervisor | 17 |
| Wilmer, Cutler & Pickering (200) | Practice Area Manager | 99 |
| **Florida** | | |
| **Fort Lauderdale** | | |
| Fleming, O'Bryan & Fleming (34) | | 10 |
| Holland & Knight (284/27) | | 39/9 |
| Ruden, Barnett, McClosky (103) | | 33 |
| **Miami** | | |
| Anderson, Moss, Parks | Legal Assistant Coordinator | |
| Floyd, Pearson, Richman (31) | | 8 |
| Fowler, White, Burnett (54) | | 14 |
| Greenberg, Traurig, Hoffman (134) | Paralegal Manager | 38 |
| Mershon, Sawyer, Johnson (93) | | 12 |
| McDermott, Will & Emery (520/30) | | 90/8 |
| Mershon, Sayer, Johnston (77) | | 11 |
| Shutts & Bowen (83) | Paralegal Supervisor | 25 |
| Steel, Hector & Davis (143/111) | | 18/12 |
| Valdes-Fauli, Cobb, Petrey | Paralegal Supervisor | |
| **Orlando** | | |
| Akerman, Senterfitt & Eidson (42) | | 9 |
| Baker & Hostetler (503/35) | | 78/15 |
| Gray, Harris & Robinson (32) | | 10 |
| Lowndes, Drosdick, Doster (48) | | 9 |
| McGuire, Voorhis & Wells (59) | | 22 |
| Rumberger, Kirk, Caldwell | Legal Assistant Coordinator | |
| **Tampa** | | |
| Carlton, Fields, Ward (150/107) | | 35/22 |
| Fowler, White, Gillen (77) | Director of Personnel and Recruiting | 21 |
| Holland & Knight (284/74) | Legal Assistant Coordinator | 39/16 |
| Rudnick & Wolfe (246/17) | Personnel Manager | 37/8 |
| Shackleford, Farrior, Stallings (58) | | 10 |
| Trenam, Simmons, Kemker (75) | | 16 |

Continued

**FIGURE 2.2**   Employment in Selected Large Law Firms*—*Continued*

| Number of Attorneys | Title of Paralegal Manager | Number of Paralegals |
|---|---|---|
| **Georgia** | | |
| | **Atlanta** | |
| Alston & Bird (221/179) | Legal Assistant Coordinator | 36 |
| Arnall, Golden & Gregory (62) | Senior Litigation Paralegal | 21 |
| Hurt, Richardson, Garner (89) | Paralegal Coordinator | 16 |
| Hyatt & Rhoads (49) | | 17 |
| Jones, Day, Reavis (1259/102) | | 221/17 |
| Kilpatrick & Cody (172/124) | | 35 |
| King & Spalding (270/230) | Paralegal Coordinator | 73 |
| Long, Aldridge & Norman (90) | Human Resources Manager | 22 |
| Neely & Player (42) | | 14 |
| Parker, Johnson, Cook | Coodinator, Paralegal Program | |
| Powell, Goldstein, Frazer (241/197) | Paralegal Manager | 53 |
| Schwall, Ruff & Goodman | Director of Administration | |
| Smith, Gambrell & Russell (90) | Paralegal Coordinator | 10 |
| Stokes, Shapiro, Fussell | Senior Legal Assistant | |
| Sutherland, Asbill & Brennan (244/110) | Paralegal Specialist | 51/29 |
| Troutman, Sanders, Lockerman (165) | | 28 |
| **Hawaii** | | |
| Cades, Schutte, Fleming (74) | | 16 |
| Goodsill, Anderson, Quinn (81) | | 20 |
| **Illinois** | | |
| | **Chicago** | |
| Altheimer & Gray (179) | Director, Corporate Support Group | 27 |
| Baker & McKenzie (1580/174) | Paralegal Coordinator | 20 |
| Bell, Boyd & Lloyd (206/165) | | 27/23 |
| Cassiday, Schade & Gloor | Paralegal Director | |
| Chapman & Cutler (257/241) | | 18/16 |
| Clausen, Miller, Gorman (121) | | 18 |
| Coffield, Ungaretti, Harris (90) | | 17 |
| Gardner, Carton & Douglas (204/163) | | 28/23 |
| Hinshaw, Culbertson, Moelmann (279/155) | Paralegal Coordinator | 32/16 |
| Hopkins & Sutter (287/182) | Paralegal Coordinator | 31/19 |
| Jenner & Block (289/248) | Paralegal Manager | 101/91 |
| Jones, Day, Reavis (1259/83) | | 221/13 |
| Katten, Muchin & Zavis (341/283) | | 42 |
| Keck, Mahin & Cate (351/212) | Legal Assistant Coordinator | 39/29 |
| Kirkland & Ellis (425/259) | Manager of Legal Assistants; Legal Assistant Coordinator | 110/77 |
| Latham & Watkins (570/67) | | 174/12 |

Continued

**FIGURE 2.2**    Employment in Selected Large Law Firms*—*Continued*

| Number of Attorneys | Title of Paralegal Manager | Number of Paralegals |
|---|---|---|
| **Illinois** | | |
| **Chicago** | | |
| Levin & Funkhouser (18) | | 14 |
| Lord, Bissel & Brook (275/227) | | 41/33 |
| Mayer, Brown & Platt (566/381) | Paralegal Coordinator | 113/91 |
| McDermott, Will & Emery (520/309) | | 90/57 |
| Peterson, Ross, Schloerb (163/147) | | 35 |
| Phelan, Pope & John (74) | | 18 |
| Pretzel & Stouffer | Supervisor of Litigation Paralegals | |
| Ross & Hardies (166/128) | | 15 |
| Rudnick & Wolfe (246/219) | Personnel Manager | 37/31 |
| Sachnoff & Weaver (103) | | 23 |
| Schiff, Hardin & Waite (213/198) | | 31 |
| Seyfarth, Shaw, Fairweather (318/176) | | 29/14 |
| Sidley & Austin (707/414) | Paralegal Recruiting Coordinator | 174/89 |
| Skadden, Arps, Slate (1133/106) | Legal Assistant Supervisor | |
| Sonnenschein, Nath (300/207) | Paralegal Administrator | 24 |
| Vedder, Price, Kaufman (155/138) | | 17 |
| Wildman, Harrold, Allen (194/191) | Paralegal Coordinator | 24 |
| Winston & Strawn (404/298) | Paralegal Manager; Legal Assistant Supervisor | 33 |
| **Indiana** | | |
| **Indianapolis** | | |
| Baker & Daniels (182/139) | | 33 |
| Barnes & Thornburg (202/118) | | 27/18 |
| Bingham, Summers, Welsh (54) | Legal Assistant Supervisor | 12 |
| Bose, McKinney & Evans (48) | | 13 |
| Ice, Miller, Donadio (165) | Chief Operating Officer | 19 |
| **Kentucky** | | |
| **Lexington** | | |
| Greenebaum, Doll & McDonald | Paralegal Coordinator | |
| Stoll, Keenon & Park (63) | | 14 |
| Wyatt, Tarrant & Combs (162/35) | | |
| **Louisville** | | |
| Brown, Todd & Heyburn (131/100) | Paralegal Coordinator | 22 |
| Greenebaum, Doll & McDonald (67) | Administrative Paralegal Coordinator | 11 |
| Stites & Harbison (100) | Paralegal Administrator | |
| Wyatt, Tarrant & Combs (162/89) | Professional Personnel Administrator | 28 |

Continued

**FIGURE 2.2**    Employment in Selected Large Law Firms*—*Continued*

| Number of Attorneys | Title of Paralegal Manager | Number of Paralegals |
|---|---|---|
| **Louisiana** | | |
| **New Orleans** | | |
| Adams & Reese (86) | | 50 |
| Chaffe, McCall, Phillips | Paralegal Coordinator | |
| Carmouche, Gray, Hoffman (55) | | 13 |
| Deutsch, Kerrigan & Stiles | Senior Paralegal | |
| Jones, Walker, Waechter (161/153) | Paralegal Manager, General Litigation Section | 41 |
| McGlinchey, Stafford, Cellini (137/123) | | 58 |
| Milling, Benson, Woodward (71) | | 22 |
| Phelps, Dunbar, Marks (161/95) | | 36/25 |
| Stone, Pigman, Walther (62) | | 13 |
| **Maine** | | |
| **Bangor** | | |
| Eaton, Peabody, Bradford (30) | | 14 |
| **Portland** | | |
| Bernstein, Shur, Sawyer (50) | | 17 |
| Drummond, Woodsum, Plimpton (41) | | 8 |
| Poerce, Atwood, Scribner (83) | | 18 |
| Verrill & Dana (70) | | 16 |
| **Maryland** | | |
| **Baltimore** | | |
| Frank, Bernstein, Conaway (200/133) | Assistant Director of Recruitment | 35/25 |
| Gordon Feinblatt, Rothman (72) | | 16 |
| Melnicove, Kaufman, Weiner (78) | | 8 |
| Miles & Stockbridge (192/107) | | 39/25 |
| Montedonico & Mason (52) | | 10 |
| Ober, Kalor, Grimes (107) | | 21 |
| Piper & Marbury (269/195) | Recruiting Administrator | 44/36 |
| Semmes, Bowen & Semmes (165/144) | | 44 |
| Smith, Somerville & Case (89) | | 18 |
| Tydings & Rosenberg (32) | Paralegal Supervisor | 12 |
| Venable, Baetjer & Howard (295/167) | | 53 |
| Weinberg & Green (146/134) | | 18 |
| Whiteford, Taylor & Preston (138) | | 41 |
| **Massachusetts** | | |
| **Boston** | | |
| Bingham, Dana & Gould (236/225) | | 41 |
| Brown, Rudnick, Freed (114) | Corporate Paralegal Coordinator; Litigation Paralegal Supervisor | 23 |

Continued

**FIGURE 2.2**  Employment in Selected Large Law Firms*—*Continued*

| Number of Attorneys | Title of Paralegal Manager | Number of Paralegals |
|---|---|---|
| **Massachusetts** | | |
| **Boston** | | |
| Burns & Levinson (103) | | 34 |
| Campbell & Associates (31) | | 12 |
| Choate, Hall & Stewart (165) | | 23 |
| Fish & Richardson (38) | | 21 |
| Foley, Hoag & Eliot (149/138) | | 28/25 |
| Gaston & Snow (272/174) | Paralegal Coordinator | 55/30 |
| Goodwin, Proctor & Hoar (288) | Director of Administration & Human Resources | 39 |
| Goulston & Storrs (91) | | 16 |
| Hale & Dorr (324/293) | Manager of Paralegal Services | 63 |
| Hill & Barlow (93) | | 22 |
| Hutchins & Wheeler (83) | | 13 |
| Mintz, Levin, Cohn (188/167) | | 36 |
| Nutter, McClennen & Fish (168/160) | Paralegal Coordinator | 20 |
| Palmer & Dodge (144) | Legal Assistant Coordinator | 22 |
| Rackemann, Sawyer & Brewster (60) | Paralegal Administrator | 17 |
| Ropes & Gray (312/289) | Director of Paralegal Services; Senior Legal Assistant Coordinator | 47/44 |
| Sullivan & Worcester (133/114) | Paralegal Manager | 28/23 |
| Testa, Hurwitz & Thiebeault (82) | Paralegal Manager | 13 |
| Warner & Stackpole (49) | Executive Director | 10 |
| Widett, Slater & Goldman (83) | Director of Personnel | 15 |
| **Worcester** | | |
| Bowditch & Dewey (59) | Paralegal Administrator | 16 |
| Fletcher, Tilton & Whipple | Paralegal Manager | |
| **Michigan** | | |
| **Detroit** | | |
| Butzel, Long, Gust (85) | Legal Assistant Coordinator | 16 |
| Clark, Klein & Beaumont (86) | | 10 |
| Dickinson, Wright, Moon (213/138) | | 37 |
| Dykema Gossett (312/162) | | 37 |
| Honigman, Miller, Schwartz (236/182) | Manager of Legal Assistants | 55/40 |
| Kitch, Saurbier, Drutchas (90) | | 23 |
| Miller, Canfield, Paddock (239/123) | | 43 |
| Plunkett & Cooney (150/105) | | 25 |
| Vandeveer, Garzia, Tonkin (48) | | 28 |
| **Grand Rapids** | | |
| Miller, Johnson, Snell (77) | | 13 |
| Varnum, Riddering, Schmidt (119) | | 18 |
| Warner, Norcross & Judd (96) | Director of Administration | 16 |

Continued

**FIGURE 2.2**   Employment in Selected Large Law Firms*—*Continued*

| Number of Attorneys | Title of Paralegal Manager | Number of Paralegals |
|---|---|---|
| **Minnesota** | | |
| **Minneapolis** | | |
| Bowman & Brooke (23) | | 19 |
| Dorsey & Whitney (352/269) | Senior Legal Assistant Supervisor | 70/45 |
| Faegre & Benson (233/184) | | 47/39 |
| Fredrikson & Byron (100) | | 22 |
| Gray, Plant, Mooty (86) | | 19 |
| Larkin, Hoffman, Daly (84) | | 22 |
| Leonard, Street & Deinar (89) | | 17 |
| Lindquist, Vennum (94) | Human Resources Manager | 15 |
| Mackall, Crounse & Moore (49) | | 11 |
| Maslon, Edelman, Borman (43) | | 20 |
| Oppenheimer, Wolff & Donnelly (251/178) | Legal Assistant Manager | 36/27 |
| Popham, Haik, Schnobrich (175/129) | Legal Assistant Manager | 39/33 |
| Robins, Kaplan, Miller (190/117) | Legal Assistant Manager | 60/52 |
| **St. Paul** | | |
| Briggs & Morgan (143/76) | Paralegal Coordinator | 24 |
| Doherty, Rumble & Butler (77) | | 13 |
| **Mississippi** | | |
| **Jackson** | | |
| McDavid, Noblin & West (8) | | 8 |
| Thomas, Price, Alston (27) | | 15 |
| Watkins, Ludlam & Stennis (50) | Legal Assistant Coordinator | 18 |
| **Missouri** | | |
| **Kansas City** | | |
| Blackwell, Sanders, Matheny (72) | | 12 |
| Polsinelli, White, Vardeman | Legal Assistant Coordinator | |
| Shook, Hardy & Bacon (151/127) | Paralegal Supervisor | 44 |
| Shughart, Thomson & Kilroy | Paralegal Coordinator | |
| Stinson, Mag & Fizzell (146/133) | Litigation Paralegal Coordinator | 23 |
| **St. Louis** | | |
| Armstrong, Teasdale, Schlafly (162/118) | | 22 |
| Bryan, Cave, McPheeters (367/181) | | 76/37 |
| Coburn, Croft & Putzell (70) | | 14 |
| Greensfelder, Hemker & Gale (81) | | 11 |
| Husch, Eppenberger, Donohue (74) | | 10 |
| Lewis, Rice & Fingersh (141/90) | | 18 |
| Peper, Martin, Jensen (80) | | 14 |
| Sandberg, Phoenix & von Gontard (37) | | 10 |
| Stolar Partnership (44) | | 12 |
| Thompson & Mitchell (176/124) | | 20/16 |

Continued

**FIGURE 2.2**　Employment in Selected Large Law Firms*—*Continued*

| Number of Attorneys | Title of Paralegal Manager | Number of Paralegals |
|---|---|---|
| **Nebraska** | | |
| **Omaha** | | |
| Fraser, Stryker, Vaughn (31) | | 7 |
| Kutak, Rock & Campbell (205/90) | Manager of Litigation Support Services | 44/14 |
| **Nevada** | | |
| **Las Vegas** | | |
| Lionel, Sawyer & Collins (52) | | 12 |
| **Reno** | | |
| Hill, Cassas, deLipkau (135) | | 23 |
| **New Hampshire** | | |
| **Concord** | | |
| Sullivan, Hollis & Soden (40) | | 26 |
| **Manchester** | | |
| Devine, Millimet, Stahl (48) | | 16 |
| McLane, Graf, Raulerson (50) | | 16 |
| Sheehan, Phinney, Bass (52) | | 19 |
| **New Jersey** | | |
| **Morristown** | | |
| Pitney, Hardin, Kipp (155) | Administrator of Litigation Paralegals | 15 |
| Porzio, Bromberg & Newman (30) | Paralegal Coordinator | 40 |
| Riker, Danzig, Scherer (116) | Paralegal Manager | 20 |
| Stanely & Fisher (116) | Paralegal Manager, Litigation | 32 |
| **Newark** | | |
| Carpenter, Bennett & Morrissey (78) | | 13 |
| Crummy, Del Deo, Dolan (105) | Paralegal Administrator | 25 |
| McCarter & English (182/159) | Paralegal Coordinator | 48/34 |
| Sills, Cummis, Zuckerman (138/128) | Paralegal Coordinator | 40 |
| **Roseland** | | |
| Hannoch Weisman (150/128) | Director of Paralegal Service | 33 |
| Lowenstein, Sandler, Kohl (132/115) | Corporate Supervisor; Litigation Paralegal Supervisor | 27 |
| **Woodbridge** | | |
| Greenbaum, Rowe, Smith (81) | Legal Assistant Coordinator | 21 |
| Wilentz, Goldman & Spitzer (138/122) | Paralegal Manager | 34/28 |

Continued

**FIGURE 2.2**   Employment in Selected Large Law Firms*—*Continued*

| Number of Attorneys | Title of Paralegal Manager | Number of Paralegals |
|---|---|---|
| **New Mexico** | | |
| **Albuquerque** | | |
| Eaves, Darling & Porter | Supervising Paralegal | |
| Modrall, Sperling, Roehl (68) | Legal Assistant Coordinator | 21 |
| Poor Law Firm (37) | | 10 |
| **New York** | | |
| **Buffalo** | | |
| Damon & Morey (55) | | 17 |
| Hodgson, Russ, Andrews (135/108) | | 34 |
| Jaeckle, Fleischmann & Mugel (81) | | 17 |
| Moot & Sprague (61) | | 15 |
| Phillips, Lytle, Hitchcock (136/98) | | 52/34 |
| Saperston & Day (80) | | 17 |
| **New York City** | | |
| Anderson, Kill, Olick (182/150) | | 100 |
| Battle, Fowler (127) | | 21 |
| Bower & Gardner (218/212) | | 54 |
| Breed, Abbott & Morgan (117) | Legal Personnel Coordinator | 20 |
| Brown & Wood (242/195) | Legal Assistant Supervisor | 49 |
| Cadwalader, Wickersham & Taft (295/208) | Director of Legal Assistants | 40/36 |
| Cahill, Gordon & Reindel (287/273) | Legal Assistant Coordinator | 76/68 |
| Carter, Ledyard & Milburn (76) | Paralegal Supervisor | 27 |
| Chadbourne & Parke (276/220) | Legal Assistant Manager | 55 |
| Cleary, Gottlieb, Steen (429/270) | Coordinator of Paralegal Services | 66 |
| Coudert Brothers (360/172) | Legal Personnel Manager | 61/33 |
| Cravath, Swaine & Moore (309/301) | Manager of Legal Assistants | 117 |
| Davis, Polk & Wardwell (433/378) | Manager, Corporate Assistants; Manager, Litigation Assistants | 123/114 |
| Debevoise & Plimpton (349/288) | Manager, Legal Assistant Department | 81 |
| Dewey, Ballantine (394/287) | Legal Assistant Administrator | 81/53 |
| Dilworth, Paxson, Kalish (145) | Paralegal Supervisor | 20 |
| Dreyer & Traub (95) | | 37 |
| Fish & Neave (102) | | 35 |
| Fitzpatrick, Cella, Harper (49) | | 27 |
| Fried, Frank, Harris (397/250) | Legal Assistant Manager | 143/75 |
| Hughes, Hubbard & Reed (244/179) | | 35/27 |
| Kaye, Scholer, Fierman (399/305) | Manager of Legal Assistants | 88/65 |
| Kramer, Levin, Nessen (140) | Paralegal Coordinator | 33 |
| LeBoeuf, Lamb, Leiby (405/218) | Paralegal Supervisor | 110/80 |
| Lord, Day, Lord (205/193) | | 45 |

Continued

**FIGURE 2.2**   Employment in Selected Large Law Firms*—*Continued*

| Number of Attorneys | Title of Paralegal Manager | Number of Paralegals |
|---|---|---|
| **New York** | | |
| | **New York City** | |
| Milbank, Tweed, Hadley (504/350) | | 116/91 |
| Milgram, Thomajan & Lee (85) | | 21 |
| Morgan & Finnegan (76) | Paralegal Coordinator | 34 |
| Mudge, Rose, Guthrie (304/237) | | 72/52 |
| Patterson, Belknap, Webb (144/138) | Paralegal Manager | 40/35 |
| Parker, Chapin, Flattau (130) | | 21 |
| Paul, Weiss, Rifkind (411/382) | Paralegal Supervisor | 116 |
| Proskauer, Rose, Goetz (425/350) | Corporate Paralegal Supervisor | 90/84 |
| Reid & Priest (203/159) | | 28/20 |
| Rogers & Wells (337/255) | Litigation Legal Assistant Supervisor; Corporate Legal Assistant Coordinator; Real Estate Legal Assistant Coordinator | 40 |
| Rosenman & Colin (229/223) | Paralegal Coordinator | 40 |
| Rubin, Baum, Levin (54) | | 24 |
| Schulte, Roth & Zabel (162/161) | Litigation Legal Assistant/ Supervisor | 34 |
| Shey & Gould (292/252) | Legal Assistant Manager; Corporate Paralegal Supervisor | 82/69 |
| Shearman & Sterling (624/478) | Legal Assistant Manager | 112/105 |
| Sidley & Austin (707/66) | Paralegal Manager | 174/20 |
| Simpson, Thacher & Bartlett (442/431) | Paralegal Coordinator | 128 |
| Skadden, Arps, Slate (1133/583) | Director of Legal Assistant Services | 433 |
| Stroock, Stroock & Lavan (339/250) | Litigation Paralegal Supervisor | 74/29 |
| Sullivan & Cromwell (366/303) | Director of Paralegal Services | 73/60 |
| Weil, Gotshall & Manges (552/392) | Legal Assistant Manager | 137/108 |
| White & Case (462/311) | Manager of Legal Assistants; Coordinator of Evening Legal Assistants | 64 |
| Whitman & Ransom (255/149) | | 34/24 |
| Willkie, Farr & Gallagher (350/281) | Corporate Supervisor; Director of Litigation Services | 74/58 |
| Wilson, Elser, Moskowitz (379/222) | Legal Assistant Supervisor | 30 |
| Winthrop, Stimson, Putnam (289/222) | Legal Assistant Manager | 42/29 |
| Winston & Strawn (404/91) | Legal Assistant Manager | 62 |
| | **Rochester** | |
| Chamberlain, D'Amanda, Oppenheimer (31) | | 13 |
| Harter, Secrest & Emery (93) | | 30 |
| Harris, Beach, Wilcox (96) | | 15 |
| Nixon, Hargrave, Devans (259/142) | Manager of Paralegal Services | 46 |
| Phillips, Lytle, Hitchcock (136/24) | | 52/10 |
| Woods, Oviatt, Gilman (40) | | 11 |

Continued

**FIGURE 2.2**   Employment in Selected Large Law Firms*—*Continued*

| Number of Attorneys | Title of Paralegal Manager | Number of Paralegals |
|---|---|---|
| **New York** | | |
| *Syracuse* | | |
| Bond, Schoeneck & King (143/98) | | 29/19 |
| Hiscock & Barclay (95) | | 26/11 |
| **North Carolina** | | |
| *Charlotte* | | |
| Kennedy, Covington, Lobdell (74/68) | | 17/13 |
| Moore & Van Allen (62) | Legal Assistant Coordinator | 18 |
| Robinson, Bradshaw & Hinson (66) | | 14 |
| Smith, Helms, Mulliss (147/64) | | 60/19 |
| *Greensboro* | | |
| Smith, Helms, Mulliss (147/69) | | 60/41 |
| *Raleigh* | | |
| Hunton & Williams (471/33) | | 142/10 |
| Maupin, Taylor, Ellis (59) | | 12 |
| Moore & Van Allen | Legal Assistant Coordinator | |
| Poyner & Spruill (106/70) | | 28/17 |
| *Winston-Salem* | | |
| Petree, Stockton & Robinson (70) | | 10 |
| Womble, Carlyle, Sandridge (182/125) | | 48 |
| **Ohio** | | |
| *Cincinnati* | | |
| Dinsmore & Shohl (133/122) | Paralegal Administrator | 38 |
| Frost & Jacobs (167/141) | | 49 |
| Graydon, Heed & Ritchey (63) | | 12 |
| Keating, Muething & Klekamp (61) | | 15 |
| Taft, Stettinius & Hollister (154/133) | Administrator | 26 |
| Thompson, Hine & Flory (348/65) | | 61/20 |
| *Cleveland* | | |
| Arter & Hadden (337/126) | Paralegal Coordinator | 77/20 |
| Baker & Hostetler (503/173) | Paralegal Manager | 78/29 |
| Benesch, Friedlander, Coplan (174/127) | | 28/19 |
| Calfee, Halater & Griswold (150/147) | | 24 |
| Hahn, Laeser & Parks (73) | | 16 |
| Jones, Day & Reavis (1259/228) | Administrative Assistant | 221/41 |
| McDonald, Hopkins, Burke (62) | | 18 |
| Squire, Sanders & Dempsey (430/185) | Chairman, Legal Assistant Personnel Committee | 80/33 |
| Thompson, Hine & Flory (348/166) | Legal Assistant Manager | 61/29 |

Continued

**FIGURE 2.2**   Employment in Selected Large Law Firms*—*Continued*

| Number of Attorneys | Title of Paralegal Manager | Number of Paralegals |
|---|---|---|
| **Ohio** | | |
| **Columbus** | | |
| Arter & Hadden (337/61) | | 77/10 |
| Baker & Hostetler (503/84) | | 78/10 |
| Bricker & Eckler (82) | | 22 |
| Carlile, Patchen, Murphy (33) | | 9 |
| Emens, Hurd, Kegler (63) | | 11 |
| Porter, Wright, Morris (214/134) | Paralegal Administrator | 40 |
| Schottenstein, Zox & Dunn (79) | | 10 |
| Schwartz, Kelm, Warren (39) | Director, Paralegal Services | 12 |
| Squire, Sanders & Dempsey (430/87) | | 80/18 |
| Thompson, Hine & Flory (348/36) | | 61/13 |
| Vorys, Sater, Seymour (255/203) | Paralegal Administrator | 56 |
| **Toledo** | | |
| Fuller & Henry (53) | | 10 |
| Nathan & Roberts | Paralegal Administrator | |
| Schumaker, Loap & Kendrick (69) | | 7 |
| **Oklahoma** | | |
| **Oklahoma City** | | |
| Crowe & Dunlevy (91) | | 22 |
| **Tulsa** | | |
| Conner & Winters (45) | | 9 |
| Gable & Gotwals (46) | | 7 |
| Hall, Estill, Hardwick (79) | | 32 |
| **Oregon** | | |
| **Portland** | | |
| Bullivant, Houser (61) | Paralegal Manager | 14 |
| Davis, Wright, Tremaine (238/60) | | 22/9 |
| Miller, Nash, Wiener (104) | Coordinator, Litigation Legal Assistants | 15 |
| Schwabe, Williamson & Wyatt (151/125) | | 21 |
| Sears, Lubersky, Bledsoe (86) | | 15 |
| Stoel, Rives, Boley (220/153) | Legal Assistant Manager | 40/11 |
| **Pennsylvania** | | |
| **Philadelphia** | | |
| Ballard, Spahr, Andrews (218/158) | Senior Legal Assistant | 51/32 |
| Blank, Rome, Comisky (227/204) | | 35 |
| Clark, Ladner, Fortenbaugh (51) | | 17 |
| Cohen, Shapiro, Polisher (83) | | 14 |
| Cozen & O'Connor (136/106) | | 46 |

Continued

**FIGURE 2.2**   Employment in Selected Large Law Firms*—*Continued*

| Number of Attorneys | Title of Paralegal Manager | Number of Paralegals |
|---|---|---|
| **Pennsylvania** | | |
| | **Philadelphia** | |
| Dechert, Price & Rhoades (384/254) | Paralegal Coordinator | 82/58 |
| Dilworth, Paxson, Kalish (155/116) | Paralegal Supervisor, Litigation Department | 27/20 |
| Drinker, Biddle & Reath (217/178) | Senior Legal Assistant | 56/36 |
| Duane, Morris, Heckscher (223/167) | | 56/42 |
| Fox, Rothchild, O'Brien (118) | | 25 |
| Hoyle, Morris & Kerr (60) | Legal Assistant Administrator | 36 |
| Mesirov, Gelman, Jaffe (102) | | 33 |
| Montgomery, McCracken, Walker (160/146) | Paralegal Coordinator | 35/32 |
| Morgan, Lewis & Bockius (672/173) | | 113/50 |
| Pechner, Dorfman, Wolffe (62) | | 11 |
| Pepper, Hamilton & Scheetz (355/177) | Legal Assistant Administrator | 73/39 |
| Rawle & Henderson (72) | | 19 |
| Reed, Smith, Shaw (387/61) | Paralegal Coordinator | 24 |
| Saul, Ewing, Remick (183/152) | Litigation Support Manager | 42 |
| Schnader, Harrison, Segal (245/199) | Supervisor of Legal Assistants | 45 |
| Stradley, Ronon, Stevens (80) | | 19 |
| White & Williams (101) | | 42 |
| Wolf, Block, Schorr (244/221) | | 40/38 |
| | **Pittsburgh** | |
| Buchanan Ingersoll (190/174) | Legal Assistant Coordinator | 33 |
| Eckert, Seamans, Cherin (201/155) | Paralegal Coordinator | 27/24 |
| Kirkpatrick & Lockhart (315/190) | Legal Assistant Coordinator | 83 |
| Klett, Lieber, Rooney (63) | Director of Paralegal Services | 13 |
| Reed, Smith, Shaw (387/201) | Paralegal Manager | 85/37 |
| | **Wilkes-Barre** | |
| Rosenn, Jenkins & Greenwald (46) | | 18 |
| **Rhode Island** | | |
| | **Providence** | |
| Edwards & Angell (170/93) | | 34 |
| Hinckley, Allen, Snuder (78) | | 22 |
| Gamma Law Associates | Paralegal Manager | |
| Roberts, Carroll, Feldstein | Paralegal Manager | |
| Tillinghast, Collins & Graham (51) | | 14 |
| **South Carolina** | | |
| | **Charleston** | |
| Sinkler & Boyd (50/19) | Legal Assistant Coordinator | 15/9 |
| Young, Clement, Rivers | Paralegal Coordinator | |

Continued

**FIGURE 2.2**   Employment in Selected Large Law Firms*—*Continued*

| Number of Attorneys | Title of Paralegal Manager | Number of Paralegals |
|---|---|---|
| **South Carolina** | | |
| *Columbia* | | |
| Nelson, Mullins, Riley (86) | Legal Assistant Coordinator | 35 |
| *Greenville* | | |
| Leatherwood, Walker, Todd (40) | | 13 |
| Wyche, Burgess, Freeman (22) | | 8 |
| **Tennessee** | | |
| *Nashville* | | |
| Baker, Worthington, Crossley (94/34) | | 16 |
| Bass, Berry & Sims (80/77) | | 25 |
| Boult, Cummings, Conners (33) | Administrator/Paralegal Coordinator | 13 |
| Farris, Warfield, Kanaday (46) | | 13 |
| Hartwell, Martin & Stegall (24) | | 10 |
| Manier, Herod, Hollabaugh (41) | | 11 |
| **Texas** | | |
| *Austin* | | |
| Brown, Maroney, Oaks (81) | Legal Assistant Coordinator | 32 |
| Clark, Thomas, Winters (74) | | 17 |
| Graves, Dougherty, Hearon (71) | | 13 |
| Fulbright & Jaworski (685/33) | | 160/12 |
| Johnson & Gibbs (312/32) | | 40/13 |
| Small, Craig, Werkenthin (63) | | 25 |
| Vinson & Elkins (503/33) | | 174/21 |
| *Dallas* | | |
| Akin, Gump, Strauss (485/167) | Legal Assistant Staff Manager | 109/32 |
| Arter & Hadden (337/61) | Paralegal Coordinator | 24 |
| Baker & Botts (407/76) | Legal Assistant Coordinator | 13 |
| Baker, Mills, Glast (88) | | 22 |
| Carrington, Coleman, Sloman (81) | Legal Assistant Administrator | 18 |
| Cowles & Thompson (69) | | 25 |
| Fulbright & Jaworski (685/66) | | 160/16 |
| Gardere & Wynne (200) | | 46 |
| Gibson, Dunn & Crutcher (738/33) | | 165/11 |
| Goodwin, Carlton & Maxwell (100) | | 20 |
| Haynes & Boone (246/161) | Legal Assistant Coordinator; Litigation Support Coordinator | 47 |
| Hughes & Luce (156/133) | | 30/26 |
| Jackson & Walker (216/144) | Legal Assistant Manager | 35/25 |
| Jenkins & Gilchrist (199/148) | | 32/24 |
| Johnson & Gibbs (312/230) | | 40 |

Continued

**FIGURE 2.2**   Employment in Selected Large Law Firms*—*Continued*

| Number of Attorneys | Title of Paralegal Manager | Number of Paralegals |
|---|---|---|
| **Texas** | | |
| **Dallas** | | |
| Jones, Day, Reavis (1259/162) | Administrative Assistant | 221/40 |
| Locke, Purnell, Rain (190/183) | | 33 |
| Page & Addison (28/24) | | 16/14 |
| Riddle & Brown (50) | | 20 |
| Shank, Irwin, Conant | Paralegal Coordinator | |
| Strasburger & Price (183/169) | Legal Assistant Coordinator | 51 |
| Thompson & Knight (213/198) | Legal Assistant Coordinator | 46 |
| Vial, Hamilton, Koch (85) | | 29 |
| Wendel Turley (21) | | 24 |
| Winstead, McGuire, Sechrest (180/128) | Paralegal Coordinator | 41/37 |
| **El Paso** | | |
| Grambling & Mounce (37) | | 11 |
| Kemp, Smith, Duncan (82) | | 18 |
| Scott, Hulse, Marshall (40) | | 15 |
| **Fort Worth** | | |
| Cantey & Hanger (75) | | 16 |
| Kelly, Hart & Hallman (76) | | 14 |
| **Houston** | | |
| Andrews & Kurth (287/202) | Legal Assistant Coordinator for Litigation | 93/27 |
| Arnold, White & Durkee (67) | Paralegal Coordinator | 27 |
| Baker & Botts (407/259) | Legal Assistant Manager | 95/62 |
| Baker, Brown, Sharman (60) | Legal Assistant Coordinator | 15 |
| Beirne, Maynard & Parsons (21) | | 12 |
| Bracewell & Patterson (207/155) | | 40/36 |
| Butler & Binion (171/140) | Legal Assistant Coordinator | 45/28 |
| Davis & McFall (33) | Paralegal Coordinator | 20 |
| Fulbright & Jaworski (685/337) | Coordinator, Legal Assistants | 160/68 |
| Hutcheson & Grundy (66) | Legal Assistant Coordinator | 14 |
| Jackson & Walker (216/54) | | 35/13 |
| Liddell, Sapp, Zivley (178/130) | | 35/27 |
| Lorance & Thompson (33) | | 11 |
| Mayer, Day, Caldwell (70) | | 16 |
| Porter & Clements (47) | | 11 |
| Sewell & Riggs (53) | | 11 |
| Sheinfeld, Maley & Key (71) | | 17 |
| Vinson & Elkins (495/387) | Legal Assistant Manager; Legal Assistant Recruiter | 174/146 |
| Weil, Gotshal & Manges (552/60) | Legal Assistant Coordinator | 22 |

Continued

**FIGURE 2.2**   Employment in Selected Large Law Firms*—*Continued*

| Number of Attorneys | Title of Paralegal Manager | Number of Paralegals |
|---|---|---|
| **Texas** | | |
| *San Antonio* | | |
| Cox & Smith (82) | | 19 |
| Fulbright & Jaworski (685/48) | | 160/12 |
| Groce, Locke & Hebdon (82) | Personnel Administrator | 27 |
| Matthews & Branscomb (82) | Legal Assistant Supervisor | 19 |
| **Utah** | | |
| *Salt Lake City* | | |
| Ray, Quinney & Nebeker (73) | | 11 |
| Van Cott, Bagley, Cornwall (78) | | 11 |
| **Virginia** | | |
| *Fairfax* | | |
| Hazel & Thomas (166/61) | | 32 |
| Wilkes, Artis, Hedrick (40) | | 13 |
| *McLean* | | |
| McGuire, Woods, Battle (336/67) | | 94/19 |
| Watt, Tieder, Killian (46) | | 13 |
| *Richmond* | | |
| Browder & Russell (44) | Paralegal Manager | 17 |
| Hunton & Williams (471/241) | Legal Services Manager; Human Resources Administrator | 146/77 |
| Mays & Valentine (131/111) | | 29 |
| McGuire, Woods, Battle (336/180) | Legal Assistant Administrator | 111/58 |
| Sands, Anderson, Marks (42) | | 12 |
| Williams, Mullen, Christian (58) | Personnel Manager | 18 |
| **Washington** | | |
| *Seattle* | | |
| Betts, Patterson & Mines (51) | Paralegal Coordinator | 15 |
| Bogle & Gates (235/159) | | 78/53 |
| Davis, Wright, Tremaine (238/125) | Legal Assistant Coordinator | 20 |
| Foster, Pepper & Shefelman (138/105) | | 21 |
| Gibson, Dunn & Crutcher | | 18 |
| Helsell, Fetterman, Martin (49) | | 13 |
| Lane, Powell, Spears (241/133) | Paralegal Manager | 43/37 |
| Oles, Morrison & Rinker (32) | | 10 |
| Perkins Coie (336/178) | Legal Assistant Coordinator | 85/47 |
| Preston, Thorgrimson, Shidler (207/125) | Coordinator/Litigation Legal Assistants and Clerks | 41/25 |
| Reed, McClure, Moceri (46) | | 18 |
| Riddall, Williams, Bullitt (73) | Personnel Manager | 14 |

Continued

**FIGURE 2.2**   Employment in Selected Large Law Firms*—*Continued*

| Number of Attorneys | Title of Paralegal Manager | Number of Paralegals |
|---|---|---|
| **Washington** | | |
| Seattle | | |
| Stoel, Rives, Boley (220/60) | | 40/11 |
| Williams, Kastner & Gibbs (80) | Paralegal Coordinator | 18 |
| Wilson, Smith, Cochran | | 18 |
| **West Virginia** | | |
| Charleston | | |
| Bowles, Rice, McDavid (66/47) | | 17/12 |
| Huntington | | |
| Jenkins, Fenstermaker, Krieger (16) | | 5 |
| **Wisconsin** | | |
| Milwaukee | | |
| Foley & Lardner (410/210) | | 56/25 |
| Geofrey & Kahn (88) | | 23 |
| Quarles & Brady (207/162) | | 27/22 |
| Whythe & Hirschboeck (60) | | 10 |

*Sources: West's Legal Directory; National Association of Legal Placement Directory; National Law Journal (September 26, 1988; September 18, 1989; September 24, 1990); PIC's National Law Network; California Lawyer (November 1990); Legal Assistants Management Association Directory (1990); and independent checking.

- In the general counsel's office of individual agencies
- In other departments of individual agencies, e.g., enforcement department, civil rights division
- In the office of individual legislators, legislative committees, legislative counsel, or the legislative drafting office of the legislature

### Federal Government

Thousands of paralegals work for the federal government in the capital (Washington, D.C.) and the main regional cities of the federal government (Boston, New York, Philadelphia, Atlanta, Chicago, Kansas City, Dallas, Denver, Seattle, and San Francisco). The most important job classification for this position is the *Paralegal Specialist* (GS-950).[4] This position is described in the following excerpt from the *Office of Personnel Management Handbook,* X-118. Note the extensive responsibility that these individuals have. The ending of this description is quite remarkable: paralegals perform "duties requiring discretion and independent judgment" which "may or may not be performed under the direction of a lawyer." There is no doubt that government paralegals have a range of responsibility that is broader than paralegals working anywhere else in the country.

---

[4]GS stands for *General Schedule,* which is the main pay-scale system used by the federal government. The number 950 is the occupational code for the Paralegal Specialist.

### Description of Work

Paralegal specialist positions involve such activities as (a) legal research, analyzing legal decisions, opinions, rulings, memoranda, and other legal material, selecting principles of law, and preparing digests of the points of law involved; (b) selecting, assembling, summarizing and compiling substantive information on statutes, treaties, contracts, other legal instruments, and specific legal subjects; (c) case preparation for civil litigation, criminal law proceedings or agency hearings, including the collection, analysis and evaluation of evidence, e.g., as to fraud and fraudulent and other irregular activities or violations of laws; (d) analyzing facts and legal questions presented by personnel administering specific Federal laws, answering the questions where they have been settled by interpretations of applicable legal provisions, regulations, precedents, and agency policy, and in some instances preparing informative and instructional material for general use; (e) adjudicating applications or cases on the basis of pertinent laws, regulations, policies and precedent decisions; or (f) performing other paralegal duties requiring discretion and independent judgment in the application of specialized knowledge of particular laws, regulations, precedents, or agency practices based thereon. These duties may or may not be performed under the direction of a lawyer.

The largest numbers of Paralegal Specialists are employed in the following units of the federal government:[5]

> U.S. Department of Health & Human Services
> U.S. Department of Justice
> U.S. Court System
> U.S. Department of Treasury
> U.S. Department of Transportation
> U.S. Department of the Army
> U.S. Department of the Interior
> U.S. Equal Employment Opportunity Commission
> U.S. General Services Administration
> U.S. Department of Energy
> U.S. Department of State
> U.S. Department of Labor

Paralegal Specialists are not the only individuals using special legal skills in the federal government. The following law-related occupations, filled mainly by nonattorneys, should be considered:

Legal Clerk
Legal Technician
Immigration Specialist
Foreign Affairs Analyst/Officer
Civil Rights Analyst
Social Services Representative
Equal Employment Opportunity
  Specialist
Hearings and Appeals Officer
Legal Instruments Examiner
Public Utilities Specialist
Tax Law Specialist
Patent Advisor
Patent Examiner

Contract Specialist
Contract Representative
Labor Relations Specialist
Employee Relations Specialist
Wage & Hour Compliance Specialist
Mediation Specialist
Investigator
Regulatory Analyst
Legislative Analyst
Land Law Examiner
Copyright Examiner
Copyright Technician
Railroad Retirement Claims
  Examiner

[5] J. Harris, *The Paralegal's Guide to U.S. Government Jobs,* 3 (Federal Reports, 1986).

Patent Technician
Intelligence Analyst
Internal Revenue Officer
Import Specialist
Environmental Protection Specialist
Security Specialist
Freedom of Information Act
    Specialist

Estate Tax Examiner
Workers Compensation Claims
    Examiner
Unemployment Compensation
    Claims Examiner

When there is an opening for a Paralegal Specialist or for one of the positions listed above, the individual agency with this opening may do its own recruiting or may recruit through the Office of Personnel Management[6] (formerly called the Civil Service Commission), which oversees hiring procedures throughout the federal government. For a list of job information centers in your area where you can inquire about paralegal and other law-related positions in the federal government, see Appendix H.

### State Government

When looking for work as a paralegal in the *state* government, find out if your state has established civil service classification standards for paralegal positions. See Figure 2.3 for some of this data. In addition, locate a directory of agencies, commissions, boards, or departments for your state, county, and city governments. You want to find a list of all (or most of the major) government offices. Many local public libraries will have a government directory. Alternatively, check the offices of state and local politicians, such as governor, mayor, commissioner, alderman, representative, or senator. They will probably have such a directory. Finally, check your local phone book for the sections on government offices. Contact as many of them as you can to find out whether they employ paralegals. If you have difficulty obtaining an answer to this question, find out where their attorneys are located. Sections or departments that employ attorneys will probably be able to tell you about paralegal employment opportunities. In your search, include a list of all the courts in the state. Judges and court clerks may have legal positions open for nonattorneys.

In addition to the statewide personnel departments listed in Figure 2.3, many government offices have their own personnel department that will list employment openings. Also, whenever possible, talk with attorneys and paralegals who already work in these offices. They may know of opportunities that you can pursue.

Do not limit your search to paralegal or legal assistant positions. Legal jobs for nonattorneys may be listed under other headings, such as research assistant, legal analyst, administrative aide, administrative officer, executive assistant, examiner, clerk, and investigator. As we have seen, this is also true for employment in the federal government.

## 4.  Legal Service/Legal Aid Offices (Civil Law)

Community or neighborhood legal service offices and legal aid offices exist throughout the country. (See *Directory of Legal Aid & Defender Offices*, published by the National Legal Aid & Defender Association.) They obtain most of their funds from the government, often in the form of yearly grants to provide

[6]1900 E. St. NW, Wash. D.C. 20415 (202-606-1800).

**FIGURE 2.3**   Summary Chart—Survey of State Government Job Classifications for Paralegals

| GOVERNMENT | POSITION | RESPONSIBILITIES | QUALIFICATIONS | SALARY |
|---|---|---|---|---|
| **Alabama**<br>Personnel Dept.<br>64 N. Union St., Rm. 402<br>Montgomery, AL 36130-2301<br>205-261-3389 | Legal Assistant<br>10/22/82<br>(11503) | ■ Perform legal research<br>■ Draft pleadings<br>■ Interview witnesses in preparation for trial<br>■ Conduct routine investigations<br>■ Prepare and interpret legal documents in noncomplex cases<br>■ Prepare summaries of documents<br>■ Perform office administrative duties | Graduation from an accredited legal assistant program<br>OR<br>possession of a legal assistant certificate | $15,366–$23,369 per year |
| Other positions to check in Alabama: Docket Clerk (11501); Legal Opinions Clerk (11505); Contract Clerk (119.267-018); Legal Investigator (119.267-022); Title Examiner (119.287-010); Appeals Referee (119.267-014). | | | | |
| **Alaska**<br>Department of Administration<br>Division of Personnel<br>Pouch C<br>Juneau, AK 99811<br>907-465-4430 | Paralegal Assistant I<br>4/1/84<br>(7105-13) | ■ Interview clients<br>■ Obtain statements and affidavits<br>■ Conduct investigations<br>■ Perform legal research<br>■ Coordinate witness scheduling<br>■ Represent clients at hearings | Certificate from a state paralegal training program<br>OR<br>Associate of Arts program with a major in paralegal, criminal justice, or law studies<br>OR<br>3 years experience as legal secretary, court clerk, etc. | $26,460–$36,048 per year |
| Other positions to check in Alaska: Legal Assistant II (7106); Investigator II (7767); Latent Fingerprint Examiner (7756). | | | | |
| **American Samoa**<br>Department of Human Resources<br>American Samoa Government<br>Pago Pago, AS 96799<br>684-633-4489 | Legal Assistant I<br>(E2-09-7524) | ■ Conduct routine investigations<br>■ Perform legal research<br>■ Review citations for traffic court cases<br>■ Interview witnesses<br>■ Present traffic cases in court<br>■ Prepare orders to show cause | A bachelor's degree with a major in police science, corrections, or a related field | $9,317–$15,167 per year |
| Other positions to check in American Samoa: Legal Assistant II (E2-10-7525); Legal Assistant III (E2-11-7526); Paralegal (12-13-7552). | | | | |
| **Arizona**<br>Dept. of Administration<br>Personnel Division<br>1831 West Jefferson St.<br>Phoenix, AZ 85007<br>602-542-5482 | Legal Assistant<br>1/11/77<br>(74510) | ■ Perform legal research<br>■ Help prepare briefs and pleadings<br>■ Take statements and depositions<br>■ Interview complainants<br>■ Index laws | 2 years of college study in relevant courses (experience involving legal terminology and legal research procedures can substitute for the education requirement) | $16,618–$23,937 per year |

Continued

**FIGURE 2.3**   Summary Chart—Survey of State Government Job Classifications for Paralegals—*Continued*

| GOVERNMENT | POSITION | RESPONSIBILITIES | QUALIFICATIONS | SALARY |
|---|---|---|---|---|
| **Arizona** | | ■ Serve papers<br>■ Help answer court calendars | | |
| *Other positions to check in Arizona: Legal Assistant I, Legal Assistant II (Child Support Enforcement Administration)* | | | | |
| **Arkansas**<br>Office of Personnel<br>  Management<br>P.O. Box 3278,<br>1509 West 7th St.<br>Little Rock, AR 72203<br>501-682-1507 | Legal Assistant<br>7/1/77<br>7/1/79-R<br>(R177) | ■ Receive legal questions from agency attorneys<br>■ Collect and evaluate information on the questions<br>■ Provide reports (orally or in memo form) to attorneys<br>■ File pleadings and briefs<br>■ Maintain law library | The education equivalent of completion of 1 year of law school, including a course in legal bibliography | $14,118 per year |
| **California**<br>State Personnel Board<br>801 Capitol Mall<br>P.O. Box 944201<br>Sacramento, CA 94244-<br>  2010<br>916-445-5291<br>ALSO:<br>Dept. of Personnel<br>  Administration<br>1115 11th St., 1st Fl.<br>Sacramento, CA 95814-<br>  3860<br>916-322-5193 | Legal Assistant<br>3/13/75<br>9/20/78<br>(CW55, 1820) | ■ Assist in reviewing legal documents to determine if they comply with the law<br>■ Analyze proposed legislation<br>■ Digest and index opinions, testimony, depositions, and other trial documents<br>■ Perform research of legislative history<br>■ Assist in drafting complaints and other pleadings<br>■ Perform routine legal research | 2 years of legal clerical experience in California government<br><u>OR</u><br>3 years in a law office | $2,009–$2,418 per month |
| | Legal Analyst<br>7/2/81<br>(LE18, 5237) | ■ Investigate and analyze facts<br>■ Coordinate witnesses<br>■ Draft interrogatories<br>■ Draft pleadings<br>■ Summarize discovery documents<br>■ Supervise other staff | 1 year as a state Legal Assistant<br><u>OR</u><br>2 years in another paralegal job and 15 semester hours or 22 quarter units in a paralegal curriculum or equivalent to graduation from college | $2,278–$2,700 per month |
| **Colorado**<br>Dept. of Personnel<br>State Centennial Bldg.<br>1313 Sherman St.<br>Denver, CO 80203<br>303-866-2321 | Legal Assistant<br>6/23/82<br>("A" 77500)<br>("B" 77501) | ■ Provide discovery and investigation assistance<br>■ Digest and index legal documents<br>■ Check legal citations<br>■ Take notes during deposition | Bachelor's degree and approved paralegal studies program (experience can substitute for general education) | Legal Assistant A $2,025–$2,713 per month |

Continued

**FIGURE 2.3**   Summary Chart—Survey of State Government Job Classifications for Paralegals—*Continued*

| GOVERNMENT | POSITION | RESPONSIBILITIES | QUALIFICATIONS | SALARY |
|---|---|---|---|---|
| Colorado | | ▪ Prepare simple pleadings and briefs<br>▪ Maintain case files<br>▪ Prepare statistical reports<br>▪ Perform legal research | | Legal Assistant B $2,344–$3,141 per month |
| Connecticut<br>Personnel Div.<br>Dept. of Administration Services<br>165 Capital Ave.<br>Hartford, CT 06106-1630<br>203-566-3081 | Paralegal Specialist I<br>10/1/87<br>(6140)(NL16) | ▪ Act as liaison between legal and clerical staff<br>▪ Perform legal research<br>▪ Assist in drafting legal documents<br>▪ Maintain tickler systems<br>▪ Present written and oral argument at administrative hearings<br>▪ Maintain records | 2 years of experience working for a lawyer<br>OR<br>A designated number of college courses in law or paralegal studies<br><br>(Note: substitutions are allowed) | $970–$1,168 biweekly |
| Other positions to check in Connecticut: Paralegal Specialist II (6141, NL 20); Legal Office Administrator (5373, 9389c, MP 18). | | | | |
| Delaware<br>State Personnel Office<br>Townsend Bldg.<br>P.O. Box 1401<br>Dover, DE 19901<br>302-736-4195 | Legal Assistant<br>8/75<br>(12846) | ▪ Review documents to assess consistency with law<br>▪ Summarize cases<br>▪ Draft pleadings, deeds, and other documents<br>▪ Interview clients and witnesses<br>▪ Assist in investigations<br>▪ File documents in court | Enough education and/or experience to demonstrate competence in research, drafting, filing, interviewing, record keeping, and communication (oral and written) | $17,400 per year |
| Other positions to check in Delaware: License Investigator (Dept. of Administrative Services); Clerk of Court I (Family Court) (12311); Law Library Assistant. | | | | |
| District of Columbia<br>D.C. Personnel Office<br>613 G St. NW, Rm 306<br>Wash. D.C. 20001-3798<br>202-727-6406 | Paralegal Specialist | Similar to Paralegal Specialist positions in the federal government. (See page 82.) | | |
| Florida<br>Dept. of Administration<br>Division of Personnel Management Services<br>330 Carlton Bldg.<br>Tallahassee, FL 32399<br>904-488-5823 | Paralegal Specialist<br>1/1/84<br>(7703) (0807) | ▪ Take affidavits from victims and witnesses<br>▪ Perform legal research under supervision<br>▪ Maintain case files and tickler system | Completion of legal assistant training course<br>OR<br>Bachelor's degree with major in allied legal services<br>OR | $1,220–$1,975 per month |

Continued

**FIGURE 2.3**   Summary Chart—Survey of State Government Job Classifications for Paralegals—*Continued*

| GOVERNMENT | POSITION | RESPONSIBILITIES | QUALIFICATIONS | SALARY |
|---|---|---|---|---|
| Florida | | ▪ Perform notary functions<br>▪ Prepare case summaries<br>▪ Draft pleadings | 4 years of experience as a paralegal or legal secretary | |
| Other positions to check in Florida: Appeals Coordinator/Clerk (Public Employees Relations Commission) (7704); Legal Trainee (7706) | | | | |
| Georgia<br>State Merit System of Personnel Administration<br>200 Piedmont Ave.<br>Atlanta, GA 30334-5100<br>404-656-2705 | Legal Assistant<br>1/1/81<br>(44330) | ▪ Perform legal research<br>▪ Review litigation documents<br>▪ Summarize law<br>▪ Develop forms and procedures | 2 years of legal experience involving legal research, interpreting laws, or relevant administrative responsibilities | $20,310–$32,052 per year |
| Other positions to check in Georgia: Law Clerk (44340)—requires a law degree OR two years of legal assistant experience; Para-Legal (nonmerit position in State Law Department); Research Assistant (nonmerit position in State Law Department). | | | | |
| Guam<br>Civil Service Commission<br>Kumision I Setbision Sibit<br>P.O. Box 3156<br>Agana, GU 96910<br>011-671-649-NORM<br><br>Department of Administration<br>Division of Personnel<br>P.O. Box 3156<br>Agana, GU 96910<br>011-671-472-8194 | Paralegal I<br>12/83<br>(2.810) | ▪ Perform legal research<br>▪ Index public laws<br>▪ Prepare updates to administrative laws<br>▪ Draft bills and simple pleadings<br>▪ Compile laws by subject matter<br>▪ Interview clients and witnesses | 3 years of experience working with laws and procedures<br>OR<br>A bachelor's degree<br>OR<br>Completion of a course leading to certification as a paralegal<br>OR<br>Equivalent experience and training | Pay Range:<br>28<br>$13,930–$18,610 per year |
| Other position to check in Guam: Legal Clerk I (2.805). | | | | |
| Hawaii<br>Dept. of Personnel Services<br>830 Punchbowl St.<br>Honolulu, HI 96813<br>808-548-7405 | Legal Assistant II<br>4/15/83<br>(2.141) | ▪ Act as conduit between attorneys and client, e.g., provide legal information<br>▪ Perform legal research<br>▪ Summarize laws<br>▪ Collect and evaluate evidence for trial<br>▪ Perform cite checks<br>▪ Index depositions | 4 years of legal experience<br>OR<br>Graduation from an accredited legal assistant training program | $1,690–$2,326 per month |
| Idaho<br>Personnel Commission<br>700 West State<br>Boise, ID 83720<br>208-334-2263 | Idaho currently does not have any job classifications for paralegal work. The Legal Assistant position (05916) was phased out. The Office of the Attorney General does, however, employ a paralegal in its Consumer Protection Unit and in its Natural Resource Division. | | | |

Continued

**FIGURE 2.3** Summary Chart—Survey of State Government Job Classifications for Paralegals—*Continued*

| GOVERNMENT | POSITION | RESPONSIBILITIES | QUALIFICATIONS | SALARY |
|---|---|---|---|---|
| **Illinois** Department of Central Management Services Bureau of Personnel 505 Stratton Office Bldg. Springfield, IL 62706 217-782-2141 312-917-2141 (Chicago) | Paralegal Assistant 11/17/83 (1887, 30860) (RC-062-12) | ■ Write legal memoranda and other documents for attorneys ■ Analyze hearing transcripts ■ Excerpt data from transcripts ■ Prepare statistical reports ■ Edit, index, and proofread decisions ■ Perform legal research | Knowledge and skill equivalent to four years of college and knowledge and skills relevant to job responsibilities | $1,643–$2,102 per month |
| Other position to check in Illinois: Legal Research Assistant (1888) (23350) (MC-02) (RC-028-13). | | | | |
| **Indiana** State Personnel Dept. Rm. 513, State Office Bldg. 100 North Senate Ave. Indianapolis, IN 46204 317-232-3056 | The state has no special classifications for paralegals working in the state government. In the Offices of Attorney General, however, the Consumer Protection Division now has Complaint Analyst positions that have been filled with paralegals. Complaint Analysts act as a mediator between the consumer and the business against which the consumer has a complaint. Each Complaint Analyst handles at least 200 cases. | | | |
| **Iowa** Department of Personnel Grimes State Office Building E. 14th St. & Grand Ave. Des Moines, IA 50319 515-281-3351 | Paralegal (Office of Attorney General) (45004) | ■ Represent the state at revocation hearings ■ Write administrative appeal briefs ■ Resolve appeals not needing a hearing ■ Initiate suggestions to improve hearing procedures | 2-year paralegal degree | $787–$1,024 biweekly |
| Other position to check in Iowa: Administrative Assistant I (00708) | | | | |
| **Kansas** Dept. of Administration Div. of Personnel Services Landon State Office Bldg. 900 SW Jackson St. Topeka, KS 66612-1251 913-296-4278 | Legal Assistant 6/83 (D3 1961) | ■ Perform legal research ■ Draft pleadings ■ Compile administrative transcript ■ Conduct investigations | Completion of a Legal Assistant training program of at least 60 semester hours. | $1,630–$2,294 per month |
| **Kentucky** Dept. of Personnel Capitol Annex, Rm. 373 Frankfort, KY 40601 502-564-4460 | Paralegal 12/1/85 (9856) | ■ Conduct analytical research ■ Investigate cases ■ Interview complainants and witnesses ■ Draft documents | Bachelor's degree in paralegal science OR Post-baccalaureate certificate in paralegal studies | $1,139–$1,826 per month |

Continued

**FIGURE 2.3**   Summary Chart—Survey of State Government Job Classifications for Paralegals—*Continued*

| GOVERNMENT | POSITION | RESPONSIBILITIES | QUALIFICATIONS | SALARY |
|---|---|---|---|---|
| **Kentucky** | | ■ Provide general assistance to attorneys in litigation | OR<br>Completion of a 2-year program in paralegal studies<br><br>(Note: paralegal experience can be substituted) | |
| Other positions to check in Kentucky: Paralegal Senior (9857); Law Clerk (9801). | | | | |
| **Louisiana**<br>Dept. of Civil Service<br>P.O. Box 94111<br>Capitol Station<br>Baton Rouge, LA<br>  70804-9111<br>504-342-8083 | Paralegal Assistant<br>6/3/86<br>(113470) (C1 PA) | ■ Perform legal research<br>■ Draft pleadings<br>■ Interview potential trial witnesses<br>■ Compose briefs and memoranda<br>■ Collect delinquent payments<br>■ Index legal opinions<br>■ Maintain law library | 1 year of law school<br>OR<br>Paralegal certification<br>OR<br>A baccalaureate degree and 30 semester hours of paralegal courses<br>OR<br>2 years of paralegal school with 30 semester hours of paralegal courses | $1,180–$1,770 per month |
| Other position to check in Louisiana: Legal Research Assistant (70490). | | | | |
| **Maine**<br>Bureau of Human<br>  Resources<br>State Office Bldg.<br>State House Station 4<br>Augusta, ME 04333<br>207-289-3761 | Paralegal Assistant<br>(0016/U336) | ■ Assist attorney in title search<br>■ Perform legal research<br>■ Assist attorney at hearings<br>■ Conduct investigations | 4 years of college and 1 year of paralegal experience<br>OR<br>Graduation from an approved paralegal course | $21,507–$28,787 per year |
| Other positions to check in Maine: Legal Researcher (0018, 02045, 0979, 20E); Law Clerk (secretarial position with paralegal duties)(0061, 41255, 202.362-014, 0380, 0880, 18R; Workers Compensation Assistant (036900) | | | | |
| **Maryland**<br>Department of<br>  Personnel<br>State Office Bldg. #1<br>301 W. Preston St.<br>Baltimore, MD 21201<br>301-225-4715<br>800-492-7845 | Legal Assistant I<br>(10/31/47) (9/3/68)<br>0589 | ■ Perform legal research<br>■ Conduct investigations<br>■ File pleadings<br>■ Prepare affidavits<br>■ Maintain docket file<br>■ Coordinate employee activities | High school diploma or certificate and 4 years of experience as a clerk or secretary in a law office<br><br>(Note: One year of paralegal education can substitute for two years of experience) | $17,261–$22,609 per year |
| Other positions to check in Maryland: Legal Assistant (209, 13); Legal Assistant II (1292); Para-Legal I (e.g., Howard County Office of State's Attorney). | | | | |

Continued

**FIGURE 2.3**   Summary Chart—Survey of State Government Job Classifications for Paralegals—*Continued*

| GOVERNMENT | POSITION | RESPONSIBILITIES | QUALIFICATIONS | SALARY |
|---|---|---|---|---|
| **Massachusetts**<br>Department of Personnel Administration<br>One Ashburton Pl.<br>Boston, MA 02108<br>617-727-3555 | Paralegal Specialist<br>5/11/88<br>(10-R39) (Group 31) | ■ Perform legal research<br>■ Analyze statutes<br>■ Digest the law<br>■ Prepare briefs and answers to interrogatories<br>■ Interview parties<br>■ Evaluate evidence<br>■ Develop case tracking systems<br>■ Schedule appointments | 2 years of experience in legal research or legal assistant work.<br><br>(Note: An associate's degree or a higher degree with a major in paralegal studies can be substituted for the required experience) | $24,490–$32,691 per year |
| **Michigan**<br>Dept. of Civil Service<br>Capitol Commons Center<br>400 South Pine St.<br>P.O. Box 30002<br>Lansing, MI 48909<br>517-373-3020 | Paralegal III<br>5/81<br>(8020403, BA, 7) | ■ Perform legal research<br>■ Conduct investigations<br>■ Draft legal documents<br>■ Prepare interrogatories<br>■ Digest and index laws<br>■ Serve and file legal papers | Associate degree in a paralegal program<br>OR<br>Equivalent combination of experience and education to perform the job | Pay range (023):<br>$10.43–$12.78 per hour |
| Other positions to check in Michigan: Paralegal IV (8020404, BA, 7); Paralegal VB (8020405, BA, 7); Paralegal VI (8031106, BA, 7). Note: The Legal Assistant I position requires a law degree. |||||
| **Minnesota**<br>Dept. of Employee Relations<br>520 LaFayette Rd.<br>St. Paul, MN 55101<br>612-296-8366 | Legal Technician<br>2/75<br>3/76<br>(17526C) | ■ Perform legal research<br>■ Prepare legal documents<br>■ Collect documents for attorney | Completion of paralegal training program<br>OR<br>2 years of varied paralegal experience<br>OR<br>1 year of law school | $20,609–$25,829 per year |
| Other positions to check in Minnesota: Legal Technician-Farm Real Estate (Dept. of Agriculture); Legal Text Edit Specialist (001936, 206). |||||
| **Mississippi**<br>State Personnel Board<br>301 N. Lamar St.<br>Jackson, MS 39201<br>601-359-1406 | Paralegal Specialist<br>7/83<br>(1848-PR 188-269, D) | ■ Interpret and explain laws to staff<br>■ Assist in preparing legal documents<br>■ Review reports<br>■ Assist in referring cases for prosecution<br>■ Train and supervise staff in research<br>■ Perform research | Bachelor's degree in paralegal studies or a related field and 1 year of experience | $17,323 per year |
| Other position to check in Mississippi: Legal Clerk I (1962-PR 081-162, B) (clerical position with paralegal duties). |||||
| **Missouri**<br>Office of Administration<br>Division of Personnel<br>P.O. Box 388<br>Jefferson City, MO 65102<br>314-751-4162 | Paralegal or legal assistant positions are not found under the Missouri Merit System. Individual agencies not covered by the Merit System, however, may have such positions. ||||

*Continued*

**FIGURE 2.3**   Summary Chart—Survey of State Government Job Classifications for Paralegals—*Continued*

| GOVERNMENT | POSITION | RESPONSIBILITIES | QUALIFICATIONS | SALARY |
|---|---|---|---|---|
| **Montana**<br>Dept. of Administration<br>Personnel Division<br>Mitchell Bldg., Rm. 130<br>205 Roberts St.<br>Helena, MT 59620<br>406-444-3871 | Paralegal Assistant I<br>1/80<br>(119004) | ■ Perform legal research<br>■ Compile citations and references; check cites<br>■ Assemble exhibits<br>■ Explain laws<br>■ Arrange interviews and depositions<br>■ File pleadings<br>■ Supervise clerical staff | Examples of how applicant can qualify: completion of paralegal training program; education and experience equivalent to a bachelor's degree with courses in business, economics, law, etc. | Grade 11<br>$16,092–$22,236 per year |
| Other positions to check in Montana: Paralegal Assistant II (119005); Agency Legal Services Investigator (168155). | | | | |
| **Nebraska**<br>Dept. of Personnel<br>Box 94905<br>Lincoln, NE 68509-4905<br>402-471-2075 | Legal Aide I<br>5/1/78<br>C318131 | ■ Perform legal research<br>■ Proofread legal material<br>■ Help draft regulations<br>■ Help maintain hearing room tapes and films | Any combination of training and/or experience that will enable the applicant to possess the required knowledge, ability, and skills | $13,054 per year |
| Other position to check in Nebraska: Legal Aide II (C318132). | | | | |
| **Nevada**<br>Department of Personnel<br>209 E. Musser St.<br>Capitol Complex<br>Carson City, NV 89710<br>702-885-4050<br>800-992-0900 | Legal Assistant<br>7/1/89<br>(2.155) | ■ Digest information in files<br>■ Explain status of case to clients or to the public<br>■ Offer advice on procedures<br>■ Interview clients and witnesses<br>■ Schedule depositions<br>■ Organize and prepare exhibits | Completion of 1 year or 2 year paralegal course <u>AND</u> Legal secretarial experience or training <u>OR</u> Any combination of education and experience to demonstrate entry level knowledge, skills, and abilities | $18,803–$25,136 per year |
| Other positions to check in Nevada: Legal Assistant II (2.159); Legal Research Assistant (7.750). | | | | |
| **New Hampshire**<br>Division of Personnel<br>State House Annex<br>25 Capitol St., Rm. 1<br>Concord, NH 03301<br>603-271-3261 | Paralegal I<br>2/4/76<br>1/27/87<br>(6793-15) | ■ Evaluate complaints of violations of state law<br>■ Interview business owners and consumers<br>■ Perform legal research<br>■ Examine contracts, agreements, and related legal documents to insure they comply with the law | 4 years of college with 9 semester credits in law topics related to paralegal studies, plus 6 months experience in research or investigation | $19,110–$22,542 per year |
| Other positions to check in New Hampshire: Paralegal II (6792-18); Legal Coordinator and Contracts Monitor (5668-22); Legal Research Assistant (5676-23); Legal Research Aide I (5670-16); Legal Research Aide II (5671-18); Legal Aide (5660-14). | | | | |

Continued

**FIGURE 2.3**   Summary Chart—Survey of State Government Job Classifications for Paralegals—*Continued*

| GOVERNMENT | POSITION | RESPONSIBILITIES | QUALIFICATIONS | SALARY |
|---|---|---|---|---|
| **New Jersey**<br>Department of<br>  Personnel<br>Front & Montgomery<br>  Sts.<br>CN 317<br>Trenton, NJ 08625<br>609-292-4144 | Paralegal<br>Technician Assistant<br>2/4/87<br>(A13-30459) | ■ Perform legal re-<br>  search under close<br>  supervision<br>■ Help draft noncom-<br>  plex memoranda<br>■ Help prepare<br>  correspondence<br>■ Help prepare<br>  pleadings<br>■ Perform cite checks<br>■ Proofread legal<br>  documents | Completion of an ap-<br>proved course of para-<br>legal training | $25,535–<br>$35,266 per<br>year |
| Other positions to check in New Jersey: Legal Services Assistant I (A18-72743); Paralegal Technician, Law and Public Safety (A17-30461); Paralegal Technician, Casino Control Commission (X17-98648); Research Analyst (A18-03171); Research Analyst—Civil Service (A18-03171); Supervising Research Analyst—Div. of Youth and Fam. Services (A28-03184B). | | | | |
| **New Mexico**<br>State Personnel Office<br>810 W. San Mateo Rd.<br>Santa Fe, NM 87503<br>505-827-8190 | Legal Assistant I<br>8/29/79<br>(1330) | ■ Provide help in legal<br>  research<br>■ Prepare affidavits and<br>  exhibits<br>■ Serve legal papers<br>■ Prepare and maintain<br>  records<br>■ Handle routine legal<br>  correspondence | Education and legal ex-<br>perience equaling 4<br>years. The experience<br>can be gained as a<br>paralegal. An Associ-<br>ate's Degree in parale-<br>gal studies can substi-<br>tute for 3 years of<br>experience. | $14,891–<br>$24,760 per<br>year |
| Other position to check in New Mexico: Legal Assistant II (1331). | | | | |
| **New York**<br>Dept. of Civil Service<br>One Harriman State Of-<br>  fice Bldg.<br>Albany, NY 12239<br>518-457-3701 | Legal Assistant I<br>2/10/84<br>(26-880) | ■ Compile and organize<br>  documents<br>■ Help prepare legal<br>  documents and forms<br>■ Respond to inquiries<br>  and complaints<br>■ Maintain files<br>■ Monitor legislation<br>■ Perform legal<br>  research | Associate's degree in<br>paralegal studies<br>OR<br>completion of general<br>practice legal specialty<br>training<br>AND<br>passing a test on law<br>and procedure | $25,786 per<br>year |
| Other positions to check in New York: Legal Assistant Trainee I (00-107); Legal Assistant II (26-881). | | | | |
| **North Carolina**<br>Office of State<br>  Personnel<br>116 West Jones St.<br>Raleigh, NC 27603-8004<br>919-733-7108 | Paralegal I<br>6/82<br>(NC 1422)<br>(INCAC 8G.0402) | ■ Draft legal<br>  instruments<br>■ Prepare routine<br>  opinions<br>■ Handle complaints<br>  and inquiries from the<br>  public<br>■ Administer the law<br>  office<br>■ Perform legal<br>  research | Graduation from a certi-<br>fied paralegal school<br>and 1 year of paralegal<br>experience | $19,783–<br>$31,428 per<br>year |
| **North Dakota**<br>Central Personnel<br>  Division | Legal Assistant I<br>4/87<br>(0701) | ■ Perform legal<br>  research<br>■ Maintain case files | The equivalent of 2<br>years of college in a<br>curriculum appropriate | $1,219–<br>$1,882 per<br>month |

Continued

**FIGURE 2.3**   Summary Chart—Survey of State Government Job Classifications for Paralegals—*Continued*

| GOVERNMENT | POSITION | RESPONSIBILITIES | QUALIFICATIONS | SALARY |
|---|---|---|---|---|
| **North Dakota**<br>Office of Management &<br>  Budget<br>State Capitol, 14th Fl.<br>Bismarck, ND 58505<br>701-224-3290 | | ■ Maintain law library<br>■ Assist attorneys in<br>  litigation<br>■ Perform general sec-<br>  retarial duties | to prelaw and 2 years of<br>related experience | |
| Other position to check in North Dakota: Legal Assistant II (0702). | | | | |
| **Ohio**<br>Dept. of Administrative<br>  Services<br>Div. of Personnel<br>30 E. Broad Street<br>Columbus, OH 43266<br>614-466-3455 | Legal Aide<br>8/84<br>(63810) | ■ Perform legal<br>  research<br>■ Conduct<br>  investigations<br>■ Draft legal documents<br>■ Draft responses to le-<br>  gal questions<br>■ Assist attorneys at<br>  hearings<br>■ File legal papers<br>■ Maintain legal<br>  records | Completion of certifica-<br>tion program for<br>paralegals<br>OR<br>Completion of desig-<br>nated courses, e.g., le-<br>gal research, case anal-<br>ysis, legal analysis, civil<br>procedure | $9.01–<br>$10.58 per<br>hour |
| Other positions to check in Ohio: Hearing Assistant (63821); Hearing Officer (63831). | | | | |
| **Oklahoma**<br>Office of Personnel<br>  Management<br>2101 N. Lincoln Blvd.<br>Oklahoma City, OK<br>  73105<br>405-521-2171<br>800-522-8122 | Legal Research<br>Assistant<br>7/1/81<br>(K101 FC: K10) | ■ Perform legal<br>  research<br>■ Conduct<br>  investigations<br>■ Assist attorneys in<br>  litigation<br>■ File pleadings<br>■ Maintain law library | Completion of approved<br>legal research assistant<br>program<br>OR<br>Completion of 18 se-<br>mester hours of law<br>school | $1,691–<br>$2,256 per<br>month |
| Other positions to check in Oklahoma: Legal Assistant I; Legal Assistant II (Office of the Municipal Counselor, Okla-<br>homa City). | | | | |
| **Oregon**<br>Executive Dept.<br>Personnel & Labor Rela-<br>  tions Div.<br>155 Cottage St. N.E.<br>Salem, OR 97310-0310<br>503-378-3020 | Paralegal Specialist<br>(1526) | ■ Organize complex<br>  facts<br>■ Communicate with<br>  experts<br>■ Analyze cases<br>■ Assist attorneys in<br>  litigation<br>■ Arrange for case<br>  settlements<br>■ Answer<br>  interrogatories | Experience and training<br>that demonstrate the<br>knowledge and skills re-<br>quired for the position | $2,140–<br>$2,845 per<br>month |
| Other positions to check in Oregon: Paralegal I (1523); Paralegal II (1524); Paralegal III (1525); Investigator (C1031);<br>Special Investigator (X 1032); Legal Assistant (C0680). | | | | |
| **Pennsylvania**<br>Office of Administration<br>Bureau of Personnel<br>517 Finance Bldg.<br>Harrisburg, PA 17105<br>717-787-5545 | Legal Assistant I<br>6/89<br>(0701) | ■ Review work of field<br>  personnel for possi-<br>  ble legal implications<br>■ Summarize cases<br>■ Prepare reports | 1 year of experience as<br>legal assistant trainee<br>OR<br>4 years of experience in<br>clerical work, investiga-<br>tion, or enforcement | $16,919–<br>$26,171 per<br>year |

Continued

| GOVERNMENT | POSITION | RESPONSIBILITIES | QUALIFICATIONS | SALARY |
|---|---|---|---|---|
| **Pennsylvania**<br>Other positions to check in Pennsylvania: Legal Assistant II (07020); Legal Assistant Supervisor (07030); Legal Assistant Manager (07040). | | | | |
| **Rhode Island**<br>Office of Personnel Administration<br>289 Promenade St.<br>Providence, RI 02908<br>401-277-2160 | Paralegal Aide<br>11/24/85<br>(02461300) | ■ Perform legal research<br>■ Conduct investigations<br>■ Answer questions by interpreting laws<br>■ Assist in litigation<br>■ Maintain files | Completion of an approved paralegal training program<br>OR<br>Paraprofessional experience in an extensive legal service program | $18,380–$19,965 per year |
| **South Carolina**<br>Budget and Control Board<br>Division of Human Resource Management<br>1201 Main St.<br>P.O. Box 12547<br>Columbia, SC 29211<br>803-737-0900 | Paralegal Assistant I<br>4/84<br>(2066) | ■ Obtain and assemble witness statements, reports, and exhibits<br>■ Draft and proofread pleadings<br>■ Maintain tickler system<br>■ Assist in document control | Certification from an approved paralegal program<br>OR<br>High school diploma and 1 year of experience with a South Carolina attorney | $17,821–$26,731 per year |
| Other positions to check in South Carolina: Paralegal Assistant II (2067); Legal Aide (2065). | | | | |
| **South Dakota**<br>Bureau of Personnel<br>500 E. Capitol<br>Pierre, SD 57501-5070<br>605-773-3148 | Does not have positions within state government specifically titled paralegal, legal assistant, legal technician, or legal aide. Individuals performing these functions are usually classified as administrative assistants, secretaries, or exempt professionals. | | | |
| **Tennessee**<br>Dept. of Personnel<br>505 Deaderick St.<br>Nashville, TN 37243-0635<br>615-741-2958 | Legal Assistant<br>7/1/84<br>(02350) | ■ Perform legal research e.g., cite checking<br>■ Draft regulations<br>■ Maintain law library<br>■ Answer routine inquiries on laws and regulations | Completion of an approved curriculum in paralegal studies | $1,128–$1,677 per month |
| **Texas**<br>State Auditor's Office<br>P.O. Box 12067<br>419 Reagan State Office Bldg.<br>Austin, TX 78711-2067<br>512-463-5788 | Legal Assistant I<br>9/1/89<br>(3570) | ■ Perform legal research<br>■ Compile citations and references<br>■ Research land titles<br>■ Assemble exhibits<br>■ Help prepare legal documents<br>■ File pleadings in court | Completion of a paralegal training program<br>OR<br>The equivalent in experience | $20,772–$26,160 per year |
| Other positions to check in Texas: Legal Assistant II (3572); Legal Assistant III (3574); Administrative Technician II (Office of Attorney General). | | | | |
| **Utah**<br>Department of Human Resource Management<br>2229 State Office Bldg.<br>Salt Lake City, UT 84114<br>801-538-3025 | Paralegal<br>9/30/89<br>(18750) | ■ Digest pretrial data<br>■ Maintain calendar/docket systems<br>■ Draft subpoenas, motions, etc.<br>■ Assist at depositions and hearings<br>■ Interview witnesses | Certificate of paralegal studies, plus 2 years work experience, preferably in a legal field | $18,325–$27,165 per year |

**FIGURE 2.3** Summary Chart—Survey of State Government Job Classifications for Paralegals—*Continued*

| GOVERNMENT | POSITION | RESPONSIBILITIES | QUALIFICATIONS | SALARY |
|---|---|---|---|---|
| **Utah**<br>Other position to check in Utah: Paralegal (18751). | | | | |
| **Vermont**<br>Agency of<br>  Administration<br>Dept. of Personnel<br>110 State St.<br>Montpelier, VT 05602<br>802-828-3497 | Paralegal<br>Technician<br>8/11/89<br>(081800)<br>(P.G. 18) | ▪ Assist attorneys in litigation<br>▪ Conduct investigations<br>▪ Interview parties<br>▪ Perform legal research<br>▪ Audit records<br>▪ Interpret laws<br>▪ Draft briefs and legal documents | 1 year of experience in investigatory, analytical, research or paralegal duties; plus 3 years of additional experience at or above a senior clerical or technical level.<br><br>(Note: 30 college credits in legal or paralegal studies can substitute for the 3 years of additional experience.) | $20,072–$30,305 per year |
| **Other position to check in Vermont: State Investigator—Civil Rights.** | | | | |
| **Virginia**<br>Office of Compensation<br>  Management<br>Dept. of Personnel and<br>  Training<br>101 N. 14th St.<br>Richmond, VA 23219-<br>  3657<br>804-225-2131 | Legal Assistant<br>11/1/83<br>(21521) | ▪ Help supervise clerical staff<br>▪ Monitor compliance requirements<br>▪ Draft briefs and fact narratives<br>▪ Perform legal research<br>▪ Prepare witnesses and exhibits<br>▪ Manage law library | Paralegal course work or training preferred, plus experience in judicial and quasi-judicial systems and in the application of legal principles | $18,723–$25,572 per year |
| **Washington D.C. (See District of Columbia)** | | | | |
| **Washington State**<br>Department of<br>  Personnel<br>600 S. Franklin<br>P.O. Box 1789<br>Olympia, WA 98504<br>206-586-0194 | Legal Examiner I<br>9/14/89<br>(4661) | ▪ Assist in litigation<br>▪ Assist in investigations<br>▪ Perform legal research<br>▪ Collect and organize economic data<br>▪ Help organize large volume of documents | 2 years of experience as a legal assistant<br>OR<br>Completion of approved 2 year paralegal or legal assistant course<br>OR<br>4 year college degree and either completion of a 10-month legal assistant program or 1 year of experience as paralegal or legal assistant | $1,647–$2,081 per month |
| **Other positions to check in Washington: Legal Examiner II (4662); Legal Examiner III (4663).** | | | | |
| **West Virginia**<br>Civil Service System<br>1900 Washington St.<br>  East, Rm. B-456<br>Charleston, WV 25305<br>304-348-3950 | Para-Legal Assistant<br>10/7/74<br>10/21/80<br>(0550) | ▪ Perform legal research<br>▪ Write abstracts of evidence<br>▪ Supervise clerical staff<br>▪ Maintain case records<br>▪ Summarize legal literature | Completion of approved Para-Legal Assistant program<br>OR<br>2 years of relevant legal experience under the supervision of an attorney | $1,064–$1,920 per month |

Continued

**FIGURE 2.3**   Summary Chart—Survey of State Government Job Classifications for Paralegals—*Continued*

| GOVERNMENT | POSITION | RESPONSIBILITIES | QUALIFICATIONS | SALARY |
|---|---|---|---|---|
| **West Virginia** | | ■ Maintain statistical records<br>■ Monitor pending legislation<br>■ Prepare legal documents | | |
| Other position to check in West Virginia: Child Advocate Para-Legal (8098). | | | | |
| **Wisconsin**<br>Dept. of Employment Relations<br>149 East Wilson St.<br>P.O. Box 7855<br>Madison, WI 53707<br>608-266-9820 | Legal Assistant I<br>4/79<br>(PR2-08) | ■ Abridge transcripts of testimony<br>■ Prepare appendices for appellate briefs<br>■ Paginate appeal records<br>■ Collect and organize facts for trial preparation<br>■ Draft routine pleadings<br>■ Conduct elementary research | There must be reasonable assurance that the applicant has the skills and knowledge to perform the tasks. "Under current civil service statutes, the state of Wisconsin does not require specific credentials unless it can be established that the position needs professional licensing." | $10.03–$14.02 per hour |
| Other positions to check in Wisconsin: Legal Assistant II (PR2-09); Legal Assistant I—Confidential (PR1-08) (Dept. of Justice, Attorney General); Administrative Assistant IV (PR1-13). | | | | |
| **Wyoming**<br>Personnel Division<br>Department of Administration and Fiscal Control<br>2001 Capitol Ave.<br>Cheyenne, WY 82002<br>307-777-6713 | There are no paralegal or legal assistant classifications in state government. The closest may be the positions of Executive Secretary and Legal Investigator (LE52). | | | |

legal services to the poor. The clients do not pay fees. These offices make extensive use of paralegals with titles such as:

Administrative Benefits Representative

Administrative Hearing Representative

AFDC Specialist (Aid to Families with Dependent Children)

Bankruptcy Law Specialist

Case Advocate

Case Specialist

Community Law Specialist

Disability Law Specialist

Domestic Relations Specialist

Employment Law Specialist

Food Stamp Specialist

Generalist Paralegal

Health Law Specialist

Housing/Tenant Law Specialist

Immigration Paralegal

Information and Referral Specialist

Legal Assistant

Legal Research Specialist

Legislative Advocate

Paralegal

| | |
|---|---|
| Paralegal Coordinator | Social Security Specialist |
| Paralegal Supervisor | Tribal Court Representative |
| Public Entitlement Specialist | Veterans Law Specialist |
| Senior Citizen Specialist | Wills Procedures Specialist |

As we will see in Chapter 4, many administrative agencies permit nonattorneys to represent citizens at hearings before those agencies. Legal service and legal aid offices take advantage of this authorization. Their paralegals undertake extensive agency representation. (See Figure 2.4 for a sample job announcement that lists paralegal duties, including work at hearings, on behalf of clients.) The distinction between attorneys and paralegals in such offices is less pronounced than in any other setting. Unfortunately, however, such paralegals are among the lowest paid because of the limited resources of the offices where they work.

Another way in which legal services are provided to poor people (sometimes referred to as *indigents*) is through *judicare*. This is a system of paying private attorneys for legal services to the poor on a case-by-case basis. Instead of receiving a government grant to open up an office that will serve only the poor, the Judicare attorney maintains a private office and bills the government whenever legal services are delivered to the poor. These attorneys often employ paralegals.

Further variations on methods by which paralegals are used to deliver legal services to the poor include:

- Paralegals who work in special institutions such as mental health hospitals or prisons
- Paralegals who are senior citizens providing legal services to senior citizens at nursing homes, neighborhood centers, and similar locations

## 5. Law Departments of Corporations, Banks, Insurance Companies, and Other Businesses

Not every corporation or business in the country uses a law firm to handle all of its legal problems. Many have their own in-house law department under the direction of an attorney who is often called the *general counsel* or *corporate counsel*.[6] The attorneys in this department have only one client—the corporation or business itself. Examples include manufacturers, retailers, transportation companies, publishers, general insurance companies, real estate and title insurance companies, estate and trust departments of large banks, hospitals, universities, etc. In increasing numbers, paralegals are being hired in these settings. The average corporate law department employs seventeen attorneys, two paralegals, two nonattorney professionals, and fourteen legal support personnel.[7] Paralegal salaries are relatively high because the employer (like the large traditional private law office) can afford to pay good wages.

---

[6]Even if a corporation has its own law department, however, it may still occasionally hire an outside law firm in special situations such as complex litigation.

[7]Stanton, *Stepping Up to the Bar*, 35 Occupational Outlook Quarterly 3, 7 (Spring 1991).

**FIGURE 2.4**

Sample Job
Description for
Paralegal in Legal
Service Office

---

**Gulf Coast Legal Foundation**

**Positions Open for Paralegals Experienced in Welfare**

The Gulf Coast Legal Foundation, formerly the Houston Legal Foundation, has three positions open for paralegals with experience in welfare law. However, if experienced persons do not apply, we will seriously consider applicants with no more educational qualifications than a GED. We are discouraging law students and law graduates from applying. Our program has five neighborhood offices in Houston and Galveston and will expand to Fort Bend and Brazoria Counties. Our paralegals are assigned to specialty units. These positions are for the welfare unit where the goal is to increase the number of AFDC (Aid to Families with Dependent Children) families by 12,000 in the county and the number of SSI (Supplemental Social Security Income) recipients by 1,500 in the county, and to increase the level of benefits. The welfare unit represents the local welfare rights organization, which has ten years of history, parent councils of Title XX day care centers, and in cooperation with another unit, groups of handicapped people. The paralegal would maintain a direct service caseload of state welfare appeals and SSI hearings as well as some unemployment, health claims and other administrative matters. Each paralegal will be expected to handle six pending hearings and perform one research task each month after a training period of half a year. And do their own typing. The paralegal would also maintain a library of state manuals and social security materials. The paralegal would also be expected to participate in saturation leafleting, to attend some group meetings, and to perform minor educational services. The supervising attorney of the welfare unit would supervise the paralegal. The unit will have a total of five lawyers and six paralegals.

Because of inadequate public transportation, the paralegal would be responsible for transporting clients to welfare centers and maintaining a personal automobile.

Applicants should furnish their scores on the SAT or GRE exam, a writing sample, and detailed information concerning any prior legal services experience. We will weigh mathematical skills over writing skills. Our program will give preference to experienced paralegals who intend to continue a career as a paralegal. Our program also has an affirmative action policy for the hiring of women and members of minority groups. Our program serves a substantial Mexican-American population and must give an additional preference to applicants who speak Spanish fluently.

The salary range can go up to the equivalent of a moderately experienced attorney.

---

## 6.  Special Interest Groups or Associations

Many special interest groups exist in our society: unions, business associations, environmental protection groups, taxpayer associations, consumer protection groups, trade associations, citizen action groups, etc. The larger groups have their own offices, libraries, and legal staff, including paralegals. The legal work often involves monitoring legislation, lobbying, preparing studies, etc. Direct legal services to individual members of the groups are usually not provided. The legal work relates to the needs (or a cause) of the organization as a whole. Occasionally, however, the legal staff will litigate test cases of individual members that have broad impact on the organization's membership.

A different concept in the use of attorneys and paralegals by such groups is *group legal services.* Members of unions or groups of college students, for example, pay a monthly fee to the organization for which they are entitled to designated legal services, such as preparation of a will or divorce representation. The members pay *before* the legal problems arise. Group legal service systems are a form of legal insurance. The group legal service office will usually employ paralegals.

## 7.  Criminal Law Offices

Criminal cases are brought by government attorneys who are called prosecutors, district attorneys, or attorneys general. Defendants are represented by private attorneys if they can afford the fees. If they are indigent, they are assigned private counsel whose fees are paid by the government, or they are represented by public defenders who work in a special office set up by government funds to represent the poor. The use of paralegals in the practice of criminal law is increasing, particularly due to the encouragement of organizations such as the National District Attorneys Association and the National Legal Aid & Defender Association.

## 8.  Freelance Paralegals

As we learned in Chapter 1, most *freelance paralegals* are self-employed individuals who sell their services to attorneys. They are also called independent paralegals and contract paralegals. They perform their services in their own office or in the offices of the attorneys who hire them for special projects. Often they advertise in publications read by attorneys, such as legal newspapers and bar association journals. Such an ad might look something like this:

> **Improve the quality and**
> **\*\*\*\*cost-effectiveness\*\*\*\***
> **of your practice with the help of:**
> **Lawyer's Assistant, Inc.**

In addition, these paralegals will usually have a flyer or brochure that describes their services. Here is an excerpt from such a flyer:

> Our staff consists of individuals with formal paralegal training and an average of five years of experience in such areas as estates and trusts, litigation, real estate, tax, and corporate law. Whether you require a real estate paralegal for one day or four litigation paralegals for one month, we can provide you with reliable qualified paralegals to meet your specific needs.

The attorneys in a law firm may be convinced of the value of paralegals but not have enough business to justify hiring a full-time paralegal employee. A freelance paralegal may be an alternative.

For an overview on how to start a freelance business, see Appendix I.

As we saw in Chapter 1, there are also self-employed paralegals who sell their services directly to the public. They, too, are sometimes called freelance paralegals, although the terms legal technician and independent paralegal are more common. Relatively few paralegals are engaged in this kind of business. This may change, however, as a number of states seriously consider a form of limited licensing to authorize what they do. We will examine this possibility in Chapter 4.

## 9.  Service Companies/Consulting Firms

*Service companies* and consulting firms also sell services to attorneys, but usually on a broader and more sophisticated scale than the freelance paralegal does. Examples include:

- Selecting a computer system for a law office
- Designing and managing a computer-assisted document control system for a large case
- Digesting discovery documents

- Helping a law firm establish a branch office
- Designing a filing or financial system for the office
- Incorporating a new company in all fifty states
- Conducting a trademark search
- Undertaking a UCC (Uniform Commercial Code) search and filing in all fifty states

In order to accomplish such tasks, these service companies and consulting firms recruit highly specialized staffs of management experts, accountants, economists, former administrators, etc. More and more paralegals are joining these staffs, particularly paralegals with prior law office experience.

## 10.  Related Fields

Experienced paralegals have also been using their training and experience in a number of nonpractice legal fields. Many are becoming law librarians at firms. Paralegal schools often hire paralegals to teach courses and to work in administration, in such areas as admissions, internship coordination, placement, etc. Law offices with large numbers of paralegals have hired paralegal administrators or supervisors to help recruit, train, and manage the paralegals. Some paralegals have become legal administrators or office managers with administrative responsibilities throughout the firm. It is clear that we have not seen the end of the development of new roles for paralegals within the law firm or in related areas of the law. At the end of the chapter, a more extensive list of such roles will be provided. (See Figure 2.14.)

## ■ Section C. Paralegal Specialties: A Dictionary of Functions

"The question so often asked of us is, 'what exactly do you do?' "
Douglas Parker, Paralegal, Pasadena, California, 1989.

We now examine forty-five areas of specialty work throughout the ten categories of paralegal employment just discussed. Paralegals often work in more than one of these specialties, and there is considerable overlap in the functions performed. The trend, however, is for paralegals to specialize. This follows the pattern of most attorneys.

### Paralegal Specialties

1. Administrative law
2. Admiralty law
3. Advertising law
4. Antitrust law
5. Banking law
6. Bankruptcy law
7. Civil rights law
8. Collections law
9. Communications law
10. Construction law
11. Contract law
12. Corporate law
13. Criminal law
14. Employee benefits law
15. Entertainment law
16. Environmental law
17. Estates, trusts, and probate law
18. Ethics and professional responsibility
19. Family law
20. Government contract law
21. Immigration law
22. Insurance law
23. Intellectual property law
24. International law
25. Judicial administration

26. Labor and employment law
27. Landlord and tenant law
28. Law librarianship
29. Law office administration
30. Legislation
31. Litigation
32. Military law
33. Municipal finance law
34. Oil and gas law
35. Parajudge
36. Pro bono work
37. Public sector
38. Real estate law
39. Social security law
40. Tax law
41. Tort law
42. Tribal law
43. Water law
44. Welfare law
45. Worker's compensation law
Note: Paralegal in the White House

## 1. Administrative Law

### I. Government Employment

Many paralegals work for specific administrative agencies. (See also Figure 2.3 for a list of paralegal functions in state agencies.) They might:

A. Handle questions and complaints from citizens.
B. Draft proposed regulations for the agency.
C. Perform legal research.
D. Provide litigation assistance in the agency and in court.
E. Represent the government at administrative hearings where authorized.
F. Manage the law office.
G. Train and supervise other nonattorney personnel.

### II. Representation of Citizens

Some administrative agencies authorize nonattorneys to represent citizens at hearings and other agency proceedings. (See also *immigration law, pro bono work, public sector, social security law,* and *welfare law.*)

A. Interview client.
B. Conduct investigation.
C. Perform legal research.
D. Engage in informal advocacy at the agency.
E. Represent the client at agency hearing.
F. Draft documents for submission at hearing.
G. Monitor activities of the agency—for example, attend rule-making hearings to take notes on matters relevant to particular clients.
H. Prepare witnesses, reports, and exhibits designed to influence the drafting of regulations at the agency.

■ *Comment on Paralegal Work in This Area:*

We "have a great deal of autonomy and an opportunity to develop expertise in particular areas." We have our "own caseloads, interview clients and then represent those clients at administrative hearings." Georgia Ass'n of Legal Assistants, *Sallye Jenkins Sapp, Atlanta Legal Aid; Sharon Mahaffey Hill, Georgia Legal Services,* 10 ParaGraph 5 (1987).

When I got my first case at a hearing before the State Department of Mental Health, I was "scared to death!" But the attorneys in the office were very supportive. "They advised me to make a good record, noting objections for the transcript, in case of future appeal. Making the right objections was scary." Milano, *New Responsibilities Being Given to Paralegals,* 8 Legal Assistant Today 27, 28 (November/December 1990).

## 2. Admiralty Law

This area of the law, also referred to as maritime law, covers accidents, injuries, and death connected with vessels on navigable waters. Special legislation exists in this area, such as, the Jones Act. (See also *international law, litigation,* and *tort law.*)

### I. Investigation

A. Obtain the facts of the event involved.
B. Arrange to board the vessel to photograph the scene of the accident.
C. Collect facts relevant to the seaworthiness of the vessel.
D. Take statements from witnesses.

### II. Legal Research

A. Research liability under the applicable statutes.
B. Research special procedures to obtain compensation.

### III. Subrogation

A. Handle small cargo subrogation files.
B. Prepare status reports for clients.

### IV. Litigation

A. Draft complaints and other pleadings.
B. Respond to discovery requests.

C.  Monitor maritime files to keep track of discovery deadlines.

D.  Coordinate projects by expert witnesses.

E.  Provide general trial assistance.

■ *Comment on Paralegal Work in This Area:*

Jimmie Muvern, CLA (Certified Legal Assistant), works for a sole practitioner in Baton Rouge, Louisiana who specializes in maritime litigation: "If there is a doubt regarding the plaintiff's status as a Jones Act seaman, this issue is generally raised by a motion for summary judgment filed well in advance of trial, and it is good practice for the legal assistant who may be gathering facts regarding the client's accident to also gather facts from the client and from other sources which might assist the attorney in opposing summary judgment on the issue of the client's status as a Jones Act seaman." J. deGravelles & J. Murvin, *Who Is a Jones Act Seaman?* 12 Facts & Findings 34 (NALA, April 1986).

## 3.  Advertising Law

(See also *administrative law* and *intellectual property law*.)

I.  Compliance Work

A.  *Advertising:* Review advertising of company products in order to identify possible claims made in the advertising about the product. Collect data needed to support the accuracy of claims made in advertising pursuant to regulations of the Federal Trade Commission and company guidelines.

B.  *Labels:* Review labels of company products to insure compliance with the regulations on deception of the Federal Trade Commission. Insure compliance with the Food & Drug Administration and company policy on:

1.  Product identity,

2.  New weight statement,

3.  Ingredient list,

4.  Name and address of manufacturer/distributor,

5.  Nutrition information.

C.  *Product promotions:* Review promotions for company products (coupons, sweepstakes, bonus packs, etc.) to insure compliance with Federal Trade Commission guidelines, state laws, and company policy.

II.  Inquiries and Complaints

A.  Keep up-to-date on government regulations on advertising.

B.  Help company attorney respond to inquiries and complaints from the public, a competitor, the

Federal Trade Commission, the Food & Drug Administration, the state's attorney general, etc.

■ *Comment on Paralegal Work in This Area:*

"On the surface, my job certainly does not fit the 'traditional' paralegal role. If a fortune teller had ever read my coffee grounds, I might have learned that my paralegal career would include being part of the production of commercials and labels for household products I had grown up with." "My employer, the Proctor & Gamble Company, is one of the largest consumer product companies in the United States." Its "Legal Division consists of forty attorneys and nine paralegals. Advertising law is challenging. It requires ingenuity, fast thinking and mastery of tight deadlines." Kothman, *Advertising Paralegal Finds Own Label,* National Paralegal Reporter 12 (NFPA, Spring 1990).

## 4.  Antitrust Law

(See also *administrative law, corporate law, criminal law,* and *litigation.*)

I.  Investigation/Analysis

A.  Accumulate statistical and other technical data on a company or industry involved in litigation. Check Securities & Exchange Commission (SEC) filings, annual reports, advertising brochures, etc.

B.  Prepare reports on economic data.

C.  Obtain data from government bodies.

D.  Find and interview potential witnesses.

II.  Administrative Agency

A.  Monitor the regulations and decisions of the Federal Trade Commission.

B.  Prepare drafts of answers to requests for information from the Federal Trade Commission.

III.  Litigation

A.  Assist in drafting pleadings.

B.  Request company witness files in preparation for deposition.

C.  Schedule depositions.

D.  Draft form interrogatories.

E.  Prepare special exhibits.

F.  Organize, index, and digest voluminous records and lengthy documents.

G.  Prepare trial notebook.

H.  Attend trial and take notes on testimony of witnesses.

I.  Cite check briefs of attorneys.

J.  Provide general trial assistance.

■ *Comment on Paralegal Work in This Area:*

When Mitchell became a permanent employee at the firm, "he was given three days' worth of files to read in order to familiarize himself with the [antitrust] case. At this point in the case, the firm had already gone through discovery of 27,000 documents. Mitchell analyzed and summarized documents with the other ten paralegals hired to work on the case. With a major case such as this one, paralegals did not have a regular nine to five work day. Mitchell frequently worked seventy hours a week (for which he was paid overtime). In January, Mitchell and his team were sent across the country to take depositions for the case. His air transportation, accommodations, and meals were all 'first class,' but this was not a vacation; he worked around the clock." R. Berkey, *New Career Opportunities in the Legal Profession,* 47 (Arco, 1983).

## 5. Banking Law

Paralegals employed by banks often work in the bank trust department. They also work in bank legal departments, where they become involved with litigation, real estate, bankruptcy, consumer affairs, and securities law. In addition to banks, paralegals work for savings and loan institutions and other commercial lenders. Finally, some paralegals are employed in law firms that specialize in banking law. The following overview of duties is limited to the paralegal working for the legal department of a bank. (See also *administrative law, corporate law, estates law,* and *municipal finance law.*)

### I. Claims

Assist legal staff in assessing bank liability for various claims, such as negligence and collection abuse.

### II. Compliance Analysis

Determine whether the bank is complying with the regulations and statutes that regulate the banking industry.

### III. Monitoring

Keep track of the activities of the various banking regulatory agencies and of the legislative committees with jurisdiction over banks.

### IV. Litigation

Assist attorneys litigating claims.

### V. Miscellaneous

A. Draft and/or review loan applications and accompanying credit documents.

B. Perform document analysis on
1. Financial statements,
2. Mortgages,
3. Assignments,
4. Security agreements.

C. Conduct UCC (Uniform Commercial Code) searches.

D. Assemble closing documents.

E. Arrange for and attend loan closings.

F. Prepare notarization of documents.

G. Monitor recordation.

H. Act as liaison among supervising attorney at the bank, the loan officer, and the customer.

I. Perform routine legal research and analysis for the Compliance Department.

■ *Comment on Paralegal Work in This Area:*

Ruth Sendecki is "the first legal assistant" at Merchants National Bank, one of the Midwest's largest bank holding companies. Most paralegals employed at banks today work in the trust department; Ruth, however, works with "general banking" at Merchants. Before this job, she worked at a bank, but not in a legal capacity. "You don't have to limit yourself to a law firm. You can combine being a legal assistant with other interests." Her "primary responsibility is in the commercial loan department. . . . She also serves the mortgage loan, correspondent banking and the international banking departments." According to her supervisor at the bank, "She is readily accessible for the benefit of the attorney, the loan officer and the customer to facilitate completion of the arrangements for both sides." Furthermore, she "is expanding her knowledge base, and other departments are drawing on her knowledge." Kane, *A Banker with the $oul of a Legal Assistant,* 5 Legal Assistant Today 65 (July/August 1988).

## 6. Bankruptcy Law

Paralegals in this area of law may be employed by a law firm that represents the debtor (e.g., an individual, a business); a creditor (e.g., a bank-mortgagee); or the trustee in bankruptcy. (A trustee in bankruptcy does not have to be a lawyer. Some paralegals with bankruptcy experience have in fact become trustees.) A few paralegals work directly for a bankruptcy judge as a clerk or deputy in Bankruptcy Court. The following overview assumes the paralegal works for a firm that represents the debtor. (See also *banking law, collections law, contract law,* and *litigation.*)

### I. Interviewing/Data Collection

A. Help client fill out an extensive questionnaire on assets and liabilities. May visit client's place of business to determine the kinds of records kept there.

B. Help client assemble documents:
  1. Loan agreements,
  2. Deeds of trust,
  3. Security agreements,
  4. Creditor lists,
  5. Payables lists,
  6. Employment contracts,
  7. Financial statements,
  8. Leases, etc.

## II. Investigation

A. Confirm amounts of indebtedness.
B. Identify secured and unsecured claims of creditors.
C. Check UCC (Uniform Commercial Code) filings at the secretary of state's office and at county clerk's office.
D. Check real property records in the clerk's office of the county where the property is located.
E. Verify taxes owed; identify tax liens.
F. Identify exempt property.

## III. Asset Control

A. Open bankruptcy file.
B. Prepare inventories of assets and liabilities.
C. Arrange for valuation of assets.

## IV. Creditor Contact

A. Answer inquiries of creditors on the status of the case.
B. Request documentation from creditors on claims.

## V. Drafting

A. Original bankruptcy petition.
B. Schedule of liabilities.
C. Statement of affairs.
D. Status reports.
E. Final account.

## VI. Coordination

A. Serve as liaison with trustee in bankruptcy.
B. Coordinate meeting of creditors.
C. Prepare calendar of filing and other deadlines.

■ *Comment on Paralegal Work in This Area:*

"As a legal assistant, you can play a major role in the representation of a Chapter 11 debtor. From prefiling activities through confirmation of the plan of reorganization, there are numerous duties which you can perform to assist in the successful reorganization of the debtor." Morzak, *Organizing Reorganization,* 5 Legal Assistant Today 33 (January/February).

"Bankruptcy work is unusual in a number of ways—extremely short statutes of limitation, for example. . . . The field is one in which there's lots of opportunity for paralegals. The paralegal does everything except sign the papers. . . . Most attorneys do not like bankruptcy, but if you do all the legwork for them, you can make a lot of money for them." Johnson, *The Role of the Paralegal/Legal Assistant in Bankruptcy and Foreclosure,* AALA News 7 (Alaska Ass'n of Legal Assistants, March 1987).

# 7. Civil Rights Law

(See also *labor and employment law, pro bono work,* and *public sector.*)

## I. Government Paralegal

A. Help identify and resolve discrimination complaints (based on sex, race, age, etc.) made by government employees against the government.
B. Help government attorneys litigate discrimination complaints (based on sex, race, age, etc.) brought by citizens against the government, against other citizens, or against companies.

## II. Representation of Citizens

Assist law firms representing citizens in their discrimination complaints against the government, other citizens, or companies:

A. In court.
B. In special agencies created to hear discrimination cases, such as the Equal Employment Opportunity Commission or the Human Rights Commission.

■ *Comment on Paralegal Work in This Area:*

"One aspect that Matthews likes is that each case is a different story, a different set of facts. 'There is a lot of interaction with people in the courts and with the public. We do a great deal of civil rights litigation, everything from excessive police force to wrongful termination. Sometimes there are as many as 60 witnesses. The lawyers depend on me to separate the witnesses out and advise them which ones would do best in the courtroom. A lot of time the lawyer does not know the witness and has not seen the witness until the person is in the courtroom testifying.' For one case, Matthews reviewed more than 1,000 slides taken in a nightclub, looking for examples of unusual or rowdy behavior. The slides include everything from male strippers to people flashing. Autopsy and horrible injury photographs are also part of the job." *Broadening into the Paralegal Field,* 39 The Docket 7 (NALS, January/February 1991).

## 8.  Collections Law[8]

(See also *banking law, bankruptcy law, contract law,* and *litigation.*)

### I.  Acceptance of Claims

**A.**  Open file.

**B.**  Prepare index of parties.

**C.**  Prepare inventory of debts of debtor.

### II.  Investigation

**A.**  Conduct asset check.

**B.**  Verify address.

**C.**  Verify filings at secretary of state's office and county clerk's office (e.g., UCC filings).

**D.**  Contact credit bureau.

**E.**  Verify information in probate court, registry of deeds, etc.

### III.  Litigation Assistant (Civil Court, Small Claims Court)

**A.**  Draft pleadings.

**B.**  Arrange for witnesses.

**C.**  File documents in court.

**D.**  Assist in settlement/negotiation of claim.

**E.**  Assist in enforcement work, such as:

    **1.**  Wage attachment (prejudgment attachment),

    **2.**  Supplementary process,

    **3.**  Execution,

    **4.**  Seizure of personal property.

■ *Comment on Paralegal Work in This Area:*

"O.K.—So, it [collections work] is not the nicest job in the world, but somebody has to do it, right? If the attorney you work for does not want to do it, there are plenty more in town who will. For a paralegal working in this area, there is always something new to learn. . . . It is sometimes difficult to see the results of your labor right away in this kind of work, as very few files are paid in full and closed in a short period of time. It is disheartening to go through many steps and possibly spend a great deal of time just trying to get someone served or to locate someone, and then end up with nothing. I will admit that collections can be very frustrating, but boring they are not!" Wexel, *Collections: Persistence Pay$ Off,* The Paraview (Metrolina Paralegal Ass'n, April 1987).

"I currently have responsibility for some 400 collection cases. My days are spent on the phone talking to debtors, drafting the necessary pleadings, executing forms, and hopefully depositing the money collected.

---

[8]See Commercial Law League of America, Seminar, *A Paralegal Approach to the Practice of Commercial Law* (11/14/75).

The exciting part of collection is executing on a judgment. We were successful in garnishing an insurance company's account for some $80,000 when they refused to pay a judgment that had been taken against them. We have also gone with the Sheriff to a beer distributorship two days before St. Patrick's Day to change the locks on the building housing gallons and gallons of green beer. The debtor suddenly found a large sum of money to pay us so that we would release the beer in time for St. Patrick's day." R. Swoagerm, *Collections Paralegal,* The Citator 9 (Legal Assistants of Central Ohio, August 1990).

## 9.  Communications Law

(See also *administrative law* and *entertainment law.*)

### I.  Government Paralegal

Assist attorneys at the Federal Communications Commission (FCC) in regulating the communications industry—for example, help with rule-making, license applications, hearings.

### II.  Representation of Citizens or Companies

**A.**  Draft application for licenses.

**B.**  Prepare compliance reports.

**C.**  Prepare exemption applications.

**D.**  Prepare statistical analyses.

**E.**  Monitor activities of the FCC.

**F.**  Assist in litigation.

    **1.**  Within the FCC,

    **2.**  In court.

■ *Comment on Paralegal Work in This Area:*

The current specialty of Carol Woods is the regulation of television and radio. "I am able to do work that is important and substantive, and am able to work independently. I have an awful lot of contact with clients, with paralegals at the client's office, and with government agencies. One of the liabilities of private practice for both attorneys and paralegals is that there is so much repetition and you can get bored. A lot of times as a paralegal you can't call the shots or know everything that goes into the planning of a project. However, when you can participate in all facets of a project, it's great!" A. Fins, *Opportunities in Paralegal Careers,* 84 (Nat'l Textbook Co., 1979).

## 10.  Construction Law

(See also *contract law, litigation,* and *tort law.*)

### I.  Claims Assistance

**A.**  Work with engineering consultants in the preparation of claims.

## II. Data Collection

**A.** Daily manpower hours,

**B.** Amount of concrete poured,

**C.** Change of orders.

## III. Document Preparation

**A.** Prepare graphs.

**B.** Prepare special studies—for example, compare planned with actual progress on construction project.

**C.** Prepare documents for negotiation/settlement.

**D.** Help draft arbitration claim forms.

## IV. Assist in litigation.

■ *Comment on Paralegal Work in This Area:*

"Because of the complex factual issues that arise with construction disputes, legal assistants are critical in identifying, organizing, preparing, and analyzing the extensive relevant factual information. In many cases, whether a party wins or loses depends on how effectively facts are developed from documents, depositions, interviews, and site inspections. Thus, a successful construction litigation team will generally include a legal assistant skilled in organization and management of complex and voluminous facts. . . . Construction litigation also provides legal assistants with a very distinctive area for expertise and specialization." M. Gowen, *A Guide for Legal Assistants* 229 (Practicing Law Institute, 1986).

## 11.  Contract Law

The law of contracts is involved in a number of different paralegal specialties. See *advertising law, antitrust law, banking law, bankruptcy law, collections law, construction law, corporate law, employee benefits law, entertainment law, family law, government contract law, insurance law, intellectual property law, international law, labor and employment law, landlord-tenant law, municipal finance law, oil and gas law, real estate law,* and *tax law.*

## I. Contract Review

**A.** Review contracts to determine compliance with terms.

**B.** Investigate facts involving alleged breach of contract.

**C.** Do legal research on the law of contracts in a particular specialty.

## II. Litigation Assistance

## III. Preparation of Contract Forms

**A.** Separation agreements,

**B.** Employment contracts,

**C.** Contracts for sale,

**D.** Etc.

■ *Comment on Paralegal Work in This Area:*

"The . . . paralegal also assists two attorneys in drafting reviewing, researching, revising and finalizing a variety of contracts, including Entertainment, Participant and Operational Agreements. Much of the . . . paralegal's time is spent studying existing contracts looking for provisions that may answer any inquiries or disputes. With hundreds of agreements presently active, researching, reviewing, amending, terminating, revising and executing contracts is an everyday activity for [the] . . . Legal Department." Miquel, *Walt Disney World Company's Legal Assistants: Their Role in the Show,* 16 Facts and Findings 29, 30 (NALA, January 1990).

"Initially, my primary job was to review contracts, and act as Plan Administrator for the 401(k). I was also involved in the negotiation and development of a distributor agreement to market SPSS software to the Soviet Union. Most contract amendments were to software license agreements. The pace picked up when I was promoted to Manager of Human Services, while retaining all of my previous responsibilities." Illinois Paralegal Ass'n, *Spotlight on . . . Laurel Bauer,* 20 Outlook 21 (Winter 1991).

## 12.  Corporate Law

Paralegals involved in corporate law mainly work in one of two settings: law firms that represent corporations and legal departments of corporations. Corporate legal departments are often run by an attorney called the general counsel. (See also *banking law, employee benefits law, insurance law, labor and employment law, real estate law,* and *tax law.*)

## I. Incorporation and General Corporate Work

**A.** Preincorporation.

   **1.** Check availability of proposed corporate name and, if available, reserve it.

   **2.** Draft preincorporation subscriptions and consent forms for initial board of directors where required by statute.

   **3.** Record Articles of Incorporation.

   **4.** Order corporate supplies.

**B.** Incorporation.

   **1.** Draft and file Articles of Incorporation with appropriate state agency:

     **a.** Subchapter S corporation,

     **b.** Close corporation,

     **c.** Nonprofit corporation.

   **2.** Draft minutes of initial meetings of incorporators and directors.

3. Draft corporate bylaws.

4. Obtain corporate seal, minute book, and stock certificate book.

5. Prepare necessary documents to open a corporate bank account.

C. Directors meetings.

1. Prepare and send out waivers and notices of meetings.

2. Draft minutes of directors meetings.

3. Draft resolutions to be considered by directors:

   a. Sale of stock,
   b. Increase in capitalization,
   c. Stock splits,
   d. Stock option,
   e. Pension plan,
   f. Dividend distribution,
   g. Election of officers.

D. Shareholders meetings (annual and special).

1. Draft sections of annual report relating to business activity, officers, and directors of company.

2. Draft notice of meeting, proxy materials, and ballots.

3. Prepare agenda and script of meeting.

4. Draft oath and report of judge of elections when required.

5. Maintain all of the corporate minute books and resolutions.

E. Draft and prepare general documents:

1. Shareholder agreement,
2. Employment contract,
3. Employee benefit plan,
4. Stock option plan,
5. Trust agreement,
6. Tax return,
7. Closing papers on corporate acquisition.
8. See also drafting tasks listed above in reference to directors and shareholders meetings.

## II. Public Sale of Securities

A. Compile information concerning officers and directors for use in Registration Statement.

B. Assist in research of blue sky requirements.

C. Closing:

1. Prepare agenda,

2. Obtain certificates from state agencies with respect to good standing of company and certified corporate documents,

3. Prepare index and organize closing binders.

## III. Research

A. Legislative reporting: keep track of pending legislation that may affect office clients.

B. Extract designated information from corporate records and documents.

C. Assemble financial data from records on file at SEC and state securities regulatory agencies.

D. Undertake short- and long-term statistical and financial research on companies.

E. Perform legal research.

## IV. General Assistance

A. Maintain tickler system (specifying, for example, next corporate meeting, upcoming trial, appellate court dates, etc.).

B. Monitor the daily law journal or newspaper in order to identify certain cases on calendars of courts, current court decisions, articles, etc. and forward such data in the journal or newspaper to appropriate office attorneys.

C. Act as file managers for certain clients (index, digest, and monitor documents in the file, prepare case profiles, etc.).

D. Maintain corporate forms file.

## V. Miscellaneous

A. Prepare documents for qualification to do business in foreign jurisdictions.

B. Prepare filings with regulatory agencies.

C. Assist in processing patent, copyright, and trademark applications.

D. Coordinate escrow transactions.

E. Work on certificates of occupancy.

F. Prepare documents needed to amend bylaws or articles of incorporation.

G. Prepare interrogatories.

H. Digest deposition testimony.

I. Perform cite checks.

■ *Comment on Paralegal Work in This Area:*

"When the majority of people describe a legal assistant or a paralegal, they often think of courtroom battles, million dollar lawsuits and mountains of depositions. For those of us in the corporate area, these sights are replaced with board room battles, million dollar mergers and mountains of prospectus. Some of us have NEVER seen the inside of a courtroom or have never touched a pleading. I guess it can be said that 'we don't do windows, we don't type, and we don't do litigation.' A corporate paralegal is never without a multitude of projects that offer excitement or anxiety. This isn't to say, however, that the corporate field is without its fair share of boredom. . . . The future is only limited by your imagination. Not every paralegal wants the drama of a landmark case. Some of us are quite content seeing a client's company written up in the *Wall Street Journal* for the first time!" D. Zupanovich, *The Forming of a Corporate Paralegal,* 2 California Paralegal 4 (July/September 1990).

"The company I work for is a major worldwide producer of chemicals. . . . I recently had to obtain some technical information about the computer system at a hotel in a foreign country in order to set up documents on a diskette that would be compatible with the computer system in that country before one of the attorneys went there for contract negotiations." "One of the most thrilling experiences I have had since working for the company was that of working on the closing of a leveraged buyout of a portion of our business in Delaware. To experience first-hand the intensity of the negotiating table, the numerous last-minute changes to documents, the multitudinous shuffle of papers, and the late, grueling hours was both exhausting and exhilarating." Grove, *Scenes from a Corporate Law Department,* The Paraview 2 (Metrolina Paralegal Ass'n, February 1990).

"Even 'dream jobs' have their moments of chaos. After only two months on the job [at Nestle Foods Corporation] Cheryl had to prepare for a Federal Trade Commission Second Request for Production of Documents relating to an acquisition. She suddenly was thrown into the job of obtaining and organizing over 6,000 documents from around the world, creating a document database and managing up to 10 temporary paralegals at a time. Of course, this preparation included weekends and evenings for a six-week period. Cheryl calls December the 'lost month.' " Scior, *Paralegal Profile: Corporate Paralegal,* Post Script 14 (Manhattan Paralegal Ass'n, April/May 1990).

■ *Quotes from Want Ads:*

Law firm seeks paralegal for corporate work: "Ideal candidate is a self-starter with good communications skills and is willing to work overtime." "Ability to work independently is a must." Paralegal needed to assist corporate secretary: "Analytical, professional attitude essential. Knowledge of state and/or federal regulatory agencies required." "Ability to work under pressure." "All candidates must possess excellent writing and drafting skills." "Ideal candidate is a self-starter with good communication/research skills and is willing to work overtime." "Candidate having less than three years experience in general corporate legal assistance need not apply." Position requires "word processing experience and ability to manage multiple projects." Position requires "intelligent, highly motivated individual who can work with little supervision." "Great opportunity to learn all aspects of corporate business transactions." Position requires "career-minded paralegal with excellent organizational and communications skills, keen analytical ability and meticulous attention to detail." Position

requires "an experienced paralegal with a strong blue-sky background particularly in public and private real estate syndication." Applicant must have "excellent academic credentials, be analytical, objective, and dedicated to performing thorough quality work and to displaying a professional attitude to do whatever it takes to get the job done and meet deadlines."

## 13.  Criminal Law[9]

(See also *litigation* and *military law.*)

I. Paralegal Working for Criminal/Civil Division Prosecutor

A.  Log incoming cases.

B.  Help office screen out cases that are inappropriate for arrest, cases that are eligible for diversion, etc.

C.  Act as liaison with police department and other law enforcement agencies.

D.  Prepare periodic, statistical, caseload reports.

E.  Interview citizens seeking the prosecution of alleged wrongdoers; prepare case files.

F.  Help the Consumer Fraud Department resolve minor consumer complaints—for instance, contact the business involved to determine whether a settlement of the case is possible without prosecution.

G.  Conduct field investigations as assigned.

H.  Prepare documents for URESA cases (Uniform Reciprocal Enforcement of Support Act).

I.  Monitor status of URESA cases.

J.  Help office maintain its case calendar.

K.  Act as liaison among the prosecutor, the victim, and witnesses while the case is being prepared for trial and during the trial.

L.  Act as general litigation assistant during the trial and the appeal.

II. Paralegal Working for Defense Attorney

A.  Interview defendants to determine eligibility for free legal defense (if the paralegal works for a public defender).

B.  Conduct comprehensive interview of defendant on matters relevant to the criminal charge(s).

C.  Help the defendant gather information relevant to the determination of bail.

---

[9]See J. Stein & B. Hoff, *Paralegals and Administrative Assistants for Prosecutors* (Nat'l District Attorneys Ass'n, 1974); and J. Stein, *Paralegals: A Resource for Defenders and Correctional Services* (1976).

D. Help the defendant gather information relevant to eligibility for diversion programs.

E. Conduct field investigations as assigned; interview witnesses.

F. Help obtain discovery, particularly through police reports and search warrants.

G. Act as general litigation assistant during the trial and the appeal.

■ *Comment on Paralegal Work in This Area:*

"Ivy speaks with an obvious love for her current job in the State Attorney's office. In fact, she said she would not want to do anything else! She also said there is no such thing as a typical day in her office, which is one of the many aspects of her job she enjoys. She not only helps interview witnesses and prepare them for trial, but she often must locate a witness, requiring some detective work! Ivy assisted in a case involving an elderly woman who was victimized after the death of her husband. The woman was especially vulnerable because of her illiteracy. Through the help of the State Attorney's office, the woman was able to recover her money and get assistance with housing and learning to read. Ivy continues to keep in touch with the woman and feels the experience to be very rewarding." Frazier, *Spotlight on Ivy Hart-Daniel,* JLA News 2 (Jacksonville Legal Assistants, Inc., January 1989).

"Kitty Polito says she and other lawyers at McClure, McClure & Kammen use the firm's sole paralegal not only to do investigations but 'to pick cases apart piece by piece.' Polito credits legal assistant Juliann Klapp with 'cracking the case' of a client who was accused by a co-defendant of hitting the victim on the back of the head. At trial, the pathologist testified that the victim had been hit from left to right. Klapp passed a note to the attorneys pointing out that such a motion would have been a back-handed swing for their right-handed client. Thus it was more likely that the co-defendant, who is left-handed, was the one who hit the victim. The defendant won." Brandt, *Paralegals' Acceptance and Utilization Increasing in Indy's Legal Community,* 1 The Indiana Lawyer 1 (June 20, 1990).

## 14. Employee Benefits Law[10]

Employee benefits paralegals work in a number of different settings: in law firms, banks, large corporations, insurance companies, or accounting firms. The following overview of tasks covers a paralegal working for a law firm. (See also *contract law, corporate law, labor and employment law, social security law,* and *worker's compensation law.*)

---

[10]Rocky Mountain Legal Assistants Association, *The Use of the Legal Assistant* (1975).

I. Drafting of Employee Plans

A. Work closely with the attorney, the plan sponsor, the plan administrator, and the trustee in preparing and drafting qualified employee plans, such as:

1. Stock bonus plans,
2. Profit sharing plans,
3. Money purchase pensions,
4. Other pension plans,
5. Trust agreements,
6. Individual Retirement Account (IRA) plans,
7. Annuity plans,
8. HR-10 or Keogh plans,
9. Employee stock ownership plans,
10. Life and health insurance plans,
11. Worker's compensation plans,
12. Social security plans.

II. Document Preparation and Program Monitoring

A. Gather information.
B. Determine eligibility for participation and benefits.
C. Notify employees of participation.
D. Complete input forms for document assembly.
E. Assemble elections to participate.
F. Determine beneficiary designations.
G. Record elections to contribute.
H. Allocate annual contributions to individual participant accounts.
I. Prepare annual account statements for participants.
J. Identify any potential discrimination problems in the program.

III. Government Compliance Work Pertaining To:

A. Tax requirements for qualifications, amendment, and termination of plan.
B. Department of Labor reporting and disclosure requirements.
C. Insurance requirements.
D. Welfare and Pension Plans Disclosure Act requirements.
E. ERISA requirements (Employee Retirement Income Security Act).
F. Pension Benefit Guaranty Corporation requirements.

IV. Miscellaneous

A. Help draft summary plan descriptions for distribution to employees.
B. Help prepare and review annual reports of plans.

C. Continue education in current law of the field—for instance, become a Certified Employee Benefit Specialist (CEBS).

■ *Comment on Paralegal Work in This Area:*

"Michael Montchyk was looking to use his undergraduate degree in statistics. . . . He now works for attorneys specializing in employee benefits, where understanding numbers and familiarity with the law are key skills." Lehren, *Paralegal Work Enhancing Careers of Many,* Philadelphia Business Journal 9B (August 6, 1990).

"This area is not for everybody. To succeed, you need considerable detail orientation, solid writing skills, self-motivation, the ability to keep up with a legal landscape that is never the same, and a knack for handling crisis situations which arise when least expected." Germani, *Opportunities in Employee Benefits,* SJPA Reporter 7 (South Jersey Paralegal Ass'n, January 1989).

## 15. Entertainment Law

(See also *contract law, corporate law,* and *intellectual property law.*)

### I. Types of Client Problem Areas

A. *Copyright and trademark law:* Applying for government protection for intellectual property, such as plays, films, video, music, and novels.

B. *Contract law:* Help negotiate and draft contracts, and ensure their enforcement.

C. *Labor law:* Assist in compliance with the contracts of unions or guilds.

D. *Corporate law:*
   1. Assist in formation of business organizations.
   2. Work on mergers.
   3. Maintain compliance with federal and state reporting laws and regulations.

E. *Tax law:* planning and compliance.
   1. Report passive royalty income, talent advances, residuals, etc.
   2. Allocate expenditures to specific projects.

F. *Family law:* Assist with prenuptial agreements, divorces, child custody, etc.

### II. Tasks

A. Register copyrights.

B. Help a client affiliate with his or her guild.

C. Monitor remake and sequel rights to films.

D. Prepare documents to grant a license to use client's music.

E. Check title registrations with the Motion Picture Association of America.

F. Read scripts to determine whether clearances are needed for certain kinds of material and references.

G. Apply for permits and licenses.

H. Calculate costs of property rights.

■ *Comment on Paralegal Work in This Area:*

"I am a paralegal in the field of entertainment law, one of the fastest growing, and, to me, most exciting areas of the paralegal profession, and one whose duties are as varied as the practices of the lawyers for whom we work. . . . I started in a very large Century City firm whose entertainment practice covers everything from songwriters to financing of major motion pictures, and from major recording stars and producers to popular novelists. . . . My specialty (yes, a specialty within a specialty) is music. . . . My husband is also an entertainment paralegal who works for 20th Century Fox. . . . Never, ever a dull moment!" Birkner, *Entertainment Law: A Growing Industry for the Paralegal,* 2 California Paralegal Magazine 7 (April/June 1990).

## 16. Environmental Law[11]

(See also *legislation, litigation, oil and gas law, real estate law,* and *water law.*)

### I. Research

A. Research questions pertaining to the environment, land use, water pollution, and the National Environmental Policy Act.
   1. Locate and study pertinent state and federal statutes, case law, regulations, and law review articles.
   2. Obtain secondary materials (maps, articles, books) useful for broadening the information base.
   3. Contact, when appropriate, government officials or other informants for data or answers.
   4. Obtain and develop personality profiles of members of Congress, members of relevant bureaucracies, and other political figures.
   5. Help prepare memoranda of findings, including citations and supporting documents.

B. Develop research notebooks for future reference. When new topics arise in environmental law, prepare notebooks to facilitate future research on similar topics.

C. Prepare bibliographies on environmental topics.

### II. Drafting

A. Draft memoranda regarding new federal and state laws, regulations, or findings of research.

---

[11]Colorado Bar Association Legal Assistant Committee. These tasks have been approved by the Committee, not by the Board of Governors of the Colorado Bar.

B. Draft memoranda discussing pertinent issues, problems, and possible solutions regarding public policy developments.

C. Draft narrative histories of legislation regarding political impulses, the impact of administrative and court rulings, and substantive and technical differences between drafts of legislation or results of amendments.

D. Draft and edit articles on coastal management programs and problems, conservation, water pollution, and the National Environmental Policy Act.

E. Edit environmental impact statements.

F. Assist in the preparation of briefs.

   1. Check citations for pertinence and accuracy.

   2. Develop table of contents, list of authorities, and certificate of service.

III. Hearing Participation

A. Locate and schedule witnesses.

B. Gather pertinent research materials (including necessary local documents, maps, and specific subject matter).

IV. Litigation: Provide General Trial Assistance

■ *Comment on Paralegal Work in This Area:*

Mary Peterson's firm has made a specialty of environmental and land use law. In a recent major hazardous waste case, "we will try to prove that the paint companies, dry cleaning stores and even the federal government, which used the property to build aircraft during the war" are responsible. "Some of the toxic waste dumped there were cited by federal agencies even back to 1935." Her job is to investigate the types of hazardous wastes and, with the help of the Freedom of Information Act, gather all available evidence. Then she studies it, duplicates, indexes, and writes summaries, which she distributes to the partners and associates. It's a case that has taken eight months so far and may go on for several years "because you don't know what you will uncover tomorrow. The toxins and pollutants could be different. There is no standard, just a constantly changing picture." Edwards, *The General Practice Paralegal* 8 Legal Assistant Today 49, 55 (March/April 1991).

## 17. Estates, Trusts, and Probate Law

(See also *banking law, collections law, employee benefits law, family law,* and *social security law.*)

I. Estate Planning

A. Collect data (birth dates, fair market value of assets, current assets and liabilities, etc.).

B. Prepare preliminary drafts of wills or trusts from sample forms.

C. Perform investment analysis in order to provide attorney who is fiduciary of estate with information relevant to investment options.

II. Office Management

A. Maintain tickler system.

B. Maintain attorney's calendar.

C. Open, index, monitor, and keep current all components of the client's trust and estate office file.

D. Operate computer in connection with accounting aspects of trusts and estates administered by the office.

E. Act as office law librarian (keeping loose-leaf texts up-to-date, etc.).

F. Train secretaries and other paralegals in the system used by the office to handle trusts, estates, and probate cases.

G. Selectively discard certain mail and underline significant parts of other mail.

III. Estate of Decedent

A. Assets phase.

   1. Collect assets (such as bank accounts, custody accounts, insurance proceeds, social security death benefits, safety deposit box contents, and apartment contents).

   2. Assist in the valuation of assets.

   3. Maintain records (for example, record and file wills and trusts, vault inventories, powers of attorney, property settlements, fee cards, bill-payment letters).

   4. Notify beneficiaries.

   5. Prepare profiles of wills and trusts for attorney review.

B. Accounting phase.

   1. Prepare preliminary drafts of federal and state death tax returns.

   2. Apply the income-principal rules to the estate.

   3. Organize data relevant to the tax implications of estates.

   4. Prepare accountings: final and accounts current (this involves setting up a petition for a first and final accounting).

C. Termination-distribution phase.

   1. Apply for the transfer of securities into the names of the people entitled.

   2. Draw checks for the signature of executors.

   3. Monitor legacies to charitable clients.

   4. File and prepare tax waivers.

5. Assist with the closing documents.

6. Calculate distributable net income.

7. Follow up on collection and delivery.

## IV. Litigation

1. Perform legal research.

2. Conduct factual research (investigation)—for instance, track down the names and addresses of all possible claimants and contact them.

3. Prepare sample pleadings.

4. Digest depositions (review, condense, point out inconsistencies, etc.).

5. Prepare drafts of interrogatories.

6. Prepare drafts of answers to interrogatories.

7. Notarize documents.

8. Act as court witness as to decedent's signature and other matters.

9. Assist with litigation.

■ *Comment on Paralegal Work in This Area:*

"What I like best about estate planning is that you work with people on a very individual basis. I don't think that in many other areas of law you get that one-on-one contact with the client. . . . You're working with people while they are thinking about the most important things in their lives—their families, their wealth and how to distribute it, and what they want to happen after they pass on. A lot of the clients contact me directly with their questions for the attorneys. Some of the widows especially are more comfortable calling me with their questions. They seem to think their questions might be 'stupid' and they're embarrassed to ask the attorneys directly. I can take their questions and see that the attorneys respond to them promptly." Bassett, *Top Gun Patricia Adams: Legal Assistant of the Year,* 6 Legal Assistant Today 70, 74 (July/August 1990).

"The position can be very stressful. But it is seldom boring. My typical day involves responding to many telephone inquiries from clients, dictating memos, or letters requesting additional information concerning life insurance policies, valuation of assets, or simply sending notice of an upcoming hearing "to all persons entitled," etc. I draft virtually all documents needed in the administration of an estate, beginning with the initial petition for probate. . . . The decedent may have had an interest in a closely-held business, or leave minor or handicapped children, or leave a spouse with no knowledge of the family assets; these all require additional attention. Every case is different. Probate paralegals to some extent must be 'snoopy,' because you do learn a great deal about people, both deceased and living. In most cases your client is facing a difficult time with trepidation and it is your role to provide confidence. The end results are very rewarding." Rose, *Still a Probate Paralegal,* 12 The Journal 5 (Sacramento Ass'n of Legal Assistants, August 1990).

■ *Quotes from Want Ads:*

Law firm seeks someone with "good communication and organizational skills, [who] is self-motivated, relates well with attorneys, clients, and staff, is detail oriented, has a teamwork attitude, a pleasant personality, and is a non-smoker." Bank has opening for "trust tax administrator, with emphasis on personal and trust planning." Paralegal must have "technical understanding of wills and estate plans and terminology. Must be self-starter." "This is a full-time position with extensive responsibility for both court-supervised and noncourt-supervised estates and trusts." Position requires a person who "enjoys writing and proofreading, and who has excellent grammatical skills." Job is "for individual who enjoys the complexity and detail of accounting and bookkeeping in a legal environment." "Applicants must be prepared to handle tax work."

## 18. Ethics and Professional Responsibility

Paralegals in this area work in two main settings: (1) in large law firms as a conflicts specialist, helping the firm determine whether conflicts of interest exist and (2) in state disciplinary agencies that investigate complaints against attorneys for unethical behavior.

### I. Law Firm (*Conflicts Specialist* or *Manager*)

A. Research

1. Identify all persons or companies related to the prospective client.

2. Determine whether the firm has ever represented the prospective client and/or any of its related parties.

3. Determine whether the firm has ever represented an opponent of the prospective client and/or any of its related parties.

B. *Reports:* Notify attorney in charge of professional-responsibility matters of data indicating possible conflicts.

C. *Database work:* update information in client-list database on current and past clients.

### II. Disciplinary Agency

A. Screen incoming data on new ethical complaints against attorneys.

B. Help investigate complaints.

C. Provide general litigation assistance to disciplinary attorneys during the proceedings at the agency and in court.

■ *Comment on Paralegal Work in This Area:*

Jane Palmer "does all the research on every prospective client, identifying all the related parties." Her computerized database tells her if the firm has ever represented a party on either side, or been adverse to them. "The most valuable thing has been my experience with the firm, developing somewhat of a corporate memory. The job takes extreme attention to detail. You may not always have all the information you need, so you have to be a detective. Quick response is important; so is making sure to keep things confidential." Sacramento Ass'n of Legal Assistants, *New Responsibilities Given to Paralegals*, The Journal 5 (February 1991).

## 19. Family Law[12]

(See also *contract law, employee benefits law, estates law, litigation, pro bono work,* and *public sector.*)

I. Telephone Screening of Clients

II. Commencement of Action

A. Interview client to obtain initial information for pleadings.

B. Prepare initial pleadings, including petition, summons and waiver of service, affidavit as to children, and response.

C. Draft correspondence to clients, courts, and other attorneys.

D. Arrange for service of process.

III. Temporary Orders

A. Prepare motions for temporary orders or temporary injunctions.

B. Draft notice and set hearings.

C. Assist in settlement negotiations.

D. Draft stipulations for temporary orders after negotiations.

IV. Financial Affidavits

A. Work with clients to gather and compile financial information.

B. Analyze income and expense information provided by client.

C. Work with accountants, financial advisors, brokers, and other financial experts retained by client.

D. Retain appraisers for real estate, business, and personal property.

E. Prepare financial affidavits.

V. Discovery

A. Prepare discovery requests.

B. Assist clients—gather documents and data to respond to discovery requests.

C. Help prepare responses to discovery requests.

D. Organize, index, and summarize discovered materials.

VI. Settlement Negotiations

A. Assist attorney in analysis of proposed settlements.

B. Research legal questions and assist in drafting briefs and memoranda.

C. Assist in drafting separation agreements.

VII. Hearings

A. Help prepare for final orders hearings.

B. Research legal questions and assist in drafting briefs and memoranda.

C. Assist in the preparation of trial exhibits and trial notebooks.

D. Arrange for expert witnesses and assist in preparing witnesses and clients for trial.

E. Attend hearings.

F. Prepare decree.

VIII. Post-Decree

A. Prepare documents for transfers of assets.

B. Arrange for the filing and recording of all transfer documents.

C. Review bills for tax-deductible fees and help prepare opinion letters to client.

D. Draft pleadings for withdrawal from case.

IX. Special Projects

A. Develop forms for gathering information from client.

B. Maintain files on the following: separation-agreement provisions, current case law, resource materials for clients, and experts in various fields (e.g., custody, evaluation, and business appraisals).

■ *Comment on Paralegal Work in This Area:*

Karen Dunn, a family law paralegal, "draws considerable satisfaction from a divorce case where the client was a woman in her sixties whose husband had left her, a situation which created predictable distress, notably during discussion of financial aspects. She was able to tell me things she couldn't tell the attorney. I found out she had a thyroid condition, so she was able to get more money in the end. I worked with her on the financial affidavit and drafted temporary orders to provide child support and spousal maintenance until the decree was entered." Edwards, *The General Practice Paralegal* 8 Legal Assistant Today 49, 54 (March/April 1991).

"As the only paralegal in a one-attorney family law practice, my job responsibilities are numerous. I work for an attorney who believes her paralegal should handle nearly all the legal functions she does, with the exception

[12]See footnote 11.

of appearing in court on behalf of clients, taking depositions and giving legal advice. My skills are used to the maximum, as I gather and organize all case information, allowing the attorney to prepare for court and be more cost-effective. I am the liaison person between clients and the attorney. I am able to deal with the human, emotional aspects of our clients, and not just the technical aspects of the law. As each person is different, so is every case, which makes this job a continuing challenge." Lenihan, *Role of the Family Law Paralegal,* 10 Paragram 6 (Oregon Legal Assistants Ass'n, August 1987).

■ *Quotes from Want Ads:*

Position is "excellent for a highly motivated person with excellent organizational skills and the ability to interface with clients." "Two swamped attorneys need reliable paralegal to work in fully computerized office. Must have excellent research and writing skills." Applicant must be "self-motivated, well-organized person who has initiative and can assume responsibility." Position requires "ability, experience, and attention to detail." "Looking for very professional applicants."

## 20. Government Contract Law[13]

(See also *administrative law, construction law, contract law, litigation,* and *water law.*)

### I. Calendar

A. Maintain calendar for court and appeals board appearances.

B. Record dates briefs are due, etc.

### II. Claims

A. Gather, review, summarize, and index client files.

B. Assist in drafting contract claims.

C. Conduct preliminary research on selected legal issues.

### III. Appeals

A. Draft and answer interrogatories and requests for production of documents.

B. Summarize and index answers to discovery.

C. Assist in drafting appeal.

D. Prepare questions for witnesses and summarize prior testimony.

E. Maintain documents during hearing.

### IV. Post-Hearing Briefs

A. Summarize and index transcripts.

B. Assist with analysis of government's brief.

C. Conduct preliminary research on selected issues.

D. Assist in drafting the post-hearing brief.

## 21. Immigration Law

(See also *administrative law, family law, international law, labor and employment law,* and *public sector.*)

### I. Problem Identification

A. Help individual who has difficulty in obtaining:
   1. Visa,
   2. Permanent residency based on occupation,
   3. Nonimmigrant status,
   4. Citizenship status.

B. Help individuals who are faced with deportation proceedings.

### II. Providing Information on

A. Visa process,

B. Permanent residency process,

C. Nonimmigrant status process,

D. Registration process,

E. Citizenship process,

F. Deportation process.

### III. Investigation

Assist the individual in obtaining data and documentation on birth, travel, residency, etc.

### IV. Referral

Refer individuals to foreign consulates, nationality organizations, government officials, etc., for assistance concerning their immigration status.

### V. Applications/Forms

Assist the individual in filling out visa applications, permanent residency applications, etc.

### VI. Monitor Consular Processing Procedure

■ *Comment on Paralegal Work in This Area:*

"This is not a specialty for the faint-hearted or the misanthrope. The immigration paralegal may deal with much more than the timely filing of paperwork. One distinguishing feature of immigration work is our knowledge of intensely personal aspects of the client's life. We know his criminal record, the success and failure of his personal life, how much money he makes, and his dreams and aspirations. ... Some clients have a very laissez-faire attitude towards perjury, and may invite the paralegal to participate without a blush. In America, [said one client] you lie *to* your attorney. In my country, you cook up the lie *with* your attorney." Myers & Raman, *Sweet-Talking Clients and Intransigent Bureaucrats,* 15 National Paralegal Reporter 4 (NFPA, Winter 1991).

---

[13]Berg, C. *Annual Survey* (San Francisco Association of Legal Assistants, Dec. 19, 1973).

## 22. Insurance Law

Paralegals in this area work for law firms that represent insurance companies who are defendants in litigation, often personal injury litigation. They also work for insurance companies themselves. The following overview covers the latter. (See also *corporate law, employee benefits law, litigation, social security law,* and *worker's compensation law*.)

### I. Compliance

A. Analyze government regulations on the insurance industry.

B. Prepare applications for new insurance products to obtain approval from department of insurance.

### II. Claims

A. Assist in processing disputed claims.

B. Provide trial assistance by coordinating activities of company attorneys with outside counsel representing the company.

### III. Monitoring and Research

A. Monitor regulations of agencies and statutes of the legislatures that affect the insurance industry, including the committees of the legislature with jurisdiction over the industry.

B. Provide factual and legal research on inquiries that come into the office from agents and brokers.

■ *Comment on Paralegal Work in This Area:*

"Compliance is an insurance industry term which refers to keeping the company and its products in compliance with state and federal law, and procuring licenses for the company in unlicensed states. Compliance is a good field for paralegals because there is opportunity to work autonomously and also to advance within most companies." I am a "Senior Compliance Analyst" at a life insurance company. "I have met many paralegals who are compliance analysts, compliance specialists, and compliance managers." Maston, *Insurance,* The Citator 8 (Legal Assistants of Central Ohio, August 1990).

## 23. Intellectual Property Law

(See also *contract law* and *entertainment law*.)

### I. Copyrights

A. Application

   1. Help client apply for registration of copyright for a novel, play, or other work with the Copyright Office.

   2. Collect data, such as nature of the work, date completed, name of creator/author, name of the work, owner, etc., for application.

   3. Help identify the classification for the copyright.

   4. Examine the certificate of copyright registration for accuracy.

   5. File the application.

B. Marketing

   1. Identify potential users/licensees of the copyright.

   2. Help prepare contracts.

C. Infringement

   1. Conduct investigations to determine whether an infringement exists—for example, compare the copyrighted work with the alleged infringing work.

   2. Provide general litigation assistance.

### II. Patent

A. Application

   1. Help the inventor apply for a patent with the U.S. Patent and Trademark Office.

   2. Help the inventor describe the invention—for example, assemble designs, diagrams, and notebooks.

   3. Conduct a patent search. Check technical libraries to determine the current state of the art.

   4. Determine filing fees.

   5. Help the client apply for protection in foreign countries.

   6. Monitor the responses from government offices.

   7. Examine certificate of patent for accuracy.

B. Marketing the invention

   1. Help identify licensees. Solicit bids, conduct financial checks, study the market, etc.

   2. Help prepare contracts.

C. Infringement

   1. Conduct investigation on products that may have violated the patent.

   2. Provide general litigation assistance.

### III. Trademarks

A. Registration

   1. Research trademark files or order search of trademark or trade name preliminary to an application before the U.S. Patent and Trademark Office.

   2. Examine indexes and directories.

   3. Conduct investigations to determine when the mark was first used, where, on what products, etc.

   4. Prepare foreign trademark applications.

   5. Respond to official actions taken by government offices.

6. Examine the certificate of trademark for accuracy.
7. Maintain files for renewals.

**B.** Infringement
1. Conduct investigations into who else used the mark, when, where, in what market, etc.
2. Provide general litigation assistance.

■ *Comment on Paralegal Work in This Area:*

"With the right training, trademark paralegals can find richly rewarding experiences waiting for them, whether they remain in paralegal work or go on to build careers in some other facet of trademark law. Trademark work is very dynamic." Wilkinson, *The Case for a Career in Trademark Law,* 7 Legal Professional 29 (November/December 1989).

"Paula Rein was a trademark paralegal before such a job title was even invented. Her career has spanned over 19 years, leading her to some of the biggest corporations and law firms in New York City. Her extensive knowledge of trademark administration has made her one of the most resourceful trademark paralegals in her occupation. In her current 'diversified position,' at a law firm that specializes in intellectual property, she works on the cases of clients in the food and service industries and professional associations. Paula thrives in her current position." Scior, *Paralegal Profile,* Postscript 13 (Manhattan Paralegal Ass'n, December 1989).

## 24. International Law

Example: a paralegal working on a "dumping" case in international trade.

**I. Investigation**

**A.** Examine the normal behavior in the industry/market affected.

**B.** Do statistical research (cost and price data).

**C.** Prepare profiles of domestic competitors.

**II. Preparation of Documents**

**A.** Help prepare for presentation before the Commerce Department.

**B.** Help prepare for presentation before the Court of International Trade.

**III. Accounting Research**

**IV. Coordination of Data From:**

**A.** Members of Congress,

**B.** Foreign embassies,

**C.** State Department,

**D.** U.S. Special Trade Representative.

■ *Comment on Paralegal Work in This Area:*

Steven Stark works "40–50 hours a week, specializing in international legal assisting, a hot area, while the Japanese are busy buying up American properties. [Steve became the liaison for the firm's Tokyo branch office. He originally expected to stay at the firm only three years, but found that] the longer you're here, the more they value you. New things still come up. You work with the constant tension of everyone being expected to perform at a very high level, at all times. This is a high-stakes game, with million and billion dollar deals. It's a peaked, emotional atmosphere, with long hours." Milano, *Career Profiles,* 8 Legal Assistant Today 35, 38 (September/October 1990).

## 25. Judicial Administration

Most courts have clerks to help with the administrative aspects of deciding cases. In addition, a few courts have paralegals that work for the court. They perform some of the functions of the administrative clerks, such as determining whether the parties have been properly notified of trial dates, checking filings and proposed orders from attorneys to determine whether anything appears inappropriate or premature, or obtaining additional information for a judge.

■ *Comment on Paralegal Work in This Area:*

"The Shreveport City Court has employed me as its paralegal in the civil department for the past six years. The Baton Rouge City Court employs several paralegals." We handle many matters such as determining if the legal delays for pleading have expired "before initialing the pleading and passing it on to the clerk or judge for signature. The most important task is the handling of default judgments. I must certify that proper service has been made. Perhaps I could be called a 'nitpicker' about these cases, but the judge acts on my certificate that everything is in order. It is always challenging to stay informed on our constantly changing procedural laws; I must keep a set of the Civil Procedure at my desk." Waterman, *The Court's Paralegal,* 3 NWLPA News 5 (Northwest Louisiana Paralegal Ass'n, November 1990).

## 26. Labor and Employment Law

(See also *civil rights law, contract law, employee benefits law,* and *worker's compensation law.*)

**I. Investigation**

Look into:
**A.** Sexual harassment.
**B.** Wrongful discharge.
**C.** Violation of occupational safety and health laws.

D. Violation of labor laws involving collective bargaining, union organization, grievance and arbitration procedures.

E. Violation of Civil Rights Act protecting against discrimination on the basis of race, national origin, sex, or physical handicap.

F. Violation of Age Discrimination in Employment Act.

G. Violation of Americans with Disabilities Act.

## II. Compliance

Assist companies in the design and implementation of policies on:

A. Drug and alcohol testing.

B. AIDS in the workplace.

C. Race, sex, and age discrimination.

## III. Litigation Assistance

A. Help handle labor disputes before the National Labor Relations Board, State Labor Relations Board, Civil Service Commission, Human Rights Board, and the courts.

B. Perform a variety of tasks:
   1. Maintain the files.
   2. Digest and index data in files.
   3. Arrange for depositions.
   4. Help draft petition and other pleadings.
   5. Maintain tickler system of due dates.
   6. Prepare exhibits.
   7. Prepare statistical data.
   8. Help prepare appeal.

■ *Comment on Paralegal Work in This Area:*

"My experience in the labor and employment area has proven to be both diverse and unique. It is diverse because of the various labor-related issues accessible to me as a paralegal. It is unique because it is an area of specialty which involves very few paralegals in my part of the state." Batke, *Labor and Employment Paralegal,* The Citator 3 (Legal Assistants of Central Ohio, August 1990).

"In the labor law area, I was responsible for doing background research, preparing witnesses and drafting arbitration briefs. I also assisted with the drafting of revised language during contract negotiations with unions." Diebold, *A Paralegal of Another Kind,* 16 Facts and Findings 38 (NALA, March 1990).

## 27. Landlord and Tenant Law

Paralegals in real estate law firms occasionally become involved in commercial lease cases, such as a dispute over the interpretation of the lease of a supermarket at a large shopping mall. Such landlord-tenant cases, however, are not as common as the cases that arise between landlords and tenants who live in the apartments they rent. For example, a landlord of a small apartment seeks to evict a tenant for nonpayment of rent. Many of these cases are handled by publicly funded legal service or legal aid offices which do not charge fees. (See *public sector, oil and gas law,* and *real estate law.*)

■ *Comment on Paralegal Work in This Area:*

"The Legal Action Center is the largest non-governmental social service agency in the state. As a paralegal, Virginia Farley handles all eviction calls to the landlord-tenant unit. Three afternoons a week are designated intake times. She screens all eviction cases, determines whether the applicant is eligible for free assistance according to the Center's guidelines, recommends a plan once a case is accepted and assists in carrying out the plan under an attorney's supervision. [After arriving in the city], Virginia made a commitment to work directly with the poor and started serving as a volunteer in five organizations until a job opened up for her at the Legal Action Center." Roche, *Paralegal Profile,* 4 Findings and Conclusions 5 (Washington Ass'n of Legal Assistants, November 1987).

## 28. Law Librarianship

There is a separate degree that a law librarian can obtain. This degree, however, is not a requirement to be a law librarian. There are a number of small or medium-sized law offices that are hiring paralegals to perform library chores exclusively or in combination with paralegal duties on cases. (See also *law office administration* and *litigation.*)

## I. Administration

A. Order books for law library.

B. File loose-leaf material and pocket parts in appropriate volumes.

C. Pay bills of library vendors.

D. Test and recommend computer equipment, software, and services for the law library.

E. Prepare budget for library.

## II. Cite Checking

A. Check the citations in briefs, speeches, articles, opinion letters, and other legal documents to determine the accuracy of quoted material.

B. Check the citations to determine the accuracy of citation format according to the Uniform System of Citation (the Bluebook), local court rules, or other system required by the office.

## III. Research

A. Undertake factual research projects as information resource.

B. Perform legal research.

## IV. Training

A. Train office staff in traditional legal research techniques.

B. Train office staff in computer research, for example, WESTLAW.

C. Train office staff in cite checking.

■ *Comment on Paralegal Work in This Area:*

"I suppose my entry into the law librarianship profession might be considered unorthodox because I had no formal educational courses in librarianship. My experience was that of working first as a legal secretary and later evolving into a legal assistant. My job in a small general practice firm included taking care of the office library such as filing supplements and pocket parts (because no one else would do it!!); doing the bookkeeping and paying the bills." I did some legal research "as an extension of legal drafting." "In all my working years (and they are many) I had the greatest satisfaction from my work as a law librarian because each day I learned new things." Lewek, *The Legal Assistant as Law Librarian,* 17 Facts & Findings 28 (NALA, March 1991).

## 29. Law Office Administration

At the beginning of Chapter 14, you will find a detailed job description of the legal administrator and of the legal assistant manager. (See Figures 14.2 and 14.3.) Some experienced paralegals move into management positions at a law office. This might involve helping to administer the *entire* office, or *one component* of it, such as the administration of all the legal assistants in the office, the administration of the legal assistants and other support personnel working on a large case, or the administration of the computer operation in the office. There are some smaller law offices that seek paralegals to perform office management duties along with paralegal duties. (See also *law librarianship* and *litigation.*)

■ *Comment on Paralegal Work in This Area:*

In 1984, the partners at the firm decided to upgrade their legal assistant program and needed a nonlawyer to run it. They offered Linda Katz the new position. "The firm is segmented into practice areas, with legal assistants dispersed throughout the areas. They report to supervising attorneys for work assignments each day. I serve as administrative supervisor, assuring consistency in how legal assistants are treated and utilized, and what opportunities they have for benefits and advancement." Milano, *Career Profiles,* 8 Legal Assistant Today 35 (September/October 1990).

"A good paralegal litigation manager [in a large document case] has both strong paralegal skills and strong management skills. Such a manager must be able to analyze the case's organizational needs, develop methods to cope with them effectively, and often must act as paralegal, office manager and computer expert—all in a day's work." Kaufman, *The Litigation Manager,* 6 Legal Professional 55 (July/August 1989).

## 30. Legislation

### I. Monitoring

Keep track of all events, persons, and organizations involved in the passing of legislation relevant to the clients of the firm.

### II. Legislative History

Compile the legislative history of a statute.

### III. Drafting of Proposed Legislation

### IV. Lobbying

A. Prepare reports and studies on the subject of proposed legislation.

B. Arrange for and help prepare witnesses who will testify at legislative hearings.

■ *Comment on Paralegal Work in This Area:*

Margo Horner "is a legislative analyst for the Nat'l Federation of Independent Business (NFIB). With paralegal training and a masters degree in history, her job is research, creating legislative strategy, working with [legislators] and their staffs to produce legislation favorable to [NFIB]. Margo likes the frenetic tempo of her life." Smith, *Margo,* 1 Legal Assistant Today 14 (Summer 1984).

## 31. Litigation

### I. File Monitoring

A. Index all files.

B. Write case profile based on information in the files.

C. Read attorney briefs to check accuracy of the information in the litigation file.

D. Organize and index documents obtained through discovery.

E. Code documents into the computer.

### II. Investigation

A. Gather documents:

1. Medical records,

2. Police records,

3. Birth and death records,

4. Marriage records,

5. Adoption and custody records,

6. Incorporation records.

B. Research records. For instance:

1. Prepare a profit history report of a company.
2. Identify corporate structure of parent and its subsidiaries.
3. Trace UCC (Uniform Commercial Code) filings.
4. Find out from court dockets if a particular merchant is being sued, has sued before, etc. Does any pattern exist?
5. Identify the "real owner" of an apartment building.
6. Check housing code agency to find out if a landlord has other building code violations against it on record.

C. Gather facts (other than documents). In a wide range of cases (such as real estate, corporate, criminal, divorce, and custody), the investigator substantiates facts, follows leads for possible evidence in connection with litigation, etc.

## III. Discovery

A. Draft interrogatories.
B. Draft answers to interrogatories.
C. Draft deposition questions.
D. Prepare witnesses for deposition.
E. Prepare witness books for deposition.
F. Arrange time and place of deposition.
G. Draft requests for admissions.
H. Draft requests for production of documents.
I. Index and digest discovery data.
J. Work with computer programmer in the design of a system to manage discovery documents.

## IV. Filings/Serving

In court, at agencies, on parties, on attorneys, etc.

## V. General Assistance

A. Arrange for clients and others to be interviewed.
B. Arrange for expert witnesses to appear in court or at depositions.
C. Reconstruct (from a large collection of disparate records and other evidence) what happened at a particular time and place.
D. Assist clients in completing information questionnaire, especially in class-action cases.
E. Help organize the trial notebook containing items the attorney will need during the trial, such as charts and tables to be used as exhibits at trial.
F. Sit at counsel's table at trial to take notes and suggest questions for attorney to ask witnesses.
G. Attend (and report on) hearings in related cases.
H. Supervise document encoding on a computer project related to a case in litigation.

I. Prepare and evaluate prospective jurors from jury book and during voir dire.
J. Help prepare appeal documents—for example, the notice of appeal.

## VI. Legal Research

A. Shepardize; perform cite check.
B. Write preliminary memos and briefs.
C. Prepare bibliographies of source materials related to litigation.

## VII. Pleadings

Write preliminary draft of pleadings using standard forms and/or adapting other pleadings written by attorneys on similar cases.

## VIII. Expert Analysis

Assist in obtaining expert opinions for attorneys on:
A. Taxation.
B. Accounting.
C. Statistics.
D. Economics (for example, calculation of damages).

## IX. Court Witness

A. Act as witness as to service of process.
B. Act as witness as to data uncovered or photographed (such as, the condition of an apartment building).

■ *Comment on Paralegal Work in This Area:*

"There are boxes and boxes with an infinite number of documents to be indexed. There are depositions to be summarized. There are cases whose cites need checking. There are trips to the courthouse downtown. There is red-lining of documents to determine changes between two documents. There is Bates-stamping of documents. And there are the exciting trips to visit clients." Lasky, *Impressions of a New Paralegal,* 17 Reporter 5 (Los Angeles Paralegal Ass'n, February 1988).

"I organized. I tabbed and tagged, listed and labelled, hoisted and hole-punched, folded and filed, boxed and Bates-stamped, indexed and itemized, sorted and summarized." Klinkseick, *Aim High,* 16 On Point 4 (Nat'l Capital Area Paralegal Ass'n, July/August 1990).

"Initially, it was overwhelming with the number of files and the names to learn and things to remember, but with help, I learned skills and techniques and polished them day after day as each new case brought with it new quirks and new challenges. I've attended depositions, PTO shaft inspections, and pig farm operations. I've calculated medical expenses, reviewed medical records, and been baffled at how salesmen keep time records! But the ultimate of all experiences, I have to admit, are the trials. You prepare and prepare and hope that you haven't missed any of the details. Then before you know it, the jury has been selected and you're off! The trials keep your adrenaline flowing. They frazzle your patience. They show you your limitations. They elevate you when you win. They shake your confidence when you lose." Riske, *In the Limelight,* 7 Red River Review 4 (Red River Valley Legal Assistants, North Dakota, August 1990).

"For almost six years now . . . , I've experienced the variety (and the drudgery) of preparing civil cases for trial. I've spent countless hours photocopying documents never read by any judge or jury, or worst of all, by anyone else. I've tracked down witnesses and encouraged them to talk only to find out that they know nothing about the case. In this business of endless paper where no two cases are alike, I've come to understand . . . that flexibility is essential and a sense of humor is invaluable in dealing with people, be they stressed-out attorneys or reluctant witnesses." Vore, *A Litigation Recipe* 16 On Point 4 (Nat'l Capital Area Paralegal Ass'n, November 1990).

Rebecca McLaughlin tells of a particularly memorable event during her experience as a paralegal. "It was a few minutes after 12:00 noon on Friday, and presiding Judge Barbour always recesses court at precisely 12:30 on Fridays. The Government's star witness was on the stand and denied he had ever seen a certain letter. One of the trial attorneys motioned me to counsel table and asked if we had any proof that the witness had, in fact, seen this letter." Since there were well over 900 defense exhibits, almost 300 Government exhibits, and well over 40 file cabinets filled with supporting documents, Rebecca felt little hope for success [in finding out quickly]. "She hurried across the street to the office, found the witness' original copy of the letter with his handwritten notes in the margin, and returned to the courtroom with a BIG SMILE. The witness was impeached with his own document minutes before recess." "Later, Rebecca received a well-deserved standing ovation from the attorneys, and all the trial team members. It was the highlight of her career." Johnson, *MALA Spotlight: Rebecca McLaughlin,* 8 The Assistant 17 (Mississippi Ass'n of Legal Assistants, July 1989).

■ *Quotes from Want Ads:*

"Excellent writing skills and attention to detail are absolute requirements." "Plaintiff's medical malpractice firm seeks non-smoker with word processing abilities." Position requires "extensive writing, document summarizing, and medical records research." Must have an ability "to work independently in handling cases from inception through trial preparation; familiarity with drafting law motions pleadings essential." High-energy candidate "needs to be assertive and should have an excellent academic background." "Wanted: a sharp, take-charge litigation paralegal." "Knowledge of computerized litigation support is a plus; good communications and organizational skills are a must." "Applicant must possess a thorough working knowledge of all phases of trial work." "Successful candidate will be professional, prompt, pleasant and personable. No egomaniacs or job hoppers, please." "Overtime flexibility required." "Defense litigation paralegal needed. Must be a self-starter with the ability to accept unstructured responsibility." "Applicant must have a thorough knowledge of state and federal court procedures." Position requires an ability "to organize and manage documents in large multi-party litigation." "Applicants must possess strong supervisory, analytic, writing, and investigative skills, and an ability to perform under pressure." "Position requires good analytical and writing skills, and the ability to organize and control several projects simultaneously." "Deposition summarizer needed; work in your own home on your own computer." "Part-time proofreader for deposition summaries needed."

## 32. Military Law

In the Navy, a nonattorney who assists attorneys in the practice of law is called a *legalman.* Depending upon the assignment, the legalman can work in a large variety of areas of the law—for example, admiralty law, contracts, and military justice. The following job functions, however, are not limited to any particular branch of the armed services.

### I. Military Proceedings

**A.** Assist in processing the following proceedings:
  1. Special court-martial.
  2. General court-martial.
  3. Courts of inquiry.
  4. Line of duty investigations.
  5. Reclassification board proceedings.

**B.** Prepare all special orders designating membership of special and general court-martial and courts of inquiry.

**C.** Assure that charges are properly prepared and that specifications are complete and accurate.

**D.** Make initial determination on jurisdiction of court, status of accused, and subject matter of offenses.

**E.** Examine completed records of investigations and other records requiring legal review to ensure that they are administratively correct.

**F.** Prepare all special court-martial orders promulgating sentence.

**G.** Assure that records of court-martial are correct and complete before disposing of case.

**H.** Transmit bad-conduct discharge court-martial cases to appropriate officials.

## II. Claims Against the Government

**A.** Conduct examinations.

**B.** Process claims against the United States—for instance, federal tort claims.

**C.** Manage claim funds.

**D.** Undertake research on FLITE (Federal Legal Information Through Electronics).

**E.** Write briefs.

## III. Administrative Duties

**A.** Maintain control records of all court-martial and claims cases within command.

**B.** Maintain law library.

**C.** Examine and distribute incoming correspondence, directives, publications, and other communications.

**D.** Supervise cataloging and filing of publications, books, periodicals, journals, etc.

**E.** Maintain records of discipline within command.

**F.** Administer office budget.

**G.** Orient new personnel and monitor their training.

## IV. Court Reporting

**A.** Use the steno-mask for recording legal proceedings.

**B.** Prepare charges to the jury.

**C.** Mark exhibits as they are entered into evidence.

**D.** Transcribe and assemble records of the proceeding.

■ *Comment on Paralegal Work in This Area:*

"I have been working for the Office of the Staff Judge Advocate (SJA) at Fort Ord, California. The SJA is the Army's lawyer. We serve a military community of just over 90,000 people. Staff within the SJA consists of a combination of military and civilian attorneys, paralegals, legal clerks and court reporters. I am responsible for claims filed against the federal government under the Federal Tort Claims Act. I am responsible for discovery and investigative efforts, determining legal issues, writing memorandums of law and recommending settlement or denial. Job satisfaction for paralegal professionals is high in the U.S. government. I know that, should I desire to re-enter the civilian work sector, my experience and knowledge of the government legal systems will uniquely qualify me to work for any firm which deals with the government." Richards, *Marching to a Different Drummer: Paralegal Work in the Military,* 2 California Paralegal Magazine 8 (October/December 1990).

## 33. Municipal Finance Law[14]

(See also *banking law* and *corporate law*.)

[14]See footnote 11.

## I. Document Preparation

**A.** Basic documents:

   **1.** Prepare first drafts of basic documents, including bonds, indentures of trust, financing agreements, and all other related documents.

   **2.** Attend drafting sessions and note changes required to initial drafts.

   **3.** Prepare second and subsequent drafts by incorporation of revisions and red-line changes.

**B.** Closing documents:

   **1.** Prepare first drafts of all closing documents.

   **2.** Prepare second and subsequent drafts by incorporation of revisions and red-line changes.

**C.** Draft official statement/private offering memorandum:

   **1.** Prepare first drafts.

   **2.** Attend drafting sessions.

   **3.** Perform due diligence to verify the information and data contained in the offering document.

   **4.** Prepare second and subsequent drafts by incorporation of revisions and red-line changes.

## II. Coordination

**A.** Establish timetables and list of participants.

**B.** Distribute documents to participants.

**C.** Coordinate printing of bonds and offering documents.

**D.** File all documents as required.

**E.** Coordinate publication of notices of meetings and elections, ordinances, public hearing notices, etc.

## III. Closing

**A.** Prepare checklist.

**B.** Arrange and assist in preclosing and closing.

**C.** File any documents necessary to be filed prior to closing.

**D.** Secure requisite documents to be prepared or furnished by other participants.

**E.** Perform all post-closing procedures, including:

   **1.** File all documents or security agreements.

   **2.** Supervise preparation of closing binders.

## IV. Formation of Special Districts

**A.** Prepare documents necessary to organize the district.

**B.** File documents with municipality or county and district court.

**C.** Prepare documents for organizational meeting of district.

## V. Elections (Formation of District or for Bond Election)

Draft election documents and obtain all necessary election materials.

## VI.  Develop and Maintain Research Files

A.  IDB procedures for municipalities.
B.  Home rule charters.
C.  Demographic and economic statistics.
D.  Memoranda noting statutory changes.
E.  Interoffice research memoranda.
F.  Checklists for each type of financing.

## 34.  Oil and Gas Law

Some paralegals who work in the area of oil and gas law are referred to as *land technicians* or *landmen*. (See also *real estate law*.)

I.   Collect and analyze data pertaining to land ownership and activities that may affect the procurement of rights to explore, drill for, and produce oil or gas.
II.  Help acquire leases and other operating rights from property owners for exploration, drilling, and producing oil, gas, and related substances.
III. Monitor the execution of the leases and other operating agreements by ensuring that contract obligations are fulfilled (e.g., payment of rent).
IV.  Help negotiate agreements with individuals, companies, and government agencies pertaining to the exploration, drilling, and production of oil or gas.
V.   Assist in acquiring oil and gas producing properties, royalties, and mineral interests.
VI.  Process and monitor the termination of leases and other agreements.
VII. Examine land titles.

■ *Comment on Paralegal Work in This Area:*

"As an oil and gas paralegal, my practice encompasses many different areas of law including real estate, litigation, bankruptcy, and securities, as well as contact with various county, state, and federal government agencies. I frequently spend time searching real estate records in counties . . . for information on leases to determine such things as who has been assigned an interest in the lease. I have worked in mechanic's lien foreclosures, partition actions, and bankruptcy cases. While researching such things as regulatory information and oil prices, I have obtained information from the Federal Energy Regulatory Commission offices in Washington. The variety of work requires a working knowledge of several areas of law, and is always challenging and interesting." Hunt,

*Oil and Gas,* The Citator (Legal Assistants of Central Ohio, August 1990).

## 35.  Parajudge

In many states, the judge presiding in certain lower courts does not have to be an attorney. Such courts include justice of the peace courts and local magistrates courts.

Administrative agencies often hold hearings conducted by hearing officers, referees, or administrative law judges (ALJ). Frequently, these individuals are not attorneys, particularly at state and local agencies.

## 36.  Pro Bono Work

Pro bono work refers to services provided to another person at no charge. Law firms often give their attorneys time off in order to take pro bono cases—for example, to defend a poor person charged with a crime. Paralegals are also encouraged to do pro bono work. This is done on their own time or on law firm time with the permission of their supervisor. The following are examples of pro bono work performed by paralegals:

### I. Abused Women

A.  Draft request for protective order.
B.  Draft divorce pleadings.

### II. AIDS Patients

A.  Interview patients and prepare a memorandum of the interview for the pro bono attorney supervising the paralegals.
B.  Assist patients with guardianship problems.
C.  Draft powers of attorney.

### III. Homeless

A.  Handle Supplemental Social Security claims (SSI).
B.  Make referrals to shelters and drug programs.

■ *Comment on Paralegal Work in This Area:*

"Asked to share her favorite pro bono experience, Therese Ortega, a litigation paralegal, answered that to choose was too difficult; any time her efforts result in a benefit to the client, 'I get a warm glow.' One occasion she obviously cherishes was the fight on behalf of some low-income kidney dialysis patients whose eligibility for transportation to and from treatment was threatened. 'Perseverance and appeals paid off,' she says. Rides were re-established through the hearing process, then by information conferences. Finally, the cessation notices stopped." *Spotlight on Therese Ortega*, 13 The Journal 3 (Sacramento Ass'n of Legal Assistants, March 1991).

## 37. Public Sector

A paralegal in the *private sector* works in an office whose funds come from client fees or from the budget of the corporate treasury. Every other setting is generally considered the *public sector*. More specifically, the latter refers to those law offices that provide civil or criminal legal services to the poor for free. Often, the services consist of helping clients obtain government benefits such as public housing, welfare, medical care, etc. Such services are referred to as *public benefits,* and providing such assistance is called practice of public benefits law. Some of the paralegals who are employed by these offices are called Public Benefits Paralegals. The offices operate with government grants, charitable contributions, and the efforts of volunteers. They are called Legal Aid Society, Legal Aid Foundation, Legal Services Office, Office of the Public Defender, etc. For examples of the kinds of functions performed by paralegals in these offices, see *administrative law, bankruptcy law, civil rights law, criminal law, family law, landlord and tenant law, litigation, pro bono work, social security law, welfare law,* and *worker's compensation law.*

■ *Comment on Paralegal Work in This Area:*

"If someone asked me what I disliked most about my job, I would have to answer: the size of my paycheck. That is the only drawback of working for a nonprofit law firm—[the Community Legal Aid Society which represents elderly and handicapped persons]. Everything else about my job is positive." For example, to "be an integral part of a case where a landlord is forced by the Courts to bring a house up to code and prevent a tenant from being wrongfully evicted is a great feeling." The positive aspects of the job "more than compensate for the size of the paycheck." Hartman, *Job Profile,* Delaware Paralegal Reporter 5 (Delaware Paralegal Ass'n, November 1988).

"Mr. Watnick stressed that the organization doesn't have the luxury of using paralegals as "xeroxers" or errand runners. Staff paralegals have their own caseloads and represent clients before Administrative Law Judges—with a dramatically high rate of success." Shays, *Paralegals in Human Service,* Postscript 16 (Manhattan Paralegal Ass'n, March/April 1990).

## 38. Real Estate Law

(See also *banking law, contract law,* and *landlord and tenant law.*)

### I. General

Assist law firms, corporations, and development companies in transactions involving land, houses, condominiums, shopping malls, office buildings, redevelopment projects, civic centers, etc.

A. Research zoning regulations.

B. Prepare draft of the contract of sale.

C. Title work:
1. If done outside, order title work from the title company; arrange title insurance.
2. If done in-house:
   a. Examine title abstracts for completeness,
   b. Prepare a map based on a master title plat or the current government survey map,
   c. Help construct a chain of title noting defects, encumbrances, liens, easements, breaks in the chain, etc.,
   d. Obtain releases of liens, payoff statements for existing loans, etc.
   e. Help draft a preliminary title opinion.

D. Mortgages:
1. Assist in obtaining financing,
2. Review mortgage application,
3. Assist in recording mortgage.

E. Closing:
1. Arrange for a closing time with buyer, seller, brokers, and lender. Obtain letter confirming date of closing.
2. Collect the data necessary for closing. Prepare checklist of expenses:
   a. Title company fee,
   b. Lender's fee,
   c. Attorney's fee,
   d. Taxes and water bills to be prorated,
   e. Tax escrow, discharge of liens.
3. Prepare and organize the documents for closing:
   a. Deed,
   b. Settlement statement,
   c. Note and deed of trust,
   d. Corporate resolutions,
   e. Performance bond,
   f. Waivers.
4. Check compliance with the disclosure requirements of the Real Estate Settlement Act.
5. Arrange for a rehearsal of the closing.
6. Attend and assist at the closing—for example, take minutes, notarize documents.

F. Foreclosure:
1. Order foreclosure certificate.
2. Prepare notice of election and demand for sale,
3. Compile a list of parties to be notified,
4. Monitor publication of the notice.
5. Assist with sale documents—for example, prepare bid letter.

G. Eminent Domain:
  1. Photograph or videotape the property taken or to be taken by the state,
  2. Prepare inventory of the property taken,
  3. Help client prepare business records pertaining to the value of the property,
  4. Arrange for appraisals of the property,
  5. Order and review engineering reports regarding soil,
  6. Review tax appeals records on values claimed by the property owner,
  7. Mail out notice of condemnation.
H. Office management:
  1. Maintain office tickler system,
  2. Maintain individual attorney's calendar,
  3. Be in charge of the entire client's file (opening it, keeping it up-to-date, knowing where parts of it are at all times),
  4. Train other staff in the office system of handling real estate cases.

II. Tax-exempt Industrial Development Financing

A. Undertake a preliminary investigation to establish facts relevant to:
  1. Project eligibility,
  2. The local issuer,
  3. Cost estimates of the financing.
B. Prepare a formal application to the issuer.
C. Prepare a timetable of approvals, meetings, and all other requirements necessary for closing.
D. Prepare a preliminary draft of portions of the proposal memorandum (relating to the legal structure of the financing) that is submitted to prospective bond purchasers.
E. Obtain confirmation from the Treasury Department that the company is in compliance with the financing covenants of current external debt instruments.
F. Obtain insurance certificates.
G. Write the first draft of the resolutions of the board of directors.
H. Write the preface and recital of documents for the legal opinion of the company.
I. Contact the bank to confirm the account numbers, amount of money to be transferred, and investment instructions.
J. Prepare a closing memorandum covering the following documents:
  1. Secretary's certificate including resolutions of the board of directors, the certified charter and bylaws of the company, and the incumbency certificate,
  2. UCC-1 financing statements,
  3. Requisition forms,
  4. Certificate of authorized company representative,
  5. Deed,
  6. Legal opinion of the company,
  7. Transfer instruction letter,
  8. Officer's certificate.
K. Confirm that the money has been transferred to the company's account on the day of closing.
L. Order an updated good-standing telegram.
M. Send a copy of the IRS election statement.
N. Assemble, monitor, and distribute documents to appropriate departments.

■ *Comment on Paralegal Work in This Area:*

"Although it may look boring to the untrained eye, and sound boring to the untrained ear, for those of us whose livelihoods depend upon it, real estate law is *interesting* and *exciting*. There is always something new to learn or a little flaw to resolve. What can be better than having clients come to you and thank you for your assistance in what would have been a complete disaster without your knowledge and expertise to get them through? I call that total job satisfaction. I am now capable of doing everything in a real estate settlement from opening the file to walking into the settlement room and disbursing the funds. It is not uncommon for me to receive calls from attorneys in the area asking me how certain problems can be solved. That boosts my ego more than any divorce case every could!" Jaeger, *Real Estate Law Is a Legal Profession Too!*, 14 On Point 9 (Nat'l Capital Area Paralegal Ass'n, June 1988).

At a paralegal conference, Virginia Henderson made a seminar presentation on her duties as a paralegal. Her "candor and energetic enthusiasm concerning her profession were encouraging and motivating. She was very explicit about her duties as a commercial real estate paralegal, explaining that attorney supervision is lessened once the paralegal assumes more responsibility and exhibits initiative as far as his/her duties are concerned. It was refreshing to listen to a veteran of the paralegal profession speak so optimistically about the profession's limitless potential. Here's to having more paralegals as seminar speakers!" Troiano, *Real Estate,* Newsletter 12 (Western New York Paralegal Ass'n, November/December 1987).

"As a foreclosure legal assistant, one of my worst fears is to have a client call and say, 'Remember the Jones property you foreclosed for us last year? Well, we're trying to close on this and it seems there's a problem with the title. . . .' Oh no, what *didn't* I do! Mortgage foreclosure litigation is fraught with all kinds of pitfalls for the inexperienced and the unwary. An improper or faulty foreclosure could not only be disastrous for the client, it can also be a malpractice nightmare for the law firm." Hubbell, *Mortgage Foreclosure Litigation: Avoiding the Pitfalls,* 16 Facts and Findings 10 (NALA, November 1989).

■ *Quotes from Want Ads:*

"Ideal candidate must possess exceptional organization, communication, writing and research skills and be willing to work overtime." "We need a team player with high energy." Position requires an ability to work independently on a wide variety of matters and to meet deadlines." "Experience in retail real estate or real estate financing a must." "Should be assertive and have excellent analytical skills." Position requires a "self-motivated person. We seek a TIGER who can accomplish much with a minimum of supervision." "Knowledge of state and federal securities law a plus." "Must be flexible and possess high integrity." Position requires a "self-starter able to deal effectively with executive management, outside counsel, escrow and title companies, brokers, leasing agents, and clients."

## 39. Social Security Law

(See also *administrative law, public sector,* and *welfare law.*)

### I. Problem Identification

Identify whether:
A.  Person is denied benefits.
B.  Recipient is terminated from disability payments.
C.  Recipient is charged with receiving overpayment.
D.  Medicare waivers/appeals are involved.

### II. Case Preparation

A.  Investigate relevant facts.
B.  Perform legal research.
C.  Engage in informal advocacy with Social Security employees.

### III. Representation

A.  Represent clients at administrative hearings regarding SSI (Supplemental Security Income).
B.  Represent clients at administrative hearings regarding SSD (Social Security Disability)

### IV. Appeal

A.  Help attorney prepare a court appeal of the agency's decision.

■ *Comment on Paralegal Work in This Area:*

"Paralegal representation of a claimant in a Social Security Disability hearing is the closest to a judicial setting that a paralegal may expect to become involved in. For the paralegal, this can be a very complex and challenging field. It can also be extremely rewarding, bringing with it the satisfaction of successfully representing a claimant in a quasi-judicial setting." Obermann, *The Paralegal and Federal Disability Practice in Maine,* MAP Newsletter (Maine Ass'n of Paralegals, January 1988).

## 40. Tax Law

(See also *corporate law, employee benefits law, estates law,* and *real estate law.*)

I. Compile all necessary data for the preparation of tax returns:

A.  Corporate income tax,
B.  Employer quarterly tax,
C.  Franchise tax,
D.  Partnership tax,
E.  Sales tax,
F.  Personal property tax,
G.  Individual income tax,
H.  Estate tax,
I.  Gift tax.

II. Communicate with client to obtain missing information.

III. Compile supporting documents for the returns.

IV. Draft extensions-of-time requests.

V. Make corrections in the returns based upon new or clarified data.

VI. Compute the tax liability or transfer client information to computer input sheets for submission to a computer service that will calculate the tax liability.

VII. Organize and maintain client binder.

VIII. Compute cash flow analysis for proposed real estate syndication.

IX. Compile documentation on the valuation of assets.

X. Maintain the tax law library.

XI. Read loose-leaf tax services and other periodic tax data to keep current on tax developments. Bring such developments to the attention of others in the office.

XII. Supervise and train other nonattorney staff within the tax department of the office.

■ *Comment on Paralegal Work in This Area:*

"A legal assistant with the firm for the past thirteen years, Pat [Coleman] spends a lot of time in her office. She is surrounded by her work, and one gets the idea that Pat knows exactly what is in every file and could put her hand on any information that is needed. Notes are taped next to the light switch; the firm's monthly calendar highlighting important meetings is readily available, and helps her track her many deadlines. Pat is an Enrolled Agent (which permits her to practice before the Treasury Department) and has a lot of tax background, and is competent in that area as well as bookkeeping. One of her least favorite tax forms is the 990 required of not-for-profit organizations. The 990 tax form is second only to private foundation returns when it comes to being pesky and tricky." Howard, *Patricia Coleman of Chicago Creates Her Niche in Taxes, Trusts and ERISA*, 3 Legal Assistant Today 40 (Winter 1986).

## 41.  Tort Law

A tort is a civil wrong that has injured someone. Paralegals who work on PI (personal injury) cases are mainly litigation assistants. The major torts are negligence, defamation, strict liability, and wrongful death. Paralegals in this area are also often involved in worker's compensation cases for injuries that occur on the job. (See *admiralty law, litigation,* and *worker's compensation.*)

■ *Comment on Paralegal Work in This Area:*

"Personal injury/products liability cases can be fascinating, challenging, and educational. They also can be stressful, aggravating and very sad. I have been involved in a great many cases in my career, on both sides of the plaintiff/defendant fence. Some of the cases seemed frivolous and somewhat 'ambulance chasing' in nature. Others were significant cases in which the plaintiff had wrongfully suffered injury. There are many talents a good personal injury/products liability paralegal must have. He or she must be creative, tenacious, observant and able to communicate well with people." Lee, *Personal Injury/Products Liability Cases*, 11 Newsletter 7 (Dallas Ass'n of Legal Assistants, November 1987).

"Recently, Mary Mann, a paralegal who works on product liability litigation, was asked by her attorney to track down a specific medical article [on a subject relevant to a current case]. The attorney only had a vague description of the article, a possible title, and the name of the organization that might have published it. In her search Mary spoke by phone to people in New York, Atlanta, Washington, and finally to a doctor in Geneva, Switzerland, who spoke very little English. In her effort to make herself understood by the doctor, Mary continued to speak louder and louder in very simplistic and basic English phrases, as people tend to do when con-

fronted by a language barrier. She is sure her efforts to maintain a professional demeanor were humorous to those passing by her office. However, she did succeed in getting the article and in the process gained a friend in Switzerland!" Fisher, *Spotlight: Mary Mann,* 7 The Assistant 14 (Mississippi Ass'n of Legal Assistants, April/June 1988).

"Asbestos litigation . . . opened up in the late 1970's with the law suits initiated against the Johns-Mansville Corporation. In 1982 Mansville filed a Chapter 11 bankruptcy to protect its assets from the thousands of claims being filed against it." Huge numbers of paralegals were employed in this litigation. For those paralegals working *for* Johns-Mansville on the defense team, "the question of morality arose. I get asked about the morality of my job constantly. For me, personal moral judgment does not enter into it. Our legal system is based on the availability of equal representation for both sides. I think I play a small part in making that system work." Welsh, *The Paralegal in Asbestos Litigation,* 10 Ka Leo O' H.A.L.A. 6 (Hawaii Ass'n of Legal Assistants, February/March 1987) (reprint from newsletter of the East Bay Ass'n of Legal Assistants).

■ *Quotes from Want Ads:*

"Medical malpractice law firm seeks paralegal who is a self-starter, has good communication skills, is organized and detail-oriented." Position in PI [personal injury] firm requires "a take-charge person to handle case details from beginning to end." "Prefer person with experience in claims adjustment, medical records, or nursing." Position requires "dynamic, highly-motivated individual who will enjoy the challenge of working independently and handling a wide variety of responsibilities." "Excellent writing skills a must." "Should be able to perform under pressure." Manufacturer of consumer products "seeks paralegal with engineering background." Must be mature enough to handle "heavy client contact." Position requires "ability to read and summarize medical records."

## 42.  Tribal Law

Tribal courts exist on Indian reservations that have jurisdiction over many civil and criminal cases in which both parties are Native Americans. Parties are often represented by tribal court advocates who are nonattorney Native Americans. In addition, the judges are often nonattorneys. (See *litigation.*).

## 43.  Water Law[15]

(See also *administrative law* and *real estate law.*)

---

[15]See footnote 11.

## I. Water Rights

Investigate and analyze specific water rights and water rights associated with property:

**A.** Do research at Department of Water Resources regarding decrees, tabulations, well permits, reservoirs, diversion records, maps, and statements.

**B.** Communicate in writing and orally with Department of Water Resources personnel regarding status of water rights and wells.

**C.** Communicate in writing and orally (including interviews) with District Water Commissioners regarding status of water rights and wells, historic use, and use on land.

**D.** Communicate in writing and orally (including interviews) with property owners and managers, ranch managers, ditch company personnel, etc. regarding status of water rights and wells, historic use, and use on land.

**E.** Do research at other agencies and offices (such as the Bureau of Land Management, state archives, historical societies, public libraries).

**F.** Prepare historic use affidavits.

**G.** Prepare reports regarding investigation and analysis of the status of water rights and wells, historic use, and use on land.

**H.** Prepare maps, charts, diagrams, etc. regarding status of water rights and wells, historic use, and use on land.

## II. Real Estate Transactions

**A.** Draft documents for the purchase and sale, encumbrance, or lease of water rights and wells.

**B.** Perform standup title searches in county clerk and recorder's offices.

**C.** Perform due diligence investigations.

**D.** Prepare for and assist at closings.

## III. Well Permit Applications

**A.** Prepare well permit documents for filing— applications, land ownership affidavits, statements of beneficial use, amendments to record, extensions of time.

**B.** Coordinate and monitor the well permitting and drilling process.

**C.** In writing and orally, communicate with Department of Water Resources personnel, well drillers, and client.

## IV. Water Court Proceedings—

Certain district courts have special jurisdiction over water right proceedings. Proceedings are governed by the Rules of Civil Procedure for District Courts and by local water court and district court rules.

**A.** Prepare water court documents for filing— applications, statements of opposition, draft rulings and orders, stipulations, withdrawals of opposition and affidavits.

**B.** Maintain diligence filing tickler system. Work with client to record and maintain evidence of diligence.

**C.** Review, route, and maintain a file of water court resumes.

**D.** Review, route, and maintain file of term day notices and orders. Prepare attorneys for term day and/or attend term day.

## V. Monitor Publications

Read *Reporter,* water court resumes, and register for new water law cases and Department of Water Resources regulations.

## 44. Welfare Law

(See also *administrative law, pro bono work, public benefits,* and *social security law.*)

## I. Problem Identification

**A.** Perform preliminary interview:

   1. Identify nonlegal problems for referral to other agencies,

   2. Open a case file or update it,

   3. Using a basic fact sheet (or form), record the information collected during the interview,

   4. Determine next appointment,

   5. Instruct client on what to do next, such as obtain medical and birth records, etc.,

   6. Arrange for client to see office attorney.

**B.** Categorize welfare problems:

   1. Help client learn what benefits exist in programs such as:

     a. Welfare

     b. Social Security

     c. Medicare

   2. Help client fill out application forms.

   3. Deal with client who objects to home visits by caseworkers or attempt by welfare department to force him or her to take a job or enter a training program.

   4. Help client when welfare department wants to reduce the amount of client's welfare check or terminate public assistance altogether.

## II. Problem Resolution

**A.** Consult with attorney immediately:

   1. Summarize facts for the attorney,

   2. Submit the case record to the attorney,

  **3.** Obtain further instructions from attorney.

**B.** Refer nonlegal problems to other agencies:

  **1.** Give name and address of agency to client,

  **2.** Search for an appropriate agency,

  **3.** Contact agency for the client.

**C.** Investigate:

  **1.** Verify information (call caseworker, visit welfare office, etc.)

  **2.** Search for additional information.

  **3.** Record relevant facts.

  **4.** Consult with attorney on difficulties encountered.

**D.** Analyze laws:

  **1.** Check office welfare law manual,

  **2.** Consult with office attorneys,

  **3.** Contact legal service attorneys outside office,

  **4.** Do research in law library.

**E.** Be an informal advocate (to determine if the problem can be resolved without a hearing or court action).

  **1.** Make sure everyone (welfare department, client, etc.) understands the issue,

  **2.** Provide missing information,

  **3.** Pressure the welfare department (with calls, letters, visits, etc.),

  **4.** Maintain records such as current and closed files.

**F.** Be a formal advocate:

  **1.** Prior hearing (administrative review)

   **a.** Determine if such hearing can be asked for and when request must be made,

   **b.** Draft letter requesting such hearing,

   **c.** Prepare for hearing (see "Fair Hearing" below).

   **d.** Conduct hearing (see "Fair Hearing" below),

   **e.** Follow-up (see "Fair Hearing" below).

  **2.** Fair Hearing

   **a.** Determine if the hearing can be asked for and when request must be made,

   **b.** Draft letter requesting the hearing,

   **c.** Prepare for the hearing:

    **i.** In advance of hearing, request that the welfare department send a paralegal the documents it will rely on at the hearing.

    **ii.** In advance of hearing, make sure that everyone (department representatives, client, etc.) is going to the hearing on the same issues.

    **iii.** Organize other relevant documents such as cancelled check stubs.

    **iv.** Find witnesses (other than client).

    **v.** Prepare all witnesses (for example, explain what hearing will be about; conduct a brief role-playing experience to acquaint them with the format and what the paralegal will be seeking from the witnesses).

    **vi.** Map out a preliminary strategy to use in conducting the hearing.

    **vii.** Make a final attempt to resolve the issues without a hearing.

    **viii.** Make sure client and other witnesses will appear (e.g., give address of the hearing, take them to the hearing on the date of the hearing).

   **d.** Conduct the hearing:

    **i.** Make sure the name, address, and title of everyone present is identified for the record.

    **ii.** Make opening statement summarizing client's case.

    **iii.** Ask for a postponement if the client has not appeared or if an emergency has arisen requiring more time to prepare.

    **iv.** Clearly state what relief the client is seeking from the hearing.

    **v.** If confusion exists on the issues, fight for a statement of the issues most favorable to the client.

    **vi.** Take notes on the opening statement of the welfare department representative.

    **vii.** Complain if welfare department failed to provide sufficient information in advance of the hearing.

    **viii.** Present the client's case.

     **a.** submit documents.

     **b.** conduct direct examination of own witnesses.

     **c.** conduct re-direct examination of own witnesses (if allowed).

     **d.** cite the law.

    **ix.** Rebut case of welfare department.

     **a.** object to their documents.

     **b.** object to their use of jargon.

     **c.** object to their interpretation of the law.

     **d.** cross-examine their witnesses.

     **e.** re-cross-examine their witnesses (if allowed).

x. Make closing statement summarizing the case of the client and repeating the result the client is seeking.

e. Follow up:

i. Pressure the hearing officer to reach a result without undue delay.

ii. Request a copy of the transcript of the hearing.

iii. When a result is reached, pressure the welfare department to abide by it.

iv. Consult with attorney to determine whether the hearing result should be appealed in court.

3. Court

a. Prepare preliminary draft of the legal argument to be made on appeal,

b. Assist the attorney in gathering the documents for appeal; interview the witnesses for appeal, etc.,

c. Be a general assistant for the attorney at court proceedings,

d. File papers in court,

e. Serve the papers on opponents.

G. Miscellaneous

1. Train other paralegals.

2. Write pamphlets on welfare law for distribution in the community.

3. Organize the community around welfare issues.

# 45.  Worker's Compensation Law

(See also *administrative law, labor and employment law,* and *litigation.*)

## I.  Interviewing

A. Collect and record details of the claim (date of injury, nature and dates of prior illness, etc.).

B. Collect or arrange for the collection of documents, such as medical records, employment contract.

C. Schedule physical examination.

## II.  Drafting

A. Draft claim for compensation.

B. Draft request for hearing.

C. Draft medical authorization.

D. Draft demand for medical information in the possession of respondent or insurance carrier.

E. Draft proposed summary of issues involved.

## III.  Advocacy

A. Informal: Contact (call, visit, write a letter to) the employer and/or the insurance carrier to determine whether the matter can be resolved without a formal hearing or court action.

B. Formal: Represent claimant at the administrative hearing.

## IV.  Follow-up

A. Determine whether the payment is in compliance with the award.

B. If not, draft and file a statutory demand for proper payment.

C. If such a statutory demand is filed, prepare a tickler system to monitor the claim.

### ■ *Comment on Paralegal Work in This Area:*

"I have been working as a paralegal in this area for more than seven years. This is one of the areas of the law [in this state] in which a paralegal can perform almost all of the functions to properly process a Workers' Compensation claim. A Workers' Compensation practice must be a very high volume in order to be [profitable]. Thus paralegal assistance in handling a large case load is an absolute necessity. An extensive volume of paperwork is processed on a daily basis. Client contact is a major portion of a paralegal's responsibilities. With a large case load, it is physically impossible for an attorney to communicate with each and every client on a regular basis. It is not unusual for a paralegal in this field to work on several hundred files each week." Lindberg, *Virtually Limitless Responsibilities of a Workers' Compensation Paralegal,* Update 6 (Cleveland Ass'n of Paralegals, July 1989).

"The Company's two worker's compensation paralegals are responsible for reviewing each claimant's file, preparing a summary of medical reports, outlining the issues, and reviewing with the adjusters any questions or circumstances of the case before the claimant's disposition. In addition, they draft any necessary subpoenas, witness lists and settlement stipulations for their respective attorneys, and collect information and draft letters to the Special Disability Trust Fund outlining the Company's theory of reimbursement for second injury cases." Miquel, *Walt Disney World Company's Legal Assistants: Their Role in the Show,* 16 Facts and Findings 29, 30 (NALA, January 1990).

---

**Note**

### A PARALEGAL IN THE WHITE HOUSE
### MEG SHIELDS DUKE
### NEW ROLES IN THE LAW CONFERENCE REPORT, 93 (1982)

[After working as a paralegal on the Reagan-Bush Campaign Committee], I'm a paralegal in the White House Counsel's office. I believe I'm the first paralegal in this office, in the White House. They've had law clerks in the past, but never have they hired a paralegal. There's one paralegal to nine attorneys at the moment. I think that's ridiculous and I hope we'll change that in the next several months to a year. But my responsibilities here are varied. Everybody is still trying to determine what their turf is. But for the first couple of months I've worked on a lot of transition matters, which might be expected. I was the coordinator for our transition audit, congressional transition audit, from the hill, which just ended a few weeks ago. I have engaged in drafting correspondence concerning the use of the president's name; the use of his image; our policy on gifts acceptance by public employees; drafting standards of conduct for public employees in the White House; job freeze litigation; those few controversial things. The last few weeks of my time have been devoted to the Lefever nomination. It's all been fascinating. Anyway, there are a number of areas that we also get involved in, the ethics of government act, for example. It's the first time it has been applied across the board to a new administration. It has been very, very time consuming for all our staff. I've been assisting in that, reviewing each individual file for high level government employees. As I said, I'm in the counsel's office now and intend to stay for a couple of years. But I would like to start my own paralegal firm. I have a close friend who started her own paralegal firm in Florida and we've talked often in the past of expanding it to Washington and a few other cities West where we'd like to spend some time. We're investigating the possibilities of reopening another firm here in Washington at some point, maybe in the next year and a half. But I think there is a place for more paralegals in the public sector, at least in the White House area, and I understand the Department of Justice of course has many, but I'd like to see it expanded and I'd also like to see more people branching out and trying this independent approach because I think it's fun. It's risky, but it's worth it.

---

■

"In my experience, most entry-level candidates are unprepared to effectively market themselves to law firms and corporations in this increasingly competitive marketplace. It is no longer enough simply to have a paralegal certificate. An individual must be able to sell him or herself effectively through the use of a well-written resume and cover letter, and be prepared to develop strong interviewing skills."
Tami M. Coyne, May 1990.

■

■

"Getting the job you want requires planning, determination, hard work, and follow-through. Don't give up!"
Lindi Massey, January 1991.

■

## ■ Section D.  Finding a Job: Employment Strategies

The following strategies are primarily for individuals who have never worked with attorneys or held a paralegal job. Many of the strategies, however, are also relevant to people who have worked in law offices as secretaries or who are paralegals and wish to find other employment opportunities in the field.

### General Strategies for Finding Employment

1. Begin now
2. Start compiling a Job Hunting Notebook
3. Organize an employment workshop
4. Locate working paralegals
5. Go on informational interviews
6. Locate potential employers
7. Prepare a resume, cover letter, and writing sample
8. Prepare for the job interview

### Strategy 1: Begin Now

You should begin preparing for the job hunt on the first day of your first paralegal class. Do *not* wait until the program is almost over. Whether or not there is a placement office at your school, you should assume that obtaining a job will be your responsibility. For most students, the job you get will be the job *you* find.

While in school, your primary focus should be on compiling an excellent academic record. *In addition,* you must start the job search now. It is not too early, for example, to begin compiling the lists called for in the Job Hunting Notebook that we will examine later. When school is over, be prepared to spend a substantial amount of additional time looking for employment. Since most students in the country will not have employment lined up before they graduate, time must be set aside for the search. How much time? There is, of course, no absolute answer to this question. It is clear, however, that a half-hearted, part-time effort will probably not be successful. Simply sitting back and sending out a stack of resumes is rarely effective! Since this is a "buyer's market" where there are many more applicants than available jobs, a conscientious search could involve four-to-six hours a day for several months. This may surprise—and disappoint—many graduates of paralegal programs. Yet this time frame is a reality throughout the legal profession. It applies to the majority of attorneys and legal administrators looking for work as well as to paralegals. *Being* a paralegal requires determination, assertiveness, initiative, and creativity. *Finding* paralegal work will require these same skills. This is not a field for the faint of heart who are easily discouraged.

It may be that there is still a lot of uncertainty in your mind about the kinds of employment options that exist. How can you begin looking for a job if you don't yet know what kind of job you would like to have? First of all, many of the suggested steps in this chapter will be helpful regardless of the kind of job you are pursuing. More important, however, the very process of going through these steps will help you clarify your employment objectives. As you begin seeking information and leads, the insights will come to you.

At this point, keep an open mind, be conscientious, and begin now.

## Strategy 2: Begin Compiling a Job Hunting Notebook

Later in this chapter, you will find an outline for a Job Hunting Notebook that you should start preparing now. Following the outline, there are sample pages for the various sections in the Notebook.

## Strategy 3: Organize an Employment Workshop

In Figure 2.1 at the beginning of this chapter, you were given a list of the major categories (and subcategories) of paralegal employment. Begin organizing an employment conference or workshop consisting of a panel of paralegals from as many of the categories and subcategories of paralegals as you can locate in your area. Try to find at least one paralegal to represent each category and subcategory. The guest paralegals could be asked to come to an evening or Saturday session to discuss the following topics:

- How I obtained my job
- My recommendations for finding work
- Dos and don'ts in the employment interview
- What I do (what a typical day consists of)
- What were the most valuable parts of my legal education
- Etc.

While you might want to ask a teacher or the director of the program at your school to help you organize the workshop, it is recommended that you make it a student-run workshop. It will be good practice for you in taking the kind of initiative that is essential in finding employment. You might want to consider asking the nearest paralegal association to co-sponsor the workshop with your class. (See question 5 in the letter found at the end of the index of this book.)

Have a meeting of your class in which a chairperson is selected to help coordinate the event. Then divide up the tasks of contacting participants, arranging for a room, preparing an agenda for the workshop, etc. You may want to invite former graduates of your school to attend as panel speakers or as members of the audience. The ideal time for such a workshop is a month or two after you begin your coursework. This means that you need to begin organizing immediately.

### Strategy 4: Locate Working Paralegals

Perhaps the most significant step in finding employment is to begin talking with paralegals who are already employed. They are the obvious experts on how to find a job! They are probably also very knowledgeable about employment opportunities in their office and in similar offices in the area. (See Job Hunting Notebook, p. 168.)

Attend paralegal association meetings. See Appendix B for a list of paralegal associations. Contact the one nearest you and ask about joining. There may be a special dues or fee structure for students.

Ask if the association has a *job bank* service. Here is what a paralegal who recently used this service had to say:

> I gained access to an opening to a wonderful job at a law firm exclusively listed in the Minnesota Association of Legal Assistants (MALA) Job Bank. . . . I would never have heard about the position if I hadn't been a member of MALA. *Merrill Advantage* (Spring 1990).

Not all associations, however, have job bank services, and those that do have them may not make them available to students.

Try to obtain copies of current and past issues of the monthly or bimonthly newsletters of all the local paralegal associations in your area. Some of these newsletters give listings of job openings that mention specific employers. If so, try to contact the employers to determine if the position is still open. If it is no longer open, ask if you could send your resume to be kept on file in the event a position becomes available in the future. Also, try to speak to the paralegal who filled the position in order to ask for leads to openings elsewhere.

Ask the local paralegal association if it has a job-finding manual for paralegals in your area. Find out about attending various association meetings. Try to participate in committees. The more active you are as a student member, the more contacts you will make. If there is no paralegal association near you, organize one—beginning with your own student body and past graduates of your school.

Paralegal newsletters often announce continuing education conferences and seminars for paralegals. Similar announcements are found in the newsletters of the two major national paralegal associations: the National Federation of Paralegal Associations *(National Paralegal Reporter),* and the National Association of Legal Assistants *(Facts and Findings).* Employed paralegals attend these events in large numbers. Hence they are excellent ways in which to meet experienced paralegals.

Paralegals sometimes attend continuing education conferences conducted by the local bar association, particularly those bar associations where paralegals are allowed to become associate members. You should also find out if there is an association of legal secretaries and of legal administrators in your area. If so, they might conduct workshops or meetings that you can attend. At such meetings and elsewhere, try to talk with individual legal secretaries and legal administrators about employment opportunities for paralegals where they work.

### Strategy 5: Go on Information Interviews

An *informational interview* is an opportunity for you to sit down with someone, preferably where he or she works, to learn about a particular kind of employment. Unlike a job interview, where you are the one interviewed, *you* do the interviewing in an informational interview. You ask questions that will help you learn what life is like working at that kind of office. Your goal is to find out if a particular kind of paralegal practice interests you.

> If, for example, you are a real "people" person who finds antitrust theory fascinating, you should listen to antitrust paralegals discussing their day-to-day work. You may hear that most of them spend years in document warehouses with one lawyer, two other paralegals and a pizza delivery man as their most significant personal contacts. That information may influence your decision about antitrust as a career path.[16]

Do *not* try to turn an informational interview into a job interview. While on an informational interview, it is inappropriate to ask a person for a job. Toward the end of the interview, you can delicately ask for leads to employment and you can ask how the person obtained his or her job, but these inquiries should be secondary to your primary purpose of obtaining information about the realities of work at that kind of office. Do not use an informational interview as a subterfuge for a job interview that you are having difficulty obtaining.

The best people to interview are employed paralegals whom you have met through the steps outlined in Strategy 4. While attorneys and legal administrators may also be willing to grant you informational interviews, the best people to talk to are those who were once in your shoes. Simply say to a paralegal you have met, "Would it be possible for me to come down to the office where you work for a brief informational interview?" If he or she is not familiar with this kind of interview, explain its limited objective. Some may be too busy to grant such interviews, but you have nothing to lose by asking, even if you are turned down. As an added inducement, consider offering to take the paralegal to lunch. In addition to meeting this paralegal, you also want to try to have at least a brief tour of the office where he or she works. Observing how different kinds of employees interact with each other and with available technology in the office will be invaluable.

Here are some of the questions you should ask on an informational interview.

- What is a typical day for you in this office?
- What kinds of assignments do you receive?
- How much overtime is usually expected? Do you take work home with you?

---

[16]Gainen, *Information Interviews: A Strategy,* Paradigm (Baltimore Ass'n of Legal Assistants, November/December 1989).

- How do the attorneys interact with paralegals in this kind of practice? Who does what? How many different attorneys does a paralegal work with? How are assignment priorities set?
- How do the paralegals interact with secretaries and other support staff in the office?
- What is the hierarchy of the office?
- What kind of education best prepares a paralegal to work in this kind of office? What courses are most effective?
- What is the most challenging aspect of the job? The most frustrating?
- How are paralegals perceived in this office?
- Are you glad you became this kind of paralegal in this kind of office? Would you do it over again?
- What advice would you give to someone who wants to become a paralegal like yourself?

Several of these questions are also appropriate in a job interview, as we will see later.

One final word of caution. Any information you learn at the office about clients or legal matters must be kept confidential, even if the person you are interviewing is casual about revealing such information to you. This person may not be aware that he or she is disclosing confidential information. Carelessness in this regard is not uncommon.

### Strategy 6: Locate Potential Employers

There are a number of ways to locate attorneys:

a. Placement office
b. Personal contacts
c. Ads
d. Through other paralegals
e. Employment agencies
f. Directories and other lists
g. Courts and bar association meetings

(See Job Hunting Notebook, p. 168).

For every attorney that you contact, you want to know the following:

- Has the attorney hired paralegals in the past?
- If so, is the attorney interested in hiring more paralegals?
- If the attorney has never hired paralegals before, might he or she consider hiring one?
- Does the attorney know of other attorneys who might be interested in hiring paralegals?

The last point is particularly important. Attorneys from different firms often talk with each other about their practice, including their experiences with paralegals or their plans for hiring paralegals. Hence always ask about other firms. If you obtain a lead, begin your contact with the other firm by mentioning the name of the attorney who gave you the lead. You might say, "Mary Smith told me that you have hired paralegals in the past and might be interested in hiring another paralegal," or "John Jones suggested that I contact you concerning possible employment at your firm as a paralegal."

*a. Placement Office.*    Start with the placement office of your paralegal school. Talk with staff members and/or check the bulletin board regularly. If your school is part of a university that has a law school, you might want to check the placement office of the law school as well. While paralegal jobs are usually not listed there, you may find descriptions of law firms with the number of attorneys and paralegals employed. (See Figure 2.2.) It would be useful for you to identify the major resources for obtaining attorney jobs, such as special directories, lists or ads in bar publications, legal newspapers, etc. In particular, try to find the following resource used by unemployed attorneys and law students: *Directory of Legal Employers,* which is published by the National Association of Law Placement. (The Directory can also be used on WESTLAW, page 585, if you have access to this computer legal research system.) Such resources might provide leads on contacting offices about paralegal employment.

*b. Personal Contacts.*    Make a list of attorneys who fall into the following categories:

- Personal friends
- Friends of friends
- Attorneys you have hired
- Attorneys your relatives have hired
- Attorneys your former employers have hired
- Attorneys your friends have hired
- Teachers
- Politicians
- Neighbors
- Etc.

You should consider contacting these attorneys about their own paralegal hiring plans as well as for references to other attorneys. Don't be reluctant to take advantage of any direct or indirect association that you might have with an attorney. Such contacts are the essence of networking. (See Job Hunting Notebook, page 168).

*c. Ads.*    You should regularly check the classified pages of your daily newspaper as well as the legal newspaper for your area. If you are seeking employment in another city, the main branch of your public library and the main library of large universities in your area may have out-of-town newspapers. If you have friends in these other cities, they might be willing to send you clippings from the classified ads of their newspapers. There are several *national* legal newspapers that sometimes have paralegal employment ads. These include the *National Law Journal* and the *American Lawyer.* Law libraries often subscribe to such newspapers.

Look for ads under the headings "Paralegal" or "Legal Assistant." For example:

```
PARALEGAL
   TRUST ACCOUNTANTS
For details see our ad in
this section headed
   ACCOUNTANT
```

```
PARALEGALS Fee Pd.
Salary Open. Corporate &
Real Estate positions. Su-
perior writing ability is a
necessity. Must be able to
work under pressure. Su-
perior opportunities. Con-
tact . . .
```

---

**PARALEGAL (CORPORATE)**
Large downtown Boston law firm seeks expd Corporate Paralegal. Oppty for responsibility & growth. Must have strong academic background. Computer literacy a plus. Salary commensurate with exp. Send resume in confidence to: X2935 TIMES

**LEGAL ASSISTANT**
Large West Palm Beach, Florida firm wishes to employ legal assistant with immigration/naturalization experience, in addition to civil litigation, research & pleading abilities. Knowledge of Germanic languages helpful. Full fringe benefits/profit sharing. Salary negotiable. Contact . . .

---

For detailed quotes from want ads for a variety of different kinds of paralegal jobs, see pages 108–126.

Some ads are placed by private employment agencies that specialize in legal placements. The ad may not give the name and address of the employer seeking the paralegal. Instead, it will direct interested parties to an intermediary, such as a newspaper, which forwards all responses to the employer. Such ads are called "blind ads."

You will find that most want ads seek paralegals with experience in a particular area of practice. Hence if you are a recent graduate of a paralegal school who is looking for a beginning or entry-level position, you may not meet the qualifications sought in the ads.[17] Should you apply for such positions nevertheless? Suppose, for example, that an add seeks "a corporate paralegal with two years of experience." You might consider answering such an ad as follows:

> I am responding to your ad for a corporate paralegal. I do not have the experience indicated in the ad, but I did take an intensive course on corporate law at my paralegal school, and I'm wondering whether I could send you my resume so that you could consider what I have to offer.

If the answer is no, you can certainly ask for leads to anyone else who might be hiring individuals like yourself.

When reading want ads, do not limit yourself to the entries for "Paralegal" and "Legal Assistant." Also look for headings for positions that may be law related, such as "Research Assistant," "Legislative Aide," "Law Library Assistant." For example:

---

**RESEARCH ASSISTANT**

**IMMEDIATE POSITION**
Social Science Research Institute in downtown looking for coder/editor of survey instruments. Post Box L3040.

**PROOFREADER**
Leading newspaper for lawyers has an immediate opening for a proofreader of manuscripts and galleys. Attention to detail, some night work. Past experience preferred. Low teens. Call Nance, 964-9700, Ext. 603.

**LEGISLATIVE ASSISTANT/SECRETARY—**
Good skills essential, dwntwn location, send resume/sal. requirements to Post Box M 8341.

---

[17]At the end of this chapter, we will examine the catch-22 problem of "no job/no experience" and "no experience/no job" when we discuss "your second job."

<table>
<tr>
<td>

**RECRUITMENT COORDINATOR**

Local office of national law firm seeks individual to coordinate attorney recruiting and paralegal program. B.A. required and 1–3 year's personnel, recruitment, or paralegal experience preferred. Salary commensurate with experience. E.O.E. Please send resume and salary requirements to LT Box 9-24-2101.

</td>
<td>

**LEGISLATIVE ASST/ADMIN**—If you are looking for that foot in the door, apply up on CAPITOL HILL, here's the job for you. Newsmaking Congressman seeks dedicated indiv to handle challenging & rewarding duties. Track legislation, handle corresp & mailing. Get involved in the fast-paced world of Capitol Hill. Good typg. Call Tues–Fri 8:30–4.

**LIBRARY/CLERICAL**—permanent, full-time pos. at lge law firm library. Duties incl. looseleaf filing, processing new books & periodicals, shelving books, and some typing. Exper. w/looseleaf filing pref. Good benefits and excel. leave policy. Respond to Post Box No. M8272.

</td>
<td>

**ADMINISTRATOR—LAW**

Medium-size established law firm seeks manager with administrative, financial, and personnel experience and EDP familiarity to supervise all non-legal office activities. Salary commensurate with experience. Equal opportunity employer. Applicants should send resumes with salary requirements to LT Box 9-17-2085.

</td>
</tr>
</table>

Of course, some of the above jobs may not be what you are looking for. They may not be directly related to your legal training and experience. Nevertheless, you should read such ads carefully. Some might be worth pursuing.

On most classified pages, you will find many ads for legal secretaries or word processors. You might want to respond to such ads as follows:

> I saw your ad for a legal secretary. I am a trained paralegal and am wondering whether you have any openings for paralegals. If not, I would greatly appreciate your referring me to any attorneys you know who may be looking for paralegals.

What about applying for a clerical position in a law office? Many paralegals take the view that this would be a mistake. In a tight employment market, however, some paralegals believe that a secretarial or typing job would be a way to "get a foot in the door," and hope that they will eventually be able to graduate into a position in the office that is commensurate with their paralegal training. Such a course of action is obviously a very personal decision that you must make on your own. It is not uncommon for clerical staff to be promoted to paralegal positions in a firm. It is also not uncommon, however, to get stuck in a clerical position.

Should you ever respond to want ads *for attorneys?* Such ads are common in legal newspapers and magazines. Of course, a paralegal cannot claim to be an attorney. But any office that is looking for attorneys obviously has a need for legal help. Hence, consider these possible reasons for responding to such ads, particularly when they give the name and address of the office seeking the attorney:

■ Perhaps the office is *also* looking for paralegal help but is simply not advertising for it (or you have not seen the want ad for paralegals).

- Perhaps the office is having difficulty finding the attorney it is seeking and would consider hiring a paralegal for a temporary period of time to perform paralegal tasks *while* continuing the search for the attorney.
- Perhaps the office has never considered hiring a paralegal *instead of* an attorney, but would be interested in exploring the idea.

Many of these employers may be totally uninterested in a response by a paralegal to an ad for an attorney. Yet none of the possibilities just described is irrational. The effort might be productive. Even if you are given a flat rejection, you can always use the opportunity to ask the person you contact if he or she knows of any other offices that are hiring paralegals.

Finally, a word about want ads placed *by a paralegal* seeking employment. Should you ever place an ad in a publication read by attorneys, such as the journal of the bar association, or the legal newspaper for your area? Such ads can be expensive and are seldom productive. Nevertheless, if you have a particular skill—for example, if you are an exnurse trained as a paralegal and are seeking a position in a medical malpractice firm, an ad might strike a responsive chord.

*d. Through Other Paralegals.*   In Strategy 4 above, we discussed methods to contact working paralegals. Once you talk with a paralegal, you can, of course, obtain information about contacting the employing attorney of that paralegal.

*e. Employment Agencies.*   There have always been employment agencies for the placement of attorneys. Many of these agencies also handle paralegal placement. Recently, a number of agencies have been opened to deal primarily with paralegal placement. Here is an example of an ad from such an agency:

---

## Help Wanted

**Paralegal Agency**                                                  **Fee Paid**

**Paralegal Placement Experts Recognized by
Over 200 Law Firms and Corporations**

**PENSIONS**

Outstanding law firm seeks 1+yrs pension paralegal exper. Major responsibilities, quality clients & liberal benefits. Salary commensurate w/exper.

**LITIGATION**

SEVERAL positions open at LAW FIRMS for litigation paralegals. Major benefits incl bonus.

**MANAGING CLERK**

Midtown law firm seeks 1+ yrs exper as a managing clerk. Work directly w/top management. Liberal benefits.

These are just a few of the many paralegal positions we have available. Call us for professional career guidance.

---

Look for such ads in the classified pages of general circulation and legal newspapers. Check your yellow pages under "Employment Agencies." If you are not sure which of the listed agencies cover legal placements, call several at random and ask which agencies in the city handle paralegal placement or legal placement in general. Caution is needed, however, in using such agencies. Some of them know very little about paralegals, in spite of their ads claiming to place paralegals. You may find that the agency views a paralegal as a secretary with a little extra training.

All employment agencies charge a placement fee. You must check whether the fee is paid by the employer or by the employee hired through the agency. Read the agency's service contract carefully before signing. Question the agency about the jobs they have available—for instance, whether evening work is expected or what typing requirements there are, if any.

Finally, you should find out if a paralegal *staffing agency* exists in your area. This is an employment agency that provides part-time employment at law offices. Most of the people placed are paralegals with experience in a particular area of practice. The paralegals are often paid by the agency, which in turn is paid by the offices. Law firms and corporate law departments may prefer part-time paralegals because of the low overhead costs involved, the availability of experienced people on short notice for indefinite periods, and the ability to end the relationship without having to go through the sometimes wrenching experience of terminating permanent employees.

*f. Directories and Other Lists of Attorneys.*   Find out whether there is a directory or list of attorneys in your area. Ask a librarian at any law library in your area. Your yellow pages will also list attorneys generally or by specialty.

Also check with a librarian about national directories of attorneys. One of the major directories is the *Martindale-Hubbell Law Directory* which gives descriptions of law firms by state and city or county (see Figure 2.5). For each firm, you are given brief biographies of the attorneys (listing bar memberships, colleges attended, etc.) as well as the areas of practice for the firm. (In 1992, Martindale-Hubbell started to include information on paralegals and other legal support personnel in law firms.) Also inquire about the availability of specialty lists of attorneys. Examples include criminal law attorneys, corporate counsel, bankruptcy attorneys, black attorneys, women attorneys, etc. Read whatever biographical data is provided on the attorneys. If there is something you have in common with a particular attorney (for example, you were both born in the same small town or you both went to the same school), you might want to mention this fact in a cover letter or phone conversation.

If you have access to either of the two major computer research systems—WESTLAW or LEXIS—you can locate attorneys online. LEXIS gives you the entire *Martindale-Hubbell Law Directory*. WESTLAW has created its own directory: *West's Legal Directory*. See Figure 2.6.

Finally, you may want to examine the *Directory of Legal Employers*, published by the National Association of Law Placement. As mentioned earlier, it lists the names and addresses of law firms and corporations that hire attorneys. But it will also indicate the number of paralegals employed by the offices listed in the directory. There are two places where you can find this directory: in the placement offices of most law schools and on WESTLAW.

*g. Courts and Bar Association Meetings.*   You can also meet attorneys at the courts of your area—for example, during a recess or at the end of the day. Bar association committee meetings are sometimes open to nonattorneys. When the other strategies for contacting attorneys do not seem productive, consider going to places where attorneys congregate. Simply introduce yourself and ask if they know of paralegal employment opportunities at their firms or at other firms. If you meet an attorney who practices in a particular specialty, it would be helpful if you could describe your course work or general interest in that kind of law. If you are doing some research in that area of the law, you might begin by asking for some research leads before you ask about employment.

**FIGURE 2.5**

Excerpt from a Page in Martindale-Hubbell Law Directory

---

### POYATT, ROYCROFT & MACDONALD
#### Established In 1968

*731 SHADY LANE*
**DALLAS, TEXAS 75202**
*Telephone: 214-555-6720*

*Fax: 214-555-6730*

*Fort Worth, Texas Office: 34 Main Street, Suite 10, 77001*
*Telephone: 817-555-9224.  Fax: 817-555-9220*

Poyatt, Roycroft & MacDonald was founded in 1968 by Kathleen Poyatt, Greg Roycroft and Julie MacDonald, former classmates and graduates of the University of Texas Law School. Starting with a local general practice, the firm now serves the entire state and maintains two fully-staffed offices offering a wide range of legal services. The firm encourages continuing professional development, and all partners and associates participate in continuing legal education seminars, professional association activities and civic affairs.

#### MEMBERS OF FIRM

KATHLEEN POYATT, born Plano, Texas, May 13, 1940; admitted to bar, 1967, Texas and U.S. Court of Appeals, Fifth Circuit. *Education:* Tulane University (B.A., with honors, 1962); University of Texas (J.D., cum laude, 1967). Phi Beta Kappa; Phi Delta Phi; Order of the Coif. Associate Editor, Texas Law Review, 1966–1967. Certified Public Accountant, Texas, 1971. Member, Advisory Board, Dallas Family Planning Council, 1982–1984. Legal Counsel, Dallas Board of Realtors, 1986–1987. *Member:* Dallas and American Bar Associations; State Bar of Texas (Chair, Committee on Trust Administration, Estate Planning and Probate Section, 1989– ); American Judicature Society. (Board Certified, Estate Planning and Probate Law, Texas Board of Legal Specialization). LANGUAGES: Spanish and French. SPECIAL AGENCIES: Texas Council on Charitable Trusts. REPORTED CASES: Mastalia v. Fairty, 145 S.E. 2d 1405. TRANSACTIONS: Bankruptcy of Braniff Airlines, 1982; The Keepwell Foundation, 1990. AREAS OF CONCENTRATION: Trust Administration, Banking and Creditors' Rights, Trial, Litigation and Real Estate.

JULIE MACDONALD, born Nashville, Tennessee, August 29, 1940; admitted to bar, 1967, Texas and U.S. District Court, Northern District of Texas. *Education:* University of Tennessee at Memphis (B.A., with honors, 1962); University of Texas (J.D., with honors, 1967). Alpha Lambda Delta; Phi Kappa Phi; Phi Beta Kappa. Member, Tennessee State Board of Professional Responsibility, 1983–1984; Dallas Association of Young Lawyers; The Association of Trial Lawyers of America. *Member:* Dallas (*Member:* Real Estate and Commercial Real Estate Morning Section; Continuing Education Committee) and American (*Member:* Real Property Section; Continuing Education Committee). Bar Associations; State Bar of Texas; Dallas Association of Young Lawyers; The Association of Trial Lawyers of America, LANGUAGES: Spanish and Italian. SPECIAL AGENCIES: Texas Council on Taxation Trusts. REPORTED CASES: Cuneo v. Banks, 466 S.E. 2d 6609; Kyle v. Smily, 432 S.E. 2d 4599. TRANSACTIONS: The Hines foundation, 1989. AREAS OF CONCENTRATION: Trials and Appeals, Estate Planning, Real Estates, Banking and Taxation.

#### LEGAL SUPPORT PERSONNEL
#### PARALEGAL

LINDA DAVIS, born Maurice, Louisiana, August 16, 1962. *Education:* Interstate Paralegal Institute. Certified Legal Assistant, Texas, 1985. President, Dallas Paralegal Association, 1987. Secretary, Texas State Paralegal Association, 1988. *Member:* National, State and Local Paralegal Association. Legal Research, Drafting Legal Pleadings, Client Correspondence, Deposition Summaries and File Investigations.

---

*h. Miscellaneous.*  Go to a recent reporter volume (page 491) or advance sheet (page 486) of a reporter volume containing court opinions of your state. At the beginning of each opinion, there is a list of the attorneys who represented the parties in that case. You can obtain their addresses from standard directories such as those mentioned above. If the opinion is on an area of law in which you have an interest, call the attorneys after you have read the opinion. Ask a question or two about the case and that area of the law. Then ask about employment opportunities for paralegals in that area.

Look for ads in legal newspapers in which an attorney is seeking information about a particular product involved in a suit that is contemplated or underway. Or read feature stories in this newspaper on major litigation that is about to begin. If the area of the law interests you, contact the law firms in-

**FIGURE 2.6**

Sample Screen from West's Legal Directory

| | |
|---|---|
| Name: | Jones, James E |
| City: | Boston |
| State: | Massachusetts |
| Position: | Partner |
| Firm: | Smith, Jones & White |
| Address: | 1000 State Street, Exchange Plaza, Boston, MA  90001 |
| Phone: | (617)722-7777 |
| Electronic Mail: | Fax Area Code (617) Phone 722-7776 |
| Born: | May 20, 1947, Dallas, TX. U.S.A. |
| Education: | Baylor University, Waco, Texas (J.D., 1973), Cum Laude |
| | University of Texas, Austin, Texas (B.A., 1969) |
| Admitted: | Massachusetts 1975 |
| | Texas 1973 |
| | Federal Court 1979 |
| Fraternities: | Phi Alpha Delta |
| Directorships: | Massachusetts Commerce Association, 1980–Present |
| Affiliations: | American Bar Association |
| | State Bar of Massachusetts |
| Representative Clients: | Semi-Conductor, Inc. |
| | BCA National Bank |
| Representative Cases: | Thayer v. Smith, 560 S.W.2d 137 (1989) |
| Practice: | 50% Patent, Trademark, Copyright |
| | 25% Corporations Law |
| | 25% Litigation |
| Foreign Languages: | Russian |
| Certified Specialty: | Patent, Trademark, Copyright--U.S. Patent & Trademark Office |
| Published Works: | *Corporations and Business Law,* 1981, CAB Publishing Company |

volved to ask about employment opportunities for paralegals. Many firms hire additional paralegals, particularly for large cases.

Find the bar journal of your local or state bar associations in the law library. The articles in the journal are often written by attorneys from the state. If the subject of an article interests you, read it and call the author. Ask a question or two about the topic of the article and the area of the law involved. Then ask about employment opportunities for paralegals in that area.

*Strategy 7: Prepare Your Resume, Cover Letter, and Writing Sample*

The cardinal principle of resume writing is that the resume must fit the job you are seeking. Hence, you must have more than one resume or you must rewrite your resume for each kind of paralegal job you are seeking. A resume is an *advocacy* document. You are trying to convince someone (a) to give you an interview and ultimately (b) to offer you a job. You are not simply communicating information about yourself. A resume is *not* a summary of your life or a one-page autobiography. It is a very brief *commercial* in which you are trying to sell yourself as a person who can make a contribution to a particular prospective employer. Hence the resume must stress what would appeal to this employer. You are advocating (or selling) yourself effectively when the form and content of the resume has this appeal. Advocacy is required for several reasons. First, there are probably many more applicants than jobs available. Second, most prospective employers ignore resumes that are not geared to their particular needs.

Before examining sample resumes, we need to explore some general guidelines that apply to *any* resume.

## Guidelines on Drafting an Effective Resume

1. Be concise and to the point. Generally, the resume should fit on one page. A longer resume is justified only if you have a unique education or experience that is directly related to law or to the particular law firm or company in which you are interested.

2. Be accurate. Studies show that about 30% of all resumes contain inaccuracies. Recently, a legal administrator felt the need to make the following comment (to other legal administrators) about job applicants: "I'm sure we have all had experiences where an applicant has lied on an application about experience, previous salary scales, length of time with previous employers, training, skills, and anything else they can think of that will make them appear more attractive." [18] While you want to present yourself in the best possible light, it is critical that you not jeopardize your integrity. All of the data in the resume should be verifiable. Prospective employers who check the accuracy of resumes usually do so themselves, although some use outside organizations such as the National Credential Verification Service.

3. Include personal data—that is, name, address, zip code, and phone (with area code) where you can be reached. (If someone is not always available to take messages while you are away, invest in an answering machine.) Do not include a personal photograph or data on your health, height, religion, or political party. You do not have to include information that might give a prospective employer a basis to discriminate against you illegally, such as your marital status or the names and ages of your children. Later we will discuss how to handle such matters in a job interview.

4. Provide a concise statement of your career objective at the top of the resume. (It should be pointed out, however, that some people recommend that this statement be included in the cover letter rather than in the resume.) The career objective should be a quick way for the reader to know whether your goal fits the needs of the prospective employer. Hence, *the career objective should be targeted to a particular employer.* An overly general career objective gives the unfortunate effect of a "mass-mailing resume." Suppose, for example, you are applying for a position as a litigation paralegal at a forty-attorney law firm that is looking for someone to help with scheduling and document handling on several cases going on simultaneously.

Don't say: **Career Objective**—A position as a paralegal at an office where there is an opportunity for growth.

Do say: **Career Objective**—A position as a litigation paralegal at a medium-sized law firm where I will be able to use and build on the organization skills I developed in my prior employment and the case management skills that I have learned to date.

---

[18]Jacobi, *Back to Basics in Hiring Techniques,* The Mandate, 1 (Ass'n of Legal Administrators, San Diego Chapter, October 1987).

The first statement is too flat and uninformative. Its generalities could fit just about *any* paralegal job. Even worse, its focus is on the needs of the applicant. The second statement is much more direct. While also referring to the needs of the applicant, the second statement goes to the heart of what the employer is looking for—someone to help create order out of the complexity of events and papers involved in litigation.

5. Next, state your prior education and training.[19] (See Job Hunting Notebook, page 164, page 165.) List each school or training institution and the dates attended. Use a reverse chronological order—that is, start the list with the most current and work backwards. Do not include your high school unless you attended a prestigious high school, you have not attended college, or you are a very recent high school graduate. When you give your legal education:

a. List the major courses.

b. State specific skills and tasks covered in your courses that are relevant to the job you are applying for. Also state major topic areas covered in the courses that demonstrate a knowledge of (or at least exposure to) material that is relevant to the job. For example, if you are applying for a corporate paralegal job, relevant courses could be stated as follows:

> **Corporate Law:** This course examined the formation of a corporation, director and shareholder meetings, corporate mergers, and the dissolution of corporations; we also studied sample shareholder minutes and prepared proxy statements. Grade received: B+.

> **Legal Bibliography:** This course covered the basic law books relevant to researching corporate law, including the state code. We also covered the skills of using practice books, finding cases on corporate law through the digests, etc. Grade received: A−.

c. List any special programs in the school, such as unique class assignments, term papers, extensive research, moot court, internship, or semester projects. Give a brief description if any of these programs are relevant to the job you are applying for.

d. State any unusually high grades: give overall grade point average (GPA) if it is distinctive.

List any degrees, certificates, or other recognition that you earned at each school or training institution. Include high aptitude or standard test scores. If the school or institution has any special distinction or recognition, mention this as well.

6. State your work experience. (See Job Hunting Notebook, pages 160–163.) List the jobs you held, your job title, the dates of employment, and the major duties that you performed. (Do not state the reason you left each job, although you should be prepared to discuss this if you are granted an interview.) Again, work backwards. Start with the most current (or your present) employment. The statement of duties is particularly important. If you have legal experience, emphasize specific duties and tasks that are directly relevant to the position you are seeking—for example, include that you drafted corporate minutes or prepared incorporation papers. Give prominence to such skills and tasks on the resume. Nonlegal experience, however, can also be relevant. Every

---

[19]If you already have experience as a paralegal and are seeking to change jobs, the next section of the resume should be work experience, followed by education and training.

prior job says something about you as an individual. Phrase your duties in such jobs in a manner that will highlight important personality traits. (See p. 163.) In general, most employers are looking for people with the following characteristics:

- Emotional maturity
- Intelligence
- Willingness to learn
- Ability to get along with others
- Ability to work independently (someone with initiative and self-reliance who is not afraid of assuming responsibility)
- Problem-solving skills
- Ability to handle time pressures and frustration
- Loyalty
- Stability, reliability
- Energy

As you list duties in prior and current employment settings, do *not* use any of the language just listed. But try to state duties that tend to show that these characteristics apply to you. For example, if you had a job as a camp counselor, state that you supervised eighteen children, designed schedules according to predetermined objectives, prepared budgets, took over in the absence of the director of the camp, etc. A listing of such duties will say a lot about you as a person. You are someone who can be trusted, you know how to work with people, you are flexible, etc. These are the kind of conclusions that you want the reader of your resume to reach. Finally, try to present the facts to show a growth in your accomplishments, development, and maturity. Note that *action verbs* were used in examples just given: supervised, designed, prepared, took over. Concentrate on such verbs. Avoid weak verbs such as "involved in" or "was related to."

7.  State other experience and skills that do not fall within the categories of education and employment mentioned above. (See Job Hunting Notebook, p. 163.) Perhaps you have been a homemaker for twenty years, you raised five children, you worked your way through college, you were the church treasurer, a cub scout volunteer, etc. In a separate category on the resume called "Other Experience," list such activities and state your duties in the same manner mentioned above to demonstrate relevant personality traits. Hobbies can be included (without using the word "hobby") when they are distinctive and illustrate special talents or achievement.

8.  State any special abilities (for example, that you can design a database or speak a foreign language), awards, credentials, scholarships, membership associations, leadership positions, community service, publications, etc., that have not been mentioned elsewhere on the resume.

9.  No one has a perfect resume. There are facts about all of us that we would prefer to downplay or avoid, e.g., sudden change in jobs, school transfer because of personal or family difficulties, low aptitude test scores. There is no need to point out these facts, but in a job interview you must be prepared to discuss any obvious gaps or problems that might be evident from your resume. Thus far we have been outlining the format of a *chronological resume* in which your education, training, and experience are presented in a chronological se-

quence from the present backwards. (See Figure 2.8.) Later we will examine how a *functional resume* might be more effective than a chronological resume in handling difficulties such as sudden changes or gaps in employment. (See Figure 2.9.)

10. At the end of the resume, say, "References available on request." On a separate sheet of paper, type the names and addresses of people who know your abilities and who could be contacted by a prospective employer. If the latter is seriously considering you for a position, you will probably be asked for the list. This will most likely occur during a job interview. Generally, you should seek the permission of people you intend to use as references. Call them up and ask if you can list them as references in your job search.

11. Do not include salary requirements or your salary history on the resume. Leave this topic for the interview.

12. The resume should be neatly typed, grammatically correct, and readable. Be sure that there are no spelling errors or smudge spots from erasures or fingerprints. In this regard, if you can't make your resume *perfect,* don't bother submitting it. Avoid abbreviations except for items such as street, state, degrees earned, etc. Do not make any handwritten corrections. Proofread carefully. Ask someone else to proofread the resume for you to see if you missed anything.

You do not have to use complete sentences in the resume. Sentence fragments are adequate as long as you rigorously follow the grammatical rule on parallelism. For example, say, "research*ed* securities issues, draft*ed* complaints, serv*ed* papers on opposing parties." Do not say, "researched securities, drafting complaints, and I served papers on opposing parties." When you present a series or a list, be consistent in using words ending in "ed" or ending in "ing," etc. Do not suddenly change from an "ed" word to an "ing" word or add personal pronouns on only some of the items in the series or list.

Leave generous margins. Cluster similar information together and use consistent indentation patterns so that readers can easily scan the resume and quickly find those categories of information in which they are most interested.

The resume should have a professional appearance. Consider having your resume typeset on quality paper (with matching envelopes) by a commercial printing company or word processing service. Obtain multiple copies of your resume. Avoid submitting a resume that was obviously reproduced on a poor-quality Xerox machine at a corner drugstore. The resume is often the first contact that a prospective employer will have with you. You want to convey the impression that you know how to write and organize data. Furthermore, it is a sign of respect to the reader when you show that you took the time and energy to make your resume professionally presentable. Law offices are *conservative* environments. Attorneys like to project an image of propriety, stability, accuracy, and order. Be sure that your resume also projects this image.

13. Again, the resume concentrates on those facts about you that show you are particularly qualified *for the specific job you are seeking.* The single most important theme you want to convey in the resume is that you are a person who can make a contribution to *this* organization. As much as possible, the reader of the resume should have the impression that you prepared the resume for the particular position that is open. In style and content, the resume should emphasize what will be pleasing to the reader and demonstrate what you can contribute to a particular office. (See Figure 2.7.)

The last guideline is very important. You cannot comply with it unless you have done some *background research* on the law office where you are applying

**FIGURE 2.7**

The Resume as an
Advocacy
Document

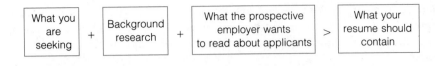

and, if possible, on the person who will be receiving the resume. How do you do this background research? First and foremost, you want to try to contact employees, particularly paralegals, who work there now or who once worked there. That's why Strategy 4, outlined above, on ways to locate working paralegals is so important.

In addition, consult one of the directories of attorneys, such as the *Martindale-Hubble Law Directory* or *West's Legal Directory*, discussed earlier. Ask a librarian for a current directory of attorneys used in your state. Many large firms have brochures on their firms which are part of marketing strategies to find new clients. They may also have newsletters that they send to their current clients. Such brochures and newsletters may not be available to the general public unless someone within the firm gives you access to them.

If you are applying for a position in the law department of a large corporation, call the public relations office of the corporation and ask for promotional literature and a copy of its annual report. Many law libraries have directories of corporate counsel which you should check. In addition, most general libraries have directories, such as *Standard & Poor's Register of Corporations, Directors and Executives* and *Moody's Bank and Finance Manual,* that provide information on such companies. Ask the librarian what other sources provide profiles of businesses.

Here is a partial checklist of information you want to obtain through background research on a prospective employer or job (see also page 156):

- Why has the office decided to hire a paralegal now? What needs or problems prompted this decision?
- What kind of law is practiced at the office? What are its specialties?
- How is the office structured and governed? By management committee?
- How old is the office? Has it expanded recently? If so, in what areas?
- What kinds of clients does the office have? A variety of small clients? Several large clients that provide most of the fees?
- If the office is the law department of a corporation, what are the company's main products or services?
- How many attorneys are in the office?
- How many paralegals? What kind of work do they do? Does the office understand the role of paralegals? What kinds of complaints have the paralegals had about the office? What are the advantages and disadvantages of working in the office?
- Has the office had personnel problems? High turnover?
- Does the office operate through systems? If not, how does it feel about developing such systems?

If you do your homework on a prospective employer, you will have begun collecting answers to such questions so that you can tailor your resume to these answers. You will select those aspects of your prior employment or education, for example, that suggest or demonstrate you are able to handle the demands of the job.

Of course, for many jobs, you will *not* be able to obtain answers to these questions, no matter how much background research you do. You will simply have to do the best you can to predict what the "correct" answers are and structure your resume, cover letter, and writing sample accordingly.

The main point, however, is that a lot of preparation is needed before you approach a prospective employer. Much time and energy must be expended. A conscientious and organized job search will be good preparation for the career ahead of you. *The same kind of motivation, creativity, and aggressiveness that is needed to find a good job is also needed to perform effectively as a paralegal and to advance in this field.* The cornerstone of achievement and success is a heavy dosage of old-fashioned hard work.

Figure 2.8 is an example of a *chronological resume,* the most common and traditional format used by many applicants today. As indicated earlier, this re-

**FIGURE 2.8**

Sample Chronological Resume

**JOHN J. SMITH**
**43 BENNING ROAD SE**
**SALEM, MARYLAND 21455**
**(301) 456-0427**

**Career Objective**

Position as a paralegal at a small law firm in the area of probate, trusts, and estates in a firm where my accounting and legal skills will be used and where there are opportunities for growth.

**Education**

Jan. 1989–Jan. 1990 Maynard Paralegal Institute.
Courses:

Trusts and Estates: The course presented an overview of probate procedure in Maryland. We covered how to conduct a client conference to collect the basic facts and how to prepare the 105 short form.

Tax I: An introduction to the taxation of estates and general income tax; fundamentals of accounting; valuation of personal and real assets.

Introduction to Law   Civil Procedure
Family Law   Legal Research
Litigation

Internship: Part of the curriculum at Maynard involved a six-week internship placement at a law firm; I was placed at Donaldson and Tannance, a general practice firm in Salem. Tasks undertaken at the internship: drafted answers to interrogatories in a divorce case on the ground of mental cruelty; maintained the office's tickler system; completed cite checking and shepardizing for an appellate brief.

Sept. 1987–June 1988 Jefferson Junior College Courses:
Business Law   Sociology
English I, II   Chemistry
Introduction to Psychology   Creative Writing
French I

**Employment**

1985–1988 Teller, Salem National Bank
Responsibilities: receiving deposit and withdrawal requests; training new tellers, supervising note department in the absence of the assistant manager.

1980–1984 Driver, ABC Biscuit Company

**Honors**

1985 Junior Achievement Award for Outstanding Marketing

**Associations**

Financial Secretary, Salem Paralegal Association
Regional Representative, National Federation of Paralegal Associations
Member, National Association of Legal Assistants

**References**

Available on request.

**FIGURE 2.9**

Sample Functional
Resume[20]

Jane Doe
18 East 7th Avenue
Denver, Colorado 80200
303-555-1198

**JOB OBJECTIVE**

A position in a legal office requiring skills in communications, research, and organization, leading toward training for and work as a paralegal.

**BRIEF SUMMARY OF BACKGROUND**

Bachelor of Arts and Bachelor of Science (Education) with major in English and minor
in Library Science. Taught creative writing and communications to high school jun-
iors and seniors; worked several years as research and index assistant in records
and research department of large, international organization; worked part-time on a
volunteer basis in schools and libraries as librarian and reading tutor.

**PROFESSIONAL SKILLS RELATED TO CAREER OBJECTIVE**

**Communications Skills**

Taught communications to high school seniors; read extensively in international publications during nonworking years; conducted workshops on library skills and sto-
rytelling to children and young adults; participated in workshops with educators on
reading skills; served as Circulation Representative for *The Christian Science Monitor,* which included promoting and selling subscriptions by telephone and in person.
Gained considerable writing experience while working toward college degrees in
English.

**Clerical Skills**

Facility with [a] vocabulary and spelling; [b] rules of diction and usage; [c] typing
(80 wpm); [d] filing (helped revise and maintain many files including administrative,
subjective, alpha-chrono combinations); [e] systems (maintained and circulated library collections and maintained catalog card files).

**Research Skills**

As librarian: helped students and teachers research and retrieve information and
materials on various subjects; ordered, received, processed, and shelved library
materials.

As research assistant: indexed correspondence; researched files for information using subject index; collated information on various subjects.

**Analytical and Organizational Skills**

Handled all phases of management of school library; planned for materials needed;
ordered to meet those needs; supervised assistants; set up revised filing systems;
helped engineer departmental move to new quarters.

**EMPLOYMENT HISTORY**

| | |
|---|---|
| 9/84–Present | Lincoln Elementary School<br>100 Oak Street, Denver, Colorado 80000<br>*Title:* Teacher's Aide (Part-time) |
| 6/76–6/84 | International Church Center<br>Executive Department, Records and Research Section<br>465 E. 8th St., Boston, Massachusetts 02127<br>*Title:* Research and Index Assistant (1 year full-time; 7 years part-time) |
| 4/84–6/84 | Latin Preparatory School<br>16 Adams Court, Dorchester, Massachusetts 02139<br>*Title:* School Librarian (substitute) |
| 2/83–6/84 | James P. O'Reilly Elementary School<br>74 Statler Road, Boston, Massachusetts 02140<br>*Title:* School Librarian (volunteer) |
| 9/74–6/75 | Roosevelt High School<br>16 Main St., Minneapolis, Minnesota 55162<br>*Title:* English Teacher |

Continued

**EDUCATION**

| 1983–1984 | University of Massachusetts, Boston Campus<br>Special courses included: Library and Urban Children; Design Management |
| 1979–1980 | Harvard Extension, Problems in Urban Education |
| 1969–1973 | University of Minnesota, Minneapolis,<br>B.S. and B.A., *Major:* English<br>*Minor:* Library Science |

**SCHOOL ACTIVITIES**

National Honor Society; Dramatic Club; Creative Writing Club; YWCA; Member, Minnesota Dance Company, 1969–1973.

**REFERENCES**

Available on request.

**FIGURE 2.9**

Sample Functional Resume[20]
—*Continued*

sume presents your education, training, and work history in reverse chronological sequence, beginning with the most recent events and working backwards.

A *functional resume,* on the other hand, clusters certain skills or talents together regardless of the period in which they were developed. See Figure 2.9. This style of resume can be particularly useful when you want to downplay large gaps in education, when you are making a radical change of careers, or when your skills were not gained in paralegal education, training, or employment. The functional resume should not, however, ignore the chronological sequence of the major training and work events of your life, since a prospective employer will want to know what this sequence is. Note that the functional resume in Figure 2.9 has a skill cluster early in the resume, after which there is the historical overview in reverse chronological order. Because of this format, the emphasis of the resume is on the skills or abilities highlighted at the beginning.

### Cover Letter

The *cover letter* should state how you learned of the office. It should also highlight and amplify those portions of the resume that are relevant to the position you are seeking. Without being unduly repetitive of the resume, explain how you are qualified for the job. Like the resume itself, the cover letter should give the impression that you are a professional. It is also important that you communicate a sense of enthusiasm about the position.

Note that the cover letter in Figure 2.10 is addressed to a specific person. It would be inappropriate to send a "To Whom It May Concern" letter. Find out the exact name of the person to whom the resume should be sent. If you are not sure, call the office and ask.

One final, critically important point about the cover letter: it must be grammatically correct and contain no spelling errors. Your standard must be perfection. While this is also true of the resume, it is particularly true of the cover letter. When the envelope is opened, the first thing that is read is the cover letter. The vast majority of us are *unaware of how poor our grammar is.* We have been lulled into a sense of security because readers of what we write—including

[20]Rocky Mountain Legal Assistants Association, *Employment Handbook for Legal Assistants,* 26–8 (1979).

**FIGURE 2.10**
Cover Letter

> 43 Benning Road SE
> Salem, Maryland 21455
> 301/456-0427
> March 13, 1990
>
> Linda Stenner, Esq.
> Stenner, Skidmore & Smith
> 438 Bankers Trust Bldg.
> Suite 1200
> Salem, Maryland 21458
>
> Dear Ms. Stenner:
>
>     Michael Diamond, Esq. told me that your firm may have an opening for a trusts and estates paralegal. I am enclosing my resume for your consideration. I am very interested in working in the field of probate, trusts, and estates. The course work that I did at Maynard Institute and my prior work at the Salem National Bank provided me with an appreciation of the complexity of this area of the law. I find the field fascinating.
>
>     I am fully aware of the kind of attention to detail that a paralegal in this field must have. If you decide to check any of my references, I am confident that you will be told of the high level of discipline and responsibility that I bring to the tasks I undertake.
>
>     I have two writing samples that may be of interest to you: a draft of a will that I prepared in my course on trusts and estates, and a memorandum of law on the valuation of stocks. These writing samples are available on request.
>
>     I would appreciate the opportunity to be interviewed for the paralegal position at your firm. I feel confident that my training and experience have prepared me for the kind of challenge that this position would provide.
>
>                               Sincerely,
>
>                               John J. Smith

teachers—seldom complain unless we make an egregious error. People read primarily for content; they do not focus on grammar and spelling. Hence you must provide this focus on your own. In the section on studying at the beginning of this book, there are suggestions for improving your writing skills. In the meantime, proofread, proofread, proofread; and then find others to proofread everything that you intend to submit in writing to a prospective employer.

### Writing Samples

You should be constantly thinking about writing samples based upon the course work you do and any legal employment or internship experiences you have had. If your writing sample comes from a prior job or internship, be sure that the confidentiality of actual parties is protected by "whiting out" or changing their names.[21] In addition, consider preparing other writing samples *on your own.* For example:

- a brief memorandum of law on the application of a statute to a set of facts that you make up (see Chapter 12)

---

[21] "It is always inappropriate to hand a prospective employer anything that has current, active case information anywhere in it: case names and numbers, court and internal file numbers, names, addresses, telephone numbers of deponents, names of plaintiffs, defendants, and third parties in the body of the document." Fitzgerald, *Ethics and the Job Hunting Paralegal,* 18 Reporter (Los Angeles Paralegal Ass'n, November 1989).

- a pleading such as a complaint (see Chapter 10)
- a set of interrogatories (see Chapter 10)
- articles of incorporation and bylaws for a fictitious corporation
- an analysis of a recent court opinion (see Chapters 7 and 11)
- an in-take memorandum of law based on an interview that you role-play with another student (see Chapter 8)
- an annotated bibliography on a particular topic (see Chapter 11)
- a brief article that you write for a paralegal newsletter on an aspect of your legal education or work experience as a paralegal (see Appendix B)

Prepare a file of all your writing samples. (See Job Hunting Notebook, page 167.) If possible, try to have a teacher, practicing attorney, or paralegal review each sample. Rewrite it based on their comments. You must take the initiative in preparing writing samples and in soliciting feedback from knowledgeable contacts that you make. You need to have a large pool of diverse writing samples from which to choose once you begin the actual job hunt. Start preparing these samples now.

### Strategy 8: The Job Interview

Once you have overcome the hurdles of finding a prospective employer who will read your cover letter and resume, the next problem is to arrange for a job interview. In your cover letter, you may want to add the following sentence at the end: "Within the next two weeks, I will give you a call to determine whether an interview would be possible." This strategy does not leave the matter entirely up to the prospective employer as to whether there will be further contact with you. You must be careful, however, not to appear too forward. Some may resent this approach. On the other hand, you have little to lose by trying it several times to see what response you obtain.

Always try to have a paralegal, attorney, administrator, or secretary in the office arrange the interview for you with the person who will be doing the hiring and/or interviewing. Hopefully, your background research into the office will enable you to identify such an in-house person who will put in a word for you.

## Job Interview Guidelines

(See Job Hunting Notebook, page 169.)

"Attired in your best interviewing suit, you nervously navigate your way to the reception area of what you hope will be your future employer's office. You are a comfortable ten minutes early. Upon arrival you are directed to the office of the interviewer, whom you greet with a smile and pleasant handshake. She offers you a cup of coffee, which you wisely refuse, since you may spill it. She then looks you in the eye and poses her first question. 'Why are you interested in working for this company?' [Suddenly you go blank!] All thoughts leave your mind as you pray for the ability to speak." Cunningham, *A Planned Approach to Interviewing*, 5 The LAMA Manager 1 (Legal Assistants Management Association, Fall 1989).

1. Be sure you have the exact address, room number, and time of the interview. Give yourself sufficient time to find the office. If the area is new to you, be sure that you have precise directions. It would be unfortunate to start your contact with the office by having to provide excuses for being late. Arrive at least

ten minutes early. You will probably be nervous and will need to compose your-self before the interview. It is important that you are as relaxed as possible.

2.  Try to find out in advance who will be interviewing you. Don't be sur-prised, however, if the person who greets you is a substitute for the person orig-inally scheduled to conduct the interview. There are a number of different kinds of people who might conduct the interview: the law office manager, the man-aging attorney, the supervising attorney for the position, the paralegal supervi-sor, a staff paralegal, or a combination of the above if you are interviewed by different people on the same day or on different days. The style of the interview may be quite different depending on who conducts it. Someone with manage-ment responsibility might stress the interpersonal dimensions of the position, whereas a trial attorney might give you the feeling that you are being cross-examined. Try to determine whether you are being interviewed by the person who has the final authority to hire you. In many offices, you will be interviewed by someone whose sole task is to screen out unacceptable applicants. If you make it through this person, the next step will usually be an interview with the ultimate decision-maker. Whenever you know or suspect that you will be inter-viewed by an attorney, try to obtain his or her professional biography through *Martindale-Hubbell* or other directories. You might be lucky enough to get to talk with someone who has been interviewed by this person before (such as a paralegal now working at the office, a fellow job seeker, or someone at the local paralegal association) so that you can obtain a sense of what to expect.

3.  Although relatively uncommon, you may have to face a *group inter-view*. There could be several interviewers questioning you at once. Alterna-tively, one or more interviewers could interview you along with, and at the same time as, other candidates for the job.

4.  Make sure that you are prepared for the interview. Review the guide-lines discussed above on writing your resume. In the resume and in the inter-view, you are trying to sell yourself. Many of the principles of resume writing apply to the interview. Know the kinds of questions you will probably be asked. Rehearse your responses. Write down a series of questions (tough ones) and ask a friend to role-play an interview with you. Have your friend ask you the ques-tions and critique your responses. Also take the role of the interviewer of your friend so that you can gauge both perspectives. Be prepared to handle a large variety of questions. See Figure 2.11. Keep in mind, however, that no matter how much preparation you do, you may still be surprised by the course the interview takes. Be flexible enough to expect the unexpected. If you are relaxed, confident, *and prepared,* you will do fine.

5.  You are not required to answer potentially illegal questions—for in-stance, "Are you married?" Some employers use the answers to such irrelevant questions to practice illegal sex discrimination. You need to decide in advance how you will handle them if they are asked. You may want to ask why the question is relevant. Or you may simply decide to steer the interview back to the qualifications that you have and the commitment that you have made to a professional career. A good response might be, "If you're concerned that my marital status may affect my job performance, I can assure you that it will not." Follow this up with comments about dedication and job commitment. It may be the perfect time to offer references.[22] Whatever approach you take, be sure to remain courteous.

---

[22]Reitz, *Be Steps Ahead of Other Candidates: Understand the Interview Game,* 5 Legal Assistant Today 24, 84 (March/April 1988).

FIGURE 2.11

The Six Categories
of Job Interview
Questions

- **Open-Ended Questions** (which are calculated to get you to talk, giving the listener an idea of how you organize your thoughts)

    (1)  Tell me about yourself.

    (2)  What kind of position are you seeking?

    (3)  What interests you about this job?

- **Closed-Ended Questions** (which can be answered by one or two words)

    (4)  When did you receive your paralegal certificate?

    (5)  Did you take a course in corporate law?

- **Soft-Ball Questions** (which should be fairly easy to answer if you are prepared)

    (6)  What are your interests outside of school and work?

    (7)  What courses did you enjoy the most? Why? Which were least rewarding? Why?

    (8)  Do your grades reflect your full potential? Why or why not?

    (9)  Why did you leave your last job?

    (10)  How have you grown or developed in your prior jobs? Explain.

    (11)  How were you evaluated in your prior jobs?

    (12)  What are your strengths as a worker?

    (13)  Describe an ideal work environment. What would your "dream job" be?

    (14)  What factors make a job frustrating? How would you handle these factors?

    (15)  What do you hope to be doing in ten years? What are your long-term goals?

    (16)  If you are hired, how long are you prepared to stay?

    (17)  Are you interested in a job or a career? What's the difference?

    (18)  Why did you become a paralegal?

    (19)  What problems do you think a paralegal might face in a busy law office? How would you handle these problems?

    (20)  Can you work under pressure? When have you done so in the past?

    (21)  How flexible are you in adapting to changing circumstances? Give examples of your flexibility in the last year.

    (22)  How do you feel about doing routine work?

    (23)  Do you prefer a large or a small law office? Why?

    (24)  What accomplishment in your life are you most proud of? Why?

    (25)  What salary expectations do you have? What was your salary at your last position?

    (26)  What other questions do you think I should ask in order to learn more about you?

    (27)  What questions would you like to ask me about this office?

- **Tension Questions** (which are calculated to put you on the spot in order to see how you handle yourself)

    (28)  No one is perfect. What are your weaknesses as a worker?

    (29)  Have you ever been fired from a position? Explain the circumstances.

    (30)  Why have you held so many jobs?

    (31)  Name some things that would be unethical for an attorney to do. What would you do if you found out that the attorney supervising you was doing these things?

    (32)  Are you a competitive person? If not, why not? If you are, give some examples over the last six months that demonstrate this characteristic.

    (33)  Is there something in this job that you hope to accomplish that you were not able to accomplish in your last job?

Continued

**FIGURE 2.11**

The Six Categories
of Job Interview
Questions—
*Continued*

(34) Do you type? If not, are you willing to learn?

(35) Do you smoke? If so, how would you handle a work environment that is totally smoke-free, including the wash rooms?

(36) Where else have you interviewed for a job? Have you been turned down?

(37) Why wouldn't you want to become an attorney now?

(38) Everyone makes mistakes. What is the biggest mistake that you made in any of your prior jobs and how did you handle it?*

(39) No job is perfect. What is the least appealing aspect of the job you are seeking?

(40) There are over fifty applicants for this one position. Why do you think you are the most qualified?

(41) If you are offered this position, what are the major concerns that you would have about taking it?

(42) What would make you want to quit a job?

(43) Give some examples of when you have shown initiative over the last six months in school or at your last job.

▪ **Hypothetical Questions** (in which you are asked how you would handle a stated fact situation)

(44) If you were told, "This isn't any good, do it again, and get it right this time," what would you do?

(45) If you find out on Friday afternoon that you're expected to come in on Saturday, what would you do?**

(46) Assume that you are given the position here and that you work very closely on a day-to-day basis with an attorney. After a six-month period, what positive and negative comments do you think this attorney would make about you as a worker?

(47) Suppose that your first assignment was to read through and summarize 4,000 documents over an eight-month period. Could you do it? Would you want to do it?

(48) Assume that two airplanes crash into each other and that your firm represents one of the passengers who was killed. What kind of discovery would you recommend?

▪ **Potentially Illegal Questions** (because the questions are not relevant to the candidate's fitness and ability to do most jobs)

(49) Are you married? Do you plan to marry?

(50) Do you have any children? If so, how old are they? Who takes care of your children?

(51) If you do not have any children now, do you plan to have any in the future?

(52) How old are you?

(53) What is your religion?

(54) What is your political affiliation?

---

*Moralez, *Sample Interview Questions,* 11 Paragram (Oregon Legal Assistant Ass'n, May 1988).
**Wendel, *You the Recruiter,* 5 Legal Assistant Today 31 (September/October 1987).

6. Avoid being critical of anyone. Do not, for example, "dump on" your prior employer or school. Criticizing or blaming other organizations, even if justified, is likely to give the interviewer the impression that you will probably end up blaming *this* organization if you get the job and difficulties arise.

7. What about being critical of yourself? You will be invited to criticize yourself when you are asked the seemingly inevitable question, "What are your weaknesses?" You may want to pick a *positive* trait and express it as a negative.

For example: "I tend to get frustrated when I'm not given enough to do. My goal is not just to collect a paycheck. I want to make a contribution." Or: "I think I sometimes have expectations that are too high. There is so much to learn, and I want it all now. I have to pace myself, and realize that the important goal is to complete the immediate task, even if I can't learn every conceivable aspect of that task at the present time." Or: "I get irritated by carelessness. When I see someone turn in sloppy work, or work that is not up to the highest standards, it bothers me."

If you use any of these approaches, be sure that you are able to back them up when you are asked to explain what you mean. You will probably be asked to give concrete examples of such "weaknesses."

8.  If you have done the kind of background research on the office mentioned earlier, you will have a fairly good idea what the structure and mission of the office is. Interviewers are usually impressed by applicants who demonstrate this kind of knowledge during the interview. It will be clear to them which applicants have done their homework. A major goal of the interview is to relate your education and experience to the needs of the office. To the extent possible, you want to know what these needs are before the interview so that you can quickly and forcefully demonstrate that you are the person the office is looking for. Most offices decide to hire someone because they have a problem—for example, they need someone with a particular skill, they need someone to help them expand, or they need someone who can get along with a particularly demanding supervising attorney. If you are not sure, ask the interviewer directly why the office has decided to add a paralegal. The success of the interview is directly related to your ability to identify the problem of the office and to demonstrate how you can solve it for them.

9.  If the paralegal job is in a certain specialty, such as probate or corporate law, you must be prepared to discuss that area of the law. You may be asked questions designed to assess your familiarity with the area. Prior to the interview, spend some time reviewing your class notes. Skim through a standard practice book for that area of the law in the state. Be sure that you can back up anything you said in your resume about prior involvement with the area in your school or work experience. Such discussions are always an excellent opportunity for you to present writing samples in that field of the law. (Be sure to bring extra copies of such writing samples and of your resume).

10.  Dress conservatively. "It is recommended that a man be clean shaven, wear a dark suit (gray or navy blue), a white shirt, and a muted-tone tie. Shoes should be polished. A woman should wear a skirt-suit or a blazer and skirt, plain blouse, neutral-colored stockings, and a simple hairdo. A minimal amount of jewelry and no perfume are the rule." "To complete these 'uniforms,' a briefcase is a necessity. It symbolizes that you are a professional. Women may want to keep their purses in their briefcases." [23]

11.  Be sure that you project yourself positively. Take the initiative in greeting the interviewer. A firm handshake is recommended. Maintain good posture and eye contact. Remember that everything you do will be evaluated. The interviewer will be making mental notes on your body language. Avoid appearing ill at ease or fidgety. Many feel that the practice of law is a battlefield. The interviewer will be forming an opinion of whether you "fit in."

12.  Try to avoid the topic of salary until the end of the interview when you have completed the discussion of the job itself. Preferably, let the interviewer

[23]Berkey, *Successful Interviewing*, 5 Legal Assistant Today 66 (September/October 1987).

raise the issue. Think through how you will handle the topic, but try to avoid discussing it until the appropriate time arises. If asked what salary you are seeking, give a salary range rather than a single rigid figure. Always relate salary to the specific skills and strengths that you would be able to bring to the office, rather than to the "going rate." You need to know what the going rate is—check recent salary surveys of local and national paralegal associations—so that the salary range you seek is realistic. But avoid using the going rate as the first and sole reason for your position on salary.

13.  Be an active participant in the interview even though you let the interviewer conduct the interview. Help keep the discussion going.

14.  Be enthusiastic, but not overly so. You want to let the office know that you really want the job, not because you are desperate but because you see it as a challenge offering professional development. You are qualified for the job and you feel that the office is the kind of place that recognizes valuable contributions from its workers.

15.  Be yourself. Do not try to overwhelm the interviewer with your cleverness and charm.

16.  Be prepared to leave the following documents with the interviewer: extra copies of your resume, a list of references, and writing samples.

17.  Ask the interviewer if you can be given the opportunity to talk with one or more paralegals currently working at the office. It will be another sign of your seriousness.

18.  Ask your own questions of the interviewer. In effect, you are interviewing the office as much as the other way around. Come with a written list and don't be afraid to let the interviewer see that you have a checklist of questions that you want to ask. It is a sign of an organized person. There is a great deal of information about the job that you could inquire about. From your background research about the job, you should already have some of this information, but you can now verify what you know. You want to ask pertinent and intelligent questions that will communicate to the interviewer that you are serious about the paralegal field, that you are prepared, and that you grasp what the interviewer has been telling you about the job and the office.

Below are some of the topics that you could cover in your own questions. See also Figure 2.12 and Figure 2.13 for ideas on questions.

- What type of person is the office seeking to hire?
- What prompted the office to seek this type of person?
- What are some examples of paralegal responsibilities? Will the paralegal specialize in certain tasks or areas of the law? (Ask for a description of a typical workday of a paralegal at the firm.)
- What skills will the paralegal need for the job? Digesting? Investigation? Research? Drafting? Interviewing?
- How many attorneys are in the firm? Is the number growing, declining, remaining constant?
- How is the firm managed or governed? Managing partner? Management committees? Legal administrator? Is there a policy manual for the firm?
- How many paralegals are in the firm? Is the number growing, declining, remaining constant? Are all the paralegals at the firm full-time? Does the firm use part-time or freelance paralegals? Has the firm considered hiring a paralegal coordinator?
- Is there a career ladder for paralegals in the firm?

- How long has the firm used paralegals? What is the average length of time a paralegal stays with the firm? What are the feelings of firm members on the value of paralegals to the firm? Why is this so? How would firm members describe an ideal paralegal employee? Do all members of the firm feel the same about paralegals? What reservations, if any, do some members of the firm have about paralegals?

- What other personnel does the firm have (secretaries, computer staff, library staff, clerks, messengers, part-time law students, etc.)? How many of each are there? What relationship does the paralegal have with each?

- What kind of supervision does a paralegal receive? Close supervision? From one attorney? Several?

- Will the paralegal work for one attorney? Several? Will the paralegal have his or her own case load? Is there a paralegal pool available to many attorneys?

- What kind of client contact will the paralegal have? Phone? Meetings? Interviews? Document inspection at client's office?

- What kind of correspondence will the paralegal be preparing? Letters that the paralegal will sign? Letters for attorney to sign? Memos?

- What opportunities does a paralegal have for further learning? Office training programs? (Do paralegals attend new-attorney training sessions?) Does the firm encourage outside training for paralegals, e.g., from paralegal associations, bar associations, area schools?

- Will the paralegals be attending staff meetings? Strategy sessions with attorneys?

- How are paralegals evaluated in the office? Written evaluations? Oral? How often?

- Are paralegals required to produce a set number of billable hours? Per day? Per week? Per month? Annually? What is the hourly rate at which a paralegal's time is billed to a client? Do different paralegals in the office bill at different rates? If so, what determines the difference?

- How often are paralegals required to record their time? Daily, hourly, in ten-minute segments, etc.?

- What secretarial assistance is available to the paralegal? None? A personal secretary? Secretary shared with an attorney? Use of a secretarial pool? Will the paralegal do any typing? Light typing? His or her own typing? Typing for others?

- Does the job require travel?

- What equipment will the paralegal be using? Word processor, typewriter, copier, dictaphone, research computer?

- Office space for the paralegal? Private office? Shared office? Partitioned office?

- Compensation and benefits—See Figure 2.12, Checklist of Possible Paralegal Fringe Benefits.

19. After you have thoroughly explored the position during the interview, if you still want the job, ask for it. Be sure that you make a specific request. Some interviewers go out of their way to stress the difficult aspects of the job in order to gauge your reaction. Don't leave the interviewer with the impression

**FIGURE 2.12**

Checklist of
Possible Paralegal
Fringe Benefits

**Compensation:**

____ Salary Increase Policy (amount? criteria for determining? frequency of review? who reviews?)

____ Overtime (frequency? method of compensation?)

____ Bonus (method for determining? frequency?)

____ Cost-of-Living Adjustment (frequency? method for determining?)

____ Other Incentive Programs, like Profit Sharing Plan

____ Pension/Retirement Plan (defined benefit? defined contribution? other?)

____ Tax Deferred Savings Plan

____ Other Investment Plan

**Insurance:**

____ Basic Medical (full coverage? partial?)

____ Major Medical (full coverage? partial?)

____ Dependent Medical Insurance (fully paid? partially paid?)

____ Supplemental Medical (fully paid? partially paid?)

____ Dental (full coverage? partial?)

____ Maternity Leave (full coverage? partial?)

____ Eye Care/Glasses (full coverage? partial?)

____ Life Insurance (full coverage? partial?)

____ Physical Disability (short term? long term? full coverage? partial?)

____ Sick Days (number? carry-over of unused sick leave allowed?)

**Professional Activities:**

____ Time Off for Association Events

____ Association Dues Paid

____ Association Dinner Events Paid

____ Tuition Reimbursement for Paralegal Classes

____ Tuition Reimbursement for Law School

**Other:**

____ Vacation (number of days? carry over of unused vacation allowed?)

____ Personal Leave Days (number allowed?)

____ Child Care Assistance

____ Paid Holidays (number?)

____ Parking (fully paid? partially paid?)

____ Leased Car

____ Mileage Allowance

____ Club Membership

____ Fitness Center

____ Refreshments on the Job

____ Sports Tickets

____ Entertainment Allowance

____ Free Legal Advice and Representation by the Firm on Personal Matters

**Comparability:**

____ Paralegal Fringe Benefits Similar to Those of New Attorneys?

____ Paralegal Fringe Benefits Similar to Those of Secretaries?

_____ Policy Manual on Paralegal Use in Office (available?)

_____ Evaluation (method? frequency?)

_____ Career Ladder for Paralegals in Office (criteria for advancement?)

_____ Supervision of Paralegal (by attorney? by paralegal manager? by legal administrator?)

_____ Supervision by Paralegal (secretary? assistant to paralegal?)

_____ Work Assignments (who delegates? one attorney? several? paralegal manager?)

_____ Availability of Secretarial Assistance

_____ Paralegal Turnover in Office (low? high?)

_____ Client Contact (frequent? rare?)

_____ Attendance at Trials (frequent? rare?)

_____ Sit at Counsel's Table (frequent? rare?)

_____ Billable Hours: hourly rate?

_____ Billable Hours: quota? (monthly quota? annual quota?)

_____ Time Spent on Non-Billable Matters (frequent? rare? type?)

_____ Office Space (private? shared?)

_____ Use of Computers (frequent? rare?)

_____ Availability of Word Processing Department to Paralegal (frequent? rare?)

_____ Typing (own work? attorney's work?)

_____ How Management Perceives Paralegals (professionals? administrative? support staff? combination?)

_____ Flexible Work Schedule

_____ Travel Required (frequent? rare? type?)

_____ Attendance at Attorney Strategy Meetings (frequent? rare?)

_____ Attendance at Management Meetings (frequent? rare?)

_____ Office Training for Paralegals (kind? frequency?)

_____ In-House Attorney Training Available to Paralegals (frequent? rare?)

_____ CLE (Continuing Legal Education) for Attorneys Available to Paralegals (frequent? rare?)

_____ Business Cards Provided

_____ Name on Door

_____ Name on Letterhead Stationery of Law Office

_____ Has Own Letterhead Stationery

_____ Office Correspondence (does paralegal ever sign under own name?)

_____ Attendance at Attorney Retreats (frequent? rare?)

_____ Attendance at Attorney Social Functions (frequent? rare?)

**FIGURE 2.13**

Checklist of Factors that Help Determine the Quality of the Work Environment of a Paralegal

that you may be having second thoughts if in fact you still want the job after you have had all your questions answered.

### Follow-Up Letter

After the interview, always send a letter to the person who interviewed you. In a surprising number of cases, the follow-up letter is a significant factor in obtaining the job. In the letter:

■ Thank the person for the interview.

- Tell the person that you enjoyed the interview and the opportunity to learn about the office.
- State that you are still very interested in the position.
- Briefly restate why you are qualified for the position.
- Clarify any matters that arose during the interview.
- Submit references or writing samples that may have been asked for during the interview.

Keep a copy of all such letters. In a notebook, maintain accurate records on the dates you sent out resumes, the kinds of resumes you sent, the dates of interviews, the names of people you met, your impressions, the dates when you made follow-up calls, etc. (See page 171.)

If you are turned down for a job, find out why. Call the office to try to obtain more information than is provided in standard rejection statements. Politely ask what could have improved your chances. Finally, use the occasion to ask for any leads to other prospective employers.

---

### ■ ASSIGNMENT 2.1

Role-play an interview in class. The instructor will decide what kind of job the interview will be for, and will select students to play the role of interviewer and interviewee. The interviewer should ask a variety of questions such as those presented above in the guidelines for handling a job interview. The rest of the class will evaluate the performance of the interviewee. What mistakes did he or she make? How should he or she have dealt with certain questions? Was he or she confident? Overconfident? Did he or she ask the right questions of the interviewer? Were these questions properly timed? What impressions did the interviewee convey of himself or herself? Make a list of dos and don'ts for such interviews.

---

## ■ Section E. The Job Hunting Notebook

Purchase a large three-ring, loose-leaf notebook for your Job Hunting Notebook. Include in it the outline of sections listed below. Following the outline, create at least one page for each section.

There are a number of purposes for the Notebook:

- To help you identify your strengths based on past legal or nonlegal employment, training, and other life experience.
- To help you organize this data for your resumes.
- To provide you with checklists of contacts that you should start making immediately.
- To help you prepare for job interviews.
- To provide a place to store copies of resumes, cover letters, writing samples, follow-up letters, notes on job leads and strategies, personal impressions, etc.
- To keep a calendar on all aspects of the job search.

The Notebook is your own personal document. No one else will see it unless you choose to share its contents with others.

## Outline of Job Hunting Notebook

*Part I. Resume & Writing Sample Preparation*

1. Prior and Current Nonlegal Employment—Analysis Sheet
2. Prior and Current Legal Employment—Analysis Sheet
3. Prior and Current Volunteer Activity—Analysis Sheet
4. Other Life Experiences—Analysis Sheet
5. Nonlegal Education & Training—Analysis Sheet
6. Legal Education & Training—Analysis Sheet
7. Notes on Resume Writing
8. Draft of General Resume
9. Drafts of Specialized Resumes
10. Writing Samples

*Part II. Contacts for Employment*

11. Contacts—Attorneys You Already Know or With Whom You Have Indirect Association
12. Contacts—Employed Paralegals
13. Contacts and Tasks—General

*Part III. Legwork in the Field*

14. Job Interview Checklist
15. Job Interview—Analysis Sheet
16. Record Keeping     . . . . . . . . . . . . . .

*1. Prior and Current Nonlegal Employment—Analysis Sheet*

*2. Prior and Current Legal Employment—Analysis Sheet*

*3. Prior and Current Volunteer Activity—Analysis Sheet*

We begin by analyzing your experience in nonlegal jobs (e.g., cashier, truck driver); then in legal jobs (e.g., legal secretary, investigator); and finally in volunteer activity (e.g., church sale coordinator, political campaign assistant). Make a list of these jobs and volunteer activities. Start a separate sheet of paper for each entry on your list, and then do the following:

- State the name, address, and phone number of the place of employment or location of the volunteer work.
- State the exact dates you were there.
- State the names of your supervisors there. (Circle the name of supervisors who had a favorable impression of you. Place a double circle around the name of each supervisor who would probably write a favorable recommendation for you, if asked.)
- Make a list of every major task you performed there. Number each task, starting with number 1. (As you write this list, leave a three-inch *left-hand margin* on the paper. In front of the number for each task, place as many of the following letters that apply to that task. When an explanation or description is called for, provide it on attached sheets of paper.)

B    The task required you to conform to a *budget*. (Briefly describe the budget, including its size and who prepared it.)

C    There was some *competition* in the office about who is the person most qualified to perform it. (Briefly describe why you were the most qualified.)

E    You were *evaluated* on how well you performed the task. (Briefly describe the evaluation of you.)

EI    To perform the task, you occasionally or always had to *exercise initiative*; you did not just wait for detailed instructions. (Briefly describe the initiative you took.)

ET    You occasionally or frequently had to devote *extra time* to perform the task. (Briefly describe the circumstances.)

J/C    It was not a mechanical task; you had to exercise some *judgment* and/or *creativity* to perform it. (Briefly describe the kind of judgment or creativity you exhibited.)

M    *Math* skills were involved in performing the task. (Briefly describe what kind of math you had to do).

OD    *Others depended* on your performing the task well. (Briefly describe who had to rely on your performance and why.)

OT    You always or regularly performed the task *on time*.

OW    To perform the task, you had to coordinate your work with *other workers*; you did not work alone. (Briefly describe the nature of your interaction with others.)

P    You had some role in *planning* how the task would be performed; you were not simply following someone else's plan. (Briefly describe your planning role.)

PI    You did not start out performing the task; you were formally or informally *promoted into* it. (Briefly describe what you did before being asked to perform this task and the circumstances of the promotion.)

PP    You are *personally proud* of the way you performed the task. (Briefly describe why.)

R    You made *recommendations* on how the task could be more efficiently performed or better integrated into the office. (Briefly describe the recommendations you made and what effect they had.)

RR    You *received recognition* because of how well you performed the task. (Briefly describe what recognition you received and from whom.)

SE    To perform the task, you had to operate *some equipment* such as computers or motor vehicles. (Briefly describe the equipment and the skills needed to operate it.)

SO    To perform the task, you had to *supervise others* or help supervise others. (Briefly describe whom you supervised and what the supervision entailed.)

T    You *trained* others to perform the task. (Briefly describe this training.)

TP    You had to work under *time pressures* when you performed the task; you didn't have forever to perform it. (Briefly describe these pressures.)

W    There was some *writing* involved in performing the task. (Briefly describe what kind of writing you did.)

Include other characteristics of the task that are not covered in this list.

## 4. Other Life Experiences—Analysis Sheet

Circle *each* of the following experiences that you have had. Do not include experiences that required schooling, since these experiences will be covered elsewhere in the Notebook. Do not include experiences that involved volunteer work unless you have not already included them elsewhere in the Notebook. Attach additional sheets as indicated and where more space is needed.

- Raised a family alone
- Helped raise a family
- Traveled extensively
- Read extensively in a particular field on your own
- Learned to operate a computer on your own
- Learned a language on your own

- Learned a craft on your own, such as weaving or fixing cars
- Learned an art on your own, such as painting or sculpture
- Developed a distinctive hobby requiring considerable skill
- Other life experiences (list each)

Attach a separate sheet of paper for *each* of the life experiences or activities that you listed above. Write the activity at the top of the sheet. Answer the following questions for each activity:

a. How long did you engage in this activity?

b. Have you ever tried to teach this activity to someone else? If so, describe your efforts.

c. Do you think you could teach this activity to others? Explain your answer.

d. Which of the following characteristics do you think are necessary or helpful in being able to perform the activity competently? Do not focus at this point on whether you possess these characteristics. Simply compile a list of what would be helpful or necessary.

| | | |
|---|---|---|
| Intelligence | Compassion | Patience |
| Creativity | Responsibility | Dependability |
| Perseverance | Punctuality | Determination |
| Drive | Self-confidence | Stamina |
| Independence | Poise | Self-control |
| Talent | Efficiency | Grace |
| Understanding | Skill | Dexterity |
| Cleverness | Competitiveness | Sophistication |
| Spirit | Congeniality | Stick-to-itiveness |
| Conviction | Judgment | Will power |
| Fortitude | Strength | Zeal |
| Ambition | Know-how | Experience |
| Ability to work with others | Imagination | Others? (list) |

e. Ask *someone else* (whom you trust and who is familiar with you) to look at the list. Ask this person if he or she would add anything to the list. Then ask him or her to identify which of these characteristics apply to *you* for this activity.

f.  Now it's your turn. Which of these characteristics do *you* think apply to you for this activity?

g.  If there are any major differences in the answers to (e) and (f) above, how do you explain the discrepancy? Are you too hard on yourself? Do you tend to put yourself down and minimize your strengths?

## 5. *Nonlegal Education and Training—Analysis Sheet*

On a separate sheet of paper, list every school or training program *not* involving law that you have attended or are now attending (whether or not you completed it), starting with the most recent. Include four-year colleges, two-year colleges, vocational training schools, weekend seminars, work-related training programs, internships, church training programs, hobby training programs, self-improvement training, etc. Include everything since high school.

Devote a separate sheet of paper to each school or training program, writing its name at the top of the sheet and answering the following questions for it. If more than one course was taught, answer these questions for two or three of the most demanding courses.

a.  What were the exact or approximate dates of attendance?

b.  Did you complete it? What evidence do you have that you completed it? A grade? A certificate? A degree?

c.  Were you required to attend? If so, by whom? If not, why did you attend?

d.  How did you finance your attendance?

e.  What requirements did you meet in order to attend? Was there competition to attend? If so, describe in detail.

f.  Describe the subjects taught. What was the curriculum?

g.  How were you evaluated?

h.  What evidence of these evaluations do you have? Could you obtain copies of them?

i.  Describe in detail any writing that you had to do, such as exams or reports. Do you have copies of any of these written items? If not, could you obtain copies? Could any of these items be rewritten now for use as a writing sample?

j.  What skills other than writing did you cover, such as organization, research, speaking, reading, manual dexterity, machine operation, interpersonal relations?

k.  What evidence do you have or could you obtain that shows you covered these skills and how well you did in them?

l.  Did you receive any special award or distinction? If so, describe it and state what evidence you have or could obtain that you received it.

m.  Make a list of every favorable comment you can remember that was made about your work. What evidence of these comments do you have or could you obtain?

n.  Was the experience meaningful in your life? If so, explain why. How has it affected you today?

o.  What, if anything, did you do that called for extra effort or work on your part beyond what everyone else had to do?

p.  Have you ever tried to teach someone else what you learned? If so, describe your efforts. If not, could you? Describe what you could teach.

q.  List each teacher who knew you individually. Circle the name of each teacher who would probably write you a letter of recommendation if asked.

r.  Would any other teacher or administrator be able to write you a letter of recommendation based on the records of the school or program? If so, who?

s.  Does the school or program have a reputation for excellence? If so, describe its reputation.

## 6. *Legal Education and Training—Analysis Sheet*

On a separate sheet of paper, list every *legal* course or training program that you have ever taken—formal or informal. Include individual classes, seminars, internships, etc., at formal schools, on the job, or through associations. Devote a separate sheet of paper to each course or program, writing its name at the top of the sheet and answering the following questions for it.

a.  What were the exact dates of attendance?

b.  Did you complete it? What evidence do you have that you completed it? A grade? A certificate?

c.  What requirements did you meet in order to attend? Was there competition to attend? If so, describe in detail.

d.  What text(s) did you use? Photocopy the table of contents in the text(s) and circle those items that you covered.

e.  Attach a copy of the syllabus and circle those items in the syllabus that you covered.

f.  Make two lists: a list of the major themes or subject areas that you were required to *know* or understand (content) and a list of the things that you were asked to *do* (skills).

g.  Make a detailed list of everything that you were asked to write for the course or program, such as exams, memos, research papers, other reports. For every written work product other than exams, give the specific topic of what you wrote. Describe this topic in at least one sentence.

h.  Which of these written work products could you now *rewrite* as a writing sample? Whom could you ask to evaluate what you rewrite to insure that it meets high standards?

i.  Describe in detail everything else you were asked to do other than mere reading assignments. Examples: role-play a hearing, visit a court, verbally analyze a problem, interview a client, evaluate a title abstract, search a title, operate a computer, find something in the library, investigate a fact.

j.  How were you evaluated? What evidence do you have or could you obtain of these evaluations?

k.  Did you receive any special award or distinction? If so, describe it and state what evidence you have or could obtain that you received it.

l.  Make a list of every favorable comment you can remember that was made about your work. What evidence of these comments do you have or could you obtain?

m.  What, if anything, did you do that called for extra work or effort on your part beyond what everyone else had to do?

n.  Describe the most valuable aspect of what you learned.

o.  Have you ever tried to teach anyone else what you learned? If so, describe your efforts. If not, could you? Describe what you could teach.

p.  Describe every individual who evaluated you. Could you obtain a letter of recommendation from these individuals?

## 7. Notes on Resume Writing

It is important that you have an open mind about resumes. There is no correct format. Different people have different views. In the best of all worlds, you will be able to do some background research on the law office where you are applying for work and you will learn what kind of resume (in form and content) that office prefers. When this type of research is not possible, you must do the best you can to predict what kind of a resume will be effective .

On this page in the Notebook, you should collect ideas about resumes from a wide variety of people such as:

| | |
|---|---|
| Teachers | Program administrators |
| Working paralegals | Unemployed paralegals |
| Paralegal supervisors | Legal administrators |
| Fellow students | Attorneys whom you know |
| Personnel officers | Authors of books and articles on |
| Placement officers | finding employment |
| Legal secretaries | Others? |

You want to collect divergent viewpoints on questions such as the following:

- What is an ideal resume?
- What are the major mistakes that a resume writer can make?
- What is the best way to phrase a career objective?
- How long should the resume be?
- In what order should the data in the resume be presented?
- How detailed should the resume be?
- What kind of personal data should be included and omitted?
- How do you phrase educational experiences to make them relevant to the job you are seeking?
- How do you phrase employment experiences to make them relevant to the job you are seeking?
- How do you show that nonlegal experiences (school or work) can be relevant to a legal job?
- How do you handle potentially embarrassing facts, e.g., frequent job changes, low course grades?
- What should the cover letter for the resume say?

## 8. Draft of General Resume

Prepare a general resume and include it here. We are calling it general because it is not directed at any specific job. It should be comprehensive with no page limitation. Use the guidelines, questions, and checklists in this Notebook to help you identify your strengths. The resumes you write for actual job searches will be shorter, specialized, and tailored to the job you are seeking.

Before you write specialized resumes, however, you should write a general one that will be your main point of reference in preparing these other resumes. The general resume will probably never be submitted anywhere. Take at least one full day to compile and carefully think about the data needed for the general resume.

## 9. Drafts of Specialized Resumes

Every time you write a resume that is tailored to a specific job, include a copy here. Also include several practice copies of specialized resumes. While taking a course in corporate law, for example, write a resume in which you pursue an opening at a law office for a corporate paralegal. For each resume that you write (practice or real), solicit the comments of teachers, administrators, fellow students, working paralegals, attorneys, etc. Include these comments in this section of the Notebook.

## 10. Writing Samples

The importance of collecting a large pool of writing samples cannot be overemphasized. Even if you eventually use only a few of them, the value of preparing them is enormous. The following characteristics should apply to *each* writing sample:

- It is your own work.
- It is clearly and specifically identified. The heading at the top tells the reader what the writing is.
- It is typed (handwritten work should be typed).
- There are no spelling or grammatical errors in it.
- Its appearance is professional.
- Someone whom you respect has evaluated it before you put it in final form.
- You feel that it is a high-quality product.
- It does not violate anyone's right to privacy or confidentiality. (If the sample pertains to real people or events, you have disguised all names or other identifying features.)

There are two main kinds of writing samples: those that are assigned in school or at work and those you generate on your own.

Examples of Required Work That You
Could Turn into a Writing Sample

- A memorandum of law (page 618)
- A legal research report or memo (page 608)
- An answer to a problem in a textbook
- An exam answer
- An intake memorandum of law (page 368)
- A complaint (page 468)
- An answer to a complaint
- A motion

- A set of interrogatories (page 466)
- Answers to a set of interrogatories
- An index to discovery documents (page 461)
- A digest of one or more discovery documents (page 462)
- Other memos, studies, or reports
- Articles of incorporation and bylaws

Any of the above writing samples could be generated on your own if they are not required in your coursework. Ask your teachers or supervisors to help you identify written pieces that you could create. Also consider writing an article for one of the many newsletters of paralegal associations (see Appendix B). The article could cover an aspect of your education or work experience. Or consider writing a review of a recent paralegal book. Even if what you write is not published in a newsletter, it might still become a writing sample if it meets the criteria listed above.

### 11.  Contacts—Attorneys You Already Know or With Whom You Have Indirect Association

Make a list of attorneys as described in Strategy 6 in this chapter, page 134. Not only do you want to know whether any of these attorneys are interested in hiring paralegals, but equally important, you want to know if they can give you any leads to other employers who might be interested in hiring.

### 12.  Contacts—Employed Paralegals

You want to talk with as many employed paralegals as you can in order to obtain leads to possible positions, as well as general guidelines for the job search. Make a list of all the paralegals that you contact and what they tell you. If they have nothing useful to say at the present time, ask them if you could check back with them in several months and if you could leave your name and number with them in the event that they come across anything in the future. See page 132 for ideas on how to locate employed paralegals.

### 13.  Contacts and Tasks—General

Below you will find a general checklist of contacts and tasks that you should consider in your job search. Take notes on the results of these contacts and tasks and include these notes here if they are not included elsewhere in the Notebook. Your notes should include what you did, when, whom you contacted, what was said, what follow-up is still needed, etc.

- Attorneys with whom you already have a direct or indirect association
- Employed paralegals
- Other paralegals searching for work; they may be willing to share leads that were unproductive for them, especially if you do likewise
- Contacts provided by your placement office
- Want ads in general circulation newspapers
- Want ads in legal newspapers
- Want ads and job bank openings listed in paralegal newsletters
- General directories of attorneys, such as *Martindale-Hubbell*
- Special directories of attorneys, such as the *Directory of Corporate Counsel*
- Information from placement offices of local law schools
- Employment agencies specializing primarily in attorney placement
- Employment agencies specializing in paralegal placement
- Staffing agencies specializing in support staff and paralegal placement
- Bar association meetings open to the public

- Legal secretaries who may have leads
- Legal administrators who may have leads
- Local attorneys of record printed in reporter volumes (page 355)
- Local attorneys who have written articles in bar journals
- Stories in legal newspapers on recent large cases that are in litigation or are about to go into litigation (page 140)
- Local and national politicians who represent your area
- Service companies and consulting firms (page 99)

### 14. *Job Interview Checklist*

1. _____ Exact location of interview
2. _____ Time of arrival
3. _____ Professional appearance in dress
4. _____ Extra copies of resume
5. _____ Extra copies of writing samples
6. _____ Name of person(s) who will conduct interview
7. _____ Background research on the firm or company so that you know the kind of law it practices, why it is considering hiring paralegals, etc.
8. _____ Role-playing of job interview in advance with a friend
9. _____ Preparation for difficult questions that might be asked, such as why you left your last job so soon after starting it
10. _____ Preparation of questions that you will ask regarding:
    - _____ Responsibilities of position
    - _____ Skills needed for the position
    - _____ Methods of supervision
    - _____ Office's prior experience with paralegals
    - _____ Career ladder for paralegals
    - _____ Relationship between paralegals, secretaries, and other clerical staff
    - _____ Client contact
    - _____ Opportunities for growth
    - _____ Methods of evaluating paralegals
    - _____ Continuing education
    - _____ Billable hours expected of paralegals
    - _____ Availability of systems
    - _____ Working conditions (typing, photocopying, office, etc.)
    - _____ Travel
    - _____ Overtime
    - _____ Equipment use
    - _____ Compensation and fringe benefits (see Figure 2.12)
11. _____ Follow-up letter

### 15. Job Interview—Analysis Sheet

Write out the following information *after* each job interview that you have.

1. Date of interview
2. Name, address, and phone number of firm or company where you interviewed
3. Name(s) and phone number(s) of interviewer(s)
4. Kind of position that was open
5. Date you sent the follow-up letter
6. What you need to do next (send list of references, send writing samples, provide missing information that you did not have with you during the interview, etc.)
7. Your impressions of the interview (how you think you did, what surprised you, what you would do differently the next time you have an interview)
8. Notes on why you did not get the job

### 16. Record Keeping

You need a system to keep track of the steps taken to date. See Figure 2.14, Record Keeping & the Job Search. In addition, keep a calendar in which you record important future dates, such as when you must make follow-up calls, when the local paralegal association meets, etc.

## ■ Section F. Your Second Job

If you examine want ads for paralegals (p. 136), you will find that most prospective employers want paralegals with experience. The market for such individuals is excellent. But if you are *new* to the field, you are caught in the dilemma of not being able to find a job without experience and not being able to get experience without a job. How do you handle this classic Catch-22 predicament?

- You work even harder to compile an impressive resume. You make sure that you have collected a substantial writing-sample file. Such writing samples are often the closest equivalent to prior job experience available to you.
- When you talk to other paralegals, you seek specific advice on how to present yourself as an applicant for the first job.
- You consider doing some volunteer work as a way to acquire experience for your resume. Legal service offices (page 83) and public interest law firms (page 98) often encourage volunteer work. A recent law school graduate struggling to start a practice may be another option.
- You may have to reassess what you will accept for your first job. Perhaps you can eventually turn the first job into a more acceptable position. You may simply use it to gain the experience necessary for landing a better second job.
- Pray for luck.

**FIGURE 2.14**   Record Keeping & the Job Search

| CALLS MADE TO: | DATE | RESUME SENT TO: | DATE | FOLLOW-UP | DATE | WRITING SAMPLES PROVIDED TO: | DATE | INTERVIEW | DATE | FOLLOW-UP | DATE |
|---|---|---|---|---|---|---|---|---|---|---|---|
| | | | | | | | | | | | |
| | | | | | | | | | | | |
| | | | | | | | | | | | |

**FIGURE 2.15**

Positions for
Experienced
Paralegals

- Paralegal supervisor
- Law office administrator (Legal administrator)
- Law firm marketing administrator
- Paralegal consultant
- Freelance/independent paralegal
- Law librarian/assistant
- Paralegal teacher
- Paralegal school administrator
- Placement officer
- Bar association attorney referral coordinator
- Court administrator
- Court clerk
- Sales representative for legal publisher/vendor
- Investigator
- Customs inspector
- Compliance and enforcement inspector
- Occupational safety and health inspector
- Lobbyist
- Legislative assistant
- Real estate management consultant
- Real estate specialist
- Real estate portfolio manager
- Land acquisitions supervisor
- Title examiner
- Independent title abstractor
- Abstractor
- Systems analyst
- Computer analyst
- Computer sales representative
- Bank research associate
- Trust officer (Trust administrator)
- Trust associate
- Assistant loan administrator
- Fiduciary accountant
- Financial analyst/planner
- Investment analyst
- Assistant estate administrator
- Enrolled agent
- Equal employment opportunity specialist
- Employee benefit specialist/consultant
- Pension specialist
- Pension administrator
- Compensation planner
- Corporate trademark specialist

Continued

- Corporate manager
- Securities analyst
- Securities compliance officer
- Insurance adjustor
- Actuarial associate
- Claims examiner
- Claims coordinator
- Director of risk management
- Environmental specialist
- Editor for a legal or business publisher
- Recruiter, legal employment agency
- Personnel director
- Administrative law judge
- Arbitrator
- Mediator
- Internal security inspector
- Evidence technician
- Demonstrative evidence specialist
- Fingerprint technician
- Polygraph examiner
- Probation officer
- Parole officer
- Corrections officer
- Politician
- Etc.

**FIGURE 2.15**

Positions for Experienced Paralegals— *Continued*

Once you have had several years of experience and have demonstrated your competence, you will find many more employment options available to you. You will find it substantially easier to negotiate salary and articulate your skills in a job interview. You can also consider other kinds of employment where your legal training, skills, expertise, and experience are valuable. It is not uncommon for a paralegal to be recruited by former or active clients of a first employer. Numerous business contacts are made in the course of a job; these contacts could turn into new careers. In Figure 2.15 you will find a list of some of the types of positions that paralegals have taken after they demonstrated their ability and acquired legal experience.

In short, you face a different market once you have acquired a record of experience and accomplishment. You are in greater demand in law firms and businesses. Furthermore, your legal skills are readily transferable to numerous law-related positions.

## ☐ Chapter Summary

Someone once said that finding a job is a job in itself. This is especially true in the current market. It will take determination to find what you want. The first step is to become informed about where paralegals work and what they do at those locations. The first part of this chapter was designed to provide you with this information. The major employers of paralegals are private law firms, the government, legal service offices, corporations, and other businesses. While other settings also exist, these are the largest. After examining these settings, we looked at approximately forty-five specialties such as bankruptcy and criminal law. Our focus was the identification of paralegal functions in the specialties and a paralegal perspective of what life is like in each. For the specialties where most paralegals work—litigation, corporate law, estates, and real estate—quotations from job ads identified traits and skills employers want.

In the second half of the chapter, we turned to strategies for finding employment. The strategies addressed the following questions: When should you begin the search? How do you compile a job hunting notebook? How do you organize an employment workshop? How do you locate working paralegals in order to obtain leads to employment? How do you arrange an informational interview? How can you use local paralegal associations as a resource? How do you locate potential employers? How do you do background research on potential employers? What should your resume contain? What is an effective cover letter? What kinds of writing samples should you prepare, and when should you start preparing them? How should you prepare for a job interview? What kinds of questions should you anticipate? What kinds of questions should you ask? How can you organize all of the contacts, events, and pieces of paper that are involved in a comprehensive job search?

Finally, we examined alternative career opportunities for paralegals, particularly for those who have gained paralegal experience on the job.

## Key Terms

private law firm
legal clinic
paralegal manager
paralegal specialist
general schedule (GS)
Office of Personnel
    Management
neighborhood legal service
    office
judicare
indigents
corporate counsel
special interest groups
group legal services
assigned counsel
legal insurance

public defender
freelance paralegal
service company
consulting firm
paralegal specialties
conflicts specialist
legalman
landmen
private sector
public sector
public benefits
PI cases
tort
job bank
National Paralegal Reporter
Facts & Findings

informational interview
networking
blind ad
staffing agency
*Martindale-Hubbell*
chronological resume
functional resume
cover letter
group interview
open-ended question
closed-ended question
hypothetical question
CLE

## 3

# On-the-Job Realities: Assertiveness Training for Paralegals

## ■ Chapter Outline

Section A. The Ideal
Section B. The Big Three Employment Problems
Section C. Communication
Section D. Expectations
Section E. The Environment of a Law Office
Section F. Office Politics
Section G. Self-Assessment and Employer Evaluations
Section H. Characteristics of Some Attorneys
Section I. Assertive/Nonassertive/ Aggressive Behavior

Section J. Keeping a Diary and a Career Development File
Section K. The "Swoose Syndrome"
Section L. Paralegal CLE
Section M. Responsibilities of Supervisors
Section N. Relationship with Secretaries
Section O. Sex Harassment
Section P. Working with Systems
Section Q. Career Ladders
Section R. Your Next Job
Section S. Paralegal Associations and Networking

## ■ Section A. The Ideal

The practice of law is not for the faint of heart. Before exploring paralegal survival in a legal environment, we pause to examine the ideal. What is a "perfect" paralegal job? Perhaps it is impossible to describe perfection in its fullest sense, but if we made the attempt, what would the description contain? Figure 3.1 presents such an attempt: it tries to identify seventy-five factors of an ideal paralegal job environment. The factors are not of equal importance, and there is some overlap among them. Nor would every paralegal agree that all seventy-five are needed. In general, however, these are the factors (not necessarily listed in order of priority) that must be considered according to most working paralegals:

**FIGURE 3.1**

Seventy-Five Factors That Affect Paralegal Job Satisfaction

1. Your pay is satisfactory.

2. You receive satisfactory bonuses.

3. Your fringe benefits are satisfactory (e.g., health plan, life insurance, pension; see Figure 2.12).

4. Your compensation is fair in relation to that of attorneys, other paralegals, and secretaries.

5. You receive overtime pay or sufficient "comp time" when you work extra hours.

6. You are given financial support and time off to participate in activities of paralegal associations.

7. You are given financial support and time off to attend training sessions outside the office at paralegal schools, paralegal associations, bar associations, etc.

8. Adequate supplies are readily available.

9. Your hours are satisfactory.

10. You have your own office.

11. You have adequate access to secretarial help.

12. You have adequate access to word processing equipment.

13. You have your own business card.

14. You are challenged by your job.

15. You like your job.

16. Your privacy is respected.

17. No sexism or racism exists.

18. People in the office share the same basic values.

19. The office has high standards of performance; there are many good role models.

20. You are respected.

21. You are not taken advantage of.

22. You are not unduly pressured to fill billable-hour quotas.

23. You are not unduly pressured to work evenings or weekends.

24. You are encouraged to develop new skills.

25. Your paralegal training is being used by the office.

26. You have meaningful client contact.

27. Your name is in the office directory.

28. You do not feel isolated; there are few or no "attorney only" social events.

29. The office politics are manageable.

30. The secretaries, clerks, and other support personnel understand your job and accept your role in the office.

31. Your supervisors are not afraid of delegating tasks to paralegals.

32. The attorneys in the office understand your job and accept your role.

33. You are not in competition with anyone else in the office.

34. You have good rapport with other paralegals in the office.

35. You respect others in the office.

36. The office functions as a team; employees are not obsessed with a niche or territory that they are protecting.

37. People in the office are willing to compromise on personnel methods and procedures.

38. The office has high standards of ethics and moral responsibility.

39. There is a career ladder in the office for paralegals.

40. You are not constantly being relegated to someone else's deadline; it is recognized that you have deadlines of your own that others must respect.

41. You are viewed and treated as a professional.

42. People in the office know how to listen; employees do not simply *talk at* everyone else.

43. You feel that you are making a contribution to the office.

44. You have the feeling that your office is offering a social service; it is not "just a business."

45. There is an adequate flow of communication in the office; you know what is going on because the office makes it known; you don't have to rely on the grapevine.

46. There is a clear line of authority; you know who your supervisors are.

47. The importance of profit is never emphasized at the expense of people's lives.

48. At all times, you know which people you can go to for help and you are encouraged to seek this help.

Continued

49. You are adequately supervised by attorneys and other senior personnel.

50. You are encouraged to do self-evaluations, which are given serious consideration.

51. You are regularly evaluated in a constructive manner.

52. You are given credit for the contributions you make.

53. The roof does not cave in if you disagree with your supervisors.

54. If you make a mistake it's not the end of the world.

55. You attend regular staff meetings.

56. You participate in office training programs for new attorneys.

57. You attend strategy meetings for cases to which you are assigned.

58. You are not constantly being asked why you don't become an attorney.

59. There is low turnover in your office; people feel comfortable enough about the office to make a long-term commitment to it.

60. You are not the first paralegal in the office; the office has had experience working with paralegals.

61. You are not constantly interrupted with new assignments, new priorities, new crises; you are not the dumping ground for everyone else's problems.

62. You are kept busy all the time without feeling overburdened; "the time flies by."

63. You are permitted to see the end product of your work, for example, you observe or are in contact with a case from beginning to completion.

64. You are encouraged to make use of the law library.

65. Office manuals or procedure guides are available on many assignments.

66. A personnel manual clearly spells out employee policies.

67. Your advocacy of positions on office policy or case strategy is not resented; it is encouraged.

69. You have some independence; there are opportunities to work alone in the office.

70. You are given authority.

71. You are encouraged to make decisions within your competence, and there is someone to back you up on these decisions.

72. There is reasonable variety in your assignments.

73. You are given a reasonable amount of time to complete your assignments.

74. You are not given assignments beyond your present capacity.

75. You are given reasonable time and training to learn new areas.

**FIGURE 3.1**

Seventy-Five Factors That Affect Paralegal Job Satisfaction

■ **ASSIGNMENT 3.1**

(a) Which of the seventy-five factors in Figure 3.1 do you think are *not* important for job satisfaction? Why?

(b) Select what you feel are the fifteen most important factors. Write out your list and make a copy. Indicate whether you have ever had any law office work experience as a secretary, a paralegal, etc.

(c) Give the copy of your list to a person in the class whom your instructor will designate as the statistician. The latter will collect all the copies from the students and make the following tabulations: (1) which factors received the most votes on the "top fifteen" list by the students who have had prior law office experience; (2) which received the most votes from the other students.

In class, discuss the results of these tabulations. Are there significant differences in the opinions of the two groups? Can you explain the differences or similarities?

We move now to the *reality* of paralegal employment. The seventy-five factors obviously do not exist in every paralegal job. To be candid, there are paralegals who are quite dissatisfied with their job. As of the late 1970s and early 1980s:

- Paralegal turnover was high; the average length of a paralegal's first job was two to three years.
- Approximately 25% of working paralegals indicated that they did not plan to remain in the paralegal career.

In examining such realities, this chapter will focus on the negative, since it is a chapter about *problems* on the job. Do not get the impression, however, that gloom is the order of the day. A large majority of paralegals express substantial satisfaction with their work and career. While even these paralegals point to areas in need of improvement, they will tell you that they find their work stimulating and even fascinating at times. Most paralegals are satisfied with the career they have chosen. These are not the paralegals, however, that this chapter is primarily about.

It should also be pointed out that many of the problems we will be discussing are not peculiar to paralegalism. Sexism, for example, and the hassles of worker coexistence are certainly not unique to the law office. It is probably true that this chapter is as much about human nature as it is about this new career in law.

Some of the discussion will be directed at attorneys and what they must do to solve a particular employment problem. Yet a major concern of this chapter is what the *paralegal* can do to overcome difficulties, even those that appear to be beyond the control of the paralegal. According to Beth King, president of the Oregon Legal Assistant Association:

> Job satisfaction is one of life's most important assets. As such, it is something we should cherish and cultivate. We may blame a lack of job satisfaction on our employer or those with whom we work. In truth, satisfaction with our jobs lies within our control.[1]

## ■ Section B. The Big Three Employment Problems

The most frequently mentioned problems are: inadequate opportunity for advancement, inadequate compensation, and underutilization.

### Inadequate Opportunity for Advancement

Once paralegals have become successful on the job, they need opportunities for internal advancement. Some large law offices have begun to create *career-ladder* structures, as we saw in Chapter 1. In the smaller offices, however, there is seldom a "next step" in the development of one's career. In a 1989 survey of all paralegals in Oregon, eighty-five percent of the paralegals responding to the survey said that their firm or company had not developed a career path for paralegals.[2] Too often, a paralegal has no place to go other than to another paralegal job or to law school. Later in this chapter, we will examine how this problem is being addressed.

---

[1]King, *President's Message*, 10 Newsletter 1 (Oregon Legal Assistant Ass'n, February 1987).
[2]Michaelis, *The Legal Assistant Profession, Part II*, 13 Paragraph 10 (Oregon Legal Assistants Ass'n, May 1991).

## Inadequate Compensation

Some paralegals are not satisfied with their compensation. When used effectively, they can be *"profit centers"* primarily because of the paralegal fees that attorneys charge clients; yet there are paralegals who are dissatisfied with the pay and fringe benefits that they receive. The consequences to the law office can be unfortunate. A candid bar association article on ways to make paralegals more profitable gives employers the following advice:

> Hire the level of experience you need and pay accordingly. There are very few bargains in the paralegal job market. If you do find people at a bargain salary, be aware that you stand the risk of losing them to a higher paying position after you have trained them.[3]

Not all employers, however, follow this advice.

## Underutilization

Unfortunately, the following description of a paralegal's job does *not* apply to every paralegal in the country:

> Attorney Ron Bliss of Bradbury, Bliss & Riordan did not hire his legal assistant to do a few narrow, limited tasks. "She does everything that she's capable of doing."[4]

The paralegal at this firm probably does not feel underutilized. Many paralegals, however, complain they have skills that are not being used. The result is mounting frustration. A paralegal should not be stuck doing the same task over and over. Yet this does occur, particularly in law offices handling very large cases where there may be thousands of documents that must be identified, read, organized, stamped, coded, indexed, digested, etc. In extreme situations, paralegals have referred to such offices as "sweatshops."[5] There are a few law offices that *expect* their paralegals to become bored with relatively tedious tasks and then to move on. While some offices use part-time paralegals or independent paralegals for such tasks, a significant number of full-time paralegals find themselves in the middle of document avalanches.

This problem of *underutilization* is most acute in larger law firms where the practice of law is often compartmentalized into specialty areas (such as litigation, corporate law, real estate) with little crossover among the specialties. The more specialized the supervising attorney, the more specialized his or her paralegal will probably be. And it is within the specialties—particularly the litigation specialty—that paralegals often find themselves performing the same tasks over and over. It must be emphasized, however, that this is not universally so. There are paralegals in the so-called "megafirms" who have fascinating and challenging careers.

When underutilization does exist, regardless of the size of the law office, the problem cannot be solved unless attorneys are willing to delegate meaning-

---

[3]Wesemann, *Ten Ways to Make Paralegals More Profitable*, 134 Pittsburgh Legal Journal 20 (April 1986).

[4]Johnson, *Attorneys and the Use of Legal Assistants*, AALA News (Alaska Ass'n of Legal Assistants, August 1987).

[5]Fenn, *Letters to the Editor*, 10 National Paralegal Reporter 6 (Nat'l Federation of Paralegal Associations, June 1986).

ful tasks to paralegals. Paralegals also have a role in bringing about change. Here is the advice of two experienced paralegals:

> It is frustrating to beginning paralegals to be assigned "menial tasks"; however, we cannot run until we have learned to walk. Therefore, even assignments that seem menial must be done well. Once we prove ourselves in small assignments, large assignments will follow, as will increased responsibility and job satisfaction.[6]

> It is common today in any group of paralegals to find a vast disparity in job responsibility. It is equally common to find a vast difference in job duties among paralegals from the same firm. This is not good, but it happens. Don't despair. Sometimes this occurs because entry-level paralegals must pay their dues (much like their predecessors) before they secure the really challenging assignments. You must accept these mundane responsibilities and demonstrate your willingness to complete the task to the best of your ability. Once you are perceived as a team player and a professional, you will receive the meaty assignments you prepared for during your paralegal education or training.[7]

Later we will discuss assertiveness techniques that should help you make this transition.

While underutilization is a problem for many paralegals, the opposite problem of *over*utilization also exists. There are paralegals who are given tremendous amounts of responsibility, particularly in smaller law firms. The constant pressure and tension can be extreme. One paralegal, who loves her job, describes her life this way:

> I am trusted to the extent that I have nightmares about what I may have forgotten to do. I generally work ten to twelve hours a day, five days a week, and another five hours on Saturday. I have children who want to know why I am home so early if I come in the door at seven.[8]

Another paralegal, who was once a litigation specialist, commented, "I miss the pressure. I miss being overworked."[9] For most paralegals, however, such an environment can become overwhelming. In addition to covering techniques to combat underutilization, we also need to explore ways to handle work overloads.

##  Section C. Communication

There is nothing leisurely about the practice of law, particularly in a litigation practice where most paralegals work. The atmosphere can be highly charged because of the high stakes and egos involved. In such an environment, communication can easily break down.

> Here is a case in point. A senior partner thinks he has told his paralegal to take care of an important filing. In actuality, all he told the paralegal to do was to draft the necessary documents to make the filing. The paralegal drafts the documents and puts them in the senior partner's in-box for his review. The filing deadline is missed. The senior partner blames his paralegal. The worst part of

---

[6]*Paralegal Pride: Is There Such a Thing?*, 10 Precedent (Indiana Paralegal Ass'n, April 1987).

[7]Sova, *Bridging the Gap from Student to Professional,* 7 Legal Professional 47 (January/February 1990).

[8]Slate, *Mousebites,* 9 Newsletter 3 (Dallas Ass'n of Legal Assistants, March 1985).

[9]Frank, *Paralegal Burnout,* 70 American Bar Association Journal 30 (December 1984).

**Source:** Sheila Swanson, 14 At Issue 8 (San Francisco Ass'n of Legal Assistants, January 1987)

this scenario is that the paralegal is never told what happened or that she is being blamed. Perhaps the senior partner wishes to avoid a confrontation; perhaps he fears being told that the problem is not only his responsibility, but also his fault. In any event, the paralegal's reputation is smeared among the professional staff.[10]

Solving a communication problem is never as satisfactory as preventing the problem from arising in the first place. Many factors—time pressures, personality conflicts, ego needs, sloppiness, equipment breakdown—can account for a failure of communication. A paralegal must become astute in identifying whatever the weak spots might be in a particular office. It's a little like crossing the street. The busier the intersection, the more caution you must use to avoid an accident. Most law offices are very busy intersections.

## ■ Section D. Expectations

A fair amount of paralegal frustration on the job is due to unrealistic expectations about the career in general and about a particular job. Frustration is mainly generated by surprise: "I never thought the job would be like this!"

One of the objectives of this chapter is to provide you with the information that is needed to prevent this surprise. You need a candid account of what you might find. In Chapter 2, steps were outlined on doing background research on a potential employer *before* you accept a job, such as talking with paralegals who have worked or who still work at the office. Following these steps, whenever possible, should give you an accurate picture of what lies ahead if you take the job.

[10]Sgarlat, *The Scape Goat Phenomenon,* 6 The Journal 10 (Sacramento Ass'n of Legal Assistants, June 1986).

In a seller's market where there are more applicants than jobs, you may be so anxious to obtain a job that you will overlook potential negative aspects. This is unfortunate. It is essential that you walk into a job, or any situation, with open eyes. Not only will accurate information help reduce any frustration that may eventually develop, but the information will also be the foundation for corrective steps that you can begin taking as soon as possible.

There is a lot of information that you need. In the best of all possible worlds, you want information relevant to each of the seventy-five factors listed in Figure 3.1 that affect potential job satisfaction. (At a minimum, you would like information on the fifteen factors that you identified as most important in Assignment 3.1.) Of course there are limitations on what you can learn now. Furthermore, even the information that you receive can at best be a guide to your own prediction of how these factors might apply to you as an individual once you are on the job. This should not deter you, however, from going after whatever information is available. Some investigation is needed on your part.

## Section E. The Environment of a Law Office

When you walk into a law office, some of your first impressions might be as follows:

- The office is very formal and organized.
- The people here know what they are doing and are set in their ways.

These impressions can be very misleading. A law office is in a stage of perpetual *becoming*. The environment is always changing. New people are added, new clients come in, old clients are lost, new ways of doing things are developed, personality conflicts arise—numerous factors interact to produce an office that is in constant transition. Furthermore, you go through a process of change along with everyone else as the office continues to grow. On the surface, the office may appear to be a model of stability, but underneath all the layers of order and permanence, there is a *live* office that is in motion.

The consequences of this reality for the new paralegal are twofold:

- Do not be deceived by appearances.
- Recognize your own responsibility and *power* to help create the environment in which you are working.

If you become dissatisfied with your job, avoid being passive or defeatist. Everyone else in the office is trying to mold the environment to his or her own needs. Join the club! You may not succeed the first time. You may not succeed the fifth time. You may not even be aware of when your advocacy for yourself is having an impact. *Yet you must assert yourself and do so regularly.* Change usually does *not* occur within the timetable of the person trying to bring about the change. Occasionally you will get the impression that everyone is resisting what you feel is right. You must be prepared to lose on some points. But you must stick with it. The person who wins is often the person who outlasts the others. The losers are those who demand instant success—whether or not there is justice behind their positions.

Three things must happen before change can occur:

- You convince yourself that you have the power to create change.
- Your mind generates ten to fifteen ways of creating the change.

"It is difficult to explain to outsiders the pressures of a law firm environment. Client demands are never ending, equipment failures send staff into a frenzy, messengers run throughout the city like maniacs, paralegals pore through documents to find 'the one' to save the day or hour, receptionists cannot find various personnel because they did not check in or out, the accounting [department] is complaining about time and billing, and priorities change every minute."
Mary Ryan, Human Resources Consultant, 1988.

- You have the stamina and perspective to live through the unsuccessful attempts until you finally hit upon the strategy that produces the change.

This is not to say that you must live through misery indefinitely. There are times when you will reach the conclusion that it would be best to leave. But this should occur only after you have stretched your creativity to the point where you have thought of and exhausted a variety of strategies that ultimately prove unproductive. Don't view a law office in black-and-white terms. View it in changing shades of gray. No environment is static; an environment is simply an opportunity to be molded.

##  Section F. Office Politics

Few people like office politics. Most of us want to work where office politics does not exist. If this is not possible, our instinct is to blame others. We do what is right; others play politics.

These attitudes are illusions and interfere with your chances of bringing about change. Whenever two people work together, politics is involved. When fifty people work together, politics is the order of the day. The "people you work with become your second family, complete with squabbles and jealousies. It is not possible to completely avoid confrontations or politics." [11] Everyone cannot possibly agree about everything. Hence conscious or unconscious *negotiation* is the mechanism by which things get done. Bargaining takes place all the time. More to the point, bargaining in the context of egos takes place all the time. There is simply no alternative to this process.

If there is harmony in an office, it is because people are engaged in *effective* office politics. People are trading what others want. Disharmony usually results from the fact that people are not responding to each other's needs. A cardinal principle of human relations is that you cannot get anyone to do anything well until you have found a way of making them happy about doing it. Coercion and management-by-might have within them the seeds of their own defeat. They may work for a while, but at great cost. People generally want to do their jobs well, but this will not happen unless they strive hard to help *other* people do their jobs well.

The following dimensions of office politics may at first appear to be unpleasant to some paralegals:

- You must make sure that the decision-makers in the office learn about your work.

- You must make sure that everyone with whom you work has a good opinion of you.

This is distasteful to some because good work should speak for itself and be its own reward. Why make a campaign about it?

Unfortunately, there is a danger, particularly in a large firm, of the paralegal getting lost in the shuffle. The remedy is to be constantly looking for ways to sell yourself without appearing to do so. This goes against the grain of many paralegals. They don't like to sell themselves, especially after they have been at an office for a while. They want to settle in and not be obsessed with getting ahead. Yet you can't have it both ways. You can't complain about conditions

---

[11]McLaverty, *Office Politics and Communication*, 24 WALS State Journal 50 (January 1990).

of employment and refuse to assert your most valuable asset—yourself. This means establishing credibility and making sure that people know your worth.

> Blow your own horn: let the attorney know how you saved the client thousands of dollars, how you found the hard-to-locate witness, how you organized a huge file in mere hours, how the information you gathered helped win the case, etc. (Attorneys do this all the time.) Make sure your colleagues know of your special areas of expertise. For example, perhaps you are a good photographer, know everything there is to know about stocks and bonds, or speak several languages. (One paralegal I know dabbles in handwriting analysis; her firm found out and now she is a 'handwriting expert.') Show an interest in other matters your firm is handling. Compliment an attorney with whom you are not presently working when you hear he/she won in court, closed a complicated big dollar deal, negotiated brilliantly, etc. . . . Be a real team player.[12]

What do you think of the following advice from another successful paralegal? "Set your goals and aim for them. Open your mouth and let people know that you're headed up. Search out greater responsibility. Work your tail off—and let everyone know about it?[13] Too extreme? Too risky? People really don't get ahead this way? You don't have to advertise talent because it will eventually be discovered? Maybe. Talk with successful and satisfied paralegals around you. Make inquiries. Take a long look at people you respect in a competitive environment. Try to assess whether their abilities might have gone untapped without a healthy, effective, measured dose of self-assertiveness.

## ◼ Section G. Self-Assessment and Employer Evaluations

None of the techniques and strategies discussed in this chapter can ever be a substitute for your own competence as a paralegal. The techniques and strategies are designed to combat unrecognized and unrewarded competence.

Are you competent? To answer this question, you must evaluate yourself and receive the evaluations of others. Here are some suggestions in making both kinds of evaluations more meaningful, now and on the job.

■ Carefully read the evaluation form presented in Figure 3.2.[14] First, note the standards used to earn a "Superior" rating and a "Very Good" rating in the eight categories being evaluated. These standards should be the day-to-day employment goals of every paralegal. Second, apply the form now to your present job or to any of your prior jobs, regardless of the kind of work involved. What ratings would you give yourself in the eight categories? What ratings do you think your supervisor would give you? (If you have never worked in a law office, simply substitute the word *supervisor* every time the word *attorney* is used in the form.)

■ When you become a paralegal, the ideal will be for you and your supervisor to design an evaluation form *together*. The goal is to have a form that is specifically geared to the tasks you perform in the office. Even if the office

---

[12]Chernowsky, *Toward Greater Visibility*, 15 Reporter (Los Angeles Paralegal Ass'n, August 1986.)

[13]Oder, *Paralegal Upward Mobility*, 6 National Paralegal Reporter 6 (Nat'l Federation of Paralegal Associations, Fall/Winter, 1981); Los Angeles Paralegal Ass'n, *Reporter* (September 1981).

[14]Reprinted with the permission of Heller, Ehrman, White & McAuliffe, San Francisco, California.

Personal and Confidential

Legal Assistant _____   Hire Date _____
Review Period _____   Department _____
Evaluating Attorney _____

**A. CONTACT.** Indicate the contact you have had with the legal assistant during the review period.

_____ *Substantial.* Regular, daily, or weekly contact. Included in most attorney briefing/ strategy meetings.

_____ *Occasional.* Specific assignments and routine maintenance work requiring occasional personal instruction.

_____ *Infrequent.* Limited contact.

**B. WORK PERFORMED.** Describe the work performed by the legal assistant for you, listing some examples. Specify the degree of difficulty and expertise required.

_____
_____
_____
_____
_____

**C. PERFORMANCE EVALUATION.** Evaluate the legal assistant in each of the following areas. Check the blank to the left of the rating description that best summarizes the legal assistant's performance. Use the space on the back of the last page for additional comments.

1. **Work Product.** (Consider the legal assistant's ability to understand what is required and to provide a work product that is both thorough and complete. Consider the speed and efficiency with which the work product is returned.)

   _____ *Superior.* In most cases, needs little instruction. Takes initiative in asking questions if aspects of the task are unclear. Is resourceful in developing more efficient ways to complete projects. Demonstrates ability to consider factors not indicated by attorney that make the work product more useful.

   _____ *Very good.* Needs instruction once or twice. Legal assistant completes task thoroughly and keeps attorney informed as to work progress.

   _____ *Good.* Sometimes needs to do a task several times before he or she feels comfortable. Substantial attorney supervision is necessary during first attempts at project. Once legal assistant is comfortable with the job requirements, he or she does a thorough and complete work product.

   _____ *Marginal.* Has difficulty understanding what kind of work product is required. Sometimes does an incomplete job and takes more time than should be needed.

   _____ *Unacceptable.* Seldom masters what is required, and hence cannot do a thorough and complete work product.

   _____ *No opportunity to form an opinion.*

2. **Efficient Management of Workload.** (Consider the volume of work produced and the efficient use of time in order to meet deadlines.)

   _____ *Superior.* Highly efficient. Completes all assignments successfully, on time, and without prompting.

   _____ *Very good.* Efficient. Most assignments completed successfully. Rarely misses deadlines.

   _____ *Good.* Basically efficient. Assignments are generally completed successfully within a reasonable amount of time.

   _____ *Marginal.* Needs to improve efficiency. Assignments sometimes go uncompleted. Needs substantial attorney supervision.

   _____ *Unacceptable.* Inefficient. Deadlines are rarely met. Assignments often uncompleted.

   _____ *No opportunity to form an opinion.*

**FIGURE 3.2**

Legal Assistant Evaluation Form

Continued

**FIGURE 3.2**

Legal Assistant
Evaluation Form—
*Continued*

3. **Ability to Work Well Under Pressure.** (Consider the ability of the legal assistant to make sound judgments and to organize work under pressure.)

_____ *Superior.* Nearly always works well under pressure. Maintains organization and control over assignments; continues to make sound judgments.

_____ *Very good.* In most cases works well under pressure; rarely makes unsound judgments or becomes disorganized.

_____ *Good.* Generally works fairly well under pressure; sometimes makes judgments that are not carefully considered or becomes slightly disorganized.

_____ *Marginal.* Frequently fails to work well under pressure. Tends to become disorganized and to exercise poor judgment.

_____ *Unacceptable.* Rarely works well under pressure. Allows pressure to interfere with effective management of assignments, and often uses poor judgment.

_____ *No opportunity to form an opinion.*

4. **Analytical Skill.** (Consider the legal assistant's ability to digest and analyze the facts of a particular case or assignment and the thoroughness of factual research.)

_____ *Superior.* Is exceptionally thorough in gathering facts and quick to master the facts. Depth of understanding is evidenced by high-quality work product.

_____ *Very good.* Is thorough in gathering information. Masters facts quickly and uses them well in preparation of work product.

_____ *Good.* Generally thorough in gathering information. Masters facts over an acceptable period of time. Sometimes needs attorney direction in developing the information required for work product.

_____ *Marginal.* Sometimes misses essential information during factual investigation. Knowledge of facts is incomplete. Needs substantial attorney direction in order to analyze facts correctly.

_____ *Unacceptable.* Often misses essential information during factual investigation. Knowledge of facts is seriously deficient. Work product needs substantial revision in order to ensure completeness. Sometimes careless in presentation of facts to attorney.

_____ *No opportunity to form an opinion.*

5. **Professionalism.** (Consider the extent to which the legal assistant is personally involved in his or her work; the extent to which he or she takes the job requirements seriously; and the extent to which he or she demonstrates responsibility for high-quality work in all instances.)

_____ *Superior.* Exhibits exceptionally high level of personal involvement in assignments and is extremely responsible. Takes initiative.

_____ *Very good.* Highly involved in assignments. Demonstrates strong commitment to his or her work. Very dependable.

_____ *Good.* Generally dependable and involved in assignments. Demonstrates average commitment to his or her work.

_____ *Marginal.* Frequently appears to lack interest in assignments. Needs substantial follow-up by attorney as to both deadlines and quality of work.

_____ *Unacceptable.* Unwilling to assume the necessary responsibility.

_____ *No opportunity to form an opinion.*

6. **Ability to Work Independently.** (Consider the legal assistant's ability to exercise good judgment by making well-reasoned choices and then to maintain necessary communication with attorney.)

_____ *Superior.* Considers all options and makes good decisions. Always keeps attorney well informed.

_____ *Very good.* In most cases makes good decisions. Occasionally needs attorney assistance in defining options. Keeps attorney well informed.

_____ *Good.* Usually considers options before making a decision. May not recognize the need to request attorney assistance in defining options.

_____ *Marginal.* Has difficulty making well-reasoned choices after options are defined. Fails to cover necessary material with attorney and does not readily call upon attorney for assistance or explanation.

Continued

FIGURE 3.2

Legal Assistant Evaluation Form— *Continued*

_____ *Unacceptable.* Is not able to make reasonable choices after options are defined. Rarely keeps attorney informed and lacks understanding as to appropriate area of legal assistant work as defined by attorney.

_____ *No opportunity to form an opinion.*

7. **Quality of Written Work.** (Consider the ability of the legal assistant to express himself or herself in a clear, precise language; thoroughness; organization; accuracy and neatness; grammar.)

_____ *Superior.* Exceptionally clear, precise, and thorough work that is neat and free from errors.

_____ *Very good.* In most cases, precise, clear, and thorough.

_____ *Good.* Generally acceptable but occasionally needs improvement.

_____ *Marginal.* Frequently lacking in one or more respects.

_____ *Unacceptable.* Work product is almost always lacking in one or more respects.

_____ *No opportunity to form an opinion.*

8. **Outside Contact.** (Consider the extent to which the legal assistant is required to work with persons outside the firm, such as co-counsel, clients, state and federal agencies, state and federal court personnel.)

_____ *Superior.* Consistently demonstrates ability to readily gain the cooperation and confidence the assignment requires. Establishes excellent working relationships.

_____ *Very good.* Generally gains cooperation and confidence. Establishes cooperation and confidence.

_____ *Good.* Needs occasional assistance but is able to gain the necessary cooperation and confidence.

_____ *Marginal.* Unable to handle outside assignments without substantial attorney assistance. Has difficulty developing necessary confidence and cooperation.

_____ *Unacceptable.* No understanding of what is required in order to gain necessary cooperation and confidence. Complaints received with regard to legal assistant's behavior.

_____ *No opportunity to form an opinion.*

**COMMENTS.** On the back of this form, space is provided to allow for elaboration of any of the ratings checked under the preceding categories. You are encouraged to comment in general on the legal assistant's performance: strengths, weaknesses, and suggestions for improvement.

already has an evaluation form, think about ways to adapt it more closely to you as an individual. Make notes on what you would like to see in such a form. Discuss it with your supervisor. Your initiative in this regard will be much appreciated, especially if you make clear that your goal is to use the evaluation to improve communication and to find ways to increase your skills and productivity.

■ Start preparing for your evaluation on the first day of your employment, *and* on the day after your last evaluation. Do not wait until a few days before the evaluation itself.[15]

■ When you work on large projects, ask for a "project evaluation" at the conclusion of the project. This evaluation should be in *addition* to regularly scheduled evaluations.

■ Before an evaluation, write a *"pre-evaluation memo"* and submit it to your supervisor. The memo should list the major cases or projects you have worked on since the last evaluation, your functions on each, names of your

---

[15]Wojt, *Making the Most of Your Performance Review*, 38 The Docket 22 (May/April 1990).

supervisors and co-workers on each, special accomplishments, events showing initiative (such as weekend work), written or oral quotations from individuals commenting on your work, etc.[16]

- Before an evaluation, review the criteria by which you will be evaluated, if available.

- Before an evaluation, review your job description. If your duties have been slowly changing, rewrite your job description to reflect these changes. Submit this to your supervisor.

- If this is your first formal evaluation by a particular supervisor, try to talk with others in the office who have been evaluated by this supervisor before. Find out what you might expect from this person.

- After an evaluation, set some *measurable* goals. Do not simply pledge that you will "work harder." Establish goals that are much more concrete. For example:

    - "Before January, attend a bar-association seminar or a paralegal-association conference covering an aspect of my job."

    - "For the next ten weeks, spend a minimum of ten minutes a day studying paragraph structure in grammar/writing books."

    - "Once a month for the next six months, go to lunch with a paralegal whose professionalism I respect in order to brainstorm techniques of improvement."

    - "Within five weeks, reread the word-processing software manual from cover to cover."

    Note that each of these goals can be placed on a calendar. You can determine whether or not each has been met. Of course, you should also commit yourself to broader goals, like learning how to digest interrogatories or improving your research skills. Yet be sure to include more objective, short-term, self-measurable goals as well.

- If you receive a negative evaluation, ask for a follow-up evaluation *before* your next regularly scheduled evaluation in order to determine whether you have made any progress on what was considered negative.

We will have more to say about evaluations later when we discuss ways to support your request for a salary increase.

## Section H. Characteristics of Some Attorneys

The personality of a particular attorney has a great deal to do with the effectiveness of a paralegal–attorney working relationship. Many paralegals speak in glowing terms about their attorney–supervisor. Not only is the attorney easy to work with, but he or she also provides a challenging environment within which the paralegal can grow. Other attorneys, however, fall short of this standard; they do not function well as the leader of a team. According to

---

[16]In some offices, the employee will be asked to fill out a *self*-evaluation form before any formal evaluations by a supervisor take place.

two experts on the practice of law, there are a number of characteristics common to many attorneys that do not encourage effective team-building:[17]

*Autonomy.*   Attorneys are less likely to collaborate than people in other occupations. Often they adhere to their preferred approach even when another is equally desirable.

*Critical.*   The successful attorney is highly critical. Typically, the focus of the attorney is on what is wrong with an idea. The merits of the idea are often ignored.

*Competitive.*   Like the very nature of the legal system, the attorney is competitive and adversarial. In policy questions and in personal relationships, progress and truth are achieved through varying degrees of confrontation.

It may not be easy to work with attorneys that fit these characteristics. The key to survival is assertiveness. According to one expert, "attorneys prefer to work with assertive paralegals who are competent and knowledgeable. If you are not assertive with attorneys, they will lose confidence in you, and you may find yourself burdened with problems [including] . . . boring work, poor raises, and poor working conditions."[18]

Thus far in the chapter, we have referred to the importance of initiative and assertiveness several times. We now turn to a closer examination of this topic.

# Section I. Assertive/Nonassertive/Aggressive Behavior

Nonassertive behavior is the easiest of the three behaviors discussed here to define. It is passiveness or undue silence. A nonassertive person rarely, if ever, complains to a person causing a problem.

Aggressive behavior is at the other extreme; it is constant complaining. An aggressive person is a negative person who cannot express dissatisfaction without depressing someone else. Aggressive people may be right in many of the things they are saying, but they are so unpleasant that supervisors and co-workers seldom listen to them.

In between these two extremes is *assertive* behavior. Assertive people:

- are competent, and display competence
- are prepared
- show initiative (do not always wait to be told what to do)
- act like they belong in the office
- are always willing to learn
- respect the competence of others
- are problem-solvers
- know that one of the best ways to help others solve problems is to provide them with options

[17]Allen & Williams, *Team-Building Frenzy Reaches Law Firms,* The National Law Journal 20 (December 17, 1990).
[18]Wagner, *Tips and Traps for the New Paralegal,* 8 Legal Assistant Today 78, 82 (March/April 1991).

- appreciate the value of timing ("now" is not always the best time to resolve a problem)
- act like professionals
- do not shy away from office politics
- know the difference between griping and negotiating
- understand the necessity of compromise
- know the difference between little concerns and major ones (do not allow every problem to become a crisis)
- know when and how to lose gracefully
- advocate with resolve, not fanfare
- are self-assured enough to give credit to subordinates
- are willing to help others do their job well
- are secure enough to be able to say *no*
- are not offensive
- can express an opinion without putting someone down

Assertive paralegals make themselves known. The backbone of assertiveness is competence—you know that you are capable. The trump card of assertiveness is timing—you watch for the right moment to come forward. The foundation of assertiveness is preparation—you have collected all the facts that support your position.

Suppose, for example, you feel that you are not earning what you are worth. What do you do? You can take one of a number of approaches:

### Nonassertive

You hope that things will get better, but you don't want to rock the boat. After all, your salary isn't *that* bad; it could be worse. You talk with fellow paralegals about your salary, and you are very frank with your aunt when the two of you talk on the phone about your work. But there's no sense in trying to get the firm to pay you more. The firm probably doesn't earn that much. And Mr. Smith, the head of the firm, is very pleasant to work with. Money isn't that important. Maybe next year will be better.

### Aggressive

Three weeks after you begin your job, you tell your boss that your salary is ridiculous. "With inflation, how do you expect me to live on this salary?" When your boss is not responsive, you send a memo to all the attorneys in the firm demanding that "something be done about paralegal salaries." When you walk the corridors of the firm, you are always visibly angry.

### Assertive

- You prepare a fact sheet of paralegal salaries in your area after you talk with paralegals at other firms and examine salary surveys conducted by local and national paralegal associations, such as *Legal Assistant Managers and Legal Assistants Compensation* (published by the Legal Assistant Management Association); and *National Utilization and Compensation Survey Report* (published by the National Association of Legal Assistants).

■ You make sure that your supervisors have evaluated you regularly in writing. You summarize these evaluations and add them to the fact sheet.

■ You make a list of the various projects you have worked on. You highlight special projects, like helping design part of the office manual or training a new paralegal or attorney.

■ You make sure that the decision-makers in the firm know who you are and what you have accomplished.

■ You add up your billable hours over a designated period. This is added to the fact sheet.

■ You make note of every nonbillable task you performed which freed an attorney to devote more time to billable tasks.

■ You discuss strategies for seeking a raise with other paralegals in the firm, other paralegals in the area, and perhaps with some attorneys in the firm with whom you have developed considerable rapport.

■ When others have made a favorable comment about your work, you asked them to put it in writing so that it could go into your personnel file.

■ You select the right time to meet with your supervisor. You may decide to wait until the supervisor is not hassled with a difficult case.

■ You may adopt a two-part strategy: you first ask for a meeting with your supervisor to discuss ways of increasing your contribution and productivity. At a follow-up meeting, you raise the question of a salary increase.

■ Months before you ask for a raise, you ask your supervisor to identify those factors that will be taken into consideration in evaluating your overall performance and in recommending a salary level. In the months that follow, you make sure that you organize your efforts and your notes in accordance with the criteria the supervisor initially identified.

■ You let your supervisor know what increase you are requesting, phrasing it as a range rather than as a rigid single figure.

■ If you are unsuccessful in obtaining the amount you are seeking, you have a fall-back position ready—for example, you seek: a performance bonus in lieu of a raise; additional insurance, educational tuition, or other fringe benefits; perhaps a different office setting; or flex time.

If you ask successful paralegals their secret of success (see Figure 3.3), one message will come through loud and clear: *Seize the initiative.* No one is going to hand you anything simply because you are smart or because you have a certificate. You must prove yourself. You must be assertive.

## ■ Section J. Keeping a Diary and a Career Development File

Keep a daily diary or journal in which you record:

■ the assignments you are given

■ the dates the assignments are given and the due dates for completion

■ the dates when the assignments are actually completed

■ favorable and unfavorable comments (written or oral) that have been made about your work

**FIGURE 3.3**

Taking the
Initiative:
Recommendations
of Successful
Paralegals

**Tami Coyne:**

I have heard this tired refrain many times: "I am a hard worker and just don't get the recognition or the responsibility I deserve." This attitude gets you nowhere. If you believe that it is up to your employer to pick you out of the crowd and reward you just because you do your job, you will be sorely disappointed. In order to advance as a paralegal, you must prove that you are capable of taking on greater responsibility by performing your present duties exceptionally well. Show your initiative by anticipating the next stage of any assignment and completing it before you are asked to do it. Do not wait for recognition or feedback. You must be the one to initiate a feedback discussion after you have completed an assignment.[19]

**Renee Sova:**

Volunteer to draft the next document. Say, "I can do that; will you let me try?" Patience is a virtue. If the lawyer doesn't accommodate your first request, keep asking. Upon receiving and ultimately completing the assignment, there is nothing wrong with asking: "What could I have done differently to make it better?" This shows you truly care about your work product. Always do more than is expected. Few professionals became successful [by leaving] their careers to fate.[20]

**Laurie Roselle:**

If you feel like a second-class citizen, that's the way you will be treated—and that's how you should be treated. However, if you want respect in this profession, you must command it. To command this respect, you must be an intelligent professional willing to take on responsibility without having to be asked. Find ways to make yourself even more valuable than you already appear to be. Don't sit and complain about the way things are. Take charge and change them.[21]

**Chere Estrin:**

Be assertive. Take an attorney to lunch![22]

**Carol Musick:**

Stay current on file status. Don't wait to be told to do something. Attorneys don't have time to spoon feed their paralegals. Stay current and find out "what comes next" on your own initiative.[23]

**Marian Johnson:**

The greatest key to success is something no one can give you—a good attitude! Enthusiasm has nothing to do with noise; it has more to do with motivation. It deals with our attitude. An attitude is something you can do something about. I can choose to be enthusiastic or I can choose not to be. Excitement is infectious. It's sort of like a case of the measles. You can't infect someone unless you have the real thing![24]

[19]Coyne, *Strategies for Paralegal Career Development,* Nat'l Paralegal Reporter 20 (NFPA, Winter 1990).
[20]Sova, *Bridging the Gap from Student to Professional,* 7 Legal Professional 47 (January/February 1990).
[21]Roselle, *I Don't Get No Respect!,* 9 Nat'l Paralegal Reporter 2 (NFPA, November/December 1984).
[22]Estrin, *10 Easy Steps to Leveraging Your Career,* 10 TALA Newsletter 7 (Toledo Ass'n of Legal Assistants, October 1989).
[23]Musick, *Productivity,* 5 FWPA Newsletter 3 (Fort Worth Paralegal Ass'n, May 1987).
[24]Johnson, President's Message, *Newsletter* 1 (Arizona Paralegal Ass'n, July 1988).

- total billable hours per day attributable to your work
- total nonbillable hours devoted to assigned tasks
- the dates when you work evenings and weekends
- the dates when you work on something at home

- the dates you were late, absent, or had to leave early
- the dates when you came in early or worked through lunch hour
- the names of any clients you referred to the firm
- the amount of time you spent doing your own typing or photocopying
- the time you spend in courses, seminars, or other ventures to improve your skills.

You need to have the facts of your employment at your command. The diary is your personal record; you keep it to yourself for use as needed. Not only will the facts be valuable when you are making an argument for a raise, they also might be essential when misunderstandings arise about what you have or have not done.

The diary may be burdensome for you at first, and it may take a while before you make use of it. It is worth the burden and the wait. A law firm respects someone who has the facts, particularly with dates!

In addition, start a *career development file* which contains everything that is relevant to your employment and growth as a paralegal. It should include:

- *Resumes.* A copy of every resume you have written, including a current one which you update every two or three months.
- *Job history.* A record of the dates you were hired in previous and current jobs; who hired you; who supervised you; a copy of your job descriptions; starting salary; amounts and dates of raises, bonuses, and other benefits received; the dates and reasons you left.
- *Work accomplishments.* A copy of every written evaluation; letters received from clients commenting on your work; verbal comments made about your work by supervisors which you later write down.
- *Professional activities.* Evidence of your involvement with paralegal associations; attendance at conferences, seminars, and classes (including names of major teachers, copies of syllabi, etc.); speaking engagements; articles you have written for paralegal newsletters; significant events at church or other community groups.
- *Conflict-of-interest data.* A list of the cases on which you worked, including the exact names of all clients, opposing parties, and opposing attorneys; a brief description of your role in each case; the dates of your involvement in these cases. (This data may be needed when you seek employment with another law office that wants to avoid being disqualified from a case because of your involvement with a particular party at a prior job. See page 292).

. . . . . . . . . . . . . . .

Now you are ready. If the job you are waiting for opens up, you have almost everything ready to present to the prospective employer; or you are armed and ready to sit down with management to show you deserve the raise you have been so patiently waiting for; or you are prepared to show your supervisor you are ready to take on that new case that just came into the firm. Document everything. Be prepared.[25]

[25]Kunz, *Personal Management File*, WDALA Summons (Western Dakota Ass'n of Legal Assistants, August 1990).

Section K. The "Swoose Syndrome"

Is a paralegal part of the clerical staff or part of the professional staff? In some offices, the answer is both. See Figure 3.4. If someone is part swan and part goose, they are experiencing the *swoose syndrome*.[26] A paralegal in this position has also been referred to as a "tweener:" one who performs both clerical and paralegal tasks, and hence falls somewhere in be*tween* these two employment categories.[27]

One of the traditional hallmarks of a professional is the absence of *overtime compensation*. When professionals work more than forty hours a week, they do not expect "time-and-a-half" compensation. They work the number of hours required to do the job. If they happen to work a great number of hours, this fact is taken into consideration in the form of a bonus at the end of the year. Clerical staff, on the other hand, are less likely to receive significant bonuses. Their extra time is compensated primarily by overtime pay or by time off ("comp time").

What happens when *paralegals* work overtime? Should they receive overtime compensation, or are they part of the professional staff and hence not entitled to overtime pay? Paralegals are divided on this issue. Some find themselves in the dilemma of wanting to receive overtime pay, yet resenting any suggestion that they are not professionals. They appear to be trying to have it both ways, in effect perpetuating the schizophrenia of "swoosism." Other paralegals are

**FIGURE 3.4**

Factors Affecting Professional vs. Clerical Status

| PROFESSIONAL STATUS | CLERICAL STATUS |
|---|---|
| 1. Does not do typing for anyone else | 1. Does typing for others |
| 2. Only occasionally types own material | 2. Often types own material |
| 3. Has own office | 3. Does not have own office |
| 4. Has own computer (used primarily for database management) | 4. Has own computer (but used primarily for word processing) |
| 5. Does not do own photocopying | 5. Photocopies for others |
| 6. Has secretarial help | 6. Does not have secretarial help |
| 7. Has a business card | 7. Does not have a business card |
| 8. Has name printed on letterhead of firm | 8. Does not have name printed on letterhead |
| 9. Is paid a bonus rather than overtime | 9. Is paid overtime but not a bonus |
| 10. Is paid a salary comparable to attorneys | 10. Is paid a salary comparable to that of secretaries and other clerical staff |
| 11. Always attends strategy meetings on cases | 11. Never or only occasionally attends strategy meetings on cases |
| 12. Is given financial support and time off to attend association meetings and training sessions. | 12. Is not given financial support or time off to attend association meetings and training sessions |
| 13. Can become an associate member of a bar association | 13. Is not eligible to become an associate member of a bar association |
| 14. Clients can be separately billed for time | 14. Clients cannot be separately billed for time; services are part of overhead |

[26]Brandom, *Comments on Educating the Attorney to Employ, Utilize and Retain Legal Assistants,* 5 Facts & Findings 1, 10 (NALA, January/February 1979).
[27]Zavalney, *The Price of Success,* 6 Texas Lawyer 10, 11 (January 21, 1991).

"Good morning Mr. Davis. Here is the deposition summary I worked on till midnight, plus your coffee and danish."

less ambivalent; they are offended by the notion of overtime pay. They prefer to receive bonuses rather than overtime pay since the latter would clearly categorize them as nonprofessionals.

As we shall see in Chapter 4, the choice is not in the hands of paralegals or their employers. There is a law governing who *must* receive overtime pay, the *Fair Labor Standards Act*. For purposes of this Act, paralegals are *not* considered professionals and hence must receive overtime pay unless they have clear management duties. An office may *also* pay them a bonus, but this cannot be in lieu of overtime pay.

Hence one of the realities of paralegalism is that for some purposes (for example, paralegal billing), a paralegal is not part of the clerical staff. Yet for other purposes (such as overtime pay) the paralegal *is* part of the clerical staff. An attorney can bill a client for paralegal time, but only if the paralegal is engaged in nonclerical functions for that client. Yet, like secretaries and filing clerks, the attorney must pay paralegals overtime compensation.

Welcome to the sometimes strange world of the law. A cynic once said: "The person who asked a simple question and received a simple answer did not ask a lawyer!" The question "Is a paralegal a professional?" is not simple. The answer is *yes* for some purposes, and *no* for others.

## Section L. Paralegal CLE

Elsewhere in this book we have stressed the reality that your legal education never ends. There is always something to learn. This is true for attorneys, and it is certainly true for paralegals. Education after employment is referred to as CLE—continuing legal education. CLE is offered mainly by paralegal associations and by bar associations. It usually consists of relatively short seminars that take place on a workday afternoon at a downtown hotel, or over a two- or three-day period in another city. CLE is often significantly different from the paralegal education you initially received. Since CLE occurs while you are employed, you are able to select seminars that directly and immediately relate to

"I'm headed out for a show tonight, and tomorrow I'll be at the golf tournament. I know the report is due tomorrow. I'll ask Helen, my paralegal, to do the report. She needs something to do."

your day-to-day job responsibilities. Here is an example of this reality from Felicia Garant, a paralegal in Maine:

> I had an experience where I attended a half-day title insurance seminar and passed around a memo to attorneys in my section of the firm summarizing what I had learned there. A few minutes after I circulated the memo, an attorney flew out of his office exclaiming, "There's a new law on this subject?" He asked me to help him get a copy of the law since he had a case at that time that would be directly affected. You are the attorney's extra pair of eyes and ears, and you may pick up something at these seminars which will be new to the attorney. Your attendance at seminars, educating yourself, then passing the information on to the attorney not only increases your qualifications as a legal assistant, but also makes you a valuable employee.[28]

Often, but not always, the employer is willing to pay all or part of your expenses in attending such seminars and to give you time off if they occur during work hours. Even if your employer refuses to pay for them, you should go on your own time and at your own expense. There are few things that are more important than CLE to the professional development of a paralegal.

## Section M. Responsibilities of Supervisors

What is a good attorney supervisor? The checklist in Figure 3.5 lists the factors that constitute effective supervision. You might consider showing this checklist to your supervisors so that they might evaluate themselves as supervisors. Do not do this, however, until you are well established in your job. Considerable tact is needed when suggesting that something might be less than perfect about a supervisor.

---

[28]Garant, *Speech to USM Paralegal Program Graduates*, Newsletter 3 (Maine Ass'n of Paralegals, April 1990).

**FIGURE 3.5**

Checklist for
Effective
Supervision
of Paralegals

(Grade each factor on a scale of 1 to 5 with a 5 indicating that the supervisor is excellent in this factor and 1 indicating an unsatisfactory rating.)

| FACTOR | RATING (on a scale of 1–5) |
|---|---|
| a.  You give clear instructions to the paralegal on assignments. | a. _____ |
| b.  You do not overburden the paralegal with assignments. Before you give a new assignment, you determine what the paralegal already has to do. If the demands on a paralegal are great, you consider hiring temporary paralegal help. | b. _____ |
| c.  You provide reasonable deadlines on assignments, with adequate time built in for review and redrafting where appropriate. | c. _____ |
| d.  You take affirmative steps to inquire about the paralegal's progress on assignments to determine if you should offer more guidance or if deadline extensions are needed. You do not simply wait for the paralegal to come to you with problems. | d. _____ |
| e.  You provide adequate training for each assignment given. You take the time to make sure the paralegal can perform the task. | e. _____ |
| f.  You are not afraid to delegate tasks to the paralegal. | f. _____ |
| g.  You delegate meaningful tasks, not just the drudgery. Also, you do not ask the paralegal to do personal errands for you. | g. _____ |
| h.  You make sure that the paralegal has some variety in his or her work. | h. _____ |
| i.  You are supportive when the paralegal makes a mistake: your corrective suggestions for the future are constructive. | i. _____ |
| j.  You permit paralegals to experience the end product of cases on which they are working—for example, you give them a copy of the finished product, or you invite them to your court presentation. | j. _____ |
| k.  You include the paralegal in strategy meetings on cases. | k. _____ |
| l.  You encourage the paralegal to use the law library in order to increase his or her knowledge and to appreciate the legal context of a case. | l. _____ |
| m.  You use the paralegal's skills and regularly look for ways the paralegal can increase his or her skills. | m. _____ |
| n.  You encourage paralegals to give their opinion on cases and on office policy. | n. _____ |
| o.  You design systems with instructions, checklists, forms, etc. for the performance of tasks involving paralegals. | o. _____ |
| p.  You encourage the paralegal to help you write these systems. | p. _____ |
| q.  You regularly evaluate the paralegal, informally and in writing. | q. _____ |
| r.  You encourage the paralegal to help you design a relevant paralegal evaluation form. | r. _____ |
| s.  You encourage the paralegal to evaluate you as a supervisor. | s. _____ |
| t.  You give credit to the paralegal where credit is due. | t. _____ |
| u.  You make sure others in the firm know about the contribution of the paralegal. | u. _____ |
| v.  You lobby with other attorneys who do not use paralegals or do not appreciate their value in order to change their attitude. | v. _____ |
| w.  You make yourself aware of any tension that may exist among paralegals, secretaries, and other staff members in the office in order to help end the tension. | w. _____ |

Continued

**FIGURE 3.5**

Checklist for
Effective
Supervision
of Paralegals
—*Continued*

| | | |
|---|---|---|
| x. | You back the paralegal's reasonable requests on salary and working conditions. | x. _____ |
| y. | You introduce your clients to the paralegal, explain the latter's role, and express your confidence in your employee. | y. _____ |
| z. | You do not pressure the paralegal about producing a quota of billable hours. | z. _____ |
| aa. | You make sure the paralegal has suitable office space, supplies, secretarial support, access to word processing, etc. | aa. _____ |
| bb. | When changes in office procedures are made that affect paralegals, you let them know in advance so that they can make suggestions about the changes. | bb. _____ |
| cc. | You support the paralegal's need for financial help and time off to attend outside training programs (CLE). | cc. _____ |
| dd. | You support the paralegal's need for financial help and time off to participate in the activities of paralegal associations. | dd. _____ |
| ee. | You recognize that the paralegal, like any employee, will need reasonable time off to attend to pressing personal matters. | ee. _____ |
| ff. | You consider letting the paralegal have reasonable time off to do some *pro bono* work (e.g., time donated to poverty law offices or public interest law firms). | ff. _____ |
| gg. | You don't assume that the paralegal is happy about his or her job simply because you have no complaints and the paralegal hasn't expressed dissatisfaction; you take the initiative to find out what is on the paralegal's mind. | gg. _____ |
| hh. | You treat the paralegal as an individual. | hh. _____ |
| ii. | You treat the paralegal as a professional. | ii. _____ |

## Section N. Relationship with Secretaries

There was a time when many secretaries resented the hiring of paralegals, particularly in smaller law offices. A number of reasons accounted for this friction:

> Historically, the legal secretary was "queen" of her territory. The more competent she was, the more control she had over her immediate environment—how the office looked, how the work was done, how the clients were handled, and for that matter, how the lawyer was trained. The longer she worked with one lawyer, the more responsibility she was given, and the better she got at her job. In the office of the sole practitioner, the practice could go on smoothly even if the lawyer was in court or out of town. She was just about as indispensable as one person could be. There was a relationship of mutual trust and respect between the legal secretary and the lawyer that was practically impenetrable. Then along came the legal assistant, intruding on the legal secretary's territory, doing many of the things that the legal secretary had been doing for years. To add insult to injury, the legal secretary was expected to perform secretarial work for the legal assistant![29]

Fortunately, this problem is less prevalent today, even in smaller law offices. But the paralegal still needs to be sensitive to the needs of the secretary, partic-

---

[29]*The Legal Assistant and the Legal Secretary: Friend or Foe,* 8 The Journal 4 (Sacramento Ass'n of Legal Assistants, April 1988).

ularly the veteran secretary who was a valuable fixture in the office long before the paralegal arrived.[30]

When you start working with legal secretaries, consider the following recommendations for a smooth working relationship:[31]

- Give the secretary accurate, detailed instructions along with a reasonable timetable for completion.
- Make sure your written instructions are legible.
- Avoid waiting until the last minute to assign work that you know about beforehand.
- Don't pawn off undesirable chores that are rightly yours.
- Limit interruptions.
- Make yourself available to discuss problems or questions that arise during the performance of a task.
- Provide all the tools necessary to complete a job.
- Look for ways to recognize the contribution of secretaries. (The Rhode Island Paralegal Association, for example, conducts an annual secretary-appreciation luncheon.) "Remember that a pat on the back is just a few vertebrae removed from a kick in the pants, but miles ahead in results." [32]
- A cheerful demeanor can go a long way toward making your relationship more pleasant. Treat your secretary the way you wish to be treated, and don't forget basic courtesies, such as saying "good morning" and "have a nice evening."

Paralegals sometimes complain that attorneys do not treat paralegals with respect. How ironic that an insensitive paralegal could become subject to this same criticism.

##  Section O. Sexual Harassment

There are two kinds of sexual harassment on the job:

### Quid Pro Quo Harassment:

Submission to or rejection of unwelcome sexual conduct by an individual is used as the basis for employment decisions affecting that individual, such as promotion or other job-related benefits.

### Hostile Environment Harassment:

Pervasive unwelcome sexual conduct or sex-based ridicule unreasonably interferes with an individual's job performance or creates an intimidating, hostile, or offensive working environment, even if it leads to no tangible or eco-

---

[30]The largest organization of legal secretaries is NALS, the National Association of Legal Secretaries (see Appendix B for address). It administers the Professional Legal Secretary (PLS) exam. Passing the exam entitles the secretary to use the designation "Certified PLS" after his or her name. Many legal secretaries do not consider themselves significantly different from paralegals. In fact, a number of paralegals are members of NALS. One of the major *paralegal* associations, the National Association of Legal Assistants (NALA), was originally formed as a breakaway group from NALS.
[31]Rosen, *Effective Delegation,* 13 Update 8 (Cleveland Ass'n of Legal Assistants, June/July 1990).
[32]Guinn, *Personnel Management Techniques,* 8 Legal Assistant Today 56, 58 (March/April 1991).

**FIGURE 3.6**

Incidents of Sexual Harassment

| PERCENTAGE OF RESPONDENTS WHO REPORT HAVING EXPERIENCED VARIOUS TYPES OF SEXUAL HARASSMENT ON THE JOB | | | |
|---|---|---|---|
| Incident | By Superior | By Colleague | By Client |
| Unwanted sexual teasing, jokes, remarks, or questions | 36 | 30 | 32 |
| Unwanted pressure for dates | 8 | 6 | 10 |
| Unwanted letters, telephone calls, or materials of a sexual nature | 4 | 3 | 4 |
| Unwanted sexual looks or gestures | 21 | 11 | 16 |
| Unwanted deliberate touching, leaning over, cornering, or pinching | 14 | 6 | 9 |
| Unwanted pressure for sex | 6 | 3 | 4 |
| Unwanted pressure for sex in return for promotions or business | 1 | 0 | 1 |
| Actual or attempted rape or assault | 1 | 0 | 0 |

**Source:** *National Law Journal/West Publishing Company Survey on Women and Law,* National Law Journal S2 (December 11, 1989).

nomic job consequences. The work environment is significantly pervaded by sexual commentary, dirty jokes, offensive pictures, or generalized sexual conduct even if there is no direct trading of sexual favors for employment benefits.[33]

. . . . . . . . . . . . . .

A recent study indicated that the harassment can come from a superior, a colleague, or a client of the law office. See Figure 3.6. Here are some concrete examples:

> The paralegal . . . told of one incident in which a partner placed his hand on her knee and asked if she had thought about her future with the firm. "Harassment of women lawyers is only the tip of the iceberg," according to the paralegal. "The support staff has it much, much worse."[34]

> Recently a female paralegal began working with an insecure male lawyer who was a first year associate at the firm. He started "making the moves" on her by constantly asking if she was dating anyone. One day he called her in his office, closed the door, dialed a number on the phone, and handed the receiver to the paralegal. "What I heard was an obscene recording. I laughed, opened the door, and left." She did not believe in pursuing office relationships. Resentment developed when they began working on the same case together. He falsely accused the paralegal of lying and of not completing assignments on time. He made derogatory comments to her co-workers. When she confided in a female lawyer at the firm, she was told that the associate acts that way with all the women at the firm, that the paralegal supervisor and the associate are very good friends, and that the partner in charge "sticks to this associate like glue" and does not want to be bothered by "petty personnel problems."[35]

---

[33]Wapner, *Sexual Harassment in the Law Firm,* 16 Law Practice Management 42, 43 (September 1990); Smith, *Sexual Harassment Discussed at Litigation Sectional,* MALA Advance 19 (Minnesota Ass'n of Legal Assistants, Summer, 1989); 29 CFR § 1604.11(a)(2) and (a)(3); 47 Federal Register 74,676 (November 10, 1980).

[34]Goldberg, *Law's "Dirty Little Secret,"* 76 ABA Journal 34 (October 1990).

[35]Nat'l Federation of Paralegal Associations, *Harassment: Personnel Problem or Worse?* 9 Nat'l Paralegal Reporter 7 (February 1985).

What should a paralegal do in such a predicament? A passive response would be to ignore the problem and hope that it will go away. Another response would be to blame yourself. Phyllis Schlafly told the Senate Labor and Human Resources Committee that "Men hardly ever ask sexual favors of women from whom the certain response is *no*."[36] It is highly unlikely, however, that blaming yourself is either correct or productive.

For isolated and less serious problems, all that may be needed is a firm comment to the offender such as:

> Mr. Smith, you know that I respect your ability and authority in the firm. But I want you to know that I do not appreciate the comment you made at that meeting about women. I did not think it was appropriate.

Unfortunately, this approach may be inadequate when the problem becomes more complicated and persists. Clearly, all internal avenues of trying to resolve the problem should be attempted. Hopefully, *somebody* in a position of responsibility will lend a sympathetic ear. Local paralegal associations should be a source of ideas and support. Speak with officers of the association. Go to general meetings. Ask for advice. It is highly likely that you will find others who have had similar experiences and who can provide concrete suggestions.

If all else fails, you have a powerful weapon at your disposal: the law. Harassment on the basis of sex is a violation of Title VII of the Civil Rights Act. The federal *Equal Employment Opportunity Commission (EEOC)* as well as state departments of civil rights are available to enforce the law.

It is not enough for a law office to say that any sexual harassment in the office is forbidden. The employer must actively combat such harassment by informing employees of their right to raise (and telling them how to raise) the issue of harassment under Title VII, establishing a written policy against harassment and distributing it throughout the office, investigating all allegations of harassment promptly, and developing appropriate sanctions for actual harassment. An office that ignores the problem or that adopts an attitude that "men will be men" could be subject to liability.

## Section P. Working with Systems

Some paralegal employment problems are attributed to the fact that the firm has not carefully examined how paralegals can be effectively used in the office. Paralegals should be part of an attorney-paralegal-secretary team. The difficulty, however, is that the office may not have done the necessary planning to design the *system* that the team will execute.

A system is an organized way of accomplishing a task. Each participant is supposed to perform those functions that they are capable of handling and for which they are not overtrained. Here is how many systems are created:

■ Select the task that is to be systematized. It will usually be a task that the office performs regularly, such as incorporating a business, probating an estate, filing for divorce, engaging in discovery. (According to some studies, attorneys perform over 75% of their tasks more than once.)

■ The task is carefully studied in order to identify the various components of the task. What are the pieces that must always be performed? What facts

---

[36]Baca, *Speech to Nat'l Capital Area Paralegal Ass'n* (April 29, 1981).

must always be obtained? What letters must always be sent? What forms must always be prepared?

- A systems or procedural manual is then prepared containing a description of the task, instructions or checklists of things to be done, standardized letters, pleadings, forms and other documents that are customarily used for that task, etc. The manual might be placed in a three-ring notebook and/or on a computer.
- Photocopies of statutes, court rules, or other laws frequently used to perform the task are placed in a section of the manual, often in an appendix.
- Performance of the components of the task is then delegated to various members of the team.

It takes considerable sophistication to *design* a system. Even more sophistication is sometimes needed to *implement* the system and make it work. The participants must believe in the system, and ideally have had a role in its design if it requires changes in their work habits. Many attorneys are notoriously resistant to change, particularly if they believe that the system fails to recognize the role of professional judgment. If you have been doing something the same way for 15 years, you tend to be suspicious of suggestions that more efficient ways are possible. Furthermore, in the transition from blueprint to operation, there may have to be modifications made in the system in order to work out the "bugs." Again, a precondition for success is a willingness of the participants to make the new system work.

When paralegals walk into an office for the first time, they may confront a number of situations:

- There are no systems; everybody practices law in their own individualistic way.
- There is talk of systemization, but no one has yet done any serious design work.
- An ineffective system is in place.
- A system is in place, but the participants do not believe in it.
- A system exists on paper, but no one has expended the time and energy to make the system work.

All these environments can make life difficult for the paralegal. A disorganized office can be very frustrating.

One of the most valuable things a paralegal can do is to observe an effective system in place. One or more may exist in other parts of the firm where you work. It may be possible for you to visit other firms in the area. There are systems described in formbooks, manuals, and legal periodical literature on law office management, but they are no substitute for seeing the real thing.

Don't be reluctant to try to design your own system. You might want to begin with a system for a portion of one of your tasks. Start out on a small scale with instructions or checklists for functions that you regularly perform. Write the system so that a new paralegal would be able to read it and know what to do. Here is an example of how a project led to the creation of a system:

Diedre Wilton's organizational skills were really put to the test during a recent assignment which required her to file fictitious business name statements for a client in every county in California. "Almost every county had a different form!" lamented Diedre. "And I had to arrange for publication in fifty-eight different newspapers." She is creating an extensive file on the project so that . . . when the filings come up for renewal, the next person won't have to start from scratch.[37]

Supervisors will be *very* impressed by such efforts to create systems. A paralegal with this much initiative will soon become a prized member of the office.

 ## Section Q. Career Ladders

In the early days of the paralegal movement, a common complaint among paralegals was the absence of career ladders. Once a paralegal demonstrates competence by making a significant contribution to the office, what comes next? Higher salaries, a better office, more variety in assignments—these are all helpful, but they are not the same as promotion. Yet what can a paralegal be promoted to? The only next step was lawyerdom. But going to law school is a rather drastic step. Taking this step means, of course, leaving the field of paralegalism entirely. Hence, in those early days, the only way up was out!

Although some progress has been made in developing career ladders, the progress has been primarily limited to law offices that employ relatively large numbers of paralegals. Most of the paralegals in small offices still have no career ladder. For this and related reasons, surveys show that between ten and fifteen percent of working paralegals today say that they intend to go to law school—eventually.

Yet there are paralegals who resent the following question put to them by attorneys: "So when are you going to law school?" or "Why don't you become an attorney?" Here is another example of this mentality:

One day I accompanied an attorney to a deposition, at the request of our client. When we arrived at the opposing counsel's office, the attorney I was working with introduced me as the paralegal working on the case. The opposing counsel responded with, "Oh, so you're an aspiring attorney." "No," I responded, "I'm an aspiring paralegal." [38]

Such paralegals see paralegalism as an end in itself, not a stepping stone to becoming an attorney. Attorneys are not always asked, "When are you going to become a judge?" And nurses do not constantly hear, "When are you going to become a doctor?" Paralegals deserve the same respect. Many wish that they could stop having to answer "the law-school question."

The solution, of course, is the creation of meaningful career ladders for paralegals within a particular law office. As indicated, the larger law offices have responded. The *Legal Assistants Management Association (LAMA),* for example, has defined six different levels within the world of the legal assistant:

*Legal assistant clerk*

*Legal assistant*

*Senior legal assistant*

*Supervising legal assistant*

*Case manager*

*Legal assistant manager*

---

[37]*Paralegal Profile,* 12 Points & Authorities 9 (San Joaquin Ass'n of Legal Assistants, March 1991).
[38]Burdett, *Rodney Dangerfield: You're Not Alone,* 12 Nat'l Paralegal Reporter 12 (Nat'l Federation of Paralegal Associations, Spring 1988).

These levels were defined in Chapter 1 (see Figure 1.1). Under this tiered structure, the lowest position is called the legal assistant clerk. Not all offices, however, use this terminology. An office might call the position *case clerk, document clerk,* or some similar term.

It must be emphasized again, however, that this kind of career ladder does *not* apply to all law offices. Many paralegals begin work in a law office as a paralegal or legal assistant, and end their work there with the same title. If they want to experience a different level of work, they must try to obtain a job at another office that employs more paralegals and is enlightened enough to have instituted a meaningful career ladder.

## ■ Section R. Your Next Job

It is extremely important to remember that throughout your current employment, you will be creating a record for your *next* job. While it is possible that you will remain in one position for your entire paralegal career, the likelihood is that you will one day become employed at another law firm, corporation, or other law office. You should assume that everyone in a position of authority where you now work will one day be called by a prospective employer who will ask a series of questions about you:

- What kind of a worker were you?
- How did you get along with coworkers?
- Did you show initiative?
- Did you function well under pressure? etc.

The legal profession is conservative by nature. Attorneys like to stay with winners; they are often reluctant to take chances. The most attractive candidate for a paralegal job is someone who has been successful at a previous paralegal job. Attorneys are hesitant to hire people who have run into difficulty at an earlier job—even if it was not their fault. Hence, *treat all supervisors in the office as potential references.*

## ■ Section S. Paralegal Associations and Networking

Your greatest ally in confronting any of the on-the-job problems discussed in this chapter is the paralegal association at the local and national level. (See Appendix B). Not only are the associations a source of excellent information about paralegal practice in your area and across the nation, they are also a potential gold mine of ideas and strategies. It is probably impossible for you to have a problem on the job that has not been experienced by numerous other paralegals within an association. Tap into this resource as soon as possible. You can learn a great deal by listening to the problems of others and finding out how they tried to solve them. What worked? Why? What didn't work? Why not? What is the next thing that should be tried? Answers to such questions will be readily available to you through the paralegal associations. (To begin your contact with them now, use the forms at the end of the index of this book.)

*Networking* is the process of establishing a large number of social and professional contacts with people, making notes on what they do and how to reach them, and organizing these notes so that you can renew the contacts in the future if the need arises. For a paralegal, the nucleus of networking is the paralegal association.

---

■ **ASSIGNMENT 3.2**

Examine the following fact situations. For each situation:

- Identify the problem or problems that you see.
- What strategies do you think would be helpful in resolving the problem or problems? Why?
- What strategies do you think would be counterproductive? Why?
- What do you think could have been done to prevent the problem or problems from occurring in the first place? How could they have been avoided?
- In your responses, specify what you think would be assertive, nonassertive, and aggressive behavior.

(a) Tom has been a paralegal at a firm for three years. His paralegal training in school was in drafting, legal research, investigation, etc. For the entire three years, however, he has been collating and digesting numerous documents in a big antitrust case. It is a very important case, and the firm is reluctant to take him off it due to his familiarity with these documents. The problem, however, is that Tom is becoming bored. He is satisfied with his pay but dreads coming to work each day. He tried to explain this to his supervisor, but he was simply told how important he was to the case. The supervisor said, "If you decide to leave the firm, I hope you will give us six months' lead time so that you can train a replacement." This made Tom all the more depressed since he does not want to leave.

(b) Ellen is a probate paralegal at a firm. She has worked there two years. At a recent paralegal association meeting, she discovered that other probate paralegals in the city with the same experience are making at least $4,000 more per year than she. She wants to talk with her supervisor about this, but is not sure if this is the right time. The last three months have been difficult for her. She has been out of work a lot due to illness. She also recently began work on a new complex case. She is struggling to keep up with the new work involved in the case and must constantly ask her supervisor for help. The supervisor appears to be irritated with her progress on the case. Her next scheduled salary review is ten months away.

(c) Jim, Janet, Brenda, Helen, and Pat are paralegals at a law firm. They are all unhappy about their job: low pay, long hours, sexism, menial tasks, etc. On a number of occasions they have met with the senior partners in the firm to discuss ways of improving their situation. Minor changes were made, but the problems persist. They are approached by a local union about joining the union.

(d) Fran is a paralegal in a firm where she works for the senior partner—the most powerful person in the firm. Fran receives excellent pay and fringe benefits. She loves her work. Other paralegals in the firm, however, resent her because their benefits are much lower and they receive assignments that they dislike.

(e) Same situation as in (d) above. Fran's boss is currently going through a divorce, and the strain on him has been enormous. One consequence of this is that Fran's workload is increasing. More of his work is being shifted to her. The boss is extremely sensitive to any criticism about the way he practices law, so Fran is reluctant to talk with him about the extra work—particularly when he is under so much pressure due to the divorce. Yet Fran is worried about her ability to do her job competently in view of the increased work. She hopes that things will get back to normal when the divorce is over.

(f) Mary works in a law firm that charges clients $125 an hour for attorney time and $55 an hour for paralegal time. She and another paralegal, Fred, are working with an attorney on a large case. She sees all of the time sheets that the three of them submit to the firm's accounting office. She suspects that the attorney is *padding* his time sheets by overstating the number of hours he works on the case. For example, he lists thirty hours for a four-day period when he was in court every day on another case. Furthermore, Fred's time is being billed at the full $55-an-hour-rate even though he spends about 80% of his time typing correspondence, filing, and performing other clerical duties.

(g) Tom has been a paralegal at the firm for six years. He works for three attorneys. One day he is told by a memo from the office administrator that an outside consultant has been hired to study Tom's job in order to find ways "to increase productivity." The letter instructs Tom to spend the next two days permitting the consultant to follow Tom around and ask questions about what he does. Tom is furious.

(h) Mary has been a paralegal at the firm for two years. She works for one attorney, Mr. Getty. One day a client calls Mary and says, "I'm sending you another copy of the form that Mr. Getty said you lost." This is news to Mary. She works with the client's file every day and knows that she has never lost anything. She pauses, trying to think of what to say to this client over the phone before hanging up.

(i) Veronica works for a law firm where none of the supervisors give formal evaluations of the paralegals. The supervisors feel that formal evaluations would be too time-consuming and too general to be helpful. Veronica has received yearly raises, and according to her supervisor, this is the best indication of what the firm thinks of her. Veronica is unhappy, however, with the feedback she has gotten about her work.

(j) How would you handle the fact situation presented at the bottom of page 200 involving sexual harassment? Assume the paralegal does not want to quit and is afraid that she will lose her job if she institutes legal action.

## ■ ASSIGNMENT 3.3

Karen considers herself a quiet, nonaggressive person. She has two job offers: (a) a large law firm (seventy-five attorneys and twenty-two paralegals) and (b) a one-attorney/one-secretary office. She likes the type of work both offices do. The pay and benefits in both offices are roughly the same. How would you advise Karen on which job to take?

## ■ ASSIGNMENT 3.4

According to Douglas McGregor in *The Human Side of Enterprise* (1960), there are two basic views of human behavior at work. "Theory X" says that a person has a natural dislike of work and will avoid it whenever possible. "Theory Y" says that physical and mental work are as natural to a person as any other activity. Under theory Y, workers do not naturally shy away from responsibility.

- Describe a law office using paralegals that is managed under theory X. How would it function? How would the office handle paralegal problems?
- Describe a law office using paralegals that subscribes to theory Y. How would it function? How would the office handle paralegal problems?
- Which theory do you think is correct?
- Which theory describes you?

## ■ ASSIGNMENT 3.5

What needs does a paralegal or any worker have? What is our "hierarchy of needs"? Rearrange the following needs so that you think they reflect the conscious or unconscious priorities of most human beings: the need to be fulfilled; the need to be respected; the need to eat, sleep, and be clothed; the need to be safe; the need to be respected; the need to be admired; the need to belong; the need to have self-worth. See Maslow, A., *Motivation and Personality* (1970).

## ☐ Chapter Summary

A major theme of Chapter 3 is the critical importance of paralegal initiative. Every occupation has its problems. This chapter covered problems in the paralegal arena and how initiative is a primary vehicle for resolving them. After listing seventy-five factors that influence job satisfaction, we turned to some of the major on-the-job difficulties that some paralegals face. The following topics were examined: the need for career ladders, the adequacy of compensation, the inability of some attorneys to use paralegals effectively, the breakdown of communication in the hectic environment of a law practice, the lack of realistic expectations of what it means to work with attorneys, the characteristics of some attorneys that do not make them good supervisors, the inevitability of office politics, the central role of self-evaluation and employer evaluation, the question of professional status, the tensions that can exist in the attorney-paralegal-secretary relationship, and finally the problem of sexual harassment.

While initiative cannot solve all of the problems that may exist, it appears to be a central ingredient in the success of competent paralegals. Such paralegals take advantage of opportunities for continuing legal education; they know how to work with—and to help create—systems; they know what it means to be prepared; and they understand the value of networking.

## Key Terms

career ladder
profit center
underutilization
office politics
pre-evaluation memo
assertive
billable/nonbillable
career development file
swoose syndrome

overtime compensation
Fair Labor Standards Act
CLE
pro bono
NALS
Certified PLS
quid pro quo harassment
hostile environment
    harassment

EEOC
systems
LAMA
legal assistant clerk
case clerk
document clerk
networking
padding

# 4

# The Regulation of Paralegals

## ■ Chapter Outline

Section A. Kinds of Regulation
Section B. Unauthorized and
   Authorized Practice of Law
   Defining the Practice of Law
   Authorized Practice of Law
Section C. Licensing of Paralegals
   Broad-Based Licensing
   Limited Licensing
Section D. Bar Association Control of
   Paralegal Education

Section E. Should Paralegals Become
   Part of Bar Associations?
Section F. Self-Regulation by
   Paralegals: The Certification
   Debate
Section G. Fair Labor Standards Act
Section H. Tort Liability of
   Paralegals
Section I. Malpractice Insurance

## ■ Section A. Kinds of Regulation

The activities of paralegals could be regulated in seven important ways:

■ Laws on the unauthorized practice of law and on the *authorized* practice of law by nonattorneys

■ State licensing

■ Regulation of education

■ Self-regulation

■ Fair Labor Standards Act

■ Tort Law (e.g., the negligence of paralegals and of attorneys who employ them)

■ Ethical rules

The first six of these methods of regulation are covered in this chapter. Ethics will be examined in the next chapter. As we explore these methods, you should keep in mind the terminology of regulation outlined in Figure 4.1.

**FIGURE 4.1**

The Terminology of Regulation

*Accreditation* is the process by which an organization evaluates and recognizes a program of study (or an institution) as meeting specified qualifications or standards.

*Approval* means the recognition that comes from accreditation, certification, licensure, or registration. As we will see, the American Bar Association uses the word "approval" as a substitute for "accreditation" of paralegal education programs.

*Certification* is the process by which a nongovernmental organization grants recognition to an individual who has met qualifications specified by that organization. Three of the most common qualifications are:

- Graduating from a school or training program, or

- Passing a standard examination, or

- Completing a designated period of work experience.

Once certification has been bestowed by one or a combination of these methods, the individual is said to have been *certified*. If the certification comes from a school or training program, some prefer to say that the person has been *certificated*. (Occasionally a government agency will have what it calls a certification program. This program may be similar to those described above, or it may in fact be a license program.)

*Code* is any set of rules that regulates conduct.

*Ethics* are rules that embody standards of behavior to which members of an organization are expected to conform.

*Guideline* is suggested conduct that will help an applicant obtain accreditation, certification, licensure, registration, or approval.

*Licensure* is the process by which an agency of government grants permission to persons meeting specified qualifications to engage in an occupation and/or to use a particular title.

*Limited Licensure* (also called *specialty licensure*) is the process by which an agency of government grants permission to persons meeting specified qualifications to engage in designated activities that are customarily (but not always exclusively) performed by another license holder. (If, in the future, paralegals are granted a limited license in a particular state, they will be authorized to sell designated services—now part of the attorney monopoly—directly to the public in that state.)

*Registration* or *enrollment* is the process by which individuals or institutions list their names on a roster kept by an agency of government or by a nongovernmental organization. There may or may not be qualifications that must be met before one can go on the list.

*Regulation* is any governmental or nongovernmental method of controlling conduct.

# ■ Section B. Unauthorized and Authorized Practice of Law

## (a)  Defining the Practice of Law

Every state has laws on who can be an attorney and on the *unauthorized practice of law*. In many states it is a *crime* to practice law illegally. It is not a crime to represent yourself, but you risk going to jail if you practice law on behalf of someone else. Why such a harsh penalty? Legal problems often involve complicated, serious issues. A great deal can be lost if citizens do not receive competent legal assistance. To protect the public, the state has established a system of licensing attorneys to provide this assistance and to punish anyone who tries to provide it without the license.

The *practice of law* involves three major kinds of activities:

- Representing someone in court or in an agency proceeding

- Preparing and drafting legal documents for someone

- Providing legal advice on someone's rights and obligations

The essence of legal advice is to relate the law to an individual's specific legal problem.

Suppose that you write a self-help book on how to sue your landlord. The book lists all the laws, provides all the forms, and gives precise guidelines on how to use the laws and the forms. Are you practicing law? No, since you are not addressing the *specific* legal problem of a *specific* person. It is not the practice of law to sell legal books or similar materials to the general public even if a member of the public uses them for his or her specific legal problem. Now suppose that you open an office in which you sell the book and even type the forms for customers. Practice of law? No, *unless you provide individual help in filling out the forms.* You can type the forms so long as the customer does all the thinking about what goes in the forms! So too:

■ It is proper for a nonattorney to charge citizens a fee to type legal forms in order to obtain a divorce. But it is the unauthorized practice of law to provide personal assistance on how to fill out the forms.

■ It is proper for a nonattorney to charge citizens a fee to type their will or trust. But it is the unauthorized practice of law to provide personal assistance on what should go in the will or trust.

For years, attorneys have complained that large numbers of individuals were crossing the line by providing this kind of personal assistance. Bar associations often asked the state to prosecute many of them. Yet some charged that the attorneys were less interested in protecting the public than in preserving their own monopoly over the practice of law. Perhaps the most famous recent case involving this controversy was that of Rosemary Furman and the Florida Bar.

---

### Rosemary Furman: Folk Hero?

Rosemary Furman, a former legal secretary, believes that you should be able to solve simple legal problems without hiring an attorney. Hence she established the Northside Secretarial Service in Jacksonville, Florida. She compiled and sold packets of legal forms (for $50) on divorce, name changes, and adoptions. The price *included her personal assistance in filling out and filing the forms.* The Florida Bar Association and the Florida courts moved against her with a vengeance for practicing law illegally. She was convicted and sentenced to 30 days in jail.

Widespread support for Ms. Furman developed. Her case soon became a cause célèbre for those seeking increased access to the legal system for the poor and the middle class.[1] Many were outraged at the legal profession and the judiciary for their treatment of Ms. Furman.

The CBS program *60 Minutes* did a story that was favorable to her cause. Other national media, including *Newsweek,* covered the case. Warner Brothers considered doing a docudrama on the story. Rosemary Furman struck a responsive chord when she claimed that for every $50 she earned, an attorney lost $500. An editorial in the *Gainesville Sun* said, "Throw Rosemary Furman in jail? Surely not after the woman forced the Florida bar and the judiciary to confront its responsibility to the poor. Anything less than a 'thank you' note would indeed show genuine vindictiveness on the part of the legal profession" (Nov. 4, 1984). There were, however, other views. An editorial in *USA Today* said, "If she can give legal advice, so can charlatans, frauds, and rip-off artists" February 2, 1984).

The events in the Rosemary Furman story are as follows:

■ 1978 & 1979: The Florida Bar Association takes Rosemary Furman to court, alleging that she is practicing law without a license.

■ 1979: The Florida Supreme Court rules against her. She is enjoined from engaging in the unauthorized practice of law.

---

[1] Peoples & Wertz, *Update: Unauthorized Practice of Law,* 9 Nat'l Paralegal Reporter 1 (Nat'l Federation of Paralegal Associations, February 1985).

- 1982: The Florida Bar Association again brings a complaint against her business, alleging that she was continuing the unauthorized practice of law.
- 1983: Duval County Circuit Judge A. C. Soud, Jr. finds her in contempt of court for violating the 1979 order. The judge makes this decision in a nonjury hearing. She is then ordered to serve 30 days in jail.
- 1984: The United States Supreme Court refuses to hear the case. This has the effect of allowing the state jail sentence to stand. The Court is not persuaded by her argument that she should have been granted a jury trial of her peers rather than have been judged solely by members of a profession (attorneys and judges) that was biased against her.
- Her attorneys ask the Florida Supreme Court to vacate the jail sentence if she agrees to close her business.
- The Florida Bar Association tells the Florida Supreme Court that the jail term is a fitting punishment and should be served.
- November 13, 1984: The Florida Supreme Court orders her to serve the jail sentence for practicing law without a license. (451 So.2d 808)
- November 27, 1984: Rosemary Furman is granted clemency from the 30-day jail term by Florida Governor Bob Graham and his Clemency Board. She does not have to go to jail.
- Furman and her attorneys announce that they will work on a constitutional amendment defining the practice of law to make it easier for citizens to avoid dependency on attorneys in civil cases. Says Ms. Furman, "I have only begun to fight."

This case has had an impact in Florida and elsewhere in the country. Recently, for example, Florida has been considering a dramatic change in the definition of unauthorized practice of law. Under this proposal, it "shall not constitute the unauthorized practice of law for nonlawyers to engage in limited oral communications to assist a person in a completion of a legal form approved by the Supreme Court of Florida. Oral communications by nonlawyers are restricted to those communications reasonably necessary to elicit factual information to complete the form and inform the person how to file the form."[2] Later in this chapter, we will discuss the even more dramatic concept of *limited licensing* for paralegals, which is being considered in a number of states. Some have referred to these developments as "the long shadow of Rosemary Furman."

---

[2] Florida Bar News 12 (August 1, 1989).

---

## ■ ASSIGNMENT 4.1

**(a)** Define the practice of law in your state. Quote from your state code, court rules, or other official authority that is available.

**(b)** Would Rosemary Furman have been prosecuted for the unauthorized practice of law in your state today?

---

■
Legal Assistant regulation is on the horizon in one form or another, [and possibly in many forms]. It is imperative that we approach the regulation "can of worms" from an informed and knowledgeable vantage point, and that we participate in the formative process.
Gail White Nicholson, Vice-President, Greenville Association of Legal Assistants, 1991
■

The Furman case involved direct competition with attorneys. More indirect competition comes from people engaged in law-related activities, such as accountants, claims adjusters, real estate agents, life insurance agents, and officers of trust departments of banks. For years, bar associations complained about such activities. In many instances, they challenged the activities in court as the unauthorized practice of law. The problem was so pervasive that some bar associations negotiated a "statement of principles" (sometimes called a treaty) with these occupations in an attempt to identify boundary lines and methods of resolving difficulties. Most of these treaties, however, have been ineffective in defining the kinds of law-related activities that can and cannot be performed by nonattorneys. A tremendous amount of effort and money is needed to negotiate, monitor, and enforce the treaties. The resources are simply not available. Furthermore, there is a concern that such efforts by attorneys to restrain competition might violate the antitrust laws, as we will see later in the chapter.

Some practitioners of law-related occupations have gone directly to the legislature to seek enactment of statutes that authorize what would otherwise be the unauthorized practice of law. In many instances, they have been successful. For example:

**Ga.Code Ann. § 9-401 (Supp. 1970).**  § 9-401. . . . Provided that, a title insurance company may prepare such papers as it thinks proper, or necessary, in connection with a title which it proposes to insure, in order, in its opinion, for it to be willing to insure such title, where no charge is made by it for such papers.

**Utah Code Ann. 1968, 61-2-20.**  § 61-2-20. Rights and privileges of real estate salesmen—brokers.—It is expressly provided that a real estate salesman shall have the right to fill out and complete forms of legal documents necessary to any real estate transaction to which the said broker is a party as principal or agent, and which forms have been approved by the commission and the attorney general of the state of Utah. Such forms shall include a closing real estate contract, a short-form lease, and a bill of sale of personal property.

**Tenn. Code Ann. § 62-1325 (1955).**  § 62-1325. Licensed Real Estate Brokers may draw contracts to option, buy, sell, or lease real property.

The effect of such statutes is to allow members of designated occupations to perform certain legal tasks that are intimately related to their work without having to hire attorneys or without forcing their clients to hire them.

## (b)  Authorized Practice of Law

Examine the following phrase closely: unauthorized practice of law by non-attorneys. If there is such a thing as the *un*authorized practice of law, then, by implication, there must be an *authorized* practice of law. And indeed there is. The treaties and statutes discussed above are examples of this. There are also other areas where nonattorneys are given a special authorization to practice law. Occasionally attempts are made to call what they do something other than the *practice of law,* but as we will see, these attempts conflict with reality since the nonattorneys are doing what attorneys do within the sphere of the special authorization. These special authorizations have been vigorously opposed by attorneys on the ground that the authorizations conflict with the privileged domain of attorneys. The latter are not always this blunt in stating their opposition. The objection is usually couched in terms of "protection of the public," but in large measure, the opposition has its roots in turf protection. Attorneys are not above engaging in battles for economic self-preservation.

Some members of the public view attorneys as fighters, people who will pursue an issue to the bitter end. While this trait may place attorneys in a favorable light in the eyes of clients for whom they are doing battle, many feel that the aggressive inclination of the attorney can be counterproductive. Administrative agencies, for example, are often suspicious of the involvement of attorneys. They are viewed as combatants who want to turn every agency decision into an adversarial proceeding. Agencies often see courtroom gymnastics and gimmicks as the attorney's primary mode of operation. The attorney is argumentative to a fault.

This image of the attorney as someone who complicates matters is best summed up by an old accountant's joke that taxation becomes more and more complex in direct proportion to attempts by attorneys to *simplify* the tax law. Whether or not this view of the attorney is correct, it has accounted for some erosion of the legal profession's monopoly over the practice of law.

The unavailability of attorneys has also helped produce this result. A vast segment of our population has legal complaints that are never touched by lawyers. This is due, in part, to the fact that most of these complaints do not involve enough money to attract attorneys.

We now turn to a fuller exploration of these themes under the following headings:

1. Court "representation" by nonattorneys

2. Attempted restrictions on the activities of the "jailhouse lawyer" and the broader policy considerations raised by such restrictions

3. Agency representation by nonattorneys

### (1)  Court Representation

In the vast majority of courts in this country, only attorneys can represent someone in a judicial proceeding. There are, however, some limited—but dramatic—exceptions.

In Maryland, a nonattorney employee of a nonprofit legal service office can represent tenants in a summary ejectment proceeding in the District Court of Maryland! A special Lay Advocacy Program oversees this form of court advocacy by nonattorneys.[3] Another extraordinary example exists in North Dakota where lay advocates assist women who are petitioners seeking protective orders in domestic violence cases. Some judges "encourage and allow" the lay advocate "to conduct direct and cross-examination of witnesses and make statements to the court." A proposal has been made to formalize this activity by creating a new position called a Certified Domestic Violence Advocate. Under this proposal, the following activities of this nonattorney would *not* be considered the unauthorized practice of law: helping a petitioner fill out printed forms, sitting with the petitioner during court proceedings, and making written or oral statements to the court.[4]

There are some lower courts in the country, particularly in the West, where parties can have nonattorneys represent them. Examples include Justice of the Peace Courts, Magistrates Courts, and Small Claims Courts. It is relatively rare, however, for parties to have any representation in such courts.

---

[3]*Lay Advocacy Program Defends Indigent Tenants,* 6 Bar Bulletin 3 (Maryland Bar Ass'n, January 1991). Annotated Code of Maryland § 10–101 (1991 Supp).
[4]*Role of Lay Advocates in Domestic Violence Proceedings,* 15 Note Pad 1 (State Bar Ass'n of North Dakota, April 5, 1991).

As we learned in Chapter 2, Tribal Courts on Indian reservations have jurisdiction over designated civil and criminal matters involving Native Americans. In many of these courts, both parties are represented by nonattorney advocates.

Government employees occasionally act in a representative or semi-representative capacity in court proceedings, even though they are not attorneys. In North Carolina cases involving the termination of parental rights, for example, the United States Supreme Court has noted the role of nonattorneys:

> In fact, . . . the North Carolina Departments of Social Services are themselves sometimes represented at termination hearings by social workers instead of by lawyers.[5]

It is well known that attorneys waste a good deal of pretrial time traveling to court and waiting around simply to give documents to the judge and to set dates for the various stages of pretrial and trial proceedings. Another problem is that an attorney may have to be in two different courtrooms at the same time. For example, the time spent at an early morning hearing may be unexpectedly extended so that the attorney cannot appear at a previously scheduled mid-morning proceeding in another courtroom on a different case. In such situations, wouldn't it be helpful if the attorney's paralegal could "appear" in court for the limited purpose of delivering papers to the judge, asking for a new date, or presenting some other message? *In most states, such activity is strictly prohibited.*

On August 16, 1982, a Kentucky paralegal learned about this prohibition in a dramatic way. Her attorney was involved in a trial at the Jefferson Circuit Court. He asked the paralegal to go to another courtroom during "Motion Hour," where attorneys make motions or schedule future proceedings on a case. He told her to ask for a hearing date on another case that he had pending. She did so. When the case was called during "Motion Hour," she rose, identified herself as the attorney's paralegal, and gave the message to the judge, asking for the hearing date. Opposing counsel was outraged. He verbally assaulted the paralegal in the courtroom and filed a motion to hold the paralegal and her attorney in contempt of court for the unauthorized practice of law. When a hearing was later held on this motion, members of a local paralegal association packed the courtroom. Tensions were high. When the judge eventually *denied* the motion, after a hearing on the matter, the audience broke out into loud applause. "Apparently the judge concluded that [the paralegal] had rendered no service involving legal knowledge or advice, but had merely transmitted to the court [the attorney's] message regarding disposition of the motion, that is, she had been performing a function that was administrative, not legal in nature."[6]

About twenty years earlier, a celebrated Illinois opinion, *People v. Alexander,*[7] took a position similar to this Kentucky court. In this opinion, the defendant was an unlicensed law clerk who appeared before the court to state that his employing attorney could not be present in court at the moment because he was trying a case elsewhere. On behalf of his employer, the law clerk requested a continuance. The defendant's actions were challenged. It was argued that any

[5]*Lassiter v. Dept. of Social Services,* 452 U.S. 18, 29, 101 S.Ct. 2153, 2161, 68 L.Ed.2d 640, 651 (1981).
[6]Winter, *No Contempt in Kentucky,* 7 Nat'l Paralegal Reporter 8 (Nat'l Federation of Paralegal Associations, Winter 1982).
[7]53 Ill. App. 2d 299, 202 N.E.2d 841 (1964).

### People v. Alexander

Appellate Court of Illinois, First District
53 Ill. App. 2d 299, 202 N.E.2d 841 (1964)

. . .

In the case of People ex rel. Illinois State Bar Ass'n v. People's Stock Yards State Bank, 344 Ill. 462, at page 476, 176 N.E. 901, at page 907, wherein a bank was prosecuted for the unauthorized practice of law, the following quotation is relied upon:

"According to the generally understood definition of the practice of law in this country, it embraces the preparation of pleadings, and other papers incident to actions and special proceedings, and the management of such actions and proceedings on behalf of clients before judges and courts * * *."

Since this statement relates to the appearance and management of proceedings in court on behalf of a client, we do not believe it can be applied to a situation where a clerk hired by a law firm presents information to the court on behalf of his employer.

We agree with the trial judge that clerks should not be permitted to make motions or participate in other proceedings which can be considered as "managing" the litigation. However, if apprising the court of an employer's engagement or inability to be present constitutes the making of a motion, we must hold that clerks may make such motions for continuances without being guilty of the unauthorized practice of law. Certainly with the large volume of cases appearing on the trial calls these days, it is imperative that this practice be followed.

In Toth v. Samuel Phillipson & Co., 250 Ill.App. 247 (1928) the court said at page 250:

"It is well known in this county where numerous trial courts are sitting at the same time the exigencies of such a situation require that trial attorneys be represented by their clerical force to respond to some of the calls, and that the court acts upon their response the same as if the attorneys of record themselves appeared in person."

After that opinion was handed down, the number of judges was substantially increased in the former Circuit and Superior Courts and the problem of answering court calls has at least doubled. We cannot add to the heavy burden of lawyers who in addition to responding to trial calls must answer pre-trial calls and motion calls—all held in the morning—by insisting that a lawyer must personally appear to present to a court a motion for a continuance on grounds of engagement or inability to appear because of illness or other unexpected circumstances. To reduce the backlog, trial lawyers should be kept busy actually trying lawsuits and not answering court calls.

appearance by nonattorneys before a court in which they give information as to the availability of counsel or the status of litigation constitutes the unauthorized practice of law. The Illinois court took the unique position that this was not the practice of law. The reasoning of the court is presented in the excerpt from the opinion printed above.

It must be emphasized that most states would *not* agree with Kentucky and Illinois. Most states would prohibit nonattorneys from doing what was authorized in these two states. Fortunately, however, there are at least a few additional states that have begun to move in the direction of the minority view.

The Allen County Bar Association of Indiana has taken the bold move of permitting paralegals to perform what hitherto had been considered attorney functions in court. A paralegal is authorized:

- To "take" default judgments
- To "set" pretrial conferences, uncontested divorces, and all other hearing dates
- To "file" stipulations or motions for dismissal
- Etc.

The paralegal, however, must perform these tasks with court personnel other than judges; nonattorneys cannot communicate directly with judges.

The vast majority of attorneys in the country would be amazed to learn what is going on in Allen County. Once the shock subsides, however, these attorneys will probably see the wisdom and common sense of what Allen County has done and begin to think of ways to try it themselves.

The rules of the Allen County program are as follows:

---

**Paralegal Rules of Practice**
**Allen County Bar Association (Indiana)**

1. Generally, a legal assistant employee shall be limited to the performance of tasks which do not require the exercising of legal discretion or judgment that affects the legal right of any person.

2. All persons employed as legal assistants shall be registered [see Figure 4.2] by their employer law firm with the Allen County Circuit and Superior Court Administrator and the Clerk of the Allen Superior and Circuit Courts. Said law firm shall, by affidavit, state that it shall be bound and liable for the actions of its legal assistant employee, and that any and all actions or statements made by such personnel shall be strictly and completely supervised by his employer member of the Bar. All documents the legal assistant presents or files must contain the attorney's signature, either as an attorney for the petitioning party, or a statement affixed indicating that the documents were prepared by said attorney. Each law firm shall certify in writing that the legal assistant employee is qualified in each field in which they will act with the Courts (probate, dissolution of marriage, collection, etc.). A copy of such statement and certification shall be given to such legal assistant and shall be carried by such person whenever activity with the Court is pursued by such person. There shall be one legal assistant certified by each law office desiring same, but [an] alternate shall be allowed in case of illness, vacation or unavailability. However, in those instances where a single law firm has more than one full time legal assistant, each of whom operate in separate specialized areas, a certification can be had by more than one person, showing that such person's specialization on a full time basis is limited to one specific area. Otherwise, there should be a limit of one person certified as a legal assistant per law firm.

3. Such employee shall be limited to the following acts:

(a) Such employee may take default judgments upon the filing of an affidavit in each case stating the amount of damages and that proper service was obtained sworn to by affidavit.

(b) Such employee shall have authority to set Pre-Trial Conferences, Uncontested Divorces, and all other hearing dates.

(c) Such employee shall have authority to obtain trust account deposits at the Allen County Clerk's Office but only in the name of his employer firm.

(d) Such employee shall have authority to file stipulations or motions for dismissal.

(e) Such an employee shall have the authority to do all filing of documents and papers with the Clerk of the Allen Superior Courts and Circuit Court where such documents and papers are not to be given to anyone authorized to affix a judge's signature or issue Court orders.

(f) Notwithstanding the limitations of subparagraph (e) above, such employee shall have the authority to obtain from the law clerk the signature stamp of the judge on non-discretionary standard orders and notices, such as notice of hearing, and orders to appear and to answer interrogatories on the filing of a Verified Motion for Proceedings Supplemental. Note: Standard orders which depart from the usual format, restraining orders, suit and support orders, bench warrants, and body attachments must be secured by an attorney.

(g) Such employee is not to negotiate with opposing litigants within the Courthouse nor confer with a judge on legal matters. Matters requiring communications with a judge, require an attorney.

(h) Where circumstances permit, attorneys shall take precedence over such employees in dealings with courts and clerks.

---

Note again that the above program does not allow the paralegal to talk directly with a judge in performing the authorized tasks. ("Matters requiring communications with a judge, require an attorney.") Why such a restriction? Wouldn't it make sense to allow paralegal-judge communication on some procedural matters that are of a routine nature? *No*, would be the response of most bar associations.

*Yes*, however, is the refreshing response of several county bar associations in the state of Washington. Under the sponsorship of the Seattle-King County

**FIGURE 4.2**

Allen County
Circuit and
Superior Court
Certification of
Legal Assistants

---

**STATEMENT OF CERTIFICATION**

This is to certify that _____
is employed by the law firm of _____.
Said law firm binds itself and takes full responsibility and liability for the actions of its legal
assistant employee above-named and that any and all actions or statements made by such
personnel shall be strictly and completely supervised by a member of the Bar of the State
of Indiana. This is to certify that the above-mentioned legal assistant is qualified to assist
an attorney in the _____ area of law.

**LAW FIRM OF:**_____

        **BY:**_____

**STATE OF INDIANA, COUNTY OF ALLEN, SS:**

Subscribed and sworn to before me, a Notary Public in and for said County and State, this
_____ day _____ , 19_____ .

_____
                                    **Notary Public**

---

Bar Association and the Tacoma-Pierce County Bar Association, paralegals are allowed to "present" certain orders to judges. The orders must be those that the parties have already agreed on, or must be ex parte (which means involving one party only). In presenting such orders to a judge, the paralegal must obviously deal directly with—and perhaps even communicate with—an almighty judge! The prohibition in Allen County, Indiana on communicating with a judge does not exist in these two counties of Washington state.

## (2)  The Jailhouse Lawyer

A *jailhouse lawyer* is a nonattorney who helps fellow prisoners with their legal problems. Some prisons attempted to prevent the jailhouse lawyer from providing this legal assistance even though no meaningful alternatives for such assistance were provided by the prisons. This prohibition was struck down, however, by the United States Supreme Court in *Johnson v. Avery* in 1969. The basis of the opinion was that without the jailhouse lawyer, prisoners may not have access to the courts. The concurring opinion of Justice Douglas has become one of the most widely quoted and influential statements in the field of paralegalism.

---

**Johnson v. Avery**
Supreme Court of the United States, 1969.
393 U.S. 483, 89 S.Ct. 747, 21 L.Ed.2d 718

. . .

Mr. Justice DOUGLAS, concurring.

While I join the opinion of the Court [in striking down the prohibition on the activities of jailhouse lawyers] I add a few words in emphasis of the important thesis of the case.

The increasing complexities of our governmental apparatus at both the local and the federal levels have made it difficult for a person to process a claim or even to make a complaint. Social security is a virtual maze; the hierarchy that governs urban housing is often so intricate that it takes an expert to know what agency has jurisdiction over a particular complaint; the office to call or official to see for noise abatement, for a broken sewer line, or a fallen tree is a mystery to many in our metropolitan areas.

A person who has a claim assertable in faraway Washington, D.C., is even more helpless, as evidenced by the increasing tendency of constituents to rely on their congressional delegation to identify, press, and process their claims.

We think of claims as grist for the mill of the lawyers. But it is becoming abundantly clear that more and more of the effort in ferreting out the basis of claims and the agencies responsible for them and in preparing the almost endless paperwork for their prosecution is work for laymen. There are not enough lawyers to manage or supervise all of these affairs; and much of the basic work done requires no special legal talent. *Yet there is a closed-shop philosophy in the legal profession that cuts down drastically active roles for laymen. . . . That traditional, closed-shop attitude is utterly out of place in the modern world where claims pile high and much of the work of tracing and pursuing them requires the patience and wisdom of a layman rather than the legal skills of a member of the bar.* [Emphasis added.]

"If poverty lawyers are overwhelmed, some of the work can be delegated to sub-professionals. New York law permits senior law students to practice law under certain supervised conditions. Approval must first be granted by the appellate division. A rung or two lower on the legal profession's ladder are laymen legal technicians, comparable to nurses and lab assistants in the medical profession. Large law firms employ them, and there seems to be no reason why they cannot be used in legal services programs to relieve attorneys for more professional tasks." Samore, Legal Services for the Poor, 32 Albany L.Rev. 509, 515–516 (1968).

The plight of a man in prison may in these respects be even more acute than the plight of a person on the outside. He may need collateral proceedings to test the legality of his detention or relief against management of the parole system or against defective detainers lodged against him which create burdens in the nature of his incarcerated status. He may have grievances of a civil nature against those outside the prison. His imprisonment may give his wife grounds for divorce and be a factor in determining the custody of his children; and he may have pressing social security, workmen's compensation, or veterans' claims.

While the demand for legal counsel in prison is heavy, the supply is light. For private matters of a civil nature, legal counsel for the indigent in prison is almost nonexistent. Even for criminal proceedings, it is sparse. While a few States have post-conviction statutes providing such counsel, most States do not. Some States like California do appoint counsel to represent the indigent prisoner in his collateral hearings, once he succeeds in making out a prima facie case. But as a result, counsel is not on hand for preparation of the papers or for the initial decision that the prisoner's claim has substance.

## Notes

1. "Jailhouse lawyers, or *writ writers,* as they are sometimes called, have always been part of prison society. But in recent years their numbers as well as the amount of litigation they generate, his increased substantially. In 1985, prisoners filed 33,400 petitions in federal and state courts, . . ." One

Jailhouse lawyer,
Fernando Jackson,
Soledad Prison, California

jailhouse lawyer at Soledad prison "devotes 16 hours a day to his legal work, subscribes to dozens of legal publications (at a cost of $1,800 a year), and files a steady stream of lawsuits." Suing "has become almost a national pastime. Prisoners act no differently from other citizens in a litigious society." Kroll, *Counsel Behind Bars: Jailhouse Lawyers . . .* , 7 California Lawyer 34 (June 1987).

2. The *Johnson* opinion stressed that the prison provided *no* alternative to the jailhouse lawyer. If alternatives had been available, the inmate would not be allowed to practice law. In *Williams v. U.S. Dep't of Justice*, 433 F.2d 958 (5th Cir. 1970), the court held that the presence of law students in the prison could be an alternative, but only if it is demonstrated that the students are meeting the need for inmate legal services. If the inmates had to wait a considerable period of time, for example, before they could be interviewed by the law students, then no alternative existed and the jailhouse lawyer could not be prevented from helping other inmates.

3. In *Gilmore v. Lynch*, 319 F. Supp. 105 (N.D. Cal. 1970), affirmed by the United States Supreme Court in *Younger v. Gilmore*, 404 U.S. 15 (1971), the court held that California either had to satisfy the legal needs of its prisoners or expand the prison law library to include a more comprehensive collection of law books. See also *Bounds v. Smith*, p. 221.

4. Finally, the right of an inmate to assist a fellow inmate in legal matters does *not* extend to representing the inmate in court. *Guajardo v. Luna*, 432 F.2d 1324 (5th Cir. 1970). Nor can a nonattorney represent an inmate in court even if this nonattorney is not an inmate himself or herself. This latter point was decided by the United States Supreme Court in *Hackin v. Arizona*, 389 U.S. 143 (1967).

5. How far can the rationale of *Johnson* be extended? Suppose, for example, it is demonstrated that many claimants before state administrative agencies are not receiving legal services because attorneys cannot be afforded. Would the *Johnson* opinion permit paralegal representation before such agencies even if the latter prohibited it? What is the difference between an inmate's right to have access to the courts and *anyone's* right to complain to an agency? How do you think Justice Douglas would handle the case if it came before him?

"Although the *Johnson* case is admittedly narrow in scope, it does nevertheless, give aid and comfort to the view that whenever lawyers are unavailable for whatever reason, society will sanction alternative systems for the delivery of legal services. The paramount consideration will not be ethics nor the exclusivity of the right to practice law, but rather it will be the facilitation of access routes to the grievance machinery set up for the resolution of claims. If lawyers are not available to assist the citizenry with these claims, then the question arises as to whether skilled nonlawyers represent a viable alternative. The inevitability of this question becomes clear when we listen to the statistics on the demand for the services of a lawyer. Estimates have been made to the effect that if every lawyer devoted full time to the legal needs of the poor, there would still be a significant shortage of lawyers for the poor. If the legal needs of the middle class are added, the legal service manpower shortage becomes overwhelming." Statsky, W. and Lang, P., *The Legal Paraprofessional as Advocate and Assistant: Roles, Training Concepts and Materials*, 49–50 (1971).

See also Statsky, W., *Inmate Involvement in Prison Legal Services: Roles and Training Options for the Inmate as Paralegal* (American Bar

## Procunier v. Martinez

Supreme Court of the United States, 1974.
416 U.S. 396, 94 S.Ct. 1800, 40 L.Ed.2d 244

. . .

The District Court also enjoined continued enforcement of Administrative Rule MV-IV-02, which provides in pertinent part:

"Investigators for an attorney-of-record will be confined to not more than two. Such investigators must be licensed by the State or must be members of the State Bar. Designation must be made in writing by the Attorney."

By restricting access to prisoners to members of the bar and licensed private investigators, this regulation imposed an absolute ban on the use by attorneys of law students and legal paraprofessionals to interview inmate clients. In fact attorneys could not even delegate to such persons the task of obtaining prisoners' signatures on legal documents. The District Court reasoned that this rule constituted an unjustifiable restriction on the right of access to the courts. We agree.

The constitutional guarantee of due process of law has as a corollary the requirement that prisoners be afforded access to the courts in order to challenge unlawful convictions and to seek redress for violations of their constitutional rights. This means that inmates must have a reasonable opportunity to seek and receive the assistance of attorneys. Regulations and practices that unjustifiably obstruct the availability of professional representation or other aspects of the right of access to the courts are invalid. Ex parte Hull, 312 U.S. 546, 61 S.Ct. 640, 85 L.Ed. 1034 (1941).

The District Court found that the rule restricting attorney-client interviews to members of the bar and licensed private investigators inhibited adequate professional representation of indigent inmates. The remoteness of many California penal institutions makes a personal visit [by attorneys] to an inmate client a time-consuming undertaking. The court reasoned that the ban against the use of law students or other paraprofessionals for attorney-client interviews would deter some lawyers from representing prisoners who could not afford to pay for their traveling time or that of licensed private investigators. And those lawyers who agreed to do so would waste time that might be employed more efficaciously in working on the inmates' legal problems. Allowing law students and paraprofessionals to interview inmates might well reduce the cost of legal representation for prisoners. The District Court therefore concluded that the regulation imposed a substantial burden on the right of access to the courts.

## Bounds v. Smith

Supreme Court of the United States, 1977
430 U.S. 817, 97 S.Ct. 1491, 52 L.Ed.2d 72

[In this opinion the Supreme Court is again concerned with the need of prisoners to have access to the courts and the use of nonlawyers in helping to obtain that access. The Court held that prisons must assist inmates in the preparation and filing of meaningful legal papers by providing the inmates with adequate law libraries or adequate assistance from persons trained in the law. The Court rejected the claim that nonlawyer inmates were ill-equipped to use the "tools of the trade of the legal profession." In the Court's experience, nonlawyer petitioners are capable of using law books to file cases raising claims that are "serious and legitimate" whether or not such petitioners win the cases. In outlining the options available to a prison, the Court specifically referred to paralegals:]

It should be noted that while adequate law libraries are one constitutionally acceptable method to assure meaningful access to the courts, our decision here, . . ., does not foreclose alternative means to achieve that goal. Nearly half the States and the District of Columbia provide some degree of professional or quasi-professional legal assistance to prisoners. . . . Such programs take many imaginative forms and may have a number of advantages over libraries alone. Among the alternatives are the training of inmates as para-legal assistants to work under lawyers' supervision, the use of paraprofessionals and law students, either as volunteers or in formal clinical programs, the organization of volunteer attorneys through bar associations or other groups, the hiring of lawyers on a part-time consultant basis, and the use of full-time staff attorneys, working either in new prison legal assistance organizations or as part of public defender or legal services offices.

Association, Commission on Correctional Facilities and Services, Resource Center on Correctional Law and Legal Services, 1974).

. . . . . . . . . . . . . . .

Two other important Supreme Court cases involving nonattorneys in prison need to be considered: The *Procunier* case and the *Bounds* case. See page 221.

---

### ■ ASSIGNMENT 4.2

Jim Mookely is an attorney who represents fifty inmates on a consolidated case in the state court. The inmates are in fourteen different institutions throughout the state. Jim asks the director of the state prison system to allow his paralegal, Mary Smith, to interview all fifty inmates at a central location. The director responds as follows:

- He refuses to transport the inmates to one location. The inmates would have to be interviewed at the institutions where they are currently living.
- He refuses to let anyone in any institution unless the individual has either a law degree *or* has been through the prison's two-week orientation program totaling twenty hours in the evening at the state capital.

Mary Smith has not taken the orientation program, and it would be very inconvenient for her to do so since she lives 150 miles from the capital. How would *Johnson, Procunier,* or *Bounds* apply to this problem?

---

### (3) Agency Representation

A considerable number of administrative agencies will permit a paralegal or other nonattorney to represent clients at the agency. These individuals are usually called agents, practitioners, or representatives. They engage in informal advocacy for their clients at the agency or formal advocacy, including representation at an adversarial administrative hearing. (A proceeding is adversarial if another side appears in the controversy, whether or not the other side is represented. If there is no other side present in the matter before the agency, the proceeding is considered nonadversarial.) Often the issues before the agency are economic, statistical, or scientific, but legal issues are also involved. It is clear that in conducting an adversarial hearing before an agency, the nonattorney can be practicing law in a manner that is remarkably similar to an attorney's representation of a client in court. Our study of this phenomenon will begin with federal administrative agencies, and then we will cover state agencies.

*Nonattorney Practice before Federal Administrative Agencies.* For federal agencies, Congress has passed a statute, the Administrative Procedure Act, that gives each federal agency the power to decide for itself whether only attorneys can represent clients before it:

> **Administrative Procedure Act 5 U.S.C.A. § 555 (1967).** (b) A person compelled to appear in person before an agency is entitled to be accompanied, represented, and advised by counsel or, if permitted by the agency, by other qualified representative. . . .

See Appendix E on the extent of nonattorney representation in federal agencies.

When an agency decides to use this power to permit nonattorney representation, it can simply allow anyone to act as the agent or representative of another before the agency, or it can establish elaborate qualifications or standards of admission to practice before it. If the agency takes the latter course, its qualifications or standards could include a specialized test to demonstrate competency in the subject matter regulated by the agency, minimum educational or experience requirements, registration or enrollment on the agency's approved roster of representatives, and an agreement to abide by designated ethical rules of practice—a violation of which could result in suspension and "disbarment."

The United States Patent Office has established criteria for individuals to practice (as *registered agents*) before this agency by drafting and filing applications for patents, searching legal opinions on patentability, etc.[8] In 1982, there were approximately 12,000 registered agents who had met this criteria at the agency. Of this number, about 1,900 (or 15.8%) were nonattorneys. At the Interstate Commerce Commission, close to 10,000 nonattorney "practitioners" have been authorized to represent clients at ICC proceedings that often involve issues such as rate increases and service extensions for railroads and other transportation carriers.[9] Perhaps the largest use of nonattorneys in federal agencies is at the Internal Revenue Service within the Treasury Department.[10] Any certified public accountant is authorized to practice before the IRS. There are over 190,000 members of the American Institute of Certified Public Accountants, most of whom are not attorneys.[11] In addition, the IRS has enrolled, i.e., registered, thousands of nonattorneys to represent taxpayers at all administrative proceedings within the IRS. These individuals, called *enrolled agents,* charge clients fees for their services. (Once a dispute goes to court, however, an attorney must take over.) To become an enrolled agent, an individual must either pass a written IRS examination or prove that he or she once worked at the IRS for five years interpreting and applying tax laws. In most states there are organizations of enrolled agents; the major national organization is the National Association of Enrolled Agents.

While many federal agencies allow nonattorney representation, it is not true that extensive numbers of nonattorneys actually use the authority they have. A recent study by the American Bar Association of thirty-three federal administrative agencies reached the following conclusion: "We found that the overwhelming majority of agencies studied permit nonlawyer representation in both adversarial and nonadversarial proceedings. However, most of them seem to encounter lay practice very infrequently (in less than 5% of adjudications), while only a few encounter lay practice as often as lawyer practice. Thus, although universally permitted, lay practice before federal agencies rarely occurs."[12]

One agency where nonattorney representation is fairly high (about 15%) is the Social Security Administration. Paralegals are frequently appointed by clients (see Figure 4.3) to represent them before the agency. In 1983, a study compared the success of clients at hearings based upon the kind of representation they received. The results were as follows:

- 59% of clients were successful when they were represented by attorneys.

- 54.5% of clients were successful when they were represented by nonattorneys.

---

[8]37 C.F.R. 1.341–1.348 (1983).

[9]49 C.F.R. 1103.1–1103.5 (1983).

[10]31 C.F.R. 10.3–10.75 (1983); 20 U.S.C. 1242 (1975).

[11]Rose, *Representation by Non-Lawyers in Federal Administrative Agency Proceedings* (Administrative Conference of the United States, 1984); Vom Baur, *The Practice of Non-Lawyers before Administrative Agencies,* 15 Federal Bar Journal 99 (1955).

[12]ABA Standing Committee on Lawyers' Responsibility for Client Protection, *Report of 1984 Survey of Nonlawyer Practice before Federal Administrative Agencies* (October 19, 1984).

**FIGURE 4.3**

Appointment of Representative

```
                        DEPARTMENT OF
                    HEALTH AND HUMAN SERVICES
                    SOCIAL SECURITY ADMINISTRATION

NAME (Claimant) (Print or Type)              SOCIAL SECURITY NUMBER

WAGE EARNER (if different)                   SOCIAL SECURITY NUMBER

Section I                    APPOINTMENT OF REPRESENTATIVE

I appoint this individual _____
                                      (Name and Address)

to act as my representative in connection with my claim or asserted right under:

  ☐ Title II        ☐ Title XVI       ☐ Title IV FMSHA      ☐ Title XVIII
    (RSDI)             (SSI)             (Black Lung)          (Medicare Coverage)

I authorize this individual to make or give any request or notice; to present or elicit evidence; to obtain information; and to
receive any notice in connection with my pending claim or asserted right wholly in my stead.

SIGNATURE (Claimant)                         ADDRESS

TELEPHONE NUMBER                             DATE
(Area Code)

Section II                    ACCEPTANCE OF APPOINTMENT

I, _____ , hereby accept the above appointment. I certify
that I have not been suspended or prohibited from practice before the Social Security Administration; that I am not, as a current
or former officer or employee of the United States, disqualified from acting as the claimant's representative; and that I will not
charge or receive any fee for the representation unless it has been authorized in accordance with the laws and regulations referred
to on the reverse side hereof. In the event that I decide not to charge or collect a fee for the representation, I will notify the Social
Security Administration. (Completion of Section III satisfies this requirement.)

I am a / an _____
                       (Attorney, union representative, relative, law student, etc.)

SIGNATURE (Representative)                    ADDRESS

TELEPHONE NUMBER                             DATE
(Area code)

Section III (Optional)                WAIVER OF FEE
I waive my right to charge and collect a fee under Section 206 of the Social Security Act, and I release my client (the claimant)
from any obligations, contractual or otherwise, which may be owed to me for services I have performed in connection with
my client's claim or asserted right.

SIGNATURE (Representative)                    DATE


                              WAIVER OF DIRECT PAYMENT

I ONLY waive my right to direct certification of a fee from the withheld past-due benefits of my client (the claimant). I do
NOT, however, waive my right to petition for and be authorized to charge and collect a fee directly from my client.

SIGNATURE (Representative)                    DATE

Form SSA-1696-U4 (3-88)      (See Important Information on Reverse)
Detroy prior editions
                                                              FILE COPY
```

■ 43.7% of clients were successful when they represented themselves.[13]

Fees can be charged by attorneys or paralegals for these services, but the agency must specifically approve the fee. This is not to say, however, that attorneys and paralegals are treated alike. If an attorney successfully represents a claimant, the agency will deduct up to 25% of the claimant's award, which will be paid directly to the attorney to cover fees. On the other hand, if a paralegal successfully represents a claimant, the paralegal must collect the fee directly from the client, since the Social Security Administration will not deduct anything from the award in such cases.[14]

*Nonattorney Practice before State Administrative Agencies.* At the *state* level, there is often a similar system for authorizing nonattorneys to provide represen-

---

[13]DSS/OHA *Participant Involvement in Request for Hearing Cases for Fiscal 1983*, Table 6, (May, 1984).
[14]42 U.S.C. 406 (1975).

tation at many, but by no means all, state administrative agencies. Many states have their own version of the federal Administrative Procedure Act quoted above.

Of course, the organized bar has never been happy with this special authorization given to nonattorneys within federal or state administrative agencies. Since there are state statutes on who can practice law (and often criminal penalties for nonattorneys who practice law in violation of these statutes), how can an administrative agency allow a nonattorney to engage in activity that is clearly the practice of law? The answer to this question is somewhat different for federal and state agencies.

If the agency permitting nonattorney representation is a *federal* agency (for example, the United States Patent Office, the Interstate Commerce Commission, the Internal Revenue Service, and the Social Security Administration), its authorization takes precedence over any *state* laws on the practice of law that would prohibit it. This principle was established in the United States Supreme Court case of *Sperry v. State of Florida ex rel the Florida Bar.*[15] The case involved a nonattorney who was authorized to represent clients before the United States Patent Office. The Florida Bar claimed that the nonattorney was violating the state practice-of-law statute. The Supreme Court ruled that the *Supremacy Clause* of the United States Constitution gave federal laws supremacy over conflicting state laws. The Court also said:

> Examination of the development of practice before the Patent Office and its governmental regulation reveals that: (1) nonlawyers have practiced before the Office from its inception, with the express approval of the Patent Office and to the knowledge of Congress; (2) during prolonged congressional study of unethical practices before the Patent Office, the right of nonlawyer agents to practice before the Office went unquestioned, and there was no suggestion that abuses might be curbed by state regulation; (3) despite protests of the bar, Congress in enacting the Administrative Procedure Act refused to limit the right to practice before the administrative agencies to lawyers; and (4) the Patent Office has defended the value of nonlawyer practitioners while taking steps to protect the interests which a State has in prohibiting unauthorized practice of law. We find implicit in this history congressional (and administrative) recognition that registration in the Patent Office confers a right to practice before the Office without regard to whether the State within which the practice is conducted would otherwise prohibit such conduct.
>
> Moreover, the extent to which specialized lay practitioners should be allowed to practice before some 40-odd federal administrative agencies, including the Patent Office, received continuing attention both in and out of Congress during the period prior to 1952. The Attorney General's Committee on Administrative Procedure which, in 1941, studied the need for procedural reform in the administrative agencies, reported that "[e]specially among lawyers' organizations there has been manifest a sentiment in recent years that only members of the bar should be admitted to practice before administrative agencies. The Committee doubts that a sweeping interdiction of nonlawyer practitioners would be wise. . . ."

. . . . . . . . . . . . . .

Suppose, however, that a *state* agency permits nonattorney representation. Can this be challenged by the bar? The issue may depend on who has the *power* to regulate the practice of law in a particular state. If the state legislature has this power, then the agency authorization of nonattorney representation is valid, since the agency is under the jurisdiction and control of the legislature. So

---

[15] 373 U.S. 379, 83 S.Ct. 1322, 10 L.Ed.2d 428 (1963).

long as the nonattorney representation is based on a statute of the legislature, it is valid. If, however, the state judiciary has the power to control the practice of law in a state, then the courts may be able to invalidate any nonattorney representation that is authorized by the agency.

Nonattorneys who have the authority to provide representation at an administrative agency may do so as independent paralegals, or as full-time employees of attorneys. The following ethical opinion from California involves the latter—a paralegal employee of a law firm. The opinion discusses some of the issues that are involved when the law firm wants its paralegal to use the special authorization for nonattorney representation at a particular administrative agency—the Worker's Compensation Appeals Board. Later in Chapter 5 we will examine the ethical issues involved in this opinion in greater depth.

---

### Formal Opinion 1988–103
State Bar Committee on
Professional Responsibility and Conduct
California

#### Issue

May a law firm, having advised its clients of its intention to do so, delegate authority to a paralegal employee to make appearances at Workers' Compensation Appeals Board hearings and to file petitions, motions or other material?

#### Digest

A law firm may delegate such authority, provided that the paralegal employee is adequately supervised.

#### Authorities Interpreted

Rules 3-101, 3-103 and 6-101 of the Rules of Professional Conduct of the State Bar of California.

\* \* \*

#### Issue

A client has contracted for the services of a law firm for representation in a matter pending before the Workers' Compensation Appeals Board (hereinafter "WCAB"). The law firm employs and intends to utilize the services of the paralegal in connection with the proceedings pending before the WCAB to make appearances, file petitions and present motions.

The client has consented to the law firm utilizing the services of the paralegal, after being informed as to the potential consequences of representation by a person of presumably lesser qualification and skill than may be reasonably expected of an attorney. In addition, the status of the employee as a paralegal rather than an attorney will be fully disclosed at all proceedings at which the paralegal appears and on all documents which the paralegal prepares.

#### Discussion

It is unlawful for any person to practice law in this state without active membership in the State Bar of California. (Bus. & Prof. Code, ¶6125) The practice of law includes the performing of services in any matter pending in a court or administrative proceeding throughout its various stages, as well as the rendering of legal advice and counsel in the preparation of legal instruments and contracts by which legal rights are secured. (cf. *Smallberg v. State bar* (1931) 212 Cal. 113.)

It has been held that the representation of claimants before the Industrial Accident Commission (predecessor to the WCAB) constitutes the performance of legal services. (*Bland v. Reed* (1968) 261 Cal.App.2d 445, 448.) However, the representation by a nonattorney of an applicant before the WCAB is expressly authorized by Labor Code 5501 and 5700 as follows:

> The application may be filed with the appeals board by any party in interest, his attorney, or other representative authorized in writing . . .,
> . . . Either party may be present at any hearing, in person, by attorney, or by any other agent, and may present testimony pertinent under the pleading.

Thus, the principal issue is whether an attorney may hire a nonattorney to engage in conduct on behalf of the attorney's client which the employee is authorized to perform independently, but which, if performed by the attorney, would constitute the practice of law.

It is the opinion of the Committee that because the client has been informed about, and has consented to the involvement of the paralegal, no violation occurs with respect to dishonesty or deceit. (See Bus. & Prof. Code, ¶6106, 6128, subd.(a).) In addition, if the status of the employee as a paralegal rather than attorney is fully disclosed at all proceedings at which the paralegal appears and on all documents which the paralegal prepares, no violation of the prohibition on an attorney lending his or her name to be used as an attorney by a person not licensed to practice law will occur. (See Bus. & Prof. Code, ¶6105.)

In addition, because Labor Code sections 5501 and 5570 expressly authorize nonattorneys to represent applicants before the WCAB, the proposed arrangements would not constitute a violation of Rule of Professional Conduct 3-101(A), which provides as follows:

> A member of the State Bar shall not aid any person, association, or corporation in the *unauthorized* practice of law. (Emphasis added.)

Further, there is no indication that the facts presented that the relationship between the paralegal and the law firm would constitute a partnership in violation of Rule of Professional Conduct 3-103, which provides as follows:

> A member of the State Bar shall not form a partnership with a person not licensed to practice law if any of the activities of the partnership consist of the practice of law.

The pivotal consideration is that the client contracted for the services of the law firm, rather than a paralegal, for representation. However, since the safeguards mentioned above have been taken to avoid misleading or deceiving the client or any one else regarding the status of the paralegal, the Committee finds no ethical insufficiency inherent in the participation of paralegals.

A lawyer or law firm contemplating entering into such an arrangement should remember that an attorney stands in a fiduciary relationship with the client. (*Krusesky v. Baugh* (1982) 138 Cal.App.3d 562, 567.) When acting as a fiduciary, the law imposes upon a member the strictest duty of prudent conduct as well as an obligation to perform his or her duties to the best of the attorney's ability. (*Clark v. State Bar* (1952) 39 Cal.2d 161, 167; and cf. Bus. & Prof. Code, ¶6067; Rule of Professional Conduct 6-101(A). However, an

attorney does not have to bear the entire burden of attending to every detail of the practice, but may be justified in relying to some extent on nonattorney employees. (*Moore v. State Bar* (1964) 62 Cal.2d 74, 80; *Vaughn v. State Bar* (1972) 6 Cal.3d 847, 857.)

The attorney who delegates responsibilities to his or her employees must keep in mind that he or she, as the attorney, has the duty to adequately supervise the employee. In fact, the attorney will be subject to discipline if the lawyer fails to adequately supervise the employee. (*Chefsky v. State Bar* (1984) 36 Cal.3d 116, 123; *Palomo v. State bar* (1984) 36 Cal.3d 785; *Gassman v. State Bar* (1976) 18 Cal.3d 125.)

What constitutes adequate supervision will, of course, depend on a number of factors, including, but not limited to, the complexity of the client matter, the level of experience of the paralegal and the facts of the particular case.

It is the opinion of the Committee that, even though the paralegal will be providing substantive legal services to the client, adequate supervision under these unique facts does not require the attorney to ensure that the paralegal performs the services in accordance with the level of competence that would be expected of the attorney under rule 6-101.

So long as the paralegal is adequately supervised and the law firm does not mislead the client that the services will be performed in accordance with the attorney level of competence or that an attorney will be handling the matter, the Committee does not believe the attorney would be in violation of the Rules of Professional Conduct.

This opinion is issued by the Standing Committee on Professional Responsibility and Conduct of the State Bar of California. It is advisory only. It is not binding upon the courts, the State Bar of California, its Board of Governors, or any persons or tribunals charged with regulatory responsibility or any member of the State Bar.

---

## ■ ASSIGNMENT 4.3

Make a list of every state and local administrative agency in your state. Have a class discussion in which students identify as many state and local agencies as they can. Then divide the total number of agencies by the number of students in the class so that each student will be assigned the same number of agencies. For your agencies, find out whether nonattorneys can represent citizens. What are the requirements, if any, to provide this representation informally (e.g., calling or writing the agency on behalf of someone else) or formally (e.g., representing someone else at an agency hearing)? Check your state statutes. Check the regulations of the agency. If possible, call the agency to ask what its policy is and whether it can refer you to any statutes or regulations on the policy.

■ **ASSIGNMENT 4.4**

Paul is a nonattorney who works at the Quaker Draft Counseling Center. One of the clients of the center is Dan Diamond. Paul says the following to Mr. Diamond:

> You don't have anything to worry about. The law says that you cannot be drafted until you have had an administrative hearing on your case. I will represent you at that hearing. If you are drafted before that hearing, I will immediately draft a habeas corpus petition that can be filed at the United States District Court.

Any problems with Paul's conduct?

 Section C. Licensing of Paralegals

Many occupations (electricians, brokers, nurses, etc.) are licensed by the government. To date, *no* federal, state, or local government has imposed a licensing requirement on traditional paralegals. Proposals for licensing have been made in some legislatures, but none has been enacted into law. For paralegals who work under the supervision of attorneys, licensing is arguably unnecessary, since the public is protected by this supervision. But what about the relatively small number of independent paralegals who work directly with the public without attorney supervision? Many have argued that there *is* a need to license them in order to protect the public. The phrase *limited licensing* refers to a government authorization to perform a designated number of activities that are now part of the attorney monopoly. While no limited licensing proposal has yet been enacted into law, the likelihood of passage is very real in spite of substantial attorney opposition. Before covering limited licensing, let's examine efforts to enact broad-based licensing schemes covering all activities of all paralegals.

### Broad-Based Licensing

A number of states have proposed legislation to license all paralegals. Many of these proposals confuse the word *certification* with *licensure*. Certification is usually a statement by a *non*governmental organization that a person has met certain qualifications. Licensure, on the other hand, is a permission or authorization *by a government* to engage in a certain activity.

In 1977, for example, the Michigan legislature gave serious consideration to passing the Legal Assistant Act to "regulate the practice of legal assistants." Under this proposal, a nine-member commission would be created to establish the requirements for the "certification" of legal assistants. Even though the proposal uses the word *certification*, it was a licensure program, since it would establish the qualifications to engage in a particular occupation. If this legislation had been enacted, a person could not be a legal assistant in Michigan without passing a statewide examination and having the educational credentials identified by the commission.

This plan was *not* adopted in Michigan. Such licensing schemes are usually vigorously opposed by paralegal associations as being premature, unnecessary, and unduly restrictive. A commonly voiced fear is that the license might limit what paralegals are now authorized to do without a license, and that some competent paralegals who now work in law offices might not fit within rigid eligibility criteria that might be established for the license. The organized bar is also opposed to broad-based licensing. The following excerpts from bar association reports give some of the reasons why:

**North Carolina Bar,** *Report of Special Committee on Paralegals* 3 (1980)

Several states have considered the possibility of adopting a licensing statute for paralegals, but none has done so. Licensing itself is subject to great public and legislative concern at present. So long as the work accomplished by non-lawyers for lawyers is properly supervised and reviewed by a licensed and responsible attorney, there would seem to be no need for a further echelon of licensing for the public's protection. Furthermore, licensing might be more dangerous than helpful to the public. The apparent stamp of approval of a license possibly could give the impression to the public that a person having such a license is qualified to deal directly with and give legal advice to the public. Although the Committee would not attempt to close the door on licensing of paralegals in the future if circumstances change and if, for example, the use of independent, non-lawyer employee paralegals were to become widespread, present conditions, at least, do not call for any program of licensing for paralegals.

**Illinois State Bar Association,** *Report on the Joint Study Committee on Attorney Assistants* 6 (6/21/77)

Our Joint Committee arose because there was a suggestion that attorney assistants be licensed. After due consideration we recommend no program of licensure or certification of attorney assistants or other lay personnel.

We are opposed to licensure because the standards on which licensure are to be based are difficult or impossible to formulate. Furthermore, we have started with a premise that precedes this conclusion; to wit: no delegation of any task to an attorney assistant shall diminish the responsibility of the attorney for the services rendered. We believe that any program which purports to say who is "licensed" and who is "not licensed" creates a standard which will diminish the attorney's responsibility. It furthermore may exclude from useful and desirable employment people who, under the supervision and control of an attorney, may perform useful tasks but who may not meet the standards of licensure involved.

We are further opposed to licensure because of the danger that it poses to the public. If a group of persons appears to be authorized to perform tasks directly for the public, without the intervening control of an attorney, it would be humanly inevitable that many of the licensed persons would try to deal directly with the public. We think these risks would be substantially increased by licensure.

---

## ■ ASSIGNMENT 4.5

How would you characterize the opposition to licensure expressed in the above excerpts from the bar reports? Do you think there is a conflict of interest in attorneys making these judgments about paralegal control? Explain.

---

## Limited Licensing

As we saw earlier, some independent, or freelance, paralegals have their own businesses, through which they sell their services to attorneys. A smaller number work directly for the public without attorney supervision. For example, a paralegal might sell divorce forms and type them for clients. This is not the illegal practice of law, so long as no legal advice is given in the process. One of the reasons Rosemary Furman got into trouble was that she gave such advice along with the forms she typed, and hence was charged with the unauthorized practice of law by the Florida bar.

Some have argued that the law that led to the prosecution of people like Rosemary Furman should be changed. Why not grant them a limited license (sometimes called a specialty license) to practice law? Remarkably, a suggestion to this effect was actually made by a Commission of the American Bar Association! The ABA does not favor broad-based licensing of all paralegals. In a 1986 report, however, an ABA Commission on Professionalism cautiously suggested—on page 52 of the report—that there be "limited licensing of paralegals" and "paraprofessionals" to perform certain functions such as handling some real estate closings, drafting simple wills, and performing certain tax work. The report argued that such a proposal could help reduce the cost of legal services:

> No doubt, many wills and real estate closings require the services of a lawyer. However, it can no longer be claimed that lawyers have the exclusive possession of the esoteric knowledge required and are therefore the only ones able to advise clients on any matter concerning the law.[16]

This remarkable proposal caused quite a stir. Many refer to the controversy it created as the "page 52 debate." For years, many attorneys were suspicious of paralegalism because of a fear that paralegals might eventually be licensed and compete with attorneys. Then along comes a report of an ABA Commission that recommends licensing! Yet it must be remembered that neither the report nor the Commission speaks for the entire ABA. In fact, the proposal in the report "drew the ire" of other ABA members *and is unlikely to be given serious consideration by the ABA as a whole any time soon.* This will not, however, prevent continued suggestions in favor of some form of licensing—even from within segments of the ABA itself.

Before paralegals had time to recover from the drama of the "page 52 debate," another shock wave arrived. In 1989, the State Bar of California stated that there was "an overwhelming unmet need" for better access to legal services, and created a *Commission on Legal Technicians* to study whether independent paralegals can help meet this need. Its answer was *yes!* The Commission recommended that the California Supreme Court adopt a Rule of Court authorizing nonattorneys to engage in the practice of law in the following three areas: bankruptcy law, family law, and landlord-tenant law. (Other areas might be added later.) As "licensed independent paralegals," they would not be required to have attorney supervision. They could open an office and sell their services directly to the public. In effect, the state's rules on the unauthorized practice of law would be abolished for those services. Court representation, however, would not be included. If a client needed to go to court, an attorney would have to be hired. This "limited license" program would be administered by the California State Department of Consumer Affairs with help from an Advisory Committee consisting of two independent paralegals, one attorney, and four members of the public who are not independent paralegals or attorneys.

Here are some of the other features of the proposal:

■ Applicants for the license must be at least 18 years of age.

■ Applicants must submit fingerprints.

---

[16]*In the Spirit of Public Service: A Blueprint for Rekindling of Lawyer Professionalism*, 52 (ABA, Comm'n on Professionalism, 1986).

- Applicants must take and pass a two-part written examination: (1) a general knowledge examination, including an ethics section, and (2) a specialty exam in an area of practice. In order to be licensed, an applicant must take and pass both the general and specialty examinations within a two-year period.

- Applicants must meet minimum levels of education and/or experience, as recommended by the Advisory Committee. However, as of the date of implementation of the enabling legislation, persons who have practiced in the field for two years should have the right to take the examination without additional entry requirements. (The last sentence constitutes the grandfathering provision of the proposal.)

- For license renewal, licensees must fulfill annual continuing education requirements.

- Complaints and investigations would be handled by the Department of Consumer Affairs' centralized services.

- A client security fund would be established to provide compensation to victims of independent paralegal thefts. The initial annual fee would be $25.00 per licensee and the Advisory Committee would develop recommended guidelines for disbursement, including an appropriate cap to be placed on each claim paid by the fund.

- Standards for denial of licensure and for discipline would be established.

- The Supreme Court would approve a code of professional conduct for licensed independent paralegals.

The reaction among paralegals to this proposal has been surprisingly mixed. The two national paralegal associations—the National Association of Legal Assistants (NALA) and the National Federation of Paralegal Associations (NFPA)—have taken very different positions. As we will see later, this is not the first time that these two giants have clashed over the issue of regulating paralegals.

The National Association of Legal Assistants is *against* the California proposal for a number of reasons. First, the proposal does not provide guidelines to determine the kinds of bankruptcy, family law, or landlord-tenant cases an independent paralegal is competent to handle. Many of these cases are complex at the outset or become complex as they unfold. Such cases require the attention of an attorney. Independent paralegals are not in the best position to determine when a case is beyond their skills. Second, the licensing of independent paralegals could eventually lead to a climate in which traditional paralegals and legal assistants who work for attorneys would have to become licensed. Third, the licensing of independent paralegals will lead to open warfare with attorneys and to public disillusionment with the legal system. "For all practical purposes . . ." the independent paralegals covered by the California proposal, ". . . will become direct and fierce competitors of . . . lawyers who will not look kindly upon these untrained 'mini-lawyers.' It is only a matter of time . . . [until] the inevitable will occur; the public will have a bad experience working with one of these untrained, inadequately educated non-lawyers and it will become further disillusioned with the legal system. Thus the results will further blacken the public's image of lawyers and the law profession."[17] Finally, NALA objects to the use

---

[17]National Ass'n of Legal Assistants, *Statement to . . . State Bar of California* (1991).

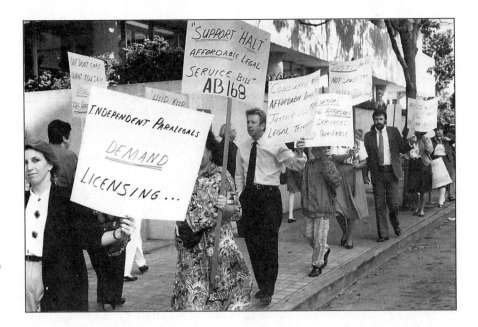

Demonstration in front of
the California State Bar
Association on the issue
of limited licensing

of the word *paralegal* for anyone who does not work under the supervision of an attorney.

The National Federation of Paralegal Associations, on the other hand, has taken a different approach. While not directly endorsing or opposing the California proposal, the NFPA has laid out the conditions under which it will support "regulation of paralegals who deliver legal services directly to the public." The conditions are as follows:

- the regulation expands the utilization of paralegals to deliver cost-efficient legal services,
- there is a demonstrated public need,
- the regulation includes minimum criteria for performing independent paralegal services such as experience under the supervision of an attorney or of a licensed paralegal,
- the paralegals pass a performance-based proficiency examination.

Applying these conditions to the California proposal, the NFPA would probably favor the proposal, although, as indicated, no formal position has been taken on it.

As revolutionary as this proposal is, there is another proposal in California from *HALT (Help Abolish Legal Tyranny)* that is even more radical. HALT is a national legal consumer group. It has proposed that nonattorneys be allowed to practice law in fourteen specialty areas.[18] A Board of Legal Technicians in the Department of Consumer Affairs would decide which of these specialty areas require registration (involving little more than providing information about yourself), and which require licensing (involving passing an examination).

---

[18]The areas are: Immigration law, family law, housing law, public benefits law, litigation support law, conservatorship and guardianship law, real estate law, liability law, estate administration law, consumer law, corporate/business law, intellectual property law, estate planning law, bankruptcy law. (Under the HALT proposal, other specialty areas might be added later.)

Other states are also considering proposals for limited licensing. In Illinois, for example, an Independent Paralegal Licensing Act was introduced in the legislature. The origin of this plan is quite interesting. A paralegal student designed a regulation plan as part of a class assignment. When this student went to work for an Illinois state legislator, the plan eventually became the basis of the licensing plan that was actually introduced in the legislature!

As you might expect, many attorneys have been intensely opposed to any form of limited licensing. A former president of the State Bar of California said, "It's like letting nurses do brain surgery." Here are some other comments from attorneys: "This is the worst thing since the plague!" They think "just about everybody should be able to practice law. I guess they think everybody should be able to slice open a belly and remove an appendix." "I cannot think of anything that would be more injurious to the public." This is an idea "whose time has not yet come." And "this is potentially the most fractious and controversial issue ever confronted" by the bar association. So far, such opposition has been successful since none of the limited license proposals have been enacted into law.

A much more modest form of limited licensing, however, has in fact been enacted into law in the state of Washington. A totally new category of worker has been created in the real estate industry, the *Limited Practice Officer* (LPO), also referred to as a Closing Certified Officer. This individual is a nonattorney with the authority "to select, prepare and complete legal documents incident to the closing of real estate and personal property transactions."[19] The State Supreme Court has created a Limited Practice Board to which applicants apply for "admission" to become an LPO. (See Figure 4.4.) The Board approves the form of the documents that the LPO can "select, prepare, and complete" in a closing, e.g., deeds, promissory notes, guaranties, deeds of trust, reconveyances, mortgages, satisfactions, security agreements, releases, Uniform Commercial Code documents, assignments, contracts, real estate excise tax affidavits, and bills of sale. Like the system for regulating attorneys, an LPO applicant must demonstrate "good moral character" and pass a combined essay and multiple-choice examination on the law. Once certified, LPOs can be disciplined for violating their authority. At present, there are no educational requirements to become an LPO, although such requirements are anticipated. LPOs must provide proof of financial responsibility by such means as purchasing a liability insurance policy ("errors and omissions insurance coverage") or showing that coverage exists under a bond taken out by their employer.

---

### ■ ASSIGNMENT 4.6

(a) Compare the LPO program in Washington with the two proposals for limited licensing in California.

(b) Do you agree with NALA's position on limited licensing, or that of NFPA? Why?

---

What are the chances of a licensing requirement becoming law? Even though proposals for broad-based licensing continue to appear, passage is unlikely in view of widespread opposition from attorneys and paralegals. Limited licensing, on the other hand, may eventually become a reality, in spite of the

---

[19]Washington Supreme Court Rule 12(a).

**FIGURE 4.4**

Application for Admission to Limited Practice as a Limited Practice Officer in the State of Washington under the Admission to Practice Rule 12

**To the Washington State Limited Practice Board:**

**I hereby apply for a limited license to practice law in the State of Washington as a limited practice officer under the Admission to Practice Rule 12.**

**Applicant's Name in Full** _____

Last                          First                          Middle

**Applicant's Date of Birth** _____

Month                       Day                          Year

**Applicant's Business Address** _____

Address

_____

City                          State                          Zip Code

**Applicant's Business Phone**   ( )_____

Area Code                   Number

**Applicant's Home Address**   _____

Address

_____

City                          State                          Zip Code

**Applicant's Home Tel. No.**   ( )_____

Area Code                   Number

**Applicant's Social Security Number** _____

Please list:

| **Employers/Supervisors** | **From** | **To** | **Telephone Number** |
|---|---|---|---|
| (Past five years) Attach separate sheet if needed. | | | |

position of NALA. The LPO program in Washington represents a small crack in the door. Will current proposals, such as those under serious consideration in California and Illinois, eventually kick the door through?

It is becoming increasingly difficult for attorneys to oppose limited licensing on the basis of the need to protect the public. A system now exists for identifying and punishing unscrupulous and incompetent attorneys; a similar system could be designed to regulate independent paralegals. And, of course, no one is proposing the equivalent of allowing nondoctors to perform brain surgery. The proposals for limited licensing simply try to identify services that do not require all of the skills of an attorney.

Perhaps the most compelling argument for limited licensing is the fact that attorneys have priced themselves out of the market. Recent studies continue to document a vast unmet need for legal services in our society. Attorneys, however, point to the reforms that have made legal services more accessible at a lower cost. See Figure 4.5. Yet, in spite of these reforms and in spite of the dramatic increase in the number of attorneys coming out of our law schools, the unmet need for legal services among the poor and middle class continues to grow. Here, for example, are some of the conclusions of legal-needs studies covering two large states:

> Each year in Illinois, by conservative estimates, 300,000 low-income families face approximately 1,000,000 civil legal problems for which they do not receive legal help.[20]

---
[20]Illinois State Bar Association and Chicago Bar Association, *Illinois Legal Needs Study* 5 (1989).

- *Pro bono work.* Many law firms and corporations give their attorneys time off to provide free legal services to the poor.
- *Simplified forms.* Bar associations have helped create legal forms that are relatively easy for the public to use without the assistance of an attorney.
- *Prepaid legal services.* Some companies and unions have developed programs of legal insurance under which participants pay a set amount each month for designated legal services that might be needed while the participant is in the program.
- *Attorney advertising.* Advertising has arguably made the public more aware of legal services and more inclined to use such services.
- *Publicly funded legal services.* The bar associations have consistently supported increased funding by the government for organizations that provide free legal services to the poor.
- *Traditional paralegals.* The increased use of paralegals by attorneys can lead to lower client costs since the billing rate for paralegal time is considerably lower than the billing rate for most attorneys.

**FIGURE 4.5**

Reforms in the Practice of Law

The poor in New York face nearly 3,000,000 civil legal problems per year without legal help. Not more than 14% of their overall need for legal assistance is being met.[21]

The statistics are even more alarming if the legal needs of the middle class are included. In the light of these numbers, critics are calling for drastic reform.

In areas such as divorce and bankruptcy, an increasingly large underground network of nonattorneys are providing low-cost legal services to citizens. Why not bring these nonattorneys out into the open? Subject them to testing and other license requirements to help ensure competence and honesty. While many attorneys see this cure as worse than the disease, others are more receptive to the idea.

Each state must make its own determination of whether limited licensing should be adopted. It is quite possible that one or two states will take the plunge in the near future and enact limited licensing. Will your state do so? Keep in mind that even if it does, it will probably affect very *few* paralegals in your state. The likelihood is that the requirement will apply only to those paralegals who do not work for attorneys. This means that the vast majority of paralegals in the state who work for attorneys would continue as they are—with no license requirement. It is true that some paralegals favor limited licensing for traditional paralegals who work under the supervision of attorneys in order to expand what they are allowed to do for attorneys. But any movement toward such expansion is considerably weaker than the current momentum toward licensing independents.

. . . . . . . . . . . . . .

When a licensing proposal—or a proposal for any kind of paralegal regulation—comes before the legislature, here are some of the steps that should be taken immediately:

## What to Do When the Legislature Proposes Legislation to Regulate Paralegals

(In general, see also *How to Monitor Proposed Legislation,* p. 599.)

1. Obtain a copy of the proposed legislation or bill as soon as possible. If you know the name of the legislator sponsoring the bill, write or call him or her

[21]New York State Bar Association, *New York Legal Needs Study: Draft Final Report,* 196 (1989).

directly. Otherwise contact the office of the Speaker of the House, Speaker of the Assembly, President of the Senate, etc. Ask how you can locate the proposed bill.

2. Find out the exact technical status of the bill. Has it been formally introduced? Has it been assigned to a committee? What is the next scheduled formal event on the bill?

3. Immediately inform the sponsoring legislator(s) and the relevant committee(s) that you want an opportunity to comment on the bill. Find out if hearings are going to be scheduled on the bill. Make known your interest in participating in such hearings. Your goal is to slow the process down so that the bill is not rushed into enactment. Be particularly alert to the possibility that the paralegal bill may be buried in proposed legislation on a large number of related or unrelated topics. Again, there is a real danger that the bill will get through relatively unnoticed.

4. Determine why the paralegal bill is being proposed. What is the *public* reason given for the proposal of the bill? More important, what is the underlying *real* reason for the proposal? Perhaps some special interest or small group (real estate agents, for instance) is seeking a special privilege in a law-related field. Yet the language of the bill they are proposing may be so broad that paralegals will be adversely affected.

5. Alert your local paralegal association. It needs to be mobilized in order to express an organized position on the bill. Contact the major national paralegal associations: NFPA and NALA (see Appendix B). Do they know about the proposed legislation? Have they taken a position? They need to be activated.

6. If your local bar association has a paralegal committee, seek its support.

7. Launch a letter-writing campaign. Make sure that large numbers of paralegals in the area know about the bill and know how to express their opinion to the legislature.

8. Ask local paralegal schools to take a position.

. . . . . . . . . . . . . . .

Keep in mind that we are talking about mandatory *licensing* by the state, not voluntary *certification* by entities such as paralegal associations. The certification debate will be covered later in the chapter.

---

### ■ ASSIGNMENT 4.7

(a) Do you favor broad-based licensing for every paralegal? Limited licensing? Will licensing advance or restrict the development of paralegalism?

(b) If all attorneys in the country drastically cut their fees, would there be a need for paralegal licensing?

(c) There are some tasks that even paralegals who work for attorneys cannot perform, such as taking the deposition of a witness. Should there be limited licensing to authorize such tasks?

---

### ■ ASSIGNMENT 4.8

Evaluate the following observation: "The emerging professions and the more established professions have frequently sought greater regulation of their occupational group. They are often motivated, despite the obligatory language on protection of the public interest, to do so in efforts to establish their 'territorial imperative' or to establish barriers to entry into the profession and thereby enhance their economic self-interest." Sapadin, *A Comparison of the Growth and Development of the Physician Assistant and the Legal Assistant,* in Journal of the American Association for Paralegal Education: Retrospective 1983, 142 (1983).

# Section D. Bar Association Control of Paralegal Education

Since the early 1970s, the American Bar Association has been "approving" paralegal training programs after a recommendation is made by its standing Committee on Legal Assistants, all of whose members are attorneys. There is no requirement that a school be ABA-approved in order to train paralegals. In fact, most training programs are not so approved. The approval process is voluntary, and the majority of programs have decided *not* to apply for approval. A program must meet state government accreditation standards, but it does not have to seek the approval of the ABA or of any other bar association.

The ABA approval process has been controversial from its inception. Those who oppose total attorney control of paralegalism feel that the bar associations are inappropriate mechanisms to regulate training institutions. Since a major objective of attorneys is to increase their profits by employing paralegals, critics argue that it is a conflict of interest for attorneys to control the field totally. When regulatory decisions must be made on matters such as the approval of schools, whose interest would the attorneys be protecting in making these decisions? The interest of the paralegals? The interest of the public? Or the profit interest of the attorney-regulators?

The ABA has been somewhat sensitive to this criticism, and, as we will see, at one time considered withdrawing from the approval process. In recent years, challenges have been made to the monopoly that bar associations exercise over the practice of law. In 1975, the United States Supreme Court sent shock waves throughout the legal profession when the Court ruled that attorneys were no longer exempt from the *antitrust* laws, and that some minimum fee schedules are a violation of these laws.[22] In 1979, an antitrust charge was brought against the ABA on the ground that its paralegal-school approval process was designed to eliminate competition from, and restrict entry into, the market for recruitment, training, and placement of paralegals. The ABA won this case.[23] Despite the victory, the ABA remains vulnerable to future challenge.

Note that the ABA uses the word "approval" rather than accreditation in describing its process of exercising control over educational institutions. Yet the process meets the accepted definition of accreditation presented in Figure 4.1 at the beginning of this chapter. The use of the more euphemistic word "approval" may be an indication that the ABA is itself not sure whether it should be in the business of regulating paralegal education. Indeed, in 1981, the House of Delegates of the ABA instructed its Committee on Legal Assistants to terminate ABA involvement in the approval process. However, some schools that had al-

[22]Goldfarb v. Virginia State Bar, 421 U.S. 773 (1975).

[23]*Paralegal Institute, Inc. v. American Bar Association*, 475 F. Supp. 1123 (E.D.N.Y. 1979).

ready received approval objected. As a result, the Committee proposed and the House of Delegates accepted an alternative system of approving schools.

The alternative was the creation of an ABA Approval Commission to implement the approval process. The final decision on approval of individual schools is still left in the hands of the ABA. The Commission makes its recommendations on approval to the Committee on Legal Assistants, which in turn makes it recommendations to the House of Delegates of the ABA. The major difference between the Committee and the Commission is that the latter must contain nonattorney members. There are eleven members of the Commission, all of whom are appointed by the president of the ABA on advice from the Committee:

- Three attorneys (one of whom has taught in a paralegal program)
- One attorney who represents the ABA Committee on Legal Assistants
- One paralegal nominated by the National Federation of Paralegal Associations (NFPA)
- One paralegal nominated by the National Association of Legal Assistants (NALA)
- Two representatives nominated by the American Association for Paralegal Education (AAfPE)
- One representative nominated by the Association of Legal Administrators (ALA)
- One nonlegal educator
- One representative of the general public

The ABA does not view the Commission as a permanent institution. The plan is to phase it out over a period of years and to replace it with an *independent* accrediting body that is equally broad based. It is unclear, however, whether this replacement is feasible. It depends on the willingness of paralegal schools to submit themselves to this still-voluntary approval process. Furthermore, an independent body would be very expensive to run. Its revenues would come from fees paid by the schools that apply for approval and for renewals of approval. If large numbers of schools continue to bypass a national accrediting or approval entity, the process will lose both the political and financial support it needs. Since there is no realistic hope that an independent accrediting body will be formed, the ABA will probably continue its approval program indefinitely.

---

### ■ ASSIGNMENT 4.9

Who should control accreditation? Are there too many attorneys on the ABA Approval Commission? Too few paralegals? Could there be too many paralegals on such a body? Do you favor an independent accrediting entity? Who should run it? Should it be voluntary?

---

Only one thing is sure: change is on the horizon. The legal profession can no longer feel secure in its privileged position, as the following speech demonstrates.

## The Legal Profession:
## A Bow to the Past—a Glimpse of the Future
### by J. Sims

[Mr. Sims was the Deputy Assistant Attorney General in the Antitrust Division of the United States Department of Justice. The following are excerpts from a speech he delivered on February 11, 1977, before a conference of the Federation of Insurance Counsel in Arizona.]

Today, in Los Angeles, legal services are being advertised on television. That fact alone gives us some idea of how much change has come to the legal profession in the last few years.

That change has not always come easy, but the fact that it has come so far, so fast, tells us quite a bit about what will happen in the future. We lawyers as a group have grumbled and argued, fought and yelled, struggled and been confused—but there are now lawyers advertising on television. Even a casual observer cannot fail to appreciate the significance of this change.

Competition, slowly but surely, is coming to the legal profession. This opening of traditional doors, the breaking of traditional barriers is the result of many forces—the number of new lawyers, the awakening of consumerism, the growing realization that the complexity of our society requires legal assistance in more and more areas. But one contributing factor has been antitrust litigation and the Department of Justice. . . .

[T]he Supreme Court fired the shot heard 'round the bar [o]n June 16, 1975. [I]n a unanimous decision [Goldfarb v. Virginia State Bar, 421 U.S. 773 (1975)], the Court held that the minimum fee schedule challenged by the Goldfarbs violated Section 1 of the Sherman Act. This decision broke the dam and released the flood of change that we see engulfing the profession today. For better or worse, the Goldfarbs had set in motion a series of events that were to change the character of the legal profession forever.

The Court decided several things in *Goldfarb,* but the most important was that the legal profession was subject to the antitrust laws—there was no "professional exemption." The response to *Goldfarb* was fascinating. A large number of private suits were filed challenging various aspects of bar regulation. . . .

[An] area sure to be controversial in the future is unauthorized practice. There is already at least one antitrust challenge, against the Virginia State Bar,

seeking to prohibit the bar from promulgating unauthorized practice opinions. This case, which involves title insurance, is a direct challenge to the extraordinary power that the legal profession now has—in most states—to define the limits of its own monopoly. It would be strange indeed for a state to hand over to, say its steel industry, not only the power to regulate entry into the industry and the conduct of those within it, but also the power to define what the industry was. In many states, that is exactly the power the organized bar now has, and that power is being challenged as inconsistent with the antitrust laws.

The heart of this challenge is that lawyers shouldn't be deciding what is the practice of law—defining the scope of the legal monopoly. The papers filed in that case . . . indicate that the objection is not to such a decision being made; the objection is to the State's delegation of that power to the profession.

In fact, of course, the principle behind this lawsuit could be expanded not only to other subject matter areas, but also to arrangements between the organized bar and other professions which have as their basic result the division of commercial responsibilities.

For example, the American Bar Association has entered into "statements of principles" with respect to the practice of law with a variety of other professions and occupations ranging from accountants to claim adjusters, publishers, social workers, and even professional engineers [page 212]. These documents generally set forth the joint views of the professions as to which activities fall within the practice of law and which activities are proper for members of the other profession. They nearly all provide that each profession will advise its clients to seek out members of the other profession in appropriate circumstances.

As a general rule, two competitors may not agree with each other to allocate markets, or bids, or even functions; if they do, they violate the antitrust laws. At the least, this traditional antitrust principle raises some questions about the legal effect of such "statements of principles." . . .

[T]he efforts of the bar to limit the scope of paralegal responsibilities and, in some jurisdictions, to seek a certification requirement for paralegals are seen by many as simply another effort to preserve and protect the legal services monopoly. Many believe that non-lawyers could perform many tasks reserved today for people with law degrees. . . .

■ **ASSIGNMENT 4.10**

What are the implications of Mr. Sims' remarks on the role of bar associations in regulating paralegal education?

## ■ Section E. Should Paralegals Become Part of Bar Associations?

At present, no paralegals are full members of any bar associations. In 1981, however, the State Bar of Texas created a Legal Assistant Division of the bar. Its unique aspect is that all of its regular members *must* be paralegals. Hence, while paralegals cannot become members of the bar association, they can become members of a *Division* of the bar association. The Division is not a mere advisory committee of the bar; it is part of the bar association itself, which means that it is under the ultimate control of the Board of Directors of the State Bar of Texas.

The qualifications for membership in the Division are as follows:

■ The applicant must *not* be a Texas attorney.

■ The applicant must perform "substantial paralegal services in rendering direct assistance to an attorney." (Someone who does occasional paralegal work would not qualify.)

■ The applicant's supervising attorney must certify that the applicant performs substantial paralegal services for that attorney.

Members pay annual dues of $25.

The bylaws of the Division state its purpose as follows: "to enhance legal assistants' participation in the administration of justice, professional responsibility and public service in cooperation with the State Bar of Texas." All the officers of the Division are paralegals elected by the membership. The budget of the Division, however, must be approved by the State Bar of Texas.

The Division has been very popular among paralegals in Texas; by the middle of 1990, almost 2,000 paralegals had joined. The State Bar of Michigan recently adopted a similar program by creating a Legal Assistant Section of the bar consisting of legal assistants who are *affiliate members* of the bar. Other bar associations have also created special membership categories. There are, for example, *associate members* of the Columbus Bar Association (Ohio), associate members of the Bar Association of San Francisco, paralegal affiliate members of the Association of Trial Lawyers of America, and associate members of the American Immigration Lawyers Association.[24] Not all bar associations, however, have moved in this direction. The Louisiana State Bar Association, for example, voted in 1989 *not* to offer associate membership to paralegals because "the occupation of paralegals has not been sufficiently defined so as to provide guidance as to who is a trained and qualified paralegal, and who is not."[25]

---

[24]As of 1991, associate membership status existed or was under serious consideration in the following states either in the bar itself or in one of its committees or sections: Alaska, Arizona, Colorado, Connecticut (pending), District of Columbia, Florida, Illinois, Massachusetts, Michigan, Missouri (St. Louis County Bar only), New Jersey, New Mexico, North Dakota, Ohio (pending), Pennsylvania (pending), Texas, Wisconsin (pending), and West Virginia. Maze, *Bar Associate Membership Status for Legal Assistants,* 17 Facts & Findings 6 (NALA, March 1991).

[25]Landers, *Louisiana State Bar Association Decides Against Associate Membership for Paralegals,* 4 The Advocate (Louisiana State Paralegal Ass'n, August 1989).

---

■ **ASSIGNMENT 4.11**

Does the state, city, or county bar association where you live have a membership category for paralegals? If so, what are the eligibility requirements for membership and what are the benefits of membership?

---

What about the major national bar association—the American Bar Association (ABA)? For a long time, many argued that paralegals should become affiliated with the ABA in some way. In 1982 the ABA Committee on Legal Assistants proposed that the ABA create a new category of membership for paralegals. The National Association of Legal Assistants (NALA) warmly endorsed the proposal, while the National Federation of Paralegal Associations (NFPA) opposed it. Initially the House of Delegates of the ABA rejected the proposal of the Committee on the ground that the addition of this nonattorney membership category would further "dilute" the primary attorney category. Eventually, however, this objection was overcome. The House of Delegates agreed to accept a *legal assistant associate* category of membership. (For an application form, see Figure 4.6.) An ABA member who supervises the legal assistant must sign the latter's application for associate membership. As of 1991, there were 1200 Legal Assistant Associates in the ABA.

As indicated, not all paralegals endorsed the concept of associate or affiliate membership in bar associations when the idea was first proposed. Here are some typical comments in opposition:

I haven't been able to understand why paralegals would want to become second class members of an organization that represents the interests of another profession. [Some paralegals view associate membership] as a positive development, while the very idea is enough to raise the blood pressure of other paralegals.[26]

[It is] in the public interest that the allied legal professions remain autonomous. [It is] necessary and advisable that paralegals retain primary control in the development of the paralegal profession.[27]

It is a recognized and uncontested fact that the purpose of any bar association is to promote and protect attorneys and their practice of law, rather than legal assistants. Further, associate members do not participate in the administrative and substantial legal decisions which are made by the Bar Association, e.g., no vote on dues, by-laws, budget or substantive issues of membership requirements. [A separate identity may] eliminate possible conflicts of interest on issues where attorneys and legal assistants hold differing perspectives and opinions regarding the future of legal practice.[28]

Those who viewed paralegals as an autonomous, self-directed profession tended to disagree with the effort to join bar associations in any form. Yet this point of view is *not* shared by the majority of paralegals today. The momentum is toward more and more bar associations creating membership categories for paralegals. The reasons are best summed up by the following comment made

---

[26]Whelen, *An Opinion: Bar Association's Paralegal Non-Voting Membership*, 15 At Issue 9 (San Francisco Ass'n of Legal Assistants, May 1987).

[27]*NFPA Findings*, 8 The Journal 3 (Sacramento Ass'n of Legal Assistants, January 1986).

[28]Heller, *Legal Assistant Associate Membership in the ABA*, 14 On Point 1, 14 (Nat'l Capital Area Paralegal Ass'n, August 1988).

**FIGURE 4.6**

ABA Associate Membership Application

Legal Assistant Associate** Persons who, although not members of the legal profession, are qualified through education, training, or work experience, are employed or retained by a lawyer, law office, governmental agency, or other entity in a capacity or function which involves the performance, under the direction and supervision of an attorney, of specifically-delegated substantive legal work, which work, for the most part, requires a sufficient knowledge of legal concepts such that, absent that legal assistant, the attorney would perform the task.

**An ABA member who supervises you <u>MUST</u> sign your application under Annual Associate Dues on page 3.

---

**ABA ASSOCIATE APPLICATION**

Membership Department • American Bar Association • 750 North Lake Shore Drive, Chicago, Illinois 60611, (312) 988-5522 FAX: (312) 988-6281

**ADDRESS**

Please print the way you wish your name and address to appear in the ABA records and on your Associate card and certificate. All materials will be sent to this address.

Name _____

Firm/Agency/Organization _____

Address _____

_____

City _____ State _____ Zip Code _____

Country _____

This address is my ☐ Home   ☐ Business   ☐ Both

Home Phone ( ) _____   Business Phone ( ) _____

Birth Date ____/____/____   Gender ☐ Male ☐ Female

**EMPLOYMENT**

Employer _____

Your Title _____

Number of Years in this position _____

For Judicial Associate applicants only, please indicate:
☐ Judge   ☐ Court administrator   ☐ Federal court executive

Employment Setting (Check one):
1 Law Firm   2 Corporate Law Dept.   3 Gov't.   4 Judiciary
5 Law School   6 Legal Service/Public Defense Agency   7 Military
9 Other _____

Number of attorneys at this office:
A Solo   B 2-5   C 6-9   D 10-19   E 20-99   F 100+

**EDUCATION**

Institution _____

Type of Degree or Certificate _____

**REQUIRED CERTIFICATION**

I certify that I meet the criteria for the category of Associate affiliation I have selected (as defined on page 2).

If elected an Associate of the American Bar Association, I will abide by its Constitution and Bylaws, and the authority of the Board of Governors with respect to Associates.

Signature _____
(required)

**ANNUAL ASSOCIATE DUES ARE $75**

The ABA year runs from Sept. 1 to Aug. 31. Associates who join after October 1st receive a pro-rated credit toward next year's dues. Section dues are not pro-rated. *Some Associate categories REQUIRE you to join an ABA section. They are indicated by an *. These required section dues are reflected in the total annual dues.*

Check your selection(s):                                    **Total Annual Dues**

☐  Administrative Law Associate
    Administrative Law and
    Regulatory Practice Section* ($25.00)...................$100.00
☐  Bar Executive Associate ...............................$ 75.00
☐  Criminal Justice Associate
    Criminal Justice Section* ($25.00).......................$100.00
☐  Educational Associate
    Legal Education and Admissions
    to the Bar Section* ($25.00)...........................$100.00
☐  Governmental Business Associate .......................$ 75.00
☐  Industrial Organization Economist Associate .............$ 75.00
☐  International Associate ................................$ 75.00
    Jurisdiction(s) in which admitted to practice _____

    _____ Admission year(s): _____
    Bar associations or legal organizations of which applicant is a
    member, and any offices held in them _____

☐  Judicial Associate
    Judicial Administrative Division* ($25.00) ...............$100.00
☐  Law Librarian Associate ...............................$ 75.00
☐  Law Office Administrative Associate
    Law Practice Management Section* ($27.50)............$102.50
☐  Legal Assistant Associate ..............................$ 75.00
    Supervising Attorney Verification: I, _____,
    ABA Membership I.D. Number: _____,
    a member of the Bar of the State of _____ verify that the
    above applicant for Legal Assistant Associate does or has
    performed for me in a capacity which meets the requirements
    described on page 2.
    Attorney
    Signature _____
    (required)

                              **Subtotal** (from above)  $ _____
                 **Subtotal** for additional sections (from page 4)  $ _____
                                    **Total**  $ _____

**FULL PAYMENT (Must be enclosed)**

☐ Check enclosed (payable to ABA)
☐ VISA   ☐ MasterCard
Card Number _____        Exp. Date _____

Signature _____

**International Associates:**
Please make payment in U.S. funds drawn on a U.S. bank, or a wire transfer through the First National Bank of Chicago, Account Number 50-03997 (include your name, address and "New Applicant" on the transfer for reference). **Your application CANNOT otherwise be processed.**

Associate Dues for the American Bar Association and ABA sections, divisions and forum committees are not deductible as charitable contributions for federal income tax purposes. However, such dues may be deductible as business expense.

Associate dues include a basic subscription to the *ABA Journal*, and Section dues include basic subscriptions to the section publications as shown on page 4.

---

**AMERICAN BAR ASSOCIATION ASSOCIATE AFFILIATION**

Article Three of the ABA Constitution and Bylaws provides for the establishment of classes of Associates, composed of non-members with whom affiliation is considered to be in the interest of the Association. Associates are not members of the Association and do not, as a group, constitute a membership classification. Associates of the American Bar Association, except for International Associates, are non-lawyers who are not eligible for membership within the Association, but serve within the legal profession. Pursuant to Article 21.12 of the Association Bylaws, persons who are ineligible to be members of the Association may qualify for election by the Board of Governors as Associates if they are in one of the classifications listed above, and satisfy such further eligibility requirements as may be approved by the Board.

**PRIVILEGES OF ASSOCIATES**

1. To attend meetings of the Association, including sessions of the House of Delegates and the Assembly, and to enjoy any floor privileges extended to non-members.

2. To receive Association publications that are regularly provided to all members of the Association.

3. To be appointed to any Committee or Commission of the Association for which non-members are eligible for appointment.

4. To participate in the economic benefit programs available to ABA members, with the exception of the insurance programs of the American Bar Endowment.

5. To affiliate with one or more of the sections of their choice, upon application and payment of the annual section dues then in effect. All Associates under the age of 36 shall automatically become Associates of the Young Lawyers Division (see page 4).

before the ABA created the associate membership category:

> It is time our profession stopped being paranoid about ABA Associate Membership and open our eyes to opportunities presented to us. [We should not be spending time] dreaming up reasons to reject a chance for growth and improved relations within the established legal community. No guarantees have been given to assure us that associate membership would be beneficial, but why close *any* doors opened to us? If just a few paralegals would like to take advantage of this opportunity, why slam the door in their faces? The spirit of cooperation and teamwork within the legal community are the key reasons to encourage associate membership.[29]

---

## ■ ASSIGNMENT 4.12

**(a)** Should paralegals become a formal part of bar associations? What effect do you think associate membership would have on existing paralegal associations? Strengthen them? Destroy them? Is it healthy or unhealthy for paralegals to organize themselves as independent entities? Is it healthy or unhealthy for them to be able to challenge the organized bar? What is the conflict-of-interest argument against associate membership? Do you agree with this argument?

**(b)** Should a paralegal association allow *attorneys* to become associate members of the *paralegal* association? Why or why not?

**(c)** Under the ABA associate membership category, what kinds of paralegals are excluded from membership? Is such exclusion a good idea?

**(d)** To become an associate or affiliate member of a bar association, the applicant usually must obtain the signed statement of an attorney-employer asserting or attesting certain facts about the applicant—for instance, that he or she is a paralegal who works for the attorney. The statement is called an attorney attestation. For example, to obtain affiliate membership in the State Bar of Michigan, the attorney must "hereby attest" that the applicant "is employed by me and is recognized as a legal assistant (paralegal) and that he/she, under the supervision and direction of a lawyer, performs the services" specified elsewhere on the application. Some *paralegal* associations require the same kind of attorney attestation as a condition of allowing paralegals to join the paralegal association. Do you think attorney attestation is a good idea for associate/affiliate membership in a bar association? For full membership in a paralegal association?

**(e)** As indicated elsewhere in this book, there are a fairly large number of paralegals who have moved on to management positions as paralegal coordinators or legal assistant managers. Should these individuals become members of traditional paralegal associations?

---

# ■ Section F. Self-Regulation by Paralegals: The Certification Debate

As we have seen, there are two major national associations of paralegals:

■ National Federation of Paralegal Associations (NFPA): An association of associations; its membership consists of state and local paralegal associations

■ National Association of Legal Assistants (NALA): an association of individuals, plus a number of state and local paralegal associations, and several student paralegal associations

---

[29]Anderson, *ABA Associate Membership: A Different Perspective,* 3 Findings and Conclusions 7 (Washington Ass'n of Legal Assistants, August 1987).

In Appendix B, there is a list of state and local paralegal associations, with a notation of whether they are part of NFPA, part of NALA, or unaffiliated.

NALA is *not* a member of NFPA, and vice versa. In fact, the two groups take very different positions on a number of issues, two of the most important of which are limited licensing of independent paralegals and certification of all paralegals. Earlier in this chapter we examined the clash of views on limited licensing. We turn now to the older and perhaps more bitter debate over certification. NALA has created two major certification programs for paralegals—the Certified Legal Assistant (CLA) program and the Certified Legal Assistant Specialist (CLAS) program. The major opponent of the very existence of these programs has been NFPA. The following two excerpts present a detailed description of the position of both associations on certification. At the end of the descriptions, you will be asked which side is correct.

---

### The Case for Certification[30]

#### by Jane H. Terhune

[Jane H. Terhune is a past president of the National Association of Legal Assistants. She is employed as a legal assistant for the firm of Hall, Estill, Hardwick, Gable, Collingsworth & Nelson, Tulsa, Oklahoma.]

Professional competence of an *individual* can be assessed by two recognized mechanisms: licensing or certification. Accreditation or approval, on the other hand, examines educational *programs* to determine whether they meet established standards of quality. Although the ABA has an institutional approval process, this paper is concerned only with the assessment of *individual* competence and therefore will not deal with the issue of institutional accreditation or approval.

Since the early 1970s legal assistants have obtained employment by means of formal training, in-house training, or other law office experience. While each method of training has certain advantages, no one method has proven superior to the others. Thus the dilemma: how can prospective employers or clients assess or legal assistants demonstrate paralegal skills and knowledge when there is no standard for performance?

Is licensing the appropriate mechanism to assure professional competence of legal assistants at this time? Several states have recently considered it, but none has yet adopted it. It is generally agreed that requirements for licensing would either severely limit the growth and development of the still new paralegal field or be so weak as to be meaningless. Licensing,

by definition, is a mandatory requirement and is usually administered and controlled by government entities or well-established and strong professional associations. It is doubtful that state legislatures can define the legal assistant profession well enough to regulate it effectively at this time. Therefore, licensing appears to be impractical as well as premature.

*Certification,* on the other hand, is a voluntary professional commitment that appears to be a practical alternative, and the National Association of Legal Assistants believes that one national certification program is preferable to a multitude of possible state programs. Certification is not new or unique. Many professions and paraprofessions have developed and supported certification as an alternative to licensing or other forms of regulation. Certification recognizes expertise and proven ability without limiting entrance into or employment in the field, and the same standards are applied regardless of the individual's background or training. Furthermore, a certification program can help guide educational institutions in developing and evaluating their legal assistant curricula. It is argued that certification would limit the development of the paralegal field, but the PLS (Professional Legal Secretary) certification of legal secretaries has in no way interfered with their employment. To the contrary, secretaries with the Certified PLS title are regarded as professionals in their respective fields.

In 1974, as part of an effort to set high professional standards for legal assistants while the field was in its early development, the NALA Certifying Board for Legal Assistants was created. It was composed of nine members—five legal assistants (working in different areas of the law), two paralegal educators, and two attorneys. The composition of the Board has remained the same to date, and in number is similar to many certification boards or committees in other fields. During the first year of its existence the Certifying Board

[30] American Bar Association, Standing Committee on Legal Assistants, *Legal Assistant Update '80* 5–16 (1980). This article has been updated to reflect current positions of NALA and NFPA.

acted mainly as a feasibility study group. All known national professional associations with certification programs were contacted for advice and guidance. Paralegal educators were contacted for information about their programs as well as entrance and graduation requirements. Legal assistant duties and responsibilities in various areas of the law were surveyed, and correspondence with the Institute of Legal Executives in England began. Our English counterparts were anxious to share their ten years of experience with NALA. After several months of gathering information, replies were tabulated and summarized and the NALA Certifying Board for Legal Assistants was ready to embark on its task. Its first task was to create an examination. Passing this examination would enable a legal assistant to become a CLA—Certified Legal Assistant.

Although many legal assistants work in special areas of law rather than as generalists, there are general skills and knowledge which apply to all legal fields and, for this reason, general subjects or topics were selected for inclusion in the examination.

### The CLA Examination—Outline

The two-day CLA examination contains objective questions, such as multiple choice, true/false, and matching. There are also essay questions and short answer questions. The examination covers the follow areas:

*Communications.* This section of the CLA examination contains questions on:

| | | |
|---|---|---|
| word usage | capitalization | grammar |
| number usage | vocabulary | correspondence |
| punctuation | word division | nonverbal communication |
| sentence structure | concise writing | |

*Ethics.* This section deals with ethics in the legal assistant's contacts with employers, clients, co-workers, and the general public. Unauthorized practice, ethical rules, practice rules, and confidentiality are among the topics tested by this section. Knowledge of the American Bar Association Rules of Professional Conduct and the National Association of Legal Assistants, Inc., Code of Ethics and Professional Responsibility is required for this examination.

*Human Relations and Interviewing Techniques.* The Human Relations portion encompasses professional and social contacts with the employer, clients, and other office visitors, co-workers, including subordinates, and the public outside of the law office. For this reason, the legal assistant should be familiar with: authorized practice, ethical rules, practice rules, delegation of authority, consequences of delegation, and confidentiality.

Interviewing techniques cover basic principles, as agreed upon by most authors on the subject, definitions of terms of basic principles, and handling of specialized interviews. Subject areas included in this section of the examination are:

| | |
|---|---|
| General considerations for the interviewing situation: courtesy, empathy, and physical setting | Manner of questions |
| | Use of checklists for specific matters |
| Initial Roadblocks—lapse of time, prejudice, etc. | Special-handling situations: the elderly, the very young |

The test covers initial and subsequent interviews as well as both client and witness interviews.

*Judgment and Analytical Ability.*   The sections of this part deal with (1) analyzing and categorizing facts and evidence; (2) the legal assistant's relationship with the lawyer, the legal secretary, the client, the courts, and other law firms; (3) the legal assistant's reactions to specific situations; (4) handling telephone situations; and (5) reading comprehension and data interpretation.

*Legal Research.*   It is extremely important for the legal assistant to be able to use the most important "tool" of the legal profession—the law library. The purpose of the legal research section of the CLA Examination is to test your knowledge of the use of state and federal codes, the statutes, the digests, case reports, various legal encyclopedias, court reports, shepardizing, and research procedure.

*Legal Terminology.*   The sections of this part deal with (1) Latin phrases; (2) legal phrases or terms in general; and (3) utilization and understanding of common legal terms. The questions involve legal terminology and procedures used in general practice.

*Substantive Law.*   The substantive law section of the CLA examination is divided into nine parts: (1) general (which includes American Legal System); (2) bankruptcy; (3) corporate; (4) estate planning and probate; (5) contract; (6) litigation; (7) real estate; (8) criminal; and (9) administrative law. Each examinee will be required to take the first part and must select four out of the remaining eight parts.

---

After passing the examination, a legal assistant may use the *CLA (Certified Legal Assistant)* designation, which signifies certification by the National Association of Legal Assistants, Inc. CLA is a service mark duly registered with the U.S. Patent and Trademark Office (No. 1131999). Any unauthorized use is strictly forbidden.

Based on the premise that education, a commitment of all professionals, is a never ending process, Certified Legal Assistants are required periodically to submit evidence of continuing education in order to maintain certified status. The CLA designation is for a period of five years, and if the CLA submits proof of continuing education in accordance with the stated requirements, the certificate is renewed for another five years. Lifetime certification is not permitted.

Continuing education units are awarded for attending seminars, workshops or conferences in areas of substantive law or a closely related area. The seminars, etc., do not have to be sponsored by NALA, although all NALA seminars and workshops qualify.

The development of the specific test items was a time-consuming and difficult project. Rather than employ professional testing companies unfamiliar with the legal assistant field, it was decided that the Certifying Board, composed of legal assistants, attorneys, and educators from the legal assistant field, was best qualified to prepare the exams. Then followed a series of meetings to review, refine, and evaluate the proposed exams. The exams were pilot-tested, testing times were noted, results were systematically analyzed, and problems were identified. Every question in each section was carefully scrutinized for "national scope," and questions which did not apply to all states were removed from the exam.

**Eligibility Requirements for CLA Examination**

Applicants for the Certified Legal Assistant examination must meet one of the following three requirements at the time of filing the application.

1. Graduation from a legal assistant program that is:

   a) Approved by the American Bar Association; or

   b) An associate degree program; or

   c) A post-baccalaureate certificate program in legal assistant studies; or

   d) A bachelor's degree program in legal assistant studies; or

   e) A legal assistant program which consists of a minimum of 60 semester hours (or equivalent quarter hours) of which at least 15 semester hours (or equivalent quarter hours) are substantive legal courses.

2. A bachelor's degree in any field plus one (1) year's experience as a legal assistant.

3. A high school diploma or equivalent plus seven (7) years' experience as a legal assistant under the supervision of a member of the Bar plus evidence of a minimum of twenty (20) hours of continuing legal education credit to have been completed within a two (2) year period prior to the application date.

Applicants meeting any one of these criteria may take the exam. They need not be members of the National Association of Legal Assistants to apply for or receive the CLA (Certified Legal Assistant) certification.

The CLA examination was first offered in November, 1976, at regional testing centers. Approximately 50 percent of the first group of applicants passed the entire exam, and the board was particularly pleased that the passing percentage was uniform throughout the country, a fact which seemed to indicate that the test was free of state or regional bias. Although the passing rate has fluctuated slightly in subsequent testing, the uniformity has been maintained. In the March 1990 exam, there was a 51.5% pass rate, as 504 of 977 legal assistants passed the test. As of April 1991, there were 4,265 CLAs in the country. The following states have the most CLAs:

| Florida: | 1120 | Colorado: | 122 |
|---|---|---|---|
| Texas: | 967 | Kansas: | 106 |
| Arizona: | 316 | Iowa: | 77 |
| Oklahoma: | 202 | Louisiana | 73 |
| California: | 157 | New Mexico: | 63 |

Certification is an ambitious and expensive project for a young professional association. Over $20,000 and thousands of hours were initially invested in the CLA program, but the National Association of Legal Assistants believes it has been a wise investment. Traditionally, where new professions do not set their own standards, related professions or governments have done so for them. NALA felt a responsibility to develop a quality national certification program for legal assistants desiring professional recognition. The CLA exam has been in use for a number of years, but work on the project continues. The question bank is continually expanded so that an indefinite number of exam versions can be created, and questions are being reviewed and updated constantly.

## Specialty Certification

Recently NALA launched a major new component of its CLA program. It is now possible for someone who has already achieved CLA status to take additional examinations in order to receive *Specialty Certification* in one or more of the following areas:

- **Civil Litigation** covers Federal Rules of Civil Procedure, Federal Rules of Evidence, and Federal Rules of Appellate Procedure; document control; drafting pleadings; abstracting information; and general litigation procedures.

- **Probate and Estate Planning** covers general probate and trust law, federal estate tax, fiduciary income tax, drafting wills and trusts, and estate planning concepts.

- **Corporate and Business Law** covers the knowledge and applications of those principles of contract, tort, property, agency, employment, administrative, corporate, and partnership law which commonly constitute the subject matter known as business law. Examinees must be thoroughly familiar with the Uniform Commercial Code, Uniform Partnership Act, Uniform Limited Partnership Act, Model Business Corporate Act, as well as with the regulatory authority of those federal agencies which affect the business relationship such as the SEC, FTC, OSHA, and EPA.

- **Criminal Law and Procedure** covers an applicant's knowledge in the area of criminal procedure and law from arrest through trial. The examination covers components of substantive criminal law, procedural matters, and constitutional rights guaranteed to defendants. Applicants must be thoroughly familiar with the Federal Rules of Criminal Procedure, Federal Rules of Evidence, the Model Penal Code, and major United States Supreme Court cases.

- **Real Estate** covers the applicant's knowledge in the area of real estate purchases, sales, terminology, actions affecting title, landlord-tenant relations, oil and gas, easements, abstracts, title insurance, liens, cluster developments, types of conveyances, methods of passing title included in conveyances, legal remedies associated with real estate, and legal descriptions of real estate.

Each of these specialty examinations takes four hours to complete. Upon passing one of them, the legal assistant becomes a *CLAS—a Certified Legal Assistant Specialist*. The CLA examination tests broad *general* skills required of *all* legal assistants. Specialty certification, on the other hand, recognizes significant competence in a *particular* field. Yet both the CLA exam and the CLAS exam are similar in that they do not test the law of any particular state. They are national in scope, since NALA believes that standard national examinations will ensure uniformity of professional standards as well as permit legal assistants to move from one state to another without loss of certified status.

From the inception of the CLAS program in 1982 to 1990, 298 legal assistants have achieved CLAS status in the country.

---

### The Case Against Certification
#### by Judith Current

[Judith Current is a past president of the National Federation of Paralegal Associations. She is employed as a legal assistant in the firm of Holme, Roberts & Owen, Denver, Colorado.]

The National Federation of Paralegal Associations (NFPA) is a professional organization composed of fifty-two state and local paralegal associations representing over 17,000 paralegals across the country. NFPA was founded in 1974 and adopted the following purposes in 1975:

- to constitute a unified national voice of the paralegal profession
- to advance, foster, and promote the paralegal concept
- to monitor and participate in developments in the paralegal profession
- to maintain a nationwide communications network among paralegal associations and other members of the legal community

NFPA has continued to foster these goals through its established policies and activities. In 1977 NFPA adopted its Affirmation of Responsibility (p. 313).

NFPA recognizes that certification of paralegals is of national concern, but it feels that there has been insufficient study as to the impact of certification and the means by which certification should be administered. NFPA will only support a certification program which is coordinated by a national, broadly based, autonomous body in which paralegals have at least equal participation with attorneys and other members.

The topic of certification of legal assistants has been of concern to NFPA since its inception. It has found every certificate proposal advanced to date to be seriously lacking in the understanding of the true nature of the profession, particularly its diversity, and the proposals have offered a structure that provides little or no representation to the persons most affected, the legal assistants themselves.

Specifically, its reservations fall within the following areas:

#### Need/Prematurity

Since there is tremendous diversity in the functions and classifications of paralegals, it is extremely difficult to create generalized standards that can be fairly applied. This problem may eventually find an acceptable solution; but it will require much study and considerable input from all affected sectors.

No studies have been conducted that have demonstrated a need for certification. A study conducted by the American Bar Association in 1975 concluded that certification was premature. The California State Bar in 1978 rejected a proposal for certification and accreditation after nearly two years of study. Other states have similarly rejected certification. Until a need for certification is clearly demonstrated, certification will be premature.

Premature regulation runs a risk of foreclosing yet unseen avenues of development, as well as creating yet another layer of costly bureaucracy when, in fact, none may be needed. NFPA sees nothing to prevent, and everything to encourage, an extremely cautious approach to the enactment of any program of certification. Meanwhile, the normal mechanisms of the marketplace, the existing unauthorized practice laws and ethical guidelines, the increasing numbers of legal assistants with demonstrable experience, and the ever-growing reputations of various training programs can serve as guidelines for those who seek the sorts of yardsticks that certification might provide.

## Impact of Certification

No studies have been conducted that satisfactorily assess the potential impact of certification on the delivery of legal services. Some of the possible negative effects include:

1. *The growth, development, and diversity of the paralegal profession could be diminished by certification.* The paralegal profession has been developing steadily without a demonstrated need for such regulation. Regulating the profession could curtail development into new areas, stifling the potential growth of the field and unnecessarily limiting the role of the paralegals in the delivery of legal services.

2. *Certification could result in a decrease of the availability of legal services to the poor.* Legal aid offices [page 83] are economically dependent upon paralegals who represent clients at various administrative hearings. Most of these paralegals are in-house trained specialists who are paid lower salaries than private sector paralegals. If certification is implemented, it is conceivable that administrative agencies may initiate a system in which only certified paralegals, or attorneys, would be allowed to represent clients at the hearings. Many paralegals successfully working in this area might not meet the educational or testing requirements imposed by certification, and the legal aid offices would not be able to meet the salary demands that would be made by certified paralegals.

3. *Innovation in paralegal education programs could diminish as a result of certification.* Schools would be forced by necessity to gear their courses to a certification examination rather than to the needs of the legal community and the marketplace. While some standardization of training programs might be desirable in the future, it would be premature at this time because the training programs have not been in existence long enough to determine which types of programs are most effective and because the paralegal profession is still in a dynamic stage of development. Experimentation and variety are currently essential to the field of paralegal education.

4. *Entry into the profession could be curtailed by certification.* At the present time, a paralegal can enter the profession in a variety of ways, including formal education, in-house training, promotion from legal secretary, or a combination thereof. Certification could limit these entry paths by establishing prescribed educational requirements.

## No Acceptable Model for Certification

In the opinion of NFPA, no acceptable model or program of certification has yet been devised. Oregon is the only state to have adopted a certification program, but it was discontinued shortly after it began because of a lack of interest from paralegals and attorneys in the state. NFPA questions the propriety of the Oregon State Bar controlling the certification of paralegals, and deplores the fact that the paralegals were denied equal representation on the certifying board. The Oregon program failed adequately to recognize specialization and failed to make any distinctions between the tasks which may be performed by a certified paralegal and those which may be performed by an uncertified paralegal. Thus, certification did not enhance the position of paralegals in Oregon.

NFPA feels that the certification program conducted by the National Association of Legal Assistants (NALA) is unacceptable. The criteria for eligibility to take the certification examination is not based on objective data. The examination, in the Federation's opinion, contains questions irrelevant to a practicing paralegal and is not an effective measure of a person's ability to work successfully as a paralegal. The NALA certification program is not officially recognized by a governmental body, and a person certified under this program is not allowed to perform any tasks other than those which may also be performed by uncertified paralegals.

## Control and Representation

No certification program will be acceptable to NFPA unless it is developed, implemented, and controlled by an autonomous group which is composed of an equal number of attorneys, paralegals, paralegal educators, and members of the public. Self-regulation is unacceptable to NFPA since self-regulation can become self-interest, and self-interest can conflict with the public interest. NFPA strongly believes that bar control of paralegals is inappropriate in that such regulation may meet the interests of the organized bar and lawyers but not necessarily the interests of the public or the paralegal profession. NFPA also questions the propriety of the organized bar attempting to regulate another profession.

## National Coordination

NFPA believes that any program of certification will be most efficient and equitable if it is developed as a national program rather than on a state-by-state basis. A national program would eliminate duplication of effort on the part of each individual state. It would allow for mobility and would avoid a conflict of standards between states.

NFPA recommends that the need for and possible methods of certification be studied in much greater depth, and that this study be conducted by an autonomous group which provides equal representation to paralegals, attorneys, paralegal educators, and members of the public. NFPA also recommends that bar associations work with paralegals and educators to educate lawyers in the proper and effective utilization of paralegals and that paralegals work to promote the growth and the development of the profession through support of and participation in the local and national paralegal associations.

---

### ■ ASSIGNMENT 4.13

(a) Which side is correct? Conduct a debate in your class on the advantages and disadvantages of certification.

(b) Do you agree with NFPA that self-regulation is unacceptable?

---

### Certification in Florida

Florida Legal Assistants (FLA) is a statewide paralegal association that is affiliated with the National Association of Legal Assistants. Florida is a big NALA state; over 25% of all CLAs in the country live in Florida. Several years ago, FLA began its own exam on Florida law for those legal assistants who had passed the CLA exam of NALA. In 1984, FLA launched the Certified Florida Legal Assistant Examination. A person who is a CLA and passes this exam on Florida law can become a *CFLA—a Certified Florida Legal Assistant*. Like the CLA exam, the CFLA exam is voluntary; no one is required to take it. The program is not endorsed by any of the bar associations in Florida. It is run exclusively by FLA. "Some legal assistants view the CFLA designation as a step up from NALA's CLA designation." [31]

### Certification in Texas?

The Florida certification program was inaugurated with relative calm. The exact opposite occurred when certification proposals emerged in Texas. As we saw earlier, there is a *Legal Assistant Division* within the State Bar of Texas. A survey of the members of the Division revealed very high interest in adopting a voluntary certification program specifically for Texas. Over 76% of the members indicated that they would take a certification exam if it were offered. Consequently, the Division drafted two certification proposals and conducted a series of hearings on them in 1986. The proposals were as follows:

*Proposal 1.* The Division would develop and administer its own two-day exam on generic topics (such as legal analysis and communications) and on Texas law. Only legal assistants with at least two years working experience as a legal assistant would be eligible to take the exam.

*Proposal 2.* The Division would join forces with NALA and give two exams. NALA would administer its two-day Certified Legal Assistant (CLA) exam. Then the Division would administer its half-day exam designed with a focus on Texas law. Anyone who had previously passed the CLA exam would be required to have worked as a legal assistant in Texas for one year before taking the Division's Texas exam.

---

[31]Morris, *State Certifying Test for Legal Assistants in Florida: Is Arizona Next?*, The Digest, p. 1 (Arizona Paralegal Ass'n, October 1989).

These two proposals stirred great controversy in Texas and throughout the country. The National Federation of Paralegal Associations (NFPA) vigorously opposed both proposals, raising many of the same arguments against certification discussed earlier. But the Dallas Association of Legal Assistants (which is a member of NFPA) criticized NFPA for its opposition. The National Association of Legal Assistants (NALA) endorsed the Texas move toward certification. Of course, this is not surprising in view of NALA's history of supporting certification. And NALA would play a major role if the second proposal were adopted.

The debate was not limited to NFPA and NALA. Eight public hearings were held throughout Texas, and 187 persons submitted written comments. *But no clear consensus emerged from the hearings on the two proposals.* There was considerable confusion about the nature, purpose, and scope of the two proposals, and indeed, about the value of certification itself.

In spite of these difficulties, there is continued interest in developing a state-specific certification program in Texas within the structure of the state bar association. The most recent proposal under consideration is the establishment of a series of voluntary specialty examinations on Texas law to recognize "advanced professional competency" within a particular specialty. The likelihood of enacting such a proposal is very high. The bar's Legal Assistants Committee has appointed a Certification Committee to study it.

## Position of the American Bar Association on Certification

The ABA has taken the following positions on paralegal certification:

1. Certification of *minimal,* or *entry-level,* paralegal competence is *not* appropriate.

2. Voluntary certification of *advanced* paralegal competence or proficiency in specialty areas of the law *might* be appropriate *if* it were administered by the appropriate body.

3. The ABA is *not* the appropriate body to undertake a program of certifying paralegals in advanced competence or proficiency in specialty areas of the law.

4. A voluntary program of certifying advanced paralegal competence or proficiency in specialty areas of the law, if undertaken at all, should be undertaken on a national basis by a board that includes attorneys, paralegals, educators, and members of the general public.

5. Since such a board does not presently exist, there should not be any certification at this time.

According to the ABA, certification of minimal competence does not have the benefits that would justify the time, expense, and effort to implement it. Furthermore, any of the benefits would be outweighed by potential detriment from it. A major danger the ABA sees is that such certification could evolve into licensure, which the ABA opposes.

But the ABA does see benefit in certifying paralegals in areas of specialization *after* they have been on the job. This kind of advanced certification would be a way of recognizing professional advancement. "Such certification would be a measure of quality of work and experience. Its function would be to demonstrate to employers or prospective employers a high degree of legal assistant competence in a particular area of practice that has already been obtained, rather than just the potential for such competence." [32]

The ABA feels, however, that advanced certification must be administered by the appropriate body. This body should be broad based, including attorneys, paralegals, educators, and members of the public. The ABA recognizes that it is *not* such a body. Neither is the National Association of Legal Assistants nor the National Federation of Paralegal Associations. In fact, such a body simply does not exist. It would take a great deal of money, energy, and political skill to create one. Beyond a lot of rhetoric, no one is even trying.

Hence, as a practical consequence, it can be said that the ABA is opposed to *any* certification at this time.

---

### ■ ASSIGNMENT 4.14

When a new local paralegal association is formed, it is often lobbied by NALA and by NFPA to become a part of one of these national organizations. The local association will usually make one of three decisions: affiliate with NALA, affiliate with NFPA, or remain unaffiliated. If you were a member of a local association faced with the decision of whether to join NALA, NFPA, or stay unaffiliated, what would your vote be? Why?

---

### ■ ASSIGNMENT 4.15

Is it a good idea to have two national associations? Why or why not?

---

Throughout this book the importance of paralegal associations has been stressed. They have had a major impact on the development of paralegalism. Many state and local bar associations as well as the ABA have felt the effect of organized paralegal advocacy through the associations.

As soon as possible, you should join a paralegal association. Find out if the association allows students to become members. (See the form at the end of this book after the index.) If an association does not exist in your area, you should form one and decide whether you want to become part of the National Federation of Paralegal Associations or the National Association of Legal Assistants. The paralegal association is your main voice in the continued development of the field. Join one now and become an active member. In addition to the educational benefits of membership and the job placement services that many associations provide, you will experience the satisfaction of helping shape your career in the years to come. Attorneys and the bar associations should not be the sole mechanism for controlling paralegals.

## ■ G. Fair Labor Standards Act

Yes, I am paid overtime. I am paid at time and a half rate. I agree with being paid overtime. If the attorney asks me to work additional long hours and weekends, then yes I do believe I should be compensated for yielding my free time

---

[32] ABA Standing Committee on Legal Assistants, *Position Paper on the Question of Legal Assistant Licensure or Certification,* 5 Legal Assistant Today 167 (1986).

for work. This does not make me any less of a professional. My professionalism will show through my work product.[33]

My firm doesn't pay paralegals overtime, and I don't want to be classified as a person eligible for overtime. For one thing, people paid overtime are non-professionals, and I don't think of myself as a non-professional. I feel that my salary, salary increases, and bonuses reflect a degree of compensation for the extra hours I work.[34]

One of the "hot topics" in the field is GOD: the Great Overtime Debate. "The mere mention of the subject of overtime in any group of working legal assistants is guaranteed to spark a prolonged session of horror-story telling." [35] The topic is so controversial that one paralegal association recently established a hotline to answer questions confidentially. Some paralegals have filed—and won—lawsuits against their employers for failure to pay *overtime compensation* for hours worked beyond forty hours in a week.

There is a definite body of law that determines whether overtime compensation must be paid; the issue is not dependent on the preferences of individual paralegals. The governing law is the federal *Fair Labor Standards Act,*[36] which is enforced by the Wage and Hour Division of the U.S. Department of Labor. Under the Act, overtime compensation must be paid to employees unless they fall within one of the three "white collar" exemptions. Exempt employees are those who work in a professional, administrative, or executive capacity.[37] The vast majority of traditional paralegals do *not* fit within any of these exemptions. Since they are nonexempt, they *are* entitled to the protection of the Act. Phrased another way, they are not considered professionals, administrators, or executives under the Act and must therefore be paid overtime compensation. If, however, the paralegal is a supervisor with extensive management responsibilities over other employees, an exemption may apply. But this would cover only a small segment of the paralegal population. The following opinion letter explains the position of the government on this issue. As you will see, the criteria

---

[33]*The Member Connection,* 14 Facts & Findings 7 (NALA, June 1988).

[34]*The Membership Responds,* 9 The ParaGraph (Georgia Ass'n of Legal Assistants, September/October 1987).

[35]Acosta, *Let's Talk About Overtime!,* 10 Ka Leo O' H.A.L.A. 6 (Hawaii Ass'n of Legal Assistants, August/September 1987).

[36]29 U.S.C.A. §§ 201 *et seq.* (1976).

[37]The Professional Employee Exemption:

- Primary duty consists of work requiring knowledge of an advanced type in a field customarily acquired by a prolonged course of specialized intellectual instruction and study. (Such course of study means at least a baccalaureate degree or equivalent.)
- Work requires the consistent exercise of judgment and discretion.
- Work is predominantly intellectual and varied in character, as opposed to routine, mental or physical work.

The Administrative Employee Exemption:

- The employee's primary duty consists of work related to management policies or general business operations.
- The employee regularly exercises discretion and independent judgment.

The Executive Employee Exemption:

- The employee's primary duty consists of the management of the enterprise.
- The employee regularly supervises two or more other employees. 29 C.F.R. part 541 (1983).

used to distinguish exempt from nonexempt employees are the actual job responsibilities of the employee, not the job title or compensation policy of the office.

---

### ■ ASSIGNMENT 4.16

(a) If you had a choice, would you want to receive overtime compensation as an entry-level paralegal?

(b) Surveys have shown that between twenty and forty percent of nonexempt paralegals today do *not* receive overtime compensation. Can you explain this startling fact?

---

**Wage and Hour Division**
**United States Department of Labor**
September 27, 1979

This is in further reply to your letter of July 12, 1979, . . . concerning the exempt status under section 13(a)(1) of the Fair Labor Standards Act of paralegal employees employed by your organization, . . .

The specific duties of the paralegal employees (all of which occur under an attorney's supervision) are interviewing clients; identifying and refining problems; opening, maintaining, and closing case files; acting as the liaison person between client and attorney; drafting pleadings and petitions, and answering petition, and interrogatories; filing pleadings and petitions; acting as general litigation assistant during court proceedings; digesting depositions, and preparing file profiles; conducting formal and informal hearings and negotiations; preparing and editing newsletters and leaflets for community development and public relations purposes; performing outreach services; coordinating general activities with relevant local, State, and Federal agencies; assisting in establishing and implementing community legal education programs; and working as a team with other employees to deliver quality legal services. You state that the job requires at least two years of college and/or equivalent experience.

[The Fair Labor Standards] Act provides a complete minimum wage and overtime pay exemption for any employee employed in a bona fide executive, administrative, or professional capacity . . . . An employee will qualify for exemption if all the pertinent tests relating to duties, responsibilities and salary . . . are met. In response to your first question, the paralegal employees you have in mind would not qualify for exemption as bona fide professional employees as discussed in section 541.3 of the regulations, since it is clear that their primary duty does not consist of work requiring knowledge of an advanced type in a field of science or learning customarily acquired by a prolonged course of specialized intellectual instruction and study, as distinguished from a general academic education and from an apprenticeship and from training in the performance of routine mental, manual, or physical processes.

With regard to the status of the paralegal employees as bona fide administrative employees, it is our opinion that their duties do not involve the exercise of discretion and independent judgment of the type required by section 541.2(b) of the regulations. The outline of their duties which you submit actually describes the use of skills rather than discretion and independent judgment. Under section 541.207 of the regulations, this requirement is interpreted as involving the comparison and evaluation of possible courses of conduct and acting or making a decision after the various possibilities have been considered. Furthermore, the term is interpreted to mean that the person has the authority or power to make an independent choice, free from immediate direction or supervision with respect to matters of significance.

The general facts presented about the employees here tend to indicate that they do not meet these criteria. Rather, as indicated above, they would appear to fit more appropriately into that category of employees who apply particular skills and knowledge in preparing assignments. Employees who merely apply knowledge in following prescribed procedures or determining whether specified standards have been met are not deemed to be exercising independent judgment, even if they have some leeway in reaching a conclusion. In addition, it should be noted that most jurisdictions have strict prohibitions against the unauthorized practice of law by lay persons. Under the American Bar Association's Code of Professional Responsibility, a delegation of legal tasks to a lay person is proper only if the lawyer maintains a direct relationship with the client, supervises the delegated work and has complete professional responsibility for the work produced. The implication of such strictures is that the paralegal employees you describe would probably not have the amount of authority to exercise independent judgment with regard to legal matters necessary to bring them within the administrative exemption. . . .

With regard to your [other] questions, all nonexempt employees, regardless of the amount of their wages, must be paid overtime premium pay of not less than one and one-half times their regular rates of pay for all hours worked in excess of 40 in a workweek. The fact that an employee did not obtain advanced approval to work the overtime does not relieve the employer from complying with the overtime provisions of the Act.

We hope this satisfactorily responds to your inquiry. However, if you have any further questions concerning the application of the Fair Labor Standards Act to the situation you have in mind please do not hesitate to let us know.

Sincerely,

C. Lamar Johnson
Deputy Administrator

## Section H. Tort Liability of Paralegals

Thus far we have discussed a number of ways that paralegal activities are or could be regulated:

- Criminal liability for violating the statutes on the unauthorized practice of law
- Special authorization rules on practice before administrative agencies and other tribunals
- Licensing
- Bar rules on paralegal education
- Self-regulation
- Labor laws

Finally, we come to *tort liability,* which is another method by which society defines what is and is not permissible. A tort is a private wrong or injury other than a breach of contract or the commission of a crime, although some breaches of contract and crimes can also constitute torts.

Two questions need to be kept in mind. First, when are paralegal employees *personally liable* for their torts? Second, when are employers *vicariously liable* for the torts of their paralegal employees? (As we will see, vicarious liability simply means being liable because of what someone else has done or failed to do.) The short answer to the first question is: *always.* The short answer to the second question is: *when the wrongdoing by the paralegal was within the scope of employment.* After covering both questions, we will then examine the separate question of when malpractice insurance will pay for such liability.

Several different kinds of wrongdoing are possible. The paralegal might commit:

- The tort of negligence
- An intentional tort, such as battery.
- An act which is both a crime (such as embezzlement) *and* an intentional tort (such as conversion).

A client who is injured by any of these torts can sue the paralegal in the same manner that a patient in a hospital can sue a nurse. Paralegals are not relieved of liability simply because they work for, and function under the supervision of, an attorney. Every citizen is *personally* liable for the torts he or she commits. The same is true of criminal liability.

Next we turn to the employers of paralegals. Are they *also* liable for wrongdoing committed by their paralegals? Assume that the supervising attorneys did nothing wrong themselves. For example, the attorney did not commit the tort or crime as an active participant with the paralegal, or the attorney was not careless in selecting and training the paralegal. Our question is: Can an attorney be liable to a client solely because of the wrongdoing of a paralegal? When such liability applies, it is called *vicarious liability,* which exists when one person is liable solely because of what someone else has done or failed to do. The answer to our question is found in the doctrine of *respondeat superior,* which makes employers responsible for the torts of their employees or agents when the wrongdoing occurs within the scope of employment.[38]

Hence, if a tort is committed by a paralegal within the scope of employment, the client can sue the paralegal or the attorney, or both. This does not mean that the client recovers twice; there can be only one recovery for a tort. The client is simply given a choice in bringing the suit. In most cases, the primary target of the client will be the employer, who is the so-called *deep pocket,* meaning the one who has resources from which a judgment can be satisfied.

Finally we need to examine what is meant by "scope of employment." Not every wrongdoing of a paralegal is within the scope of employment simply because it is employment related. The test is as follows: Paralegals act within the scope of employment when they are furthering the business of their employer, which for our purposes is the practice of law. Slandering a client for failure to pay a law firm bill certainly furthers the business of the law firm. But the opposite is probably true when a paralegal has an argument with a client over a football game and punches the client during their accidental evening meeting at a bar. In the latter example, the client could not sue the paralegal's employer for the intentional tort of battery under the doctrine of *respondeat superior,* because the battery was not committed while furthering the business of the employer. Only the paralegal would be liable for the tort under such circumstances.

The most common tort committed by attorneys is negligence. This tort occurs when a client is injured because of a failure to use the ordinary skill, knowledge, and diligence normally possessed and used, under similar circumstances, by a member of the profession in good standing. In short, the tort is committed by failure to exercise the reasonable care expected of an attorney. An attorney is not, however, an insurer. Every mistake will not lead to negligence liability even if it causes harm to the client. The harm must be due to an unreasonable mistake, such as forgetting to file an action in court before the statute of limitations runs out.

When a paralegal commits negligence for which the attorney becomes liable under *respondeat superior,* the same standard applies. Since the work product of the paralegal blends into the work product of the supervising attorney, the attorney becomes as fully responsible for what the paralegal did as if the attorney had committed the negligence. Unreasonableness is measured by what a

---

[38]We are talking here of vicarious *civil* liability, or more specifically, the tort liability of employers because of the torts committed by their employees. Employers are not subject to vicarious *criminal* liability. If a paralegal commits a crime on the job, only the paralegal goes to jail (unless the employer actually participated in the crime).

reasonable attorney would have done, not what a reasonable paralegal would have done.

There have not been many tort cases in which paralegals have been sued for wrongdoing in a law office. Yet as paralegals become more prominent in the practice of law, more are expected to be named as defendants. The most common kinds of cases involving paralegals have occurred when the paralegal was a notary and improperly notarized signatures under pressure from the supervising attorney.

---

### ■ ASSIGNMENT 4.17

Mary Smith is a paralegal at the XYZ law firm. One of her tasks is to file a document in court. She negligently forgets to do so. As a result, the client has a default judgment entered against her. What options are available to the client?

---

### ■ ASSIGNMENT 4.18

Go to the *American Digest System*. For information on this digest and its use, see pages 498 and 557. Give citations to and brief summaries of court cases on the topics listed in (a) and (b) below. Start with the Descriptive Word Index volumes of the most recent Decennial. After you check the appropriate key numbers (page 555) in that Decennial, check those key numbers in all the General Digest volumes that follow the most recent Decennial. Then check for case law in at least three other recent Decennials. Once you obtain citations to case law in the digest paragraphs, you do not have to go to the reporters to read the full text of the opinions. Simply give the citations you find and brief summaries of the cases as they are printed in the digest paragraphs.

**(a)** Cases, if any, dealing with the negligence of attorneys in the hiring and supervision of legal secretaries, law clerks, investigators, and paralegals. (If there are many, select any five cases.)

**(b)** Cases, if any, dealing with the negligence of doctors and/or hospitals in the hiring and supervision of nurses, paramedics, and other medical technicians. (If there are many, select any five cases.)

---

## ■ Section I. Malpractice Insurance

Legal *malpractice* generally refers to wrongful conduct by an attorney for which an injured party (the attorney's client) can receive damages. Just as doctors purchase malpractice insurance against suits by their patients, so too attorneys can buy such insurance to cover suits against them by their clients for alleged errors and omissions. We need to examine how paralegals fit into this picture.

Until the 1940s, not many attorneys bought malpractice insurance because suits by clients were relatively rare. Today, the picture has changed radically; cautious attorneys do not practice law without such insurance against their own malpractice. "Statistically, the new attorney will be subjected to three claims before finishing a legal career." [39] Hence, very few attorneys are willing to *go bare,*—that is, practice without insurance. This change has been due to a num-

---

[39] R. Mallen & J. Smith, *Legal Malpractice*, 3rd ed., 2 (1989).

**FIGURE 4.7**

Malpractice
Liability Claims
Against Attorneys

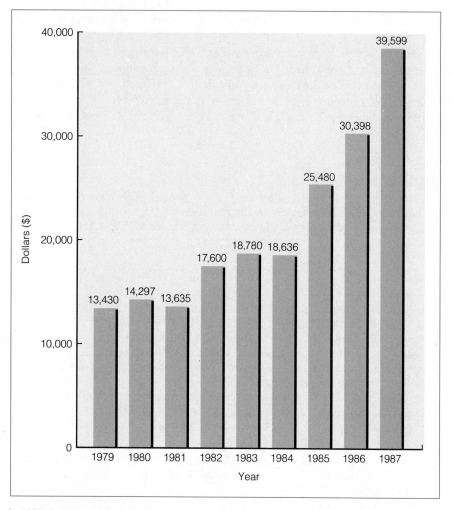

In 1979 the average claim paid, including all expenses, was $13,430. By 1987 this amount rose 295% to a new average of $39,599.

**Source:** St. Paul Fire & Marine Insurance Company

ber of factors. As the practice of law becomes more complex, the likelihood of error increases. Furthermore, the public is becoming more aware of its right to sue. In spite of disclaimers by attorneys that they are not guaranteeing any results, client expectations tend to be high, and hence clients are more likely to blame their attorney for an unfavorable result. And attorneys are increasingly willing to sue each other. In fact, some attorneys have developed a legal malpractice specialty in which they take clients who want to sue other attorneys. As malpractice awards against attorneys continue to rise (see Figure 4.7), the market for malpractice insurance has dramatically increased. And so has the cost. In some cities, the premium for insurance is over $6,000 per year per attorney.

There are two kinds of professional liability insurance policies covering attorney malpractice: occurrence policies and claims-made policies. An *occurrence policy* covers all occurrences (such as negligent error or omission) during the period the policy is in effect, even if the claim on such an occurrence is not actually filed until after the policy expires. Insurance companies are reluctant to write such policies because of the length of time it sometimes takes to uncover the existence of the negligent error or omission. Here's an example: An attorney makes a careless mistake in drafting a will that is not discovered until the person who hired the attorney dies many years later. Under an occurrence policy, the attorney is protected if the mistake occurred while the policy was in effect, even if the actual claim was not filed in court until after the policy terminated. The most common kind of policy sold by insurance companies today is the *claims-made policy* under which coverage is limited to claims actually filed (made) during the period in which the policy is in effect.[40]

Malpractice policies usually cover all the attorneys *and* the nonattorney employees of the law office. One policy, for example, defines the individuals covered—"the insured"—as follows:

> The insured includes the firm, all lawyers within the firm, and all non-lawyer employees, as well as former partners, officers, directors and employees solely while they acted on behalf of the insured firm.[41]

Such inclusion of employees is not always automatic, however. The policies of some insurance companies do not include paralegals or secretaries unless the law firm specifically requests coverage for them and pays an additional premium for their inclusion. Paralegals should therefore ask their employers if their malpractice policy explicitly covers paralegals.

What about freelance or independent paralegals who sell their services to attorneys? Although they may not be considered employees of the firm, they will usually be covered under the firm's policy in the same manner as full-time, in-house paralegal employees. So long as the employing attorney supervises and is responsible for the conduct of the paralegal, the malpractice policy usually provides coverage. In the language of one widely used policy, coverage is provided for "any other person for whose acts, errors or omissions the insured is legally responsible," [42] which would include freelance paralegals.

Nevertheless, some freelance paralegals have explored the possibility of obtaining their own malpractice insurance policies. To date, most traditional insurance companies have not made such policies available, although there are exceptions. Complete Equity Markets, Inc., for example, offers "Paralegals Professional Indemnity Insurance" as a claims-made policy. For approximately $1,800 a year, a paralegal can purchase $250,000 worth of malpractice insurance. Since most paralegals work for an attorney and are already covered under the attorney's policy, few paralegals have purchased their own policy. Yet if paralegals are eventually granted a form of limited license that authorizes them to sell their services directly to the public, separate paralegal malpractice policies will become common and may even be mandated as a condition of receiving the license.[43]

---

[40]It is possible for a claims-made policy to cover a negligent error or omission that took place *before* the effective date of the policy, but most companies exclude coverage for prepolicy claims that the attorney knows about or could have reasonably foreseen at the time the policy is applied for.

[41]Home Insurance Companies, Professional Liability Insurance.

[42]American Home Assurance Company, Lawyers Professional Liability Policy.

[43]As we saw earlier, most Enrolled Agents are nonlawyers who are authorized to provide certain tax services to the public. The National Association of Enrolled Agents offers a "Professional Liability Insurance Plan" through the St. Paul Fire and Marine Insurance Company. The Association's brochure says, "You can now secure protection against an unexpected lawsuit or penalty for damages arising from services you provide as an Enrolled Agent." Attorneys are not eligible to purchase this insurance.

# Chapter Summary

Criminal prosecution may result from violating statutes on the unauthorized practice of law. In general, they prohibit nonattorneys from appearing for another in a representative capacity, drafting legal documents, and giving legal advice. Nonattorneys can sell forms and other legal materials but cannot give individual help in using them.

There are some major exceptions to the prohibitions on nonattorney conduct. In a limited number of circumstances, nonattorneys are authorized to do what would otherwise constitute the unauthorized practice of law. For example:

- In most states, a real estate broker can draft sales contracts.

- Several specialized courts allow nonattorneys to represent clients in court, although this is rare.

- A few states allow paralegals to "appear" in court to request a continuance or a new date for the next hearing in a case.

- An inmate can "practice law" in prison—for example, he or she can draft court documents for and give legal advice to another inmate if the prison does not offer adequate alternative methods of providing legal services.

- Many administrative agencies, particularly at the federal level, allow nonattorneys to represent clients before the agencies.

A number of states have considered broad-based licensing (which would cover all activities of all paralegals), and limited licensing (which would cover specified activities of those paralegals, often called legal technicians, who are not supervised by attorneys). To date, neither kind of licensing has been enacted. Relatively soon, however, a limited-license requirement will probably be enacted in one or two states. While this would be a dramatic event, it would affect very few paralegals, since limited licensing would not apply to paralegals who work for attorneys.

All paralegal schools in the country must be licensed by their state. There is no requirement that they be accredited by the bar association. The American Bar Association, however, has an "approval" process whereby a school can be approved by the ABA.

A number of bar associations allow paralegals to become associate or affiliate members. For example, the American Bar Association has a membership category called Legal Assistant Associate.

Certification has been a major point of disagreement between the National Association of Legal Assistants (NALA) and the National Federation of Paralegal Associations (NFPA). NALA has instituted a national test that leads to certification as a Certified Legal Assistant (CLA). Even though this is a voluntary program, NFPA opposes its very existence.

The Fair Labor Standards Act requires employers to pay overtime compensation to employees unless they function in an executive, administrative, or professional capacity. Paralegal managers with major responsibility for the supervision of other paralegals would fall within one of the exceptions, and hence would not be entitled to overtime compensation. All other paralegals, however, do not fall within an exception and therefore must be paid overtime compensation.

If a paralegal commits a tort, such as negligence, he or she is personally liable to the defendant. Under the theory of *respondeat superior,* the supervising attorney is also liable for the wrong committed by the paralegal if it occurred within the scope of employment. Most attorneys have a claims-made malpractice insurance policy that covers their employees.

# Key Terms

accreditation
approval
certification
certified
certificated
ethics
guideline
licensure

limited licensure
specialty licensure
registration
regulation
practice of law
unauthorized practice of law
authorized practice of law
statement of principles

treaties
certified domestic violence
    advocate
ex parte order
jailhouse lawyer
writ writer
*Johnson v. Avery*
Administrative Procedure Act

registered agent
agency practitioner
enrolled agent
supremacy clause
page 52 debate
legal technician
licensed independent
    paralegal
HALT
limited practice officer
pro bono
prepaid legal services
legal insurance
approval commission

antitrust
monopoly
associate members
affiliate members
attorney attestation
CLA
CLAS
CFLA
specialty certification
legal assistant division
entry-level certification
advanced certification
GOD
Fair Labor Standards Act

overtime compensation
Wage and Hour Division
exempt paralegal
nonexempt paralegal
tort liability
personal liability
vicarious liability
respondeat superior
deep pocket
malpractice
go bare
occurrence policy
claims-made policy

# 5

# Attorney Ethics and Paralegal Ethics

## ■ Chapter Outline

**Section A. The Ten Commandments of an Ethical Conservative**

**Section B. Enforcing Ethics**

Ethics and Sanctions

Paralegals and Attorney Ethics

Courts, Legislatures, and Bar Associations

Accusation of Unethical Conduct

**Section C. The Ethical Rules**

Competence

Diligence/Unwarranted Delay

Fees

Crime or Fraud by an Attorney

Crime or Fraud by a Client

Frivolous Legal Positions

Safekeeping Property

False Statements/Failure to Disclose

Withdrawal

Confidentiality of Information

Conflict of Interest

Communication with the Other Side

Solicitation

Advertising

Reporting Professional Misconduct

Appearance of Impropriety

Unauthorized Practice of Law

Paralegals

**Section D. Doing Research on an Ethical Issue**

**Section E. Ethical Codes of the Paralegal Associations**

**Section F. An Ethical Dilemma: Your Ethics or Your Job!**

## ■ Section A. The Ten Commandments of an Ethical Conservative

When it comes to ethics, *a paralegal must be conservative.* To an ethical conservative, the question is not, "What can I get away with?" but rather, "What is the right thing to do?" With this guideline in mind, we will examine many ethical principles in this chapter. Some of the most important are presented in Figure 5.1.

## ■ Section B. Enforcing Ethics

### 1. Ethics and Sanctions

*Ethics* are rules that embody standards of behavior to which members of an organization must conform. The organization is often an association of individuals in the same occupation—for example, attorneys, paralegals, stockbrokers, or accountants. The ethical rules of some organizations are enforced by *sanctions.* A sanction is any penalty or punishment imposed for unaccepta-

**FIGURE 5.1**

Paralegal Ethics:
The Ten
Commandments of
a Conservative

1. Know the ethical rules governing attorneys. If you understand when attorneys are vulnerable to charges of unprofessional conduct, you will be better able to help them avoid such charges.

2. Know the ethical rules governing paralegals. At the start of your paralegal career, promise yourself that you will adhere to rigorous standards of professional ethics, even if these standards are higher than those followed by people around you.

3. Never tell anyone who is not working on a case anything about that case. This includes your best friend, your spouse, and your relative.

4. Assume that people outside your office do not have a clear understanding of what a paralegal or legal assistant is. Make sure that everyone with whom you come in contact (clients, attorneys, court officials, agency officials, the public) understand that you are not an attorney.

5. Know what legal advice is and refuse to be coaxed into giving it, no matter how innocent the question asked of you appears to be.

6. Never make contact with an opposing party in a legal dispute, or with anyone closely associated with that party, unless you have the permission of your supervising attorney and of the attorney for the opposing party, if the latter has one.

7. Don't sign your name to anything if you are not certain that what you are signing is 100% accurate and that the law allows a paralegal to sign it.

8. Never pad your time sheets. Insist that what you submit is 100% accurate.

9. Know the common rationalizations for misrepresentation and other unethical conduct:
   - it's always done
   - the other side does it
   - the cause of our client is just
   - if I don't do it, I will jeopardize my job.

   Promise yourself that you will not allow any of these rationalizations to entice you to participate in misrepresentation or other unethical conduct.

10. If what you are asked to do doesn't feel right, don't proceed until it does.

ble conduct.[1] Other organizations, however, have ethical rules that are not tied to any system of enforcement.

All of the major national paralegal associations have adopted ethical rules, as we shall see later in the chapter. But none are enforced by sanctions. No paralegal, for example, has ever been thrown out of a paralegal association for unethical conduct. It could happen, but it is unlikely since it is very expensive to establish and operate an enforcement system. Paralegal associations simply do not have the resources that would be required.

Attorneys, on the other hand, *are* subject to enforceable ethical rules. These rules attempt to govern everything an attorney does in the practice of law. Of course, one of the things an attorney does is employ paralegals. Hence, as we will see, there are rules on how an attorney can use paralegals ethically. Unethical use of paralegals can subject the attorney to sanctions.

## 2. Paralegals and Attorney Ethics

Can a paralegal *also* be sanctioned for violating these ethical rules? No. The rules govern attorney conduct only.[2] Since paralegals cannot join a bar associ-

---

[1]Another meaning of the word sanction is to authorize or to give formal approval. Example: the court *sanctioned* the payment of attorney fees.

[2]Remarkably, there is one jurisdiction—the District of Columbia—that allows a nonattorney to become a full owner/partner of a law firm! This individual must agree to abide by the ethical code that governs attorneys. In D.C., therefore, the ethical rules governing attorneys *do* apply to nonattorneys. (The first nonattorney to become a partner of a law firm was an accountant.)

ation as full members, they cannot be sanctioned by a bar association or by any other agency set up to monitor attorney conduct. Serious wrongdoing by paralegals may result in their being fired and might subject them to negligence suits or to criminal prosecution (as we saw in Chapter 4,) but they cannot be punished for unethical conduct by the entity that regulates attorneys.

This does not mean, however, that paralegals can ignore the ethical rules governing attorneys. Quite the contrary. *One of the paralegal's primary responsibilities is to help an attorney avoid being charged with unethical conduct.* (A recent seminar conducted by the Los Angeles Paralegal Association was entitled "Law Firm Ethics: How to Keep Your Attorneys off '60 Minutes'!") Hence, the paralegal must be intimately familiar with ethical rules. Our goal in this chapter is to provide you with that familiarity.

## 3. Courts, Legislatures, and Bar Associations

In most states, the regulation of attorneys is primarily under the control of the highest court in the state (often called the Supreme Court), which determines when an attorney can be granted a license to practice law and under what conditions the license will be taken away or suspended because of unethical conduct. Since the state legislature may also exert some regulatory authority over attorneys, a dispute occasionally arises over which branch of government can control a particular aspect of the practice of law. The judiciary often wins this dispute and becomes the final authority. In practice, however, the judicial branch and the legislative branch usually share regulatory jurisdiction over the practice of law, with the dominant branch being the judiciary. The day-to-day functions of regulation are delegated to an entity such as a state bar association and a disciplinary board or grievance commission.

There are three kinds of bar associations:

- National (for example, American Bar Association, Association of Trial Lawyers of America, Hispanic National Bar Association)
- State (for example, Illinois State Bar Association, State Bar of Montana) and
- Local (for example, Boston Bar Association, San Diego County Bar Association).

All national and local bar associations are voluntary; no attorney is required to be a member. The majority of state bar associations in the country are *integrated,* which simply means that membership is required as a condition of practicing law in the state. (Integrated bar associations are also referred to as *mandatory* or *unified* bar associations. See Figure 5.2.) There is a state bar association in every state. Most, but not all, are mandatory.

Under the general supervision of the state's highest court, the state bar association has a large role in regulating most aspects of the practice of law. For example, dues charged by integrated bar associations are used to fund the state's system of enforcing ethical rules. States that do not have integrated bar associations often have a *registration* requirement. Each attorney in the state registers to practice law and pays a registration fee that is used to fund that state's system of enforcing the ethical rules. Even in these states, the state bar association has a great influence over the regulation of attorneys. Given this dominant role of bar associations, the method of regulating attorneys in America is essentially that of self-regulation: attorneys regulating attorneys.[3]

---

[3]This is so even in states that allow nonattorneys to serve on boards or commissions that regulate an aspect of the legal profession.

**FIGURE 5.2**

States with Unified
Bar Associations
(1991)

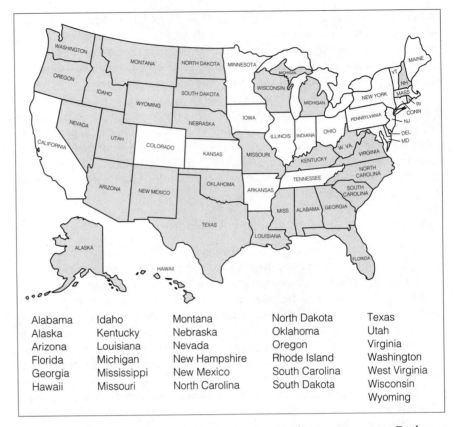

| | | | | |
|---|---|---|---|---|
| Alabama | Idaho | Montana | North Dakota | Texas |
| Alaska | Kentucky | Nebraska | Oklahoma | Utah |
| Arizona | Louisiana | Nevada | Oregon | Virginia |
| Florida | Michigan | New Hampshire | Rhode Island | Washington |
| Georgia | Mississippi | New Mexico | South Carolina | West Virginia |
| Hawaii | Missouri | North Carolina | South Dakota | Wisconsin |
| | | | | Wyoming |

There is no national set of ethical rules that applies to every state. Each state can adopt its own rules to regulate the attorneys licensed in that state. The rules are found in documents with various names, such as code of ethics, canons of ethics, code of professional responsibility, model rules. In fact, however, there is considerable similarity in the rules that the states have adopted. The reason for this similarity is the influence of the American Bar Association.

As indicated, the American Bar Association is a voluntary national bar association; no attorney must belong to it. Yet approximately 55% of the attorneys in America do belong to the ABA. It publishes ethical rules but does *not* discipline attorneys for unethical conduct. The role of the ABA in this area is to write ethical rules and to *propose* to the individual states that they be accepted. A state is free to adopt, modify, or reject them. The current recommendation of the ABA is found in a document called the *Model Rules of Professional Conduct*.[4] This document has been very influential throughout the country. Many states adopted it with relatively minor changes.

## 4. Accusation of Unethical Conduct

When an attorney is charged with unethical conduct, the case is investigated by a disciplinary body appointed by the state's highest court. The name

---

[4]The *Model Rules of Professional Conduct* is a 1983 revision of the ABA's *Model Code of Professional Responsibility*. The latter document consists of three main parts. First, there are nine *canons*, which are general statements of norms that express the standards of professional conduct expected of attorneys. Second, and more important, there are *disciplinary rules* (abbreviated DR), which are mandatory statements of the minimum conduct below which no attorney can fall without being subject to disciplinary action. Third, there are *ethical considerations* (abbreviated EC) which represent the objectives toward which each member of the profession should strive.

for this body differs from state to state, e.g., the Grievance Commission, the Attorney Registration and Disciplinary Commission, the Committee on Professional Conduct, the Board of Professional Responsibility.

A hearing is held to determine whether unethical conduct was committed by the accused attorney. The commission, committee, or board then makes its recommendation to the state's highest court which makes the final determination of whether to accept this recommendation. A number of sanctions can be imposed by the court. See Figure 5.3.

## Section C. The Ethical Rules

We turn now to an overview of specific ethical rules that apply to attorneys. Where appropriate, a paralegal perspective on the rules will be presented. At the end of the overview, there will be a more concentrated focus on paralegals, particularly on ethical issues not covered earlier in the chapter. The overview is based on the ABA *Model Rules of Professional Conduct*. The rule numbers used in the discussion (such as Model Rule 1.5) refer to these *Model Rules,* which will either be quoted or summarized.

### 1. Competence

*An attorney shall provide competent representation to a client.* Model Rule 1.1

A *competent* attorney uses the *knowledge* and *skill* that are reasonably necessary to represent a particular client. What is reasonably necessary depends on the complexity of the case. A great deal of knowledge and skill, for example, may be needed when representing a corporate client accused of complicated antitrust violations.

How do attorneys obtain this knowledge and skill? They draw on the general principles of legal analysis and legal research learned in law school. But more importantly, they take the time needed to *prepare* themselves. They spend time in the law library. They talk with their colleagues. In some instances, they formally associate themselves with more experienced attorneys in the area. Attorneys who fail to take these steps are acting unethically if their failure means that they do not have the knowledge and skill reasonably necessary to represent a particular client.

Some attorneys have so many clients that they could not possibly give proper attention to each. Always looking for more lucrative work, they run the risk of neglecting the clients they already have. As a consequence, they might miss court dates or other filing deadlines, lose documents, fail to determine what law governs a client's case, etc. Such an attorney is practicing law "from the hip"—incompetently and unethically.

Example: Mary Henderson, Esq. has a large criminal law practice. She agrees to probate the estate of a client's deceased son. She has never handled such a case before. Five years go by. No progress is made in determining who is entitled to receive the estate. If some minimal legal research had been done, Henderson would have been able to close the case within six months of taking it.

Henderson has probably acted unethically. The failure to do basic research on a case is a sign of incompetence. The need for such research is clear in view

**FIGURE 5.3**

Attorney Sanctions
for Unethical
Conduct

| | |
|---|---|
| DISBARMENT: | The termination of the right to practice law. The disbarment can be permanent or temporary. If it's temporary, the attorney will be allowed to apply for readmission after a designated period. |
| SUSPENSION: | The removal of an attorney from the practice of law for a specified minimum period, after which the attorney can apply for reinstatement. An *interim suspension* is a temporary suspension pending the imposition of final discipline. |
| REPRIMAND: | A public declaration that the attorney's conduct was improper. This does not affect his or her right to practice. Reprimand is also called *censure* or *public censure*. |
| ADMONITION: | A nonpublic declaration that the attorney's conduct was improper. The mildest form of punishment that can be imposed, it does not affect his or her right to practice. An admonition is also known as a *private reprimand*. |
| PROBATION: | Allowing the attorney to continue to practice but under specified conditions, such as submitting to periodic audits of client funds controlled by the attorney or making restitution to a client whose funds were wrongly taken by the attorney. |

of the fact that she has never handled a probate case before. Either she must take the time to find out how to probate the estate, or she must contact another attorney with probate experience and arrange to work with this attorney on the case. Not doing either is unethical.

The vast majority of graduates of law schools need a good deal of on-the-job study and guidance before they are ready to handle cases of any complexity. A law school education does little more than help ensure that the attorney is equipped to go out and *continue* learning through experience and legal research. A good attorney is always learning the law—long after law school is over. The first day on the job for new attorneys is often a very nervous event because they are acutely aware of how much they do *not* know.

In addition to sanctions for unethical conduct, an attorney's incompetence may have other consequences as well. The client might try to sue the attorney for negligence in a legal malpractice case. (Such suits were discussed in Chapter 4.) If the client is a criminal defendant who was convicted, he or she may try to appeal the conviction on the ground that the attorney's incompetence amounted to a denial of the effective "Assistance of Counsel" guaranteed by the 6th Amendment of the U.S. Constitution.

*Paralegal Perspective:*

- "An attorney who utilizes a legal assistant's services is responsible for determining that the legal assistant is competent to perform the tasks assigned, based on the legal assistant's education, training, and experience . . . ."[5] While the attorney has this supervisory responsibility, paralegals also have a responsibility to maintain their own competence.

- If you are given assignments that are beyond your knowledge and skill, let your supervisor know. Either you must be given training with close supervision, or you must be given other assignments. A "lawyer should explain to

---

[5]ABA Standing Committee on Legal Assistants, *Model Guidelines for the Utilization of Legal Assistant Services,* Draft, Comment to Guideline 1 (March 1991). (Hereinafter cited as ABA *Model Guidelines.*)

the legal assistant that the legal assistant has a duty to inform the lawyer of any assignment which the assistant regards as beyond his capability." [6]

■ After you complete an assignment, look for an opportunity to ask your supervisor how you could have improved your performance on the assignment. Do not wait for a year-end evaluation to learn what you can do to become a more competent paralegal.

■ Find out which attorneys, administrators, paralegals, and secretaries in the office have a reputation for explaining things well. Spend time with such individuals even if you do not work with them on a daily basis. Take them to lunch. Find time to sit with them on a coffee break. Ask lots of questions. Let them know you respect high-quality work and appreciate anything they can tell you to help you increase your competence.

■ Take the initiative in continuing your formal paralegal education after you are employed. Do not wait for someone to suggest further training. Find out what seminars and conferences are being conducted by paralegal associations and bar associations in your area. Attend those that are relevant to your job even if you must pay for them yourself.

## 2. Diligence/Unwarranted Delay

*An attorney shall act with reasonable diligence and promptness in representing a client.* Model Rule 1.3

*An attorney must make reasonable efforts to expedite litigation.* Model Rule 3.2

Angry clients often complain that attorneys take forever to complete a case, and keep clients in the dark about what is happening. "He never answers my calls." "It took months to file the case in court." "He keeps telling me that everything is fine, but nothing ever gets done." Such complaints do not necessarily indicate unethical behavior by the attorney. Events may be beyond the control of the attorney. For example, the court calendar is crowded, the other side is not responding. Yet this does not excuse a lack of regular communication with clients to keep them reasonably informed about the status of their case.

Other explanations for a lack of diligence and promptness, however, are more serious:

■ The attorney is disorganized. The law office has not developed adequate systems to process cases. The delays are due to careless mistakes and a lack of skill.

■ The attorney is taking many more cases than the office can handle. Additional personnel should be hired to do the needed work, or new cases should not be accepted.

Often, the failure to use reasonable diligence and promptness causes harm to the client. For example, the attorney neglects to file a suit before the statute of limitations has run against the client. Unreasonable procrastination, however, can be unethical even if such harm does not result.

Another problem is the attorney who intentionally seeks numerous delays in an effort to try to wear the other side down. It is unethical to engage in such

---

[6]Section 20–110, Committee Commentary, *New Mexico Rules Governing the Practice of Law* (Judicial Pamphlet 16).

dilatory practices. Attorneys must use reasonable efforts to expedite litigation, consistent with protecting the interests of their clients.

## Paralegal Perspective:

- An overloaded attorney probably works with an overloaded paralegal. Successful paralegals often take the initiative by asking for additional work. But reason must prevail. If you have more work than you can handle, you must let your supervisor know. Otherwise, you might be contributing to the problem of undue procrastination.

- Learn everything you can about office systems. Find out how they are created. (See Chapter 3.) After you have gained some experience in the office, you should start designing systems on your own initiative.

- When a busy attorney is in court or cannot be disturbed because of pressing work on another case, someone in the office should be available to communicate with clients who want to know the status of their case. In many offices, the paralegal is in a position to provide this information. The role is delicate, however, since in addition to asking about the status of their case, clients often asks questions that call for legal advice. Giving such advice may constitute the unauthorized practice of law. Later we will examine in greater depth the temptations and pressures on a paralegal to give legal advice.

## 3. Fees

*An attorney's fee shall be reasonable.* Model Rule 1.5(a)

There is no absolute standard to determine when a fee is excessive and therefore unreasonable. A number of factors must be considered: the amount of time and labor involved, the complexity of the case, the experience and reputation of the attorney, the customary fee in the locality for the same kind of case, etc.

> Examples: In 1979, a court ruled that $500 an hour was excessive in a simple battery case involving a guilty plea and no unusual issues. In 1984, a court ruled that a fee of $22,500 was excessive in an uncomplicated real estate case involving very little time. The case was settled through the efforts of someone other than the attorney.

The basis of the fee should be communicated to the client before or soon after the attorney starts to work on the case. This is often done in the contract of employment called a *retainer*.[7]

At one time, bar associations published a list of "recommended fees" that should be charged for designated kinds of services. These *minimum-fee schedules* have now been prohibited by the United States Supreme Court. They constitute illegal price fixing by the bar in violation of the antitrust laws.

*Contingent fees* can sometimes present ethical problems. A contingent fee is a fee that is dependent on the outcome of the case. (Other kinds of fees will be examined in Chapter 14.)

---

[7]Another meaning of the word *retainer* is the amount of money or other assets that will serve as an advance payment for services. Depending on the agreement reached, the retainer may or may not be refundable in the event that the attorney-client relationship ends before all the legal services are performed.

> Example: An attorney signs a retainer to represent a client in an automobile negligence case. If the jury awards the client damages, the attorney will receive 30% of the award. If the client loses the case, the attorney receives no fee.

This is a contingent fee since it is dependent on the outcome of the negligence case.

The benefit of a contingent fee is that it provides an incentive for an attorney to take the case of a client who does not have funds to pay an attorney while the case is pending. But contingent fees are not ethical in every case, even if the amount to be received by the successful attorney is otherwise reasonable. A contingent fee in a criminal case, and in most divorce cases, for example, is unethical.

> Example: Gabe Farrell is a client of Sam Grondon, Esq. in a criminal case where Gabe is charged with murder. Gabe agrees to pay Grondon $100,000 if he is found innocent. Grondon will receive nothing if Gabe is convicted of any crime.

This fee agreement is unethical. Contingent fees are not allowed in criminal cases. Note the pressures on Grondon. He arguably has no incentive to try to negotiate a guilty plea to a lesser charge, since such a plea would mean a conviction and, hence, no fee. In such a situation, the attorney's own personal interest (obtaining the $100,000) could conflict with the interest of the client (receiving a lesser penalty through a negotiated plea). Similar pressures can arise in family-law cases.

> Example: To obtain a divorce from his wife, a client hires an attorney. The fee is $25,000 if the divorce is granted.

As the case develops, suppose there is a glimmer of hope that the husband and wife might reconcile. Hence, the attorney's interest (obtaining the $25,000) could conflict with the interest of the client (reconciling). This might lead the attorney to discourage the reconciliation or to set up roadblocks to it. Reconciliation obviously removes the possibility of the contingency—obtaining the divorce—from occurring. In family law cases, therefore, contingent fees are unethical if the fee is dependent on securing a divorce, on the amount of alimony obtained, on the amount of support obtained, or on the amount of a property settlement in lieu of alimony or support. Model Rule 1.5(d). This is so even if the terms of the contingent fee are otherwise reasonable.

One final theme should be covered: *fee splitting*. The splitting or division of a fee refers to a single client bill covering the fee of two or more attorneys who are not in the same firm.

> Example: John Jones, Esq. is hired by a singer who is charging her record company with copyright infringement and breach of contract. Jones calls in Randy Smith, Esq., a specialist in copyright law from another firm. Both work on the case. The singer receives one bill for the work of both attorneys even though they work for different law firms.

The attorneys are splitting or dividing the fee between them.[8] This arrangement is proper under certain conditions. For example, the total fee must be reasonable, and the client must be told about the participation of all the attorneys and not object.

Suppose, however, that the attorney splits the fee with a nonattorney.

---

[8]The attorney who refers a case to another attorney receives what is called a *referral fee* or *forwarding fee* from the latter.

> Example: Frank Martin is a freelance investigator. He refers accident victims to a law firm. For every client he refers to the firm, he receives 25% of the fee collected by the firm.

> Example: Helen Gregson is a chiropractor. She refers medical malpractice cases to a law firm which compensates her for each referral.

These are improper divisions of fees with nonattorneys—even if the amount of the division is reasonable and the clients brought in by Martin or Gregson consent to their receiving a part of the fee. An attorney cannot share with a nonattorney a portion of a fee paid by particular clients. The rationale behind this prohibition is that the nonattorney might exercise some control over the attorney and thereby jeopardize the attorney's independent judgment.

For the same reason, an attorney cannot form a partnership with a nonattorney if any of the activities of the partnership consist of the practice of law. If the office practices law as a corporation, a nonattorney cannot own any interest in the company or be a director or officer.[9]

### Paralegal Perspective:

- An attorney or law firm may include paralegals and other nonattorney employees in a compensation or retirement plan, even though the plan is based in whole or in part on a profit-sharing arrangement. Model Rule 5.4(a)(3).

> Example: Frank is a paralegal at a law firm. The firm has a retirement plan under which the firm contributes a portion of its profits into the plan. Frank is a member of this retirement plan.

The firm is not acting unethically. In most states, paralegals can receive compensation and retirement benefits that are based on the fees received by the firm so long as they are not receiving all or part of *particular* legal fees. "The linchpin of the prohibition [against splitting fees with a legal assistant] seems to be the advance agreement of the lawyer to 'split' a fee based on a preexisting contingent arrangement. There is no general prohibition against a lawyer who enjoys a particularly profitable period recognizing the contribution of the legal assistant to that profitability with a discretionary bonus. Likewise, a lawyer engaged in a particularly profitable specialty of legal practice is not prohibited from compensating the legal assistant who aids materially in that practice more handsomely than the compensation generally awarded to legal assistants in that geographic area who work in law practices that are less lucrative. Indeed, any effort to fix a compensation level for legal assistants and prohibit greater compensation would appear to violate the federal antitrust laws." [10]

- A related restriction in many states is that an attorney cannot give a paralegal any compensation for referring business to the attorney. "It appears clear that a legal assistant may not be compensated on a contingent basis for a particular case or paid for 'signing up' clients for a legal practice." [11]

---

[9] Wolfram, C., *Modern Legal Ethics,* § 9.2.4 (1986). In the District of Columbia, however, where nonattorneys are allowed to be owner-partners in law firms, nonattorneys can obviously share legal fees with attorneys. See footnote 2.

[10] ABA *Model Guidelines,* Comment to Guideline 9, see footnote 5.

[11] Ibid.

■ Attorneys must not allow their paralegals to accept cases, to reject cases, or to "set fees." The responsibility "for establishing the amount of a fee to be charged for a legal service" may not be delegated to a paralegal.[12]

■ "A lawyer may include a charge for the work performed by a legal assistant in setting a charge for legal services." [13] As we saw in Chapter 1, most attorneys bill clients for paralegal time. Paralegals record their time on time sheets that become the basis of bills sent to clients. The amount that an attorney bills for paralegal time must be reasonable. Reasonableness is determined by a number of factors, such as the experience of the paralegal, the nature of the tasks the paralegal undertakes, and the market rate for paralegals in the area.

■ *Double billing* must be avoided. The paralegal's time should not have already been figured into the attorney's hourly rate. Some states ask the attorney to submit an affidavit to support the amount claimed for the paralegal's time. The affidavit must give a detailed statement of the time spent and services rendered by the paralegal, a summary of the paralegal's qualifications, etc. In New Mexico, the attorney must disclose to the client the amount to be charged for the services of the paralegals in the office.

■ As a paralegal, your time records should be contemporaneous, that is, made at approximately the same time as the events you are recording. Try to avoid recording time long after you perform tasks that require time records.

■ Time sheets must also be accurate; padding is clearly unethical. Padding occurs when someone records time that was not in fact spent. When a client is billed on the basis of time sheets that have been padded, fraud has been committed. Padding is a serious problem in the practice of law:

> [It] occurs most typically when attorneys are under the gun to bill a large number of hours. Everyone knows of lawyers who begin work at 8:00, leave the office at 6:00 and yet bill 10 hours a day—a feat that utterly amazes me. Whether it be eating lunch, talking to a spouse, working with support staff, reading advance sheets or just taking a break, some portion of every day is spent on non-billable matters. [A young Midwestern associate at a medium-sized firm says] padding or fabrication of entries is encouraged, or at the very least tolerated, at his firm, and many others, to judge from his friends' experiences. The pressure to pad is intense. [14]

Unfortunately, paralegals can find themselves under a similar pressure, which, of course, should be resisted.

> One of the most common temptations that can corrupt a paralegal's ethics is to inflate billable hours, since there is often immense pressure in law firms to bill high hours for job security and upward mobility. Such "creative billing" is not humorous; it's both morally wrong and illegal. It's also fraudulent and a plain and simple case of theft.[15]

---

[12]ABA *Model Guidelines*, Guideline 3(b), see footnote 5.
[13]ABA *Model Guidelines*, Guideline 8, see footnote 5.
[14]Doe, *Billing: Is "Padding" Widespread?*, 76 American Bar Ass'n Journal 42 (December 1990).
[15]Smith, *AAfPE National Conference Highlights*, 8 Legal Assistant Today 103 (January/February 1991).

## 4. Crime or Fraud by an Attorney

*An attorney must not engage in criminal or fraudulent conduct.* Model Rule 8.4

Sadly, it is not uncommon for an attorney to be charged with criminal conduct, such as theft of client funds, *insider trading* and securities fraud, falsifying official documents, or tax fraud. Since such conduct obviously affects the attorney's fitness to practice law, sanctions for unethical conduct can be imposed in addition to prosecution in a criminal court. Once an attorney is convicted of a serious crime in court, a separate disciplinary proceeding is often instituted to suspend or disbar the attorney for unethical conduct growing out of the same incident.

### Paralegal Perspective:

- Value your integrity above all else. A paralegal in Oklahoma offers the following advice: "Insist on the highest standards for yourself and for your employer. One small ethical breach can lead to a series of compromises with enormous" disciplinary and "legal malpractice consequences."[16]

- If your supervisor is charged with criminal conduct, the chances are good that you will be questioned by prosecutors, and you might become a suspect yourself.

- In the highly charged, competitive environment of a law office, there are attorneys who are willing to violate the law in the interest of winning. Be sensitive to the overt and subtle pressures on you to participate in such violations. Talk with other paralegals who have encountered this problem. Don't sit in silence. If there is no one in the office with whom you can frankly discuss the elimination of these pressures, you must consider quitting. (See Section F of this chapter.)

- Paralegals who are also notaries are sometimes asked by their supervisors to notarize documents that should *not* be notarized. In fact, paralegals "are most often named as defendants for false notarization of a signature."[17] Such acts may not be covered in malpractice liability insurance policies since they are intentional acts. Be extremely cautious of what you are asked to sign.

- At some law firms, employees have succumbed to the temptation of using a "hot tip" that crosses their path in a corporate takeover case.[18] Assume that Company X is planning to merge with Company Y. The news is not yet public. When it does become public, the value of the stock in Company X is expected to rise dramatically. You work at a law firm that represents Company X and you find out about the planned merger while at work. If you buy stock in Company X before the announcement of the merger, you would benefit from the increased value of the stock that would result after the announcement. This might be an illegal use of inside information. In a dramatic recent case, a paralegal who worked at a securities law firm in Boston was charged with insider trading by the Securities and Exchange Com-

---

[16]Tulsa Ass'n of Legal Assistants, *Hints for Helping Your Attorney Avoid Legal Malpractice,* TALA Times (August 1989).

[17]Race, *Malpractice Maladies,* Paradigm 12 (Baltimore Ass'n of Legal Assistants, July/August 1989).

[18]Milford, *Law Firms Expected to Take Steps to Avert Insider Trading Scandals,* The News Journal D3 (October 16, 1989).

mission (SEC). While working on a case involving a proposed merger, she learned certain information which she gave to outside investors who used it to make illegal profits in the stock market. The story made national news. One headline read, "SEC Says Boston Paralegal Gave Tip Worth $823,471." Soon after the incident, she was fired. All employees of law firms must be extremely careful. Innocently buying stock as a personal investment could turn into a nightmare. One attorney "recommends that any paralegal who would like to buy or sell securities should check first with a corporate attorney in the firm to see if the firm represents the issuer or a company negotiating with the issuer. If it does, an accusation of 'insider trading' might later be made." [19] The same caution applies when a member of the paralegal's immediate family buys or sells such securities.

■ Another problem area is the use of so-called *pirated software*. Many businesses buy one copy of computer software and then copy it so that other employees in the office can use it on other terminals. This is illegal, and can subject violators to fines and other criminal penalties.

■ In all aspects of your career as a paralegal, adopt the motto, "If it doesn't feel right, it probably isn't."

## 5. Crime or Fraud by a Client

*An attorney shall not counsel a client to engage in conduct the attorney knows is criminal or fraudulent.* Model Rule 1.2(d)

The client hires the attorney and controls the purpose of the attorney-client relationship. Furthermore, the client is entitled to know the legal consequences of any action he or she is contemplating. This does not mean, however, that the attorney must do whatever the client wants.

Example: The president of a corporation hires Leo Richards, Esq. to advise the company on how to dump toxic waste into a local river.

Note that the president has not asked Richards *if* the dumping is legal. It would be perfectly ethical for Richards to answer such a question. In the example, the president asks *how* to dump. If Richards feels that the dumping can legally take place, he can so advise the president. Suppose, however, that it is clear to Richards that the dumping would violate the federal or state criminal code. Under such circumstances, it would be unethical for Richards to advise the president on how to proceed with the dumping. The same would be true if the president wanted help in filing an environmental statement that misrepresented the intentions of the company. Such an application would be fraudulent, and an attorney must not help someone commit what the attorney knows is fraudulent conduct.

When attorneys are later charged with unethical conduct in such cases, their defense is often that they did not know the conduct proposed by the client was criminal or fraudulent. If the law applicable to the client's case is unclear, an attorney can make a good faith effort to find a legal way for the client to achieve his or her objective. The point at which the attorney crosses the ethical line is when he or she *knows* the client is trying to accomplish something criminal or fraudulent.

---

[19]Shays, *Ethics for the Paralegal*, Postscript 15 (Manhattan Paralegal Ass'n, August/September 1989).

*Paralegal Perspective:*

■ An attorney will rarely tell paralegals or other staff members that he or she knows the office is helping a client do something criminal or fraudulent. But you might learn that this is so, particularly if there is a close, trusting relationship between you and your supervising attorney. You must let this attorney or some other authority in the office know you do not feel comfortable working on such a case.

## 6. Frivolous Legal Positions

*An attorney must not bring a frivolous claim or assert a frivolous defense.* Model Rule 3.1

A client has a right to an attorney who is a vigorous advocate. But there are limits on what this can entail. It is unethical, for example, for an attorney to assert *frivolous positions* as claims or defenses. There are two major tests for determining when a legal position is frivolous: the good-faith test and the intentional-injury test. First, a position is frivolous if the attorney is unable to make a good-faith argument that existing law supports the position, or the attorney is unable to make a good-faith argument that existing law should be changed or reversed to support the position. A position is not necessarily frivolous simply because the attorney happens to think that the client will ultimately lose. The key is whether there is a good-faith argument to support the position. If the attorney can think of absolutely no rational support for the position, it is frivolous. Since the law is often unclear, it is difficult to establish that an attorney is acting unethically under the test of good faith.

Second, a position is frivolous if the client's primary purpose in having the position asserted is to harass or maliciously injure someone.

*Paralegal Perspective:*

■ In the heat of controversy, tempers can run high. Attorneys do not always exhibit the detachment expected of professionals. They may so thoroughly identify with the interests of their clients that they lose perspective. Paralegals working for such attorneys may get caught up in the same fever, particularly if there is a close attorney-paralegal working relationship on a high-stakes case that has lasted a considerable time. The momentum is to do whatever it takes to win. While this atmosphere can be exhilarating, it can also create an environment where less and less attention is paid to the niceties of ethics.

## 7. Safekeeping Property

*An attorney shall hold client property separate from the attorney's own property.* Model Rule 1.15

A law office often receives client funds or funds of others connected with the client's case—for example, attorneys receive money as trustees of a will or trust, as escrow agents in closing a business deal, or as settlement of a case. Such funds should be held in separate accounts, with complete records kept on each. The attorney should not *commingle* (i.e., mix) law firm funds with client funds. It is unethical to place everything in one account. This is so even if the firm maintains accurate records on what amounts in the single account belong to which clients and what amounts belong to the firm. In a commingled account, the danger is too great that client funds will be used for nonclient purposes.

*Paralegal Perspective:*

■ Use great care whenever your responsibility involves client funds, such as receiving funds from clients, opening bank accounts, depositing funds in the proper account at a bank, and making entries in law firm records on such funds. It should be fairly obvious to you whether an attorney is violating the rule on commingling funds. It may be less clear whether the attorney is improperly using client funds for unauthorized purposes. Attorneys have been known to "borrow" money from client accounts and then return the money before anyone discovers what was done. They may even arrange to pay the account interest while using the money. Elaborate bookkeeping and accounting gimmicks might be used to disguise what is going on. Such conduct is unethical even if the attorney pays interest and eventually returns all the funds. In addition, the attorney may eventually be charged with theft or criminal fraud. Of course, anyone who knowingly assists the attorney could be subject to the same consequences.

## 8. False Statements and Failure to Disclose

*An attorney shall not knowingly:*

*(1) make a false statement of material fact or law to a tribunal,*

*(2) fail to disclose a material fact to a tribunal when disclosure is necessary to avoid assisting a client commit a criminal or fraudulent act,*

*(3) fail to tell a tribunal about laws or other authority directly against the position of the attorney's client if this law or authority is not disclosed by opposing counsel, or*

*(4) offer evidence that the attorney knows is false.* Model Rule 3.3(a)

One of the reasons the general public holds the legal profession in low esteem is their perception that attorneys seldom comply with the above rules. Our legal system is *adversarial,* which means that legal disputes are resolved by neutral judges after listening to fiercely partisan opponents. In effect, the parties do battle through their attorneys. This environment does not always encourage the participants to cooperate in court proceedings. In fact, quite the opposite is often true. In extreme cases, attorneys have been known to lie to the court, to offer knowingly false evidence, etc. Under Model Rule 3.3(a), such conduct is unethical.

Subsection (3) of Model Rule 3.3(a) is particularly startling.

Example: Karen Singer and Bill Carew are attorneys who are opposing each other in a bitter case involving a large sum of money. Singer is smarter than Carew. Singer knows about a very damaging but obscure case that goes against her client. But because of sloppy research, Carew does not know about it. Singer never mentions the case and it never comes up during the litigation.

Singer must pay a price for her silence. She is subject to sanctions for a violation of her ethical obligation of disclosure under Model Rule 3.3(a)(3).

Another controversial part of Model Rule 3.3(a) is subsection (2) requiring disclosures that involve criminal or fraudulent acts. Since this raises issues of confidentiality, we will discuss such disclosures later when we cover confidentiality.

*Paralegal Perspective:*

■ Be aware that an attorney who justifies the use of deception in one case will probably repeat such deceptions in the future on other cases. To excuse the deception, the attorney will often refer to the necessity of protecting the client or to the alleged evilness of the other side. Deceptions are unethical despite such justifications.

- Chances are also good that employees of such an attorney will be pressured into participating in deception—for example, give a false date to a court clerk, help a client lie (commit perjury) on the witness stand, help an attorney alter a document to be introduced into evidence, or improperly notarize a document.

- Do not compromise your integrity no matter how much you believe in the cause of the client, no matter how much you detest the tactics of the opposing side, no matter how much you like the attorney for whom you work, and no matter how important this job is to you.

## 9.  Withdrawal

*An attorney must withdraw from a case: if continuing would result in a violation of ethical rules or other laws; if the client discharges the attorney, or if the attorney's physical or mental condition materially impairs his or her ability to represent the client.* Model Rule 1.16(a)

Attorneys are not required to take every case. Furthermore, once they begin a case, they are not obligated to stay with the client until the case is over. If, however, the case has already begun in court after the attorney has filed a notice of appearance, *withdrawal* is usually improper without the permission of the court.

There are circumstances in which an attorney *must* withdraw from a case that has begun:

- Representation of the client would violate ethical rules—for example, the attorney discovers that he or she has a conflict of interest with the client which cannot be cured (i.e., corrected or overcome) by the consent of the client.

- Representation of the client would violate the law—for example, the client insists that the attorney provide advice on how to defraud the Internal Revenue Service.

- The client fires the attorney. (An attorney is an agent of the client. Clients are always free to dismiss their agents.)

- The attorney's physical or mental condition has deteriorated (through problems with alcohol, depression due to marital problems, etc.) to the point where the attorney's ability to represent the client has been materially impaired.

An attorney has the option of withdrawing if the client insists on an objective that the attorney considers repugnant (such as pursuing litigation solely to harass someone), or imprudent (such as refiling a motion the attorney feels is an obvious waste of time and likely to incur the anger of the court). Model Rule 1.16(b)(3).

### Paralegal Perspective:

- When you have a close working relationship with an attorney, you become aware of his or her professional strengths and personal weaknesses, particularly in a small law office. Bar associations around the country are becoming increasingly concerned about the *impaired attorney,* someone who's not functioning properly due to alcohol, drugs, or related problems. A paralegal with such an attorney for a supervisor is obviously in a predicament. Seemingly small problems have the potential of turning into a crisis. If it is not practical to discuss the situation directly with the attorney involved, you need to seek the advice of others in the firm.

## 10. Confidentiality of Information

*An attorney must not reveal information relating to the representation of a client unless (a) the client consents to the disclosure or (b) the attorney reasonably believes the disclosure is necessary to prevent a client from committing a criminal act that is likely to result in imminent death or substantial bodily harm.* Model Rule 1.6

Information is confidential if others do not have a right to receive it. When access to information is restricted in this way, the information is considered *privileged.* While our primary focus in this section is on the ethical dimensions of confidentiality, we also need to examine confidentiality in the related contexts of attorney-client privilege and the attorney work-product rule.

### Ethics and Confidentiality

The ethical obligation to maintain *confidentiality* applies to *all* information that relates to the representation of a client, whatever its source. Note that the obligation is broader than so-called secrets or matters explicitly communicated in confidence. Confidentiality has been breached in each of the following examples:

> At a party, an attorney tells an acquaintance from another town that the law firm is representing Jacob Anderson, whose employer is trying to force him to retire.

> At a bar association conference, an attorney tells an old law school classmate that a client named Brenda Steck is considering a suit against her brother over the ownership of property left by their deceased mother.

> A legal secretary carelessly leaves a client's file open on his desk where a stranger (e.g., another client) can and does read parts of it.

The rule on confidentiality is designed to encourage clients to discuss their case fully and frankly with their attorney, including embarrassing and legally damaging information. Arguably, a client would be reluctant to be open with an attorney if he or she had to worry about whether the attorney might reveal the information to others. The rule on confidentiality makes it unethical for attorneys to do so.

Of course, a client can always consent to an attorney's disclosure about the client—*if* the client is properly consulted about the proposed disclosure in advance. Furthermore, sometimes the client implicitly authorizes disclosures because of the nature of his or her case. In a dispute over alimony, for example, the attorney would obviously have to disclose certain financial information about the client to a court or to opposing counsel during the settlement negotiations.

Disclosure can also be ethically permissible in cases involving future criminal conduct.

> Example: An attorney represents a husband in a bitter divorce action against his wife. During a meeting at the law firm, the husband shows the attorney a gun which he says he is going to use to kill his wife later the same day.

Can the attorney tell the police what the husband said? Yes. It is not unethical for an attorney to reveal information about a crime if the attorney reasonably believes that disclosure is necessary to prevent the client from committing a criminal act that could lead to someone's imminent death or substantial bodily harm.

Finally, some disclosures can be proper in suits between attorney and client. Suppose, for example, that the attorney later sues the client for nonpayment of a fee, or the client sues the attorney for malpractice. In such proceedings, an attorney can reveal information about the client if the attorney reasonably believes disclosure is necessary to present a claim against the client or to defend against the client's claim.

### Attorney-Client Privilege

The *attorney-client privilege* serves a similar function as the ethical rule on confidentiality. The two doctrines overlap. The attorney-client privilege is an *evidentiary* rule that applies to judicial and other proceedings in which an attorney may be called as a witness or otherwise required to produce evidence concerning a client. Under the attorney-client privilege, the attorney can refuse to disclose communications with his or her client whose purpose was to facilitate the provision of legal services for the client. The privilege also applies to employees of an attorney with respect to the same kind of communication—those whose purpose was to facilitate legal services.

---

**Who May Not Testify Without Consent**
Colorado Revised Statutes (1984 Cum. Supp.)
13-90-107 (1)(b)

An attorney shall not be examined without the consent of his client as to any communication made by the client to him or his advice given thereon in the course of professional employment; nor shall an attorney's secretary, paralegal, legal assistant, stenographer, or clerk be examined without the consent of his employer concerning any fact, the knowledge of which he has acquired in such capacity.

---

The *ethical* rule on confidentiality tells us when sanctions can be imposed on attorneys for disclosing confidential client information to anyone outside the law office. The *attorney-client privilege* tells us when attorneys (and their employees) can refuse to answers questions pertaining to confidential client information.

### Attorney Work-Product Rule

Suppose that, while working on a client's case, an attorney prepares a memorandum or other in-house document that does *not* contain any confidential communications. The memorandum or document, therefore, is *not* protected by the attorney-client privilege. Can the other side force the attorney to provide a copy of the memorandum or document? Are they *discoverable*, meaning that an opposing party can obtain information about it during discovery? This question leads us to the work-product rule.

Under this rule, the *work product* of an attorney is considered confidential. Work product consists of any notes, working papers, memoranda, or similar documents and tangible things prepared by the attorney in anticipation of litigation. An example is a memorandum the attorney writes to the file indicating his or her strategy in litigating a case. Attorneys do not have to disclose their work product to the other side. It is not discoverable.[20] To the extent that such documents are not discoverable, they are privileged. (The work-product rule is sometimes referred to as the work-product privilege.)

## Inadvertent Disclosure of Confidential Material

The great fear of law office personnel is that the wrong person will obtain material that should be protected by ethics, by the attorney-client privilege, or by the work-product rule. This can have devastating consequences. For example, if a stranger overhears a confidential communication by a client to the attorney or to the attorney's paralegal, a court might rule that the attorney-client privilege has been waived. At a recent paralegal conference, a speaker told a stunned audience that a paralegal in her firm accidentally "faxed" a strategy memo on a current case to the opposing attorney! The paralegal punched in the wrong phone number on the fax machine!

*Paralegal Perspective:*

- Attorneys must instruct their paralegals and other nonattorney assistants on the obligation not to disclose information relating to the representation of a client. "It is the responsibility of a lawyer to take reasonable measures to ensure that all client confidences are preserved by a legal assistant."[21]
- As we shall see later, the two major national paralegal associations also stress the ethical obligation of confidentiality in their own ethical codes:
  - "A legal assistant must protect the confidences of a client, and it shall be unethical for a legal assistant to violate any statute . . . controlling privileged communications." Canon 7. National Association of Legal Assistants, Code of Ethics and Professional Responsibility (page 314).
  - "A paralegal shall preserve client confidences and privileged communications. Confidential information and privileged communications are a vital part of the attorney, paralegal, and client relationship. The importance of preserving confidential and privileged information is understood to be an uncompromising obligation of every paralegal." IV. National Federation of Paralegal Associations, Affirmation of Professional Responsibility (page 314).
- There are *many* temptations on paralegals to violate confidentiality. For example, a paralegal inadvertently reveals confidential information:
  - while networking with other paralegals at a paralegal-association meeting;
  - during animated conversation with another paralegal at a restaurant or on an elevator;

---

[20]An exception exists if the "party seeking discovery has substantial need of the materials in the preparation of his case" and is unable to obtain them without undue hardship by other means. This test is rarely met. Federal Rule of Civil Procedure 26(b)(3).
[21]ABA *Model Guidelines,* Guideline 6, see footnote 5.

- after returning home from work during casual discussions with a relative, spouse, or roommate about interesting cases at the office.

Recall the scope of the rule: *all* information relating to the representation of a client must not be revealed. Some paralegals make the mistake of thinking that the rule applies only to damaging or embarrassing information or that the rule simply means you should not reveal things to the other side in the dispute. Not so. The rule is much broader. *All* information relating to the representation of a client must not be revealed to *anyone* who is not working on the case in the office.

- In Missouri, the obligation of silence is even broader. The paralegal must not disclose information—"confidential or otherwise"—relating to the representation of the client.[22] In Texas, confidential information includes both privileged information and unprivileged client information. An attorney must "instruct the legal assistant that all information concerning representation of a client (indeed even the fact of representation, if not a matter of public record) must be kept strictly confidential."[23] In Philadelphia, paralegals are warned that it is "not always easy to recognize what information about your firm's clients or office is confidential. Moreover, a client of your office might be offended to learn that a . . . firm employee has discussed the client's business in public, even if the information mentioned is public knowledge. The easiest rule is to consider *all* work of the office to be confidential: do not discuss the business of your office or your firm's clients with any outsider, no matter how close a friend, at any time, unless you are specifically authorized by a lawyer to do so."[24] Under guidelines such as these, there is very little that paralegals can tell someone about their work!

- During the war, sailors were told that "loose lips sink ships." The same applies to law firms. One law firm makes the following statement to all its paralegals, "Throughout your employment, you will have access to information that must at all times be held in strictest confidence. Even the seemingly insignificant fact that the firm is involved in a particular matter falls within the orbit of confidential information. Unless you have attorney permission, do not disclose documents or contents of documents to anyone, including firm employees who do not need this information to do their work."[25]

- If you attend a meeting on a case outside the law office, ask your supervisor whether you should take notes or prepare a follow-up memorandum on the meeting. Let the supervisor decide whether your notes or the memo might be discoverable.[26]

- Be *very* careful when you talk with clients in the presence of third persons. Overheard conservations might constitute a waiver of the attorney-client privilege.

- Use a stamp marked *privileged* on protected documents.

[22]*Guidelines for Practicing with Paralegals,* Missouri Bar Ass'n (1987).
[23]State Bar of Texas, *General Guidelines for the Utilization of the Services of Legal Assistants by Attorneys* (1981). Rule 1.01, Texas Disciplinary Rules of Professional Conduct (1990).
[24]*Professional Responsibility for Nonlawyers,* Professional Responsibility Committee of the Philadelphia Bar Ass'n (1989) (emphasis added).
[25]*Orientation Handbook for Paralegals* 2 (Lane, Powell, Moses & Miller, 1984).
[26]Daniels, *Privileged Information for Paralegals,* 17 At Issue 15 (San Francisco Ass'n of Legal Assistants, November 1990).

■ During a job interview, be very careful about submitting writing samples that contain confidential information, such as privileged communications or the identity of clients at law offices where you may have worked or volunteered in the past.[27] Your lack of professionalism in carelessly referring to confidential information during an interview will probably destroy your chances of getting the job.

## 11. Conflict of Interest

*An attorney should avoid a conflict of interest with his or her client.*

"Like obscenity, *conflicts of interest* are difficult to define, but easy to recognize."[28] A conflict of interest is divided loyalty that actually or potentially places one of the participants to whom undivided loyalty is owed at a disadvantage. Such conflicts can exist in many settings.

> Example: Bill Davenport is a salesman who does part-time work selling the same type of product manufactured by two competing companies.

Davenport has a conflict of interest. How can he serve two masters with the same loyalty? Normally, a company expects the undivided loyalty of people who work for it. How can Davenport apportion his customers between the two companies? There is an obvious danger that he will favor one over the other. The fact that he may try to be fair in his treatment of both companies does not eliminate the conflict of interest. A *potential* certainly exists that one of the companies will be disadvantaged. It may be that the two companies are aware of the problem and are not worried. This does not mean that there is no conflict of interest; it simply means that the affected parties have consented to take the risks involved in the conflict.

The same kind of conflict can exist in other settings.

> Example: Frank Jones is the head of the personnel department of a large company. Ten people apply for a job, one of whom is Frank's cousin.

Frank has a conflict of interest. He has loyalty to his company (pressuring him to hire the best person for the job) and a loyalty to his cousin (pressuring him to help a relative). There is a potential that the company will be disadvantaged, since Frank's cousin may not be the best qualified for the job.

The conflict exists even if the cousin *is* the best qualified, and even if Frank does *not* hire his cousin for the job, and even if the company *knows* about the relationship but still wants Frank to make the hiring decision. For conflict of interest to exist, all you need is the potential for disadvantage due to *divided loyalties;* you do not have to show that disadvantage actually resulted.

In a law office, a number of conflict-of-interest issues can arise:

(a)  Business transactions with a client

(b)  Loans to a client

(c)  Gifts from a client

---

[27]As we will see later, you may have to disclose the names of cases and clients in order to help the office decide whether you are "tainted" with a conflict of interest and hence could cause the disqualification of the office if you are hired. But this disclosure should occur only when the employment discussions are getting serious *and* with the knowledge of your former employers.

[28]Holtzman, *Conflicts of Interest,* 14 Legal Economics 55 (October 1988).

(d)  Multiple representation

(e)  Former client/present adversary

(f)  Law firm disqualification

(g)  Switching jobs and "the Chinese wall"

As we examine each of these topics, our central concern is whether the independence of the attorneys' professional judgment is compromised in any way because of conflicting interests.

### (a)  Business Transactions with a Client

Attorneys sell professional legal advice and representation. When they go beyond such services and enter a business transaction with the client, a conflict of interest can arise.

> Example: Janet Bruno, Esq. is Len Oliver's attorney in a real estate case. Oliver owns an auto repair business for which Bruno has done legal work. Oliver sells Bruno a 30% interest in the repair business. Bruno continues as Oliver's attorney.

Serious conflict-of-interest problems may exist here. Assume that the business runs into difficulties and Oliver considers bankruptcy. He goes to Bruno for legal advice on bankruptcy law. Bruno has dual concerns: to give Oliver competent legal advice and to protect *her own* 30% interest in the business. Bankruptcy may be good for Oliver but disastrous for Bruno's investment. How can an attorney give a client independent professional advice when the advice may go against the attorney's own interest? Bruno's concern for her investment creates the potential that Oliver will be placed at a disadvantage. Divided loyalties exist.

This is not to say, however, that it is always unethical for an attorney to enter a business transaction with a client. If certain strict conditions are met, it can be proper.

> *An attorney shall not enter a business transaction with a client, unless*
> *(i) the terms of the business transaction are fair and reasonable to the client and are fully disclosed to the client in understandable language in writing, and*
> *(ii) the client is given reasonable opportunity to seek advice on the transaction from another attorney who is not involved with the transaction or the parties, and*
> *(iii) the client consents to the business transaction in writing.* Model Rule 1.8(a)

In our example, Oliver must be given the chance to consult with an attorney other than Bruno on letting Bruno buy a 30% interest in the business. Bruno would have to give Oliver a clear, written explanation of their business relationship. And the relationship must be fair and reasonable to Oliver.

### (b)  Loans to a Client

An attorney, like all service providers, wants to be paid. Often a client does not have the resources to pay until *after* the case is over.

> Example: Harry Maxell, Esq. is Bob Stock's attorney in a negligence action in which Stock is seeking damages for serious injuries caused by the defendant. Since the accident, Stock has been out of work and on welfare. While the case is pending, Maxell agrees to lend Stock living expenses and court-filing fees.

The loan covering *living expenses* creates a conflict-of-interest problem. Suppose that the defendant in the negligence case makes an offer to settle the case with Stock. Should he accept the offer? There is a danger that Maxell's advice on this will be colored by the fact that he has a financial interest in Stone—he wants to have his loan repaid. The amount of the offer to settle may not be enough to cover the loan. Should he advise Stock to accept the offer? It may be in Stock's interest to accept the offer but not in Maxell's own interest. Such divided loyalty is an unethical conflict of interest. Model Rule 1.8(e).

The loan covering *litigation expenses,* such as filing fees and other court costs, is treated differently. The amount of such a loan is usually relatively small, and hence unlikely to interfere with the independence of the attorney's judgment. In our example, Maxell's loan to cover the cost of the filing fees is proper.

## (c)  Gifts from a Client

Clients sometimes make gifts to their attorneys or to the spouse or relative of their attorneys. Such gifts rarely create ethical problems except when a document must be prepared to complete the gift.

> Example: William Stanton, Esq. has been the family attorney of the Tarkinton family for years. At Christmas, Mrs. Tarkinton gives Stanton a television set and tells him to change her will so that Stanton's ten-year-old daughter would receive funds for a free college education.

If a document is needed to carry out the gift, it is unethical for the attorney to prepare that document. Its preparation would create a conflict of interest. In our example, the gift of money for college involves a document—Mrs. Tarkinton's will. Note the conflict. It would be in Mrs. Tarkinton's interest to have the will written so that she, and the executor of her will, retained considerable flexibility when questions arise on how much to pay for the college education. (For example, is there to be a maximum amount? Is room and board included?) And they need flexibility on the effect of contingencies, such as a delay or an interruption in going to college. (What happens if the daughter does not go to college until after she marries and raises her own children?) Other questions could arise as well. Stanton, of course, would want the will drafted so that his daughter received the most money possible; he does not want any contingencies in the will that might threaten receipt of the funds. It is in his interest to prepare the will so that Mrs. Tarkinton and her executor have very little flexibility.

Because of this conflict, an attorney cannot prepare a document such as a will, trust, or contract that results in any substantial gift from a client to the attorney or to the attorney's children, spouse, parents, or siblings. If a client wants to make such a gift, *another* attorney must prepare the document.[29] There is, however, one exception. If the client is *related* to the person receiving the gift, the attorney can prepare the document. Model Rule 1.8(c).

There does not appear to be any ethical problem in taking the gift of the television set from Mrs. Tarkinton. No documents are involved.

## (d)  Multiple Representation

A client is entitled to the independent professional judgment and vigorous representation of an attorney. Rarely can this occur in a case of *multiple repre-*

---

[29]This other attorney should not be a member of the same law firm. See the related discussion (later) on imputed disqualification.

*sentation* (also referred to as *common representation*), where the same attorney represents both sides in a legal dispute.

> Example: Tom and Henry have an automobile accident. Tom wants to sue Henry for negligence. Both Tom and Henry ask Mary Franklin, Esq. to represent them in the dispute.

Franklin has a conflict of interest. How can she give her undivided loyalty to both sides? Tom needs to prove that Henry was negligent; Henry needs to prove that he was not negligent, and perhaps that Tom was negligent himself. How can Franklin vigorously argue that Henry was negligent and at the same time vigorously argue that Henry was not negligent? How can she act independently for two different people who are at odds with each other? Since Tom and Henry have *adverse interests,* she cannot give each her independent professional judgment. (Adverse interests are simply opposing purposes or claims.) The difficulty is not solved by Franklin's commitment to be fair and objective in giving her advice to the parties. Her role as attorney is to be a *partisan advocate* for the client. It is impossible for Franklin to play this role for two clients engaged in a dispute where they have adverse interests. An obvious conflict of interest would exist. In every state, it would be unethical for Franklin to represent Tom and Henry in this case.

Furthermore, this is a case in which consent is *not* a defense. Even if Tom and Henry agree to allow Franklin to represent both of them, it would be unethical for her to do so. The presence of adverse interests between the parties makes it unethical for an attorney to represent both sides.

Suppose, however, that the two sides do not have adverse interests. There are cases that must go before a court even though the parties are in agreement about everything.

> Example: Jim and Mary Smith are separated, and both want a divorce. They have been married only a few months. There are no children and no marital assets to divide. George Davidson, Esq. is an attorney that Jim and Mary know and trust. They decide to ask Davidson to represent both of them in the divorce.

Can Davidson ethically represent both sides here? There are some states that *will* allow him to do so, on the theory that there is not much of a conflict between the parties. Jim and Mary want the divorce, there is no custody battle, and there is no property to fight over. All they need is a court to decree that their marriage is legally over. Hence the potential for harm caused by multiple representation in such a case is almost nonexistent. Other states, however, disagree. They frown on multiple representation in so-called "friendly divorces" of this kind.

There is no absolute ban on all multiple representation in the Model Rules, although such representation is certainly discouraged.

> *An attorney shall not represent a client if the representation of that client will be directly adverse to another client, unless*
>
> *(i) the attorney reasonably believes the representation will not adversely affect the relationship with the other client, and*
>
> *(ii) both clients consent after consultation about the risks of the multiple representation.* Model Rule 1.7

In the Smith example, both conditions can probably be met. Such a divorce is little more than a paper procedure since there is no real dispute between the parties. Hence Davidson would be reasonable in believing that his representation of Jim would not adversely affect Mary, and vice versa. Davidson can represent both sides so long as Jim and Mary consent to the multiple representation after Davidson explains whatever risks might be involved.

Nevertheless, attorneys are urged *not* to engage in multiple representation even if it is ethically proper to do so under the standards listed above. The case may have been "friendly" at the outset, but years later when everything turns sour, one of the parties inevitably attacks the attorney for having had a conflict of interest. Cautious attorneys always avoid multiple representation.

### (e)  Former Client/Present Adversary

As indicated earlier, clients are encouraged to be very open with their attorney since the latter needs to know favorable and unfavorable information about the client in order to evaluate the legal implications of the case. The more trust that exists between them, the more frank the client will usually be. Assume that such a relationship exists and that the case is eventually resolved. Months later, another legal dispute arises between the same parties, but this time the attorney represents the other side!

> Example: Helen Kline, Esq. represented Paul Andrews in his breach-of-contract suit against Richard Morelli, a truck distributor. Andrews claimed that Morelli failed to deliver five trucks that Andrews ordered. A court ruled in favor of Morelli. Now, a year later, Andrews wants to sue Morelli for slander. After accidentally meeting at a conference, they started discussing the truck suit. Morelli allegedly called Andrews a liar and a thief. In the slander suit, Andrews hires Michael Manna, Esq. to represent him. Morelli hires Helen Kline, Esq.

A former client is now an adversary. Kline once represented Andrews; she is now representing a client (Morelli) who is an adversary of Andrews. Without the consent of the former client (Andrews), it is unethical for Kline to *switch sides* and represent Morelli against him. Model Rule 1.9(a). Consent is needed *when the second case is the same as the first one* or *when the two are substantially related.* The slander suit is substantially related to the breach-of-contract suit, since they both grew out of the original truck incident.

If the cases are the same or are substantially related, the likelihood is strong that the attorney will use information learned in the first case to the detriment of the former client in the second case. Kline undoubtedly found out a good deal about Andrews when she represented him in the breach-of-contract case. She would now be in a position to use that information *against* him while representing Morelli in the slander case.

Kline had a duty of loyalty when she represented Andrews. This duty does not end once the case is over and the attorney fees are paid. The duty continues if the same case arises again or if a substantially related case arises later—even if the attorney no longer represents the client. A conflict of interest exists when Kline subsequently acquires a new client who goes against Andrews in the same case or in a substantially related case. This, of course, is what happened in our example. Her duty of undivided loyalty to the second client would clash with her *continuing* duty of undivided loyalty to the former client in the original case.

Suppose, however, that an attorney *can* take the second case against a former client because the second case is totally unrelated to the first. There is still an ethical obligation to refrain from using any information relating to the representation in the first case to the disadvantage of the former client in the second case. There is no ethical ban on taking the case, but if there is any information in the office relating to the first case, that information cannot be used against the former client in the second case.[30]

### (f)  Law Firm Disqualification

If an attorney is disqualified from representing a client because of a conflict of interest, every attorney in the *same law firm* is also disqualified unless the client being protected by this rule consents to the representation.

> **Example:** Two years ago, John Farrell, Esq. of the law firm of Smith & Smith represented the stepfather in a custody dispute with the child's grandmother. The stepfather won the case, but the grandmother was awarded limited visitation rights. The grandmother now wants to sue the stepfather for failure to abide by the visitation order. John Farrell no longer represents the stepfather. The grandmother asks John Farrell to represent her. He declines because of a conflict of interest, but sends her to his law partner, Diane Williams, Esq., down the corridor at Smith & Smith.

The *stepfather* would have to consent to the representation of the grandmother by Williams. There would certainly be a conflict of interest if John Farrell tried to represent the grandmother against the stepfather. The custody dispute and the visitation dispute are substantially related. Once one attorney in a firm is disqualified because of a conflict of interest, every other attorney in that firm is also disqualified. (This is known as *imputed disqualification* or *vicarious disqualification*.) The entire firm is treated as one attorney. The disqualification of any one "tainted" attorney in the firm contaminates the entire firm. In our example, Farrell's partner (Williams) is disqualified because Farrell would be disqualified. Model Rule 1.10.

### (g)  Switching Jobs and "the Chinese Wall"

Finally we need to consider the conflict-of-interest problems that can arise from changing jobs. We just saw that there can be an imputed disqualification of an entire law firm because one of the attorneys in the firm has a conflict of interest with a client. If that attorney now goes to work for a *new* firm, can there be an imputed disqualification of the new firm because of the same conflict of interest?

> **Example:** Kevin Carlson, Esq. works at Darby & Darby. He represents Ajax, Inc. in its contract suit against World Systems, Inc. The latter is represented by Polk, Young & West. Carlson quits his job at Darby & Darby and takes a job at Polk, Young & West.

While Carlson was at Darby and Darby, he obviously acquired confidential information about Ajax. Clearly, he cannot now represent World Systems in the contract litigation against Ajax. Blatant side-switching of this kind is highly unethical. But what about other attorneys at Polk, Young & West? Is the *entire* firm contaminated and hence disqualified from continuing to represent World Systems because of the hiring of Carlson? If other attorneys at Polk, Young & West are allowed to continue representing World Systems against Ajax, there would be pressures on Carlson to tell these attorneys what he knows about Ajax. Must Polk, Young & West therefore withdraw from the case? The states do not all answer this question in the same way.

---

[30]While this duty might exist, it is not easy to enforce. Think of how difficult it might be to prove that the attorney in the second case used information obtained in the first case.

In many states, the answer is *yes,* because the tainted attorney[31]—Carlson—possesses confidential information about Ajax, and the case at the new firm involves the same or substantially the same matter as at the prior firm. The confidential information learned at the prior firm would be material to the matter being handled by the new firm. In these states, the only way to avoid disqualification is if Ajax waives its right to object. Ajax must be told that Carlson now works at Polk, Young & West, which represents World Systems, and must consent to allowing an attorney at Polk, Young & West (other than Carlson) to continue to represent World Systems in the case. It is unlikely, however, that Ajax will give this consent. Why would it want to take the chance that Carlson will reveal confidential communications to his new colleagues at Polk, Young & West?

To avoid the drastic penalty of imputed disqualification, law firms often promise to build a *Chinese wall* (sometimes called an *ethical wall* or *cone of silence*) around the attorney who created the conflict of interest—the *tainted* or *contaminated* attorney. The goal of the wall is to screen the tainted attorney from any contact with a case where earlier confidentiality could be compromised. In many states, however, this promise is *ineffective* to avoid the disqualification. Yet there are states that are more sympathetic to a firm that wants to avoid the disqualification, depending on how involved the tainted attorney was in the case while at the previous firm and on the quality of the wall at the new firm.

The screening of the Chinese Wall should take several forms. For example:

- The tainted attorney promises not to discuss what he or she knows with anyone in the new firm.

- Those working on the case in the new firm promise not to discuss it with the tainted attorney.

- The tainted attorney works in an area that is physically segregated from work on the case in the new firm.

- The files in the case are locked so that the tainted attorney will have no access to the files. In addition, colored labels or "restricted flags" are placed on each of these files to indicate that they are off limits to the tainted attorney.

- All employees in the new firm are formally told that if they learn anything about the case, they must not discuss it with the tainted attorney.[32]

A tainted employee around whom a Chinese Wall is built is called a *quarantined* employee.

As indicated, there are states where a Chinese Wall will *not* be successful in preventing the imputed disqualification of the new firm.[33] There is skepticism that the tainted attorney will be able to resist the pressure to disclose what he or she knows in spite of these screening mechanisms. "Whether the screen is breached will be virtually impossible to ascertain from outside the firm."[34]

Yet again, not all states take this position. There are states that will not order a disqualification if the court can be convinced that harm to the former

---

[31] Also called the *contaminated* attorney or *infected* attorney.

[32] Another dimension of the Chinese Wall is to forbid the tainted attorney from earning any profit or financial gain from the case in question.

[33] The Model Rules explicitly recognize a Chinese Wall to prevent imputed disqualification only where the attorney has moved from a government position to private employment. Model Rule 1.11.

[34] C. Wolfram, *Modern Legal Ethics* § 7.6.4 (1986).

**FIGURE 5.4**

Computer Software
Used for Conflicts
Checks

```
┌─────────────────────────────────────────────────────────┐
│              LEGALMASTER Conflicts Found                  │
│ Conflicts checked for case: SAMUE—(10 matches on 3 names) │
│ Rubin (2 matches)                                         │
│     CSP-          CLNT Rubin Phillip                      │
│     FFIC-5        JUDGE Rubin Laurie                      │
│ Samuel* (6 matches)                                       │
│     GREGS-1       OPATT Samuels Fritz                     │
│     SCOTT-1       EXPRT Samuels Phillip J.                │
│     SMITH-PI      JUDGE Samuels Norman I.                 │
│     IBM-          OPATT Samuels Jacob                     │
│     CSP-          OPATT Samuels Jacob                     │
│     ISIS-2        EXPRT Samuelson Juan                    │
│ Savag* (2 matches)                                        │
│     IBM-          CLNT Savage Norm                        │
│     GRUPE-7       CLNT Savage Emily                       │
│              Press any key to exit.                       │
└─────────────────────────────────────────────────────────┘
```

Legalmaster's Conflicts Module. Computer Software for Professionals, Inc.

client can be avoided. This is most likely to happen if the Wall was in place at the new firm at the outset of the employment transfer, if the new firm built the Wall before the other side raised the conflict-of-interest issue, and, most important, if the tainted attorney's involvement in the case at the old firm was relatively minor. This, of course, was not true for Kevin Carlson, Esq. in our example, since he actually represented Ajax while at Darby & Darby.

Imputed disqualification is a drastic consequence of job switching. In the Carlson example, somebody at Polk, Young & West made a major blunder in hiring Carlson. Before hiring him, a *conflicts check* should have been performed in order to determine whether he might taint the new firm and, if so, whether a Chinese Wall could prevent disqualification. This is done by obtaining the names of the clients Carlson and his old law firm (Darby & Darby) worked for and by determining whether the new firm (Polk, Young & West) ever worked *against* any of them.[35] Unfortunately, law firms often perform such conflicts checks carelessly or not at all.

Some large firms assign paralegals to perform the check under the supervision of an attorney. This paralegal will enter data on parties into a "conflicts index system" and compare it with data already in the system to identify potential conflicts. Computer programs (such as the one shown in Figure 5.4.) have been developed to assist in the task.

Insurance companies that issue malpractice policies to attorneys are very concerned about conflicts of interests that can arise from a *lateral hire,* in which a law firm hires an attorney from another law firm. The same concerns exist when one law firm buys or merges with another law firm. In Figure 5.5, you will find a series of questions one insurance company asks of all law firms applying for malpractice insurance.

*Paralegal Perspective:*

- "A lawyer should take reasonable measures to prevent conflicts of interest resulting from a legal assistant's other employment or interests insofar as

[35]For each client that is a corporation, the firm should also cross-check the names of the parent corporation, all subsidiary corporations, and the names of chief executive officers. If the client is a partnership, the same kind of check is needed for the names of all general partners.

**FIGURE 5.5**

Questions on Malpractice Insurance Application about Conflict-of-Interest Avoidance

| ADMINISTRATIVE SYSTEMS AND PROCEDURES—CONFLICT OF INTEREST | YES | NO |
|---|---|---|
| 22. Do you have a written internal control system for maintaining client lists and identifying actual or potential conflicts of interest? .................................................................... | ☐ | ☐ |
| 23. How does the firm maintain its conflict of interest avoidance system?<br>☐ Oral/Memory   ☐ SIngle Index Files   ☐ Multiple Index Files   ☐ Computer | | |
| 24. Have the firm members disclosed in writing, all actual conflicts of interest and conflicts they reasonably believe may exist as a result of their role as director, officer, partner, employee or fiduciary of an entity or individual other than the applicant firm? ................................... | ☐ | ☐ |
| 25. Do firm members disclose to their clients, in writing, all actual conflicts of interest and conflicts they reasonably believe may exist? .................................................................... | ☐ | ☐ |
| 26. Upon disclosure of actual or potential conflicts, do firm members always obtain written consent to perform ongoing legal services?.............................................................. | ☐ | ☐ |
| 27. Has the firm acquired, merged with or terminated a formal business relationship with another firm within the last three years? ............................................................... | ☐ | ☐ |
| 28. Does the firm's conflict of interest avoidance system include attorney-client relationships established by predecessor firms, merged firms and acquired firms? ................................... | ☐ | ☐ |
| **Source:** The St. Paul Companies, Professional Liability Application for Lawyers. | | |

such other employment or interests would present a conflict of interest if it were that of the lawyer." [36] Many paralegals change jobs one or more times in the course of their careers. Such changes can create the same kind of conflicts problems that result when attorneys change jobs:

> Example: Paul Benton is a paralegal who works for Sands, Leonard & Wiley. One of the cases Paul works on is Mary Richardson v. Jane Quigly. Sands, Leonard & Wiley represents Richardson. The law firm of Neeley & Neeley represents Quigly. Before the case is resolved, Paul quits in order to take a job as a paralegal with Neeley & Neeley.

Neeley & Neeley is now in a position to determine what Paul found out about Richardson while he worked for Sands, Leonard & Wiley. The latter firm will probably ask a court to force Neeley & Neeley to withdraw from the case because it hired a tainted paralegal—Paul. The courts in some states will do just that. In these courts, imputed disqualification can result from tainted paralegals as well as from tainted attorneys. Yet other states say that paralegals should not be treated the same as attorneys. Under this view, a court is more likely to accept a Chinese Wall built around a tainted paralegal (who becomes a quarantined paralegal) as an alternative to disqualifying the law firm this paralegal recently joined. This view is represented in the ethics opinion of the American Bar Association (Informal Opinion 88-1526) printed below. It must be emphasized, however, that not all states follow this opinion.

■ In a recent, dramatic case, a San Francisco law firm was disqualified from representing nine clients in asbestos litigation involving millions of dollars.

---

[36]ABA *Model Guidelines*, Guideline 7, see footnote 5.

The sole reason for the disqualification was that the firm hired a paralegal who had once worked for a law firm that represented the opponents in the asbestos litigation. Soon after the controversy arose, the disqualified firm laid off the tainted paralegal who brought this conflict to the firm. He was devastated when he found out that he was being let go. "I was flabbergasted, totally flabbergasted." He has not been able to find work since.[37] The case was widely reported throughout the legal community. A front-page story in the *Los Angeles Daily Journal* said that it "could force firms to conduct lengthy investigations of paralegals and other staffers before hiring them." [38]

■ One law firm makes the following statement to all its paralegals, "If you or a temporary legal assistant working under your supervision were formerly employed by opposing counsel, this could be the basis for a motion to disqualify" this law firm. "So also could personal relationships such as kinship with the opposing party or attorney or dating an attorney from another firm. Make your attorney aware of such connections." [39]

■ If you have worked (or volunteered) for an attorney in the past in *any* capacity (as a paralegal, as an investigator, as a secretary, etc.), you should make a list of all the clients and cases with which you were involved. When you apply for a new job, your list may be relevant to whether the law firm will be subject to disqualification if you are hired. You must be careful, however, with the list. Do not attach it to your resume and randomly send it around town! Until employment discussions have become serious, do not show it to the prospective employer. Furthermore, try to notify prior attorneys with whom you have worked that you are applying for a position at a law firm where its "conflicts check" on you must include knowing what cases you worked on with previous attorneys. Giving them this notice is not always practical, and may not be required. Yet it is a safe procedure to follow whenever possible.

■ Freelance paralegals who work for more than one attorney on a part-time basis are particularly vulnerable to conflict-of-interest charges. For example, in a large litigation involving many parties, two opposing attorneys might unknowingly use the same freelance paralegal to work on different aspects of the same case, or might use two different employees of this freelance paralegal. Another example is the freelance paralegal who worked on an earlier case for a client and now works on a different but similar case in which that client is the opponent. The California Association of Freelance Paralegals has attempted to address this problem in Article 11 of its proposed Code of Ethics: "A freelance paralegal shall avoid conflicts of interest relating to client matters. The freelance paralegal shall not accept any case adverse to the client of [an attorney who hires the paralegal] if the latter case bears a substantial connection to the earlier one or if there is a possibility that the two cases are substantially related, regardless of whether confidences were in fact imparted to the freelance paralegal by the attorney or the attorney's client in the earlier case." [40] There are practical problems with such rules. It is not always easy

[37]Motamedi, *Landmark Ethics Case Takes Toll on Paralegal's Career, Family,* 7 Legal Assistant Today 39 (May/June 1990). *In re Complex Asbestos Litigation,* 232 Cal.App.3d 572, 283 Cal.Rptr. 732 (Cal.Ct.App. 1991).

[38]M. Hall, *S.F. Decision on Paralegal Conflict May Plague Firms,* 102 Los Angeles Daily Journal 1, col. 2 (September 25, 1989).

[39]Orientation Handbook for Paralegals 3 (Lane, Powell, Moses & Miller, 1984).

[40]California Ass'n of Freelance Paralegals, "CAFP's Proposed Code of Ethics," Article 11, *Freelancer* 9 (July/August 1991).

to determine whether two cases are "adverse" or bear a "substantial connection" with each other. If there is doubt, it is in the economic self-interest of the freelance paralegal *not* to tell the attorney since he or she will most likely refuse to hire the paralegal rather than take the risk of later disqualification because of contamination injected into the case by this paralegal. Finally, conducting a conflicts check could be somewhat difficult for a busy, experienced freelance paralegal who has worked for scores of attorneys and hundreds of clients over the years.

---

### Standing Committee on Ethics and Professional Responsibility of the American Bar Association
#### Informal Opinion 88-1526

*A law firm that employs a nonlawyer who formerly was employed by another firm may continue representing clients whose interests conflict with the interests of clients of the former employer on whose matters the nonlawyer has worked, as long as the employing firm screens the nonlawyer from information about or participating in matters involving those clients and strictly adheres to the screening process described in this opinion and as long as no information relating to the representation of the clients of the former employer is revealed by the nonlawyer to any person in the employing firm. In addition, the nonlawyer's former employer must admonish the nonlawyer against revelation of information relating to the representation of clients of the former employer.*

The Committee is asked whether, under the ABA Model Rules of Professional Conduct (1983, amended 1987), a law firm that hires a paralegal formerly employed by another lawyer must withdraw from representation of a client under the following circumstances. The paralegal has worked for more than a year with a sole practitioner on litigation matters. One of those matters is a lawsuit which the sole practitioner instituted against a client of the law firm that is about to hire the paralegal and wishes to continue to defend the client. The paralegal has gained substantial information relating to the representation of the sole practitioner's client, the plaintiff in the lawsuit. The employing firm will screen the paralegal from receiving information about or working on the lawsuit and will direct the paralegal not to reveal any information relating to the representation of the sole practitioner's client gained by the paralegal during the former employment. The Committee also is asked whether the paralegal's former employer must take any actions in order to comply with the Model Rules.

#### Responsibilities of Employing Firm

The Committee concludes that the law firm employing the paralegal should not be disqualified from continuing to defend its client in the lawsuit, as long

as the law firm and the paralegal strictly adhere to the screening process described in this Opinion, and as long as no information relating to the representation of the sole practitioner's client is revealed by the paralegal to any person in the employing firm.

The Model Rules require that a lawyer make reasonable efforts to ensure that each of the lawyer's nonlawyer employees maintains conduct compatible with the professional obligations of the lawyer, including the nondisclosure of information relating to the representation of clients. This requires maintaining procedures designed to protect client information from disclosure by the lawyer's employees and agents. . . .

It is important that nonlawyer employees have as much mobility in employment opportunity as possible consistent with the protection of clients' interests. To so limit employment opportunities that some nonlawyers trained to work with law firms might be required to leave the careers for which they are trained would disserve clients as well as the legal profession. Accordingly, any restrictions on the nonlawyer's employment should be held to the minimum necessary to protect confidentiality of client information.

Model Rule 5.3 imposes general supervisory obligations on lawyers with respect to nonlawyer employees and agents. The obligations include the obligation to make reasonable efforts to ensure there are measures in effect to assure that the nonlawyer's conduct is compatible with the professional obligations of the lawyer. With respect to new employees who formerly worked for other lawyers, these measures should involve admonitions to be alert to all legal matters, including lawsuits, in which any client of the former employer has an interest. The nonlawyer should be cautioned: (1) not to disclose any information relating to the representation of a client of the former employer; and (2) that the employee should not work on any matter on which the employee worked for the prior employer or respecting which the employee has information relating to the representation of the client of the former employer. When the new firm becomes aware of such matters, the employing firm must also take reasonable steps to ensure that the employee takes no action and does no work in relation to matters on which the nonlawyer worked in the prior employment, absent client consent after consultation.

Circumstances sometimes require that a firm be disqualified or withdraw from representing a client when the firm employs a nonlawyer who formerly was employed by another firm. These circumstances are present either: (1) where information relating to the representation of an adverse party gained by the nonlawyer while employed in another firm has been revealed to lawyers or other personnel in the new firm . . .; or (2) where screening would be ineffective or the nonlawyer necessarily would be required to work on the other side of the same or a substantially related matter on which the nonlawyer worked or respecting which the nonlawyer has gained information relating to the representation of the opponent while in the former employment. If the employing firm employs the nonlawyer under those circumstances, the firm must withdraw from representing the client, unless the client of the former employer consents to the continued representation of the person with conflicting interests after being apprised of all the relevant factors.

### Responsibilities of Former Employer

Under Model Rule 5.3, lawyers have a duty to make reasonable efforts to ensure that nonlawyers do not disclose information relating to the representation of the lawyers' clients while in the lawyer's employ and afterwards. On the facts presented to the Committee here, once the lawyer learns that the paralegal has joined the opposing law firm, the lawyer should consider advising the employing firm that the paralegal must be isolated from participating in the matter and from revealing any information relating to the representation of the lawyer's client. If not satisfied that the employing firm has taken adequate measures to prevent participation and disclosures, the lawyer should consider filing a motion in the lawsuit to disqualify the employing law firm from continuing to represent the opponent. . . .

Therefore, the lawyer who hires the paralegal, under the circumstances before the Committee, must screen the paralegal from participating in the lawsuit with the employing law firm. Both the employing firm and the sole practitioner should admonish the paralegal not to disclose information relating to the representation of the plaintiff in the lawsuit and also of any other client of the sole practitioner for whom the paralegal formerly worked while with the former employer.

The standards expressed in this Opinion apply to all matters where the interests of the clients are in conflict and not solely to matters in litigation. The Committee also notes that these standards apply equally to all nonlawyer personnel in a law firm who have access to material information relating to the representation of clients and extends also to agents who technically may be independent contractors, such as investigators.

## 12.  Communication with the Other Side

*In representing a client, an attorney shall not communicate with a party on the other side about the subject of the case if the attorney knows that the party is represented by another attorney. The latter attorney must consent to such a communication.* Model Rule 4.2

*If the other side is not represented, an attorney must not give him or her the impression that the attorney is uninvolved. The attorney should not give this person advice other than the advice to obtain his or her own attorney.* Model Rule 4.3

The ethical concern here is that an attorney will take an unfair advantage of the other side.

**Example:** Dan and Theresa Kline have just separated and are thinking about a divorce. Each claims the marital home. Theresa hires Thomas Farlington, Esq. to represent her. Farlington calls Dan to ask him if he is interested in settling the case.

It is unethical for Farlington to contact Dan about the case if Farlington knows that Dan has his own attorney. Farlington must talk with Dan's attorney. Only the latter can give Farlington permission to communicate with Dan. If Dan does not have an attorney, Farlington can talk with Dan, but he must not allow Dan to be misled about Farlington's role. Farlington works for the other side; he is not disinterested. Dan must be made to understand this fact. The only advice Farlington can give Dan in such a situation is to seek his own attorney.

### Paralegal Perspective:

■ The ethical restrictions on communicating with the other side apply to the employees of an attorney as well as to the attorney. "The lawyer's obligation is to ensure that the legal assistants do not communicate directly with parties known to be represented by an attorney, without that attorney's consent, on the subject of such representation."[41] You must avoid improper communication with the other side. If the other side is a business or some other large organization, do not talk with anyone there unless your supervisor tells you that it is ethical to do so. Never call the other side and pretend you are someone else in order to obtain information.

■ If your office allows you to interview someone who is not represented by an attorney, you cannot give this person any advice other than the advice to secure his or her own attorney.

## 13.  Solicitation

*In person, an attorney may not solicit employment from a prospective client with whom the attorney has no family or prior professional relationship when a significant motive for doing so is the attorney's monetary gain.[42] Model Rule 7.3*

People in distress are sometimes so distraught that they are not in a position to evaluate their need for legal services. They should not be subjected to pressures from an attorney who shows up wanting to be hired, particularly if the attorney is not a relative or has never represented them in the past.[43] Such in-person solicitation is unethical.

Example: Rachael Winters, Esq. stands outside the police station and gives a business card to any individual being arrested. The card says that Winters is an attorney specializing in criminal cases.

Winters is obviously looking for prospective clients. Doing so in this manner is referred to as *ambulance chasing*, which is a pejorative term for aggressively tracking down anyone who probably has a legal problem in order to drum up business. There is no indication either that Winters is related to any of the people going into the police station or that she has any prior professional relationship with them, (for example, they are *not* former clients). Winters appears to have one goal: finding a source of fees. Hence her conduct is unethical. Such direct, in-person, one-on-one solicitation of clients in this way is not allowed. The concern is that an attorney who approaches strangers in trouble

---

[41]Section 20-104, Committee Commentary, *New Mexico Rules Governing the Practice of Law* (Judicial Pamphlet 16).

[42]This prohibition also applies to *live* telephone conversations in which the attorney seeks to be hired.

[43]Furthermore, the improper solicitation of clients and promotion of litigation constitutes the crime of *barratry* in some states. For example, in 1990 three attorneys and an employee of a law firm were indicted in Texas on charges that they illegally sought clients at hospitals and funeral homes after twenty-one students were killed and sixty-nine were injured in a school bus accident. *4 Said to Have Used Bus Crash to Get Business for Law Firm*, New York Times 8, col. 5 (April 7, 1990).

may exert undue influence on them. This is less likely to occur if the solicitation comes in the mail, even if it is sent to individuals known to need legal services.

> Example: An attorney obtains the names of homeowners facing foreclosure and sends them the following letter: "It has come to my attention that your home is being foreclosed on. Federal law may allow you to stop your creditors and give you more time to pay. Call my office for legal help."

While critics claim that such solicitation constitutes "ambulance chasing by mail," the technique is ethical in most states so long as it is truthful and not misleading.[44] *In-person* solicitation, however, is treated differently because of the obvious pressure that it imposes. It is "easier to throw out unwanted mail than an uninvited guest."[45]

## Paralegal Perspective:

■ An unscrupulous attorney may try to use a paralegal to solicit clients for the office.

> Example: Bill Hill is a senior citizen who lives at a home for senior citizens. Andrew Vickers, Esq. hires Bill as his "paralegal." His sole job is to contact other seniors with legal problems and to refer them to Vickers.

Andrew Vickers is engaging in unethical solicitation through Bill Hill. Attorneys cannot hire a paralegal to try to accomplish what they cannot do themselves. Nor can they use a *runner*[46]—an employee or independent contractor who contacts personal-injury victims or other potential clients in order to solicit business for an attorney.

■ See also the related discussion above on splitting fees with nonattorneys.

## 14.  Advertising

> *An attorney may advertise services on radio, on TV, in the newspaper, or through other public media so long as the ad is neither false nor misleading and does not constitute improper in-person solicitation.* Model Rule 7.2

There was a time when almost all forms of advertising by attorneys were prohibited. Traditional attorneys considered advertising to be highly offensive to the dignity of the profession. In 1977, however, the United States Supreme Court stunned the legal profession by holding that truthful advertising cannot be completely banned.[47] The First Amendment protects such advertising. Furthermore, advertising does not pose the same danger as in-person solicitation by an attorney. A recipient of advertising is generally under very little pressure to buy the advertised product—in this case, an attorney's services. Hence, attorneys can ethically use truthful, nonmisleading advertising to the general public in order to generate business.

Studies have shown that over one third of all attorneys in the country engage in some form of advertising. Most of it consists of listings in the Yellow

---

[44]*Shapero v. Kentucky Bar Ass'n,* 486 U.S. 466, 108 S.Ct. 1916, 100 L.Ed.2d 475 (1988). Some states impose additional requirements on mail solicitations—for example, the phrase "Advertising Material" must be printed on the outside of the envelope, and the word "advertisement" must be printed at the top of each page of the letter.

[45]Metzner, *Strategies That Break the Rules,* National Law Journal, 16 (July 15, 1991).

[46]Also called a *capper* if the person uses fraud or deception in the solicitation.

[47]*Bates v. State Bar of Arizona,* 433 U.S. 350, 97 S.Ct. 2691, 53 L.Ed.2d 810 (1977).

Pages. The use of other marketing tools is also on the rise. Revenue for television advertising, for example, was more than $89 million in 1989.[48] Former Chief Justice Warren Burger commented that some attorney ads "would make a used-car dealer blush with shame." Proponents of attorney advertising, however, claim that it has made legal services more accessible to the public and has provided the public with a better basis for choosing among available attorneys.

## 15.  Reporting Professional Misconduct

*Attorneys with knowledge that another attorney has committed a serious violation of the ethical rules must report this attorney to the appropriate disciplinary body.* Model Rule 8.3

Attorneys may pay a price for remaining silent when they become aware of unethical conduct. The failure of an attorney to report another attorney may mean that both attorneys can be disciplined for unethical behavior. Not every ethical violation, however, must be reported. The ethical violation must raise a substantial question of the attorney's honesty, trustworthiness, or fitness to practice law.

### *Paralegal Perspective:*

■ If a paralegal is aware of unethical conduct of his or her own attorney supervisor, is it unethical for the paralegal to fail to report the attorney to the bar association? No. As indicated earlier, the ethical rules under consideration here apply only to attorneys. Yet the paralegal is still in a predicament. If there is no one to talk to at the firm, he or she must decide whether to remain at this job. Sooner or later, unethical attorneys will probably ask or pressure their paralegal to participate in unethical conduct.

## 16.  Appearance of Impropriety

How would you feel if you were told that, even though you have not violated any rule, you are still going to be punished because what you did *appeared* to be improper? That would be the effect of an obligation to avoid even the appearance of impropriety. In some states, however, it *is* unethical for attorneys to engage in such appearances.[49] The ABA Model Rules, however, does not list appearance of impropriety as an independent basis of determining unethical conduct. To be disciplined in states that have adopted the Model Rules, an attorney must violate one of the specific ethical rules. Yet even in these states, there are conservative attorneys who are as worried about apparent impropriety as they are about specific, actual impropriety.

## 17.  Unauthorized Practice of Law

*An attorney shall not assist a nonattorney in the unauthorized practice of law.* Rule 5.5(b)

In Chapter 4, we saw that it is a crime in many states for a nonattorney to engage in the *unauthorized practice of law.* Our main focus in Chapter 4 was

---

[48]Hornsby, *The Complex Evolution of Attorney Ad Regs,* Nat'l Law Journal S4 (August 6, 1990).
[49]See Canon 9 of the *ABA Code of Professional Responsibility* (1981). "A lawyer should avoid even the appearance of professional impropriety."

the nonattorney who works for an office other than a traditional law office. An example would be a do-it-yourself divorce office that sells kits and typing services. Now our focus is the nonattorney who works under the supervision of an attorney in a law office. We want to explore the ways in which attorneys might be charged with unethically assisting *their own paralegals* engage in the unauthorized practice of law. For example, an attorney might allow a paralegal to give legal advice, to conduct depositions, or to sign court documents. These areas will be discussed below along with an overview of other major ethical issues involving paralegals.

## 18.  Paralegals

We turn now to a more direct treatment of when attorneys can be disciplined for the unethical use of paralegals. We will cover the following topics:

(a)  Paralegals, the ABA Model Code, and the ABA Model Rules

(b)  Misrepresentation of paralegal identity or status

(c)  Doing what only attorneys can do

(d)  Absentee, shoulder, and environmental supervision

### (a)  Paralegals, the ABA Model Code, and the ABA Model Ru.

The first major statement by the American Bar Association on the ethical use of paralegals by attorneys came in its *Model Code of Professional Responsibility:*

> DR 3-101(A): A lawyer shall not aid a nonlawyer in the unauthorized practice of law.

> EC 3-6: A lawyer often delegates tasks to clerks, secretaries, and other lay persons. Such delegation is proper if the lawyer maintains a direct relationship with his client, supervises the delegated work, and has complete professional responsibility for the work product. This delegation enables a lawyer to render legal services more economically and efficiently.[50]

A 1967 opinion elaborated on these standards:

**American Bar Association**

Formal Opinion 316 (1967)

A lawyer can employ lay secretaries, lay investigators, lay detectives, lay researchers, accountants, lay scriveners, non-lawyer draftsmen or non-lawyer researchers. In fact, he may employ non-lawyers to do any task for him except counsel clients about law matters, engage directly in the practice of law, appear in court or appear in formal proceedings as part of the judicial process, so long as it is he who takes the work and vouches for it to the client and becomes responsible for it to the client. In other words, we do not limit the kind of assistance that a lawyer can acquire in any way to persons who are admitted to the Bar, so long as the non-lawyers do not do things that lawyers may not do or do the things that lawyers only may do.

From these documents we learn that an attorney can hire a paralegal and is responsible for what the paralegal does. There are two levels of this responsibility: civil liability for malpractice and ethical liability for violation of ethical rules.

---

[50]See footnote 4 on the meaning of DR and EC in the ABA Model Code.

Example: The law firm of Adams & Adams represents Harold Thompson in his negligence suit against Parker Co. At the firm, Elaine Stanton, Esq. works on the case with Peter Vons, a paralegal whom she supervises. Peter neglects to file an important pleading in court, and carelessly gives confidential information about Thompson to the attorney representing Parker. All of this causes Thompson great damage.

Stanton is fully responsible to the client, Thompson, who might decide to bring a malpractice suit in court against her. She cannot hide behind the fact that her paralegal was at fault. (See the discussion of malpractice liability and respondeat superior in Chapter 4.)

What about ethics? Can Stanton be reprimanded, suspended, or disbarred because of what her paralegal did? None of the materials quoted above answer this question. Responsibility to a client for malpractice often raises separate issues from responsibility to a bar association (or other disciplinary body) for unethical conduct. The two kinds of responsibility can be closely interrelated because the same alleged wrongdoing can be involved in the malpractice suit and in the disciplinary case. Yet the two proceedings are separate and should be examined separately.

In 1983, the ABA replaced the *Model Code of Professional Responsibility* with its *Model Rules of Professional Conduct.* The Model Rules, which have been our main focus in this chapter, are more helpful in telling us when attorneys are subject to ethical sanctions because of their paralegals. This is done in *Model Rule 5.3,* covering paralegals. All attorneys in the law firm are not treated the same in Rule 5.3. As you read this rule, note that different standards of ethical responsibility are imposed on the following three categories of attorneys:

- Any attorney in the firm
- A partner in the firm
- An attorney in the firm with direct supervisory authority over the paralegal

### Model Rules of Professional Conduct
### Rule 5.3. Responsibilities
### Regarding Nonlawyer Assistants

With respect to a nonlawyer employed or retained by or associated with a lawyer:

(a) a partner in a law firm shall make reasonable efforts to ensure that the firm has in effect measures giving reasonable assurance that the person's conduct is compatible with the professional obligations of the lawyer;

(b) a lawyer having direct supervisory authority over the nonlawyer shall make reasonable efforts to ensure that the person's conduct is compatible with the professional obligations of the lawyer; and

(c) A lawyer shall be responsible for conduct of such a person that would be a violation of the Rules of Professional Conduct if engaged in by a lawyer if:

(1) the lawyer orders or ratifies the conduct involved; or

(2) the lawyer is a partner in the law firm in which the person is employed, or has direct supervisory authority over the person, and knows of the conduct at a time when its consequences can be avoided or mitigated but fails to take reasonable remedial action.

**Comment:**

Lawyers generally employ assistants in their practice, including secretaries, investigators, law student interns, and paraprofessionals. Such assistants, whether employees or independent contractors, act for the lawyer in rendition of the lawyer's professional services. A lawyer should give such assistants appropriate instruction and supervision concerning the ethical aspects of their employment, particularly regarding the obligation not to disclose information relating to representation of the client, and should be responsible for their work product. The measures employed in supervising nonlawyers should take account of the fact that they do not have legal training and are not subject to professional discipline.

Let us analyze Rule 5.3 by applying it to Elaine Stanton, Esq. in our example. First of all, under 5.3(c)(1), *any* attorney in the firm who "orders" the paralegal to commit the wrongdoing in question is ethically responsible for that conduct. The same is true if the attorney "ratifies" (that is, approves or endorses) the wrongdoing after the paralegal commits it. There is no indication in the example that Stanton or any other attorney in the firm told Peter not to file the pleading in court, or told him to give confidential information about Thompson to the other side. Nor is there any indication that an attorney approved of Peter's conduct after it occurred.[51] Therefore, Rule 5.3(c)(1) does not apply.

We need to know whether Stanton is a partner in the firm. If so, she has an ethical obligation under 5.3(a) to "make reasonable efforts to ensure that the firm has in effect measures giving reasonable assurance" that the paralegal's conduct "is compatible with the professional obligations of the lawyer." Hence a partner cannot completely ignore office paralegals in the hope that someone else in the firm is monitoring them. Reasonable steps must be taken by every partner to establish a system of safeguards. Here are some examples:

- Make sure that all paralegals in the firm are made aware of the ethical rules governing attorneys in the state.
- Make sure that all paralegals in the firm are made aware of the importance of deadlines in the practice of law and of the necessity of using date-reminder (tickler) techniques.

In the example, Peter Vons is supervised by Elaine Stanton, Esq. Hence she is an attorney with "direct supervisory authority" over Peter. Rule 5.3(b) governs the conduct of such attorneys. This section requires her to "make reasonable efforts to ensure" that the paralegal's conduct "is compatible with the professional obligations of the lawyer."

Assume that Stanton is charged with a violation of Rule 5.3(b) because her paralegal, Peter, failed to file an important pleading in court and disclosed confidential information about a client. At Stanton's disciplinary hearing, she would be asked a large number of questions about how she supervised Peter. For example:

- How do you assign tasks to Peter?
- How do you know if he is capable of handling an assignment?
- How often do you meet with him after you give him an assignment?
- How do you know if he is having difficulty completing an assignment?
- Has he made mistakes in the past? If so, how have you handled them?

Peter might be called as a witness in her disciplinary hearing and be interrogated extensively. For example:

- How were you trained as a paralegal?
- What kinds of assignments have you handled in your paralegal career?
- How long have you worked for Elaine Stanton?
- How does she evaluate your work?
- What do you do if you have a question on an assignment but she is not available in the office?

---

[51]By Peter's conduct, we mean both what he did (disclose confidential information) and what he failed to do (file the papers in court).

- Why didn't you file the court document on time?

- Describe the circumstances under which you revealed confidential information to the opponent in the Thompson case.

All of these questions of Stanton and of Peter would be designed to find out if Stanton made "reasonable efforts" to ensure that Peter did not violate ethical standards. Note that attorney supervisors do not have to guarantee that a paralegal will act ethically. They simply have to "make reasonable efforts" that this will occur. The above questions are relevant to whether Stanton exerted such efforts with respect to Peter.

Another basis of ethical liability under the Model Rules is Rule 5.3(c)(2). Both a partner and a supervisory attorney can be subject to discipline if they knew about the paralegal's misconduct yet failed to take reasonable corrective steps at a time when such steps would have avoided or minimized ("mitigated") the damage. At their disciplinary hearing, a partner and/or a supervising attorney would be asked questions such as:

- When did you first find out that Peter did not file the court document?

- What did you do at that time? Why didn't you act sooner?

- When did you first find out that Peter spoke to opposing counsel?

- What did you do at that time? Why didn't you act sooner?

So, too, Peter might be asked questions at the hearing relevant to when his supervising attorney (Stanton) or any partner in the firm found out about what he had done—and what they did when they found out.

### (b) Misrepresentation of Paralegal Identity or Status

"It is the lawyer's responsibility to take reasonable measures to ensure that clients, courts, and other lawyers are aware that a legal assistant, whose services are utilized by the lawyer in performing legal services, is not licensed to practice law." [52] People who come into contact with paralegals must not think that they are attorneys. Paralegals should not misrepresent their status intentionally or accidentally. The following status issues need to be covered:

- Titles
- Disclosure of status
- Business cards
- Letterhead
- Signature on correspondence
- Advertisements, announcement cards, signs, lists, and directories
- Name on court documents

*What Title Can Be Used?*   There are no ethical problems with the titles *paralegal* or *legal assistant*. No one is likely to think that persons with such titles are attorneys. There are some bar associations that prefer titles that are even more explicit in communicating nonattorney status—for example, *lawyer's assistant* and *nonattorney assistant*. Yet, they are seldom used because of the widespread acceptance and clarity of the titles *paralegal* and *legal assistant*. Some years ago,

---

[52]ABA *Model Guidelines*, Guideline 4, see footnote 5.

the Philadelphia Bar Association[53] said that the latter titles should be given only to employees that possessed "the requisite training and education." No state, however, is this explicit in stating who can use the titles.

It is unethical to call a paralegal an "associate" or to refer to a paralegal as being "associated" with a law firm. The title, "paralegal associate," for example, should not be used. The common understanding is that an associate is an attorney. In Iowa, similar problems exist with the title, "Certified Legal Assistant," as we shall see shortly. (See Figure 5.7).

*Note on Disbarred or Suspended Attorney as Paralegal.*   When attorneys have been disbarred or suspended from the practice of law for ethical improprieties, they may try to continue to work in the law as a paralegal for an attorney willing to hire them. Some states will not allow this because it shows disrespect for the court that disciplined the attorney and because of the high likelihood that the individual will engage in the unauthorized practice of law by going beyond paralegal duties. Other states are more lenient but impose other restrictions, such as not allowing a disbarred or suspended attorney to have any client contact while working as a paralegal.

*Should Paralegals Disclose Their Nonattorney Status to Clients, Attorneys, Government Officials, and the General Public?*   Yes, this disclosure is necessary. The more troublesome questions are: What kind of disclosure should you make and when must you make it? Compare the following communications by a paralegal:

- "I work with attorney Ward Brown at Brown & Tams."
- "I am a paralegal."
- "I am a legal assistant."
- "I am not an attorney."

The fourth statement is the clearest expression of nonattorney status. The first is totally unacceptable since you have said nothing about your status. For most contacts, the second and third statements will be ethically sufficient to overcome any misunderstanding about your nonattorney status. Yet there might be members of the public who are confused about what a paralegal or legal assistant is. Hence, the only foolproof communication in all circumstances is the fourth.

In some states, the disclosure of nonattorney status is necessary only if a client, an attorney, a government official, or a member of the public is unaware of this status. Other states say that the paralegal should always disclose his or her nonattorney status at the outset of the contact. "Common sense suggests a routine disclosure at the outset of the conversation." Furthermore, the failure to provide an oral clarification of status is *not* cured simply by handing over a business card that says you are a paralegal or a legal assistant.

Do not assume that a person with whom you come in contact knows you are not an attorney; the safest course is to assume the opposite!

*May a Paralegal Have a Business Card?*   Every state allows paralegals to have their own *business cards* as long as their nonattorney status is clear. (See Figure 5.6.) At one time, some states wanted the word "nonlawyer" used along

---

[53]Throughout this discussion, there will be references to the opinions of specific bar associations. For a summary of these opinions and their citations, see Appendix F.

**ABEL MUSSER SOKOLOSKY &CLARK**

**ATTORNEYS AT LAW**

DEBRA J. HOBBS
LEGAL ASSISTANT

ONE LEADERSHIP SQUARE
211 N. ROBINSON, SUITE 600
(405) 239-7046  OKLAHOMA CITY, OK 73102

Ethically proper in every state.

**FIGURE 5.6**
Paralegal
Business Card

John Simpson, CLA
PARALEGAL

JONES, DAY, OVERTON & DAVIS, P.C.
8262 PRESTWICK DR.
PHONE  WATERLOO, IA 50702
(319) 456-9103

Ethically proper in every state *except* in Iowa.

**FIGURE 5.7**
Paralegal
Business Card

with the paralegal's office title. This is rarely required today. Since paralegals are not allowed to solicit business for their employer, the card may not be used for this purpose. The primary focus of the card must be to identify the paralegal rather than the attorney for whom the paralegal works. Finally, there must be nothing false or misleading printed on the card. In most states, a paralegal who is a *Certified Legal Assistant (CLA)* can include this fact on their card. In Iowa, however, this is not permitted, as we will see when we discuss signatures on correspondence. (See Figure 5.7.)

*May the Letterhead of Law Firm Stationery Print the Name of a Paralegal?* States differ in their answer to this question, although most now agree that nonattorneys' names can be printed on *law-firm letterhead* if their title is also printed so that their nonattorney status is clear. (See Figure 5.8.) Before 1977, almost all states did *not* allow attorney stationery to print the names of nonattorney employees. The concern was that the letterhead would be used as a form of advertising by packing it with names and titles in order to make the office look impressive. This concern, however, evaporated in 1977 when the Supreme Court held that all forms of attorney advertising could not be banned.[54] After this date, most states withdrew their objection to the printing

---

[54]See footnote 47 above.

**FIGURE 5.8**

Attorney
Letterhead that
Prints Paralegal
Names

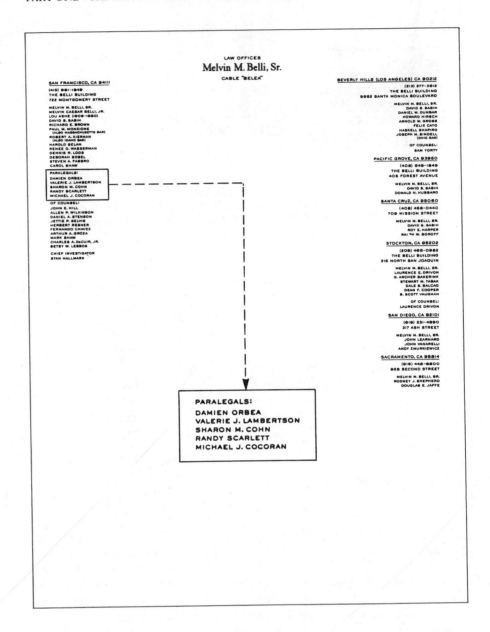

of paralegal names on attorney letterhead as long as no one would be misled into thinking that the paralegals were attorneys. In Michigan, it was recommended, but not required, that attorneys and nonattorneys be printed on different sides of the stationery to "enhance the clarification that the paraprofessional is not licensed to practice law." A few states adhere to the old view that only attorney names can be printed on law-firm letterhead. Yet, to the extent that it is still based on a prohibition of attorney advertising, this view is subject to challenge.

*May a Paralegal Write and Sign Letters on Attorney Stationery?* There is never an ethical problem with a paralegal writing a letter that will be reviewed and signed by an attorney. Suppose, however, that the attorney wants the paralegal to sign his or her own name to the letter. Most states will permit this if certain conditions are met. For example, a title must be used that indicates the signer's nonattorney status, and the letter must not give legal advice.

The following formats are proper:

| Sincerely, | Sincerely, | Sincerely, |
|---|---|---|
| Leonard Smith<br>Paralegal | Pauline Jones<br>Legal Assistant | Jill Strauss<br>Legal Assistant<br>   for the Firm |

The following formats, however, pose difficulties:

| Sincerely, | Sincerely, | Sincerely, |
|---|---|---|
| William Davis | John Simpson, CLA | Mary Page<br>Certified Legal<br>Assistant |

The first format is ethically improper. The lack of a title could mislead the reader into thinking that William Davis is an attorney. In most states, using the designations "CLA" or "Certified Legal Assistant" is also proper. (See Chapter 4 for a discussion of the CLA program.) In Iowa, however, they cannot be used. "A reader might think that CLA was a legal degree;" and if "Certified Legal Assistant" is used, "the public might be misled about his or her nonlawyer status." Hence, the second and third formats just shown cannot be used in Iowa. Presumably this also applies to a business card with the CLA designation. (See Figure 5.7.) This is an extreme view and is unlikely to be followed elsewhere.

In most states, there are no limitations on the persons to whom a paralegal can send letters. Yet there are a few states (such as New Jersey) where only an attorney can sign a letter to a client, to an opposing attorney, or to a court. A very minor exception to this rule would be "a purely routine request to a court clerk for a docket sheet." A paralegal can sign such a letter. This also is an extreme position. So long as the paralegal's nonattorney status is clear, and so long as an attorney is supervising the paralegal, restrictions on who can be the recipient of a paralegal-signed letter make little sense.

*May an Attorney Print the Name of a Paralegal in an Advertisement, an Announcement Card, a Door Sign, an Outdoor Sign, a Law Directory or Law List, an Office Directory, or a Telephone Directory?*   Attorneys communicate to the public and to each other through advertisements, law directories or lists (that print the names of practicing attorneys), office directories, general telephone directories, door signs, outdoor signs, and announcement cards (that announce that the firm has moved, opened a new branch, merged with another firm, taken on a new partner, etc.). It is relatively rare that an attorney will want to print the name of his or her paralegal in one of these vehicles of communication. In a small city or town, however, a solo practitioner or small law firm might want to do so. While several states will not allow attorneys to do this, most states that have addressed the issue say it is ethically permissible if nothing false or misleading is said about the paralegal and the latter's nonattorney status is clear.

*May an Attorney Print the Name of a Paralegal on a Court Document?* Formal documents that are required in litigation, such as appellate briefs, memoranda supporting a motion, complaints, or other pleadings, must be signed by an attorney representing a party in the dispute. With rare exceptions, the document cannot be signed by a nonattorney, no matter how minor the formal document may be. In most states, a paralegal can sign a letter on a routine matter to a clerk or other nonjudge, but formal litigation documents require an attorney's signature.

Suppose, however, that the attorney wishes to print on a document the name of a paralegal who worked on the document *in addition to* the attorney's name and signature. The attorney may simply want to give a measure of recognition to the efforts of this paralegal. Most states permit this as long as there is no misunderstanding as to the paralegal's nonattorney status, and no attempt is made to substitute a nonattorney's signature for an attorney's signature.

Occasionally, a court opinion will recognize the contribution of a paralegal. Before the opinion begins, the court lists the names of the attorneys who represented the parties. The name of a paralegal might be included with these attorneys. Here, for example, is the list of attorneys that includes the name of a paralegal (Becky Strickland) in the case of *United States v. Cooke*, 625 F.2d 19 (4th Cir. 1980):

> Thomas J. Keith, Winston-Salem, N.C., for appellant.
> David B. Smith, Asst. U.S. Atty. (H. M. Michaux, Jr., U.S. Atty., Durham, N.C., Becky M. Strickland, Paralegal Specialist on brief), for appellee.
> Before HALL and PHILLIPS, Circuit Judges, and HOFFMAN, Senior District Judge.

### (c) Doing What Only Attorneys Can Do

There are limitations on what attorneys can ask their paralegals to do. We just examined one such limitation: paralegals should never be asked to sign court documents. The failure to abide by these limits might subject the attorney to a charge of unethically assisting a nonattorney to engage in the unauthorized practice of law. The areas we need to examine are as follows:

- Legal advice
- Nonlegal advice
- Drafting documents
- Real estate closings
- Depositions
- Executions of wills
- Settlement negotiations
- Court appearances
- Counsel's table
- Administrative hearings

*May a Paralegal Give Legal Advice?*   Unfortunately, it is not easy to define legal advice or the practice of law. According to the American Bar Association:

> It is neither necessary nor desirable to attempt the formulation of a single, specific definition of what constitutes the practice of law. Functionally, the practice of law relates to the rendition of services for others that call for the professional judgment of a lawyer. The essence of the professional judgment of the lawyer is his educated ability to relate the general body and philosophy of law to a specific legal problem of a client. . . . Where this professional judgment is not involved, non-lawyers, such as court clerks, police officers, abstracters, and

many governmental employees, may engage in occupations that require a special knowledge of law in certain areas. But the services of a lawyer are essential in the public interest whenever the exercise of *professional judgment* is required.[55]

The major way that an attorney communicates this professional judgment is through *legal advice*. According to the ABA, it occurs when "the general body and philosophy of law" is related or applied "to a specific legal problem." You are giving legal advice when you tell a particular person how the law might affect a particular legal problem or how to achieve a particular legal result that solves or avoids such a problem. Giving such advice is the unauthorized practice of law, whether or not you charge for the advice, and whether or not your advice is correct.

Compare the following sets of statements:

| General Information about the Law | Information about the Law as Applied to a Specific Person |
|---|---|
| "The Superior Court is located at 1223 Via Barranca." | "Your case must be heard in the Superior Court which is located at 1223 Via Barranca." |
| "There are several different kinds of bankruptcy." | "There are several different kinds of bankruptcy, but you should file under Chapter 13." |
| "The failure to pay child support will lead to prosecution." | "Your failure to pay child support will lead to prosecution." |

Arguably, the statements in the second column constitute legal advice; general information about the law has been related or applied to a particular legal problem of a particular person. The legal questions or problems addressed are: What court can hear (has jurisdiction over) *your* case? What kind of bankruptcy should *you* file? Can *you* be prosecuted for not paying child support?

The statements in the first column do not appear to focus on any particular person's legal problem. Hence such statements do not constitute legal advice, at least not explicitly. But we need to examine some of these statements more closely. When you tell someone that there are "several different kinds of bankruptcy," are you, by implication, telling that person that he or she should consider, and may qualify for, at least one of the kinds of bankruptcy? When you tell someone that the "failure to pay child support will lead to prosecution," are you, by implication, telling that person that his or her failure to pay child support will lead to his or her prosecution? The moment there is a focus on a particular person's legal problem, you are in the realm of legal advice. This focus can be express or implied. Hence, whenever *any* statement about the law is made, you must ask yourself two questions:

- Am I trying to relate legal information to any particular person's legal problem? (If so, I am giving express legal advice.)
- Could a person reasonably interpret what I am saying as relating legal information to a particular person's legal problem even if this is not my intent? (If so, I am giving implied legal advice.)

Great care is sometimes needed to avoid giving legal advice.

---

[55]EC 3–5, *ABA Model Code of Professional Responsibility* (1981).

There are a number of circumstances that increase the likelihood that statements can reasonably be interpreted as giving implied legal advice. For example:

- The statement is made by someone who works in the law, such as an attorney, paralegal, or legal secretary.
- The statement is made by someone who has helped the person with his or her legal problems in the past.
- The statement is made by someone who knows that the person has a current legal problem.
- The person is distressed about his or her current legal problem.

Under such circumstances, the person is likely to interpret *any* statement about the law as being relevant to his or her particular legal problem.

A number of paralegals have pointed out how easy it is to fall into the trap of giving legal advice:

> Legal assistants should be alert to all casual questions [since your answers] might be interpreted as legal advice.[56]

> Most of us are aware of the obvious, but we need to keep in mind that sometimes the most innocent comment could be construed as legal advice.[57]

> A ... typical scenario, particularly in a small law office where legal assistants have a great deal of direct client contact, is that the clients themselves will coax you to answer questions about the procedures involved in their cases, and lead you into areas where you would be giving them legal advice. Sometimes this is done innocently—because the attorney is unavailable and they are genuinely unaware of the difference between what you can do for them and what their legal counsel is authorized to do. ... They will press you for projections, strategy, applicable precedents—in short, legal advice. Sometimes you are placed in situations where you are not adequately supervised and your own expertise may be such that you know more about the specialized area of law than the attorney does anyway. ... We have all walked the thin line between assisting in the provision of legal services and actually practicing law.[58]

When a paralegal gives legal advice in these circumstances, he or she is engaged in the unauthorized practice of law. An attorney who permits this to occur, or who fails to take the preventive steps required by Model Rule 5.3, is aiding the paralegal in the unauthorized practice of law—and hence is acting unethically.

There are a number of situations, however, in which a paralegal *can* give legal advice. First, a paralegal can tell a client precisely what the attorney tells the paralegal to say, even if the message constitutes legal advice. The paralegal, however, cannot elaborate on or explain this kind of message from the attorney. Paralegals "may be authorized to communicate legal advice so long as they do not interpret or expand on that advice." [59] Second, the paralegal may be working in an area of the law where nonattorneys are authorized to represent clients, such as social security hearings. (See Chapter 4.) In such areas, the authorization includes the right to give legal advice.

---

[56]King, *Ethics and the Legal Assistant,* 10 ParaGram 2 (Oregon Legal Assistants Ass'n, August 1987).

[57]DALA Newsletter 2 (Dallas Ass'n of Legal Assistants, December 1990).

[58]Spiegel, *How to Avoid the Unauthorized Practice of Law,* 8 The Journal 8–10 (Sacramento Ass'n of Legal Assistants, February 1986).

[59]ABA *Model Guidelines,* Comment to Guideline 3, see footnote 5.

*May a Paralegal Give a Client Nonlegal Advice?*   Yes. An attorney may allow a paralegal to render specialized advice on scientific or technical topics. For example, a qualified paralegal can give accounting advice or financial advice. The danger is that the nonlegal advice might also contain legal advice or that the client might reasonably interpret the nonlegal advice as legal advice.

*May a Paralegal Draft Legal Documents?*   Yes. A paralegal can draft any legal document as long as an attorney supervises and reviews the work of the paralegal. Some ethical opinions say that the document must lose its separate identity as the work of a paralegal and must leave the office as the work product of an attorney. In West Virginia, for example, "anything delegated to a nonattorney must lose its separate identity and be merged in the service of the lawyer." The key point is that an attorney must stand behind and be responsible for the document.

*May a Paralegal Attend a Real Estate Closing?*   The sale of property is finalized at an event called a real estate closing. Many of the events at the closing are formalities, such as signing and exchanging papers. Occasionally, however, some of these events turn into more substantive matters where negotiation, legal interpretation, and legal advice are involved.

In most states, paralegals can attend closings in order to assist their attorney-supervisor. The real question is whether they can attend alone and conduct the closing themselves. Chicago has one of the most liberal rules. There, paralegals can conduct the closing without the attorney-supervisor being present if no legal advice is given, if all the documents have been prepared in advance, if the attorney-supervisor is available by telephone to provide help, and if the other attorney consents. In some states, additional conditions must be met before allowing paralegals to act on their own. For example, the closing must take place in the attorney's law office with the attorney readily accessible to answer legal questions. It must be noted, however, that this is a minority position. Most states would say that it is unethical for an attorney to allow a paralegal to conduct a real estate closing alone.

*May a Paralegal Conduct a Deposition?*   No. Paralegals can schedule depositions, can assist in preparing a witness who will be deposed (called the deponent), can take notes at the deposition, and can summarize deposition transcripts, but they cannot conduct the deposition. Asking and objecting to questions are attorney-only functions.

*May a Paralegal Supervise the Execution of a Will?*   In Connecticut, the execution of a will must be supervised by an attorney. A paralegal can act as a witness to the execution, but an attorney must direct the procedure. Most other states would probably agree, although few have addressed this question.

*May a Paralegal Negotiate a Settlement?*   Some states allow a paralegal to negotiate with a nonattorney employee of an insurance company, such as a claims adjuster, as long as the paralegal is supervised by an attorney. Most states, however, limit the paralegal's role to exchanging messages from the supervising attorney, and do not allow any actual give-and-take negotiating by the paralegal.

*May a Paralegal Make a Court Appearance?*   In the vast majority of courts, a paralegal cannot perform even minor functions in a courtroom, such as asking a judge for a hearing date. As we saw in Chapter 4, very few exceptions to this rule exist. Only attorneys can act in a representative capacity before a judge. There are, however, a small number of specialized courts, like the small claims court of some states, where you do not have to be an attorney to represent parties. This exception, however, is rare. And, as mentioned earlier, a paralegal should not sign a formal court document that is filed in litigation.

*May a Paralegal Sit at Counsel's Table During a Trial?* In many courts, only attorneys can sit at counsel's table during a trial. Yet, in some courts a paralegal is allowed to sit with the attorneys if permission of the presiding judge is obtained. When allowed, it is sometimes referred to as sitting *second chair* in the courtroom.

*May a Paralegal Represent Clients at Administrative Hearings?* Yes, when this is authorized at the particular state or federal administrative agency. (See Chapter 4 and Appendix E.)

### (d) Absentee Supervision, Shoulder Supervision, and Environmental Supervision

It is difficult to overestimate the importance of attorney supervision in the arena of ethics. Almost every ethical opinion involving paralegals (and almost every attorney malpractice opinion involving paralegals) stresses the need for effective supervision. The justification for the very existence of perhaps 95% of paralegal activity is this supervision. Indeed, one of the main reasons many argue that paralegal licensing is not necessary is the protective cover of attorney supervision.

What is meant by supervision? The extremes are easy to identify. Figure 5.9 provides this spectrum of extremes. *Absentee supervision* refers to the attorney who is either never around or never available. Once tasks are assigned, paralegals are on their own. At the other extreme is *shoulder supervision,* practiced by attorneys who are afraid to delegate. When they do get up enough courage to delegate something, they constantly look over the shoulder of the paralegal, who is rarely left alone for more than two-minute intervals. Such attorneys suffer from *delegatitis,* the inordinate fear of letting anyone do anything for them.

Both kinds of supervision are misguided. If you work for an attorney who practices absentee supervision, disaster is just around the corner. You may feel flattered by the confidence placed in you; you may enjoy the challenge of independence; you may be highly compensated because of your success. But you are working in an office that is traveling 130 miles per hour in a 50 miles per hour zone. Any feeling of safety in such an office is illusory. Shoulder supervision, on the other hand, provides safety at the expense of practicality. Perpetual step-by-step surveillance will ultimately defeat the economy and efficiency motives that originally led the office to hire paralegals.

Perhaps the most effective kind of supervision is *"environmental supervision,"* or what might be called *holistic supervision.* It is far broader in its reach than the immediate task delegated to a paralegal. It addresses the essential question: What kind of environment will lead to a high-quality paralegal work product without sacrificing economy? The components of this kind of supervision

**FIGURE 5.9**
Levels of Supervision: The Spectrum of Extremes

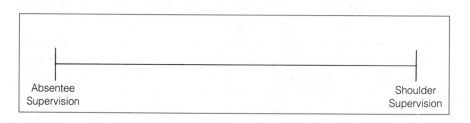

are outlined in Figure 5.10. Environmental supervision requires *hiring* the right people, *training* those people, *assigning* appropriate tasks, *providing* the needed resources, *monitoring* the progress, *reviewing* the end product, and *rewarding* competence.

---

1. Before paralegals are hired, the office undertakes a study of its practice in order to identify what tasks paralegals will perform and what levels of ability will be required to perform those tasks.

2. As part of the interview process, the office conducts background checks on applicants for paralegal jobs in order to ensure that competent people are hired who already have the needed skills or who are trainable so that they can acquire these skills on the job.

3. A program of orientation and training is created to introduce paralegals to the office and to prepare them for the tasks ahead.

4. Paralegals are given a copy of the ethical rules governing attorneys in the state. In addition to reading these rules, they are given training on the meaning of the rules.

5. Paralegals are told what to do if they feel that an ethical problem exists. Lines of authority are identified if the paralegal needs to discuss the matter with someone other than, or in addition to, his or her immediate supervisor.

6. The office does not assume that every attorney knows how to supervise paralegals. Paralegals are assigned to attorneys who have the required supervisory sensitivity and skill. Furthermore, the office is always looking for ways to increase this sensitivity and skill.

7. An attorney reviews all paralegal work. While paralegals may be given discretion and asked to exercise judgment in the tasks assigned, this discretion and judgment is always subjected to attorney review.

8. No task is assigned that is beyond the capacity of the paralegal. Specialized instruction always accompanies tasks the paralegal has not performed before.

9. Once a task is assigned, the paralegal is told where to receive assistance if the immediate supervisor is not available. This lack of availability, however, is relatively rare.

10. For tasks that the office performs on a recurring basis, manuals, office procedures, checklists, or other written material are available to the paralegal to explain how the tasks are performed and where samples or models can be found. If such *systems* material does not currently exist, the office has realistic plans to create such material.

11. To cut down on misunderstanding, every paralegal assignment includes the following information:

    ■ A *specific due date*. ("Get to this when you can" is unacceptable and unfair.)

    ■ A *priority assessment*. ("Should everything else be dropped while I do this assignment?")

    ■ A *context*. ("How does this assignment fit into the broader picture of the case?") and

    ■ A *financial perspective*. ("Is this billable time?")

12. At reasonable times before the due date of selected assignments, the supervisor monitors the progress of the paralegal to ensure that the work is being done professionally and accurately.

13. A team atmosphere exists at the office among the attorneys, paralegals, secretaries, and other employees. Everyone knows each other's functions, pressures, and potential as resources. A paralegal never feels isolated.

14. Evaluations of paralegal performance are constructive. Both the supervisor and paralegal feel that there are opportunities for further learning.

15. The office sends the paralegal to training seminars conducted by paralegal associations and bar associations to maintain and to increase the paralegal's skills.

16. The office knows that an unhappy employee is prone to error. Hence the office ensures that the work setting of the paralegal encourages personal growth and productivity. This includes matters of compensation, benefits, work space, equipment, and advancement.

**FIGURE 5.10**

"Environmental Supervision": The Ethical Ideal

Unfortunately, most law offices do *not* practice environmental supervision as outlined in Figure 5.10. The chart represents the ideal. Yet you need to know what the ideal is so that you can advocate for the conditions that will bring it about.

Thus far, our discussion on supervision has focused on the traditional paralegal who works full time in the office of an attorney. We also need to consider the freelance paralegal who works part-time for one or more attorneys. Very often this freelance or independent paralegal works in his or her own office. (See Chapters 1 and 4, and Appendix I.) How can attorneys fulfill their ethical obligation to supervise such paralegals?

> Example: Gail Patterson has her own freelance business. She offers paralegal services to attorneys who hire her for short-term projects which she performs in her own office.

Arguably, attorneys who hire Gail often do not provide the same kind of supervision that they can provide to a full-time paralegal who works in their office. We saw earlier that Model Rule 5.3(c)(2) says that an attorney has the responsibility to take steps to avoid the consequences of an ethical violation by a paralegal or to mitigate the consequences of such a violation. Suppose that Gail commits an ethical impropriety—for example, she reveals confidential communications. Since she works in her own office, the attorney who hired her may not learn about this impropriety in time to avoid or mitigate its consequences. Conflict of interest is another potential problem. Gail works for many different attorneys and hence many different clients of those attorneys. It is possible that she could accept work from two attorneys who are engaged in litigation against each other without either attorney knowing that the other has hired Gail on the same case. (See the earlier discussion of this problem on page 292.)

A few bar associations have declared that it is ethically improper for an attorney to hire a freelance paralegal because of the difficulties of providing meaningful supervision. It is not enough that the attorney vouches for, and takes responsibility for, the final product submitted by the freelance paralegal. Ongoing supervision is also needed under Model Rule 5.3. Not many states, however, have addressed this area of ethics. In the future, we will probably see the creation of new standards to govern this kind of paralegal.

## ■ Section D. Doing Research on an Ethical Issue

1. At a law library, ask where the following two items are kept:
   - The code or rules of ethics governing the attorneys in your state
   - The ethical opinions that interpret the code or rules

2. Contact your state bar association. Ask what committee or other body has jurisdiction over ethics. Contact it to find out if it has published any opinions, guidelines, or other materials on paralegals. Also ask if there is a special committee on paralegals. If so, find out what it has said about paralegals.

3. Do the same for any other bar associations in your area, such as city or county bar associations.

4. At a law library, ask where the following two items are kept:
   - The ABA's Model Rules of Professional Conduct
   - The ethical opinions that interpret these Model Rules as well as the earlier Model Code of Professional Responsibility of the ABA

5. Examine the *ABA/BNA Lawyers' Manual on Professional Conduct.* This is a loose-leaf book containing current information on ABA ethics and the ethical rules of every state.

6. Other material to check in the library:
   - C. Wolfram, *Modern Legal Ethics* (1986) (treatise)
   - *The Georgetown Journal of Legal Ethics* (periodical)
   - *Lawyers' Liability Review* (newsletter)

7. Computer research in either WESTLAW or LEXIS will enable you to do legal research on the law of ethics in your state. (See Chapters 11 and 13.) Here, for example, is a query (question) you could use to ask WESTLAW to find cases in your state in which a paralegal was charged with the unauthorized practice of law:

   > paralegal "legal assistant" /p "unauthorized practice"

   After you instructed WESTLAW to turn to the database containing the court opinions of your state, you would type this query at the keyboard in order to find out if any such cases exist.

8. Another way to find court opinions on ethics in your state is to go to the digest covering the courts in your state. Use its index to find cases on ethical issues.

## Section E. Ethical Codes of the Paralegal Associations

As indicated at the beginning of this chapter, there are no binding ethical rules published by paralegal associations. Yet the two major national associations—the National Federation of Paralegal Associations (NFPA) and the National Association of Legal Assistants (NALA)—have written ethical codes. These important documents of NFPA and of NALA are presented below, followed by a broader document of NALA, its Model Standards and Guidelines.

---

### Affirmation of Professional Responsibility
of the National Federation of Paralegal Associations

**Preamble**

The National Federation of Paralegal Associations recognizes and accepts its commitment to the realization of the most basic right of a free society, equal justice under the law.

In examining contemporary legal institutions and systems, the members of the paralegal profession recognize that a redefinition of the traditional delivery of legal services is essential in order to meet the needs of the general public. The paralegal profession is committed to increasing the availability and quality of legal services.

The National Federation of Paralegal Associations has adopted this *Affirmation of Professional Responsibility* to delineate the principles of purpose and conduct toward which paralegals should aspire. Through this Affirmation, the National Federation of Paralegal Associations places upon each paralegal the responsibility to adhere to these standards and encourages dedication to the development of the profession.

**I. Professional Responsibility**

A paralegal shall demonstrate initiative in performing and expanding the paralegal role in the delivery of legal services within the parameters of the unauthorized practice of law statutes.

*Discussion:* Recognizing the professional and legal responsibility to abide by the unauthorized practice of law statutes, the Federation supports and encourages new interpretations as to what constitutes the practice of law.

**II. Professional Conduct**

A paralegal shall maintain the highest standards of ethical conduct.

*Discussion:* It is the responsibility of a paralegal to avoid conduct which is unethical or appears to be unethical. Ethical principles are aspirational in character and embody the fundamental rules of conduct by which every paralegal should abide. Observance of these standards is essential to uphold respect for the legal system.

### III. Competence and Integrity

A paralegal shall maintain a high level of competence and shall contribute to the integrity of the paralegal profession.

*Discussion:* The integrity of the paralegal profession is predicated upon individual competence. Professional competence is each paralegal's responsibility and is achieved through continuing education, awareness of developments in the field of law and aspiring to the highest standards of personal performance.

### IV. Client Confidences

A paralegal shall preserve client confidences and privileged communications.

*Discussion:* Confidential information and privileged communications are a vital part of the attorney, paralegal and client relationship. The importance of preserving confidential and privileged information is understood to be an uncompromising obligation of every paralegal.

### V. Support of Public Interests

A paralegal shall serve the public interests by contributing to the availability and delivery of quality legal services.

*Discussion:* It is the responsibility of each paralegal to promote the development and implementation of programs that address the legal needs of the public. A paralegal shall strive to maintain a sensitivity to public needs and to educate the public as to the services that paralegals may render.

### VI. Professional Development

A paralegal shall promote the development of the paralegal profession.

*Discussion:* This Affirmation of Professional Responsibility promulgates a positive attitude through which a paralegal may recognize the importance, responsibility and potential of the paralegal contribution to the delivery of legal services. Participation in professional associations enhances the ability of the individual paralegal to contribute to the quality and growth of the paralegal profession.

---

## Code of Ethics and Professional Responsibility
of the National Association of Legal Assistants

### Preamble

It is the responsibility of every legal assistant to adhere strictly to the accepted standards of legal ethics and to live by general principles of proper conduct. The performance of the duties of the legal assistant shall be governed by specific canons as defined herein in order that justice will be served and the goals of the profession attained.

The canons of ethics set forth hereinafter are adopted by the National Association of Legal Assistants, Inc., as a general guide, and the enumeration of these rules does not mean there are not others of equal importance although not specifically mentioned.

### Canon 1

A legal assistant shall not perform any of the duties that lawyers only may perform nor do things that lawyers themselves may not do.

### Canon 2

A legal assistant may perform any task delegated and supervised by a lawyer so long as the lawyer is responsible to the client, maintains a direct relationship with the client, and assumes full professional responsibility for the work product.

### Canon 3

A legal assistant shall not engage in the practice of law by accepting cases, setting fees, giving legal advice or appearing in court (unless otherwise authorized by court or agency rules).

### Canon 4

A legal assistant shall not act in matters involving professional legal judgment as the services of a lawyer are essential in the public interest whenever the exercise of such judgment is required.

### Canon 5

A legal assistant must act prudently in determining the extent to which a client may be assisted without the presence of a lawyer.

### Canon 6

A legal assistant shall not engage in the unauthorized practice of law and shall assist in preventing the unauthorized practice of law.

### Canon 7

A legal assistant must protect the confidences of a client, and it shall be unethical for a legal assistant to violate any statute now in effect or hereafter to be enacted controlling privileged communications.

## Canon 8

It is the obligation of the legal assistant to avoid conduct which would cause the lawyer to be unethical or even appear to be unethical, and loyalty to the employer is incumbent upon the legal assistant.

## Canon 9

A legal assistant shall work continually to maintain integrity and a high degree of competency throughout the legal profession.

## Canon 10

A legal assistant shall strive for perfection through education in order to better assist the legal profession in fulfilling its duty of making legal services available to clients and the public.

## Canon 11

A legal assistant shall do all other things incidental, necessary, or expedient for the attainment of the ethics or responsibilities imposed by statute or rule of court.

## Canon 12

A legal assistant is governed by the *American Bar Association Model Code of Professional Responsibility* and the *American Bar Association Model Rules of Professional Conduct*.

---

## Model Standards and Guidelines for Utilization of Legal Assistants

of the National Association of Legal Assistants

### Preamble

Proper utilization of the services of legal assistants affects the efficient delivery of legal services. Legal assistants and the legal profession should be assured that some measures exist for identifying legal assistants and their role in assisting attorneys in the delivery of legal services. Therefore, the National Association of Legal Assistants, Inc., hereby adopts these Model Standards and Guidelines as an educational document for the benefit of legal assistants and the legal profession.

### Definition

Legal assistants* are a distinguishable group of persons who assist attorneys in the delivery of legal services. Through formal education, training, and experience, legal assistants have knowledge and expertise regarding the legal system and substantive and procedural law which qualify them to do work of a legal nature under the supervision of an attorney.

### Standards

A legal assistant should meet certain minimum qualifications.The following standards may be used to determine an individual's qualifications as a legal assistant:

1. Successful completion of the Certified Legal Assistant (CLA) examination of the National Association of Legal Assistants, Inc.;

2. Graduation from an ABA approved program of study for legal assistants;

3. Graduation from a course of study for legal assistants which is institutionally accredited but not ABA approved, and which requires not less than the equivalent of 60 semester hours of classroom study;

4. Graduation from a course of study for legal assistants, other than those set forth in (2) and (3) above, plus not less than six months of in-house training as a legal assistant;

5. A baccalaureate degree in any field, plus not less than six months in-house training as a legal assistant;

6. A minimum of three years of law-related experience under the supervision of an attorney, including at least six months of in-house training as a legal assistant; or

7. Two years of in-house training as a legal assistant.

For purposes of these standards, "in-house training as a legal assistant" means attorney education of the employee concerning legal assistant duties and these Guidelines. In addition to review and analysis of assignments, the legal assistant should receive a reasonable amount of instruction directly related to the duties and obligations of the legal assistant.

### Guidelines

These guidelines relating to standards of performance and professional responsibility are intended to aid legal assistants and attorneys. The responsibility rests with an attorney who employs legal assistants to

---

*Within this occupational category some individuals are known as paralegals.

educate them with respect to the duties they are assigned and to supervise the manner in which such duties are accomplished.

Legal assistants should:

1. Disclose their status as legal assistants at the outset of any professional relationship with a client, other attorneys, a court or administrative agency or personnel thereof, or members of the general public.
2. Preserve the confidences and secrets of all clients; and
3. Understand the attorney's Code of Professional Responsibility and these Guidelines in order to avoid any action which would involve the attorney in a violation of that Code, or give the appearance of professional impropriety.

Legal assistants should not:

1. Establish attorney-client relationships; set legal fees; give legal opinions or advice; or represent a client before a court; nor
2. Engage in, encourage, or contribute to any act which could constitute the unauthorized practice of law.

Legal assistants may perform services for an attorney in the representation of a client, provided:

1. The services performed by the legal assistant do not require the exercise of independent professional legal judgment;
2. The attorney maintains a direct relationship with the client and maintains control of all client matters;
3. The attorney supervises the legal assistant;
4. The attorney remains professionally responsible for all work on behalf of the client, including any actions taken or not taken by the legal assistant in connection therewith; and
5. The services performed supplement, merge with and become the attorney's work product.

In the supervision of a legal assistant, consideration should be given to:

1. Designating work assignments that correspond to the legal assistants' abilities, knowledge, training and experience;
2. Educating and training the legal assistant with respect to professional responsibility, local rules and practices, and firm policies;
3. Monitoring the work and professional conduct of the legal assistant to ensure that the work is substantively correct and timely performed;
4. Providing continuing education for the legal assistant in substantive matters through courses, institutes, workshops, seminars and in-house training; and
5. Encouraging and supporting membership and active participation in professional organizations.

Except as otherwise provided by statute, court rule or decision, administrative rule or regulation, or the attorney's Code of Professional Responsibility; and within the preceding parameters and proscriptions, a legal assistant may perform any function delegated by an attorney, including, but not limited to the following:

1. Conduct client interviews and maintain general contact with the client after the establishment of the attorney-client relationship, so long as the client is aware of the status and function of the legal assistant, and the client contact is under the supervision of the attorney.
2. Locate and interview witnesses, so long as the witnesses are aware of the status and function of the legal assistant.
3. Conduct investigations and statistical and documentary research for review by the attorney.
4. Conduct legal research for review by the attorney.
5. Draft legal documents for review by the attorney.
6. Draft correspondence and pleadings for review by and signature of the attorney.
7. Summarize depositions, interrogatories, and testimony for review by the attorney.
8. Attend executions of wills, real estate closings, depositions, court or administrative hearings and trials with the attorney.
9. Author and sign letters, provided the legal assistant's status is clearly indicated and the correspondence does not contain independent legal opinions or legal advice.

## ■ Section F. An Ethical Dilemma: Your Ethics or Your Job!

Throughout this chapter we have stressed the importance of maintaining your integrity through knowledge of and compliance with ethical rules. There may be times, however, when this is much easier said than done. Consider the following situations:

- You are not sure whether an ethical violation is being committed. Nor is anyone else in the office sure. Like so many areas of the law, ethical issues can be complex.

- You are sure that an ethical violation exists, and the violator is your supervisor!

- You are sure that an ethical violation exists, and the violators are everyone else in the office!

You face a potential dilemma (1) if no one seems to care about the ethical problem or, worse, (2) if your supervising attorney is the one committing the ethical impropriety or (3) if the entire office appears to be participating in the impropriety. People do not like to be told that they are unethical. Rather than acknowledge the fault and mend their ways, they may turn on the accuser, the one raising the fuss about ethics. Once the issue is raised, it may be very difficult to continue working in the office.

You need someone to talk to. In the best of all worlds, it will be someone in the same office. If this is not practical, consider contacting a teacher whom you trust. Paralegal associations are also an excellent source of information and support. A leader in one paralegal association offers the following advice:

> I would suggest that if the canons, discipline rules, affirmations, and codes of ethics do not supply you with a clear-cut answer to any ethical question you may have, you should draw upon the network that you have in being a member of this association. Getting the personal input of other paralegals who may have been faced with similar situations, or who have a greater knowledge through experience of our professional responsibilities, may greatly assist you in working your way through a difficult ethical situation.[60]

Of course, you must be careful not to violate client confidentiality during discussions with someone outside the office. Never mention actual client names or any specific information pertaining to a case. You can talk in hypothetical terms. For example, "an attorney working on a bankruptcy case asks a paralegal to. . . ." Once you present data in this sterilized fashion, you can then ask for guidance on the ethical implications of the data.

If handled delicately, most ethical problems that bother you can be resolved without compromising anyone's integrity or job. Yet the practice of law is not substantially different from other fields of endeavor. There will be times when the clash between principle and the dollar cannot be resolved to everyone's satisfaction. You may indeed have to make a choice between your ethics and your job.

---

## ■ ASSIGNMENT 5.1

**(a)** What is the name of the code of ethics that governs attorneys in your state?

**(b)** To what body or agency does a client initially make a charge of unethical conduct against his or her attorney in your state?

**(c)** List the steps required to discipline an attorney for unethical conduct in your state. Begin with the complaint stage and conclude with the court that makes the final decision. Draw a flow chart that lists these steps.

---

[60]Harper, *Ethical Considerations for Legal Assistants,* Compendium (Orange County Paralegal Ass'n, April 1987).

### ■ ASSIGNMENT 5.2

Paul Emerson is an attorney who works at the firm of Rayburn & Rayburn. One of the firm's clients is Designs Unlimited, Inc. (DU), a clothing manufacturer. Emerson provides corporate advice to DU. Recently Emerson made a mistake in interpreting a new securities law. As a consequence, DU had to postpone for six months the issuance of a stock option. Has Paul acted unethically?

### ■ ASSIGNMENT 5.3

(a) Three individuals in Connecticut hire a large New York law firm to represent them in a proxy fight in which they sought control of a Connecticut bank. They lose the proxy fight. The firm then sends these individuals a $358,827 bill for 895 hours of work over a one month period. Is this bill unethical? What further facts would you like to have to help you answer this question?

(b) Victor Adams and Len Patterson are full partners in the law firm of Adams, Patterson & Kelly. A client contacts Patterson to represent him on a negligence case. Patterson refers the case to Victor Adams who does most of the work. (Under an agreement between them, Patterson will receive 40% and Adams will receive 60% of any fee paid by this client.) Patterson does not tell the client about the involvement of Adams in the case. Any ethical problems?

(c) An attorney establishes a bonus plan for her paralegals. A bonus will be given to those paralegals who bill a specified number of hours in excess of a stated minimum. The amount of the bonus will depend on the amount billed and collected. Any ethical problems?

### ■ ASSIGNMENT 5.4

Mary works in a law firm that charges clients $125 an hour for attorney time and $55 an hour for paralegal time. She and another paralegal, Fred, are working with an attorney on a large case. She sees all of the time sheets that the three of them submit to the firm's accounting office. She suspects that the attorney is padding his time sheets by overstating the number of hours he works on the case. For example, he lists thirty hours for a four-day period when he was in court every day on another case. Furthermore, Fred's time is being billed at the full $55-an-hour rate even though he spends about 80% of his time typing correspondence, filing, and other clerical duties. Mary also suspects that her attorney is billing out Mary's time at the attorney rate rather than the paralegal rate normally charged clients for her time. Any ethical problems? What should Mary do?

### ■ ASSIGNMENT 5.5

Smith is an attorney who works at the firm of Johnson & Johnson. He represents Ralph Grant, who is seeking a divorce from his wife, Amy Grant. In their first meeting, Smith learns that Ralph is an experienced carpenter but is out of work and has very little money. Smith's fee is $150 an hour. Since Ralph has no money and has been having trouble finding work, Smith tells Ralph that he won't have to pay the fee if the court does not grant him the divorce. One day while Smith is working on another case involving Helen Oberlin, he learns that Helen is looking for a carpenter. Smith recommends Ralph to Helen, and she hires him for a small job. Six months pass. The divorce case is dropped when the Grants reconcile. In the meantime, Helen Oberlin is very dissatisfied with Ralph's carpentry work for her; she claims he didn't do the work he contracted to do. She wants to know what she can do about it. She tries to call Smith at Johnson & Johnson but is told that Smith does not work there anymore. Another attorney, Georgia Quinton, Esq. helps Helen. Any ethical problems?

# ■ ASSIGNMENT 5.6

John Jones is a paralegal working at the XYZ law firm. The firm is handling a large class action involving potentially thousands of plaintiffs. John has been instructed to screen the potential plaintiffs in the class. John tells those he screens out (using criteria provided by the firm) in writing or verbally that "unfortunately, our firm will not be able to represent you." Any ethical problems?

# ■ ASSIGNMENT 5.7

A paralegal quits the firm of Smith & Smith. When she leaves, she takes client documents she prepared while at the firm. The documents contain confidential client information. The paralegal is showing these documents to potential employers as writing samples.

(a) What is the ethical liability of attorneys at Smith & Smith under Model Rule 5.3?

(b) What is the ethical liability of attorneys at law firms where she is seeking employment under 5.3?

(c) What is the paralegal's liability?

# ■ ASSIGNMENT 5.8

(a) Mary Smith is a paralegal at the ABC law firm. She has been working on the case of Jessica Randolph, a client of the office. Mary talks with Ms. Randolph often. Mary receives a subpoena from the attorney of the party that is suing Ms. Randolph. On the witness stand, Mary is asked by this attorney what Ms. Randolph told her at the ABC law office about a particular business transaction related to the suit. Randolph's attorney (Mary's boss) objects to the question. What result?

(b) Before Helen became a paralegal for the firm of Harris & Derkson, she was a chemist for a large corporation. Harris & Derkson is a patent law firm where Helen's technical expertise in chemistry is invaluable. Helen's next-door neighbor is an inventor. On a number of occasions he discussed the chemical makeup of his inventions with Helen. Regarding one of these inventions, the neighbor is being charged by the government with stealing official secrets to prepare the invention. Harris & Derkson represent the neighbor on this case. Helen also works directly on the case for the firm. In a prosecution of the neighbor, Helen is called as a witness and is asked to reveal the substance of all her conversations with the neighbor concerning the invention in question. Does Helen have to answer?

# ■ ASSIGNMENT 5.9

Bob and Patricia Fannan are separated, and they both want a divorce. They would like to have a joint-custody arrangement in which their son would spend time with each parent during the year. The only marital property is a house, which they agree should be sold, with each to get one half of the proceeds. Mary Franklin, Esq. is an attorney whom Jim and Mary know and trust. They decide to ask Franklin to represent both of them in the divorce. Any ethical problems?

## ■ ASSIGNMENT 5.10

Alice is a freelance paralegal with a specialty in probate law. One of the firms she has worked for is Davis, Ritter & Boggs. Her most recent assignment for this firm has been to identify the assets of Mary Steck, who died six months ago. One of Mary's assets is a 75% ownership share in the Domain Corporation. Alice learns a great deal about this company, including the fact that four months ago it had difficulty meeting its payroll and expects to have similar difficulties in the coming year.

Alice's freelance business has continued to grow because of her excellent reputation. She decides to hire an employee with a different specialty so that her office can begin to take different kinds of cases from attorneys. She hires Bob, a paralegal with four years of litigation experience. The firm of Jackson & Jackson hires Alice to digest a series of long deposition documents in the case of Glendale Bank v. Ajax Tire Co. Jackson & Jackson represents Glendale Bank. Peterson, Zuckerman & Morgan represents Ajax Tire Co. Alice assigns Bob to this case. Ajax Tire Co. is a wholly owned subsidiary of the Domain Corporation. Glendale Bank is suing Ajax Tire Co. for fraud in misrepresenting its financial worth when Ajax Tire Co. applied for and obtained a loan from Glendale Bank.

Any ethical problems?

## ■ ASSIGNMENT 5.11

Assume that you owned a successful freelance business in which you provided paralegal services to over 150 attorneys all over the state. How should your files be organized in order to avoid a conflict of interest?

## ■ ASSIGNMENT 5.12

Joan is a paralegal who works for the XYZ law firm, which is representing Goff in a suit against Barnard, who is represented by the ABC law firm. Joan calls Barnard and says, "Is this the first time that you have ever been sued?" Barnard answers, "Yes it is. Is there anything else that you would like to know?" Joan says *no* and the conversation ends. Any ethical problems?

## ■ ASSIGNMENT 5.13

Mary is a paralegal who is a senior citizen. She works at the XYZ legal service office. One day she goes to a senior citizens center and says the following:

All of you should know about and take advantage of the XYZ legal service office where I work. Let me give you just·one example why. Down at the office there is an attorney named Armanda Morris. She is an expert on insurance company cases. Some of you may have had trouble with insurance companies that say one thing and do another. Our office is available to serve you.

Any ethical problems?

## ■ ASSIGNMENT 5.14

(a) What restrictions exist on advertising by attorneys in your state? Give an example of an ad on TV or in the newspaper that would be unethical. On researching an ethical issue, see page 312.

**(b)** In *Bates v. State Bar of Arizona,* 433 U.S. 350 (1970), the United States Supreme Court held that a state could not prohibit all forms of lawyer advertising. Has *Bates* been cited by state courts in your state on the advertising issue? If so, what impact has the case had in your state? To find out, shepardize *Bates.* The specific techniques of shepardizing a case are found in Checklist 4a, page 569.

## ■ ASSIGNMENT 5.15

Mary Jackson is a paralegal at Rollins & Rollins. She is supervised by Ian Gregory. Mary is stealing money from the funds of one of the firm's clients. The only attorney who knows about this is Dan Roberts, Esq., who is not a partner at the firm and who does not supervise Mary. Dan says and does nothing about Mary's actions. What ethical obligations does Dan have under Model Rule 5.3?

## ■ ASSIGNMENT 5.16

John Smith is a paralegal who works for the firm of Beard, Butler, and Clark. John's immediate supervisor is Viola Butler, Esq. With the full knowledge and blessing of Viola Butler, John Smith sends a letter to a client of the firm (Mary Anders). Has Viola Butler acted unethically in permitting John to send out this letter? The letter is as follows:

---

Law Offices of
**Beard, Butler, and Clark**
310 High St.
Maincity, Ohio 45238
512-663-9410

*Attorneys at Law*                                              *Paralegal*

Ronald Beard                                                    John Smith
Viola Butler
Wilma Clark

                                                        May 14, 1991

Mary Anders
621 S. Randolph Ave.
Maincity, Ohio 45238

Dear Ms. Anders:

   Viola Butler, the attorney in charge of your case, has asked me to let you know that next month's hearing has been postponed. We will let you know the new date as soon as possible. If you have any questions don't hesitate to call me.

                                                        Sincerely,


                                                        John Smith
                                                        Legal Intern

JS:wps

---

## ■ ASSIGNMENT 5.17

Under what circumstances, if any, would it be appropriate for you to refer to a client of the office where you work as "my client"?

## ■ ASSIGNMENT 5.18

John Jones is a paralegal who works for an attorney named Linda Sunders. Linda is away from the office one day and telephones John, who is at the office. She dictates a one-line letter to a client of the office. The letter reads, "I advise you to sue." Linda asks John to sign the letter for her. The bottom of the letter reads as follows:

_____

Linda Sunders
by John Jones

Any ethical problems?

## ■ ASSIGNMENT 5.19

Mary is a paralegal who works at the XYZ law firm. She specializes in real estate matters at the firm. Mary attends a real estate closing in which her role consists of exchanging documents and acknowledging the receipt of documents. Analyze this problem on the basis of the following variations:

(a) The closing takes place at the XYZ law firm.

(b) The closing takes place at a bank.

(c) Mary's supervising attorney is not present at the closing.

(d) Mary's supervising attorney is present at the closing.

(e) Mary's supervising attorney is present at the closing except for thirty minutes, during which time Mary continued to exchange documents and acknowledge the receipt of documents.

(f) During the closing, the attorney for the other party says to Mary, "I don't know why my client should have to pay that charge." Mary responds: "In this state that charge is always paid in this way."

## ■ ASSIGNMENT 5.20

John is a paralegal who works for the XYZ law firm, which is representing a client against the Today Insurance Company. The Company also employs paralegals who work under the Company's general counsel. One of these paralegals is Mary. In an effort to settle the case, Mary calls John and says, "We offer you $200.00." John says, "We'll let you know." Any ethical problems?

## ■ ASSIGNMENT 5.21

John Smith is a paralegal who works for Beard, Butler, and Clark. He sends out the following letter. Any ethical problems?

**John Smith**

Paralegal
310 High St.
Maincity, Ohio 45238
512-663-9410

June 1, 1991

State Unemployment Board
1216 Southern Ave.
Maincity, Ohio 45238

Dear Gentlepeople:

I work for Beard, Butler, and Clark, which represents Mary Anders, who has a claim before your agency. A hearing originally scheduled for June 8, 1991 has been postponed. We request that the hearing be held at the earliest time possible after the 8th.

Sincerely,

John Smith

JS:wps

## ■ ASSIGNMENT 5.22

In Section C of Chapter 2, there is a long list of tasks that paralegals have performed, and comments by paralegals working in the specialties covered. Identify any three tasks or paralegal comments that *might* pose ethical problems or problems of unauthorized practice. Explain why.

## ■ ASSIGNMENT 5.23

Compare the Affirmation of Professional Responsibility of NFPA with the Code of Ethics and Professional Responsibility of NALA, page 313. Make a list of the topics or themes covered in one of the documents but not in the other. Is there a difference in emphasis between the two documents?

## ■ ASSIGNMENT 5.24

Draft your own paralegal code as a class project. First, have a meeting in which you make a list of all the issues that you think should be covered in the code. Divide up the issues by the number of students in the class so that every student has roughly the same number of issues. Each student should draft a proposed rule on each of the issues to which he or she is assigned. Accompany each rule with a brief commentary on why you think the rule should be as stated. Draft alternative versions of the proposed rule if different versions are possible and you want to give the class the chance to examine all of them. The class then meets to vote on each of the proposed rules. Students will make presentations on the proposed rules they have drafted. If the class is not happy with the way in which a particular proposed rule was drafted by a student, the latter will redraft the rule for later consideration by the class. One member of the class should be designated the "code reporter," who records the rules accepted by the class by majority vote.

After you have completed the code, you should consider inviting attorneys from the local bar association to your class in order to discuss your proposed code. Do the same with officials of the closest paralegal association in your area.

## ■ Chapter Summary

Attorneys are regulated by the highest court in the state, often with the extensive involvement of the state bar association. Since paralegals cannot practice law and cannot become full members of a bar association, they cannot be punished for a violation of the ethical rules governing attorneys. The American Bar Association is a voluntary association; no attorney must be a member. The ABA publishes ethical rules which the states are free to adopt, modify, or reject.

The current rules of the ABA are found in its *Model Rules of Professional Conduct.* These ethical rules require attorneys to be competent, to act with reasonable diligence and promptness, to charge fees that are reasonable, to avoid conduct that is criminal and fraudulent, to avoid asserting claims and defenses that are frivolous, to safeguard the property of clients, to avoid making false statements of law and fact to a tribunal, to withdraw from a case for appropriate reasons, to maintain the confidentiality of client information, to avoid conflicts of interest, to avoid improper communications with an opponent, to avoid improper solicitation of clients, to avoid improper advertising, to report serious professional misconduct of other attorneys, to avoid assisting nonattorneys engage in the unauthorized practice of law, and to supervise paralegal employees appropriately.

Ethical opinions and guidelines exist in almost every state on the proper use of a paralegal by an attorney. All states agree that the title used for this employee must not mislead anyone about his or her nonattorney status, and that the employee must disclose his or her nonattorney status when necessary to avoid misunderstanding. Rules also exist on other aspects of the attorney-paralegal relationship, but not all states agree on what these rules should be. The following apply in most states:

Under attorney approval and supervision, paralegals in most states:

- can have their own business card
- can have their name printed on the law firm letterhead
- can sign law firm correspondence
- can give nonlegal advice
- can draft legal documents
- can attend a real estate closing
- can represent clients at agency hearings if authorized by the agency

With few exceptions, paralegals in most states:

- cannot give legal advice
- cannot conduct a deposition
- cannot sign formal court documents
- cannot supervise the execution of a will
- cannot make an appearance in court

Separate ethical rules and guidelines have been adopted by the National Association of Legal Assistants and by the National Federation of Paralegal Associations.

## Key Terms

ethics
sanctions
national bar association
state bar association
local bar association

integrated bar association
mandatory bar association
unified bar association
registration
self-regulation

Model Rules of Professional Conduct
Model Code of Professional Responsibility
DR

EC
disbarment
suspension
interim suspension
reprimand
private reprimand
censure
public censure
admonition
probation
competence
malpractice
6th amendment
reasonable diligence
reasonable fee
retainer
minimum fee schedule
antitrust law
contingent fee
fee splitting
referral fee
forwarding fee
double billing
padding time sheets
insider trading
pirated software
frivolous positions
commingle funds
adversarial system

withdrawal
cured
impaired attorney
privileged
confidentiality
attorney-client privilege
work-product rule
discoverable
waiver
conflict of interest
divided loyalty
multiple representation
common representation
adverse interests
friendly divorce
switching sides
imputed disqualification
vicarious disqualification
Chinese wall
ethical wall
cone of silence
tainted/contaminated
    employee
quarantined paralegal
conflicts check
lateral hire
disinterested
in-person solicitation
barratry

ambulance chasing
attorney advertising
runner/capper
unauthorized practice of law
model rule 5.3
tickler
associate/associated
business card
CLA
law-firm letterhead
law directory
legal advice
professional judgment
separate identity of document
real estate closing
deposition/deponent
supervision
delegatitis
second chair
freelance paralegal
Affirmation of Professional
    Responsibility (NFPA)
Code of Ethics and
    Professional
    Responsibility (NALA)
Model Standards and
    Guidelines for Utilization
    of Legal Assistants
    (NALA)

# CHAPTER

6

# Introduction to the Legal System

## ■ Chapter Outline

**Section A. Basic Terminology**
   Levels and Branches of Government
   Kinds of Law
**Section B. Judicial Systems**
   Jurisdiction
   State Court Systems
   Federal Court System
**Section C. Administrative Agencies**

**Section D. The Legislative Process**
   Proposal
   Initial Committee
   Floor Debate
   Conference Committee
   Floor Debate
   Chief Executive

## ■ Section A. Basic Terminology

Our legal system is really *three* systems consisting of independent but inter-connected governments: federal government, state governments, and local (city or county) governments. The interrelationship among these levels of govern-ment is what is known as *federalism*. Each level of government has three *branches*: one that makes laws (legislative branch), one that carries out laws (executive branch), and one that interprets laws and resolves disputes that arise under them (judicial branch).

*Federal Government.*
*Legislative branch:* Congress
*Executive branch:* The President and the federal administrative agencies (see chart in Appendix D.)
*Judicial branch:* The U.S. Supreme Court, the U.S. Courts of Appeal, the U.S. District Courts, and other federal courts (see Figure 6.3).

*State Government.*
*Legislative branch:* The state legislature
*Executive branch:* The governor and the state administrative agencies
*Judicial branch:* The state courts (see Figure 6.2).

*Local Government.*
*Legislative branch:* City Council or County Commission
*Executive branch:* Mayor or County Commissioner and the local administrative agencies
*Judicial branch:* The local courts (see Figure 6.2).

Figure 6.1 provides an overview of the basic kinds of law that govern and that are produced by the above institutions.

#  Section B. Judicial Systems

## 1. Jurisdiction

There are fifty state court systems and a federal court system. Each court within a system is identified by its *jurisdiction.* The word jurisdiction has three meanings.

First, the word is often used to refer to the *geographic* area over which a particular court has authority. A state trial court, for example, has *geographic jurisdiction* to hear cases arising in a specific county or district of the state. A state supreme court, in contrast, may have geographic jurisdiction to hear appeals in cases arising anywhere in the state. Thus a state supreme court will often say "in this jurisdiction" when referring to its own state. The phrase has the same meaning as "in this state."

Secondly, the word jurisdiction is used to refer to the *power* of a court to adjudicate a dispute. *Adjudication* is the process by which a court (or administrative agency) resolves a legal dispute through litigation. In order for the court to have the power to order the defendant to do anything (or to refrain from doing something), the court must have *personal jurisdiction* over the defendant. This is also called *in personam jurisdiction.* Personal jurisdiction is acquired through service of process on the defendant.

Thirdly, jurisdiction means the power that a court must have over the *subject matter* or over the particular kind of dispute that has been brought before it. Some of the more common classifications of *subject-matter jurisdiction* are:

(a)  *Limited jurisdiction*

(b)  *General jurisdiction*

(c)  *Exclusive jurisdiction*

(d)  *Concurrent jurisdiction*

(e)  *Original jurisdiction*

(f)  *Appellate jurisdiction*

*(a) Limited Jurisdiction.*   A court of *limited* (or *special*) *jurisdiction* can hear only certain kinds of cases. A criminal court is not allowed to take a noncriminal case, and a small claims court is authorized to hear only cases in which the plaintiff claims less than a certain amount of money as damages from the defendant.

Another way to look at a court of limited jurisdiction is to say it has a specified *subject matter jurisdiction.* Its subject-matter jurisdiction is limited to cases that deal with designated subject matters only, such as criminal cases.

*(b) General Jurisdiction.*   A court of *general jurisdiction* can, with some exceptions, hear any kind of case as long as the case arises within the geographic

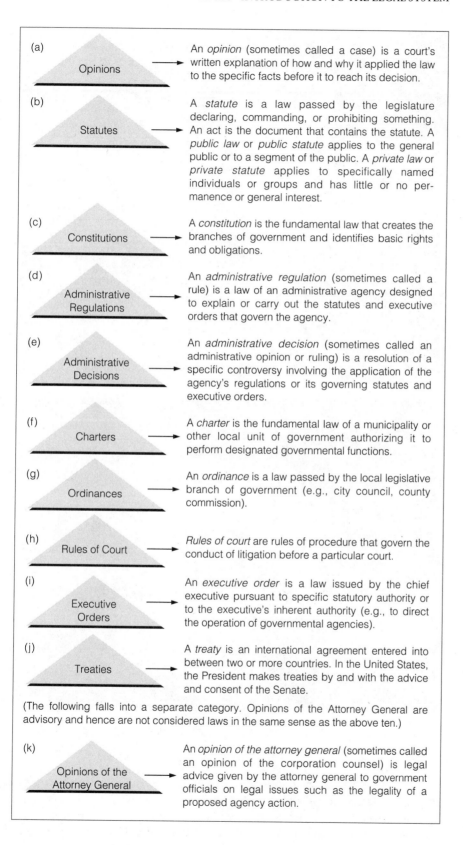

**FIGURE 6.1**
Kinds of Law

(a) Opinions — An *opinion* (sometimes called a case) is a court's written explanation of how and why it applied the law to the specific facts before it to reach its decision.

(b) Statutes — A *statute* is a law passed by the legislature declaring, commanding, or prohibiting something. An act is the document that contains the statute. A *public law* or *public statute* applies to the general public or to a segment of the public. A *private law* or *private statute* applies to specifically named individuals or groups and has little or no permanence or general interest.

(c) Constitutions — A *constitution* is the fundamental law that creates the branches of government and identifies basic rights and obligations.

(d) Administrative Regulations — An *administrative regulation* (sometimes called a rule) is a law of an administrative agency designed to explain or carry out the statutes and executive orders that govern the agency.

(e) Administrative Decisions — An *administrative decision* (sometimes called an administrative opinion or ruling) is a resolution of a specific controversy involving the application of the agency's regulations or its governing statutes and executive orders.

(f) Charters — A *charter* is the fundamental law of a municipality or other local unit of government authorizing it to perform designated governmental functions.

(g) Ordinances — An *ordinance* is a law passed by the local legislative branch of government (e.g., city council, county commission).

(h) Rules of Court — *Rules of court* are rules of procedure that govern the conduct of litigation before a particular court.

(i) Executive Orders — An *executive order* is a law issued by the chief executive pursuant to specific statutory authority or to the executive's inherent authority (e.g., to direct the operation of governmental agencies).

(j) Treaties — A *treaty* is an international agreement entered into between two or more countries. In the United States, the President makes treaties by and with the advice and consent of the Senate.

(The following falls into a separate category. Opinions of the Attorney General are advisory and hence are not considered laws in the same sense as the above ten.)

(k) Opinions of the Attorney General — An *opinion of the attorney general* (sometimes called an opinion of the corporation counsel) is legal advice given by the attorney general to government officials on legal issues such as the legality of a proposed agency action.

Courtrooms in America

boundaries of that court. A *state* court of general jurisdiction can handle any
case that raises *state questions* (i.e., questions arising from the state constitution, state statutes, state regulations, or state common law); a *federal* court of
general jurisdiction can handle any case that raises *federal questions*, (i.e., questions arising from the federal constitution, federal statutes, federal regulations,
or other federal laws).

*(c) Exclusive Jurisdiction.*   A court of *exclusive jurisdiction* is the only court that can handle a certain kind of case. For example, it may be that the Juvenile Court has exclusive jurisdiction over all cases involving children under a certain age who are charged with acts of delinquency. If this kind of case is brought in another court, there could be a challenge on the ground that the court lacked jurisdiction over the case.

*(d) Concurrent Jurisdiction.*   Sometimes two courts have jurisdiction over a case; the case could be brought in either court. In such a situation, both courts are said to have *concurrent jurisdiction* over the case. For example, it could be that both the Family Court and a County Court have jurisdiction to enforce a child-custody order.

*(e) Original Jurisdiction.*   A court of *original jurisdiction* is the first court to hear and decide a case. It is also called a trial court or a court of first instance. In addition, it can be classified as a court of limited jurisdiction (if it can try only certain kinds of cases), or of general jurisdiction (if it can try cases involving any subject matter), or of exclusive jurisdiction (if the trial can take place only in that court), or of concurrent jurisdiction (if the trial can take place either in that court or in another kind of court).

*(f) Appellate Jurisdiction.*   A court with *appellate jurisdiction* can hear appeals from lower tribunals. An appeal is a review of what a lower court or agency has done to determine if there was any error. Sometimes a party who is dissatisfied with a lower court ruling can appeal as a matter of right to the appellate court (the court must hear the appeal); in other kinds of cases, the appellate court has discretion as to whether it will hear the appeal.

## 2. State Court Systems

*(a) Courts of Original Jurisdiction.*   Depending on the particular state, there may be one or more levels of trial courts (courts of original jurisdiction). These courts hear the dispute, determine the facts of the case, and make the initial determination or ruling. In addition, they may sometimes have the power to review cases that were initially decided by an administrative agency.

The most common arrangement is a two-tier system of trial courts. At the lower level are courts of limited or special jurisdiction, the so-called *inferior courts.* Local courts, such as city courts, county courts, or justice of the peace courts, often fall into this category. These courts may have original jurisdiction over relatively minor cases, such as violations of local ordinances and lawsuits involving small sums of money. Also included in this category are special courts that are limited to specific matters, such as surrogate courts or probate courts which are limited to hearing matters involving the estates of deceased or mentally incompetent persons.

Immediately above the trial courts of limited jurisdiction are the trial courts of general jurisdiction, which usually handle more serious cases, such as violations of state laws or lawsuits involving large sums of money. The name given to the trial courts at this second level varies greatly from state to state. They are known as superior courts, courts of common pleas, district courts, or circuit courts. New York is especially confusing. There the trial court of general jurisdiction is called the *supreme court,* a label reserved in most states for the court of final appeals, the highest court in the system.

This two-tier system is not invariable. Some states may have only one court of original jurisdiction. Moreover, the individual levels may be segmented into divisions. A court of general, original jurisdiction, for example, may be broken up into specialized divisions such as landlord-tenant, family, juvenile, and criminal divisions.

*(b)  Courts of Appeal.*    These courts rarely make the initial decision in a case. Their primary function is to *review* decisions made by lower courts in order to correct *errors of law.* That is, they will look to see if the lower court correctly interpreted and applied the law to the facts of the dispute. In this review process, appellate courts do not make their own findings of fact. No new evidence is taken, and no witnesses are called. The court limits itself to an analysis of the *trial court record* (transcripts of testimony and copies of the various documents that were filed, etc.) to determine if that lower court made any errors of law. Attorneys submit *appellate briefs* containing their arguments on the correctness or incorrectness of what the lower court did.

Depending on the state, there may be not one but two levels of appellate courts. The first level is the court of middle appeals, sometimes called an *intermediate appellate court.* The decisions of this court may in turn be reviewed by a second-level appellate court, the court of final appeals. This latter court, often known as the supreme court, is the highest court in the state, the court of final or last resort.

Figure 6.2 illustrates the organization of and the lines of appeal in many state court systems.

## 3.  Federal Court System

The federal court system, like those of the states, consists of two basic kinds of courts: courts of original jurisdiction (trial courts) and appellate courts.

*(a)  Courts of Original Jurisdiction.*    The basic federal court at the trial level is the *United States District Court.* There are districts throughout the country, at least one for every state, the District of Columbia, Guam, the Virgin Islands, and Puerto Rico. The District Courts exercise original jurisdiction over most federal litigation and also serve as courts of review for many cases that were initially decided by federal administrative agencies.

In addition to the District Courts, there are several federal courts that exercise original jurisdiction over specialized cases. These include the United States Tax Court, the United States Claims Court, and the United States Court of International Trade. (See Figure 6.3).

*(b)  Courts of Appeals.*    The federal system, like almost half of the fifty state judicial systems, has two levels of appellate courts: middle appeals and final appeals. The primary courts at the middle level are the *United States Courts of Appeals.* These courts are divided into twelve geographic circuits, eleven of which are made up of groupings of various states and territories, with a twelfth for the District of Columbia. Their primary function is to review the decisions of the federal courts of original jurisdiction. In addition, the decisions of certain federal agencies, notably the National Labor Relations Board, are reviewed directly by the Court of Appeals without first going to the District Court. Finally, there is a specialized Court of Appeals called the Court of Appeals for the Federal Circuit. This court, created in 1982, reviews decisions of the United States Claims Court and the United States Court of International Trade, rulings of the Patent and Trademark Office, and some decisions of the federal District Courts where the United States government is a defendant.

**FIGURE 6.2**   Hierarchy of State Judicial System

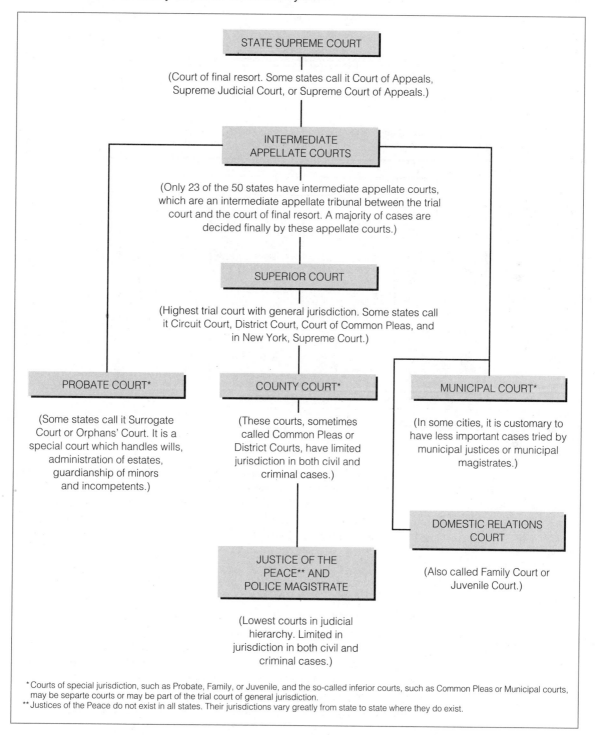

**STATE SUPREME COURT**

(Court of final resort. Some states call it Court of Appeals, Supreme Judicial Court, or Supreme Court of Appeals.)

**INTERMEDIATE APPELLATE COURTS**

(Only 23 of the 50 states have intermediate appellate courts, which are an intermediate appellate tribunal between the trial court and the court of final resort. A majority of cases are decided finally by these appellate courts.)

**SUPERIOR COURT**

(Highest trial court with general jurisdiction. Some states call it Circuit Court, District Court, Court of Common Pleas, and in New York, Supreme Court.)

**PROBATE COURT\***

(Some states call it Surrogate Court or Orphans' Court. It is a special court which handles wills, administration of estates, guardianship of minors and incompetents.)

**COUNTY COURT\***

(These courts, sometimes called Common Pleas or District Courts, have limited jurisdiction in both civil and criminal cases.)

**MUNICIPAL COURT\***

(In some cities, it is customary to have less important cases tried by municipal justices or municipal magistrates.)

**DOMESTIC RELATIONS COURT**

(Also called Family Court or Juvenile Court.)

**JUSTICE OF THE PEACE\*\* AND POLICE MAGISTRATE**

(Lowest courts in judicial hierarchy. Limited in jurisdiction in both civil and criminal cases.)

\* Courts of special jurisdiction, such as Probate, Family, or Juvenile, and the so-called inferior courts, such as Common Pleas or Municipal courts, may be separte courts or may be part of the trial court of general jurisdiction.
\*\* Justices of the Peace do not exist in all states. Their jurisdictions vary greatly from state to state where they do exist.

**Source:** *Law and the Courts,* 20 (American Bar Association, 1974).

The federal court of final appeals is, of course, the *United States Supreme Court,* which provides the final review of the decisions of all federal courts and agencies. The Supreme Court may also review certain decisions of the state

**FIGURE 6.3**   Federal Judicial System and Flow of Cases to U.S. Supreme Court

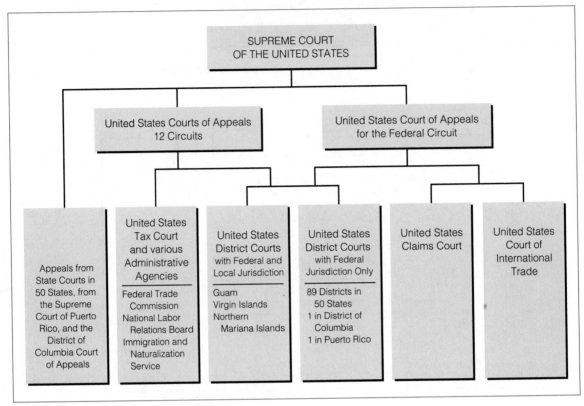

**Source:** United States Administrative Office of Courts.

courts when these decisions raise questions involving the United States Constitution or a federal statute. (See Figure 6.3.)

Figure 6.4 illustrates the division of the federal court system into twelve geographic circuits. Each circuit has its own United States Court of Appeals. The United States District Courts exist within these circuits.

## ▇ Section C. Administrative Agencies

An *administrative agency* is a unit of government whose primary mission is to carry out—or administer—the statutes of the legislature and the executive orders of the chief of the executive branch of government. At the federal level, the chief is the president; at the state level, it is the governor; and at most local levels, it is the mayor. As we will see in a moment, many agencies also have rule-making and dispute-resolution responsibilities.

Administrative agencies can have a wide variety of names. Here are some examples:

- Fire Department
- Board of Licenses and Occupations
- Civil Service Commission
- Agency for International Development

**FIGURE 6.4**   United States Courts of Appeals and United States District Courts

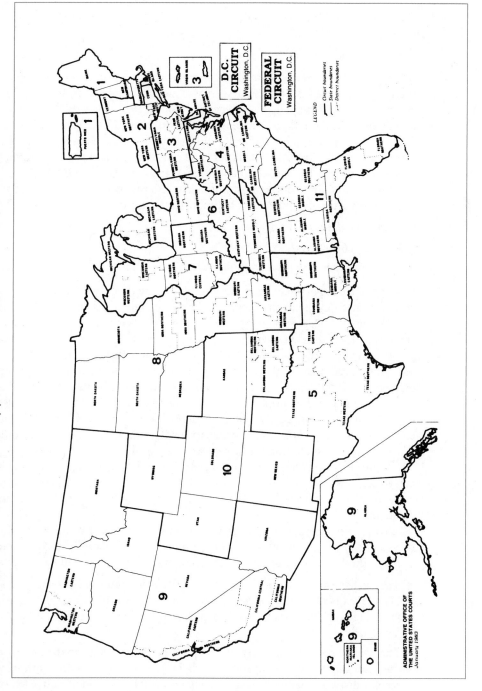

- Department of Defense
- Office of Management and Budget
- Legal Services Corporation
- Bureau of Taxation
- Internal Revenue Service
- Division of Child Support and Enforcement
- Social Security Administration

Certain types of agencies exist at all three levels of government. For example, there is a separate tax collection agency in each of the federal, state, and local governments. Other agencies, however, are unique to one of the levels. For example, only the federal government has a Department of Defense (DOD) and a Central Intelligence Agency (CIA). Nothing comparable exists at the state and local levels of government. The latter have police departments and the highway patrol, but their role is significantly different from the DOD and CIA.

For a list of some of the most important federal agencies, see Appendix D.

There are three main kinds of administrative agencies:

- *Executive department agencies*
- *Independent regulatory agencies*
- *Quasi-independent regulatory agencies*

Executive department agencies exist within the executive branch of the government, often at the cabinet level. Examples include the Department of Agriculture and the Department of Labor. These agencies are answerable to the chief executive, who usually has the power to dismiss those in charge of them.

Independent regulatory agencies exist outside the executive department and, therefore, outside the day-to-day control of the chief executive. Examples include the Interstate Commerce Commission, the Securities and Exchange Commission, and the Public Utilities Commission. Their function is usually to regulate an aspect of society—often a particular industry such as railroads, securities, and public utilities. In order to insulate these agencies from politics, those in charge usually cannot be removed at the whim of the chief executive.

A quasi-independent regulatory agency is a hybrid agency, often with characteristics of the two kinds just described. It often has more independence than an executive department agency, yet it might exist within the executive department.

In addition to carrying out laws, administrative agencies (particularly independent agencies) have *rule-making* functions and *dispute-resolution* functions. In this sense, the agency is acting like the legislature and like the courts:

- The agency often has the authority to write rules and regulations, which are laws. This is the agency's rule-making function. In this sense, the agency is "making law" like a legislature. Such laws are sometimes referred to as *quasi-legislation.*
- The agency has the authority to interpret the laws governing the agency and the laws created by the agency. Furthermore, it often has the authority to resolve disputes that arise over such laws. It will hold administrative hearings and issue administrative decisions. In this sense, the agency is acting like a court when the latter resolves, or adjudicates, disputes. The phrase *quasi-adjudication* means the process by which agencies act like courts in interpreting laws and resolving disputes.

- The agency's primary function, as we have seen, is to carry out or execute designated statutes and executive orders.

For example, the SEC (Securities and Exchange Commission):

- Makes laws, e.g., the SEC will write administrative regulations on insider stock trading.

- Resolves disputes, e.g., the SEC will hold a hearing to decide whether a company has violated a securities law. The end product of the hearing will be an administrative decision.

- Carries out laws, e.g., the SEC will accept filings of registration statements containing financial data on issuers of securities pursuant to statutes written by Congress and to securities regulations written by the SEC.

Later in Chapter 10 we will take a closer look at the dispute-resolution (quasi-adjudication) responsibility of a state agency.

 ## Section D. The Legislative Process

Figure 6.5 contains an outline of the steps that a bill goes through before it becomes a statute. The chart assumes that the legislature considering the bill is *bicameral*, i.e., consists of two houses. The two houses are referred to as the House and the Senate. (In some legislatures the houses may have different names, such as the Assembly and the Senate.) Legislatures with only one house are called *unicameral*. Very few state legislatures are unicameral. Local legislatures, however, such as city councils, are often unicameral.

The process of enactment can involve six major stages:

- Proposal
- Initial committee consideration
- Floor debate
- Conference committee consideration
- Floor debate
- Signature of the chief executive

The *legislative history* of a statute is what occurs at each of these stages.

*(a) Proposal.*   The idea for a statute can come from many sources. The chief executive of the government (for example, the president or governor) may initiate the process by sending the legislature a message in which the reasons for a proposed law are stated. Frequently an administrative agency has made a study of a problem, which is the impetus for the proposal. The agency will usually be the entity with responsibility for administrating the proposal if it is enacted into law.

The bar association may prepare a report to the legislature calling for the new legislation. The legislature or chief executive may have established a special commission to study the need for changes in the law and to propose changes where appropriate. The commission might consist of members of the legislature and outside experts. In some states there are ongoing law-revision commissions that frequently make proposals for legislation. In many areas there are councils of government made up of neighboring governments. Such councils often study problems and propose legislative changes. The National Conference of Com-

FIGURE 6.5   The Legislative History of a Statute—How a Bill Becomes a Law

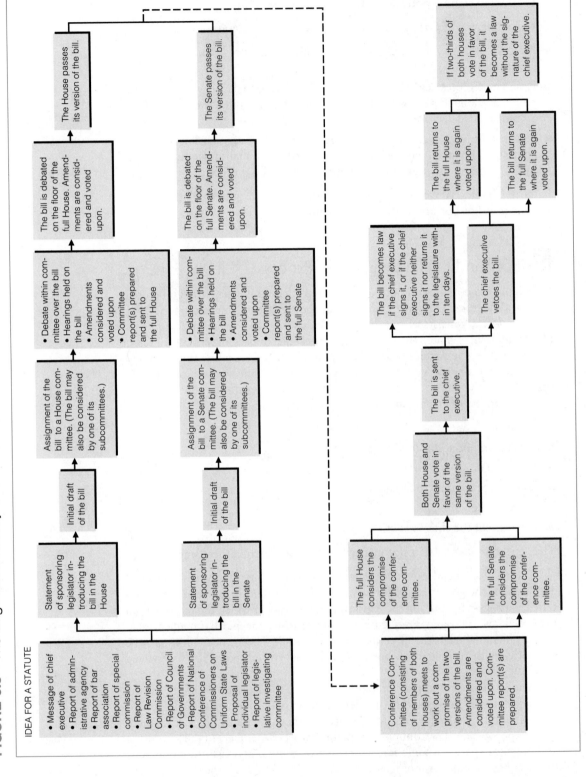

missioners on Uniform State Laws is an organization with members from each state. The conference makes proposals to the state legislatures for the enactment of laws where it deems uniformity to be desirable.

Finally, the idea for the legislation may be generated within the legislature itself. An individual legislator can always propose a *bill*. One or both houses of the legislature may have established an investigating committee to examine a problem and propose legislation where needed.

*(b) Initial Committee Consideration.*   The next step is for a member of the legislature to introduce the bill. This introduction is usually accompanied by a statement as to why the bill should be enacted. The bill may be introduced in only one of the houses or in both houses simultaneously by a member of each house. If the latter option is not used, the bill will often be introduced in the other house after it has been considered by the first house. As bills are introduced, they are assigned a consecutive number (S 250 is the 250th bill introduced in the Senate during the current session; HR 1753 is the 1753rd bill introduced in the House of Representatives during the current session).

Once the bill is introduced, it follows a similar procedure in each house. The bill is sent to the committee with responsibility over the subject matter of the bill—for example, a bill to change the criminal law might go to the Judiciary Committee. The initial draft of the bill might be considered by this committee and by one of its subcommittees. Hearings are held. Citizens and public officials give testimony for or against the bill. In some legislatures this testimony is transcribed so that a word-for-word record is made available. Legislators often propose amendments to the bill, which are voted on by the committee. The committee then issues a report summarizing why the bill is needed and what its major provisions are. If there is disagreement on the committee, a minority report is often prepared.

*(c) Floor Debate.*   The bill with its accompanying report(s) then goes to the floor of the house of which the committee is a part. The bill is debated by the full house. During the debate, which will usually be recorded or transcribed, questions are asked by members as to the meaning of certain provisions in the bill: what is covered and what is not. Amendments are often made from the floor and voted upon.

*(d) Conference Committee Consideration.*   Since both houses act independently of each other in considering the bill, it is rare that they will both produce exactly the same bill. Inevitably, the amendment process leads to different versions of the proposed law. To resolve these differences, a *conference committee* is established, consisting of key members of both houses, such as the chairpersons of the committees that initially considered the bill or the members who first introduced or sponsored the bill. A compromise is attempted in the conference committee. Amendments are considered and a final report of the conference committee is issued. Dissenting members of the committee might prepare a minority report. The majority report summarizes the major terms of the compromise and explains why it should be enacted by each house.

*(e) Floor Debate.*   The conference committee compromise then goes back to the floor of each house where more debate, explanations, and amendments are considered. Again, usually everything is recorded or transcribed. If both houses pass the same version of the bill, usually by a majority vote, it goes to the chief executive.

*(f) Chief Executive.*   The bill becomes law if the chief executive signs it. When it is signed, the chief executive will sometimes make a statement as to why this action is being taken. If he or she *vetoes* the bill, it goes back to the legislature, often with an explanation as to why it is being disapproved. If a designated number of legislators (usually two-thirds) in each house still vote in favor of the bill, it becomes law over the objection of the chief executive. Finally, if the chief executive neither signs nor vetoes the bill, and fails to return it to the legislature within ten days (excluding Sundays) before the legislature adjourns, the bill automatically becomes law.

## ☐ Chapter Summary

There are ten main categories of laws: opinions, statutes, constitutions, administrative regulations, administrative decisions, charters, ordinances, rules of court, executive orders, and treaties. (In a special category are opinions of the attorney general.) These laws are written by one or more of the three branches of government (legislative, executive, and judicial) that exist within the three levels of government (federal, state, and local).

An understanding of jurisdiction is key to understanding our judicial system. Two of the main kinds of jurisdiction are: geographic jurisdiction, which specifies an area of the country over which a court can exercise its power, and subject-matter jurisdiction, which specifies the kinds of cases over which a court can exercise its power. There are six main kinds of subject-matter jurisdiction: limited, general, exclusive, concurrent, original, and appellate. Courts of original jurisdiction are the trial courts. There may be two levels of trial courts within a judicial system. There may also be two levels of courts with appellate jurisdiction.

There are three kinds of administrative agencies: executive department agencies, independent regulatory agencies, and quasi-independent regulatory agencies. Agencies serve three main functions: to carry out statutes and executive orders, to write rules and regulations, and to resolve disputes that arise under laws over which the agency has responsibility.

The federal legislature (Congress) and most state legislatures are bicameral, that is, they consist of two houses. For a bill to become a statute, it must go through approximately six stages. First, the bill is proposed, and then introduced into one of the houses of the legislature. It may be introduced into the other house simultaneously or at a later date. Second, a committee of each house gives the bill initial consideration. If the committee votes in favor of the bill, it goes to the next stage. Third, all of the members of one of the houses debate and vote on the bill, and then all of the members of the other house debate and vote on the bill. Fourth, a conference committee made up of members of both houses considers the bill. The role of this committee is to try to reconcile any differences in the two versions of the bill passed by each house. Fifth, the bill goes back to the full membership of each house for a vote on what the conference committee produced. Sixth, the chief executive signs or vetoes the bill. If he or she vetoes the bill, it can still become a statute if two-thirds of each house vote to override the chief executive. The legislative history of a statute consists of what happens during these six stages.

# Key Terms

federalism
legislative branch
executive branch
judicial branch
opinion
case
statute
act
public law/public statute

private law/private statute
constitution
administrative regulation
administrative decision
ruling
charter
ordinance
rules of court
executive order

treaty
opinion of the attorney
   general
geographic jurisdiction
personal jurisdiction
in personam jurisdiction
adjudication
subject-matter jurisdiction
limited jurisdiction

special jurisdiction
general jurisdiction
state question
federal question
exclusive jurisdiction
concurrent jurisdiction
original jurisdiction
court of first instance
appellate jurisdiction
appeal as a matter of right
inferior court
surrogate court
review

trial court record
appellate brief
intermediate appellate court
supreme court
superior court
United States District Court
United States Court of
    Appeals
United States Supreme Court
administrative agency
executive department agency
independent regulatory
    agency

quasi-independent agency
rule-making function
quasi-legislation
quasi-adjudication
bicameral/unicameral
legislative history
uniform state laws
bill
floor debate
conference committee
veto

# II

# The Skills of a Paralegal

## Contents

7  Introduction to Legal Analysis      345

8  Legal Interviewing      365

9  Investigation in a Law Office      401

10  Litigation Assistantship      435

11  Legal Research      477

12  Legal Writing      619

13  Computer Literacy for Paralegals: An Introduction to the Use of Computers in a Law Office      639

14  Introduction to Law Office Administration      685

15  Informal and Formal Administrative Advocacy      719

# 7

# Introduction to Legal Analysis

## ■ Chapter Outline

**Section A. The Structure of Legal Analysis**

**Section B. The Element-Identification Skill**

**Section C. The Issue-Statement Skill**

**Section D. The Definitions Skill**

**Section E. Briefing Court Opinions**

**Section F. Applying Court Opinions**

## Section A. The Structure of Legal Analysis

*Legal analysis* is the process of connecting a rule of law to a set of facts in order to determine how that rule might apply to a particular situation. The goal of the process is to solve a legal dispute or to prevent one from arising. Here is a relatively simple example:

| Rule + | Facts + | Issue + | Connection = (rule and facts) | Conclusion |
|---|---|---|---|---|
| § 10. "Any business within the city must apply for and obtain a license to do business within the city limits." | Fran owns a grocery store in the city. | Is a grocery store in the city a "business" under § 10 requiring a license "to do business"? | A grocery store is a business. Fran runs this business within the city. | § 10 requires Fran to have a license. |

Of course, not all legal analysis is this simple. *Yet the basic structure of a legal argument will always have this format.* Note the following characteristics of the process:

■ You start with a specific rule, such as a statute or regulation. You quote the relevant language exactly.

■ The major facts are stated.

■ The legal issue states the controversy in terms of specific language in the rule and specific facts that raise the controversy.

■ You draw the *connection* between specific language in the rule and specific facts. The analysis *is* this connection.

■ You reach a conclusion based on the above steps. The conclusion is phrased in terms of the rule.

More complicated example:

| Rule + | Facts + | Issue + | Connection (rule and facts) = | Conclusion |
|---|---|---|---|---|
| § 10. "Any business within the city must apply for and obtain a license to do business within the city limits." | Bill and his neighbors in the city have formed a food co-op through which members buy their food collectively from a wholesale company. All funds received by the co-op go for expenses and the purchase of food. | Is a non-profit co-op a "business" within the meaning of § 10 requiring a license "to do business"? | The city argues that the co-op is a business in the city. The co-op concedes that it is in the city but argues that it does not "do business," since the co-op does not earn a profit. | The co-op has the better argument. § 10 was not intended to cover non-profit ventures. Hence, the co-op does not have to have a license. |

The following is a more detailed statement of the analysis, which is referred to as the "connection" in the above charts:

§ 10 provides as follows:

"Any business within the city must apply for and obtain a license to do business within the city limits."

There are two main *elements* to § 10:

1. Any business
2. Within the city

When the facts fit within these two elements, the entity in question must apply for and obtain a license to do business. The consequence of the rule is the need to be licensed. This consequence is mandated once both elements exist.

*1. Any Business.*    The city claims that the co-op is a business. It does not matter to the city that profits in the traditional sense are not earned by the co-op. According to the city, the co-op members are "selling" goods to each other. A business is any entity that engages in any form of selling.

The co-op, on the other hand, argues that § 10 was not intended to cover co-ops. A business is an enterprise that makes a profit over and above expenses. Nothing of this kind occurs in the co-op. Everything taken in by the co-op goes out in the form of food purchases and expenses. Hence, the co-op is not a business and does not have to have a license.

*2. Within the City.*    There is no dispute between the parties on this element. The city and the co-op agree that the co-op operates within the city limits. The only dispute in this case concerns whether the co-op is a business.

. . . . . . . . . . . . . . .

If you had included legal research data on the meaning of § 10, the analysis would *also* have contained:

- A discussion of court opinions, if any, that interpret § 10
- A discussion of administrative regulations, if any, that implement § 10
- A discussion of the legislative history, if available, of § 10
- A discussion of secondary authority, if any, that interprets § 10, such as legal periodical literature and treatises

■ A discussion of constitutional provisions, if any, that affect the applicability of § 10

■ Etc.

The analysis, the facts, the issues, etc., are often presented in the format of a *memorandum of law*, which will be examined in greater detail in chapter 12 on Legal Writing.

We turn now to three skills that are important in legal analysis: the element-identification skill, the issue-statement skill, and the definitions skill.

## Section B. The Element-Identification Skill

All rules have consequences. There are rules that impose punishments, require payments, establish norms of behavior, institute procedures, etc. How do you determine when the consequence of a particular rule must be followed? The answer is: When *all* of the *elements* of that rule apply. In our example on § 10, note that the analysis proceeded through a discussion of the elements of § 10. An element is a component or portion of a rule. If you can show that all of the elements of a rule apply to a fact situation, then the rule itself—and its consequence—applies to the fact situation. The failure of any one of the elements to apply means that the entire rule cannot apply. In effect, each element is a precondition of the applicability of the entire rule.

The elements of § 10 were relatively short (business; within the city). This is not always so. How long should an element be? There is no absolute answer to this question. The two main criteria to keep in mind are these: (1) each element must be a precondition to the consequence of the entire rule, and (2) you should be able to discuss each element separately with relative ease.

Let us examine some additional examples:

> **§ 971.22. Change of place of trial.** The defendant may move for a change of the place of trial on the ground that an impartial trial cannot be had in the county. The motion shall be made at the time of arraignment.

Step one is to break the rule into its elements. The effect or consequence of the rule is to change the place of the trial. Ask yourself what must happen before this consequence will follow. Ask yourself what conditions or preconditions must exist before the result will occur. The answer will provide you with the elements of the rule:

1. Defendant

2. May move for a change of the place of trial

3. On the ground that an impartial trial cannot be had in the county

4. The motion must be made at the time of the arraignment

Hence, there are four elements to § 971.22. All four must exist before the place of the trial will be moved.

Suppose you are analyzing the following rule found in a statute:

> **§ 25–403.** A pharmacist must not sell prescription drugs to a minor.

As with almost all rules, this one is not already broken down into elements. You must identify the elements on your own. Ask yourself what conditions must exist before § 25–403 is violated, which would be the consequence of its applicability. Your answer will consist of its elements:

1. Pharmacist
2. Must not sell
3. Prescription drugs
4. To a minor

No violation exists unless all four elements of the statute are established. If, for example, a pharmacist sells simple aspirin (a nonprescription drug), he or she has not violated the statute. The third element cannot be established. Hence no violation, since one of the elements (preconditions) cannot be met.

For a number of reasons, rules such as statutes and regulations can be difficult to break into elements. For example, the rule may be long or may contain:

- Lists
- Alternatives
- Exceptions or provisos

Nevertheless, the same process is used. You must take the time to dissect the rule into its component elements. Examine the following rule as we try to identify its elements.

> § 5. While representing a client in connection with contemplated or pending litigation, a lawyer shall not advance or guarantee financial assistance to his client, except that a lawyer may advance or guarantee court costs, expenses of investigation, expenses of medical examination, and costs of obtaining and presenting evidence provided the client remains ultimately liable for such expenses.

Elements of § 5:

1. A lawyer
2. Representing a client in connection with contemplated litigation or in connection with pending litigation
3. Shall not advance financial assistance to his client or guarantee financial assistance to his client, except that the following is proper:
   a. lawyer advances or guarantees court costs, or
   b. lawyer advances or guarantees expenses of investigation, or
   c. lawyer advances or guarantees expenses of medical examination, or
   d. lawyer advances or guarantees costs of obtaining and presenting evidence

   *as long as the client remains ultimately liable for all expenses ("a"–"d").*

When an element is stated in the alternative, list all the alternatives within the same element. Alternatives related to one element should be kept within the phrasing of that element. The same is true of exception or proviso clauses. State them within the relevant element, since they are intimately related to the applicability of that element.

In the above example, the most complicated element is the third—(3). Within it there are lists, alternatives, an exception, and a proviso. But they all relate to the same point—the propriety of financial assistance. None of the subdivisions of the third element should be stated as a separate element. Sometimes you must do some unraveling of a rule in order to identify its elements. This certainly had to be done with the third element of § 5. Do not be afraid to pick the rule apart in order to cluster its thoughts around unified themes that should stand alone as elements. Diagram the rule for yourself as you examine it.

If more than one rule is involved in a statute, regulation, constitutional provision, charter, ordinance, etc., treat one rule at a time. Each rule should have its own elements, and, when appropriate, each element should be subdivided into its separate components, as in the third element of § 5.

Once you have broken the rule down into its elements, you have the structure of the analysis in front of you. Each element becomes a separate section of your analysis. You discuss one element at a time, concentrating on those that pose the greatest difficulties.

Element identification has many benefits in the law, as demonstrated in Figure 7.1.

To a very large extent, as you can see in Figure 7.1, legal analysis proceeds by *element analysis*. A major characteristic of sloppy legal analysis is that it does not clearly take the reader (or listener) through the important elements of rules that must be analyzed.

**FIGURE 7.1**
The Benefits of Element Identification

- *Identifying Issues*. Once you identify the elements of a rule, the next step is to find the *elements* that are most likely to be in contention. These elements become the basis of legal issues (as we shall see in the next section).

- *Drafting a Complaint*. When drafting a legal complaint, you often organize your factual allegations around the *elements* of each important rule in the controversy. (The most important rule is called the *cause of action*, which is a legally acceptable reason for suing someone; negligence is an example.)

- *Drafting an Answer*. When drafting an answer to a complaint, you often state your defenses by alleging facts that support the *elements* of each defense. (Most defenses, such as the statute of limitation, are nothing more than rules designed to defeat the claims of another.)

- *Organizing an Interview of a Client*. One of the goals of interviewing a client is to obtain information on facts relevant to each of the *elements* of the potential causes of action and defenses in the case. Element analysis, therefore, helps you organize the interview and give it direction.

- *Organizing an Investigation*. One of the goals of investigation is to obtain information on facts relevant to each of the *elements* of the potential causes of action and defenses in the case. Element analysis, therefore, helps you organize the investigation and give it direction.

- *Conducting a Deposition*. During a deposition, many of the questions are designed to determine what facts the other side may be able to prove that support the *elements* of the potential causes of action and defenses in the case.

- *Organizing a Memorandum of Law*. One of the purposes of a memorandum of law is to tell the reader what rules might apply to the case, what *elements* of these rules might be in contention, and what strategy should be undertaken as a result of this analysis.

- *Organizing an Examination Answer*. Many essay examinations in school are organized around the key *elements* of the rules that should be analyzed.

- *Charging a Jury*. When a judge charges (that is, instructs) a jury, he or she will go over each of the *elements* of the causes of action and defenses in the case in order to tell the jury what standard to use to determine whether facts in support of those elements have been proven during the trial.

### ■ ASSIGNMENT 7.1

Break the following rules into their elements:

**(a)** § 75(b). A lawyer shall not enter into a business transaction with a client if they have differing interests therein and if the client expects the lawyer to exercise his professional judgment therein for the protection of the client.

**(b)** § 38. A person or agency suing or being sued in an official public capacity is not required to execute a bond as a condition for relief under this section unless required by the court in its discretion.

**(c)** § 1.2. A lawyer may not permit his legal assistant to represent a client in litigation or other adversary proceedings or to perform otherwise prohibited functions unless authorized by statute, court rule or decision, administrative rule or regulation or customary practice.

**(d)** § 179(a)(7). If at any time it is determined that application of best available control technology by 1988 will not assure protection of public water supplies, agricultural and industrial uses, and the protection and propagation of fish, shellfish and wildlife, and allow recreational activities in and on the water, additional effluent limitations must be established to assure attainment or maintenance of water quality. In setting such limitations, EPA must consider the relationship of the economic and social costs of their achievement, including any economic or social dislocation in the affected community or communities, the social and economic benefits to be obtained, and determine whether or not such effluent limitations can be implemented with available technology or other alternative control strategies.

## ■ Section C. The Issue-Statement Skill

After you have broken a rule into its elements, the next step is to identify the *element in contention*. That element then becomes the basis of a *legal issue*. An element is in contention when you can predict that the other side in the controversy will probably not agree with your interpretation of that element and/or with whether the facts support that element. If a rule has five elements and you anticipate disagreement over all of them, phrase five separate issues. If, however, only one of the five elements will probably be in contention, phrase only one issue. There is no need to waste time over elements that will most likely not be the basis of disagreement.

Legal issues are often phrased in *shorthand* such as "Does § 34 apply?" "Can a van be burglarized?" A more *comprehensive* phrasing of a legal issue would consist of:

■ A brief quote from the element in contention, and

■ Several of the important facts relevant to that contention

For example, suppose that you are analyzing the following rule and facts:

> § 92. The operator of any vehicle riding on a sidewalk shall be fined $100.
>
> *Facts:* Fred rides his ten-speed bicycle on the sidewalk. He is charged with violating § 92.

The element breakdown and issue statement would be as follows:

Elements of § 92:

1. Operator
2. Any vehicle

3. Riding

4. On a sidewalk

*Issue:* Is a ten-speed bicycle a "vehicle" under § 92?

The parties will probably agree that Fred rode his bicycle on a sidewalk and that Fred was the operator of his bicycle. The first, third, and fourth elements, therefore, should not be be made into legal issues. The only disagreement will be over the second element. Hence it is the basis of an issue. Note the quote marks around the element in contention (vehicle) and the inclusion of an important fact that is relevant to this contention (it was a ten-speed bicycle).

---

### ■ ASSIGNMENT 7.2

Provide a comprehensive phrasing of the legal issue or issues in each of the following situations:

(a) *Facts:* Harry Franklin works for the XYZ Agency. In one of the Agency's personnel files there is a notation that Paul Drake, another Agency employee, was once arrested for fraud. Harry obtains this information from this file and tells his wife about it. (She also knows Paul.) Harry is unaware that Paul has told at least three other employees of his fraud arrest.

   *Regulation: . 20(d).* It shall be unlawful for any employee of the XYZ Agency to divulge confidential material in any file of the Agency.

(b) *Facts:* Jones has a swimming pool in his backyard. The pool is intended for use by the Jones family members and guests who are present when an adult is there to supervise. One hot summer night, a neighbor's child opens an unlocked door of a fence that surrounds the Jones' yard and goes into the pool. (There is no separate fence around the pool.) The child knows that he should not be there without an adult. No one else is at the pool. The child drowns.

   *Statute: § 77.* Property owners are liable for the foreseeable harm that occurs on their property.

---

## ■ Section D. The Definitions Skill

Language can frequently be defined broadly or narrowly. Assume that Jim meets a friend in a parking lot and says to him, "You can use my car." Jim is quite upset, however, when the friend returns five months later after driving the car through about twenty states. The friend asserts that he did nothing more than "use" the car. The question becomes: What is the definition of "use?"

*Broad Definition:* Use means to operate or employ something for any purpose and for any length of time.

*Narrow Definition:* Use means to operate or employ something for a reasonable purpose within a reasonable time.

The same dynamic is found when interpreting ambiguous language within elements in contention. Recall the bicycle example discussed in the preceding section:

§ 92. The operator of any vehicle riding on a sidewalk shall be fined $100.

*Facts:* Fred rides his ten-speed bicycle on the sidewalk. He is charged with violating § 92.

*Issue:* Is a ten-speed bicycle a "vehicle" under § 92?

This controversy may well turn on whether "vehicle" can be defined broadly or narrowly. Fred will argue that it should be interpreted narrowly, whereas the government will argue for a broad definition:

> *Broad Definition:* Vehicle means any method of transportation.

> *Narrow Definition:* Vehicle means any motorized method of transportation.

Whenever you have an element in contention that contains ambiguous language, you should put yourself in the shoes of each person in the controversy to try to identify what definition of the language each would propose. Think of a broad and a narrow definition, and state which side would argue which definition.

To help resolve a definition dispute, you would undertake some legal research—for example, you would try to find cases interpreting "vehicle" under § 92 and trace the legislative history of § 92. Often, however, you will *not* find the answer in the library. The precise question may never have arisen before. This is particularly true of recent statutes and regulations.

---

### ■ ASSIGNMENT 7.3

In each of the following problems, identify any ambiguous language in elements in contention. Give broad and narrow definitions of this language and state which side would argue which definition. Do not do any legal research.

**(a)** *Facts:* Alice Anderson is nine months pregnant. A police officer gives her a ticket for driving in a car-pool lane in violation of § 101. The officer said he gave her the ticket because she was alone in the car at the time.

*Regulation:* § 101. Car-pool lanes can be used only by cars in which there is at least one passenger in the car with the driver.

**(b)** *Facts:* Mary is arrested for violating § 55. She is charged as a felon. She forced open the lock on the driver's side of a van at 5 P.M. Mary didn't know that the door on the passenger side was unlocked. She went into the back of the van and fell asleep on the floor. The police arrested her after waking her up at 9 P.M. The owner of the van claims that a $20 bill is missing. Mary had a $20 bill on her, but she said it was her own.

*Statute:* § 55. A person who breaks and enters a dwelling at night for the purpose of stealing property therein shall be charged as a felon.

---

### ■ ASSIGNMENT 7.4

Analyze the problem in the following situations. Do not do any legal research. Simply use the facts and rules you are given. Be sure to include in your analysis what you have learned about elements, issues, and definitions.

**(a)** Susan is arrested for carrying a dangerous weapon. While in a hardware store, she got into an argument with another customer. She picked up a hammer from the counter and told the other customer to get out of her way. The customer did so and Susan put the hammer back. She was later arrested and charged with violating § 402(b), which provides: "It is unlawful for anyone to carry a dangerous weapon."

**(b)** It is against the law in your state "to practice law without a license" (§ 39). Fred is charged with violating this law. He told a neighbor that a certain parking ticket received by the neighbor could be ignored since the police officer was incorrect in issuing the ticket. In gratitude, the neighbor buys Fred a drink. (Assume that what Fred told the neighbor about the ticket was accurate and that Fred is *not* an attorney.)

**(c)** Ted and Ann are married. Ted is a carpenter and Ann is a lawyer. They buy an old building that Ted will repair for Ann's use as a law office. Ted asks Ann to handle the legal aspects of the purchase of the building. She does so. Soon after the purchase, they decide to obtain a divorce. Ted asks Ann if she will draw up the divorce papers. She does so. Ted completes the repair work on the building for which Ann pays him a set amount. Has Ann violated the rule stated in problem (a) in Assignment 7.1, page 350, above?

# Section E. Briefing Court Opinions

The word *brief* has several meanings.

First, to *brief* a court opinion is to summarize its major components (e.g., key facts, issues, reasoning, disposition). Such a brief is your own summary of the opinion for later use. Second, a *trial brief* is an attorney's set of notes on how to conduct the trial. The notes (often placed in a *trial notebook*) will be on the opening statement, witnesses, exhibits, direct and cross-examination, closing argument, etc. This trial brief is sometimes called a trial manual or trial book. Third, the *appellate brief* is the formal written argument to a court of appeals on why a lower court's decision should be affirmed, modified, or reversed. It is submitted to the appellate court and to the other side.

Here our concern is the first meaning of the word brief—a summarization of the major components of a court opinion. Before we examine these components, we will study an opinion as it might appear in a library reporter volume.

The circled numbers are explained after the opinion.

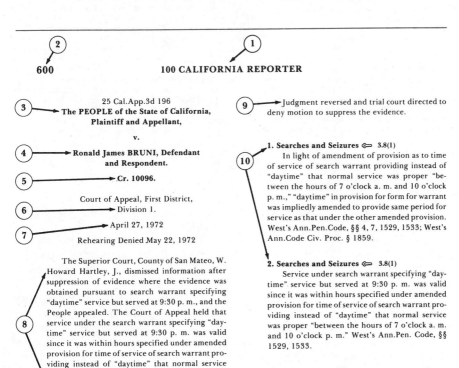

**2**

**600**

**1**

**100 CALIFORNIA REPORTER**

**3**  25 Cal.App.3d 196
**The PEOPLE of the State of California,
Plaintiff and Appellant,**

v.

**4**  **Ronald James BRUNI, Defendant
and Respondent.**

**5**  **Cr. 10096.**

**6**  Court of Appeal, First District,
Division 1.

**7**  April 27, 1972

Rehearing Denied May 22, 1972

**8**  The Superior Court, County of San Mateo, W. Howard Hartley, J., dismissed information after suppression of evidence where the evidence was obtained pursuant to search warrant specifying "daytime" service but served at 9:30 p. m., and the People appealed. The Court of Appeal held that service under the search warrant specifying "daytime" service but served at 9:30 p. m. was valid since it was within hours specified under amended provision for time of service of search warrant providing instead of "daytime" that normal service was proper "between the hours of 7 o'clock a. m. and 10 o'clock p. m."

**9**  Judgment reversed and trial court directed to deny motion to suppress the evidence.

**1. Searches and Seizures ⟾ 3.8(1)**

**10**  In light of amendment of provision as to time of service of search warrant providing instead of "daytime" that normal service was proper "between the hours of 7 o'clock a. m. and 10 o'clock p. m.," "daytime" in provision for form for warrant was impliedly amended to provide same period for service as that under the other amended provision. West's Ann.Pen.Code, §§ 4, 7, 1529, 1533; West's Ann.Code Civ. Proc. § 1859.

**2. Searches and Seizures ⟾ 3.8(1)**

Service under search warrant specifying "daytime" service but served at 9:30 p. m. was valid since it was within hours specified under amended provision for time of service of search warrant providing instead of "daytime" that normal service was proper "between the hours of 7 o'clock a. m. and 10 o'clock p. m." West's Ann.Pen.Code, §§ 1529, 1533.

Evelle J. Younger, Atty. Gen. of California, Edward P. O'Brien, Robert R. Granucci, Deputy Attys. Gen., San Francisco, for appellant. (11)

William F. DeLucchi, Regalado & Lindquist, Redwood City, for respondent.

Smith, Judge. (12)

The People appeal from a judgment dismissing an Information after suppression of evidence, (13) where the evidence was obtained pursuant to a search warrant specifying "daytime" service, but (14) which was served at 9:30 p. m. at night.

In 1970, section 1533 of the Penal Code was amended to eliminate the provision for "daytime" service for normal service of a search warrant. Instead of "daytime," the statute now specifies normal service as proper "between the hours of 7 (15) o'clock a. m. and 10 o'clock p. m." Apparently by oversight, the Legislature neglected to also amend the mandatory provisions under section 1529 of the Penal Code, which continues to require "daytime" service. An inconsistency exists as to the mandatory requirements of search warrants unless section 1529 of the Penal Code is read as having been amended by implication when section 1533 of the Penal Code was expressly amended. Otherwise, the only warrant an issuing magistrate could authorize, without possibly violating one or the other statute, would be one for unlimited service at any hour of day or night upon a showing of good cause. Nothing suggests that this was the legislative intent.

The provisions of the Penal Code "are to be construed according to the fair import of their terms, with a view to effect its objects and to pro- (16) mote justice." (Pen.Code. § 4.) "In the construction of a statute the intention of the Legislature. . . is to be pursued, if possible; and when a (18) general and particular provision are inconsistent, the latter is paramount to the former." (Code (16) Civ.Proc., § 1859.)

[1]  Under the definition in Section 7 of the (10a) Penal Code, daytime is defined as "the period between sunrise and sunset." This general provision is clearly inconsistent with the particular provision relating to service of search warrants between the hours of 7 o'clock a. m. and 10 o'clock p. m. estab- (18) lished under the amendment of section 1533 of the Penal Code. Under the general rules of statutory construction, we interpret "daytime" in the particular provisions of section 1529 of the Penal Code

as having been impliedly amended to provide the (19) same period for service as that under amended section 1533 of the Penal Code.

(18) ". . . 'where the language of a statute is reasonably susceptible of two constructions, one of which in application will render it reasonable, fair and harmonious with its manifest purpose, and another which would be productive of absurd consequences, the former construction will be adopted.' (citation); and 'if certain provisions are repugnant, effect should be given to those which best comport with the end to be accomplished and render the statute effective, rather than nugatory.'" (Dept. of (17) Motor Vehicles of California v. Indus. Acc. Com. (1939) 14 Cal.2d 189, 195, 93 P.2d 131, 134.)

(10a)
(19)  [2]  We hold that the People are correct in their assertion that service was valid since it was within the hours specified under amended section 1533 of the Penal Code. See Tidwell v. Superior Court (1971) 17 Cal.App.3d 780, 786-787, 95 (17) Cal.Rptr. 213.

This court has always been scrupulous in demanding a high standard for the admission of evidence pursuant to warrants. Our ruling today does not violate this standard. The integrity of our trial system in large measure depends upon the integrity of the evidence admitted at trial. The case before us deals with the timing of serving a warrant. (21) If the case had involved other aspects of the warrant such as its specificity, our result would probably have been different.

The judgment is reversed, and the trial court (20) is directed to deny the motion to suppress the evidence.

Jones, Judge (Concurring in result only). (22)

Thomas, Judge (Dissenting). (23)
If the California legislature intended to amend section 1529 of the Penal Code, it should have done so expressly. It is not the function of the judiciary to amend the statutes passed by the legislature. The public has a right to rely on the written language of statutes; in fact, we frequently admonish the citizenry if they ignore that language. For the courts to alter the language after the fact not only infringes upon the right of the legislature to be the sole entity under our system that can enact and amend legislation, but also is a signal to the public and to government officials that they can no longer trust the law as validly passed by the legislative branch. Both results are intolerable.

I would affirm the judgment below.

---

① The *California Reporter* is an unofficial reporter of state opinions in California. The "100" indicates the volume number of the reporter.

② The *Bruni* case begins on page 600. The citation of this case is *People v. Bruni*, 25 Cal. App. 3d 196, 100 Cal. Rptr. 600 (1972). The official cite is given at the top of the caption above the word PEOPLE. (We will cover citations in Chapter 11.)

③ When the *People* or the state brings an action, it is often a criminal case. This is an appellate court decision. Trial court decisions are appealed to the appellate court. The *appellant* is the party bringing the appeal because of dissatisfaction with the ruling or decision of the lower court. The state of California brought the case as the plaintiff and prosecutor in the lower court (Superior Court, County of San Mateo) and is now the appellant in the higher court (Court of Appeal, First District, Division 1).

④ Bruni was the defendant in the lower court since he was being sued or, in this case, charged with a crime. The appeal is taken against him by the People (appellant), because the lower court ruling was favorable to Bruni, to the dissatisfaction of the People. The party against whom a case is brought on appeal is called the *respondent.* Another word for respondent is *appellee.*

⑤ "Cr. 10096" refers to the *docket,* or calendar number of the case. "Cr." stands for *criminal.*

⑥ Make careful note of the name of the court writing the opinion. As soon as possible, you must learn the hierarchy of state courts in your state. In many states, there are three levels of courts: trial level, middle appeal level, and supreme level. (Most cases are appealed from the trial court to the middle appeal level, and then to the supreme level.) Here, we know from the title of the court (Court of Appeal) that it is an appellate court. It is not the supreme court, because in California the highest court is the California Supreme Court.

The name of the court is significant because of "legal authority." If the court is the highest or supreme court of the state, then the case would be applicable throughout the state. A middle appeals court case, on the other hand, applies only in the area of the state over which it has jurisdiction. When you see that the case was written by a trial or middle appeals court, you are immediately put on notice that you must check to determine whether the case was ever appealed subsequent to the date of the case. The main system for checking is called shepardizing (see Chapter 11).

⑦ When a case is being cited, only the year (here, 1972) is used, not the month or day (April 27). Sometimes, the date of the hearing or rehearing will be given as well as the date of the decision. The year of the decision is still the critical one for citation purposes.

⑧ Here the editors provide the reader with a summary of what the case says. The court did not write this summary; the editors did. It, therefore, is not an official statement of the law. It is merely an aid to the reader, who can quickly read this summary to determine whether the case covers relevant areas of law. This summary paragraph is often called the *syllabus.*

⑨ Here continues the unofficial summary, providing the reader with what procedurally must happen as a result of the April 27 case.

⑩ These are editor's *headnotes,* which are small-paragraph summaries of portions of the case. When the editors first read the case, they decide how many major topics or issues are covered in the case. Each of these topics is summarized in a headnote, all of which are then given consecutive numbers, here 1 and 2. These numbers correspond with the bracketed numbers [1] and [2] in the case itself. (See ⑩a.) If, for example, you wanted to read the portion of the case that was summarized in the second headnote of the case, you would go to the text of the case that begins with the bracketed [2].

The headnotes also have *a topic and a key number,* here "Searches and Seizures ☞3.8(1)." Each headnote will also be printed in the *digests* of West Publishing Company. Digests are volumes that contain nothing but the headnotes of court opinions. You can find out what other courts have said about the same or similar points by going to the digest volumes, looking up the key topic and number of a headnote (e.g., Searches and Seizures ☞ 3.8(1)), and reading summary paragraphs from many court cases such as our case, *People v. Bruni.*

⑪ Here are the attorneys that represented the appellant and respondent on appeal. Note that the attorney general's office represented the People. The attorney general or the district attorney's office represents the state in criminal cases.

⑫ The opinion begins with the name of the judge who wrote the opinion, Judge Smith. In this spot you will sometimes find the words "The Court," *"Per curiam,"* or *"Memorandum Opinion,"* which simply means that the court decided not to mention the name of the individual judge who wrote the opinion for the court.

⑬ In reading or briefing a case, make note of the judicial history of the case to date. The lower court dismissed the information (similar to an indictment) against

Bruni after certain evidence was suppressed (declared inadmissible), and the People appealed this dismissal judgment.

If the words *information* or *suppression* are new to you, look them up in a legal dictionary before proceeding. Do this for every new word.

⑭ It is critical to state the facts of the case accurately. Here the facts are relatively simple: A search warrant that said "daytime" service was served at 9:30 P.M., and evidence was taken pursuant to this search warrant. Defendant objected to the admission of this evidence at trial. In most cases, the facts are not this simple. The facts may be given at the beginning of the case, or they may be scattered throughout the case. If you confront the latter situation, you must carefully read the entire case to piece the facts together. The facts are critical because you must assess how analogous or similar the facts of your own problem are to those of the case you are reading (assuming that the issues in the problem are covered in the case at all). If your facts are the same or substantially the same as the key facts of the case, then the law of the case will probably apply to your problem. If the facts of your problem are somewhat the same and somewhat different from those of the case, then it is much more debatable whether the case is analogous and therefore whether the law of the case applies.

⑮ The next critical stage of reading a case is to state the issue (or issues) that the court was deciding in the case. This can sometimes be a difficult task, since many cases are long and complicated. Judges often ramble. The issue in *People v. Bruni* is not difficult to state: Is evidence that was obtained pursuant to a daytime warrant but served at 9:30 P.M. admissible when there is an inconsistency in the statutes as to when service must take place?

According to the court, § 1533 is inconsistent with § 1529. Section 1529 requires a "daytime" service. The legal issue, stated another way, is whether § 1529 was amended by implication when § 1533 was amended to allow service up to 10:00 P.M. so that the evidence obtained at 9:30 P.M. would be admissible in court (if otherwise valid).

⑯ The court refers to other statutes to support the conclusion it will reach. Note the interrelationship of the statutory sections. One statute is interpreted by interpreting other statutes. Section 4 of the Penal Code ("Pen.Code") says that the sections of the Penal Code are to be interpreted ("construed") rationally in order to carry out their purpose or objective and to promote justice. Section 1859 of the Code of Civil Procedure ("Code Civ.Proc.") says that when there is a general and a particular section that are inconsistent, the latter is preferred.

The sequence of statutory interrelationship in this case is as follows:

- Section 1529 of the Penal Code says "daytime."
- Section 7 of the Penal Code defines daytime as sunrise to sunset.
- Section 1533 of the Penal Code, as amended, says between 7:00 A.M. and 10:00 P.M.
- Section 4 of the Penal Code and § 1859 of the Code of Civil Procedure provide principles of interpreting statutes that are inconsistent.

⑰ In the same manner, a court will refer to other cases to support its ruling. In this way, the court argues that the other cases are *precedents* for the case before the court. The court in *People v. Bruni* is saying that *Dept. of Motor Vehicles of California v. Indus. Acc. Com.* and *Tidwell v. Superior Court* are precedents for its own ruling.

⑱ Here is the reasoning of the court to support its ruling: If there is a general statute and a specific statute that are inconsistent, the court will adopt the interpretation that is consistent with the purpose of the statutory scheme. Specific provisions are preferred over general ones. This is what the legislature must have intended.

⑲ The result, or holding, of the court's deliberation of the issue must then be identified. The holding is that § 1529 was impliedly amended to authorize service up to 10:00 P.M. The holding is also called the court's ruling.

㉑  The procedural consequences of the court's resolution of the issue are then usually stated, as here, toward the very end of the case. The judgment of the lower court is reversed. The lower court cannot continue to suppress (i.e., declare inadmissible) the evidence seized at the 9:30 P.M. search.

An appeals court could take a number of positions with respect to a lower court's decision. It could affirm it; modify it (reverse it only in part); *remand* the case (send it back to the lower court) with instructions on how to proceed or how to retry the case, etc.

㉑  In theory, a judge must be very precise in defining the issue before the court—and in resolving only that issue. The judge should not say more than *must* be said to decide the case. This theory, however, is sometimes not observed. Judges will go off on tangents, giving long dissertations or speeches through their opinions. As indicated, this can make your job more difficult; you must wade through all the words to identify (1) the key facts, (2) the precise issues, (3) the precise reasoning, and (4) the precise holdings.

The worst tangent that a judge can stray into is called *dictum.* Dictum is a judge's or court's view of what the law is, or might be, on facts that are *not* before the court. Judge Smith indicated that the result of the case might be different if the warrant were not specific, that is, if it did not name the individual to be searched or what the investigator was looking for. This was not the situation in the *Bruni* case; therefore, Judge Smith's commentary or speculation is dictum.

㉒  On any court there may be several judges. They do not always agree on what should be done in a case. The majority controls. In *Bruni,* Judge Smith wrote the *majority opinion.* A *concurring opinion* is one that votes with the majority but adds its own views about the case. In *Bruni,* Judge Jones concurred but specified that he accepted only the result of Judge Smith's opinion. Normally, judges in such situations will write an opinion indicating their own point of view. Judge Jones did not choose to write an opinion. He simply let it be known that he did not necessarily agree with everything Judge Smith said; all he agreed with was the conclusion that the warrant was validly served. To reach this result, Judge Jones might have used different reasoning, relied on different cases as precedent, etc.

㉓  A *dissenting opinion* disagrees with part or with all of the opinion of the majority. Dissenting opinions are sometimes heated. Of course, the dissenter's opinion is not controlling. It is often valuable to read, however, in order to determine what the dissenter thinks that the majority decided.

Having studied the *Bruni* case in this way, you should prepare a seven-part *brief:*

1. Facts: A search warrant that said "daytime" service was served at 9:30 P.M. Evidence was obtained during this search. The People (state) attempted to introduce this evidence at trial. Defendant Bruni objected.

2. Judicial History: The trial court dismissed the information against Bruni after refusing to consider the evidence seized pursuant to an improperly served warrant.

3. Issue: When § 1533 of the Penal Code was amended to allow service between 7:00 A.M. and 10:00 P.M., did the legislature impliedly also amend § 1529, which continued to require daytime service, so that evidence obtained pursuant to a warrant served at 9:30 P.M. can be admitted into evidence?

4. Result or Holding: Section 1529 was impliedly amended to conform to § 1533. The evidence seized pursuant to the search warrant can be admitted.

5. Reasoning: Courts will try to reconcile statutes that are inconsistent. If a general statute is inconsistent with a specific statute, the court will prefer the latter. The intent and purpose of the legislature is to be followed.

6. Procedural Consequences: The trial court's dismissal of the information is reversed. The trial must resume, and the evidence cannot be excluded on the basis of the time of service.

**7.** Subsequent Judicial History: As of the date of this brief, [here state whether there have been any subsequent decisions in this litigation; you obtain this information by shepardizing (page 566) the case you are briefing].

---

■ **ASSIGNMENT 7.5**

Brief the Quinn opinion at the end of this chapter. Do first six parts of the seven-part brief.

---

#  Section F. Applying Court Opinions

As we have seen, a court opinion interprets one or more rules of law that are applied to the fact situation before the court. There are two main kinds of rules of law that are interpreted and applied in this way:

■ Enacted law

■ Common law

**Enacted law** consists of: *constitutional provisions* (created by a constitutional convention and by a combination of legislative and voter approval), *statutes* (created by the legislature), *administrative regulations* (created by agencies), *ordinances* (created by city councils and county boards), etc. **Common law** is judge-made law created by the courts when there is no controlling enacted law that governs the controversy before the court. For example, most of the law on negligence was initially created as common law by the courts because the legislature had not provided any statutes in this area. If, however, such statutes did exist, the courts would have to apply them. Since statutes are superior in authority to common law, new statutes can always change common law. Statutes that bring about such change are called *statutes in derogation of the common law.*

The starting point in your analysis is a set of facts presented to you by a client or by your instructor for a school assignment. The goal is to apply the court opinion to this set of facts. The opinion reached a certain result, called a holding, or ruling. The conclusion of your legal analysis of the opinion will be your assessment of whether this holding applies to the set of facts presented to you. How do you reach this assessment?

■ First, you *compare* the rule that was interpreted and applied in the opinion with the rule that you have uncovered through legal research as potentially applicable.

■ Second, you *compare* the facts given to you by the client or by your instructor with the key facts in the opinion.

### Rule Comparison

Suppose your client is charged with a violation of § 23(b) of the state code on the payment of certain taxes. One of your first steps is to go to the law library and find § 23(b). You want to know whether § 23(b) applies to your client. You do an element analysis of the statute, you identify the issue(s), and you do a definitions analysis in the manner discussed earlier in this chapter. In the library you also look for court opinions. Your search is for court opinions that interpreted and applied § 23(b). You would not try to find opinions that interpreted housing or pollution statutes. You focus on opinions that cover the *same* rule involved in the case of the client—here, § 23(b). This is also true of the common law. If the client has a negligence case, for example, you search for opinions that interpret the law of negligence.

Rule comparison in the analysis of opinions is fairly simple. The general principle is: you compare the rule involved in your client's case (or school assignment) with the rule interpreted and applied in the opinion, and you proceed only if the rule is exactly the same. While there are some exceptions, this principle will be sufficient to guide you most of the time.

## Fact Comparison

Here is the heart of the analysis. Before the holding of an opinion can apply, you must demonstrate that the key facts of the opinion are substantially the same as the facts in the client's case (or school assignment). If the facts are exactly the same or almost exactly the same, the opinion is said to be *on all fours* with your facts. If so, then you will have little difficulty convincing someone that the holding of the opinion applies to your facts. It is rare, however, that you will find an opinion on all fours. Consequently, careful analysis of factual similarities and differences must be made. In general, if the facts are substantially similar, the ruling applies; if they are substantially different, it does not.

You must make a determination of what the *key facts* are in the opinion, since it is these facts alone that are the basis of the comparison. A key fact is a very important fact—a fact that was crucial to the conclusion or holding of the court. In a divorce opinion, for example, it will probably not be key that a plaintiff was thirty-three years old. The court would have reached the same result if the plaintiff was thirty-two or thirty-four. Age may have been irrelevant or of very minor importance to the holding. What *may* have been key is that the plaintiff beat his wife, since without this fact the court may not have reached the ruling that the ground of cruelty existed. You carefully comb the opinion to read what the judge said about the various facts. Did the court emphasize certain facts? Repeat them? Label them as crucial or important? These are the kinds of questions you must ask yourself to determine which facts in the opinion were key.

Let us assume that you have been able to identify the key facts of opinion. Your next concern is comparing these facts and the facts of your own problem. For example:

| Your Facts | The Case: Smith v. Apex Co. |
|---|---|
| Client sees an ad in the paper announcing a sale at a local store. He goes to the back of the store and falls into a pit. There was a little sign that said *danger* near the pit. The client wants to sue the store owner for negligence in failing to use reasonable care in preventing his injury. The law office assigns a paralegal to research the case. The paralegal finds the case of Smith v. Apex Co. and wants to argue that it applies. | This case involved a man (Smith) who is looking for an address. He is walking down the street. He decides to walk into an office building to ask someone for help. While coming down the corridor, he slips and falls on a wet floor. There was a small sign in the corridor that said *wet floor,* which Smith saw. Smith sued the owner of the building (Apex Co.) for negligence. The court held that the owner was negligent for failure to exercise reasonable care for the safety of users of the building. |

First, identify all factual similarities:

■ The client was in a public place (a store). Smith was also in a public place (an office building).

- Both situations involved some kind of warning (the *danger* sign and the *wet floor* sign).
- The warning in both situations was not conspicuous (the *danger* sign was "little"; the *wet floor* sign was "small").

Next, identify all factual differences:

- The client was in a store, whereas Smith was in an office building.
- Your case involved a hole or pit, whereas Smith v. Apex Co. involved a slippery surface.
- The client was there about a possible purchase whereas Smith was not trying to transact any business in the office building.

Next, identify any factual gaps:

- Smith saw the *wet floor* sign, but we do not know whether the client saw the *danger* sign.

Ninety percent of your legal analysis is complete if you have been able to make the above identifications. Most students do a sloppy job at this level. They do not carefully pick apart the facts in order to identify similarities, differences, and gaps.

Once you have done this properly, you make your final arguments about the opinion:

- If you want the holding in the opinion to apply, you emphasize the similarities between your facts and the key facts in the opinion. If any of your facts differs from a fact in the opinion, you try to point out that this is not significant since the latter was not a key fact in the opinion.
- If you do not want the holding in the opinion to apply, you emphasize the differences between your facts and the key facts in the opinion. If any of your facts is similar to a fact in the opinion, you try to point out that this is not significant since there is still a dissimilarity with at least one of the key facts in the opinion.

. . . . . . . . . . . . . .

*Factual gaps* sometimes pose a problem. If the factual gap is in the facts of your client's case, you simply go back to the client and ask him or her about the fact. In the above case, for example, the paralegal asks the client whether he saw the "danger" sign. Suppose, however, that the factual gap is in the opinion itself. Assume that your client was running when he fell into the pit, but that the opinion does not tell you whether Smith was running, walking, etc. You obviously cannot go to Smith or to the judge who wrote the opinion and ask. You must make a guess of what the judge would have done in the opinion if Smith was running at the time he slipped on the corridor floor. You may decide that it would have changed the result or that this additional fact would have made no difference to the ruling reached.

We turn now to an overview of how Smith v. Apex Co. would be applied to the client's case in a memorandum of law. The client's case and the opinion involve exactly the same rule—the law of negligence. Assume that the element in contention in this rule is the failure to use reasonable care.

*Issue.*   Did the store use "reasonable care" for the safety of users of the store when the only warning of a pit in the store was a small *danger* sign near the pit?

*Facts.*    The client saw an ad in the newspaper announcing a sale. He went to the back of the store and fell into a pit. There was a small sign that said *danger* near the pit.

*Analysis.*    An opinion on point is Smith v. Apex Co., 233 Mass. 578, 78 N.E.2d 422 (1980). In this opinion, the court found the owner of an office building liable for negligence when Smith slipped on a wet corridor floor in the building. There was a small *wet floor* sign in the corridor. This opinion is substantially similar to our own client's case. Both were in public buildings where owners can expect people to be present. In both situations, the warning was insufficient. The *wet floor* sign in the opinion was "small." The *danger* sign in our situation was "little." Because of all these important similarities, it can be argued that the holding in Smith v. Apex Co. applies.

It is true that in the opinion the judge pointed out that Smith saw the sign. Our facts do not state whether the client saw the *danger* sign in the store. This should not make any difference, however, since the judge in the opinion would probably have reached the same result if Smith had not seen the *wet floor* sign. In fact, the case would probably have been stronger for Smith if he did *not* see the sign. The building was dangerous in spite of the fact that users of the building such as Smith could see the sign. Obviously, the danger would be considered even greater if such users could not see the sign. We should find out from our client whether he saw the *danger* sign, but I do not think that it will make any difference in the applicability of the holding in Smith v. Apex Co.

The store owner will try to argue that the opinion does not apply. The argument might be that a pit is not as dangerous as a wet floor, since a pit is more conspicuous than a wet floor and hence not as hazardous. A user is more likely to notice a hole in the floor than to know whether a floor is slippery enough to fall on. Our client could respond by pointing out that the pit was in the back of the store where it may not have been very noticeable. Furthermore, the wet floor in the opinion was apparently conspicuous (Smith saw the *wet floor* sign), yet in the opinion the judge still found the defendant liable.

---

## ■ ASSIGNMENT 7.6

In the following situations, point out any factual similarities, differences, and gaps between the client facts and the facts of the opinion.

**(a)** *Client Facts:* Jim is driving his car 30 MPH on a dirt road at night. He suddenly sneezes and jerks the steering wheel slightly, causing the car to move to the right and run into Bill's fence. Bill sues Jim for negligence.

*Opinion:* A pedestrian brings a negligence action against Mary. Mary is driving her motorcycle on a clear day. A page of a newspaper unexpectedly flies into Mary's face. Since she cannot see where she is going, she runs into a pedestrian crossing the street. The court finds for Mary, ruling that she did not act unreasonably in causing the accident.

**(b)** *Client Facts:* Helen is the mother of David, age four. The state is trying to take David away from Helen on the ground that Helen has neglected David. Helen lives alone with David. She works part time and leaves David with a neighbor. Helen's job occasionally requires her to travel. At one time she was away for a month. During this period, David was sometimes left alone, since the neighbor had to spend several days at the hospital. When David was discovered alone, the state began proceedings to remove David on the ground of neglect.

*Opinion:* The state charged Bob Thompson with the neglect of his twins, aged ten. The state wishes to place the twins in a foster home. Bob is partially blind.

One day he accidentally tripped and fell on one of the twins, causing severe injuries to the child. Bob lives alone with the twins but refuses to hire anyone to help him run the home. The court ruled that Bob did not neglect his children.

## ■ ASSIGNMENT 7.7

Salem is a factory town of 500 inhabitants in Hawaii. The factory employs 95% of the workers in the town. The town has only two private attorneys: Ann Grote and Timothy Farrell. Forty of the employees have decided to sue the factory over a wage dispute. Ann Grote represents all these employees. She works alone except for her only employee, Bob Davis, a paralegal. In this litigation, the factory is represented by Timothy Farrell who has no employees—no secretaries and no paralegals. Grote and Farrell are young attorneys who have just begun their practices. Their only clients are the forty employees and the factory, respectively. The litigation has become quite complicated. Several months before the case is scheduled to go to trial, Farrell offers Davis a job as a paralegal at double the salary he is earning with Grote. He accepts the offer. Grote goes to court seeking a preliminary injunction against Davis and Farrell, which would bar them from entering this employment relationship.

Apply *Quinn v. Lum and Cronin, Fried, Sekiya & Kekina,* printed below, to the facts of the case of *Grote v. Davis and Farrell.* Do not do any legal research. Limit yourself to the application of this one opinion based on the guidelines of this chapter. (*Quinn* is an actual opinion from a state court in Hawaii.)

---

## Quinn v. Lum and Cronin, Fried, Sekiya & Kekina

Civ. No. 81284
Hawaii Court of Appeals

On January 25, 1984, Richard K. Quinn, Attorney at Law, a Law Corporation, filed suit against Rogerlene Lum, a member of the Hawaii Association of Legal Assistants (HALA) and formerly legal secretary with the Quinn firm, for injunctive relief based on the allegation that Mrs. Lum possesses confidential client information from her work as Quinn's legal secretary, which information would be transmitted to the co-defendant, Mrs. Lum's new employer, Cronin, Fried, Sekiya & Kekina, Attorneys at Law, if she were to begin her employment with the Cronin firm as a legal assistant.

On or about January 3, 1984 Mrs. Lum notified Quinn that she had accepted a position as a paralegal with the Cronin firm. Quinn subsequently discussed and corresponded with Mr. Cronin regarding the hiring of Mrs. Lum, who was scheduled to begin work with the Cronin firm on January 30, 1984. Mr. Cronin repeatedly refused Quinn's request that she not be hired by the Cronin firm.

On January 26, a hearing on the application for a temporary restraining order was heard by Judge Philip T. Chun of the Circuit Court of the First Circuit, State of Hawaii. The application was denied.

Quinn alleges in the pleadings filed with the Court in Civil No. 81284 that Mrs. Lum's employment with the Quinn firm from December 1, 1982 to January 17, 1984, and as Mr. Quinn's secretary from April 25, 1983 to January 17, 1984, included attendance at the firm's case review committee meetings. Confidential discussions occurred concerning case evaluation, settlement evaluation, strategy and tactics between Quinn, his associates, and their clients.

Cronin et al. are attorneys of record for the plaintiffs in *Firme v. Honolulu Medical Group and Ronald P. Peroff, M.D.* Quinn's firm represents the defendants. The case was set for trial on March 19, 1984. According to exhibits attached to the records filed in the instant case, Mr. Cronin recognized the *Firme* situation and agreed that Mrs. Lum would not be involved in the *Firme* case in her new employment, nor would his firm "[ever] seek to obtain any information from her concerning cases with which she was involved while in [Quinn's] office, nor would we have her work on any while here." Mr. Cronin goes on to say in his January 24 letter to Quinn that Quinn should consult with his clients in the *Firme* case as to whether Quinn's "attempt . . . to stop Mrs. Lum from working for [the Cronin firm] is with their approval."

Quinn also alleges that while his firm is known in the Honolulu legal community as one which represents hospitals, doctors and other health care providers, the Cronin firm is known as a plaintiff medical malpractice firm. Quinn lists in several pleadings that on more than one occasion, these firms found themselves adversaries in the same cases.

[Quinn contends] that this action was brought not to "bar Lum from working as a legal secretary or even as a paralegal, since that would be ludicrous given the size of Hawaii's legal community." In fact, Quinn states he would have "no objection to Lum's working for any other law firm in Hawaii other than one which specializes in medical malpractice plaintiffs' work, like [Cronin's]."

A subsequent hearing on the original complaint for injunctive relief was then held in Judge Ronald Moon's court on February 6. Plaintiff's motion for a preliminary injunction that would bar such employment "for at least two years" was denied, with the judge noting *Quinn v. Lum* as a case of first impression.

The Court explained its decision in light of the standards to be met before a preliminary injunction could be issued, as dealt with in depth by Mrs. Lum's attorney, David L. Fairbanks, who is also the current President of the Hawaii State Bar Association.

The standards which must be met in order to obtain a preliminary injunction, as listed by Judge Moon, follow:

1. The Court did not feel there was a substantial likelihood that plaintiff would prevail on the merits. If an injunction were to be issued, it would:

   "[E]ssentially prevent a paralegal or legal secretary, [or] attorney from joining any law firm that may have had some case in the past, . . . cases pending at the present time, or potential cases which may be worked on in the future" (Transcript of the Hearing, page 82).
2. The evidence is lacking regarding irreparable damage to Richard Quinn's clients.

3. The public interest would not be served by issuing such an injunction.

When an attorney enters practice in the State of Hawaii, he or she agrees to abide and be governed by the Hawaii Code of Professional Responsibility. This code does not attempt to govern the ethical actions of the non-attorneys. While Canon 37 of the American Bar Association's Code of Professional Responsibility, adopted pre-1971, states that a lawyer's employees have the same duty to preserve client confidences as the lawyer, this Canon is not included in the Hawaii code. Compliance, therefore, with the same rules of ethics guiding the Hawaii attorney is currently left to the discretion—and conscience—of the non-attorney.

If an attorney in Hawaii breaches the Code of Professional Responsibility, the office of Disciplinary Counsel may choose to investigate the matter and may pass the matter on to the Disciplinary Board and possibly, to the Hawaii Supreme Court for adjudication.

If an employee of a law office becomes suspect of some breach of ethics or acts of omission, the employing attorney becomes responsible for the employee's deeds. For example, if a legal secretary fails to file the complaint the day the Statute of Limitations expires thinking the next day would suffice, it is the attorney who is responsible to the client. The attorney can fire the secretary "for cause" but the attorney, nevertheless, stands responsible. It appears the only way for an attorney to further censor the employee directly is via a civil suit for tortious damages.

Whether a permanent injunction can or will be granted has yet to be seen in this case. What is clear is that neither the office of Disciplinary Counsel nor the Hawaii Supreme Court would or could become involved; they have no jurisdiction over the non-attorney working in a law office.

## ☐ Chapter Summary

Legal analysis is the process of connecting a rule of law to a set of facts in order to determine how that rule might apply to a particular situation. The goal of the process is to solve a legal dispute or to prevent one from arising. The structure of legal analysis is always the same: a rule and facts lead to a legal issue, which is generally phrased as a question. That question is answered by drawing a connection between the language of the rule and the facts, producing a conclusion.

An important skill in legal analysis is the ability to break a rule down into its elements. An element is simply a component or portion of a rule. If all the elements apply to a fact situation, then the rule applies to the fact situation. If one element does not apply, then the rule does not apply. Hence each element of a rule is one of the preconditions of the applicability of the entire rule. A legal issue is often phrased to ask whether one of the elements applies to the facts. (This element is sometimes re-

*(Continued on next page)*

## ☐ Chapter Summary *(Continued)*

ferred to as the element in contention or the element in controversy.) The answer may depend on whether the element is to be interpreted broadly or narrowly.

To brief an opinion means to identify its major components: facts, judicial history, issue, holding, reasoning, and the procedural consequences of the holding. In addition, it is often essential to determine the subsequent history of the opinion. There are two main steps in applying an opinion to a set of facts from a client's case. First, you compare the rule (which will either be an enacted law or a common law) that was interpreted in the opinion with the rule you are considering in the client's case. With limited exceptions, the opinion cannot apply unless these two rules are the same. Second, you compare the key facts in the opinion with the facts of the client's case. In general, the opinion will apply if these facts are the same or are substantially similar.

## Key Terms

legal analysis
elements
cause of action
defense
memorandum of law
legal issue
element in contention
shorthand issue
comprehensive issue
broad/narrow definition
brief
trial brief
trial notebook
trial manual
trial book
appellate brief

People
appellant
respondent
appellee
docket number
shepardizing
syllabus
headnote
topic and key number
digests
attorney general
per curiam
memorandum opinion
precedent
holding
ruling

remand
dictum
majority opinion
concurring opinion
dissenting opinion
enacted law
common law
statute in derogation of the
    common law
rule comparison
fact comparison
on all fours
key fact
fact similarities
fact differences
fact gaps

# 8

# Legal Interviewing

## ■ Chapter Outline

**Section A. The Context of Interviewing in Litigation**

**Section B. The Format of an Intake Memo**

**Section C. What Facts Do You Seek? Guides to the Formulation of Questions**

The Instructions of the Supervisor for the Interview

Checklists

Legal Analysis

Fact Particularization

Common Sense

Flexibility

**Section D. What Does the Client Want?**

**Section E. Human Relations and Communications Skills in Interviewing**

**Section F. Analysis of a Legal Interview**

## ■ Section A. The Context of Interviewing in Litigation

There are at least three kinds of legal interviews:

1. The initial client interview
2. The follow-up client interview
3. The field interview involving someone other than the client

In the initial client interview, the interviewer introduces the client to the kind of legal services offered by the office, identifies legal problems, and explains the way in which the office will handle the case. Follow-up interviews occur after the initial interview. The client is asked about additional facts and is consulted on a variety of matters that require his or her attention, consent, and participation. Finally, there is the field interview conducted during investigation, in which the interviewer seeks out a great diversity of people for a wide range of purposes. Investigation will be examined in the next chapter. Here our focus will be the *initial client interview.*

Interviewing is among the most important skills used in a law office. Since it appears to be relatively easy to engage in interviewing (all you need is a person to interview and some time), it is commonly assumed that legal interviewing, like good conversation, requires little more than intelligence and a pleasing personality. This misconception often leads to incomplete and sloppy interviewing. Legal interviewing is much more than conversation. They are similar in that both frequently involve building a relationship and exchanging information. In legal interviewing, however, the goal is to help solve a client's problem. In order to do this, a relationship must be established between the interviewer and client that is warm, trusting, professional, and goal-oriented.

Paralegals in different settings have varied duties and authority. In a private law office, an attorney will usually conduct the initial interview and assign the paralegal the limited task of gathering detailed information from the client on a specific topic. For example, a paralegal may be asked to help a bankruptcy client detail debts and financial entanglements by listing them all on a worksheet. On the other hand, in a government agency or in a government-funded legal service office, the paralegal's interviewing responsibilities can be extensive. For example, a paralegal may conduct the initial interview with a client and remain the primary office contact for the client throughout the resolution of the case.

The initial client interview is critical because it sets the foundation for the entire litigation process. (See Figure 8.1.) The facts obtained from this interview are further pursued through field *investigation;* the laws governing these facts are *researched* in the law library; the facts and the governing law are informally argued between counsel for the parties in an effort to *settle* the case through *negotiation;* if there is no settlement, a *trial* is held in which the facts are formally established; finally, the process ends with an *appeal.* Everything begins with the facts obtained through the initial client interview.

## ■ Section B. The Format of an Intake Memo

Before analyzing the interviewing process, we should look briefly at one of the end products of the interview—the *intake memo.* This is the document the paralegal writes on the basis of notes taken at the interview. The intake memo

**FIGURE 8.1**
Interviewing in
Context

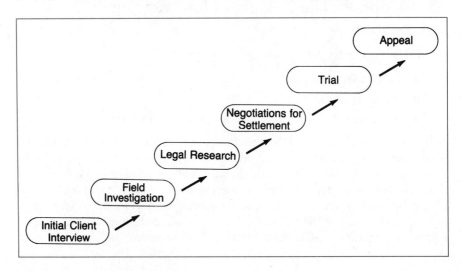

goes first to the supervisor and then into a newly opened case file on the client. The memo often has five parts:

*1. Heading.*    The heading provides the following information at the top of the first page:

- Who wrote the memo
- The supervisor in charge of the case
- The date the memo was written
- The date the interview was conducted
- The name of the case
- The office file number of the case
- The kind of case (general area of the law)
- The subject matter of the memo following the notation "RE"

*2. Personal Data.*

- Name of the client
- Home address
- Phone numbers where client can be reached
- Age of client
- Marital status
- Place of employment of client
- Etc.

*3. Statement of the Assignment.*    The first paragraph of the memo should state the precise objective the paralegal was given in conducting the interview.

*4. Body of the Memo.*    Here the facts are presented in a coherent, readable manner according to a number of possible organizational principles:

- A chronological listing of the facts so that the events are unfolded as a story with a beginning, middle, and end
- A categorizing of the facts according to the major topics or issues of the case, each with its own subject heading under which the relevant facts are placed
- Any other format called for by the supervisor

*5. Conclusion.*    Here a number of things could be included:

- A brief summary of the major facts listed in the body of the memo
- The impressions of the paralegal of the client, such as
  - how knowledgeable the client appeared to be
  - how believable the client appeared to be
- A list of the next steps, for example:
  - what further facts should be sought through investigation
  - what legal research should be undertaken
  - any other recommendations on what should be done on the case based on what was learned during the interview
- A list of anything the paralegal told the client to do, for example:
  - bring in specified documents relevant to the case

**FIGURE 8.2**
Intake Memo

---

### Inter-Office Memo

**To:** Ann Fuller, Supervisor                     **Case:** John Myers vs. Betsy Myers
**From:** Jim Smith, Paralegal                     **File Number:** 91-102
**Date of Memo:** March 13, 1991                   **Kind of Case:** Child Custody
**Date of Interview:** March 12, 1991              **Re:** Intake Interview of John Myers

**Personal Data:**

**Name of Client:** John Myers
**Address:** 34 Main Street, Salem, Massachusetts 01970
**Phone:** 966-3954 (H) 297-9700 (x 301) (W)
**Age:** 37
**Marital Status:** Married but separated from his wife, Betsy Myers
**Employment:** ABC Construction Co., 2064 South Street, Salem, Massachusetts 02127

   You asked me to conduct a comprehensive intake interview of John Myers, our client, in order to obtain a listing of his assets and the facts surrounding his relationship with his children.

   A. ASSETS
      John Myers owns . . .

---

   ▪ check on further facts and call back

   ▪ return for another interview

In Figure 8.2 there is a sample of the introductory parts of an intake memo:

## ▪ Section C. What Facts Do You Seek? Guides to the Formulation of Questions

   Unless the paralegal knows what to accomplish in an interview, valuable time will be wasted. For example, suppose a client is being interviewed concerning the grounds (legally sufficient reasons) for a divorce. The paralegal does not simply write down *all* the facts about the marriage and the client's problems in it. The facts must be clustered or arranged in categories that are relevant to grounds for divorce. Unless paralegals have this objective in mind before and during the interview, they may end up with such a confusing collection of facts they'll have to conduct a second interview to go over matters that should have been covered initially. This does not mean that the paralegal cannot talk about anything other than what is directly related to the objective, but it does mean that each interview must have a definite *focus*.

   There are six major ways a paralegal can achieve focus in the formulation of questions to be asked of a client:

▪ Instructions of the supervisor for the interview

▪ Checklists

▪ Legal analysis

▪ "Fact particularization"

▪ Common sense

▪ Flexibility

These methods are designed to help you avoid all the following examples of an *ineffective* interview:

▪ You fail to seek the information that the supervisor wanted you to obtain.

---

▪

"If you don't know where you're going, when you get there you'll be lost."
Yogi Berra

▪

■ You miss major relevant facts.

■ You fail to obtain sufficient detail on the major relevant facts.

■ You fail to ask questions about (and record) the extent to which the client was sure or unsure about the facts given you.

■ You fail to pursue leads the client provides about other relevant themes or topics that may not have been part of the supervisor's explicit instructions.

## The Instructions of the Supervisor for the Interview

These instructions, of course, control what you do in the interview. As indicated above, you may be asked to do a limited interview or a comprehensive one. Be sure to write down what the supervisor wants from the interview. One concern that frequently arises is the amount of detail desired. Attorneys like facts. During three years of law school, they were constantly asked by their law professors, "What are the facts?" The likelihood is that the attorney for whom you work will want considerable detail from the interview. Even if you are told to limit yourself to obtaining the basic facts from the client, you may find that the supervisor wants a lot of detail about those basic facts. When in doubt, the safest course is to be detailed in your questioning. If possible, try to sit in on an interview conducted by your supervisor in order to observe his or her method of questioning and the amount of detail sought. Also, examine some closed case files that contain intake memos. Ask the supervisor if any of these memos are exemplary, and if so, why. Once you have a model, it can be very useful as a guide.

## Checklists

The office where you work may have checklists that are used in conducting interviews. For some kinds of cases, such as probate or estate matters, the checklists may be extensive. If such checklists are not available, you should consider writing your own for the kinds of cases in which you do a good deal of interviewing.

Caution is needed, however, in using checklists:

■ You should find out why individual questions were inserted in the checklist.

■ You should be flexible enough to ask questions not on the checklist when your interview assignment calls for such adaptation.

A checklist must be viewed as a guide that should be adjusted to adapt to the case and client in front of you rather than as a rigid formula from which there can never be deviation.

## Legal Analysis

Extensive legal analysis does not take place while the interview is being conducted. Yet *some* legal analysis may be needed to conduct an intelligent interview.

Most of the questions you ask in the interview must be *legally relevant*, which means that the answer is needed in order to determine whether a particular legal principle governs. It takes some understanding of legal analysis to apply the concept of legal relevance intelligently. It could be dangerous for the paralegal to be asking questions by rote, even if checklists are used. The question-and-answer process is a little like a tennis match—you go where the ball is hit or it passes you by.

Suppose that you are interviewing a client on an unemployment compensation claim. The state denied the claim because the client is allegedly not "available for work." You cannot conduct a competent interview unless you know the legal meaning of this phrase. From this understanding you can formulate questions that are legally relevant to the issue of whether the client has been and is "available for work." You will ask obvious questions such as:

What is your present health?

Where have you applied for work?

Were you turned down, and if so, why?

Did you turn down any work, and if so, why?

Suppose that during the interview, the client tells you the following:

There were some ads in the paper for jobs in the next town, but I didn't want to travel that far.

At this point you must decide whether to pursue this matter by inquiring about the distance to the town, whether public transportation is available, the cost of such transportation, whether the client owns a car, etc. Again, legal analysis can be helpful. Does "available for work" mean available in the same area? Is one *un*available for work because of a refusal to make unreasonable efforts to travel to an otherwise available job in another area? What does unreasonable mean? Definitional questions such as these must go through your mind as you decide whether to seek more details about the ads for work in the other town. These are questions of legal analysis. *You must be thinking while questioning.* Some instant mental analysis should be going on all the time. This does not mean you must know the answer to every legal question that comes to mind while interviewing the client. But you must know something about the law and must be flexible enough to think about legal questions that should be generated by unexpected facts provided by the client.

When in doubt about whether to pursue a line of questions, check with your supervisor. If he or she is not available, the safest course is to pursue it. As you acquire additional interviewing experience in particular areas of the law, you will be better equipped to know what to do. Yet you will never know everything. There will always be fact situations that you have never encountered before. Legal analysis will help you handle such situations.

## Fact Particularization (FP)

"Fact particularization" is perhaps one of the most important concepts in this book. To *particularize a fact* means to ask an extensive series of questions

**FIGURE 8.3**

Fact
Particularization

The investigator must *particularize* facts collected thus far:

1. By assuming that the facts are woefully incomplete, and

2. By assuming that there is more than one version of the facts, and

3. By identifying a large number of basic who, what, where, why, when, and how questions which, if answered, would provide as complete a picture of what happened as is possible to obtain at this time

about that fact in order to explore its uniqueness. Fact assessment is critical to practice of the law; fact particularization is critical to the identification of the facts that must be assessed. FP is a fact-collection technique. It is the process of viewing every person, thing, or event as unique—different from every other person, thing, or event. Every important fact a client tells you in an interview should be particularized. You do this by asking a large number of follow-up questions once you have targeted the fact you want to explore.

FP can be a guide to the formulation of questions in a number of situations:

- In a client interview (our focus in this chapter)
- In investigations (see Chapter 9)
- In drafting interrogatories (see Chapter 10)
- In preparing for a deposition (see Chapter 10)
- In examining witnesses on the stand at trial (see Chapters 10 and 15)

In legal interviewing, the starting point for the FP process is an important fact that the client has told you during the interview. Examples include: "I tried to find work"; "the car hit me from the rear"; "the pain was unbearable"; "the company was falling apart"; "he told me I would get the ranch when he died"; "he fired me because I am a woman"; etc. Then you ask the client eight categories of questions about the fact that is being particularized. (See Figure 8.4.)

The eight categories are not mutually exclusive, and all eight categories are not necessarily applicable to every fact that you will be particularizing. There is no definite order in which the questions must be asked as long as you are comprehensive in your search for factual detail. The point of FP is simply to get the wheels of your mind rolling so that you will think of a large number of questions and avoid conducting a superficial interview.

### Time Details

When did the fact occur or happen? Find out the precise date and time. The interviewer should be scrupulous about all dates and times. If more than one event is involved, ask questions about the dates and times of each. If the client is not sure, ask questions to help jog the memory and ask the client to check his or her records or to contact other individuals who might know. Do not be satisfied with an answer such as, "It happened about two months ago." If this is what the client says, record it in your notes, but then probe further. Show the client a calendar and ask about other events going on at the same time in an effort to help him or her be more precise.

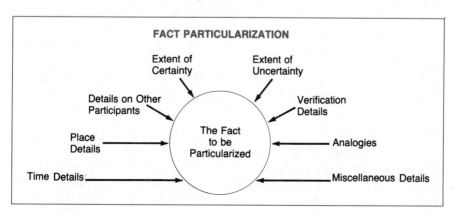

**FIGURE 8.4**

The Categories of Fact Particularization

## Place and Environment Details

Be equally scrupulous about geography. Where did the event occur? Where was the thing or object in question? Where was the client at the time? Ask the client to describe the surroundings. Ask questions with such care that you obtain a verbal photograph of the scene. If relevant, ask the client to approximate distances between important objects or persons. You might want to have the client draw a diagram, or you can draw a diagram on the basis of what you are told and ask the client if the drawing is accurate. Ask questions about the weather or about lighting conditions. You want to know as much as you can about the environment or whatever the client could observe about the environment through the senses of touch, sight, hearing, and smell.

## Details on Other Participants

Who else was involved? Ask questions about who they were, their roles, their age, appearance, etc., if relevant. Where were they at the time? When did they act? Why did they act? Why did they fail to act? Could you have anticipated what they did or failed to do? Why or why not? Have they ever acted or failed to act in this way before? Ask questions designed to obtain a detailed picture of who these other participants were and their precise relationship to the fact being particularized.

## Extent of Certainty/Uncertainty

Everything the client tells you can be placed somewhere on the spectrum of certainty:

| Absolutely Certain | Substantially Certain | Fairly Certain | Have A Vague Certainty | Unsure | Do Not Know |
|---|---|---|---|---|---|
| | | | | | |

It would be a big mistake, for example, to record that the client said a letter was received two weeks ago when in fact the client said. "I think it came two weeks ago." Do not turn uncertainty into certainty by sloppy listening and sloppy recording in your intake memo of what the client said. Of course, it may be possible for a client to be uncertain about a fact initially but then become more certain of it with the help of your questioning. If so, record this transition by saying, "The client was first unsure of who else was present, but then said she was fairly certain that Fred was there."

Explain to the client right at the beginning how critical it is for you to obtain accurate information. Encourage the client to say "I'm not sure" when that's the case. It is important that the client be relaxed and unthreatened. It would not be wise for you to keep asking, "Are you sure?" following every fact the client tells you. Yet you must find out where on the spectrum of certainty a fact falls. Temper your probe with tact and sensitivity.

## Verification Details

The fact that the client tells you something happened is *some* evidence that it happened. Verification data is evidence that supports what the client has said. Verification data is *additional* evidence to support the client. Always pursue such verification details. Ask yourself how you would establish the truth of what the client has said if the client suddenly disappeared and you had to rely exclusively on other sources. Inquire about documents (such as letters or check stubs) that support the client's statements. Inquire about other people who might be available to testify to the same subject. Ask the client questions that will lead you to such verification details. This approach does not mean that you do not trust the client, or that you think the client is lying. It is simply a good practice to view a fact from many perspectives. You are always seeking the strongest case possible. This calls for questioning about verification details.

## Analogies

Some facts that you are particularizing (e.g., "the pain was unbearable"; "I was careful"; "it looked awful"; "I was scared") are difficult to pin down. In the interview, you should ask the client to explain such statements. Sometimes it is helpful to ask the client to use analogies to describe what is meant. An analogy is simply explaining something by comparing it to something else. For example, you ask the client:

What would you compare it to?

Was it similar to anything you have ever seen before?

Have you observed anyone else do the same thing?

Have you ever been in a similar situation?

Did it feel like a dentist's drill?

You ask the client to compare the fact to something else. Then you ask about the similarities and differences. Through a series of directed questions you are encouraging the client to analogize the fact he or she is describing to some other fact. This is done in a further attempt to obtain as comprehensive a picture as possible of what the client is saying.

## Miscellaneous Details

Here you simply ask about any details that were not covered in the previous categories of questions. Include questions on anything else that might help in particularizing the fact under examination.

---

### ■ ASSIGNMENT 8.1

In this assignment, FP will be role-played in class. One student will be selected to play the role of the client and another, the role of the paralegal interviewer. The rest of the class will observe and fill out the FP Score Card on the interview.

*Instructions to Interviewer.* You will not be conducting a complete interview from beginning to end. You will be trying to particularize a certain fact that's given to you. Go through the eight categories of FP described above. Use any order of questioning that you want. Probe for comprehensiveness. Your instructor will select one of the following facts, which will be used as the basis of the interview:

**(a)** "I was hit in the jaw by Mary."

**(b)** "He neglects his children."

**(c)** "I have not been promoted because I am a woman."

Your opening question to the client will be, "What happened?" The client will make one of the three statements above. You then use the process of FP to particularize this statement.

*Instructions to Client.* The interviewer will ask you what happened. Simply make one of the three statements above as selected by the instructor. Then the interviewer will ask you a large number of questions about the statements. Make up the answers—ad lib your responses. Do not, however, volunteer any information. Answer only the questions asked.

*Instructions to Class.* Observe the interview. Use the following score card to assess how well you think the interviewer particularized the fact.

### FP SCORE CARD

| Precision in obtaining time details | 5 4 3 2 1 | Sloppiness in obtaining time details |
| Precision in obtaining place details | 5 4 3 2 1 | Sloppiness in obtaining place details |
| Precision in obtaining details on other participants | 5 4 3 2 1 | Sloppiness in obtaining details on other participants |
| Precision in finding out where the client's statements fall on the spectrum of certainty | 5 4 3 2 1 | Sloppiness in finding out where the client's statements fall on the spectrum of certainty |
| Precision in seeking verification details | 5 4 3 2 1 | Sloppiness in seeking verification details |
| Effectiveness in using analogies to obtain greater detail | 5 4 3 2 1 | Ineffectiveness in using analogies to obtain greater detail |
| Precision in obtaining miscellaneous details | 5 4 3 2 1 | Sloppiness in obtaining miscellaneous details |

Following the interview, put a check on the appropriate number for each of the above categories of assessment. A "5" score means you thought the interview was very precise or effective in fulfilling the goal of FP. A "1" score means the opposite. Also, make notes of questions that you think the interviewer should have asked. These questions, and your scores, will be discussed in class after the interview.

## Common Sense

Common sense is another major guide to determining what questions to ask, achieving comprehensiveness, and giving the interview a focus. Though law is full of legalisms and technicalities, good judgment and common sense are still at the core of the practice of law. It is common sense, for example, to organize an interview by having the client tell the relevant events chronologically in the form of a story with a beginning, middle, and end. It is common sense to follow up on a topic the client mentions with further questioning even though you had not anticipated the topic. If the client says something you do not understand, common sense dictates that you ask what the client means before continuing with the interview. At times, it may be common sense to stop the interview for a moment to obtain further guidance from your supervisor.

## Flexibility

In the previous discussion, the importance of flexibility was mentioned a number of times. You must be prepared to expect the unexpected and you must be relaxed. Although you lead the interview and give it direction, you must be ready to go where the interview takes you. It would be potentially disastrous for you to block out topics that arise simply because they were not part of your game plan in conducting the interview or are not on your checklist. As with so many areas of the law, you may not know what you are looking for until you find it. In interviewing a client about incorporating a business, for example, you may stumble across a lead from something the client says that could involve fraud or criminal prosecution on a matter unrelated to the incorporation. Don't block this out. Pursue what appears to be reasonably related to the law office's relationship with the client. Check with your supervisor. Again, let common sense be your guide. Flexibility is one of the foundations of common sense.

---

### ■ ASSIGNMENT 8.2

Interview a classmate for the purpose of writing his or her resume. Assume that this person wants to work for a law firm eventually. After you conduct the interview, write the resume. It should include the following categories of information:

- *Basic data* (name, address, phone, marital status, etc.)
- *Career objective* (what does the person hope to be doing—hope to be accomplishing—in the immediate future? five years from now?)
- *Education* (begin with current school and work back, including names of schools, dates of attendance, degrees or certificates awarded, etc.)
- *Prior employment* (begin with most recent and work back, including names of employers, addresses, dates of employment, titles, responsibilities, etc.)
- *Community activities* (volunteer work, etc.)

The trouble with most resumes in that they focus only on events and rarely spend enough space listing specific skills and accomplishments. To identify them, you need to ask questions such as:

- Have you ever supervised other people? How many? To do what tasks?
- Have you had responsibility for handling someone else's money?
- Have you ever had to write a budget?
- Have you ever had the responsibility of evaluating someone else?
- Have you ever written a proposal?
- What kind of reports have you written?
- What work products have resulted from your previous employment and schooling? For instance, have you ever drafted a complaint? In what area of the law and under what circumstances? Have you done any legal research? On what specific issues and under what circumstances?
- Have you ever written a speech and delivered it?
- Have you ever run for any elective office in a club or other organization?
- Etc.

Ask questions such as these to try to identify items that should be considered for the resume. When someone reads the resume, what impression would they get of the individual? A self-starter? Someone who can act without constant supervision? An unstable person who moves from job to job to job? A doer? A person with enthusiasm? A live person or a collection of statistics? When you are conducting the interview, be sure to bring out facts that will enable you to place the person in a positive light in the resume.

There is no length limitation to the resume you prepare after the interview. Your goal is to particularize the person you are interviewing. (A resume that is actually used in a job search will have to be relatively brief. See Chapter 2.)

Type the resume and make at least one photocopy. Give the copy to the person you interviewed. Ask that person to read the resume and give it *as many* of the following ratings as he or she feels are applicable:

Rating I:    The resume describes me to a "T."

Rating II:   I would definitely hire me on the basis of this resume!

Rating III:  The resume is substantially accurate, but there are some factual errors in it.

Rating IV:   The facts in the resume are fairly accurate, but it's rather flat; it doesn't describe me as a live person.

Rating V:    I hardly recognized myself.

Rating VI:   The person described in this resume is impersonating me!

Rating VII:  Nice try, but. . . .

Before you hand the resume in to the teacher, indicate on the top of the front page the rating(s) your interviewee gave the resume.

 Section D. What Does the Client Want?

There are a number of assumptions that can be made about many clients:

- They are not sure what they want.
- They are not aware of what legal and nonlegal options are available to help solve the problem that exists.
- The problem probably involves other legal problems about which the client is unaware and about which even you may be unaware at the outset.

Suppose that a client walks into the office and says "I want a divorce." The following observations *might* be possible about the client:

- The client has an incorrect understanding of what a divorce is.
- The client says she wants a divorce because she thinks that this is the only legal remedy available to solve her problem.
- If the client knew that other remedies existed (e.g., annulment, judicial separation, a support order) she would consider these options.
- What the client is really troubled about is the fact that her husband beats the kids; a divorce is the only way she thinks she can stop it.
- The client does not want a divorce. She is being pressured by her husband to institute divorce proceedings. He threatened her with violence if she refuses.
- The client consciously or unconsciously wants and needs an opportunity to tell someone how badly the world is treating her, and if given this opportunity, she may not want to terminate the marriage.
- If the client knew that marriage counseling was available in the community, she would consider using it before taking the drastic step of going to a law office for a divorce.

If any of these observations is correct, think of how damaging it would be for someone in the law office to take out the standard divorce forms and quickly fill them out immediately after the client says, "I want a divorce." This response would not be appropriate without first probing beneath the statement to determine what in fact is on the client's mind. Some clients who speak only of divorces and separation agreements are receptive to and even anxious for reconciliation. The danger exists that the client might be steered in the direction of divorce because no other options are presented to her or because no one takes the time to help her express the ideas, intentions, and desires that are lurking beneath the otherwise clear statement, "I want a divorce."

This is not to say that you must psychoanalyze every client or that you must always distrust what the client tells you initially. It is rather a recognition of the fact that *most people are confused about the law and make requests based on misinformation about what courses of action are available to solve problems.* Common sense tells us to avoid taking all statements at face value. People under emotional distress need to be treated with sensitivity. In view of the emotions involved and the sometimes complicated nature of the law, we should not expect them to express their intentions with clarity all the time.

---

### ■ ASSIGNMENT 8.3

A client walks into the office where you work and makes the statements that follow. What areas do you think it would be reasonable to probe to determine if the statement is an accurate reflection of what the client wants? What misunderstandings do you think the client might have? What further questions should you ask to be sure that you have identified what the client wants?

(a) "I want to commit my husband to a mental institution."

(b) "I can't control my teenage son anymore. I want him placed in a juvenile home."

(c) "I want to put my baby daughter up for adoption."

(d) "I want to dissolve my business."

(e) "I want to sell my house."

(f) "I'm fed up with that department store. I want to sue the store so that it goes out of business."

---

## ■ Section E. Human Relations and Communication Skills in Interviewing

---

### ■ ASSIGNMENT 8.4

Write down your answers to the following questions. When you have finished this chapter, come back to what you have written and ask yourself whether your perspective has changed.

(a) List some of the times you have interviewed someone. List some of the times you have been interviewed by someone.

(b) Describe what you feel are the central ingredients of a good interview in any setting.

(c) Describe a bad interview. From your experience, what are some of the worst mistakes an interviewer can make?

(d) Describe what you think are some of your strong and weak points as an interviewer.

---

Thus far our main emphasis has been on obtaining the facts. We now pursue this theme in the broader context of human relations and communications skills. This will raise some basic questions about who you are, how you view other people, how you are perceived by others, how you handle sensitive problems in the lives of others, etc.

Interviewing is a reflection of your personality. There are no absolute answers to interviewing problems; there is no such thing as the "perfect interview." There is such a thing, however, as an interview that works, that achieves its purpose. We need to find out what works in a legal interview.

In the following assignment, you will observe an interview role-played in class. After watching this interview, you will be asked to deduce some principles of communication involved in interviewing.

---

### ■ ASSIGNMENT 8.5

In this assignment, two students will role-play a legal interview in front of the class. The rest of the class will observe the interview and comment on it.

*Instructions to Client.* You will role-play the part of a client. A month ago you sprained your back while lifting a computer and carrying it from one room to another. You are an accountant. When you came into work that day you found the computer on your desk. It did not belong there and you did not know how it got there. You decided to move it to another desk. That was when you sprained your back.

You have come to the law office for legal advice. You have already seen an attorney in this office who has agreed to take your case. An interviewer has been assigned to conduct an interview with you to obtain a complete picture of what happened. This interview will now be role-played in front of the class.

The basic facts involve the computer, as indicated above. You can make up all other facts to answer the questions that will be put to you by the interviewer. Make up the name of the company for which you work, make up the details surrounding the accident, etc. You can create *any* set of facts as long as your answers are reasonably consistent with the basic facts given to you above.

*Instructions to Interviewer.* You will play the role of the interviewer in the case involving the sprained back. You are a paralegal in the office. All you know about the case thus far is that the office has agreed to represent the client and you have been assigned to interview the client for detailed information about the client and about the accident. Start off by introducing yourself and stating the purpose of the interview. Then proceed to the questions that you need to ask.

You do not need to know any law in order to conduct the interview. Let common sense be your guide. To compile a comprehensive picture of the facts as this client is able to convey them, what questions would you ask? Consult the material on fact particularization (FP) as you prepare and formulate questions.

The class will observe you in order to assess the manner and content of the interview. A good deal of constructive criticism may develop from the class discussion. As you listen to the criticism, try to be as objective as you can. It is difficult to conduct a comprehensive interview and probably impossible to conduct one flawlessly. For every question that you ask, there may be twenty observations on how you could have asked it differently. Hence, try not to take the comments personally.

*Instructions to Class.* You will be watching the interview involving the sprained back. You have two tasks:

1. Fill out a LICS (Legal Interview Communications Score) form. After the interview, take a moment to score the interview according to the LICS form that follows. The teacher will ask you to state the total score you gave the interview or to submit this score to someone who will calculate the average score from all students' scores.

2. Identify as many dos and don'ts of interviewing as you can. If you were writing a law office manual on *How to Interview,* what would you include? What guidance would you give an interviewer on taking notes during the interview, asking follow-up questions, maintaining eye contact with the client, etc.? After you observe the interview, discuss specific suggestions on what an interviewer should or should not do. Ideas will come to mind while you are filling out the LICS form. Following

---

## Legal Interviewing Communications Score (LICS)

**How to Score:** You will be observing the role-playing of a legal interview and evaluating the interviewer on a 100-point scale. These 100 points will be earned in the four categories listed below. The score is not based on scientific data. It is a rough approximation of someone's oral communication skills in a legal interview. The interpretation of a score is as follows:

90–100 Points: Outstanding Interviewer
80–89 Points: Good Interviewer
60–79 Points: Fair Interviewer
0–59 Points: A Lot More Work Needs to Be Done

(Of course, the LICS does *not* assess the interviewer's ability to *write* an intake memorandum of law for the file. See Section B of this chapter.)

---

### Category I: Factual Detail

On a scale of 0–80, how would you score the interviewer's performance in asking enough questions to obtain factual comprehensiveness? How well was FP performed?
(An 80 score means the interviewer was extremely sensitive to detail in his or her questions. A 0 score means that the interviewer stayed with the surface facts, with little or no probing for the who-what-where-why-when-how details. The more facts you think the interviewer did *not* obtain, the lower the score should be.)

**Category I Score:** _____

### Category II: Control

On a scale of 0–10 how would you score the interviewer's performance in controlling the interview and in giving it direction?
(A 10 score means the interviewer demonstrated an excellent sense of control and direction in terms of knowing what his or her objectives were while asking the questions and in using the interview to meet those objectives. A 0 score means the interviewer rambled from question to question or let the client ramble from topic to topic.)

**Category II Score:** _____

### Category III: Earning the Confidence of the Client

On a scale of 0–5 how would you score the interviewer's performance in gaining the trust of the client and in setting him or her at ease?
(A 5 score means the interviewer appeared to do an excellent job of gaining the trust and confidence of the client. A 0 score means the client seemed to be suspicious of the interviewer and probably doubted his or her professional competence. The more the interviewer made the client feel that he or she was genuinely concerned about the client, the higher the score. The more the client obtained the impression that the interviewer was "just doing a job," the lower the score.)

**Category III Score:** _____

### Category IV: Role Identification

On a scale of 0–5 how well did the interviewer explain his or her role and the purpose of the interview?
(A 5 score means the interviewer took the time to explain clearly what his or her job was in the office and what he or she hoped to accomplish in the interview. A 0 score means either that the interviewer gave no explanation at all or mumbled through an explanation without being sensitive to whether the client understood.)

**Category IV Score:** _____

**Total Score:** _____

the class discussion on the dos and don'ts of interviewing, your teacher may ask you to make a written list of these dos and don'ts to hand in later. Also include thoughts that come to you after class.

After observing an interview, discussing it in class, and thinking about it, your class might collect all the written dos and don'ts and consolidate them into a manual of legal interviewing principles that reflects the best thinking of your class.

---

## ■ ASSIGNMENT 8.6

In your area there are probably many television programs in which some form of interviewing takes place—news programs, talk shows, etc. The instructor will select a program to be aired within the next few days. It should be a program that everyone in the class will be able to watch. Take notes on the communications skills of the interviewer for the program. Make comments on the following topics:

- *The setting of the interview*. How did it facilitate or detract from communication?
- *Focus*. What techniques or mannerisms of the interviewer facilitated or detracted from the interview's focus or direction?
- *Listening*. Was the interviewer a good listener? Explain.
- *Style of questioning*. How would you characterize the interviewer's style?
- *Self-image*. What image was the interviewer trying to project of himself or herself? Why? Did it work? Why or why not?
- *Achieving the purpose of the interview*. What purpose do you think the interviewer had in conducting the interview? Was it achieved? Why or why not?
- *Handling resistance*. Did the person being interviewed appear to resist any of the questions? If so, how was this handled by the interviewer? How should it have been handled?
- Make a list of dos and don'ts of interviewing that you deduced from watching the interview.

Make a copy of your comments and send it to the person who conducted the television program along with an explanation of this class assignment interview. If you receive a reply, share it with the class.

---

### Communications Checklist
### for Legal Interviewing

Purpose: There are no absolute rules on how to interview. There are, however, a number of considerations that you should have in mind while interviewing. The following questions are designed to increase your sensitivity about the manner in which an interview is conducted. *The more aware an interviewer is of the factors that might affect communication, the greater the likelihood that an effective interview will result.* These factors are posed below as questions or as a communications checklist. The checklist items are not mutually exclusive. Nor is there universal agreement on how some of these questions should be answered.

_____ Do I fully understand the purpose of this interview? Do I know what my supervisor wants me to accomplish?

_____ How do I prepare for this interview? From an office manual checklist? By talking with others who have conducted similar interviews in the past? Trial and error?

_____ Do I want to conduct this interview? Do I view this interview as my thousandth? Do I wish someone else would do this interview? Do I feel that I am doing the office a favor in conducting the interview? Do I feel that I am doing the client a favor? Has the day long passed when I view each interview as a potential learning experience?

_____ Where should the interview be conducted? In my office? At the client's home or place of work? Would it make any difference?

_____ How am I dressed? Do I dress to suit *my* personal taste? Have I thought about the impact my clothes and appearance may have on the client and on the effectiveness of the interview? Am I secure enough to ask the opinion of a colleague? How could I encourage a colleague to give me an honest opinion on how I come across to people?

_____ Do I have enough time to conduct this interview? If not, on whom will I take out my frustration?

_____ How should I introduce myself to the client? I understand my title and everyone else in the law office understands my title. Does this automatically mean that the client will understand my title? Should I assume that the client won't care? Does the client think I am an attorney? Does the client think that I am experienced and competent in this kind of case? After the interview, if the client were asked by a friend or relative who I was, what would the client say other than "someone who works in the office"? To what extent does the client need to know my job description and background?

_____ How is my office arranged? Professionally? Casually? How private is the interview? Can anyone overhear my conversation with the client?

_____ Do I know what client confidentiality means? Do I have a clear understanding of when confidentiality is violated? Do I appreciate the gray areas? Does the client understand his or her confidentiality rights? Should I make specific assurances to the client about confidentiality?

_____ Do I know what legal advice is? Do I know how to answer questions that directly or indirectly ask me for legal advice?

_____ Do I use a questionnaire in the interview? If so, do I know why each question is on the questionnaire? How closely do I follow the questionnaire? Do I know when I can deviate from it? Is it only a guide or is it something that I must follow rigorously?

_____ What should I say, if anything, to the client about the questionnaire?

_____ Do I take notes on what the client says? If so, what do I say to the client, if anything, about the fact that I am taking notes?

_____ How extensive are my notes? What am I doing to increase the speed of my note-taking?

_____ In answering questions, clients are certain about some facts, but uncertain about others. Do I know how to take notes about *both* kinds of answers? Do I fall into the trap of taking notes on only concrete answers of the client? Do I understand the importance of articulating on paper (in my client intake memo) when the client *thinks* something happened, or *probably* did something on a given date?

_____ How do I help the client recall factual details?

_____ How do I help the client unravel complicated facts so that the "story" of the case can be told coherently—for instance, chronologically?

_____ Do I know how to *particularize* a fact by asking all the appropriate who-what-where-why-when-how questions concerning the fact? Am I scrupulous about dates, places, verification details, etc.?

_____ Do I ask follow-up questions to help the client give more specific factual detail? Or do I let the interview wander from topic to topic, question to question, answer to answer?

_____ When the client answers a question by saying, "I'm not sure," or "maybe," do I ask questions designed to help the client remember with greater specificity? (If no greater specificity is possible, see the standard above on the importance of stating when the client was ambiguous or unsure about a fact.)

_____ Do I make the distinction between facts that establish what happened and facts that help verify someone's version of what happened? Do I ask questions that elicit both kinds of facts?

_____ Is the client answering my questions? If not, is it due to the manner in which I am asking the questions?

_____ Am I condescending to the client? Do I know when I am condescending?

_____ Do I talk distinctly?

_____ Do I use words the client cannot understand, such as legal jargon or terms of art? Since most people do not want to admit that they don't understand a word or phrase, how do I know whether the client understands everything I am saying?

_____ Interviewers have a mental picture or at least a general idea of the topic of the interview, such as a car accident. What do I do when something comes up during the interview that does not fall into the pigeonhole of this mental picture or general idea? Do I block it out of my mind? How do I know that I *don't* block it out?

_____ Have I made the client feel welcome?

_____ Am I aware of the impact and importance of attentive listening? Am I one of the few attentive listeners around?

_____ Do I build the client's ego? Do I understand that ego building is not achieved merely by praising someone?

_____ Am I offended if the client does not build my ego? Am I aware of my ego needs in an interview?

_____ Am I willing to say to the client, "I don't know"?

_____ How do I handle the client's embarrassment over one of my questions?

_____ How do I handle my own embarrassment over one of my questions or over one of the client's answers? Am I aware of the embarrassment?

_____ How do I handle the client's irritation over one of my questions?

_____ How do I handle my own irritation over an answer to one of my questions? Am I aware of the irritation?

_____ How do I handle a client who is telling me something I do not believe?

_____ When I have personal knowledge of some aspect of what the client is saying, do I record the client's perspective or my own? Do I know the difference?

_____ When, if ever, should I role-play with the client? (For example, if I am trying to help the client recall a conversation, I might take the role of the other party in the conversation to see if it aids recollection.)

_____ Have I determined what the client wants? Do I know what his or her expectations are?

_____ At the conclusion of the interview, have I made it clear to the client what I will do, what the office will do, and what the client is to do as the next step?

_____ Am I a good interviewer? How do I know? Who has evaluated me? How can I obtain feedback on the quality of my interviewing skill? Who is around whom I respect enough to give me this feedback? How can I approach this person? For 99% of us, intensive criticism is unsettling and threatening to us—even if it is constructive. What makes me think that I fall into the 1% category?

## ▉ Section F. Analysis of a Legal Interview

What follows is an analysis of a hypothetical interview involving Sam Donnelly, a senior citizen who walks into a law office seeking legal assistance. He will be interviewed by Jane Collins, a paralegal in the office. We will assume that her attorney–supervisor has instructed her to find out as much as possible about his problem. Since the office is government funded, the question of fees will not be involved. In analyzing this interview, our central concern will be the techniques or principles of communication that can be effective in interviewing.

**[Setting: There is a knock at Jane Collins' door. She gets up from her chair, goes over to the door, opens it, and says to the man facing her (as she extends her hand for a handshake):]**

Paralegal: *Hello, my name is Jane Collins. Won't you come in?*

Suppose that the paralegal did not go to the door to greet the client, and instead merely called from her chair, "Come in," in a loud voice. Do you think that it makes any difference whether the interviewer walks over to the client or not? When an individual walks with someone into a room, is the individual saying "come share my room with me"? If, on the other hand, the individual is seated at her desk and calls the visitor in, is the message to the visitor likely to be: "This is my room; I am in control of it; you may enter"? Consciously or unconsciously, the interviewer may want to project herself as a figure of authority to the client.

The interviewer cannot assume that the client will approve of and be receptive to everything the interviewer does simply because the interviewer is trying to help. It may be more appropriate to assume that the client is confused about who the interviewer is, and therefore will be somewhat suspicious of what the interviewer does until trust has been established.

**Principle: The interviewer has the responsibility of building a relationship of trust with the client.**

Studies have shown that clients rate "evidence of concern" as being even more significant than the results they obtain from a law office.[1] Furthermore, for the relationship between office personnel and the client to work, the client must feel that the office has a genuine interest in the client as a person.

Paralegal: *Let me take your coat for you. Won't you have a seat? [The paralegal points the client toward a chair that is at the opposite end of the desk where the paralegal sits. They face each other.]*

Note the seating arrangement the paralegal selects as illustrated in diagram A. "I" stands for interviewer and "C" stands for client.

Diagram A

---

[1]H. Freeman & H. Weihofen, *Clinical Law Training, Interviewing and Counseling: Text and Cases,* 13 (1972).

A number of other seating arrangements could have been used:

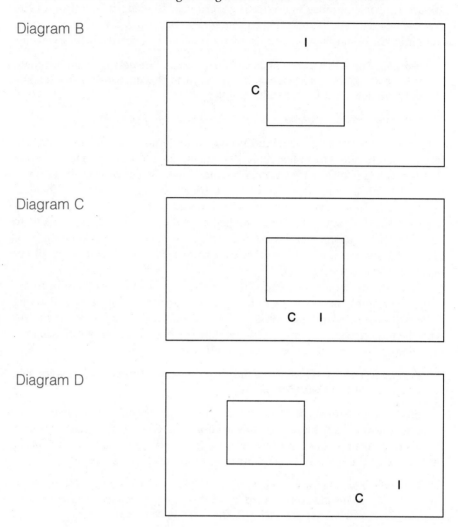

Diagram B

Diagram C

Diagram D

The chairs can be arranged so that the interviewer and the client sit at op-posite ends of a desk (diagram A), diagonally across a desk (diagram B), at the same end of a desk (diagram C), or at another end of the room away from the desk altogether (diagram D). Seating arrangements are usually made at the con-venience of the "owner" of the office. Rarely is enough thought given to how a particular arrangement may help or hurt the flow of communication. Some-times the seating arrangement will create an austere and official atmosphere; other settings may be close and warm.

**Principle: Select a seating arrangement that will maximize communication.**

Of the four seating arrangements diagrammed above, which do you think would be most effective? Which would you feel most comfortable with? Which do you think the client would be most comfortable with? A number of factors can help you answer these questions. First, there is probably no single seating arrangement that will be perfect for all situations. The interviewer must be flex-ible enough to experiment with different arrangements. Will you be taking notes while interviewing? If so, do you want the client to be able to see what you are writing? Would this make him more at ease? If so, which arrangements would facilitate this? Do you want to project yourself as an authority figure? Do you, on the other hand, want the client to feel closer to you and not to have the impression that you are hiding behind a desk? Do you think it would ever be wise to change a seating arrangement in the middle of an interview? If a particular arrangement is used for the initial interview, do you think a different arrangement might ever be appropriate for follow-up interviews with the same client? When the client lifts his head, do you want him to be looking straight at you (diagram A) or do you think that it might be more comfortable for him to be able to face his head in other directions (diagram B) without appearing to scatter his attention?[2]

Of course, an office is much more than an arrangement of desks and chairs. Describe the potential benefits or disadvantages of the following:

1. Numerous posters on the wall contain political slogans
2. A half-dozen citations, certificates, and degrees are on the wall
3. The desk is cluttered with papers and books
4. The room is completely bare except for two chairs and a desk
5. The interviewer is dressed very casually
6. The interviewer is wearing a formal three-piece suit
7. The interviewer is smoking, eating lunch, or drinking coffee
8. The interviewer has no ashtray in the room
9. A "Please don't smoke" sign is on the wall
10. An open case file of another client is on the interviewer's desk
11. The secretary keeps knocking on the door or calling the paralegal on the phone for emergencies that require immediate attention
12. The paralegal does not have her own office and talks to the client with secretaries or other personnel around

Generally speaking, room settings that are extreme should always be avoided. Furthermore, the paralegal must be scrupulous in preserving the *confidentiality* of a client's case. Item 10 is therefore totally inappropriate. What about item 12?

**Principle: Always be sensitive to the client's right to confidentiality.**

Client: *It's a little hard getting around lately.*
Paralegal: *What do you mean?*
Client: *Oh, I just ache all over, you know, and on a hot day like this . . . my asthma gets up and, you know, I can hardly breathe sometimes. I'm sorry. I'm just a little out of breath coming up the stairs and all.*
Paralegal: *Well, just take your time and relax a bit.*
Client: *It's these bus drivers . . . I don't have a car; I lost it. It's not easy to get around . . . [Pause] Well, I feel a little better now.*
Paralegal: *Uh-huh.*
Client: *My wife is sick, and me, I'm not feeling too good. I've been sick going on three years. It goes back about eight or nine years. The last two or three years, I honestly haven't been able to do anything.*
Paralegal: *Sir, I didn't get your name.*
Client: *Donnelly, Sam Donnelly, the wife's name is Sarah.*

---

[2]See also White, *Architectural Suggestions for a Law Office Building,* 9 Practical Lawyer 66 (No. 8, 1956).

In this sequence, it's perhaps more significant to note what the paralegal did *not* say than what she did say. It may have been very tempting for the paralegal to have begun by asking the client, "What's the problem?" as soon as he sat down. Instead, the paralegal allowed the client to talk about what was on *his* mind. The interview did not begin by the paralegal directing the course of the interview through questions or comments. There are a number of benefits to this approach. First, the client is given an opportunity to relax; he is not immediately pressured by questions. Second, the message that comes across is that the paralegal is interested in the client as a person. The client obviously wants someone to listen to his story of how the world is mistreating him. He's sick; he can't get around, etc. Avoid dismissing such talk as either irrelevant to the interview or as typically senile. Much more sensitivity is required. Apparently this client is old and without substantial means. Perhaps to him the most significant information about his life is that he is old and sick. It is an extremely important event to him to be able to share this with someone else and to have his story listened to with concern. Third, by letting the client talk, indeed, by letting him ramble on a bit, the paralegal may be able to collect information not as easily obtained by pointed questioning at the outset.

There are, of course, limitations in this approach. The paralegal does not have all day to interview this client. Other tasks may be waiting to be done. In the interview under analysis, however, the exchange was relatively short; it took a matter of seconds before the paralegal began to direct the attention of the client to such basic data as his name. It is not always easy to break off the conversation in this way. The interruption must be handled with tact.

> **Principle: The interviewer should consider the advantages of permitting the client to say what is on his mind at the outset instead of beginning with a series of questions.**

If the client has nothing to say at the outset, then of course the paralegal will have to take the initiative with questions such as, "How are you today?" "Is there anything I can help you with?" or "I understand you've come to this office about a legal matter."

Soon after the interview begins, the paralegal should be taking notes on what the client is saying. The notes should be extensive. The paralegal should say something about the notes to the client such as, "I hope you don't mind if I make a few notes on what you say so that I don't forget anything." This should set the client's mind at ease about her writing. The client will probably respect the paralegal for this thoroughness and consideration in explaining the writing to him. In addition to aiding the paralegal's memory, the notes serve another important function: recordkeeping. In a law office, every case must be adequately documented. Personnel other than the paralegal will probably be working on the case at many stages. A well-kept case record can save a great deal of time and ensure accuracy. After the interview, the paralegal should take the time to compose a coherent report (intake memo) on the interview from her notes.

> **Principle: The interviewer should take notes and explain to the client why she is doing so.**

The paralegal is always looking for clues (or flags) of potential legal problems. From the brief exchange between the paralegal and Mr. Donnelly, a number of such problems may have surfaced. At some point in the interview, the paralegal must ask questions about them if the client does not volunteer further information. Note that the client may not know which of his problems are legal and which are not. He may have come in with one problem on his mind but reveal a number of others as he speaks. Here again we see the value of letting the client talk. This approach is much more beneficial than saying to the client, "Tell me all your legal problems." It is the job of the interviewer to assist the client in identifying such problems. What are some of his potential legal problems that require further inquiry?

- He lost his car. Was it stolen or repossessed?
- He is sick. Is he getting proper medical attention? Is he receiving all the public medical services to which he is entitled?
- His wife is sick; same questions as to her.
- Is there an emergency that requires immediate attention?

The last question is essential. Very early in the interview, the paralegal must determine whether a crisis exists with respect to such matters as health or housing. If so, then the office must act immediately either through legal proceedings or by helping the client obtain government emergency social services.

> **Principle: The interviewer is always alert to the flags indicating potential legal problems.**

Paralegal: *Mr. Donnelly, I am a paralegal . . .*
Client: *A what?*
Paralegal: *A paralegal. I am not an attorney. My job is to get some preliminary information so that when you do see a lawyer, he'll be able to help you a lot more quickly.*

Do you think that the client understands who Jane Collins is? If he were asked what a paralegal is, what do you think he would answer? What obligation does the interviewer have, if any, to be sure that the client knows whom he is talking to before asking him for personal information?

> **Principle: It should be made absolutely clear to the client that the paralegal is not an attorney.**

Client: *I don't have any money, and I went to these welfare people and they won't put me on the program. They say I'm not sick enough. And I haven't been able to do a solid day's work in, oh, two and a half years now. Every once in a while I do a little bit and I have to lay down for hours. Go to the doctor a couple times a month. I've been to the hospital two or three times. So, you know, I don't really know how or what you can do about this. I really don't. I don't know what to do. My wife has been sick too.*
Paralegal: *Everything's been hitting you at once, it seems.*

Note again how the client's story is beginning to unfold. The paralegal learns for the first time that Mr. Donnelly has been to a welfare department and has been told that he does not qualify for a program because he is not sick enough. Most assuredly, this information should go into the paralegal's notes for further questioning. Clients sometimes tell their stories piecemeal rather than in a coherent fashion. The job of the interviewer is to put these pieces together.

How would you characterize the paralegal's statement that, "Everything's been hitting you at once, it seems"? Patronizing? Sympathetic? Unprofessional? What effect do you think it had on the client? Do you think that, with this statement, the paralegal is taking sides? Suppose the paralegal said, "It sounds like the government is really trying to do you in," or "Well, of course, you know, Mr. Donnelly, the government is made up of a large group of people and it's almost impossible for them to please everyone." Would these be appropriate opinions for the paralegal to express, if she believes either of them? Shouldn't she be honest about her feelings?

Generally, it is more appropriate for the paralegal to be *neutral* in the expression of personal opinions. It is not the paralegal's job to comment on the evils of government or to be apologetic about government. This does not mean, however, that she should always refrain from expressing personal feelings about subjects. If the client is telling a horror story about his life, it would be only natural for the paralegal to react with surprise or dismay. This is fine as long as the paralegal does not lose perspective and objectivity in trying to gather all the facts.

> **Principle: The interviewer should exercise self-restraint in the expression of personal opinions or feelings. Remain neutral unless it would be awkward and unnatural not to express oneself in the context of the interview.**

It is all too tempting for a paralegal to become overly involved in the emotional aspects of assisting people with legal problems. The paralegal must retain composure in a milieu where tempers can run high and where facts can change rapidly. The best legal service can be provided by someone with a cool head. Again, this does not necessarily mean that the paralegal cannot identify with the very real frustrations and problems of the client. Objectivity is not inconsistent with empathy.

Paralegal: *Mr. Donnelly, before we get down to the specifics of your case, I need to ask you a few questions. As you may know, this office does not charge clients for its services as long as the client lives within the area served by this office and does not have income above a certain level. We provide free service to low-income clients.*

Client: *Well, I'll tell you, I think I could pass the test, yes ma'am! I have a little nest egg, but I haven't been able to work over the years . . .*

Paralegal: *How much do you have left?*

Client: *I have about $500, $600 in the bank.*

Paralegal: *Uh-huh.*

Client: *But I'll tell you, that's about to be eaten up. I don't have a car. It's really hard to get around on the bus. Other than that, the wife's got a little bit of jewelry, a wedding ring, stuff like that. And that's about it.*

Paralegal: *Do you rent an apartment?*

Client: *Yes, we do.*

Paralegal: *What about Social Security. Do you receive any income there?*

Client: *Well, we get a little bit of Social Security.*

Paralegal: *How much is that?*

Client: *$305 a month. I can't live on that. My wife is taking work into the house like . . . She's been sick lately. We don't have the money coming in.*

Paralegal: *Do you have any children?*

Client: *No.*

Paralegal: *Okay, Let me ask you a couple of other questions. I want to make sure that I have the street right. You want to give that to me?*

Client: *Delores, 1429 Delores Street, Apartment 7B.*

Paralegal: *What about a phone? Still have it?*

Client: *Yes. The number is 824-8027.*

Paralegal: *824-8027. Fine. Well, it's pretty clear that you're eligible for our services.*

Client: *Very good, I sure do need it.*

Paralegal: *Okay, I've got some other questions that I want to ask you, and if there are things that you want to say, just stop me. If you have any questions, just stop me and ask.*

Client: *Okay.*

The paralegal was correct in stating that government-funded legal service offices do not charge clients for their services as long as they live within a designated geographical area and meet an income test. Regulations exist on how much income and assets a family can have in order to be eligible. The paralegal (or sometimes the receptionist) has the job of determining eligibility based on office charts.

Matters of income and wealth are intensely personal and must be approached with great delicacy. A rapid-fire series of questions such as, "Do you work?" "How much do you make?" "How much do you have in the bank?" "Do your relatives give you money?" can be very demoralizing. The common complaint against bureaucracy is the distance and impersonality with which it deals with the public. There is absolutely no reason why a law office must act in the same manner, no matter how busy it is.

Note that the client was somewhat hesitant about answering some of the questions and took every opportunity to demonstrate how poor he was. This is understandable. Perhaps he was not aware of the fact that the office was *not* actively looking for ways to disqualify people and that he will normally be taken at his word on eligibility. The dignity of the client requires that the interviewer not assume that everything said is a lie until proven otherwise.

> **Principle: Whenever an interviewer is asking a client for personal information, the client should clearly know why the information is needed. It should be taken with great sensitivity.**

Paralegal: *Mr. Donnelly, do you have any papers with you . . . anything that was sent to you concerning the problem that you want some help with?*

Client: *Yes, I brought it along here. I'm not sure I understand it all.*

Paralegal: *Okay, let's take a look at it.*

Now the paralegal has gotten through the preliminaries, and the central core of the interview is about to begin. There are a number of options available. Here the paralegal began concretely by asking a directed or close-ended question, one that required the client to focus on a very specific area—the legal papers. This is usually a good way to begin. The event that convinces clients that they should receive legal help is often the receipt of papers, either through the mail or delivered (served) to them in person. The papers may be confusing and upsetting.

> **Principle: As soon as possible, the interviewer should try to focus on concrete matters that are bothering the client.**

There are other ways that the paralegal could have proceeded. The paralegal could have asked, "What's the problem?" or "What's on your mind?" These are *open-ended questions.* They invite the client to respond in a wide variety of ways within the general confines of the question. Unlike the directed or *close-ended question,* the client is given control of the situation when asked an open-ended question. The danger of such a question is that the client will ramble on at great length, providing irrelevant as well as relevant data. It may be difficult for the paralegal to follow the answer. On the other hand, the client may have a need to vent his frustrations in this way. It is often important to "get it off his chest" and have someone listen to the complete story. Once the client has been allowed to experience this catharsis, he may be better able to relate to the more directed questions of the interviewer.

> **Principle: Interviewers must be sensitive to when clients are ready to answer directed questions.**

Another approach would be to refer back to something the client said earlier in the interview. For example, the paralegal could have said, "Mr. Donnelly, you said earlier that you applied for a program. Could you tell me a little bit more about that?" It can be reassuring for the client to know that the interviewer has been listening to what he has been saying and wants to know more.

One of the most effective ways to assist a client is to help him give the facts in sequence. "When did you become ill?" "How was the illness treated?" "When did you apply at the welfare department?" "What happened next?" The client has one large story to tell and perhaps a series of substories. Each story can be conceived of as a unit with a beginning, middle, and end. Helping the client reconstruct the stories chronologically will aid him in recalling details and will assist the paralegal in later organizing notes for the office file.

> Paralegal: *This is a letter from the welfare department denying your application for disability payments. When did you get this, Mr. Donnelly?*
> Client: *Oh, just a couple of weeks ago. They don't know what they are talking about! I can't understand why they are lying. They are not giving me the respect I am entitled to.*

Clients are very much inclined to think in terms of opinions, conclusions, and characterizations, as opposed to facts. A primary objective of the interviewer is to identify the *facts*. The client's interpretations of the facts may be important. However, the discussion must go beyond or behind the interpretations to cover the basic factual questions: who, when, where, how, etc.? When a client gives an opinion or a characterization of a fact or series of facts, the interviewer must ask the client to talk about what led to the interpretation. When and if a client becomes involved in an agency proceeding or a court hearing, the referee or judge will focus primarily on the facts that are alleged. Hence it is the job of the interviewer, as early as possible, to uncover as many underlying relevant facts as she can.

> **Principle: An interviewer should always encourage a client to spell out all the facts that led him to a particular conclusion or interpretation of what happened or is happening.**

The paralegal asked the client when he had received the letter. From the paralegal's study of welfare law, she knows that there are certain requirements that must be met whenever the welfare department makes decisions. One such requirement relates to the time span between the date of the decision and the date the client is notified of the decision. Another problem is the length of time the client has to appeal after receiving written notice of a decision.

> Paralegal: *Why did you wait two weeks to come in?*
> Client: [Mr. Donnelly slumps a little in his chair and looks around the room].
> Paralegal: *Well, it's not that important.*

Here the paralegal has asked a "why question," potentially calling into question either the client's motives or his competence. Luckily, the paralegal picked up on the inappropriateness of the question right away from the client's nonverbal cues (change in seating posture and apparent loss of attention). If the "why information" is important, it may be better to wait until later to try to obtain it. The paralegal must always be alert to *nonverbal communication*: mannerisms, gestures, silence, etc.

**Principle: The interviewer must be able to interpret nonverbal forms of communication.**

Paralegal: *Well, Mr. Donnelly, what I'd like to do is find out a little bit more about what happened. When did you first apply?*
Client: [A long silence].
Paralegal: *Mr. Donnelly, when did . . .*
Client: *I'm not sure.*

This particular client is very opinionated and may have taken offense at the interviewer's sudden shift from his (the client's) opinions ("they are lying") to the "why inquiry" and the cold facts ("When did you first apply?"). A client who is silent or who uses comments such as "I'm not sure" or "I don't know" may be on a different wavelength from the interviewer. The client often has his own agenda and expectations from the interview. Of course, the statement "I don't know" may mean nothing more than the absence of knowledge, just as silence may simply mean that the client needs more time or guidance to remember the facts. On the other hand, they could be a signal to the interviewer that communication is breaking down. There are a number of ways to deal with this. The interviewer could change the topic for the moment. She could ask the client if anything is troubling him. Or, she could simply proceed and try to play it by ear. In Mr. Donnelly's case, all that may be required is giving him the opportunity to express his opinions as often as possible. This is fine as long as they do not interfere with the fact-gathering function of the interview.

**Principle: Interviewers must be able to recognize client discomfort or non-cooperation and to deal with it flexibly.**

Paralegal: *Could I ask you what you mean when you say that they are not treating you with respect?*
Client: *I am disabled and they tell me I'm not. It's plain for anyone to see.*
Paralegal: *What we would have to do then, Mr. Donnelly, is to try to show that they are wrong.*
Client: *Yes, very wrong.*
Paralegal: *And to do it, what we need to do is get a complete picture of all the facts so that when we challenge them, we will be able to do it correctly. So, I'd like to start by your giving me an estimate (in days, weeks, or even months) of how long ago you first applied.*
Client: *I think it was a month ago. I have it written down at home.*

How would you analyze this exchange? What do you think the paralegal did that was or was not effective? Note the sensitivity with which the paralegal is questioning the client. The first time the paralegal asked him when he initially applied, she got no response. When she asked the same question less directly (in terms of estimates), she had greater success.

**Principle: The style or manner of questioning should flexibly fit the unfolding and often shifting context of the interview.**

Paralegal: *Looking at your letter here, I see that it was signed by Ralph Smith of the welfare department. After you leave, I will call him and ask him*

> *about things such as the date you applied. In addition, I'd appreciate it if you would call me when you get home and have had time to look at your own notes of when you applied. Could you do that?*
Client: *Yes, I will.*

Whenever practical, it is wise to have the client take some steps on his own behalf. This tends to ensure a sense of involvement and cooperation between office staff and client. It also is a step in the direction of accuracy, since the client is often in the best position to collect certain facts or perform certain tasks.

**Principle: Whenever practical, the interviewer should ask the client to perform tasks on his own to aid the office in handling the case.**

Exactly how much you can ask a client to do depends on the circumstances. Some clients may be willing and able to do a good deal, such as help locate a lost relative or make a written list of all known debts. Again, however, this aspect of legal services must be handled with care. The client cannot be asked to do the job of the paralegal or the attorney.

The paralegal told the client that she was going to call the welfare department. The client should be told what steps the office proposes on his behalf. A client needs to know what action will be taken.

**Principle: As often as possible, the concrete steps the office proposes to take on behalf of the client should be explained to the client.**

Paralegal: *Time and again, here in the office, we have clients who are unsure about such basic things as dates, amounts, what was signed, and so on. Of course, you can't be expected to have a record of everything. We have to be practical. All I'm saying is that it's a good idea for a person to keep a record of as many basic things as possible.*

Here we have the paralegal stepping out of her role as interviewer and becoming a teacher. This can be upsetting to some clients; others will appreciate it very much. Here, the lecture on keeping records is fundamental, since documentation is fundamental in the law.

Paralegal: *Okay, fine. Just as soon as you can call me, please do it. Now I want to ask you some questions about your medical history. First, let's get back to this letter. It says that your application for Aid for the Totally Disabled was denied because they say you are not disabled. It also says that they examined the medical records you brought with you. Is that right?*
Client: *Yes, I brought my papers there.*
Paralegal: *Do you have these papers with you now?*
Client: *No, they are at home. Do you want me to bring them to you?*
Paralegal: *Yes, would you? Why don't you take this piece of paper and make a note of the things you should do. First, you are going to call me to let me know the date you first applied. Then you are going to bring me the medical records that the welfare department looked at when they were deciding on your application. Do you have all that?*
Client: *Yes, I think so.*
Paralegal: *Could you give me the name and address of the doctor who most recently examined you?*
Client: *Dr. Edward Zuder of 7th Avenue; I don't know the exact address.*
Paralegal: *What other doctors have examined you?*
Client: *Well, I'm not sure. There was one that I saw a few months ago in Mason County.*
Paralegal: *Do you remember the doctor's name?*

Client: *Johnson, or Thompson, I don't recall fully. I think my wife would know. I'll ask her. She's better at names than me.*

Paralegal: *That would be fine. Have her do that. In fact, Mr. Donnelly, what I am going to need is a list of every doctor that you have seen within the last five years. When you bring me your medical records, a lot of the names and addresses will be there. Some may not be. Just try to remember—you and your wife—as many as you can. Why don't you add that to the list of things you are going to do? With your permission, I will call some of them for some basic information.*

Client: *For five years? Why do you need all that?*

Paralegal: *I know it's a lot of information, but from experience we know that old medical records are often very important. We should be prepared.*

Client: *Well, I'll get what I can.*

The paralegal is probing for information. Probing is important but sometimes difficult to do. The client should never feel that he is being interrogated or cross-examined. It is obvious that Mr. Donnelly cannot be pushed much further. He cannot be expected to recall all the information the paralegal is seeking. When he was surprised at being asked for information dating back five years, he may have been reacting not simply to the difficulty of obtaining such data but also to the possible implication that the paralegal doubted his claim. Do you think that the client felt that he had to prove something *to the paralegal?*

**Principle: Probing is a valid technique of data-gathering, but it must be used with care to avoid making the client uncomfortable.**

The paralegal did not simply rely on probing the client to obtain information. Jane Collins has a talent for trying different approaches to data-gathering. She asked the client to check his records and call her, and she also asked him to bring records to her. Finally, *she* will take the *initiative* in making some calls herself. These are a series of comprehensive steps calculated to obtain facts and to cross-check the validity of facts.

The steps used by the paralegal demonstrate the intimate relationship between interviewing and investigation. The interviewer lays the groundwork for the investigative function (which in this office may or may not be performed by the same paralegal). Both the interviewer and the investigator seek relevant facts that can be verified or documented. If names, dates, and witnesses must be tracked down in the field by the investigator, the process is begun by a thorough interview.

The same is true of the informal and formal advocacy function. At some later point, the office may try to negotiate the case with the welfare department through informal advocacy (see Chapter 15) in order to obtain what the client wants without resorting to a formal agency hearing or a court proceeding. If informal advocacy does not work, formal advocacy at agency hearings (see Chapter 15) or in court may be tried. All these steps begin with and are dependent on a competent initial client interview. The groundwork is established at this level with fact and problem identification, on the one hand, and a trustful, cooperative client on the other.

**Principle: Interviewing is intimately connected with and is the foundation for investigation, negotiation, and formal advocacy.**

Client: *Do you think I have a chance of winning?*

Paralegal: *Well, we're going to study your case carefully. I can tell you definitely that you do have a right to fight the department for denying your application. This could mean forcing them into a fair hearing. Before any final decision on strategy is made, however, I and one of the attorneys here in the office will be checking with you.*

Client: *I see.*

Has the paralegal given the client legal advice? The paralegal is interpreting administrative regulations on challenging welfare decisions in reference to a particular client's case.

Generally, if an administrative agency authorizes a lay person to represent clients before it, this authorization includes the right to give legal advice in preparation for such representation. The welfare department provides such authorization. Hence, the paralegal can give legal advice to Mr. Donnelly in this case. If there is no specific authorization for lay representation at agency hearings, then the paralegal cannot give legal advice. Normally, no such authorization exists when the case involves traditional divorce, landlord-tenant, consumer fraud, or other court cases. In such cases, the role of the paralegal is limited to fact-gathering in interviewing and investigation, preliminary drafting of legal documents for attorneys, legal research, etc. Of course, in every case, a paralegal can give clients legal advice when the advice is specifically dictated by an attorney. In such situations, the paralegal is merely relaying a message from the attorney to the client.

**Principle: The paralegal must know what legal advice is and when she can and cannot give it to clients.**

The paralegal properly instructed the client on how the office functions in handling cases: paralegals work closely with attorneys and both are in regular communication with the client.

The paralegal used the phrase "fair hearing" without explaining that this is the technical procedure used by the welfare department to permit clients to challenge its actions. The client, on the surface, appeared to understand when he said, "I see." It is more probable, however, that the client was simply covering up his confusion by being polite.

**Principle: Technical terms (i.e., jargon) should either be rejected in favor of understandable English or explained clearly to clients.**

Paralegal: *Well, I think that we have gone about as far as we can today. Is there anything else that you want to tell me, anything that I should know? Are you sure you've told me everything?*

Client: *What do you mean?*

Here again it is possible that the client could take offense to this last question. The client might be thinking, "Doesn't she trust me? I've tried to tell her everything." On the other hand, experienced interviewers know that clients have a natural inclination to overstate their case, to highlight what they feel are the good points of their case, and to minimize anything negative about their case. They may fear that the office will not take their case if it knew the whole story. Furthermore it may take more than one interview for the client to place his full trust in the paralegal or in the office as a whole. Nevertheless, the interviewer must pursue every aspect of the case, even that which may be damaging. Better to learn everything now so that the office can be prepared for potentially negative factors than to be surprised at a hearing with information that is damaging.

While it is true that the paralegal must try to uncover everything, there are effective and ineffective ways of going about it. The approach taken by the paralegal here does *not* appear to be effective. The blanket question she asked is not likely to communicate the message that she needs to know everything. She was indirect, vague, and potentially condescending. If the paralegal suspected that there were aspects of the case that the client was concealing, she should have asked specific questions designed to determine whether her suspicions were valid. Furthermore, she should have explained to the client why it is important to provide all the facts. Perhaps this would necessitate some explanation to the client of how our *adversarial system* of justice works. When advocates for clients go before referees, judges, or juries, it is their duty to present the best case possible for the client. It is the job of the advocate for the other side to point up the negative aspects of the case. The advocate for the client, however, must be ready in advance to respond to what the other side will say. Hence the necessity of knowing everything as soon as possible. The key point that must be made to the client is that the office will not refuse to serve a client simply because he doesn't have a perfect case.

**Principle: Interviewers must uncover both the positive and damaging aspects of a case.**

Paralegal: *I have a few forms here that I would like you to sign. They simply give this office your authority to represent you and to look at your welfare and medical records. You'll sign these here, won't you?*
Client: *You want me to sign this here?*
Paralegal: *Yes, would you?*
Client: *Okay, should my wife sign?*
Paralegal: *No, that won't be necessary.* [Client signs.] *Fine.*

Asking the client to sign papers is always a delicate matter. Very often, the client does not know what he is signing. The interviewer should assume that the client is confused about the signing. The client should be given the chance to read over what he is being asked to sign and encouraged to ask questions about what he doesn't understand. Not only is this good practice as a matter of courtesy, but it is also good training for the client to read carefully and ask questions about *any* papers *before* signing.

**Principle: Before a client is asked to sign anything, the interviewer should be sure that the client knows what he is signing, why he is being asked to sign, and that it is up to the client to decide whether he wants to sign.**

Whenever a question is asked and the answer is strongly stated or implied in the question, we have a *leading question*. Leading questions are potentially dangerous because of the manipulative way in which words are put into the mouth of the person being asked the question. Here are some examples: "Mr. Jones, you knew that it was past midnight when you called, isn't that right?" "Wasn't it past midnight when you called?" Leading questions attempt to pressure the individual to answer in a certain way. This is not to say that a person asking leading questions is always devious. People can ask leading questions without even realizing it. They may feel that they are helping out by asking the question in this manner.

Now, look again at the statement "You'll sign these here, won't you?" Is this a leading question? Should the question have been asked in this way?

**Principle: Interviewers must be able to recognize their own leading questions and to understand the dangers of such questions.**

Paralegal: *Just a couple of points before we conclude, Mr. Donnelly. You said something earlier about having lost your car. What did you mean?*

Client: *Well, I had to give it to my nephew. It wasn't safe for me to drive, you know. I've been very ill lately.*

Paralegal: *I see. What about your wife? You said that she was sick. Has she applied to the welfare department for the same benefits that you applied for?*

Client: *Why, no. I never thought of her going ahead. Do you think I should?*

Paralegal: *You certainly can't lose anything. It's up to you if you want to give it a try.*

Here the paralegal is going back to her notes to ask about matters that she noted earlier. This is the sign of a thorough interview. The office is interested in all legal aspects of the client's needs. The paralegal may have suspected creditor or car repair problems. It was totally appropriate to check this out. The law is critical, however, of attorneys who try to stir up legal problems and who go on so-called fishing expeditions to discover legal problems of citizens in order to generate business for themselves. Such stirring up of litigation is frowned on. This was not the case here, however. The paralegal properly inquired about issues suggested by what the client told her.

The suggestion to the client that his wife apply for benefits raises another question about the role of the paralegal and the office. Clients should not be pressured, persuaded, or urged to take courses of action. The task of the office is to lay out *options* for the client, explain the merits and demerits of each option, and leave it for the client to decide what he wants to do. If the client asks for a recommendation on what option to choose, an answer should be given, but it should always be made clear to the client that he has the final responsibility to decide what he wants to do. The paralegal in this case acted properly. She did not urge Mr. Donnelly to do anything. She made the client aware of the option concerning his wife and responded to the client's specific request for her opinion about whether he should take the option.

**Principle: The interviewer should not pressure the client to take any course of action.**

Paralegal: *Okay, Mr. Donnelly, let's leave it at that. If you don't have any more questions, we can conclude now. I will be talking to an attorney about your case shortly. You will call me concerning the date we spoke about, bring me your medical records, and put together a list of the doctors who treated you in the last five years. I will call Mr. Smith at the welfare department to find out what I can from him. If your wife wants to talk to me about applying, have her come by or call me. We'll be glad to help her in any way we can.*

Client: *Okay, and I thank you.*

Paralegal: *Thank you for coming by. I hope we can help you. Good-bye.*

Client: *Good-bye.*

The paralegal's final comment is very significant. It is important not to leave the client with the impression that the office is definitely going to win the case. It would be easy to raise this expectation in the mind of the client, since undoubtedly this is what he wants to believe. More realistically, all the office can say is that it will do the best it can for the client and that no guarantees of success can be given. The comment "I hope we can help you" is appropriate to convey this message.

> **Principle: The interviewer must not raise false expectations in the mind of the client about what the office will be able to do.**

---

### ■ ASSIGNMENT 8.7

Form a circle of chairs centered around a single chair in the middle. The student sitting in the middle will play the role of the client. The students in the circle (numbering about ten) will be the interviewers, in rotation. The instructor will ask one of the students to begin the interview. As this student runs into difficulty during the interview, the student to his or her right picks up the interview, tries to resolve the difficulty in his or her own way, and then proceeds with the interview. If *this* student cannot resolve the difficulty, the student to his or her right tries, and so on. The objective is to identify as many diverse ways of handling difficulties as possible in a relatively short period. No interviewer should have the floor for more than a minute or two at any one time. The student playing the role of the client is given specific instructions about how to play the role—that is, sometimes he or she is asked to be shy; other times, demanding. The client should not overdo the role, however. He or she should respond naturally within the role assigned. Here are four sets of instructions to attempt this "interview in rotation."

(a) The interviewer greets the client and says, "I am a paralegal." The client is confused about what a paralegal is. The interviewer explains. The client is insistent upon a comprehensive definition that he or she can understand.

(b) The client comes to the law office because he or she is being sued for negligent driving. The interviewer asks the client if he or she must wear eyeglasses to drive. The answer is *yes.* The interviewer then asks if he or she was wearing eyeglasses during the accident. The client is very reluctant to answer. (In fact, the client was not wearing glasses at the time.) The client does not appear to want to talk about this subject. The interviewer persists.

(c) The client is being sued by a local store for $750.00 in grocery bills. The client has a poor memory and the interviewer must think of ways to help him or her remember. The client wants to cooperate but is having trouble remembering.

(d) The client wants to sue an auto mechanic. The client gives many opinions, conclusions, and judgments (such as: "The mechanic is a crook," "I was their best customer," "The work done was awful.") The interviewer is having difficulty encouraging the client to state the facts underlying the opinions. The client insists on stating conclusions.

After each exercise, the class should discuss principles, guidelines, and techniques of interviewing.

---

### ■ ASSIGNMENT 8.8

Below are two additional role-playing exercises to be conducted in class.

(a) The instructor asks the class if anyone was involved, in any way, in a recent automobile accident. If someone says *yes,* this student is interviewed by another class member whose job is to obtain as complete a picture as possible of what happened. At the outset the interviewer knows nothing other than that some kind of an automobile accident occurred.

(b) The instructor asks the class if anyone has recently had trouble with any government agency (like the post office or sanitation department). If someone says *yes,* this student is interviewed by another class member whose job is to obtain as complete a picture as possible of what happened. The interviewer at the outset knows nothing other than the fact that the person being interviewed has had some difficulty with a government agency.

---

## ■ ASSIGNMENT 8.9

When an office represents a debtor, one of the paralegal's major responsibilities may be to interview the client in order to write a comprehensive report on the client's assets and liabilities. Assume that your supervising attorney has instructed you to conduct a comprehensive interview of the client in order to write such a report. Assets are everything the client *owns* or has an interest in. Liabilities are everything *owed;* they are debts. These are the only definitions you need; you do not need any technical knowledge of law to conduct this interview. All you need is common sense in the formulation of questions.

Your instructor will role play the client in front of the room. It will be a collective interview. Everyone will ask questions, but you will each write individual reports on the interview based on your own notes. Raise your hand to be recognized. Be sure to ask follow-up questions when needed for factual clarity and comprehensiveness. You can repeat the questions of other students if you think you might elicit a more detailed response. Any question is fair game as long as it is directly or indirectly calculated to uncover assets or liabilities. There may be information the client does not have at this time, such as bank account numbers. Help the client determine how such information can be obtained later. In your notes, state that you asked for information that the client didn't have and state what the client said he or she would do to obtain the information. To achieve comprehensiveness, you must obtain factual detail. This means that you go after names, addresses, phone numbers, dates, relevant surrounding circumstances, verification data, etc. In short, we want Fact Particularization. Take detailed notes on the questions asked by every student (not just your own) and the answers provided in response. You will have to write your report based on your own notes.

The heading of your report will be as follows:

### Inter-Office Memorandum

**To:**     [name of your instructor]
**From:**   [your name]
**Date:**   [date you prepared the report]
**RE:**     Comprehensive Interview of
_____

**Case File Number:** _____

(Make up the case file number.) The first paragraph of your report should state what your supervisor has asked you to do in the report. Simply state what the assignment is. Organization of the data from your notes is up to you. Use whatever format you think will most clearly communicate what you learned from the client in the interview.

---

# ☐ Chapter Summary

Interviewing is conversation for the purpose of obtaining information. In a law office, legal interviewing is designed to obtain facts that are relevant to the identification and eventual resolution of a legal problem. These facts are often reported in a document called an intake memo. Six major guides exist to the kinds of questions that should be asked during a legal interview. The most important is the instructions of the supervisor on the goals of the interview. Other guides include preprinted checklists for certain kinds of interviews, legal analysis to help you focus on issues such as relevance, "fact particularization" as a device to achieve comprehensiveness, and finally, common sense and flexibility to help you remain alert and responsive as the interview unfolds.

A good deal of sensitivity is needed when interviewing clients. They are sometimes confused about the law and about what they want from the law.

There are a large number of factors that inhibit or facilitate communication. For example, the professional appearance of the office and of the interviewer, the seating arrangement in the office, the preservation of confidentiality, the explanation of the paralegal's role and status, the readiness of the client to answer open-ended and directed questions, the use of leading questions, the timing of probing questions, the exploration of damaging and favorable aspects of the case, the sequencing of questions designed to elicit a chronological recitation of the facts, sensitivity when covering personal matters, and the use of jargon. Finally, the paralegal must be alert to the danger of giving legal advice during the interview.

# Key Terms

initial client interview
follow-up interview
field interview
intake memo
RE
grounds
checklists

legal analysis
legally relevant
fact particularization
analogies
confidentiality
directed question
close-ended question

open-ended question
nonverbal communication
probing
legal advice
jargon
adversarial system
leading question

# 9

# Investigation in a Law Office

## ■ Chapter Outline

Section A. The Nature and Context
  of Investigation
Section B. Fact Analysis: Organizing
  the Options
Section C. Distortions in
  Investigation
Section D. Sources of Evidence/
  Sources of Leads
Section E. Gaining Access to Records
Section F. Evaluating Testimonial
  and Physical Evidence

Section G. Interviewing Witnesses
Section H. Special
  Investigative Problems
    Judgment Collection
    Missing Persons
    Background Investigations
Section I. Evidence and Investigation
Section J. Taking a Witness
  Statement
Section K. The Settlement Work-Up

## ■ Section A. The Nature and Context of Investigation

Investigation is the process of gathering additional facts and verifying presently known facts in order to advise a client about solving a legal problem or about preventing a legal problem from occurring. In Chapter 8 on legal interviewing, we examined six major guides to fact gathering:

- Instructions of the supervisor
- Checklists
- Legal analysis
- Fact Particularization (FP)
- Common sense
- Flexibility

You should review these guides now since they are equally applicable to investigation. Fact Particularization (FP) is especially important.

. . . . . . . . . . . . . . .

*1. Investigative techniques are often very individualistic.* Styles, mannerisms, and approaches to investigation are often highly personal. Through a sometimes arduous process of trial and error, the investigator develops effective techniques. While some of these techniques come from the suggestions of fellow investigators, most are acquired from on-the-job experience.

*2. It is impossible to overemphasize the importance of hustle, imagination, and flexibility.* If there is one characteristic that singles out the effective investigator, it is a willingness to dig. While many investigation assignments may be relatively easy (e.g., photograph the ceiling of a bathroom that a tenant claims is falling down), most assignments are open-ended in that the range of options and possible conclusions to a problem are extensive. The answer is not always there for the asking. For such assignments, investigators must be prepared to identify and pursue leads, be unorthodox, and let their feelings, hunches, and intuition lead where they will. In short, the formal principles of investigation must give way to hustle, imagination, and flexibility.

Good investigators are always in pursuit. They are on the offensive and don't wait for the facts to come to them. They know that legwork is required. They know that 50% of their leads will become dead ends. They are not frightened by roadblocks and therefore do not freeze at the first hurdle. They know that there are no perfect ways of obtaining information. They know that they must take a stab at possibilities and that it takes persistent thinking and imagination to come up with leads. At the same time, good investigators are not fools. They do not pursue blind alleys. After being on the job for a while, they have developed "a feel" for what is or is not a reasonable possibility or lead. They have been able to develop this feel because, when they first started investigating, they had an open mind and were not afraid to try things out.

*3. Investigators may not know what they are looking for until they find it.* As with legal interviewing and legal research, good investigation may sometimes live a life of its own in terms of what it uncovers. There are two kinds of investigation assignments: the closed-ended assignment (where the end product is carefully defined in advance, such as the photograph assignment mentioned in the tenant case), and the open-ended assignment (where the investigator begins with only the general contours of a problem and is asked to fill in the facts). An example of an open-ended assignment is to find out as much as possible about the case of a client charged with burglary. In the open-ended assignment (and in some closed-ended ones), investigators are walking into the unknown. They may have no idea what they will uncover. Suppose in the burglary assignment, the investigator sets out to focus on whatever is relevant to the burglary charge and in the process discovers that a homicide was involved, as yet unknown to the police. The investigator had no idea that she would find this until she found it. Suppose that the law firm has a client who is charging his employer with racial discrimination, and in the process of working on the case the investigator discovers that this employee had a managerial job at the company and that several of the workers under him have complained that *he* practiced sex discrimination against them. The investigator had no idea that she would uncover this until it was uncovered. In short, an open mind is key when undertaking an assignment.

*4. Investigation and interviewing are closely related.* The interviewer conducting the initial client interview has two responsibilities: to help identify legal problems and to obtain from the client as many relevant facts on those problems as possible. The starting point for the investigator is the report or intake memo (see Chapter 8) prepared by the interviewer on what the client said. It is either clear from this report what the investigation needs are, or they become clear only after the investigator and his or her supervisor have defined them more precisely.

The investigator should approach the interview report with a healthy skepticism. Thus far, all the office may know is what the client has said. The perspective of the office is therefore narrow. Without necessarily distrusting the client's word, the investigator's job is to verify the facts given during the interview and to determine whether new facts exist that were unknown or improperly identified during the interview. The interview report should not be taken at face value. New facts may be revealed or old facts may for the first time be seen in a context that gives them an unexpected meaning. The investigator must approach a case almost as if the office knows nothing about it or as if what the office knows is invalid. By adopting this attitude, the investigator will be able to give the case an entirely different direction when the product of the investigation warrants it.

*5. The investigator must be guided by goals and priorities.* It is one thing to say that the investigator must be open-minded enough to be receptive to the unexpected. It is quite another to say that the investigator should start in a void. The starting point is a set of instructions from the supervisor. How clear a supervisor is about an investigation assignment may vary with each assignment. For example:

- Supervisors may have a very definite idea of what they want.
- Supervisors think they know what they want but are not sure.
- Whatever conception supervisors have about what they want, they are not effective in explaining it to the investigator.
- Supervisors have no idea what they want other than a desire to obtain as many facts about the case as possible.

The first responsibility of the investigator is to establish communication with the supervisor. With as much clarity as possible, determine what the supervisor wants accomplished through the investigation.

*6. There is a close relationship among investigation, negotiation, and trial.* There are two ultimate questions that should guide the investigator's inquiry into every fact being investigated:

- How will this fact assist or hurt the office in attempting to settle or negotiate the case without a trial?
- How will this fact assist or hurt the office in presenting the client's case at trial?

A large percentage of legal claims never go to full trial; they are negotiated in advance. Opposing counsel have a number of bargaining sessions in which attempts are made to hammer out a settlement acceptable to their clients. Very often they discuss the law that they think will be applicable if the case goes to trial. Even more often they present each other with the facts that they think they will be able to establish at trial. Here the investigator's report becomes invaluable. As a result of this report, the attorney should be able to suggest a wide range of facts that could be used at trial ("we have reason to believe . . ." or "we are now pursuing leads that would tend to establish that . . ." etc.). The attorney's bargaining leverage is immeasurably increased by a thorough investigation report.

If negotiations do not produce a settlement, the investigator's report can help the attorney in a number of ways:

- Determining whether or not to go to trial
- Deciding what witnesses to call
- Choosing questions to ask of witnesses

■ Deciding how to impeach (i.e., contradict or attack the credibility of) opposing witnesses

■ Determining what tangible or physical evidence to introduce

■ Deciding how to attack the tangible or physical evidence the other side will introduce

The investigator should be familiar with the standard, pretrial *discovery devices:* depositions, interrogatories, requests for admissions, medical examination reports, etc. (See Chapter 10.) A *deposition* is a pretrial question-and-answer session conducted outside of court, usually in the office of one of the attorneys. The attorney asks questions of the other party (or of a witness of the other party) in order to obtain facts that will assist in preparing for trial. Depositions are often transcribed so that typed copies of the session are available. The same objective exists with the use of *interrogatories,* except that the questions and answers are usually submitted in writing rather than in person. An interrogatory is simply a question. A *request for admission* is a statement of fact submitted by one party to another. The latter is asked to admit or deny the statement. Those that are admitted do not have to be proven at trial. A request for a medical examination will be granted by the judge when medical issues are relevant to the trial.

Investigators can be of assistance during this discovery stage by helping the attorney decide what questions to ask in a deposition or in an interrogatory, what admissions to request, whether to ask for a medical examination, etc.

After the discovery devices have been used, the investigator should carefully study all the facts these devices disclosed in order to:

■ Cross-check or verify these facts, and

■ Look for new leads (names, addresses, incidents) that should be the subject of future investigation.

*7. It is important to distinguish between absolute proof of a fact and some evidence of a fact.*    Investigators must not confuse their role with that of a judge or jury in deciding truth or falsity. The function of investigators is to identify reasonable options or fact possibilities. To be sure, they can speculate on whether a judge or jury would ever believe a fact to be true. But the presence or absence of absolute proof is not the test that should guide them in their investigations. The tests that an investigator should apply in determining whether to pursue a fact possibility are:

■ Am I reasonable in assuming that a particular fact will help establish the case of the client? Am I reasonable in assuming that if I gather enough evidence on such a fact, a judge, jury, or hearing officer *might* accept it as true?

■ Am I reasonable in assuming that a particular fact will help to challenge or discredit the case of the opposing party? Am I reasonable in assuming that if I gather enough evidence on such a fact (evidence that will challenge or discredit the case of the other side) a judge, jury, or hearing officer *might* accept it as true?

You should also approach the case from the perspective of the opponent, even to the point of assuming that you work for the other side! What facts will the opponent go after to establish its case? What is the likelihood that such facts will be accepted? Again, do not confuse proof with evidence.

*8. The investigator must know some law.*    Investigators do not have to be experts in every area of the law or in any particular area of the law in order to perform their job. For their field work to have a focus, however, they must have at least a general understanding of evidence, civil procedure, and the areas of the law governing the facts of the client's case. They must know, for example, what *hearsay* and *relevance* mean. They must understand basic procedural steps in litigation in order to see where fact gathering can be used and how it is often used in different ways at different steps in the litigation process. Some substantive law is also needed. In a divorce case, for example, the investigator must know what the grounds for divorce are in the state. The same kind of basic information is needed for every area of the law involved or potentially involved in the client's case. Such knowledge can be obtained:

- In paralegal courses or seminars
- Through brief explanations from the supervisor
- By talking to experienced attorneys and paralegals whenever they have time to provide their perspective on the law.
- By reading a chapter in a legal treatise or a section in a legal encyclopedia that provides an overview of the relevant area of the law. (See Chapter 11.)

*9. The investigator must know the territory.*   When you are on the job as an investigator, it is important to begin acquiring a detailed knowledge on the makeup of the city, town, or state where you will be working. Such knowledge should include:

- The political structure of the area: Who is in power? Who is the opposition? In what direction is the political structure headed?
- The social and cultural structure of the area: Are there racial problems? Are there ethnic groupings that are diffuse or unified? Are there different value systems at play?
- The contacts that are productive: If you want something done at city hall, whom do you see? Does the director of a particular agency have any control over the staff? What agencies have "real services" available? What court clerk is most helpful?

It is usually very difficult for the investigator to acquire this knowledge in any way other than going out into the field and obtaining it through experience. Others can provide guidance, and often will. In the final analysis, however, you will probably discover that what others say is biased or incomplete. You must establish your own network of contacts and sources of information. First and foremost, you must establish your credibility in the community. People must get to know and trust you. Simply by announcing yourself as an investigator (or by presenting a printed card indicating title and affiliation), you will not find instant cooperation from the community. You must *earn* this cooperation. If you gain a reputation as arrogant, dishonest, opportunistic or insensitive, you will quickly find that few people want to deal with you. An investigator could be in no worse predicament.

   Often the best way to learn about an area and to begin establishing contacts is by being casual and unassuming. Have you ever noticed that insurance agents often spend three fourths of their time talking about the weather, sports, politics, the high cost of housing, etc., *before* coming to their sales pitch? Their approach is to relax you, to find out what interests you, to show you that they are human. Then they hit you with the benefits of buying their insurance. The investigator can learn from this approach not only in establishing contacts at agencies and in the community generally, but also in dealing with prospective witnesses on specific cases.

##  Section B. Fact Analysis: Organizing the Options

The process of structuring or organizing fact options may initially appear to be complex and cumbersome. But the process can become second nature to you once you understand it, try it out, evaluate it, modify it, and find it helpful. It is, of course, perfectly proper to adopt any process that you find effective. Whatever method you use, you need to develop the *discipline* of fact analysis as soon as possible.

There are a number of fundamental characteristics of facts that should be kept in mind:

- Events take place.
- Events mean different things to different people.
- Different people, therefore, have different versions of events.
- Inconsistent versions of the same event do not necessarily indicate fraud or lying.
- Although someone's version may claim to be the total picture, it probably will contain only a piece of the picture.
- In giving a version of an event, people usually mix statements of *why* the event occurred with statements of *what* occurred.
- Whenever it is claimed that an event occurred in a certain way, one can logically expect that certain signs, indications, or traces (evidence) of the event can be found.

Given these truisms, the investigator should analyze the facts along the lines indicated in Figure 9.1. It is possible for a single client's case to have numerous individual facts that are in dispute. Furthermore, facts can change, or people's versions of facts can change in the middle of a case. Each new or modified fact demands the same comprehensive process of fact analysis that is outlined in Figure 9.1.

Obtaining different versions of a fact may be difficult because the differences may not be clear on the surface. Of course, every fact will not necessarily have multiple versions. It is recommended, however, that you assume there will be more than one version until you have demonstrated otherwise to yourself. Undoubtedly, you must do some probing in order to uncover the versions that exist. Better to do so now than to be confronted with a surprise at trial or at an agency hearing.

People will not always be willing to share their accounts or versions of facts with you. If you are not successful in convincing them to tell their story, you may have to make some assumptions of what their story is *likely* to be and to check out these assumptions.

##  Section C. Distortions in Investigation

Investigators are not mere newspaper reporters or photographers who simply report what they see, hear, or otherwise experience. You have a much more dynamic role. In a very significant sense, you sometimes have the power of controlling what someone else says about the facts. This can have positive and negative consequences.

**FIGURE 9.1**

Fact Analysis in
Investigation

| **Starting Point:** |
| --- |
| All the facts you presently have on the case. |

| **Procedure:** |
| --- |
| ■ Arrange the facts chronologically.<br>■ Place a number before each fact that must be established in a legal proceeding. |

| **State the Following Versions of Each Fact:** |
| --- |
| Version I:  The client's<br>Version II:  The opponent's (as revealed to you or as assumed)<br>Version III:  A witness's<br>Version IV:  Another witness's<br>Version V:  Any other reasonable version (e.g., from your own deductions) |

| **As to Each Version:** |
| --- |
| ■ State precisely (with quotes if possible) what the version is.<br>■ State the evidence or indications that tend to support the version according to persons presenting the version.<br>■ State the evidence or indications that tend to contradict this version.<br>■ Determine how you will verify whether the evidence or indications exist. |

At its worst, this can mean that you are not listening to the person or that you are asking questions in such a manner that you are putting words into the person's mouth. The primary technique that can bring about this result is the *leading question.* A leading question is a pressure question, one that contains (or suggests) the answer in the statement of the question. For example, "You were in Baltimore at the time, isn't that correct?" "You earn over $200 a week?" "Would it be correct to say that when you drove up to the curb, you didn't see the light?"

Questions can intentionally or unintentionally manipulate someone's answer by including a premise that has yet to be established. It takes an astute person to say to such questions, "I can't answer your question (or it is invalid) because it assumes another fact that I haven't agreed to." In the following examples of questions and answers, the person responding to the question refuses to be trapped by the form of the question:

Q: How much did it cost you to have your car repaired after the accident?
A: It's not my car and it wasn't an accident; your client deliberately ran into the car that I borrowed.

. . . . . . . . . . . . . . .

Q: Have you stopped beating your wife?
A: I never beat my wife!

. . . . . . . . . . . . . . .

Q: Can you tell me what you saw?
A: I didn't see anything; my brother was there and he told me what happened.

The last leading question containing the unestablished premise can be highly detrimental. Suppose the question and answer went as follows:

Q: Can you tell me what you saw?
A: The car was going about 70 MPH.

In fact, the person answering the question did not see this himself; his brother told him that a car was traveling at this speed. There are a number of reasons why this person may have failed to tell the investigator that he didn't see anything first-hand:

- Perhaps he did not hear the word "saw" in the investigator's question.

- He may have wanted the investigator to think that he saw something himself; he may want to feel important by conveying the impression that he is special because he has special information.

- He may have felt that it was not significant enough to correct the investigator's false assumption; he may have thought that the investigator was more interested in *what* happened than in *who* saw what happened.

Whatever the reason, the investigator has carelessly put himself or herself in the position of missing a potentially critical fact, namely that the person is only talking from hearsay.

Another way to blur communication is by completely avoiding some topics and concentrating only on selected ones. If you do not ask questions about certain matters, intentionally or otherwise, you are likely to end up with a distorted picture of a person's version of the facts. For example, assume that Smith and Jones have an automobile collision. The investigator, working for the attorney that represents Jones, finds a witness who says that she saw the accident. The investigator asks her to describe what she saw, but fails, however, to ask her where she was at the time she saw the collision. In fact, she was sitting in a park over two blocks away and could see the collision only through some shrubbery. The investigator didn't ask questions to uncover this; it wasn't volunteered. The investigator, therefore, walks away with a potentially distorted idea of how much light this individual can shed on what took place. This is similar to the distortion that can result from the use of questions that contain an unestablished premise.

Yet there may be instances in which these techniques have beneficial results. First of all a leading question can help jar someone's memory so that they are better able to recall the facts. If, however, this individual is constantly in need of leading questions in order to remember, you have strong reason to suspect that, rather than being merely shy, inarticulate, or in need of a push now and then, the person knows little or nothing.

Suppose that the witness being questioned is uncooperative or has a version of the facts that is damaging to the client of the investigator's office. It may be that the techniques described in this section as normally improper can be used to challenge a version of the facts. A leading question with an unestablished premise, for example, may catch an individual off guard and give the investigator reasonable cause to believe that the person is not telling the truth.

Suppose that the person being questioned is not hostile but is neutral, or seemingly so. The way in which such individuals are questioned may help them emphasize certain facts as opposed to others. Once witnesses have committed themselves to a version of the facts, either completely on their own or with some subtle help from the questioner, there is a good chance that they will stick by this version because they do not want to appear to be vague, uncertain, or inconsistent later. An investigator who takes such a course of action, however, must be extremely careful. You are taking certain risks, not because your conduct is illegal or unethical, but because a witness who needs subtle pressuring in order to state a version of the facts in a certain way is probably going to be a weak witness at trial or at an agency hearing. On cross-examination, the witness may fall apart.

 ## Section D. Sources of Evidence/Sources of Leads

*Evidence* is that which is used to prove or disprove a fact. Testimonial evidence is what someone says. Physical or tangible evidence is what can be seen or touched. A *lead* is simply a path to potentially admissible evidence. Of course, evidence is often its own lead to other evidence.

In Figure 9.2, there is a partial checklist containing some of the standard sources of evidence and leads at the investigator's disposal. (The list is not presented in order of priority.)

---

- Statements of the client
- Documents the client brings or can obtain
- Information from attorneys involved with the case in the past
- Interrogatories, depositions, other discovery devices; letters requesting information
- Pleadings (such as complaints) filed thus far in the case
- Newspaper accounts; notices in the media requesting information
- General records of municipal, state, and federal administrative agencies
- Business records (such as cancelled receipts)
- Employment records, including job applications
- Photographs
- Hospital records
- Informers or the "town gossip"
- Surveillance of the scene
- Reports from the police and other law enforcement agencies (see Figure 9.3)
- Fingerprints
- School records
- Military records
- Information that may be voluntarily or involuntarily provided by the attorney for the other side
- Use of alias
- Bureau of vital statistics and missing persons

- Court records
- Worker's Compensation records
- Office of politicians
- Records of Better Business Bureaus and consumer groups
- Telephone book
- Boat register
- *Polk Directory*
- *Reverse Directory*
- Accounts of eyewitnesses
- Hearsay accounts
- Automobile register (DMV)
- County assessor (for real property)
- Tax assessor's offices
- County election records
- Post office (record of forwarding addresses)
- Object to be traced (such as an auto)
- Credit bureaus
- Reports of investigative agencies written in the past
- Resources of public library
- Associations (trade, professional, etc.)
- *Who's Who* directories
- Insurance Company Clearing House
- Standards and Poor's *Register of Directors and Executives*
- Telling your problem to a more experienced investigator and asking for other leads
- Shots in the dark

**FIGURE 9.2**

Checklist on the Standard Sources of Evidence and Leads

Section E. Gaining Access to Records

It is easy to say that the investigator should check records for evidence and leads; but sometimes it is quite difficult to gain access to these records. There are four categories of records:

1. Those already in the possession of the client or of an individual willing to turn them over to you on request

2. Those in the possession of a governmental agency or of a private organization and available to anyone in the public

**FIGURE 9.3**

Request for Copy of Peace Officer's Accident Report

---

**REQUEST FOR COPY OF PEACE OFFICER'S ACCIDENT REPORT**
**(PLEASE SUBMIT IN DUPLICATE)**

Statistical Services                                          Date of Request _____
Texas Department of Public Safety
P.O. Box 15999                                               Claim or Policy No. _____
Austin, Texas 78761–5999

Enclosed is a (check)(money order) payable to the Texas Department of Public Safety in the amount of

$_____ for (check service desired):

☐ Copy of Peace Officer's Accident Report - $4.00 each

☐ Certified Copy of Peace Officer's Accident Report - $8.00 each

for the accident listed below:

---

Please provide as accurate and complete information as possible.

ACCIDENT DATE _____
              MONTH     DAY     YEAR

ACCIDENT LOCATION _____  _____  _____
                     COUNTY              CITY          STREET OR HIGHWAY

WAS ANYONE
KILLED IN THE ACCIDENT? _____ If So, Name of one Deceased _____

INVESTIGATING AGENCY AND/OR OFFICER'S NAME (IF KNOWN) _____

| DRIVER'S FULL NAME | DRIVER INFORMATION (If Available) DATE OF BIRTH | TEXAS DRIVER LICENSE NO. | ADDRESS |
|---|---|---|---|
| 1. | | | |
| 2. | | | |
| 3. | | | |

---

Texas Statutes allow the investigating officer 10 days in which to submit his report.
**Requests should not be submitted until at least 10 days after the accident date to allow time for receipt of the report.**

The Law also provides that if an officer's report is not on file when a request for a copy of such report is received, a certification to that effect will be provided in lieu of the copy and the fee shall be retained for the certification.

Mail To _____

Mail Address _____

City _____ State _____ Zip _____

Requested By _____ Phone # _____

3. Those in the possession of a governmental agency or of a private organization and available only to the client or to the individual who is the subject of the records

4. Those in the possession of a governmental agency or of a private organization and claimed to be confidential except for in-house staff

There should obviously be no difficulty in gaining access to the first category of records unless they have been misplaced or lost, in which event the person who once had possession would ask the source of the records to provide another copy. As to records in the latter three categories, the checklist in Figure 9.4 should provide some guidelines on gaining access.

## ■ Section F. Evaluating Testimonial and Physical Evidence

At all times, you must make value judgments on the usefulness of the evidence that you come across. There are a number of specific criteria that can be used to assist you in assessing the worth of what you have. The checklists in Figures 9.6 and 9.7 may be helpful in determining this worth.

## ■ Section G. Interviewing Witnesses

*1. Know what image you are projecting of yourself.*  In the minds of many people, an investigator is often involved in serious and dangerous undertakings.

---

**FIGURE 9.4**

Guidelines to Gaining Access to Records

1. Write, phone, or visit the organization and ask for the record.
2. Have the client write, phone, or visit and ask for it.
3. Draft a letter for the client to sign that asks for it.
4. Have the client sign a form that states that he or she gives you authority to see any records that pertain to him or her and that the client specifically waives any right to confidentiality with respect to such records.
5. Find out if one of the opposing parties has the record, and if so, ask them to send you a copy.
6. Find out if others have it (such as a relative of the client or a co-defendant in this or in a prior court case) and ask them if they will provide you with a copy.
7. For records available generally to the public, find out where these records are and go use them.
8. If you meet resistance (fourth category of records), make a basic fairness pitch to the organization as to why you need the records.
9. Find out (by legal research) if there are any statutes, regulations, or cases that arguably provide the client with the right of access to the records—for example, through the *Freedom of Information Act* (FOIA). (See Figure 9.5).
10. Let the organization know that your office is in the process of establishing a legal basis to gain access to the records and that the office is contemplating initiating litigation to finalize the right.
11. Solicit the intervention of a politician or of some other respectable and independent person in trying to gain access.
12. If the person who initially turns down the request for access is a line officer, appeal the decision formally or informally to his or her supervisor, and up the chain of command to the person with final authority.

**FIGURE 9.5**

Sample FOIA Letter

Agency Head or FOIA Officer
Title
Name of Agency
Address of Agency
City, State, Zip

Re: Freedom of Information Act (FOIA) Request.

Dear _____:

   Under the provisions of the Freedom of Information Act, 5 U.S.C. 552, I am requesting access to (identify the records as clearly and specifically as possible).

   If there are any fees for searching for, or copying, the records I have requested, please inform me before you fill the request. (Or: . . . please supply the records without informing me if the fees do not exceed $_____.)

[Optional] I am requesting this information (state the reason for your request if you think it will assist you in obtaining the information.)

[Optional] As you know, the FOIA permits you to reduce or waive fees when the release of the information is considered as "primarily benefiting the public." I believe that this request fits that category and I therefore ask that you waive any fees.

   If all or any part of this request is denied, please cite the specific exemption(s) that you think justifies your refusal to release the information, and inform me of the appeal procedures available to me under the law.

   I would appreciate your handling this request as quickly as possible, and I look forward to hearing from you within 10 days, as the law stipulates.

Sincerely,

Signature<br>Name<br>Address<br>City, State, Zip

**Source:** U.S. Congress. House. Committee on Government Operations. *A Citizen's Guide on How to Use the Freedom of Information Act and the Privacy Act Requesting Government Documents,* 95th Congress, 1st sess. (1977).

What reaction would you have if a stranger introduced himself or herself to you as an investigator? Would you be guarded and suspicious? You may not want to call yourself an investigator at all. You may want to say "My name is _____, I work for (name of law office) and we are trying to get information on _____." On the other hand, you may find that you are most effective when you are direct and straightforward.

   Can you think of different people who would respond more readily to certain images of investigators? The following is a partial list of some of the images that an investigator could be projecting by dress, mannerisms, approach, and language:

- A professional
- Someone who is just doing a job
- Someone who is emotionally involved in what he or she is doing
- A neutral bystander
- A friend
- A manipulator or opportunist
- A salesperson
- A wise person
- An innocent and shy person

| Checklist to Use If the Witness Is Speaking from First-Hand (Eyewitness) Information | Checklist to Use If the Witness Is Speaking from Second-Hand (Hearsay) Information |
|---|---|
| ■ How long ago did it happen?<br>■ How good is the memory of this witness?<br>■ How far from the event was the witness at the time?<br>■ How good is the sight of the witness?<br>■ What time of day was it and would this affect vision?<br>■ What was the weather at the time and would this affect vision?<br>■ Was there a lot of commotion at the time and would this affect vision or ability to remember?<br>■ What was the witness doing immediately before the incident?<br>■ How old is the witness?<br>■ What was the last grade of school completed?<br>■ Employment background?<br>■ What is the reputation of the witness in the community for truthfulness?<br>■ Was the witness ever convicted of a crime? Are any criminal charges now pending against him or her?<br>■ Is the witness an expert on anything?<br>■ What are the qualifications of the witness?<br>■ Is the witness related to, an employee of, or friendly with the other side in the litigation? Would it be to this person's benefit, in any way, to see the other side win?<br>■ Does any direct evidence exist to corroborate what this witness is saying?<br>■ Does any hearsay evidence exist to corroborate it?<br>■ Is the witness willing to sign a statement covering what he or she tells the investigator? Is he or she willing to say it in court?<br>■ Is the witness defensive when asked about what he or she knows? | ■ How well does the witness remember what was told to him or her by the other person (the declarant) or what the witness heard him or her say to someone else?<br>■ How is the witness sure that it is exact?<br>■ Is the declarant now available to confirm or deny this hearsay account of the witness? If not, why not?<br>■ Under what conditions did the declarant allegedly make the statement (for example, was declarant ill)?<br>■ Is there other hearsay testimony that will help corroborate this hearsay?<br>■ Does any direct evidence exist to corroborate this hearsay?<br>■ How old is the witness? How old is the declarant?<br>■ What are the educational and employment backgrounds of both?<br>■ Is either of them related to, an employee of, or friendly with the other side in the litigation? Would it be to the benefit of either of them to see the other side win?<br>■ Is the witness willing to sign a statement covering what he or she tells the investigator? Is he or she willing to say it in court?<br>■ Is the witness defensive when asked about what he or she was told by the declarant or what he or she heard the declarant say to someone else?<br>■ Are there any inconsistencies in what the witness is saying?<br>■ How does the witness react when confronted with the inconsistencies? Defensively?<br>■ Are there any gaps in what the witness is saying?<br>■ Does the witness appear to exaggerate? |

**FIGURE 9.6**

Checklist on the Validity of Testimonial Evidence

Continued

**FIGURE 9.6**

Checklist on the Validity of Testimonial Evidence
—*Continued*

| Checklist to Use If the Witness Is Speaking from First-Hand (Eyewitness) Information | Checklist to Use If the Witness Is Speaking from Second-Hand (Hearsay) Information |
| --- | --- |
| ■ Are there any inconsistencies in what the witness is saying?<br>■ How does the witness react when confronted with the inconsistencies? Defensively?<br>■ Are there any gaps in what the witness is saying?<br>■ Does the witness appear to exaggerate?<br>■ Does the witness appear to be hiding or holding anything back? | ■ Does the witness appear to be hiding or holding anything back?<br>■ What is the reputation of the witness in the community for truthfulness? |

You must be aware of (a) your own need to project yourself in a certain way, (b) the way in which you think you *are* projecting yourself, (c) the way in which the person to whom you are talking perceives you, and (d) the effect that all this is having on what you are trying to accomplish.

2. *There are five kinds of witnesses: hostile, skeptical, friendly, disinterested or neutral, and a combination of the above.* Hostile witnesses want your client to lose; they will try to set up roadblocks in your way. Skeptical witnesses are not sure who you are or what you want in spite of your explanation of your role. They are guarded and unsure of whether they want to become involved. Friendly witnesses want your client to win and will cooperate fully. *Disinterested* or neutral witnesses don't care who wins. They have information that they will tell anyone who asks.

If the hostile witness is the opposing party who has retained counsel, it is unethical for the investigator to talk directly with this person without going through his or her counsel (see Chapter 5). If the hostile witness is not a party but is closely associated with a party, you should check with your supervisor on how, if at all, to approach such a witness.

To complicate matters, it must be acknowledged that witnesses are seldom totally hostile, skeptical, friendly, or neutral. At different times during the investigation interview, and at different times throughout the various stages of the case, they may shift from one attitude to another. While it may be helpful to determine what general category witnesses fit into, it would be more realistic to view any witness as an individual in a state of flux in terms of what he or she wants to say and what he or she is capable of saying.

3. *The investigator must have the trust of the witness.* You have the sometimes difficult threshold problem of sizing up the witness from whom you are trying to obtain information. What are some of the states of mind that such witnesses could have?

■ They may want to feel important.

■ They may want to be "congratulated" for knowing anything, however insignificant, about the case.

■ They may want absolute assurance from you that they won't get into trouble by talking to you. They shy away from talk of courts, lawyers, and law.

| Checklist for Written Material | Checklist for Nonwritten Material |
|---|---|
| ■ Who wrote it? <br> ■ Under what circumstances was it written? <br> ■ Is the original available? If not, why not? <br> ■ Is a copy available? <br> ■ Who is available to testify that the copy is in fact an accurate copy of the original? <br> ■ Is the author available to testify on what he or she wrote? If not, why not? <br> ■ Is there any hearsay testimony available to corroborate the authenticity of the writing? <br> ■ Is there any other physical evidence available to corroborate the authenticity of the writing? <br> ■ What hearsay, direct evidence, or physical evidence is available to corroborate or contradict what is said in the writing? <br> ■ Can you obtain sample handwriting specimens of the alleged author? | ■ Who found it and under what circumstances? <br> ■ Where was it found? <br> ■ Why would it be where it was found? Was it unusual to find it there? <br> ■ Who is available to identify it? <br> ■ What identifying characteristics does it have? <br> ■ Who owns it? Who used it? <br> ■ Who owned it in the past? Who used it in the past? <br> ■ Who made it? <br> ■ What is its purpose? <br> ■ Does it require laboratory analysis? <br> ■ Can you take it with you? <br> ■ Can you photograph it? <br> ■ Is it stolen? <br> ■ Is there any public record available to trace its history? <br> ■ What facts does it tend to establish? <br> ■ Was it planted where it was found as a decoy? |

**FIGURE 9.7**

Checklist on the Validity of Physical (Tangible) Evidence

■ They may be willing to talk only after you have given full assurance that you will never reveal the source of the information they will give you.

■ They may be willing to talk to you only in the presence of their friends.

■ If they know your client, they may want to be told that you are trying to keep the client out of trouble.

■ They may want the chance to meet you first and then have you go away in order to decide whether they want to talk to you again.

■ They may not be willing to talk to you until you fulfill some of their needs— for example, listen to their troubles; act in a fatherly or motherly manner; play subtle, seductive games; etc.

In short, the investigator must gain the trust of individuals by assessing their needs and by knowing when they are ready to tell you what they know. If you take out your notebook immediately upon introducing yourself, you are probably too insensitive to establish the communication that's needed.

*4. The investigator must assess how well the witness would do under direct and cross-examination.*   As witnesses talk, ask yourself a number of questions:

■ Would they be willing to testify in court? Whatever the answer to this question is now, are they likely to change their mind later?

■ Would they be effective on the witness stand?

■ Do they know what they are talking about?

- Do they have a reputation for integrity, credibility, or truthfulness in the community?
- Are they defensive?
- Would they know how to say "I'm not sure" or "I don't understand the question," as opposed to giving an answer for the sake of giving an answer (e.g., to avoid being embarrassed)?
- When they talk, are they internally consistent?
- Do they know how to listen as well as talk?
- Do they understand the distinction between right and wrong, truth and lying?

## ■ Section H. Special Investigative Problems: Some Starting Points

### Judgment Collection

The person who wins a money judgment in court is called the *judgment creditor*. Unfortunately, collecting that judgment can be a difficult undertaking. An investigator may be asked to assist the law firm in ascertaining the financial assets of a particular individual or corporation against whom the judgment was obtained, called the *judgment debtor*.

One of the best starting points for such an investigation is government records. The following is a partial list of records available from the county clerk's or court office:

- Real property tax assessments
- Personal property tax assessments
- Filings made under the Uniform Commercial Code
- Federal tax liens
- Court dockets—to determine whether the judgment debtor has been a plaintiff or defendant in prior litigation
- Inheritance records—to determine whether the judgment debtor has inherited money or other property (determined by checking records of surrogate's court or probate court that handles inheritance and trust cases)

Such records could reveal a good deal of information on the financial status of the party under investigation.

For corporations that are judgment debtors, check the records of state and federal government agencies (such as the Secretary of State and the Securities and Exchange Commission) with whom the corporation must file periodic reports or disclosures on its activities and finances. You should also check with people who have done business with the corporation (customers or other creditors) as well as with its competitors in the field. These records and contacts could provide good leads.

### Missing Persons

An investigator may be asked to locate a missing heir, a relative of a client, a person who needs to be served with process in connection with current litigation, etc. A missing person is generally not difficult to locate—unless this person does not want to be found. The first step is to send a registered letter to the person's last-known address, "return receipt requested," which asks the post office to send you back a notice of who accepted the letter. Other possible leads:

- Relatives or friends
- Former landlord, neighbors, mail carrier, and local merchants in the area of the last-known address
- Local credit bureau
- Police department, hospitals
- References listed on employment applications
- Naturalization certificate, marriage record, drivers license, car registration
- Ad in the newspaper

## Background Investigations

Figure 9.8 presents a form used by a large investigative firm for its general background investigations on individuals. The first part of the form seeks information regarding identification of the subject. The antecedent data covers prior history.

---

### ■ ASSIGNMENT 9.1

Which of the following statements do you agree or disagree with? Why? For those statements that you are unsatisfied with, how would you modify them to reflect your own view?

**(a)** Investigation is a separate profession.

**(b)** There is a great difference between investigation conducted by the police and that conducted by a paralegal working for a law office.

**(c)** An investigator is an advocate.

**(d)** It is impossible for the investigator to keep from showing his or her own personal biases while in the field investigating.

**(e)** There is often a need for a separate investigation to verify the work of another investigation.

**(f)** A good investigator will probably be unable to describe why he or she is effective. There are too many intangibles involved.

**(g)** It is a good idea for an investigator to specialize in one area of the law, such as automobile negligence cases.

**(h)** If someone is willing to talk to and cooperate with an investigator, there is reason to suspect that this person is trying to manipulate the investigator.

---

### ■ ASSIGNMENT 9.2

If you were Tom in each of the following situations, what specific things would you do to deal with the situation?

**(a)** On September 1st, Tom decides that he wants to enter a community college. School opens in five days. There are only two colleges that still allow time for registration. Both are about the same distance from his home and he can afford both. Tom's problem is that he doesn't know enough about either college to make a decision. He works full-time from 9 to 6 and *must* continue to work right up to the first day of school in order to be able to finance his education.

Continued

**FIGURE 9.8**
Background
Investigations

### Identification of Subject

1. Complete Name _____ Age _____ SS# _____ Marital Status _____

Spouse's Name; Pertinent Info _____

_____

Children's Names and Ages _____

_____

_____

2. Current Residence Address and Type of Neighborhood _____

_____

_____

How Long at Present Address—Prior Residence Info _____

_____

_____

3. Business Affiliation and Address, Position, Type of Bus. _____

_____

_____

_____

### Antecedent History

1. Place & Date of Birth _____

Parents' Names & Occupations _____

_____

Where Did They Spend Their Youth? _____

_____

2. Education—Where, Which Schools, Dates of Attendance _____

_____

_____

Degree? What Kind? _____Any Other Info Pertaining to Scholastic Achievement,
Extracurric. Activities _____

_____

_____

_____

3. First Employer, to Present—F/T or P/T, Position or Title, Job Description, Exact Dates of
Employment, Type of Company _____

_____

_____

_____

_____

_____

4. Relationship with Peers, Supervisors, Subordinates—Where Do His or Her Abilities Lie?
Any Outside Activities? Reputation for Honesty, Trustworthiness, Integrity? Does He or She
Work Well Under Pressure? Anything Derogatory? If So, What Are Details? Reasons for
Leaving? Would They Rehire? Salaries? Health? Reliability? Job Understanding? Willing-
ness to Accept Responsibility? _____

_____

Continued

_____
_____
_____
_____
_____
_____

If Self-Employed—What Was the Nature of the Business? With Whom Did He or She Deal? Corp. Name? _____
_____

Date & Place of Incorporation _____
Who Were Partners, If Any? _____
What % of Stock Did Subj. Own? _____Was Business Successful? _____What Happened to It? _____
If Sold, to Whom? _____Any Subsid. or Affiliates? _____
_____
_____

5. What Is His or Her Character or Personality Like? Did Informer Know Him or Her Personally? _____
Hobbies? _____
Family Life? _____
Even-Tempered? _____ Loner or Joiner? _____
Introverted, Extroverted? _____ Written or Oral Abilities? _____
Does Informer Know Anyone Else Who Knows Subj.? _____
_____

6. Credit Information _____
_____
_____

7. Litigation _____Civil _____Criminal _____Bankruptcy _____
State _____Federal _____Local _____
_____

8. Banking—Financial: Bank _____
Types of Accounts—Average Bal. _____
How Long Did Subj. Have Accounts? _____Any Company Accounts?
_____

Is He or She Personally Known to Officers of the Bank? _____Any Borrowing?_____
Secured or Unsecured? _____If Secured, by What? Do They Have Financial Statement on the Subj.? _____
What Is His or Her Net Worth? _____Other Assets? Real Estate _____
Stocks _____
Equity in His or Her Co., etc. _____
_____

**FIGURE 9.8**

Background Investigations —*Continued*

### ■ ASSIGNMENT 9.2—*Continued*

(b) Tom teaches a second-grade class. It is the end of the school day on Friday and the bus is in front of the school ready to take his class home. If the students are not out in time for the bus, it will leave without them. It is 2:50 p.m. and the bus is scheduled to leave at 3:05 p.m. Tom discovers that his briefcase is missing from the top of his desk.

(c) Tom is the father of two teenagers, Ed and Bill. He comes home one day and finds a small package of marijuana in the front hall. He immediately suspects that Ed or Bill left it there. He turns around and goes out to look for them.

(d) Tom's son, Bill, has been accused of using abusive language in front of his teacher. Tom calls the teacher, who refuses to talk about it. The teacher refers Tom to the principal. The principal refuses to talk about it and refers Tom to the assistant superintendant at the central office.

(e) Tom's sister is ill. She received a letter from a local merchant where she often buys goods on credit. The letter informs her that she owes $122.00 and that unless she pays within a week "legal proceedings will be instituted" against her. She calls Tom and tells him that she paid the bill by sending $122.00 in cash last week. She asks Tom to help her.

(f) Tom works for a local legal service office. The office has a client who wants to sue her landlord because the kitchen roof is falling down. Tom is assigned to the case.

(g) A welfare department has told a client that it is going to terminate public assistance because the client's boyfriend is supporting her and her family. The client denies this. Tom is assigned to the case.

(h) A client has been to the office seeking help in obtaining a divorce. She claims that her husband beat her. Tom is assigned to the case.

(i) Sam owes Tom $1,000. When Tom asks for his money, Sam tells him that he is broke. Tom suspects differently.

(j) Tom's uncle once lived in Boston. After spending two years in the Army, he started traveling across the country; he has not been heard from for five years. Tom wants to locate his uncle.

---

### ■ ASSIGNMENT 9.3

How would you find the following information:

(a) The average life span of a lobster.

(b) The maiden name of the wife of the first governor in your state's history.

(c) The assessed property tax value of the tallest commercial building in your city in 1980.

(d) The number of vehicles using diesel fuel that drove in or through the state last month.

(e) The salary of the air traffic controller with the most seniority on duty on the day last year when the nearest airport experienced the largest rainfall of the year.

---

### *Note on the Need for a License*

In some states, investigators must be licensed. What about paralegals who are assigned investigation tasks by their supervising attorneys? A literal reading of the licensing statute might lead to the conclusion that such paralegals must be licensed along with traditional, self-employed private investigators. Often, however, the legislature will make an exception to the licensing requirement for employees of attorneys who engage in investigation under the attorney's supervision. Paralegal associations have been active in seeking these exemptions for paralegals. The main opposition to such exemptions has come from organizations of private investigators, who allegedly seek to impose roadblocks to paralegal investigation in order to secure more business for themselves.

 ## Section I. Evidence and Investigation

There is a close relationship between investigation and the law of evidence. One of the aims of investigation is to uncover and verify facts that will eventually be *admissible* in court. Admissibility is determined by the law of evidence. When attorneys are negotiating a case to try to reach a settlement in order to avoid a trial, they frequently talk (and argue) about the admissibility of the facts in the event that a trial does occur.

### Evidence in General

*Evidence* is that which is used to prove or disprove a fact, as indicated earlier.

*Admissible evidence* is evidence that the judge will permit the jury to consider. Admissible evidence does not mean that the evidence is true. It simply means that there are no valid objections to keep the evidence out. The jury is free to conclude that it does not believe the evidence that the judge ruled admissible.

*Direct evidence* is evidence (usually from personal observation or knowledge) that tends to establish a fact (or to disprove a fact) without the need for an inference.

*Circumstantial evidence* is evidence of one fact from which another fact can be inferred.

*Example:*   The police officer says, "I saw skid marks at the scene of the accident." This statement is:

Direct evidence
- that the police officer spoke these words.
- that skid marks were at the scene of the accident.

Circumstantial evidence
- that the driver of the car was speeding (this is the inference that can be drawn from the officer's statement).

Examples of *direct* evidence that someone was speeding would be: an admission by the driver that he or she was speeding, radar results, testimony of people who saw the car being driven, etc.

**Investigation Guideline:**
Direct evidence is preferred over circumstantial, although both kinds of evidence may be admissible. It is important that you are able to identify the inference in the circumstantial evidence. Then try to find direct evidence of whatever was inferred.

### Relevance

*Relevant evidence* is evidence that reasonably tends to make the existence of a fact more probable or less probable than it would be without that evidence. Relevancy is a very broad concept. It simply means that the evidence may be helpful in determining the truth or falsity of a fact involved in a trial. The test of relevancy is common sense and logic. If, for example, you want to know whether a walkway is dangerous, it is relevant that people have slipped on this walkway in the immediate past. Prior accidents under the same conditions make it more reasonable for someone to conclude that there is danger.

All relevant evidence is not necessarily admissible evidence. It would be highly relevant, for example, to know that the defendant told his attorney he was driving 80 MPH at the time of the accident, yet the attorney-client privilege would make such a statement inadmissible. Also, relevant evidence is not necessarily conclusive evidence. The jury will usually be free to reject certain relevant evidence and to accept other relevant evidence that is more believable. Relevancy is a *tendency* of evidence to establish or disestablish a fact. It may be a very weak tendency. Prior accidents may be relevant to show danger, but the jury may still conclude, in the light of all the evidence, that there was no danger.

> **Investigation Guideline:**
> Let common sense be your main guide in pursuing relevant evidence. So long as there is some logical connection between the fact you are pursuing and a fact that must be established at trial, you are on the right track.

### ■ ASSIGNMENT 9.4

Examine the following four situations. Discuss the relevance of each item of evidence being introduced.

**(a)** Mrs. Phillips is being sued by a department store for the cost of a gas refrigerator. Mrs. Phillips claims that she never ordered and never received a refrigerator from the store. The attorney for Mrs. Phillips wants to introduce two letters: (1) a letter from Mrs. Phillips' landlord stating that her kitchen is not equipped to handle gas appliances and (2) a letter from another merchant stating that Mrs. Phillips bought an electric refrigerator from him a year ago.

**(b)** Phil Smith has been charged with burglary in Detroit on December 16, 1986. His attorney tries to introduce testimony into evidence that on December 7, 8, 11, 15, and 22, 1986, the defendant was in Florida.

**(c)** Al Neuman is suing Sam Snow for negligence in operating his motor vehicle. Al's attorney tries to introduce into evidence the fact that Snow currently has pending against him four other automobile negligence cases in other courts.

**(d)** Jim is on trial for the rape of Sandra. Jim's attorney wants to introduce into evidence (1) the fact that Sandra subscribes to *Cosmopolitan* magazine, (2) the fact that Sandra is a member of AA, and (3) the fact that Sandra is the mother of Jim's child, who was born three years ago when they were dating. They separated in bitterness five months after the birth and never married.

## Competence of Witnesses

A witness is competent to testify if the witness:

■ understands the obligation to tell the truth
■ has the ability to communicate
■ has knowledge of the topic of his or her testimony

Children or mentally ill persons are not automatically disqualified. They are competent to testify if the judge is satisfied that the above criteria are met.

The competence of a witness must be carefully distinguished from the credibility of the witness. *Competency* is simply a ticket into the trial. *Credibility* goes to the *weight* of the evidence. This weight is assessed by the trier of fact—usually the jury. Competence goes to whether that witness will be allowed to testify at all. The jury may decide that everything said by a competent witness has little weight or is unworthy of belief.

## Lay Opinion Evidence

An opinion is an inference from a fact. For example, after you watch George stagger down the street and smell alcohol on his breath, you come to the conclusion that he is drunk. The conclusion is the inference. The facts are the observation of staggering and the smell of alcohol on his breath. Technically, a lay witness should not give opinion evidence. He or she must state the facts and let the trier of fact form the opinions. (Under certain circumstances, expert witnesses *are* allowed to give opinions on technical subjects not within the understanding of the average layperson.) The problem with the opinion rule, however, is that it is sometimes difficult to express oneself without using opinions, as when a witness says it was a sunny day or the noise was loud. Courts are therefore lenient in permitting opinion testimony by lay witnesses when the witness is talking from his or her own observations and it would be awkward for the witness not to express the opinion. If people regularly use opinions when discussing the topic in question, it will be permitted.

> **Investigation Guideline:**
> Know when a person is stating an opinion. Even though an opinion may be admissible, you should assume that it will *not* be admissible. Pursue all of the underlying facts that support the inference in the opinion. In the event that the person is not allowed to testify by using the opinion, be prepared with a list of the underlying facts the person relied on for the opinion.

---

■ **ASSIGNMENT 9.5**

Make a list of the questions that you would ask in order to uncover the underlying facts that formed the basis of the following opinions:

(a) He was insane.

(b) She couldn't see.

(c) It was cold out.

(d) He was traveling very fast.

---

## Hearsay

If evidence is *hearsay,* it is inadmissible unless one of the exceptions to the hearsay rule applies. Hearsay is testimony in court, or written evidence, of a statement made out of court when the statement is offered to show the truth of matters asserted therein and thus resting for its value on the credibility of the out-of-court asserter.[1]

> **Example:**
> Sam, a witness on the stand, says, "Fred told me on the street that he was speeding."

Note the conditions for the presence of hearsay:

---

[1]E. Cleary, ed., McCormick's *Handbook of the Law of Evidence,* 584 (1972).

| | |
|---|---|
| *Testimony in court* | The witness, Sam, is on the stand. |
| *Statement made out of court* | The statement by Fred was made on the street and not in court. |
| *Offered to assert the truth of the matter in the statement* | Assume that the purpose of the attorney questioning Sam is to show that Fred was speeding—that is, that the statement is true. |
| *The value of the statement depends on the credibility of the out-of-court asserter* | Fred is the out-of-court asserter. The value of the statement depends on how believable or credible *Fred* is. |

If the statement is not offered to prove the truth of the matters asserted in the statement, it is not hearsay. Suppose, for example, that the attorney wants to prove that Fred was alive immediately after the accident—that death was not instantaneous. The above statement would be admitted to prove that Fred actually said something, in other words, that Fred was alive enough to make a statement. If the testimony of the witness is offered to prove simply that the words were spoken by Fred rather than to prove that Fred was speeding, then the statement is not hearsay. The testimony that "Fred told me on the street that he was speeding" would therefore be admissible. The jury would have to be cautioned to examine the testimony for the limited purpose for which it is offered and not to consider it evidence that Fred was speeding.

Conduct intended as a substitute for words can also be hearsay. For example, the witness is asked, "What did Fred say when you asked him if he was speeding?" The witness answers, "He nodded his head yes." This testimony is hearsay if it is offered to prove that Fred was speeding. Conduct—nodding the head—was intended as a substitute for words.

**Investigation Guideline:**
Know when hearsay exists so that you can try to find alternative, nonhearsay evidence to prove the truth of the assertions made in the hearsay.

---

### ■ ASSIGNMENT 9.6

Is hearsay evidence involved in the following situations? Examine the four conditions of hearsay in each.

**(a)** Tom is suing Jim for negligence. On the witness stand, Tom says, "Jim was speeding at the time he hit me."

**(b)** Tom is suing Jim for negligence. While Tom is on the stand, his attorney introduces into evidence a mechanic's bill showing that the repair of the car cost $178.

**(c)** Mary and George were passengers in Tom's car at the time of the collision with Jim. George testifies that just before the collision, Mary shouted, "Look out for that car going through the red light!"

**(d)** He told me he was God.

---

### ■ ASSIGNMENT 9.7

Smith is being sued for assaulting Jones, who later died. Smith is on the stand when the following exchange occurs. How would you rule on the objection?

*Counsel for Smith:* "Did you strike the decedent, Jones?"
*Smith:* "Yes."
*Counsel for Smith:* "Did Jones say anything to you before you struck him?"

*Smith:* "Yes, he told me that he was going to kill me."
*Counsel for Jones's estate:* "Objection, your honor, on the grounds of hearsay. Smith cannot give testimony on what the decedent said since the decedent is obviously not subject to cross-examination."

There are a limited number of exceptions to the hearsay rule that have the effect of making evidence admissible even if it fulfills all the conditions of hearsay.

*1. Admissions.*   An *admission* is an out-of-court statement made by a party to the litigation that is inconsistent with a position the party is taking in the litigation. Example: Tom is being sued for negligence in driving a car that resulted in a collision at night. After the accident, Tom told the victim that he was driving. (Before the trial, Tom died of unrelated causes.) At the trial, the attorney for Tom's estate is claiming that Tom was only a passenger in the car. The victim's testimony that Tom said he was driving is admissible hearsay since it is an admission by a party—Tom.

*2. Declarations against Interest.*   A *declaration against interest* is an out-of-court statement made by a nonparty (who is now unavailable) when the statement is against the interest of the nonparty. Example: Fred sues Bob for stealing Fred's car. Bob introduces a statement of Kevin, who is now dead, that he (Kevin) stole the car. The testimony is admissible hearsay, since it is a declaration by Kevin, who is unavailable, that is against the interest of Kevin.

*3. Dying Declaration.*   A *dying declaration* is an out-of-court statement concerning the causes or circumstances of death when made by a person whose death is imminent. Example: Tom dies two minutes after he was hit over the head. Seconds before he dies, he says, "Linda did it." Tom's statement is admissible hearsay since it is a dying declaration. Some courts limit this exception to the hearsay rule to criminal cases. Other states would also allow it to be used in a civil case, such as in a civil battery or wrongful death case against Linda.

*4. Business Entry.*   A *business entry* is an out-of-court statement found in business records made in the regular course of business by someone whose duty is to make such entries. (This also applies to records of non-businesses such as universities, government agencies, or associations.) Example: A party seeks to introduce into evidence a hospital record containing a description of the plaintiff's condition when admitted to the emergency room. The record was made by the supervising nurse who is not in court. The record containing the description of the plaintiff's condition is admissible hearsay as a business entry made in the regular course of business by someone whose duty is to make such a report (assuming that the supervising nurse has this duty).

*5. Spontaneous Declaration.*   A *spontaneous declaration* is an out-of-court statement or utterance made spontaneously during or immediately after an exciting event by an observer of the event. Example: On the witness stand, Fred says, "I heard John say 'Oh my God, the truck just hit the child.' " This testimony is admissible hearsay as a spontaneous declaration.

*6. Declaration of Bodily Feelings, Symptoms, and Conditions.*   A *declaration of bodily feelings, symptoms, and conditions* is an out-of-court statement or utterance made spontaneously about the person's present bodily condition. Example: On the witness stand, Carol says, "My husband told me he had a sharp pain in his stomach." This testimony is admissible hearsay as a declaration of present bodily condition.

7. *Declaration of Mental State of Mind.*   A *declaration of mental state of mind* is an out-of-court statement made about the person's present state of mind. Example: On the witness stand, Len says, "The manager said she knew about the broken railing and would try to fix it." This testimony is admissible hearsay as a declaration of mental state of mind.

8. *Declaration of Present Sense Impression.*   A *declaration of present sense impression* is an out-of-court statement that describes an event while it is being observed by the person making the statement. Example: On the witness stand, Bill says, "As the car turned the corner, a bystander turned to me and said, 'She'll never make it.' " This testimony is admissible hearsay as a declaration of present sense impression.

NOTE: Exceptions 5–8 are referred to as the *res gestae* exceptions; the statements or utterances are all closely connected or concurrent with an occurrence.

## Privilege

A *privilege* in the law of evidence is the right to refuse to testify or the right to prevent someone else from testifying on a matter.

1. *Privilege against Self-Incrimination.*   An accused person cannot be compelled to testify in a criminal proceeding or answer incriminating questions that directly or indirectly connect the accused to the commission of a crime.

2. *Attorney-Client Privilege.*   A client and an attorney can refuse to disclose any communications between them whose purpose was to facilitate the provision of legal services for that client. The attorney cannot disclose the communication without the permission of the client.

3. *Doctor-Patient Privilege.*   A patient and doctor can refuse to disclose any confidential (private) communications between them that relate to medical care. The doctor cannot disclose the communication without the permission of the patient.

4. *Clergy-Penitent Privilege.*   A penitent and a member of the clergy can refuse to disclose any confidential (private) communications between them that relate to spiritual counseling or consultation. The minister, priest, or rabbi cannot disclose the communication without the permission of the penitent.

5. *Marital Communications.*   A husband and wife can refuse to disclose confidential (private) communications between them during the marriage. One spouse can also prevent the other from making such disclosures. Both spouses must agree to the disclosure. This privilege does not apply to litigation between spouses, e.g., divorce litigation.

6. *Government Information.*   Some information collected by the government about citizens is confidential and privileged. Examples include adoption records and tax records. The privilege would not prevent use of the information to prosecute the citizen in connection with the citizen's duty to provide accurate information. It would, however, prevent third parties from gaining access to the confidential information.

**Investigation Guideline:**
When a privilege applies, look for alternative, nonprivileged sources of obtaining the information protected by the privilege.

### Best Evidence Rule

To prove the contents of a private (nonofficial) writing, you should produce the original writing unless it is unavailable through no fault of the person now seeking to introduce a copy of the original e.g., it was destroyed in a storm.

### Authentication

Authentication is evidence that a writing (or other physical item) is genuine and that it is what it purports to be—for example, the testimony of witnesses who saw the document being prepared.

### Parol Evidence Rule

Oral evidence cannot be introduced to alter or contradict the contents of a written document if the parties intended the written document to be a complete statement of the agreement.

##  Section J. Taking a Witness Statement

There are four major kinds of *witness statements:*

1. Handwritten statement
2. Recorded statement in question-and-answer format (on audio or video tape)
3. Responses to a questionnaire that is mailed to the witness to answer
4. A statement taken in question-and-answer format with court reporters

The most common kind of statement is the first, which we shall consider here.

In a handwritten statement, the investigator writes down what the witness says, or the witness writes out the statement himself or herself. There is no formal structure to which the written statement must conform. The major requirements for the statement are clarity and accuracy.

The statement should begin by identifying (1) the witness (name, address, place of work, names of relatives, and other identifying data that may be helpful in locating the witness later); (2) the date and place of the taking of the statement; and (3) the name of the person to whom the statement is being made. See the example of a witness statement in Figure 9.9.

Then comes the body of the statement, in which the witness provides information about the event or circumstance in question (an accident that was observed, what the witness did and saw just before a fire, where the witness was on a certain date, etc.) It is often useful to have the witness present the facts in a chronological order, particularly when many facts are involved in the statement. It is important that the witness give detailed facts, such as facts demonstrating that the witness was in a good position to observe the event, to lend credibility to the statement.

At the end of the statement, the witness should say that he or she is making the statement of his or her own free will, without any pressure or coercion from anyone. The witness then signs the statement. The signature goes on the last page. Each of the other pages is also signed or initialed. If others have watched the witness make and sign the statement, they should also sign an *attestation clause,* which simply states that they observed the witness sign the statement.

**FIGURE 9.9**
Witness Statement

---

**Statement of John Wood**

I am John Wood. I am 42 years old and live at 3416 34th Street, N.W., Nashua, New Hampshire 03060. I work at the Deming Chemical Plant at region circle, Nashua. My home phone is 966-3954. My work phone is 297-9700 ×301. I am married to Patricia Wood. We have two children, Jessica (fourteen years old) and Gabriel (eleven years old). I am making this statement to Rose Thompson, a paralegal at Fields, Smith and Farrell. This statement is being given on March 13, 1986 at my home, 3416 34th Street, NW.

On February 15, 1986, I was standing on the corner of. . . .

---

Before the witness signs, he or she should read the entire statement and make any corrections that need to be made. Each correction should be initialed by the witness. Each page should be numbered with the total number of pages indicated each time. For example, if there are four pages, the page numbers would be "1 of 4," "2 of 4," "3 of 4," and "4 of 4." The investigator should not try to correct any spelling or grammatical mistakes made by the witness. The statement should exist exactly as the witness spoke or wrote it. Just before the signature of the witness at the end of the statement, the witness should say (in writing), "I have read all _____ pages of this statement, and the facts within it are accurate to the best of my knowledge."

Investigators sometimes use various tricks of the trade to achieve a desired effect. For example, if the investigator is writing out the statement as the witness speaks, the investigator may *intentionally* make an error of fact. When the witness reads over the statement, the investigator makes sure that the witness catches the error and initials the correction. This becomes added evidence that the witness carefully read the statement. The witness might later try to claim that he or she did not read the statement. The initialed correction helps rebut this position.

Not all witness statements are eventually admitted into evidence at the trial. They may be admitted to help the attorney demonstrate that the pretrial statement of the witness is inconsistent with the testimony of this witness during the trial itself. The main value of witness statements is thoroughness and accuracy in case preparation. Trials can occur years after the events that led to litigation. Witnesses may disappear or forget. Witness statements taken soon after the event can sometimes be helpful in tracking down witnesses and in helping them recall the details of the event.

---

■ **ASSIGNMENT 9.8**

Select any member of the class and take a witness statement from this person. The statement should concern some accident in which the witness was a participant or an observer. The witness, however, should not be a party to any litigation growing out of the accident. You write out the statement from what the witness says in response to your questions. Do not submit a statement handwritten by the witness except for his or her signature, initials, etc. Assume that you (the investigator–paralegal) work for the law firm of Davis and Davis, which represents someone else involved in the accident.

---

■ Section K. The Settlement Work-Up

One of the end products of investigation is the *settlement work-up,* which is a summary of the major facts obtained through investigation, client interviewing, answers to interrogatories, deposition testimony, etc. The work-up, in one form or another, is used in negotiation with the other side or with the other side's liability insurance company in an effort to obtain a favorable settlement in lieu of trial.

In Figure 9.10, there is a memo containing data for a proposed settlement work-up.[2] Note its precision and attention to detail. Excellent FP (Fact Particularization, see Chapter 8) had to be used as the basis of this report.

---

[2]Prepared by Katherine Webb, Legal Assistant at Cartwright, Sucherman, Slobodin & Fowler, Inc., San Francisco, California.

---

**FIGURE 9.10**

**Settlement Work-Up**

**Interoffice Memorandum**

To: Mary Jones, Esq.
From: Katherine Webb, Paralegal
Date: June 12, 1975
Re: Joseph Smith vs. Dan Lamb et al.
    Case Summary—Settlement Work-Up

**I. Facts of Accident:**

The accident occurred on September 6, 1973, in Orange, California. Joseph Smith was driving westbound on Chapman Avenue, stopped to make a left turn into a parking lot, and was rear-ended by the one-half-ton panel truck driven by Dan Lamb.

The defendant driver, Mr. Lamb, was cited for violation of Vehicle Code Sections 21703 and 22350, following too close, and at an unsafe speed for conditions.

**II. Injuries:**

Severe cervical and lumbar sprain, superimposed over pre-existing, albeit asymptomatic, spondylolisthesis of pars interarticulus at L5-S1, with possible herniated nucleus pulposus either at or about the level of the spondylolisthesis; and contusion of right knee.

Please see attached medical reports for further details.

**III. Medical Treatment:**

Mr. Smith felt an almost immediate onset of pain in his head, neck, back, and right knee after the accident and believes that he may have lost consciousness momentarily. He was assisted from his car and taken by ambulance to the St. Joseph Hospital emergency room, where he was initially seen by his regular internist, Raymond Ross, M.D.

Dr. Ross obtained orthopedic consultation with Brian A. Ewald, M.D., who reviewed the multiple X-rays taken in the emergency room and found them negative for fracture. Lumbar spine X-rays did reveal evidence of a spondylolisthesis defect at the pars interarticulus of L5, but this was not felt to represent acute injury. Dr. Ewald had Mr. Smith admitted to St. Joseph Hospital on the same day for further evaluation and observation.

On admission to the hospital, Mr. Smith was placed on complete bed rest, with a cervical collar and medication for pain. On September 10, neurological consultation was obtained with Michael H. Sukoff, M.D., who, although he did not find any significant objective neurological abnormality, felt that there might be a herniated disc at L4-L5, with possible contusion of the nerve roots.

Drs. Ewald and Sukoff followed Mr. Smith's progress throughout the remainder of his hospitalization. He was continued on bed rest, physiotherapy, and medication, and fitted with a lumbosacral support. He was ultimately ambulated with crutches and was discharged from the hospital on September 25, 1973, with instructions to continue to rest and wear his cervical collar and back brace.

On discharge from the hospital, Mr. Smith was taken by ambulance to the Sky Palm Motel in Orange, where his wife and children had been staying during his hospitalization. Arrangements were made for home physiotherapy and rental of a hospital bed, and Mr. Smith was taken by ambulance on the following day to his residence at the Riviera Country Club in Pacific Palisades.

After returning home, Mr. Smith continued to suffer from headaches, neck pain, and severe pain in his lower back, with some radiation into both legs, especially the right. He

Continued

**FIGURE 9.10**
Settlement
Work-Up—
*Continued*

was totally confined to bed for at least two months following the accident, where he was cared for by his wife. Daily physical therapy was administered by Beatrice Tasker, R.P.T.

Mr. Smith continued to receive periodic outpatient care with Dr. Ewald. By the end of December, 1973, Mr. Smith was able to discontinue the use of his cervical collar and was able to walk, with difficulty, without crutches. At the time of his office visit with Dr. Ewald on December 21, he was noted to be having moderate neck discomfort, with increasingly severe low back pain. At the time, Dr. Ewald placed Mr. Smith on a gradually increasing set of Williams exercises and advised him to begin swimming as much as possible.

Mr. Smith continued to be followed periodically by Dr. Ewald through March 1974, with gradual improvement noted. However, Mr. Smith continued to spend the majority of his time confined to his home and often to bed, using a cane whenever he went out. In addition, he suffered periodic severe flareups of low back pain, which would render him totally disabled and would necessitate total bed rest for several days at a time.

During this period of time, Mr. Smith also experienced headaches and blurred vision, for which Dr. Ewald referred him to Robert N. Dunphy, M.D. Dr. Dunphy advised that the symptoms were probably secondary to his other injuries and would most likely subside with time.

On April 1, 1974, Mr. Smith consulted Dr. Ewald with complaints of increased back pain following an automobile ride to San Diego. Dr. Ewald's examination at that time revealed bilateral lumbar muscle spasm, with markedly decreased range of motion. Due to his concern about the extremely prolonged lumbar symptoms, and suspecting a possible central herniated nucleus pulposus, Dr. Ewald recommended that Mr. Smith undergo lumbar myelography. This was performed on an inpatient basis at St. Joseph Hospital on April 4, 1974 and reported to be within normal limits.

Mr. Smith continued conservative treatment with Dr. Ewald through February 1974, following the prescribed program of rest, medication, exercise, and daily physiotherapy administered by his wife. He was able to graduate out of his lumbosacral support by approximately October 1974, resuming use of the garment when he experienced severe flareups of low back pain.

In his medical report dated January 2, 1975, Dr. Ewald stated that he expected a gradual resolution of lumbar symptomatology with time. However, in his subsequent report, dated January 10, 1975, Dr. Ewald noted that since his original report, Mr. Smith had suffered multiple repetitive episodes of low back pain, secondary to almost any increase of activity. At an office visit on February 25, Mr. Smith was reported to have localized his discomfort extremely well to the L5-S1 level, and range of motion was found to have decreased to approximately 75%. Since his examination in February, Dr. Ewald has discussed at length with both Mr. Smith and his wife the possibility of surgical intervention, consisting of lumbar stabilization (fusion) at the L5-S1 level, secondary to the spondylolisthesis present at that level. Dr. Ewald has advised them of the risks, complications, and alternatives with regard to consideration of surgical stabilization, noting that surgery would be followed by a 6-to-9-month period of rehabilitation, and further warning that even if the surgical procedure is carried out, there is no guarantee that Mr. Smith will be alleviated of all of his symptomatology.

As stated in Dr. Ewald's medical report dated March 10, 1975, Mr. Smith is himself beginning to lean toward definite consideration with regard to surgery, although he is presently continuing with conservative management.

Dr. Ewald recommends that in the event Mr. Smith does choose to undergo surgery, a repeat myelogram should be performed in order to rule out, as much as possible, the presence of a herniated nucleus pulposus either above or at the level of the spondylolisthesis.

### IV. Residual Complaints

Mr. Smith states that his neck injury has now largely resolved, although he does experience occasional neck pain and headaches. However, he continues to suffer from constant, severe pain in his low back, with some radiation of pain and numbness in the right leg.

Mr. Smith notes that his low back pain is worse with cold weather and aggravated by prolonged sitting, walking, driving, or nearly any form of activity. He finds that he must rest frequently and continues to follow a daily regimen of swimming, Williams exercises,

Continued on next page

pain medication, and physiotherapy administered by his wife. He has also resumed the use of his lumbosacral brace.

Mr. Smith was an extremely active person prior to the accident, accustomed to working 12 to 16 hours per day and engaging in active sports such as tennis. Since the accident, he has had to sell his business and restrict all activities to a minimum, because he has found that any increase in activity will trigger a flareup of low back pain so severe that he is totally incapacitated for several days at a time.

As stated by Dr. Ewald, Mr. Smith is now seriously considering the possibility of surgical stabilization, despite the risks and complications involved. He has always viewed surgery as a last resort but is now beginning to realize that it may be his only alternative in view of his prolonged pain and disability. However, he currently intends to delay any definite decision until after the summer, during which time he intends to increase his swimming activity and see if he can gain any relief from his symptomatology.

## V.  Specials

(Copies of supporting documentation attached hereto.)

### A.  Medical:

| | |
|---|---|
| 1. Southland Ambulance Service (9/6/73) | $    37.00 |
| 2. St. Joseph Hospital (9/6–9/25/73) | 2,046.29 |
| 3. Raymond R. Ross, M.D. (Emergency Room, 9/6/73) | 25.00 |
| 4. Brian A. Ewald, M.D. (9/6/73–4/28/75) | 604.00 |
| 5. Michael H. Sukoff, M.D. (9/10–9/22/75) | 140.00 |
| 6. Wind Ambulance Service (9/25/73) | 39.50 |
| 7. Wind Ambulance Service (9/26/73) | 89.00 |
| 8. Beatrice Tasker, R.P.T. (9/21–10/22/73) | 825.00 |
| 9. Abbey Rents (Rental of hospital bed and trapeze bar, 9/25–11/25/73) | 222.00 |
| 10. Allied Medical & Surgical Co. (Purchase of cane, 1/10/73) | 10.45 |
| 11. Rice Clinical Laboratories (2/1/74) | 4.00 |
| 12. Robert N. Dunphy, M.D. (2/1–4/15/74) | 95.00 |
| 13. St. Joseph Hospital (X-rays and lab tests, 2/9/74) | 156.00 |
| 14. St. Joseph Hospital (Inpatient myelography, 4/23–4/24/74) | 251.60 |
| 15. Medication | 357.70 |
| Total Medical Expenses | $4,902.54 |

### B.  Miscellaneous Family Expenses

(During plaintiff's hospitalization, 9/6–9/25/75.)

| | |
|---|---|
| 1. Sky Palm Motel (Lodging for wife and children) | $1,050.50 |
| 2. Taxicab (9/6/73) | 2.45 |
| Total Miscellaneous Expenses | $1,052.95 |

### C.  Wage Loss

At the time of the accident, Mr. Smith was employed as president and co-owner, with Mr. George Frost, of the Inter Science Institute, Inc., a medical laboratory in Los Angeles.

**FIGURE 9.10**

Settlement Work-Up— *Continued*

Continued on next page

**FIGURE 9.10**

Settlement
Work-Up
—*Continued*

As stated in the attached verification from Mr. Mamikunian, Mr. Smith was earning an annual salary of $48,000.00, plus automobile, expenses, and fringe benefits.

In a telephone conversation with Mr. Frost on May 6, 1975, he advised me that the Inter Science Institute had grossed $512,000.00 in 1973 and $700,000.00 in 1974. He further confirmed that prior to the accident of September 6, 1973, both he and Mr. Frost had been approached on at least two to three different occasions by companies, including Revlon and a Canadian firm, offering substantial sums of money for purchase of the business. On the basis of the foregoing, both Mr. Smith and Mr. Frost place a conservative estimate of the value of the business at $2,000,000.00.

Due to injuries sustained in the subject accident, Mr. Smith was unable to return to work or perform the necessary executive and managerial functions required in his position as president and part owner of the business. As a result, on or about October 26, 1973, while still totally incapacitated by his injuries, Mr. Smith was forced to sell his 50% stock interest in the Inter Science Institute for a total sum of $300,000.00.

On the basis of the prior estimated value of the business at $2,000,000.00, *Mr. Smith sustained a loss of $700,000.00 in the sale of his one-half interest in Inter Science Institute, Inc., in addition to the loss of an annual salary of $48,000.00, plus automobile, expenses, and fringe benefits.*

Even if one were to assume that the sale of his interest in the business was reasonable value, Mr. Smith has sustained a loss in salary only in the sum of *$84,000.00* to date, based on an annual salary of $48,000.00 for one year and nine months up to today's date, June 12, 1975.

## Chapter Summary

The goal of investigation is to obtain new facts and to verify facts already known by the office. It is a highly individualistic skill where determination, imagination, resourcefulness, and openness are critical. A good investigator has a healthy suspicion of preconceived notions of what the facts are when this might interfere with uncovering the unexpected. In the search for the facts, the investigator is concerned with truth in the context of the evidence that will be needed to establish that truth in court. But the standard that guides the search is not absolute truth or proof; the guideline of the investigator is to pursue whatever degree of evidence (large or small) that is reasonably available.

People often have different perspectives on what did or did not happen, particularly in regard to emotionally charged events. When different versions of facts exist, the investigator must seek them out.

Competent investigation requires a knowledge of the standard sources of information; an ability to use the techniques of gaining access to records, and an ability to evaluate the trustworthiness of testimonial and physical evidence.

Investigators must be aware of the image they project of themselves, be prepared for witnesses with differing levels of factual knowledge, be ready for witnesses who are unwilling to cooperate, and be able to gain the trust of witnesses.

The law of evidence is an important part of the investigator's arsenal. This should include an understanding of: admissible evidence, the distinction between direct evidence and circumstantial evidence, the nature of relevance, when a witness is competent to give testimony and to state an opinion, the nature of hearsay and the eight exceptions that allow hearsay to be admitted. Investigators need to understand the effect of the privilege against self-incrimination, the attorney-client privilege, the doctor-patient privilege, and the confidentiality of some government information. They must also understand the best evidence rule, the authentication of evidence, and the parol evidence rule.

Two important documents that are the products of competent investigation are: a witness statement, which is taken to preserve the testimony of an important witness, and a settlement work-up, which is an advocacy document that compiles and organizes facts in an effort to encourage a favorable settlement.

# Key Terms

impeach
discovery devices
deposition
interrogatories
request for admissions
evidence
testimonial evidence
physical evidence
tangible evidence
Freedom of Information Act
disinterested witness
admissible evidence
direct evidence
circumstantial evidence
relevant evidence

competency
credibility
lay opinion evidence
hearsay
admissions
declaration against interest
dying declaration
business entry
spontaneous declaration
declaration of bodily feelings
declaration of mental state of
   mind
declaration of present sense
   impression
res gestae exceptions

privilege
privilege against self-
   incrimination
attorney-client privilege
doctor-patient privilege
clergy-penitent privilege
marital communications
best evidence rule
authentication
parol evidence rule
witness statement
attestation clause
settlement work-up

# 10

# Litigation Assistantship

## ■ Chapter Outline

**Section A. Overview of Litigation**
    An Anatomy of the Litigation Process
    *Civil Liability*
    *Criminal Liability*
    *Administrative Dispute*
**Section B. Alternative Dispute
    Resolution**
**Section C. Litigation Assistantship:
    Pretrial Stage**
    Data Retrieval
    Digesting and Indexing

Calendar Control and Scheduling
Drafting Interrogatories and Replies to
    Interrogatories
Drafting Pleadings
Preparation of Trial Notebook
**Section D. Litigation Assistantship:
    Trial Stage**
**Section E. Litigation Assistantship:
    Appeal Stage**
**Section F. Litigation Assistantship:
    Enforcement Stage**

## ■ Section A. Overview of Litigation

*Litigation* is the formal process of resolving legal controversies through special tribunals established for this purpose. The main tribunals are courts and administrative agencies acting in their *quasi-judicial* capacity.[1] Paralegals can perform many functions in assisting attorneys who are litigating cases. The following overview of litigation will help you place these functions in context. The overview is presented in the form of a story—the litigation woes of Michael Brown, who finds himself embroiled in civil and criminal disputes.

A *civil dispute* consists of (a) one private party suing another private party, or (b) a private party suing the government, or (c) the government suing a private party for a matter other than the commission of a crime. A *criminal dispute* is a suit brought by the government for the alleged commission of a crime. Most civil and criminal disputes are resolved in court. Occasionally, however, some of these disputes (particularly civil ones) are first heard by an administrative agency.

### The Legal Odyssey of Michael Brown: An Anatomy of the Litigation Process

Michael Brown is a truck driver for the Best Bread Company. Several years ago, as Brown was walking home from work, Harold Clay, an old friend from the past, stopped and offered him a ride. They had not seen each other since

---

[1]*Quasi-judicial* means like or similar to a court. When an administrative agency holds a hearing to resolve a dispute, it is acting quasi-judicially. See Chapter 6.

Clay had moved cross-country a number of years ago. They carried on an excited conversation as Clay drove. After a few blocks, a car driven by George Miller, a resident of a neighboring state, ran through a red light and struck Clay's car. All three individuals were seriously injured and were taken to a local hospital. Clay died two weeks later from injuries received in the crash.

Several days after the accident, Brown's boss, Frank Best, wrote Brown a letter. In it, Best said that he had learned that the police had found about one-half ounce of heroin under the front passenger seat of Clay's car and were planning to charge Brown with possession of narcotics with intent to distribute. Best also stated that several thefts had occurred at the company warehouse recently and that he now suspected Brown of having been involved in them. For these reasons, he decided to fire Brown, effective immediately.

There are at least three different legal disputes involving Brown that could arise out of this fact situation:

1. A dispute among Brown, Miller, and Clay's estate regarding civil liability for the accident
2. A dispute between Brown and the government regarding the criminal charges
3. A dispute among Brown, the Best Bread Company, and the State Unemployment Compensation Board concerning Brown's entitlement to unemployment compensation benefits

Each of these disputes could lead to a number of court opinions. The third dispute might involve an administrative decision, possibly followed by one or more court opinions, all concerning Brown's claim for unemployment compensation.

## 1. Civil Liability

Brown suffered substantial injury as a result of the crash. From whom could he collect *damages?* Who was *liable* for the accident? Was Miller at fault? Clay? Was each of them *jointly and severally* liable?

Damages:   An award of money (paid by the wrongdoer) to compensate the person who has been harmed.

Liable:   Legally responsible.

Joint and several liability:   When two or more persons are jointly and severally liable, they are legally responsible, together and individually. Each wrongdoer is individually responsible for the entire judgment. The person who has been wronged can collect from one of them or from all of them.

Brown hired Brenda Davis, Esq. to represent him. Once Brown signed the *retainer,* David would later enter an *appearance* and become the *attorney of record.*

Retainer:   A contract between attorney and client stating the nature of the services to be rendered and the cost of the services. (A retainer can also refer to an amount of money or other assets given to an attorney to insure that the attorney will remain available to represent the client.)

Appearance:   Going to court to act on behalf of a party to the litigation. The attorney usually appears by filing a *notice of appearance* in court, which is often accomplished through a *praecipe.* A praecipe is a formal request to the court (usually made through the court clerk) that something be done. Here the request is that the attorney become the attorney of record.

Attorney of record:   An attorney of record is the attorney who has filed a notice of appearance (through a praecipe or other means) and who is formally mentioned in court records as the official attorney of the party. Once this occurs, the attorney may not be able to withdraw from the case without court permission.

The attorney explained that a number of factors had to be considered before deciding on the *forum* in which to sue Miller and Clay's *estate*. Brown might be able to bring the suit in a number of places: (a) in a state trial court where Brown lives, (b) in a state trial court where Miller lives, (c) in a state trial court where Clay's estate is located, (d) in the federal trial court sitting in Brown's state, (e) in the federal trial court sitting in Miller's state, or (f) in the federal trial court sitting in the state where Clay's estate is located. The reason Brown could sue in a federal court is the existence of *diversity of citizenship*: all the parties involved in the litigation came from different states. Davis advised Brown to sue in federal court. The suit would be brought in the U.S. District Court sitting in Brown's own state, since this would be the most convenient *venue* for Brown.

Forum:   The court where the case is to be tried.

Estate:   All the property left by a decedent (one who has died), from which any obligations or debts of the decedent must be paid.

Diversity of citizenship:   A kind of jurisdiction giving a federal court the power to hear a case based upon the fact that (a) the parties to the litigation are from different states, and (b) the amount of money involved exceeds the amount specified by federal statute.

Venue:   The place of the trial. In most judicial systems, there is more than one trial court. For example, there may be one for each county or district. The selection of a particular trial court within a judicial system is referred to as a *choice of venue*.

Having decided on a court, Davis was ready to begin the lawsuit. She drafted a *complaint*, naming Brown as the *plaintiff* and *stating a cause of action* for negligence against Miller and Clay's estate as *codefendants*. The complaint was the first *pleading* of the case. In the complaint, Davis stated the facts she felt constituted a cause of action for negligence. Some of the factual *allegations* were based on personal knowledge of Brown, while others were based on *information and belief*. The *ad damnum* clause of the complaint asked for $100,000. When she finished drafting the complaint, Ms. Davis signed the pleading, attached a written demand for a *jury trial*, and *filed* both documents with the clerk of the court.

Complaint:   A pleading (see definition below) filed by the plaintiff that tries to state a claim or *cause of action* (see definition below) against the defendant.

Plaintiff:   The party initiating the lawsuit.

Cause of action:   A legally acceptable reason for suing.

Stating a cause of action:   Including in the complaint those facts which, if proved at trial, would entitle the plaintiff to win (assuming the defendant could not establish any defenses that would defeat the case).

Codefendants:   More than one defendant being sued in a civil case (or prosecuted in a criminal case) in the same litigation.

Pleading:   A paper or document filed in court, such as a complaint or an answer, stating the position of one of the parties on the cause(s) of action or on the defenses.

Allegation:   A claimed fact; a fact that a party will try to prove at trial.

Information and belief:   A standard legal term used to indicate that the allegation is not based on the firsthand knowledge of the person making the allegation but that the person, nevertheless, believes in good faith that the allegation is true.

Ad damnum:   A statement in the complaint in which the plaintiff asks for a specified sum of money as damages.

Jury trial:   A jury is a group of citizens who will decide the issues or questions of fact at the trial. The judge decides the issues or questions of law. If there is no jury at the trial, then the judge decides both the questions of law and the questions of fact..

Filed:   Formally presented to a court (usually to the clerk of the court) or to an opposing party.

*Service of process* came next. It was accomplished when a copy of the complaint, along with the *summons,* was served on both Miller and on the legal representative of Clay's estate. Davis did not serve these parties herself. She used a *process server* who then had to file with the court an *affidavit* of service indicating the circumstances under which service was achieved. Service was made before the *statute of limitations* on the negligence cause of action had run out. Once the defendants were properly served, the court acquired *in personam jurisdiction* over them.

Service of process:   The delivery of the summons which is a formal notice to a defendant ordering him or her to appear in court in order to answer the allegations made by the plaintiff.

Summons:   The formal notice from the court ordering the defendant to appear and answer the plaintiff's allegations. The summons is *served* on the defendant. The words summons and process are often used interchangeably..

Process server:   A person who charges a fee for serving process.

Affidavit:   A written statement of fact in which a person (called the *affiant*) swears that the written statement is true.

Statute of limitations:   The law establishing the period within which the lawsuit must be commenced; if it is not brought within that time, it can never be brought..

In personam jurisdiction:   Personal jurisdiction: the power of the court over the person of the defendant obtained in part by proper service of process.

Both Miller and Clay's estate filed *motions to dismiss* for *failure to state a cause of action*. The motions were denied by the court.

Motion to dismiss:   A request that the court decide that a party may not further litigate a claim—that is, that the claim be dropped.

Failure to state a cause of action:   Failure of the plaintiff to allege enough facts in the complaint. Even if the plaintiff proved all the facts alleged in the complaint, the facts would not establish a cause of action entitling the plaintiff to recover against the defendant. The motion to dismiss for failure to state a cause of action is sometimes referred to as (a) a *demurrer* or (b) a *failure to state a claim upon which relief can be granted*.

Because the case had been filed in a federal court, the *procedural law* governing the case would be found in the *Federal Rules of Civil Procedure*. (The *substantive law* of the case would be the state law of negligence.) According to the Federal Rules of Civil Procedure, Miller and Clay's estate were each required to file an *answer* to Brown's complaint within twenty days. Miller filed his answer almost immediately. Since Clay was dead and unable to tell his attorney what had happened at the accident, the attorney for the estate had some difficulty in *drafting* an answer and was unable to file it within the twenty days. In order to avoid a *default judgment* against the estate, the attorney filed a *motion* asking for an extension of thirty days within which to file the answer. The motion was granted by the court, and the answer was filed within the new deadline.

Procedural law:   The technical rules setting forth the steps required to resolve a dispute in court or in an administrative agency.

Federal Rules of Civil Procedure (FRCP):   The technical rules governing the manner in which civil cases are brought in and progress through the federal trial courts.

Substantive law:   The rights and duties imposed by law (such as the duty to use reasonable care) other than procedural rights and duties.

Answer:   The pleading that responds to or answers allegations of the complaint.

Draft:   To write.

Default judgment:   An order of the court deciding the case in favor of the plaintiff because the defendant failed to appear or to file an answer before the deadline.

Motion:   A request made to the court, such as a motion to dismiss. The party making the motion is called the *movant*. The verb is *move*, as in "I move that the court permit the demonstration."

The answer filed on behalf of Clay's estate denied all allegations of negligence and raised an *affirmative defense* of contributory negligence against Brown on the theory that if Clay had been partially responsible for the collision, it was because Brown had distracted him through his conversation in the car. Finally, the answer of Clay's estate raised a *cross-claim* against the codefendant Miller, alleging that the accident had been caused solely by Miller's negligence. The estate asked $1,000,000 in damages.

Defense:   A response to the claims of the other party, setting forth reasons why the claims should not be granted. The defense may be as simple as a flat denial of the other party's factual allegations or may involve entirely new factual allegations. (In the latter situation, the defense is an *affirmative defense*.)

Affirmative defense:   A defense that is based on new factual allegations by the defendant not contained in the plaintiff's allegations.

Cross-claim:   Usually, a claim by one codefendant against another codefendant.

Miller's answer also raised the defense of contributory negligence against Brown and stated a cross-claim against Clay's estate, alleging that the accident had been caused solely by the negligence of Clay, or of Clay and Brown together. On this same theory, that Brown together with Clay had negligently caused the accident, Miller's answer also stated a *counterclaim* against Brown. Miller sought $50,000 from Brown and $50,000 against Clay's estate as damages.

Counterclaim:   A claim or a cause of action against the plaintiff stated in the defendant's answer.

For a time, Miller and his attorney considered filing a *third-party complaint* against his own insurance company since the company would be liable for any judgment against him. They decided against this strategy since they did not want to let the jury know that Miller was insured. If the jury knew this fact, it might be more inclined to reach a verdict in favor of the plaintiff and for a high amount of damages. The strategy was also unnecessary because there was no indication that Miller's insurer would *contest* its obligation to compensate

Miller for any damages that he might have to pay Brown or Clay's estate in the event that the trial resulted in an *adverse judgment* against him.

Third-party complaint:   A complaint filed by the defendant against a third party (that is, a person not presently a party to the lawsuit). This complaint alleges that the third party is or may be liable for all or part of the damages that the plaintiff may win from the defendant.

Contest:   To challenge.

Adverse judgment:   A judgment or decision against you.

At this point, five assorted claims, cross-claims and counterclaims had been filed by the parties. A sixth, Miller's third-party claim against his insurer, had been considered but ultimately had not been filed. These claims and their relationship to each other are illustrated in Figure 10.1.

1. Brown's original complaint for negligence against Miller and
2. against Clay's Estate, as codefendants
3. Defendant Miller's counterclaim for negligence against plaintiff, Brown
4. Defendant Miller's cross-claim for negligence against his codefendant, the Estate
5. Defendant Estate's cross-claim for negligence against its codefendant, Miller
6. Third-party complaint which defendant Miller considered but ultimately decided *not* to file against his insurance company

Once the pleadings were filed, all three parties began to seek *discovery*. Each attorney first served written *interrogatories* on the opposing parties. These were followed by *depositions* and *requests for admissions*. Miller refused to answer several questions during his deposition in his attorney's office. As a result, Brown's attorney had to file a discovery motion, seeking an *order* from the court compelling Miller to answer. A *hearing* was subsequently held on the motion, and after listening to arguments by all of the attorneys, the judge granted the motion in full, ordering Miller to answer the questions. Faced with the court's order, Miller answered the remaining questions.

Each party then filed a *motion for summary judgment*. The judge denied these motions, and the case was ready for trial.

**FIGURE 10.1**

Diagram of the Claims in the Brown/Miller/Estate Litigation

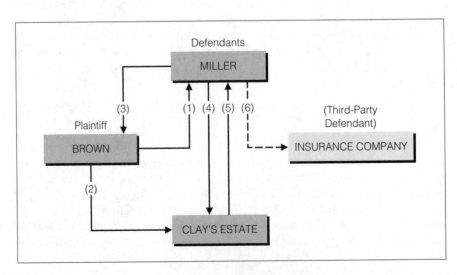

Discovery:   The pretrial devices that can be used by one party to obtain facts and information about the case from the other party in order to assist in preparing for trial.

Interrogatories:   A discovery device consisting of written questions about the case submitted by one party to the other party. The answers to the interrogatories are usually given under oath—that is, the person answering the questions signs a sworn statement that the answers are true.

Deposition:   A discovery device by which one party asks oral questions of the other party or of a witness for the other party. The person who is *deposed* is called the *deponent.* The deposition is conducted under oath outside of the courtroom, usually in one of the attorney's offices. (A recording or transcript—a word-for-word account—is made of the deposition.)

Requests for admissions:   Written statements of fact concerning the case which are submitted to an adverse party and which that party is required to admit or deny; those statements that are admitted will be treated by the court as having been established and need not be proven at trial.

Order:   An official command by the court requiring, allowing, or forbidding some act to be done.

Hearing:   A proceeding in which the judge or presiding officer examines some aspect of the dispute. An *adversary hearing* exists when both parties are present at the hearing to argue their respective positions. An *ex parte hearing* exists when only one party is present at the hearing. Hearings occur in court as well as in administrative agencies.

Summary:   Done relatively quickly and informally without going through an entire adversary hearing or an entire trial.

Motion for a summary judgment:   A request by a party that a decision be reached on the basis of the pleadings alone without going through an entire trial. A summary judgment is normally allowed only when there is no dispute between the parties as to any of the material or significant facts. Summary judgment can be granted on the entire case or on some of the claims raised within it.

As the trial date neared, each of the attorneys received a notice asking them to appear before a *magistrate* for a *pretrial conference.* On the appointed day, the attorneys met with the magistrate to prepare the case for trial. During the conference, the magistrate, with the help of the attorneys, prepared a pretrial statement for the trial judge on the case. It contained a statement of those facts that had been *stipulated* by the attorneys, the facts that were still *in issue,* and a list describing the *tangible evidence* and witnesses that each attorney intended to *introduce* at the trial.

Magistrate:   A judicial officer having some but not all of the powers of a judge. In the federal trial courts (the U.S. District Courts), the magistrate may conduct many of the preliminary or pretrial proceedings in both civil and criminal cases.

Pretrial conference:   A meeting between the judge (or magistrate) and the attorneys to prepare the case for trial. At this conference, the presiding officer often encourages the parties to settle the dispute on their own in order to avoid a trial.

Stipulated:   Agreed to. A *stipulation* of fact will not be *contested* or disputed. Hence, no evidence need be presented as to the truth or falsity of that fact at trial.

In issue:   In question. A *question* or issue *of fact* means that the truth or falsity of that fact must be established at the trial. A question or issue *of law* means that the judge must rule on what the law is or how the law applies to the facts.

Tangible evidence:   Physical evidence; evidence that can be seen or touched, such as letters, photographs, or skeletons. *Testimonial evidence* is evidence of what someone says, such as the statements made by anyone sitting in the witness box.

**Introduce:**   To place *evidence* formally before the court so that it will become part of the record for consideration by the judge and jury

After some delay, the case was finally *set for trial.* All of the parties, their attorneys, and the witnesses assembled in the courtroom. The judge entered, took the bench, and ordered the *bailiff* to summon a *jury panel* for the trial. Once the potential or prospective jurors were seated in the courtroom, *voir dire* began. Several jurors were *challenged for cause* and dismissed—one because she worked for the insurance company that had issued the policy on Miller's car. The position as to this prospective juror was that she might be *biased.* Several other jurors were dismissed as a result of *peremptory challenges.* A panel of twelve jurors plus two *alternates* was eventually selected and seated in the jury box.

**Set for trial:**   To schedule a date when the trial is to begin.

**Bailiff:**   A court employee who keeps order in the courtroom and renders general administrative assistance to the judge.

**Jury panel:**   A group of citizens who have been called to jury duty. From this group, juries for particular trials will be selected.

**Voir dire:**   The oral examination of prospective jurors by the attorneys, by the judge, or by both the attorneys and the judge for the purpose of selecting a jury.

**Challenge for cause:**   A request from a party to a judge that a prospective juror *not* be allowed to become a member of this jury because of specified causes or reasons.

**Peremptory challenge:**   A request from a party to a judge that a prospective juror *not* be allowed to become a member of this jury. No reason or cause need be stated for this type of challenge. Both sides are allowed a limited number of peremptory challenges, but they will be granted as many challenges for cause as they can establish.

**Bias:**   Unfairly leaning in favor of or against someone; the potential for unfairness because of prior knowledge or involvement leading to possible preconceptions and a lack of open-mindedness.

**Alternate:**   An extra juror who will sit with the regular jurors and who will take the place of a regular juror if one becomes incapacitated during the trial.

When the jury was seated, Brown's attorney rose and told the judge that she wished to invoke the *rule on witnesses.* The judge nodded to the bailiff, who then led all of the witnesses (except for the parties themselves) out of the courtroom. Brown's attorney then began the trial with her *opening statement* to the jury. When she finished, Miller's attorney also delivered an opening statement. The attorney for Clay's estate, however, decided to reserve his opening statement until it was time for him to present the estate's case.

**Rule on witnesses:**   A rule that requires certain witnesses to be removed from the courtroom until it is time for their individual testimony so that they will not be able to hear each other's testimony.

**Opening statement:**   A speech or presentation made by each attorney to the jury summarizing the facts the attorney intends to try to prove during the trial.

Brown's attorney, whose client had the *burden of proof,* called her first witness, a ten-year-old boy who had seen the accident. Miller's attorney immediately rose and requested a *bench conference.* When all the attorneys had gathered around the bench, he stated that he *objected* to the witness on the basis of *competency.* The judge then *excused the jury* temporarily while he conducted a brief *examination* of the witness. The judge *overruled* the objection upon being satisfied that the boy was old enough to understand the obligation to tell the truth and had the ability to communicate what he knew.

Burden of proof:   The responsibility of proving a fact at the trial. Generally, the party making the factual allegation has the burden of proof as to that allegation.

Bench conference:   A discussion between the judge and the attorneys held at the judge's bench so that the jury cannot hear what is being said.

Objection:   A formal challenge usually directed at the evidence that the other side is trying to pursue or introduce.

Competency:   Legal capacity to testify.

Excused the jury:   Asked the jury to leave the room.

Examination:   Questioning, asking questions of.

Overrule:   Deny. (The word *overrule* is also used when a court repudiates the holding of a prior opinion written by the same court.)

The jury was brought back into the courtroom, and Brown's attorney began her *direct examination*. After a few questions, Miller's attorney again objected, this time on the *ground* that the child's answer had been *hearsay*. The judge *sustained* the objection and, after instructing the jury to disregard the boy's answer, ordered it *stricken from the record*. Brown's attorney continued her examination of the witness for a few minutes before announcing that she had no further questions. The attorney for the estate then rose to conduct a brief *cross-examination* of the boy. He was followed by Miller's attorney, whose cross-examination was also brief. There was no *redirect examination*.

Direct examination:   Questioning the witness first. Normally the attorney who *calls* the witness to the stand conducts the direct examination.

Ground:   Reason.

Hearsay:   Testimony in court on a statement asserted or made by someone else out of court when the statement is being offered to establish the truth of the statement, and thus its value is based on the credibility of the out-of-court asserter.

Sustain:   To affirm the validity of.

Strike from the record:   To remove the testimony or evidence from the written record or *transcript* of the trial.

Cross-examination:   Questioning the witness after the other side has completed the direct examination. Generally, the person conducting the cross-examination must limit himself or herself to the topics or subject matters raised during the direct examination of this witness by the other side.

Redirect examination:   Questioning the witness after the cross-examination. The attorney who conducted the direct examination conducts the redirect examination.

Brown's attorney, Davis, called several other witnesses who had seen the accident occur. Each witness was examined and cross-examined in much the same fashion as the boy had been. Davis was about to call her fourth witness, Dr. Hadley, when the judge announced a brief recess for lunch. The judge admonished the jury not to discuss the case with anyone, even among themselves, and ordered everyone to be back in the courtroom by 2:00 P.M.

Dr. Hadley was called to the stand immediately after the lunch recess. Brown's attorney began her direct examination with a series of questions about the doctor's medical training and experience in order to *qualify* him as an *expert*

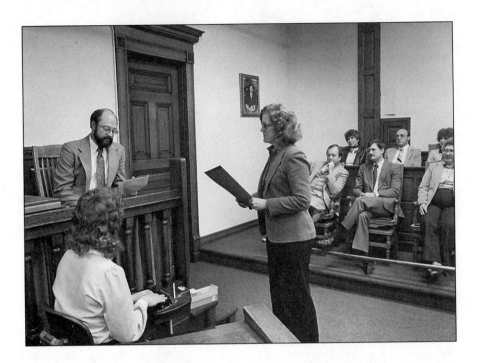

Attorney examines an expert witness during a trial

*witness.* She then moved that Dr. Hadley be recognized as an expert witness. The *court,* with no objections by either defense counsel, granted the motion.

Qualify:   To demonstrate background and experience sufficient to convince the court that the witness has expertise in a particular area.

Expert witness:   A witness who has been *qualified* as an expert and who, therefore, will be allowed to give his or her expert opinion in order to assist the jury in understanding those technical subjects not within the understanding of the average lay person.

Court:   Here refers to the judge trying the case.

Brown's attorney then asked the doctor to testify as to the nature and extent of the injuries that the plaintiff, Brown, had suffered as a result of the accident. In addition to multiple cuts and bruises, the doctor stated that Brown had suffered a broken knee. The knee, in the doctor's opinion, had been permanently injured, and Brown would continue to suffer periodic pain and stiffness due to the injury. In order to show the expense that these injuries had cost Brown, the attorney produced the original copies of the bills that the doctor had sent to Brown. She handed the bills to the *clerk,* who marked them as plaintiff's *exhibit* number one. After allowing defense counsel to inspect the bills, Brown's attorney handed them to the doctor, who promptly identified them. The attorney then *moved the bills into evidence* and turned the witness over to defense counsel for cross-examination.

Clerk:   The court employee who assists the judge in recordkeeping at the trial.

Exhibit:   An item of physical or tangible evidence that is to be or has been offered to the court for inspection.

Move . . . into evidence:   To request that the items be formally declared *admissible* (which is not the same as declaring them to be true; admissible means that the items will be admitted simply for consideration as to their truth or falsity).

It was late in the afternoon when Brown's attorney finished with her final witness, Brown himself. The judge did not want to recess for the day, however, until the attorneys for the defendants completed their cross-examination of Brown. After about an hour, all the defense attorneys completed their questioning of Brown, and Brown's attorney *rested her case.* The judge *adjourned* the trial until the following morning.

Rest one's case:   To announce formally that you have concluded the presentation of evidence (through the introduction of tangible evidence, through direct examination of your own witnesses, etc.). While the other side presents its case, however, you will be entitled to cross-examine its witnesses.

Adjourn:   To halt the proceedings temporarily.

On the following morning, the attorney for Clay's estate advised the judge that he had a preliminary matter to bring up before the jury was brought into the courtroom. He then proceeded to make a motion for a *directed verdict* in favor of the estate on Brown's claim of negligence. Miller's attorney made a similar motion on behalf of his client. The judge listened to arguments by the attorneys and then stated his decision. As to defendant Miller, the motion was denied because the plaintiff had introduced sufficient evidence to make out a *prima facie case* of negligence that should go to the jury. As to the estate, the judge would neither grant nor deny the motion but would *take it under advisement.*

Directed verdict:   An order by the court that the jury reach a verdict for the party making the motion for a directed verdict on the ground that the other side, who has just rested its case, has failed to produce enough convincing evidence to establish a cause of action.

Prima facie case:   The party's evidence, if believed by the jury, would be legally sufficient to support a verdict in favor of that party—that is, the party has introduced evidence which, if believed, would include all the facts necessary to establish a cause of action. If the plaintiff *fails* to establish a prima facie case, the judge will decide the case in favor of the defendant without any further proceedings. If the judge finds that there *is* a prima facie case, the defendant will be allowed an opportunity to produce contrary evidence. The case will then go to the jury to decide which version of the facts meets the *Standard of proof* (see definition on page 446).

Take under advisement:   To delay ruling on the motion until another time.

The jury was summoned into the courtroom and seated in the jury box for the second day of the trial. The attorney for the estate began his case by making an opening statement to the jury, reserved from the previous day. He then proceeded to call his witnesses. He had only a few witnesses and was able to conclude his case just before noon, at which time he introduced Clay's death certificate into evidence. The judge then declared a recess for lunch.

Miller's attorney began to present his case in the afternoon, and by late afternoon he too had rested his case. The judge dismissed the jury until the following morning and told the attorneys to be prepared for *closing arguments* at that time. He also asked them to submit any *jury instructions* that they would like to request, so that he could review them. Brown's attorney requested an instruction that the codefendants had to overcome a *presumption* of negligence against them. The judge denied this request. Finally, he announced that he had decided to deny the estate's earlier motion for a directed verdict.

Closing argument:   The final statements by the attorneys summarizing the evidence that they think they have established and the evidence that they think the other side has failed to establish.

Jury instructions:   A statement of the guidelines and law given by the judge to the jury, which they are to use in deciding the issues of fact. The instructions to the jury are also referred to as the *charge* to the jury. The attorneys are usually allowed to submit proposed instructions for consideration by the judge.

Presumption:   An assumption that a certain fact is true. A *rebuttable presumption* is an assumption that can be overcome or changed if the other side introduces enough facts to overcome it. If the other side does not rebut the presumption, then the assumption stands. A *nonrebuttable* presumption cannot be overcome no matter how convincing the evidence of the other side against the assumption.

Closing arguments began late the following morning. Each attorney carefully reviewed the evidence for the jury and argued for a *verdict* in favor of his or her client. Following a brief recess for lunch, the judge thanked the alternate jurors for their time and dismissed them. He then began to instruct the remaining twelve jurors as to the law they were to follow in finding the facts and in reaching a verdict. He said that they, as jurors, were the finders of fact and were to base their decision solely upon the testimony and exhibits introduced during the trial. He explained the concept of burden of proof and stated which party had to carry this burden as to each of the various *elements* of negligence. Each element had to be proved by a *preponderance of the evidence*. This was the *standard of proof* for this kind of case. Finally, he described the manner in which they should compute the amount of damages, if any, suffered by the parties. The jury was then led out of the courtroom to deliberate on its verdict. The judge retired to his chambers, and the attorneys settled back with their clients to wait.

Verdict:   The final conclusion of the jury.

Elements:   Here, the components of a cause of action. (An element is a component or portion of a rule which is a precondition of the applicability of the entire rule.)

Preponderance of the evidence:   A standard of proof (used in many civil suits) that is met when a party's evidence on a fact indicates that it is "more likely than not" that the fact is as the party alleges it to be.

Standard of proof:   A statement of how convincing a version of a fact must be before the trier of facts (jury or judge) can accept it as true. The main standards of proof are proof *beyond a reasonable doubt* (in criminal cases only), proof *by clear and convincing evidence,* and proof by *preponderance of the evidence.*

After about an hour, the judge received a note from the foreman of the jury, asking that the jury be allowed to view several of the exhibits. The items requested consisted largely of the various medical bills allegedly incurred by Brown and Clay. The attorneys for Brown and for the estate took this as a good sign—the jury had probably decided the case against Miller and was now trying to compute damages.

A second note arrived in another hour, announcing that the jury had reached a verdict. The bailiff summoned everyone back to the courtroom, and the jury came in a few minutes later. At the clerk's request, the foreman rose to read the verdict. On Brown's original complaint against Miller for negligence, the jury found for Brown and against Miller, awarding Brown $30,000 in damages. However, on Brown's complaint against Clay's estate (the codefendant), the jury decided in favor of the estate, finding that Clay had not been negligent. The jury found for the estate on its cross-claim against its codefendant, Miller, awarding $750,000 in damages to the estate. Finally, the jury found against Miller on his own cross-claim against the estate, as well as on his counterclaim against Brown. The judge entered a judgment against Miller in the amounts awarded by the jury. After denying a motion by Miller for a *judgment notwithstanding the verdict*, he thanked the jurors and dismissed them.

Judgment:   The decision of the court resolving the dispute and determining the rights and obligations of the parties. Many judgments order the losing party to do something (such as pay damages) or to refrain from doing something. A *declaratory judgment* establishes the rights and obligations of the parties, but it does not order the parties to do or refrain from doing anything.

Judgment notwithstanding the verdict:   A judgment by the court that is contrary or opposite to the verdict reached by the jury, in effect, overruling the jury. (Also referred to as *a judgment n.o.v.*)

Miller's attorney immediately made a *motion for a new trial*, arguing several possible grounds. When this motion was denied by the trial judge, he moved for a *reduction of the verdict* on the grounds that the amounts awarded were excessive. This motion was also denied, and the attorney announced his intention to *appeal*. The judge did, however, grant Miller a *stay* of the judgement, conditioned upon his filing a *timely notice of appeal* and posting the appropriate *bond*.

Motion for a new trial:   A request that the judge set aside the judgment and order a new trial on the basis that the trial was improper or unfair due to specified prejudicial errors that occurred.

Reduction of the verdict:   Lowering the amount of the damage award reached by the jury.

Appeal:   To ask a court of *appellate jurisdiction* (a higher court within the same judicial system as the trial court) to *review* or examine the decision of the lower court on the basis that the lower court made some errors of law in conducting the trial.

Stay:   To delay enforcement or *execution* of the court's judgment.

Timely:   On time, according to the time specified by law.

Notice of appeal:   A document announcing an intention to appeal which is filed with the appellate court and served on the opposing party.

Bond:   A sum of money deposited with the court to insure compliance with some requirement.

Miller asked his attorney what the $30,000 verdict against him meant. Since Brown had originally sued for $100,000, could Brown later sue Miller again for the rest of the amount he claimed? The attorney explained that, because of the stay granted by the judge, Miller would not have to pay anything until a decision on appeal had been reached. Furthermore, Brown could not sue Miller again on the same cause of action, because Brown had received a *judgment on the merits* which would be *res judicata* and would *bar* any later suit on the same negligence cause of action. The same would be true of a later negligence action by Clay's estate against Miller.

Judgment on the merits:   A decision on the substance of the claims raised. Normally, a judgment of dismissal based solely on some procedural error is *not* a judgment on the merits. A judgment that is not on the merits is called a *dismissal without prejudice*. A party who has received a judgment on the merits cannot bring the same suit again. A party whose case has been dismissed without prejudice can bring the same suit again so long as the procedural errors are corrected (i.e., cured) in the later action.

Res judicata:   The legal doctrine that a judgement on the merits will prevent the same parties from relitigating the same cause of action on the same facts; the parties have already had their day in court.

Bar:   Prevent or stop.

Miller's attorney filed his notice of appeal with the United States Court of Appeals and posted bond the following week. As attorney for the *appellant*, it was also his duty to see to it that the *record*, including *transcripts* and copies of exhibits, was transmitted to the Court of Appeals and that the case was *docketed* by the clerk of that court. Miller's attorney then had forty days in which to draft and file his *brief* with the Court of Appeals. He served copies of the brief on the attorneys for the *appellees*, Brown and Clay's estate, who in turn filed their briefs concerning the *issues on appeal*.

Appellant:   The party initiating the appeal; the party who is complaining of error(s) made by the lower court.

Record:   The official collection of all the trial pleadings, exhibits, orders, and word-for-word testimony that took place during the trial.

Transcript:   Word-for-word typed record of everything that was said during the trial. The court reporter types this transcription, which is paid for by the parties requesting it.

Docket:   The court's official calendar of pending cases. Once all of the necessary papers have been filed, the appeal is "docketed" by the clerk—that is, placed on the court's official calendar.

Brief:   An appellate brief is a written argument presented to the appeals court by a party stating the legal issues on appeal and the positions of the party on those issues—all relating to the claimed errors that occurred during the trial.

Appellee:   The party against whom the appeal is brought (also called the *respondent*). Generally the appellee is satisfied with what the trial court did and wishes the appellate court to approve of or *affirm* the trial court's judgment.

Issues on appeal:   The claimed errors of law committed by the trial judge below. The appellate court does not retry the case. No witnesses are called, and no testimony is taken by the appellate court. The court examines the record and determines whether errors of law were committed by the trial judge.

Several months passed before the attorneys finally received a notice from the clerk of the Court of Appeals that the appeal had been scheduled for *oral argument* before a three-judge *panel* of the court. The arguments were heard a few weeks later. Six months after oral argument, the attorneys received the decision of the court in its written *opinion*. By a vote of two to one (one judge *dissenting*), the court *affirmed* the judgments against Miller. The only error which the majority found was the admission of certain testimony offered by Brown's expert witness. However, because Miller's attorney had not objected to this testimony at trial, the opinion stated, he had *waived* this defect.

Oral argument:   A verbal presentation made by the attorneys before the appellate court, during which arguments about the validity or invalidity of what the trial judge did are presented.

Panel:   The group of appellate judges, usually three, who preside over the appeal of the case and who vote on the result.

Opinion:   The written decision of the majority of judges on the court, which includes the reasons for the decision. One case can contain several opinions: a majority opinion, a concurring opinion (see the definition that follows), and a dissenting opinion. Opinions are often collected in official and unofficial *reporters*.

Dissent:   Disagree with the decision (the result and the reasons) of the *majority* on the court. If a judge agrees with the result reached by the majority but disagrees with reasons the majority used to support that result, the judge would cast a *concurring* vote and might write a separate concurring opinion.

Affirm:   To agree with or uphold the lower court judgment. If the appellate court *remanded* the case, it would be sending it back to the lower court with instructions to correct the irregularities specified in the appellate opinion. If the appellate court *reversed* the court below, it would have changed the result reached below.

Waive:   To lose a right or privilege because of an explicit rejection of it or a failure to claim it at the appropriate time. Here the court is referring to the well-established rule that failure to object during trial is an implied waiver of the right to complain about the alleged error on appeal.

Miller, undaunted, *petitioned* for a *rehearing* by the court *en banc.* The petition was denied. Miller then discussed the possibility of further appeal with his attorney. The attorney explained that Miller could, if he desired, try to appeal to the United States Supreme Court. He cautioned Miller, however, that he could not *appeal as a matter of right* in this case, but would be limited to a petition for a *writ of certiorari.* He advised Miller that it was extremely unlikely that the Supreme Court would grant the petition and that it probably would not be worth the expense. Miller agreed, and no further appeal was attempted. Shortly thereafter the Court of Appeals issued its *mandate,* and the case was returned to the District Court, where Miller, through his insurance company, *satisfied* the judgment.

Petition:   To make a formal request; similar to a motion. (The word *petition* is sometimes synonymous with the word *complaint,* the plaintiff's pleading that attempts to state a cause of action.)

Rehearing:   A second hearing by the appellate court to reconsider the decision it made after the first appellate hearing.

En banc:   By the entire court. The *panel* of judges that heard the first appeal may have consisted of only three judges, yet the number of judges on the full court may be much larger.

Appeal as a matter of right:   An appeal in which the appellate court has no discretion on whether to hear the appeal and thus is *required* to review the decision below.

Writ of certiorari:   An order by the appellate court (here the highest court) which is used when the court has discretion on whether to hear an appeal. If the writ is denied, the court refuses to hear the appeal, and, in effect, the judgment below stands unchanged. If the writ is granted, then it has the effect of ordering the lower court to certify the record and send it up to the higher court which has used its discretion to hear the appeal.

Mandate:   The order of the court. Here the mandate of the appellate court was to affirm the trial court's judgment.

Satisfy:   To comply with a legal obligation, here to pay the judgment award.

## 2. Criminal Liability

Brown was involved in a second legal dispute during the same period of time that the negligence suit was under way. In addition to suing Clay's estate and Miller, Brown was defending himself in a criminal *prosecution* for possession of narcotics.

Prosecution:   The bringing and processing of a criminal charge by the government. (Prosecution also sometimes means going through the steps to litigate a civil case.)

As Brown was leaving the hospital after having recovered from his injury, he was met at the door by two police officers. The officers produced a *warrant* and advised Brown that he was under arrest. After he was read his rights, he was taken to the police station.

Warrant:  An order from a judicial officer authorizing an act such as the arrest of an individual or the search of property.

The following morning Brown was taken before a judge for his *initial appearance*. The judge advised Brown that he has been charged with a *felony,* "possession of narcotics with intent to distribute." He then advised Brown of his rights, including his right to be represented by an attorney. Since Brown was unemployed and without adequate funds to pay an attorney, the judge asked him if he would like the court to appoint an attorney to handle the case. Brown said yes. An attorney was *assigned* to represent Brown. The judge, at the attorney's request, then agreed to give Brown a chance to confer with his new attorney before continuing the hearing.

Initial appearance:  A court proceeding during which (a) the accused is told of the charges, (b) a decision on bail is made, and (c) arrangements for the next court proceeding are specified.

Felony:  A crime that is punishable by a sentence of one year or more. A *misdemeanor* is a crime that is punishable by a sentence of less than a year.

Assigned counsel:  An attorney appointed to represent an *indigent* (impoverished) defendant.

When the case was recalled, Brown and his court-appointed attorney again approached the bench and stood before the judge. The attorney handed the clerk a praecipe formally entering his name as attorney of record for Brown and advised the judge that he was prepared to discuss the matter of *bail*. He proceeded to describe for the judge the details of Brown's background—his education, employment record, length of residence in the city, etc. He concluded by asking that he be released on his own *personal recognizance*. The prosecutor was then given an opportunity to speak. He recommended a high *bond*, pointing out that the defendant was unemployed and had no close relatives in the area. These facts, he argued, coupled with the serious nature of a felony charge, indicated a very real risk that the defendant might try to flee. The judge nevertheless agreed to release Brown on his personal recognizance and set a date for a *preliminary hearing* the following week.

Bail:  Property or a sum of money deposited with the court in order to insure that the defendant will reappear in court at designated times.

Personal recognizance:  The defendant's sworn promise that he or she will return to court at the designated times. No bail money is required.

Bail bond:  A written obligation to pay a sum of money to the court in the event that the defendant fails to appear at designated times.

Preliminary hearing:  A hearing during which the state is required to produce sufficient evidence to establish that there is *probable cause* (see definition below) to believe that the defendant committed the crimes charged.

The only witness at the preliminary hearing was the police officer who had been at the scene of the accident. The officer testified that when he helped pull Brown out of the car, he noticed a small paper sack sticking out from under the passenger's side of the front seat. Several glassine envelopes containing a white powdery substance, the officer said, had spilled out of the sack. The substance, totaling about one-half ounce, was tested and proved to be 80% pure heroin. Brown's attorney cross-examined the officer briefly, but little additional information came out. The judge found that there was *probable cause* to hold the defendant and ordered the case *bound over* for *grand jury* action. He continued Brown's release on personal recognizance.

Probable cause:   A reasonable basis to believe that the defendant is guilty of the crime(s) charged.

Bound over:   Submitted.

Grand jury:   A special jury whose duty is to hear evidence of felonies presented by the prosecutor to determine whether there is sufficient evidence to return an *indictment* (see definition that follows) against the defendant and cause him or her to stand trial on the charges.

Shortly after the preliminary hearing, Brown's attorney went to the prosecutor to see if he could work out an informal disposition of the charge. He tried to convince the prosecutor to enter a *nolle prosequi* on the charge, explaining that Brown had simply been offered a ride home and was not aware of the fact that the heroin was in the car. The prosecutor was unwilling to drop the charge. However, he was willing to "nolle" the felony charge of possession with intent to distribute if Brown would agree to *plead* guilty to the lesser offense of simple possession of a dangerous drug, a misdemeanor. The attorney said he would speak to his client about it.

Nolle prosequi:   A statement by the prosecutor that he or she is unwilling to prosecute the case. The charges, in effect, are dropped.

Plead:   To deliver a formal statement or response. In a criminal case, to *plead* means to admit or deny the charges made by the prosecutor.

He spoke to Brown that same afternoon, told him about the *plea bargaining* session, and advised him of the prosecutor's offer. Brown was not interested. He felt he was innocent and was unwilling to plead guilty, even to a misdemeanor.

Plea bargaining:   Negotiation between the prosecution and defense counsel during which an attempt is made to reach a compromise in lieu of a criminal trial. Generally the defendant agrees to plead guilty to a lesser charge in return for the state's willingness to drop a more serious charge.

Several weeks went by before Brown's attorney was notified that the grand jury had returned an *indictment* against his client. The next step would be the *arraignment* on the following Monday. On this date, Brown and his attorney appeared before the judge, and Brown was formally notified of the indictment. He entered a plea of not guilty to the charge. The judge set a trial date about two-and-one-half months away and again agreed to continue Brown's release on personal recognizance.

Indictment:   A formal document issued by a grand jury accusing the defendant of a crime. (If the state has no grand jury, the accusation is often contained in a document called an *information*.)

Arraignment:   A court proceeding in which the defendant is formally charged with a crime and enters a plea. Arrangements are then made for the next proceeding.

The day for the trial arrived, and both sides (Brown's attorney and the prosecutor) announced that they were ready. Voir dire was held, and a jury was *impaneled.* The trial itself was relatively uneventful, lasting less than a day. The prosecutor, following a brief opening statement, presented only two witnesses: the police officer who had been at the scene, and an expert from the police lab who identified the substance as heroin. He then rested his case. Brown's attorney then made his opening statement and presented his only witness, Brown himself. The jury listened attentively as Brown, on direct examination, explained the events leading up to the accident and his subsequent arrest. Not only had he been unaware of the heroin, he testified, but he had never even seen it, since he had been knocked unconscious by the accident and had not revived until he was in the ambulance. Brown had a previous conviction for shoplifting, and the prosecutor on cross-examination attempted to use this conviction to *impeach* Brown's testimony. Brown's attorney successfully objected, arguing that the conviction, which had occurred eight years previously, was too remote to be *relevant.* The judge agreed and prohibited any mention of the prior conviction. After a few more questions, the prosecutor concluded his cross-examination, and the defense rested its case.

Impaneled:   Selected, sworn in, and seated.

Impeach:   To attack or discredit by introducing evidence that the testimony of the witness is not credible (believable).

Relevant:   Tending to prove or disprove a fact in issue.

Both sides presented their closing arguments following the lunch recess. The judge then instructed the jury; he described the elements of the offense and explained that the burden of proof in a criminal case is on the *government.* That burden, he continued, is to prove each element of the offense *beyond a reasonable doubt.* The jury took less than forty-five minutes to reach its verdict. All parties quickly reassembled in the courtroom to hear the foreman announce the verdict *acquitting* Brown of the offense. A *poll* of the jury, requested by the prosecutor, confirmed the result, and the judge advised Brown that he was free to go.

Government:   Here, the prosecutor.

Beyond a reasonable doubt:   The standard of proof required for conviction in a criminal case. If any reasonable doubt exists as to any element of the crime, the defendant cannot be convicted.

Acquit:   Find not guilty; absolve of guilt.

Poll:   To question jurors individually in open court as to whether each agrees with the verdict announced by the foreman.

Generally, criminal cases in which the defendant is acquitted may not be appealed by the prosecutor. Hence, in this case, there was no appeal of the trial judgment.

## 3. Administrative Dispute

The day after his indictment on the felony charge, Brown went down to the state unemployment office to apply for benefits. After being interviewed by a clerk, he filled out an application form. The clerk told Brown that he would receive a letter in about a week notifying him of the agency's initial determination of his eligibility. If he were eligible, his benefits would start in about ten days.

Brown received the letter a few days later. It advised him that, although he was otherwise eligible for benefits, a routine check with his former employer had disclosed that he had been fired for misconduct. For this reason, the letter stated, he would be deemed disqualified for a nine-week period. Moreover, the benefits due for those nine weeks would be deducted from the total amount to which he would otherwise have been entitled. If he wished to appeal this decision, the letter went on, he could request an *administrative hearing* within ten days.

Administrative hearing:   A proceeding at an administrative agency presided over by a hearing officer (called a hearing examiner, an administrative law judge, a referee, etc.) to resolve a controversy. The hearing is usually conducted less formally than a court hearing or trial.

Brown felt that he needed some legal advice, but he was still out of work and broke. (The lawsuit in the civil action had not been filed yet—it would be well over a year before the case would be tried, appealed, and the judgment award actually paid.) Brown therefore decided to obtain help from the local legal aid office. He explained his problem to a receptionist and was introduced to the paralegal who would be handling his case. The paralegal, an expert in unemployment compensation law, discussed the case with Brown and agreed to represent Brown at the hearing. He helped Brown fill out a form requesting a hearing and promised to let him know as soon as the date was set. Brown left and the paralegal immediately began to research and draft a *memorandum* to submit to the *hearing examiner* on Brown's behalf.

Memorandum:   Here, a written presentation of a party's arguments on facts and legal issues in the case.

Hearing examiner:   A hearing examiner is someone who presides over the hearing and makes findings of fact and rulings of law, or who recommends such findings and rulings to someone else in the agency who will make the final decision.

The hearing, held ten days later, lasted about an hour and a half. The only witnesses were Brown and his former boss, Frank Best. Best told the examiner about Brown's arrest and about the thefts from the warehouse. Taken together, he argued, these events made it impossible for him to trust Brown on the job any longer. Brown, in turn, denied any participation in the thefts and maintained his innocence on the drug charge. (As of this time, Brown had not been acquitted of the felony.) The hearing examiner, at the close of the proceedings, thanked the parties and promised a decision within a few days.

The hearing examiner's decision arrived shortly thereafter in a document labeled "Proposed Findings and Rulings." The last paragraph contained the examiner's recommended decision. The hearing examiner agreed with Brown that his boss's mere suspicion that Brown was involved in the thefts was not enough to justify a finding of misconduct. However, the decision went on, the pending criminal charges for a drug-related offense did provide the employer with good cause to fire Brown, since drug involvement could affect his ability to operate a truck safely. The paragraph concluded by recommending a finding of misconduct and the imposition of a nine-week penalty period.

Proposed findings and rulings:   Recommended conclusions presented to someone else in the agency who will make the final decision.

A second letter arrived ten days later giving the *administrative decision* of the agency. The letter, signed by the director of the local agency, adopted the recommended decision of the hearing examiner. This decision, the letter concluded, could be appealed within fifteen days to the State Unemployment Compensation *Board of Appeals*. Brown immediately appealed.

**FIGURE 10.2**
Civil Litigation

| (Possible proceedings where administrative decisions, court rulings, and opinions could be written. The events and their sequence presented below are examples only.) | | |
|---|---|---|
| **EVENT** | **DEFINITIONS** | **DECISIONS, RULINGS, AND OPINIONS** |
| **I. Agency Stage** | | |
| (If no agency is involved, the litigation begins in court at the pretrial stage.)<br>1. Someone protests an action taken by the *administrative agency*<br>2. *Agency hearing*<br>3. *Intra-agency appeal* to a Commission, Board, Director, or Secretary within the agency | *Administrative Agency:* a governmental body whose primary function is to carry out or administer statutes passed by the legislature<br>*Agency hearing:* a proceeding, similar to a trial, in which the hearing examiner of the agency listens to evidence and legal arguments before deciding the case<br>*Intra-agency appeal:* a review within the agency of the earlier decision to determine if that decision was correct | A mid-level agency official, e.g., hearing examiner, writes a *recommended decision*.<br>The Commission, Board, Director, or Secretary issues an *administrative decision*. |
| **II. Pretrial Stage** | | |
| 4. Plaintiff files a *complaint*<br>5. Clerk issues a *summons*<br>6. *Service of process* on defendant<br>7. Defendant files an *answer*<br>8. *Discovery* by written *interrogatories*<br>9. *Discovery* by *deposition*<br>10. Pretrial *motions*<br>11. *Settlement* efforts<br>12. *Voir dire* | *Complaint:* a pleading in which the plaintiff states claim(s) against defendant<br>*Summons:* a court notice requiring the defendant to appear and answer the complaint<br>*Service of process:* the delivery of the summons to the defendant<br>*Answer:* a pleading in which the defendant gives a response to the plaintiff's complaint<br>*Discovery:* methods by which one party obtains information from the other party about the litigation prior to trial<br>*Interrogatories:* a method of discovery through written questions submitted by one party to another before trial<br>*Deposition:* a method of discovery through a question-and-answer session, usually conducted in | The trial court will often be making rulings concerning these events but rarely will write an opinion on any of the rulings.<br>Occasionally, a party may be allowed to appeal a pretrial ruling to an appeals court, which may write an opinion affirming, modifying, or reversing the ruling. Such an appeal is called an *interlocutory* appeal. It takes place before the trial court reaches a final judgment. |

Continued

**FIGURE 10.2**
Civil Litigation
—*Continued*

| EVENT | DEFINITIONS | DECISIONS, RULINGS, AND OPINIONS |
|---|---|---|
| II. Pretrial Stage—*Continued* | | |
| | the offices of one of the attorneys. Parties and prospective witnesses are questioned by the attorneys without a judge being present. Their testimony is recorded or transcribed for possible later use.<br><br>*Motion:* a formal request to the court, such as a motion to dismiss<br><br>*Settlement:* a resolution of the dispute, making the trial unnecessary<br><br>*Voire dire:* Selection of the jury (not all cases are tried by a jury) | |
| III. Trial Stage | | |
| 13. *Opening statement* of plaintiff<br><br>14. *Opening statement* of defendant<br><br>15. Plaintiff presents its case<br>   **(a)** *evidence introduced*<br>   **(b)** *direct examination*<br>   **(c)** *cross-examination*<br><br>16. *Motions* to dismiss<br><br>17. Defendant presents its case<br>   **(a)** *evidence introduced*<br>   **(b)** *direct examination*<br>   **(c)** *cross-examination*<br><br>18. Closing arguments to jury by attorneys<br><br>19. *Charge* to jury<br><br>20. *Verdict* of jury<br><br>21. *Judgment* of court | *Opening statement:* a summary of the facts the attorney will try to prove during the trial<br><br>*Evidence:* that which is offered to help prove or disprove a fact involved in the dispute<br><br>*Direct examination:* questioning by an attorney of his or her own witnesses<br><br>*Cross-examination:* questioning of witness by an attorney for the other side<br><br>*Charge:* the judge's instructions to the jury on how it should go about reaching its verdict<br><br>*Verdict:* the results of the jury's deliberation<br><br>*Judgment:* the final statement of the trial court on the rights and responsibilities of the parties | The trial court will often be making rulings concerning these events, but rarely will write an opinion on any of the rulings.<br><br>After the trial, the trial court will deliver its judgment. Usually an opinion (explaining the judgment) will *not* be written. Several trial courts, however, do sometimes write opinions, such as federal trial courts (U.S. District Courts) and New York State trial courts. |

Continued

**FIGURE 10.2**

Civil Litigation
—*Continued*

| IV. Appeal Stage | | |
|---|---|---|
| 22. Filing of *notice of appeal*<br><br>23. Filing of *appellant's appellate brief*<br><br>24. Filing of *appellee's appellate brief*<br><br>25. Filing of appellant's reply brief<br><br>26. Oral argument by attorneys<br><br>27. Decision of court | *Notice of appeal:* a statement of the intention to seek a review of the trial court's judgment<br><br>*Appellant:* the party bringing the appeal because of dissatisfaction with the trial court's judgment<br><br>*Appellee:* the party against whom the appeal is brought<br><br>*Appellate brief:* written arguments by the attorney on why the trial court acted correctly or incorrectly | An opinion of the middle appeals court (intermediate appellate court) will often be written.<br><br>This opinion of the middle appeals court might be further appealed to the highest court, in which event another opinion could be written.<br><br>[Note that in some states there is no middle appeals court; the appeal goes directly from the trial court to the highest state court.] |

**Administrative decision:** An administrative agency's resolution of a controversy involving the application of the agency's regulations or its governing statutes and executive orders. In this case, the decision refers to a determination by a superior of the hearing examiner adopting, modifying, or rejecting the recommended decision of the hearing examiner.

**Board of Appeals:** A nonjudicial, administrative tribunal that reviews the decision made by the hearing officer or by the head of the agency.

Copies of the hearing transcript along with memoranda from both sides were filed with the Board of Appeals. The Board, exercising its *discretion*, refused to allow oral arguments before it and *summarily* reversed the decision reached *below*. It issued a short written decision which noted that, while Best may have had cause to be suspicious of Brown, there wasn't sufficient evidence of actual misconduct on Brown's part. The Board, in this final administrative decision, ordered the local office to begin paying benefits immediately, including back benefits to cover the period since he had first applied.

**Discretion:** The power to choose among various courses of conduct based solely on one's reasoned judgment or preference.

**Summarily:** Quickly, briefly, without formal proceedings such as a hearing.

**Below:** The lower tribunal that heard the case before the appeal was brought.

Best decided to appeal this administrative decision to a court. He was allowed to do so since he had *exhausted* his *administrative remedies*. He filed a complaint in a county court seeking review of the Board's decision. He submitted the entire record from the proceedings below and asked the court for a *trial de novo*. Brown, now represented by an attorney from the legal aid office, filed his answer and immediately made a motion for summary judgment. The court, upon a review of the record and the pleadings, granted the motion and affirmed the judgment of the Board of Appeals. Best, after discussing the case at length with his attorney, decided against a further appeal of the case to the court of appeals.

**Exhausting one's administrative remedies:** Pursuing *all* available methods of resolving a dispute within the administrative agency before asking a court to review

| EVENT | DEFINITIONS | RULINGS AND OPINIONS |
|---|---|---|
| (Possible proceedings where court rulings and opinions could be written. The events and their sequence presented below are examples only.) | | |

**FIGURE 10.3**
Criminal Litigation

| EVENT | DEFINITIONS | RULINGS AND OPINIONS |
|---|---|---|
| **I. Pretrial Stage** | | |
| 1. *Arrest*<br>2. *Initial appearance* before a judge or a magistrate<br>3. *Preliminary hearing*<br>4. *Indictment* by grand jury<br>5. *Arraignment*<br>6. Limited pretrial discovery<br>7. Pretrial motions<br>8. *Voir dire* | *Arrest:* to take someone into custody in order to bring him or her before the proper authorities<br><br>*Initial appearance:* a court proceeding during which the accused is told of the charges, a bail decision is made, and arrangements for the next proceeding are specified<br><br>*Preliminary hearing:* a court proceeding during which a decision is made as to whether there is probable cause to believe that the accused committed the crime(s) charged<br><br>*Indictment:* a formal charge issued by the grand jury accusing the defendant of a crime. (If no grand jury is involved in the case, the accusation is contained in a document called an *information*.)<br><br>*Arraignment:* a court proceeding in which the defendant is formally charged with the crime and enters a plea. Arrangements are then made for the trial.<br><br>*Voir dire:* Selection of the jury (not all cases are tried by a jury) | The trial court will often be making rulings concerning these events but rarely will write an opinion on any of the rulings.<br><br>Occasionally, a party may be allowed to appeal a pretrial ruling immediately to an appeals court, which may write an opinion affirming, modifying, or reversing the ruling. This interlocutory appeal takes place before the trial court reaches a final judgment. |
| **II. Trial Stage** | | |
| 9. *Opening statements* of attorneys<br>10. Government presents its case against the defendant<br>  **(a)** *evidence* introduced<br>  **(b)** *direct examination*<br>  **(c)** *cross-examination* | *Opening statements:* a summary of the facts the attorney will try to prove during the trial<br><br>*Evidence:* that which is offered to help prove or disprove a fact involved in the dispute | The trial court will often be making rulings concerning these events but rarely will write an opinion on any of the rulings.<br><br>After the trial, the trial court will deliver its judgment. Usually no opinion (explaining the judgment) will be written. |

Continued

**FIGURE 10.3**

Criminal Litigation
—*Continued*

| EVENT | DEFINITIONS | RULINGS AND OPINIONS |
|---|---|---|
| II. Trial Stage—*Continued* | | |
| 11. Motions to dismiss <br> 12. Defendant presents its case <br>   (a) *evidence* introduced <br>   (b) *direct examination* <br>   (c) *cross-examination* <br> 13. Closing arguments to jury by attorneys <br> 14. *Charge* to jury <br> 15. *Verdict* to jury <br> 16. *Judgment* of court, including the sentence if defendant is convicted | *Direct examination:* questioning by an attorney of his or her own witnesses <br> *Cross-examination:* questioning of witness by an attorney for the other side <br> *Charge:* the judge's instructions to the jury on how it should go about reaching its verdict <br> *Verdict:* the results of the jury's deliberation <br> *Judgment:* the final statement of the trial court disposing of the criminal charges stated in the indictment or information | Several trial courts, however, do sometimes write opinions, e.g., federal trial courts (U.S. District Courts) and New York State trial courts. |
| III. Appeal Stage | | |
| 17. Filing of *notice of appeal* <br> 18. Filing of *appellant's appellate brief* <br> 19. Filing of *appellee's appellate brief* <br> 20. Filing of appellant's reply brief <br> 21. Oral argument by attorneys <br> 22. Decision of court | *Notice of appeal:* a statement of the intention to seek a review of the trial court's judgment. <br> *Appellant:* the party bringing the appeal because of dissatisfaction with the trial court's judgment <br> *Appellee:* the party against whom the appeal is brought <br> *Appellate brief:* written arguments by the attorney on why the trial court acted correctly or incorrectly | An opinion in the middle appeals court (intermediate appellate court) will often be written. <br> This opinion in the middle appeals court might be appealed to the highest court, in which event another opinion could be written. <br> [Note that in some states, there is no middle court; the appeal goes directly from the trial court to the highest state court.] |

what the agency did. A court generally will not allow a party to appeal an administrative decision until this process has been completed.

Trial de novo:   A totally new fact-finding hearing.

 ## Section B. Alternative Dispute Resolution (ADR)

As you can see, litigation can be an involved and costly process. If the parties cannot resolve the dispute on their own, an increasingly popular option is alternative dispute resolution *(ADR)*. Many disputants try it before resorting to traditional litigation. ADR may take several forms:

*Arbitration.*   Both sides agree to submit their dispute to a neutral third party who will listen to the evidence and make a decision. This individual is usually a professional arbitrator hired through organizations such as the American Arbitration Association. An arbitration proceeding is not as formal as a court trial. Generally, the decision of an arbitrator is not appealable to a court. If a party is dissatisfied, he or she must go to court and start all over again. In certain kinds of cases, such as medical malpractice, some states require the parties to try arbitration before they can use the court system.

*Rent-a-Judge.*   This is actually another form of arbitration. A retired judge is hired by both sides to listen to the evidence and to make a decision which has no more or less validity than any other arbitrator's decision.

*Mediation.*   Both sides agree to submit their dispute to a neutral third party who will help the disputants reach a negotiated settlement on their own. The mediator does not render a decision, although sometimes he or she may make suggestions or recommendations.

*Med-Arb.*   First mediation is tried. If it is not successful, the proceeding becomes an arbitration, and the mediator switches roles. He or she then makes a decision as an arbitrator.

*Neighborhood Justice Center (NJC).*   In many localities, an NJC exists to offer mediation and arbitration services for disputes involving ongoing relationships in the community, such as between landlord and tenant, or among neighbors. The NJC could be sponsored by the government, a foundation, or an existing community organization.

##  Section C. Litigation Assistantship: Pretrial Stage

For a list of paralegal functions in litigation, see the overview in Chapter 2, page 100. At the pretrial stage, some of the most important paralegal functions are as follows:

1. Data retrieval
2. Digesting and indexing
3. Calendar control and scheduling
4. Drafting interrogatories and answers to interrogatories
5. Drafting pleadings
6. Preparation of trial notebook
7. Interviewing and investigation
8. Legal research

The remainder of this section will primarily cover the first six of these tasks. Some of the tasks mentioned at the top of the list will also be discussed in Chapter 14 on law office administration, and in Chapter 13 on computerization. Interviewing, fact investigation, and legal research are treated in Chapters 8, 9, and 11.

### 1. Data Retrieval

Finding or retrieving data from a file can sometimes be a difficult task. As soon as a lawsuit starts, letters, memoranda, affidavits, and other documents are collected at a rather fast pace. The filing problems presented by this volume of documents can be enormous. A usable index system should exist to let everyone know what is in a file. Even with a good index, however, portions of an active file may be scattered throughout the office on the desks of different people working on the case.

Several basic guidelines should be part of the paralegal's standard practice when engaged in any data retrieval assignment:

- Have a comprehensive knowledge of the office's filing system. Be sure you know who in the office already has this knowledge so that they can be consulted. Is there an index system? Is there a cross-index system? Are there file summaries available?

- Have a comprehensive knowledge of the different stages of litigation and the most common documents involved in each stage.

- If possible, find out who wrote the document that contains the data you are trying to retrieve. Ask him or her for leads.

- Determine whether the data you are seeking may be found in more than one document and, if so, look for each document.

- Recognize that data in a document may be contradicted by other data in other documents. To determine the most current status of data, start examining the most recent documents in the file and work back.

## 2. Digesting and Indexing

Many paralegals are given the assignment of digesting or summarizing discovery documents, particularly depositions. Here is how Dana Nikolewski describes a recent experience with this seemingly never-ending task:

> It's Thursday and I'm on page 20 of a 300-page deposition which I really should have finished summarizing last week. The phone rings and I relish the thought of this brief interruption, until I recognize the voice on the other end as none other than our local courier announcing the arrival of 200 more depositions which I know need to be summarized ASAP.[2]

Litigation paralegals do indeed spend a good deal of time digesting. Occasionally you will see a want ad for paralegals to digest depositions full-time. Such individuals are sometimes called *depo summarizers*. While all paralegals do not perform the task full time, the experience of Dana Nikolewski is not unusual.

To *digest* a document, you summarize it according to a given organizational principle. To *index* a document, you state where certain topics are covered in the document. The complexity of the task depends on the complexity of the case and the volume of paper generated before and during discovery. Computer programs, such as SUMMATION II, have been developed to provide assistance.

Some of the basic objectives of digesting and indexing include:

- Creating order out of what might be hundreds or thousands of pages of data
- Providing ready access to selected topics in these pages once the summaries are correlated by subject matter
- Providing a way of comparing testimony, verifying facts, spotting inconsistencies, and identifying evidentiary holes that need to be filled by further interviewing, investigation, and discovery

---

[2]Nikolewski, *Just Call Me Dorothy*, 13 Newsletter 5 (Dallas Ass'n of Legal Assistants, April 1989).

**FIGURE 10.4**
Deposition Index

```
                  INDEX OF DEPOSITION OF IAN SMITH
                              3/13/93

TOPIC                                      PAGES IN DEPOSITION

Leg injuries ........................................... 2, 24, 33, 35, 45
Medical payments ................................... 1, 7, 19
Tax payments ....................................... 40, 43, 50
Wage history ........................................ 1, 2, 4, 7, 25, 29
```

■ Assisting the attorney in organizing the trial, particularly by suggesting questions to be used in the direct and cross-examination of witnesses on the stand; such strategy considerations will often go into the attorney's trial notebook which you may be asked to help prepare.

The starting point in *indexing* any document is to find out what topics in the document your supervisor wants you to index, such as leg injuries, wage history, medical payments, or tax assessments. Every time these topics appear in the document, you note the page number so that someone else can find these topics easily in that document. For an example of an index of a deposition, see Figure 10.4.

The method of *digesting* or summarizing data is also fairly simple. Suppose, for example, the following material comes from page 65 of the transcript of a deposition of Mr. Smith:

```
Line
1. Q. Could you tell me please exactly how long after the accident you
2.    first felt the pain in your leg?
3. A. Well, it's hard to say precisely because everything happened so
4.    fast and my head was spinning from. . . .
5. Q. Was it an hour, a day, a week?
6. A. Oh no, it wasn't that long. I'd say the pain started about ten min-
7.    utes after the collision.
```

The above transcript testimony could be digested into:

```
Began feeling pain in leg about 10 min. after collision: page 65, lines 1–7
```

Your supervisor might want you to present this digest in a three column format. For example:

| PAGE/LINE | SUMMARY | TOPIC |
|---|---|---|
| 65:1–7 | Began feeling pain in leg about 10 min. after collision | Injury, Leg Pain |

As you can see, considerable space can be saved by eliminating the question-and-answer format and by focusing directly on the information sought. Such summaries could be placed on small file cards under the heading "Injury" or on summary sheets that are categorized by such headings. Alternatively, the summaries can be entered into computer programs. You then can collate all statements made by the same witness on a particular topic. You can compare what this same deposition witness said about a particular topic in his or her answers to interrogatories. You can compare what other witnesses have said about the same topic. The possibilities are endless once you have prepared careful, readable summaries.

Before examining some of the major kinds of digesting that are used in a law office, read the general guidelines on digesting in Figure 10.5.

There are two major kinds of summaries:

- *Digest by person*
- *Digest by subject matter*

### Digest by Person

In a digest by person, you focus on a particular witness, such as the person questioned in a deposition. Your instructions may be to provide a page-by-page summary of what the witness said. If so, you simply go through the entire document and summarize everything (see Figure 10.6). Include a table of contents at the beginning of the report you prepare that provides the summary (see Figure 10.7).

### Digest by Subject Matter

Here you are asked to focus on a particular topic only. For example:

- Everything the witness said about the dismissal
- Everything that all the witnesses said about the condition of the car after the accident
- Everything that all the witnesses said about events after 6 P.M. on 5/30/90
- All statements made to the police after the accident
- All references to the meeting of 7/23/90

The subject-matter inquiry can be limited to a particular discovery document, such as a deposition, or it can cover a large number of documents:

- The complaint
- The answer
- Interrogatory answers
- Deposition transcript
- Responses to requests for admission
- Reports obtained via a motion to produce documents or other things
- Medical examination reports
- Other investigation reports
- Etc.

Hence, one digest summary can pull together everything on a particular topic from all of the above sources so that comparisons, correlations, and commentaries can be made.

1.  Obtain clear instructions from your supervisor. What precisely have you been asked to do? What have you expressly or by implication been told not to do? It is a good idea to write down the supervisor's instructions. If you have never worked with a particular supervisor before, show him or her your work soon after you begin the assignment in order to make sure you have understood the instructions.

2.  Know the difference between paraphrasing testimony and quoting testimony. To *paraphrase* is to put the testimony into your own words. To quote is to use the words of the witness even though you may leave out part of what the witness said. Supervisors may not want you to do any paraphrasing. They may want to do their own paraphrasing. Again, you need to know precisely what is expected.

3.  Know the case inside and out. You cannot digest something you do not understand. You must understand the causes of action and the defenses so that you can grasp the meaning of the testimony. Read the client file, including interview and investigation reports, pleadings, other discovery documents, etc.

4.  The answers given in a deposition often ramble. (The same may be true of some interrogatories.) Given this reality, act on the assumption that the same topic is covered in more than one place in the discovery document. Look for this diversity and record it in your summary by pointing out *each* time the same topic is mentioned.

5.  Don't expect the answers to be consistent—even from the same witness. Do not consciously or unconsciously try to help the witness by blocking out potential inconsistencies. If on page 45 the witness said she saw a "car" but on page 104 said she saw a "van" do not blot out the distinction by saying she saw a "motor vehicle," or by failing to mention both. The danger of doing this is more serious than you think, particularly when you are reading hundreds of pages and are getting a little red in the eyes.

6.  Always think in terms of categories as you summarize. Place your summaries into categories. The categories may be as broad as the name of a given witness. Other categories include:

    ■ Background information

    ■ Education

    ■ Past employment

    ■ Present employment

    ■ Medical history

    ■ Insurance

    ■ Prior claims

    ■ Facts of the accident

    ■ Medical injuries from this accident

    ■ Damage to property

    ■ Prior statements made

    Your supervisor may tell you what categories or topics to use in organizing your summaries. If not, use your common sense and create your own.

7.  Each summary should include the specific document you used (e.g., deposition), the page, and, if possible, the lines on the page that are the basis of the summary.

8.  Find out if the law firm has an office manual that gives you instructions on digesting. If not, check closed case files for samples of the kind of digesting and indexing that the firm has done in the past. Ask your supervisor if you should use such samples as models.

9.  Prepare summaries of your summaries whenever you have an extensive digesting assignment that requires the examination of numerous documents for numerous topics.

10. Update the summaries. After you finish your digest, more facts may become known through further investigation and discovery. Supplement your earlier summary reports by adding the new data.

11. Keep a list (or know where to find a list) of every piece of paper in a file. Some digesting/indexing assignments will require you to examine everything in the file.

**FIGURE 10.5**
Guidelines for Digesting Discovery Documents

**FIGURE 10.6**

Digest by Person

| PAGE/LINE | SUMMARY | TOPIC |
|---|---|---|
| 1:1–35 | John R. Smith, 12 Main St. Buffalo N.Y. 14202; 456-9103. | Personal Data |
| 1:36–40 | Mechanic, XYZ Factory, 3/13/73; became supervisor 3/87. | Employment |
| 2:1–28 | Met plaintiff 7/31/81 at factory; was plaintiff's superior; trained plaintiff to operate equipment. | Relationship to Plaintiff |
| 2:29–47 | Was working on date of accident (9/1/90); saw plank fall on plaintiff. | Accident |

**FIGURE 10.7**

Digest by Person with Table of Contents

**DIGEST OF DEPOSITION OF JOHN R. SMITH**

**CASE:** Jones v. XYZ Factory                **OFFICE FILE NUMBER:** 90-341
**DEPONENT:** John R. Smith, supervisor of       **COURT DOCKET NUMBER:** Civ. 2357-1
    plaintiff                                **ATTORNEY ON CASE:** Linda Stout

**DATE OF DEPOSITION:** 2/24/91
**DATE SUMMARY PREPARED:** 5/16/91
**SUMMARY PREPARED BY:** George Henderson, Paralegal

**TABLE OF CONTENTS**

| Topic | Pages in Deposition |
|---|---|
| Background Information | 1–4, 9 |
| Smith's Knowledge of Accident | 2–3, 5, 7–10 |
| Company Report Filed by Smith | 23 |
| Smith's Instructions to Plaintiff Just Before Accident | 15–17 |

## 3. Calendar Control and Scheduling

The central focus of calendar control is the office *tickler system,* which is used to record important dates and to remind everyone to take appropriate action on these dates. Attorneys need constant reminders of due dates, particularly when they are working on more than one case, or when more than one attorney is working on a single case. Here are some examples of tasks and events about which attorneys need to be "tickled:" client meetings, filing complaint before the running of the statute of limitations, sending demand to insurance company, requesting a jury trial, filing interrogatories, responding to interrogatories, filing requests for production of documents, responding to requests for production of documents, conducting depositions, filing pretrial motions, appearing at hearings on pretrial motions, conducting settlement negotiations, etc.

Scheduling is often a secretarial responsibility, although in complex cases, paralegals can become involved. Arrangements must be made for expert witnesses to prepare reports and to give deposition and trial testimony; timely notifications of discovery events must be made; medical examinations must be arranged, etc.

## 4. Drafting Interrogatories and Replies to Interrogatories

Considerable skill is required in drafting and replying to interrogatories. These tasks have opposite objectives: in drafting interrogatories you want to obtain as much information as possible from the other side, while in responding to interrogatories, you usually want to say as little as possible. See Figures 10.8 and 10.9 for guidelines on drafting and responding to interrogatories.

---

### Excerpt from a Set of Interrogatories

**Injuries and Damages**

551. State the name of each person for whom you claim damages for personal injuries.

552. Describe in detail all injuries and symptoms, whether physical, mental, or emotional, experienced since the occurrence and claimed to have been caused, aggravated, or otherwise contributed to by it.

553. As to each medical practitioner who has examined or treated any of the persons named in your answer to Interrogatory 551, above, for any of the injuries or symptoms described, state:
    (a) The name, address, and specialty of each medical practitioner;
    (b) The date of each examination or treatment;
    (c) The physical, mental, or emotional condition for which each examination or treatment was performed.

554. Has any person named in your answers to Interrogatory 551, above, been hospitalized since the occurrence? _____ If so, state:
    (a) The name and location of each hospital in which each was confined;
    (b) The dates of each hospitalization;
    (c) The conditions treated during each hospitalization;
    (d) The nature of the treatment rendered during each hospitalization.

555. Have any diagnostic studies, tests, or procedures been performed since the accident? _____ If so, state:
    (a) The nature thereof;
    (b) The name, address, and occupation of the person performing same;
    (c) The place where performed, and, if in a clinic, laboratory, or hospital, the name and address thereof;
    (d) The name and present or last-known address of each party now in possession or control of any records prepared in connection with each study, test, or procedure.

556. Is any person named in your answer to Interrogatory 551, above, still under the care of any medical practitioner? _____ If so, state:
    (a) The name and address of each practitioner;
    (b) The nature of each condition for which care is being rendered;
    (c) Which of the conditions are related to the accident.

557. State as to each item of medical expense attributable to the accident:
    (a) The amount;
    (b) The name and address of the person or organization paid or owed therefor;
    (c) The date of each item of expense (attach copies of itemized bills).

---

## 5. Drafting Pleadings

The major pleadings in litigation are the complaint answer, reply, and counterclaim. Very often you will use standard forms as the starting point in drafting pleadings. Closely examine the guidelines in Figure 10.10, on page 467, on using standard forms.

Here, we will concentrate on drafting a complaint through an examination of its basic structure. The components of a complaint are illustrated in Figure 10.11, on page 468.[3]

---

[3]Adapted from MacDonald, Pick, DeWitt & Volz, *Wisconsin Practice Methods, 2d ed.*, section 1530, page 239 (West, 1959).

**FIGURE 10.8**

Guidelines on
Drafting
Interrogatories

1. Obtain general and specific instructions from your supervisor on the questions to be asked in the interrogatories.

2. Read all the documents on the case that have been prepared thus far (such as the client interview report (intake memo), field investigation report, complaint, and answer).

3. Look at drafts of other interrogatories that have been used in other cases that are similar to your case. Determine whether courts in your area have approved any standard-form interrogatories.

4. Recognize the need to adapt interrogatories from other cases to the peculiar needs of your case.

5. Start out with requests for basic data (name, address, age, occupation, etc.).

6. Try to avoid questions that call for simple *yes/no* answers unless you also ask questions about the factual basis for such answers.

7. Try to avoid questions that call for an opinion from the respondent unless the opinion is relevant or might provide leads to other facts.

8. Phrase the questions so as to elicit facts.

9. Know what facts will be necessary to establish your client's case, and ask specific questions focusing on those facts. Know the elements of the causes of action and defenses in the case. Ask questions designed to uncover facts for each element.

10. As to each fact, ask questions calculated to elicit the respondent's ability to comment on the fact. (How far away was he? Does he wear glasses? etc.)

11. Phrase the fact questions so that the respondent will have to indicate clearly whether he or she is talking from firsthand knowledge or hearsay.

**FIGURE 10.9**

Guidelines on
Responding
to Interrogatories

1. Obtain general and specific instructions from your supervisor on drafting the answers.

2. Check all proposed answers with available documents (such as the client interview report (intake memo), field investigation report, complaint, and answer).

3. Do not volunteer information beyond the confines of the question unless necessary to clarify a position (when, for example, a simple answer would be damagingly misleading without the clarification).

4. When an answer to a question is not known, say so.

5. Preface most answers by saying "to the best of my knowledge" or "as far as I can recall" in order to provide some leeway if the answer later proves to be invalid.

6. Recognize that the other side will try to use the answers against you. For example, opposing counsel may try to get the client to say something on cross-examination that will contradict the answers given by the client in the interrogatories.

7. Recognize the kinds of improper questions that a party does not have to answer. For example:

   ■ Clearly irrelevant questions

   ■ Unduly repetitive or burdensome questions

   ■ Questions inquiring into the *attorney's work product*, e.g., questions that ask for the attorney's legal opinion or that ask for copies of legal memoranda.

   ■ Questions that expressly or implicitly call for a violation of the attorney-client privilege, e.g., "what did your attorney tell you?"

*Caption of Complaint*

A caption is the heading of a document. For the caption of a complaint, see Figure 10.11, on page 468. A complaint is the pleading that tries to state a cause of action against the defendant. (A cause of action is a legally acceptable reason for suing.) The caption of a complaint should contain the name of the court, the name of the parties, and the number assigned to the case by the court.

**FIGURE 10.10**

How to Avoid
Abusing a
Standard Form

1. A standard form is an example of the document or instrument that you need to draft, such as a pleading, contract, or other agreement.

2. Standard forms are found in a number of places—for example, formbooks, manuals, practice texts, in some statutory codes, and in some court rules.

3. Most standard forms are written by private attorneys. Occasionally, however, a standard form will be written by the legislature or by the court as the suggested or required format to be used.

4. Considerable care must be exercised in the use of a standard form. Such forms can be deceptive in that they appear to require little more than filling in the blanks. The intelligent use of these forms usually requires much more.

5. The cardinal rule is: *adapt* the form to the particulars of the client's case.

6. Do not be afraid of changing the printed language in the form if you have a good reason. Whenever you make such a change, bring it to your supervisor for approval.

7. You should never use a standard form unless and until you have satisfied yourself that you know the meaning of *every* word and phrase on the form. This includes *boilerplate,* which is standard language that is often used in the same kind of document. The great temptation of most form users is to ignore what they do not understand because the form has been used so often in the past without any apparent difficulty. Do not give in to this temptation. Find out what everything means by:

    ■ Using a legal dictionary

    ■ Asking your supervisor

    ■ Asking other knowledgeable people

    ■ Doing other legal research

8. You need to know whether the entire form or any part of it has ever been litigated in court. To find this out, do some legal research in the area of the law relevant to the form.

9. Once you have found a form that appears useful, look around for another form that attempts to serve the same purpose. Analyze the different or alternative forms available. Which one is preferable? Why? The important point is: keep questioning the validity of the form. Be very skeptical about the use of any form.

10. Do not leave any blank spaces on the form. If a question does not apply, make a notation to indicate this, such as N.A.

11. If the form was written for another state, be sure that the form is adapted to the law of your state.

12. Occasionally you may go to an old case file to find a document that might be used as a model for a similar document that you need to draft on a current case. All the above cautions apply to the adaptation of documents from closed case files.

## Designation of the Pleading

The title of the pleadings should be clearly stated at the top. In the example in Figure 10.11, the pleading is a Complaint for Negligence.

## Statement of Jurisdiction

Not all states require a statement of the court's subject-matter jurisdiction—its power or authority to hear this kind of case. A complaint filed in federal court, however, usually contains a statement of the U.S. District Court's jurisdiction.

For purposes of determining venue—the place of the trial—the complaint may also have to allege the residence of the parties, where the accident or wrong allegedly occurred, etc.

**FIGURE 10.11**

Structure of a Complaint

**Caption**

STATE OF _____ COUNTY OF _____
_____ COURT

John Doe, Plaintiff

v.                                    Civil Action No. _____

Richard Roe, Defendant

**Designation of Pleading →**          COMPLAINT FOR NEGLIGENCE

**Statement of Jurisdiction →** Plaintiff alleges that:

**Body**

1. The jurisdiction of this court is based on section _____, title _____ of the [State] Code.

2. Plaintiff is a plumber, residing at 107 Main Street in the City of _____, _____ County, State of _____ .

3. Upon information and belief, defendant is a traveling salesman, residing at 5747 Broadway Street in the City of Chicago, Cook County, Illinois.

4. On or about the second day of January, 1989 an automobile driven by defendant, on Highway 18 in the vicinity of Verona, _____, struck an automobile being driven by the plaintiff on said highway.

5. Defendant was negligent in the operation of said automobile at the aforesaid time and place as to:

a. Speed,

b. Lookout,

c. Management and control.

6. As a result of said negligence of defendant, his automobile struck plaintiff's automobile and caused the following damage:

a. Plaintiff was subjected to great pain and suffering.

b. Plaintiff necessarily incurred medical and hospital expense.

c. Plaintiff suffered a loss of income.

d. Plaintiff's automobile was damaged.

**Prayer for Relief →**   Wherefore plaintiff demands judgment in the amount of one hundred thousand dollars ($100,000), together with the costs and disbursements of this action.

**Subscription →**
_____
Plaintiff's Attorney
1 Main Street

_____ , _____

**Verification**

State of _____

                                                                          ss

County of _____

John Doe, being first duly sworn on oath according to law, deposes and says that he has read the foregoing complaint and that the matters stated therein are true to the best of his knowledge, information, and belief.

_____
John Doe

Subscribed and sworn to before me on this_____ day of _____, 19 _____ .

_____
Notary Public

My commission expires:

## Body

The claims of the plaintiff are presented in the *body of the complaint.* A claim is a cause of action. Every separate cause of action being used by the plaintiff should be stated in a separate "count," e.g., Count I, Count II, or simply as First Cause of Action, Second Cause of Action, etc. The paragraphs should be consecutively numbered. Each paragraph should contain a single fact or a closely related grouping of facts.

With what factual detail must the complaint state the cause of action? There are two main schools of thought on this question.

*1. Fact Pleading*   There must be a statement of the *ultimate facts* that set forth the cause of action. Not every detail that the plaintiff intends to try to prove at trial is pleaded. The complaint need not contain a catalog of the evidence that the plaintiff will eventually introduce at the trial. Only the ultimate facts are pleaded. There is, however, no satisfactory definition of an ultimate fact. Generally, it is one that is essential to the establishment of an element of a cause of action.

The complaint must *not* state conclusions of law, such as "Jones assaulted Smith" or Jones "violated section 23 of the state code." The problem, however, is that it is as difficult to define a conclusion of law as it is to define an ultimate fact. Some statements are mixed statements of fact and law—for example, "Jones negligently drove his car into. . . ." As a matter of common sense and practicality, if the conclusion of law (here, "negligently") is also a convenient way of stating facts, it will be permitted.

The only reliable guide for a pleader is to determine what the prior decisions of the courts in the state have concluded are proper and improper statements of fact in a complaint.

*2. Notice Pleading.*   Under the federal system and under states that have adopted the lead of the federal courts, the goal of the complaint is say enough to notify or inform the defendant of the nature of the claims against him or her. There is no requirement that ultimate facts be alleged. The plaintiff must simply provide a "short and plain statement of the claim showing the pleader is entitled to relief."

It is not improper to fail to plead an ultimate fact. The critical point is that the complaint will not be thrown out if it *fails* to plead an ultimate fact or if it *includes* conclusions of law—as long as the complaint gives adequate notice of the nature of the claim. The technicalities of pleading facts, conclusions of law, etc. are unimportant in notice pleading.

Notice pleading does not necessarily require a different kind of pleading from fact pleading; notice pleading is simply more liberal or tolerant in what is acceptable.

. . . . . . . . . . . . . . .

When the plaintiff lacks personal knowledge of a fact being alleged, the fact should be stated "upon information and belief" as in the third paragraph of Figure 10.11.

There are times when the law requires specificity in the pleading. For example, allegations of fraud must be stated with specificity or particularity. Also, when special damages are required in defamation cases, the facts must be pleaded with some specificity.

### Prayer for Relief

In the prayer, the complaint asks for a specific amount of damages, or for some other form of relief such as an injunction against a nuisance. In the event that the defendant fails to appear and answer the complaint, a default judgment is entered against the defendant. The relief given the plaintiff in a default judgment cannot exceed what the plaintiff asked for in the prayer for relief.

### Subscription

The subscription is the signature of the attorney who prepared the complaint and who represents the plaintiff. If the plaintiff wrote the complaint and is acting as his or her own attorney in the case, the plaintiff signs.

### Verification

A verification is an affidavit that is submitted with the pleading. It is signed by a party on whose behalf the pleading was prepared, who swears that he or she has read the pleading and that it is true to the best of his or her knowledge, information, and belief. (Not all states require that complaints be verified.)

## 6.  Preparation of Trial Notebook

A *trial notebook,* also called a trial book, is a collection of documents, arguments, and strategies that an attorney plans to use during a trial. It is often organized as a loose-leaf binder for easy use by the attorney. The notebook becomes the attorney's checklist for conducting the trial. Many trial notebooks contain the following sections:[4]

- Table of Contents to Notebook
- Things to Do
- Trial Schedule/Deadlines
- Trial Team (addresses, phone numbers)
- Case Outline
- Statement of Facts
- Pleadings
- Trial Briefs/Trial Memoranda (submitted to the court)
- Law
- Outline of Liability
- My Exhibits
- Opposition Exhibits
- My Witnesses
- Opposition Witnesses
- Witness Statements
- Requests for Production and Responses
- Requests for Admission and Responses

---

[4]Hollins, *Assignment: Trial Prep,* 2 California Paralegal 30 (April/June 1990); Feder, *Translating Professional Competence into Performance Competence,* 15 Legal Economics 44 (April 1989).

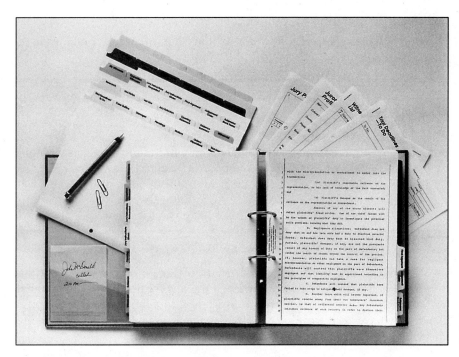

LawFiles Trial Notebook.
Courtesy of Bindertek,
Sausalito, California.

- Direct Examination Outline of Questions
- Anticipated Cross-Examination Questions
- Outline of Damages
- Motions
- Deposition Index and Outlines
- Voir Dire Questions
- Juror Information
- Jury Chart
- Records
- Opening Statements
- Plaintiff Testimony
- Jury Instructions Requests
- Defendant Testimony
- Final Arguments

It's often the paralegal's job to collect the material that will go into the note-book, organize it, keep it current, and help make it useful to the attorney as a vehicle for trial preparation and trial management. Specifically, the paralegal might:

- Prepare summaries of deposition testimony
- Prepare a list of every party and witness plus people who are expected to be mentioned during testimony; index this list to the rest of the trial notebook
- Prepare sample questions to ask witnesses, particularly when needed to lay the foundation for evidence to be introduced
- Prepare a summary description or log of all the exhibits to be used

- Prepare an abstract of the contents of every document
- State the location of documents and exhibits that will not be contained in the trial notebook itself
- Cross-index material on particular witnesses or legal theories
- Collect all the information known about each juror, from voir dire and by other means
- Prepare end tabs for each section of the notebook
- Color-code different kinds of documents and information, such as with blue sheets for citations to authorities supporting claims, and yellow sheets for deposition testimony and other statements of the opposing party

## ■ Section D. Litigation Assistantship: Trial Stage

The role of paralegals at trials depends, in part, on the involvement that they have had with the case up to trial. If the involvement has been minimal, then they may not have much to do to assist the attorney at trial. If, on the other hand, they have been working closely with the attorney on the case all along, their role at trial could include a number of tasks:

- Monitoring all the files, documents, and evidence that the attorney will need to present the case, to plan and to replan strategy as outlined in the trial notebook
- Doing some spot legal research on issues that come up during the trial that require an answer fairly quickly
- Preparing preliminary drafts of certain motions and other documents that are required during the course of the trial
- Assuring the presence of witnesses; assisting the attorney in preparing them for direct examination, and in anticipating what may be asked of them on cross-examination
- Taking notes on the testimony of certain witnesses. The attorney may be able to use these notes in preparing for other segments of the trial. A typed transcript of the testimony may not be available until after the trial.
- Making suggestions to the attorney on what questions to ask a witness based on the paralegal's close following of what has happened thus far in the trial, and based on his or her involvement with the documents and files prepared during the pretrial stage

## ■ Section E. Litigation Assistantship: Appeal Stage

After the trial, the losing attorney plans appeal strategies. He or she must review all of the documents and testimony in the trial in order to identify grounds for an appeal. The paralegal may be asked to go back over the record and do the following:

- Make a list of every time I objected to something during the trial. Include the page number where my objection is found, a brief summary of what my objection was, and the ruling of the judge on my objection.

- Make a list of every time opposing counsel made reference to a particular topic, such as the plaintiff's prior involvement in other litigation.
- Make a list of every time the judge asked questions of witnesses.

    Other paralegal tasks can include:

- Researching the legislative history of relevant statutes
- Shepardizing cases, and conducting cite checking (see Chapter 11)
- Reading over appellate briefs to cross-check the accuracy of quoted testimony from the typed transcript of the trial
- Conducting legal research on assigned issues of law
- Monitoring the typing, printing, and filing of appellate briefs

## Section F. Litigation Assistantship: Enforcement Stage

If a money judgment was awarded to the client, considerable work may be required in collecting it from the *judgment debtor,* the party obligated by the court to pay the judgment. (The person who won the judgment and must be paid is the *judgment creditor.*) The paralegal can arrange for the sheriff to begin execution, which is the process of carrying out or enforcing a judgment. The judgment debtor may be ordered by the court to submit to an examination of what his or her assets are. Investigation work will probably be required to determine what assets exist, where they are, and how they might be reached. In some cases, the attorney may be able to petition the court for a contempt order against the judgment debtor for noncompliance. The paralegal can help by assembling the factual basis to support this charge and in drafting some of the court papers involved.

## Chapter Summary

Civil litigation begins with the filing of a complaint, to which the defendant responds with an answer. In these pleadings, the parties state their causes of action and defenses. The next major event is discovery, which can include interrogatories, depositions, requests for admissions, etc. If motions for summary judgment are denied, the trial proceeds. After voir dire and opening statements to the jury, the party with the burden of proof puts on its case through the introduction of evidence and the direct examination of witnesses. The latter can be cross-examined by the other party. When the first party rests, the other goes through the same steps. A motion for a directed verdict will be granted (thus ending the case), if there was a failure to establish a prima facie case. After closing statements to the jury and the instructions of the judge, the case goes to the jury. Its verdict (if ac-

cepted by the court) becomes the basis of the court's judgment.

If dissatisfied with the judgment, the appellant files a notice of appeal and an appellate brief. The appellee also files an appellate brief. After oral argument, the appellate court affirms, modifies, or reverses the judgment of the lower court. A further appeal to a higher appellate court might also be possible.

Criminal litigation often begins with an arrest warrant, followed by an initial appearance. Once the decision on bail is made, the prosecution proceeds to the preliminary hearing to determine whether probable cause exists. If so, the grand jury will then determine whether to issue an indictment. The arraignment is next. If plea bargaining is unsuccessful, the case goes to trial, where guilt must be established beyond a reasonable doubt. The

*(Continued on next page)*

## ☐ Chapter Summary (Continued)

criminal trial then proceeds in a manner similar to a civil trial: voir dire, opening statements, etc. The appeal process is also similar: notice of appeal, appellate briefs, etc.

In an administrative hearing, a hearing examiner makes a decision on the dispute within the agency. His or her decision will usually be in the form of a recommendation to a higher official or body within the agency. When a party has exhausted administrative remedies, he or she can appeal the agency's decision to a court.

Alternatives to litigation include arbitration, rent-a-judge, mediation, med-arb, and neighborhood justice centers.

Among the roles fulfilled by paralegals during litigation are the following: retrieving and organizing data from the files; indexing and digesting discovery documents; maintaining the calendar; drafting interrogatories and replies to interrogatories; drafting complaints and other pleadings; helping prepare the trial notebook; providing assistance as needed during the trial; retrieving and digesting facts in preparation for appeal; and providing general assistance in collecting a judgment.

## Key Terms

litigation
quasi-judicial
civil dispute
criminal dispute
damages
liable
joint and several liability
retainer
appearance
notice of appearance
attorney of record
praecipe
forum
estate
diversity of citizenship
venue
complaint
plaintiff
cause of action
stating a cause of action
codefendant
pleading
allegation
information and belief
ad damnum
jury trial
filed
service of process
summons
process server
affidavit
affiant
statute of limitations
in personam jurisdiction

personal jurisdiction
motion to dismiss
failure to state a cause of
    action
demurrer
procedural law
FRCP
substantive law
answer
draft
default judgment
motion/movant/move
defense
affirmative defense
cross-claim
counterclaim
thirty-party complaint
contest
adverse judgment
discovery
interrogatories
oath
deposition/deponent/depose
transcript
requests for admissions
order
hearing
adversarial hearing
ex parte hearing
summary
motion for summary judgment
magistrate
pretrial conference
stipulated

in issue
question of fact
question of law
tangible evidence
testimonial evidence
introduce evidence
set for trial
bailiff
jury panel
voir dire
challenge for cause
peremptory challenge
bias
alternate
rule on witnesses
opening statement
burden of proof
bench conference
objection
competency
excuse the jury
overrule
direct examination
ground
hearsay
sustain
strike
cross examination
redirect examination
qualify a witness
expert witness
clerk
exhibit
move into evidence

rest
adjourn
directed verdict
prima facie
take under advisement
closing argument
jury instructions
charge to jury
presumption
rebuttable presumption
nonrebuttable presumption
verdict
elements
preponderance of the
    evidence
standard of proof
judgment
declaratory judgment
judgment nov
motion for a new trial
appeal
review
stay
execution
timely
notice of appeal
bond
judgment on the merits
dismissal without prejudice
cured
res judicata
bar
appellant
record
transcript
docket/docketed
appellate brief
appellee
issues on appeal
respondent
oral argument
panel
opinion
reporters

dissent
majority opinion
concurring opinion
affirm
remand
reverse
waive
petition
rehearing
en banc
writ of certiorari
mandate
satisfy
prosecution
warrant
initial appearance
felony
misdemeanor
assigned counsel
indigent
bail
personal recognizance
bail bond
preliminary hearing
probable cause
bound over
grand jury
nolle prosequi
plead
plea bargaining
indictment
information
arraignment
impaneled
impeach
credible
relevant
beyond a reasonable doubt
acquit
poll
administrative hearing
hearing examiner
administrative law judge
intra-agency appeal

board of appeals
discretion
summarily
below
exhausting administrative
    remedies
trial de novo
interlocutory appeal
arrest
ADR
arbitration
rent-a-judge
mediation
med-arb
NJC
data retrieval
digesting
depo summarizers
indexing
paraphrasing
digest by person
digest by subject
tickler system
attorney work product
pleadings
standard forms
boilerplate
complaint
caption
subject-matter jurisdiction
venue
cause of action
body of complaint
fact pleading
ultimate fact
notice pleading
upon information and belief
prayer for relief
subscription
verification
trial notebook
judgment debtor
judgment creditor

# CHAPTER

## 11

# Legal Research

## ■ Chapter Outline

Section A. Strategy for Studying Legal Research

Section B. The Importance of Legal Research

Section C. Frustration and Legal Research

Section D. Flexibility in Legal Research

Section E. The Vocabulary of Legal Research: A Checklist

Section F. Finding Law Libraries

Section G. A Glossary of Law and Law Books

Section H. Authority in Research and Writing
1. Introduction
2. Mandatory Authority
3. Court Opinions as Persuasive Authority
4. Secondary Authority as Persuasive Authority

Section I. Citation Form
Basic Citation Rules

Section J. Cite Checking
Guidelines for Cite Checking

Section K. Components of a Law Book

Section L. The CARTWHEEL

Section M. The First Level of Legal Research: Background

Section N. Checklists for Using the Ten Major Search Resources
1. Card Catalog
2. Digests
3. Annotations
4. Shepard's
5. Loose-leaf Services
6. Legal Periodical Literature
7. Legal Encyclopedias
8. Treatises
9. Phone and Mail
10. Computers

Section O. Finding Case Law

Section P. Reading and Finding Statutes

Section Q. Legislative History
1. Why Search for Legislative History
2. Finding Legislative History

Section R. Monitoring Proposed Legislation

Section S. Reading and Finding Constitutional Law

Section T. Finding Administrative Law

Section U. Finding Local Law

Section V. Finding Rules of Court

Section W. Finding International Law

Section X. The Third Level of Research: Validation

Section Y. Annotated Bibliography

## ■ Section A. A Strategy for Studying Legal Research

This chapter does not cover every aspect of legal research, nor does it treat every conceivable law book that could be found in a law library. Rather, the chapter examines the major components of legal research with the objective of identifying effective starting points.

**FIGURE 11.1**

A Strategy for
Studying Legal
Research

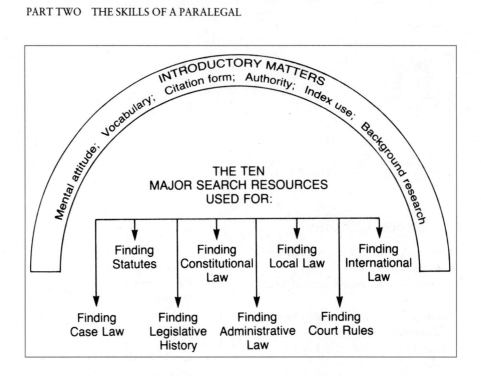

A great deal of information is provided in the pages that follow. You should first read the chapter through quickly to obtain an overview and to begin seeing where some concepts are covered in more than one place. The second time you read the chapter, you should begin collecting the terminology called for in Assignment 11.1. The best way to avoid becoming overwhelmed is to start feeling comfortable with terminology as soon as possible.

When you walk into a law library, your first impression is likely to be one of awe. You are confronted with row upon row of books, most of which seem unapproachable; they do not invite browsing. To be able to use the law library, your first responsibility as a legal researcher is to break down any psychological barrier that you may have with respect to the books in it. This is done not only by learning the techniques of research but also by understanding the limitations of the law library.

A major misunderstanding about the law library is that it contains the answer to every legal question. In many instances, legal problems have no definitive answers. The researcher often operates on the basis of "educated guesses" of what the answer is. To be sure, your guess is supported by what you uncover through legal research in the law library. The end product, however, is only the researcher's opinion of what the law is, rather than the absolute answer. No one will know for sure what the "right" or final answer is until the matter is litigated in court. If the problem is never litigated, then the "right" answer will be whatever the parties accept among themselves through negotiation or settlement. The researcher will not know what answer carries the day for the client until the negotiation process is over.

Many simple problems, however, can be answered by basic (easy) legal research. If someone wants to know, for example, the name of the government agency in charge of incorporating a business or the maximum number of weeks one can receive unemployment compensation, finding the answer is not difficult if the researcher knows what books to go to and how to use their indexes. Most legal research problems, however, are not this simple.

Perhaps the most healthy way to approach the law library is to view it not as a repository of answers but as a storehouse of ambiguities that are waiting to be identified, clarified, manipulated, and applied to the facts of a client's case. You may have heard the story of a client who walked into a law office and asked to see a one-armed attorney. When asked why he required an attorney meeting such specifications, he replied that he was tired of presenting problems to attorneys and having them constantly tell him that "on the one hand" he should do this but "on the other hand" he should do that; he hungered for an attorney who would give him an answer. This concern is well taken. A client is entitled to an answer, to clear guidance. At the same time (or, on the other hand), part of the attorney's job is to identify alternatives or options and to weigh benefits and liabilities of any one particular course of action. Good attorneys are so inclined because they understand that our legal system is infested with unknowns and ambiguities. Good legal researchers also have this understanding. They are not frightened by ambiguities; they thrive on them.

## Section B. The Importance of Legal Research

You will eventually forget most of the law that you learn in school. If you do not forget most of it, you should! No one can know all of the law at any given time, even in a specialty. Furthermore, the law is always changing. Nothing is more dangerous than someone with out-of-date "knowledge" of the law. Law cannot be practiced on the basis of the rules learned in school, since those rules may no longer be valid by the time you try to use them in actual cases. Thousands of courts, legislatures, and administrative agencies spend considerable time writing new laws and changing or adapting old ones.

The law library and the techniques of legal research are the indispensable tickets of admission to current law. School teaches you to think. *You teach yourself the law through the skill of legal research.* Every time you walk into a law library, you are your own professor. You must accept nothing less than to become an expert on the topic of your research, no matter how narrow the topic. The purpose of the law library is to enable you to become an expert on the current law of your topic. Do not fall into the trap of thinking that you must be an expert in an area of the law to research it properly. The reverse is true. A major way for you to become an expert in an area is through what you discover in the law library on your own.

Never be reluctant to undertake legal research on a topic simply because you know very little about the topic. Knowing very little is often the most healthy starting point for the researcher! Preconceptions about the law can sometimes lead you away from avenues in the library that you should be traveling.

To become an expert through comprehensive legal research does not necessarily mean that you will know everything. Experts are not simply people who know the answers; they also know how to *formulate the questions that remain unanswered even after comprehensive legal research.* An expert is someone who can say:

This is what the current law says, and these are the questions that the law has not yet resolved.

Of course, you cannot know what is unresolved until you know what is resolved. The law library will help tell you both.

## Section C. Frustration and Legal Research

You are in the position of the king who sadly had to be told that there is no royal road to geometry. If he wanted to learn geometry, he had to struggle through it like everyone else. Legal research is a struggle and will remain so for the rest of your career. The struggle will eventually become manageable and even enjoyable and exciting—but there is no way out of the struggle no matter how many short cuts you learn. The amount of material in a law library is simply too massive for it to be otherwise, and the material is growing every day with new laws, new formats for law books, and new law publishers offering different services that must be mastered.

Unfortunately, many cannot handle the pressure that the law library sometimes seems to donate in abundance. Too many attorneys, for example, stay away from the library, and consequently practice law "from the hip." Such attorneys need to be sure that they have extensive malpractice insurance!

Legal research will be difficult for you at the beginning, but with experience in the law library, the difficulties will become manageable. The most important advice you can receive is *stick with it.* Spend a lot of time in the library. Be inquisitive. Ask a lot of questions of fellow students, teachers, librarians, lawyers, paralegals, legal secretaries, etc. Be constantly on the alert for tips and techniques. Take strange books from the shelf and try to figure out what they contain, what they try to do, how they are used, and how they duplicate or complement other law books that are not strange to you. Do not wait to be taught how to use sets of books that are new to you. Strike out on your own.

The coming of computer technology to legal research is of some help, but computers cannot eliminate your need to learn the basics. The struggle does not disappear if you are lucky enough to study or work where computers are available. Intelligent use of computers requires an understanding of the fundamental techniques of legal research.

At this stage of your career, most of the frustration will center on the question of how to *begin* your legal research of a topic. Once you overcome this frustration, the concern will then become how to *end* your legal research. After having located a great deal of material, you will worry about when to stop. In this chapter, our major focus will be the techniques of beginning. Techniques of stopping are more troublesome for the conscientious researcher. It is not always easy to determine whether you have found everything that you should find. Although guidelines do exist and will be examined, a great deal of experience with legal research is required before you can make the judgment that you have found everything available on a given topic. Don't be too hard on yourself. The techniques will come with time and practice. You will not learn everything now; you can only begin the learning that must continue throughout your career.

Keep the following "laws" of legal research in mind:

1. *The only books that will be missing from a shelf are those that you need to use immediately.*

2. *A vast amount of information on law books and research techniques exists, most of which you will forget soon after learning.*

3. *Each time you forget something, relearning it will take half the time it previously took.*

4. *When you have relearned something for the fourth time, you own it.*

At times you will walk away from a set of law books that you have used and wonder what you have just done—even if you obtained an answer from the books. At times you will go back to a set of books that you have used before and draw a blank on what the books are and how to use them again. These occurrences are natural. You will forget and you will forget again. Stay with it. Be willing to relearn. You cannot master a set of books after using them only a few times. Learning legal research is a little like learning to play a musical instrument: a seat is waiting for you in the orchestra, but you must practice. A royal road does not exist.

##  Section D. Flexibility in Legal Research

Researchers have reached an enviable plateau when they understand the following paradox: You sometimes do not know what you are looking for until you find it. Since simple answers are rare, researchers are constantly confronted with frustration and ambiguity. As they pursue avenues and leads, they invariably come upon new avenues and thoughts that never occurred to them initially. An entirely new approach to the problem may be uncovered that radically changes their initial perceptions. They reached this stage not because they consciously sought it out but because they were flexible and open-minded enough to be receptive to new approaches and perceptions. This phenomenon is by no means peculiar to legal research. Take the situation of the woman in need of transportation. She sets herself to the task of determining the most economical way to *buy* a good car. In her search, she stumbles upon the practice of leasing cars. After studying this option, she concludes that leasing is the most sensible resolution of her transportation problem. She did not know what she was looking for—a car *leasing* deal—until she found it. Compare this situation with that of a client who comes into a law office for advice on how to write a will so that a certain amount of money will pass to designated individuals upon death. The attorney asks you to do some legal research in the area of wills. While in the law library studying the law of wills, you see reference to life insurance policies as a substitute for wills in passing cash to beneficiaries at death. You bring this to the attention of the attorney, who decides that this option is indeed worth pursuing. You did not know what you were looking for—a will substitute— until you found it.

## ■ Section E. The Vocabulary of Legal Research: A Checklist

This section includes a list of 175 words and phrases, most of which are examined in the remainder of the chapter. The page number in parentheses indicates where the item is covered in the text. The list is the vocabulary of legal research. Before you are finished with this text, one of your goals should be to know the meaning or function of everything on the list. You must learn to speak the language of legal research, as well as to do legal research. See Figure 11.2.

---

### ■ ASSIGNMENT 11.1

For each of the words and phrases in Figure 11.2, prepare a three-by-five-inch index card on which you include the following information:

- The word or phrase
- The pages in this text where the word or phrase is discussed (begin with the page number given in parentheses, then add other page numbers as the word or phrase is discussed elsewhere in the text)
- The definition of the word or phrase, or the function of the word or phrase
- Other information about the word or phrase that you obtain as you use the law library
- Comments by your instructor in class about any of the words and phrases

Some words and phrases will call for more than one card. You should strive, however, to keep the information on the cards brief. Place the cards in alphabetical order. The cards will become your own file system on legal research that you can use as a study guide for the course and as a reference tool when you do legal research in the library. Be sure to add cards for words and phrases as you come across new ones in class and in the library.

See also Assignment 11.7 for other data that you can add to your cards.

---

## ■ Section F. Finding Law Libraries

The availability of law libraries depends to a large degree on the area in which you live, study, or work. Rural areas have fewer possibilities than larger cities or capitals.

Twelve different law library possibilities are listed below. Find out which ones exist in your area. You may need permission to use some of them. (This is certainly true of a private law firm's library.) If a law school or university library is a *depository library,* you must be allowed to use it, or at least those sections of the library that contain the law books that the library receives free of charge from the federal government.

- Law school library
- General university library (may have a law section)
- Law library of a bar association
- State law library (in the state capital and perhaps in branch offices in counties throughout the state)
- Local public library (may have a small law section)
- Law library of a court

FIGURE 11.2

The Vocabulary of
Legal Research:
A Checklist*

1. Act (486)
2. Administrative code (486)
3. Administrative decision (329)
4. Administrative regulation (329)
5. Advance Sheet (for reporters) (486)
6. Advance Sheet (for Shepard's) (487)
7. A.L.R. Blue Book of Supplemental Decisions (560)
8. A.L.R. Digest to 3d, 4th, Federal (559)
9. A.L.R. First, A.L.R.2d, A.L.R.3d, A.L.R.4th, A.L.R. Fed (487)
10. ALR Index (559)
11. A.L.R.2d Digest (559)
12. A.L.R.2d Later Case Service (560)
13. American Digest System (498)
14. American Law Institute (508)
15. Am. Jur. 2d (487)
16. Amicus curiae brief (491)
17. Annotated reporter (487)
18. Annotation (487)
19. Annotation History Table (A.L.R.) (561)
20. Appellant (448)
21. Appellate brief (491)
22. Appellate court (331)
23. Appellee (448)
24. Atlantic Digest (499)
25. Atlantic 2d (A.2d) (494)
26. Authority, mandatory (517)
27. Authority, persuasive (517)
28. Authority, primary (517)
29. Authority, secondary (517)
30. Auto-Cite (586)
31. Bill (490)
32. Bluebook (citations) (490)
33. Blue and White Book (490)
34. Brief of a case (353)
35. California Reporter (Cal. Rptr.) (491)
36. CALR (585)
37. Case (491)
38. Casebook (495)
39. Case on point (518)
40. CCH U.S. Supreme Court Bulletin (492)
41. CD ROM (495)
42. Century Digest (498)
43. Certiorari (Cert.) (449)
44. Charter (329)
45. CARTWHEEL (544)
46. Citation (496)
47. Citator (496)
48. Cite checking (539)
49. Cited material (Shepard's) (510)
50. Citing material (Shepard's) (510)
51. Code, codify (496)
52. Code of Federal Regulations (C.F.R.) (496)
53. Common law (358)
54. Concurring opinion (357)
55. Congressional Record (496)
56. Constitution (329)
57. Corpus Juris Secundum (C.J.S.) (496)
58. Cumulative (497)
59. Current Law Index (579)
60. Decennial Digest (499)
61. Descriptive Word Index (DWI) (556)
62. DIALOG (587)
63. Dicta, dictum (357)
64. Digests (for reporters) (497)
65. Digests (for A.L.R. annotations) (559)
66. Docket Number (355)
67. Et. Seq. (573)
68. Executive Order (329)
69. Federal Digest (498)
70. Federal Practice Digest 2d (499)
71. Federal Practice Digest 3d (499)
72. Federal Practice Digest 4th (499)
73. Federal Supplement (F. Supp.) (492)
74. Federal Register (502)
75. Federal Reporter 2d (F.2d) (492)
76. Federal Rules Decisions (F.R.D.) (502)
77. General Digest (499)
78. Headnote (503)
79. Hornbook (504)
80. Index Medicus (581)
81. Index to Legal Periodicals (578)
82. Index to Annotations (A.L.R.) (559)
83. Insta-Cite (657, 659)
84. Key topic and number (497)
85. Law review (505)
86. Lawyer's Edition (L. Ed.) (491)
87. Legal dictionary (504)
88. Legal encyclopedia (504)
89. Legal newspaper (505)
90. Legal periodical (578)
91. Legal Resource Index (581)
92. Legal thesaurus (505)
93. LegalTrac (581)
94. Legislative history (337)
95. LEXIS (585)
96. Loose-leaf service (506)
97. Majority opinion (357)
98. Maroon Book (539)
99. Martindale-Hubbell (506)
100. Memorandum opinion (355)
101. Military Justice Reporter (492)
102. Modern Federal Practice Digest (499)
103. National Reporter System (493)
104. National Reporter Blue Book (490)
105. New York Supplement (N.Y.S.) (507)
106. NEXIS (587)
107. Nominative reporter (531)
108. North Eastern 2d (N.E.2d) (494)
109. North Western Digest (499)
110. North Western 2d (N.W.2d) (494)
111. Notes of decisions (591)
112. Official citation (491)
113. Opinion (court) (329)

*The numbers in parentheses refer to pages in this book.

Continued

**FIGURE 11.2**

The Vocabulary of
Legal Research:
A Checklist
—*Continued*

| | |
|---|---|
| 114. Opinion of the Attorney General (329) | 148. Superseded annotation (A.L.R.) (561) |
| 115. Ordinance (329) | 149. Supplemented Annotation (A.L.R.) (561) |
| 116. Pacific 2d (P.2d) (494) | 150. Supreme Court Reporter (S. Ct.) (491) |
| 117. Pacific Digest (499) | 151. Syllabus (355) (567) |
| 118. Parallel Cite (526) | 152. Table of Authorities (628) |
| 119. Parallel Table of Authorities and Rules (in C.F.R.) (596) | 153. Table of Courts and Circuits (A.L.R.) (560) |
| 120. Per Curiam (355) | 154. Table of Jurisdictions Represented (A.L.R.) (560) |
| 121. Permanent A.L.R. Digest (559) | 155. Table of Laws, Rules, and Regulations (A.L.R.) (559) |
| 122. Pocket part (508) | 156. Total Client-Service Library (514) |
| 123. Popular Name Table (595) | 157. Treatise (515) |
| 124. Public Law (PL) (329) | 158. Treaty (329) |
| 125. Record (508) | 159. A Uniform System of Citation (490) |
| 126. Remand (449) | 160. Unofficial citation (491) |
| 127. Regional digest (499) | 161. U.S. Code (U.S.C.) (514) |
| 128. Reporter (491) | 162. U.S. Code Annotated (U.S.C.A.) (514) |
| 129. Respondent (448) | 163. U.S. Code Service (U.S.C.S.) (514) |
| 130. Restatements (508) | 164. U.S. Code Congressional and Administrative News (USCCAN) (515) |
| 131. Rules of court (329) | 165. U.S. Court of Appeals (332) |
| 132. Scope Note (556) | 166. U.S. District Court (332) |
| 133. Series (509) | 167. U.S. Law Week (U.S.L.W.) (516) |
| 134. Session Law (571) | 168. U.S. Reports (U.S.) (491) |
| 135. Shepardize (510) | 169. U.S. Statutes at Large (516) |
| 136. Slip law (510) | 170. U.S. Supreme Court Digest (L. Ed.) (500) |
| 137. Slip opinion (513) | 171. U.S. Supreme Court Digest (West) (500) |
| 138. South Eastern Digest (499) | 172. VERALEX (586) |
| 139. South Eastern 2d (S.E.2d) (494) | 173. WESTLAW (585) |
| 140. Southern 2d (So.2d) (494) | 174. WILSONLINE (587) |
| 141. South Western 2d (S.W.2d) (494) | 175. Words and Phrases (504) |
| 142. Squib (497) | |
| 143. Star paging (491) | |
| 144. Statute, private (329) | |
| 145. Statute, public (329) | |
| 146. Statutes at Large (513) | |
| 147. Statutory code (513) | |

- Law library of the legislature or city council
- Law library of the city solicitor or corporation counsel
- Law library of a private law firm
- Law library of the district attorney or local prosecutor
- Law library of the public defender
- Law library of a federal, state, or local administrative agency (particularly in the general counsel's office of the agency)

　　You may need some ingenuity to locate these libraries and to gain access to them. Try more than one avenue of entry. Do not become discouraged when the first person you contact tells you that the library is for members or private use only. Some students adopt the strategy of walking into a library—particularly a library supported by public funds—and acting as if they belong. Rather than asking for permission, they wait for someone to stop them or to question their right to be there. Other students take the wiser course of seeking permission in advance. Yet, even here, some creativity is needed in the way that you ask for permission. The bold question, "Can I use your library?" may be less effective than an approach such as, "Would it be possible for me to use a few of your law books for a short period of time for some important research that I must do?"

There is one other law library that you need to consider: your own. It is not too soon for you to start collecting your own law books, beginning with your course books on law. But never buy a practice book or manual without checking with at least two attorneys or paralegals on the *practical* value of the book. Ask them how often they consult the book. It is not necessarily wise to purchase a book simply because it treats an area of the law you need to know something about. Also, be prepared for sticker shock when you find out what many of these books cost.

Once you gain access to a law library, you may face another problem. There are library employees who resent spending a great deal of time answering the questions of students. At a recent conference of the American Association of Law Libraries, an entire session was devoted to the theme of student paralegal requests for assistance which "can take a tremendous amount of the law librarian's time and energy." Even if an employee at the desk is willing to give you all the time you need, the supervisor of that employee may be opposed to the attention you are getting. Use your common sense in such situations. Keep your requests to a minimum, particularly if there are other students seeking the same kind of help. Before you ask a question, reread the textbook. Many questions can be answered on your own.

## ◼ Section G. A Glossary of Law and Law Books: Introduction

There are ten major categories of law. The purpose of legal research is to find these laws, to check their current validity, and to apply them to the facts of the research problem. Step one is to know the definitions of the categories.

Categories of Law

| | |
|---|---|
| Opinions | Ordinances |
| Statutes | Rules of court |
| Constitutions | Executive orders |
| Administrative regulations | Treaties |
| Administrative decisions | Opinion of attorney general |
| Charters | |

These categories of law (plus opinions of the attorney general) were defined in Chapter 6. See page 329. You should review these definitions now.

A word of caution on the vocabulary of law and legal research: The same word or phrase can often have a different meaning depending on the context in which it is used. *Supreme Court,* for example, refers to the *highest* court in our federal judicial system as well as to the *trial* court in New York State; and the word *opinion* can refer to the judicial decisions of courts and to the administrative decisions of agencies. Although standard definitions are generally used, you should be prepared to find variations.

We now begin examining the sets of books in the library that are relevant to these categories of laws. For each category, four types of books should be kept in mind:

- Sets of books that contain the full text of a certain kind of law
- Sets of books that can be used to locate that kind of law
- Sets of books that can be used to help explain that kind of law
- Sets of books that can be used to help determine the current validity of that kind of law

Some sets of books cover more than one category of law and serve more than one of these four functions. The chart in Figure 11.3 presents a catalog of research materials according to their functions.

The following is a glossary of some of the major legal research books and terms, including many used in Figure 11.3.

### Act; Acts and Resolves

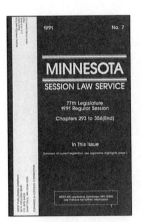

Example of a pamphlet containing session laws

An *act* is the official document that contains the statute passed by the legislature. *Acts and Resolves* is the set of books that contain all the acts of the legislature. They are also sometimes called Session Laws, Statutes, Statutes at Large, Laws, etc. A major characteristic of all of these books is that the statutes in them are printed chronologically as they are passed. They are not classified or organized by subject matter. (See *Code.*)

### Administrative Code

An *administrative code* is a collection of the regulations of one or more agency. The regulations in a code are organized by subject matter. Generally, the regulations of state and local administrative agencies are poorly organized and difficult to obtain. Not so for the federal agencies.

### Advance Sheet

An *advance sheet* is a pamphlet printed before (in advance of) a bound volume, or a thicker pamphlet, that will consolidate the material in several of the earlier advance sheets. When the bound volume or thicker pamphlet comes out, the advance sheet is thrown away. There are two kinds of advance sheets in the law library: an advance sheet for reporters and one for Shepard's.

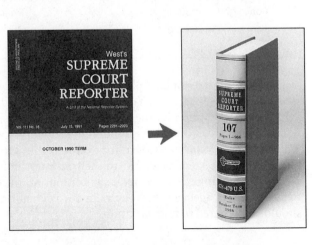

Advance sheet for a reporter (here the *Supreme Court Reporter*). The advance sheet contains the full text of court opinions that will later be printed in a bound *Supreme Court Reporter* volume.

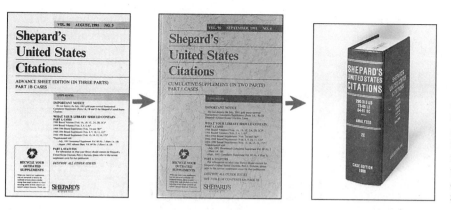

Advance sheet for Shepard's (here *United States Citations* covering cases of the U.S. Supreme Court). The advance sheet contains the "shepardizing" data that will later be printed in thicker pamphlets and eventually in a bound Shepard's volume.

## A.L.R., A.L.R.2d, A.L.R.3d, A.L.R.4th, A.L.R. Fed.

- A.L.R.: *American Law Reports,* First Series
- A.L.R.2d: *American Law Reports,* Second Series
- A.L.R.3d: *American Law Reports,* Third Series
- A.L.R.4th: *American Law Reports,* Fourth Series
- A.L.R. Fed.: *American Law Reports,* Federal Series

These sets of books contain the complete text of *selected* court opinions followed by extensive commentary or research papers on issues within the opinions selected. These research papers are called annotations. The sets of books are therefore called annotated reports. They are published by Lawyers Co-operative Publishing Company (Lawyers Co-op.). As we shall see later, annotations are excellent case finders. Recently, all of the annotations (except for those in A.L.R. First Series) were placed "online" so that they can now be found and read on a computer screen. The two computer systems that provide this service are LEXIS and VERALEX. (Although the abbreviation A.L.R. refers primarily to the First Series, it sometimes refers to all of the sets collectively.)

**American Law Reports, Fourth Series**

### American Digest System

A multivolume set of digests. *See* Digests (p. 497, p. 553).

### American Jurisprudence 2d (Am. Jur. 2d)

Am. Jur. 2d is a national legal encyclopedia (published by Lawyers Co-op.) that summarizes almost every area of the law. It is particularly useful (a) as background reading before beginning legal research on a topic, and (b) as a case finder because of the extensive footnotes. (Am. Jur. 2d is the second edition of Am. Jur. First.) The main competitor of Am. Jur. 2d is *Corpus Juris Secundum.*

### Annotation

To *annotate* means to provide notes or commentary. An annotated bibliography, for example, is a list of references (citations) plus brief summaries or comments on each entry in the list. (See p. 608.) An annotated reporter is a volume containing the full text of court opinions plus notes or commentary on the opinions in it. The word *annotation* mainly refers to the notes and commentary that follow the opinions found in A.L.R., A.L.R.2d, A.L.R.3d, A.L.R.4th,

**FIGURE 11.3**

A Catalog of Research Materials

| Kind of Law | Materials That Contain the Full Text of This Kind of Law | Materials That Can Be Used to Locate This Kind of Law | Materials That Can Be Used to Help Explain This Kind of Law | Materials That Can Be Used to Help Determine the Current Validity of This Kind of Law |
|---|---|---|---|---|
| (a) Opinions | Reports<br>Reporters<br>A.L.R., A.L.R.2d,<br>A.L.R.3d,<br>A.L.R.4th,<br>A.L.R. Fed.<br>Legal newspapers<br>Loose-leaf services<br>Slip opinion<br>Advance sheets<br>WESTLAW<br>LEXIS | Digests<br>Annotations in<br>A.L.R., A.L.R.2d,<br>A.L.R.3d,<br>A.L.R.4th,<br>A.L.R. Fed.<br>Shepard's<br>Legal periodicals<br>Legal encyclopedias<br>Legal treatises<br>Loose-leaf services<br>Words and Phrases | Legal periodicals<br>Legal encyclopedias<br>Legal treatises<br>Annotations in<br>A.L.R., A.L.R.2d,<br>A.L.R.3d,<br>A.L.R.4th,<br>A.L.R. Fed.<br>Loose-leaf services | Shepard's<br>Insta-Cite<br>Auto-Cite |
| (b) Statutes | Statutory Code<br>Statutes at Large<br>Session Laws<br>Laws<br>Compilations<br>Consolidated Laws<br>Slip Laws<br>Acts & Resolves<br>WESTLAW<br>LEXIS | Index volumes of<br>statutory code<br>Loose-leaf services<br>Footnote references<br>in legal<br>encyclopedias,<br>legal periodicals,<br>etc. | Legal periodicals<br>Legal encyclopedias<br>Legal treatises<br>Annotations in<br>A.L.R., A.L.R.2d,<br>A.L.R.3d,<br>A.L.R.4th,<br>A.L.R. Fed.<br>Loose-leaf services | Shepard's |
| (c) Constitutions | Statutory Code<br>Separate volumes<br>containing the<br>constitution<br>WESTLAW<br>LEXIS | Index volumes of<br>statutory code<br>Loose-leaf services<br>Footnote references<br>in legal<br>encyclopedias,<br>legal periodicals,<br>etc. | Legal periodicals<br>Legal encyclopedias<br>Legal treatises<br>Annotations in<br>A.L.R., A.L.R.2d,<br>A.L.R.3d,<br>A.L.R.4th,<br>A.L.R. Fed.<br>Loose-leaf services | Shepard's |
| (d) Administrative Regulations | Administrative Codes<br>Separate volumes<br>containing the<br>regulations of<br>certain agencies<br>Loose-leaf services<br>WESTLAW<br>LEXIS | Index volumes of the<br>administrative<br>code<br>Loose-leaf services<br>Footnote references<br>in legal<br>encyclopedias,<br>legal periodicals,<br>etc. | Legal periodicals<br>Legal treatises<br>Annotations in<br>A.L.R., A.L.R.2d,<br>A.L.R.3d,<br>A.L.R.4th,<br>A.L.R. Fed.<br>Loose-leaf services | Shepard's (for some<br>agencies only)<br>List of Sections<br>Affected |
| (e) Administrative Decisions | Separate volumes of<br>decisions of some<br>agencies<br>Loose-leaf services<br>WESTLAW<br>LEXIS | Loose-leaf services<br>Index or digest<br>volumes to the<br>decisions<br>Footnote references<br>in other materials | Legal periodicals<br>Legal treatises<br>Annotations in<br>A.L.R., A.L.R.2d,<br>A.L.R.3d,<br>A.L.R.4th,<br>A.L.R. Fed.<br>Loose-leaf services | Shepard's (for some<br>agencies only) |

Continued

**FIGURE 11.3**

A Catalog of Research Materials —*Continued*

| Kind of Law | Materials That Contain the Full Text of This Kind of Law | Materials That Can Be Used to Locate This Kind of Law | Materials That Can Be Used to Help Explain This Kind of Law | Materials That Can Be Used to Help Determine the Current Validity of This Kind of Law |
|---|---|---|---|---|
| (f) Charters | Separate volumes containing the charter<br>Municipal Code<br>State session laws<br>Official journal<br>Legal newspaper | Index volumes to the charter or municipal code<br>Footnote references in other materials | Legal periodicals<br>Legal treatises<br>Annotations in A.L.R., A.L.R.2d, A.L.R.3d, A.L.R.4th, A.L.R. Fed. | Shepard's |
| (g) Ordinances | Municipal Code<br>Official journal<br>Legal newspaper | Index volumes of municipal code<br>Footnote references in other materials | Legal periodicals<br>Legal treatises<br>Annotations in A.L.R., A.L.R.2d, A.L.R.3d, A.L.R.4th, A.L.R. Fed. | Shepard's |
| (h) Rules of Court | Separate rules volumes<br>Statutory code<br>Practice manuals | Index to separate rules volumes<br>Index to statutory code<br>Index to practice manuals<br>Footnote references in other materials | Practice manuals<br>Legal treatises<br>Annotations in A.L.R., A.L.R.2d, A.L.R.3d, A.L.R.4th, A.L.R. Fed.<br>Legal encyclopedias<br>Loose-leaf services | Shepard's |
| (i) Executive Orders | Federal Register<br>Code of Federal Regulations<br>U.S. Code Congressional and Administrative News<br>U.S.C./U.S.C.A./U.S.C.S.<br>WESTLAW<br>LEXIS | Index volumes to the sets of books listed in the second column<br>Footnote references in other materials | Legal periodicals<br>Legal treatises<br>Annotations in A.L.R., A.L.R.2d, A.L.R.3d, A.L.R.4th, A.L.R. Fed. | Shepard's Code of Federal Regulations Citations |
| (j) Treaties | Statutes at Large (up to 1949)<br>United States Treaties and Other International Agreements<br>Department of State Bulletin<br>International Legal Materials<br>United Nations Treaty Series | Index within the volumes listed in second column<br>World Treaty Index<br>Current Treaty Index<br>Footnote references in other materials | Legal periodicals<br>Legal treatises<br>Annotations in A.L.R., A.L.R.2d, A.L.R.3d, A.L.R.4th, A.L.R. Fed. | Shepard's<br>U.S. Code Service (Notes to Uncodified Laws and Treaties) |
| (k) Opinions of the Attorney General | Separate volumes containing these opinions<br>WESTLAW<br>LEXIS | Digests<br>Index in separate volumes of the opinions<br>Footnote references in other materials | | |

and A.L.R. Fed. You are being directed to these sets of books when someone asks you to "find out if there are any annotations on this issue." The phrase *annotated code* or *annotated statutes* is also sometimes used (e.g., United States Code Annotated). Annotated codes or statutes are sets of statutes that contain the full text of the statutes organized by subject matter, plus research references such as summaries of opinions interpreting the statutes. The abbreviation for annotated is "Ann." (e.g., Del. Code Ann. for Delaware Code Annotated) or "A" (e.g., U.S.C.A. for United States Code Annotated).

### Atlantic Digest

A digest that summarizes cases in the *Atlantic Reporter. See* Digests (page 497).

### Atlantic Reporter 2d (A.2d)

A regional reporter. *See* Cases (page 493).

### Ballentine's Law Dictionary

*See* Legal Dictionary (page 504).

### Bill

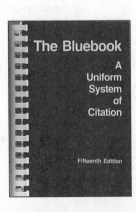

A *bill* is a proposed statute (one that has not yet been enacted into law). A bill is printed in a small booklet or pamphlet called a slip law. (Federal bills are also printed in the *Congressional Record*.)

### Black's Law Dictionary

*See* Legal dictionary (page 504).

### Blue Book

The phrase *blue book* will usually refer to one of the three following books or sets of books:

- *Bluebook: A Uniform System of Citation*
- *National Reporter Blue Book*
- *A.L.R. Blue Book of Supplemental Decisions*

**Bluebook: A Uniform System of Citation.** A small blue pamphlet published by the law reviews of several law schools. The pamphlet covers the "rules" of citation form. It is considered by many to be the bible of citation form.

**National Reporter Blue Book.** A set of books published by West Publishing Company that will enable you to find a parallel cite to a court opinion. The *National Reporter Blue Book* covers every state. Some states have a *Blue and White Book*, which provides parallel cites for one state only.

*The A.L.R. Blue Book of Supplemental Decisions* will enable you to update the annotations found in *A.L.R. First Series.*

## Brief, Appellate

An *appellate brief* is a written document prepared by a party for submission to an appellate court in which arguments are presented on the correctness or incorrectness of what a trial court or lower court of appeals did or failed to do.

*Amicus curiae* means friend of the court. An *amicus curiae brief* is also an appellate brief, but it is prepared and submitted by a nonparty. A court must give permission for the nonparty to submit such a brief.

It is often possible to locate appellate briefs written on recent cases. The briefs are found in the clerk's office of the court where they were submitted, in large law school libraries, in court libraries, and in state law libraries. They can provide excellent research leads for cases with similar issues.

Front cover of an appellate brief submitted to the U.S. Supreme Court

## Bulletin

A bulletin is a publication issued on an ongoing or periodic basis (such as *Internal Revenue Bulletin*).

## California Reporter (Cal. Rptr.)

A court reporter containing selected California cases. *See* Cases (page 493).

## Cases

A *case* is a dispute that has been litigated in court or that is now in litigation. The word is sometimes used interchangeably with the word *opinion,* although the latter word is more often used to mean the court's written explanation for reaching a particular result. The full text of cases is found in volumes called reports or reporters. An *official reporter* is published under the authority of the government and is often printed by the government itself. An *unofficial reporter* is printed by a private or commercial publishing company (such as West) without special authority from the government. We will now examine the reporters containing opinions of the federal courts. Then we look at the reporters for state courts.

*Federal Court Opinions.*    The opinions of the United States Supreme Court are printed in an official report, *United States Reports* (abbreviated "U.S."), and in several unofficial reporters: the *Supreme Court Reporter* published by West (abbreviated "S. Ct.") and *United States Supreme Court Reports,* Lawyers' Edition, published by Lawyers Co-op. (abbreviated "L. Ed.").

When an opinion is printed in the *United States Reports,* it will also be printed word-for-word in S. Ct. and in L. Ed., the unofficial reporters—but not necessarily on the same page numbers. Suppose that you are reading an opinion in an unofficial reporter and you want to quote from it. The standard practice is to give the reference or citation to the quote as it appears in the *official* reporter. Suppose, however, that the latter is simply not available in your library, but one of the unofficial reporters is. How do you quote a page number in an official reporter when all you have available is an unofficial reporter? You use a technique called "star-paging." While you are reading a page in an unofficial reporter, you will find a notation of some kind provided by the printer (an asterisk, a star, or a special indentation) plus a page number, usually in black bold

The three major reporters containing opinions of the United States Supreme Court

print. The latter is a reference to a page number of the same case in the official reporter. *Star paging* therefore enables you to determine on what pages the same court language can be found in official and unofficial reporters.

Two loose-leaf services (page 506) also print the text of all U.S. Supreme Court opinions:

- *United States Law Week* (U.S.L.W.) published by Bureau of National Affairs (BNA).

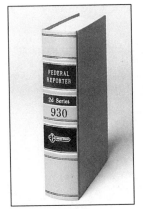

**Federal Reporter, Second Series (F.2d).** Currently contains the full text of the opinions written by the United States Courts of Appeals.

- *United States Supreme Court Bulletin* published by Commerce Clearing House. S. Ct. Bull. (CCH).

. . . . . . . . . . . . . . . .

We turn now to reporters for the *lower* federal courts. Two major reporters contain the full text of opinions from lower federal courts:

- Federal Reporter (abbreviated "F.")
  Federal Reporter, Second Series (abbreviated "F.2d")
- Federal Supplement (abbreviated "F. Supp.")

These are all unofficial reporters published by West. They do *not* print every opinion written by the courts that they cover. The courts decide which opinions are sufficiently important to submit to West for publication.

In addition to F., F.2d, and F. Supp., West publishes several specialty or topical reporters that also cover federal courts. For example:

*Federal Rules Decisions* (F.R.D.)
- Contains opinions of the U.S. District Courts on the Federal Rules of Civil and Criminal Procedure, and also
- Contains articles, speeches, and conference reports on procedural issues

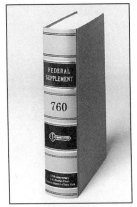

**Federal Supplement (F. Supp.)** Currently contains the full text of the opinions written by the United States District Courts and the United States Court of International Trade.

*Military Justice Reporter* (M.J.)
- Contains opinions of the United States Court of Military Appeals and the Courts of Military Review for the army, navy-marines, air force, and coast guard

*Bankruptcy Reporter* (B.R.)
- Contains opinions of the United States Bankruptcy Courts and selected bankruptcy opinions of other federal courts

*Education Law Reporter*

*Social Security Reporting Service*

*United States Claims Court Reporter*

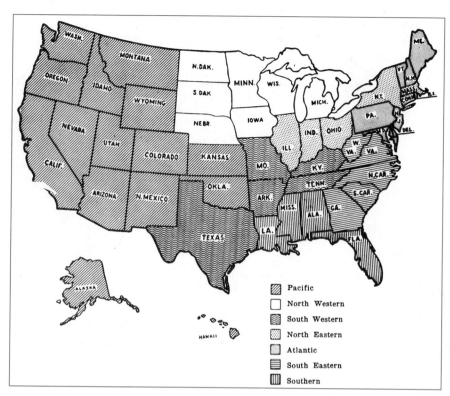

**FIGURE 11.4**
National Reporter
System Map

Legend:
- Pacific
- North Western
- South Western
- North Eastern
- Atlantic
- South Eastern
- Southern

Example of an official state reports volume

*State Court Opinions.*    At one time, all states had official reports containing the opinions of their highest state courts. A large number of states, however, have discontinued their official reports. For such states, the unofficial reporters are the main or only source where you can find the opinions of their state courts.

The major publisher of unofficial state reports is West Publishing Company through its *National Reporter System.* There are seven *regional reporters* in the System. For a photo of each reporter, see page 494.

The seven regional reporters and the states they cover can be seen on the map in Figure 11.4.

If a law office subscribes to a regional reporter covering its own state, the office is also receiving opinions of other states in the same region. These other opinions may be of little practical value to the office. West therefore publishes special state editions for many of the states. These special edition state reporters contain only the opinions of an individual state that are also printed in the regional reporter. For example, you saw that the opinions of the highest court in Kansas are printed in the *Pacific Reporter.* A Kansas attorney who does not want to subscribe to the *Pacific Reporter* can subscribe to the special edition Kansas reporter, called *Kansas Cases.*

Finally, West publishes three separate reporters for New York, California, and Illinois:

- New York Supplement (N.Y.S.)
- California Reporter (Cal. Rptr.)
- Illinois Decisions (Ill. Dec.)

Each contains the opinions of the highest court in the state as well as selected opinions of its lower courts.

A volume of **Kansas Cases** (a special edition state reporter) containing all the Kansas opinions printed in *Pacific Reporter, 2d*

## The Seven Regional Reporters in the National Reporter System

**Atlantic Reporter (A.), Atlantic Reporter, Second Series (A.2d).** The opinions of the highest state court and some intermediate appellate courts in the following states: Conn., Del., D.C., Me., Md., N.H., N.J., Pa., R.I., Vt.

**North Eastern Reporter (N.E.), North Eastern Reporter, Second Series (N.E.2d).** The opinions of the highest state court and some intermediate appellate courts in the following states: Ill., Ind., Mass., N.Y., Ohio.

**North Western Reporter (N.W.), North Western Reporter, Second Series (N.W.2d).** The opinions of the highest state court and some intermediate appellate courts in the following states: Iowa, Mich., Minn., Neb., N.D., S.D., Wis.

**Pacific Reporter (P.), Pacific Reporter, Second Series (P.2d).** The opinions of the highest state court and some intermediate appellate courts in the following states: Alaska, Ariz., Cal., Colo., Haw., Idaho, Kan., Mont., Nev., N.M., Okla., Or., Utah, Wash., Wyo.

  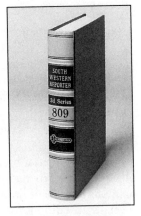

**South Eastern Reporter (S.E.), South Eastern Reporter, Second Series (S.E.2d).** The opinions of the highest state court and some intermediate appellate courts in the following states: Ga., N.C., S.C., Va., W. Va.

**Southern Reporter (So.), Southern Reporter, Second Series (So. 2d).** The opinions of the highest state court and some intermediate appellate courts in the following states: Ala., Fla., La., Miss.

**South Western Reporter (S.W.), South Western Reporter, Second Series (S.W.2d).** The opinions of the highest state courts and some intermediate appellate courts in the following states: Ark., Ky., Mo., Tenn., Tex.

*Major Characteristics of West Reporters*

- **The reporters contain the full text of court opinions.**
- The opinions are arranged in roughly chronological order according to the date of decision.

- The reporters have advance sheets that come out before the bound volumes.
- There is a Table of Cases at the beginning of each reporter volume.
- There is a Table of Statutes Construed in many reporters, listing the statutes interpreted within an individual reporter volume.
- There is *no* traditional subject-matter index in any reporter volume (the main index to the opinions in reporters is the separate set of books called digests).
- At the beginning of each opinion there are small-paragraph summaries of the opinion. As we will see later, these are headnotes which are also printed in digests, and at the beginning of the advance sheet containing the opinion, and at the end of the reporter volume containing the opinion.

## Casebook

A *casebook* is a law school textbook. It consists mainly of a collection of edited court opinions and other materials relating to a particular area of the law, e.g., Lockhart, Kamisar, Choper, and Shiffrin, *Constitutional Law: Cases, Comments, Questions.*

## CD ROM

*CD ROM* ("computer disc read-only memory") is an optical information-storage system that operates much like a compact disc sold in music stores. Through your computer system, you gain access to the vast amount of information stored on the disc. Up to 60 large volumes of law books can be stored on one disc! Users cannot add any information to the disc; they can only read the information on it through their computer screen or monitor. (Hence the phrase *read only*.) Unlike more traditional computer-assisted research systems, you do not need a modem (see Chapter 13) to use CD ROM. Everything you need is on the disc.

## Century Digest

A digest that is part of the American Digest System. *See* Digests (p. 498).

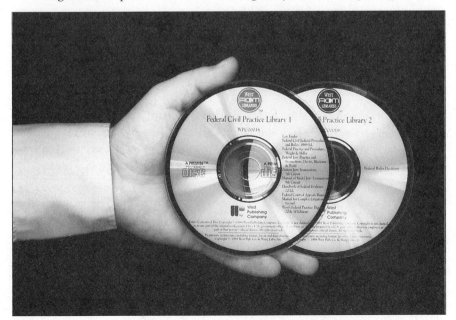

A CD ROM product of West Publishing Co.

## Citation

A *citation* (also called a cite) is a reference to any written material, such as a case, statute, law review article, treatise, treaty, annotation or report. It is the "address" where that material can be found in the library. The reference tells you how to locate the item by volume number, name of book, edition, page number, or section number. A *parallel cite* is an additional reference to the *same* material. If there are two parallel cites to a case, for example, you will be able to find the same case—word for word—in two different reporters. The major book on citation form is A Uniform System of Citation.

## Citator

A *citator* is a book containing lists of citations that serve two functions: first and foremost, to help you assess the current validity of a case, statute, or other law; and secondarily, to provide you with leads to additional laws. Citators often provide other features as well, e.g., they will give you a parallel citation. The major citator in legal research is Shepard's. The columns of Shepard's contain nothing but citations that are relevant to whatever you are "shepardizing" (pp. 509, 563). There are also citators on computer systems, such as Insta-Cite and Auto-Cite.

## Code

A code is a collection of laws or rules classified by subject matter. To *codify* something means to rearrange it by subject matter. The arrangement of *un*codified material is chronological by date of enactment; the arrangement of *codified* material is by subject matter or topic. When statutes are first passed by the legislature, they are placed in uncodified books called Session Laws, Acts and Resolves, Statutes at Large, etc. Most of these statutes are later codified into statutory codes. (See Statutory Code.) Administrative regulations are also often codified. (See Administrative Code.)

## Code of Federal Regulations (C.F.R.)

The C.F.R. is a set of pamphlets containing many of the regulations of federal agencies. *See* Administrative Code.

Code of Federal
Regulations

## Congressional Record

The *Congressional Record* is an official collection of the day-to-day happenings of Congress. It is one source of legislative history (p. 596) for federal statutes. It also contains many relatively trivial items that are relevant only to the districts of individual legislators.

## Corpus Juris Secondum (C.J.S.)

*Corpus Juris Secondum* (C.J.S.) is a national legal encyclopedia (published by West) that summarizes almost every area of the law. (C.J.S. is the second edition of *Corpus Juris*.) It is very useful (a) as background reading before beginning legal research on a topic and (b) as a case finder because of the extensive footnotes. Its main competitor is *American Jurisprudence 2d*.

Corpus Juris Secundum

## Cumulative

*Cumulative* means that which repeats earlier material and consolidates it with new material. A cumulative supplement, for example, is a pamphlet or volume that repeats, updates, and consolidates all earlier pamphlets or volumes. Because of the repetition, the earlier pamphlets or volumes can be thrown away. Similarly, pocket parts (containing supplemental material at the end of a book) are often cumulative. When the most recent pocket part comes out, the old one can be thrown away.

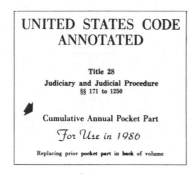

## Decennial Digest

A digest that is part of the American Digest System. *See* Digests.

## Digests

Our goals in this section are to define *digest,* to identify the major digests, and to explain the relationship between digests and reporters. Later in the chapter, we will cover the techniques of using digests in research (page 553).

Digests are volumes containing small-paragraph summaries of court opinions organized by subject matter. (These summaries are sometimes called *abstracts* or *squibs.*) The primary purpose of digests is to serve as case finders. The major publisher of digests is West. Its *key topic and number system* is the organizational principle used to classify the millions of small-paragraph summaries in the digests. Every topic and subtopic in the law is assigned a key topic and number by West. For example:

> ⌐290. Strikes and lockouts.
>
> ⌐984. Sentence on conviction on dif-
>        ferent counts.
>
> ⌐406.3(9). Clearly erroneous findings
>          of court or jury.

Once you find a key topic (and subtopic)—plus its key number—relevant to your research problem, you are given paragraph summaries of cases under that topic and number. For example, the following excerpt from a digest contains cases that are digested under the topic of "Obscenity" and the subtopics of "Nature and elements of offenses in general" and "Statutory provisions":

## OBSCENITY

**☞1. Nature and elements of offenses in general.**

**Ill.App. 1973.**   Obscenity vel non is not constitutionally protected.   People v. Rota, 292 N.E.2d 738.

**Iowa 1973.**   Knowledge of obscene material is an essential element in obscenity prosecutions.   I.C.A. § 725.5.   State v. Lavin, 204 N.W.2d 844.

**☞2. Statutory provisions.**

**D.C.Md. 1972.**   Although Maryland motion picture censorship statute did not provide disseminator of motion picture film with an adversary hearing before board of censors on issue of obscenity, disseminator was not constitutionally prejudiced in this regard because the statute requires an adversary judicial determination of obscenity with circuit court for Baltimore City exercising de novo review of the board's finding of obscenity, and with burden of proving that the film is unprotected expression resting on the board.   Code Md. 1957, art. 66A, §§ 6(c, d), 19(a); 28 U.S. C.A. § 100.   Star v. Preller, 352 F.Supp. 530.

Beneath each summary paragraph is a citation to the case being summarized. For example, see the citation for *People v. Rota* in the first paragraph listed.

There are a few digests that are *not* published by West. For example, the United States Supreme Court Digest, L. Ed. is published by Lawyers Co-op. Such digests also contain small-paragraph summaries of court opinions, but since they are not published by West, they are not organized by the key topic system. They use their own organizational principle. (See photo at top of page 500.)

We now turn to an overview of the West digests. There are four main kinds:

- A national digest covering most state and federal courts
- Federal digests covering only federal courts
- Regional digests covering the courts found in the regional reporters
- Digests of individual courts or states

*National Digest*   There is one national digest: the *American Digest System* published by West. This massive set (containing over 100 volumes) gives you small-paragraph summaries of the court opinions of most appellate state and federal courts and some lower state and federal courts. The American Digest System has three main units: (a) *Century Digest,* (b) *Decennial Digests,* and (c) *General Digests.*

*Federal Digests Covering Only Federal Courts*   There are five large digests that cover the main federal courts: the U.S. Supreme Court, the U.S. Courts of Appeal, and the U.S. District Courts:

- *Federal Digest*
- *Modern Federal Practice Digest*
- *Federal Practice Digest* 2d
- *Federal Practice Digest* 3d
- *Federal Practice Digest* 4th

(a) Here is a sample volume from the **Century Digest,** covering summaries of opinions written between 1658 and 1896 (part of the American Digest System).

(b) The **Decennial Digests** cover summaries of opinions for ten-year periods starting in 1897. Here is a sample volume from the Ninth Decennial. It is printed in two parts, each covering five years. Part I covers the period from 1976 to 1981. Part II covers 1981–1986. (Prior to the Ninth Decennial, all of the *Decennial Digests* were issued in one part only—covering the entire ten years.)

(c) The **General Digests** cover summaries of opinions since the last Decennial was published. The *General Digest* volumes are kept on the shelf only until they are eventually consolidated (cumulated) into the next *Decennial Digest* unit. At that time, all of the General Digest volumes are thrown away.

**Modern Federal Practice Digest.** Contains small-paragraph summaries of federal cases decided between 1939 and 1961.

**Federal Practice Digest 2d.** Contains small-paragraph summaries of federal cases decided from 1961 to 1975.

**Federal Practice Digest 3d.** Contains small-paragraph summaries of federal cases decided from 1975.

**Federal Practice Digest 4th.** This is the most recent set. Its coverage begins where *Federal Practice Digest 3d* leaves off.

Finally, West publishes a number of special digests that cover specific federal courts or specific topics of federal law:

- West's *Bankruptcy Digest*
- West's *Military Justice Digest*
- *United States Claims Court Digest*

Given the tremendous importance of the U.S. Supreme Court, there are two extensive digests covering only its opinions. These two digests (shown at the top of page 500) are published by competing companies.

*Regional Digests*   A regional digest contains small-paragraph summaries of those court opinions that are printed in its corresponding regional reporter. The opinions in the *Pacific Reporter,* for example, are digested in the *Pacific Digest.* As we shall see in Figure 11.5, only four of the seven regional reporters have corresponding regional digests. Those digests are: *Atlantic Digest, North Western Digest, Pacific Digest,* and *South Eastern Digest.* (Regional digests for the other three regions either do not exist or have been discontinued.)

One of the regional digests

**United States Supreme Court Digest.** Published by West, containing small-paragraph summaries of every opinion of the U.S. Supreme Court (uses the key topic system).

**United States Supreme Court Digest, L. Ed.** Published by Lawyers Co-op., containing small-paragraph summaries of every opinion of the U.S. Supreme Court (does not use key topic system).

*Digests of Individual States*    A state digest contains small-paragraph summaries of the opinions of the state courts within that state, as well as the opinions of the federal courts that are relevant to that state. The following are examples of state digests:

Now let us summarize. In Figure 11.5, there is a list of reporters, the names of the courts whose full opinions are currently printed in those reporters, and the names of the digests that give small-paragraph summaries of those opinions.

### Federal Cases

*Federal Cases* is the name of the reporter that contains very early opinions of the federal courts (up to 1880) before F., F.2d, and F. Supp. came into existence.

### Federal Digest

*See* Digests.

| NAME OF REPORTER | THE COURTS WHOSE OPINIONS ARE CURRENTLY PRINTED IN FULL IN THIS REPORTER | THE DIGESTS THAT CONTAIN SMALL-PARAGRAPH SUMMARIES OF THE OPINIONS IN THIS REPORTER |
|---|---|---|
| United States Reports (U.S.)<br>Supreme Court Reporter (S.Ct.)<br>United States Supreme Court Reports, Lawyers Edition (L.Ed.)<br>United States Law Week (U.S.L.W.)<br>United States Supreme Court Bulletin (CCH) | United States Supreme Court | American Digest System<br>United States Supreme Court Digest (West)<br>United States Supreme Court Digest, L.Ed.<br>Federal Digest<br>Modern Federal Practice Digest<br>Federal Practice Digest, 2d<br>Federal Practice Digest, 3d<br>Federal Practice Digest, 4th<br>Individual state digests (for Supreme Court cases relevant to that state) |
| Federal Reporter, 2d (F.2d) | United States Courts of Appeal | American Digest System<br>Federal Digest<br>Modern Federal Practice Digest<br>Federal Practice Digest, 2d<br>Federal Practice Digest, 3d<br>Federal Practice Digest, 4th<br>Individual state digests (for federal cases relevant to that state) |
| Federal Supplement (F.Supp.) | United States District Courts<br>United States Court of International Trade | American Digest System<br>Federal Digest<br>Modern Federal Practice Digest<br>Federal Practice Digest, 2d<br>Federal Practice Digest, 3d<br>Federal Practice Digest, 4th<br>Individual state digests (for federal cases relevant to that state) |
| Atlantic Reporter 2d (A.2d) | The highest state court and some intermediate appellate courts in Conn., Del., D.C., Me., Md., N.H., N.J., Pa., R.I., Vt. | American Digest System<br>Atlantic Digest<br>Individual state digests for Conn., Del., D.C., Me., Md., N.H., N.J., Pa., R.I., Vt. |
| North Eastern Reporter 2d (N.E.2d) | The highest state court and some intermediate appellate courts in Ill., Ind., Mass., N.Y., Ohio | American Digest System<br>Individual state digests for Ill., Ind., Mass., N.Y., Ohio<br>(There is *no* North Eastern Digest) |
| North Western Reporter 2d (N.W.2d) | The highest state court and some intermediate appellate courts in Iowa, Mich., Minn., Neb., N.D., S.D., Wis. | American Digest System<br>North Western Digest<br>Individual state digests for Iowa, Mich., Minn., Neb., N.D., S.D., Wis. |

**FIGURE 11.5**

Reporters and Digests: A Checklist

Continued

**FIGURE 11.5**
Reporters and
Digests:
A Checklist
—*Continued*

| NAME OF REPORTER | THE COURTS WHOSE OPINIONS ARE CURRENTLY PRINTED IN FULL IN THIS REPORTER | THE DIGESTS THAT CONTAIN SMALL-PARAGRAPH SUMMARIES OF THE OPINIONS IN THIS REPORTER |
| --- | --- | --- |
| Pacific Reporter, 2d (P.2d) | The highest state court and some intermediate appellate courts in Alaska, Ariz., Cal., Colo., Haw., Idaho, Kan., Mont., Nev., N.M., Okla., Or., Utah., Wash., Wyo. | American Digest System Pacific Digest Individual state digests for Alaska, Ariz., Cal., Colo., Haw., Idaho, Kan., Mont., Nev., N.M., Okla., Or., Utah., Wash., Wyo. |
| South Eastern Reporter, 2d (S.E.2d) | The highest state court and some intermediate appellate courts in Ga., N.C., S.C., Va., W. Va. | American Digest System South Eastern Digest Individual state digests for Ga., N.C., S.C., Va., W. Va. |
| Southern Reporter, 2d (So. 2d) | The highest state court and some intermediate appellate courts in Ala., Fla., La., Miss. | American Digest System Individual state digests for Ala., Fla., La., Miss. (There is *no* Southern Digest) |
| South Western Reporter, 2d (S.W.2d) | The highest state court and some intermediate appellate courts in Ark., Ky., Mo., Tenn., Tex. | American Digest System Individual state digests for Ark., Ky., Mo., Tenn., Tex. (There is *no* South Western Digest) |

### *Federal Practice Digest 2d; Federal Practice Digest 3d; Federal Practice Digest 4th*

*See* Digests.

### *Federal Register (Fed. Reg.)*

The *Federal Register* is a daily publication of the federal government that prints proposed regulations of the federal administrative agencies; executive orders and other executive documents; and news from federal agencies, such as announcements calling for applications for federal grants. Many of the proposed regulations that are adopted by the federal agencies are later printed in the *Code of Federal Regulations* (C.F.R.). (See photo at top of page 503.)

### *Federal Reporter*

A reporter containing opinions of the United States Courts of Appeal. *See* Cases.

### *Federal Rules Decisions (F.R.D.)*

A reporter containing opinions of United States District Courts on issues of

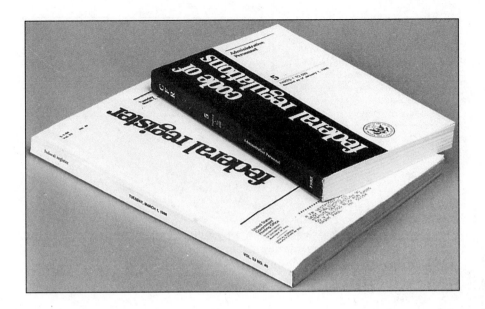

civil and criminal procedure, plus articles and speeches on procedural issues. *See* Cases.

## Federal Supplement

A reporter containing opinions of the United States District Courts. *See* Cases.

## Formbook

A *formbook* is a manual written by private individuals (or by a public official writing in a private capacity) giving practical information on how to practice law in a given area. It contains summaries of the law, checklists, sample forms, etc. Formbooks are how-to-do-it texts. They can be single-volume or multivolume. Other names for a formbook are *practice manual, handbook,* etc.

Example of a formbook

## General Digest

A digest that is part of the American Digest System. *See* Digests.

## Handbook

A practical text on an area of the law. See *formbook*.

## Headnote

A headnote is a summary of a portion of an opinion, printed just before the opinion begins. In West reporters, each headnote is numbered consecutively and is assigned a key topic and number. The headnote is later printed in the digests of West.

Here is the third headnote printed at the beginning of an opinion from a West reporter. It summarizes a portion of the opinion. West also prints this headnote in one or more of its digests. If you went to these digests and looked up Libel and Slander 28, you would find this headnote plus headnotes from other opinions on the same point of law,

---

**3. Libel and Slander** ⊕⊸ **28**

One may not escape liability for defamation by showing that he was merely repeating defamatory language used by another person, and he may not escape liability by falsely attributing to others the ideas to which he gives expression.

---

## Hornbook

A hornbook is a treatise (page 515) that summarizes an area or topic of the law. It may contain commentaries, extensive footnote references, etc. Hornbooks differ somewhat from formbooks in that hornbooks are often less practical than formbooks.

## Interstate Compact

An *interstate compact* is an agreement between two or more states governing a problem of mutual concern, such as the resolution of a boundary dispute. The compact is passed by the legislature of each state and is therefore part of the statutes of the states involved. Also, Congress must give its approval.

Example of a hornbook

## Kardex

*Kardex* is a file in which the library records the volume numbers and dates of incoming publications that are part of subscriptions. If, for example, you are not sure whether certain volumes or supplements on the shelf are the most current ones received by the library, you would ask the library staff to check Kardex. Not all libraries use Kardex. A library might use another system of recording subscription material received by the library.

## Legal Dictionary

A *legal dictionary* contains definitions of words and phrases used in the law. Examples include: *Black's Law Dictionary* (West), *Ballentine's Law Dictionary* (Lawyers Co-op.), and *Statsky's Legal Thesaurus/Dictionary* (West). The major multivolume legal dictionary is *Words and Phrases* from West. The definitions in this set consist of thousands of excerpts from court opinions that have treated the word or phrase. Hence, this set of volumes can also serve as an excellent case finder.

## Legal Encyclopedia

Multivolume legal dictionary

A *legal encyclopedia* is a multivolume set of books that summarizes almost every legal topic (page 582). It is valuable (a) as background reading for a research topic that is new to you, and (b) as a case finder (due to its extensive footnotes). The two competing national encyclopedias are *American Jurisprudence 2d* published by Lawyers Co-op., and *Corpus Juris Secundum* published by West. A number of states have their own encyclopedias covering the law of that state, e.g. *Florida Jurisprudence* and *Michigan Law and Practice.*

## Legal Newspaper

A *legal newspaper* is a local newspaper published (often daily) by a private company that lists court calendars, legal announcements, the full text of some opinions of local courts, new court rules, job announcements, etc. Most large cities have their own legal newspaper. It may be called the daily law journal, the daily law reporter, etc.

## Legal Periodical

A *legal periodical* (often called a *law review* or a *law journal*) is an ongoing publication of scholarly commentary published by law students of specific law schools. In addition, there are some periodicals published by private companies and by bar associations that tend to be more practice-oriented (and more expensive). Periodicals are first published as small pamphlets, and are later bound by most libraries.

As we will see later (page 578), the major general indexes to legal periodical literature are:

- Index to Legal Periodicals (ILP)
- Current Law Index (CLI)
- Legal Resource Index (LRI)

In addition, there are special indexes to legal periodical literature on topics such as tax law.

## Legal Thesaurus

A *legal thesaurus* provides word alternatives for words used in legal writing. The thesaurus may also be helpful in forming queries for computer-assisted legal research (page 655). Two examples: Burton's *Legal Thesaurus* (Macmillan, 1980); and Statsky's *Legal Thesaurus/Dictionary: A Resource for the Writer and Legal Researcher* (West, 1985).

## Legislation

*Legislation* is the process of making statutory law by the legislature. The word legislation also refers to the statutes themselves.

## LEXIS

LEXIS is a legal research computer system. (See pages 585 and 656.)

## Loose-Leaf Service

Most law books come in one of three forms:

- Pamphlet
- Bound volume
- Loose-leaf

A *loose-leaf* text or *service* is a three-ring (or post) binder containing pages that can easily be inserted or taken out. As new material is written covering the subject matter of the loose-leaf text, it is placed in the binder, often replacing the pages that the new material has changed or otherwise supplemented. Since this kind of updating can sometimes occur as often as once a week, loose-leaf services frequently contain the most current material available.

There are few areas of the law that are *not* covered by one or more loose-leaf services. Examples of such services include: *Employment Practices Guide, Standard Federal Tax Reports, United States Law Week, Criminal Law Reporter, Family Law Reporter, Media Law Reporter, Sexual Law Reporter, Environmental Law Reporter, Labor Relations Reporter.*

While some loose-leaf services do little more than print the most current cases in their speciality, most have more varied features:

- The full text plus summaries of court opinions in the area of the specialty
- The full text plus summaries of administrative regulations and decisions in the area of the specialty (some of which may not be available elsewhere)
- Summaries of the major statutory provisions of the specialty
- Suggestions on how to practice in the specialty

Examples of a loose-leaf service

The major publishers of loose-leaf services are Commerce Clearing House (CCH), Bureau of National Affairs (BNA), Prentice-Hall (PH), and Matthew Bender.

## Martindale-Hubbell Law Directory

The *Martindale-Hubbell Law Directory* (see excerpt on page 140) is a multivolume set of books that serves three major functions:

- Gives an alphabetical listing of attorneys and law firms by state and city (for some firms, the listing includes paralegals and other nonattorney personnel)
- Gives short summaries of the law of all fifty states (in its separate Digest volume)
- Gives short summaries of the law of many foreign countries (in its separate Digest volume)

## Microforms

Microforms are images or photographs that have been reduced in size. Among the material stored on microforms are pages from reporters, codes, trea-

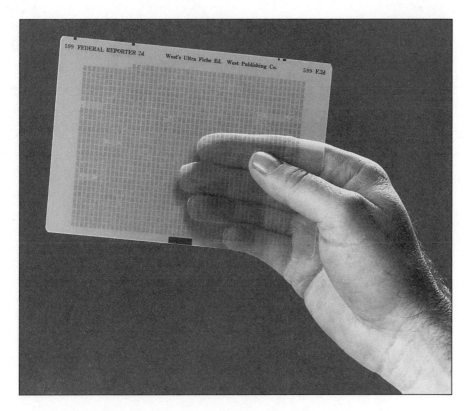

Example of West's ultrafiche, containing a volume of the *Federal Reporter 2d*

tises, periodicals, etc. Vast amounts of material can be stored in this way. An entire volume of a 1,000-page law book can fit on a single plastic card! Special machines (reader-printers and fiche readers) magnify the material so that it can be read. Several kinds of microforms are available. (a) *Microfilms* store the material on film reels or cassettes. (b) *Microfiche* stores the material on single sheets of film. (c) *Ultrafiche* is microfiche with a considerably greater storage capacity.

### New York Supplement (N.Y.S.)

A reporter containing New York cases. *See* Cases.

### North Eastern Reporter 2d (N.E.2d)

A regional reporter. *See* Cases.

### North Western Digest

A digest that summarizes cases in the North Western Reporter. *See* Digests.

### North Western Reporter 2d (N.W.2d)

A regional reporter. *See* Cases.

### Pacific Digest

A digest that summarizes cases in the Pacific Reporter. *See* Digests.

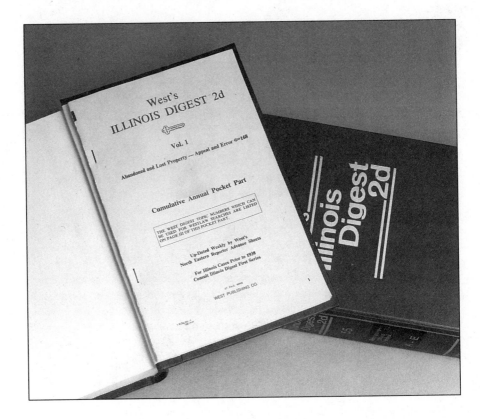

Example of a law book
with a pocket part

### Pacific Reporter 2d (P.2d)

A regional reporter. *See* Cases.

### Pocket Part

A *pocket part* is a small-pamphlet addition placed in a special pocket built into the inside cover of a bound volume. The purpose of the pamphlet is to update the material in the bound volume.

### Record

When referring to a trial, the *record* is the official collection of what happened during the trial. It includes a word-for-word transcript of what was said, the pleadings, all the exhibits, etc.

### Regional Digest

A digest that summarizes cases in a regional reporter. *See* Digest.

### Restatements

Restatements are scholarly *treatises* (see page 515) published by the American Law Institute (ALI) which attempt to formulate (that is, restate) the existing law of a given area. Occasionally the Restatements also state what the ALI thinks the law *ought* to be.

Examples of Restatements:

| | |
|---|---|
| *Restatement of Agency* | *Restatement of Property* |
| *Restatement of Conflicts of Law* | *Restatement of Restitution* |
| *Restatement of Contracts* | *Restatement of Security* |
| *Restatement of Foreign Rela-* | *Restatement of Torts* |
| *tions Law* | *Restatement of Trusts* |
| *Restatement of Judgments* | |

Restatements are not law, but they are extensively relied on and cited by courts.

## Rules of Court

*Rules of Court,* also called *Court Rules,* are the rules of procedure that govern the conduct of litigation before a particular court. They are often found in the statutory code and in separate volumes or pamphlets.

## Series

An *edition* is a *revision* of an earlier version of a book or set of books. The word *series,* on the other hand, refers to a new numbering order for new volumes within the *same* set of books. Reporters, for example, come in series. Federal Reporter, First Series (abbreviated "F.") has 300 volumes. After the last volume was printed, the publisher decided to start a new series of the same set of books—Federal Reporter, Second Series (abbreviated "F.2d"). The first volume of F.2d is volume 1. After a large number of F.2d volumes are printed, we will probably see an F.3d, which will begin again with volume 1. There is no consistent number of volumes that a publisher will print before it decides to start a new series for a set of books.

## Session Law

An uncodified printing of statutes. *See* Act; Acts and Resolves.

## Shepard's

Our goal here is to provide a brief overview of Shepard's and shepardizing by identifying the major sets of Shepard's volumes that exist. Later in the chapter we will learn how to use Shepard's—how to *shepardize.* (See page 563.)

Excerpt from a page in a Shepard's volume

*Shepard's Citations* are citators (page 496). To *shepardize* an item means to use the volumes of Shepard's to collect the research references provided for that item. The references differ depending on what you are shepardizing. If, for example, you are shepardizing a case, you will be given the parallel cite (if one exists) for this case, the history of the case, such as appeals within the same litigation, other cases that have interpreted or mentioned the case you are shepardizing, legal periodical literature on the case, etc. If you are shepardizing a statute, you may be given the session law cite for the statute, amendments, repeals or additions to the statute, court opinions that have interpreted the statute, legal periodical literature on the statute, etc.

What can you shepardize? Here is a partial list:

- Court opinions
- Statutes
- Constitutions
- Some administrative regulations
- Some administrative decisions
- Ordinances
- Charters

- Rules of court
- Some executive orders
- Some treaties
- Patents, trademarks, copyrights
- Restatements
- Some legal periodical literature

As we shall see later, the items in this list constitute the *cited* material—that which you are shepardizing. When you go to the references to these cited materials in the volumes of Shepard's, you will be given a variety of other references on the cited materials, such as cases that have interpreted statutes, annotations on statutes, and cases that have overruled prior cases. These other references are called the *citing* material. (See page 565.)

On pages 511–513, there is an overview of some of these items that can be shepardized with the appropriate sets of Shepard's that you would use to shepardize them.

Shepard's Citations are also available online through WESTLAW and LEXIS.

### Slip Law

A *slip law* is a single act passed by the legislature. It is printed separately, often in a small pamphlet. It is the first official publication of the act. All slip laws are later printed in volumes that may be called Session Laws, Acts, Statutes at Large, etc. Finally, if the slip law is a public law or statute, it is also printed in a *statutory code*.

Example of
a slip law

> **Public Law 87-17**
> **87th Congress, H. R. 4363**
> **April 7, 1961**
>
> **AN ACT**                                                     75 STAT. 41.
>
> To amend Public Law 86–272 relating to State taxation of interstate commerce.
>
> *Be it enacted by the Senate and House of Representatives of the United States of America in Congress assembled,* That section 201 of Public Law 86–272 (73 Stat. 556) is amended to read as follows:    Interstate commerce.
> "Sec. 201. The Committee on the Judiciary of the House of Representatives and the Committee on Finance of the United States Senate, acting separately or jointly, or both, or any duly authorized subcommittees thereof, shall make full and complete studies of all matters pertaining to the taxation of interstate commerce by the States, territories, and possessions of the United States, the District of Columbia, and the Commonwealth of Puerto Rico, or any political or taxing subdivision of the foregoing."     Taxation studies. 15 USC 381 note.
>
> **Approved April 7, 1961.**

Assume that you want to shepardize an opinion of the United States Supreme Court:

*Supreme Court Reporter*

Assume that you want to shepardize opinions found in *Federal Reporter, 2d:*

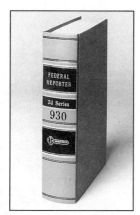

*Federal Reporter, 2d (F.2d)*

Assume that you want to shepardize opinions found in *Federal Supplement:*

*Federal Supplement (F. Supp.)*

Here is the set of Shepard's you use to shepardize an opinion of the United States Supreme Court:

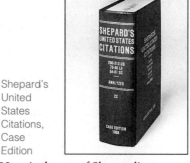

*Shepard's United States Citations, Case Edition*

Here is the set of Shepard's you use to shepardize an F.2d opinion:

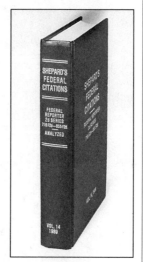

*Shepard's Federal Citations*

Here is the set of Shepard's you use to shepardize an F. Supp. opinion:

*Shepard's Federal Citations*

An Overview of Major Items That Can Be Shepardized

An Overview of
Major Items That
Can Be
Shepardized
—*Continued*

Assume that you want to shepardize a federal statute of Congress: a statute found in U.S.C.A. *(United States Code Annotated)* or in U.S.C.S. *(United States Code Service)* or in U.S.C. *(United States Code):*

Assume that you want to shepardize a regulation of a federal agency found in C.F.R.:

Assume that you want to shepardize opinions found within the following regional reporters:

> *Atlantic Reporter 2d*
>
> *Pacific Reporter 2d*
>
> *South Western Reporter 2d*
>
> *South Eastern Reporter 2d*
>
> *North Eastern Reporter 2d*

At right are the sets of Shepard's that you use to shepardize the opinions in these regional reporters.

Here is the set of Shepard's that you use to shepardize a federal statute:

*Shepard's United States Citations, Statute Edition*

Here is the set of Shepard's that will enable you to shepardize a regulation in C.F.R.:

*Shepard's Code of Federal Regulations Citations*

You want to shepardize the following:

A Rhode Island court opinion

A Rhode Island statute

A Rhode Island constitutional provision

A New Hampshire court opinion

A New Hampshire statute

A New Hampshire constitutional provision

Here are the sets of Shepard's that you would use:

Note: Every state has its own set of Shepard's similar to Shepard's Rhode Island Citations and Shepard's New Hampshire Citations above.

An Overview of Major Items That Can Be Shepardized —*Continued*

### Slip Opinion

When a court first announces a decision, it is usually published in what is called a *slip opinion* or slip decision. It contains a single case in pamphlet form. The slip opinions are later printed in advance sheets for reporters, which in turn become bound reporters.

### South Eastern Digest

A digest that summarizes cases in the South Eastern Reporter. *See* Digests.

### South Eastern Reporter 2d (S.E.2d)

A regional reporter. *See* Cases.

### Southern Reporter 2d (So. 2d)

A regional reporter. *See* Cases.

### South Western Reporter 2d (S.W.2d)

A regional reporter. *See* Cases.

### Statutes at Large

An uncodified printing of statutes. *See* Act; Acts and Resolves. *See also* United States Statutes at Large.

### Statutory Code

A *statutory code* is a collection of the statutes of the legislature organized by subject matter. For example, the statutes on murder are together, the statutes on probate are together, etc. Statutory codes are often annotated, meaning that there are research references provided along with the full text of the statute. The references might include summaries of cases that have interpreted the statute and information on the legislative history of the statute such as the dates of earlier amendments.

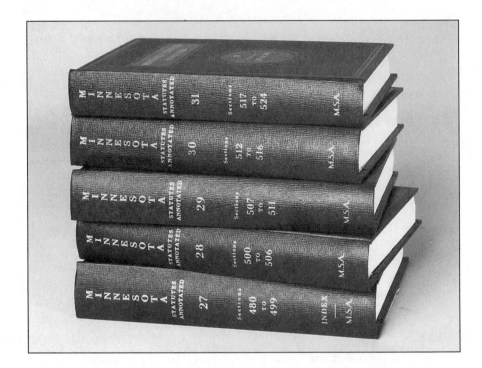

Example of a state
statutory code

The three major federal
statutory codes

**U.S.C.A.**—United States Code Annotated (published by West)
**U.S.C.S.**—United State Code Service (published by Lawyers Co-op.)
**U.S.C.**—United States Code (published by the U.S. Government Printing Office)

### *Supreme Court Reporter (S. Ct.)*

An unofficial reporter that prints every opinion of the United States Supreme Court. *See* Cases.

### *Total Client-Service Library*

The *Total Client-Service Library* is the system by which Lawyers Co-op refers you to many of the books and materials it publishes. If, for example, you are reading an annotation in A.L.R., A.L.R.2d, A.L.R.3d, A.L.R.4th, or A.L.R. Fed, you may be referred to other Lawyers Co-op. books on the same subject matter, such as *American Jurisprudence 2d,* U.S.C.S. (United States Code Service), *Am Jur Pleading and Practice Forms,* etc. Note that the following example also refers you to the Auto-Cite computer service of Lawyers Co-op., which we will examine later.

---

**Total Client-Service Library® References**

50 Am Jur 2d, Landlord and Tenant §§ 1168–1171

Annotations: See the related matters listed in the annotation, infra.

16 Am Jur Pl & Pr Forms (Rev). Landlord and Tenant §§ 161:724–161:727

US L Ed Digest, Landlord and Tenant § 10

ALR Digests, Landlord and Tenant §§ 52.57

L Ed Index to Annos, Buildings; Landlord and Tenant; Real Property

ALR Quick Index, Adequacy Sufficiency; Buildings; Extension or Renewal; Landlord and Tenant; Leases; Perpetuities and Restraints on Alienation; Real Property

Federal Quick Index, Buildings; Landlord and Tenant; Leases; Real Property; Renewal

Auto-Cite®: Any case citation herein can be checked for form, parallel references, later history, and annotation references through the Auto-Cite computer research system

---

### Treatise, Legal

A *treatise* (not to be confused with treaty) is any book written by a private individual (or by a public official writing as a private citizen) that provides an overview, summary, or commentary on a topic of law. The treatise will usually attempt to give an extensive treatment of that topic. Hornbooks and formbooks are also treatises.

### Ultrafiche

*See* microforms.

### United States Code (U.S.C.)

Volumes containing federal statutes. *See* Statutory Code.

### United States Code Annotated (U.S.C.A.)

Volumes containing federal statutes. *See* Statutory Code.

### U.S. Code Congressional and Administrative News (U.S.C.C.A.N.

U.S.C.C.A.N., published by West, will enable you to:

- Obtain the complete text of public laws or statutes of Congress before they are published in U.S.C./U.S.C.A./U.S.C.S.

- Obtain the complete text of some congressional committee reports (important for legislative history)

- Translate a Statute at Large cite into a U.S.C./U.S.C.A./U.S.C.S. cite (through Table 2)

- Obtain leads to the legislative history of federal statutes (primarily through its Table 4)

- Obtain the complete text of some federal agency regulations (duplicating what is found in the *Federal Register—Fed. Reg.*, and in the *Code of Federal Regulations—C.F.R.*)
- Obtain the complete text of executive orders and other executive documents
- Obtain the complete text of all current United States Statutes at Large (see below)

### United States Code Service (U.S.C.S.)

Volumes containing federal statutes. *See* Statutory Code.

### United States Law Week (U.S.L.W.)

U.S.L.W. is a loose-leaf service published by the Bureau of National Affairs (BNA) that prints the full text of every U.S. Supreme Court case on a weekly basis. It also prints other data on cases in the Supreme Court and summarizes important cases from other courts.

### United States Reports (U.S.)

An official reporter that prints every opinion of the United States Supreme Court. *See* Cases.

### United States Statutes at Large

The United States Statutes at Large (abbreviated "Stat.") contains the full text of every public law or statute and every private law or statute of Congress. The statutes within it are printed chronologically. All current statutes at large are now also printed in *U.S. Code Congressional and Administrative News* as well as in separate Stat. volumes. (The public laws of general interest are later codified and printed in each of the three sets of codified federal statutes: U.S.C., U.S.C.A., U.S.C.S.)

### United States Supreme Court Reports, L. Ed.

An unofficial reporter that prints every opinion of the United States Supreme Court. *See* Cases.

*WESTLAW*

WESTLAW is a legal research computer system. (See pages 585 and 656).

 Section H. Authority in Research and Writing

## 1. Introduction

*Authority*

*Authority* is anything that a court can rely on in reaching its conclusion.

*Primary and Secondary Authority.*    *Primary authority* is any *law* that the court can rely on in reaching its conclusion. Examples include statutes, regulations, constitutional provisions, executive orders, charters, ordinances, treaties, and other court opinions.

*Secondary authority* is any *nonlaw* that the court can rely on in reaching its conclusion. Examples include legal and nonlegal periodical literature, legal and nonlegal encyclopedias, legal and nonlegal dictionaries, legal and nonlegal treatises.

*Mandatory Authority and Persuasive Authority.*    *Mandatory authority* is whatever the court *must* rely on in reaching its conclusion. Only primary authority, such as another court opinion, a statute, or a constitutional provision can be mandatory authority. A court is never required to rely on secondary authority, such as a law review article or legal encyclopedia. Secondary authority cannot be mandatory authority.

*Persuasive authority* is whatever the court relies on when it is not required to do so. There are two main kinds of persuasive authority: (a) a prior court opinion that the court is not required to follow but does so because it finds the opinion persuasive and (b) any secondary authority that the court is not required to follow but does so because it finds the secondary authority persuasive.

*Nonauthority.*    *Nonauthority* is (a) any primary or secondary authority that is not "on point" because it does not cover the facts of the client's case, (b) any invalid primary authority, such as an unconstitutional statute, or (c) any book that is solely a finding aid, such as Shepard's Citations or digests.

## 2. Mandatory Authority

Courts *must* follow mandatory authority. There are two broad categories of mandatory authority: (a) *enacted law* such as a statute, a constitutional provision, an ordinance, or a regulation, and (b) other court opinions. Each category will be considered separately.

### (a) Enacted Law as Mandatory Authority

Any enacted law is mandatory authority and must be followed if the following two tests are met:

- It was the intention of the authors of the enacted law (e.g., the legislature that wrote the statute) to cover the facts that are currently before the court; and
- The application of this enacted law to these facts does not violate some other law that is superior in authority (e.g., the statute does not violate the constitution).

Suppose that Smith is arrested for burglarizing a house. Section 14 of the state code provides, "It shall be a felony to break and enter a dwelling for the purpose of stealing property therein." Section 14 is mandatory authority for the court as long as it is clear that the statute was intended to cover this kind of situation, and the statute does not violate a higher law—the constitution. Suppose, however, that Smith was arrested for breaking into a car. Is a car a "dwelling" for purposes of § 14? Did the legislature intend to include motor vehicles within the meaning of "dwellings?" Would it depend on whether the owner ever slept in the car? These are questions of legislative intent. If the statute was not intended to cover these facts, it is not applicable; it cannot be mandatory authority.

Even if the enacted law was intended to cover the facts before the court, it is not mandatory authority if it violates some higher law. The authors of a regulation, for example, may intend to cover a particular individual's activities, but if this regulation is inconsistent with the statute that the regulation is supposed to be carrying out, the regulation is not mandatory authority; it is invalid. Similarly, a statute may clearly cover a given set of facts but be invalid because the statute is unconstitutional. For example, a statute that prohibits marriage between the races is clearly intended to prevent whites from marrying blacks, but the statute is not mandatory authority because it is in violation of the constitution.

*State* enacted law is usually mandatory only in the state that enacted that law. Suppose, however, that a state court is considering a *federal* enacted law.

*Federal* enacted law can sometimes be mandatory authority in *state* courts. The United States Constitution is the highest authority in the country. If a provision of this Constitution applies, it controls over any state law to the contrary. Federal statutes and the regulations of federal agencies are also superior in authority to state laws in those areas entrusted to the federal government by the United States Constitution, such as the regulation of interstate commerce, patents, bankruptcy, or foreign affairs. Federal statutes and regulations in these areas are mandatory authority in state courts.

Can the enacted law of one state ever be mandatory authority in another state? Generally no, with two exceptions involving the principles of conflict of law, and full faith and credit. We will consider these principles when we examine court opinions as mandatory authority.

## (b) Court Opinions as Mandatory Authority

When is a court *required* to follow an opinion? Two conditions must be met:

- The opinion must be *on point,* that is, it must be *analogous* and
- The opinion must have been written by a court that is superior to the court currently considering the applicability of the opinion.

For an opinion to be on point, or analogous, there must be a sufficient similarity between the key facts of the opinion and the facts of the client's case, and between the rule of law (e.g., statute, common-law principle) that was interpreted and applied in the opinion and the rule of law that must be interpreted and applied in the client's case.

If the opinion is not on point or is not analogous because the similarity listed above does not exist, then the opinion cannot be mandatory authority; it is nonauthority.

The second condition for the existence of mandatory authority requires us to examine the relationship between the court that wrote the opinion and the court that is currently considering that opinion. Six variations will be covered briefly:

1. The highest court in the judicial system is considering an opinion written by a lower court in the same judicial system.
2. A lower court is considering an opinion written by the highest court in the same judicial system.
3. A court is considering an opinion written in the past by the same court.
4. A court in one state is considering an opinion written by a court from another state.
5. A state court is considering an opinion written by a federal court.
6. A federal court is considering an opinion written by a state court.

In each of these six situations a court is attempting to determine whether a prior opinion is binding in the litigation currently before the court. Assume that each opinion *is* analogous: the facts currently before the court are similar to the key facts in the opinion under consideration, and the rules of law are also the same or similar.

*1. The highest court is considering an opinion written by a lower court in the same judicial system.*   A higher court is never required to follow an opinion written by a lower court in the same judicial system, whether or not the opinion is analogous. If the opinion is analogous, it can only be persuasive authority; the higher court can follow it if it chooses to do so.

*2. A lower court is considering an opinion written by the highest court in the same judicial system.*   An opinion written by the highest court in a judicial system is mandatory on every lower court in the same judicial system—if that opinion is analogous. An analogous opinion by the Supreme Court of Montana, for example, must be followed by every lower state court in Montana.

*3. A court opinion is being considered by the same court that wrote the opinion.*   Does a court have to follow its *own* prior opinions? If, for example, the Florida Supreme Court wrote an opinion in 1970, is that opinion mandatory authority for the Florida Supreme Court in 1992 if the opinion is analogous? No. A court is always free to *overrule* its own prior opinions.

Suppose that the opinion was written by an intermediate or middle appeals court. Does that same court have to follow this opinion later if the opinion is analogous? No. *Any* court can later overrule itself and reach a holding that differs from the holding it reached in the earlier opinion as long as there is no opinion in existence written by a higher court that is contrary to the result the middle appeals court now wants to reach.

*4. One state court is considering an opinion written by a state court in another state.*   One state court, generally, does not have to follow an opinion written by another state court no matter how similar the opinion is. An Idaho court, for example, does not have to follow an opinion written by a Massachusetts court.

There are two main exceptions to the principle that an opinion of one state is not mandatory authority in another state. The first involves conflicts of law and the second, full faith and credit:

(a) *Conflicts of Law.* Suppose that an accident occurs in New York, but the negligence suit based on this accident is brought in an Ohio state court. Assume that the Ohio court has subject-matter jurisdiction over the dispute and personal jurisdiction over the parties. What negligence law does the Ohio court apply? Ohio negligence law or New York negligence law? The negligence law of the two states may differ in significant respects. This is a conflicts-of-law problem. Under the principles of the conflicts of law, a court of one state may be required to apply the law of another state. For example, the law to be applied may be the law of the state where the injury occurred or the law of the state that is at the center of the dispute. If this state is deemed to be New York, then the Ohio court will apply New York negligence law. Analogous opinions of New York courts on the law of negligence will be mandatory authority in the Ohio court.

(b) *Full Faith and Credit.* The United States Constitution provides that "Full Faith and Credit shall be given in each State to the public Acts, Records, and judicial Proceedings of every other State." art. IV, § 1. Suppose that Richards sues Davis for breach of contract in Delaware. Davis wins. Richards cannot go to another state and bring a breach-of-contract suit arising out of the same facts against Davis in the other state. If the Delaware court had proper jurisdiction when it rendered its judgment, the Delaware opinion must be given full faith and credit in every other state. The case cannot be relitigated. The Delaware opinion is mandatory authority in every other state.

*5 and 6. A state court is considering an opinion written by a federal court and vice versa.* The general rule is that state courts have the final say on what the state law is, and federal courts have the final say on what the federal law is. State courts do *not* have to follow opinions written by federal courts *unless* the issue before the state court involves a federal question—one arising out of the United States Constitution or out of a statute of Congress. Federal courts do not have to follow state court opinions *except to the extent that* the federal court needs to know what the state law is on a given topic.

## 3. Court Opinions as Persuasive Authority

Review the two conditions mentioned earlier on when an opinion is mandatory authority: the opinion must be analogous, or on point, *and* it must have been written by a court that is superior to the court currently considering that opinion. If *both* these tests are not met, the opinion is either nonauthority or it might be *persuasive authority.*

Assume that the holding in the *X v. Y* opinion is not analogous to the legal issues currently being considered by a court in the *A v. B* litigation. Assume also that within *X v. Y* there is some *dictum* that has relevance or some bearing on the issues before the *A v. B* court. By definition, the dictum cannot be part of the *X v. Y* holding, since dictum is a statement by a judge that was not necessary to resolve the narrow legal issues before the court in *X v. Y.* Dictum, therefore, can never be mandatory authority. The *A v. B* court is not *required* to follow the *X v. Y* dictum. The *A v. B* court, however, has the discretion of adopting the *X v. Y* dictum, since it does relate to the issues before the *A v. B* court. If the court does adopt it, it has become persuasive authority.

Suppose that you are reading an opinion that *is* analogous, or on point, but is not mandatory because:

- It was written by an inferior court and is now being considered by a court within the same judicial system that is superior to the court that wrote the opinion; or

- It was written by a court from a judicial system that is different from the judicial system where the court considering that opinion sits.

If either of these two situations exists, the court, as we have seen, does *not* have to follow the opinion; it is not mandatory authority. If, however, the opinion is on point, the court would be free to adopt it as persuasive authority.

A number of factors go into a court's determination of whether a prior opinion is persuasive enough to adopt. A judge will usually be interested in knowing how many other courts have adopted the result of this opinion. Is there a "majority rule" or school of thought that has developed around that result? Has the opinion been frequently cited with approval? How well reasoned is the opinion? These considerations will help a judge decide whether to adopt an opinion as persuasive. Finally, it is human nature for judges to gravitate toward those opinions that are most in tune with their personal philosophies and biases—although preferences on this basis are never acknowledged.

## 4. Secondary Authority as Persuasive Authority

Secondary authority is not the law itself. It is *not* written by the legislature, a court, an agency, a city council, etc. Secondary authority can never be mandatory authority; it can only be persuasive. The chart in Figure 11.6 provides an overview of the major kinds of secondary authority that a court could decide to rely on in reaching its conclusion.

Some of these secondary authorities quote from the law itself, that is, they quote primary authority. As a general rule, *you should never use someone else's quotation of the law*. Quote *directly* from the primary authority. Use the secondary authority to bolster your arguments on the interpretation of the primary authority. This is the main function of secondary authority: to help you persuade a court to adopt a certain interpretation of primary authority. You are on very dangerous ground when you use secondary authority as a substitute for primary authority.

Secondary authority will frequently *paraphrase* or summarize primary authority, e.g., a hornbook or legal encyclopedia will summarize the law of a particular state on a topic. You will be *very* tempted to use such summaries in your own legal writing. There are serious dangers, however, in relying on excerpts containing such summaries. While they can be used and sometimes *should* be used (with proper citation to avoid the charge of plagiarism), the difficulties with using quotes from such excerpts are as follows:

- The excerpts are secondary authority, and the goal of your writing is to use primary authority to support your arguments.

- The excerpts may contain summaries of court opinions; these opinions should be *individually* analyzed before you use any of them in your writing.

- The excerpts may be based on opinions from different states, and your legal writing must focus on the law of the state in which the client is litigating the case.

In short, too much reliance on such excerpts from secondary authority amounts to laziness in legal research and analysis. It is sometimes difficult to find and

**FIGURE 11.6**

Categories of
Secondary
Authority

| KIND | CONTENTS | EXAMPLES |
|------|----------|----------|
| 1. Legal Encyclopedias | Summaries of the law, organized by topic | *Corpus Juris Secundum* *American Jurisprudence 2d* |
| 2. Nonlegal Encyclopedias | Summaries of many topics on science, the arts, history, etc. | *Encyclopedia Britannica* |
| 3. Legal Dictionaries | Definitions of legal terms taken almost exclusively from court opinions | *Words and Phrases* |
| 4. Legal Dictionaries | Definitions of legal terms that come from a variety of sources | *Black's Law Dictionary* *Ballentine's Law Dictionary* West's *Legal Thesaurus/ Dictionary* |
| 5. Nonlegal Dictionaries | Definitions of all words in general use | *Webster's Dictionary* |
| 6. Legal Periodicals (general) | Pamphlets (later often bound) containing articles written on a variety of legal topics | *Harvard Law Review* *American Bar Association Journal* |
| 7. Legal Periodicals (specialized) | Pamphlets (later often bound) containing articles written on a specialized area or aspect of the law | *Journal of Family Law* *Journal of Legal Education* |
| 8. Nonlegal Periodicals | Pamphlets on general topics | *Newsweek* *Foreign Affairs* |
| 9. Legal Treatises | Summaries of and commentaries on areas of the law | *McCormick on Evidence* Johnstone and Hopson, *Lawyers and Their Work* *Restatement of the Law of Torts* |
| 10. Nonlegal Treatises | Perspectives on a variety of topics | Samuelson, *Economics* |
| 11. Loose-Leaf Services | Collections of materials in three-ring binders covering current law in designated areas | *Pollution Control Guide* *Accountancy Law Reports* *Products Liability Reporter* |
| 12. Formbooks, Manuals, Practice Books | Same as legal treatises with a greater emphasis on the "how-to-do-it" practical dimensions of the law | Dellheim, *Massachusetts Practice* Moore's *Federal Practice* *Am. Jur. Pleading and Practice Forms Annotated* |
| 13. Legal Newspapers | Daily or weekly compilations of information relevant to practice | *Daily Washington Law Reporter* *National Law Journal* |
| 14. Nonlegal Newspapers | General circulation newspapers | *New York Times* *Detroit Free Press* |

apply the law. If someone else at least appears to have done all the work for you in secondary authority, why not use it? The answers to this question are found in the three difficulties mentioned above.

Before covering the *proper* use of secondary authority in your legal writing, the value of secondary authority *as a research tool* should be reemphasized. Often the most valuable parts of these texts are the footnotes. The citations in the footnotes to court opinions (and to other authority) can be invaluable to you as you pursue your search for relevant law. If the secondary authority has led you to laws that you eventually use in your writing (after proper legal analysis), the secondary authority will have been of tremendous service to you.

Secondary authority can provide another service, independent of whether you use it directly in your writing. You will often be doing legal research in areas of the law that are new to you. You may need help trying to make sense of what might appear to be quite formidable and esoteric areas of the law— with or without the inevitable Latin phrases. One approach is to read a chapter in a hornbook, a section in a legal encyclopedia, or material in any other secondary authority in order to obtain an overview of the law. Armed with this general understanding, you will be better equipped to resume your research and analysis in the unfamiliar area of law. See page 550 on doing such background research.

Suppose that you want to *use* a quote from the secondary authority *in your legal writing*. What steps must you take in order to do so properly? What is the proper *foundation* for the use of secondary authority in legal writing? Figure 11.7 presents the steps that provide this foundation. The secondary authority mentioned in the chart is a treatise, although the steps apply equally to *any* type of secondary authority that you are thinking about using in your legal writing as possible persuasive authority. You cannot avoid extensive research and analysis simply by quoting from secondary authority—no matter how tempting. Unless you have researched and analyzed the relevant *mandatory* authority, you will be unable to establish the necessary foundation to use *secondary* authority.

Many well-written and comprehensively researched legal memoranda and appellate briefs make very few references to secondary authority. Experienced advocates know that judges are suspicious of secondary authority. It is true that some secondary authorities are highly respected (such as *Prosser on Torts* or any of the *Restatements* of the American Law Institute). Yet even these must be used with caution. The preoccupation of a court is on primary authority. Before you use secondary authority in your writing, you must be sure that (a) the secondary authority is not used as a substitute for the primary authority, (b) the

---

1. You must satisfy yourself through independent legal research that the quote from the treatise that you want to use does not contradict any law (opinion, statute, constitutional provision, etc.) that exists in the jurisdiction where the client is litigating the case. Stated more simply: there must be no contrary mandatory authority.

2. If the quote from the treatise *does* contradict any such law, you cannot use the quote *unless* you satisfy yourself:

   ■ that the court before which the client is litigating the case has the power to change the law that contradicts what the treatise says and, in effect, adopt the treatise's statement as new law in the jurisdiction, and

   ■ that there is a reasonable likelihood that a court with such power is inclined to change the law.

**FIGURE 11.7**

The Foundation for the Use of Secondary Authority in Legal Writing as Possible Persuasive Authority secondary authority is not unduly repetitive of the primary authority, (c) the secondary authority will be helpful to the court in adopting an interpretation of primary authority, particularly when there is not a great deal of primary authority on point, (d) you discuss the secondary authority after you have presented the primary authority, and (e) the foundation for the use of secondary authority (see Figure 11.7) can be demonstrated if needed.

## ■ Section I. Citation Form

A citation, or cite, is a reference to any written material. The cite gives you the "address" where you can go in the library to find the cited document.

Are there any consistent rules on citation form? If you pick up different law books and examine the citations of similar material within them, you will notice great variety in citation form. You will find that people abbreviate things differently, they do not include the same order of information in the cite, they use parentheses differently, they use punctuation within the cite differently, they include different amounts of information in the same kind of cite, etc. There does not appear to be any consistency. Yet, in spite of this diversity and confusion, you are often scolded by supervisors for failing to use "proper citation form." What, you may well ask, is "proper"?

Start by checking the court rules of the court that will have jurisdiction over the problem you are researching. There may or may not be citation rules within them. If such rules exist, they must obviously be followed in spite of what any other citation rule book may say. These are, in effect, citation *laws*.

Suppose, however, that there are no official citation laws in the court rules for your court or that these citation rules do not cover the citation question that you have. In such circumstances, *ask your supervisor what citation form you should use.* You will probably be told, "Use the Bluebook." This is a reference to A Uniform System of Citation we looked at earlier (page 490). It is a small blue pamphlet (although in earlier editions, white covers were used). The Bluebook is published by a group of law students on the law reviews of their law schools. Caution is needed, however, in using the Bluebook. It is a highly technical and sometimes difficult-to-use pamphlet because it packs so much information in a relatively small space. Primary users of the Bluebook are law

---

**GENERAL GUIDELINES ON CITATION FORM**

1. Find out if there are citation laws in the rules of court.

2. Ask your supervisor if he or she has any special instructions on citation form.

3. Consult the Bluebook.

4. Consult the basic citation rules presented below (I–VII). Most of these rules are based on the Bluebook.

5. Remember that the *functional* purpose of a citation is to enable readers to locate your citation in a library. You must give enough information in the cite to fulfill this purpose. Courtesy to the reader in providing this help is as important as compliance with the niceties of citation form.

6. Often a private publisher of a book will tell you how to cite the book. ("Cite this book as. . . .") Ignore this instruction! Instead, follow guidelines 1–5 above.

7. When in doubt about whether to include something in a citation after carefully following guidelines 1–5 above, resolve the doubt by including it in the cite.

schools that wish to have their law reviews typeset by professional printers. What about those of us who use regular typewriters or word processors and do not typeset what we produce? While the Bluebook does cover many of our citation needs, keep in mind that we are not the main audience of the Bluebook. Also, be aware that many courts do *not* follow the Bluebook even if there are no court rules on citation form for that court. Judges often simply use their own "system" of citation without necessarily being consistent.

## Basic Citation Rules

Use the following citation forms unless General Guidelines 1–3 above tell you otherwise:

   I.  Citing Opinions

  II.  Citing Constitutions and Charters

 III.  Citing Federal Statutes

 IV.  Citing State Statutes

  V.  Citing Administrative Regulations

 VI.  Citing the Documents of Legislative History

VII.  Citing Secondary Authority

### I. *Citing Opinions*

The following are the most common kinds of opinions and decisions that you will be citing:

Example A: Format of a Citation to an Opinion of the Highest Federal Court (the United States Supreme Court):

> *Taglianetti v. United States,* 394 U.S. 316, 89 S. Ct. 1099, 22 L. Ed.2d 302 (1969). [As indicated below, there is a disagreement over the proper citation form for this Court. The Bluebook says the correct cite would be: *Taglianetti v. United States,* 394 U.S. 316 (1969).]

Example B: Format of a Citation to an Opinion of a Federal Middle Appeals Court (the United States Court of Appeals, Second Circuit):

> *Sterling Nat'l Bank & Trust Co. of N.Y. v. Fidelity Mortgage Investors,* 510 F.2d 870 (2d Cir. 1975).

Example C: Format of a Citation to an Opinion of a Federal Trial Court (the United States District Court, Western District in Wisconsin):

> *Stone v. Schmidt,* 398 F. Supp. 768 (W.D. Wis. 1975).

Example D: Format of a Citation to an Opinion of the Highest State Court (New Jersey Supreme Court):

> *Petlin Associates, Inc. v. Township of Dover,* 64 N.J. 327, 316 A.2d 1 (1974).

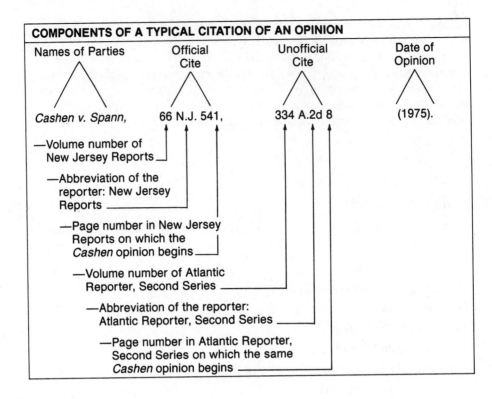

**COMPONENTS OF A TYPICAL CITATION OF AN OPINION**

| Names of Parties | Official Cite | Unofficial Cite | Date of Opinion |
|---|---|---|---|
| *Cashen v. Spann,* | 66 N.J. 541, | 334 A.2d 8 | (1975). |

—Volume number of New Jersey Reports

—Abbreviation of the reporter: New Jersey Reports

—Page number in New Jersey Reports on which the *Cashen* opinion begins

—Volume number of Atlantic Reporter, Second Series

—Abbreviation of the reporter: Atlantic Reporter, Second Series

—Page number in Atlantic Reporter, Second Series on which the same *Cashen* opinion begins

Example E: Format of a Citation to an Opinion of a Lower State Court (Connecticut Superior Court, Appellate Session):

*Huckabee v. Stevens,* 32 Conn. Supp. 511, 338 A.2d 512 (Super. Ct. 1975).

Example F: Format of a Citation to an Administrative Decision (National Labor Relations Board):

*Standard Dry Wall Products, Inc.,* 91 N.L.R.B. 544 (1950).

Example G: Format of a Citation to an Opinion of the Attorney General:

40 Op. Att'y Gen. 423 (1945).

*Guidelines:*

1. You will note that some of the citations in the above examples have *parallel cites* (see Examples A, D, and E) and some do not. Before examining the rules of providing parallel cites and the techniques of finding such cites, some basics need to be covered.

2. The same opinion can be printed in more than one reporter. A parallel cite is a reference to an *additional* reporter where the same opinion (word-for-word) can be found. In Example D, the *Petlin* opinion can be found in New Jersey Reports (abbreviated "N.J.") and in Atlantic 2d ("A.2d").

3. Do not confuse (a) the parallel cite with (b) the same case on appeal. Examine the following three citations:

- *Smith v. Jones,* 24 Mass. 101, 19 N.E.2d 370 (1920).
- *Jones v. Smith,* 26 Mass. 228, 21 N.E.2d 1017 (1922).
- *Smith v. Jones,* 125 F.2d 177 (2d Cir. 1925).

Assume that these three opinions involve the same litigation—the same parties and the same issues. The case went up on appeal three times: twice to the Massachusetts Supreme Judicial Court and once to the United States Court of Appeals for the Second Circuit. The first two opinions have parallel cites. For example, the first opinion is printed in both Massachusetts Reports (24 Mass. 101) and in North Eastern Reporter, 2d (19 N.E.2d 370). The third opinion has no parallel cite. The second and third opinions are citations to the "same case on appeal." They are *not* parallel cites to the first opinion. While the same litigation is involved, the citations are to three distinct opinions, two of which have parallel cites.

4. There are four main techniques of finding a parallel cite:
   - Shepardize the case. The first cite in parentheses in Shepard's is the parallel cite. If you find no cite in parenthesis, it means (a) that no parallel cite exists, (b) that the reporter containing the parallel cite has not been printed yet, or (c) the parallel cite was given in one of the earlier volumes of Shepard's and was not repeated in the volume you are examining.

```
 – 717 –
(439US438)    | o,
592F2d²288    | e61.
f615F2d¹739   | f473t
f615F2d²739   | 94Æ3.1b
f615F2d⁵739   | 94Æ3.19:
471FS⁵101     | 94Æ3.211
f476FS¹92     | 94Æ3.24‘
477FS961
⁴77FS⁴969

    ⁷33
```

Finding a parallel cite through Shepard's

   - *National Reporter Blue Book.* Go to this set of books published by West to try to locate a parallel cite. The National Reporter Blue Book will also tell you which official reporters have been discontinued. (If your state has a Blue and White Book, you can also use it to try to find a parallel cite.)
   - Top of the caption. Go to the reporter that contains the opinion. At the beginning of the opinion, there is a caption giving the names of the parties, the court, etc. At the top of this caption, see if there is a parallel cite. (This technique does not always work, but it is worth a try.)

```
       169 Conn. 677
Application of Verne Freeman SLADE
     for Admission to the Bar.

 Supreme Court of Connecticut.

       Dec. 2, 1975.
```

Finding a parallel cite by checking the top of the caption

- Table of Cases in Digest. Go to every digest that gives small-paragraph summaries of court opinions for the court that wrote the opinion, e.g., the American Digest System. Go to the table of cases in these digests. See if there is a parallel cite for your case. In the following excerpt from a digest table of cases, you find two cites for *Ames v. State Bar*—106 Cal. Rptr. 489 and 506 P.2d 625:

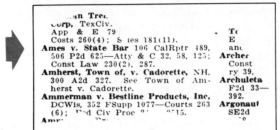

Finding a parallel cite by checking the table of cases in digests

5. When submitting a document (e.g., an appellate brief) to a state court, provide available parallel cites to all cases written by state courts in that state. According to the Bluebook, the unofficial cite is sufficient in all other situations. (The better practice, however, is always to provide a parallel cite, with the exceptions listed below.)

6. Although an opinion may eventually be printed in more than one reporter, the reporters are rarely, if ever, printed at the same time. The publication of an official reporter, for example, can be as much as a year behind the unofficial reporter. At the time you want to cite a recent opinion, you may have only the unofficial reporter available. Hence, you could not provide a parallel cite if you wanted to include one. Simply provide the cite that you have.

7. As indicated earlier, loose-leaf services often provide the most current legal material available. Some services will send out opinions within a week of their issuance by the court. Generally, however, you do *not* include the citation to the loose-leaf service *unless* no other citation to the opinion is available at the time.

8. Court opinions are found in traditional library volumes (reporters) and on computerized legal research services. Some opinions, however, are found *only* online in these services. An example is *Bucknum v. Bucknum,* which was decided on February 19, 1991 by the Minnesota Court of Appeals. Its docket number is No. C6-90-1798. This opinion is found on WESTLAW and on LEXIS but not in a traditional library reporter volume. Here is how the case is cited in WESTLAW and LEXIS respectively:

   *Bucknum v. Bucknum,* 1991 WL 17881 (Minn. App.).

   *Bucknum v. Bucknum,* 1991 Minn. App. LEXIS 145.

   The number 17881 is an internal WESTLAW number, and 145 is an internal LEXIS number.
     The Bluebook does *not* follow these citation formats. The Bluebook has its own format for citing cases found in WESTLAW and LEXIS:

   *Bucknum v. Bucknum,* No. C6–90–1798, 1991 WL 17881 (Minn. App. Feb. 19, 1991).

   *Bucknum v. Bucknum,* No. C6–90–1798, 1991 Minn. App. LEXIS 145 (Feb. 19, 1991).

Note that in these Bluebook cites, the docket number and the WESTLAW/LEXIS cite are given, along with the full date of the decision in parentheses at the end. You should not cite a case in WESTLAW or LEXIS unless it is not readily available in traditional library volumes such as reporters.

9. There is some disagreement as to whether parallel cites are needed for opinions of the U.S. Supreme Court. The Bluebook says you should not provide a parallel cite for such opinions if you have the official cite ("U.S.") available, even if the parallel cites in "S. Ct." and "L. Ed." are also available. The better view, however, is to give all three cites when they are available. (See Example A.)

10. When parallel cites are to be cited, always place the official cite first before the unofficial cite. (See Examples A, D, and E.)

11. There is no parallel cite for Federal Reporter 2d cases (F.2d). (See Example B.) Abbreviate the circuit in parentheses at the end of the cite before the year. 2d Cir. means the opinion was decided by the U.S. Court of Appeals for the Second Circuit. D.C. Cir. would mean the case was decided by the U.S. Court of Appeals for the District of Columbia Circuit. The caption of the opinion will tell you which circuit court wrote the opinion.

12. There is no parallel cite for Federal Supplement cases (F. Supp.). (See Example C.) Abbreviate the U.S. District Court in parentheses at the end of the cite before the year. W.D. Wis. means the opinion was written by the United States District Court, Western District, sitting in Wisconsin. The caption of the opinion will tell you which U.S. District Court wrote the opinion.

13. In Example D, the parentheses at the end of the cite to the *Petlin* case contain the date of the decision, but nothing more. There is no need to indicate the name of the court in the parentheses if the court is the highest court of the state, and if it is clear from the reporter abbreviation what state is involved. In Example D, the *Petlin* case was written by the highest court (the Supreme Court) in the state of New Jersey. You know this by examining the abbreviation of the official reporter in the cite (64 N.J. 327). When the abbreviation of the reporter (here, N.J.) is the abbreviation of the state, you can assume that the case was written by the highest court in that state. Suppose, however, that you did not have this official reporter cite. If all you had was the unofficial Atlantic 2d cite (316 A.2d 1), you would cite the case as follows:

*Petlin Associates, Inc. v. Township of Dover,* 316 A.2d 1 (N.J. 1974).

By looking at the abbreviation of the reporter (A.2d), you cannot tell which state wrote this opinion. Therefore, you must indicate the name of the state in the parentheses before the date. Since the case was written by the highest court in the state, there is no need to abbreviate the name of this court. Using the abbreviation of the state alone (N.J.) tells you that it was the highest.

14. In Example E, there is an abbreviation of the court that wrote the opinion (Superior Court) in parentheses before the date at the end of the cite. This is necessary because the opinion was written by a state court other than the highest court in the state. Note that it is not necessary to tell the reader

that this court is in Connecticut because it is clear from the abbreviation of the reporter (32 Conn. Supp. 511) that it is a Connecticut case.

15. Include only the last name of parties who are people. For example, if the parties are listed as "Frank Taylor v. Mary Smith" by the court, your cite should list them as *Taylor v. Smith*.

16. If a party is a business, use the full name of the business, but abbreviate words such as Corporation (Corp.), Incorporated (Inc.), Company (Co.), Limited (Ltd.), and Brothers (Bros.). If, for example, a party is listed by the court as "John J. Dover, Incorporated," your cite would read *John J. Dover, Inc.* (If, however, John J. Dover was a party suing or being sued as a human person rather than as a business, your cite would simply list this party as *Dover*.)

17. When the United States is a party, do not use the abbreviation "U.S." See Example A.

18. Assume that New York State is a party. Your cite should say "State" (rather than "State of New York" or "New York") *if and only if* the opinion was written by a New York state court. Suppose, however, that New York is a party in a case written by an Ohio court. In such a case, use "New York" (not "State of New York" or "State") in your cite as the name of this party. This same guideline applies for the words "Commonwealth" and "People." These words are used alone in a cite only if the court that wrote the opinion you are citing is in the same state referred to by the words "Commonwealth" and "People." Example: You are citing an opinion of the California Supreme Court, which describes the parties as follows:

*People of California v. Gabriel S. Farrell*

Your cite of this opinion would be *People v. Farrell*.

19. If your printer can print in italics, you should italicize the names of the parties. For example:

*Steck v. Farrell*

If you cannot italicize, underline or underscore. For example:

Steck v. Farrell

20. Some opinions consolidate more than one litigation. A supreme court, for example, may use one opinion to resolve similar issues raised in several different lower court cases. The caption of the opinion written by the supreme court will probably list all the parties from these different lower court cases, for example, *A v. B; C v. D; E v. F.* When you cite this opinion, include only the *first* set of parties listed in the caption—here, *A v. B.* On the other hand, the court may not list all the multiple parties but may simply say *et al.* (and others) after the name of a party. Do not include the phrase *et al.* in your cite.

21. Often the court will tell you the litigation status of the parties, such as plaintiff, defendant, appellant, or appellee. Generally, you should not include this information in your cite.

22. Titles of individual parties (such as administrator or secretary) should be omitted from your cite. One exception is the Commissioner of Internal Revenue. Cite this party simply as "Commissioner"—for example, *Jackson v. Commissioner*.

23. Include the phrase *in re* (meaning "in the matter of") in your cite—for example, *In re Jones.*

24. Include the year of the decision at the end of the cite in parentheses. If more than one date is given in the caption of the opinion, use the year from the date the opinion was decided.

25. Do not include the *docket number* of the case in the cite unless the case is not printed in a traditional reporter (see guideline #8), or unless the case is still pending.

26. The reporter volumes that contain current opinions are conveniently arranged by volume number. All the volumes of the same set have the same name, e.g., Atlantic Reporter, 2d. There was a time, however, when life was not this simple. Volumes of opinions were identified by the name of the individual person who had responsibility for compiling the opinions written by the judges. These individuals were called reporters. "7 Cush. 1," for example, refers to an opinion found on page 1 of volume 7 of Massachusetts cases when Mr. Cushing was the official reporter. When he ended his employment, Mr. Gray took over, and the cite of an opinion in the volume immediately after "7 Cush." was "1 Gray." Simply by looking at the cover of the volume, you *cannot* tell what court's opinions were inside unless you happen to be familiar with the names of these individuals and the courts for which they worked. These volumes are called *nominative reporters* because they are identified by the name of the individual person who compiled the opinions for the court.

27. Assume that all you know are the names of the parties and the name of the court that wrote the opinion. How do you obtain the full cite?

    ■ Go to every digest that covers that reporter. Check its table of cases.

    ■ Call the court clerk for the court that wrote the opinion. If it is a recent case, the clerk may be able to send you a copy. Occasionally, the clerk will give you the cite of the case. (It will help if you can tell the clerk the docket number of the case.)

    ■ Go to the reporter volumes that cover the court that wrote the opinion. Since you do not have a volume number, you cannot go directly to the volume that has the opinion. If, however, you can *approximate* the date of the case, you can check the table of cases in each reporter volume that probably covers that year. You may have to check the table of cases in 10 to 15 volumes before achieving success. The opinions are printed in the reporters in roughly chronological order.

28. When quoting from or referring to specific language in an opinion, you must list both the number of the page on which the opinion begins *and* the number of the page on which the quoted language begins. The latter page number is inserted in the citation immediately following the former and is set off with a comma. If a parallel cite is included, do the same for the parallel cite. In the following example, the quote is from page 20 of *Maryland Reports* ("Md.") and from p. 379 of Atlantic 2d ("A.2d"):

### EXAMPLE

"Even though laches may not apply, one must use reasonable promptness when availing himself of judicial protection." *Bridgeton Educ. Ass'n v. Bd. of Educ.,* 147 Md. 17, 20, 334 A.2d 376, 379 (1975).

## II.  *Citing Constitutions and Charters*

Constitutions and charters are cited to (a) the abbreviated name of the constitution or charter, (b) the article, and (c) the section.

EXAMPLE

U.S. Const. art. I, § 9.
N.M. Const. art. IV, § 7.

In citing constitutions and charters, the date of enactment should *not* be given unless the provision you are citing has been amended or repealed.

## III.  *Citing Federal Statutes*

1. All federal statutes of Congress are collected in chronological order of passage as session laws in the *United States Statutes at Large*. If the statute is of general public interest, it is also printed in *each* of three codes:

   - United State Code (U.S.C.)
   - United States Code Annotated (U.S.C.A.)—West Publishing Co.
   - United States Code Service (U.S.C.S.)—Lawyers Co-operative Publishing Co.

   The preferred citation format is to U.S.C. For example:

   42 U.S.C. § 3412(a)(1970).
   *or*
   Narcotic Rehabilitation Act of 1966, 42 U.S.C. § 3412(a)(1970).

   While it is not necessary to give the popular name of the statute (as in the second version of the above example), citing the popular name when known is often helpful.

2. A new edition of the U.S.C. comes out every six years. The date you use in citing a statute in U.S.C. is the date of the edition you are using unless your statute is found in one of the annual Supplements to the U.S.C., which come out in between editions. If your statute is in a Supplement, you cite the volume and year of this Supplement. Suppose your statute is found in the sixth Supplement published in 1983. Your cite would be as follows:

   29 U.S.C. § 169 (Supp. VI 1983).

   The date you use in citing a statute in U.S.C. is not the year the statute was enacted or passed by the legislature. It is the date of the edition of the code or of the Supplement year.

3. Although citation to U.S.C. is preferred, it is not uncommon to find citations to the other codes: U.S.C.A. and U.S.C.S. (There is never a need, however, to cite more than one of the three codes.) The format is as follows:

   29 U.S.C.A. § 169 (West 1983).
   29 U.S.C.S. § 169 (Law. Co-op. 1982).

   In parentheses before the date, include the name of the publisher. Use the year that appears on the title page of the volume, or its latest copyright year, in this order of preference. If your statute is in one of the annual pocket parts of either of these two codes, include "Supp." and give the year of the pocket part—for example, (West Supp. 1984).

4. There is one instance in which you *must* cite to the *United States Statutes at Large* ( abbreviated Stat.) rather than to U.S.C. The rule is as follows: Cite to the statute in Statutes at Large if (a) there is a difference in the language of the statute in Stat. and in the U.S.C. and (b) the statute in U.S.C. is in a title that has *not* been enacted into positive law by Congress.

   It is highly unlikely that you will find a difference in language between Stat. and U.S.C. Yet the conscientious researcher must check this out before relying on any statutory language.

   All the statutes in U.S.C. fall within one of fifty titles—for example, title 11 on Bankruptcy, title 39 on the Postal Service. If Congress goes through all the statutes in a particular title and formally declares that all of them are valid and accurate, then that title has been enacted into positive law. You can rely exclusively on the language of such statutes even if the language is different from the statute as it originally appeared in Statutes at Large. At the beginning of the first volume of U.S.C., you will be told which titles of the U.S.C. have been enacted into positive law.

5. A Statute at Large cite, when needed, should include (a) the name of the statute if one exists; if one does not exist, include "Act of" and give the full date of enactment—month, day, and year, (b) the Public Law number of the statute or its chapter number, (c) the section of the statute you are citing, (d) the volume number of the Statutes at Large used, (e) the abbreviation "Stat.," (f) the page number on which your statute is found in the Stat. volume, (g) in parentheses, the year the statute was enacted or passed by the legislature. Do not include the year, however, if you used the "Act of" option referred to in (a).

## EXAMPLE

Narcotic Addict Rehabilitation Act, Pub. L. No. 80–793, § 9, 80 Stat. 1444 (1966).

Note that the year in parentheses at the end of the cite is the year the statute was passed. Guideline 2 above said that you do not use the date of enactment when citing a statute in U.S.C. The rule is different when giving a Stat. cite.

   Note the section number (9) of this Public Law in the example. The statute might also have several title numbers. If so, § 9 would be found within one of these titles. Assume, for example, that § 9 is in title III of the Public Law. It is important to remember that these section and title numbers are found in the original *session law* edition of the statute. When this statute is later printed in U.S.C. (assuming it is a public law of general interest), it will *not* go into § 9 of the third title. The U.S.C. has its own title and section number scheme. (For example, title III, § 9 of the above statute might be found in title 45, § 1075(b) of the U.S.C.) This can be very frustrating for the researcher new to the law. If you are reading a statute in its original session or Public Law form, you cannot find this statute under the same title and section number in U.S.C. You must *translate* the Public Law or Stat. cite into a U.S.C. cite. Phrased another way, you must translate the session law cite into a code cite. Later, we will see that this is done by using one of two tables: Table III in a special Tables volume of USC/USCA/USCS, or Table 2 in U.S. Code Congressional and Administrative News.

6. Of course, if the statute is a private law or is a public law that is deemed to be of no general public interest, it will not be printed in the U.S.C. It will be found only in Statutes at Large.

7. The Internal Revenue Code is within the U.S.C. Hence, you use guideline 1 above in citing a tax statute. For example:

26 U.S.C. § 1278 (1976).

For tax statutes in the Internal Revenue Code (I.R.C.), however, there is *another* option that is considered acceptable:

I.R.C. § 1278 (1976).

8. There is a special format for citing Federal Rules of Civil Procedure, Federal Rules of Criminal Procedure, Federal Rules of Appellate Procedure, and the Federal Rules of Evidence. Examples:

Fed. R. Civ. P. 15
Fed. R. Crim. P. 23
Fed. R. App. P. 3
Fed. R. Evid. 310

## IV. *Citing State Statutes*

1. Like federal statutes, the statutes of the various states are compiled in two kinds of collections: state *codes* (arranged by subject matter) and *session laws* (arranged in chronological order of enactment).
2. Citations to state codes vary from state to state. On page 535, there are examples of standard citation formats. Use these as guides unless local rules of court dictate otherwise. The year at the end of the cite should be the year that appears on the spine of the code, or the year that appears on the title page, or the latest copyright year—in this order of preference.

## V. *Citing Administrative Regulations*

1. Federal administrative regulations are published in the *Federal Register* (Fed. Reg.). Many of these regulations are later codified by subject matter in the *Code of Federal Regulations* (C.F.R.).
2. Federal regulations that appear in the *Code of Federal Regulations* are cited to (a) the title number in which the regulation appears, (b) the abbreviated name of the code, (c) the number of the particular section to which you are referring, and (d) the date of the code edition which you are using.

### EXAMPLE

29 C.F.R. § 102.60(a)(1975).

3. Federal regulations that have not yet been codified into the *Code of Federal Regulations* are cited to the *Federal Register* using (a) the volume in which the regulation appears, (b) the abbreviation "Fed. Reg.," (c) the page on which the regulation appears, and (d) the year of the *Federal Register* you are using.

### EXAMPLE

27 Fed. Reg. 2,092 (1962).

## Examples of State Statutory Code Citations

| | |
|---|---|
| Alabama: | Ala. Code § 37–10–3 (1977). |
| Alaska: | Alaska Stat. § 22.10.110 (1962). |
| Arizona: | Ariz. Rev. Stat. Ann. § 44–1621 (1956). |
| Arkansas: | Ark. Code Ann. § 20–316 (Michie 1968). |
| California: | Cal. Prob. Code § 585 (West 1956). |
| | Cal. Prob. Code § 585 (Deering 1956). |
| Colorado: | Colo. Rev. Stat. Ann. § 32–7–131 (West 1971). |
| | Colo. Rev. Stat. § 32-7-131 (1971). |
| Connecticut: | Conn. Gen. Stat. § 34–29 (1989). |
| | Conn. Gen. Stat. Ann. § 53a–135 (West 1972). |
| Delaware: | Del. Code Ann. tit. 18, § 2926 (1974). |
| District of Columbia: | D.C. Code Ann. § 16–2307 (1981). |
| Florida: | Fla. Stat. ch. 2.314 (1986). |
| | Fla. Stat. Ann. ch. 6.341 (Harrison 1985). |
| Georgia: | Ga. Code Ann. § 110–118 (Michie 1973). |
| | Ga. Code Ann. § 22–1414 (Harrison 1977). |
| Hawaii: | Haw. Rev. Stat. § 431:19–107 (1988). |
| Idaho: | Idaho Code § 18–3615 (1987). |
| Illinois: | Ill. Rev. Stat. ch. 85, para. 8–103 (1985). |
| | Ill. Ann. Stat. ch. 40, para. 501 (Smith-Hurd 1980). |
| Indiana: | Ind. Code § 9–8–1–13 (1976). |
| | Ind. Code Ann. § 9–8–1–13 (Burns 1983). |
| | Ind. Code Ann. § 9–8–1–13 (West 1979). |
| Iowa: | Iowa Code § 455.92 (1958). |
| | Iowa Code Ann. § 98.14 (West 1984). |
| Kansas: | Kan. Stat. Ann. § 38–1506 (1986). |
| | Kan. Corp. Code Ann. § 17–6303 (Vernon 1975). |
| Kentucky: | Ky. Rev. Stat. Ann. § 208.060 (Baldwin 1988). |
| | Ky. Rev. Stat. Ann. § 44.072 (Michie/Bobbs-Merrill 1986). |
| Louisiana: | La. Rev. Stat. Ann. § 15:452 (West 1981). |
| | La. Code Civ. Proc. Ann. art. 3132 (West 1961). |
| Maine: | Me. Rev. Stat. Ann. tit. 36, § 1760 (West 1964). |
| Maryland: | Md. Fam. Law Code Ann. § 7–106 (1984). |
| | Md. Ann. Code art. 78, § 70 (1957). |
| Massachusetts: | Mass. Gen. L. ch. 106, § 2–318 (1984). |
| | Mass. Gen. Laws Ann. ch. 156, § 37 (West 1970). |
| | Mass. Ann. Laws ch. 123, § 15 (Law. Co-op. 1988). |
| Michigan: | Mich. Comp. Laws § 550.1402 (1980). |
| | Mich. Comp. Laws Ann. § 211.27 (West 1986). |
| | Mich. Stat. Ann. § 28.1070 (Callaghan 1987). |
| Minnesota: | Minn. Stat. § 336.1–101 (1988). |
| | Minn. Stat. Ann. § 104.08 (West 1987). |
| Mississippi: | Miss. Code Ann. § 19–13–57 (1972). |
| Missouri: | Mo. Rev. Stat. § 545.010 (1986). |
| | Mo. Ann. Stat. § 334.540 (Vernon 1989). |
| Montana: | Mont. Code Ann. § 37–5–313 (1989). |
| Nebraska: | Neb. Rev. Stat. § 44–406 (1983). |
| Nevada: | Nev. Rev. Stat. § 463.150 (1987). |
| | Nev. Rev. Stat. Ann. § 679B.180 (Michie 1986). |

Continued

---

**Examples of State Statutory Code Citations**—*Continued*

| | |
|---|---|
| New Hampshire: | N.H. Rev. Stat. Ann. § 318:25 (1984). |
| New Jersey: | N.J. Rev. Stat. § 40:62–127 (1961).<br>N.J. Stat. Ann. § 14A:5–20 (West 1969). |
| New Mexico: | N.M. Stat. Ann. § 31–6–2 (Michie 1978). |
| New York: | N.Y. Penal Law § 155.05 (McKinney 1988).<br>N.Y. Town Law § 265 (Consol. 1978). |
| North Carolina: | N.C. Gen. Stat. § 15A–1321 (1988). |
| North Dakota: | N.D. Cent. Code § 23–12–11 (1989). |
| Ohio: | Ohio Rev. Code Ann. § 2935.03 (Anderson 1987).<br>Ohio Rev. Code Ann. § 2305.131 (Baldwin 1975). |
| Oklahoma: | Okla. Stat. tit. 42, § 130 (1979).<br>Okla Stat. Ann. tit. 21, § 491 (West 1983). |
| Oregon: | Or. Rev. Stat. § 450.870 (1987). |
| Pennsylvania: | 1 Pa. Cons. Stat. § 1991 (1972).<br>18 Pa. Cons. Stat. Ann. § 3301 (1983).<br>Pa. Stat. Ann. tit. 24, § 7–708 (1949). |
| Puerto Rico: | P.R. Laws Ann. tit. 7, § 299 (1985). |
| Rhode Island: | R.I. Gen. Laws § 34–1–2 (1956). |
| South Carolina: | S.C. Code Ann. § 16–23–10 (Law. Co-op 1976). |
| South Dakota: | S.D. Codified Laws Ann. § 15–6–54(c) (1984). |
| Tennessee: | Tenn. Code Ann. § 33–1–204 (1984). |
| Texas: | Tex. Penal Code Ann. § 19.06 (West 1989).<br>Tex. Rev. Civ. Stat. Ann. art. 5336 (West 1962). |
| Utah: | Utah Code Ann. § 41–3–8 (1953). |
| Vermont: | Vt. Stat. Ann. tit. 19, § 708 (1987). |
| Virginia: | Va. Code Ann. § 18.2–265.3 (Michie 1950). |
| Washington: | Wash. Rev. Code § 7.48A.010 (1987).<br>Wash. Rev. Code Ann. § 11.17.110 (West 1967). |
| West Virginia: | W. Va. Code § 23–1–17 (1985). |
| Wisconsin: | Wis. Stat. § 52.28 (1967).<br>Wis. Stat. Ann. § 341.55 (West 1971). |
| Wyoming: | Wyo. Stat. § 26–18–113 (1977). |

---

## VI. *Citing the Documents of Legislative History*

1. The main documents of legislative history (page 596) are: copies of the bills and amendments introduced, copies of the reports and hearings of congressional committees, the *Congressional Record* that contains transcripts of floor debates and material submitted from the floor, etc.

2. Bills and amendments are cited by referring to (a) the number assigned to the bill by the House or Senate, (b) the number and session of Congress during which the bill was introduced, and the year of the bill.

### EXAMPLES

H.R. 3055, 94th Cong., 2d Sess. (1976).
S. 1422, 101st Cong., 1st Sess. (1989).

3. Reports of congressional committees are cited by reference to (a) the number of the report, (b) the number and session of the Congress during which the report was published, (c) the number of the page to which you are referring, and (d) the year in which the report was published.

## EXAMPLES

H.R. Rep. No. 238, 92d Cong., 1st Sess, 4 (1979)
S. Rep. No. 415, 92d Cong., 1st Sess., 6 (1971).

4. Hearings held by congressional committees are cited by reference to (a) the title of the hearing, (b) the number and session of Congress during which the hearing was held, (c) the number of the page in the published transcript to which you are referring, and (d) the year in which the hearing was held.

## EXAMPLE

*Hearings on S. 631 Before the Subcomm. on Labor of the Senate Comm. on Labor and Public Welfare,* 92d Cong., 1st Sess., 315 (1971).

5. The *Congressional Record* is issued on a daily basis and later collected into bound volumes. The *bound* volumes are cited by referring to (a) the number of the volume in which the item appears, (b) the abbreviation "Cong. Rec.," (c) the number of the page on which the item appears, and (d) the year. The *unbound* daily volumes are cited in the same manner except that (a) the page number should be preceded by the letter "H" or "S" in order to indicate whether the item appeared in the House pages or the Senate pages of the volume, (b) the date should include the exact day, month, and year, and (c) the phrase "daily ed." should go before the date.

## EXAMPLES

Bound volumes:
103 Cong. Rec. 2,889 (1975).
Unbound volumes:
122 Cong. Rec. S2,395 (daily ed. Feb. 26, 1976)
132 Cong. Rec. H1,385 (daily ed. Mar. 13, 1990).

## VII.  *Citing Secondary Authority*

1. Treatises and other books are cited to (a) the number of the volume being referred to (if part of a set), (b) the full name of the author, (c) the full title of the book as it appears on the title page, (d) the number of the section and/or page to which you are referring, (e) the edition of the book, if other than the first, and (f) the date of publication. The title of the book should be italicized or underscored. The name of the publisher is almost never given.

## EXAMPLES

6 Melvin Belli, *Modern Trials* § 289 (1963).
George Osborne, *Handbook on the Law of Mortgages* 370 (2d ed. 1970).

2. Law review *articles* are cited by reference to (a) the full name of the author, (b) the title of the article, (c) the number of the volume in which the article appears, (d) the abbreviated name of the law review, (e) the number of the page on which the article begins, and (f) the year of publication. The title of the article should be italicized or underscored.

## EXAMPLE

Robert Catz & Susan Robinson, *Due Process and Creditor's Remedies,* 28 Rutgers L.Rev. 541 (1975).

3. Law review *notes* and *comments* written by law students are cited in the

same manner as the law review articles (see #2) except that the word "Note," "Comment," or "Special Project" is placed after the author's name just before the title.

4. Legal encyclopedias are cited by reference to (a) the number of the volume, (b) the abbreviated name of the encyclopedia, (c) the subject heading to which you are referring—in italics or underscored, (d) the number of the section to which you are referring, and (e) the date of publication of the volume you are citing.

### EXAMPLES

83 C.J.S., *Subscriptions* § 3, (1953)
77 Am. Jur. 2d, *Vendor and Purchaser* § 73 (1975).

6. *Restatements of the Law* published by the American Law Institute are cited by reference to (a) the title of the Restatement, (b) the edition being referred to (if other than the first edition), (c) the number of the section being referred to, and (d) the date of publication.

### EXAMPLE

*Restatement (Second) of Agency* § 37 (1957).

7. Annotations in A.L.R., A.L.R.2d, A.L.R.3d, A.L.R.4th, and A.L.R. Fed. are cited by (a) the full name of the author, if available, (b) the word, "Annotation," (c) the title of the annotation—in italics or underscored, (d) the volume number, (e) the abbreviation of the A.L.R. unit, (f) the page number where the annotation begins, and (g) the date of the volume.

### EXAMPLE

James J. Watson, Annotation, *Attorney's Fees: Cost of Services Provided by Paralegals or the Like as Compensable Element in Award in State Court*, 73 A.L.R.4th 938 (1989).

---

### ■ ASSIGNMENT 11.2

There is one or more things wrong with each of the following citations. Describe the errors and gaps in format. For example, a parallel cite is missing or something is abbreviated incorrectly. You do not have to go to the library to check any of these cites. Simply use the guidelines presented above.

(a) Smith v. Jones, 135 Mass. 37, 67 N.E.2d 316, 320 (1954).
(b) *Paul Matthews v. Edward Foley, Inc.,* 779 F.2d 729 (W.D.N.Y., 1979).
(c) *Jackson v. Jackson,* 219 F.Supp. 1276, 37 N.E.2d 84 (1980).
(d) *Davis v. Tompson,* et al, 336 P.2d 691, 210 N.M. 432 (1976).
(e) *Washington Tire Company v. Jones,* 36 N.J.Super. 222, 351 A.2d 541 (1976).
(f) *State of New Hampshire v. Atkinson,* 117 N.H. 830, 228 A.2d 222 (N.H.Super., 1978).
(g) *Richardson v. U.S.,* 229 U.S. 220 (1975).
(h) American Law Institute, *Restatement of Torts* (2d ed 1976).
(i) U.S.Const. Art. III (1797).
(j) Smith, F., Products Liability (3rd ed. 1985).
(k) 42 USC 288 (1970).
(l) 17 U.S.C.A. 519 (1970).
(m) 40 Fed. Reg. § 277 (1976).

---

■ **ASSIGNMENT 11.3**

**(a)** For your state, check the state code and rules of court of the highest state court in the state to find out whether there are any special citation rules that must be followed in documents submitted to the courts.

**(b)** Find a court opinion written by any state court in your state. (See Figures 11.4 and 11.5.) Pick an opinion that is at least ten pages long.

    (i)  Write down every citation in this opinion (up to a maximum of twenty-five).

    (ii)  State whether these citations conform to the Bluebook citation rules outlined in this section of Chapter 11. Point out any differences.

    (iii)  State whether these citations conform to the special citation rules, if any, you identified in answering question (a) above. Point out any differences.

---

### Note on the Maroon Book

For years, many have criticized *A Uniform System of Citation*—the Bluebook. People find its citation rules too arbitrary and the book itself difficult to use. In 1989, a major challenger to the Bluebook appeared: *The University of Chicago Manual of Legal Citation,* also known as the Maroon Book because of the color of its cover. Whereas the Bluebook tries to include citation rules for almost every situation, the Maroon Book adopts a substantially different point of view. Because "it is neither possible nor desirable to write a particular rule for every sort of citation problem that might arise," the citation rules in the Maroon Book "leave a fair amount of discretion to practitioners, authors, and editors." To a devotee of the Bluebook, such discretion is very distasteful. It is too early to tell what impact the Maroon Book will have on the world of citation. Because the Bluebook is so firmly entrenched, it is unlikely that a competitor will replace it any time soon.

##  Section J. Cite Checking

In a *cite-checking* assignment, you are given a document written by someone else and asked to check the citations provided by the author of the document. The assignment is quite common in law firms, particularly when the document to be checked is an appellate brief. Students on law review in law school also do extensive cite checking on the work of fellow students and outside authors.

While our focus in this section will be the writing of others, the guidelines discussed here are in large measure equally applicable to your own writing.

### Guidelines for Cite Checking

1. The first step is to obtain clear instructions from your supervisor on the scope of the assignment. Should you do a "light check" or a comprehensive one? Should you focus solely on citation form, or should you determine the accuracy of all quotes used by the writer of the document? On citation form, what Rules should you use? The Bluebook?

    . . . . . . . . . . . . . .

The following guidelines assume that you have been asked to undertake a comprehensive check.

2. Make sure that you have a *copy* of the document on which you can make comments. Avoid using the original.

3.  If the pages of the document already have pencil or pen markings made by others (or by the author who made last-minute insertions), use a pencil or pen color that is different from any other markings on the pages. In this way it will be clear to any reader which corrections, notations, or other comments are your own. If you find that you do not have enough room to write in the margins of the pages, use separate sheets of paper. You can increase the size of the margins by photocopying the document on a machine that will reduce the size of what is copied.

4.  If the document is an appellate brief, be sure that you have in front of you any citation rules that are required by the court where the brief will be submitted. If such rules exist, they must be followed. Then determine from your supervisor what citation system should be used for citations that are not governed by court rules, e.g., the Bluebook.

5.  Before you begin, try to find a model. By going through the old case files of the office, you may be able to locate a prior document, such as an old appellate brief, that you can use as a general guide. Ask your supervisor to direct you to such a document. While it may not cover all the difficulties you will encounter in your own document, you will at least have a general guide approved by your supervisor.

6.  Check the citation form of *every* cite in the document. This includes any cites in the body of the text, the footnotes, appendix material, and in the introductory pages of the document, such as the Table of Authorities (page 627) at the beginning of a brief.

7.  For longer documents, you need to develop your own system for ensuring the completeness of your checking. For example, you might want to circle every cite that you have checked and found to be accurate, and place a small box around (or a question mark next to) every cite that is giving you difficulties. You will want to spend more time with the latter, seeking help from colleagues and your supervisor.

8.  When you find errors in the form of the citation, make the corrections in the margin of the pages where they are found.

9.  For some errors, you will not be able to make the corrections without obtaining additional information, such as a missing date or a missing parallel cite. If you can obtain this data by going to the relevant library books, do so. Otherwise make a notation in the margin of what is missing or what still needs correction.

10. Consistency in citation format is extremely important. On page 2 of the document, for example, the author may use one citation form, but on page 10, he or she may use a completely different format for the same kind of legal material. You need to point out this inconsistency, and make the corrections that are called for.

11. Often your document will quote from legal materials such as cases, statutes, etc. Check the accuracy of these quotations. Go to the material being quoted, find the quote, and check it against the document line by line, word by word, and punctuation mark by punctuation mark. Be scrupulous about the accuracy of quotations.

12. Shepardize anything that can be shepardized, such as cases and statutes. Examples of what you need to determine through shepardizing:

    ▪ Whether any of the cited cases have been overruled

- Whether any of the cited statutes have been repealed, amended, or changed in any way

13. Check the accuracy of all "*supra*'s" and "*infra*'s." The word *supra* means "above" or "earlier." It is a reference to something mentioned earlier in the document. For example, on page 23 of the document, there might be a footnote that says, "See *Smith v. Jones*, *supra* p. 9." Go to page 9 and verify that *Smith v. Jones* is discussed or mentioned there. *Infra* means "below" or "later" and refers the reader to something that will come later in the document. In the same manner as you checked the *supra*'s, determine whether the *infra* references are accurate.

### Cite-Checking Software

Two kinds of cite-checking software have been produced by computer companies. First, there is *format* software that tells you whether a particular citation conforms to *A Uniform System of Citation*—the Bluebook. The developers placed the entire Bluebook into the program so that it can recognize discrepancies between the rules of the Bluebook and citations that are typed into the computer. In addition to pointing out citation errors, the program will refer you to specific rules in the Bluebook that have been violated. Two examples of such software are Cite Checker from Legal Software, Inc., and CiteRite II from Jurisoft, Inc. The second kind of cite-checking software provides *validation* data on citations. You will be told, for example, whether a particular court opinion has been overruled and whether a particular statute has been repealed. Two examples of such software are WESTcheck, used in conjunction with WESTLAW, and CheckCite, used in conjunction with LEXIS. Unlike the format cite-checking software, the validation programs are online and hence are used through a modem.

## Section K. Components of a Law Book

There are similarities in the structure of many law books. To be sure, some books, such as *Shepard's Citations*, are totally unique. In the main, however, there is a pattern to the texts. The following is a list of components that are contained in many:

*1. Outside Cover.*    On the outside cover you will find the title of the book, the author(s) or editor(s), the name of the publisher (usually at the bottom), the edition of the book (if more than one edition has been printed), and the volume number (if the book is part of a series of books). After glancing at the outside cover, the researcher should ask the following questions:

- Is it a book *containing* law (written primarily by a court, a legislature, or an administrative agency), or is it a book *about* the law (written by a scholar who is commenting on the law)? Is the book a combination of both?

- Is this book the most current available? Look at the books on the shelf in the area where you found the book that you are examining. Is there a replacement volume for your book? Is there a later edition of the book? Check your book in the card catalog to see if other editions are mentioned.

*2. Publisher's Page.*    The first few pages of the book often include a page or pages about the publisher. The page may list other law books published by the same company.

*3. Title Page.*   The title page repeats most of the information contained on the outside cover: title, author, editor, publisher. It also contains the date of publication.

*4. Copyright Page.*   The copyright page (often immediately behind the title page) has a copyright mark © plus a date or series of dates. The most recent date listed indicates the timeliness of the material in the volume. Given the great flux in the law, it is very important to determine how old the text is. If the book has a pocket part (see item 14 below), it has been updated to the date on the pocket part.

COPYRIGHT © 1974, 1979, 1985, 1989 WEST PUBLISHING CO.

COPYRIGHT © 1992
By
WEST PUBLISHING CO.

The dates on this copyright page indicate that the material in the book is current up to 1992, the latest copyright date.

*5. Foreword, Preface, or Explanation.*   Under such headings, the reader may find some basic information about the book, particularly material on how the book was prepared and guidance on how to use it.

*6. Summary Table of Contents.*   On one or two pages, the reader may find the main topics treated in the book.

*7. Detailed Table of Contents.*   When provided, the detailed table can be very extensive. The major headings of the summary table of contents are repeated, and detailed subheadings and sub-subheadings are listed. This table can be used as an additional index to the book.

*8. Table of Cases.*   The table of cases lists, alphabetically, every case that is printed or referred to in the text, with the page(s) where the case is found or discussed. This table is sometimes printed at the end of the book.

*9. Table of Statutes.*   The table of statutes gives the page numbers where every statute is interpreted or referred to in the text. This table is sometimes printed at the end of the book.

*10. List of Abbreviations.*   The abbreviation list, if provided, is critical. A reader who is unfamiliar with law books should check the list immediately. It may be the only place in the book that spells out the abbreviations used in the body of the text. In *Shepard's Citations,* for example, abbreviations are found in the first few pages of bound volumes and in most of the pamphlets covering case citations. (See example at the top of page 543.)

*11. Statutory History Table.*   In statutory codes, there may be a table that lists every statute cited in the book and indicates whether it has been repealed or whether there is a new section number and title for the statute. The legislature may have changed the entire name of the statutory chapter (from Prison Law to Correction Law, for instance) and renumbered all the sections. Without this table, the researcher can become lost. In the example below, note that former Prison Law sections 10–20 are now found in Correction Law sections 600–610. You may find a citation to a Prison Law section in a book that was published

| History of Case | | |
|---|---|---|
| a | (affirmed) | Same case affirmed on appeal. |
| cc | (connected case) | Different case from case cited but arising out of same subject matter or intimately connected therewith. |
| D | (dismissed) | Appeal from same case dismissed. |
| m | (modified) | Same case modified on appeal. |
| r | (reversed) | Same case reversed on appeal. |
| s | (same case) | Same case as case cited. |
| S | (superseded) | Substitution for former opinion. |
| v | (vacated) | Same case vacated. |
| US cert den | | Certiorari denied by U. S. Supreme Court. |
| US cert dis | | Certiorari dismissed by U. S. Supreme Court. |
| US reh den | | Rehearing denied by U. S. Supreme Court. |
| US reh dis | | Rehearing dismissed by U. S. Supreme Court. |

| Treatment of Case | | |
|---|---|---|
| c | (criticised) | Soundness of decision or reasoning in cited case criticised for reasons given. |
| d | (distinguished) | Case at bar different either in law or fact from case cited for reasons given. |
| e | (explained) | Statement of import of decisions in cited case. Not merely a restatement of the facts. |
| f | (followed) | Cited as controlling. |
| h | (harmonized) | Apparent inconsistency explained and shown not to exist. |
| j | (dissenting opinion) | Citation in dissenting opinion. |
| L | (limited) | Refusal to extend decision of cited case beyond precise issues involved. |
| o | (overruled) | Ruling in cited case expressly overruled. |
| p | (parallel) | Citing case substantially alike or on all fours with cited case in its law or facts. |
| q | (questioned) | Soundness of decision or reasoning in cited case questioned. |

Example of abbreviations used by Shepard's

## TABLE OF PRISON LAW SECTIONS

Showing the distribution of those sections of the former Prison Law in effect prior to the general amendment by L.1929, c. 243, which are contained wholly or in part in the Correction Law, or which have been omitted or repealed.

| Prison Law Section | Correction Law Section |
|---|---|
| 1 | 1 |
| 10–20 | 600–610 |
| 21 | Repealed |
| 22 L.1919, c. 12 | 611 |
| 22 L.1920, c. 933 | 612 |
| 23–32 | 613–622 |
| 40–50 | 40–50 |

Example of a statutory history table

before the state changed to Correction Law sections. When you go to look up the Prison Law section, you will find nothing unless you have a way to translate the section into a Correction Law section. The statutory history table may be one way to do it.

*12. Body of the Text.* The fundamental characteristic of the body of many legal texts is that it is arranged according to units such as parts, subparts, divisions, subdivisions, chapters, subchapters, sections, subsections, etc. Often each unit covers a similar subject matter, and is numbered or lettered in sequence. You should thumb through the entire book to obtain a feel for the numbering and classification system used by the author or editor.

*13. Footnotes.* Footnotes are very important in law books; researchers place great emphasis on them. They often give extensive citations to cases and other cross-references, and hence can be an excellent lead to additional law.

*14. Pocket Parts.* A unique and indispensable feature of many law books is the pocket part. It is a small-booklet addition to the text, placed at the very end of the text in a specially devised "pocket" built into the inside of the rear cover. (See page 508.) The pocket part is published after the book is printed and is designed to bring the book up-to-date with the latest developments in the field covered by the book. Of course, a pocket part can also grow out of date. Normally it is replaced once a year. On the front cover of the pocket-part booklet, there is a date telling you what period is covered. The title page (see above) may say that the last edition of the book was published in 1990, but the front page of the pocket part may say "for use during 1992–1993."

Normally the organization of the pocket part exactly parallels the organization of the main text. To find out, for example, if there has been anything new in the area covered by chapter 7, part 2, section 714 of the main text, you go to chapter 7, part 2, section 714 of the pocket part. If nothing is found there, then nothing new has happened. If changes or additions have occurred, they will be found there.

Pocket parts are cumulative in that, whenever a pocket part is replaced by another pocket part, everything in the early pocket part is consolidated into the most recent one. The earlier pocket part is thrown away.

*15. Appendix.*   The text may include one or more appendixes. Normally, they include tables, charts, or the entire text of statutes or regulations, portions of which are discussed in the body of the book.

*16. Glossary.*   The book may include a glossary, which is a dictionary that defines a selected number of words used in the body of the book.

*17. Bibliography.*   A brief or extended bibliography of the field covered by the book may be included at the end of each chapter or at the end of the book.

*18. Index.*   The index is a critical part of the book. Unfortunately, some books either have no index or do a sloppy job of indexing. (Some sets of administrative regulations and loose-leaf services fall into this category.) The index is arranged alphabetically and should refer the reader to the page number(s) or to the section number(s) where the item is treated in the body of the text. The index is found at the end of the book. If there are many volumes in the set, you may find more than one index. For example, there may be a general index for the entire set and a series of smaller indexes covering individual volumes.

## ■ Section L. The CARTWHEEL: A Technique of Using Indexes and Tables of Contents

We now come to one of the most important skills in legal research: the creative use of indexes and tables of contents in law books. If you have mastered this skill, 70 percent of the research battle is won. The CARTWHEEL is a technique designed to assist you in acquiring the skill. (See Figure 11.8.)

The objective of the CARTWHEEL can be simply stated: to develop the habit of phrasing every word involved in the client's problem *fifteen to twenty different ways!* When you go to the index or table of contents of a law book, you naturally begin looking up the words and phrases that you think should lead you to the relevant material in the book. If you do not find anything relevant to your problem, two conclusions are possible:

- There is nothing relevant in the law book.
- You looked up the wrong words in the index and table of contents.

While the first conclusion is sometimes accurate, nine times out of ten, the second conclusion is the reason you fail to find material in a law book that is relevant to the client's problem. The solution is to be able to phrase a word in

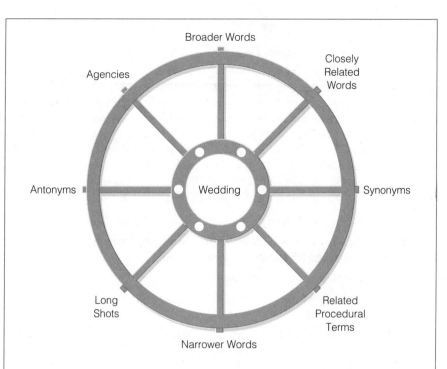

**FIGURE 11.8**

The CARTWHEEL:
Using the Index
and Table of
Contents of
Law Books

1. Identify all the *major words* (such as *wedding*) from the facts of the client's problem. (Most of these facts can be obtained from the intake memorandum (see page 366) written following the initial interview with the client.) Place each word or small set of words in the center of the CARTWHEEL.

2. In the index and table of contents, look up all of these major words.

3. Identify the *broader* categories of the major words.

4. In the index and table of contents, look up all of these broader categories.

5. Identify the *narrower* categories of the major words.

6. In the index and table of contents, look up all of these narrower categories.

7. Identify all *synonyms* of the major words.

8. In the index and table of contents, look up all of these synonyms.

9. Identify all of the *antonyms* of the major words.

10. In the index and table of contents, look up all of these antonyms.

11. Identify all words that are *closely related* to the major words.

12. In the index and table of contents, look up all of these closely related words.

13. Identify all *procedural* terms related to the major words.

14. In the index and table of contents, look up all of these procedural terms.

15. Identify all *agencies,* if any, with some connection to the major words.

16. In the index and table of contents, look up all of these agencies.

17. Identify all *long shots.*

18. In the index and table of contents, look up all of these long shots.

**Note:** The above categories are not mutually exclusive.

as many different ways and in as many different contexts as possible. Hence, the CARTWHEEL.

Suppose that the problem of the client involved, among other things, a wedding. The first step would be to look up the word *wedding* in the index and table of contents of any law book. Assuming that you are not successful with this word (either because the word is not in the index and table or because the page or section references do not lead you to relevant material in the body of the book), the next step is to think of as many different phrasings and contexts of the word *wedding* as possible. This is where the eighteen steps of the CARTWHEEL can be useful.

If you applied the steps of the CARTWHEEL to the word *wedding,* here are some of the words and phrases that you would check:

- *Broader words:* celebration, ceremony, rite, ritual, formality, festivity, etc.
- *Narrower words:* civil wedding, church wedding, golden wedding, proxy wedding, sham wedding, shotgun wedding, etc.
- *Synonyms:* marriage ceremony, nuptial, etc.
- *Antonyms:* alienation, annulment, divorce, separation, legal separation, judicial separation, etc.
- *Closely related words:* remarriage, antenuptial, prenuptial, matrimony, marital, conjugal, domestic, husband, wife, bride, license, anniversary, custom, children, blood test, premarital, spouse, relationship, family, home, consummation, cohabitation, sexual relations, betrothal, minister, wedlock, consent, oath, contract, religion, community property, name change, domicile, residence, etc.
- *Procedural terms:* action, suit, statute of limitations, complaint, discovery, defense, petition, jurisdiction, court, superior court, county court, etc.
- *Agencies:* Bureau of Vital Statistics, County Clerk, Department of Social Services, License Bureau, Secretary of State, Justice of the Peace, etc.
- *Long shots:* dowry, common law, single, blood relationship, fraud, illegitimate, alimony, bigamy, pregnancy, gifts, chastity, impotence, incest, virginity, support, custody, paternity, etc.

As indicated in Figure 11.8, there may be some overlapping of categories; they are not mutually exclusive. Also, it is not significant whether you place a word in one category or another so long as the word comes to your mind as you comb through the index and table of contents. The CARTWHEEL is, in effect, a *word association game* that should become second nature to you with practice. Perhaps some of the word selections seem a bit far-fetched. You will not

---

■ **ASSIGNMENT 11.4**

CARTWHEEL the following words or phrases:

1. Paralegal
2. Woman
3. Rat bite
4. Rear-end collision
5. Monopoly

---

know for sure, however, whether a word is fruitful until you try it. Be imaginative, and take some risks.

Indexes and tables of contents are often organized into headings, subheadings, sub-subheadings and perhaps even sub-sub-subheadings. In the following excerpt from an index, "Burden of proof" is a sub-subheading of "Accidents" and a subheading of "Unavoidable accident or casualty." The latter is a subheading of "Accidents," which is the main heading of the index entry. If you were looking for law on burden of proof, you might be out of luck unless you *first* thought of looking up "accidents" and "unavoidable accident."

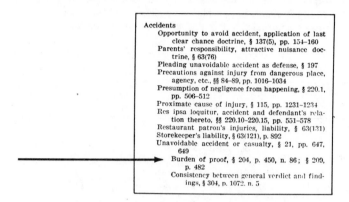

Suppose that you identify the following words to check in an index:

|         |          |
|---------|----------|
| minor   | sale     |
| explosion | warranty |
| car     | damage   |

The index may have no separate heading for "minor," but "minor" may be a subheading under "sale." If so, you would not find "minor" unless you first thought of checking "sale." Under each of the above six words, you should be alert to the possibility that the other five words may be subheadings for that word. Hence the process of pursuing these six words in an index (or table of contents) would be as follows: (The word in bold letters is checked first and then the five words *under it* are checked to see if any of them are subheadings.)

| **Car**   | **Damage**  |
|-----------|-------------|
| damage    | car         |
| explosion | explosion   |
| minor     | minor       |
| sale      | sale        |
| warranty  | warranty    |

| **Explosion** | **Minor**   |
|---------------|-------------|
| car           | car         |
| damage        | damage      |
| minor         | explosion   |
| sale          | sale        |
| warranty      | warranty    |

| **Sale**   | **Warranty** |
|------------|--------------|
| car        | car          |
| damage     | damage       |
| explosion  | explosion    |
| minor      | minor        |
| warranty   | sale         |

## ■ ASSIGNMENT 11.5

One way to gain an appreciation for the use of indexes is to write one of your own. Be sure to use headings, subheadings, sub-subheadings, etc. in each index you write.

**(a)** Write a comprehensive index of your present job or the last job that you had.

**(b)** Pick one area of the law that you have covered in class or read about. Write your own comprehensive index on what you have learned.

**(c)** Write a comprehensive index of the following statute:

> **§ 132. Amount of force.** The use of force against another for the purpose of effecting the arrest or recapture of the other, or of maintaining custody of him, is not privileged if the means employed are in excess of those which are reasonably believed to be necessary.

**FIGURE 11.9**

Excerpt from Index

---

### EVIDENCE

**Dealers,**
  Securities, judicial notice, § 29, p. 890
  **Value,**
    Household goods, opinion evidence, § 546(121), p. 479, n. 95
    Property, § 546(115), p. 430
    Opinion evidence, § 546(122), p. 483
**Death,**
  Autopsy, generally, ante
  Best evidence rule, § 803, p. 136
  Book entries,
    Entrant, proof of handwriting, § 693, p. 942
    Supplemental testimony respecting entries by clerks and third persons, § 693, p. 939
    Supporting entries by deceased persons by oath of personal representative, § 684, p. 910
  Clerk or employee making book entries, § 692
  Copy of record, certification by state registrar, § 664, p. 865, n. 69
  Declaration against interest, death of declarant, § 218, p. 604
  Declarations, § 227, p. 624
    Death of declarant as essential to admission, § 230
  Dying declarations, generally, post
  Experiments, object or purpose, § 588(1)
  Former evidence, death of witness, § 392
  General reputation, § 1048
  Hearsay, § 227, p. 624
    Death certificates, § 194, pp. 561, 562; § 766, p. 66
    Death of declarant, § 205
    Impossibility of obtaining other evidence, § 204
  Letters, § 703, p. 976
  Maps and diagrams of scenes of occurrence, § 730(1), p. 1045
  Memorandum, § 696, p. 955
  Mortality tables, generally, post
  Newspaper announcement, § 227, p. 625
  Opinion evidence,
    Animals, § 546(68)
    Cause and effect, § 546(11), p. 129
    Effect on human body, § 546(97), p. 374
    Fixing time, § 546(91), n. 16
  Owners, admissions, § 327
    Personal property, § 334
  Parol or extrinsic evidence, rule excluding, action to recover for, § 861, p. 230
  Photographs, personal appearance or identity, § 710
  Presumptions, ancient original public records, official making, § 746, p. 37
  Prima facie evidence, record of, § 644
  Private documents, recitals, § 677
  Public records and documents, registers of, § 623
  Reputation, § 227, p. 626
  Res gestae, statements, § 410, p. 991
  Rumor, § 227, p. 625
  Self-serving declarations, effect of death of declarant, § 216, p. 591
  Services, value, opinion evidence in death action, § 546(124), p. 489, n. 96
  Statements, weight of evidence, § 266
  Value of service rendered by claimant, opinion evidence, § 546(125), p. 493, n. 41

**Death—Continued**
  Witness, unsworn statements, circumstances tending to disparage testimony, § 268
  Wrongful death,
    Admissions, husband and wife, § 363
    Admissions of decedent, privity, § 322, n. 96.5
    Declarations against interest, § 218, p. 607
    Loss of life, value, opinion evidence, § 546 (121), p. 473, n. 54
    Municipal claim, evidence of registry, § 680, n. 21
    Value of decedent's services, opinion evidence, § 546(124), p. 489, n. 96
**Death certificates,**
  Certified copies, § 651, p. 851
    Officer as making, § 664, p. 865, n. 69
    Prima facie evidence, § 773
  Church register, competency, § 727
  Conclusiveness, § 766, p. 64
  Expert testimony, supporting opinion, § 570
  Foreign countries, authenticated copies, § 675, p. 885
  Hearsay, § 194, pp. 561, 562; § 766, p. 66
  Kinship, § 696, p. 949, n. 2
  Official document, § 638, pp. 823, 824
  Prima facie case or evidence, post
**Debate,** judicial notice, United States congress, § 43, p. 995
**Debs,** judicial notice, § 67, p. 56, n. 17
**Debtor and creditor,** admissions, § 336
**Debts.** Indebtedness, generally, post
**Decay,**
  Judicial notice, vegetable matter, § 88
  Opinion evidence, buildings, § 546(73), p. 290
**Decedents' estates,**
  Judicial admissions, claim statements, § 310
  Judicial records, inferences from, § 765
  Official documents, reports and inventories of representatives, § 638, p. 818
  Value, opinion evidence, § 546(121), p. 478
**Deceit.** Fraud, generally, post
**Decisions,** judicial notice, sister states, § 18, p. 861
**Declaration against interest,** §§ 217–224, pp. 600–615
  Absence of declared from jurisdiction, § 218, p. 604
  Account, § 224
  Admissions, distinguished, § 217, p. 603
  Adverse character, § 222
  Affirmative proof as being best evidence obtainable, § 218, p. 604
  Apparent interest, § 219, p. 608
  Assured, § 219, p. 611
  Best evidence obtainable, necessity of, § 218, p. 604
  Boundaries, § 219, p. 611
  Coexisting, self-serving interest, § 221
  Contract, § 224
  Criminal prosecution, statement subjecting declarant to, § 219, p. 608
  Death action, § 218, p. 607
  Death of declarant, § 218, p. 605
  Dedication to public use, § 219, p. 611
  Deeds, § 224
  Disparagement of title § 219, p. 611
  Distinctions, § 217, p. 603
  Enrollment of vessel § 224

■ **ASSIGNMENT 11.6**

Examine the index in Figure 11.9 from a legal encyclopedia. It is an excerpt from the heading of "Evidence." "Death" is the subheading of "Evidence." What sub-subheadings or sub-sub-headings of "Evidence" would you check to try to find material on the following?

**(a)** Introducing a death certificate into evidence.

**(b)** The weight that a court will give to the personal conclusions of a witness.

**(c)** Introducing the last words of a decedent into evidence.

**(d)** A statement by the person who died disclaiming ownership of land around which he or she had placed a fence.

## ■ Section M. The First Level of Legal Research: Background

There are three interrelated levels of researching a problem:

*Background Research*   provides you with a general understanding of the area of law involved in your research problem.

*Specific Fact Research*   provides you with primary and secondary authority that covers the specific facts of your research problem.

*Validation Research*   provides you with the most up-to-date information on the current validity of all the primary authority you intend to use in your research memorandum on the problem.

．．．．．．．．．．．．．．

At times all three levels of research go on simultaneously. If you are new to legal research, however, it is recommended that you approach your research problem in the three stages just listed. Our concern in this section is the first level: background research. See Figure 11.10. The other two levels are covered throughout the remainder of the chapter.

Our assumption here is that you are researching a topic that is totally new to you. Spend an hour or two (depending on the complexity of the area) doing some reading in law books that will provide you with an overview—a general understanding of the area. This will help you identify the major terminology, the major agencies involved, if any, and some of the major issues. Of course, while doing this background research, you will probably also come up with leads that will be helpful in the second and third levels of research.

All this background research will be in the secondary sources—legal encyclopedias, treatises, legal periodical literature, legal dictionaries, etc. Caution must be exercised in studying these materials. As we have seen, they must never be used as a substitute for mandatory primary authority, which is the objective of your research. In your research memorandum, try to avoid quoting from a legal dictionary or a legal encyclopedia. Many courts do not consider them very persuasive. Treatises and periodical literature are considered somewhat more persuasive (depending on the author), but again, even these secondary sources should be quoted infrequently once you have laid the proper foundation for their use. (See Figure 11.7 on when you can use secondary authority.) As we noted, judges want to know what the primary authority is—opinions, statutes, constitutional provisions, regulations, etc. Use the secondary material for the

**FIGURE 11.10**

Techniques for
Doing Background
Research on
a Topic

---

1. **LEGAL DICTIONARY**

   Have access to a legal dictionary throughout your research. For example:

   > *Black's Law Dictionary*
   > *Ballentine's Law Dictionary*
   > *Oran's Law Dictionary*
   > Statsky's *Legal Thesaurus/Dictionary*

   Look up the meaning of all important terms that you come across in your research. These dictionaries are starting points only. Eventually you want to find primary authority that defines these terms.

---

2. **LEGAL ENCYCLOPEDIAS**

   Find discussions of your topic in the major national legal encyclopedias:

   > *American Jurisprudence 2d*
   > *Corpus Juris Secundum*

   Also check encyclopedias, if any, that cover only your state. Use the CARTWHEEL to help you use their indexes and tables of contents.

---

3. **TREATISES**

   Find discussions of your topic in legal treatises. Go to your card catalog. Use the CARTWHEEL to help you locate cards on treatises such as hornbooks, handbooks, formbooks, practice manuals, scholarly studies, etc. Many of these books will have KF call numbers. Use the CARTWHEEL to help you use the indexes and tables of contents of these books.

---

4. **ANNOTATIONS**

   Find discussions of your topic in the annotations of A.L.R., A.L.R.2d, A.L.R.3d, A.L.R.4th, and A.L.R. Fed. Use the Quick Index and the *ALR Index*. The CARTWHEEL will help you use these indexes.

---

5. **LEGAL PERIODICAL LITERATURE**

   Find discussions of your topic in legal periodical literature. The three main indexes to such literature are:

   > *Index to Legal Periodicals*
   > *Current Law Index*
   > *Legal Resource Index*

   Use the CARTWHEEL to help you use these indexes to locate legal periodical literature on your topic. (Later we will cover computer index systems.)

---

6. **AGENCY REPORTS/BROCHURES**

   If your research involves an administrative agency, call or write the agency. Find out what brochures, reports, or newsletters the agency has available to the public. Such literature often provides useful background information.

---

7. **COMMITTEE REPORTS**

   Before statutes are passed, committees of the legislature often write reports that comment on and summarize the legislation. In addition to being good sources of legislative history on the statute, the reports are excellent background reading. If practical, contact both houses of the legislature to find out which committees acted on the statute. If the statute is fairly recent, they may be able to send you copies of the committee reports or tell you where to obtain them. If you live near the library of the legislature, you may be able to find committee reports there. The committee reports of many federal statutes are printed in *U.S. Code Congressional and Administrative News*.

Continued

FIGURE 11.10
Techniques for
Doing Background
Research on
a Topic
—Continued

**8. REPORTS/STUDIES OF SPECIAL INTEREST GROUPS**

There are special interest groups for almost every area of the law, e.g., unions, bar associations, environmental associations, tax associations, insurance and other business associations. They often have position papers and studies that they could send you. Although one-sided, such literature should not be ignored.

**9. MARTINDALE-HUBBELL LAW DIRECTORY**

The Digest volume of Martindale-Hubbell provides concise summaries of the law of the fifty states and many foreign countries. (See page 506.)

limited purposes of (1) background reading and (2) providing leads to primary authority—particularly through the footnotes in the secondary sources. Of course, you will not have time to use all of the nine techniques on background research presented in Figure 11.10. Usually one or two of the techniques is sufficient for the limited purpose of providing an overview and getting you started.

## Section N. Checklists for Using the Ten Major Search Resources

We have said that the main objective of legal research is to locate mandatory primary authority. There are three levels of government—federal, state, and local. An overview of their primary authority is as follows:

| KINDS OF PRIMARY AUTHORITY | | |
| --- | --- | --- |
| **FEDERAL LEVEL OF GOVERNMENT** | **STATE LEVEL OF GOVERNMENT** | **LOCAL LEVEL OF GOVERNMENT (CITY, COUNTY, ETC.)** |
| U.S. Constitution | State constitution | Charter |
| Statutes of Congress | State statutes | Local ordinances |
| Federal court opinions | State court opinions | Local court opinions |
| Federal agency regulations | State agency regulations | Local agency regulations |
| Federal administrative decisions | State administrative decisions | Local administrative decisions |
| Federal rules of court | State rules of court | Local rules of court |
| Executive orders of the president | Executive orders of the governor | Executive orders of the mayor |
| Opinions of the U.S. attorney general | Opinions of the state attorney general | Opinions of the corporation counsel |
| Treaties | | |

Later in this chapter, we examine methods of finding most of these kinds of primary authority. Throughout our examination, you will be referred back to the ten checklists for the major finding tools presented in this section. These ten findings tools (or search resources) are often useful for locating more than one kind of primary authority. Hence they are presented together here.

Many of the ten search resources are also helpful in doing background research in the secondary sources. Indeed, some of the search resources *are* secondary sources themselves. Finally, some of the search resources are helpful in doing the third level of research—validation research, particularly Shepard's.

In short, the following ten search resources, or finding tools, are the foundation of legal research itself:

1. Card catalog
2. Digests
3. Annotations
4. Shepard's
5. Loose-leaf services
6. Indexes to legal periodical literature
7. Legal encyclopedias
8. Treatises
9. Phone and mail
10. Computers

The tenth resource—computers—will be introduced here, but covered in greater depth in Chapter 13.

## 1. Card Catalog

A well-organized card catalog is one of the researcher's best friends. If the law library has not switched over to a completely computerized catalog, you need to learn some of the basics of the manual card catalog. Most law libraries use the Library of Congress (LC) classification system. Under this system, many law books have KF call numbers. The following is an example of a card from a card catalog:

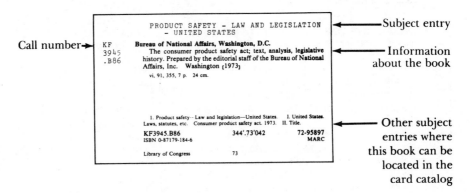

Checklist #1

| Checklist for Using the Card Catalog |
|---|
| **1.** Find out if your law library has more than one card catalog. Is there a catalog with entries by subject matter and another with entries by author? Are there different catalogs for different topics or areas of the law? |
| **2.** Find out if the library has any descriptive literature on how to use the catalog. |
| **3.** Pull out a tray from the catalog at random. Thumb through the KF cards in this tray. Put a paper clip on an example of each kind of card that appears to be organized differently or that contains different kinds of information. Pick any two of these cards. Try to figure out why the cards are different. If you can't, ask a staff member of the library to briefly explain the differences. |

Continued

Checklist #1—*Continued*

| **Checklist for Using the Card Catalog—*Continued*** |
|---|
| **4.** Be sure you understand all the information on the cards that tells you where the books are located in the library. Some books may be on reserve, in special rooms, or in other buildings. |
| **5.** Select several KF cards at random, particularly on books housed in different locations. Try to find these books. Ask for help if you cannot locate them. |
| **6.** Now try the reverse process. Select at random three different kinds of books from the library shelves (not the same books you looked at in #5 above). Take these books to the card catalog and try to find their card. Your goal is to become as proficient in the structure and use of the card catalog as possible. Steps #3–6 are designed to help you achieve this goal before you experience the pressure of actual research. |
| **7.** Ask a staff member what kinds of research material, if any, are *not* cataloged, such as microfilm, ultrafiche, appellate briefs, or old exams. |
| **8.** Ask a staff member what special lists of law books, if any, are in the library (lists of legal periodicals, lists of reserve books, etc.). |
| **9.** Ask a staff member to explain the difference between the library's card catalog and Kardex. (The latter is the place where many libraries keep records of current serial publications that come into the library every day.) If the library does not use Kardex, ask what it uses instead. |
| **10.** When using any card catalog, the CARTWHEEL will help you think of words and phrases to check. |
| **11.** Never antagonize the employees of a law library! You are going to need all the help you can get! But do not abuse their availability. For example do not ask any questions until you first try to find the answer on your own. |

■ **ASSIGNMENT 11.7**

Assignment 11.1 asked you to organize a system of three-by-five-inch index cards for each of the legal research words and phrases listed there. For each card that contains the name of a law book on it, find out where the book or set of books is located in a law library near you. Obtain this information from the card catalog or other library list, and enter it on the index cards.

## 2. Digests

We have already examined the major digests and the names of reporters whose opinions are summarized (in small paragraphs) in the digests. You should review this material now. See Figure 11.5.

Our focus here is on the digests of West, which are organized by the key topic and number system. Lawyers Co-operative Publishing Company also has digests for Supreme Court opinions and for its annotations in A.L.R., A.L.R.2d, etc., which are organized differently.

The beauty of the West digests is that once you know how to use one of the digests, you know how to use them all. A good way to begin this understanding is to follow the journey of a court opinion from the time it arrives at West. (See Figure 11.11.)

Keep the following points in mind about Figure 11.11:

■ Most state court opinions printed in the reporters of West go through the same process or journey as outlined in the *first* column of Figure 11.11. Of

**FIGURE 11.11**

Journey of a
Court Opinion

| JOURNEY OF A STATE COURT OPINION, e.g., CALIFORNIA | JOURNEY OF A FEDERAL COURT OPINION, e.g., A U.S. COURT OF APPEALS |
|---|---|
| 1. The California Supreme Court sends a copy of its opinion to West Publishing Company in Minnesota. | 1. The U.S. Court of Appeals sends a copy of its opinion to West Publishing Company in Minnesota. |
| 2. West editors write brief paragraph headnotes for the opinion. Each headnote summarizes a portion of the opinion. | 2. West editors write brief paragraph headnotes for the opinion. Each headnote summarizes a portion of the opinion. |
| 3. The headnotes go at the beginning of the full text of the opinion in the reporter—here, the Pacific Reporter 2d (P.2d). The editors assign each of these headnotes a key topic and number, e.g., Criminal Law    1064(5). | 3. The headnotes go at the beginning of the full text of the opinion in the reporter—here, the Federal Reporter 2d (F.2d). The editors assign each of these headnotes a key topic and number, e.g., Appeal and Error    1216. |
| 4. In addition to being printed at the beginning of the opinion in P.2d, the headnotes will *also* be printed at the beginning of the advance sheet for P.2d that contains the opinion, and in the back of the bound P.2d volume that contains the opinion. | 4. In addition to being printed at the beginning of the opinion in F.2d, the headnotes will *also* be printed at the beginning of the advance sheet for F.2d that contains the opinion, and in the back of the bound F.2d volume that contains the opinion. |
| 5. This headnote is *also* printed in the appropriate digests of West. The above example will go in the "C" volume of these digests where "Criminal Law" is covered. The headnote will be placed under key number 1064(5) of Criminal Law along with summaries of other opinions on the same or similar area of law. In what digests will such headnotes from a recent California opinion be printed? The list follows: | 5. This headnote is *also* printed in the appropriate digests of West. The above example will go in the "A" volume of these digests where "Appeal and Error" is covered. The headnote will be placed under key number 1216 of Appeal and Error along with summaries of other opinions on the same or similar area of law. In what digests will such headnotes from a recent F.2d opinion be printed? The list follows: |
| ■ All headnotes of P.2d cases go into the *American Digest System*. First, the headnote goes into a General Digest volume. After a ten-year period (in two five-year intervals), all the General Digests are thrown away, with the material in them printed in the next Decennial Digest. | ■ All headnotes of F.2d cases go into the *American Digest System*. First, the headnote goes into a General Digest volume. After a ten-year period (in two five-year intervals), all the General Digests are thrown away with the material in them printed in the next Decennial Digest. |
| ■ All headnotes of P.2d cases are *also* printed in its regional digest—the Pacific Digest. | ■ All headnotes of F.2d cases are *also* printed in the most current federal digest—the Federal Practice Digest 4th. |
| ■ All headnotes of California cases in P.2d are *also* printed in the individual state digest—the California Digest. | ■ If our F.2d case dealt with a particular state, the headnotes of the F.2d case will *also* be printed in the individual state digest of that state. |
| 6. Hence, the headnote from the California opinion will be printed: | 6. Hence, the headnote from the opinion of the U.S. Court of Appeals will be printed: |
| ■ at the beginning of the opinion in P.2d. | |

Continued

<table>
<tr>
<td>

- at the beginning of the P.2d advance sheet containing the opinion.

- at the end of the bound P.2d volume containing the opinion.

- in the *American Digest System* (first the General Digest and then the Decennial Digest).

- in the regional digest—*Pacific Digest.*

- in the individual state digest—*California Digest.*

   In all the above digests, the headnote will be printed in the "C" volume for Criminal Law under number 1064(5) along with headnotes from other opinions on the same or similar area of the law.

</td>
<td>

- at the beginning of the opinion in F.2d.

- at the beginning of the F.2d advance sheet containing the opinion.

- at the end of the bound F.2d volume containing the opinion.

- in the *American Digest System* (first in the General Digest and then in the Decennial Digest).

- in the *Federal Practice Digest* 4th.

- in a state digest if the F.2d case dealt with a particular state.

   In all the above digests, the headnote will be printed in the "A" volume for Appeal and Error under number 1216 along with headnotes from other opinions on the same or similar area of the law.

</td>
</tr>
</table>

**FIGURE 11.11**

Journey of a Court Opinion —*Continued*

course, different states have their own reporters and digests (see Figure 11.5), but the process is the same.

- All U.S. District Court opinions printed in *Federal Supplement* (F. Supp.) go through the same process or journey as outlined in the *second* column of Figure 11.11.

- All U.S. Supreme Court opinions printed in *Supreme Court Reporter* (S. Ct.) go through the same process or journey as outlined in the *second* column of Figure 11.11. (For additional digests that summarize all U.S. Supreme Court opinions, see Figure 11.5.)

Assume that you are doing research on the right of a citizen to speak in a public park. You find that the digests of West cover this subject under the following key topic and number:

### Constitutional Law ☞ 211

West publishes about sixty digests—state, federal, and national. You can go to the "C" volume of *any* of these sixty digests, turn to "Constitutional Law" and find number "211" under it. Do you want only Idaho case law? If so, go to Constitutional Law ☞ 211 in the *Idaho Digest.* Do you want only case law from the states in the western United States? If so, go to Constitutional Law ☞ 211 in the *Pacific Digest.* Do you want only current federal case law? If so, go to Constitutional Law ☞ 211 in the *Federal Practice Digest 4th.* Do you want only U.S. Supreme Court cases? If so, go to Constitutional Law ☞ 211 in the *U.S. Supreme Court Digest* (West).

Do you want the case law of *every* court in the country? If so, trace Constitutional Law ☞ 211 through the three units of the *American Digest System:*

- Go to Constitutional Law ☞ 211 in every General Digest volume.

- Go to Constitutional Law ☞ 211 in every Decennial Digest.

- Go to the equivalent number for Constitutional Law ☞ 211 in the Century Digest.

To *trace a key topic and number* through the *American Digest System* means to find out what case law, if any, is summarized under that key topic and number in every unit of the American Digest System. (For the Century Digest, you will need an equivalent number, since there are no key topics and numbers in the Century Digest. See step 8 in the following checklist.)

Checklist #2

---

**Checklist for Using the Digests of West**

1. Locate the right digests for your research problem. This is determined by identifying the kind of case law you want to find. State? Federal? Both? Review pages 498 ff. on the American Digest System, the four regional digests, the five major federal digests, the two digests for U.S. Supreme Court cases (only one of which is a West digest), the individual state digests, etc. You must know what kind of case law is contained in each of these digests. See the chart in Figure 11.5.

2. Find a key topic and number to cover your research problem. There are thousands of topics and subtopics in the digests. How do you find the ones relevant to your research problem? There are four techniques:

   ■ Descriptive Word Index (DWI). Every digest has a DWI. Use the CARTWHEEL to help you locate key topics and numbers in the DWI.
   ■ Table of Contents. There are approximately 400 main topics (e.g., Constitutional Law, Criminal Law), which are scattered throughout the volumes of the digest you are using. At the beginning of each main topic you will find a table of contents. If you can find one of these main topics in the general area of your research, you then use its table of contents to locate specific key numbers. These tables of contents have different names: "Scope Note," "Analysis," or "Subjects Included." Use the CARTWHEEL to help you locate key topics and numbers in them.
   ■ Headnote in West Reporter. Suppose that you already have an opinion on point. You are reading its full text in a West reporter. Go to the headnotes at the beginning of this opinion. Each headnote has a key topic and number. Use this key topic and number to go to any of the digests to try to find *more* case law on that topic and number.
   ■ Table of Cases in the Digests. Suppose again that you already have an opinion on point. You are reading its full text in a reporter. Go to the table of cases in the *American Digest System* or in any other digest that covers the reporter. Look up the name of the case in this table of cases. There you will find out what key topics and numbers that case is digested under in the digest. Go to those topics and numbers in the body of the digest to find that case summarized along with *other* cases under the same topics and numbers. (Note: the Table of Cases in some West digests is called Plaintiff-Defendant Table *or* Defendant-Plaintiff Table, depending on which party's name comes first. The Defendant-Plaintiff Table is useful if you happen to know only the name of the defendant or if you want many cases where the same party was sued, e.g., General Motors. Defendant-Plaintiff Tables usually refer you back to the Plaintiff-Defendant Table, where the key topics and numbers are listed.)

3. Assume that while using the Descriptive Word Index (DWI) in any of the digests, you come across a key topic and number that appears to be relevant to your research problem. But when you go to check that topic and number in the body of the digest, you find no case law, and the phrase "See Scope Note for Analysis." The DWI has, in effect, led you to nonexistent case law! The editors are telling you that there are no cases digested under this topic and number *at this time.* Go to the table of contents for the main topic you are in (see step #2 above). Check the Scope Note there to see if you can find a more productive key topic and number. Or, go to a different digest to see if you can be more lucky with your original key topic and number.

4. The West editors occasionally add new key topics and numbers to its system. Hence, you may find topics and numbers in the later digests that are not in the earlier digests.

---

Continued

Checklist #2—*Continued*

| **Checklist for Using the Digests of West—*Continued*** |
|---|
| 5. The first key number under most topics and subtopics is often labeled "In General." This is obviously a broad category. Many researchers make the mistake of overlooking it in their quest for more specific topic headings. Go after more specific key numbers, but do not neglect this general one. |
| 6. The West digests obviously duplicate each other in some respects. The *American Digest System,* for example, contains everything that is in all the other digests. A regional digest will duplicate everything found in the individual state digests covered in that region. (See the chart in Figure 11.5.) It is wise, nevertheless, to check more than one digest. Some digests may be more up-to-date than others in your library. You may miss something in one digest that you will catch in another. |
| 7. Be sure you know all the units of the most comprehensive digest—the *American Digest System:* Century Digest, Decennial Digests, General Digests. These units are distinguished solely by the period of time covered by each unit. Know what these periods of time are: Century Digest (1658–1896), Decennial Digests (ten-year periods), General Digests (the period since the last Decennial Digest was printed). |
| 8. At the time the Century Digest was printed, West had not invented the key number system. Hence, topics are listed in the Century Digest by *section* numbers rather than by key numbers. Assume that you started your research in the Century Digest. You located a relevant section number and you now want to trace this number through the Decennial Digests and General Digests. To do this you need a corresponding *key* number. There is a parallel table in volume 21 of the First Decennial that will tell you the corresponding *key* topic number for any section number in the Century Digest. Suppose, however, that you started your research in the Decennial Digests or the General Digests. You have a key topic and now want to find its corresponding section number in the Century Digest. In the First and Second Decennial, there is a "see" reference under the key topic number that will tell you the corresponding section number in the Century Digest. |
| 9. Tricks of the trade are also needed in using the General Digests, which cover the most recent period since the last Decennial Digest was printed. When the current ten-year period is over, all the General Digests will be thrown away. The material in them will be consolidated or cumulated into the next Decennial Digests (which is issued in two parts beginning with the Ninth Decennial). When you go to use the General Digests, there may be twenty to thirty bound volumes on the shelf. To be thorough in tracing a key topic and number in the General Digests, you must check *all* these bound volumes. There is, however, one shortcut. Look for the "Table of Key Numbers" within the General Digests. This table tells you which General Digests contain anything under the key topic and number you are searching. You do not have to check the other General Digests. |

## 3. Annotations

An annotation is a collection of notes or commentary on something. It is, in effect, a research paper. The most extensive annotations are those of the Lawyer's Co-operative Publishing Company in the following sets of books:

A.L.R.
*American Law Reports, First*

A.L.R.2d
*American Law Reports, Second*

A.L.R.3d
*American Law Reports, Third*

A.L.R.4th
*American Law Reports, Fourth*

A.L.R. Fed.
*American Law Reports, Federal*

All five sets are reporters in that they print opinions in full. They are *annotated* reporters in that notes or commentary is provided after each case in the form of an annotation. Unlike West reporters, only a selected number of opinions are printed in these A.L.R. volumes. The editors select opinions raising novel or interesting issues, which then become the basis of an annotation. The following is an example of an annotation found on page 1015, volume 91 of A.L.R.3d:

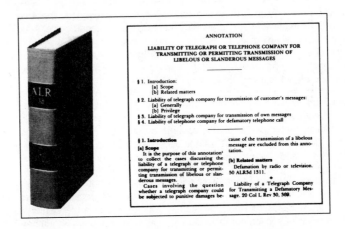

One of the joys of legal research is to find an annotation on point. A wealth of information is contained in annotations, such as a comprehensive, state-by-state survey of law on an issue. It would not be uncommon for a single annotation to contain hundreds of citations to court opinions. Picture yourself having the capacity to hire your own team of researchers to go out and spend weeks finding just about everything there is on a particular point of law. While none of us is likely to have this luxury, we do have a close equivalent in the form of annotations in the five sets of *American Law Reports*. They are a gold mine of research references. Since there are hundreds of volumes in these five sets, the chances are very good that we will find an annotation that is on point, i.e., that covers the facts of our research problem.

Most of the references in the annotations are to case law. Their primary service, therefore, is to act as a case finder. Because of this, the annotation system of Lawyers Co-operative Publishing Company is the major competitor of the other massive case finders—the digests of West. It is to our advantage that each system claims to do a better job than the other. Their competition has led to a rich source of material at our disposal.

The annotations cover both federal and state case law. A.L.R. First, A.L.R.2d, and most of A.L.R.3d cover both state and federal case law. The later volumes of A.L.R.3d and all of A.L.R.4th cover mainly state case law. A.L.R. Fed. covers only federal case law. The annotations in these five sets do not follow any particular order. There may be an annotation on burglary, for example, followed by an annotation on defective wheels on baby carriages. The annotations in A.L.R. First and A.L.R.2d are older than the annotations in the other sets, but this is not significant because all of the annotations can be updated.

We turn now to the two major concerns of the researcher:

- How do you find an annotation on point?
- How do you update an annotation that you have found?

| Index Systems for A.L.R. First | Index Systems for A.L.R.2d | Index Systems for A.L.R.3d, A.L.R.4th, A.L.R. Fed. |
|---|---|---|
| ■ *A.L.R. First Series Quick Index*<br>■ *Permanent A.L.R. Digest* | ■ *ALR Index*<br>■ *A.L.R.2d Digest*<br>■ LEXIS | ■ *ALR Index*<br>■ *A.L.R. Digest to 3d, 4th, Federal*<br>■ LEXIS |

**FIGURE 11.12**
Finding
Annotations
When You Have
No Leads

It is much easier to find and update annotations in A.L.R.3d, A.L.R.4th, and A.L.R. Fed. than in the earlier A.L.R. First and A.L.R.2d.

### (a) Finding an Annotation on Point

The major ways of finding annotations on point are outlined in Figure 11.12. These methods are most useful when you are at the very beginning of your search and have no leads.

Annotations in A.L.R. First are found by using a single-volume Quick Index.[1] The multivolume *ALR Index* is used to find annotations in A.L.R.2d, A.L.R.3d, A.L.R.4th, and A.L.R. Fed. There are also sets of digests that can be used as indexes, although they are somewhat more awkward. The digest for A.L.R. First is the *Permanent A.L.R. Digest*. The digest for A.L.R.2d is the *A.L.R.2d Digest*. There is a single digest that covers all of A.L.R.3d, A.L.R.4th, and A.L.R. Fed. It is called the *A.L.R. Digest to 3d, 4th, Federal*. Finally, you can search for annotations by computer through LEXIS, which covers all annotations except those in A.L.R. First.

Figure 11.13 tells you what to do if you are further along in your research and you already have an opinion (state or federal), a statute (state or federal), or a regulation (federal) that is on point, or potentially on point. Use the methods listed in the second column of Figure 11.13 to try to find any annotations that discuss or mention that opinion, statute, or regulation.

As we will see later, annotations are one of the "citing materials" in Shepard's. This simply means that the annotations have discussed or mentioned whatever you are shepardizing. Hence if you shepardize the items in the first column of Figure 11.13, you will be led to all annotations, if any, that have mentioned that item. If you have access to Auto-Cite (page 586), this computer service will tell you what annotations have mentioned your federal or state court opinion. Finally, use the "Table of Laws, Rules, and Regulations" to find annotations on a federal statute (in U.S.C., U.S.C.A., or U.S.C.S.), or on a federal administrative regulation (in C.F.R.). This excellent table is located in volume 6 of the *ALR Index* referred to in Figure 11.12.

As indicated earlier, some of the annotations in the five sets are very long and comprehensive. How do you find the law of a *particular* state or court within an annotation without having to read the entire annotation? At the beginning of annotations in A.L.R.3d and A.L.R.4th, you will find a "Table of

---

[1]There is also a multivolume index to the annotations in A.L.R. First. It is called *A.L.R. Word Index to Annotations*. It is seldom used today even though many libraries still keep it on the shelf. This set is different from the other multivolume index, called *ALR Index* (formerly called *Index to Annotations*), which *is* widely used today. The latter covers A.L.R.2d, A.L.R.3d, A.L.R.4th, and A.L.R. Fed.

**FIGURE 11.13**

Finding Annotations When You Already Have a Lead

| IF YOU ALREADY HAVE A CITATION TO: | USE THE FOLLOWING METHODS OF FINDING ANNOTATIONS THAT MENTION THAT CITATION: |
|---|---|
| **A State Court Opinion** | ■ Shepardize the opinion<br>■ Check Auto-Cite |
| **A Federal Court Opinion** | ■ Shepardize the opinion<br>■ Check Auto-Cite |
| **A State Statute** | ■ Shepardize the statute |
| **A Federal Statute** | ■ Shepardize the statute<br>■ Check the "Table of Laws, Rules, and Regulations" in the *ALR Index* |
| **A Federal Regulation** | ■ Shepardize the regulation<br>■ Check the "Table of Laws, Rules, and Regulations" in the *ALR Index* |

Jurisdictions Represented," which will direct you to specific sections of the annotation that cover the law of your state. At the beginning of annotations in A.L.R. Fed. there is a "Table of Courts and Circuits," which will direct you to sections of the annotation dealing with certain federal courts. In addition to these tables, there will usually be other indexes or tables of contents found at the beginning of the annotations.

| TABLE OF JURISDICTIONS REPRESENTED | TABLE OF COURTS AND CIRCUITS |
|---|---|
| Consult POCKET PART in this volume for later cases | Consult POCKET PART in this volume for later cases and statutory changes |

**TABLE OF JURISDICTIONS REPRESENTED**

US: §§ 2[b], 3, 4[a], 5[b], 6[a], 7[a], 10[b]   Miss: §§ 4[a]
Ala: §§ 2[b], 4[a], 6[a], 7[a], 8, 10[b]   Mo: §§ 4[a], 6[a], 10[b]
Cal: §§ 4[a, b], 7[a, b], 10[b], 11   NH: §§ 3, 4[b]
Fla: §§ 5[a]   NC: §§ 7[a]
Ga: §§ 3, 4[b], 5[b], 6[b], 10[a]   Ohio: §§ 4[a, b], 6[a], 7[a, b], 10[b]
Ill: §§ 4[b], 5[a, b], 6[a, b], 10[a]   Or: §§ 4[a], 10[b]
Ind: §§ 4[a], 5[b], 6[a], 7[a, b], 8, 9, 10[b]   Pa: §§ 4[a], 7[a], 10[b]
Iowa: §§ 7[a], 8   Tenn: §§ 4[a], 5[b], 6[a]
Ky: §§ 3, 4[a], 5[b]   Tex: §§ 4[a], 7[a], 10[b]
La: §§ 5[b], 7[a, b]   Vt: §§ 9
Me: §§ 5[b], 7[a], 10[b]   Wash: §§ 6[a], 7[a], 8
Md: §§ 4[b]   Wis: §§ 7[a], 8, 10[b], 11
Mich: §§ 4[a], 10[b]

**TABLE OF COURTS AND CIRCUITS**

Sup Ct: §§ 2[a], 3[a], 5, b, 14   Sixth Cir: §§ 5[b], 6[b], 10[a, b], 12[a], 13[a], 15[b]
First Cir: §§ 5[b], 6[b], 15[b], 16[a], 18[a]   Seventh Cir: §§ 2[a, b], 4[b], 5[b], 10[b], 15[b]
Second Cir: §§ 2[b], 3[a], 5[a], 5[a], 12[a], 16[a], 18[a]   Eighth Cir: §§ 3[a], 4[a, b], 5[a, b], 6[a], 12[a], 13[a], 15[b], 16[a], 17, 19
Third Cir: §§ 3[a], 5[a], 7, 11[b], 12[b], 13[a], 15[b]   Ninth Cir: §§ 2[a, b], 3[a], 4[a], 5, a, 6[b], 7, 8, 10[a], 11[a, b], 12[a, b], 13[a, b], 15[a, b], 16[b], 17, 18[a, b]
Fourth Cir: §§ 2[b], 3[a], 4[b], 5[a, b], 8, 9, 10[b], 12[a, b], 13[b], 14, 15[a, b], 16[a], 17, 18[a]   Tenth Cir: §§ 2[b], 3[a], 5[a, b], 6[a, b], 9, 11[a, b], 12[a], 14, 17, 18[b]
Fifth Cir: §§ 3[a], 5[a, b], 8, 10[a], 11[a, b], 13[a], 15[a], 16[b], 18[b]   Dist Col Cir: §§ 3[b], 5[b], 6[b], 10[a, b]
   Ct Cl: § 16[a]

### (b)  *Updating an Annotation*

Suppose that you have found an annotation on point. It has led you to very useful law. This annotation, however, may be ten, twenty, thirty, or more years old. How do you update this annotation to find the most current law on the points covered in the annotation? Of course, any opinion or statute found within the annotation can be shepardized as a technique of finding more law. But our focus here is the updating systems within A.L.R. itself. Figure 11.14 outlines these systems.

If the annotation you want updated is in A.L.R. First, you use the *A.L.R. Blue Book of Supplemental Decisions*. (Check each volume of this Blue Book.) If the annotation you want updated is in A.L.R. 2d, you use the *A.L.R. 2d Later Case Service*. (Check the volume that covers your annotation, plus the pocket part of this volume of the Later Case Service.) If the annotation you want updated is in A.L.R. 3d, or in A.L.R. 4th, or in A.L.R. Fed., you check the pocket part of the volume containing the annotation.

There are no pocket parts to the volumes of A.L.R. First and A.L.R. 2d. Hence you need the Blue Book and Later Case Service in order to perform needed updating. Thankfully, the volumes of A.L.R. 3d, A.L.R. 4th, and

**FIGURE 11.14**

How to Update an
Annotation

| Updating an Annotation in A.L.R. First | Updating an Annotation in A.L.R.2d | Updating an Annotation in A.L.R.3d, A.L.R.4th, and A.L.R. Fed. |
|---|---|---|
| ■ *A.L.R. Blue Book of Supplemental Decisions*<br><br>■ "Annotation History Table" in *ALR Index* | ■ *A.L.R.2d Later Case Service*<br><br>■ "Annotation History Table" in *ALR Index* | ■ Pocket Part of volume containing the annotation<br><br>■ "Annotation History Table" in *ALR Index* |
| Note: any case you find in an annotation can also be updated by shepardizing that case. | | |

A.L.R. Fed. *do* have pocket parts that can be used to update annotations in them. The existence of these pocket parts makes it much easier to update annotations in A.L.R. 3d, A.L.R. 4th, and A.L.R. Fed. than to update annotations in A.L.R. First or A.L.R. 2d.

There is a toll-free number that can be used to obtain additional updating information on the annotations in A.L.R. 2d, A.L.R. 3d, A.L.R. 4th, and A.L.R. Fed. Any member of the public can use this number; you do not have to be a subscriber. Currently, the number is 1-800-225-7488.

One final updating feature must be covered: the Annotation History Table. Note that Figure 11.14 lists this Table as a further method of updating annotations in all five sets of A.L.R. The law in some annotations may become so outdated that it is replaced by another annotation. The outdated annotation is called a *superseded annotation,* which should not be read. If, however, an annotation is substantially updated but not totally replaced by another annotation, the older annotation is called a *supplemented annotation,* which can be read along with the newer annotation. There are two ways to find out which annotations have been superseded or supplemented. Check the "Annotation History Table" found in volume 6 of *ALR Index.* Of course, you should also check the standard method for updating annotations in A.L.R. First (the Blue Book), in A.L.R. 2d (Later Case Service), in A.L.R. 3d (pocket parts), in A.L.R. 4th (pocket parts), and in A.L.R. Fed. (pocket parts).

*Note on Another Annotated Reporter of Lawyers Co-op.*  Lawyers Co-op. publishes *United States Supreme Court Reports, Lawyers' Edition* (abbreviated L.Ed.). This is also an annotated reporter in that it prints the full text of opinions (those of the U.S. Supreme Court) with annotations on issues following some of these opinions. (See photo of this reporter at the top of page 492.)

Checklist #3

| Checklist For Finding and Updating Annotations in A.L.R., A.L.R.2d, A.L.R.3d, A.L.R.4th, and A.L.R. Fed. |
|---|
| **1.** Your goal is to use the five sets to find annotations on your research problem. The annotations are extensive research papers on numerous points of law. |
| **2.** The most current annotations are in A.L.R.3d, in A.L.R.4th, and in A.L.R. Fed. Start with these sets. Then try to find annotations in A.L.R.2d, and in A.L.R. First. Use the CARTWHEEL to help you locate annotations in the following index resources: |

Continued

*Checklist #3—Continued*

---

**Checklist For Finding and Updating Annotations
in A.L.R., A.L.R.2d, A.L.R.3d, A.L.R.4th, and A.L.R. Fed.**

(a) To find annotations in A.L.R.3d, in A.L.R.4th, and in A.L.R. Fed.:
- Use *ALR Index*
- Use *A.L.R. Digest to 3d, 4th, Federal*
- Use LEXIS

(b) To find annotations in A.L.R.2d:
- Use *ALR Index*
- Use *A.L.R.2d Digest*
- Use LEXIS

(c) To find annotations in A.L.R. First:
- Use *A.L.R. First Series Quick Index*
- Use *Permanent A.L.R. Digest*

---

3. If you already found a particular law and you want to know if there is an annotation that mentions that law, check the following resources:

   (a) If you already have a federal opinion or a state opinion:
   - Shepardize that opinion
   - Check Auto-Cite

   (b) If you already have a state statute:
   - Shepardize that statute

   (c) If you already have a federal statute:
   - Shepardize that statute
   - Check the "Table of Laws, Rules, and Regulations" in volume 6 of *ALR Index*

   (d) If you already have a federal administrative regulation:
   - Shepardize that regulation
   - Check the "Table of Laws, Rules, and Regulations" in volume 6 of *ALR Index*

---

4. Use the tables or other indexes at the beginning of the annotation to help you locate specific sections of the annotation. (Before you spend much time with the annotation, however, check the "Annotation History Table" to determine if it has been superseded or supplemented by another annotation. See step 5 below.)

---

5. Update all annotations that are on point.

   (a) To update an annotation in A.L.R. First:
   - Check the *A.L.R. Blue Book of Supplemental Decisions*
   - Check the "Annotation History Table" in volume 6 of *ALR Index*

   (b) To update an annotation in A.L.R.2d:
   - Check the *A.L.R.2d Later Case Service*
   - Check the "Annotation History Table" in volume 6 of *ALR Index*

   (c) To update an annotation in A.L.R.3d, in A.L.R.4th, or in A.L.R. Fed.:
   - Check the pocket part
   - Check the "Annotation History Table" in volume 6 of *ALR Index*

## 4. Shepard's

There have been four great research inventions in the law:

- The key topic and number system of the West digests
- The annotations in A.L.R., A.L.R.2d, A.L.R.3d, A.L.R.4th, and A.L.R. Fed
- Computers (CALR: Computer Assisted Legal Research)
- Shepard's

The first three are extensively used as case finders. While Shepard's is not primarily designed to be a case finder, it can serve this function, along with other functions, as we shall now see.

Before we examine Shepard's and the techniques of *shepardizing*, you should review the material starting on page 511 covering the kinds of Shepard's volumes that exist, the material on page 527 covering the use of Shepard's as one of the four techniques of finding a parallel cite, and the material on page 487 describing an advance sheet for Shepard's.

Shepard's is a citator, which means that its function is to provide you with relevant citations to whatever you are shepardizing. We will examine Shepard's through the following topics:

(a) The units of a set of Shepard's

(b) Determining whether you have a complete set of Shepard's

(c) The distinction between "cited material" and "citing material"

(d) Abbreviations in Shepard's

(e) Shepardizing a case (court opinion)

(f) Shepardizing a statute

(g) Shepardizing a regulation

We will limit ourselves to shepardizing cases, statutes, and regulations. Knowing how to shepardize these items, however, will go a long way toward equipping you to shepardize other items as well (such as constitutions, administrative decisions, charters, and rules of court).

### (a) The Units of a Set of Shepard's

By "set of Shepard's" we mean the group of volumes of Shepard's that cover whatever you are trying to shepardize. There are two main units to every set of Shepard's: (a) *bound* red volumes and (b) white, gold, yellow or red *pamphlet* volumes. The bound volumes and pamphlets are sometimes broken into parts, e.g., Part 1, Part 2. The white pamphlet is the advance sheet (page 487) that is later thrown away and cumulated (or consolidated) into a larger pamphlet. Eventually all the pamphlets are thrown away and cumulated into bound red volumes. The pamphlets contain the most current shepardizing material.

### (b) Determining Whether You Have a Complete Set of Shepard's

You should not try to shepardize anything until you are satisfied that there is a complete set of Shepard's on the shelf in front of you. As we saw above, Shepard's comes in sets, e.g., the set of Shepards for United States statutes, the set for New Mexico laws. You need a complete set in order to shepardize. To determine whether you have a complete set, go through the following four steps:

1. Pick up the advance sheet or the most recently dated pamphlet for that set of Shepard's (the date is on top of the pamphlet).

2. What month and year is at the top of this advance sheet or other pamphlet? If the month is not the month of today's date or the immediately preceding month, ask the librarian for the date of the most recent pamphlet the library has received for the set of Shepard's you are using. (The librarian will check the office Kardex, (page 504), or other system of recording serial or subscription material that the library has received.)

3. Once you are satisfied that the advance sheet or latest pamphlet is the most current the library has, find the following statement on its front cover: "What Your Library Should Contain." Here you will be told what constitutes a complete set of Shepard's for the set you are using. Go down the list and make sure that the library has on the shelf everything you are told should be there.

4. The last entry in the list is always the advance sheet or other pamphlet that contains the list you are reading.

Here, for example, is the list that will allow you to shepardize the cases and statutes of the state of Kansas:

### WHAT YOUR LIBRARY SHOULD CONTAIN:

- 1986 Bound Volume, Cases (Parts 1 and 2)*
- 1986 Bound Volume, Statutes*

*Supplemented with January, 1989 Cumulative Supplement Vol. 60 No. 5 and February, 1989 Advance Sheet Vol. 60 No. 6

*DESTROY ALL OTHER ISSUES*

To be complete, the following units of *Shepard's Kansas Citations* should be on the shelf:

- a 1986 bound volume of *Shepard's Kansas Citations* covering cases (Part 1); *and,*

- a 1986 bound volume of *Shepard's Kansas Citations* covering cases (Part 2); *and,*

- a 1986 bound volume of *Shepard's Kansas Citations* covering statutes; *and,*

- a January 1989 Cumulative Supplement pamphlet of *Shepard's Kansas Citations,* Vol. 60, No. 5.; *and,*

- A February 1989 Advance Sheet of *Shepard's Kansas Citations,* Vol. 60, No. 6.

The last item on the list is always the pamphlet that contains the list you are reading. Hence, the above list is found on the February 1989 Advance Sheet pamphlet of *Shepard's Kansas Citations,* Vol. 60, No. 6.

Occasionally the list can become quite involved. For example, you may find two lists on the pamphlet. One list tells you what should be on the shelf before a certain bound Shepard's volume is received by the library, and a second list tells you what should be on the shelf after that bound volume is received by the library. Yet the same process is followed. Carefully go through the list (or lists) one unit at a time, checking to see if the library has on the shelf what the list says should be present.

### (c)  The Distinction Between "Cited Material" and "Citing Material"

■ Cited Material: whatever you are shepardizing, such as a case, statute, or regulation.

■ Citing Material: whatever mentions or discusses the cited material, such as another case, a law review article, an annotation in A.L.R., A.L.R.2d, A.L.R.3d, A.L.R.4th, A.L.R. Fed, etc.

Suppose you are shepardizing the case found in 75 F.2d 107 (a case that begins on page 107 of volume 75 of Federal Reporter 2d). While reading through the columns of Shepard's, you find the following cite: f56 S.E.2d 46. The *cited* material is 75 F.2d 107. The *citing* material is 56 S.E.2d 46, which followed (f) or agreed with the decision in 75 F.2d 107.

Suppose you are shepardizing a statute: 22 U.S.C. § 55.8 (section 55.8 of title 22 of the United States Code). While reading through the columns of Shepard's, you find the following cite: 309 U.S. 45. The *cited* material is 22 U.S.C. § 55.8. The *citing* material is 309 U.S. 45, which interpreted or mentioned 22 U.S.C. § 55.8.

Shepard's always indicates the cited material by the black bold print along the top of every page of Shepard's and by the black bold print numbers that are the volume or section numbers of the cited material. In the following excerpt, the cited material is 404 P.2d 460. The citing material follows the number **460**:

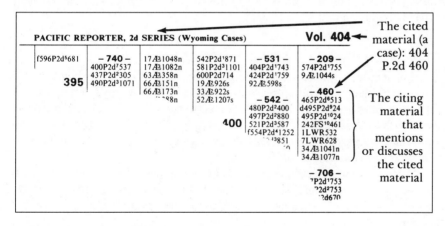

In the following excerpt, the cited material is a statute: § 37–31 of the Wyoming Statutes. The citing material is indicated beneath § 37–31.

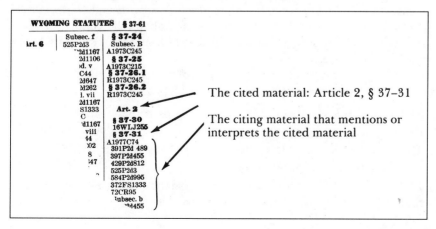

## (d) Abbreviation in Shepard's

Shepard's packs a tremendous amount of information (the cites) into every one of its pages. Each page contains about eight columns of cites for the cited and the citing materials. For the sake of economy, Shepard's uses many abbreviations that are peculiar to Shepard's. For example:

FS  → means Federal Supplement

**A3** → means American Law Reports 3d

\* → means that a regulation of a particular year was discussed

△ → means that a regulation was discussed without mentioning the year of the regulation

Most researchers do not know the meaning of every abbreviation and signal used by Shepard's. *But you must know where to find their meaning.* There are two places to go:

- The abbreviations tables at the beginning of most of the units of Shepard's (for an example, see page 543).

- The preface or explanation pages found at the beginning of most of the units of Shepard's.

Many researchers neglect the latter. Buried within the preface or explanation pages may be an interpretation of an abbreviation or symbol that is not covered in the abbreviation tables.

## (e) Shepardizing a Case (Court Opinion)

Almost every reporter has a corresponding Shepard's set, which will enable you to shepardize cases in that reporter (page 511). For example, if the case you want to shepardize is 193 Mass. 364, you go to the set of Shepard's that covers cases in Massachusetts Reports—*Shepard's Massachusetts Citations.* If the case you want to shepardize is 402 F.2d 1064, you go to the Shepard's set that covers F.2d cases—*Shepard's Federal Citations.*

Of course, many cases have parallel cites—the case is found word-for-word in more than one reporter. You can shepardize the case through *either* reporter for most cases with parallel cites. Assume you want to shepardize the following case:

Welch v. Swasey, 193 Mass. 364, 79 N.E. 745 (1907).

This case is found in two reporters: *Massachusetts Reports* and *North Eastern Reporter.* Hence, you can shepardize the case and obtain the same citing material from two different sets of Shepard's: **Shepard's Massachusetts Citations** and **Shepard's Northeastern Citations.**

To shepardize a *case* means to obtain the following six kinds of information about the cited case (the case you are shepardizing):

1. The parallel cite of the case. The first entry in parenthesis is the parallel cite. (See page 527 for the reasons why you may find no parallel cite here.)

2. The history of the case. Here you will find all cases that are part of the same litigation, e.g., appeals, reversals.

3. Citing cases that have mentioned or discussed the cited case—for example, followed it, distinguished it, or just mentioned it.

4. Citing legal periodical literature (articles or case notes) that has analyzed or mentioned the cited case.

5. Citing annotations in A.L.R., A.L.R.2d, A.L.R.3d, A.L.R.4th, or A.L.R. Fed. that have analyzed or mentioned the cited case.

6. Citing opinions of the attorney general that have analyzed or mentioned the cited case.

The great value of Shepard's as a case finder comes through items 3 to 5. If a citing case mentions or discusses the cited case, the two cases probably deal with similar facts and law. All citing cases, therefore, are potential leads to more case law on point. Similarly, a citing law review article or annotation will probably discuss a variety of cases in addition to the discussion of the cited case. Hence again, you are led to more case law through Shepard's.

Items 2 and 3 above also enable you to do validation research (page 606). They tell you if the cited case is still good law. Has it been reversed? Has it been discussed with approval by citing cases? Has it been ignored by other courts?

One final point before examining an excerpt from a Shepard's page. Recall that cases in reporters are broken down into headnotes at the beginning of the case (page 503). These headnotes are written either by the private publisher (such as West) or by the court clerk in official editions of the case. Shepard's calls these headnotes of the case the *syllabus* of the case—small-paragraph summaries of portions of the case found at the beginning of the case.

A case can involve many issues, only a few of which may be relevant to your research problem. Is it possible to narrow your sheparizing to those parts of the case that are most relevant to your research problem? Yes. It is possible to shepardize a portion of a case through its headnote or syllabus numbers. In effect, you are shepardizing the headnote! How is this done?

■ Every headnote or syllabus paragraph of the *cited* case has a consecutive number: 1, 2, 3, 4, etc.

■ When the editors of Shepard's come across a *citing* case that deals with only one of the headnotes or syllabus paragraphs of the *cited* case, they include the number of this headnote or syllabus paragraph as part of the reference to the *citing* case in the columns of Shepard's.

■ The number is printed as a small raised, or elevated, number—called a small superior figure—within the reference to the *citing* case.

Be careful. It is easy to become confused. The superior figure refers to the headnote or syllabus number of the *cited* case, not the citing case.

For example, assume again that you are sheparizing Welch v. Swasey, 193 Mass. 364. In the columns of Shepard's you find the following:

$$\text{f193Mas}^8\text{476}$$

The *citing* case is 193 Mass. 476. This case follows (agrees with) the *cited* case: Welch v. Swasey, 193 Mass. 364. Note the raised number 8—the superior figure. This 8 refers to the eighth headnote or syllabus of the *cited* case, *Welch v. Swasey*. The *citing* case dealt with that portion of *Welch* that was summarized in the eighth headnote or syllabus of the *Welch* case. Again, do not make the mistake of thinking that the small raised number refers to a headnote or syllabus in the citing case. It refers to a headnote or syllabus number of the *cited* case.

We now look at a sample or specimen page from *Shepard's Massachusetts Citations* (see Figure 11.15), where we will begin to shepardize *Welch v. Swasey*, 193 Mass. 364. Read the oval inserts on this specimen page now—before carefully studying the following comments.

Let us assume that in your legal research you have located the case of *Welch v. Swasey*, reported in volume 193 of Massachusetts Reports at page 364. This again is the cited case that we want to shepardize.

**FIGURE 11.15**

Excerpt from
Shepard's Page
(Cases)

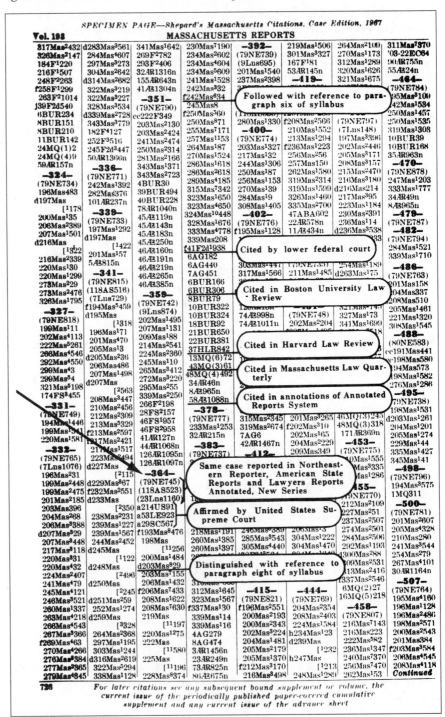

The specimen page contains a reproduction of page 726 in the 1967 Case Edition of *Shepard's Massachusetts Citations*. Note the number of the volume of reports, "Vol. 193," in the upper left corner of the page.

Find our page number in bold print "—364—" in the third column. See the arrow. This is the initial page of our cited case under consideration. Following this page number you will find the citations "(79NE745)," "(118AS523)," "(23Lns1160)," indicating that the same case is also reported in 79 *North Eastern Reporter* 745, 118 *American State Reports* 523, and 23 *Lawyers Reports Annotated, New Series* 1160. These are parallel citations. As indicated earlier, abbreviations are explained at the beginning of Shepard's volumes.

Next comes the history of the cited case. On appeal to the United States Supreme Court, our cited case was affirmed "a" in 214US91 (also printed in 53LE923 and in 29SC567). Also, the cited case has been followed "f" and distinguished "d" in subsequent cases of the Massachusetts and federal courts.

In the citation "f242 Mas⁶34" (see top of next column), the small superior figure ⁶ before the citing page number 34 indicates that the principle of law brought out in the sixth paragraph of the syllabus (i.e., of the headnotes) of 193 Mass. 364 has been followed in 242 Mass. 34.

This case has also been cited in several legal periodicals: *Harvard Law Review* "HLR," *Boston University Law Review* "BUR," and *Massachusetts Law Quarterly* "MQ."

The citations appearing in annotations of the *American Law Reports* are grouped together after the legal periodical citing references.

By examining the same volume and page number of the cited case in the other units of *Shepard's Massachusetts Citations*, more citing material for this case will be found.

## Checklist #4a

| **Checklist for Shepardizing a Case** |
|---|
| **1.** You have a case you want to shepardize. In what reporter is this case found? Go to the set of Shepard's in the library that covers this reporter. |
| **2.** If the case you want to shepardize has a parallel cite that you already have, find out if the library has a set of Shepard's for the other reporter volumes in which the case is also found. You may be able to shepardize the case through more than one set of Shepard's. (There are sets of Shepard's for the individual state official reports and for all the reporters of West's unofficial National Reporter System.) |
| **3.** Know whether you have a complete set of Shepard's in front of you by reading the "What Your Library Should Contain" list on the most recent pamphlet of that set. |
| **4.** The general rule is that you must check the cite of the case you are sheparding (the cited case) in *every* unit of a set of Shepard's. With experience you will learn, however, that it is possible to bypass some of the units of the set. There may be information on the front cover of one of the Shepard's volumes, for example, that will tell you that the date or volume number of the reporter containing your cited case will not be covered in that Shepard's volume. You can bypass it and move on to other units of the set. |
| **5.** In checking all the units of Shepard's, it is recommended that you work *backward* by examining the most recent Shepard's pamphlets first so that you obtain the latest citing materials first. |
| **6.** Suppose that in one of the units of a set of Shepard's, you find nothing listed for the cited case. This could mean one of three things: |

Continued

Checklist #4a—*Continued*

| **Checklist for Shepardizing a Case—*Continued*** |
|---|
| (a) You are in the wrong set of Shepard's. |
| (b) You are in the right set of Shepard's, but the Shepard's unit you are examining does not cover the particular volume of the reporter that contains your cited case. (See #4 above.) |
| (c) You are in the right set of Shepard's. The silence in Shepard's about your cited case means that since the time of the printing of the last unit of Shepard's for that set, nothing has happened to the case—there is nothing for Shepard's to tell you. |
| 7. Know the six kinds of information that you can obtain when shepardizing a case: parallel cites, history of the cited case, citing cases, citing legal periodical literature, citing annotations, citing opinions of the attorney general. |
| 8. The page number listed for every citing case is the page on which the cited case is mentioned. It is not the page on which the citing case begins. |
| 9. Use the abbreviations tables and the preface pages at the beginning of most units of Shepard's—and use them often. |
| 10. A small "n" to the right of the page number of a citing case (e.g., 23ALR198n) means the cited case is mentioned within an annotation. A small "s" to the right of the page number of a citing case (e.g., 23ALR198s) means the cited case is mentioned in a supplement to (or pocket part of) the annotation. |
| 11. Item #2 above said that cases with parallel cites can often be shepardized through more than one set of Shepard's. There is, however, only one set of Shepard's for U.S. Supreme Court opinions *(United States Citations, Case Edition)*. The question arises as to whether you can shepardize the Supreme Court opinion through any one of the three cites within this set of Shepards. For older opinions, the answer is *no;* you must shepardize through the U.S. cite. Today, you can shepardize through any of the three cites. It is recommended, however, that you shepardize *only* through the U.S. cite, since you may pick up some citing material through the U.S. cite that is not available when you shepardize through the S. Ct. or L. Ed. cites. |
| 12. You can also shepardize a case online through either WESTLAW or LEXIS. |

## (f) Shepardizing a Statute

You shepardize a *statute* in order to try to find the following seven kinds of information:

- A parallel cite of the statute (found in parentheses immediately after the section number of the statute). The parallel cite (if given) is to the *session law* edition of the statute (see the discussion that follows)

- The history of the statute in the legislature, such as amendments, new sections added, sections repealed, renumbered, etc.

- The history of the statute in the courts, such as citing cases that have analyzed or mentioned the statute, declared it unconstitutional, etc.

- Citing administrative decisions, such as agency decisions that have analyzed or mentioned the statute

- Citing legal periodical literature, such as law review articles that have analyzed or mentioned the statute

- Citing annotations in A.L.R., A.L.R.2d, A.L.R.3d, A.L.R.4th, and A.L.R. Fed. that have analyzed or mentioned the statute

■ Citing opinions of the attorney general that have analyzed or mentioned the statute

When a statute is passed by the legislature, it comes out as a slip law (page 510) and then is printed in volumes called Session Laws, Laws, Acts, Acts and Resolves, Statutes at Large, etc. (For convenience, all the latter items will be referred to below as session laws.) Session laws are arranged chronologically by year—the statutes are not arranged by subject matter in the session law volumes. Finally, many but not all of the session laws are later printed in statutory codes. They are *codified*, which means that they *are* organized by subject matter rather than chronologically. As indicated earlier, not all session laws are codified. The statute may not be considered of sufficient general interest to be codified. If codification has occurred, there will be two cites for the same statute. Here are examples of codified and session law cites of a state statute (Ohio) and of a federal statute.

| Session Law Cite | Codified Cite |
|---|---|
| ↓ | ↓ |
| 1975 Ohio Laws, C. 508 | Ohio Rev. Code Ann. § 45 (1978) |
| 87 Stat. 297 (1965). | 34 U.S.C. § 18(c) (1970) |

Notice the totally different numbering system in the codified and session law cites—yet they are the same statutes. Section 45 of the Ohio Revised Code Annotated is found word-for-word in Chapter (C.)508 of the 1975 session laws of Ohio. And section 18(c) of title 34 of the United States Code is found word-for-word in volume 87 of Statutes at Large (Stat.) on page 297. Notice also the different years for the same statute. The year in the *session law cite* is the year the legislature passed the statute. The year in the *codified cite,* however, is usually the year of the edition of the code.

Now the question becomes: when do you shepardize a statute through its session law cite and when do you shepardize it through its codified cite?

There are two instances when you *must* shepardize the statute through its session law cite:

■ If the statute will never be codified because it is not of general public interest and

■ If the statute has not yet been codified because it is so recent (codification will come later)

If the statute *has* been codified, you must shepardize it through its latest codified cite. But suppose you know only the session law cite of the statute. How do you find its codified cite? Go to the current code that will contain your statute. Look for special tables at the beginning or end of the code. For federal statutes in the United States Code, for example, there is a Tables volume in which you will find Table III. It will enable you to translate a session law cite into a codified law cite (page 533). (A Tables volume also exists for U.S.C.A. and for U.S.C.S.)

Shepard's has its own abbreviation system for session laws. Suppose that you are shepardizing Kan Stat Ann. § 123 (1973)—a codified cite. Section 123 is the cited statute—what you are shepardizing. In the Shepard's columns for Kansas statutes, you might find:

**Section 123**
(1970C6)
A1972C23
Rp1975C45

The parallel cite in parentheses is 1970C6, which means the 1970 Session Laws of the state of Kansas, Chapter 6. The mention of a year in Shepard's for statutes usually refers to the session laws for that year. (You find the meaning of "C" by checking the abbreviations tables at the beginning of the Shepard's volume.)

Immediately beneath the parentheses in the above example, you find two other references to session laws:

| | |
|---|---|
| A1972C23 In the 1972 Session Laws of Kansas, Chapter 23, there was an amendment to section 123 (which is what "A" means according to Shepard's abbreviation tables) | Rp1975C45 In Chapter 45 of the 1975 Session Laws of Kansas, section 123 was repealed in part (which is what "Rp" means according to Shepard's abbreviation tables) |

You will note that Shepard's does *not* tell you what the amendment was, nor what was repealed in part. How do you find this out? Two ways. First, you go to the actual session laws if your library has them. Second, you go to the cited statute (§ 123) in the codified collection of the statutes (here the Kansas Statutes Annotated). At the bottom of the statute in the code, there may be historical or legislative history notes which will summarize amendments, repeals, etc. (Also check the same kind of notes for the cited statute in the pocket part of the code volume you are using.)

Other citing material given in Shepard's for a statute is less complicated. For example, there are cites to citing cases, citing law review articles, etc., that follow a very similar pattern to the citing material for cases you are shepardizing (see Checklist #4a on shepardizing a case).

**FIGURE 11.16**

Excerpt from a Shepard's Page (Federal Statutes)

| United States Code, 1970 Edition and Supplement, 1972 TITLE 18 § 700 | |
|---|---|
| Ad82St291   1 | Citations to section "§" 700 of Title 18 of the United States Code, 1970 Edition and the 1972 Supplement are shown in the left margin of this page. |
| C302FS1112  2 | Citations for each cited statutory provision are grouped as follows: |
| 394US604 | 1. amendments, repeals, etc. by acts of Congress; |
| 22LE592 | 2. citing cases of the United States Supreme Court and the lower federal courts analyzed as to constitutionality or validity; |
| 89SC1372 | |
| 445F2d226 | |
| 462F2d96 | 3. other citing cases; |
| 479F2d1177  3 | 4. citing legal periodical literature; |
| 313FS49 | 5. citing annotations; |
| 317FS138 | 6. citing material for specific subdivisions of the statute. |
| 322FS593 | For the purpose of illustration only, this grouping has been indicated by brackets. It will be noted that as yet there is no citing material in group four. |
| 324FS1278 | |
| 343FS165 | |
| 41Æ3504n  5 | The first citation shown indicates that section 700 of Title 18 was added "Ad" by an act of Congress printed in 82 United States Statutes at Large "St" at page 291. This section is next shown to have been held constitutional "C" by a lower federal court in a case reported in 302 Federal Supplement "FS" 1112 and to have been cited in several cases before the federal courts and the United States Supreme Court. The section was also cited in an annotation "n" of the American Law Reports, Third Series "*A*3 ". |
| **Subsec. a** | |
| C454F2d972 | |
| C462F2d96 | |
| 445F2d226 | |
| 479F2d1179 | |
| 324FS1278 | |
| **Subsec. b**  6 | |
| C462F2d96 | |
| 445F2d226 | Citing references to specific subdivisions of the section are then shown. Subsection (Subsec) "a" of section 700, for example, was held constitutional in two lower federal court cases reported in 454 F2d 972 and 462 F2d 96. |
| **Subsec. c** | |
| 394US598 | |
| 22LE588 | |
| 89SC1360 | |
| 322FS585 | |

Assume that you want to shepardize a federal statute—in the United States Code (U.S.C.). As with the shepardizing of every statute, you must shepardize through the most current edition of the code. A new edition of the U.S.C. comes out every six years, e.g., 1970 Edition, 1976 Edition. In between editions, the U.S.C. is supplemented by annual Supplement volumes, e.g., Supplement 1972, Supplement 1973. Shepardize your statute through the latest code edition *and* through any of the Supplement years indicated at the top of the pages used to shepardize a federal statute in *Shepard's United States Citations, Statute Edition* (page 512).

Assume that the most current code edition is the 1970 edition and that the latest Supplement year is 1972. You want to shepardize 18 USC § 700 (1970). You trace this cite through all the units of *Shepard's United States Citations, Statute Edition*. In Figure 11.16, there is an excerpt containing one column from a page in one of these units.

## Checklist #4b

| Checklist for Shepardizing a Statute |
|---|
| 1. Go to the set of Shepard's that will enable you to shepardize your statute. For federal statutes, it is *Shepard's United States Citations, Statute Edition*. For state statutes, go to the set of Shepard's for your state. This set of Shepard's may cover both state cases and state statutes in the same units or in different case and statute editions of the set. |
| 2. If the statute has been codified, shepardize it through its latest codified cite. If all you have is the session law cite of the statute, translate it into a codified cite by using the tables in the current code, such as Table III of the Tables volume of U.S.C./U.S.C.A./U.S.C.S. (page 533). |
| 3. If the statute has not been codified, you can shepardize it through its session law cite. |
| 4. Know whether you have a complete set of Shepard's in front of you by reading the "What Your Library Should Contain" list on the most recent pamphlet of that set. |
| 5. Check your cite in *every* unit of Shepard's. It is recommended that you work *backward* by examining the most recent Shepard's pamphlets first so that you obtain the latest citing material first. |
| 6. At the top of a Shepard's page, and in its columns, look for your statute by the name of the code, year, article, chapter, title, or section, however the statute is identified in its cite. Repeat this for every unit of Shepard's. |
| 7. Know the seven kinds of information you can try to obtain by shepardizing a statute: parallel cite (not always given), history of the statute in the legislature, history of the statute in the courts, citing administrative decisions, citing legal periodical literature, citing annotations, citing opinions of the attorney general. |
| 8. The history of the statute in the legislature will give you the citing material in session law form, e.g., A1980C45. This refers to an amendment (A) printed in the 1980 Laws of the legislature, chapter (C) 45. Another example: A34St.654. This refers to an amendment (A) printed in volume 34, page 654, of the Statutes at Large. If you want to locate these session laws, find out if your library keeps the session laws. Also, check the historical note after the statute in the statutory code (page 591). |
| 9. The notation "et seq" means "and following." The citing material may be analyzing more than one statutory section. |
| 10. Use the abbreviation tables and the preface material at the beginning of most of the units of the set of Shepard's. |

Continued

| **Checklist for Sheperdizing a Statute—*Continued*** |
|---|
| 11. If your state code has gone through revisions or renumberings, read the early pages in the statutory code and in the Shepard's volumes to try to obtain an explanation of what has happened. This information may be of considerable help to you in interpreting the data provided in the Shepard's units for your state code. |

## (g) *Shepardizing a Regulation*

You cannot shepardize regulations of state agencies. No sets of Shepard's cover state regulations. Until recently, the same was true of most federal regulations. Today, however, it is possible to shepardize federal regulations in the Code of Federal Regulations (C.F.R.). This is done through *Shepard's Code of Federal Regulations Citations*. (See page 512). (It will also allow you to shepardize executive orders and reorganization plans.)

The C.F.R. comes out in a new edition every year. All the changes that have occurred during the year are incorporated in the new yearly edition. Two kinds of changes can be made:

- Those changes made *by the agency* itself, e.g., amendments, repeals, renumbering—this is the history of the regulation in the agency.

- Those changes forced on the agency *by the courts,* e.g., declaring the regulation invalid—this is the history of the regulation in the courts.

Unfortunately, Shepard's will give you only the history of the regulation *in the courts* (plus references to the regulation in legal periodical literature and in annotations). The columns of Shepard's will *not* give you the history of the regulation in the agency. (To obtain the latter, you must check elsewhere, e.g., the "CFR Parts Affected" tables in the Federal Register.) The main value of the Shepard's for C.F.R. is that it will tell you what *the courts* have said about the regulation (plus the periodical and annotation references).

When shepardizing through the Shepard's C.F.R. Citations, the cited material, of course, is the federal regulation—which we refer to as the cited regulation. There are two kinds of *citing* material provided by Shepard's:

- Citing cases, periodicals, and annotations that refer to the cited regulation *by year,* that is, by C.F.R. edition.

- Citing cases, periodicals, and annotations that refer to the cited regulation *without* specifying the year or edition of the regulation in the C.F.R.

To indicate the first kind of citing material, Shepard's gives you a small elevated asterisk just before a given year. If, for example, the cited regulation you were shepardizing is 12 C.F.R. § 218.111(j), you might find the following:

**§ 218.111(j)**
420F2d90\*1965

The citing material is a citing case—420 F.2d 90. The small asterisk means that this case specifically identified the year of the cited regulation—1965. This year is *not* the year of the citing case. It is the year of the cited regulation. We are not given the year of the citing case.

Now let us examine the second kind of citing material mentioned above. There may be citing material that mentions the regulation but does *not* tell us

**FIGURE 11.17**

Excerpts from a
Shepard's Page
(C.F.R.)

---

### Code of Federal Regulations

```
CFR
TITLE
42
§53.111
323F2d965 △1963
458F2d1117 △1972
551F2d333 *1972
Va559F2d973 △1977
327FS113 △1971
359FS911 *1973      1
Vp373FS551 △1974
373FS559 △1974
409FS711 △1976
Up453FS410 *1973
453FS680 *1976
Mass
382NE1043 *1977
NY
413S2d88 △1979      2
Ore
582P2d48 *1976
88YLJ277 *1977      3
11ALRF684n △1972    4
```

Shepard's Code of Federal Regulation Citations gives citations to the Code of Federal Regulations and to Presidential Proclamations, Executive Orders, and Reorganization Plans as cited by the United States Supreme Court, by the lower federal courts, and by state courts in cases reported in any unit of the National Reporter System, and in annotations of American Law Reports. In addition, citations appearing in articles in legal periodicals are shown.

If the citing material mentioned the year of the cited CFR regulation, that year is preceded by the symbol *. When you find a year preceded by the symbol △, the year is the date of the citing material.

Citations to each provision of the Code of Federal Regulations are grouped as follows:

1. citing federal cases;

2. citing state cases;

3. citing legal periodical literature;

4. citing annotations.

The 1973 edition of section 53.111 was held unconstitutional in part "Up" by a United States District Court case reported in 453 Federal Supplement "FS" 410. Another United States District Court decision held § 53.111 void or invalid in part "Vp." The United States Court of Appeals in 1977 determined that § 53.111 was valid, "Va."

Section 53.111 has also been cited by the Courts of Massachusetts, New York, and Oregon. A citing legal periodical is shown by the reference 88 Yale Law Journal "YLJ" 277, and a citing annotation "n" is shown by the reference 11 American Law Reports, Federal "ALRF" 684.

---

the specific year or edition of that regulation. Shepard's uses a triangle in such situations. If, for example, the cited regulation you were sheparding is 12 C.F.R. § 9.18(a)(3), you might find the following:

**§9.18(a)(3)**
274FS628△1967

The citing material is a citing case—274 F. Supp. 628. The small triangle means that the citing case did not refer to the year or edition of section 9.18(a)(3). When this occurs, the year next to the triangle is the year of the citing case and not the year of the cited regulation. The citing case of 274 F. Supp. 628 was decided in 1967.

### Checklist #4c

| Checklist for Shepardizing a Federal Regulation |
|---|
| 1. Go to *Shepard's Code of Federal Regulations Citations*. |
| 2. Know whether you have a complete set of Shepard's in front of you by reading the "What Your Library Should Contain" list on the most recent pamphlet in that set. |
| 3. Shepardize your regulation through every unit of this set of Shepard's. |
| 4. This set of Shepard's will give you two kinds of information:<br>(a) Citing material that analyzes a regulation and mentions the specific year or edition of that regulation (indicated by an asterisk next to the year) |

Continued

Checklist #4c—*Continued*

| **Checklist for Shepardizing a Federal Regulation—*Continued*** |
|---|
| **(b)** Citing material that analyzes a regulation without referring to the specific year or edition of the regulation (indicated by a triangle next to the year)<br><br>The citing material includes citing cases, citing legal periodical literature, and citing annotations. |
| **5.** This set of Shepard's does not directly tell you what amendments, revisions, or other changes were made *by the agencies* to the regulations. You are told only what *the courts* have said about the regulations. (To find out what the agencies have done to the regulations, you must check sources such as the "CFR Parts Affected" tables in the *Federal Register*.) |
| **6.** Check the abbreviation table and preface at the beginning of most of the Shepard's units. |
| **7.** All regulations in C.F.R. are based on statutes of Congress. As we will see later, you can find out what statutes in U.S.C. are the authority for particular regulations in C.F.R. by checking the "authority" reference under many of the regulations in C.F.R. Once you know the statute that is the basis for the regulation, you might want to shepardize that statute for more law in the area. (See Checklist 4b on shepardizing a statute.) |

## 5. Loose-Leaf Services

Loose-leaf services are law books with a three-ring or post-binder structure. Additions to these services are made frequently—monthly or sooner. The major publishers of the services are Bureau of National Affairs (BNA), Commerce Clearing House (CCH), Prentice-Hall (PH), and Matthew Bender. They cover numerous areas of the law, such as criminal law, taxes, corporate law, and unions. You should assume that one or more loose-leaf services exist for the topic of your research problem until you prove to yourself otherwise. The contents of loose-leaf services often include the following:

- Recent court opinions or summaries of opinions
- Relevant legislation—usually explained in some detail
- Administrative regulations and decisions, or summaries of them (some of this material may not be available elsewhere)
- References to relevant studies and reports
- Practice tips

In short, the loose-leaf services are extremely valuable. Unfortunately, however, they are sometimes awkward to use. Occasionally, library users of the loose-leaf services misfile pages that they take out for photocopying.

There is no standard format to the loose-leaf books. You may find the following, for example:

- One volume or multivolume
- Organization by page number, organization by section number, organization by paragraph number, or a combination of these
- Different colored pages to indicate more recent material
- Indexes at the end, in the middle, or at the beginning of the volumes
- Bound volumes that accompany the three-ring volumes
- Transfer binders that contain current material

You should approach the structure of each loose-leaf service as a small puzzle sitting on the shelf waiting for you to be put together.

## Checklist #5

| **Checklist for Finding and Using Loose-Leaf Services** |
| --- |
| 1. Divide your research problem into its major topics, such as family law, tax law, antitrust law, etc. Assume that one or more loose-leaf services exist for these topics until you have demonstrated to yourself otherwise. |
| 2. Find out where the loose-leaf services are located in your library. Are they all together? Are they located in certain subject areas? Does the library have a separate list of them? |
| 3. Check the card catalog. Look for subject heading cards on your topics to see if loose-leaf services are mentioned. Check the names of the major publishers of loose-leaf services—Bureau of National Affairs, Commerce Clearing House, Prentice-Hall, Matthew Bender. |
| 4. Ask library staff members if they know of loose-leaf services on the major topics of your research. |
| 5. Call other law libraries in your area. Ask the staff members there if they know of loose-leaf services on the major topics of your research. See if they can identify loose-leaf services that you could not identify through your own library. |
| 6. Speak to experts in the area of the law, e.g., professors. (See Checklist #9.) Ask them about loose-leaf services. |
| 7. Once you have a loose-leaf service in front of you, you must figure out how to use it:<br><br>(a) Read any preface or explanatory material in the front of the volumes of the loose-leaf service<br><br>(b) Ask library staff members to give you some help<br><br>(c) Ask teachers who are experts in the area if they can give you a brief demonstration on its use<br><br>(d) Ask a fellow student who is familiar with the service<br><br>(e) Read any pamphlets or promotional literature by the publishers on using their loose-leaf services<br><br>(f) Do the best that you can to struggle through the set on your own<br><br>For each loose-leaf service, you need to know the following:<br><br>■ What it contains and what it does not contain<br><br>■ How it is indexed<br><br>■ How it is supplemented<br><br>■ What its special features are<br><br>■ How many volumes or units it has and the interrelationship among them<br><br>You obtain this information through techniques (a) to (f) above. |
| 8. In your research memo, you rarely cite a loose-leaf service unless the material you found there does not exist elsewhere. Use the loose-leaf service mainly as background research and as a search tool for leads to find cases, statutes, regulations, etc.—in other words, to find primary authority. |

## 6. Legal Periodical Literature

Legal periodical literature consists of the following:

- Lead articles and comments written by individuals who have extensively researched a topic
- Case notes that summarize and comment on important court opinions
- Book reviews.

Most periodicals are published by law students who are "on law review" or "on the law journal" at their law school. There are hundreds of legal periodicals containing a wealth of information for the researcher.

How can you locate legal periodical literature on point? What index systems exist for the hundreds of periodicals and the tens of thousands of articles, case notes, comments, and other material in them? There are three major index systems:

- Index to Legal Periodicals (ILP), published by H.W. Wilson Co.
- Current Law Index (CLI), published by Information Access Corporation
- Legal Resource Index (LRI), published by Information Access Corporation

While all three systems are extensive, CLI and LRI are more comprehensive than ILP. Comprehensiveness is determined by the number of periodicals indexed. The benefit of a comprehensive index is that you obtain access to many periodicals. Unfortunately, most law libraries will *not* have all the periodicals mentioned in the index. You may be obtaining cites to periodicals that your library does not have. If so, you need to check other libraries in the area.

### (a) Index to Legal Periodicals (ILP)

- The ILP first comes out in pamphlets that are later consolidated (i.e., cumulated) into bound volumes.
- You must check each ILP pamphlet and each ILP bound volume for whatever years you want.
- ILP regularly adds new periodicals to be indexed.
- Every ILP pamphlet and bound volume has four indexes:
    - **(1)** A subject-and-author index
    - **(2)** A table of cases commented on
    - **(3)** A table of statutes commented on (added recently)
    - **(4)** A book review index
- There are abbreviations tables at the beginning of every pamphlet and bound volume.
- The "subject" portion of the subject-and-author index is easy to use; you are given full bibliographic references to periodical literature under the subjects relevant to your research topics.
- Beginning in 1983, the "author" portion of the subject-and-author index also has full bibliographic references to periodical literature by that author. Prior to 1983, however, the use of the "author" portion was more complex. If you know the name of an author but not the title of his or her article, you look for that author's name in the subject-and-author index. Under that

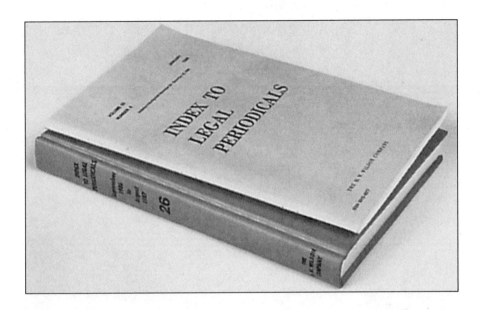

name you will find one or more subjects and capital letters in parentheses after the topics. Go to those subjects in the subject-and-author index. Under those subjects, look for articles beginning with the capital letters you initially found in parentheses until you locate the article by the author you want. This awkward procedure applies only to pre-1983 ILP volumes.

■ Toward the end of every ILP pamphlet and bound volume there is a Table of Cases Commented Upon. Suppose that elsewhere in your research you come across an important case, and you now want to know if that case was ever commented on (i.e., noted) in the legal periodicals. Go to the ILP pamphlet or bound volume that covers the year of the case and check the Table of Cases Commented Upon.

■ The Table of Statutes Commented Upon will tell you where you can find periodical literature analyzing certain statutes.

■ At the end of every pamphlet and bound ILP volume there is a book review index. If you are looking for a review of a law book you have come across elsewhere in your research, go to the ILP pamphlet or bound volume that covers the year of publication of the book for which you are seeking reviews.

■ ILP is also available:

   **(1)** On WILSONLINE, the publisher's online research system

   **(2)** On WILSONDISC, a CD-ROM system (page 495)

   **(3)** On WESTLAW

   **(4)** On LEXIS

*(b)  Current Law Index (CLI)*

■ The CLI first comes out in pamphlets that are later consolidated (i.e., cumulated) into bound volumes.

■ CLI indexes more periodical literature than ILP.

■ CLI regularly adds new periodicals to be indexed.

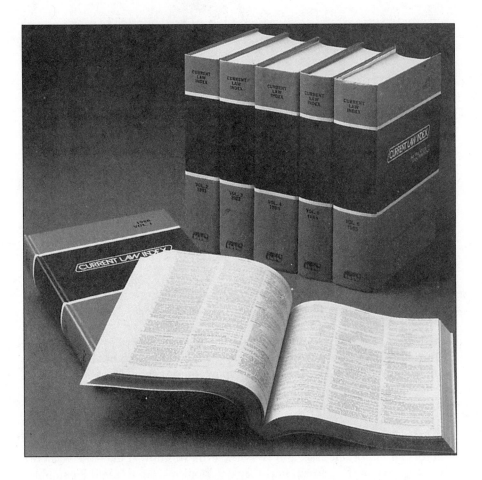

- Check all current pamphlets and all annual issues for the years you want.
- There are four indexes within each CLI unit:
  - A subject index
  - An author-title index
  - A table of cases
  - A table of statutes
- There are abbreviation tables at the beginning of every CLI unit.
- The subject index gives full citations to periodicals under a topic and under an author's name.
- Book reviews are included under the author-title index along with cites to periodical literature by the authors.
- The table of cases is valuable if you already know the name of a case located elsewhere in your research. To find out if that case was commented on, check the table of cases in the CLI unit that covers the year of the case.
- The table of statutes is equally valuable. If you already have the name of a statute from your other research (such as Atomic Energy Act; California Fair Employment Practices Act), look for the name of that statute in the table of statutes for the CLI unit that covers the approximate time the statute was passed.

- The CLI began in 1980; it does not index periodicals prior to this date. The ILP must be used for this period.

### (c) Legal Resource Index (LRI)

- LRI provides the same material as CLI; they are both published by Information Access Corporation.
- LRI can be used in several ways:
  - On microfilm with a special viewer machine (see photo below)
  - On LegalTrac, a computer using CD-ROM (page 495)
  - On WESTLAW
  - On LEXIS

### Other Index Systems.

A number of other periodical index systems exist:

- Index to Federal Tax Articles
- Index to Foreign Legal Periodicals
- Index to Canadian Legal Periodical Literature
- Jones-Chipman Index to Legal Periodical Literature (covering periodical literature up to 1937 only)
- Index Medicus (covers medical periodicals—available in medical libraries)
- MEDLINE (a computer search system for medical periodicals—available in medical libraries)

Checklist #6

| **Checklist for Finding Legal Periodical Literature** |
|---|
| **1.** Use legal periodical literature for background research and for leads to primary authority, particularly through the extensive footnotes in this literature. Scholarly articles can also be cited in your research memo. |
| **2.** There are three major index systems: Index to Legal Periodicals (ILP), Current Law Index (CLI), and Legal Resource Index (LRI). |
| **3.** The CARTWHEEL will help you locate material in these index systems. |
| **4.** Within ILP there are separate indexes. Within CLI and LRI there are also separate indexes. You should become familiar with all these internal index features. |
| **5.** Start with the subject headings index within ILP, CLI, and LRI. |
| **6.** Identify the name and date of every important case that you have found in your research thus far. Go to the table of cases in ILP, in CLI, and in LRI to find out if there is any periodical literature that has commented on that case. (Go to the ILP, CLI, and LRI units that would cover the year the case was decided. To be safe, also check their units for two years after the date of the case.) |
| **7.** If you are researching a statute, find out if there is any periodical literature that has commented on the statute. This is done in two ways:<br><br>**(a)** Check the table of statutes in ILP, CLI, and LRI.<br><br>**(b)** Break your statute down into its major topics. Check these topics in the subject indexes of ILP, CLI, and LRI to see if any periodical literature has been written on these topics. |
| **8.** If you have the name of an author who is known for writing on a particular topic, you can also check for literature written by that author under his or her name in ILP, CLI, and LRI. |
| **9.** Ask library staff members if the library has any other indexes to legal periodical literature, particularly in specialty areas of the law. |
| **10.** It is possible to shepardize some legal periodical literature. If you want to know whether the periodical article, note, or comment was ever mentioned in a court opinion, go to *Shepard's Law Review Citations*. |
| **11.** It is possible to search for legal periodical literature online in WESTLAW, LEXIS, and WILSONLINE. |

## 7. Legal Encyclopedias

Here our main concern is using the major national encyclopedias: *American Jurisprudence 2d* (Am. Jur. 2d), and *Corpus Juris Secundum* (C.J.S.).

Checklist #7

| **Checklist for Using Legal Encyclopedias** |
|---|
| **1.** Use both Am. Jur. 2d and C.J.S. for the following purposes:<br><br>**(a)** As background research for areas of the law that are new to you<br><br>**(b)** For leads in their extensive footnotes to primary authority, such as cases, statutes, etc. |

Continued

Checklist #7—*Continued*

| **Checklist for Using Legal Encyclopedias—*Continued*** |
|---|
| 2. Both legal encyclopedias have multivolume general indexes at the end of their sets. Use the CARTWHEEL to help you locate material in them. In addition to these general indexes, Am. Jur. 2d and C.J.S. have a separate index to many of the individual volumes. |
| 3. There is no table of cases in either Am. Jur. 2d or C.J.S. |
| 4. There is no table of statutes in C.J.S. In Am. Jur. 2d, however, there is a separate volume called *Table of Statutes, Rules, and Regulations Cited*. Check this table if you have found a relevant statute, regulation, or rule of court from your other research that you want to find discussed in Am. Jur. 2d. |
| 5. Am. Jur. 2d is published by Lawyers Co-op. C.J.S. is published by West. Within these legal encyclopedias, the publishers provide cross-references to other research books that they publish. In Am. Jur. 2d, for example, Lawyers Co-op will refer you to annotations in A.L.R., A.L.R.2d, A.L.R.3d, A.L.R.4th, and A.L.R. Fed. In C.J.S., West will refer you to its key number digests. |
| 6. Find out if your library has a *local* encyclopedia that is limited to the law of your state. Among the states with such encyclopedias are California, Florida, Illinois, Kentucky, Maryland, Michigan, New York, Ohio, Pennsylvania, and Texas. |

## 8. Treatises

As mentioned, a treatise is any book written by private individuals (or by public officials writing in a private capacity) on a topic of law. Some treatises are scholarly while others are more practice oriented. The latter are often called hornbooks, handbooks, formbooks, and practice manuals. Treatises give overview summaries of the law, and references to primary authority. There are single-volume treatises such as *Prosser on Torts*, as well as multivolume treatises such as *Moore's Federal Practice, Collier on Bankruptcy*, etc.

Checklist #8

| **Checklist for Finding and Using Treatises** |
|---|
| 1. Always look for treatises on the topics of your research problem. Assume, until you prove to yourself otherwise, that three or four such treatises exist and are relevant to your problem. |
| 2. Treatises are useful for background research, and for leads to primary authority. |
| 3. Many treatises are updated by pocket parts, supplemental volumes, and page inserts if the treatise has a three-ring or post-binding structure. |
| 4. Start your search for treatises in the card catalog. See Checklist #1 on using the catalog. |
| 5. Check with experts in the area of law in which you are interested, e.g., teachers, for recommendations on treatises you should examine. See Checklist #9. |
| 6. If your library has open stacks, find the treatise section (with KF call numbers, for example). Locate the areas containing treatises on your topic. Browse through the shelves in these areas of the stacks to try to find additional treatises. (Some treatises that you need may be on reserve.) |
| 7. Once you have found a treatise, check that author's name in the Index to Legal Periodicals (ILP), the Current Law Index (CLI), and the Legal Resource Index (LRI) to try to find periodical literature on the same topic by this author. You can also use these indexes to see if there are any book reviews on the treatises. (See Checklist #6 on finding legal periodical literature.) |

## 9. Phone and Mail—Speak with the Experts

Don't be reluctant to call recognized experts on the topics of your research. If you can get through to them and if you adopt a sufficiently humble attitude, they may give you leads to important laws and may even discuss the facts of your research problem. Many experts are quite willing to help you free of charge, as long as you are respectful and do not give the impression that you want more than a few moments of their time. You do not ask to come over to spend an afternoon!

Checklist #9

| **Checklist for Doing Phone and Mail Research** |
|---|
| **1.** Your goal is to contact someone who is an expert in the area of your research problem. You want to try to talk with him or her briefly on the phone. (You can try to contact experts through the mail, but this route is seldom as successful as phone contact.) |
| **2.** Do not try to contact an expert until you have first done a substantial amount of research on your own. For instance, you should have already checked the major cases, statutes, regulations, treatises, legal periodical literature, annotations, etc., that are readily available in the library. |
| **3.** Prepare the questions you want to ask the expert. Make them short and to the point. For example, "Do you know of any recent case law on the liability of a municipality for . . .?" "Could you give me any leads to literature on the doctrine of promissory estoppel as it applies to . . .?" "Do you know anyone who has done any empirical research on the new EPA regulations whom I could contact?" "Do you know of anyone currently litigating § 307?" Do *not* recite all the facts of the research problem to the expert and say, "What should I do?" If the expert wants more facts from you, let him or her ask you for them. You must create the impression that you want no more than a few moments of the expert's time. If the experts want to give your request more attention, they will let you know. |
| **4.** Introduce yourself as a student doing research on a problem. State how you got their name (see guideline below) and then state how grateful you would be if you could ask them a "quick question." |
| **5.** Your introductory comments should state how you came across their name and learned of their expertise. For example, say "I read your law review article on . . . ." "I saw your name as an attorney of record in the case of . . . ." "Mr./Ms. _____ told me you were an expert in this area and recommended that I contact you." |
| **6.** Where do you find these experts? A number of possibilities exist: <br><br> **(a)** *Special interest groups and associations* <br>      Contact attorneys within groups and associations such as unions, environmental groups, and business associations. Ask your librarian for lists of such groups and associations, for example, the *Encyclopedia of Associations*, the *Directory of Directories*. <br><br> **(b)** *Government agencies* <br>      Contact the law departments of the agencies that have something to do with the topics of your research problem. <br><br> **(c)** *Specialty libraries* <br>      Ask your librarian for lists of libraries, such as the *Directory of Special Libraries and Information Centers*. <br><br> **(d)** *Law professors* <br>      Ask a librarian if the library has the *AALS Law Teachers Directory,* which lists teachers by name and specialty across the country. <br><br> **(e)** *Attorneys of Record* <br>      If you have found a recent court opinion on point, the names of the attorneys for the case are printed at the beginning of the opinion (see page 354). Try to |

Continued

Checklist #9—*Continued*

---

**Checklist for Doing Phone and Mail Research—*Continued***

obtain the phone number and address of the attorneys in *West's Legal Directory* or *Martindale-Hubbell Law Directory*. These attorneys may be willing to send you a copy of appellate briefs on the case. Also try to find out about ongoing litigation in the courts.

    Often you are permitted to go to the court clerk's office and examine pleadings, appellate briefs, etc., on pending cases. Finally, don't forget to check the closed case files of your own office for prior research that has already been done in the same area as your problem.

**(f)** *Authors of legal periodical literature and of treatises*
    Try to contact the author of a treatise or law review article that is relevant to your research. The author's business address can often be found in sources such as the *Law Teacher's Directory, West's Legal Directory, Martindale-Hubbell,* etc.

---

## 10. Computers

If you have access to any of the computerized legal research services, ask for a demonstration on how to operate the computer from the librarian or from the company that produces the computer. *CALR* (Computer Assisted Legal Research) is becoming more and more common and essential. An overview of some legal research computer services are listed below. We will return to the major ones in Chapter 13.

### WESTLAW® by West Publishing Company

WESTLAW contains a great deal of material. Here are some examples: federal court opinions; state court opinions; United States Code; state statutes; the Code of Federal Regulations; administrative decisions; treatises published by West, Commerce Clearing House, Bureau of National Affairs, Prentice-Hall, and other publishers; legal periodical literature; a *West's Legal Directory* containing the addresses of attorneys throughout the United States; nonlegal data from Dow Jones and DIALOG, etc. You can check the current validity of cases and statutes by using Insta-Cite, QuickCite, Shepard's Preview, and Shepard's online—without leaving the computer. There are also special databases in many areas, such as international law, professional responsibility (ethics), taxation, securities, medicine, etc. Other special databases that can be of unique value to litigators contain the names and addresses of experts in the fields of science, engineering, economics, etc. Each day more material is added to WESTLAW.

### LEXIS® by Mead Data Central

LEXIS is also a massive source of *online* data. Examples include: federal and state court opinions; federal and state statutes; Code of Federal Regulations; administrative decisions; treatises, *Martindale-Hubbell Law Directory;* annotations in A.L.R.2d, A.L.R.3d, A.L.R.4th, A.L.R. Fed., and in Lawyers' Edition 2d; special libraries on taxation, insurance, and international law; treatises published by Commerce Clearing House and the Bureau of National Affairs; nonlegal databases covering medicine, patents, current news, etc.; validation data through Shepard's and Auto-Cite, etc. As with WESTLAW, materials are being added to LEXIS regularly.

In Chapter 13 when we discuss databases in general, we will examine WESTLAW and LEXIS in greater detail. In particular, we will cover the critical skill of formulating a *query,* or question to ask WESTLAW and LEXIS.

### Auto-Cite and VERALEX by Lawyers Cooperative Publishing Company

Auto-Cite permits you to check the accuracy of a legal citation. It provides parallel cites and cites to other opinions in the same litigation. Auto-Cite also gives you citations to annotations in A.L.R., A.L.R.2d, A.L.R.3d, A.L.R.4th, and A.L.R. Fed. The full text of any of these annotations can be found and read online through two computer services: LEXIS and VERALEX.

### WILSONLINE by H.W. Wilson Co.

H.W. Wilson publishes a number of periodical indexes, such as *Index to Legal Periodicals* (ILP) and *Reader's Guide*. If you want to use these indexes online, you can do so through a service called WILSONLINE. (The indexes are also available on CD-ROM as well as on a service called WILSONDISC.)

### DIALOG by Dialog Information Services

This online service provides access to a large volume of material, such as the complete text of articles from over 800 newspapers, magazines, newsletters, and trade journals; MEDLINE, a massive index to articles in medical periodicals; the complete text of selected newswires and encyclopedias; psychological abstracts; information on numerous corporations via Dun & Bradstreet, Standard & Poor's, Moody's; employee benefits data via EBIS; patent and trademarks; etc. DIALOG is also available through WESTLAW.

### NEXIS by Mead Data Central

NEXIS contains the full text of daily newspapers such as the *New York Times* and the *Los Angeles Times,* numerous magazines and trade journals, newsletters, etc.

## ▉ Section O. Finding Case Law

In Chapter 7, we covered the structure of a court opinion, the briefing of an opinion, and the application of an opinion to a set of facts. Here our focus is *finding* these opinions in the library—finding case law.

In searching for case law, you will probably find yourself in one or more of the following situations:

- You already have one opinion on point (or close to being on point) and you want to find additional ones.

- You are looking for opinions interpreting a statute, constitution, charter, ordinance, court rule, or regulation that you already have.

- You are starting from square one. You want to find case law when you do not have a case, statute, or other law to begin with. You may be looking for opinions containing common law (judge-made law in the absence of controlling statutory or constitutional law), and you have no such opinions to begin with.

The following search techniques are not necessarily listed in the order in which they should be tried. Your goal is to know how to use all of them. In practice, you can vary the order.

First, a reminder about doing the first level of legal research: background research. You should review the checklist for background research presented in Figure 11.10. While doing this research, you will probably come across laws that will be of help to you on the specific facts of your problem (which is the second level of research). If so, you may already have some case law. You now want to find more.

---

### Techniques for Finding Case Law
### When You Already Have One Case on Point

1. *Shepardize the case that you have.* (See Checklist #4a on shepardizing cases, page 569.) In the columns of Shepard's, look for cases that have mentioned your case. Such cases will probably cover similar topics.

2. *Go to the West digests.* There are two ways to do this:

   (a) Go to the table of cases in all the digests covering the court that wrote the case you already have, such as the table of cases in the *American Digest System.* The table of cases will tell you what key topics and numbers your case is digested under in the main volumes of the digest. Find your case digested under those key topics and numbers. Once you have done so, you will probably be able to find other case law under the same key topics and numbers.

   (b) Go to the West reporter that contains the full text of the case you already have. At the beginning of this case in the reporter, find the headnotes and their key topics and numbers. Take the key topics and numbers that are relevant to your problem into the digests of West to find more case law.

   (See Checklist #2 on using digests, page 556.)

3. *Find an annotation.* First identify the main topics or issues in the case you already have. Look up those topics in the *Quick Index* (to find annotations in A.L.R. First), and in the *ALR Index* (to find annotations in A.L.R.2d, A.L.R.3d, A.L.R.4th, and A.L.R. Fed.). Other ways to find annotations include shepardizing the case you have and using Auto-Cite. Once you have such an annotation, you will be given extensive citations to more case law. (See Checklist #3 on finding annotations, page 561.)

4. *Find a discussion of your case in the legal periodicals.* Go to the table of cases in the Index of Legal Periodicals (ILP), the Current Law Index (CLI), and the Legal Resource Index (LRI). There you will be told if your case was analyzed (noted) in the periodicals. If so, the discussion may give you additional case law on the same topic. (See Checklist #6 on finding legal periodical literature, page 582.)

5. *Go to Words and Phrases.* Identify the major words or phrases that are dealt with in the case you have. Check the definition of those words and phrases in the multivolume legal dictionary, *Words and Phrases.* By so doing you will be led to other cases defining the same words or phrases.

---

Now let us assume that you already have a statute and you want case law interpreting that statute. The techniques for doing so (many of which are the same when seeking case law interpreting constitutions, regulations, etc.) are as follows:

---

### Techniques for Finding Case Law Interpreting a Statute

1. *Shepardize the statute that you have.* (See Checklist #4b on shepardizing statutes, page 573.) In the columns of Shepard's, look for cases that have mentioned your statute.

2. *Examine your statute in the statutory code.* At the end of your statute in the statutory code, there are paragraph summaries of cases (often called Notes of Decisions) that have interpreted your statute. Check these summaries in the bound volume of the code, in the pocket part of this volume, and in any supplemental pamphlets at the end of the code. (For federal statutes, the codes to check are U.S.C.A. and U.S.C.S. The U.S.C. will not have such case summaries.)

---

Continued

---

### Techniques for Finding Case Law Interpreting a Statute—*Continued*

3. *Find an annotation on your statute.* To find out if there is an annotation in A.L.R, A.L.R.2d, etc. that mentions your statute, shepardize that statute. Such annotations are among the "citing materials" of Shepard's. (Also, if the statute is federal, check the Table of Laws, Rules, and Regulations in volume 6 of the *ALR Index*. See page 559.) Such annotations will probably lead you to more case law on the statute.

4. *Find legal periodical literature on your statute.* There are three ways to do this:

   (a) Shepardize the statute. (See technique 1 above.) Citing material for a statute includes legal periodical literature.

   (b) Check the table of statutes in the Current Law Index (CLI), the Legal Resource Index (LRI), and the Index to Legal Periodicals (ILP).

   (c) Go to the subject indexes in ILP, CLI, and LRI and check the topics of your statute.

5. *Go to loose-leaf services on your statute.* Find out if there is a loose-leaf service on the subject matter of your statute. Such services often give extensive cites to cases on the statute. (See Checklist #5 on loose-leaf services, page 577.)

6. *Go to treatises on your statute.* Most major statutes have treatises on them that contain extensive cites to cases on the statute. (See Checklist #8 on treatises, page 583.)

7. *Shepardize any cases you found through techniques 1–6 above.* You may be led to additional case law on the statute.

---

Finally, we assume that you are starting from scratch. You are looking for case law and you do not have a starting case or statute with which to begin. You may be looking for common law or for cases interpreting statutes that you have not found yet.

---

### Techniques for Finding Case Law When You Do Not Have a Case or Statute to Begin With

1. *West digests.* Try to find key topics and numbers in the Descriptive Word Indexes (DWI) of the West digests. (See Checklist #2 on using digests of West, page 556.)

2. *Annotations.* Try to locate annotations through the index systems for A.L.R., A.L.R.2d, A.L.R.3d, A.L.R.4th, and A.L.R. Fed. (See Checklist #3 on finding annotations, page 561.)

3. *Treatises.* Try to find treatises in the card catalog. (See Checklist #8 on finding treatises, page 583.)

4. *Loose-leaf services.* Find out if there are loose-leaf services on the topics of your research. (See Checklist #5 on finding loose-leaf services, page 577.)

5. *Legal periodical literature.* Try to find legal periodical literature in the subject indexes of ILP, CLI, and LRI. (See Checklist #6 on finding legal periodical literature, page 582.)

6. *Legal encyclopedias.* Go to the indexes for Am. Jur. 2d and C.J.S. Try to find discussions in these legal encyclopedias. (See Checklist #7 on using legal encyclopedias, page 582.)

7. *Computers* (page 585).

8. *Phone and mail research.* Find an expert. (See Checklist #9 on doing phone and mail research, page 584.)

---

Continued

---

**Techniques for Finding Case Law When You Do Not Have a Case or Statute to Begin With—*Continued***

9. *Words and Phrases.* Identify all the major words or phrases from the facts of your research problem. Look up these words or phrases in the multivolume legal dictionary, *Words and Phrases,* which gives case law definitions.

10. *Shepardizing.* If techniques 1–9 lead you to any case law, shepardize what you have found in order to look for more cases. (See Checklist #4a on shepardizing a case, page 569.)

---

# ■ P. Reading and Finding Statutes

## Reading Statutes

On page 591, there is an example of a statute from a New York statutory code. Here is an explanation of the circled numbers in this excerpt:

① This is the section number of the statute. The mark "§" before "146" means section.

② This is a heading summarizing the main topic of the statute. Section 146 covers who can visit state prisons in New York. This summarization was written by the private publishing company, not by the New York state legislature.

③ Here is the body of the statute written by the legislature.

④ At the end of a statutory section you will often find a reference to session laws (page 571), using abbreviations such as L. (laws), P.L. (Public Law), Stat. (Statutes at Large), etc. Here you are told that in the Laws (L) of 1962, chapter (c) 37, § 3, this statute was amended. The Laws referred to are the session laws. See the Historical Note ⑥ below for a further treatment of this amendment.

⑤ The amendment to . 146 was effective ("eff.") on February 20, 1962. The amendment may have been passed by the legislature on an earlier date, but the date on which it became the law of New York was February 20, 1962.

⑥ The Historical Note provides the reader with some of the legislative history (page 596) of . 146. First, the reader is again told that . 146 was amended in 1962. Note that in the second and third lines of the body of the statute, the title "commissioner of general services" is found. The 1962 amendment simply changed the title from "superintendent of standards and purchase" to "commissioner of general services."

⑦ Also, part of the Historical Note is the "Derivation" section. This tells the reader that the topic of . 146 of the Corrections Law was once contained in . 160 of the Prison Law, which dates back to 1847. In 1929 there was another amendment. The Historical Note was written by the private publisher, not by the New York state legislature.

⑧ The "Cross References" refer the reader to other statutes that cover topics similar to . 146.

⑨ The "Library References" refer the reader to other texts that address the topic of the statute. On the left-hand side, there are two topics, "Prisons" and "Reformatories," each followed by key numbers. The key numbers refer the reader to the digests of West Publishing Company. On the right column there is the abbreviation C.J.S. (*Corpus Juris Secundum*), a legal encyclopedia.

## § 146.    Persons authorized to visit prisons

The following persons shall be authorized to visit at pleasure all state prisons: The governor and lieutenant-governor, commissioner of general services, secretary of state, comptroller and attorney-general, members of the commission of correction, members of the legislature, judges of the court of appeals, supreme court and county judges, district attorneys and every minister of the gospel having charge of a congregation in the town wherein any such prison is situated. No other person not otherwise authorized by law shall be permitted to enter a state prison except under such regulations as the commissioner of correction shall prescribe. The provisions of this section shall not apply to such portion of a prison in which prisoners under sentence of death are confined.

As amended L.1962, c. 37, § 3, eff. Feb. 20, 1962.

### Historical Note

L.1962, c. 37, § 3, eff. Feb. 20, 1962, substituted "commissioner of general services" for "superintendent of standards and purchase".

**Derivation.** Prior to the general amendment of this chapter by L.1929, c. 243, the subject matter of this section was contained in former Prison Law, § 160; originally derived from R.S., pt. 4, c. 3, tit. 3, § 159, as amended L.1847, c. 460.

### Cross References

Promoting prison contraband, see Penal Law, §§ 205.20, 205.25.

### Library References

Prisons ☞13.
Reformatories ☞7.

C.J.S. Prisons §§ 18, 19.
C.J.S. Reformatories §§ 10, 11.

### Notes of Decisions

**1. Attorneys**

Warden of maximum security prison was justified in requiring that interviews of prisoners by attorney be conducted in presence of guard in room, in view of fact that attorney, who sought to interview 34 inmates in a day and a half, had shown no retainer agreements and had not stated purpose of consultations. Kahn v. La Vallee, 1961, 12 A.D.2d 832, 209 N.Y.S.2d 591.

Supreme court did not have jurisdiction of petition by prisoner to compel prison warden to provide facilities in prison which would not interfere with alleged violation of rights of prisoner to confer in private with his attorney. Mummiani v. La Vallee, 1959, 21 Misc.2d 437, 199 N.Y.S.2d 263, affirmed 12 A.D.2d 832, 209 N.Y.S.2d 591.

Right of prisoners to confer with counsel after conviction is not absolute but is subject to such regulations as commissioner of correction may prescribe, and prisoners were not entitled to confer with their attorney privately within sight, but outside of hearing of a prison guard, when warden insisted on having a guard present in order to insure against any impropriety or infraction of prison rules and regulations during interview. Id.

⑩ The most important research reference is the "Notes of Decisions." It includes a series of paragraphs that briefly summarize every court decision that has interpreted or applied § 146. Of course, the decisions cover cases decided before the book was published. For later decisions, the reader must look to the pocket part of the code volume that contains § 146, and to any supplemental pamphlets at the end of the code. The first decision that you are given is *Kahn v. La Vallee.* Next is *Mummiani v. La Vallee.* At the end of the final paragraph, you will find "Id.," which means that the paragraph refers to the case cited in the immediately preceding paragraph, the *Mummiani* case. (Of course, another way to find later decisions is to shepardize § 146. See Checklist #4b on shepardizing a statute.)

With this perspective of what an annotated statute looks like, we turn to some general guidelines on understanding statutes:

*1. Statutory codes are heavily stratified.*   A statutory code can contain anywhere from 5 to 150 volumes. If you are unfamiliar with a code, you should examine the first few pages of the first volume. There you will usually find the subject matter arrangement of all the volumes, e.g., "agency," "corrections," "corporations." Different states often have varied labels and categorization schemes.

An individual subject matter in a code may be further broken down into titles, parts, articles, or chapters, which are then broken down into sections and subsections. Here is an example of a possible categorization for the state of "X":

X Code Annotated

Title 1.  Corporate Law

Chapter 1.  Forming a Corporation

Section 1.  Choosing a Corporate Name

Subsection 1(a).  Where to File the Name Application

Subsection 1(b).  Displaying the Name Certificate

Subsection 1(c).  Changing the Corporate Name

Section 2 . . . .

Chapter 2 . . . .

Etc.

Note again, however, that each jurisdiction may adopt its own classification terminology. What is called a chapter in one state may be called a title in another.

You also need to be sensitive to the internal context of a particular statutory section. A section is often a sub-sub-subunit of larger units.

Example: Examine § 1183 in Figure 11.18. § 1183 is within Part II, which is within Subchapter II, which is within chapter 12, which is within title 8.

As indicated earlier, a legislature may completely revise its labeling system (page 542). What was once "Prison Law," for example, may now fall under the topic heading of "Correction Law." What was once section 73(b) of "Corporations Law" may now be section 13(f) of the "Business and Professions Law." If such a reordering has occurred, you should be able to find out about it either in a transfer table at the beginning of one of the code volumes or in the Historical Note at the bottom of the section.

*2. A common sequence of statutes on administrative agencies.*   Statutes are carried out mainly by administrative agencies. The agency may be a grant-making or service agency (such as the Social Security Administration) or a regulatory agency (such as the Federal Power Commission, the State Utilities Com-

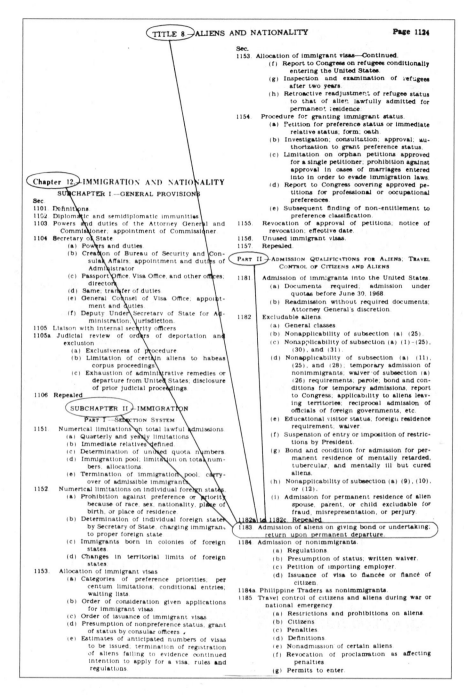

**FIGURE 11.18**
Sections, Parts, Subchapters, Chapters, and Titles in a Statutory Code

mission, etc.). Statutes that cover agencies are sometimes organized in the following sequence:

- The agency is created and named.
- The major words and phrases used in this cluster of statutes are defined.
- The administrators of the agency are given titles and powers.
- The budgetary process of the agency is specified.

- The method by which the public first comes into contact with the agency is established, such as applying for the benefits or services of the agency.
- The way in which the agency must act when a citizen complains about the agency's actions is established.
- How the agency must go about terminating a citizen from its services is established.
- The way in which a citizen can appeal to a court, if not satisfied with the way the agency handled his or her complaint, is established.

3. *All statutes must be based on some provision in the Constitution that gives the legislature the power to pass the statute.*   Legislatures have no power to legislate without constitutional authorization. The authorization may be the general constitutional provision vesting all legislative powers in the legislature, or, more often, it will be a specific constitutional provision such as the authority to raise revenue for designated purposes.

4. *Statutory language tends to be unclear.*   Seldom, if ever, is it absolutely clear what a statute means or how it applies to a given set of facts. Because of this, statutory language regularly requires close scrutiny and interpretation.

5. *Statutes are to be read line by line, pronoun by pronoun, punctuation mark by punctuation mark.*   Statutes cannot be speed read. They should be read with the same care that you would use if you were translating a foreign language to English. Sentences sometimes appear endless, and there are often so many qualifications and exceptions built into the statute that it appears incomprehensible. Don't despair. The key is perseverance and a willingness to tackle the statute slowly, piece by piece.

6. *Check to see if a statutory unit has a definition section.*   At the beginning of a cluster of statutes, look for a definition section. If it exists, the section will define a number of words used in the remaining sections of the unit. Here is an example of such a definition section:

> **§ 31.   Definitions.**—As used in this article, unless the context shall require otherwise, the following terms shall have the meanings ascribed to them by this section:
>
> 1. "State" shall mean and include any state, territory or possession of the United States and the District of Columbia.
>
> 2. "Court" shall mean the family court of the state of New York; when the context requires, it shall mean and include a court of another state defined in and upon which appropriate jurisdiction has been conferred by a substantially similar reciprocal law.
>
> 3. "Child" includes a step child, foster child, child born out of wedlock or legally adopted child and means a child under twenty-one years of age, and a son or daughter twenty-one years of age or older who is unable to maintain himself or herself and is or is likely to become a public charge.
>
> 4. "Dependent" shall mean and include any person who is entitled to support pursuant to this article.

7. *Statutes should be briefed.*   Briefing a statute simply means outlining it and breaking it down into its elements (page 347). The following are some of the questions that you should ask yourself in briefing a statute:

(a) What is the citation (the name of the statutory code, volume of the code, number of the section, date of the code edition)?

(b) To whom is the statute addressed? (To everybody? To the director of an agency? To citizens who want to do certain things?) Who is the audience?

(c) Does the statute make reference to other statutes? (If so, then the statute may be unintelligible to you unless you also study the other statutes.)

(d) Is there a condition that will make the statute operative? (Very often the statute will have a "whenever" or a "wherever" clause indicating that whenever or wherever a certain set of facts occur, the statute will be applied; without the occurrence of such facts, the statute may not apply.)

(e) What or whom does the statute specifically *include* in its provisions?

(f) What or whom does the statute specifically *exclude* from its provisions?

(g) Is the statute mandatory or discretionary? (Does it say or imply that someone "must" or "shall" do something, or does it say or imply that someone "may" or "can" do something?)

## Finding Statutes

| Techniques for Finding Statutes |
|---|
| 1. Go to the statutory code in which you are interested. Some states have more than one statutory code. For federal statutes, there is the United States Code (U.S.C.), the United States Code Annotated (U.S.C.A.), and the United States Code Service (U.S.C.S.). Know how to use all available statutory codes that cover the same set of statutes. While they contain the same statutes, the index and research features may differ. |
| 2. Read the explanation or preface pages at the beginning of the first volume of the statutory code. Also read the comparable pages at the beginning of the Shepard's volumes that will enable you to shepardize statutes in that code. These pages can be very helpful in explaining the structure of the code, particularly if there have been new editions, revisions, or renumberings. |
| 3. Most statutory codes have general indexes at the end of the set as well as individual indexes for separate volumes. Use the CARTWHEEL to help you use these indexes. Also check any tables of contents that exist. Some statutes have popular names, such as the Civil Rights Act of 1964. If you know the popular name of a statute, you can find it in the statutory code through a Popular Name Table that often exists within the code itself. |
| 4. While reading one statute in the code, you may be given a cross-reference to another statute within the same code. Check out these cross-references. |
| 5. Loose-leaf services. Find out if there is a loose-leaf service on the topics of your research. Such services will give extensive references to applicable statutes. (See Checklist #5 on finding and using loose-leaf services, page 577.) |
| 6. Treatises. Find out if there are treatises on the topics of your research. Such treatises will often give extensive references to applicable statutes. (See Checklist #8 on finding and using treatises, page 583.) |
| 7. Legal periodical literature. Consult the Index to Legal Periodicals (ILP), the Current Law Index (CLI), and the Legal Resource Index (LRI). Use these indexes to locate periodical literature on the topics of your research. This literature will often give extensive references to applicable statutes. (See Checklist #6 on finding legal periodical literature, page 582.) |
| 8. Annotations. Use the index systems for A.L.R., A.L.R.2d, A.L.R.3d, A.L.R.4th, and A.L.R. Fed. to help you locate annotations. Annotations will sometimes refer you to statutes—particularly in A.L.R. Fed. for federal statutes. (See Checklist #3 on finding and updating annotations, page 561.) |

Continued

| Techniques for Finding Statutes—*Continued* |
|---|
| 9. Legal encyclopedias. Occasionally, legal encyclopedias such as Am.Jur.2d and C.J.S. will give you references to statutes. (See Checklist #7 for using legal encyclopedias, page 582.) |
| 10. Computers. (see page 585.) |
| 11. Phone and mail research. Try to find an expert. (See Checklist #9 on doing phone and mail research, page 584.) |
| 12. For every federal statute that you find, determine whether there are federal regulations on that statute. To find out, check the Parallel Table of Authorities and Rules in the *C.F.R Index and Finding Aids* volume. |
| 13. Shepardize any statute that you locate through techniques 1–11 above. (See Checklist #4b on shepardizing a statute, page 573.) |
| 14. Check the legislative history of important statutes (page 596). |
| 15. Also update any statute that you find in the statutory code by checking the pocket part of the volume you are using, supplementary pamphlets at the end of the code, bound supplement volumes, etc. |
| 16. Occasionally in your research you will come across a statute that is cited in its session law form (page 571). To find this statute in the statutory code, you must translate the session law cite into the codified cite. This is done by trying to find transfer tables in the statutory code. For federal statutes, a session law or Statute at Large cite is translated into a U.S.C./U.S.C.A./U.S.C.S. cite by: <br><br> **(a)** Checking Table III in the Tables volume of U.S.C./U.S.C.A./U.S.C.S. <br><br> **(b)** Checking Table 2 in *U.S. Code Congressional & Administrative News* <br><br> Some session laws, however, are never printed in the statutory code. Hence there is no codified cite for such statutes. You must go directly to the session laws in the library—if the library has them. (For federal statutes, the session laws are in *United States Statutes at Large,* page 516.) It is also possible to shepardize session laws that are not codified, page 571. |

## ■ Section Q. Legislative History

In Chapter 6, we examined the six stages of the legislative process during which a bill becomes law. The documents and events of this process constitute the *legislative history* of a statute. Here we consider two themes:

- Why researchers search for legislative history
- Finding legislative history

### 1. Why Search for Legislative History: Advocacy Objectives

*Problem:* In 1975 the state legislature enacts the Liquor Control Act. Section 33 of this Act provides that "Liquor shall not be sold on Sunday or on any day on which a local, state, or federal election is being held." The Fairfax Country Club claims that § 33 does not apply to the sale of liquor on Sunday or on election day *by membership clubs;* it applies only to bars that provide service to any customers that come in off the street. The question, therefore, is whether the legislature intended to include membership clubs within the restrictions of § 33. The state liquor board says that it did. The Fairfax Country Club argues that it did not.

How can the legislative history of § 33 help resolve this controversy? An advocate has two objectives while researching the legislative history of a statute:

- To determine whether the specific facts currently in controversy were ever discussed by the legislature while it was considering the proposed statute, and

- To determine the broad or narrow purpose that prompted the legislature to enact the statute and to assess whether this purpose sheds any light on the specific facts currently in controversy

For example, when the legislature was considering § 33, was there any mention of country or membership clubs in the governor's message, in committee reports, in floor debates, etc.? If so, what was said about them? What was said about the purpose of § 33? Why was it enacted? What evil or mischief was it designed to combat? Was the legislature opposed to liquor on moral grounds? Did it want to reduce rowdyism that comes from the overuse of liquor? Did it want to encourage citizens to go to church on Sunday and to vote on election day? Were there complaints made to the legislature about the use of liquor by certain groups in the community? If so, what groups? Answers to such questions might be helpful in formulating arguments on the meaning and scope of § 33. The advocate for the Fairfax Country Club will try to demonstrate that the legislature had a narrow objective when it enacted § 33: to prevent neighborhood rowdyism at establishments that serve only liquor. The legislature, therefore, was not trying to regulate the more moderate kind of drinking that normally takes place at membership clubs where food and liquor are often served together. The opponent, on the other hand, will argue that the legislature had a broader purpose in enacting § 33: to decrease the consumption of liquor by all citizens on certain days. The legislature, therefore, did not intend to exclude drinking at a membership club.

## 2.  Finding Legislative History

In tracing legislative history, you are looking for leads to the documents of this history, such as bills, hearing transcripts, proposed amendments, and committee reports. Unfortunately, it is often very difficult to trace the legislative history of *state* statutes. The documents are sometimes poorly preserved, if at all.

| Techniques for Tracing the Legislative History of State Statutes |
|---|
| **1.** Examine the historical data beneath the statute in the statutory code (page 591). Amendments are usually listed there. |
| **2.** For an overview of codification information about your state, check the introductory pages in the first volume of the statutory code, or the beginning of the volume where your statute is found, or the beginning of the Shepard's volume that will enable you to shepardize the statutes of that state. |
| **3.** Ask your librarian if there is a book (sometimes called a legislative service) that covers your state legislature. If one exists, it will give the bill numbers of statutes, proposed amendments, names of committees that considered the statute, etc. If such a text does not exist for your state, ask the librarian how someone finds the legislative history of a state statute in your state. |

Continued

---

**Techniques for Tracing the Legislative History
of State Statutes—*Continued***

4. Contact the committees of both houses of the state legislature that considered the bill. Your local state representative or state senator might be able to help you identify these committees. If your statute is not too old, staff members on these committees may be able to give you leads to the legislative history of the statute. Ask if any committee reports were written. Ask about amendments, etc.

5. Ask your librarian (or a local politician) if there is a law revision commission for your state. If so, contact it for leads.

6. Is there a state law library in your area? If so, contact it for leads.

7. Check the law library and drafting office of the state legislature for leads.

8. Cases interpreting the statute sometimes give the legislative history of the statute, or portions of it. To find cases interpreting a statute, check the Notes of Decisions after the statute in the statutory code (page 591), shepardize the statute, etc. (See also Checklist #4b on shepardizing a statute, page 573.)

9. You may also find leads to the legislative history of a statute in legal periodical literature on the statute (see Checklist #6, page 582), in annotations on the statute (see Checklist #3, page 561), in treatises on the statute (see Checklist #8, page 583), and in loose-leaf services on the statute (see Checklist #5, page 577). Phone and mail research might also provide some leads (see Checklist #9, page 584).

---

It is easier to trace the legislative history of a *federal* statute, since the documents are generally more available.

---

**Techniques for Tracing the Legislative History of a Federal Statute**

1. Examine the historical data at the end of the statute in the United States Code (U.S.C.), in the United States Code Annotated (U.S.C.A.), and in the United States Code Service (U.S.C.S.).

2. You will also find the PL number (Public Law number) of the statute at the end of the statute in U.S.C./U.S.C.A./U.S.C.S. This PL number will be important for tracing legislative history. (Note that each amendment to a statute will have its own PL number.)

3. Step one in tracing the legislative history of a federal statute is to find out if the history has already been compiled by someone else. Ask your librarian. The Library of Congress compiles legislative histories. If the statute deals with a particular federal agency, check with the library or law department of that agency in Washington, D.C., or in the regional office nearest you to see if it has compiled the legislative history. Also check with special interest groups or associations that are directly affected by the statute. They may have compiled the legislative history, which might be available to you. (One question you can ask through phone and mail research is whether the expert knows if anyone has compiled the legislative history of the statute. See Checklist #9 on doing phone and mail research, page 584.) Ask your librarian if there is a *Union List of Legislative Histories* for your area. This list tells you what area libraries have compiled legislative histories on federal statutes.

4. The following texts are useful in tracing the legislative history of federal statutes:

   ■ *U.S. Code Congressional & Administrative News* (see table 4)
   ■ *CCH Congressional Index*
   ■ *Congressional Information Service (CIS) Annual*
   ■ Information Handling Service (legislative histories on microfiche)
   ■ *Digest of Public General Bills and Resolutions*

---

Continued

---

### Techniques for Tracing the Legislative History
### of a Federal Statute—*Continued*

- *Congressional Record* (see Index and the History of Bills and Resolutions for House and Senate)
- House and Senate Journals
- *Congressional Quarterly*
- *Congressional Monitor*
- *Monthly Catalog of U.S. Documents*

---

5. Contact both committees of Congress that considered the legislation. Ask for leads to legislative history. (They may be able to send you committee reports, hearing transcripts, etc.)

---

6. Cases interpreting the statute sometimes give the legislative history of the statute. To find cases interpreting the statute, check the Notes of Decisions after the statute in the U.S.C.A. and in the U.S.C.S. Also, shepardize the statute (see Checklist #4b on shepardizing a statute, page 573).

---

7. Find out if there is an annotation on the statute. See the "Table of Laws, Rules, and Regulations" in volume 6 of *ALR Index*. (See Checklist #3 on finding and updating annotations, page 561.)

---

8. You may also find leads to the legislative history of a statute in legal periodical literature (see Checklist #6, page 582), in treatises on the statute (see Checklist #8, page 583), in loose-leaf services on the statute (see Checklist #5, page 577), and through phone and mail research (see Checklist #9, page 584).

---

9. To try to find a discussion of your statute in Am.Jur.2d, a legal encyclopedia, check a separate volume called *Table of Statutes, Rules, and Regulations Cited.*

---

10. Examine your statute in its session law form in *United States Statutes at Large* for possible leads (page 516).

---

 ## Section R. Monitoring Proposed Legislation

Occasionally you will be asked to *monitor* a bill currently before the legislature that has relevance to the caseload of the law office where you work. To monitor a bill means to determine its current status in the legislature and to keep track of all the forces that are trying to enact, defeat, or modify the bill.

---

### Techniques for Monitoring Proposed Legislation

1. Begin with the legislature. Find out what committee in each house of the legislature (often called the Senate and House) is considering the proposed legislation. Also determine whether there are more than two committees considering the entire bill or portions of it.

---

2. Ask committee staff members to send you copies of the bill in its originally proposed form and in its amended forms.

---

3. Determine whether the committees considering the proposed legislation have written any reports on it and, if so, whether copies are available.

---

4. Determine whether any hearings have been scheduled by the committees on the bill. If so, try to attend. For hearings already conducted, see if they have been transcribed (a word-for-word recording).

Continued

---

### Techniques for Monitoring Proposed Legislation—*Continued*

**5.** Find out the names of people in the legislature who are working on the bill: legislators "pushing" the bill, legislators opposed to it, staff members of the individual legislators working on the bill, and staff members of the committees working on the bill. Ask for copies of any position papers or statements.

**6.** The local bar association may have taken a position on the bill. Call the association. Find out what committee of the bar is involved with the subject matter of the bill. This committee may have written a report on the position of the bar on the bill. If so, try to obtain a copy.

**7.** Is there an administrative agency of the government involved with the bill? Identify the agency with jurisdiction over the subject matter of the bill. Find out who in the agency is working on the bill and whether any written reports of the agency are available. Determine whether the agency has a Legislative Liaison Office.

**8.** Who else is lobbying for or against the bill? What organizations are interested in it? Find out if they have taken any written positions.

**9.** What precipitated consideration of the bill by the legislature? Was there a court opinion that prompted the legislative action? If so, you should know what the opinion said.

**10.** Are any other legislatures in the country contemplating similar legislation? Some of the ways of finding out include the following:

    **(a)** Look for legal periodical literature on the subject matter of the bill (see Checklist #6, page 582).

    **(b)** Check loose-leaf services, if any, covering the subject matter of the bill (see Checklist #5, page 577) — these services often cover proposed legislation in the various legislatures.

    **(c)** Check treatises on the area (see Checklist #8, page 583).

    **(d)** Organizations such as bar associations, public interest groups, business associations, etc. often assign staff members to perform state-by-state research on what the legislatures are doing. Such organizations may be willing to share this research with you.

    **(e)** Find out if there is a Council of State Governments in your area. It may have done the same research mentioned in (d) above.

    **(f)** Contact an expert for leads to what other legislatures are doing (see Checklist #9, page 584).

---

## ▮ Section S. Reading and Finding Constitutional Law

### Reading Constitutional Law

The constitution sets out the fundamental ground rules for the conduct of the government in the geographical area it covers. It defines the branches of the government, establishes basic rights of citizens, and covers matters that the framers considered important enough (such as limitations on the power to tax) to be included in the constitution. The United States Constitution does this for the federal government, and the state constitution does it for the state government. In reading constitutional law, a number of guidelines can be helpful:

*1. Thumb through the headings of the constitution or glance through the table of contents.* How is the document organized? What subjects did the framers want covered by the constitution? A quick scanning of the section headings or table of contents is a good way to obtain an overview of the structure of the text.

*2. The critical sections or articles are those that establish and define the powers of the legislative, judicial, and executive branches of government in the geographic area covered by the Constitution.*   Who passes, interprets, and executes the law? For the United States Constitution, "all legislative Powers granted herein shall be vested in a Congress" (art. I, § 1); "the judicial Power of the United States, shall be vested in one supreme Court, and in such inferior Courts as the Congress may from time to time ordain and establish" (art. III, § 1); and "the executive Power shall be vested in a President of the United States of America" (art. II, § 1). The exact scope of these powers, as enunciated elsewhere in the Constitution, has been and continues to be an arena of constant controversy and litigation.

*3. The amendments to the Constitution change or add to the body of the text.*   The main vehicle for changing the constitution is the amendment process, which itself is defined in the constitution. Some constitutions, for example, can be amended by a vote of the people in a general election. A condition for most amendments is that they must be approved by one or more sessions of the legislature. Constitutional amendments usually appear at the end of the document.

*4. Constitutions are written in very broad terms.*   There are, of course, exceptions to this, particularly with respect to the constitutions of local governments. In the main, however, a common characteristic of constitutional provisions is their broad language. How would you interpret the following section?

> Congress shall make no laws respecting an establishment of religion, or prohibiting the free exercise thereof; or abridging the freedom of speech, or of the press; or of the right of the people to assemble, and to petition the Government for a redress of grievances.

How many words in this provision do you *not* understand? What is an "establishment?" If the school board requires a "moment of silence" at the beginning of each day, is the school board establishing a religion? What does "abridging" mean? If a government official leaks secret documents to the press, and the government tries to sue the press to prevent the publication of the documents, has the "freedom" of the press been abridged? If the people have a right to "assemble," could the government pass a law prohibiting all gatherings of three or more people at any place within one thousand yards of the White House gates? The questions arising from the interpretation of constitutional law are endless; tens of thousands of court opinions exist on questions such as these. The broader the language, the more ambiguous it is, and therefore the greater the need for interpretation.

*5. A central question for the interpreter of constitutional law is, what meaning did the authors intend?*   Common sense dictates that when language is ambiguous, the ambiguity may be resolved in part by attempting to determine what the author of the language intended by it. What was the author's meaning? In what context was the author writing? Does the context shed any light on what was meant? This kind of analysis is fundamental to legal reasoning whether the document is a constitution, a statute, a regulation, or a case. It is particularly difficult to do, however, for a constitution written over a hundred years ago.

## Finding Constitutional Law

| Techniques for Finding Constitutional Law |
|---|
| 1. Start with the text of the constitution itself. It is usually found at the beginning of the statutory code of the jurisdiction. (The federal Constitution is in U.S.C./U.S.C.A./U.S.C.S.). |
| 2. Use the CARTWHEEL to help you use the general index of the statutory code and the separate index for the constitution itself. Also check the table of contents material for the constitution in the statutory code. |
| 3. Following the text of individual constitutional provisions there are often Notes of Decisions containing summaries of cases interpreting the constitution. Some of these notes can run hundreds of pages. Check the separate index material for these notes. |
| 4. Shepardize the constitutional provision. The set of Shepard's to use is the same set you use for shepardizing a statute. (See Checklist #4b on shepardizing a statute.) |
| 5. Annotations. Find annotations in A.L.R., A.L.R.2d, etc. on the constitutional provisions in which you are interested. (See Checklist #3 on finding and updating annotations, page 561.) |
| 6. Digests. Go to the *United States Supreme Court Digest* (West) (page 500). Also use the various digests of West that cover other jurisdictions. (The *American Digest System*, of course, covers all jurisdictions.) Use the Descriptive Word Index (DWI) of a digest to locate key topics and numbers on point. (See Checklist #2 on using West digests, page 556.) (For cases on the U.S. Constitution, you can also go to the non-West digest—the *United States Supreme Court Digest, Lawyers Ed.*, page 492.) |
| 7. Treatises. Find treatises on the entire constitution or on the specific portions of the constitution in which you are interested. (See Checklist #8 on finding treatises, page 583.) |
| 8. Legal periodical literature. Go to the three indexes to legal periodical literature: ILP, CLI, and LRI. Use them to help you locate periodical literature on the constitution. (See Checklist #6 on finding legal periodical literature, page 582.) |
| 9. Loose-leaf services. Find out if there are loose-leaf services on the area of the constitution in which you are interested. (See Checklist #5 on loose-leaf services, page 577.) |
| 10. Phone and mail research. Contact an expert. (See Checklist #9 on phone and mail research, page 584.) |
| 11. *Words and Phrases*. Identify specific words or phrases within the constitutional provision you are examining. Find court definitions of these words or phrases in the multi-volume legal dictionary, *Words and Phrases*. |
| 12. Legal encyclopedias. Find discussions of constitutional law in Am.Jur.2d and in C.J.S. (See Checklist #7 on legal encyclopedias, page 582.) |
| 13. Shepardize every case you found that interprets the constitution. (See Checklist #4a on shepardizing a case, page 569.) |

## Section T. Finding Administrative Law

A regulation is an official rule or law of an administrative agency which explains or carries out the statutes and executive orders that govern the agency.

There are many agencies writing regulations, but few of them have coherent systems of organizing and distributing the regulations. A major exception is the federal agencies whose regulations are first published in the *Federal Register;* many are then codified in the *Code of Federal Regulations.*

Normally an agency does not have the power to write regulations unless it has specific statutory authority to do so. An examination of the statute giving the agency this authority can be helpful in understanding the regulations themselves. In theory, the legislature in its statutes sets out the purpose of the agency and defines its overall policies, but leaves to the agency (through its regulations) the task of filling in the specifics of administration. Regulations, therefore, tend to be very detailed.

The other major kind of administrative law is the administrative decision, which is a written resolution of controversies brought before the administrative agency. Not many agencies publish their decisions in any systematic order; some agencies do not publish them at all. Regulatory agencies, such as the Federal Communications Commission and state environmental agencies, often do a better job at publishing their decisions than other agencies.

---

### Techniques for Finding Administrative Law

**1.** Start with the agency itself. Call or visit the agency. There may be a regional or district office near you. Contact the library, the law department, or the public information section. Ask for a list of the publications of the agency, such as regulations, decisions, annual reports. Also ask where these materials are located. Find out if you can come to the agency and use the materials. Ask about brochures describing the agency's functions, which can be sent to you.

**2.** Whenever an agency official is reluctant to let you have access to any publications of the agency, you may have to do separate research to find out whether you are entitled to access—under the federal Freedom of Information Act and its state equivalents, for example.

**3.** Many federal administrative regulations are printed in the *Code of Federal Regulations* (C.F.R.), which are usually printed first in their proposed form in the *Federal Register* before they are enacted by the agency. The C.F.R. comes out in a new edition every year. There are four main ways to locate regulations in the C.F.R.:

    **(a)** The *C.F.R. Index and Finding Aids* volume. This is a single-volume pamphlet that is reissued every year.

    **(b)** The *Index to the Code of Federal Regulations* published by Congressional Information Service (CIS).

    **(c)** The *Code of Federal Regulations Index* published by R. R. Bowker.

    **(d)** Loose-leaf services. As indicated earlier, there are numerous loose-leaf services covering many federal agencies and some state agencies. These services usually give extensive references to administrative regulations and decisions. (See Checklist #5, page 577.)

Also check the monthly and annual indexes within the Federal Register.

    If you find no federal regulations on point in the C.F.R. or in the Federal Register, you should check whether the agency has regulations, rules, bulletins, etc., that are published elsewhere. (See technique 1.)

**4.** Once you have found a federal regulation on point in the C.F.R., do the following:

    **(a)** Shepardize the regulation. (See Checklist #4c on shepardizing a regulation, page 575.)

    **(b)** Find the statute that is the authority for that regulation. Read this statute in U.S.C./U.S.C.A./U.S.C.S. Make sure the regulation does not contradict, go beyond the scope of, or otherwise violate the statute that the regulation is supposed to implement. There are two ways to find the statutory authority of a regulation:

Continued

**Techniques for Finding Administrative Law—*Continued***

- ■ Look for an "Authority" reference beneath the specific regulation in C.F.R. *or* at the beginning of the cluster of regulations of which your regulation is a part.
- ■ Check the Parallel Table of Authorities and Rules (Table II) in a volume called *Index and Finding Aids to Code of Federal Regulations,* published by Lawyer's Co-op.

(c) Once you have found a regulation in the C.F.R., you must find out if the regulation has been *affected* in any way (changed, added to, renumbered) by subsequent material printed in the *Federal Register.* This is done by checking your C.F.R. cite in:

- ■ The monthly LSA pamphlet (List of Sections Affected).
- ■ The lists of "CFR Parts Affected" in the daily *Federal Register* from the date of the LSA pamphlet to the current date

The LSA pamphlet and the "CFR Parts Affected" will tell you what pages of the *Federal Register* contain material that affects your regulation in the C.F.R. (You need to do this only until the next annual edition of the C.F.R. comes out, since anything affecting the regulation during the preceding year will be incorporated in the next edition of C.F.R.)

(d) Find out if there is an annotation on your regulation. Shepardize the regulation. Annotations in A.L.R., A.L.R.2d etc. are among the "citing materials" of Shepard's. Also, check the Table of Laws, Rules, and Regulations in volume 6 of the *ALR Index* (page 559.)

5. State administrative agency regulations are much more difficult to find and update. Very few states have an administrative code similar to the C.F.R. For most state agencies, you must check with your law library and with the agency itself (see technique 1 above) on how the regulations are printed, found, and updated.

6. When federal or state administrative *decisions* are printed, they will often be found in separate volumes for each agency. Also check loose-leaf services that cover a particular agency. (See Checklist #5, page 577.)

7. The *Federal Register* and the C.F.R. can also be found on WESTLAW and LEXIS.

## ■ Section U. Finding Local Law

Find out if there is a municipal code for your city or county containing local charters, ordinances, etc. Many charters are also printed in the state's statutory code. Check with your law librarian. Also call city hall, the city council, or the county commissioner's office. Speak with the public information officer or the law department. Ask about the local publications of your city or county. What is printed? Where is it found? How often is it printed? How is it updated?

The following are other items to check:

- ■ Legal periodical literature on local issues such as zoning, municipal bonds, etc. (see Checklist #6 on legal periodical literature, page 582).
- ■ The Shepard's volumes for a particular state will enable you to shepardize local charters and ordinances.
- ■ Digests can be used to find case law on charters and ordinances (see Checklist #2 on digests, page 556).
- ■ Annotations on local law in A.L.R., A.L.R.2d, A.L.R.3d, A.L.R.4th, and A.L.R. Fed (see Checklist #3 on annotations, page 561).
- ■ Treatises on local law (see Checklist #8 on treatises, page 583).

■ Am.Jur.2d and C.J.S. contain discussions on local law (see Checklist #7 on legal encyclopedias, page 582).

■ Loose-leaf services cover aspects of local law (see Checklist #5 on loose-leaf services, page 577).

■ Phone and mail research; contact an expert (see Checklist #9 on phone and mail research, page 584).

■ *Ordinance Law Annotations* (published by Shepard's) summarizes court opinions that have interpreted ordinances.


# ■ Section V. Finding Rules of Court

You must always check the rules of court governing practice and procedure before a *particular* court. These rules will tell you how to file a request for an extension of time, the number of days a defendant has to answer a complaint, the format of a complaint or appellate brief, etc.

---

### Techniques for Finding Rules of Court

*Rules of Court for State Courts:*

■ Check your state statutory code for the text of the rules.

■ Ask your librarian if there is a service company that publishes an updated edition of state rules of court.

■ Find out if the court itself publishes its own rules.

■ Shepardize rules of court in the same set of Shepard's you use to shepardize a statute (page 573).

■ For case law on the rules of court, check the digests for your state (see Checklist #2 on digests, page 556).

■ Check local practice books, formbooks, or other treatises (see Checklist #8 on treatises, page 583).

■ Check with an expert (see Checklist #9 on phone and mail research, page 584).

*Rules of Court for Federal Courts:*

■ Check the U.S.C./U.S.C.A./U.S.C.S., such as title 28, title 18 (appendix).

■ Shepardize federal rules of court in *United States Citations, Statute Edition* (page 512).

■ For case law on rules of court, check the digests, such as *Federal Practice Digest* 4th (see Checklist #2 on digests, page 556).

■ Check the Federal Rules Service.

■ Check special treatises on the federal rules such as:
    *Moore's Federal Practice*
    Wright and Miller, *Federal Practice and Procedure*

■ Find annotations on the federal rules of court. Check the "Table of Laws, Rules, and Regulations" in volume 6 of *ALR Index* (see Checklist #3, page 561).

■ Check legal periodical literature on the federal rules of court (see Checklist #6 on legal periodical literature, page 582).

■ Check Am. Jur. 2d and C.J.S. on the federal rules of court (see Checklist #7 on legal encyclopedias, page 582).

■ Check with an expert (see Checklist #9 on phone and mail research, page 584).

---

## Section W. Finding International Law

---

**Techniques for Finding International Law**

**1.** In general, check:

- The yearly U.S. Statutes at Large (page 516) contain U.S. treaties (page 329)
- *United States Treaties and Other International Acts*
- *Treaties and Other International Acts Series*
- *United States Treaties and Other International Agreements*
- Blaustein and Flanz, *Constitutions of the Countries of the World*
- *CCH Tax Treaties*
- *Treaties in Force*
- *Department of State Bulletin*
- United Nations Treaty Series
- Catalog of U.S. publications
- *International Legal Materials*
- Szladits, *Bibliography on Foreign and Comparative Law: Books and Articles in English*

For other texts summarizing and commenting on treaties and international law generally, see Checklist #8 on treatises, page 583.

**2.** Legal periodical literature. There is extensive periodical literature on international law, both in general legal periodicals and in specialty periodicals devoted to international law exclusively. (See Checklist #6, page 582.)

**3.** Loose-leaf services, such as CCH Tax Treaties, mentioned above. (See Checklist #5 on loose-leaf services, page 577.)

**4.** American case law on international law. Check the digests. (See Checklist #2 on digests, page 556.)

**5.** Case law of foreign countries. Statutory law of other countries. Go to the international law section of a large law library.

**6.** Annotations on international law. (See Checklist #3 on annotations, page 561.)

**7.** Legal encyclopedias. For material on international law in Am. Jur. 2d and in C.J.S., see Checklist #7, page 582.

**8.** Phone and mail research. (See Checklist #9 on contacting experts, page 584.)

**9.** See *Restatement (Second) of Foreign Relations Law of the United States.*

**10.** Shepardize all treaties. Go to *Shepard's United States Citations, Statute Edition* (page 512).

**11.** *Martindale-Hubbell Law Dictionary*—Digest volume. Contains brief summaries of the law of many countries (page 506).

---

## Section X. The Third Level of Research (Validation): Ending Your Research

Earlier (page 549) we mentioned the three levels of legal research:

- Background research

- Specific fact research
- Validation research

We already examined the steps for conducting background research on an area of law that is new to you (page 550). We also examined the techniques of specific fact research through the checklists (pages 552 ff.) presented above in section N through W of this chapter. If you have done a comprehensive job on the first two stages of research, you may also have completed most of the third stage—*validation research*.

At the validation stage, you ensure that everything you want to use from your research is still good law. This means making sure that the law is current and has not been affected by any later laws that you have not yet found. A good way to approach validation research is to take the perspective of the other side. Suppose that you have written an appellate brief. It has been filed in court and served on the attorney for the other side. Your brief is handed over to a researcher in the law office of your opponent. That person will do the following:

- Read the full text of all primary authority (page 517) on which you rely in order to see if you have interpreted the statutes, cases, regulations, etc., properly; to see whether you have taken quotations out of the context, etc.
- Shepardize the statutes, cases, regulations, etc., that you cite in order to find out whether the law is still valid (page 563)
- Read the secondary authority (page 517) that you cite in order to see whether you have interpreted the treatise, law review article, etc., properly; to see whether you have taken quotations out of context, etc.
- Look for other applicable primary authority that you failed to mention
- Look for other applicable secondary authority that you failed to mention

Proper validation research means that you will be able to predict what this imaginary researcher will find when he or she checks your research through these steps. In short, at the validation stage of your research you must ask yourself:

- Have I found everything I should have found?
- Is everything I found good law?
- Have I properly interpreted what I found?

The answer to the first two questions should be *no* if:

- You did an incomplete job of CARTWHEELING the indexes and tables of contents of all the sets of books mentioned in the checklists and techniques in this chapter.
- You failed to shepardize cases, statutes, constitutional provisions, rules of court, ordinances, treaties, etc., as called for in the checklists and techniques listed above.
- You failed to take other standard validation steps, such as checking the List of Sections Affected (LSA) material to update a regulation in the C.F.R. (page 604).

At the outset of your research, the difficulty you face is often phrased as: "Where do I begin?" As you resolve this difficulty, another one emerges: "When do I stop?" Once the research starts flowing, you are sometimes faced with a mountain of material, and yet you do not feel comfortable saying to yourself that you have found everything there is to be found. The only guidance that can be given to you is this: be comprehensive in following all the checklists and techniques presented in this chapter. With experience, you will begin to acquire a sense of when it is time to stop. But it is rare for you to know this with any certainty. You will always have the suspicion that if you pushed on just a little longer, you would find something new and more on point than what you have come up with to date. Also, there is no way around the reality that comprehensive research requires a substantial amount of time. It takes time to dig. It takes more time to dig comprehensively.

## Section Y. Annotated Bibliography

An *annotated bibliography* is a report giving a list of library material on a particular topic, with a brief description of how the material relates to the topic. An annotated bibliography on contributory negligence, for example, would list the major cases, statutes, periodical articles, etc. and would explain in a sentence or two what each says about contributory negligence. The same would be true of an annotated bibliography on a set of facts that you are researching. If the facts present more than one research issue, you would do an annotated bibliography for each issue, or you would subdivide a single annotated bibliography into sections so that it would be clear to the reader which issue you are covering at any given place in the bibliography. The annotated bibliography is, in effect, a progress report on your research. It will show your supervisor the status of your research. (The following instructions mainly cover the preparation of an annotated bibliography for a topic that requires the application of state and local law. The same instructions, however, would be used when doing the bibliography on a federal topic. The exception would be instruction #9, which calls for local ordinances. For all other instructions below, replace the word *state* with the word *federal* when researching a federal topic.)

| Instructions for Preparing an Annotated Bibliography |
|---|
| 1. CARTWHEEL the topic of your annotated bibliography. |
| 2. *Annotated* simply means that you provide some description of everything you list in the bibliography—not a long analysis, just a sentence or two explaining why you included it. If you find no relevant material in any of the following sets of books, specifically say so in your report. |
| 3. Hand in a report that will cover what you find on the topic in the sets of books mentioned in the following instructions. |
| 4. Statutes. Go to your state code. Make a list of the statutes on the topic. For each statute, give its citation and a brief quotation from it to show that it deals with the topic. |
| 5. Constitutions. Go to your state constitution (usually found within your state code). Make a list of the constitutional provisions on the topic. For each provision, give its citation and a brief quotation from it to show that it deals with the topic. |
| 6. Cases. If you found statutes or constitutional provisions on the topic, check to see if there are any cases summarized in the Notes of Decisions (page 591) *after* these statutes or provisions. Also go to the digests (page 497). Select several cases that you found through the Notes of Decisions and the digests that deal with the topic. For each case you select, give its citation and a brief quote from the case summary to show that it deals with the topic. |

Continued

## Instructions for Preparing an Annotated Bibliography—*Continued*

**7.** Key topics and numbers. In instruction #6, you went to the digests. Make a list of the key topics and numbers that you found most productive. (See page 497.)

**8.** Rules of court. Go to the rules of court that cover courts in your state (page 605). Make a list of the rules, if any, that deal with the topic. For each rule, give its citation and a brief quotation from it to show that it deals with the topic.

**9.** Ordinances. Go to the ordinances that cover your city or county (page 604). Make a list of the ordinances, if any, that deal with the topic. For each ordinance, give its citation and a brief quotation from it to show that it deals with the topic.

**10.** Agency regulations. Are there any state agencies that have jurisdiction over any aspect of the topic? If so, list the agencies. If your library has the regulations of the agencies, make a list of the regulations, if any, that deal with the topic. For each major regulation, give its citation and a brief quote from it to show that it deals with the topic (page 603).

**11.** A.L.R., A.L.R.2d, A.L.R.3d, A.L.R.4th, A.L.R. Fed. Go to these five sets of books (page 557). Try to find one annotation in *each* set that deals with your topic. Give the citation of the annotations in each set. Flip through the pages of each annotation and try to find the citation of one case from a state court of your state, or from a federal court with jurisdiction over your state. Give the citation of the case.

**12.** Legal periodical literature. Use the *Index to Legal Periodicals,* the *Current Legal Index,* and the *Legal Resource Index* to locate three law review articles that deal with the topic (page 578). Try to find at least one relevant article in each index. Give the citation of the articles. Put a check mark next to the citation if your library has the law review in which the article is located.

**13.** Treatises. Go to your card catalog (page 552). Find any two treatises (page 583) that cover your topic. Give the citation of the treatises. Sometimes you may not find entire books on the topic. The topic may be one of many subjects in a broader treatise.

**14.** Loose-leaf texts. Are there any loose-leaf services on this topic (page 577)? Check the card catalog and ask the librarian. For each loose-leaf, give its citation and explain how it covers the topic.

**15.** *Words and Phrases.* Go to this multivolume legal dictionary (page 504). In this dictionary, locate definitions, if any, of the major words and phrases involved in your topic. Limit yourself to definitions from court opinions of your state, if any.

**16.** Shepardize every case, statute, or constitutional provision you find to make sure it is still valid, and to locate other material on the topic (page 563).

**17.** Other material. If you come across other relevant material not covered in the above instructions, include it in the bibliography as well.

**18.** When in doubt about whether to include something in the bibliography, include it.

**19.** There is no prescribed format for the bibliography. One possible outline format you can use is as follows:
Topic: _____

**A.** Statutes (Instructions 4 and 16)

**B.** Constitutions (Instructions 5 and 16)

**C.** Cases (Instructions 6 and 16)

**D.** Key topics and numbers (Instruction 7)

**E.** Rules of court (Instruction 8)

**F.** Ordinances (Instruction 9)

**G.** Agency regulations (Instruction 10)

Continued

---

**Instructions for Preparing an Annotated Bibliography—*Continued***

---

**H.** A.L.R., A.L.R.2d, A.L.R.3d, A.L.R.4th, A.L.R. Fed. (Instruction 11)

**I.** Legal periodical literature (Instruction 12)

**J.** Treatises (Instruction 13)

**K.** Loose-leaf texts (Instruction 14)

**L.** *Words and Phrases* (Instruction 15)

**M.** Other material (Instruction 17)

---

## ■ ASSIGNMENT 11.8

Prepare an annotated bibliography on the following topics:

**(a)** Common-law marriage

**(b)** Negligence liability of a driver of a car to his or her guest passenger

**(c)** Negligence liability of paralegals

**(d)** Overtime compensation for paralegals

**(e)** Sex discrimination

**(f)** The felony-murder rule

**(g)** Default judgment

**(h)** Worker's compensation for injury on the way to work

**(i)** Fact situation assigned by your instructor

---

## ■ ASSIGNMENT 11.9

In the problems that follow, include citations that support every position you take in your responses. In analyzing and researching some of the problems below, you may find it difficult to proceed unless you know more facts about the problem. In such situations, clearly state the missing facts that you need to know. In order to proceed with the analysis and research, you can assume that certain facts exist as long as you state what your factual assumptions are, *and* your assumptions are reasonable given the facts that you have.

**(a)** In your state, what entity (e.g., legislature, committee, court, agency) has the authority to prescribe rules and regulations on who can and who cannot practice law?

**(b)** List the kinds (or levels) of courts (local, state, or federal) that sit in your state and identify the major powers of each court, i.e., what kinds of cases can each court hear?

**(c)** In your state, find a statute or court opinion that defines the following words or phrases:

   **(i)** Summons

   **(ii)** In personam

   **(iii)** Mandamus

   **(iv)** Exhaustion of administrative remedies

   **(v)** Judgment

**(vi)** Jurisdiction

**(vii)** Warrant

**(d)** Mary Adams works for a National Welfare Rights Organization chapter in your state. She is a paralegal. An N.W.R.O. member, Mrs. Peterson, has a complaint against a local welfare department branch concerning her welfare check. Mary Adams goes to a hearing with Mrs. Peterson to represent her. The hearing officer tells Mary that she cannot represent Mrs. Peterson since she (Mary) is not an attorney. Is the hearing officer correct?

**(e)** Using as many statutory codes of different states as are available in your law library (do not go beyond five different codes, however), find out how old a male and female must be in order to marry without consent of parent or guardian in each of the states.

**(f)** Go to any statutory code that has a pocket part. Starting with the first few pages of the pocket part, identify any three statutes that have totally repealed *or* partially modified the corresponding three statutes in the body of the bound text. Describe what the modification was. (*Note:* You may have to compare the new section in the pocket part with the old section in the body of the text in order to be able to describe the change.)

. . . . . . . . . . . . . . .

In the following problems, use the state law *of your state* whenever you determine from your research that state law governs the problem.

**(g)** John Jones was sent to a state mental hospital after being declared mentally ill. He has been institutionalized for the last five years. In his own view, he is not now mentally ill. The hospital disagrees. What can John do? What steps might he take to try to get out?

**(h)** Peter Thomas is convicted of petty larceny. At the time of sentencing, his attorney asks the court to grant probation in lieu of a prison term. The judge replies, "Since Mr. Thomas has had three prior felony convictions (one of them for attempted rape), I could not grant him probation even if I wanted to. I sentence him to a year in prison." On appeal, the attorney argues that the judge was incorrect when he ruled that he had no power to grant probation to a person with three prior convictions. Is the attorney correct?

**(i)** Mrs. Peterson invites a neighbor to her house for dinner. Mrs. Peterson's dog bites the neighbor. Is Mrs. Peterson responsible for the injury?

**(j)** Sam, age fifteen, goes to a used car lot. He signs a purchase agreement on a used car: $500 down and $100 a month for the next ten months. One day after the purchase, Sam allows a friend to drive the car. The friend demolishes the car in an accident. When Sam tells the used car dealer about the accident, he is told that he must still make all payments until the purchase price has been paid. Is the dealer right?

**(k)** An elderly woman presented the following facts to you during a legal interview. She and her husband moved into their house in 1946. Next to the house is a vacant lot. She does not know who owns the lot. She planted a small vegetable and flower garden on this lot. She built a small fence around the garden. She has continued to cultivate this garden for the past twenty-seven years. Neighbors regard this garden as hers. Since her husband's death last fall, men in the neighborhood have been trying to use the garden area as a place to store their old car parts. She is troubled by this. What are her rights?

**(l)** Dorothy Rhodes and John Samualson are the parents of Susan Samualson. (Dorothy married Robert Rhodes after divorcing John Samualson.) Dorothy died after separating from Robert Rhodes. Susan's father has disappeared.

Mr. and Mrs. Ford were neighbors of the Rhodes. Susan lived with the Fords for a long period of time while her mother was having marital difficulties. A court granted the Fords custody and guardianship in 1988. The Social Security Administration sent Susan the Social Security benefits she was entitled to on the death of her mother. In 1990, the Fords formally adopted Susan, but did not inform the Social Security office of this; they did not know that they had to. When the Social Security office learned of the adoption, they terminated the payments for Susan and informed the Fords that the money she had received since the adoption would have to be returned.

The Fords and Susan want to know what substantive and procedural rights they have.

**(m)** Jane Smith owns a small shoe repair shop. The city sanitation department determines that Jane is a carrier of a typhoid germ. She herself does not have typhoid fever, but others could become infected with the fever by coming in contact with her. The city orders Jane's shop to be closed. She and her husband are not allowed to leave the shop until arrangements can be made to transfer them to a hospital.

    **(i)**   Can the city quarantine Jane and her husband?

    **(ii)**  If the Smiths enter a hospital quarantine, can they be forced to pay the hospital bill?

    **(iii)** Can the Smiths recover loss of profits due to the closing of their business?

**(n)** The Henderson family owns a $140,000 home next door to a small grocery store. The store catches fire. In order for the firefighters to get at the fire from all angles, they decide that they must break through the Henderson home, which is not on fire. Damage to the Henderson home from the activity of the firefighters comes to $40,000. Who pays for this damage?

**(o)** Bill and Mary are married with two children. They are happily married except for one constant quarrel. Bill is upset with Mary because she goes bowling every Friday night. Mary is disturbed with Bill because he plays cards every Tuesday night. To resolve their difficulty, they reach the following agreement: Bill will give up his Tuesday night cards if Mary will give up her Friday bowling. On Friday, Mary stays home. On the following Tuesday, however, Bill plays cards. He declares that he wants to continue the card playing. Mary, on the other hand, wants him to live up to his agreement. She brings a suit in court against him, charging breach of contract. (Assume that neither wants a divorce.) What result?

**(p)** After a series of serious accidents in which numerous riders are hurt, a bill is placed before the city council that would require all motorcyclists to wear protective helmets whenever riding. Is the bill constitutional?

**(q)** As a measure to enforce a standard of dental care, a bill is proposed that all the drinking water in the state be fluoridated and every citizen be required to visit a dentist at least once a year. Is this bill constitutional?

**(r)** Tom Jones has terminal lung cancer. Modern technology, however, can keep him alive indefinitely. Tom requests that the hospital official no longer use the technology. He wants to die. What are his rights?

**(s)** Alice Brown is seventeen years old. She is a self-styled hippie. She refuses to work. Alice's parents tell her that they will fully finance a college education for her. She refuses. The parents go to court and ask that their daughter be forced to go to college and avoid ruining her life. What result?

**(t)** In 1942 James Fitzpatrick died, leaving an estate of $50,000. The executor tried to locate the heirs. In 1943 the probate court closed the estate and distributed the money to the heirs who were known at the time. In 1986, an individual claiming to be an heir appears. He wants to go to court to reopen the estate and claim his share of the inheritance. What result?

**(u)** Mary is the sole beneficiary of her father's will. Another sister is intentionally left out of the will by her father. There are no other heirs. Mary murders her father. Who gets his estate?

**(v)** The board of education is alarmed over increasing disturbances in the public schools. A board regulation currently exists that permits school principals to administer corporal punishment to unruly pupils. The superintendent of schools proposes that the board adopt a regulation that would authorize the school nurse, under the direction of the principal, to administer an oral tranquilizer to disruptive pupils so that they could be rendered "relatively passive" and responsive to school guidance. Discuss the legality of the regulation.

**(w)** The state claims that welfare costs are bringing the finances of the state to the brink of bankruptcy. It is proposed that all children of welfare parents be required to attend vocational classes as part of their regular school curriculum. Discuss the legality of the regulation.

**(x)** The United Kosher Butchers Association (UKBA) is accepted by most of the kosher meat stores as the authoritative certifier that "all the religious requirements have been thoroughly observed." Associated Synagogues (AS) certifies caterers as authentic carriers of kosher food. AS refuses to certify caterers who buy meat from stores certified by the UKBA because the latter refuses to submit to supervision by the rabbinical committee of AS. Many caterers then withdraw their patronage from stores supervised by UKBA. What legal action, if any, can UKBA take?

**(y)** The town of Salem has a population of 2,000. A group of avowed homosexuals moves into the area. They begin to run for public offices, with some success. The old-time townspeople become very upset. A state law gives courts the power to hospitalize mentally ill individuals. The mayor of Salem files petitions in court to have the homosexuals declared mentally ill and institutionalized. Discuss any law that might apply to these facts.

**(z)** Mary Perry belongs to a religion that believes that medical problems can be resolved through spiritual meditation. Her son Paul is ten years old. One day at school, Paul is rushed to a hospital after collapsing. Mrs. Perry is called at home. When she arrives at the hospital, she is told that Paul will require emergency surgery. She refuses to give her consent. The doctor tells that her if the operation is not performed within the next twenty-four hours, Paul will die. Mrs. Perry responds by saying that "God will cure my son." What legal action, if any, can be taken to protect Paul's rights and to protect Mrs. Perry's rights?

## State Legal Research References

*Alabama Practice Materials* by L. Kitchens, 82 Law Library Journal 703 (1990).

*Alaska Legal and Law-Related Publications* by A. Ruzicka (American Association of Law Libraries, 1984).

*Arizona Practice Materials* by A. Torres, 80 Law Library Journal 577 (1988).

*Survey of Arizona State Legal and Law-Related Documents* by R. Teenstra (American Association of Law Libraries, 1984).

*Arkansas Legal Bibliography* by L. Foster (American Association of Law Libraries, 1988).

*Arizona Practice Materials* by K. Fitzhugh, 81 Law Library Journal 277 (1989).

Continued

## State Legal Research References—*Continued*

*California Current State Practice Materials* by B. Ochal, 74 Law Library Journal 281 (1981).

*California Law Guide* by D. Henke (2d ed. Parker, 1976).

*Legal Research Guide for California Practice* by T. Dabagh (Hein, 1985).

*Research in California Law* by M. Fink (2d ed. Dennis, 1964).

*Colorado Legal Resources* by G. Alexander, et al. (American Association of Law Libraries, 1987). 16 Colorado Lawyer 1795 (1987).

*Colorado Legal Source Materials—1981* by S. Weinstein, 10 Colorado Lawyer 1816 (August 1981).

*Connecticut State Legal Documents* by D. Voisinet (American Association of Law Libraries, 1985).

*Sources of Connecticut Law* by S. Bysiewicz (Butterworth, 1987).

*Selected Information Sources for the District of Columbia* by C. Ahearn (2d ed. American Association of Law Libraries, 1986).

*Florida Legislative Histories* by C. Roehrenbeck (D&H, 1986).

*Guide to Florida Legal Research* by R. Reinersten & R. Brown (2d ed. Florida Bar, 1986).

*Research in Florida Law* by H. French (2d ed. Oceana, 1965).

*Reference Guide to Georgia Legal History and Legal Research* by L. Chanin (Michie, 1980).

*How To Research Constitutional, Legislative, and Statutory History in Hawaii* by R. Kahle (Hawaii Legislative Reference Bureau, 1986).

*Idaho Law-Related State Documents* by P. Cervenka (American Association of Law Libraries, 1989).

*Illinois Legal Research Manual* by L. Wendt (Butterworth, 1988).

*Illinois State Documents* by C. Nyberg (American Association of Law Libraries, 1986).

*Researching Illinois Legislative Histories: A Practical Guide* by L. Wendt, 1982 Southern Illinois University Law Journal 601.

*An Introduction to Indiana State Publications . . .* by L. Fariss (American Association of Law Libraries, 1982).

*A Guide to Kansas Legal Research* by F. Snyder (Kansas Bar Association, 1986).

*Kansas State Documents for Law Libraries* by M. Wisnecki (American Association of Law Libraries, 1984).

*Guide to Kentucky Legal Research* by W. Gilmer (2d ed. State Law Library, 1985).

*Louisiana Legal Documents . . .* by C. Corneil (American Association of Law Libraries, 1984).

*Louisiana Legal Research* by W. Chiang (2d ed. Butterworth, 1990).

*Maine Legal Research Guide* by W. Wells (Tower, 1989).

*An Introduction to Maryland State Publications . . .* by L. Davis (American Association of Law Libraries, 1981).

*Ghost Hunting: Finding Legislative Intent in Maryland* by M. Miller (Maryland State Law Library, 1984).

*Annual State Bibliography (Massachusetts)* by L. McAuliffe (American Association of Law Libraries, 1985).

*Handbook of Legal Research in Massachusetts* by M. Botsford, et al. (Massachusetts Continuing Legal Education, 1988).

*Michigan Citation Manual* by J. Doyle (1986).

*Michigan Legal Documents* by D. Yoak (American Association of Law Libraries, 1982).

*Michigan Legal Literature and Annotated Guide* by R. Beer & J. Field (2d ed. Hein, 1991).

*Michigan Practice Materials* by D. Johnson, 73 Law Library Journal 672 (1980).

*Legal Research Guide for Michigan Libraries* (Michigan Association of Law Libraries, 1982).

*Minnesota Legal Research Guide* by A. Soderberg & B. Golden (Hein, 1985).

Continued

## State Legal Research References—*Continued*

*Guide to Minnesota State Documents* . . . by M. Baum (American Association of Law Libraries, 1986).

*Mississippi Legal Documents* . . . by B. Cole (American Association of Law Libraries, 1987).

*Mississippi Legal Research Bibliography* by C. Bunnell (1983).

*A Law Librarian's Introduction to Missouri State Publications* by P. Aldridge (American Association of Law Libraries, 1980).

*A Guide to Montana Legal Research* by S. Jordan (Montana State Law Library, 1991).

*Nebraska State Documents Bibliography* by M. Fontent (American Association of Law Libraries, 1988).

*Nebraska Legal Research and Reference Manual* by P. Hall (Mason, 1983).

*Nevada State Documents Bibliography* . . . by K. Henderson (American Association of Law Libraries, 1984).

*A Guide to New Jersey Legal Bibliography and Legal History* by C. Allen (Rothman, 1984).

*New Jersey Legal Research Handbook* by P. Axel-Lute (New Jersey Institute for Continuing Legal Education, 1985).

*New Jersey State Publications* by C. Senezak (American Association of Law Libraries, 1984).

*Guide to New Mexico State Publications* by P. Wagner (American Association of Law Libraries, 1983).

*Manual for Effective New Mexico Legal Research* by A. Poldervaart (University of New Mexico Press, 1955).

*New York Legal Documents* by S. Dow (American Association of Law Libraries, 1985).

*New York Legal Research Guide* by E. Gibson (Hein, 1988).

*An Annotated Bibliography of Current New York State Practice Materials* by Brown, 73 Law Library Journal 28 (1980).

*Guide to North Carolina Legal Research* by I. Kavass (Hein, 1973).

*Survey of North Carolina State Legal and Law-Related Documents* by T. Steele (American Association of Law Libraries, 1988).

*For All Intents and Purposes: Essentials in Researching Legislative Histories* (North Dakota Legislative Council, 1981).

*Ohio Legal Research* by S. Schaefgen & M. Putnum (Professional Education Systems, 1988).

*Ohio State Legal Documents* . . . by C. Corcos (American Association of Law Libraries, 1986).

*Oklahoma Legal and Law-Related Documents* . . . by C. Corcos (American Association of Law Libraries, 1983).

*Bibliography of Law Related Oregon Documents* by L. Buhman (American Association of Law Libraries, 1984).

*An Introduction to Pennsylvania State Publications* . . . by J. Fishman (American Association of Law Libraries, 1985).

*Pennsylvania Practice Materials* by S. Fishman, 78 Law Library Journal 74 (1986).

*Research in Pennsylvania Law* by C. Moreland & E. Surrency (2d ed. Oceana, 1965).

*Legal Research in Rhode Island* (Rhode Island Law Institute, 1989).

*South Carolina Legal Research Handbook* by R. Mills (Hein, 1976).

*South Dakota Legal Documents* by D. Jorgensen (American Association of Law Libraries, 1988).

*South Dakota Legal Research Guide* by D. Jorgensen (Hein, 1988).

*Law and Government Publications of* . . . *Tennessee* by D. Picquet (American Association of Law Libraries, 1988).

*Tennessee Legal Research Handbook* by L. Laska (Hein, 1977).

Continued

## State Legal Research References—*Continued*

*An Annotated Bibliography of Texas Practice Materials* by K. Gruben, 74 Law Library Journal 87 (1981).

*A Reference Guide to Texas Law . . .*, Gruben & J. Hambleton, editors (2d ed. Butterworth, 1987).

*Texas State Documents for Law Libraries* by M. Allison (American Association of Law Libraries, 1983).

*A Bibliographical Guide to the Vermont Legal System* by V. Wise (American Association of Law Libraries, 1989).

*A Guide to Legal Research in Virginia,* D. Eure, ed. (Virginia Law Foundation, 1989).

*A Law Librarian's Introduction to Virginia State Publications* by J. Lichtman (American Association of Law Libraries, 1988).

*A Guide to Specialized Resources and Methods for Conducting Legal Research in Washington State* by J. Quinn, 44 Washington State Bar News 9 (October 1990).

*Legal Research Guide* (University of Washington Law School, 1980).

*Washington State Law-Related Publications* by S. Burson (American Association of Law Libraries, 1984).

*An Introduction to Wisconsin State Documents . . .* by J. Oberla (American Association of Law Libraries, 1987).

*Legal Research in Wisconsin* by R. Danner (University of Wisconsin, Extension Law Department, 1980).

*Wyoming State Legal Documents* by N. Greene (American Association of Law Libraries, 1985).

## ▢ Chapter Summary

The law is changing every day. The only dependable way to find out about all of these changes is through legal research. Research skills will take time and determination to master. A useful first step is to compile a list of definitions or functions of the major research terms (such as citation, citator, cumulative, and headnote), and the major sets of research materials (such as A.L.R., Corpus Juris Secundum, Federal Reporter 2d, U.S.C.A., and WESTLAW).

You need to know where to find law libraries in your community, particularly depository libraries. Within these libraries, you will find the following kinds of authority that courts consider in reaching a decision: primary authority, which consists of laws such as statutes and cases; secondary authority, which consists of nonlaws such as law review articles and legal encyclopedias; mandatory authority, which a court *must* rely on; and persuasive authority, which a court has discretion to accept or reject.

A citation is an "address" where authority can be found in a library. *A Uniform System of Citation*—the "Bluebook," tells you what to abbreviate

in the citation, where spaces and commas must be inserted, in what order the information in the citation must be provided, etc. Most courts do not follow the Bluebook; a court may have its own rules of citation that it follows. Yet a very large number of supervising attorneys and teachers will ask you to follow the Bluebook. When cite checking, you identify inaccuracies in citation form, shepardize the authorities cited, check the accuracy of any quotations referred to in the citations, etc.

There are standard features of many law books. Each time you come across a new law book or set of law books, you should check features such as the copyright page, which contains the latest copyright date; and the forward or preface, which may give a general description of how to use the book. The tables or lists at the beginning of the book will help you understand terms, symbols, or signals used in the book. Check also for updating features, (such as pocket-parts), various tables of contents, and index features that may be available.

The CARTWHEEL is a technique that helps you use the often poorly organized tables of contents and indexes of law books. The technique assumes

*(Continued on next page)*

## ☐ Chapter Summary *(Continued)*

that the entry you first check in the table or index leads you nowhere, and that you must now think of some other entries to check that might be more productive. The CARTWHEEL is designed to help you identify these other entries.

There are three levels of legal research: background research, in which you start identifying the basic vocabulary and the major principles of an area of the law that is relatively new to you; specific fact research, in which you look for primary and secondary authority covering the facts of a client's case; and validation research, in which you check the current validity of whatever authority you initially believed was relevant to the problem you are researching. Occasionally, aspects of all three levels of research will be going on simultaneously.

A competent legal researcher knows how to use the major search tools or resources:

- Card catalog (or the computer catalog) to find what is available in the library you are using
- Digests to find case law
- Annotations to find case law
- Shepard's to shepardize cases, statutes, and

regulations in order to validate cited material and to find citing material such as case law

- Loose-leaf services to give you leads to, and explanations of, primary authority
- Legal periodical literature to give you leads to, and explanations of, primary authority
- Legal encyclopedias to give you leads to, and explanations of, primary authority
- Treatises to give you leads to, and explanations of, primary authority
- Phone and mail research to give you leads to, and explanations of, primary authority.

Major CALR (computer-assisted legal research) tools include WESTLAW, LEXIS, Auto-Cite, VERALEX, WILSONLINE, DIALOG, and NEXIS. (In Chapter 13, we will cover WESTLAW and LEXIS in greater detail.)

These major search tools or resources will often lead you to more than one kind of primary authority: opinions, statutes (plus legislative history), constitutions, administrative law, local law, rules of court, and international law. (See Figure 11.1.)

## Key Terms

depository library
act
administrative code
advance sheet
legal encyclopedia
annotate
annotated
annotation
annotated code
annotated statutes
bill
Bluebook
West
appellate brief
amicus curiae brief
case
opinion
official reporter
unofficial reporter
star paging
regional reporter

special edition state reporter
casebook
CD-ROM
citation/cite
parallel cite
citator
code
codify
uncodified
cumulative
cumulative supplement
digest
abstracts
squibs
key topic and number
regional digest
formbook
practice manual
handbook
headnote
hornbook

interstate compact
kardex
legal dictionary
legal newspaper
legal periodical
law review
law journal
legal thesaurus
legislation
loose-leaf service
law directory
microform
microfilm
microfiche
ultrafiche
pocket part
record
Restatements
rules of court
edition
series

shepardize
slip law
slip opinion
statutory code
treatise
authority
primary authority
secondary authority
mandatory authority
persuasive authority
nonauthority
enacted law
on point
analogous
conflicts of law
full faith and credit
dictum
caption of opinion
reporters
online
italicize
et al.
litigation status
in re
docket number
nominative reporter

popular name
enacted into positive law
cite checking
supra
infra
title page
copyright
table of cases
table of statutes
statutory history table
footnotes
appendixes
CARTWHEEL
background research
validation research
KF call number
Library of Congress
    classification system
trace a key topic and number
DWI
scope note
superseded
supplemented
cited material
citing material
syllabus (Shepard's)

small raised number
codified cite
session law cite
et seq.
case note
online
query
CALR
common law
notes of decisions
section (§)
historical note
legislative history
Id.
mandatory statute
discretionary statute
monitoring legislation
legislative service
PL number
transcribed
constitution
regulation
validation research
annotated bibliography

# 12

# Legal Writing

## ■ Chapter Outline

**Section A. Kinds of Legal Writing**
**Section B. Memorandum of Law**
  Structure of an Interoffice Memo

**Section C. Appellate Brief**
**Section D. Some Writing Guidelines**

## ■ Section A. Kinds of Legal Writing

There are a number of different kinds of writing within a law office:

- Letters
- Instruments
- Pleadings
- Memoranda of law
- Appellate briefs

### 1. Letters

Many garden-variety letters are written in a law office every day, such as a letter requesting information, a letter demanding payment, or a letter notifying someone of the fact that the office represents a particular person or company.

In an *opinion letter,* the office writes to its client to explain the application of the law and advise the client what to do. Such letters try to clarify technical material. Unlike a brief or memorandum, the opinion letter does not make extensive reference to court opinions or statutes. The client's need is for clear, concise, practical advice.

### 2. Instruments

An *instrument* is a formal document that gives expression to a legal act or agreement. Examples of instruments include contracts, deeds, wills, leases, bonds, notes, and mortgage agreements. Many formbooks and computer programs provide models for drafting such instruments. Rarely will anyone write an instrument from scratch. The starting point is almost always a standard form or model, which is adapted to the particular facts of the client.

### 3. Pleadings

*Pleadings* are formal statements of claims and defenses that are exchanged between parties involved in litigation. The major pleadings are the complaint, answer, counterclaim, reply to counterclaim, cross-claim, and third party complaint. Formbooks are also often used as the starting point in drafting pleadings. Some high-volume litigation firms use computers or word-processing equipment to help prepare repetitive pleadings.

## ▌ Section B. Memorandum of Law

A *memorandum of law* is an analysis of legal authority governing one or more legal issues. It is generally the product of a fairly extensive research effort. There are two kinds of legal memoranda:

- The *internal* or *interoffice* memorandum
- The *external* or *adversary* memorandum

The audience of an *interoffice* memorandum is your own office. Its primary feature is its objectivity. It must present the strengths *and* weaknesses of the client's case so that the senior members of the office can make intelligent decisions based on all aspects of the law. The memo will certainly attempt to show how the law can be interpreted in the light most favorable to the client, but it must go beyond this level. The memo also must try to anticipate what the strongest arguments of the *opponent* will be. Such arguments must be presented with precision and honesty. When this is done, the reader of the memo within the office will be in the best position to design a realistic strategy.

An *external* memorandum, by contrast, is not an objective document at all. It is an *adversary* document that attempts to persuade the reader to adopt a decision favorable to the client. The audience of your external memorandum may be a hearing officer in an administrative agency (if so, it will often be called a hearing memorandum or a *points and authorities memorandum*) or a trial court judge (if so, it will often be called a *trial memorandum*). A trial memorandum is like an appellate brief (discussed below) in that both are advocacy documents directed to a court. An appellate brief, however, is more stylized in format and is not written for an agency or a trial court.

The distinguishing features of the two kinds of memoranda are outlined in the chart in Figure 12.1.

### Structure of an Interoffice Memo

Not all supervisors agree on the preferred structure of the interoffice memorandum of law. The following are common features of many memos:

1. Heading
2. Statement of the assignment
3. Legal issues
4. Facts
5. Discussion or analysis
6. Conclusion
7. Recommendations
8. Appendix

### 1. Heading

At the top of the page, state the kind of document you are writing (interoffice memorandum of law). Then list:

- The person to whom the memo is addressed
- The name of the author of the memo
- The date the memo was prepared
- The name of the client and the opponent
- The office file number of the case
- The court docket number, if the case has already been filed in court
- A very brief subject-matter entry (following the notation "RE:") in which you state what the memo is about

The following sample heading illustrates how this information might be set forth in a heading for a memorandum written on behalf of client Brown, who is suing Miller:

---

Interoffice Memorandum

TO: Jane Patterson, Esq.                    RE: Availability of the contribu-
FROM: John Jackson, Paralegal                  tory negligence defense to
DATE: April 30, 1991                           Miller
CASE: Brown v. Miller
OFFICE FILE NUMBER: 91-42
DOCKET NUMBER: CIV. 1-91-307

---

Note that the subject-matter description in this sample (RE:) briefly indicates the nature of the question that will be treated in the memorandum. This information is needed for at least two reasons. First, the average law office case file contains a large number of documents, often including several legal memoranda. A heading that at least briefly indicates the nature of the subject of each memorandum makes it much easier to locate the memorandum in the client's file. Second, it is unlikely that the usefulness of your memorandum will end when the client's case is closed. Some law offices maintain fairly extensive libraries of old office memoranda, which are cataloged and filed by subject matter for reference in future cases. This avoids unnecessary and costly duplication of research time in the event that a similar question arises in a future client's case. The subject-matter heading on your memorandum facilitates the cataloging and filing of your memorandum in such a library.

The inclusion of the date on which the memorandum was completed and submitted is important for similar reasons. While your analysis and conclusions may have been very accurate at the time the memorandum was written, subsequent changes in the law may have occurred by the time the memorandum is

| INTEROFFICE MEMORANDUM OF LAW | EXTERNAL MEMORANDUM OF LAW |
|---|---|
| ■ Emphasizes both the strengths and the weaknesses of the client's position on each issue (objective) | ■ Emphasizes the strengths but minimizes or ignores the weaknesses of the client's position on each issue |
| ■ Emphasizes both the strengths and the weaknesses of the opposing party's probable position on each issue | ■ Emphasizes the weaknesses but minimizes or ignores the strengths of the opposing party's position on each issue |
| ■ Predicts the court's or the agency's probable decision on each issue | ■ Argues for a favorable decision on each issue |
| ■ Recommends the most favorable strategy for the client to follow | |

**FIGURE 12.1**

Characteristics of Interoffice and External Memoranda of Law next referred to. On seeing the date of the memorandum, a reader will know from what date subsequent legal research is needed.

## 2.  *Statement of the Assignment*

It is a good idea early in the memo to provide an explicit statement of what your supervisor has asked you to do.

## 3.  *Statement of the Legal Issue(s)*

On phrasing issues, see page 350.

Often you must state and discuss certain issues *on the assumption* that the court or agency will decide against you on prior issues that you discuss early in the memorandum. Suppose that the client is a defendant in a negligence action. The first issue may concern the liability of the defendant: was the defendant negligent or not? In the first issue, the defendant will be covering the liability question and will attempt to demonstrate in the discussion or analysis on this issue why the defendant is *not* liable. All the evidence and authority supporting nonliability will be examined under this issue. At the time that the memorandum is written, there will, of course, be no resolution of the first issue. Hence, you must be prepared for issues that will arise *on the assumption* that the client will lose the first issue. For example, all issues concerning damages (how much money must be paid to a plaintiff who has successfully established liability) need to be anticipated and analyzed in the event that the liability issue is lost. The statement of the damage issue in the memorandum should be prefaced by language such as:

In the event that we lose the first issue, then we must discuss the issue of . . . .

*or*

On the assumption that the court finds for [the other party] on the liability issue, the damages question then becomes whether . . . .

No matter how firmly you believe in your prediction of what a court or agency will do on an issue, be prepared for what will happen in the event that your prediction eventually proves to be erroneous. This must be done in an internal memorandum, in an external memorandum (hearing or trial), and in an appellate brief.

## 4.  *Statement of the Facts*

Your statement of the facts of the client's case is one of the most important components of the memorandum. You should take great pains to see that it is concise, highly accurate, and well organized.

*Conciseness.*   An unduly long fact statement will only frustrate the reader. Try to eliminate any unnecessary facts from the statement. One way of doing this is to carefully review your fact statement *after* you have completed your analysis of the issues. If there are facts in your statement that are not subsequently referred to in your analysis, it may be that those facts are not particularly relevant to your memorandum and can be eliminated in your final draft.

*Accuracy.*   In many instances you will be drafting the memorandum for an attorney who is preparing to go before a court or agency for the first time; there may be no prior proceedings. Hence, there will be no record and no official findings of fact. The temptation will be to indulge in wishful thinking—to ignore adverse facts and to assume that disputed facts will be resolved in favor of the client. Do not give in to this temptation. You must assess the legal consequences of favorable *and* unfavorable facts. If a particular fact is presently unknown, put aside your writing, if possible, and investigate whatever evidence exists to prove the fact one way or the other. If it is not practical to conduct an investigation at the present time, then you should provide an analysis of what law will apply based on your most reasonable estimate of what an investigation may uncover. The need for accuracy does not mean that you should fail to state the facts in the light most favorable to the client. It simply means that you must be cautious in doing so in order to avoid making false or misleading statements of fact.

*Organization.*    A disorganized statement of facts not only prevents the reader from understanding the events in question but also interferes with an understanding of your subsequent analysis. In general, it is best to start with a short one- or two-sentence summary of the nature of the case, followed by a *chronologically* ordered statement of the detailed facts. Occasional variations from strict chronological order can be justified as long as they do not interfere with the flow of the story.

## 5. Discussion or Analysis

Here you present the law and explain its applicability to the facts. In other words, you try to answer the issues. For memos that require interpretation of statutes, a suggested organizational structure is as follows:

- State the entire section or subsection of the statute that you are analyzing. Include only what must be discussed in the memo. If the section or subsection is long, you may want to place it in an appendix to the memo. If you are going to discuss more than one section or subsection, treat them separately in different parts of the memo unless they are so interrelated that they must be discussed together.

- Break the statute into its elements. (An element is a portion of a rule that is a precondition of the applicability of the entire rule. See page 347.) List each element separately.

- Briefly tell the reader which elements will be in contention and why. In effect, you are telling him or her why you have phrased the issue(s) the way you did earlier in the memo.

- Go through each element you have identified, one at a time, spending most of your time on the elements that are most in contention.

- For the elements not in contention, simply tell the reader why you think there will not be any dispute about them. For example, you anticipate that both sides probably will agree that the facts clearly support the applicability or nonapplicability of the element.

- For the elements in contention, present your interpretation of each element; discuss court opinions that have interpreted the statute, if any; discuss regulations and administrative decisions that have interpreted the statute, if any; discuss the legislative history of the statute, if available (page 596); discuss scholarly interpretation of the statute, if any.

- Give opposing viewpoints for the elements in contention. Try to anticipate how the other side will interpret these elements. For example, what counter-arguments will the other side probably make through court opinions or legislative history?

## 6. Conclusion

Give your personal opinion on which side has the better arguments. Do not state any new arguments in the conclusion. Simply state your own perspective on the strengths and weaknesses of your arguments.

## 7. Recommendations

State recommendations you feel are appropriate in view of the analysis and conclusion that you have provided. For example, further facts should be investigated, further research should be undertaken, a letter should be written to the agency involved, the case should be litigated or settled, etc.

## 8. Appendix

At the end of the memo, include special items, if any, that you referred to in the memo, such as photographs, statistical tables, or the full text of statutes.

. . . . . . . . . . . . . .

What follows is an interoffice memorandum of law that conforms with this structure. Assume that the supervisor wants this memorandum within a few hours after it is given to you. You are asked to provide a preliminary analysis of a statute. Hence, at this point there has been no time to do any research on the statute, although the memo should indicate what research will be needed.

---

### INTEROFFICE MEMORANDUM OF LAW

TO: Mary Jones, Esq.                    RE: Whether Donaldson has
FROM: Tim Farrell, Paralegal                 violated § 17
DATE: March 13, 1990
CASE: Department of Sanitation v. Jim Donaldson
OFFICE FILE NUMBER: 90-114
DOCKET NUMBER: (none at this time; no action has been filed)

**A. ASSIGNMENT**
You have asked me to do a preliminary analysis of 23 State Code Ann. § 17 (1980) to assess whether our client, Jim Donaldson, has violated this statute. No research on the statute has been undertaken thus far, but I will indicate where such research might be helpful.

**B. LEGAL ISSUE**
When a government employee is asked to rent a car for his agency, but uses the car for personal business before he signs the lease, has this employee violated § 17, which prohibits the use of "property leased to the government" for nonofficial purposes?

**C. FACTS**
Jim Donaldson is a government employee who works for the State Department of Sanitation. On February 12, 1990, he is asked by his supervisor, Fred Jackson, to rent a car for the agency for a two-year

---

Continued

period. At the ABC Car Rental Company, Donaldson is shown several cars available for rental. He asks the manager if he could test drive one of the cars for about 15 minutes before making a decision. The manager agrees. Donaldson then drives the car to his home in the area, picks up a TV, and takes it to his sister's home. When he returns, he tells the manager that he wants to rent the car for his agency. He signs the lease and takes the car to the agency. The supervisor, however, finds out about the trip that Donaldson made to his sister with the TV. He is charged with a violation of § 17. Since he is a new employee at the agency, he is fearful that he might lose his job.

### D.  ANALYSIS

Donaldson is charged with violating 23 State Code Ann. § 17 (1980), which provides as follows:

§17.  Use of Government Property

An employee of any state agency shall not directly or indirectly use government property of any kind, including property leased to the government, for other than officially approved activities.

To establish a violation of this statute, the following elements must be proven:

(1)  An employee of any state agency
(2)  (a)  shall not directly use government property of any kind
          including property leased to the government, or
     (b)  shall not indirectly use government property of any kind
          including property leased to the government
(3)  for other than officially approved activities

The main problem in this case will be the second element.

(1)  Employee of a state agency

Donaldson works for the State Department of Sanitation, which is clearly a "state agency" under the statute.

(2)  Use of property leased to the government

The central issue is whether Donaldson used property leased to the government. (The rented car was not owned by the government. Hence it was not "government property." And Donaldson acted "directly" rather than "indirectly," such as by causing someone else to drive the car.) There should be no dispute that when Donaldson drove the car to his sister's, he directly used property. But was it "property leased to the government"?

Donaldson's best argument is a fairly strong one. His position will be that when he made the trip to his sister, he had not yet signed the lease. He would argue that "leased" means contractually committed to rent. Under this definition, the car did not become property leased to the government until after he returned from his sister's house. No costs were incurred by the government because of the test drive. Rental payments would not begin until the car was rented through the signing of the lease.

The supervisor, on the other hand, will argue for a broader definition of "leased"—that it means the process of obtaining a contractual commitment to rent, including the necessary steps leading up to that commitment. Under this definition, the car

Continued

was leased to Donaldson when he made the unauthorized trip. The test drive was arguably a necessary step in making the decision to sign a long-term leasing contract.

The goal of the legislature in enacting § 17 should be kept in mind when trying to determine the meaning of any of the language of § 17. The legislature was trying to avoid the misuse of government resources. Public employees should not take advantage of their position for private gain. To do so would be a violation of the public trust. Yet this is what Donaldson did. While on the government payroll, he obtained access to a car and used it for a private trip. Common sense would lead to the conclusion that leasing in § 17 is not limited to the formal signing of a leasing contract. Anything that is necessarily part of the process of signing that contract should be included. The legislature wanted to prevent the misuse of government resources in all necessary aspects of the leasing of property.

It is not clear from the facts whether the manager of the ABC Rental Company knew that Donaldson was considering the rental on behalf of a government agency when he received permission to take the test drive. The likelihood is that he did know it, although this should be checked. If the manager did know, then Donaldson probably used the fact that he was a government employee to obtain the permission. He held himself out as a reliable individual because of the nature of his employment. This reinforces the misuse argument under the broader definition of "leased" presented above.

I have not yet checked whether there are any court opinions or agency regulations interpreting § 17 on this point. Nor have I researched the legislative history of the statute. All this should be done soon.

(3) Officially Approved Activities

Nothing in the facts indicates that Donaldson's supervisor, Fred Jackson, gave him any authorization to make the TV trip. Even if Jackson had authorized the trip, it would probably not be "officially" approved, since the trip was not for official (i.e., public) business.

E. CONCLUSION

Donaldson has the stronger argument based on the language of the statute. The property simply was not "leased" at the time he made the TV trip. I must admit, however, that the agency has some very good points in its favor. Unlike Donaldson's technical argument, the agency's position is grounded in common sense. Yet on balance, Donaldson's argument should prevail.

F. RECOMMENDATIONS

Some further investigation is needed. We should find out whether the ABC Rental Company manager knew that Donaldson was a government employee at the time he asked for the test drive. In addition, legal research should be undertaken to find out if any court opinions and agency regulations exist on the statute. A check into the legislative history of § 17 is also needed.

Finally, I recommend that we send a letter to Donaldson's supervisor, Fred Jackson, explaining our position. I have attached a draft of such a letter for your signature in the event you deem this action appropriate. [See page 628.]

Continued

> There is one matter that I have not addressed in this memo. Donaldson is concerned that he might lose his job over this incident. Assuming for the moment that he did violate § 17, it is not at all clear that termination would be an appropriate sanction. The statute is silent on this point. Let me know if you want me to research this issue.

---

### ■ ASSIGNMENT 12.1

The Pepsi Cola Bottling Company is authorized to do business in Florida. It wishes to prevent another Florida company from calling itself the Pepsi Catsup Company because this name violates § 225.25. The Pepsi Catsup Company denies that its name is in violation of this statute. The Secretary of State has the responsibility of enforcing this statute.

**48 State Code Ann. § 225.25 (1979).** The name of a company or corporation shall be such as will distinguish it from any other company or corporation doing business in Florida.

Your supervisor asks you to prepare a preliminary memorandum of law on the applicability of this statute. The office represents the Pepsi Catsup Company. Do no legal research at this time, although you should point out what research might be helpful. After you complete the memo, draft a letter to the Secretary of State giving the position of your office on the applicability of the statute. (You can make up the names and addresses of the people involved as well as any dates that you need.)

---

## ■ Section C. Appellate Brief

The word *brief* has several meanings.

First, to *brief* a case is to summarize its major components, such as key facts, issues, reasoning, disposition. (See Chapter 7.) Such a brief is your own summary of a court opinion for later use.

Second, a *trial brief* is an attorney's set of notes on how to conduct the trial. The notes will be on the opening statement, witnesses, exhibits, direct and cross-examination, closing argument, etc. This trial brief is sometimes called a trial manual or trial notebook (see page 470). It is not submitted to the court nor to the other side. A *trial memorandum* on points of law might be submitted, but not the trial brief, which contains counsel's strategy. (This trial memorandum, however, is sometimes referred to as a trial brief. In such instances, the trial brief consists of arguments of law rather than the tactical blueprint for the conduct of the trial.)

Third, the *appellate brief* is the formal written argument to a court of appeals on why a lower court's decision should be affirmed, modified, or reversed. It is submitted to the appellate court and to the other side. The appellate brief is one of the most sophisticated kinds of legal writing in a law office.

The first appellate brief that is usually submitted is the *appellant's* brief. The appellant is the party initiating the appeal. Then the *appellee's* brief is filed in response. The appeal is taken against the appellee (sometimes called the *respondent*). Finally, the appellant is often allowed to submit a *reply brief* to counter the position taken in the appellee's brief.

Occasionally a court will permit a nonparty to the litigation to submit an appellate brief. This is referred to as an *amicus curiae* (friend of the court) brief

---

**Farrell, Grote, & Schweitzer**
**Attorneys at Law**
**724 Central Plaza Place**
**West Union, Ohio 45693**
**513-363-7159**

March 15, 1990

Frederick Jackson
Field Supervisor
Department of Sanitation
3416 34th St. NW
West Union, Ohio 45693

RE:  James Donaldson
90-114

Dear Mr. Jackson:

Our firm represents Mr. James Donaldson. As you know, some question has arisen as to Mr. Donaldson's use of a car prior to the time he was asked to rent it for your agency on February 12, 1990. Our understanding is that he was asked to go to the ABC Car Rental Company in order to rent a car that was needed by your agency, and that he did so satisfactorily.

Your agency became responsible for the car at the moment Mr. Donaldson signed the lease for the car rental. What happened prior to the time the lease was signed is not relevant. The governing statute (§ 17) is quite explicit. It forbids nonofficial use of property "leased" to the government. Such use did not occur in this case. No one has questioned Mr. Donaldson's performance of his duty once he "leased" the car.

If additional clarification is needed, we would be happy to discuss the matter with you further.

Sincerely,

Mary Jones, Esq.

wps: TF

---

(page 491). The *amicus* brief advises the court on how to resolve the controversies before it.

Not all appellate briefs have the same structure. Rules of court often specify what structure or format the brief should take, the print size, number of copies to be submitted, etc. The following are the major components of many appellate briefs:

*(a) Caption.* The caption states the names of the parties, the name of the court, the court file or docket number, and the kind of appellate brief it is. The caption goes on the front cover of the brief (page 491).

*(b) The Statement of Jurisdiction.* In this section of the brief, there is a short statement explaining the subject-matter jurisdiction of the appellate court. For example:

> This Court has jurisdiction under 28 U.S.C. § 1291 (1967).

The jurisdiction statement may point out some of the essential facts that relate to the jurisdiction of the appellate court, such as how the case came up on appeal. For example:

> On January 2, 1978, a judgment was entered by the U.S. Court of Appeals for the Second Circuit. The U.S. Supreme Court granted certiorari on February 6, 1978. 400 U.S. 302.

Later in the brief there is a Statement of the Case in which more detailed jurisdictional material is often included.

*(c) Table of Contents.* The table of contents is an outline of the major components of the brief, including *point headings,* and the pages in the brief on which everything begins. A point heading is the party's conclusion it wants the court to adopt for a particular issue. The function of the table of contents is to provide the reader with quick and easy access to each portion of the brief. Because the page numbers will not be known until the brief is completed, the table of contents is the last section of the brief to be written. The following excerpt from the respondent's brief illustrates the structure of a table of contents which includes the point headings as part of the "argument."

---

**TABLE OF CONTENTS**

| | Page |
|---|---|
| Opinions Below | 1 |
| Jurisdiction | 2 |
| Questions Presented | 2 |
| Constitutional Provisions, Statutes, and House Resolution Involved | 2 |
| Statement | 6 |
| Summary of Argument | 8 |

Argument:

| | |
|---|---|
| I. *Gravel v. United States* stands as a unanimous holding that the Speech or Debate clause affords absolute immunity to the legislative respondents in this case | 14 |
|   A. The challenged report | 15 |
|   B. The individual immunities of the legislative respondents | 24 |
| II. Petitioners' attempts to circumvent the unanimous holding in *Gravel* as to the immunity of the legislative activities involved here are unavailing | 30 |
|   A. There has been no invasion of the right of privacy | 31 |
|   B. The Speech or Debate immunity is dispositive of petitioners' claims | 33 |
| III. The legislative action involved here does not constitute a bill of attainder | 41 |
| IV. Separation of powers | 43 |
| Conclusion | 49 |

---

*(d) Table of Authorities.* This table lists all the cases, statutes, regulations, administrative decisions, constitutional provisions, charter provisions, ordinances, court rules, and secondary authority relied on in the brief. All the cases are listed in alphabetical order, all the statutes are listed in alphabetical and numerical order, etc. The page numbers on which each of these authorities is discussed in the brief are presented so that the table acts as an index to these authorities.

Example:

---

### Table of Authorities

| | Page |
|---|---|
| **CASES:** | |
| *Smith v. Jones*, 24 F.2d 445 (5th Cir. 1974) .................. | 2, 4, 12 |
| *Thompson v. Richardson*, 34 Miss. 650, 65 So. 109 (1930) ................................................................... | 3, 9 |
| Etc. | |
| **CONSTITUTIONAL PROVISIONS** | |
| Art. 5, Miss. Constitution ............................................. | 12, 17 |
| Art. 7, Miss. Constitution ............................................. | 20 |
| Etc. | |
| **STATUTES** | |
| Miss. Code Ann. § 23(b) (1978) .................................... | 2, 8, 23 |
| Miss. Code Ann. § 45 (1978) ........................................ | 7 |
| Etc. | |
| **LAW REVIEW ARTICLES** | |
| Colom, *Sex Discrimination in the 1980's*, 35 Miss. Law Journal 268 (1982) ..................................................... | 19 |
| ETC. | |

---

*(e) Questions Presented.*   The label used for this part of the brief varies. It may be called "Questions Presented," "Points Relied on for Reversal," "Points in Error," "Assignments of Error," "Issues Presented," etc. Regardless of the label, its substance is essentially the same: it is a statement of the legal issues that the party wishes the appellate court to consider and decide.

*(f) Statement of the Case.*   Here, the dispute and lower court proceedings to date are summarized, the essential facts of the case are presented, and (often) jurisdictional data is included.

Example:

---

These are actions based upon the Federal Tort Claims Act, 28 U.S.C. § 1346(b), initiated by the appellants, Garrett Freightlines, Inc. and Charles R. Thomas in the United States District Court for the District of Idaho. The appellant alleged that appellee's employee, Randall W. Reynolds, while acting within the scope of his employment, negligently caused injury to appellants. The United States denied that the employee was acting within the scope of his employment.

On March 27, 1973, appellant Garrett made a motion for limited summary judgment as to whether Reynolds was acting within the scope of his employment when the collision occurred. The actions of Garrett and Thomas were consolidated by order of the court, and appellee later moved for summary judgment (see trial transcript, page 204).

The District Court held that under the authority of dicta in *Berrettoni v. United States*, 436 F.2d 1372 (9th Cir. 1970), Reynolds was not within the scope of his employment when the accident occurred and granted appellee's motion for summary judgment. It is from that order and judgment that the injured now appeals.

Staff Sergeant Reynolds was a career soldier in the United States Military and, until November 9, 1970, stationed at Fort Rucker, Alabama. On or about July 30, 1970, official orders directed that Reynolds be reassigned to the Republic of Vietnam. . . .

---

*(g) Summary of Argument.*   The major points to be made in the brief are summarized in this section.

*(h) Argument.*   Here the attorney explains the legal positions of the client. All the primary and secondary authority relied on is analyzed.

*(i) Conclusion.*   The conclusion states what action the attorney is asking the appellate court to take.

*(j) Appendixes.*   The appendixes contain excerpts from statutes, or other primary authority, excerpts from the trial, charts, descriptions of exhibits entered into evidence at the trial, etc.

## Section D. Some Writing Guidelines

### 1. Words and Phrases to Avoid

■ Avoid the following terms altogether:

> above (as an adjective)
> aforementioned
> aforesaid
> and/or (say "A or B," or say "A or B or both")
> beforementioned
> provided that
> said (as a substitute for "the," "that," or "those")
> same (as a substitute for "it," "he," "her," etc.)
> to wit
> whatsoever
> whensoever
> wheresoever

■ Avoid circumlocutions, which are pairs of words having the same effect:

| | |
|---|---|
| alter and change | full force and effect |
| any and all | made and entered into |
| authorize and empower | null and void |
| by and with | order and direct |
| each and all | over and above |
| each and every | sole and exclusive |
| final and conclusive | type and kind |
| from and after | unless and until |
| full and complete | |

■ Avoid expressions such as:

> none whatever
>
> make application, make a determination
>
> shall be considered to be, shall be deemed to be, may be treated as, have the effect of (unless a fiction is intended)

## 2. Preferred Expressions

Unless there are special reasons to the contrary:

| *Do Not Say* | *Say* |
|---|---|
| (1) accorded | (1) given |
| (2) adequate number of | (2) enough |
| (3) admit of | (3) allow |
| (4) afforded | (4) given |
| (5) all of the | (5) all the |
| (6) a person is prohibited from | (6) a person shall not |
| (7) approximately | (7) about |
| (8) at least | (8) not less than (when referring to two or more) |
| (9) at such time as | (9) when |
| (10) attains the age of _____ | (10) becomes _____ years of age |
| (11) attempt (as a verb) | (11) try |
| (12) at the time | (12) when |
| (13) by means of | (13) by |
| (14) calculate | (14) compute |
| (15) category | (15) kind, class, group |
| (16) cause it to be done | (16) have it done |
| (17) contiguous to | (17) next to |
| (18) corporation organized under the laws of Ohio | (18) Ohio corporation |
| (19) deem | (19) consider |
| (20) does not operate to | (20) does not |
| (21) during such time as | (21) while |
| (22) during the course of | (22) during |
| (23) endeavor (as a verb) | (23) try |
| (24) enter into a contract with | (24) to contract with |
| (25) evince | (25) show |
| (26) expiration | (26) end |
| (27) for the duration of | (27) during |
| (28) for the purpose of holding (or other gerund) | (28) to hold (or comparable infinitive) |
| (29) for the reason that | (29) because |
| (30) forthwith | (30) immediately |
| (31) in accordance with | (31) pursuant to, under |
| (32) in case | (32) if |
| (33) in cases in which | (33) when, where |
| (34) in order to | (34) to |
| (35) in sections 2023 to 2039 inclusive | (35) in sections 2023 to 2039 |

| *Do Not Say* | *Say* |
|---|---|
| (36) in case of | (36) when, if |
| (37) in the event of | (37) if |
| (38) in the event that | (38) if |
| (39) in the interest of | (39) for |
| (40) is able to | (40) can |
| (41) is applicable | (41) applies |
| (42) is authorized to | (42) may |
| (43) is binding upon | (43) binds |
| (44) is directed to | (44) shall |
| (45) is empowered to | (45) may |
| (46) is entitled (in the sense of "has the name") | (46) is called |
| (47) is entitled to | (47) may |
| (48) is hereby authorized and it shall be his or her duty to | (48) shall |
| (49) is hereby authorized to | (49) shall |
| (50) is not prohibited from | (50) may |
| (51) is permitted to | (51) may |
| (52) is required to | (52) shall |
| (53) is unable to | (53) cannot |
| (54) it is directed | (54) shall |
| (55) it is his or her duty to | (55) shall |
| (56) it is the duty of | (56) shall |
| (57) it shall be lawful | (57) may |
| (58) it shall be unlawful for a person to | (58) a person shall not |
| (59) no later than June 30, 1990 | (59) before July 1, 1990 |
| (60) on or after July 1, 1991 | (60) after June 30, 1991 |
| (61) on or before June 30, 1989 | (61) before July 1, 1989 |
| (62) on the part of | (62) by |
| (63) or, in the alternative | (63) or |
| (64) paragraph (5) of subsection (a) of section 2097 | (64) section 2097(a)(5) |
| (65) per annum | (65) a year |
| (66) per centum | (66) percent |
| (67) period of time | (67) use period *or* time |
| (68) provision of law | (68) law |
| (69) render (in the sense of give) | (69) give |
| (70) State of Massachusetts | (70) Massachusetts |
| (71) subsequent to | (71) after |

| *Do Not Say* | *Say* |
|---|---|
| (72)  suffer (in the sense of permit) | (72)  permit |
| (73)  under the provisions of | (73)  under |
| (74)  until such time as | (74)  until |

### 3. *Action Verbs*

Wherever possible, draft your sentences to use action verbs instead of participles, gerunds, and other noun or adjective forms. Action verbs are shorter and more direct.

| *Do Not Say* | *Say* |
|---|---|
| (1)  give consideration to | (1)  consider |
| (2)  give recognition to | (2)  recognize |
| (3)  have knowledge of | (3)  know |
| (4)  have need of | (4)  need |
| (5)  in the determination of | (5)  to determine |
| (6)  is applicable | (6)  applies |
| (7)  is dependent on | (7)  depends on |
| (8)  is in attendance at | (8)  attends |
| (9)  make an appointment of | (9)  appoint |
| (10)  make application | (10)  apply |
| (11)  make payment | (11)  pay |
| (12)  make provision for | (12)  provide for |

### 4. *Active Voice*

Avoid the passive voice whenever possible.[1]

| *Do Not Say* | *Say* |
|---|---|
| It was decided by the plaintiff. | The plaintiff decided . . . |
| The motion is filed by defendant. | Defendant files the motion. |

Compare the following versions of the same sentence:[2]

| | |
|---|---|
| In neither the motion nor appellant's brief was there any reliance on ORC § 2943.39. | Appellant did not rely on ORC § 2943.39 in either his motion or his brief. |
| The testimony of the defendant was contradicted by the fact that he had the receipt showing partial payment. | The receipt showing partial payment contradicted defendant's testimony. |

---

[1]State Bar of California, *Are You Misunderstood?* (March 1990).
[2]Grey, *Writing a Good Appellate Brief,* 88 Case and Comment 44, 48–50 (No. 6, November–December 1983). Reprinted by special permission. Copyrighted © 1983 by the Lawyers Cooperative Publishing Co.

| | |
|---|---|
| The result obtained from a properly administered breathalyzer test is the percentage by weight of alcohol in a person's blood. | A properly administered breathalyzer test shows the percentage by weight of alcohol in a person's blood. |

## 5. Positive Form

Phrase something positively rather than negatively whenever possible.

| *Do Not Say* | *Say* |
|---|---|
| It is not difficult to imagine. | It is easy to imagine. |
| The paper is not without flaws. | The paper has flaws. |

## 6. Verbosity

Avoid unnecessary words. Compare the following versions of the same sentence:

| | |
|---|---|
| He consulted *with* a doctor *in regard* to his injuries. | He consulted a doctor *about* his injuries. |
| He drove to the left *due to the fact* that the lane was blocked. | He drove to the left *because* the lane was blocked. |
| This product is used for *hair-dyeing purposes*. | This product is used to *dye hair*. |
| The continuance was requested *in order to obtain the presence of a witness who was not then available.* | The continuance was requested *because a witness was unavailable.* |

Read these sentences, with and without the italicized words.

The court directed a verdict in favor of defendant *and against the plaintiff.* (Verdicts for defendants usually are against the plaintiff.)

The car was green *in color.* (This distinguishes it from the car that was green in size!)

A stipulation by *all of* the parties. (A stipulation by some of the parties is not of much use.)

A delivery was made every Tuesday *on a regular weekly basis.* (What does *every Tuesday* mean?)

## 7. Shorter Sentences

Use short sentences. A short precise sentence is often more comprehensible and more effective. What is the writer saying in the following sentence?

The Appellee contends that there is not reversible error in the trial court's sustaining the Appellant's objections given the immediate corrective instructions of the trial court as well as the weight of the evidence against the Appellant.

Divide such sentences into a series of shorter sentences:

There is no reversible error. The trial court sustained the objection and immediately cautioned the jury. Considering all the evidence, there is no prejudice to Appellant.

Compare these versions:

The deicer spray had admittedly been sprayed on the inside of the windshield. However, without knowing the name of the manufacturer or having an independent analysis made of the deicer spray, it could not possibly be ascertained what quantity of methanol was in the product and that would be essential to ascertaining what effect, if any, having breathed the chemical would have upon the intoxilizer test.

The deicer sprayed on the inside windshield contained methanol. It was not possible to analyze the product and determine the amount of methanol without knowing the name of the manufacturer. It was not possible to learn what effect, if any, inhaling the methanol would have on the intoxilizer test.

The defendant, ABC, an Ohio Corporation for profit, is engaged in the subsidized housing business and incident thereto is the owner of six dwelling units containing 46 apartment units housing 100 people. To provide for the culinary and sanitary needs of the occupants the defendant purchases from LeAx approximately 5300 gallons (22 tons) of water per day, and since opening for business in July 1975 has purchased 11,308,000 gallons of water which is all collected following use, placed in a sewage plant, treated, and discharged into a drainage ditch, which in turn discharges onto the plaintiff's property.

The defendant, ABC Corp., owns and operates a 46-unit apartment complex containing 100 residents. Water for the apartments is supplied by LeAx at the rate of 5300 gallons, 22 tons, per day. All waste water from the apartments is treated in defendant's sewage plant and discharged into a drainage ditch that runs across plaintiff's property.

This case involves an incident which occurred on November 16, 1988. The plaintiff, Oilcorp, was the owner of a drilling rig which was located in a rural section of Athens County for the purpose of drilling for petroleum. Prior to November 16, 1988, it has been determined that the drilling was completed and it was necessary to move the rig to another location. The defendant was notified of this need and was requested to bring equipment to the drill site for the purpose of moving the drilling rig and associated apparatus from that location to a new location.

The plaintiff, Oilcorp, owned an oil drilling rig located in rural Athens County. It was necessary to move the rig to another location. Oilcorp requested defendant to bring his equipment to the drill site to move the drilling rig.

## 8. Pronoun Reference

Use pronouns only where the nouns to which the pronouns refer are unmistakably clear. Using pronouns with ambiguous referents can confuse the meaning of a sentence. If the pronoun could refer to more than one person or object in a sentence, repeat the name of the person or object to avoid ambiguity.

*Do Not Say:* After the administrator appoints a deputy assistant, he shall supervise the . . .. [Who does the supervising? The administrator or the deputy? If the latter is intended, then:]

*Say:* After the administrator appoints a deputy assistant, the deputy assistant shall supervise the . . ..

## 9. *Sexism in Language*

Avoid gender-specific language when the intent is to refer to both sexes. If neutral language is not available, rewrite the sentence to avoid the problem.

| *Gender-Specific Language* | *Gender-Neutral Alternatives* |
|---|---|
| (1) businessman | (1) executive, member of the business community |
| (2) chairman | (2) chairperson, chair |
| (3) draftsman | (3) drafter |
| (4) man | (4) person, human, humankind |
| (5) man-hours | (5) worker hours |
| (6) mankind | (6) humanity |
| (7) manpower | (7) work force, personnel |
| (8) workmen's compensation | (8) worker's compensation |

# ☐ Chapter Summary

A law office prepares many different kinds of written documents. Opinion letters provide legal advice to a client. Instruments such as deeds, contracts, and other agreements are more formal documents that accomplish specific legal results. Pleadings such as complaints, answers, and cross-claims state claims, defenses, and other positions of parties in litigation. An internal memorandum of law analyzes primary and secondary authority for other members of the office. An external memorandum of law (for example, a "points and authorities" memorandum) analyzes the law for someone outside the office, such as a hearing officer. A case brief is a summary of the major parts of a court opinion. A trial brief (often called a trial manual or trial notebook) is an attorney's set of notes on how he or she intends to conduct a trial. An appellate brief is an argument submitted to an appellate court on why the decision of a lower court should be affirmed, modified, or reversed.

The major components of an internal memorandum of law are the heading, the statement of the assignment, the legal issues, the facts, the dis-

cussion or analysis, the conclusion, and the recommendations.

The major components of an appellate brief are the caption, the statement of jurisdiction, the table of contents, the table of authorities, the questions presented, the statement of the case, the summary of the argument, the argument, the conclusion, and the appendices.

There are a number of important guidelines that will increase the clarity and effectiveness of any kind of writing. Avoid overly formal language, such as aforesaid, to wit, and wheresoever. Avoid circumlocutions like "any and all," "each and every," and "unless and until." Prefer words and expressions that are less pompous and often shorter. For example, instead of saying "at such time as," say "when." Prefer action verbs. For example, instead of saying "give consideration to," say "consider." In addition, prefer the active voice to the passive voice, phrase things positively rather than negatively, avoid verbosity, use shorter sentences, make all pronoun references clear, and avoid sexism in language.

# Key Terms

opinion letter
instrument
formbook
pleading
memorandum of law
internal/interoffice
	memorandum of law
external/adversary
	memorandum of law
hearing memorandum
points and authorities
	memorandum

trial memorandum
heading
RE
legal issue
trial brief
trial manual
trial notebook
trial memorandum
appellate brief
appellant
appellee
respondent

reply brief
amicus curiae
caption of appellate brief
statement of jurisdiction
point heading
table of authorities
questions presented
statement of the case
circumlocution

# 13

# Computer Literacy for Paralegals: An Introduction to the Use of Computers in a Law Office

**with Dale Hobart***

## ■ Chapter Outline

**Section A. Law Offices, Computers, and Paralegals**
  General
  Corporate Law
  Criminal Law
  Estates and Trusts
  Insurance
  Litigation
  Professional Responsibility
  Torts

**Section B. Survival Strategies**
**Section C. Terminology**
**Section D. Hardware**
**Section E. Software**
  Word Processing Software
  Databases
  Spreadsheet Programs
  Communications
  Combinations
**Section F. The Real Investment: Time**

## ■ Section A. Law Offices, Computers, and Paralegals

It is very doubtful that you will work in an office without computers. For many medium and large law offices, computers dominate the practice of law and the management of the law office. If you flipped through the pages of a bar association magazine or legal newspaper, you would probably find that two-thirds of the advertising is from computer manufacturers, vendors, and consultants. Paralegals are an integral part of this computer environment, as demonstrated by the surveys presented in Figures 13.1 and 13.2 and by the comments of paralegals that follow these surveys.

How do paralegals feel computers have affected their professional lives? The following comments, while not representative of all paralegals, help provide an answer.

---

*Director of Legal Assistant Program and Assistant Director of Academic Computing, Ferris State College

## FIGURE 13.1

Survey on Computer Use

| Employment and Salary Survey 1990 (Rocky Mountain Legal Assistants Association, 1990) Question: Do you personally use a computer for any of the following? (Answer based on 470 responses from paralegals.) | Task | Yes | Percent Responding |
|---|---|---|---|
| | ■ Word Processing | 331 | 77 |
| | ■ Docketing | 94 | 22 |
| | ■ Conflicts Check | 24 | 6 |
| | ■ Litigation Support | 181 | 42 |
| | ■ Timekeeping/Billing | 87 | 20 |
| | ■ Other | 95 | 22 |

### PARALEGAL COMMENTS:
### General

"These amazing little machines are filled with micro-chips, circuit boards, disks, and many other magical parts about which I know nothing! What I do know is how much more efficient I am with my PC." [1]

"In the last few years, the computer has become a desirable, if not indispensable, tool of the legal profession, and, in fact, it is somewhat ironic that this new tool has caused typing skills to enjoy a comeback in popularity. Efficient use of the computer keyboard not only facilitates drafting of legal pleadings but also the use of a variety of software programs. While word processing programs are the programs most widely used by legal assistants, [other software used includes:] programs for file organization, document retrieval, calculation, spreadsheet formulation, and research. . . ." [2]

### Corporate Law

■ Not so many years ago, computers were fancy tools only big firms could afford. Even firms with computers were inclined to keep them out of sight, off the polished oak desks of their lawyers, many of whom made it a point of pride not to be able to type. Those days are gone forever.
Paul Reidinger, American Bar Association Journal (1991). ■

Some paralegals have become adept at tailoring general business programs, such as spreadsheet and database management programs, to different areas of legal practice. "When I worked . . . for a major corporation, I was responsible for the shareholder relations program. This required monthly analysis of the company's shareholder base. Rather than have a transfer agent compile the information for a handsome fee, I prepared the report on an IBM PC using Lotus 1-2-3." [3]

### Criminal Law

"We were confronted with more than 300 boxes of documents stored in a depository in Houston" that contained evidence that had to be classified so that it would be available for the trial attorney. To do that, the attorney "started building a data base, using teams of paralegals to code and input the information." The judge allowed the attorney to connect his computer and fax machine

---

[1] Eastwick, *JLA's Seminar/Workshop on Personal Computers in the Law Office*, JLA News 4, Issue 12 (Jacksonville Legal Assistants, January 1988).
[2] Schueneman, *Software Brings Typing Back to the Future*, 3 TALAFAX 3, No. 3 (Tucson Ass'n of Legal Assistants, 1991).
[3] B. Bernardo, *Paralegal* (Peterson's Guides, 1990).

**FIGURE 13.2**

Computers in the Law Office

---

**Results of 1989 Wage,
Benefit & Utilization Survey**

(Legal Assistants of New Mexico, 1989)

Question: What types of tasks do you use your computer for? (Answer based on 103 responses. Paralegals could check more than one task.)

71 Word Processing
49 Document Control
41 Case Evaluation and Management
39 Document Assembly/Forms Fill-in
39 Preparing Charts and Exhibits
36 Database Research (WESTLAW & LEXIS)
33 Full-text Data Storage and Retrieval
29 Database Research (nonlegal)
22 Calendaring/Date Reminder (tickler) System
13 Networking/E-Mail (Electronic Mail)
13 Accounting/Billing
 9 Calculating/"Number Crunching"
 5 Desktop Publishing
 4 Conflicts Checking
 5 Other

Question: Which computer do you use? (Answer based on 96 responses from paralegals.)

| Number | Computer Used |
|---|---|
| 62 | IBM or Compatible PC |
| 4 | Apple PC |
| 1 | IBM Displaywriter |
| 9 | Portable and/or laptop |
| 20 | Other |

Question: Does your firm provide you with your own PC or terminal, or do you share it with other users? (Answer based on 101 responses.)

60 Use own PC or terminal
17 Share a PC or terminal
24 N/A

Question: Which word processing software program does your office use? (Answer based on 80 responses.)

| Number | Software Used |
|---|---|
| 47 | WordPerfect |
| 14 | Wang |
| 4 | Microsoft Word |
| 3 | Displaywrite |
| 18 | Other (e.g., DEC, Lanier) |

Question: Does your firm use a computerized litigation support system? (Answer based on 103 responses.)

71 YES
29 NO
 3 N/A

Question: When your firm orders the transcript of a hearing or a deposition, is it provided on disk so that it can be used with your in-house database system? (Answer based on 95 responses.)

50 YES
40 NO
 5 N/A

Question: Has your firm used an outside computer consultant when acquiring computer hardware and/or software? (Answer based on 95 responses.)

66 YES
27 NO
 2 N/A

---

in the courtroom with the computer and fax machine in the law office. In effect, the attorney was "wired into the network back at the office, which is staffed with paralegals who have access to all kinds of information which can be faxed or sent by computer back into the courtroom immediately." [4]

---

[4] Keeva, *Document Analysis in Criminal Litigation*, 76 American Bar Ass'n Journal 80 (May 1990).

## Estates and Trusts

Ann Cook, legal assistant at Pepper, Hamilton & Scheetz of Philadelphia, saw a demonstration of a software package for fiduciary accounting and immediately began urging her firm to move in that direction. "After seeing it, I was no longer satisfied writing the same information several times for each different purpose when all I had to do was input it once and then push buttons. . . . We've now expanded our system to do estate planning calculations which manually were cumbersome and expensive to produce. Eventually, we would like to connect our system into a data bank like Standard & Poors, so that we can get instant evaluations of stock and bond values." [5]

## Insurance

In the case management area, Norman Strizek works with insurance firms. He's "created databases so they can track separately every litigation case they're involved in, and [identify] which law firm is handling each part; what they're billed each quarter; the status of the litigation; responsible attorneys and paralegals, with phone numbers; due dates of different filings and who is handling each. It helps the insurer manage all their litigation." [6]

## Litigation

"When the portable PC is not used for data retrieval, the legal assistant can use it to take notes." Julie Hoff, a litigation legal assistant for ten years, "cites an example of a legal assistant who put her portable to work in an efficient manner during a recent trial in Minneapolis. While the witness was testifying, the legal assistant summarized the proceedings on her portable computer. At the end of each day, she printed her notes and they were used in the preparation of [cross] examination for the next day and for future witnesses." [7]

"I never leave home without my laptop!" says Laurie Roselle, the Litigation Paralegal Manager at Rogers & Wells in New York. She "types in taxis, commutes with her desktop portable, pulls cases and does actual memos." She says, "You have to use every minute—and you can bill the time." [8]

## Professional Responsibility

Jane Palmer is the conflict-of-interest specialist at Hogan and Hartson in Washington D.C. Working under the supervision of an attorney, Jane spends "more than half her time at the computer on requests for information." She "does all the research on every prospective client" for the firm's offices in Washington D.C., Maryland, Virginia, London, and Brussels "to find out who are the related parties in the matter they are bringing." She "uses her database to see if Hogan and Hartson has ever represented any party on any side of the matter, or been adverse to them. The databases are a client list, accounting and

---

[5]Troop, *Paralegals Are Taking the Lead Through Computers*, 2 Legal Assistant Today 21 (Winter 1985).

[6]Milano, *Novel Way Paralegals Are Using Computers*, 8 Legal Assistant Today 22, 110 (March/April 1991).

[7]*Law Office Trends: Portable PCs in the Courtroom*, Merrill Advantage, 6 (Spring 1989).

[8]Milano, see footnote 6 at p. 23.

billing information, and addresses." "I draw on that for searches, and add to it every day, updating the information." Building on the accounting department's database, Palmer uses Informatics, software designed for conflicts, which connects to accounting and is used for both functions.[9]

## Torts

"Moving on to a tetracycline case involving five pharmaceutical firms, he computerized 40,000 documents. . . ." His "team did the coding." [10]

McCarthy, Palmer, Volkema & Becker is a plaintiff's tort litigation firm in Columbus Ohio. "Computers are an important part of the legal assistants' daily work environment. In place of the message slips and paper memos, the desks of the attorneys and paralegals are adorned with personal computers. Since the firm's beginning, all of the attorneys, legal assistants, secretaries and receptionists have been networked. All telephone messages are transferred from the receptionist via E-mail (Electronic Mail). The main function of the computer, however, is as a warehouse for client file information. The attorney and legal assistant can access the computer from the name and phone number of the judge, opposing counsel, adjuster, treating physician or expert, without pulling a large file from the filing cabinet. An electronic calendar is also available on the system. Firm members now have a means for scheduling meetings with more than one attorney and/or legal assistant without leaving their desks. The computer will notify the person . . . of any conflicts. No more telephone tag or running from one calendar to another.[11]

##  Section B. Survival Strategies

When you walk into your first paralegal job, be prepared to encounter some sophisticated equipment. Our goal in this chapter is not to make you an expert in any particular product or system, rather the goal is to provide you with some of the fundamentals so that you will be in a better position to benefit from the inevitable on-the-job training in the computer products and systems used by a particular law office. We will assume in this chapter that you are a beginner. Even if you are well-versed in computers generally, you'll be a beginner with respect to computer programs that have been (and will be) designed for law offices. Our starting point is a series of survival strategies presented in Figure 13.3. As we begin our exploration of computer use in the practice of law, keep these strategies in mind.

##  Section C. Terminology

The world of the computer, like the world of law, has its own language. Initially, this language can be very confusing. Persistence and time, however, will help rectify this problem.

---

[9]Milano, see footnote 6 at p. 24.

[10]Milano, see footnote 6 at p. 24.

[11]Overly, *Innovations in Law Office Automation*, 6 LACO Letter 12 (Legal Assistants of Central Ohio, December 1990).

**FIGURE 13.3**

Computer Survival Strategies: A Paralegal Tackles a New Program in the Law Office

---

**Stage I: Identify Your "Help" Resources**

- Find out whether there is anyone in the office who already knows how to use the program who would be willing to answer your questions about it. If possible, this should be someone other than—or in addition to—your supervisor.
- Ask if the program you will be using has an 800 number that you can call for assistance.
- Ask if the program has an *online tutorial* which explains the basics. If so, ask someone to start the tutorial for you.
- Ask if the program has a *"HELP" key* that can be used while you are running the program. If so, ask how to use it.
- Find the manual for the program (called the *documentation*). Turn to the index, if one exists. Select some familiar terms in the index, such as capitalization. Turn to the pages for such items and try to follow the instructions provided for them.
- Start a computer notebook in which you write definitions of new terms, steps to follow for certain tasks, steps you took just before you seemed to make a mistake, questions that you want to ask someone later, etc.
- Expect to learn a new vocabulary. (*Boot,* for example, has nothing to do with what goes on your foot.)

**Stage II: Learn the Big Seven Tasks**

Learn the seven essential tasks that apply to most programs:

- How to turn on the computer, *load* the program, and start using it

- How to create a new document or file with the program
- How to save a document or file
- How to call up (or retrieve) a document or file that was created and saved earlier
- How to make a copy of the document or file
- How to turn on the printer and print a document or file
- How to exit from the program and turn the computer off

**Stage III: Take the Initiative**

- Find out if your local paralegal association is offering a seminar on computer use. Attend it. If none is planned, call the president of the association and suggest that one be offered.
- Read the local bar association journals to find out what computer seminars are offered by the bar or by CLE (Continuing Legal Education). Attend some that are relevant to your job.
- Photocopy a chapter from the computer manual at the office. Take the chapter home and read it over the weekend.
- Ask librarians in your area how you can find magazine reviews of the program that you use. Read these reviews.
- Find out if there is a *users group* in your area that meets every month to discuss the program, such as a WordPerfect Users Group. Attend the meetings of this group.
- Organize a "specialty section" of your paralegal association that consists of paralegals who use the program. Members of this section would meet periodically to learn from each other and to discuss common problems with the program.

---

First we begin with some basic definitions:

*Hardware.* The computer and its physical parts. Hardware is what you take out of the box and plug together when you purchase a computer system. It is any part of the system that can be physically touched.

*Backup.* To copy information that a computer uses. The copy is made regularly just in case the original is destroyed.

*Command.* A word or character typed into the computer to tell the computer what to do next.

*Data.* Information of any type that can be used by computers. The data may consist of numbers, words, or pictures.

Typical desktop computer system

*Disk Drive (also called a disk).*    In this chapter, we will use the term *disk drive* (rather than disk) to describe the part of your hardware that is used to store and retrieve programs and information to and from diskettes (see next definition). The disk drive has the capability of placing program information on a diskette. This is often referred to as *writing information to the diskette*. The disk drive also has the capability of "reading" the information from the diskette into the computer. If the information is a program, the program can then be "run" (see definition below) by the computer. Disk drives can be hard or floppy. A *floppy disk* drive is one that can use diskettes. The diskettes can be easily inserted and removed from the disk drive. *Hard disks,* on the other hand, cannot be removed without taking the hardware apart. Furthermore, they have a much greater memory capacity than diskettes. A 40 megabyte hard disk, for example, will be

Diskette being inserted into a floppy disk drive

able to hold approximately 40 million *bytes* of information—about 20,000 pages of text. (One byte is the storage equivalent of one letter of the alphabet, or one punctuation mark, or one blank space.) It would take over one hundred regular-sized diskettes to store the same amount of data.

Sometimes these are also called disks, floppy disks, or just floppies. In this chapter, the term *diskette* will be used. A diskette is a flat piece of plastic, 3½ inch or 5¼ inch in size, that is covered with the same magnetic substance used on a magnetic tape. Information is placed on the diskette in a manner similar to the way music is stored on a cassette. The information can be a program or data to be used by a program. This information can then be read into the computer for the computer to use.

3½-inch and 5¼-inch diskettes

*File.*   A file refers to any information that a computer can use and that is stored or kept together as a group. A file can consist of data or a program. (For the meaning of file in a database program, see Figure 13.5.)

*k.*   A measure of capacity. Each k equals one kilobyte, which is 1,024 bytes (see definition of byte above). The letter k often refers to the amount of information that can be kept on your diskette. It can also refer to the work area in the computer. The work area is the amount of space available to the computer for keeping programs and information that will be used. When microcomputers were new, 64k was considered a great deal of memory (see definitions below). Today, however, many of the programs require 640k or more to function properly.

*Language.*   A program that allows a computer to understand commands and carry them out. BASIC, COBAL, and PASCAL are among the most common computer languages.

*Laptop.*   A portable computer that can be powered by rechargeable batteries.

Typical laptop computer system

*Load.*   To move or transfer a program or information from a disk drive into the computer.

*Memory.*   The area inside a computer that contains programs, and data that programs help generate.

*Microcomputer.*   A computer that is small enough to fit on a desk. The term is not clearly defined because the power of small computers has increased dramatically in the past few years.

*Monitor.*   A TV-like device that is part of the hardware of the computer. On the screen the monitor displays whatever commands you type at the keyboard—and displays information in response to those commands.

*Operating System.*   A program that is in charge of what is displayed on the screen, what is sent to the printer, and all other facets of the operation of a computer. In effect, the operating system serves the function of traffic cop or central manager. There are a variety of operating systems available, such as DOS or MS-DOS, OS/2, UNIX, GEOS, HFS (Macintosh), and NextStep. In some of the systems, you type certain commands on the keyboard. In others, you use a small pointer device called a *mouse* to point to pictures (graphics or icons) on the screen that stand for the same kind of commands that you would otherwise "type in." To execute the command, you push (or *click*) a button on the mouse. An important development in this area is *Windows* from Microsoft. This is a mouse-pointer program that allows a user to run several large programs (such as word processing, database management, spreadsheet) simultaneously. To take advantage of this *multitasking* capacity, a number of the older operating systems are issuing what they call their *windows-based* operating system. Furthermore, many software manufacturers are rushing to release versions

A monitor displaying text on screen

of their products for the *windows environment*, e.g., WordPerfect for Windows.

*Run.*    To cause a program to be loaded into the computer from a disk drive and to begin performing its task.

*Save.*    To cause a program or data that is in the computer memory to be moved or stored on a diskette or hard drive.

Computer with mouse

*Software.*  The programs that allow you to perform tasks such as word processing, database management, and spreadsheet calculations. To use a program, you must get it into the computer. This is usually done by transferring the program from a diskette or from the hard drive.

 ## Section D. Hardware

Many people make the mistake of buying a computer first and then trying to figure out what to do with it. This is not the best approach. If you know what you want to do, you should *first find the software* that can do the job and *then buy the computer* that will run that software.

When investigating available programs, you will probably discover that we live in an IBM world. At the present time, most business application programs are designed first for an IBM or *compatible* computer and then are developed for others. There are many computers that are IBM compatible.

The word *compatible,* or compatible computer, is used in several senses. At a minimum, the word simply means that the information or data files created on an IBM computer can also be used by another computer. At the other end of the spectrum of compatibility, some non-IBM computers not only will use information or data from an IBM computer but will also run most software designed for an IBM computer.

Once software has been selected, the next step is to choose a computer. One of the first considerations is how much memory should be purchased for the computer. Most come with a minimum of 640k. For multipurpose software, it is advisable to obtain considerably more.

The next item of hardware to consider is the disk drive. Disk drives are used to load programs into the computer and to store letters, documents, and other information. There are several combinations of disk drives for a microcomputer, but only two that make sense for business applications.

One choice is two floppy drives (a disk drive that uses diskettes to store data). These are disk drives that use removable diskettes that are usually 3½ or 5¼ inches in diameter. The disk drives should be *dual sided,* meaning that the disk drive is capable of writing on both sides of the diskette. It should also be able to store information on a diskette in *condensed* mode. This mode is referred to as *double-density.* Therefore, a two-floppy-drive machine should have dual-sided, double-density disk drives. This will often be abbreviated DS DD. Two disk drives are needed to make the use of a computer faster and easier. If only one disk drive is available, the user is often required to change the diskette in the drive while using the computer. This is time-consuming and frustrating.

The more common choice for business purposes is a computer with one floppy disk drive and one hard disk drive. A hard disk normally used in a microcomputer can hold much more information than a diskette. This means that most of the programs and data that are used from day to day can be kept on the hard disk, making use of the computer more convenient. There is no need to locate and insert a new diskette to change programs on a hard disk system. All the programs that you normally need can be stored on the hard disk and accessed directly. Unlike a diskette, a hard disk cannot be easily removed from the machine. If finances allow, a hard disk is preferable either in the computer itself or externally as part of a network. (A *network,* as we will see below, is created when several computers are connected together.) You will find that it is nearly impossible to have too much disk storage capacity.

You'll need a monitor as part of your system. Monitors usually come in one of two formats: monochrome or color. The monochrome may be either black and white, green, or amber. Most users prefer the green or amber screen monitors. Color is tempting, but unless the computer is going to be used for color graphics or presentations, monochrome is better. Color can be hard on the eyes, though this is beginning to change. As computers become more sophisticated, color quality will improve.

To obtain a printed copy of what has been entered into the computer, you need a printer. There are many different kinds of printers available:[12]

- *Dot Matrix Printer.* This printer uses tiny pins that press against or punch a ribbon to create a pattern of dots.

Daisy wheel

- *Daisy Wheel Printer.* This printer uses a "daisy wheel," a device (resembling a flower) that contains the alphabet and other characters on spokes. The printer spins the wheel to find the character, which then strikes the ribbon.

- *Ink Jet Printer.* This printer uses a stream of ink sprayed on paper to produce the print. The ink comes from a cartridge rather than a ribbon.

Laser printer: HP LaserJet III Printer

[12]Electronic Industries Association, *How to Buy a Personal Computer*, 14 (1990).

■ *Laser Printer.* This printer uses a laser beam of light to reproduce images. Special cartridges are needed to print text or graphics. It operates very much like a copy machine. Because of their versatility, speed, and high quality, laser printers have become standard in law offices.

A *network* is another important hardware item used by law offices. It will allow you to connect many computers together, enabling them to share (a) information, (b) a hard disk, or (c) printers. For example, a network can make it possible for everyone in a law office to have access to wills, pleadings, or other frequently used documents without each person needing separate copies on individual diskettes. A network can be cost-efficient since it can provide the means for many computers to share some of the more expensive parts of a system.

A *modem* is needed for any law office wishing to use its computer for communications. The modem makes it possible for a computer to send and receive information using regular telephone lines.

An external modem

Many other hardware options are available. The list just given covers the basics and is sufficient to satisfy the needs of most users.

## ■ Section E. Software

There are four basic types of software available:

■ Word processing
■ Database management
■ Spreadsheets
■ Communications
■ The fifth and latest kind of software consists of a combination of all four

There are two ways of making a rational choice when selecting software. One is to try out the programs *before* purchasing them. This will work best for someone with experience who knows what to look for. Testing software yourself can be very time consuming. If you have neither the background nor the time to develop the needed expertise (months are needed), consult an expert. Generally the expert should *not* be someone connected with the local computer store who has an interest in selling you the software that is in stock. A person within your own office is often the best expert. There are a surprising number of people who develop such expertise on their own.

## 1. Word Processing Software

Use a *word processor* instead of a typewriter for writing. It makes little sense to use a typewriter for anything other than addressing one envelope or filling in a simple printed form. Any letter, memo, pleading, brief, or other typed material is easier to prepare with word processing. Once you have used a good word processor, you will be very reluctant to sit at a traditional typewriter again. Since a large volume of writing is done in the law office, a word processor can be a great productivity tool.

Many law offices have used *dedicated word processing* for a long time. A dedicated word processor is one that can do only word processing and none of the other functions that a computer can perform. It is not a computer. The capabilities of the dedicated word processor, however, are now available on computers that can do word processing and other jobs for less cost than the single-purpose or dedicated word processors of old.

The most elemental difference between a word processor and the familiar manual or electric typewriter becomes apparent when you prepare a document for the first time. For example, unlike a traditional typist, the computer user does not listen for a bell in order to know whether he or she is at the end of a line. The computer will automatically move a word down to the next line when the end of a line is reached. This feature is called *word wrap*. There is no need to pause or slow down. The only time you strike the carriage return key is at the end of a paragraph. When a typing error is made at the computer keyboard, there is no need to reach for the bottle of "white out." Nor is there ever a need to worry about a messy final draft caused by insertions or corrections. With the computer you simply go back and correct the error(s). If you left out a letter or sentence, you can easily insert it. The line, in effect, opens up to allow this insertion. If you typed the wrong letter, you can quickly type the correct one directly over the wrong one. If there are too many letters, just press the delete key over the excess letters. Furthermore, there is no need to worry about what such changes will do to paragraph alignment. The computer will take care of it. The task of typing becomes infinitely easier. Someone with limited typing skills soon becomes a confident and competent typist. (See Figure 13.4 for a list of common word-processing terms.)

Easy text entry is just the beginning. Once a document has been put into the computer, it can be used over and over again. Standard paragraphs can be saved, modified, and inserted whenever needed. Documents can be designed so that names are entered once and then automatically included in the final output at fifty different locations. Standard documents can be rearranged by moving paragraphs and sentences within the document. Large or small parts of a document may be moved, deleted, or duplicated to create the final document.

A helpful feature on many word processors is the spelling checker. After a document has been typed, you can activate a spelling program. Different types of spelling programs exist, all of which are based on a large number of words in the program's dictionary. The simpler programs place a mark on any word *not* contained in the program's dictionary. You have probably misspelled such words. You can then review and correct the marked words as needed. More sophisticated spelling programs not only mark a word that is not in the program's dictionary, but also present several possible correct spellings. Spelling

**FIGURE 13.4**

Frequently Encountered Word Processing Terms

| TERM | DEFINITION |
|---|---|
| Automatic pagination | A feature that enables a word processor to number the pages of the printed copy automatically. |
| Block | A group of characters, such as a sentence or paragraph. |
| Block movement | A feature that allows the user to define a block of text and then perform a specific operation on the entire block. Common block operations include block move, block copy, block save, and block delete.. |
| Boldface | Heavy type; for example, **this is boldface**. |
| Character | A letter, number, or symbol. |
| Character enhancement | Underlining, boldfacing, subscripting, and superscripting. |
| Control character | A coded character that does not print but is part of the command sequence in a word processor. |
| Cursor | The marker on the display screen indicating where the next character can be displayed. |
| Default setting | A value used by the word processor when it is not instructed to use any other value. |
| Deletion | A feature by which a character, word, sentence, or larger block of text can be removed from the existing text. |
| Editing | The act of changing or amending text. |
| Format | The layout of a page; for example, the number of lines and the margin settings. |
| Global | An instruction that will be carried out throughout an entire document. For example, change the word "avenue" to "street" everywhere in the document. |
| Header | A piece of text that is stored separately from the text and printed at the top of each page. |
| Incremental spacing | A method by which the printer inserts spaces between words and letters to produce justified margins; also called microspacing. |
| Insertion | A feature in which a character, word, sentence, or larger block of text is added to the existing text. |
| Justification | A feature that makes lines of text even at the margins. |
| Menu | A list of commands or prompts on the display screen. |
| Print formatting | The function of a word processor that communicates with the printer to tell it how to print the text on paper. |
| Print preview | A feature that enables the user to view a general representation on the screen of how the document will look when printed. |
| Screen formatting | A function of a word processor that controls how the text will appear on the screen. |
| Scrolling | Moving a line of text onto or off the screen. |
| Search and find | A routine that searches for, and places the cursor at, a specified series or string of characters. |
| Search and replace | A routine that searches for a specified character string and replaces it with the specified replacement string. See global. |
| Status line | A message line above or below the text area on a display screen that gives format and system information. |

Continued

**FIGURE 13.4**

Frequently
Encountered Word
Processing Terms
—*Continued*

| TERM | DEFINITION |
|---|---|
| Subscript | A character that prints below the usual text baseline. |
| Superscript | A character that prints above the usual text baseline. |
| Text buffer | An area set aside in memory to hold text temporarily. |
| Text editing | The function of a word processor that enables the user to enter and edit text. |
| Text file | A file that contains text, as opposed to a program. |
| Virtual representation | An approach to screen formatting that enables the user to see on the screen exactly how the printed output will look. |
| Word wrap | The feature in which a word is moved automatically to the beginning of the next line if it goes past the right margin. |
| WYSIWYG | What you see (on the screen) is what you get (when the screen is printed). |

**Source:** S. Mandell, *Introduction to Computers Using the IBM and MS-DOS PCs with Basic*, 3d ed., 216 (West, 1991).

checkers are great for catching transposed letters, easily overlooked by a proof-reader. (You will be told, for example, that you need to change the spelling of th*ier* to th*eir*.) Be aware that a spelling checker will not tell you that you used "to" when you should have used "two" or "too." Since all these words are correctly spelled, they will not be marked by the program.

Word processors can print out a document in many formats. You can change formats if you discover that you are not satisfied with the format of your document. A variety of formats or formatting styles can be selected. The type can be *right justified* (meaning that the right-hand margin of the text is even) or have a ragged right edge. Left margins can be set at many different places throughout the document. Pages can be numbered or unnumbered, and the numbering can start with any digit you choose. Most word processors can include footnotes and keep the textual material that has been footnoted on the same page with the footnote even if you later insert a lot of material on this page. Many word processors can place the same heading at the top of each page without your having to retype the heading for all the pages in the document. A few word processors come with the capability of creating indexes for the document. You simply mark the word or phrase that is to be included in the index and run the index part of the program. An index is then created with all the page numbers for the location of the word or phrase.

Probably the most powerful capability of a word processor is called *merge printing*. It allows you to combine several whole files and to place data from one file into specific locations in another.

Merge printing whole files is very useful in creating documents with standard paragraphs. Each paragraph is usually saved in a computer file with its own name. When you wish to include the paragraph in a document, you simply enter the proper code and the name of the file. When you print out the document, the paragraph will be included at the location indicated without the necessity of retyping it.

Merging data from one file into another allows the creation of letters or other documents with appropriate names and addresses included in the finished document at all the proper places. This can be particularly useful in mailing the same document to many people. Code words are used for the placement of each bit of information such as the street address, the city, and the state. Once the code words are created, the street address, city, or whatever is represented by the code word, will be included in the final document wherever the code word is found.

When selecting a word processing program, the first step is to determine what current tasks could be done better and more efficiently with a word processing program. If the law office uses standard forms or standard language in documents or mass mailings (such as billings), a word processor with good merge capabilities is very helpful.

If you already have word processing capabilities, you may be considering a change in your system. It is critical to determine whether the current system performs all the tasks you need. If it does, you probably shouldn't change your system. The current system is known by the current users, and retraining can be very disruptive. Do not buy new software just to have the latest program. When new programs are first sold, they frequently have defects *(bugs)*. Some of the defects can be serious. If the new features are not critical to your operation, wait six months. After that time, most of the bugs will be found and fixed by the manufacturer (and the price may go down). Let someone else be the guinea pig.

Many magazines review word processors and other software programs. Go to the library and find at least three reviews on a software program that you are thinking of purchasing. Read them carefully. Usually you will find a consensus within the reviews.

Examples of computer magazines that review software programs

## 2. Databases

*Database* software is used to store and organize information. The information is entered into the database in an organized manner so that the computer can extract it, reorganize it, consolidate it, summarize it, and create reports from it. As a business management tool in a law office, a database is used for timekeeping, calendars, ticklers, billing, and client records. (See Figure 13.5.) As a case management tool, it can be used for document control in cases that have a large number of documents that must be indexed and cross-referenced. Also, as we shall see, WESTLAW and LEXIS are services that consist of hundreds of databases used for legal research.

Entering information into the database usually requires someone to sit at a terminal and manually type in the information. (Machines called *scanners* are able to enter text without typing, but they are generally more effective in taking in graphics than text.) If the database is to contain documents, each document entered will need an ID code, a brief description of the document, and index words for it. One of the major features of a database is that it can serve as a large index, thereby allowing rapid retrieval of information.

Once all the data has been entered, the database can be used to retrieve, compare, or compile information. To perform any of these functions, you need to search the database. There are two ways to search a database: *key word* searches and *full text* searches.

A *key word* search is like looking through the index of a book. The data base program will build an index using information that it is told to use for the index. The computer searches through this index and displays all information associated with the key word. For example, assume that you create a database to keep the membership list for your paralegal association, and you instruct the database program that you want an index created using the state in the address of members of the association. You could then ask the computer to list all members from Ohio or any other state. This type of search can be completed very quickly. The quality of the results of such a search depends on how well indexed the database is. If the person who made the list of index words for each document did not do a very good job, the search will not be very productive. Poor

**FIGURE 13.5**
Frequently
Encountered
Database
Management
Terms

| TERM | DEFINITION |
|---|---|
| Database | A grouping of independent files into one integrated whole that can be accessed through one central point; a database is designed to meet the information needs of a wide variety of users within an organization. |
| Data Manager | A data management software package that consolidates data files into an integrated whole, allowing access to more than one data file at a time. |
| Data Redundancy | The repetition of the same data in several different files. |
| Field | A subdivision of a record that holds a meaningful item of data, such as an employee number. |
| Record | A collection of related data fields that constitute a single unit, such as an employee record. |
| File | A group of related data records, such as employee records. |

**Source:** S. Mandell, *Introduction to Computers Using the IBM and MS-DOS PCs with Basic,* 3d ed., 514–15 (West, 1991).

indexing causes either too little or too much information to be reported from the search.

The second way to search a database is called a *full-text* search. With this type of search, the computer will examine *all* the information stored by the database program, not just the contents of an index. You might, for example, create a document-control database that contains a summary of the document, including important dates, names, and events. A full-text search would be a search of all the words in the summaries of the documents that were entered in the database. The computer will look through the summaries and display a list of documents that meet the search criteria. If, for example, the documents that were entered into the database concerned an automobile accident and you wished to find all the documents that referred to Helen Johnson (who is the chief witness for the opposition), you could make a full-text search of the document summaries and receive a list of all the documents that mention Helen Johnson.

To make a search, the computer must be told what to search for and where to search for it. This is called the *search criteria*. Many large databases allow search criteria that use the words AND, OR, and NOT. A search criteria using such words might be:

GUN AND ROBBERY AND NOT BANK

This would cause a search of the database to return a list of documents in which the summary had the words *gun* and *robbery* but exclude any summary that also contained the word *bank*. The problem with this type of search is that if the word *holdup* were used instead of *robbery* in the summary of one document, that document would not be found by the search. To find that document, the following search criteria must be used

GUN AND (ROBBERY OR HOLDUP) AND NOT BANK

The parentheses show that the OR applies only to *robbery* and *holdup*. If you did not think of the word *holdup* at the time you phrase your search request, an important document would be missed because you did not use the same words as the person who wrote the summary for the database. In a moment, we will examine how search requests are made on the major legal research services, WESTLAW and LEXIS.

Most database programs can perform several simple tasks. Calendar control is one of them. A database is very efficient in keeping trial and appointment calendars for a law office. Each attorney can receive a printed calendar of appointments for the day. All office calendars can be kept on one computer so that scheduling can be done without creating time conflicts among the attorneys.

A database could also be designed to print out a list of all the cases for the office where the statute of limitations is due to expire during the coming month.

Name, address, family status, phone numbers, case type, and other pertinent information for all the clients of a law firm can be kept in a database. This information could be used for mass mailings of informational letters about certain types of cases to those clients. The database can also be used to identify the types of cases handled by different attorneys in the office and the completion time for each type. This information is very helpful in making management and marketing decisions for the law firm.

For more complex tasks, the usefulness of the computer increases. Time-keeping and billing can be made more efficient with a good database program. There are many database programs designed specifically to perform timekeeping and billing tasks. For different clients, these programs can handle multiple rates for attorneys and paralegals. We will examine this in more detail in Chapter 14 on law office administration.

The database also makes it possible to analyze which types of cases are more profitable to the law firm and which people are more productive in terms of billed hours. Of course there are other factors that must still be evaluated subjectively. The attorney who brings in new clients for the law firm could very well show up poorly on a billable-hours evaluation. Like all other tools, the numbers produced by a computer must be evaluated in perspective.

Databases can be very useful for document control. For example, they can keep track of the content and location of thousands of documents in an antitrust case. Document-control programs were once available only for large computers and were very expensive. Consequently, document control with computers was used only in very large cases. Today, programs have been developed that enable small computers to perform many document control functions.

### WESTLAW and LEXIS

(See also page 585 in Chapter 11.) WESTLAW and LEXIS are commercial services that are available to anyone who wishes to perform (and pay for) CALR—Computer-Assisted Legal Research. As we saw in Chapter 11, these services can give you access to a vast amount of material, such as the full text of federal and state court opinions, federal and state statutes, federal and state administrative regulations, loose-leaf services, treatises, law review articles, directories of attorneys, and financial data. West Publishing Company, which offers WESTLAW,[13] and Mead Data Company, which offers LEXIS, have user agreements which must be signed before you will be allowed to use their services. The agreement establishes the fees to be paid for the different services available. You gain access to these services by using your PC, personal computer (or a custom terminal), which is connected by telephone lines to computers with vast storage capacities. Data is thereby searched *online*.

Assume that you are working on a case in which a client developed cancer after smoking for many years. You want to know if the client can bring a product-liability claim against the tobacco industry. You would need to formulate a question—called a *search query*—for the computer. The query would ask the computer to find cases involving product liability and cigarettes. Here is an example of such a query used in WESTLAW:

cigar! tobacco smok! /p product strict! /5 liab!

Later, we will examine the meaning of such queries and how to write them. For now, we simply want to give you an overview of what is available.

The screen in Figure 13.6 shows a recent case *(Forster v. R. J. Reynolds Tobacco Co.)* that would be retrieved by WESTLAW, using the above query. After looking at a large number of such cases, you might want to ask the computer to give you a list of citations of every case that fits your query. The screen in Figure 13.7 presents such a list. (It includes the *Forster* case as well as others that fit the query.) If you have a printer connected to your computer, you can ask for a printout of any of these screens.

Every citation to a case that you obtain through CALR can be taken to a traditional law library where you can read the case in a reporter volume. Of

---

[13]The assistance of Laura C. Mickelson is gratefully acknowledged for the material on WESTLAW.

**FIGURE 13.6**

```
                                                                    PAGE 1

   Citation              Rank(R)        Rank(P)       Database    Mode
   437 N.W.2d 655        R 2 OF 8       P 1 OF 37     MN–CS       T
     57 U.S.L.W. 2604, 8 UCC Rep. Serv.2d 370
   (Cite as:  437 N.W.2d 655)
                   John FORSTER, et al., Respondents,
                                  v.
   R.J. REYNOLDS TOBACCO COMPANY, Erickson Petroleum Corporation, d/b/a Holiday
                  Station Stores, Inc., Petitioners, Appellants.
                             No. C1-87-2170.
                         Supreme Court of Minnesota.
                               April 14, 1989

        Smoker who developed lung cancer brought products liability action against manu-
     facturer and retailer of cigarettes.  The District Court, Hennepin County, Jonathan Lebedoff, J.,
     granted motion of manufacturer and retailer for summary judgment on ground that claims
     were preempted, and appeal was taken.  The Court of Appeals, 423 N.W.2d 691, reversed.
     On further review, the Supreme Court, Simonett, J., held that:  (1) state tort claims based
     on state-imposed duty to warn are impliedly preempted by Federal Cigarette Labeling and
     Advertising Act, while other state tort claims are not preempted, and (2) federal Act does
     not preempt state tort claims based on failure to warn which predate its effective date.
        Affirmed in part, reversed in part, and remanded for further proceedings.

   COPR. (C) WEST 1991 NO CLAIM TO ORIG. U.S. GOVT. WORKS
```

Case retrieved in WESTLAW, with search words in bold print

course, you can also read the case on the computer screen or you can read a printout of the case, but it is usually cheaper to read material in a library volume than to read it online. The computer is excellent for searching, not necessarily for extensive reading.

The *Forster* case was decided in 1989. Suppose that you wanted to know what has happened to the case since 1989. Has it been overruled? Has it been cited by other courts? There are three different updating or validation services on WESTLAW that can give you further information about cases like *Forster*. They are Insta-Cite (see Figure 13.8), Shepard's Preview (see Figure 13.9), and Shepard's Citations (see Figure 13.10).

In litigation, there is often a need to find experts who may be able to provide consultation and, if needed, deposition or trial testimony.[14] One of the specialized searches that can be performed by computer is a search for such experts. Figure 13.11 presents an example of the results of this kind of search from the Forensic Services Directory (FSD) database in WESTLAW.

LEXIS works in a similar way, with many of the same features. Suppose, for example, that you wanted cases in which a juror concealed his or her bias.

[14]See Runde, *Computer Assisted Legal Research*, 10 Facts and Findings 13 (NALA, July/August 1983).

**FIGURE 13.7**

CITATIONS LIST                                            Total Documents: 8
Database: MN-CS

  1. Minn.App., 1991.
Andren v. White-Rodgers Co., a Div. of Emerson Elec. Co.
(To be reported at:  465 N.W.2d 102)

  2. Minn. 1989.  Forster v. R.J. Reynolds Tobacco Co.
437 N.W.2d 655, 57 U.S.L.W. 2604, 8 UCC Rep.Serv.2d 370

  3. Minn.App. 1988.  Forster v. R.J. Reynolds Tobacco Co.
423 N.W.2d 691, 56 U.S.L.W. 2664

  4. Minn.App. 1988.  Holstad v. Southwestern Porcelain, Inc.
421 N.W.2d 371, 5 UCC Rep.Serv.2d 912

  5. Minn. 1985.  Bixler by Bixler v. J.C. Penney Co., Inc.
376 N.W.2d 209

  6. Minn.App. 1984.  Dalager v. Montgomery Ward & Co., Inc.
350 N.W.2d 391

  7. Minn. 1979.  Armstrong v. Mailand  284 N.W.2d 343, 11 A.L.R.4th 583
188 N.W.2d 426, 290 Minn. 321

  8. Minn. 1971.  LEE v. CROOKSTON COCA-COLA BOTTLING COMPANY
188 N.W.2d 426, 290 Minn. 321

END OF CITATIONS LIST
            COPR. (C) WEST 1991 NO CLAIM TO ORIG. U.S. GOVT. WORKS

List of cases retrieved in WESTLAW

You would instruct LEXIS to find cases in which the word *bias* appears in proximity to the words *juror* and *conceal* or *concealing*. See Figure 13.12.

Once you have examined a number of these cases, you can ask the service to display a list of citations of all the cases discovered when LEXIS fulfilled your search request. See Figure 13.13.

## Formulating a Query

We turn now to one of the critical skills in using WESTLAW and LEXIS: formulating a research question or *query*. Our examination of this skill will explore the following topics:

(a)  Universal Character (*) and Root Expander (!) for WESTLAW and LEXIS
(b)  WESTLAW Queries:
   - The OR connector
   - The AND connector (&)
   - The sentence connector (/s)
   - The paragraph connector (/p)
   - The BUT NOT connector (%)

**FIGURE 13.8**

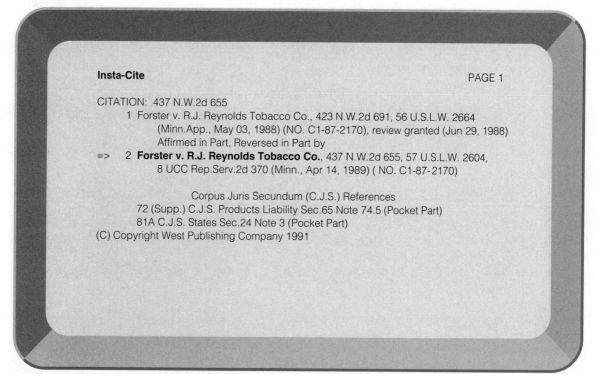

Insta-Cite, an updating or validation service in WESTLAW

- The numerical connector (/n)
- Phrase searching (" ")

(c) LEXIS Queries:
- The OR connector
- The AND connector
- The numerical connector (w/n)
- The AND NOT connector
- Phrase searching

(d) Field Searches:
- Title search
- Synopsis search
- Topic search
- Digest search
- Judge search

(e) Find and Read

## (a)  *Universal Character (\*) and Root Expander (!) for WESTLAW and LEXIS*

An important technique in the formulation of queries in either WESTLAW or LEXIS is the proper use of the asterisk (\*) as a universal character, and the exclamation mark (!) as a root expander. The discussion below of these and

**FIGURE 13.9**

**Shepard's PreView**

|  | **SHEPARDS PREVIEW** | PAGE 1 OF 2 |

Citations to: **437 N.W.2d 655**

Forster v. R.J. Reynolds Tobacco Co., (Minn. 1989)

Retrieval
No.        --------- Citation ----------
1          458 N.W.2d 417, 419

                  Mass
2          556 N.E.2d 1025, 1031
3          556 N.E.2d 1025, 1033
4          556 N.E.2d 1025, 1034

                  NJ
5          577 A.2d 1239, 1246
6          577 A.2d 1239, 1247
7          577 A.2d 1239, 1256
8          577 A.2d 1239, 1257

Note:  Citing references are only from West Reporters.  See SCOPE for a list.
       Check Shepard's, Insta-Cite, and WESTLAW as a Citator.
Copyright (c) 1991 Shepard's/McGraw-Hill, Inc. and West Publishing Company

Shepard's PreView in WESTLAW

other query-formulation techniques will cover searches for cases, although the techniques are generally applicable when searching any kind of document available in the databases and files of WESTLAW and LEXIS.

*The Universal Character (\*)*   Suppose that you asked the computer to find cases that contained the following word anywhere in the case:

> marijuana

This search will not find a case that spelled the word *marihuana*. If, however, you changed your query to:

> mari*uana

you would pick up cases under both spellings. The asterisk stands for any character or letter. Hence the above search will also pick up cases that contained the words *maribuana, marituana,* or *marizuana*—if such words existed in any of the cases in the database or file you are searching. Since the asterisk stands for any character, it is called the universal character. It is most commonly used when searching for cases that contain a proper name you are having trouble

**FIGURE 13.10**

**Shepard's**

**SHEPARD'S** (Rank 1 of 4)                  PAGE 1 of 1
CITATIONS TO:  437 N.W.2d 655
CITATOR:  NORTHWESTERN REPORTER CITATIONS
COVERAGE:  First Shepard's volume through May 1991 Supplement

| Retrieval No. | -- Analysis -- | --------- Citation ---------- | Headnote No. |
|---|---|---|---|
| 1 | SC Same Case | 423 N.W.2d 691 | |
| 2 | | 458 N.W.2d 417, 419 | |
| 3 | | 721 F.Supp. 1058, 1063 | 1 |
| 4 | | Mass | |
| | | 556 N.E.2d 1025, 1031 | |
| 5 | | NJ | |
| 6 | | 577 A.2d 1239, 1246 | |
| | | 577 A.2d 1239, 1256 | |
| 7 | | Pa | |
| | | 578 A.2d 417, 420 | |
| | N  Anno | 97 A.L.R.Fed. at 896 | |

Check Shepard's PreView, Insta-Cite, and WESTLAW as a Citator or QuickCite.
Copyright (c) 1991 McGraw-Hill, Inc.; Copyright (c) 1991 West Publishing Co.

Shepard's in WESTLAW

spelling. If, for example, you were looking for cases decided by a judge whose name is spelled *Falen* or *Falon*, you can enter the query as:

fal*n

You are not limited to one universal character per word. For example, the following search:

int**state

will give you cases containing the word *interstate* and cases containing the word *intrastate*. Similarly, the query:

s****holder

will give you cases containing the word *stockholder*, cases containing the word *stakeholder*, and cases containing the word *shareholder*.

*Root Expander (!)*   Next we consider the exclamation mark (!) as a root expander. When this mark is added to the root of a word, it acts as a substitute for one or more characters or letters. If your query is:

litig!

**FIGURE 13.11**

```
                                                              PAGE 1
Citation                Rank(R)              Database      Mode
Chapman, Judy-Anne W.   R 8 OF 14            FSD           P

              GENERAL PROFESSIONAL DISCIPLINES
                   CONSULTING SCIENTISTS
                    MEDICINE & HEALTH
                    PHYSICAL HEALTH
          Medical Research, Clinical Trials & Biostatistics

Chapman, Judy-Anne W.
11 Dayman Court
Kitchener, Ontario
Canada  N2M 3A1
(519) 579-2996

Specialties:  Biometry; Cancer research; Mortality or incidence data; Clinical trials; Case-
control studies.  Affiliations:  Independent Consultant.  Degrees and Licenses:  PhD.
END OF DOCUMENT
          COPR. (C) WEST 1991 NO CLAIM TO ORIG. U.S. GOVT. WORKS
```

Search for expert witnesses in WESTLAW

you will find cases containing one or more of the following words: litig, litigable, litigate, litigated, litigating, litigation, litigator, litigious, litigiousness. The root expander is quite powerful and can be overused. The query:

**tax!**

will lead you to cases containing any one or more of the following words: tax, taxability, taxable, taxation, taxational, taxes, taxi, taxicab, taxidermy, taxidermist, taxied, taximeter, taxing, taxis, taxiway, taxon, taxonomist, taxonomy, taxpayer. This will undoubtedly lead to cases that are beyond the scope of your research problem.

*Plurals.* Finally, it is not necessary to use universal characters or the root expander to obtain the regular plural of a word. The query:

**guest**

will give you cases containing the word *guest* and cases containing the word *guests*. Entering the singular form of a word will automatically search the plural form of that word.

Next we will focus on special guidelines for formulating WESTLAW queries and LEXIS queries.

## (b) WESTLAW Queries

When formulating a query in WESTLAW, *connectors* can be used to show the relationship between the words in the query. Connectors link query words

**FIGURE 13.12**

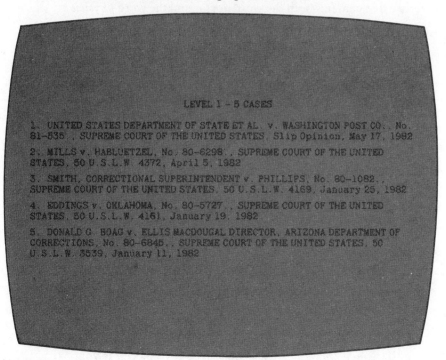

```
                    50 U.S.L.W. 4169
 O'CONNOR
CONCUR:
  JUSTICE O'CONNOR, concurring.
    I concur in the Court's opinion, but write separately to express my
view that the opinion does not foreclose the use of ''implied bias'' in
appropriate circumstances.
    I
    Determining whether a juror is biased or has prejudged a case is
difficult, partly because the juror may have an interest in concealing
his own bias and partly because the juror may be unaware of it. The
problem may be compounded when a charge of bias arises from juror
misconduct, and not simply from attempts of third parties to influence a
juror.
    Nevertheless, I believe that in most instances a post-conviction
hearing will be adequate to determine whether a juror is biased. A
hearing permits counsel to probe the juror's memory, his reasons for
acting as he did, and his understanding of the consequences of his
actions. A hearing also permits the trial judge to observe the juror's
demeanor under cross examination and to
```

Case retrieved in LEXIS, with search words highlighted

**FIGURE 13.13**

```
                    LEVEL 1 - 5 CASES

 1.  UNITED STATES DEPARTMENT OF STATE ET AL. v. WASHINGTON POST CO., No.
 81-535., SUPREME COURT OF THE UNITED STATES, Slip Opinion, May 17, 1982

 2.  MILLS v. HABLUETZEL, No. 80-6298., SUPREME COURT OF THE UNITED
 STATES, 50 U.S.L.W. 4372, April 5, 1982

 3.  SMITH, CORRECTIONAL SUPERINTENDENT v. PHILLIPS, No. 80-1082.,
 SUPREME COURT OF THE UNITED STATES, 50 U.S.L.W. 4169, January 25, 1982

 4.  EDDINGS v. OKLAHOMA, No. 80-5727., SUPREME COURT OF THE UNITED
 STATES, 50 U.S.L.W. 4161, January 19, 1982

 5.  DONALD C. BOAG v. ELLIS MACDOUGAL DIRECTOR, ARIZONA DEPARTMENT OF
 CORRECTIONS, No. 80-6845., SUPREME COURT OF THE UNITED STATES, 50
 U.S.L.W. 3539, January 11, 1982
```

List of cases retrieved in LEXIS

together to give the query more direction. The main connectors in WESTLAW are:

- The OR connector
- The AND connector (&)

- The sentence connector (/s)
- The paragraph connector (/p)
- The BUT NOT connector (%)
- The numerical connector (/n)

After explaining how to use each of these connectors, we will examine how to search for phrases on WESTLAW through the use of quotation marks (" ") in queries.

*The OR Connector*    The simplest connector in WESTLAW is OR, which can be expressed by typing the word *or* between two words, or by leaving a blank space between the words. This connector instructs WESTLAW to treat the two words as alternatives and to find cases that contain either or both words. Hence, the query:

**doctor or physician**

or the query:

**doctor physician**

will find the following cases:

- A case that contains the word *doctor,* but not the word *physician*
- A case that contains the word *physician,* but not the word *doctor*
- A case that contains both the word *doctor* and the word *physician*[15]

Similarly, the query:

**attorney or lawyer or counsel**

or the query:

**attorney lawyer counsel**

will find the following cases:

- A case that contains the word *attorney* but not the words *lawyer* or *counsel*
- A case that contains the words *attorney* and *lawyer* but not the word *counsel*
- A case that contains the words *attorney* and *counsel* but not the word *lawyer*
- A case that contains the word *lawyer* but not the words *attorney* or *counsel*
- A case that contains the words *lawyer* and *attorney* but not the word *counsel*
- A case that contains the words *lawyer* and *counsel* but not the word *attorney*
- A case that contains the word *counsel* but not the words *attorney* or *lawyer*
- A case that contains the words *counsel* and *lawyer* but not the word *attorney*
- A case that contains the words *counsel* and *attorney* but not the word *lawyer*
- A case that contains all three words: *attorney* and *lawyer* and *counsel.*

*The AND Connector* (&)    When you use the & connector in your WESTLAW query, you are asking WESTLAW to find cases that contain every word joined by &. The query:

**paralegal & fee**

---

[15]In all of these examples, remember that the service will retrieve cases containing these words and their plurals, such as physician, physicians; doctor, doctors.

will find cases in which the word *paralegal* and the word *fee* are found. The query will not find cases containing only one of these words.[16]

*The Sentence Connector (/s)*   The sentence connector (/s) requires the search words to appear in the same sentence in the case.[17] The query:

paralegal /s termin!

will find cases in which the word *paralegal* is found in the same sentence as the word *terminable* or *terminal* or *terminate* or *terminating* or *termination* or *terminator* or *terminology* or *terminus*. Here are examples of two sentences from two different cases that this query would retrieve:

Case #1:
   "The **paralegal** did not receive notice of the allegation until the letter of **termination** arrived the next day."

Case #2:
   "The patient's **terminal** condition was negligently diagnosed in a report obtained by the **paralegal** of the opposing counsel." [18]

*The Paragraph Connector (/p)*   The paragraph connector (/p) requires the search words to appear in the same paragraph in the case. The query:

paralegal /p certif!

will find cases in which the word *paralegal* is found in the same paragraph as the word *certifiable* or *certificate* or *certified* or *certification* or *certifier* or *certify* or *certifying*.

*The BUT NOT Connector (%)*   The BUT NOT connector (%) excludes everything that follows the percentage mark, %. The query:

paralegal % fee

or

paralegal but not fee

will find every case in which the word *paralegal* appears, except for those cases in which the word *fee* plus the word *paralegal* appear in the case. Perhaps you are looking for every case that mentions the word *paralegal* other than those involving paralegal fees or attorney fees.

*The Numerical Connector (/n)*[19]   The numerical connector (/n) requires search words to appear within a specified number[20] of words of each other in the case. The query:

paralegal /5 license*

---

[16]It is also possible to write this query as *paralegal and fee* (rather than use the ampersand—&), but this is not recommended.

[17]The sentence connector (/s) and the paragraph connector (/p) are referred to as the *grammatical connectors*.

[18]Note that in case #2, the order in which the search terms appear in the sentence is not the order of the words in the query itself. If you want to limit the search to cases that contain the search words in the sentence in the order presented in the query, you would phrase the query as follows: paralegal +s termin!

[19]The numerical connector can also be expressed as w/n. For example: paralegal w/5 fee. As we will see, LEXIS also uses w/n in its numerical connector. Only on WESTLAW can you use /n.

[20]Up to 255.

will retrieve any case in which the word *paralegal* appears within five words of the word *license,* or within five words of the word *licensed.* Here is an example of a line from a case that this query would retrieve:

"... the **paralegal** had no **license** from the state."[21]

A case with the following line, however, would *not* be retrieved by this query because there are more than five words between the search words of the query:

"... **paralegals** as well as notaries and process servers are not **licensed.**"

*Phrase Searching (" ")*    Thus far, our examples of queries have involved searches for individual words in cases. Suppose, however, that you wanted to search for phrases such as drug addict, habeas corpus, or legal assistant. If your query was:

legal assistant

WESTLAW would interpret the space between these two words to mean OR. Hence, it will retrieve

- Any case in which the word *legal* appears but the word *assistant* does not appear
- Any case in which the word *assistant* appears but the word *legal* does not appear
- Any case in which both the word *legal* and the word *assistant* appears

This could lead to thousands of cases, the vast majority of which would have nothing to do with legal assistants.[22] To avoid this problem, we need a way to tell WESTLAW not to interpret the space between the search words to mean OR. This is done by placing quotation marks around any phrase (or group of words) that you want WESTLAW to search as a unit. Hence our query should read:

"legal assistant"

In a moment, we will see that LEXIS does not require quotation marks when conducting a phrase search since LEXIS does not interpret every space as an OR.

## (c) LEXIS Queries

When using LEXIS, connectors are also used in formulating a query. While there are some similarities between the connectors in WESTLAW and in LEXIS, the differences are significant. The main connectors in LEXIS are:

- The OR connector
- The AND connector
- The numerical connector (w/n)
- The AND NOT connector

---

[21]In this example, the words in the sentence are presented in the order of the words in the query—paralegal before license. The query, however, would not require this order unless you use a + sign before the number: paralegal +5 license*. Another way to ensure this order would be to phrase the query: paralegal pre/5 license*.

[22]WESTLAW will probably flash a message on the screen warning you that your search query may retrieve a large number of cases and suggesting that you rephrase your query to make it narrower.

After examining these connectors, we need to compare how to search for phrases in LEXIS and in WESTLAW.

*The OR Connector*   The OR connector tells LEXIS to treat the two words joined by OR as alternatives. The query:

merger or acquisition

will find the following cases:

- A case that contains the word *merger* but not the word *acquisition*
- A case that contains the word *acquisition* but not the word *merger*
- A case that contains both the word *merger* and the word *acquisition*

Hence the OR connector in LEXIS is similar to the OR connector in WEST-LAW, except that LEXIS does not interpret a space between two words as an OR.

*The AND Connector*   When you use the AND connector in your LEXIS query, you are asking LEXIS to find cases that contain every word joined by AND. The query:

paralegal and fee

will find cases in which the word *paralegal* and the word *fee* are found. The query will not find cases containing only one of these words. (In WESTLAW, the preferred way to achieve this result is by using the & connector.)

*The Numerical Connector (w/n)*   The numerical connector (w/n) of LEXIS requires search words to appear within a designated number of words of each other in the case. The query:

paralegal w/5 license

will retrieve any case in which the word *paralegal* appears within five words of the word *license*.[23]

*The AND NOT Connector*   The AND NOT connector in a LEXIS query excludes everything that follows *and not*. The query:

paralegal and not fee

will find every case in which the word *paralegal* appears, except for those cases in which the word *fee* plus the word *paralegal* appear in the case.[24]

*Phrase Searching*   Recall that phrase searching in WESTLAW required the use of quotation marks around any phrase, since WESTLAW interprets spaces between words in a phrase to mean OR. This is not so in LEXIS, since LEXIS does not equate spaces with ORs. Hence to search for a phrase in LEXIS, you do not

---

[23]The number (n) of words that can be used as the numerical connector in LEXIS is any number up to 255. But LEXIS does not count words such as *the, be,* and *to.* LEXIS considers them "noise words." The numerical connector in WESTLAW also goes up to 255. See footnote 20. But WEST-LAW counts every word. In the LEXIS numerical query, if you wanted the words in the case to exist in the order in which the words are listed in the query, use the pre/n connector. For example: paralegal pre/5 license. See also footnote 21.

[24]Another way to phrase this query is: paralegal but not fee. The latter phrasing would make this LEXIS connector the same as the connector in WESTLAW that serves this function.

have to use quotation marks around the phrase. Simply state the phrase. The query:

legal assistant

will not lead you to any cases in which the word *legal* appeared but not the word *assistant*, and vice versa.

---

### ■ ASSIGNMENT 13.1

Below you will find five separate queries. If they were used in either WESTLAW or LEXIS, what words in the documents would they find?

(a) para!

(b) assign!

(c) crim!

(d) legis!

(e) e****e

---

### ■ ASSIGNMENT 13.2

On page 658, the following query was given as an example of a WESTLAW query:

cigar! tobacco smok! /p product strict! /5 liab!

Explain this query. State what the symbols mean. What is the query designed to find? Assume that you are using the query to find cases in one of the databases of WESTLAW.

---

### ■ ASSIGNMENT 13.3

You are looking for cases in which a paralegal is charged with the unauthorized practice of law.

(a) Write the query for WESTLAW.

(b) Write the query for LEXIS.

---

### ■ ASSIGNMENT 13.4

You are looking for cases in which a law firm illegally failed to pay overtime compensation to its paralegals.

(a) Write the query for WESTLAW.

(b) Write the query for LEXIS.

---

### ■ ASSIGNMENT 13.5

You would like to know what judges in your state have said about paralegals.

(a) Write several queries for WESTLAW.

(b) Write several queries for LEXIS.

## (d)  Field Searches

In addition to full-text searches, both WESTLAW and LEXIS allow you to conduct searches that are limited to information found in certain parts of cases or other documents. On LEXIS, these parts are called *segments*. The segments of cases are: name, court, writtenby, dissentby, counsel, number, etc. On WESTLAW, these parts are called *fields*. The fields of cases are: title, synopsis, topic, digest, judge, etc. Here is a fuller explanation and some examples of field searches on WESTLAW:

---

### Field Searches on WESTLAW

**Title** (abbreviated *ti*). The title field contains only the names of the parties to a case. Use this field to retrieve a case if you know the case name. The computer will quickly retrieve your case and display it so you can either read it online or print it to read at a later time. Suppose, for example, that the title of the case you wanted to read was *Pennzoil v. Texaco.* Once you select the database you want, a title field search for this case would be as follows:

**ti (pennzoil & texaco)**

**Synopsis** (abbreviated *sy*). The synopsis field contains a summary of the case prepared by the editorial staff of WESTLAW. This summary includes the facts presented by the case, the holding of the lower court, the issues on appeal, and the resolution of those issues. The names of majority, concurring, and dissenting judges are also included in the synopsis field. Since general legal concepts are used to describe the issues before the court, this is a good field in which to run a conceptual search. A conceptual search is helpful for finding cases that fall into a legal category or classification, such as domicile, adverse possession, or product liability. The digest field (to be considered below) also allows you to conduct a search via concepts. Hence it is often worthwhile to combine the synopsis and digest fields in a single search. For example:

**sy, di ("product liability")**

**Topic** (abbreviated *to*). Each small-paragraph summary in the West digests (page 497) is assigned a topic classification, such as criminal law, bankruptcy, and divorce. West has tens of thousands of cases summarized under these topics. If you already know

a topic classification, you can conduct a WESTLAW search that is limited to this topic field. For example:

**to (criminal)**
**to (bankruptcy)**
**to (divorce)**
**to ("product liability")**

**Digest** (abbreviated *di*). In addition to a topic classification, every small-paragraph case summary in a West digest contains the name or title of the case, the name of the court that decided it, the citation of the case, and the rest of the summary itself, known as a headnote (page 503). All of this information (topic, title, court, citation, headnote) is contained within what is called the digest field of WESTLAW. Here is an example of a search in this field:

**di (paralegal)**

This search will find every case that has the word paralegal anywhere in a small-paragraph case summary of a West digest. To make sure that your search finds cases mentioning legal assistants as well as those mentioning paralegals, the search would be:

**di (paralegal "legal assistant")**

As indicated above, it is often wise to combine searches in the digest and synopsis fields.

**Judge** (abbreviated *ju*). If you wanted to find cases written by a particular judge, e.g., Justice William Brennan, you could conduct a search in the judge field:

**ju (brennan)**

When run in the database containing opinions of the United States Supreme Court (sct), this search will give you every majority opinion written by Justice Brennan.

---

## (e) Find and Read

Suppose that you already have the citation of a case or other document, and you simply want to read it. But you are not in a traditional law library that has the bound volumes you need. If you have access to WESTLAW or LEXIS, there is a relatively easy way to retrieve what you want. On WESTLAW, use the *find* command (abbreviated *fi*). On LEXIS, use the *lexstat* command (abbreviated *lxt*) when you are looking for a statute and the *lexsee* command (abbreviated *lxe*) when you are looking for cases or any other documents available through this route.

Using the *find* command of WESTLAW, here are four examples that retrieve documents in the Supreme Court Reporter (sct), the United States Code Annotated (usca), the Code of Federal Regulations (cfr), and the Federal Register (fr). All of these examples assume that you already know the volume numbers, page numbers, section numbers, etc. indicated. You simply want to find these documents and read them on your computer screen.

```
fi 97 sct 451
fi 18 usca 1968
fi 9 cfr 11.24
fi 52 fr 22391
```

Using the *lexstat* command of LEXIS, here is an example that locates a statute in United States Code Service (uscs); and using the *lexsee* command, here are three examples that locate material in Columbia Law Review (colum l rev), American Law Reports, Federal (alrfed), and an IRS Revenue Ruling (rev rul). Again, all of these examples assume that you already know the volume numbers, pages numbers, section numbers, etc. indicated.

```
lxt 11 uscs 101
lxe 87 colum l rev 1137
lxe 44 alrfed 148
lxe rev rul 88-2
```

## 3. Spreadsheet Programs

Most law offices can clearly see the usefulness of word processing and database programs. The usefulness of a spreadsheet, however, is a little more difficult to appreciate. A spreadsheet can be helpful for almost any project that requires the use or manipulation of numbers. It is a good management tool for creating budgets and tracking expenses of a law firm. Most spreadsheet programs have built-in functions that will make intricate calculations, such as determining present net value, loan repayment schedules, averages, and many other statistical functions.

A spreadsheet allows you to create large groups of interrelated numbers. Once this is done, changing one of the numbers allows you to see what happens to all the others. A spreadsheet can quickly recalculate the values of all the numbers that are dependent on the one that was changed. (See Figure 13.14.) For example, with a spreadsheet you can create a program that will calculate the size of payments on a loan based on the amount, length, and interest rate that apply to the loan. If you change the numbers displayed on the screen for the amount, for the length, or for the interest rate of the loan, the spreadsheet will recalculate the payment size.

A spreadsheet consists of a series of boxes called cells. Numbers and other information can be placed directly into the boxes from the keyboard. Once the

| TERM | DEFINITION |
|---|---|
| Cell | A storage location within a spreadsheet used to store a single piece of information relevant to the spreadsheet. |
| Coordinates | The column letter and row number that define the location of a specific cell. |
| Formula | A mathematical expression used in a spreadsheet. |
| Label | Information used for describing some aspect of a spreadsheet. A label can be made up of alphabetic or numeric information, but no arithmetic can be performed on a label. |
| Value | A single piece of numeric information used in the calculations of a spreadsheet. |
| Window | The portion of a worksheet that can be seen on the computer display screen. |

**Source:** S. Mandell, *Introduction to Computers Using the IBM and MS-DOS PCs with Basic,* 3d ed., 409 (West 1991).

**FIGURE 13.14**

Terms Associated with Electronic Spreadsheets

information is stored in a box, it can be a source for formulas in other boxes. When a box containing a formula is displayed on the screen, the result of the formula is seen, not the formula itself. If any of the numbers in the boxes used by a formula are changed, the display for the box with the formula will reflect this change. For example, let us assume that we have a small spreadsheet program with three boxes. (Large, sophisticated spreadsheets can have thousands of boxes.) Each of our three boxes has a name that refers to the information in them. We will name our boxes A, B, and C.

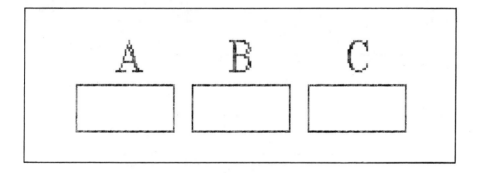

If we placed the number 5 in box A and the number 2 in box B, we could then combine this information in box C by entering the formula A + B into box C.

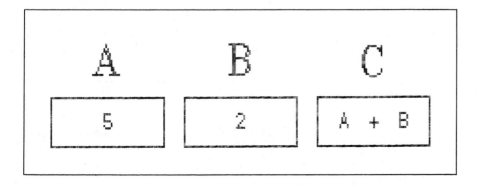

Box C would then display the number 7.

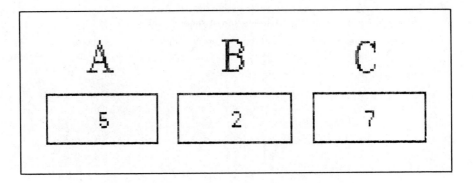

We could change the formula in box C to read (A + B) * 2 (here, the * means *times* on most computers).

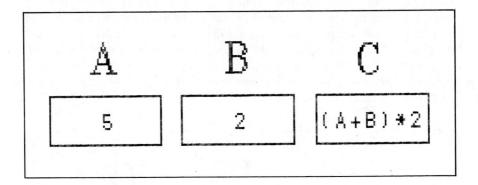

C would now read 14.

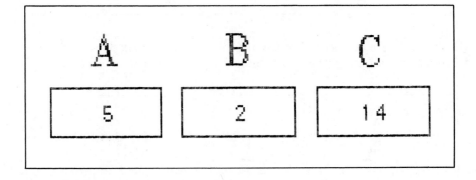

Now if we change the number in box A from 5 to 4, box C would read 12.
[(4 + 2) * 2 = 12.]

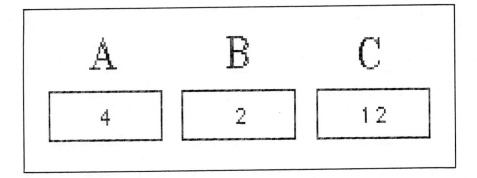

Our small spreadsheet example can be made more complicated. Let us start over. Place the number 2 in box A. Then place the formula A + 2 in box B. Box B will now contain the number 4 [2 + 2 = 4]. We could now place the formula A * B in box C. Box C would now display the number 8 [2 * 4 = 8].

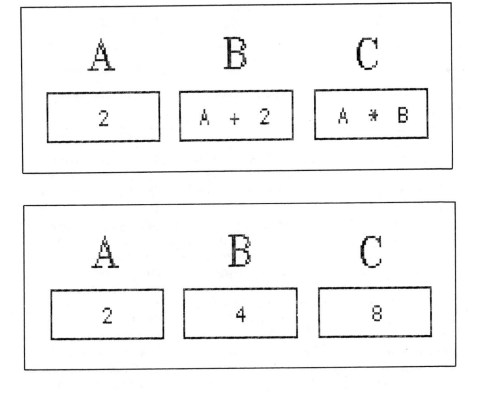

Any time we change the number that is in box A, the numbers displayed in both box B and C will change. If the number 4 is placed in box A, box B will show the number 6 [4 + 2 = 6], and box C will display the number 24 [6 * 4 = 24].

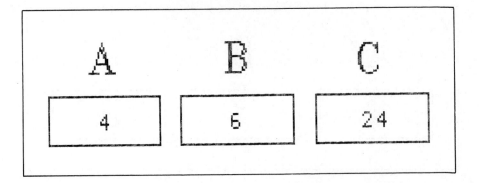

On a large spreadsheet, many cells (boxes) can depend on information from formulas in other cells. Sophisticated models and project formulas, therefore, can be created using a spreadsheet program.

When creating large models you must guard against making circular references. For example, place the formula (A * C) in box B and the formula (A * B) in box C.

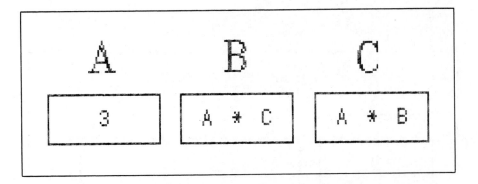

No matter what number is entered in box A, box B looks to box C for information and box C looks to box B for information. Some spreadsheet programs will get stuck on these two formulas and stop dead. Other spreadsheets will run through the calculations for the two boxes ten or twenty times and then stop.

The capability of a spreadsheet to perform a whole series of calculations based on formulas and numbers makes it possible for you to do in minutes or seconds what once took accountants hours or days. The spreadsheet is perfect for doing what users call "what ifs." Suppose you were considering the purchase of a house and wanted to figure out what the monthly payments would be. Three factors determine the size of the payments: the interest rate, the length of the mortgage, and the amount of the loan. Using the proper financial formulas, you could create a spreadsheet that would let you enter an interest rate, the number of years, and the amount that you wished to borrow. In seconds the spreadsheet would display the monthly mortgage payment based on those numbers. You can then play "what if" and change one or more of the numbers to see what happens to the payment level as the interest rate went down, the length of the mortgage increased, the amount of the loan was greater, etc. (See Figure 13.15.)

A spreadsheet used as a "what if" device can be very helpful in a law office for working out damage projections and settlement offers, particularly struc-

FIGURE 13.15
Spreadsheet
Mortgage
Cost Display

```
        Real Estate Financial Analysis

                Assumptions

House Price:              $35,900.00
Downpayment:               1,795.00
                         -------------
Amount Financed:          $34,105.00
Interest Rate %:               9.75
Number of Yrs Financed:       20.00
Calculated Payment:         $323.49
```

tured settlements where the payments are spread over a period of time and take account of the value of money in the future according to an agreed-on formula. Once the relationship of the various elements of damages is determined, different interest and inflation assumptions can be tested. You can determine how these assumptions will influence the amount of damages that would be necessary in a particular case. For example, assume you are trying to project lost wages of an injured plaintiff. Interrelated formulas can be created to determine this damage calculation. One of the formulas would project potential salary over the working life of the person, starting with the current salary and adding increases over time. The increase would be a percent of salary. The formula created can allow for changing the percent increase so that different increase assumptions may be tested quickly. Another formula can take the results from the salary calculations and determine how many dollars would be needed today to create an amount equal to the future income. Various rates of return can be tested with this formula. Used in a similar manner, a spreadsheet can be productive for estate planning and real estate projections.

Most of the current spreadsheet programs have the capability of creating graphs from the numbers they produce. They can create line, bar, and pie charts in many different formats. Bar charts can be made to appear three dimensional or can be stacked one above the other. If the computer has a color monitor, the bars representing different items can be displayed in various colors.[25]

There are many applications for spreadsheets that can be obtained by purchasing a *template* to perform the needed task. A template is a set of formulas sold with instructions on its use. A federal income tax template, for example, will contain all the lines and forms of a tax return. The template covers each part of the tax form on which information must be entered, and calculates the taxes based on the information entered. The template then prints the form as a completed tax return. Templates are available for almost any type of business calculation. There are small bookkeeping programs, purchase-lease comparison programs, linear regression programs, and many others.

Some publishers of spreadsheets claim that bookkeeping and other *database* applications can be performed using their programs. This is true to a limited extent. These bookkeeping and database systems are limited and awkward, however, and hence of little practical use in most law offices. Bookkeeping and

---

[25]When you need a hard copy of the chart, laser printers are often very effective. If high-quality charts are needed in color, a *plotter* can be used. A plotter is a device that will hold a pen to a piece of paper and draw lines as instructed by commands you enter into the computer.

database manipulation should be performed on programs designed for that purpose rather than with spreadsheet programs.

---

## ■ ASSIGNMENT 13.6

Barklay is a freelance paralegal. He shares an office with three others: Adams, Cordier, and Davis. The expenses of the office are: rent, phone, electricity, gas, postage meter, and secretarial service. They agree to the following allocation of expenses: rent will be $185 per person; the cost of electricity and gas will be split evenly among the four of them; everything else will be apportioned according to actual use and cost.

The four will have the following bill-paying responsibilities: Barklay will pay the phone and secretarial bills; Adams will pay the rent; Cordier will pay the electricity and gas bills; and Davis will pay the postage bill. At the end of every month, each will make an accounting of what was paid. They will then calculate who owes what to whom based on their agreement of how expenses are to be allocated.

Here are the figures for last month. Adams ran up $122 in phone calls, Barklay $85, Cordier $77, and Davis $19. Postage use was $22.50 for Adams, $14.20 for Barklay, $66.85 for Cordier, and $10.31 for Davis. The bill for secretarial services showed that Adams owes $118.00, Barklay $100.33, Cordier $84, and Davis $44. The electric bill was $29.03. The gas bill was $11.16.

The bills were paid on time. In Parts I and II of this assignment, you will be setting up a spreadsheet to calculate each person's share of the expenses, using the following basic structure as a guide:

| ROW | A<br>Adams | B<br>Barklay | C<br>Cordier | D<br>Davis |
|---|---|---|---|---|
| 1 Rent | | | | |
| 2 Amt. Paid | | | | |
| 3 Bal. Due | | | | |
| 4 Phone | | | | |
| 5 Amt. Paid | | | | |
| 6 Bal. Due | | | | |
| 7 Electricity | | | | |
| 8 Amt. Paid | | | | |
| 9 Bal. Due | | | | |
| 10 Gas | | | | |
| 11 Amt. Paid | | | | |
| 12 Bal. Due | | | | |
| 13 Postage | | | | |
| 14 Amt. Paid | | | | |
| 15 Bal. Due | | | | |
| 16 Secretarial | | | | |
| 17 Amt. Paid | | | | |
| 18 Bal. Due | | | | |
| 19 Grand Totals<br>Due from Each | | | | |

### Part I

For each category of expense, fill in the figures you are given for last month. Do not do any math at this time, but state the formulas that you would use to arrive at all of the mathematical calculations. For example, if you must divide $11.16 by 4, phrase the formula as follows: (11.16/4). Or, if you must add Row 13 for all four individuals, phrase the formula as follows: (A13+B13+C13+D13).

Next, do all the calculations based on your formulas.

**Part II**

Assume that there is a 3 percent tax on the phone calls over and above the amounts stated. Change your spreadsheet setup accordingly.

## 4. Communications

Finally we come to one of the most recent microcomputer developments. Communications software makes it possible to call up WESTLAW or LEXIS to do legal research over telephone lines. Such programs also make it possible to contact people or businesses and communicate with their computers. You can send or receive letters, statistical information, programs, or insults! Anything that can be put on paper or into a computer can be sent from one computer to another over telephone lines.

For successful computer communications, there are two necessary components: a modem and communications software. A *modem* is a piece of hardware that is plugged into your computer on one end and into your telephone line on the other. The modem controls the transmission of information over telephone lines. The communications software controls the information sent to the modem that is to be transmitted over telephone lines. When two computers are transmitting information to one another over telephone lines, each one must have a modem and a communications program. The two modems transmit the information that they are told to send by the communications software.

For the modems to be able to do this, they must be "speaking" with the same code and "talking" at the same speed. Most modems sold today use the same code, but they do not all communicate at the same speed. Some can communicate at more than one speed. The speed of transmission is stated in terms of *baud* or the *baud rate*. Three hundred baud is the minimum used today; most modems can transmit and receive information at this speed. If large amounts of information are being sent, however, 300 baud is very slow. The higher the baud rate, the less time it takes to send the same information. Twelve hundred baud is today's high-speed standard. As modem technology improves, 2400 baud modems are becoming available. The only drawback with higher (faster) baud rates is that the error rate goes up with the speed. When more information is squeezed into the same space, the equipment used must be more sensitive. Unfortunately sensitive equipment may be less able to distinguish static from the information being sent on the telephone line. Therefore, at higher transmission rates, the information is more likely to become garbled. This problem must be controlled by the communications software.

When selecting communications hardware, keep in mind the amount of information that you wish to send or receive. The greater the amount of bulk transmission used, the greater the need for high-speed modems. If you will be using the communications system mostly for reading or examining materials immediately on screen, 1200 is a sufficient communications speed.

When purchasing software for communications, higher cost does not necessarily mean better software. There are commercial software packages available that are expensive yet difficult to use. You may need a thick instruction manual and a degree in computer science to use them. Other communications packages are available in the *public domain,* meaning that the programs are available to the public without charge. Some are easy to use and will satisfy 90% of users requiring communications software.

Developing the skills necessary for communications can be difficult. Once you have started, however, stopping can be just as hard or harder! It is a fascinating and challenging area of the computer world. A great deal of information about sources of software, user special-interest groups, "adult" bulletin boards, etc. is available through electronic *bulletin boards.* A bulletin board is an inexpensive version of large commercial database information services, such as WESTLAW and Dialog. The bulletin board contains information centered around a common interest. Users can obtain this information, exchange messages to each other, find buyers or sellers for certain products, etc. Your phone bill could become very large if you are addicted to calling bulletin boards around the country.

## 5. Combinations

We have examined four types of programs: word processing, database management, spreadsheets, and communications. You can now obtain software packages that contain all four types in one program. These are often called *integrated* packages. They are programs that require computers with large amounts of memory. The reason for creating an integrated package is to simplify the process of moving information from one application to another. If, for example, you have information in your database that you wish to manipulate with a spreadsheet program, the task of moving the information from a format that a database understands to one that a spreadsheet understands can be monumental or impossible. An integrated package makes it possible.

The big question is, "Do you really need an integrated package?" If you are not sure, the answer is probably *no.* If you frequently find yourself wishing that you could put a graph from your spreadsheet into a letter or wishing that you could easily get your database information into a spreadsheet, then you do need integrated software.

 ## Section F. The Real Investment: Time

Thus far we have examined the relative expense of some of the hardware and software options. The greatest cost by far, however, is *time.* For the system to be implemented successfully, time must be invested both before and after acquisition of the system. Considerable time must be spent before the purchase of a system to determine what the law office needs. If this is not carefully done, the system will probably not fulfill the office's needs. After the system is acquired, time must be spent implementing the system and training all members of the staff to use its capabilities properly. If the time invested before or after installation is insufficient, the microcomputer system will be a failure.

Another costly but necessary element for the successful implementation of a computer system is a guru. The guru is the one who has a knack for figuring out and solving most of the system's problems. The guru will be a person in the office who has a system at home, or who, when introduced to the training, learns quickly and wants to take the system manuals home to see how the thing "really" works. Encourage this person. Meanwhile, other staff members need to take over some of this person's duties. Having someone present in the office who can respond to a crisis saves time and minimizes frustration.

Other cost factors that must be considered involve "down time" and lost data. *Down time* occurs when the computer breaks. No matter how good, expensive, or reliable your equipment may be, sooner or later it will fail. Many firms have discovered that microcomputers are so inexpensive they purchase one or more to keep in the closet just to replace the unit that breaks down. This is often less expensive than having to wait a day, week, month, or six months for the defective computer to be repaired.

The loss of data can be even more expensive. Some data, of course, is irreplaceable. Other data can be replaced or reconstructed only at great cost. Nothing can compare to the horror of realizing that the diskette you just erased contained the only copy of the brief you have been working on for months. Every system should have regular backup procedures. There should be at least one backup copy of all data, and for particularly valuable or difficult-to-reconstruct data, two backup copies are recommended. If possible, a backup copy of important diskettes should be kept at a place other than where the day-to-day or working copies are located. This backup is an added expense, but it's not nearly as costly as the destruction of data by fire, magnet, or other calamity.

---

## ■ ASSIGNMENT 13.7

Each student will make a presentation in front of the class on a computer product—a hardware or software product. You can select your own product, but it must be approved in advance by your teacher.

The setting will be a mock meeting of members of a law firm (attorney, paralegals, and secretaries) who have assembled to listen to you. You have come to the meeting to make a sales presentation on the product.

You have several objectives:

**(a)** *To introduce yourself.* You are the representative of the company that makes the product. Use your own name. Make up some brief facts about yourself as representative, such as how long you have been with the company.

**(b)** *To provide something visual about the product.* You do not have to bring the product with you. Try to obtain a brochure on it. If not available, try to obtain a photo of the product. For example, you might be able to photocopy an ad that has a picture of the product. At the very least, you should prepare a diagram or drawing of the product or of some important aspect of it. Circulate the brochure, photo, ad, diagram, or drawing to the group while you are talking.

**(c)** *To describe the product.* State what the product does. What is its purpose? How is it used in a law office? What are its benefits? Who is supposed to use it in the office? How will the product improve efficiency or increase profit? How does the product compare with competing products on the market? How much does it cost? Try to cover as many of these areas as possible.

The product you select must meet the following characteristics:

- It is a brand product that is currently on the market.
- It is a product that is either designed exclusively for law offices or is widely used in law offices.
- It is not a product that you work with every day (if you already work in a law office). The goal of this assignment is to force yourself to learn about a *new* product and to communicate what you have learned to others.
- It is a product that no one else in the class has covered in a presentation. (The teacher will enforce this guideline by approving the products in advance.)

The best starting point in locating a product is to go to any law library and look through ads in bar association journals (state or national) and ads in legal newspapers (state or national). Many of these ads have 800 numbers you can call for more information. Once you have identified a product, ask a librarian how you can find out if any reviews of that product have been published. (Manufacturers of the product are often very willing to send you copies of favorable reviews.) You might also obtain a lead to products by talking to someone who works in a law office.

No one is expected to have intimate familiarity with the product (although you may want to give a contrary impression as part of your sales presentation).

Your goal is give information about the product that you learn by:

- Reading ads
- Reading brochures
- Talking with company representatives (locally, if available, or via an 800 number)
- Reading reviews
- Talking with someone in a law office in your area that already uses the product

## ■ ASSIGNMENT 13.8

Smith, Smith & Smith is a forty-attorney law firm that was established thirty years ago. It employs eight paralegals, ten secretaries, a librarian, a receptionist, a file clerk, and a part-time maintenance worker. The firm handles a great variety of cases: personal injury litigation, worker's compensation, government contracts, antitrust, domestic relations, estates and trusts, taxation, bankruptcy, commercial law, etc.

The founder and leader of the firm is John Smith, who practiced law with his father in the 1920s before he set up the present firm with his two children, Mary and David Smith. They are full partners in the firm.

For years, John Smith practiced law "the old fashioned way." "If it was good enough for my father," he is fond of saying, "it's good enough for me." The consequence of this attitude is that Smith, Smith, and Smith is managed today in almost the same manner that it was run thirty years ago. Almost everything is done by hand. All the secretaries have typewriters. John agreed to purchase electric typewriters only five years ago. These machines do nothing but type. There are a few dictaphones, but they are seldom used.

Payroll, billing, document control, etc. are all done by hand. The law firm consists of a suite of fifty rooms, almost half of which contain nothing but records and files.

Six months ago John Smith died. Mary and David are now in full control of the firm. At a recent bar association meeting, Mary and David listened to a presentation on the use of computers in the practice of law. Mary was fascinated by the presentation and is ready to restructure the law firm with the introduction of computers throughout the office. David (who believed that his father and grandfather were incapable of making a mistake) is skeptical. David does not see any reason to change the way the firm practices law. Yet he agrees that the idea of computer use is worth exploring.

Mary and David agree to hire you as a computer consultant. You specialize in giving advice to attorneys in the use of computers in the management of a law firm and in the practice of law.

(a) Name some areas where you think Smith, Smith & Smith might be able to use computers in the office. Explain why.

(b) What do you think some of David's objections might be to the introduction of computers in these areas? How would you respond to these objections?

## Chapter Summary

Like almost every other aspect of our society, the law office has been substantially altered by the computer. Since there is a tremendous diversity in computer products available, it is unlikely that any paralegal will walk into a new office, particularly a large one, and be totally familiar with all of the hardware and software programs in use. Hence, you must expect to go through a large and ongoing dose of on-the-job computer training. Standard survival techniques can help, such as finding out if any of the products have an 800-number helpline that you can call, taking advantage of online tutorials, and using help keys.

Fairly soon you should learn a relatively small list of computer terms. The list includes hardware, software, backup, data, hard-disk drive, operating system, modem, laser printer, etc. The four major kinds of software programs are word processing, database management, spreadsheets, and communications. A fifth kind combines the other four.

Word processing software is a substitute for the traditional typewriter, bottle of "white-out," and scissors that were once used to cut-and-paste a report together. Now you can use the word processor to type the text of a report, to insert additional text, to move text around, and to make other corrections on a computer screen (monitor) so that you can see the finished product before the report is printed. This feature, plus many others, makes word processing the most widely used software in offices and homes throughout the country.

Database software allows you to store, organize, and retrieve a large body of information. The office can design its own database, and it can purchase access to commercial databases such as WESTLAW and LEXIS. One of the critical skills in this area is the ability to formulate a question, or query, for the computer to answer. Most queries ask the computer to find data within a designated database. In formulating a query, you need to know how to use the universal character (*) and the root expander (!). You also need to know when to use connectors (such as the OR connector, the AND connector, and the numerical connector) to specify the relationship among the search words in the query in order to give the search more direction. You also need to know how to search for phrases, how to conduct field and segment searches, and how to perform simple "find" searches when you already have the citation to something you want to read.

Spreadsheet software allows you to make financial calculations and solve mathematically oriented problems with much greater ease than with traditional calculators. Endless "what if?" questions can be answered based on variables entered into the program.

Communications software makes it possible for computers to "talk" with each other, through a modem, over telephone lines. Finally, software exists that allows the user to combine or integrate word processing, database management, spreadsheets, and communications capabilities.

## Key Terms

| | | |
|---|---|---|
| online tutorial | file | compatible |
| help key | k | dual sided |
| documentation | language | double density |
| CLE | laptop | network |
| users group | memory | dot matrix printer |
| hardware | microcomputer | daisy wheel printer |
| backup | monitor | ink jet printer |
| command | operating system | laser printer |
| data | mouse | modem |
| disk drive | windows | word processor |
| floppy disk | multitasking | dedicated word processing |
| hard disk | run | word wrap |
| byte | save | spelling checker |
| diskette | software | automatic pagination |
| floppy | hardware | block |

block movement
boldface
character
character enhancement
control character
cursor
default setting
deletion
editing
format
global
header
incremental spacing
insertion
justification
right justified
menu
print formatting
print preview
screen formatting
scrolling
search and find
search and replace
status line
subscript
superscript
text buffer
text editing
text file

virtual representation
WYSIWYG
merge printing
bugs
database
data manager
data redundancy
field
record
file
scanner
key-word search
full-text search
search criteria
WESTLAW
LEXIS
online search
search query
universal character (*)
root expander (!)
connectors
OR connector
AND connector
sentence connector
paragraph connector
grammatical connector
BUT NOT connector
numeral connector
phrase searching

noise words
AND NOT connector
segment search
field search
title search
synopsis search
topic search
digest search
headnote
judge search
fi
lexstat
lexsee
spreadsheets
cell
coordinates
formula
label
value
window
plotter
template
communications
baud rate
public domain
bulletin board
integrated packages
down time

**14**

# Introduction to Law Office Administration*

## ■ Chapter Outline

Section A. The Practice of Law in the Private Sector
  Sole Practice
  Office-Sharing Arrangement
  Partnership
  Professional Corporations
  Corporate Legal Departments
Section B. The Legal Administrator and the Legal Assistant Manager: Overview of Administration in a Large Law Firm
Section C. Expenses
Section D. Timekeeping

Section E. Billing
Section F. Administrative Reports
Section G. Procedures Manual in a Small Office: Mail, Copying, and Filing
  Incoming Mail
  Copying Charges
  Filing System
Section H. Computer-Based Records Management System in a Large Office

## ■ Section A. The Practice of Law in the Private Sector

There are over 700,000 attorneys in the United States—one for every 360 citizens. (This is double the number that existed in 1970.) By the year 2000 the number is expected to grow to 1,000,000.[1]

About 70% of attorneys practice in private law offices. Another 10% work for corporations in corporate practice. The remainder practice in the public sector for government, for legal aid and legal service offices, for organizations such as unions, trade associations, and public interest groups, or do not practice law at all. In this chapter, our primary focus will be on attorneys who practice law in relatively large private offices, although other practice settings will also be covered.

In the private sector, law is practiced in a variety of settings:

■ Sole practice

■ Office-sharing arrangement

■ Partnership

---

*Portions of this chapter were originally written with Robert G. Baylor, Business Manager at Manatt, Phelps, Rothenberg, and Tunney, Los Angeles. Others who have reviewed this chapter and provided valuable commentary include Dorothy B. Moore, Kathleen M. Reed, Michele A. Coyne, Patsy R. Pressley, Deborah L. Thompson, and Shawn A. Jones.

[1]Stanton, *Stepping Up to the Bar,* 35 Occupational Outlook Quarterly 3 (Spring 1991).

■ Professional corporation
■ Corporate law department

## Sole Practice

A *sole* (or solo) *practice* often refers to an attorney who practices alone. More accurately, it means a sole proprietorship in which one attorney owns and manages the firm. Anyone who works for this attorney, including another attorney, is an employee who receives a salary. They are not entitled to a share of the profits of the office in addition to a salary.

Sole practitioners are generalists or specialists. A generalist is the equivalent of a doctor in general practice. An attorney who is a *general practitioner* often tries to handle all kinds of cases. If, however, the case is unusually complex or if the attorney is very busy with other cases, he or she might consult with an attorney in another office or refer the case to another attorney. Other sole practitioners specialize. Their practice might be limited, for example, to tax, criminal, or patent and trademark cases, or—more commonly—to personal injury cases.

Most sole practitioners have very few employees. There is a secretary, who often performs many paralegal functions along with the traditional clerical responsibilities of typing, filing, and reception work. He or she may also perform bookkeeping chores. The most common job title of this individual is "legal secretary," although occasionally he or she will be known as a "paralegal/secretary." You will sometimes find job ads for small offices seeking paralegals with clerical skills. These skills are often phrased more positively as administrative or word processing skills, but they are, in essence, clerical. In recent years, however, many sole practitioners have begun to hire one or more paralegals who have minimal or no clerical duties.

The office may employ a part-time law clerk who is a student currently in law school. It may also employ one or more other attorneys. Again, in a sole practice these attorneys do not share in the profits of the office.

## Office-Sharing Arrangement

Occasionally, a sole practitioner will allow a newly admitted attorney to use the facilities of the office in exchange for some nonpaid help on the practitioner's cases. A more formal arrangement would be two or more attorneys with independent practices who share the use and cost of administration such as rent, copy machine, other equipment, library, secretarial help, etc. They do not practice law together as a partnership or corporation, although they may assist each other during periods of vacation, illness, or other emergencies. To avoid the conflict-of-interest and confidentiality problems discussed in Chapter 5, they must be careful in the selection of clients and in discussions about their cases with each other.

## Partnership

A law partnership is a group of individuals who practice law jointly and who share in the profits and losses of the venture. Its revenues come from client fees. If the partnership is relatively large, it will probably be organized into a series of departments based on client needs (such as an antitrust department, a litigation department, etc.) and will be managed through a series of committees (such as a recruitment committee, a library and records committee, etc.) based on the variety of support services available to the attorneys. See Figure 14.1 for an example of the organization structure of a large law firm.

There are many different categories of attorneys in a large partnership, the most common of which are:

- Partners
- Associates
- Staff attorneys
- Of counsel
- Contract attorneys

## 1. *Partners*

Partners contribute the capital that is needed to create the firm and to expand it as needed. They decide whether to merge with other firms, and, indeed,

**FIGURE 14.1**   Large Law Firm Organization Chart: An Example

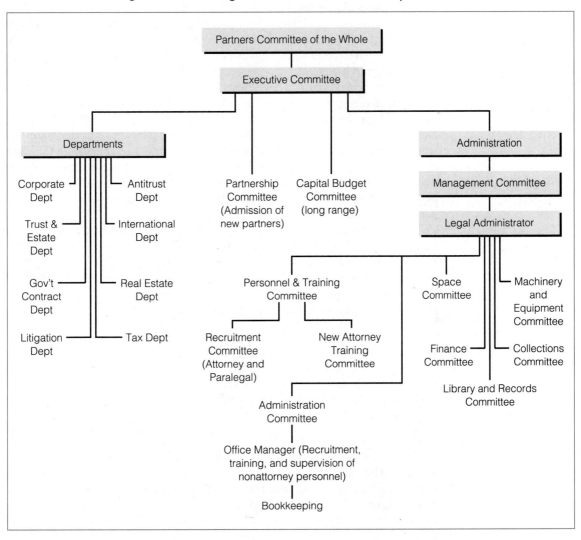

whether to go out of business altogether. Partners share the profits and losses of the firm pursuant to an elaborate partnership agreement. They decide how the firm should be managed, when to take on new partners, what attorneys, paralegals, and other employees to hire, etc. Most of this is done through a variety of administrative staff. In short, the partners own the firm. There may be different categories of partners in a firm (for example, senior partner and junior partner) depending on factors such as the amount of capital the attorney contributed to the firm and how involved he or she is in the firm's management. As we will see, a distinction is also sometimes made between equity and nonequity partners.

Generally, partners are not on salary in the traditional sense, although they do receive a periodic *draw,* which is an advance against profits in some firms and an overhead expense in others.

### 2. Associates

Associates are attorney employees of the firm. Often, they are hired right out of law school while studying for the bar examination. As students, they may have worked for the firm as a *law clerk.* Other associates, however, are hired from other law firms. They are known as *lateral hires.* (When partners and paralegals switch law firms, they also are referred to as lateral hires.) After a certain number of years at the firm, e.g. seven, associates are usually considered for partnership. If they are *passed over* for partner, they often leave the firm to practice elsewhere, although a few may be invited to stay as a *permanent associate* or a *senior associate.*

In some firms, there is a movement away from the "up-or-out" system that adds great tension to the ranks of associates. To encourage good people to stay, the firms have created different tiers of partners. For example, a firm might create the category of *nonequity partner* or *income partner,* to be distinguished from the *equity partner* or *capital partner.* The latter is a full partner in the sense of owning the firm and sharing in its profits and losses. A nonequity or income partner, on the other hand, is an individual who has not made, or who does not aspire to become, a full partner. In effect, he or she is often little more than a permanent associate with a more inviting title.

(Hence paralegals are not the only workers who are frustrated by a lack of career ladders in the legal profession. As we saw in Chapters 1 and 3, the paralegal field has been slowly developing career ladders, e.g., from case clerk to paralegal to senior paralegal and paralegal supervisor. Attorneys also want career ladders beyond the traditional associate-partner regime. Equally slowly, the profession has been responding to this need.)

### 3. Staff Attorneys

*Staff attorneys* (sometimes called *second-tiered attorneys*) are hired with the understanding that they will never be considered for partnership. This is what distinguishes them from associates.

### 4. Of Counsel

There is no fixed definition of an attorney who is *of counsel* to a firm. He or she may be a semiretired partner, a part-time attorney, or a full-time attorney who is considering a long-term relationship with the firm. Not all firms use the title "of counsel." Some prefer "special counsel" or simply "counsel."

## 5. Contract Attorneys

*Contract attorneys* (sometimes called *project attorneys*) are hired when the firm has a temporary shortage of attorneys, or needs expertise in a certain area for a limited period. Often paid on an hourly basis, the contract attorney is not a full-time employee.

## Professional Corporations

In most states, it is possible for attorneys to incorporate their practice of law as a *Professional Corporation* (P.C.), e.g., "Jamison & Jamison, P.C." This is done primarily for tax purposes. From a tax and estate-planning perspective, it is often more advantageous to organize as a corporation than as a partnership. Like any corporation, a professional corporation has stockholders (the owners), directors, and officers—all of whom are attorneys. The operation of a professional corporation is practically identical to the operation of a traditional partnership. A client would hardly notice the difference.

## Corporate Legal Departments

Many large corporations have a *law department* headed by a *general counsel* who may also be a vice-president of the company. Other attorneys in this office can include deputy or associate general counsel, senior attorneys, staff attorneys, etc. They are the in-house attorneys who handle the day-to-day tasks of advising the company on legal matters. They have one client—the corporation that hires them and that pays them a salary. Frequently, paralegals work with these attorneys. In 1983, the ratio of paralegals to attorneys was 0.15-to-1. In 1990, the ratio increased to 0.21-to-1.[2] Other support personnel may include legal administrators, legal secretaries, word processing and data processing operators, clerks, librarians, and records managers.

There are, of course, no client fees. Funds to operate the department come directly from the corporate treasury. If expertise is needed that is not available in the department, such as trial experience in a certain specialty, the general counsel will hire "outside" attorneys from law firms.

# ■ Section B. The Legal Administrator and the Legal Assistant Manager: Overview of Administration in a Large Law Firm

The practice of law is a profession, but it is also a business. The larger the practice, the more likely its business component will be managed by individuals whose main or sole responsibility is administration. While the owners of a law firm have ultimate responsibility for administration, they often delegate this responsibility to others. For example, there may be a managing partner, often an attorney with a small case load or none at all. More and more firms are hiring new categories of management personnel who are not attorneys. We will focus on two such individuals: the *legal administrator* and the *legal assistant manager*. One way to obtain an overview of management is to examine the job descriptions of such individuals.

---

[2]Wilber, *Support Staffing Ratios*, National Law Journal S6, col. 2 (May 20, 1991).

The legal administrator works under the supervision of the managing partner or of a management committee of the firm. The range of this person's responsibility, and of the business component of the practice of law, can be seen in the job description in Figure 14.2.

Again, this job description fits an individual who works for a law office that is fairly large. The support staff for such an office can also be quite extensive. Here are some examples:[3]

*Administrative Support Staff in a Large Law Office*

| | |
|---|---|
| Legal Administrator | Secretaries |
| Legal Assistant Manager | Data Processing Operators |
| Personnel Manager | Word Processing Supervisor |
| Records/File Manager | Word Processors |
| Employee Benefits Manager | Proofreaders |
| Recruiter | Docket Clerks |
| Director of Marketing | Computer Specialists |
| Facilities Manager | Equipment Managers |
| Risk Manager | File Room Clerks |
| Office Manager | Librarian |
| Financial Manager | Library Aides |
| Credit/Collections Manager | Messengers/Pages |
| Chief Financial Officer/Comptroller | Copy Room Clerks |
| Bookkeepers | Mail Clerks |
| Analysts | Purchasing Clerks |
| Payroll Specialists | Receptionists |
| Accounts Payable Clerk | Telephone Operators |
| Accounts Receivable Clerk | Reservation Clerks |
| Time and Billing Assistants | |

Prominent on this list is the legal assistant manager, whose job description is presented in Figure 14.3.

## Section C. Expenses

How does a large law firm spend the fee income that it receives? There are a number of organizations that conduct surveys to answer this question. One of the largest is the Altman Weil Pensa Survey of Law Firm Management. Some of the highlights of its 1990 survey are presented in Figure 14.4. The data was collected from 647 law firms with more than 16,000 attorneys.

## Section D. Timekeeping

Abraham Lincoln's famous statement that a "lawyer's time is his stock in trade" is still true today. Effective timekeeping is therefore critical to the success of a law firm. In some firms, it is an obsession, as typified by the following story. A senior partner in a very prestigious Wall Street law firm walked down the corridor to visit the office of another senior partner. Upon entering the room, he was startled to find his colleague on the floor writhing in pain, apparently

---

[3]R. Green, ed., *The Quality Pursuit* 69 (American Bar Association, 1989).

## Summary of Responsibilities

The legal administrator manages the planning, marketing, and business functions, as well as the overall operations, of a law office. He or she reports to the managing partner or the executive committee and participates in management meetings. In addition to general responsibility for financial planning and controls, personnel administration (including compensation), systems, and physical facilities, the legal administrator also identifies and plans for the changing needs of the organization, shares responsibility with the appropriate partners for strategic planning, practice management, and marketing, and contributes to cost-effective management throughout the organization.

**WHETHER DIRECTLY OR THROUGH A MANAGEMENT TEAM, THE LEGAL ADMINISTRATOR IS RESPONSIBLE FOR MOST OR ALL OF THE FOLLOWING:**

### Financial Management:

- [ ] Planning
- [ ] Forecasting
- [ ] Budgeting
- [ ] Variance analysis
- [ ] Profitability analysis
- [ ] Financial reporting
- [ ] Operations analysis
- [ ] General ledger accounting
- [ ] Rate analysis
- [ ] Billing and collections
- [ ] Cash flow control
- [ ] Banking relationships
- [ ] Investment
- [ ] Tax planning and reporting
- [ ] Trust accounting
- [ ] Payroll and pension plans
- [ ] Other related functions

### Systems Management:

- [ ] Systems analysis
- [ ] Operational audits
- [ ] Procedures manual
- [ ] Cost-benefit analysis
- [ ] Computer systems design
- [ ] Programming and systems development
- [ ] Information services
- [ ] Records and library management
- [ ] Office automation
- [ ] Document construction systems
- [ ] Information storage and retrieval
- [ ] Telecommunications
- [ ] Litigation support
- [ ] Conflict-of-interest docket systems
- [ ] Legal practice systems
- [ ] Other related services

### Facilities Management:

- [ ] Lease negotiations
- [ ] Space planning and design
- [ ] Office renovation
- [ ] Purchasing and inventory control
- [ ] Reprographics
- [ ] Reception/switchboard services
- [ ] Telecommunications
- [ ] Mail messenger services
- [ ] Other related functions

### Human Resource Management:

- [ ] Recruitment, selection, and placement
- [ ] Orientation, training, and development
- [ ] Performance evaluation
- [ ] Salary and benefits administration
- [ ] Employee relations
- [ ] Motivation and counseling
- [ ] Discipline
- [ ] Termination
- [ ] Worker's compensation
- [ ] Personnel data systems
- [ ] Organization analysis
- [ ] Job design, development of job descriptions
- [ ] Resource allocation
- [ ] Other human resource management functions for the legal and support staff

**AS A MEMBER OF THE LEGAL ORGANIZATION'S MANAGEMENT TEAM, THE LEGAL ADMINISTRATOR MANAGES AND/OR CONTRIBUTES SIGNIFICANTLY TO THE FOLLOWING:**

### General Management:

- [ ] Policymaking
- [ ] Strategic and tactical planning
- [ ] Business development
- [ ] Risk management
- [ ] Quality control
- [ ] Organizational development
- [ ] Other general management functions

**FIGURE 14.2**
Legal Administrator: Job Description (Association of Legal Administrators)

Continued

**FIGURE 14.2**
Legal
Administrator:
Job Description
(Association of
Legal
Administrators)
—*Continued*

| Practice Management: | Marketing: |
|---|---|
| ☐ Attorney recruiting | ☐ Management of client-profitability analysis |
| ☐ Attorney training and development | ☐ Forecasting of business opportunities |
| ☐ Legal assistant supervision | ☐ Planning client development |
| ☐ Work-product quality control | ☐ Marketing legal services: enhancement of the firm's visibility and image in the desired markets |
| ☐ Professional standards |  |
| ☐ Substantive practice systems |  |
| ☐ Other related functions |  |

**Job Requirements**

**Knowledge:** Has familiarity with legal or other professional service organizations, and experience managing business operations, including planning, marketing, financial and personnel administration, and management of professionals.

**Skills and Abilities:** Able to identify and analyze complex issues and problems in management, finance, and human relations, and to recommend and implement solutions. Able to manage office functions economically and efficiently, and to organize work, establish priorities, and maintain good interpersonal relations and communications with attorneys and support staff. Excellent supervisory and leadership skills, as well as skills in written and oral communication. Demonstrated willingness and ability to delegate.

**Education:** Graduation from a recognized college or university with major coursework in business administration, finance, data processing, or personnel management, or comparable work experience.

due to a heart attack. Standing there, he could think of only one thing to say to him: "Howard, are your time sheets in?" [5]

In some firms, the pressures of the clock on attorneys and paralegals can be enormous:

[Y]oung lawyers often are shocked to discover their new employer's time expectations. Many firms in major cities require as many as 2,400 billable hours

**FIGURE 14.3**   Legal Assistant Manager

**Legal Assistant Manager: Job Description**
**Attorneys' Guide to**
**Practicing with Legal Assistants**
(State Bar of Texas, 1986)[4]

**General Responsibilities:**

The legal assistant manager has overall responsibility for administration of the program. Formal training programs responsive to the needs of the various sections and to the professional development of legal assistants are identified and established by this individual. He or she works with the supervising attorneys, providing assistance in staffing and in resolving legal assistant-related conflicts between sections and between individuals.

**Specific Duties:**

A. Development and utilization of legal assistant skills

1. Work with the supervising attorneys. Become and remain familiar with the nature and amount of work done by each lawyer in the firm.
2. Work with the supervising attorney. Develop and submit to the Practice Management Committee a written analysis of each

[4]The job title used in the Guide is Legal Assistant Coordinator. Legal Assistant Manager or Paralegal Manager, however, is more common.
[5]Margolis, *At the Bar,* New York Times B13 (September 7, 1990).

**FIGURE 14.3**  Legal Assistant Manager—*Continued*

lawyer's work, identify the portions which should be performed by a legal assistant, and update this information on an annual basis.

3. Develop a training program for the supervising attorneys.

4. Develop a short introductory presentation for lawyers in each section to demonstrate the types of tasks for which legal assistants should be used.

5. Meet with each new attorney in the firm to explain the legal assistant program, thus ensuring the utilization of legal assistants by new attorneys.

6. Develop an orientation program for new legal assistants and conduct orientation sessions with each new legal assistant.

7. Develop an in-house training program for all new legal assistants and conduct or supervise the training provided by others.

8. Receive notice of each lawsuit docketed in the Litigation Section and assign a legal assistant to each lawsuit.

9. Assign legal assistants to all files which require the assistance of a legal assistant.

10. Receive notice of the assignment of all or major parts of "Special Projects" to attorneys, and assign a legal assistant to each "Special Project."

11. Monitor the progress of legal assistant use in each section and develop changes in the legal assistant support program as needed.

12. Consult with each legal assistant and each supervising attorney individually at appropriate intervals, perhaps quarterly, to identify problems and possible solutions.

13. Conduct monthly meetings of the legal assistants to keep them informed.

14. Work with the supervising attorney in the development of written procedures for inclusion in the firm's manual concerning the use of legal assistants.

15. Evaluate the need for support staff for legal assistants and work with firm administrator to ensure that legal assistants have adequate support.

B. Legal assistant supervision

1. Supervise the development of procedure manuals for legal assistants in each section for review by the supervising attorneys.

2. Review legal assistant time records to ensure proper preparation and to monitor workloads.

3. Coordinate evaluations of legal assistants.

4. With the respective supervising attorneys, conduct a performance interview with each legal assistant.

5. Ensure that all section staff meetings and similar meetings are open to legal assistants.

6. Monitor both quality and quantity of work assignments to legal assistants.

C. Reporting

Prepare and submit to the Practice Management Committee a quarterly report showing:

1. Approximate hours spent by each legal assistant on work from each lawyer.

2. The number of assignments carried out by each assigned legal assistant for each lawyer.

3. The same information for backup work done by the legal assistants in each section.

D. Professional development for legal assistants

1. Set objectives for and help plan in-house professional instruction for legal assistants.

2. Review all notices received in the firm regarding seminars.

3. Develop and implement schedules of continuing in-house and outside training for each legal assistant to ensure timely completion of required formal and enhancement instruction.

E. Personnel

1. Recruit, interview, and hire legal assistants.

2. Maintain a personnel file for each legal assistant.

3. Anticipate and correct unsatisfactory assignments and inadequate or inappropriate staffing.

4. Assign backup responsibility after consultation with legal assistants and supervising attorneys.

5. Provide assistance in resolving legal assistant conflicts between individuals.

6. Evaluate office space requirements for legal assistants and work with firm administration in providing office space for legal assistants.

**FIGURE 14.4**

1990 Survey of
Law Firm
Economics

During the past five years, the average overhead costs per attorney was $93,648, an increase of 51%. The average law firm spent:

- $34,121 per attorney for support staff (excluding paralegals). This constituted 16.5% of the gross revenue of the firm. This is the same percentage that existed in 1984. (Apparently, the large investment in law office automation between 1984 and 1990 did *not* result in significant net staff cost savings.)

- $28,718 per attorney for general expenses, such as insurance of all kinds, printing, meetings, postage, and office supplies not charged to clients. This constituted 13.9% of the gross revenue of the firm, an increase of 69% between 1985 and 1990.

- $8,323 per attorney for paralegals. This constituted 4.0% of gross revenue, an increase of 67% between 1984 and 1990.

- $15,462 per attorney for occupancy expenses. This constituted 7.5% of gross revenue, an increase of 49% between 1985 and 1990.

- $4,672 per attorney for equipment. This constituted 2.3% of gross revenue, an increase of 10% between 1985 and 1990.

- $2,352 per attorney for library and reference expenses. This constituted 1.1% of gross revenue, an increase of 33% between 1984 and 1990.

The median number of billable hours were:

- 1,706 for partners/shareholders (up from, 1,571 in 1984)

- 1,820 for associates (up from 1,738 in 1985)

- 1,400 for paralegals in 1989

The median billing rates were:

- $150 per hour for partners/shareholders

- $100 per hour for associates

- $55 per hour for paralegals

per year. When one considers that many full-time employees outside of the law only *work* 2,000 hours per year, the time commitment required by these firms is staggering.[6]

The cry for billable hours is thought by many to be at the heart of much of the problem. Many legal assistants as well as attorneys have quotas of billable hours. Zlaket [the President of the State Bar of Arizona] stated that some firms require 2,200 hours a year and he deems this to be outrageous. He suggested that this only leads to padding of bills and time sheets, and it leads to unnecessary work that will be paid by somebody.[7]

The ethical dimensions of this problem are considered in Chapter 5. Here our concern is the administration of the timekeeping and billing system.

. . . . . . . . . . . . . .

After the initial client interview, the accounting starting point can be a *New File Worksheet* (see Figure 14.5). It is also sometimes referred to as a *New Matter Sheet* or a *New Business Sheet*. The New File Worksheet becomes the source document for the creation of all the necessary accounting records involved in working on the case or matter of a client.

Attorneys and paralegals must keep an accurate account of the time they spend on behalf of a client. An example of a form they can use is the *Daily Time*

---

[6]Walljasper, *I Quit!*, Wisconsin Lawyer 16 (March 1990).

[7]Morris, *Join the Effort to Restore Respect to the Legal Profession*, The Digest 3 (Arizona Paralegal Ass'n, April 1989).

**FIGURE 14.5**

New File Worksheet

Billing No. _____

Date _____Opened _____Closed

New File

**Client** (Check one)

___ INDIVIDUAL _____

Last                    First                    Middle Initial

___ ENTITY _____

(Use complete name & common abbreviations; place articles [e.g., The] at end.)

___ CLASS ACTION _____

(File Name, ex.: Popcorn Antitrust Litigation)

**Matter** (Check One)

___ NON-LITIGATION _____

___ LITIGATION _____

_____ Approved for litigation by—MUST BE INITIALED by submitting attorney!!

**Nature of the Case**

Area of law code _____      Summary of work or dispute: _____

_____

**Client Contact** (N/A for Class Actions)

Name: _____

Company: _____

Street: _____

City, State, Zip: _____

Telephone: _____

**Billing Address** (N/A for Class Actions)

Name: _____

Company: _____

Street: _____

City, State, Zip: _____

Telephone: _____

**Team Information** (Use initials)

____ ____ ____    Managing Attorney(s) (for non-litigation cases only)

____ ____ ____    Bill Review Attorney(s)

____ ____ ____    Originating Attorney(s)

_____ Calendar Attorney (for litigation cases only)

_____ Legal Assistant (for litigation cases only)

_____ Secretary to Calendar Attorney (for litigation cases only)

**Referral Source** (Check one)

___ Existing Client _____

(Name)

___ Non-Firm Attorney _____

(Name)

___ Firm Attorney or Employee _____

___ Martindale-Hubbell

___ Other _____

Continued

**FIGURE 14.5**   New File Worksheet—*Continued*

---

**Fee Agreement** (Check those that apply)

___ Hourly

___ Contingent _____%

___ Fee Petition

___ Fixed Fee $_____ or Fixed Range from $_____ to $_____

___ Retainer $_____

___ Letter of Retainer sent by _____ on _____
___ ___                  (Initials)     (Date)

**Statement Format** (Check those that apply)

| | |
|---|---|
| Do you want identical disbursements grouped? | ____ Yes ____ No |
| Do you want attorney hours reflected on *each* time entry? | ____ Yes ____ No |
| Do you want fees extended on *each* time entry? | ____ Yes ____ No |

---

**Conflict Check**

**Conflict Check Completed By:** _____     **Date:**_____
                          (Initials)

**Conflict Check Not Needed:** _____
               (Initials of Submitting Person)

**Check One:**

_____ No conflicts

_____ Potential conflict with the following existing parties (from computer system):

_____

_____

*(Or attach computer printout from Conflict Check System.)*

**\*New Adverse Parties:**

_____

_____

_____

**\*New Related Parties** (for Class Actions, Named Plaintiffs Only):

_____

_____

_____

\*Will be entered into computer system by Bus. Dept. *AFTER* approval by Managing Partner.

---

**Closed File**

**Date Closed:** _____     **Atty. or Sec. Initials:** _____

_____ Attach Pleadings and/or File Indexes. If indexes are not available, attach brief description of what is contained in the file(s). SEND FILES, THIS FORM, AND INDEX TO FILE ROOM.

---

**Routing Lists**

                                        (Initial)

| | New File: | Date: | Closed File: | Date: |
|---|---|---|---|---|
| Submitted by | _____ | _____ | _____ | _____ |
| Sec. of Submitting Person | _____ | _____ | _____ | _____ |

Continued

**FIGURE 14.5**   New File Worksheet—*Continued*

| | | | | |
|---|---|---|---|---|
| Managing Partner | ——— | ——— | ——— | ——— |
| Business Department | ——— | ——— | ——— | ——— |
| File Department | ——— | ——— | ——— | ——— |
| Firm Newsletter | ——— | ——— | ——— | ——— |
| Docket for Litigation | ——— | ——— | ——— | ——— |
| EnviroLaw (Computer Center)   Add? | ——— | | | |
| IdeaLaw (Computer Center)   Add? | ——— | | | |
| JobLaw (Computer Center)   Add? | ——— | | | |
| Pulse—See Fred Farrell | | | | |

*Sheet* (see Figure 14.6). This sheet becomes the journal from which all time entries are posted to individual client ledger pages.

Law firms normally use tenths of an hour (in increments of six minutes) as the base unit for the measurement of time, although a few firms still use one-fourth of an hour as their base for recording time. *Hourly Time and Rate Charts* (see Figure 14.7) can later be used to translate these time fractions into dollars and cents for billing purposes; or this can be quickly accomplished by computer. Attorneys and paralegals note their activities on the Daily Time Sheet each time during the day that they work on a particular matter. The information from these Daily Time Sheets can then be typed on *time tickets* (see Figure 14.8) or into a computer database.

These time tickets are usually perforated or shingled. For offices still using a manual system, this facilitates easy separation so that they can be subsequently sorted into alphabetical order for quick posting to client ledger cards. The tickets can be processed in several different ways. One is to retain the individual tickets in an open tray in alphabetical order for eventual retrieval and tabulation for billing; another would be to use gummed backs for pasting directly onto a client ledger card; or the ticket may be used as a source document for transcribing onto a *Master Ledger Card* (see Figure 14.9); or the ticket could

**FIGURE 14.6**
Daily Time Sheet

| DAILY SERVICE REPORT OF: | | | DATE: | | |
|---|---|---|---|---|---|

| | | | | | | | |
|---|---|---|---|---|---|---|---|
| ANS  –Answer | DEPO –Deposition | K   –Contract | O   –Order | RES  –Research |
| APP   –Appearance or Attending | DIC  –Dictation | L   –Legal | OP  –Opinion | REV  –Revision |
| ARG   –Argue or Argument | DOC  –Document | LT  –Letter to | P   –Preparation | S   –Settlement |
| BR   –Brief | DR   –Drafting | LF  –Letter from | PL  –Plaintiff | TF   –Telephone from |
| COMP  –Complaint | F   –Facts | MT  –Memorandum to | PR  –Praecipe | TT   –Telephone to |
| CW   –Conference-Office | FL   –File | MF  –Memorandum from | PRT  –Pretrial | TR   –Trial |
| CWO  –Conference-Outside Office | H   –Hearing | MOT  –Motion | R   –Reading and Review | TRV  –Travel |
| DEF   –Defendant | INV   –Investigation | NEG  –Negotiation | REL  –Release | W   –Witness |
| DEM   –Demurrer | INT   –Interview | | | |

| CLIENT (State billing division or department) | MATTER | DESCRIPTION OF WORK (Use abbreviations above) | TIME | |
|---|---|---|---|---|
| | | | Hours | 10ths |
| | | | | |
| | | | | |
| | | | | |
| | | | | |
| | | | | |
| | | | | |
| | | | | |

**FIGURE 14.7**
Hourly Time ×
$ Hourly Rate

| TIME: | $20 | $25 | $30 | $35 | $40 | $45 | $50 | $55 | $60 | $65 | $70 | $75 |
|---|---|---|---|---|---|---|---|---|---|---|---|---|
| 0.10 hour | 2 00 | 2 50 | 3 00 | 3 50 | 4 00 | 4 50 | 5 00 | 5 50 | 6 00 | 6 50 | 7 00 | 7 50 |
| 0.20 | 4 00 | 5 00 | 6 00 | 7 00 | 8 00 | 9 00 | 10 00 | 11 00 | 12 00 | 13 00 | 14 00 | 15 00 |
| 0.30 | 6 00 | 7 50 | 9 00 | 10 50 | 12 00 | 13 50 | 15 00 | 16 50 | 18 00 | 19 50 | 21 00 | 22 50 |
| 0.40 | 8 00 | 10 00 | 12 00 | 14 00 | 16 00 | 18 00 | 20 00 | 22 00 | 24 00 | 26 00 | 28 00 | 30 00 |
| 0.50 | 10 00 | 12 50 | 15 00 | 17 50 | 20 00 | 22 50 | 25 00 | 27 50 | 30 00 | 32 50 | 35 00 | 37 50 |
| 0.60 | 12 00 | 15 00 | 18 00 | 21 00 | 24 00 | 27 00 | 30 00 | 33 00 | 36 00 | 39 00 | 42 00 | 45 00 |
| 0.70 | 14 00 | 17 50 | 21 00 | 24 50 | 28 00 | 31 50 | 35 00 | 38 50 | 42 00 | 45 50 | 49 00 | 52 50 |
| 0.80 | 16 00 | 20 00 | 24 00 | 28 00 | 32 00 | 36 00 | 40 00 | 44 00 | 48 00 | 52 00 | 56 00 | 60 00 |
| 0.90 | 18 00 | 22 50 | 27 00 | 31 50 | 36 00 | 40 50 | 45 00 | 49 50 | 54 00 | 58 50 | 63 00 | 67 50 |
| 1.00 hour | 20 00 | 25 00 | 30 00 | 35 00 | 40 00 | 45 00 | 50 00 | 55 00 | 60 00 | 65 00 | 70 00 | 75 00 |
| 2.00 | 40 00 | 50 00 | 60 00 | 70 00 | 80 00 | 90 00 | 100 00 | 110 00 | 120 00 | 130 00 | 140 00 | 150 00 |
| 3.00 | 60 00 | 75 00 | 90 00 | 105 00 | 120 00 | 135 00 | 150 00 | 165 00 | 180 00 | 195 00 | 210 00 | 225 00 |
| 4.00 | 80 00 | 100 00 | 120 00 | 140 00 | 160 00 | 180 00 | 200 00 | 220 00 | 240 00 | 260 00 | 280 00 | 300 00 |
| 5.00 | 100 00 | 125 00 | 150 00 | 175 00 | 200 00 | 225 00 | 250 00 | 275 00 | 300 00 | 325 00 | 350 00 | 375 00 |
| 6.00 | 120 00 | 150 00 | 180 00 | 210 00 | 240 00 | 270 00 | 300 00 | 330 00 | 360 00 | 390 00 | 420 00 | 450 00 |
| 7.00 | 140 00 | 175 00 | 210 00 | 245 00 | 280 00 | 315 00 | 350 00 | 385 00 | 420 00 | 455 00 | 490 00 | 525 00 |
| 8.00 | 160 00 | 200 00 | 240 00 | 280 00 | 320 00 | 360 00 | 400 00 | 440 00 | 480 00 | 520 00 | 560 00 | 600 00 |
| 9.00 | 180 00 | 225 00 | 270 00 | 315 00 | 360 00 | 405 00 | 450 00 | 495 00 | 540 00 | 585 00 | 630 00 | 675 00 |
| 10.00 hours | 200 00 | 250 00 | 300 00 | 350 00 | 400 00 | 450 00 | 500 00 | 550 00 | 600 00 | 650 00 | 700 00 | 750 00 |

**FIGURE 14.8**
Time Ticket

| DATE | NAME | CLIENT | MATTER | CLIENT REFERENCE NUMBER | TIME |
|---|---|---|---|---|---|

DESCRIPTION:

Posted: _____

**FIGURE 14.9**
Master
Ledger Card

SHEET NO. _____

TOTAL HOURS WORKED TO DATE BY LAWYER
1 2 3 4 5 6 7 8 9 0

| DATE | CHARACTER OF SERVICE | LAW-YER NO. | DAILY HOURS | N/C | CON. | | | | | | | | | | TOTAL CHARGE HOURS |

be keyed directly from the Daily Time Sheet of the attorney or paralegal and used as an input document for the firm's computerized system.

If you have never kept close track of your time, you will find that the task requires a great deal of effort and discipline; it does not come naturally to most of us. The key to performing the task effectively is to do it consistently and comprehensively until it becomes second nature. Even nonbillable activities should be accounted for, such as performing administrative chores, helping to develop standard forms, or taking a lunch break. A senior attorney or other supervisor will then be in a better position to determine the best allocation of an employee's efforts, now and in the future.

Tory Barcott, a Certified Legal Assistant in Anchorage, makes a number of important points about timekeeping:[8]

> It "sometimes" scares me a little to contemplate clients paying" $10.00 or more "for every six minutes of our time." To survive in this world, the legal assistant must possess the accuracy and efficiency of a Swiss watch. "I keep one of those small, cheap, adhesive digital clocks where it can't be missed or covered with paperwork. Sticking it to my phone, in the middle of my desk, works best for me. The first step in performing any task is to record the time on my time sheet. I do this before retrieving the file, making a phone call," or going to meet a supervising attorney. The clock is also helpful in recording the time when a task is interrupted by anything unrelated to the current client matter. "I take notes on the start and stop times exactly as displayed on my digital clock." Some Saturdays, while absently attending to household chores, "I'll glance at the clock and catch myself thinking, 'that floor took only 0.4 to clean.' " This is a sure sign that the discipline of timekeeping has been internalized!

For other recommendations on effective timekeeping, see Figure 14.10.

Computer programs have been developed to provide assistance in keeping track of time. In one program, for example, there is a menu on the screen that you use to tell the computer the following information (with relatively few keystrokes): what project you are working on, whether the time is billable, what client the project is for, the nature of the work you are doing, the time you begin the project, the times you are interrupted, and the completion time. An internal computer clock keeps track of the time until you tell it to stop and resume. You can also "input" costs connected with the case, such as postage and photocopying charges. The data you enter into the computer can be sent to the accounting department and to the supervising attorney for eventual billing. The computer can use the data in other ways as well, as the following discussion demonstrates.

> Computers . . . can take an initial item of data such as a specific transaction:
>
> Attorney RLR Met with client ACME to discuss research needs, 2 hours, July 2
>
> and use the data over and over again in various ways. For example, the data may be sorted by attorney to give a listing of all the hours worked by the attorney on that day, or in that month for all clients. It may be sorted by client to give a listing of all the hours worked for a particular client. It may be used to produce a preliminary or final bill. The data may be merged with other data to price the hours spent and to provide additional billing information. The same data may be matched with other data to list the total hours billed for the client that year or even total hours still unbilled. The Meeting With Client might be encoded as MWC and the firm, for whatever reason, might build statistics on how much meeting with clients occurred for all clients. . . .
>
> Computerization not only allows one entry to provide a great deal of output but it speeds the entry. Special codes can be used for such items as the name of the lawyer (RLR), the name of the client (ACME) and the type of work done (e.g., MWC, above). The user may not even need to enter a billing rate ($100 per hour) since some systems can automatically search the lawyer or client information to find a rate. Or the system may look at the transaction code (Processed Application for State Trademark abbreviated as AST) and disregard all hourly rates, using the $175 fixed fee automatically associated with that type of work. Some computer systems can keep track of the hours spent on all trade-

---

[8]Barcott, *Time Is Money*, AALA News (Alaska Ass'n of Legal Assistants, April 1990).

**FIGURE 14.10**

Effective
Timekeeping
Techniques[9]

- Always have your time sheet and pen at your side, ready for entries.
- If available, use a dictating machine for time only. Regularly tell the machine what you are doing—for example, as soon as you hang up the phone.
- When you begin a project, make a list of each task involved. Note the time you begin each task. Note the time of interruptions and the completion time. If additional tasks are needed for the project, add them to the list.
- In addition to a project list of tasks to be completed over a period of days, weeks, or longer, compile a **daily to-do list.** This will help you organize your day and focus on the time dimensions of what you do.
- Whenever possible, complete a project before moving on to another one. This facilitates timekeeping.
- Conduct your own study of your nonbillable hours, such as interruptions, pro bono work, interoffice conferences on administrative matters, breaks, clerical work, lunch. At the end of a pre-determined period, e.g., two weeks, identify the largest categories of your nonbillable time. Determine whether you can do anything to cut this time down. You may want to show your study to a supervisor to encourage him or her to delegate some of your nonbillable tasks to others who do not bill by the hour, or who bill at a lower rate than you do.

mark cases, multiply by the lawyer's basic rate and determine at the end of the year if the $175 fee is profitable for this type of work.

Entry by computer is also faster and easier. Computers prompt the operator for information and require it before allowing the operator to move on. The details are often immediately verified to see if they are consistent with other data in the computer. Correction speed is also improved. If a lawyer sees a printout of the work done for a client and realizes that there was an error, it can be easily corrected without much retyping. For example if an entry were made for a meeting with a client, when the meeting was actually with the client's witness, the error can usually be changed with a single entry. And all other places where the data are used are automatically changed as well.[10]

## Section E. Billing

There are least nine different methods of billing, according to the Law Practice Management Section of the American Bar Association. See Figure 14.11.

In addition to fees for services, a law firm usually recovers out-of-pocket expenses (called *disbursements* or costs) that the firm incurs while working on the case, e.g., court filing costs, witness fees, copying charges, long-distance phone calls, out-of-town transportation, and lodging for attorneys and paralegals.

The fees and costs to be paid by the client should be spelled out in the *retainer*. Unfortunately, not everyone uses this word in the same way. Its meaning should be made clear in the agreement between attorney and client. In a general sense, a retainer is the contract of employment between the attorney and client. More specifically, it sometimes refers to an amount of money paid to assure that an attorney will be available to work for a particular client, and

---

[9]Rucker, *Effective Timekeeping: A Legal Assistant's Point of View,* Newsletter (Houston Legal Assistants Ass'n, August 1987); Serrano, *The Member Connection,* Facts & Findings 7 (NALA, December 1986).

[10]P. Maggs & J. Sprowl, *Computer Applications in the Law,* 172–74 (1987).

- *Hourly Rate.* A designated amount per hour. An hourly rate is "bundled" if overhead is included in this rate. It is "unbundled" if the various charges are broken out separately.
- *Fixed Fee.* A flat fee for services.
- *Full Contingent Fee.* The amount of the fee is based on a percentage of the recovery, if any. This arrangement is often used in personal-injury cases.
- *Hourly Plus Fixed Fee.* A specified hourly rate is used until the nature and scope of the problem are defined, and a fixed fee is used thereafter.
- *Hourly Reduced or with Contingent.* A discounted hourly rate, sometimes combined with a contingent fee.
- *Blended Hourly Rate.* One rate is set depending on the mix of partners and associates working on the case.
- *Lodestar.* A lodestar is a mathematical formula used by federal courts and some state courts. It is based on a multiplier and relies on hourly rates and various other factors.
- *Value Billing.* The bill is not based solely on the time required to do the work. Instead, the amount to be paid is based on the complexity of a legal problem, the expertise it demands of an attorney, and on the sheer number of hours devoted to the matter. An estimate is often given to the client at the outset. This amount may eventually go higher or lower based on the factors used to determine value.
- *Percentage Fee.* The fee is a percentage of the amount involved in the transaction, such as the assets to be probated in an estate, the cost of real estate to be transferred, or the amount received as damages in a personal-injury case.

**FIGURE 14.11**

Methods of Billing[11]

hence unavailable to work for the client's competitor. When the attorney does work for the client, the latter pays fees in addition to the retainer, plus the out-of-pocket costs of the attorney. Another meaning of retainer is the amount of money or other assets paid by the client as a form of deposit or advance payment against future fees and costs. Additional money is paid only when the deposit or advance runs out. The agreement should specify whether money or other assets from the client are refundable if the client terminates the relationship because he or she decides not to pursue the matter.

The actual billing process differs from firm to firm, and occasionally differs from case to case within the same firm. Client billing sometimes occurs only after the matter is completed. More commonly, a client is billed monthly, quarterly, or semiannually. An administrator in the firm usually works with the billing attorney to prepare the bill. When a matter is called for billing, the administrator may prepare a billing memorandum (the *draft bill*) which specifies the disbursements of the firm in connection with the matter, plus the amount of time each attorney and paralegal has spent on the matter (along with the billing rate of each). For example:[12]

- *Attorney Jones: $1,000.* This attorney, who has a billing rate of $200 an hour, spent five hours on the matter. (5 × $200 = $1,000).

- *Attorney Smith: $800.* This attorney, who has a billing rate of $100 an hour, spent eight hours on the matter. (8 × $100 = $800).

- *Paralegal Kelly: $500.* This paralegal, who has a billing rate of $50 an hour, spent ten hours on the matter. (10 × $50 = $500).

---

[11]See Marcotte, *Billing Choices,* 75 American Bar Ass'n Journal 38 (November 1989); and *Value Billing Gaining Popularity,* Tennessee Bar Journal 9 (January/February 1990).
[12]Darby, *Of Firms and Fees: The Administrator's Role,* 8 Legal Management 34, 39 (March/April 1989).

The billing attorney has three choices: (1) Bill the total of the actual amounts. In our example, this would produce a bill of $2,300 ($1,000 + $800 + $500). (2) *Write-down* the matter by subtracting a certain amount, such as $300. This would produce a bill of $2,000. (3) *Write-up* the matter by adding an amount, such as $600. This would produce a bill of $2,900. This adjustment downwards or upwards is known as *valuing the bill.* An increase is sometimes called a premium adjustment; a decrease, a discount adjustment. The decision to adjust is based on factors such as the potential liability exposure of the firm (leading to a write-up) and the relative inexperience of an attorney or paralegal working on the matter (leading to a write-down). If, for example, recently hired attorneys or paralegals take an unusually long time to complete a task they never performed before, a write-down may be appropriate so that the client does not have to bear the full cost of their on-the-job training. See Figure 14.12 for an example of a bill sent to a client covering work of attorneys and paralegals on a matter.

##  Section F. Administrative Reports

There are different types of administrative reports that naturally "fall out" of the timekeeping and billing process. The more common reports used by law firms are:

1. Billable hours delinquent time reports
2. Billable hours analysis
3. Nonbillable time analysis
4. Accounts receivable reports
   a. Accounts receivable ledger
   b. Cash receipts journal
   c. Open invoice report
   d. Accounts receivable *aging report*[13]
      - billing by client (cumulative for a year)
      - billing by attorney (cumulative for a year)
   e. Departmental profitability analysis

These reports could be available on a regular schedule such as weekly, monthly, annually, or on request as needed. In any event, the raw data will be available and should be developed and stored in such a fashion as to accommodate easy retrieval, tabulation, and display for the legal administrator and managing partner, with summary totals being available for presentation to the entire firm. All this historical data can be compared to the results of the preceding year for the same period to measure quickly "how we are doing this year;" can be compared to the budget or any other acceptable benchmark; can be used as danger signals to prompt remedial action where appropriate; can be used as

---

[13]An *aging report* is one of the most common reports developed by accountants to provide management with the time outstanding of accounts receivables. For example, an *aged accounts receivable* will set forth how many of the total receivables are less than thirty days old, how many are thirty to fifty-nine days old, how many are sixty to ninety days old, and how many are more than ninety days old. It is a truism that the older an account receivable is, the less collectable it is. Therefore, management needs to know how old the account is in order to put the emphasis on collecting it before it becomes so old that it is worthless.

**FIGURE 14.12**
Bill Sent to Client Involving Attorney and Paralegal Services

Rubin, Rinke, Pyeumac & Craigmoyle
1615 Broadway, Suite 1400
Oakland, California 94612-2115
(415) 444-5316
Tax ID 94-2169491

April 10, 1991

IBM Corporation
Norm Savage
3133 Northside Parkway
Atlanta  GA  33033

Statement for Professional Services Rendered

Re:  Chapter 11                                                  (IBM-1)
     Reorganization

Description of services

04/17/91    Receipt and review of contracts regarding Ar-
            monk home office liquidation.

04/18/91    Meeting with opposing attorney regarding
            court appearance in Atlanta in late October
            of 1991.

04/21/91    Receipt and review of depositions from seven
            hundred forty three (743) claimants to Austin
            plant parking facilities.

04/22/91    Meeting with officers of the corporation to dis-
            cuss liquidation of office furniture in all
            branch offices. Scheduling of 2000 simultane-
            ous garage sales in marketing managers'
            driveways to be advertised during next year's
            Super Bowl.

| | | Total for legal services rendered | $797.50 |
|---|---|---|---|

| | Hours | Rate | |
|---|---|---|---|
| Partners | 4.00 | 125 | 500.00 |
| Paralegals | 3.50 | 85 | 297.50 |

Reimbursable expenses

| Date | Description | Amount |
|---|---|---|
| 04/17/91 | Lunch meeting with opposing attorney. | 185.17 |
| 04/27/91 | Atlanta Bankruptcy Court filing fee due September 1, 1990. | 55.00 |
| 04/29/91 | Photocopies. | 5.69 |
| 04/29/91 | Long distance telephone charges. | 36.90 |
| | Total expenses | $282.76 |
| | Total current charges | $1080.26 |

**Source:** Computer Software for Professionals, Inc., LEGALMASTER

the basis for compensation schedules; can provide the firm with all necessary data for complying with government regulations (such as tax laws governing the firm's income); and can be used as a general audit and control device.

A well-thought-out system should give the managers of the law firm effective control and provide additional meaningful data for:

1. Firm Management Reports
   a. Firm activity and work status
   b. Summary aging of work in progress
   c. Summary aging of uncollected bills
   d. Summary of billings and realizations
   e. Uncollected bills written off
   f. Nonlegal staff charges to work in progress
2. Practice Analysis Reports[14]
   a. Staff utilization
   b. Attorney practice experience
3. Partner Responsibility Reports
   a. Partners' work in progress summary
   b. Partners' work in progress aging
   c. Partners' uncollected bills
   d. Partners' billing and realizations
4. Work in Progress and Billing Reports
   a. Work in progress ledger—detail
   b. Work in progress disbursements—detail
   c. Billing memorandum
   d. Delinquent diaries
   e. Client billing history
5. Special Purpose Reports
   a. Billings by introducing attorney
   b. Billings by assigned attorney
   c. Allocations to prior partnerships
6. Special Management Reports as Required

One of the reports that could be generated from the basic timekeeping records is an analysis of how much time paralegals are investing in client matters. This analysis is the same kind of analysis that the firm would want regarding time invested by attorneys. Sometimes large firms also keep track of time invested by secretaries and other nonattorneys, but generally this is not done. More commonly, firms keep track of attorney time and paralegal time spent on client matters. Firms need time expenditures in order to evaluate profit centers, costs, allocation of work among attorneys and paralegals, etc.

. . . . . . . . . . . . . .

---

[14]A "practice analysis report" can be very helpful to a firm. It analyzes where the firm is investing its time, how much money it is earning from specific areas of the practice, where its costs lie, and hence how much profit is being earned from the various areas of practice. Specifically, a practice analysis could develop such information for probate practice, litigation practice, general corporate practice, banking practice, antitrust practice—any of the "specialties" that are identifiable within a firm. Beyond the economic impact, the firm can use these "practice analysis reports" to be sure that all are carrying their fair share of work.

We will now examine representative formats for some reports that are often used in law office administration.

## Work Summary

Each attorney in the firm should routinely complete a form such as that illustrated in Figure 14.13, "Work Summary," so that the managing partner of the firm can evaluate the workload of the firm each week. The managing partner should then be able to assign new work or reallocate work to attorneys on the basis of this Work Summary in conjunction with a review of time utilization reports developed from the timekeeping system. Paralegals also fill out Work Summary sheets, depending on the nature of the work they're doing. If they are working for many attorneys in one department, the department head and the paralegal supervisor, if any, often require copies of the Work Summary report in order to keep track of the work being done.

## Cash Flow Projection

Many firms have cash flow problems, but only a few use mathematical methods to determine projected needs. One approach, as suggested by the form in Figure 14.14, is to determine anticipated cash receipts for the period under consideration by adding to the ending cash balance a certain percentage of new billings (the firm can anticipate payment within thirty days from approximately 50% of new billings, with the remaining bills being paid over a sixty-day to one-year period, depending on the firm's attentiveness to receivable collections), plus the anticipated collection from the more than sixty-day old account receivables, to arrive at "total estimated cash resources," from which the firm can subtract out-of-pocket costs anticipated for the time period, and arrive at a "projected cash balance." The firm can then quickly determine whether it needs

**FIGURE 14.13**
Work Summary

**FIGURE 14.14**

Cash Flow
Projection

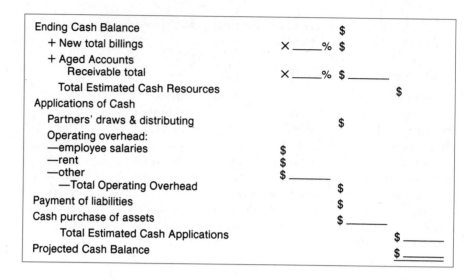

to borrow supplemental cash from the bank, or cut overhead, or take whatever remedial action may be necessary.

### Chargeable Hour Schedule

The Chargeable Hour Schedule summarizes the actual hours invested by the attorneys and paralegals on a month-by-month basis (see Figure 14.15). To refine this schedule further and make it more informative, multiply hours by billing rates to arrive at a total dollar value of an attorney's or a paralegal's investment in the practice each month.

### Aged Accounts Receivable

A list of clients, showing the amount due from each client as of a specified date, is known as a Schedule of Accounts Receivable. This schedule can be refined to indicate the number of days outstanding since the original billing date, normally into the following categories: 0–29 days old, 30–59 days old, 60–90 days old, and older than 90 days. This now becomes known as the Aged Accounts Receivable report.

The schedule in Figure 14.16 is common throughout most businesses. Law firms generally do not develop such a schedule, yet this can be a critical tool in the collection process. It should be prepared each month so that the managing partner and legal administrator can quickly determine where a special effort may be needed in the collection process, evaluate the status of receivables, and adjust cash-flow predictions in accordance with the status of the receivables.

### Budget Reports

The annual budget should be one of the very first items management develops. It can be combined with income statements to give the firm current information on the firm's financial health. See Figure 14.17. Traditionally, law firms have had little understanding or control over their financial destiny and, as a consequence, they generally tend to react to problems on a crisis basis. The use of an annual budget and other such planning tools would virtually eliminate or greatly minimize crises throughout the year. The trend is for law firms to be

**FIGURE 14.15**

Chargeable Hour Schedule

| | Jan. | Feb. | Mar. | April | May | June | July | Aug. | Sept. | Oct. | Nov. | Dec. | Total |
|---|---|---|---|---|---|---|---|---|---|---|---|---|---|
| Partners: | | | | | | | | | | | | | |
| A | | | | | | | | | | | | | |
| B | | | | | | | | | | | | | |
| C | | | | | | | | | | | | | |
| D | | | | | | | | | | | | | |
| Total Partners | | | | | | | | | | | | | |
| Associates: | | | | | | | | | | | | | |
| A | | | | | | | | | | | | | |
| B | | | | | | | | | | | | | |
| C | | | | | | | | | | | | | |
| D | | | | | | | | | | | | | |
| E | | | | | | | | | | | | | |
| F | | | | | | | | | | | | | |
| G | | | | | | | | | | | | | |
| Total Associates | | | | | | | | | | | | | |
| Paralegals: | | | | | | | | | | | | | |
| A | | | | | | | | | | | | | |
| B | | | | | | | | | | | | | |
| C | | | | | | | | | | | | | |
| Total Paralegals | | | | | | | | | | | | | |
| TOTAL FIRM | | | | | | | | | | | | | |

more and more businesslike in their management style, and many firms will probably be implementing more sophisticated budgetary procedures.

## Section G. The Procedures Manual in a Small Office: Mail, Copying, and Filing

Law offices often have a procedures manual to cover different aspects of law office administration. The following excerpts are from a manual in a relatively small firm.[15]

### Incoming Mail

Before touching sophisticated areas, the manual should start with some fairly straightforward routines. A prime candidate is incoming mail. A suggested statement for the manual begins at the top of page 709.

---

[15]Adapted from Light, *The Procedure Manual: Mail, Copying and Filing Rules*, 26 The Practical Lawyer 71 (January 1980). Copyright 1980 by the American Law Institute. Reprinted with permission of The Practical Lawyer.

**FIGURE 14.16**

Aged Accounts
Receivable
Billed—Not Yet
Collected

| Billing Attorney | Client Name | Legal Services | Disburse-ments | Total Due | | Current To 30 Days | 31– 60 Days | 61– 90 Days | 91–180 Days | More Than 6 Mos. Old |
|---|---|---|---|---|---|---|---|---|---|---|
| | (Alphabetic listing by client) " " " " " | $ | $ | $ | | $ | $ | $ | $ | $ |
| | TOTAL, ALL CLIENTS % Distribution | $ % | $ % | $ 100% | | $ % | $ % | $ % | $ % | $ % |
| | TOTAL RECAP BY BILLING ATTORNEY | | | | % to total | | | | | |
| | (Total by billing lawyer) " " " | $ | $ | $ | % % % % | $ | $ | $ | $ | $ |
| | TOTAL ALL LAWYERS | | | | 100% | | | | | |

**FIGURE 14.17**

Income Statement with Budget

```
11/16/86                      CLARK, LOWREY & SMITH
PERIOD 9                      ATTORNEYS AT LAW                              PAGE 1

                      INCOME STATEMENT WITH BUDGET
```

| ACCT NO | DESCRIPTION | CURRENT PERIOD | | | | YEAR TO DATE | | | |
|---|---|---|---|---|---|---|---|---|---|
| | | THIS YEAR | % | BUDGET | % | THIS YEAR | % | BUDGET | % |
| | INCOME | | | | | | | | |
| | INCOME ACCRUAL | | | | | | | | |
| 400 | FEES: INCOME FROM CLIENTS | 42356.00 | | 19000.00 | | 229247.57 | | 228000.00 | |
| 460 | OTHER INCOME/RECEIPTS | 1836.23 | | 700.00 | | 9232.88 | | 8400.00 | |
| 480 | INCOME PRODUCING PROPERTY | .00 | | 350.00 | | 3790.00 | | 4200.00 | |
| | TOTAL INCOME ACCRUAL | 44192.23 | | 20050.00 | | 242270.37 | | 240600.00 | |
| | EXPENSES | | | | | | | | |
| | PAYROLL | | | | | | | | |
| 500 | SALARY: SECRETARIAL | 2975.30 | 6.7 | 1500.00 | 7.5 | 17851.00 | 7.4 | 18000.00 | 7.5 |
| 501 | SALARY: WORD/DATA PROC. | 1100.00 | 2.5 | 650.00 | 3.2 | 7556.45 | 3.1 | 7800.00 | 3.2 |
| 502 | SALARY: PARALG & CLERKS | 1875.18 | 4.2 | 2000.00 | 10.0 | 20632.15 | 8.5 | 24000.00 | 10.0 |
| 503 | SALARY: ATTORNEYS | 11400.00 | 25.8 | 6000.00 | 29.9 | 68400.00 | 28.2 | 72000.00 | 29.9 |
| 504 | SALARY: OTH NON-OWN EMPL | 1050.00 | 2.4 | 700.00 | 3.5 | 7804.00 | 3.2 | 8400.00 | 3.5 |
| | TOTAL PAYROLL | 18400.48 | 41.6 | 10850.00 | 54.1 | 122244.40 | 50.5 | 130200.00 | 54.1 |
| | NON-PAYROLL EMPLOYEE COSTS | | | | | | | | |
| 510 | FICA & UNEMPLOY TAXES | 838.77 | 1.9 | 420.00 | 2.1 | 5038.77 | 2.1 | 5020.00 | 2.1 |
| 514 | RETIREMENT BENEFITS | 746.00 | 1.7 | 370.00 | 1.8 | 4446.00 | 1.8 | 4440.00 | 1.8 |
| 518 | TRAINING & EDUCATION | 250.00 | .6 | 300.00 | 1.5 | 3660.00 | 1.5 | 3600.00 | 1.5 |
| 519 | OTHER EMPLOYEE COSTS | .00 | .0 | 150.00 | .7 | 1674.00 | .7 | 1800.00 | .7 |
| | TOTAL NON-PAYROLL EMPL COST | 1834.77 | 4.2 | 1240.00 | 6.2 | 14818.77 | 6.1 | 14860.00 | 6.2 |
| | OCCUPANCY EXPENSES | | | | | | | | |
| 520 | OFFICE RENT | 2940.00 | 6.7 | 750.00 | 3.7 | 10290.00 | 4.2 | 9000.00 | 3.7 |
| 521 | PARKING | 240.00 | .5 | 80.00 | .4 | 1003.85 | .4 | 960.00 | .4 |
| 523 | REAL EST TAXES & INS | 382.00 | .9 | 185.00 | .9 | 2245.78 | .9 | 2200.00 | .9 |

**Source:** Computer Legal Systems, Inc.

## Mail: Incoming

In addition to sorting mail by addressee, the individual responsible for the morning mail should:

1. Date-stamp *everything* with the "Received" stamp. Exceptions are books received on approval or original documents such as deeds that have been mailed to the office for recording or filing elsewhere. Whenever possible, stamp the date in the same location on every document. This will make it easier for someone to read the dates when perusing through a large file.

2. When an incoming document requires reference to previous papers, place the appropriate file with it.

3. If you can draft a response to the incoming document, prepare a draft and place it with the document.

4. Return receipts for certified mail should be stapled to the copies of the documents to which they correspond.

5. File the following documents immediately without circulation:
   - Pocket parts or supplements to treatises in the library.
   - All loose-leaf page supplements.
   - The paperback supplements to the state statutes and the United States Code Annotated or United States Code Service.

6. For informational purposes, prepare a "Daily Checks and Bills Received" sheet using the format in Figure 14.18.

Incoming mail may have to be photocopied and distributed to others—for example, to paralegals for specific assignments or to clients for their information. In some firms, special stamps are used such as the following:

### FOR INFORMATION ONLY—NO ACTION REQUIRED

## Copying Charges

Failure to record legitimate copying charges for later billing to the client constitutes a drain on the firm's financial resources.

1. Register on the alphabetical list that is kept on or near the copying machine the client's name, if not already there, and the number of copies.

2. Copies that are not to be charged to any client should be noted as "office" copies or "N/C" copies.

---

**FIGURE 14.18**
Daily Checks and Bills Received

| **Received on January 6, 1991** | | |
|---|---|---|
| **CHECKS** | | |
| Hammerlee | (title search) | $380.00 |
| Mid-Penn | 136.55 C.A. | 3961.43 |
| PNB | 164.80 C.A. | 724.80 |
| Kalp, Arn | 2.25 C.A. | 62.25 |
| **BILLS** | | |
| Wagners | (clips and rubber stamps) | 12.72 |
| Rec'd vol. 97 of *Supreme Court Reporter* | | N/C |

3. On at least a monthly basis, the member of the staff who is responsible for copy charges should post them to the respective client accounts.

## Filing System

### *Rules and Comments*

The importance of a good filing system cannot be overestimated. Lost and misplaced papers are the obvious result of a poor system. But the damage can run even deeper. Deadlines can be missed, leading to one of the most common causes of malpractice claims against attorneys. Hours may be lost in ferreting through files for crucial documents that cannot be found. Appellate briefs might be poorly prepared because files are not in a readily usable form that would allow drafters to gather information and prepare the briefs in an orderly fashion. Particular tasks might be overlooked because attorneys, often subconsciously, dread having to search for needed information or simply do not know how to tell a member of the staff to compile what is needed.

Some firms use an exclusively *alphabetical filing system*. For example, all the documents for the Allen Construction Corporation case would be filed just before all the documents for the Allenson estate case. Such a system is not as effective as a *numerical filing system* accompanied by an alphabetical card index. Here is an example of the categories of cases (or client matters) that could be used in a numerical filing system:

| | |
|---|---|
| 001–099 | Large clients |
| 100–199 | Wills and estate planning |
| 200–349 | Real estate: purchase and sale |
| 350–399 | Estate administration and trusts |
| 400–499 | Domestic relations, excluding divorce and custody masterships |
| 500–549 | Personal injury, including worker's compensation |
| 600–649 | Litigation, excluding personal injury |
| 700–749 | Corporations and partnerships |
| 750–799 | Financing, bonds, industrial developments, and similar matters |
| 800–849 | Tax, excluding estate planning |
| 900–999 | Miscellaneous files not appropriate for any other category |
| 1000–1499 | Printed forms, applications, and other miscellaneous documents |
| 1500–1999 | Bar Association and non-client-related matters |
| 2000–2049 | Bankruptcy |
| 2100–2149 | Divorce and custody masterships and arbitration panels |
| 2200–2299 | Criminal matters |

These numerical categories vary widely from office to office according to size and type of practice. Large firms spread the brackets and use higher numbers. A two digit number representing the year would precede each of the number categories. Hence, 92.287 would be a real estate matter opened in 1992. Anytime a significant block of cases does not fit within a particular category, it is relatively easy to create a new category.

A numerical filing system with an alphabetical card index is preferable since it:

- Reduces the misplacement of files. For some reason, individuals are more likely to place files in correct numerical order than in correct alphabetical order. For example, a purely alphabetical system would have difficulty handling the industrial development project for a client named Jones who owns North Marine Industries involving a local development agency bearing the acronym SIFT. While someone may think of the project as "Jones: SIFT-North Marine Industries," others may look for the file under "North Marine Industries: SIFT." Cross-referencing within a card index (see below) almost eliminates this problem when a numerical filing system is used.

■ Permits the grouping of files by subject matter, such as litigation or real estate. Such a system can be useful if, for example, the firm wants to contact all clients for whom wills were prepared within the past five years.

■ Allows easier reference on memoranda, correspondence, and client lists. It is certainly simpler to jot "86.267" on a title abstract sheet than "Stankiewicz: Purchase of Real Estate (1986).

■ Allows cross-referencing within the card index. The index cards *can* be alphabetical. You can create cards under any variety of headings that you think a user might try to use. Each card would refer to the files under their numerical entry.

■ Automatically brings old files to the front of the filing system, acting almost as a tickler system.

■ Allows the immediate identification of the year of a particular file by the first two digits of the file index, such as, "86.589" for a 1986 file.

■ Facilitates the differentiation of files that may have confusingly similar designations. "Jones: Personal Injury (1981)" and "Jones: Property Settlement Agreement (1983)" would probably be stored next to one another in an *alphabetical* system and would have the tendency not only to be filed in the wrong alphabetical order but to attract each other's papers. But in a *numerical* system, although the index cards would probably be neighbors, the physical separation of the folders in the file cabinet would be more likely to prevent the misplacing of documents among the files.[16]

■ Adapts to computerization, when that time comes (see next section).

■ Eases the handling of closed files. Under an alphabetical system, when the firm is ready to "retire" a particular file, two choices are available—continue to file alphabetically, or switch to a sequential closed-file numbering system, with files placed one after the other as they are closed, regardless of their alphabetical designations. The first choice leads to the situation in which all the files from I through Z have to be moved if H grows rapidly (for example, nobody anticipated that the Half-Penny National Bank would become the firm's most active client). The second alternative requires an alphabetical card index to allow for the retrieval of particular closed files. It would already exist under the numerical system.

Depending on the size of the office, a library-like system may be needed in which files are checked out of the file room in much the same manner that books are checked out of a library. While administratively burdensome, this system at

---

[16]One possible difficulty with a numerical filing system is the confusion of file 91.325 with file 92.325. The multicolored file folders that are available from stationery suppliers offer a ready solution to this potential problem. If blue folders were used for 1991, red for 1992, and green for 1993, a file is not likely to be misplaced, and if it is in the wrong spot, it will stand out. In order to have the benefit of a fully integrated system, color-matching index cards should be used for the alphabetical index.

least ensures an ability to trace missing files. Overly strict measures, however, might backfire. For example, an attempt to prevent attorneys from ever holding files in their office might discourage them from initially storing any of their files in the filing room.

### Closed Files

The filing cabinets in the main office contain only files on which work is being done, on which work is likely to be done in the near future, or that are likely to be used for reference in a current matter. Closed file procedures are designed to save active file space as well as allow for easy retrieval of retired information. Theoretically, if the firm's practice is stable, its main filing cabinets should maintain a constant size, while the real accumulation of paper occurs in the closed file storage area.

Generally, only the billing attorney may declare a file closed. Such a decision is not crucial or irreversible because the file can be retrieved easily. It is better to close a file than to keep it around. The fewer the active files, the more manageable the filing system.

When a file is to be closed, one way to do it is to "Pendaflex" it to the individual responsible for file closings, who then:

1. Assigns a CF (closed file) number to the file. This will be the next number for the year, with the first file closed during the calendar year 1992 receiving the number CF 92.001.
2. Places the CF number on the file's alphabetical index cards.
3. Writes the CF number on the file label.
4. Places the file in the "upstairs" CF filing drawer. The upstairs CF filing drawer contains recently closed files that may be needed. These files are sent upstairs for a time, before being relegated to the basement or other permanent storage area.

The closed files are permanently stored in boxes clearly labeled with the first and last CF file number. To retrieve a closed file, simply check the alphabetical index card, obtain the CF number, and find the file in storage. In some firms, closed files are placed on microfilm after a designated time. Most of the original file is then destroyed. Future access and copying of such files are achieved through microfilm readers and printers.

## ■ Section H. Computer-Based Records Management System in a Large Office

**How One Law Firm Automated Its Records Management**

Patricia Patterson, Director of Legal Information Services,
Schiff Hardin & Waite, Chicago, Illinois
21 American Association of Law Libraries Newsletter 291 (April 1991)

By the end of the next decade, it is likely that all records managers will have considered, tested, or installed some sort of computer-based records management system. From the smallest to the most complex central file system, computer automation offers the possibility of a cost-effective method for increasing management efficiency. But for many records information managers, jumping into a computerized system may not be conceptually or economically feasible at this time. Their problems probably fall into one or more of the following categories:

1. Insufficient financial resources to purchase a completely computerized system.

2. A non-standard records system that may require a specially customized computer program.

3. Management reluctant to commit to a new way of doing business.

4. Records personnel must be retrained, at great time and expense, to become computer literate and understand a computer system.

If your situation falls into one of these categories, you can take it upon yourself to solve some of these problems.

First of all, and let me emphasize [that] a successfully Automated Records Management System is:

- User Designed and Implemented
- Easy to Use and Accessible
- Online in Real Time
- Multi-User (Multiple/Simultaneous Users)
- Application Based and Controlled
- Management Supported

Using my own experience as a working example, I would like to discuss each of these criteria.

When I assumed the responsibilities of the Schiff Hardin and Waite Records Department, I inherited a large problem. Data entry operators had been employed three years prior to my arrival to capture our 350,000 3 × 5 card file information onto magnetic tape. The Records Department was behind in its duties of opening new files, tracking file locations, and checking for conflicts of interest. In addition, the Records Department still had two people keying all of the file card and cross reference card information into batches of data onto magnetic type. Management directed me to guide the department into the twenty-first century by installing a computer system capable of using the data that the firm had spent significant time and money on over the previous four years. My background was in library management, and I was responsible for the Schiff library, so I was accustomed to working with large volumes of information.

My first task was to select a computer company to convert the data stored on nine reels of magnetic tape. We needed this data reformatted into a structure that could be loaded to an online database. Over 350,000 records of data had been keyed with very little control over checking the validity of client numbers, dates, attorney numbers, etc. Previous computer consultants employed by Schiff had not thoroughly planned for the next step. That being the case and with the keying of data nearly complete, an implementation decision was needed.

At that time, we contacted the firm of Micom Systems, Inc., of North Muskegon, Michigan. Micom had been doing custom programming and computer services work for law firms since 1969. Their proposal to convert our data to a database format and clean up the duplicate entries and as much of the erroneous

editing as possible was accepted by the firm in the fall of 1987. Micom, using its IBM 4341 computer and IBM assembler language, converted the data by January, 1988.

My next task was to select an online database on which to use our newly converted data. After researching all of the records management software packages on the market, we concluded that they were inappropriate for our application. Because of Micom's knowledge of our data and experience with online law firm systems, we selected them to develop our records management system. With our data now ready for use, and after years of keying in the data, we were naturally anxious for the system to be operational. However, Schiff's two IBM System 36s were filled to capacity with litigation support and accounting functions. There was no room for a 250 million-character records management system on either of our two computer systems. Therefore, we chose to install communications equipment and a dedicated 9600 baud line to Micom's IBM mainframe 200 miles from our Chicago office.

Micom personnel studied our information storage and reporting needs. They then designed our system to meet current, as well as future needs. Operational requirements and key functions of the system included:

1. All data from the conversion loaded and accessible.

2. User-friendly system with a short learning curve.

3. An adaptable system that could be changed quickly and easily.

4. Online interactive with additions, changes, and deletions immediately available.

5. Online conflict of interest searching with results printed on demand.

6. File cards and labels printed online using local printers.

7. Accommodation of the complex structured file identification system Schiff already had in place.

As I will list later on, the records management system has many features that address our information needs. The key ones, previously stated, were the driving force behind Micom selecting IBM CSP (Cross System Product) as its development language. Because of CSP's ability to run across IBM platforms, Micom could develop and initially run the system on their IBM mainframe. Then when Schiff installs an IBM AS/400 or networked IBM PS/2s, Micom can port the system to run on either of these computer systems. This software portability across platforms was a positive factor in our decision to use Micom to develop our system.

The Schiff requirements for an automated records management system originated from attorney needs and expectations. Accurate and thorough conflict checking is a necessity and rates the highest priority. Our system provides timely and complete new client screening based on all of the data stored in the records management system. Our attorneys need rapid opening of new files and swift retrieval of stored files. We have the ability to track folders and identify files easily and quickly with very few keystrokes or screen changes. Quick locating of a client's file folders is important whether the file is located in someone's office or in a box at an off-site storage facility. Attorney and secretary requests for file locations and identifications are handled by our staff of 11 using this system. Most requests of this type are handled by phone. New, revised, or additional file labels are printed on demand by the Records Center staff.

Our system has performed as we had hoped it would, allowing us to proceed with add-on enhancements. For example, we are now in the installation phase of a bar coding subsystem. This will enable us to print a bar code label with a unique client/matter number for each file created in the Records Center. Using a fixed scanner in our Records Department, we will scan the bar codes of all folders that leave the Records Center. Both the location and file folder identification will be scanned online directly into the computer system. All file folders leaving the Records Center at night will be batch-scanned into an IBM PS/2 and transferred to the IBM mainframe the next morning. Periodically we will scan all folders in attorneys'

offices using portable, hand-held scanners. This procedure will give us the ability to track folder movements between attorney offices.

One feature of our system which saves additional time is the box storage system. This system tracks all box storage; both on, and off-site. Folder movement into and out of boxes is monitored, as are all pick-ups and deliveries. This system provides us with reports of all pick-ups and deliveries by date to enable us to verify our warehouse service bill more easily.

The Conflict of Interest System deserves more comment. This system is fully integrated into our Records Management System. Our personnel can hot key to the full text search process at any time. Then, using . . . commands, they can completely search our file records data. The data is displayed in our record structure format with the "hits" highlighted. We also have the ability to print any or all of the occurrences immediately. This efficient system has saved us countless hours of work.

While you may not be ready to adopt the automated records system that I have described, I hope the process we went through at Schiff Hardin and Waite will alert you to the advantages offered by computerized records management systems. Just be certain that the system you select addresses your specific information needs. The future is upon us, and we must knowledgeably embrace the technology on which it is based.

Scanning coded files in records department

### ■ ASSIGNMENT 14.1

In the practice of law, time is money. Hence you must develop the discipline of recording your time. Supervisors will later decide what portions of your time are billable—and to what clients. Step one is to compile a record of your time.

To practice this discipline, fill out a Daily Time Sheet for a day that you select. On *one* sheet of paper, record (in a chart form that you design) everything (approximately) that you do *in six minute* intervals over a continuous eight-hour period. Once you design your chart, *it should take you no more than about fifteen minutes to fill it out* during the eight-hour period. You do not, however, fill it out at one time; you fill it out at appropriate times throughout the eight hours.

Select an eight-hour period in which you are engaged in a fairly wide variety of activities. If possible, avoid an eight-hour period that contains any single activity lasting over two hours. Draw a chart covering the eight-hour period. At the top of the chart, place your name, the date of the eight-hour period that you used, and the starting/ending times of the eight-hour period. The period can be within a school day, a workday, a day of leisure, etc.

Using abbreviations, make specific entries on your activities within the eight hours—in six-minute intervals. For example, "Reading a chapter in a real estate school text" might be abbreviated as RE-R. "Driving to school" might be abbreviated as D-Sch. "Purely personal matters" (such as taking a shower) might be abbreviated as PPM. You decide what the abbreviations are. On the back of the sheet of paper containing the chart, explain what the abbreviations mean. When an activity is repeated in more than one six-minute interval, simply repeat the abbreviation.

One format for the chart might be a series of vertical and horizontal lines on the sheet of paper. This will give you a small amount of space on which to insert your abbreviations for each six-minute interval. Design the chart any way that you want, keeping in mind the goal of the exercise: to enable someone else to know what you did within the eight-hour period.

On page 697, there is an example of a Daily Time Sheet (Figure 14.6) used in a law office. Note that the last column says "hours" and "10ths." A 10th of an hour is six minutes. Do *not* follow the format in Figure 14.6. Use the guidelines listed above, e.g., place your abbreviations on the other side of the sheet of paper that you submit.

### ■ ASSIGNMENT 14.2

Mary Davis is a paralegal who has been working at the law firm of Smith & Smith for five years. The firm consists of two attorneys, Sam and Karen Smith, a husband and wife attorney team. There is one other employee, Jane Jones, who has just been hired as a paralegal trainee. This person, a high school graduate, was a homemaker for fifteen years. She has had no outside employment or training. The firm has one secretary who spends most of his time typing bills to be sent to clients and acting as the receptionist.

Smith & Smith has a family-law practice, handling mostly divorces. It takes two main kinds of cases: (1) contested divorces, where the husband and wife cannot agree on one or more critical issues (such as custody, property division, or amount of alimony); and (2) uncontested divorces, where everything is agreed on. While most of the firm's clients are plaintiffs who have filed for divorce, the firm also represents defendants on occasion.

Uncontested cases involve a fair amount of paperwork plus at least one court appearance, where the attorney obtains the approval of the court on what the parties have agreed to do. Contested cases involve extensive paperwork and many court appearances in which the disputed issues are resolved by the court—unless a settlement is eventually reached by the parties.

Almost every case requires the preparation of the following documents:

- Retainer (in which the client hires the firm)
- Intake Interview Report (reporting on a long interview with the client, during which extensive information is obtained about spouses, children, addresses, employment, facts of marriage, length of time in the county, bank accounts, residences, cars, other property owned, family health conditions, kinds of insurance, stocks, bonds, pension plans, debts already incurred, budget data, etc.)
- Complaint (stating the grounds for divorce)
- Answer (responding to the complaint)
- Letters to opposing counsel requesting information
- Motions to the court requesting temporary alimony or maintenance, child custody and support, and attorney fees
- Motion for a Restraining Order (to prevent either side from transferring assets and to prevent harassment)
- Motion to Produce (a formal request that the other side turn over designated items, such as pay stubs, copies of tax returns, bank statements, and insurance policies)
- Agreement on Property Division, Custody, and Support (uncontested cases only, unless a settlement is eventually reached in contested cases)
- Interrogatories (in which one party sends written questions to the other)
- A Notice of Deposition (informing the other to appear at a designated place, such as at the office of one of the attorneys, to answer questions)
- Proposed Final Decree of Dissolution of the Marriage

In the office, Mary prepares the Intake Interview Report based on an interview that she conducts with the client. This occurs after the retainer is signed and one of the attorneys goes over the case with the client. Mary prepares the first draft of all the other documents listed above.

Mary conducts the intake interview with the client alone. Since she has done so many of these interviews, she knows from memory what questions to ask. When she was first hired, she watched the attorneys interview and so learned what to ask and how to conduct an interview on her own. Whenever anything unusual came up during the interview, she left the room to find one of the attorneys for guidance. She took extensive notes on what the client said and later typed her notes for the Intake Interview Report.

Whenever Mary needed to draft one of the documents, she went to the firm's closed-case files to try to find a model that she could adapt. Since she had legal research skills, she also sought help from texts (such as practice books) found in the law library. The more experienced Mary became, however, the less she had to resort to the old files and the law library. The attorneys were amazed at her ability to find and retain whatever she needed to prepare so many different kinds of documents. They developed tremendous trust in Mary. For many cases, the documents never seemed to vary except for the names of the parties and particular financial figures. A fair number of times, however, different situations arose—for example, the parties had prior marriages or a child was retarded and therefore required special care following the divorce. Starting from scratch, Mary used her experience and skills to draft the proper documents to accommodate these situations.

Mary was also responsible for opening case files for all new clients. Each time the firm accepted a client, she took an accordion folder and typed the name of the client on it. Scattered throughout the folder were handwritten notes (from Mary or the attorney in charge of the case) describing some event that was relevant to the case. The documents were not placed in the folder in any particular order. This, however, did not create much difficulty since Mary was so familiar with all of the files. Only occasionally were things lost or misfiled.

The reason that the firm has decided to hire another paralegal is that Mary has announced that in six months she is going to leave the firm for another position. The receptionist also gave notice that he is leaving. Neither is dissatisfied with the firm; it is simply time to move on. The firm tried to find an experienced paralegal to replace Mary, but could not. Hence it just hired Jane Jones who, as indicated, has had no experience or training. The firm will replace the receptionist with a full-time typist and a full-time receptionist who will also be available for messenger assignments.

The firm is in a panic. The caseload is increasing at a rapid pace. There is some talk of hiring an additional attorney who has just graduated from law school and passed the bar, but no definite decision has yet been made. The big worry is the effect of Mary's departure in six months.

Sam Smith's solution is to have Jane Jones, the paralegal trainee, follow Mary around, observing everything Mary does during her last six months in the hope of absorbing as much as possible.

Karen Smith has a different approach. "Why don't we create some management systems and then train everyone on them?" Sam is very skeptical, but willing to listen.

Assume that you work for a law office management consulting firm. Karen and Sam Smith have asked you to prepare a report on how the office can systematize and manage its divorce practice so that Jane Jones—and *anyone* else—can come in, learn the system on their own (or almost on their own), and become functioning members of the team.

State how you would go about handling this task. If you think more than one system is needed, describe what they are. What facts do you want to obtain on how the firm now operates? How would you go about getting these facts? State any problems that you anticipate in obtaining these facts and how these problems might be resolved. Then describe what you would do with what you learn. State how the system or systems would operate. Give examples. Detail any problems you anticipate in implementing the system or systems and how these problems might be handled. If you feel that the firm needs different kinds of equipment, describe what is needed and how it would be used within the system or systems that you propose. State the benefits that the system(s) might provide. Also describe any difficulties that might exist in the system(s). In short, provide a comprehensive but realistic report. Don't try to oversell what you propose. Assume that the main audience of your report will be attorneys who are uninformed about the management dimensions of a law office.

## ☐ Chapter Summary

Our examination of law office administration began with an overview of the different settings in which attorneys practice law in the private sector in the United States and of the different kinds of attorneys found in each setting.

A sole practice consists of one attorney who owns the practice even if he or she employs other attorneys. The others do not share in the profits and losses of the firm. To save on expenses, several sole practitioners may enter into an office-sharing arrangement under which the attorneys share expenses for office space, secretarial help, library materials, etc.

In a partnership, the equity or capital partners share in the profits and losses of the firm and control its management, often through a committee or department structure. Associates are attorneys in the firm who hope one day to be invited to become partners. There are, however, special categories of associates created for those who do not become

*(Continued on next page)*

## ☐ Chapter Summary *(Continued)*

partners, such as senior associate and permanent associate.

Other categories of attorneys who might be hired by a law firm include staff attorneys, of-counsel attorneys, and contract attorneys. For tax and estate-planning purposes, many states allow attorneys to practice law as a professional corporation. There is little practical difference, however, between the administration of a partnership and a professional corporation.

Finally, there are attorneys who practice law in the legal departments of corporations. They are employees of the corporation, which is their sole client.

Large law offices may have many nonattorney employees to help manage the office. These employees have become increasingly influential because of the sharp rise in overhead costs in recent years. Among the most prominent is the Legal Administrator. Also, if there are more than a few paralegals in the office, a Legal Assistant Manager is often hired to help administer the office's system for recruiting, hiring, training, and monitoring the progress of paralegals.

There is considerable pressure on attorneys and paralegals to keep track of their time with precision. The accounting records and financial health of the law firm depend on it. At least nine different methods of billing exist: hourly rate, fixed fee, full contingent fee, hourly plus fixed fee, hourly reduced or with contingent, blended hourly rate, lodestar, value billing, and percentage fee. The method of paying this bill (including disbursements) should be spelled out in the retainer. The amount actually paid by a client is not determined until there has been a valuing of the bill, which might result in a write-up, a write-down, or no change.

An efficient law firm uses administrative reports to help it keep track of and manage the practice. Among the most important are the practice analysis report, work summary, cash flow projection, chargeable hour schedule, aged accounts receivable, and budget reports.

A busy law firm receives a great deal of mail, does a great amount of copying, and files a great many documents. It is important for the paralegal to learn what method the firm uses for these tasks. While some offices file alphabetically, many firms have found that numerical filing is more effective. Offices with large caseloads, and hence many documents to file and store, often use a computerized system of record management.

# Key Terms

| | | |
|---|---|---|
| sole practice | professional corporation | value billing |
| general practitioner | corporate legal department | percentage fee |
| law clerk | general counsel | disbursements |
| office sharing | in-house attorney | retainer |
| partnership | legal administrator | billing memorandum |
| partner | legal assistant manager | draft bill |
| draw | timekeeping | write down |
| associate | new file worksheet | write up |
| law clerk | new matter sheet | valuing the bill |
| lateral hire | daily time sheet | premium adjustment |
| passed over | hourly time and rate chart | discount adjustment |
| permanent associate | time ticket | aging report |
| senior associate | master ledger card | practice analysis report |
| nonequity partner | hourly rate | work summary |
| income partner | bundled/unbundled | cash flow projection |
| equity partner | fixed fee | chargeable hour schedule |
| capital partner | full contingent fee | aged accounts receivable |
| staff attorney | hourly plus fixed fee | annual budget |
| second-tiered attorney | hourly reduced or with | alphabetical filing system |
| of counsel | contingent | numerical filing system |
| contract attorney | blended hourly rate | bar coding |
| project attorney | lodestar | |

# 15

# Informal and Formal Administrative Advocacy

## ■ Chapter Outline

Section A. The Nature of Advocacy
Section B. The Techniques of
   Informal Advocacy
Section C. Procedural Due Process
Section D. An Agency Problem
Section E. Preliminary Considerations
Section F. Hearsay, Opinions, and
   Relevance

Section G. Introduction to the
   Examination of Witnesses
Section H. Direct-Examination
Section I. Cross-Examination
Section J. Closing the Hearing and
   Preparing for an Appeal

## Section A. The Nature of Advocacy

*Advocacy* is the process by which an individual attempts to influence the behavior of others according to predetermined goals. Advocacy is a basic component of everyday life; we are frequently advocates for ourselves and for others. Note, for example, the advocacy involved, or potentially involved, in the following circumstances:

1. At a supermarket checkout counter, a clerk tells a customer that the price of tomatoes is 49¢ a pound. The customer replies, "But the sign back there said 39¢ a pound." The clerk says, "I'm sorry, but the price is 49¢."

2. A student goes to the teacher to say that a term paper should have been graded "A" rather than "B."

3. A tenant tells the landlord that a $50 a month rent increase is ridiculous because the building has been steadily deteriorating.

4. An individual applying for a driver's license is told that he filled out his application incorrectly and that he must wait a week before he will be allowed to fill out another one. The individual feels that his application is not incorrect and that even if it is, he should not have to wait a week to do it over.

5. An employee has been laid off from her job. She calls the unemployment insurance bureau and asks to be sent forms so that she can fill out a claim. The clerk tells her that no forms can be sent through the mail. She asks the clerk if an exception can be made in her case because she has not been feeling very well and her doctor has told her to stay in bed. The clerk says there are no exceptions.

6. A homeowner has been away on a vacation. Upon his return, he finds that his house has been burglarized. When he goes to the police station to report

the crime, he asks the desk sergeant why his neighborhood has not been receiving better protection in view of all the burglaries that have been occurring in the area lately. The sergeant replies that there are not enough police available to patrol the neighborhood adequately. The homeowner is not satisfied with this response and asks to see the precinct captain.

. . . . . . . . . . . . . . .

The customer, student, tenant, applicant, employee, and homeowner all have complaints. They are complainants. They are not satisfied with something. Their natural response it to make an *argument* for better service. In so doing, they become advocates for the goals or objectives that they are seeking. Advocacy does not always require courtrooms, judges, and attorneys; all that is needed is a complaint, a complainant, and someone who should be able to act on the complaint.

The distinction between *formal* and *informal advocacy* is primarily one of degree. Generally, the more the setting looks like a court procedure (for example, with a hearing officer present, evidence or testimony taken, or written decisions issued) the more formal it is. As we saw in Chapter 6, an administrative agency's quasi-judicial powers are often exercised through hearings that have many similarities to courtroom proceedings. A quasi-judicial proceeding is one in which the agency resolves a dispute between a citizen and the agency (such as between welfare recipient and welfare department) or between two or more citizens under the control of the agency (e.g., two students in the same school or two inmates in the same prison who are having a dispute). If you are representing yourself or someone else at such a hearing, you are engaged in formal advocacy.

Our first concern in this chapter is *in*formal advocacy that occurs (a) in connection with administrative agencies not involving formal hearings or (b) outside the realm of administrative agencies altogether, as in the supermarket case in the example at the beginning of this chapter. Our primary focus will be the informal advocacy techniques that can be used when confronting employees of *any* organization—for example, a public agency such as a social security office or a private business such as an insurance company.

Paralegals often have contact with organizations that require the application of informal advocacy techniques. The following list contains several examples:

- Determining the names and addresses of the principal shareholders of a corporation
- Gaining access to the records of an agency or of a company
- Obtaining copies of forms from the Securities and Exchange Commission on the disclosure and reporting requirements of a corporation
- Writing to or visiting an agency or company to obtain its position on a matter involving a client
- Trying to convince a caseworker or a social worker that the action the agency has taken (or that it proposes to take) is illegal or ill-advised

A paralegal can meet resistance in any and all of these situations. The basic techniques of informal advocacy should help in handling this resistance.

# Section B. The Techniques of Informal Advocacy

In Figure 15.1, on page 722, there is a summary of nineteen techniques that are sometimes used in trying to obtain action from an administrative agency or from any large organization. As you read the list, think of which ones are more likely to be effective.

Clearly, some of these techniques in Figure 15.1 will be more effective than others. Perhaps some of them should *never* be tried. A great deal would obviously depend on the circumstances confronting the paralegal at the time. In general how would you assess the nineteen techniques? If you were to list the techniques in the order in which you think that the technique would be effective in *most* situations, what would your order be?

The following outline lists the nineteen techniques in one possible order of effectiveness. The outline also presents other considerations relevant to their use: threshold concerns, evaluation of techniques, adaptation, and recording.

## Advocacy

I. *Threshold Concerns*

1. Define your goals in order of priority
2. Decide when to intervene

II. *Advocacy Techniques*

1. Put your cards on the table
2. Insist on service
3. Ask for authorization
4. Go up the chain of command
5. Insist on common sense
6. Act tired, battered, and helpless
7. Cite a precedent
8. Find the points of compromise
9. Uncover the realm of discretion
10. Demonstrate the exception
11. Cite the law
12. Be a buddy
13. Make clear that the case is important to you
14. Redefine the problem
15. Do a favor
16. Seek the support of a third party
17. Preach
18. Embarrass
19. Get angry

III. *Evaluate the Techniques Used*

1. Are you making yourself clear?

**FIGURE 15.1**

Techniques of Informal Advocacy

1. *Put your cards on the table.* Be direct and completely above board in telling the agency official what your position is and what you want.

2. *Insist on adequate service.* Point out to the agency official that the purpose of the agency is service and that this principle should guide the official's actions.

3. *Seek the support of third parties.* Before you make your position known, gather the support of individuals or groups within and outside the agency so you can demonstrate that you are not alone.

4. *Be a buddy.* Show agency officials that you are not an enemy, that you respect and like them, and that you are aware how difficult their job is.

5. *Find the points of compromise.* Ferret out the negotiable points in the dispute and determine whether you can bargain your way to a favorable result.

6. *Insist on common sense.* Convey to the agency official the impression that common sense dictates your position—in addition to or despite regulations or technicalities that might be cited against you.

7. *Demonstrate the exception.* Insist on the uniqueness of your client's situation. Show agency officials that the general rule they are using to deny your client a benefit is inapplicable.

8. *Uncover the realm of discretion.* Take the position that rules do not exist until they are applied, and that, in the application of rules, agency officials often have wide discretion despite claims that their hands are tied.

9. *Ask for authorization.* Insist that the agency official show you the regulation, law, or authority that supports the action taken or proposed by the agency.

10. *Cite the law.* Show the agency official that you know what administrative regulations apply to the case. Also cite statutes and other laws to demonstrate your point.

11. *Redefine the problem.* If you can't solve a problem, redefine it—as long as you can still achieve what the client seeks. For example, stop trying to qualify the client for program "Z" if program "Y" will serve the client equally well and the problems of qualifying the client for "Y" are not as great as you'll face by continuing to insist on "Z."

12. *Demonstrate anger and hostility.* Be completely open about the bad feelings that you have concerning what is being done or proposed.

13. *Preach.* Lecture the civil servant. Tell the agency what it should or should not be doing.

14. *Climb the chain of command.* Normally everyone has a boss who can overrule decisions made by those beneath him or her. When you are dissatisfied with the decision or action of an employee, "appeal," or complain "up the chain of command," to the employee's supervisor and to the supervisor's supervisor, if needed.

15. *Embarrass the official.* Show the agency official that you do not respect him or her. Do it in such a way that the official is made to look silly.

16. *Make clear that you and your office are going to fight this case all the way up.* Make the agency official aware of how important the case is. Point out that you are thinking about taking the case to a formal agency hearing and that your office may go to court, if necessary.

17. *Take the role of the tired, battered, helpless citizen.* Do not insist on anything. Play dumb; act exhausted; act in such a way that the agency official will think, "This person needs help;" act as if everyone else has given you the runaround and that you are praying that this official (whom you have not dealt with before) will finally give you a sympathetic ear—and some help.

18. *Do a favor to get a favor.* Be willing to do something (within reason) for the person from whom you are seeking something.

19. *Cite a precedent.* Point out to the agency official (if it is true) that your case is not unusual because the agency has granted what you want to others under the same or similar circumstances in the past.

2. Are you creating more problems than you are solving?

3. Are you accomplishing your goal?

IV. *Adaptation.*   Are you flexible enough to shift your technique?

V. *Recording*

1. Describe what you saw

2. Describe what you did

The focus of the first threshold concern is the priority of goals. This concern, of course, would not be applicable if the assignment you are given contains only one goal, such as obtaining a copy of a record at the agency. It may be, however, that the assignment contains a variety of objectives at the outset or that a single-objective assignment subsequently blossoms into tasks involving more than one goal. Priorities must be set. If you try to do everything, you may end up accomplishing nothing. Every technique of informal advocacy will probably fail if you have unrealistic expectations of what can be accomplished.

The second threshold issue is to decide when to intervene with the advocacy techniques. The decision to intervene involves a strategic judgment about when it would be most appropriate to seek what you are after at the agency. In most situations, a sense of timing is very important. For example, suppose that you must contact the complaint bureau of an agency that is relatively new to you. One approach would be simply to walk up to the complaint bureau and delve right into the matter that brought you there. Another approach would be to try to find out something about the bureau *before* going to it. There may be some literature available on the structure of the agency that will provide you with at least a general idea of what to expect. You may be able to talk to attorneys or other paralegals who have had prior contact with the bureau. Suppose you learn that there are two agency employees who rotate their work at the bureau and that one employee has a reputation of being more cooperative than the other. You may decide not to go to the bureau until this employee is on duty. In short, you decide to postpone your involvement with, or intervention at, the bureau until circumstances are most favorable to the objective you are seeking.

Next in the outline, the nineteen techniques are listed. Note that the last three are preaching, causing embarrassment, and becoming angry. These are placed at the bottom of the list because they are likely to antagonize the agency employee and perhaps set up roadblocks to your objective. Do you agree? Can you think of circumstances when anger, for example, *would* be appropriate? These questions move us to the next section (III) of the outline: evaluation of the techniques.

As you use any one of the techniques, you must simultaneously judge the *effectiveness* of the technique in light of what you are trying to accomplish. Are you making yourself clear? Are you complicating rather than resolving things? Are you getting through? Are you pacing yourself properly? Is your insistence on immediate success interfering with building a step-by-step road toward progress?

One of the major signs of ineffective advocacy is becoming so involved in the case that you begin to take roadblocks and defeat *personally*. Everyone agrees that objectivity is a good quality—and most of us claim to possess this quality in abundance. The unfortunate fact, however, is that *we tend to lose objectivity as friction increases.* We allow our careers and our lifestyles to be threatened when someone says to us, "You can't do that." Of course, we rarely admit that we can be so threatened. We justify our response by blaming someone else for insensitivity, stupidity, or unfairness.

Of course, evaluation for the sake of evaluation is worthless. Once you have disciplined yourself to identify the techniques you are using and evaluate their effectiveness, you must be flexible enough to *adapt* your techniques and shift to more effective techniques, when needed.

Finally, the paralegal usually will have a recording responsibility. Almost every case you work on will have to be heavily documented in the office files. Your efforts at informal advocacy should be included in those files.

---

### ■ ASSIGNMENT 15.1

In each role-playing exercise, there are two characters: P (the paralegal) and AE (the agency employee). Students from the class will be assigned one or the other role. As indicated, P is seeking something from AE. AE is uncooperative. The objective of AE is to antagonize P (within reason) to the point where P loses objectivity. The objective of P is to refrain from losing his or her objectivity.

(a) At 4:30 P.M., P goes to the Department of Motor Vehicles to apply for a license. AE tells P that the office closes at 5:00 P.M. and the application procedure takes forty-five minutes. AE refuses to let P apply.

(b) At the post office, P tries to buy $400.00 worth of 29¢ stamps. AE tells P that no individual customer can buy over $100.00 worth of stamps per day.

(c) P goes to the bureau of vital statistics and requests a copy of his mother's birth certificate. AE tells P that no citizen can obtain the birth certificate of another person without the written permission of the person. P's mother is ill in a hospital a thousand miles away. P wants the record without going through the bother of obtaining this permission.

Those members of the class who are not participating in the role-playing exercises should identify and evaluate the techniques of informal advocacy that P uses.

---

We now examine some of the informal advocacy techniques in the context of the following fact situation:

You are in your own home or apartment. You receive a letter from the gas company stating that your gas will be shut off in ten days if you do not pay your bill. Your spouse tells you that the bill has already been paid. You call the gas company and, when you question the clerk, she says to you, "I'm sorry sir, our records reflect an unpaid bill. You must pay the bill immediately." To try to straighten matters out, you take a trip to the utilities office.

In the dialogue that follows the complainant is his own advocate. "C" will stand for complainant and "E" will stand for the various company employees.

E: *Can I help you?*

C: *Yes, I want to see someone about my bill.*

E: *I'm sorry, sir, but the customer complaint division closed at 2 P.M. You'll have to come back or call tomorrow.*

C: *Closed! Well, let me see someone about terminating the gas service altogether.*

E: *All right, would you step right over to the desk?*

*Technique:   If you can't solve a problem, redefine the problem* to manageable proportions if, on balance, it is consistent with your objectives.

The client is taking a risk. He cannot get to the complaint division so he is going to try to achieve his objective through the termination division. He has substituted one problem (getting to the complaint division) for another problem (getting to the termination division) in the hope of expressing his grievances.

E: *Can I help you?*

C: *Yes, I want to terminate my gas if I can't get this problem straightened out.*

E: *You'll have to go over to the bill complaint division, sir.*

C: *Look, stop sending me somewhere else! Either I get this straightened out or else!*

*Technique: Demonstrate anger and hostility.* This is a dangerous tactic to employ. It is a fact of life, however, that some people respond to this kind of pressure.

C: *Aren't you here to serve the public?*

*Technique: Insist on adequate service.* Point out that the organization exists to serve and you need better service.

E: *There are rules and procedures that we all must abide by and. . . .*

C: *Your responsibility is to take care of the public!*

*Technique: Preach.* Perhaps the most common way in which people try to change other people is to lecture them, to tell them what they should or should not be doing.

*Technique: Embarrass the official.* Make the agency official look silly, unworthy of respect.

At this point, has the complainant lost all objectivity? What risks are being taken? Do you think the complainant is aware of what he is doing? If you asked him whether he's being effective, what do you think his response would be? Is he more involved with the "justice" of his case than with the effectiveness of his approach?

C: *I'd like to speak to your supervisor. Who is in charge of this office?*

E: *Well, Mr. Adams is the unit director. His office is right over there.*

C: *Fine.*

*Technique: Climb the chain of command.* Everyone has a boss who can overrule his or her subordinate's decisions. If you're unhappy about a decision, complain "up the chain of command," to the top if necessary.

E: *Can I help you?*

C: *I want to speak to Mr. Adams about a complaint. Tell him that it is very important.*

E: *Just a moment. [She goes into Mr. Adams' office for a few moments and then returns.] You can go in, sir.*

C: *Mr. Adams?*

E: *Yes, what can I do for you? I understand you are having a little problem.*

C: *It's about this bill. I have been talking to person after person in this office without getting any response. I'm going in circles. I need to talk to someone who is not going to send me to someone else!*

*Technique: Take the role of the tired, battered, helpless citizen.*

E: *Well, let me see what I can do. I've asked the secretary to get your file. . . . Here it is. The records say that you haven't paid last month's bill. Our policy here is to terminate utility service if payment is delayed thirty days or more.*

C: *What policy is that? Could I see a copy of this policy and what law it is based on?*

*Technique:   Ask for authorization.* Make the agency show you the regulation, law, or authority that allegedly backs up the action it has taken or says it will take.

What risk is the complainant taking by resorting to this technique? Is the complainant suggesting to Mr. Adams that he does not trust him? How would you have asked for authorization in this situation? Does the request for authorization always have to be made in a hostile manner?

E: *Well, I'll be glad to show you the brochure.*

C: *I would like to see it and also the law it is based on. My position, Mr. Adams, is that my wife paid the bill.*

E: *Well our records don't reflect it.*

C: *The cancelled checks have not yet come back from the bank. I would like a Xerox copy of your file on me. Under the law, I am entitled to it.*

*Technique:   Cite the law.* Demonstrate that you know what regulations and other laws apply to the case.

E: *You do have this right, but only if you make the request in writing.*

C: *Let's be reasonable. I'm making the request in person. That should be sufficient.*

*Technique:   Insist on common sense.* You need to show the agency official your position makes good common sense, even if regulations or technicalities go against you.

C: *Surely, your rule calling for a written request can't apply when the person making the request is right in front of you.*

*Technique:   Interpret the law.* Regulations, statutes, and cases often are susceptible to more than one meaning; identify and argue for the meaning most favorable to your cause.

*Technique:   Demonstrate the exception.* Insist that your situation is unique, not governed by the general rule.

C: *Don't you have the power to waive this rule in such a case?*

*Technique:   Uncover the realm of discretion.* Argue that rules do not exist until they are applied and that in the application of rules, agency officials often have a lot of latitude as to how they interpret them in spite of their claim that their hands are tied by the rules.

E: *Well, all right, I'll see if I can't get a copy run off for you while you are here, but it will take a little time and I must point out that it's highly irregular.*

C: *Now, Mr. Adams, I understand that you are a very busy man and that you have responsibilities more demanding than listening to people like me all day.*

*Technique:   Be a buddy.* Show the agency official that you are not his enemy and that you respect and like him and that you are aware of how difficult his job is.

Here the complainant has obviously shifted his tactic; he is no longer antagonistic. Consciously or unconsciously, he has made an evaluation of how successful his techniques have been thus far and has decided on a different course of action. What risk is he running in making this shift?

C: *All I want is a thirty-day extension of time so that I can collect the proof needed to show you that the bill has been paid.*

*Technique:   Put your cards on the table.* Tell the agency official, directly and openly, what your position is and what you want.

E: *Well, we seldom give extensions. The situation must be extreme. I don't know. . . .*

C: *Mr. Adams, suppose we forget my request for a copy of the records for the time being. All I want is thirty days.*

*Technique:   Find the points of compromise.* Look for the negotiable points and figure out whether you can bargain your way to a good result.

E: *I don't think so.*

C: *Well, Mr. Adams, it's either that or I'm going to go to court. All I'm asking for is some fair treatment. There's a principle involved and I intend to fight for it.*

*Technique:   Make clear that you are going to fight this case all the way up.* Make the agency official aware of how important this case is. When you have grounds to back you, point out that you are thinking about taking the case to a formal hearing and, if necessary, to court.

E: *I'm sorry you feel that way, but we have our rules here. It would be chaos if we broke them every time someone asked for it.*

C: *Good day, Mr. Adams. [You leave the office, resolved never to come back alone.]*

*Technique:   Seek the support of third parties.* Gather the support of individuals or groups within and outside of the agency so that you can demonstrate that you are not alone.

. . . . . . . . . . . . . . .

Has the complainant failed? Was he a "bad" advocate? Has he accomplished anything? Should he give up? Do you think he will? If he does not, do you think he has learned (or that he should have learned) enough about the utility company to come back next time better equipped to handle his problem? If he comes back, what approach should he take and whom should he see? Should he see the supervisor of Mr. Adams, for example?

---

### ■ ASSIGNMENT 15.2

What follows are two exercises for role-playing. The instructor will select students to play the roles indicated. The rest of the class will evaluate the role-playing through questions that follow the statement of the exercises.

(a) A paralegal is asked by his supervisor to file some papers in court. They must be filed by 5:00 P.M. that day. At 4:15 P.M. the paralegal takes the papers to the office of the court clerk. The clerk determines that the papers are in order except that the attorney forgot to sign one of them. It would take the paralegal more than an hour to go back to obtain the signature and return to court. The paralegal asks the clerk to accept the *other* papers. The clerk refuses since all the papers are closely interrelated. The paralegal tells the clerk that this happened once before and the clerk (another one) accepted the papers that were properly executed. The clerk refuses.

**(b)** A parent (acting as her own advocate) asks the principal for a meeting on her child. The child has been selected by the school to be sent to another school. The parent is opposed to this transfer. The principal tells her that she will have to go talk to an official at the City Board of Education about the matter. The parent persists in demanding a meeting with the principal. She wants to know, for example, the position of the principal on the transfer, but the principal wants to avoid controversy and therefore refers her to the City Board.

### Evaluation

1. What advocacy technique did the paralegal start out using?
2. On a scale of 1 to 10, how effective was this technique? ("10" is very effective; "1" is very ineffective.) Give reasons for your score.
3. When the sequence ended, what advocacy technique was the paralegal using? How would you score this technique?
4. What shifts in technique, if any, did the paralegal make? Score each technique.
5. On a scale of 1 to 10, how effective was the paralegal's overall performance?
6. According to the agency official, what was the problem?
7. According to the paralegal, what was the problem?
8. What, if anything, was standing in the way of communication between them?
9. How could this communication problem have been overcome?
10. Was the paralegal objective, or did the paralegal take anything personally? Explain.
11. Was the agency official taking anything personally? Explain.
12. If the agency official took anything personally, how did the paralegal deal with this?
13. What do you think the paralegal *should* have done about this?
14. Describe the most positive aspects of what you saw the paralegal do.
15. Describe the least effective aspects of what you saw the paralegal do.
16. As specifically as possible, list all the advocacy techniques that you observed the paralegal use that you haven't already mentioned.
17. Reexamine the list of nineteen informal advocacy techniques in Figure 15.1. Do you think that any techniques should be added? If so, how would you rate the effectiveness of the techniques that you would add?

---

## ▌ Section C. Procedural Due Process

Where paralegals are authorized by law to engage in *formal advocacy* by representing clients at administrative hearings (see Chapter 4), it is one of the great challenges that they enjoy. In this chapter, we will explore some of the skills required to perform this task effectively.

The subject matter of a hearing, as well as its procedure, can range from the very simple to the very complex. Our approach will be to examine a relatively simple hearing, after identifying the components of procedural due process when a government agency and a citizen have a dispute.

. . . . . . . . . . . . .

When a government agency and a citizen have a serious dispute, basic fairness may require a number of procedural safeguards for the citizen. These safeguards are known as *procedural due process.*

> Tom is a civilian employee of the army. One day he receives a call from the assistant manager of his unit who says, "I have finished examining all of the records, and it is clear to me that you have been using the agency car for your own personal use. I have decided to fire you." As a matter of common sense and fairness, what is wrong with the assistant manager's approach? (Assume that Tom denies the charge.)

Note that in this hypothetical situation, the assistant manager wanted to end the entire matter right on the phone. What visceral response would you have (if you were Tom) to the action of the assistant manager? Shock? Anger? Some of Tom's responses might be:

1. "I wasn't given a chance to explain myself before I was fired."
2. "I wasn't given a chance to talk to the assistant manager before I was fired."
3. "I wasn't give a chance to be told what records he was talking about."
4. "I wasn't given a chance to talk to the assistant manager's boss before I was fired."

These four responses can be translated into legal language:

1. Someone who is charged with wrongdoing (or who is told that he or she is not entitled to a particular benefit) should be given the opportunity to be *heard.* The *hearing* is a formal proceeding in which an individual can present his or her position on a dispute.
2. The individual should be allowed to *appear in person* at the hearing. He or she should be allowed to *confront* and *cross-examine* his or her accuser.
3. The individual should be allowed to *examine the evidence against him or her.*
4. The individual should be allowed to *appeal* the initial decision against him or her.

Note that the individual would be asking for these rights *before* the job is taken away.

Tom might have a number of other responses:

5. "Before he called me to say that I was fired, he should have let me know that I was in trouble."

Here the call, in legal terms, is for adequate *notice.* Before the phone call, and certainly before the actual firing, the employee should have been given notice that there was a grievance or complaint against him so that he could prepare a response.

6. "Since the assistant manager was the one who made the charge, he should not be the one to make the decision."

Legally, this response goes to the issue of *legal bias* and the need for an impartial decision-maker. The basic theory is that the accuser should not be the executioner. If the same person wears both hats, the likelihood is that he or she will lose objectivity. While making the ultimate decision (as executioner), his or her tendency will be to reinforce the decision he or she originally made (as accuser) rather than to approach the final decision with an open mind. In short, the person with both hats is likely to have a bias. In the hypothetical situation, the assistant manager made the original charge (accuser) of misusing the agency car and he also made the decision to fire (executioner). He appears, therefore, to have a bias.

7. "When and if I am able to confront the assistant manager, I should be able to have someone help me state my case."

Legally, the call here is for the right of *representation:* counsel or counsel-substitute.

8. "When I am able to confront the assistant manager, I should be able to bring with me some of my co-workers, who will back up my side of the case."

Legally, the call is for the right to bring *your own witnesses* to the hearing and to *present your own* counter *evidence.*

9. "When the army finally makes its decision in my case, they should give me their decision in writing with an explanation of their decision."

Legally, this is a call for a *written opinion* or a *decision with reasons.*

10. "At my hearing, they should focus only on the charge that they raised and not bring up extraneous facts, such as that I am now going through a divorce."

Legally, the call is for only *relevant evidence* to be considered in making the decision.

Hence the ten safeguards (presented in roughly chronological order) are as follows:

- Notice (#5 above)
- Examination of evidence against you (#3)
- Hearing (#1)
- No legal bias in hearing officer (#6)
- Personal appearance at hearing; confrontation and cross-examination of accuser (#2)
- Representation (#7)
- Relevance of evidence (#10)
- Presenting your own witnesses (#8)
- Written decision stating reasons (#9)
- Appeal (#4)

In constitutional law, these safeguards constitute procedural due process. Of course, an agency does not provide all ten every time it has a conflict with a citizen. The safeguards that are required differ from agency to agency, depending on the seriousness of the dispute. In a welfare hearing, for example, all ten safeguards *are* required whenever a welfare recipient wishes to challenge a decision of the welfare department to terminate public assistance. This is so because of the extreme consequences that could result from this termination. The more extreme the possible consequences, the more procedural safeguards the law imposes on the conduct of hearings to determine whether those consequences should be imposed.

 ## Section D. An Agency Problem

*Fact Situation*

George Temple was born on January 1, 1950. His parents, Mr. and Mrs. Sam Temple, live at 435 West 100th Street, New York, New York. He was graduated from high school in 1967 and spent six months at Wentworth Technical Institute in Boston before dropping out. He came back to live with his parents in February of 1968. But while in Boston, he began using drugs. He smoked pot regularly and experimented with LSD and heroin. After returning to New York on April 15, 1968, he got a job with the Thomas TV Repair Shop at 90 South Side Avenue, Queens. The boss, John Adams, fired George on June 1, 1968, because he suspected George of being an addict and of stealing.

On June 30, 1968, George married Ann Fuller. George began using drugs more often. Ann realized that he was not going to be able to support her and their expected child. When the child was born on January 2, 1969, she decided to go to the Amsterdam Welfare Center to apply for public assistance. She did so on January 10, 1969. The caseworker, Brenda Marshall, asked Ann what her husband did for a living. Ann answered that he took odd jobs "off and on," since he was sick. The caseworker asked if he was an addict. Ann was scared and answered *no*. The caseworker told her that she would need more information about her husband's employment history and condition before her application could be processed and approved. Ann left the center confused and frustrated. She never returned.

In the meantime, George was arrested on March 13, 1969 for possession of a dangerous drug in the third degree. He "took a plea" for attempted petty larceny and spent four months at Green Haven prison. When he got out on July 13, 1969, he went to live with his wife at 758 West 85th Street. While George was in prison, Ann worked as a waitress. During this time, her mother-in-law cared for the child. She was laid off from work on August 1, 1969.

George did not want to settle down with a job. He began using drugs again. He wanted to stop but couldn't.

On September 1, 1969, he went to Exodus House, a voluntary drug rehabilitation center in New York City. He stayed only two days since the program, he claimed, demanded too much from him. For example, he would have had to live at Exodus House, which he refused to do. On September 25, 1969, he went to Reality House, another voluntary rehabilitation center at 2065 Amsterdam Avenue. This was not a live-in program; members stayed there from 9 to 5. On October 1, 1969, he left this program because, when his urine was tested, it came back positive, meaning that he was still using drugs. He left rather than be confronted with the results of this urine test.

On October 2, 1969, he obtained a job with the ABC Truck Company and worked there part-time until February 15, 1970, when he was fired for being late.

On February 16, 1970, he went back to Reality House. But he failed to attend every day. On March 1, 1970, he went to the Amsterdam Welfare Center to apply for welfare for himself and his family. The caseworker, Linda Stout, asked him why he could not get a job. He said he was an addict attending Reality House. Linda Stout was skeptical. She demanded verification that he was regularly attending Reality House. George went back to Reality House to speak to his therapist, John Hughey. Mr. Hughey told him that he could not give him a letter stating that he was a member of the program until he began to attend more often.

On March 15, 1970 Linda Stout contacted Brenda Marshall, the case-worker who previously interviewed George's wife on January 10, 1969. Brenda told Linda that Mrs. Temple told her that her husband was *not* an addict.

In the meantime, George still had trouble getting a letter from Reality House stating that he was a "member" of the program. On March 17, 1970, Linda Stout called John Hughey at Reality House, who told her that George was not coming in every day. On March 18, 1970, she closed George's case, declaring him ineligible for welfare for failure to demonstrate need. She concluded that the welfare regulation authorizing public assistance to addicts attending rehabilitation programs did not apply to George.

## ◼ Section E. Preliminary Considerations

The first responsibility of the paralegal assigned to this case is to decide when and how to intervene. George comes into the law office and tells you that he wants to fight the decision of the caseworker, Linda Stout. He wants a hearing. Is this an appropriate strategy? What alternatives exist? What about informal advocacy? Would you first want to call or visit Linda Stout? Brenda Marshall? Mrs. Temple? John Hughey? Linda Stout's boss? Brenda Marshall's boss? John Hughey's boss? If so why? Is the time ripe to intervene by asking for a formal hearing?

Suppose that you decide to give informal advocacy a try, but it does not work. The welfare department still refuses to declare George eligible. Therefore, in consultation with your supervisor, you decide to ask for a hearing.

In preparing for a hearing, there are a number of preliminary considerations:

1. *Define your issues.* What are the issues in George's case? What would you have to show in order to qualify him for welfare? What are the points in doubt? Two questions should come to mind: (1) Is George an addict? And (2) is he a member of a drug rehabilitation center? If you showed that George was an addict, would he be sent to jail or to a hospital? Is this a real danger? How would you find out? Linda Stout demanded verification from George that he was a member of Reality House. Can you identify two reasons she would ask for this? Is she saying that if George is not a member of a drug rehabilitation program, he probably is not an addict? Or is she saying that he cannot obtain welfare unless he is a member of such a program even if he is an addict? Which is the case? How would you find out? What other issues exist? What legal research should be done?

2. *Draft the request for the hearing.* In welfare cases, paralegals often draft the letter to the agency requesting the *hearing*. The client signs this letter. The request is extremely important since it can be a major determinant of what the issues at the hearing will be. How broadly or narrowly should an issue be stated? How many issues should be presented? These are questions of strategy that are answered largely in the light of what the paralegal thinks he or she might be able to prove at the hearing.

When a response to the letter of request is received, the client and paralegal will know whether a hearing has been granted on the issues requested. If not satisfied with this response, the paralegal should consult with his or her supervisor on ways to challenge the response before the hearing. If satisfied, preparation should be geared accordingly.

A careful definition and a thorough understanding of what the issues are can be critical for the following reasons:

a. At the hearing, the other side or the hearing officer may raise matters outside the scope of the issues of the hearing. The paralegal can object, based on the wording of the request for the hearing and the response received to the request.

b. If an office attorney is going to appeal the final decision of the hearing in court, the starting point in preparing for the appeal is often an analysis of what the issues of the hearing were supposed to be.

3. *Engage in continuing efforts to resolve the case through informal advocacy.* It is almost always preferable to try to solve a problem informally so that the time and expense of formal hearings and court proceedings can be avoided. At the time the paralegal and his or her office decided to request a formal hearing in this case, it was determined that informal advocacy would not be or was not effective. The agency, however, can always change its mind, particularly when it realizes that the client is serious about fighting the case. Throughout preparation for the hearing, the paralegal should try to be in continued contact with employees of the agency involved in the case. In these contacts, the paralegal may be able to bring to the agency's attention new factors that may cause it to reevaluate its position. The result may be a reversal of the agency's decision or the negotiation of a settlement between agency and client, eliminating the need for a hearing altogether. The paralegal must be constantly aware of this option.

4. *Familiarize yourself with agency procedures in advance.* There is no better way to prepare for a hearing than to see one in operation before you conduct your own. You might "tag along" as the assistant of another advocate conducting a hearing. Give it a try. Take extensive notes on procedure and strategy. Later on, organize your notes into an outline covering the procedures that governed the hearing as well as the strategy that both sides used.

If the agency has more than one type of hearing, you should determine how many exist and whether you want to ask for more than one type. Some agencies have prehearing conferences, during which the advocates for both sides sit down (in advance of the hearing) to narrow the issues and determine whether a solution can be reached without a formal hearing. When available, this can be a valuable meeting. If the agency does not have prehearing conferences as a matter of course, why not ask for one anyway? Besides being a vehicle to attempt a solution, the conference is an excellent way for the paralegal to learn more about the agency's case and hence be better prepared for the hearing, if it is held.

5. *Try to respond to the client's emergency needs, if any, while waiting for a hearing decision.* In a welfare case, the recipient should not be left destitute while the agency makes a decision following a hearing. Emergency assistance of a temporary nature may be available in the interim. Suppose that the paralegal is representing a client in a worker's compensation case. While the hearing is

going on, the paralegal may be able to help this individual obtain public assistance or, possibly, union benefits. To the extent feasible, the paralegal should be alert to a client's total needs and not simply zero in on narrow legal questions. Of course, the paralegal has limited time available and must set priorities on what he or she can do. Very often the paralegal can be of help simply by referring the client to other resources in the community.

6. *Make sure that the client has given you proper authorization to act on his or her behalf.*   The law office may have a standard form for the client to sign authorizing you to represent the client at the agency proceeding. In addition, you should have the client sign a waiver-of-confidentiality statement authorizing you to examine all documents the agency possesses that pertain to the case. A similar statement may permit you to gain access to needed doctor or hospital records.

7. *Make a request in writing that the agency send you, in advance, copies of all documents that it intends to rely on at the hearing.*   Are you curious about what documents the welfare department will be using at the hearing to prove its case against George? Why not ask the department to send you copies of these documents in advance of the hearing? Would this be a fair request? In many situations, the law will back up such a request. (Suppose the agency wanted *you* to send them copies of the documents you will be using? What would you do?)

What documents would you be interested in seeing? Their entire file on George? Their most recent policy statement on addicts? What else?

8. *Find out as much as you can about the witnesses the agency intends to call at the hearing.*   Usually the agency will tell you in advance what witnesses it will call to support its position. Often these witnesses are willing to talk to you before the hearing, particularly if they are agency employees. This is frequently an excellent way to discover more details about the agency's case and how the agency intends to establish that case at the hearing. Your approach should be casual. Do not say to these witnesses, "What testimony are you going to give at the hearing next week?" Rather, deal with points of information: "I understand that you know George Temple. Could I ask when you last spoke to him?" Etc.

9. *Make sure that you have completed all necessary field investigation before the hearing.*   What facts do you think need to be checked? What are you unsure of? Are you convinced that George is an addict? What *is* an addict? Someone currently using drugs? What kinds of drugs? How would you find out? Are you also unsure about George's relationship with Reality House? What is a "member"? How many definitions of "member" might exist? Do George, Linda Stout, and John Hughey each define it differently? Would you want to check this out? How often does George go to Reality House? What other items should you investigate? Before the hearing, would you want to make a request to the agency that it state its position on George's case in writing? What would you do with such a document? Use *fact particularization* to help identify factual questions that you need to pursue through investigation and subsequent client interviews (see Chapters 8 and 9).

10. *Study the law governing your case.*   It goes without saying that the paralegal must be thoroughly familiar with the law, particularly the agency regulations that may be applicable to the case. A good deal of legal research may be necessary before the paralegal even requests a hearing. Some aspects of the law governing the case may be unclear due to ambiguities in regulations, statutes,

or cases. Part of the task of preparation is to identify these ambiguities and to map out a strategy on how to deal with them if they arise at the hearing.

Bring photocopies of relevant regulations, statutes, or cases with you to the hearing. In addition, summarize, in your own words, the sections of these documents that you believe will be most pertinent.

*11. Determine what witnesses you want to call and prepare them.*   Who should be present at the hearing to help George make his case? Should George be present? Why? Should John Hughey be present? Why? How about the boss of John Hughey? Do you want George's wife to be present? The tests that you should use in deciding whether to ask a witness to be present are: Does the witness have something to say that would help George make his case, and would the witness be able to say it? Someone may have important points to make but be so frightened at the thought of going to a hearing that he or she is, in effect, unavailable. Suppose you have a witness whom you want to call, but the person has an acute stuttering problem. How would you handle this?

Tell your witnesses what the hearing is all about to set their mind at ease. To be willing and valuable participants, they must trust you. Tell them why you want them to come. (You do not have to use words such as "witness" and "testimony" if these would frighten them.) Get them to role-play part of the proceeding with you. A brief role-playing experience can be very helpful. Explain that the other side may want to ask some questions after you introduce them and ask your own questions. Be sure that your witnesses understand what the issues are. They may try to use the occasion to begin a tirade about everything under the sun. This could be damaging, though you may determine as a matter of strategy to let the witnesses "unload" to some extent.

You must be careful not to place your witnesses in embarrassing situations. Whenever you think that a question you want to ask might be embarrassing or damaging to your witnesses, check it out with your supervisor before the hearing. What about George's addiction? Can you think of any questions you might ask that could create difficulties for him?

*12. Assemble all the documentary evidence that you want to introduce at the hearing. Determine how you will lay the foundation for each item of evidence— that is, how you will show that it is relevant to the issues of the hearing.*   What documents do you want to present at the hearing on behalf of George? Do you want a letter from Exodus House stating that he once attended the program? If so, why? What would it prove? Do you want a letter from Reality House? Saying what? Would you ask them to write down all of the dates that George did attend that program? Would it help or hurt to obtain a letter from ABC Truck Company stating that George once worked there? Is it relevant? Suppose that you could arrange a doctor's examination of George. Would you want to use the results of this examination at the hearing? What would it depend on?

*13. Draft an outline of how you intend to present your case at the hearing.*   The great danger of preplanning, of course, is that the unexpected almost always "fouls up" your preliminary plan. It nevertheless is helpful to have a tentative plan in mind, **as long as you do not slavishly try to follow it.** Flexibility is always key.

A useful approach is to arrange all the facts according to a chronological history. Every client's story has a beginning, middle, and end. Your outline should attempt to tell George's story in this way. Simple as this may seem, it is not easy to do. At the hearing, people will raise points out of sequence. These points often have to be dealt with, but if you have prepared your chronology carefully, you at least have something to come back to after this other point is treated.

Draft a preliminary outline of your strategy in conducting George's hearing. What points do you want to make? What documents or witnesses will you use to help you make these points? Arrange the entire sequence chronologically.

Confusion over the precise issue or issues of the hearing is one of the major frustrations you might experience in conducting formal hearings. This can arise in a number of ways: (a) the original request for a hearing or the agency's response to it was not precise enough; (b) the hearing officer refuses to hear testimony on an issue that you were prepared to argue; (c) your own witness raises an issue that you are not prepared to argue; (d) subissues are raised by either side, the relevance of which are dependant on the establishment of other major issues or subissues that have not yet been established; or (e) you make the dangerous assumption that everyone is focused on the same issue.

Issue control, therefore, is critical. How do you identify the issue in the most favorable light for your client? How do you make sure everyone is on the same wavelength with respect to the issues of the hearing? What do you do when new issues are raised? How do you keep from becoming paralyzed when the issue on which you have based your entire case is taken away from you, not by a failure to prove the issue but by a decision of the hearing officer about what's relevant to the hearing? Again, the answer to these questions is "preplanned flexibility." As you prepare for the hearing, you must do such a thorough job of anticipating the unexpected that you are ready to meet *any* new challenge, even if it is your own witness who poses the challenge.

Suppose that at George's hearing, the welfare department begins by making a major issue of George's poor employment record. They want to prove that he should enter a state vocational training program. What do you do? You should have anticipated this during your preparation, particularly due to the informal contacts that you had with the agency before the hearing. If for some reason this new position takes you by surprise, or if any other issue comes up that you feel is irrelevant, you have a number of options:

(a) Argue that the other side is being unfair; the agency should have let you know about its new position in advance.

(b) Argue that the issues at the hearing should conform to the issues defined in the letter granting the hearing.

(c) Ask for a postponement.

(d) After you have made your protest and lost, do the best you can with the issues that the hearing officer decides will be discussed.

14. *Make sure that the hearing officer does not have a legal bias.*   The hearing officer should not have been involved in the agency's initial decision against the client, the decision that led to the necessity of asking for a hearing. Normally this will not be a problem, since the hearing officer will usually be employed within a separate unit of the agency.

15. *If, after you request the hearing, it becomes clear that you need more time to prepare, ask for a postponement of the hearing.*   Do not be rushed into a hearing unless it is absolutely necessary. Ask for a postponement and be prepared to back up your request with reasons (e.g., you are waiting for a letter to arrive that you want to produce at the hearing).

*16.  Make sure that the client and the witnesses know when and where the hearing is to be held.*

# Section F. Hearsay, Opinions, and Relevance

Generally, the technical rules of evidence that are scrupulously followed in court proceedings (see Chapter 10) do not apply to administrative hearings. The standard rule is that hearings are conducted "informally." Nevertheless, you should have an understanding of some concepts of evidence, because they do come up in hearings despite the general rule of informality.

As we shall see when we cover direct and cross-examination, you should (1) know when your witness or a witness for the other side is speaking from firsthand or personal knowledge as opposed to second- or thirdhand knowledge *(hearsay)*, and (2) know when the witness is stating a fact as opposed to an opinion. It is important to know these distinctions not because a hearing officer will exclude hearsay evidence or opinion evidence, but because your case is always strengthened when your own witness speaks from personal knowledge of the facts. You tend to weaken the case of the other side when you can point out (through cross-examination) that a witness for the opposition is speaking from hearsay or is relating opinions as opposed to facts. If you ask your witness to state an opinion or conclusion, be sure your witness has already stated the underlying facts that support the opinion.

---

■ **ASSIGNMENT 15.3**

For each statement made by the witness below, answer the following questions:

**(a)** Is the witness talking from firsthand (personal) knowledge? Secondhand? Thirdhand?

**(b)** Is the witness stating a fact, an opinion, or a conclusion?

**(c)** What questions would you ask the witness so that the same information would come out in a different way?

   **(1)** "My case worker is rude."
   **(2)** "My caseworker called me a liar."
   **(3)** "I am eligible for public assistance."
   **(4)** "My son told me that the caseworker reported me to the supervisor."
   **(5)** "I need welfare."
   **(6)** "My mother can't pay my rent."
   **(7)** "I'm too sick to join the job training program."
   **(8)** "That job does not suit me."
   **(9)** "My husband does not contribute to the support of my family."
   **(10)** "I did report to the job employment agency."
   **(11)** "I was told that no jobs were available."
   **(12)** "You must give me seven days' notice before you terminate me."

---

Another critical concern of evidence is relevance: only evidence that is relevant to the issues at the hearing should be considered by the hearing officer. Something is relevant if it (reasonably) tends to prove or disprove a matter in dispute. Very often common sense is a clear guide on whether something is relevant. The fact that I am in Chicago is not at all relevant to whether or not it is raining in New York; but the fact that I am in Chicago is relevant to whether or not I *know* if it is raining in New York. In a large number of situations, however, the borderline between relevance and irrelevance is thin. On the question of whether or not George Temple "regularly attends" a drug rehabilitation center, is it relevant that he often plays in baseball games? Is is relevant he has an ulcer? Is it relevant that he is twenty-four years old? Hearing officers will generally lean in the direction of admitting something into evidence if its relevance is at least probable; they are more inclined to let evidence in than to exclude it.

Whenever the hearing officer or the representative of the other side objects to an item of evidence that you plan to introduce, you must be prepared to argue its relevance by explaining how it will contribute to reaching a resolution of the issues. If this approach does not seem to be successful, make a basic "fairness pitch" by asking that you be allowed to present your client's case in the best manner that you can. In effect you are saying, "Don't push me on technicalities; give me some time to show you why this is important. It may not be clear to you now why it is important, but I'll make it clear to you shortly."

Another consideration is the extent to which the evidence you want to produce would be burdensome on the proceeding. You must be reasonable. You cannot try to introduce one thousand pages of cancelled receipts and bills, for example, if it is not quite clear that every item is needed to make your case.

## ■ Section G. Introduction to the Examination of Witnesses

Before the examination of witnesses begins, be sure that you know who everyone is in the hearing room. The hearing officer may ask everyone to state his or her name and connection with the case. If the hearing officer does not, you should ask that this be done.

Another preliminary is the opening statement made by each side. When it is your turn to begin, your opening statement should briefly cover the following:

1. Your understanding of what the issues at the hearing are

2. A summary of what you are going to establish at the hearing through your witnesses and other evidence

3. The result the client is seeking from the hearing

After the opening statements, the next step is the examination of witnesses.

You *directly examine* your own witnesses (George, for example) and cross-examine the witnesses presented by the other side (the agency employee, Linda Stout, for example). After you have directly examined your own witnesses, the other side can cross-examine them. After the other side has directly examined their own witnesses, you can cross-examine them. Each side directly examines its own witnesses and cross-examines the witnesses of the other side. When you directly examine a witness, it simply means that you are the first person to ask questions of that witness.

Normally, one side presents its entire case and then the other side presents its case. The main time you talk when the other side is presenting its case is when you are cross-examining its witnesses, and vice versa.

After a side has cross-examined a witness, the other side (the one that originally examined the witness directly) is sometimes allowed to conduct a *redirect examination* to cover points raised in the cross-examination.

*Sequence:*

*I. You Present Your Side*

- You direct-examine your own witnesses.
- They cross-examine your witnesses.
- You conduct a redirect examination of your own witnesses to cover points they raised in their cross-examination.

*II. They Present Their Side*

- They direct-examine their own witnesses.
- You cross-examine their witnesses.
- They conduct a re-direct examination of their own witnesses to cover points you raised in your cross-examination.

This may all sound highly technical. Some hearings are, in fact, conducted this formally. Others are not. You must be prepared to deal with both settings.

To call a witness does not necessarily mean that the person stands in a witness box or is "sworn in." In all probability, everyone will remain in his or her own seat and will not be asked to take an oath. Furthermore, the technical words "direct," "cross," and "redirect" examination may not and need not be used. Simpler language can be used:

*Direct-Examination*

"Sir (addressed to the hearing officer) I would like to ask (name of witness) a few questions."

*Cross-Examination*

"I would like the opportunity to ask (name of witness) some questions if (name of advocate on the other side) is finished with her own questions."

*Re-Direct Examination*

"After I asked (name of witness) some questions, Ms. (name of advocate representing the other side) asked some questions of her own, and while I was listening, a few other important and pertinent points occurred to me. I would like to ask a few final questions of (name of witness), if I could."

It does not make any difference what labels are used, as long as you take every allowable opportunity to make your points.

# Section H. Direct-Examination

Reduced to its simplest level, direct examination means nothing more than interviewing or talking to someone concerning what he or she knows about an event. A direct examination has three components:

1. *Introduction:* Who is the witness, where does he or she live, where does he or she go to school or work?
2. *Connection to event:* What relationship does the witness have to the events at issue in the hearing?
3. *Testimony on event:* What does this witness have to say about the events at issue in the hearing?

## Guidelines on Conducting Direct-Examination

1. The witness on direct examination is *your* witness. You call this witness to give testimony. You are always very cordial to the witness. You never ask anything that might embarrass him or her.

2. Let the witness tell his or her own story in his or her own words. The story should flow naturally.

3. Ask the witness to speak loudly and clearly. If the witness says something that may not be clear to others, ask him or her to state it again, even though it may have been perfectly clear to *you* what was said.

4. Encourage the witness to let you know when he or she does not understand a question.

5. In the introduction of the witness, let the witness give the basic facts about himself or herself. Instead of saying, "This is John Smith of . . .," you should ask the witness to state his or her name, address, occupation, etc.

6. Before you ask the witness to state what he or she knows about an event, ask questions to establish his or her relationship or connection to the event. If the witness is a doctor, for example, before you ask his or her opinion of the client's medical condition, you should ask if the doctor has treated the patient. Before you ask a neighbor whether or not the client earns money as a private babysitter at home, you should ask the witness questions to establish that he or she is a close neighbor of the client and often visits the client during the day. By so doing, you will be **laying the foundation for the relevance of the witness's testimony.**

7. It is often helpful to structure your questions to the witness so that he or she tells the story chronologically from beginning to end. Discourage jumping from topic to topic if the narrative is becoming confusing.

8. When the witness is stating things from firsthand knowledge, emphasize the fact that it is firsthand, personal knowledge.

9. When the witness is stating things from secondhand (or hearsay) knowledge, de-emphasize the fact that it is not firsthand knowledge. When you prepare a witness to testify, encourage him or her to preface his or her statements by saying "to the best of my knowledge."

10. When your witness must state conclusions or opinions, you should structure your questions so that you first bring out all the supporting facts on which the witness has relied in forming the opinions or conclusions.

11. Be aware of the danger of open-ended questions such as, "Tell us what happened." Very often such questions are invitations to ramble. Confusion can result. The more effective kind of questions are structured to require a brief and concise answer. Use an open-ended question only when you are sure that the witness is able to handle it.

12. Very often a witness, particularly the client, has a need to vent his or her feelings. When this happens, the witness often becomes emotional and raises issues that may not be relevant. You must make a decision when this happens. On the one hand, it is the client's hearing and—as a matter of fairness—he or she should have the opportunity to speak his or her mind. It can be very frustrating if questioners keep steering the client away from what he or she has been waiting a long time to say. On the other hand, you do not want the client to say anything that may be damaging to the case. You must understand the witness psychologically. The best strategy is to determine in advance whether the witness is inclined to become emotional. If so, then the paralegal's responsibility is to make the witness aware of the consequences of this occurring at the hearing.

In the final analysis, the witness must decide; it is his or her case that's on the line, not yours.

13.  You may want to introduce certain documents into evidence after you have asked the witness questions that will reveal facts demonstrating the document's relevance. That is, you establish a foundation for the documents through your questioning. Once the foundation has been laid, you *introduce* the document by asking the hearing officer to make it part of the record and by giving a copy to the agency's representative. Then you resume your direct examination of the witness.

14.  The hearing officer may interrupt you with questions of his or her own for the witness. The officer, of course, has the right to do this. You may, however, want to tell the hearing officer politely that you will treat the subject matter of his or her question in "just a few moments."

15.  The advocate for the other side may try to interrupt you with questions. Normally, he or she does *not* have this right. Politely ask the hearing officer if you can finish your own questions before the other side asks any questions on cross-examination.

16.  Try to anticipate what the other side will want to question your witness about on cross-examination, and try to cover these points in your own direct examination.

17.  Expect the unexpected. Your witness may say things that you never anticipated. You have to be flexible enough to deal with whatever comes your way.

---

■ **ASSIGNMENT 15.4**

Role-play the following situations in class. The instructor will select one student to take the part of the person conducting the direct examination and someone else to role-play the person being questioned. The latter should make up answers that are generally consistent with the situation stated. (Review the material in Chapter 8 on fact particularization as a guide to formulating questions. See Figure 8.4.) Conduct a:

(a) Direct-examination (DE) of another student concerning the most frustrating aspect of his or her last job

(b) DE of a teenager who just drove home the family car with a big dent on the side

(c) DE of a pupil who has been charged with fighting

(d) DE of a caseworker who claims that the recipient gave her permission to enter the client's apartment (client denies it)

(e) DE of a welfare recipient on his claim that he has tried to find suitable work but has been unable to do so

(f) DE of George Temple

---

## ■ Section I. Cross-Examination

Before covering guidelines on cross-examination, you should review Chapter 9 on investigation. Restudy the evaluation of testimonial and physical evidence and the checklist on the validity of physical (tangible) evidence. (See Figures 9.6 and 9.7.) Many of the considerations discussed in the investigation chapter apply to cross-examination at hearings.

## Guidelines on Conducting Cross-Examination

1. Be courteous to the witness even though you may be tempted, and indeed baited, into attacking him or her personally.

2. Be sure that it is clear to you who the witness is and what relationship he or she has to the events at issue in the hearing. This may not have been brought out clearly enough while this witness was being direct-examined by the agency representative.

3. If during the direct examination, this witness said something based on secondhand knowledge (or if it was not clear to you whether it was said from personal or secondhand knowledge), ask about it on cross-examination. Be sure that your questions force the witness to admit that no firsthand knowledge exists when this is so.

4. If, during the direct examination, this witness stated conclusions without stating any facts to support them, ask this witness on cross-examination about these conclusions. Probe the underlying facts that support them—according to the witness. Do *not* use this tactic, however (nor the one mentioned in guideline 3 above), if you are absolutely certain that the witness has valid facts to support the conclusions or opinions even though they were not brought out on direct examination. You do *not* want to give an opposing witness the opportunity to *reinforce* damaging evidence.

5. If it is a fact (or if you are reasonable in suspecting that it is a fact) that the witness has a bias (something personal) against the client, you should try to bring this out on cross-examination. This, of course, will be very difficult and somewhat dangerous to do. No one wants to admit that he or she is not being objective. Probably the best that you can do on cross-examination is to raise some doubts about the objectivity of the witness's testimony (by asking questions about any prior hostility that may have existed between the client and the witness, for example) even though you may not be able to establish bias conclusively.

6. The point made about bias *against* someone applies to bias *in favor of* a person. A witness can lose objectivity because of partisanship and friendship as well as because of hostility.

7. If the witness is reading from any papers during cross-examination, politely ask the witness what he or she is reading from and request that you be shown a copy. If needed, ask for a few moments to read it before you continue your cross-examination. If the witness is reading from a document that was not sent to you before the hearing (and you requested that the agency send you *all* records that it was going to rely on at the hearing), you should object.

8. Sometimes the witness will read from official agency records. These records often refer to statements made by individuals who work for the agency but who are not present at the hearing. The agency representative will try to introduce these records into evidence. It has already been said that you should bring out, through your questioning, the fact that the witness is not speaking from firsthand knowledge when referring to records of which he or she is not the author. In addition, you should complain that, as a matter of fairness, authors of critically important statements in the records should be present at the hearing so that you can confront and cross-examine them. If you are not allowed to cross-examine them, you should request that their statements not become part of the hearing proceedings.

9. If, during cross-examination, the witness raises points that surprise you (for a reason other than your own sloppy preparation), you should ask the hear-

ing officer to exclude the matter because of unfair surprise or to postpone the hearing to give you more time to prepare the client's response to the new point.

10.  In courtroom proceedings, it is often the rule that you cannot raise new matters on cross-examination; you can cross-examine a witness only within the scope of the testimony this witness gave on direct examination. If, for example, the witness testifies only about food stamp eligibility on direct examination, the attorney conducting the cross-examination cannot ask questions about an invasion of privacy claim. This technical rule, however, almost *never* applies to administrative hearings. You should nonetheless be aware of it, since the advocate for the agency may improperly try to apply the technical rule against you while you are cross-examining a witness. You usually do *not* have to limit your questioning on cross-examination to the scope of what was brought out by the other side on direct examination. Normally, however, it is a good practice not to raise new matters on cross-examination unless you have no alternative. Use direct examination to make all your major points. Use cross-examination as a vehicle to challenge positions of the other side and to buttress the points you have made on direct examination.

11.  On cross-examination you are questioning witnesses who are normally hostile to your client, although this is not always so. Do not antagonize them unnecessarily. You may find that on cross-examination the witness is willing, either consciously or not, to make statements that are very favorable to your client.

12.  As a corollary to point 11, do not be unduly aggressive or defensive. Make your case positively by direct examination. Do not rely exclusively on establishing your case negatively by trying to show on cross-examination that the witnesses for the other side are fools.

13.  Do not help the other side by asking questions on cross-examination that you know (or reasonably anticipate) will produce damaging statements. (See also guideline 4 above.)

14.  You do not have to conduct a cross-examination of a witness (a) if nothing he or she said on direct examination is unclear to you or to the hearing officer or (b) if you do not think you can prompt the witness to contradict or discredit his or her position. In such a case, it would be better to rely solely on what you were able to establish on direct examination.

15.  Remain loose and flexible; anticipate the unexpected.

---

## ■ ASSIGNMENT 15.5

Role-play the following situations in class. The instructor will select students to play the roles involved. The witness should make up answers that are generally consistent with the situation stated. (Review the material in Chapter 8 on fact particularization as a guide to formulating questions. See Figure 8.4.)

(a) On direct examination, the witness testified that Mr. Smith was drunk. Conduct a cross-examination of this witness.

(b) On direct examination, the witness (a social worker) testified that she feels the client is an unfit mother. When she visited the client, the house was dirty, the children were sick, and there was no food in the refrigerator. Conduct a cross-examination of this witness.

(c) On direct examination, the witness (a social worker) testified that an unemployed client should be able to obtain employment for the following reasons: the children are old enough for daycare services, the client is basically healthy in spite of occasional headaches, and jobs are available (or at least job-training programs are available). Conduct a cross-examination of this witness.

# ■ Section J. Closing the Hearing and Preparing for an Appeal

At the end of all the questioning and presentation of evidence, ask the hearing officer to let you sum up with your version of what happened. State what you think you proved, state what you think the other side failed to prove. Specifically, state again what result you seek for the client. If you think that the hearing was inconclusive because you were unfairly surprised by what the other side did or because the other side failed to bring individuals to the hearing who were sufficiently acquainted with the case, then:

- Ask for a decision for the client because of these factors; or
- At the very least, ask for an adjournment. The hearing can resume after you have had a chance to study the matter that the other side unfairly surprised you with, or after the other side brings individuals to the hearing who should have been there.

Many hearings are either transcribed or tape recorded by the agency. Every word of the hearing, therefore, is preserved. Normally, the law office for which you work will be able to purchase a typed copy of the transcript or a copy of the tape. This record made of the hearing becomes the basis of a court appeal if the client is dissatisfied with the decision. You must understand the relationship between what happens at the hearing and a possible subsequent *court appeal*. To a very large extent, you are responsible for *making a record* for the attorney to use on appeal.

Attorneys who have litigated cases following administrative hearings should acquaint you with the mechanics of the court appeal process. If possible, you should try to read a copy of an old appellate brief that cites testimony taken at an administrative hearing so that you can see the connection between the hearing and the court action.

In some administrative hearings, an advocate waives any objection that he or she has to what takes place at the hearing *unless he or she specifically objects on the record at the agency hearing*. A *waiver* can mean that the attorney cannot later raise the point on appeal in court.

To avoid such waivers, then you must be familiar with the technique of objecting for the record. When you have an objection to make during the hearing, you should do so simply by saying to the hearing officer, "Sir, I would like to object" and briefly state what you are objecting to and the reasons. It is not necessary to object constantly to the same point. If the hearing officer decides against you and you object once, it is usually unnecessary to object again every time the agency representative brings up what you objected to.

With few exceptions, courts do not allow clients to appeal an issue in court unless the agency involved has been given the opportunity to resolve the issue within the agency's own hearing structure. This is the doctrine of *exhausting administrative remedies*. For example, at a welfare hearing, a client might claim that he or she failed to receive a check that was due *and* that the caseworker is harassing him or her with unauthorized home visits. At the hearing, if the only issue discussed concerned the check, then the visitation issue cannot be appealed in court since, as to this issue, the client has not exhausted administrative remedies. Another hearing may have to be brought on the visitation issue before it can be raised in court. You must be aware of this problem as a matter of issue control.

## ■ ASSIGNMENT 15.6

Read each situation. State whether you would raise any objection. If so, state the reasons for your objection. Also, answer any other questions asked in the problem situation.

**(a)** On direct examination, a witness of the agency representative says that your client "is a liar."

**(b)** On direct examination, a witness of the agency representative reads from a piece of paper. You are not sure what the paper is.

**(c)** On direct examination, a witness of the agency representative says that he or she was told by another caseworker that the client had a secret bank account. On cross-examination of this same witness, what line of questions should you pursue?

**(d)** Before the hearing began, you requested the agency to send you all the documents that the agency intended to rely on at the hearing. The agency never did. Should you refer to this fact at the beginning of the hearing? If so, how?

**(e)** Same as (d) above, except that when the you mention at the beginning of the hearing that the records were never sent, the agency representative hands you forty pages of records.

**(f)** Same as (d) above except that when you mention at the beginning of the hearing that the records were never sent, the agency representative responds by saying that the records are confidential.

**(g)** On direct examination of your witness, the agency representative keeps interrupting with questions of his or her own.

**(h)** While the agency representative is talking to the hearing officer, he or she uses some legal language that you do not understand.

**(i)** While talking to the hearing officer, the agency representative hands him or her a document that announces a new agency regulation.

## ■ ASSIGNMENT 15.7

Role-play the George Temple hearing in class. As a starting point, use the facts presented on page 731. Participants can make up other facts as they go along, as long as they are generally consistent with the facts given. The instructor will select students to play the parts of the various roles, such as hearing officer, paralegal for George, paralegal for the agency, and witnesses. The paralegals should review the material on fact particularization as a guide in formulating questions (see Chapter 8). The rest of the class should observe and take notes on how the paralegals conduct themselves. What did they do well? What went wrong? How should it have been handled?

## ☐ Chapter Summary

Advocacy takes place all the time. It is an everyday process by which all citizens—not just attorneys—attempt to influence or change the actions of others at one time or another. Informal advocacy occurs outside of courts or other tribunals where hearings are held to resolve controversies that the participants have not been able to resolve informally.

Advocates try many techniques of informal advocacy, with varying degrees of success. Among the most common are the following: placing your cards on the table; insisting on adequate service;

*(Continued on next page)*

## ▢ Chapter Summary (Continued)

seeking the support of third parties; being a buddy; finding the points of compromise; insisting on common sense; demonstrating the exception; uncovering the realm of discretion; asking for authorization; citing the law; redefining the problem; showing anger and hostility; preaching; climbing the chain of command; embarrassing the official; making clear that you will fight the case; taking the role of the tired, battered, helpless citizen; doing a favor to get a favor; and citing a precedent. While using any of these techniques, you need to evaluate your effectiveness and modify the techniques based on this evaluation.

Whenever the government takes an action that seriously affects a citizen, such as denying or removing a benefit, basic fairness may require a number of procedural safeguards. These requirements are referred to as *procedural due process*. While not applicable to every situation, the safeguards include notice, hearing, personal appearance at the hearing, the absence of legal bias, representation, relevance of the evidence, opportunity to examine the evidence, opportunity to present your own witnesses, a decision in writing, and an opportunity to appeal.

When paralegals are allowed to represent clients at administrative hearings, preparation requires careful defining of the issues, drafting the requests or demand for the hearing, continuation of informal advocacy, familiarity with the procedures to be used at the hearing and with the substantive law that will govern the client's case, attention to a client's emergency needs, proper authorization from the client, efforts to obtain access to agency documents and witnesses before the hearing, finalizing field investigation, preparation of your own witnesses, organization of documentary evidence, and the design of a flexible outline of your presentation. While most hearings are conducted less formally than a court proceeding, the paralegal should be familiar with the evidentiary difficulties involving hearsay, opinion testimony, and relevance. (These areas are discussed more fully in Chapter 9.)

The standard format of an administrative hearing is as follows: direct examination of a witness by the side that calls the witness; cross-examination of that witness by the other side; and redirect examination of the witness by the side that called the witness. Normally, any objections that are not made during the hearing are waived and hence cannot be the basis of a court appeal after administrative remedies have been exhausted.

# Key Terms

advocacy
formal advocacy
informal advocacy
quasi-judicial proceeding
procedural due process
hearing
confrontation
cross examination

appeal
notice
legal bias
representation
relevance
issues
hearsay
direct examination

redirect examination
appeal
making a record
waiver
exhausting administrative
    remedies

APPENDIX

A

# Bibliography

## *Abbreviations:*

AAfPE = American Association for Paralegal Education

ABA = American Bar Association

ALA = Association of Legal Administrators

F&F = Facts and Findings (a journal of NALA)

JPE&P = Journal of Paralegal Education and Practice (a journal of the AAfPE)

LAMA = Legal Assistants Management Association

LAT = Legal Assistant Today (a magazine on paralegal issues)

LAU = Legal Assistant Update (a periodical pamphlet of the ABA)

LOEM = Law Office Economics and Management (a journal)

NALA = National Association of Legal Assistants

NALS = National Association of Legal Secretaries

NFPA = National Federation of Paralegal Associations

NPR = National Paralegal Reporter (a journal of NFPA)

## Index to Bibliography

(The numbers below refer to specific entries in the bibliography.)

AAfPE, 168, 203. *See also* Paralegal Education

ABA, 1, 5, 6, 25, 46, 144, 162, 177, 181, 236, 290, 319, 489, 490

Accreditation and Approval, 2, 5, 144, 464, 489, 490

Administrative Agencies and Practice, 53, 128, 219, 311, 312, 334, 373, 420, 421, 422, 443, 457, 542, 543

Advocacy, 67, 217, 219, 267, 311, 334, 373, 542. *See also* Administrative Agencies

Alabama, 239, 246

Alaska, 390

Alternative Careers, 11, 186, 198, 285, 314, 383

American Bar Association. *See* ABA

Anger. *See* Burnout, Stress

Antitrust Law. *See* Monopoly, Unauthorized Practice of Law

Approval. *See* Accreditation

Arizona, 210, 225, 280, 296, 375, 384, 404

Arkansas, 354, 403

Army, 285, 353

Assertiveness, 32, 142

Associate Membership in Bar Associations, 3, 4, 54, 181, 418

Associates, 33, 382, 400, 441, 566

Association of Legal Administrators, 158, 172, 472, 482, 558

Attitude, 19, 279

Attorney-Client Privilege, 20, 296

Attorney General, 249, 363. *See also* Criminal Law

Attorney Fees. *See* Paralegal Fees

Australia, 389

Banking, 24

Bankruptcy, 329, 535

Bar Associations, 25, 134, 162, 347. *See also* ABA, Associate Membership

Billable Hours and Billing, 29, 109, 158, 350. *See also* Paralegal Fees

Burnout, 71, 157, 340, 499

California, 26, 34, 35, 66, 107, 122, 129, 182, 350, 362, 456, 484, 494, 569

Canada, 36

Careers, 11, 38, 39, 40, 41, 42, 69, 89, 130, 198, 301, 314, 323, 337, 338, 341, 342, 454, 497

Case Manager. *See* Management

Certification, 6, 45, 46, 47, 48, 197, 242, 315, 326, 372, 522, 523

Certified Legal Assistant. *See* CLA

Changing Jobs, Ethical Problems when, 182, 207, 378

Chicago, 412

Chinese Wall. *See* Changing Jobs

Cincinnati, 395

Cite Checking, 155

Civil Commitment, 469

CLA, 51, 58, 189, 452, 524

Clerks. *See* Law Clerks

Closings. *See* Real Estate

Collections, 175

Colorado, 44, 152, 442, 444, 463

Columbia, South Carolina, 37

Columbus, 54

Commercial Law, 97, 175

Communication, 55, 172

Community Courts, 56

Compensation, 7, 63, 163, 174, 183, 234, 322, 375, 381, 404, 463, 473, 474, 483, 503, 558, 563

Competencies, 83

Computers, 57, 72, 224, 265, 316, 323, 482, 492, 495, 549

Confidentiality, 335. *See also* Ethics

Conflict of Interest, 115, 182, 471, 495. *See also* Changing Jobs, Ethics

Connecticut, 63, 216, 229, 261, 455

Continuing Legal Education, 14. *See also* Paralegal Education

Copyright Law, 191, 232

Corporations, 39, 64, 65, 82, 125, 127, 129, 228, 271, 385, 391, 411, 470, 559

Court Interpreter, 133

Courts, 67, 68, 133, 204, 229, 250, 325, 355, 383, 533, 557

Criminal Law, 12, 75, 249, 363, 376, 380

Dallas, 74, 386

Definition, 77, 302

Delegation, 78, 167, 304, 454, 487, 504

Depositions, 220, 327

Deregulation, 194

Digesting Discovery Documents, 220, 327

Disbarred or Suspended Attorney, 300

Discovery, 86, 156, 220, 264, 307

District Attorney. *See* Attorney General, Criminal Law

District of Columbia, 141, 356, 560

Divorce, 76, 218, 537, 546

Drafting, 90, 330, 567. *See also* Legal Writing

Education. *See* Paralegal Education

Employment Law, 104

England, 90

Entertainment Law, 107, 309

Environmental Law, 309, 360

Environment of Law Firm, 448

ERISA, 412

Estates, 91, 160, 229, 248, 396, 408, 412, 488, 547, 550, 567

Ethics, 13, 50, 52, 79, 87, 88, 96, 111, 112, 113, 114, 115, 124, 126, 131, 182, 207, 209, 214, 280, 290, 291, 292, 298, 308, 310, 335, 378, 397, 438, 471, 488, 495

Evaluation, 81, 83, 98, 163, 235

Examinations and Testing, 206, 452. *See also* CLA

Exempt Employee. *See* Overtime

Family Law, 76, 88, 122, 218, 416, 537, 546

Federal Government, 53, 388, 392

Fees. *See* Paralegal Fees

Fee Shifting, 123

Fee Splitting, 124

Firing, 230

Florida, 51, 112, 126, 256, 408, 493

Foreclosure, 294

Franchise, 468

Freelance. *See* Independent Paralegals

Ft. Worth, 386

Functions, 73, 108, 143, 304, 454, 487, 504. *See also* Roles

Furman, Rosemary, 493

Government Paralegal, 49, 349, 388, 392, 443

Hiring, 161, 227, 230. *See also* Job Interviews

History, 134, 162, 212, 213

Houston, 331

Idaho, 177

Illinois, 146, 179, 466

Immigration Law, 93, 180, 508

Imputed Disqualification. *See* Changing Jobs

Income. *See* Compensation

Independent Contractor, 16, 87

Independent Paralegals, 16, 87, 131, 139, 140, 184, 185, 244, 267, 268, 269, 362, 401, 413, 419, 456, 528

Independent Secretaries, 132

Indiana, 374

Inmate. *See* Jailhouse Lawyer

Insurance Claims Adjusters, 8, 539

Insurance Defense Litigation, 399

Intellectual Property. *See also* Copyright Law, Patent Law, Trademarks

Internships, 70. *See also* Paralegal Education

Interrogatories, 90

Interviews. *See* Job Interviews, Legal Interviewing

Investigation, 160, 173, 193, 196, 264, 432, 573

Iowa, 113, 467

Jailhouse Lawyer, 66, 187, 343, 345, 465, 476
Job Descriptions, 98, 253
Job Hunting, 27, 201, 277, 331, 356, 364, 387, 388, 400, 477, 484, 527, 529
Job Interviews, 27, 59, 103, 161, 192, 227, 426, 501, 527, 570. *See also* Legal Interviewing
Job Satisfaction, 130, 165, 202, 275, 361
Judges, 204, 229, 332, 533, 543

Kansas, 33, 153
Kansas City, 215, 240
Kentucky, 205

LAMA, 565. *See also* Management
Law Clerks, 9, 208
Law Library and Librarians, 221, 222, 371, 514
Law School, 178, 212, 276
Legal Advice, 309
Legal Assistant Managers Association, 565. *See also* Management
Legal Executives, 190
Legal Interviewing, 120, 193. *See also* Job Interviews
Legal Research. *See* Computers, Law Library
Legal Technician. *See* Independent Paralegals
Legal Writing, 18, 330, 567, 577. *See also* Drafting
Leverage, 210, 270. *See also* Profitability
Licensing, 6, 84, 197, 272, 306, 320, 372, 494
Litigation, 10, 58, 73, 171, 200, 273, 274, 317, 325, 357, 399, 428, 491, 532, 551

Maine, 78
Male Paralegal, 60, 534
Malpractice, 88, 265, 358, 438, 530
Management: Managers, 10, 17, 26, 62, 102, 210, 223, 230, 231, 232, 240, 279, 280, 281, 282, 293, 295, 307, 325, 328, 393, 414, 516, 517, 568
Maryland, 488
Media's Portrayal of Paralegals, 199, 518
Mediation, 56, 286
Medical Malpractice, 317
Medical Records, 156, 359
Michigan, 154, 219, 247, 257, 263, 503
Military Law, 285, 353
Minnesota, 254, 287
Missouri, 111, 145, 248, 288, 391, 402, 424
Monopoly, 105, 425, 486
Mortgages, 294. *See also* Real Estate
Motivation, 279, 294, 366, 417, 440, 479, 480, 578

NALA, 51, 58, 121, 163, 189, 234, 283, 291, 296, 297, 298, 303, 524
National Association of Legal Assistants. *See* NALA
National Federation of Paralegal Associations. *See* NFPA
Negligence, 438, 530. *See also* Malpractice
Negotiation, 142, 174, 176
New Hampshire, 150
New Jersey, 29, 116, 481

New Mexico, 148, 252, 302
New York, 118, 149, 318, 387, 532
NFPA, 195, 297, 299, 305, 306
NLRB, 421. *See also* Employment Law
North Carolina, 106
Nurses, 317

Office Politics, 321
Ohio, 54, 395
Orange County, 569
Oregon, 214, 326
Overtime, 7, 117, 472, 558

Parajudge, 204, 332, 533
Paralegal Education, 14, 57, 70, 92, 94, 95, 136, 144, 168, 169, 177, 188, 197, 226, 236, 319, 333, 343, 344, 345, 346, 347, 348, 425, 489, 490, 505, 515, 527, 531, 532
Paralegal Fees, 21, 68, 109, 123, 225, 256, 259, 289, 384
Paralegal Malpractice, 358. *See also* Malpractice, Negligence
Patent Law, 422
Pennsylvania, 339, 521
Pittsburgh, 521
Practice of Law, 53, 77, 79, 91, 105, 128, 185, 194, 208, 214, 218, 219, 266, 300, 302, 311, 312, 457
Preventive Law, 429
Pretrial Preparation. *See* Discovery, Litigation, Trial Preparation
Prisons, 431, 512. *See also* Jailhouse Lawyer
Privilege, 20, 296
Probate, 160, 229, 248, 383, 396, 408, 547. *See also* Estates
Pro Bono, 74, 108, 379, 394, 405, 406, 433, 434, 435, 436
Productivity, 232, 246
Profession, 15, 30, 45, 52, 108, 110, 204, 305, 358, 437
Profitability, 33, 231, 241, 251, 257, 258, 263, 270, 369, 370, 381, 382, 441, 521, 548, 566
Public Sector, 249, 267

Real Estate, 179, 272, 294, 410, 446, 462, 466, 468
Registration, 449
Regulation, 194, 320, 372, 450, 451. *See also* Certification, Licensing
Responsibilities. *See* Functions
Resume, 18, 27, 28, 445, 458. *See also* Job Hunting
Retreat, 561
Rhode Island, 147, 460, 461
Roles, 72, 102, 116, 118, 119, 143, 216, 239, 249, 329, 385, 399, 455, 464, 465, 466, 467, 468, 469, 470, 515, 559. *See also* Functions

San Francisco, 26, 484
Seattle, 449
Secretaries, 132, 163, 176, 206, 284, 439, 478, 579

Senior Paralegals, 480, 481
Service Companies, 159, 411, 492
South Carolina, 37, 151
South Dakota, 47
Specialization, 143, 416, 491
Splitting Fees, 23, 397. *See also* Ethics
Status, 15, 238. *See also* Profession
St. Louis, 111, 248, 391, 402
Stress, 157, 499. *See also* Burnout
Students, 30, 92, 195. *See also* Paralegal Education
Supervision, 167, 172, 255, 517. *See also* Management
Support Staff, 17, 161, 172, 211, 503, 513
Systems, 170, 511

Tax Law, 278, 412
Teaching, 425, 505, 512, 515. *See also* Paralegal Education
Teamwork, 31, 106, 352
Temporary Paralegals, 43, 282, 519
Tennessee, 336, 352
Texas, 22, 74, 80, 137, 242, 315, 331, 386, 430, 447, 522, 523, 524, 564

Time Management, 525
Torts and Personal Injury, 10, 530. *See also* Litigation
Trademarks, 42, 191
Training. *See* Paralegal Education
Trial Preparation, 73, 171, 200, 274, 325, 407, 427, 428, 491, 509, 520, 544, 551. *See also* Litigation
Trusts. *See* Estates, Probate

Unauthorized Practice of Law, 8, 9, 77, 84, 85, 91, 194, 197, 208, 214, 218, 219, 266, 311, 312, 415, 420, 457, 475, 536, 537, 538, 539, 540, 555, 562
Unions, 541. *See also* Employment Law

Washington D.C. *See* District of Columbia
Washington State, 272, 449
Wills, 91, 408, 488, 555, 567. *See also* Estates, Probate
Wisconsin, 554
Witnesses, 173, 578
Work Product, 296
Writing. *See* Drafting, Legal Writing

## Articles, Books, Reports, etc. on Paralegals

1. *ABA Approval: Another Viewpoint* by K. Sheehy, 7 NPR 2 (NFPA, Spring 1983).

2. *ABA Associate Membership: A Paralegal's View* by J. Whalen, 10 NPR 1 (NFPA, Spring 1986).

3. *ABA Associate Membership: An Historical Review*, 10 NPR 1 (NFPA, Apr. 1986).

4. *ABA Associate Membership for Legal Assistants*, 3 LAT 32 (Winter 1986). *See also* 10 F&F 5 (Jan./Feb. 1984).

5. *ABA Commission: Historical Overview and Current Status* by R. Major, 11 NPR 18 (NFPA, Spring 1987).

6. *ABA Standing Committee on Legal Assistants: Issues Position Paper on Licensing/Certification* by K. Judd, 12 F&F 8 (NALA, Apr. 1986).

7. *The ABC's of Overtime Pay* by D. Orlik, 4 LAT 37 (July/Aug. 1987).

8. *Activities of Insurance Adjusters as Unauthorized Practice of Law*, 29 American Law Reports 4th 1156 (1967).

9. *Activities of Law Clerks as Illegal Practice of Law*, 13 American Law Reports 3rd 1137 (1967).

10. *The Administrative Legal Assistant: A Nuts and Bolts View of Complex Toxic Tort Litigation Management* by B. Gagnon, 16 F&F 24 (NALA, Mar. 1990).

11. *Alternate Career Paths* by B. Van de Mark, 16 F&F 11 (NALA, July 1989).

12. *Alternate Sentencing: A Case Study: What a Paralegal Can Do to Improve the Criminal Justice Process* by M. Courlander, 3 LAT 16 (Winter 1986).

13. *Annual Ethics and Case Law Update*, 17 F&F 36 (NALA, Fall 1990).

14. *Approaches for Continuing Legal Education of Paralegals*, by T. Calvocoressi & R. Villanova, 7 JPE&P 43 (1990).

15. *Are Paralegals Professionals?* by D. Johnson, NPR 26 (NFPA, Fall 1989).

16. *Are They Really Independent Contractors?* by D. Jackson, 17 F&F 20 (NALA, Mar. 1991) (freelance legal assistants).

17. *The Art of Managing Your Support Staff* by the Section of Economics of Law Practice (ABA, 1986).

18. *The Art of Resume Writing* by C. Jett, 7 Legal Professional 91 (renamed LAT) (Sept./Oct. 1989).

19. *Attitudes and Functions of Paralegals: Ten-Year Perspective* by M. Jennings & P. Murranka, 29 LOEM 192 (1988).

20. *Attorney-Client Privilege and the Paralegal* by K. Sheehy, 6 NPR 1 (NFPA, Fall/Winter 1981).

21. *Attorneys' Fees: Cost of Services Provided by Paralegals or the Like as Compensable Element of Award in State Court*, 73 American Law Reports 4th 938 (1989).

22. *Attorneys' Guide to Practicing with Legal Assistants* (State Bar of Texas, 1986).

23. *Attorney's Splitting Fees with Other Attorneys or Laymen as Grounds for Disciplinary Proceedings*, 6 American Law Reports 3rd 1446 (1966).

24. *A Banker with the Soul of a Legal Assistant* by C. Kane, 5 LAT 65 (July/Aug. 1988).

25. *Bar Association Involvement in the Paralegal Profession: Helpful or Harmful?* by J. Polsinelli, 6 NPR 4 (NFPA, Spring 1982).

26. *Bay Area Paralegal Administrators Speak Up About Peronnel Issues* by C. Estrin, 7 Legal Professional 36 (renamed LAT) (Sept./Oct. 1989).

27. *Be Steps Ahead of Other Candidates: Understand the Interview Game* by C. Reitz, 5 LAT 24 (Mar./Apr. 1988).

28. *Better Resumes for Attorneys & Paralegals* by A. Lewis & D. Saltman (Barron's 1986).

29. *Billing for Paraprofessional Services* by T. McCormick, New Jersey Lawyer, 20 (No. 136, Sept./Oct. 1990).

30. *Bridging the Gap from Student to Professional* by R. Sova, 7 Legal Professional 47 (renamed LAT) (Jan./Feb. 1990).

31. *Building a Strong Attorney-Paralegal Team* by N. Cattie & T. Vesper, 27 Trial 24 (Jan. 1991).

32. *Build Respect: Be an Assertive Professional* by L. Bourget, 4 LAT 40 (Jan./Feb. 1987).

33. *Calculating Profit from Associates and Paralegals*, 58 The Journal of the Kansas Bar Ass'n 5 (Apr. 1989).

34. *California Paralegal Magazine* (P.O. Box 6960, Los Osos, CA 93412) (805-772-8806).

35. *California Paralegal's Guide*, 3d ed. by Z. Mack (Parker, 1987).

36. *Canadian Legal Assistants Enjoy Growth & Recognition* by P. Hicks, 15 NPR 4 (NFPA, Spring 1991).

37. *Capitalizing on Legal Assistants in Columbia, South Carolina* by T. Howard, 5 LAT 40 (Nov./Dec. 1987).

38. *Career Paths for Legal Assistants* by D. Patrick, 8 LAT 21 (May/June 1991).

39. *Career Paths for Paralegal Assistants in Corporate Legal Departments* by R. Homes & T. Caples, 14 Legal Economics 59 (ABA, July/Aug. 1988).

40. *Career Progress* by C. Milano, 8 LAT 34 (Sept./Oct. 1990).

41. *Careers in Transition: Paralegals in Progress* by L. Jevahirian, 8 LAT 87 (Nov./Dec. 1990).

42. *The Case for Career in Trademark Law* by S. Wilkinson, 7 Legal Professional 29 (renamed LAT) (Nov./Dec. 1989).

43. *The Case for Temporary Paralegals* by D. Rothfield, 30 LOEM 305 (1989).

44. *CBA [Colorado Bar Association] Legal Assistants Committee Survey Report*, 9 Colorado Lawyer 482 (1980).

45. *Certification: A Professional Goal*, 15 F&F S1 (NALA, May 1989).

46. *Certification of Legal Assistants: A Report of the American Bar Association Survey* by R. Larson, 5 LAU 143 (ABA, 1986).

47. *Certification Proposed in South Dakota* by J. Polsinelli, 7 NPR 12 (NFPA, Spring 1983).

48. *Certification v. Certificate* by L. Klessig, 17 F&F 32 (NALA, Fall 1990).

49. *Challenges of Government Jobs: Opportunities for Paralegals* by T. Howard, 8 LAT 84 (May/June 1991).

50. *Changing Jobs: Ethical Considerations* by V. Voisin, 15 F&F 12 (NALA, Mar. 1989).

51. *CLA (Certified Legal Assistant) Study Guide* by Florida Legal Assistants, Inc. (Butterworths, 1986).

52. *Code of Ethics: Ideals of a Profession? Or Legally Enforceable Law?* by R. Major, 7 NPR 6 (NFPA, Spring 1983).

53. *Colloquium on Nonlawyer Practice Before Federal Administrative Agencies*, 37 Administrative Law Review 359 (1985).

54. *Columbus Bar Association Associate Membership for Paralegals*, 9 NPR 11 (NFPA, Feb. 1985).

55. *Communication Skills Needed by Legal Assistants* by M. Moore, 5 LAU 19 (ABA, 1986). *See also* 12 F&F 28 (NALA, Aug. 1985).

56. *Community Courts* by W. Statsky, 3 Capital University Law Review 1 (1974).

57. *A Computer Training Program for Paralegals* by R. Granat & D. Knight, 14 Legal Economics 40 (ABA, Mar. 1988).

58. *Conducting a CLA [Certified Legal Assistant] Litigation Specialty Study Group* by S. McInnis, 16 F&F 18 (NALA, Jan. 1990).

59. *Conducting an Effective Interview: How to Hire the Right Person for the Job* by J. Bassett, 7 LAT 56 (May/June 1990).

60. *Confessions of a Male Paralegal* by M. Russell, 13 NPR 15 (NFPA, Summer 1988).

61. *Confessions of Starstruck Legal Assistants* by T. Howard, 5 LAT 16 (July/Aug. 1988).

62. *Connie Burke: Legal Assistant Manager . . . Orchestrates 141 Legal Assistants* by J. Murry, 4 LAT 18 (Jan./Feb. 1987).

63. *Conn. Paralegal Wages Near U.S. Average,* 16 The Conneticut Law Tribune 13 (Feb. 26, 1990).

64. *Conoco Inc. Legal Assistant Program Job Description. . . ,* 5 Corporate Counsel's Quarterly 100 (Apr. 1989).

65. *The Corporate Paralegal* by J. Bassett, 8 LAT 21 (Nov./Dec. 1990).

66. *Counsel Behind Bars: Jailhouse Lawyers. . .* by Kroll, 7 Calif. Lawyer, 34 (June 1987).

67. *The Court Appointed Special Advocate Program* by N. Toomey, 17 F&F 16 (NALA, July 1990).

68. *Court-Awarded Paralegal Fees: An Update* by M. Lee, 5 JPE&P 11 (Oct. 1988).

69. *Create Your Own Career Path* by G. Malone, 4 LAT 33 (July/Aug. 1987).

70. *Creating Good Will Through Education: Paralegal Internships* by P. Everett, 15 NPR 10 (NFPA, Summer 1990).

71. *Creative Burnout* by M. Gorkin, 1 LAT 17 (Summer 1984).

72. *Creative Computing: A Paralegal's Key Role in Law Office Automation* by J. Gurdak & C. Bellias, 5 LAT 36 (Sept./Oct. 1987).

73. *Daily Responsibilities of Legal Assistant at Trial,* 15 F&F 24 (NALA, Mar. 1989).

74. *Dallas Paralegal Pro Bono Legal Clinics* by F. Whiteside, 15 NPR 6 (NFPA, Fall 1990).

75. *DAs [District Attorneys]: Consider Legal Assistants,* 9 NDAA Bulletin 4 (National District Attorneys Ass'n, Mar./Apr. 1990).

76. *Dealing Effectively with Divorce Clients* by M. McAuliffe, 3 LAT 39 (Summer 1986).

77. *Defining the Unauthorized Practice of Law* by A. Morrison, 4 Nova Law Journal 363 (1980).

78. *Delegate to Your Legal Assistant* by M. Gaige, 5 Maine Bar Journal 98 (Mar., 1990).

79. *The Delivery of Legal Services by Non-Lawyers* by D. Rhode, 4 Georgetown Journal of Legal Ethics 209 (1990).

80. *Demand for Paralegals Mushrooms* by R. Lee, Texas Lawyer 6 (Jan. 8, 1990).

81. *Designing an Effective Paralegal Performance Evaluation* by M. Cain, 5 LAMA Manager 3 (LAMA, Fall 1989).

82. *Developing Good Working Relations with Corporate Counsel* by E. Hourigan, 8 LAT 35 (Nov./Dec. 1990).

83. *Developing Performance Competencies for Paralegal Programs* by D. Dye, 5 LAU 51 (ABA, 1986).

84. *A Dialogue on the Unauthorized Practice of Law* by Hunter & Klonoff, 25 Villanova Law Review 6 (1979–1980) (licensing).

85. *Disciplinary Action Against Attorney for Aiding or Assisting Another Person in Unauthorized Practice of Law,* 41 American Law Reports 4th 361 (1985).

86. *Discovery Wins Recognition for Legal Assistant Sleuth* by J. Bassett, 7 LAT 71 (July/Aug. 1990).

87. *Do Independent Contractors Have Special Ethical Considerations?* by D. Brookes, 10 F&F 7 (NALA, Nov./Dec. 1982).

88. *Don't Let Your Staff Do Wrong* by D. Walther, 13 Family Advocate 40 (ABA, Spring 1991).

89. *Do You Have a Job or a Career?* by S. Brashear, 6 LAT 25 (Nov./Dec. 1988).

90. *Drafting and Answering Interrogatories* by B. De Mark, 7 LAT 62 (May/June 1990).

91. *Drafting of Will or Other Estate Planning Activities as Illegal Practice of Law,* 22 American Law Reports 3rd 1112 (1968).

92. *Educating Students about the Transition from School to Work* by J. Kaiser, 3 Journal of Paralegal Education 13 (Oct. 1986).

93. *The Education and Utilization of Paralegals in the Practice of Immigration Law* by A. Wernick, 7 JPE&P 23 (1990).

94. *The Education of Legal Paraprofessionals: Myths, Realities and Opportunities* by W. Statsky, 24 Vanderbilt Law Review 1083 (1971).

95. *Education Update 1989: The Legal Assistant & Law Office Dynamics* by G. Malone, 6 LAT 26 (Jan./Feb. 1989).

96. *Effective and Ethical Use of Legal Assistants* by T. Fagan, 15 The Colorado Lawyer 659 (1986).

97. *Effectively Using Paralegals in Commercial Litigation and Creditor's Rights Matters* by S. Stoddard, 8 LAT 74 (Sept./Oct. 1990).

98. *Effective Use of Job Descriptions and Evaluation Forms,* 15 F&F 9 (NALA, Aug. 1988).

99. *The Effective Use of Legal Assistants* by Bennett, 35 The Practical Lawyer 25 (June 1989).

100. *The Effective Utilization of Legal Assistants* by V. Kunz (Western Dakota Ass'n of Legal Assistants, 1990) (North Dakota).

101. *Effective Utilization of Legal Assistants: The Political and Economic Realities* by R. Granat, 7 LAT 25 (May/June 1990).

102. *The Emerging Role of the Case Manager* by M. Kause, 8 LAT 46 (Nov./Dec. 1990).

103. *An Employer's Assessment of Legal Assistant Candidates* by L. Wertheim & S. Sommers, 6 JPE&P 49 (1989).

104. *Employment Law Paralegals* by H. Walker, 7 Legal Professional 69 (renamed LAT) (Sept./Oct. 1989).

105. *The End of the Lawyer Monopoly: What Will It Look Like?* by S. Elias & R. Warner, 12 NPR 20 (NFPA, Spring 1988).

106. *Ensuring Attorney/Paralegal Team Excellence* by G. Green, 38 The North Carolina State Bar Quarterly 33 (Winter 1991).

107. *Entertainment Law: A Growing Industry for the Paralegal* by Birker, 2 Calif. Paralegal Magazine 7 (Apr./June 1990).

108. *Equal Professionalism, Equal Responsibility: Paralegals and Pro Bono* by T. Neiman, 17 F&F 8 (NALA, July 1990).

109. *E$$ential Nonbillable Hours* by H. Peacock, 6 LAT 33 (Jan./Feb. 1989).

110. *Establishing Yourself as a Professional* by J. Bassett, 8 LAT 41 (May/June 1991).

111. *Ethical Considerations in the Use of Paralegals in Your Office* by C. Gilsinan, 30 The St. Louis Bar Journal 14 (Summer, 1983).

112. *Ethical Considerations of Employing Paralegals in Florida* by J. Lehan, 52 The Florida Bar Journal 14 (Jan. 1979). See also *In re Petition to Amend Code of Professional Responsibility,* 327 So.2d 15 (1976).

113. *Ethical Guidelines for Legal Assistants in Iowa* (Iowa State Bar Ass'n, Mar. 1988).

114. *Ethics for the Legal Assistant* by D. Orlik (Scott, Foresman, 1986).

115. *Ethics: How Good Is Your Conflict Check?* by D. Orlik, 5 LAT 23 (July/Aug. 1988).

116. *The Evolving Role of the Paralegal* (New Jersey State Bar Ass'n, 1991).

117. *Exempt/Non-Exempt: The Debate Continues* by I. Korsack, LAMA Newsletter 8 (LAMA, Winter 1989).

118. *The Expanding Role of Legal Assistants in New York State* (N.Y. State Bar Ass'n, Subcommittee on Legal Assistants).

119. *Expanding the Role Your Paralegals Play* by C. Tokumitsu, 8 LAT 33 (Mar./Apr. 1991).

120. *Face to Face: Client Interviewing Techniques for the Legal Assistant* by R. Bilz, 5 LAT 55 (Jan./Feb. 1988).

121. *Facts and Findings* (magazine) (NALA, 1601 S. Main St., Suite 300, Tulsa, OK 74119, 918-587-6828).

122. *Family Law: Visalia's Legal Aid Paralegal* by D. Clements, 3 Calif. Paralegal Magazine 8 (Apr./June 1991).

123. *Fee-Shifting Statutes and Paralegal Services* by A. Piazza, 2 Journal of Paralegal Education 141 (Apr. 1985).

124. *Fee Splitting with Nonlawyers,* 12 Journal of the Legal Profession 139 (1987).

125. *Fitting Paralegals into the Corporate Legal Department,* 11 F&F 24 (NALA, Sept./Oct. 1984).

126. *Florida Ethics Guide for Legal Assistants* by R. Troutman (Florida Bar, Continuing Legal Education, 1986).

127. *Focus on Corporate Practice: Legal Assistants and Legal Opinion Due Diligence* by C. Drozd, 7 JPE&P 63 (1990).

128. *Focus on Law Practice before Administrative Agencies* by W. Robie, 10 NPR 5 (NFPA, Dec. 1985).

129. *The Forming of the Corporate Paralegal* by Zupanovich, 2 Calif. Paralegal Magazine 4 (July/Sept. 1990).

130. *Form Your Own Career Strategy Group: Support Comes from Others Who Are Dissatisfied or Jobless* by A. Scheele, 5 LAT 61 (July/Aug. 1988).

131. *The Free-Lance Legal Assistant and Ethics* by K. Hill, 2 LAT 15 (Winter 1985).

132. *The Freelance Legal Secretary* by P. Garcia, 38 The Docket 13 (NALS, Sept./Oct. 1989).

133. *From the Courts to the Boardroom: Legal Interpreting and Translating* by A. Adelo, 14 NPR 8 (NFPA, Spring 1990).

134. *Functional Division of the American Legal Profession: The Legal Paraprofessional* by Selinger, 22 Journal of Legal Education 22 (1960).

135. *Fundamentals of Paralegalism,* 2d ed. by T. Eimermann (Little Brown, 1987).

136. *The Future of Paralegal Education* by Q. Johnstone, 6 JPE&P 27 (1989).

137. *General Guidelines for the Utilization of the Services of Legal Assistants by Attorneys* (State Bar of Texas, 1981).

138. *The General Practice Paralegal* by I. Edwards, 8 LAT 49 (Mar./Apr. 1991).

139. *Get a Shovel* by D. Villines & L. Stailey, 17 F&F 16 (NALA, Mar. 1991) (freelance legal assistants).

140. *Getting Started as a Freelance Paralegal* by P. Everett, 8 LAT 59 (Sept./Oct. 1990).

141. *Going for Paralegal Gold* by J. Murry, 3 LAT 18 (Fall 1985) (Wash. D.C. paralegals).

142. *Griping vs. Negotiating: Techniques and Tactics for Achieving Your Goals* by S. Wendel, 4 LAT 51 (May/June 1987).

143. *A Guide for Legal Assistants: Roles, Responsibilities, Specializations,* 2d ed. by M. Gowen (Practicing Law Institute, 1991).

144. *Guidelines and Procedures for Obtaining ABA Approval for Legal Assistant Education Programs* (ABA, 1990).

145. *Guidelines for Practicing with Paralegals,* Missouri Rules of Professional Conduct (1987).

146. *Guidelines for Use of Attorney Assistants as Approved by ISBA Assembly* (1977) (Illinois State Bar Ass'n).

147. *Guidelines for Use of Legal Assistants,* Rhode Island Supreme Court, Provisional Order No. 18 (Feb. 1, 1983).

148. *Guidelines for Use of Legal Assistant Services* (State Bar of New Mexico, 1980).

149. *Guidelines for the Utilization by Lawyers of the Service of Legal Assistants,* New York State Bar Ass'n (1976).

150. *Guidelines for the Utilization by Lawyers of the Services of Legal Assistants Under the New Hampshire Rules of Professional Conduct* (Supreme Court Rule 35) (August 1987).

151. *Guidelines for the Utilization by Lawyers of the Services of Legal Assistants,* South Carolina Bar (1981).

152. *Guidelines for the Utilization of Legal Assistants,* Colorado Bar Ass'n Legal Assistant Committee. *See also* 18 Colorado Lawyer 2097 (1989).

153. *Guidelines for the Utilization of Legal Assistants in Kansas,* Kansas Bar Ass'n Committee on Legal Assistants (1988).

154. *Guidelines for Utilization of Legal Assistants Services,* 57 Michigan State Bar Journal 334 (1978).

155. *A Guide to Cite Checking* by C. Kaufman, 8 LAT 44 (Jan./Feb. 1991).

156. *A Guide to Reviewing and Summarizing Medical Records* by K. Appleby, 8 LAT 26 (Sept./Oct. 1990).

157. *Harnessing the Power of Stress* by J. Hosea, 14 NPR 7 (NFPA, Summer 1989).

158. *Helping Legal Assistants to Help Themselves* by P. Saucier, 9 Legal Management 28 (ALA, Sept./Oct. 1990) (billable hours).

159. *Help! Service Companies Come to the Rescue of Drowning Legal Assistants* by C. McKown, 4 LAT 24 (Mar./Apr. 1987).

160. *Hide & Seek for Assets: The Life of a Probate Paralegal* by H. Walker, 5 LAT 38 (Mar./Apr. 1988).

161. *Hiring Legal Staff: Determining Cost and Value* by T. Brooks & W. Hackett (ABA, 1990).

162. *A History of the American Bar* by C. Warren (Little Brown, 1966).

163. *How Much Are You Worth? Putting a Price Tag on Your Performance,* 38 The Docket 26 (NALS, Jan./Feb., 1990).

164. *How NALA Is Governed* by Favinger, 18 F&F 16 (July 1991).

165. *How Satisfied Are You with Your Job?* by J. Gurdak, 3 LAT 19 (Spring 1986).

166. *How to Analyze and Apply Case Law* by C. Smith, 8 LAT 27 (Mar./Apr. 1991).

167. *How to Assign a Task Clearly* by R. Feferman, 13 Legal Economics 62 (ABA, Apr. 1987).

168. *How to Choose a Paralegal Education Program* (AAfPE, 1990). Reprinted in 17 F&F 31 (NALA, Sept. 1990).

169. *How to Create an In-House Legal Assistant Training Program* by R. Rutherford, 7 Legal Professional 29 (renamed LAT) (Sept./Oct. 1989).

170. *How to Create-A-System for the Law Office,* R. Ramo, ed. (ABA, 1975).

171. *How to Effectively Assist at Trial* by Patrick, 8 LAT 17 (Sept./Oct. 1990).

172. *How to Improve Lawyer/Staff Communications* by E. Brown, 5 Legal Administrator 73 (ALA, Nov./Dec. 1987).

173. *How to Locate Elusive Witnesses* by E. Thorp, 8 LAT 60 (Nov./Dec. 1990).

174. *How to Negotiate a Good Raise* by I. Hill, 8 LAT 53 (May/June 1991).

175. *How to Use Legal Assistants to Enforce Commercial Secured Claims* by J. Verellen, 33 The Practical Lawyer 9 (Dec. 1987).

176. *How to Wage Peace* by T. McGowan, 2 LAT 22 (Winter 1985) (friction with secretaries).

177. *Idaho Needs ABA Approved Legal Assistants' School* by H. Moncrief, The Advocate 8 (Dec. 1989).

178. *If You're Smart, Why Aren't You in Law School?* by L. Hardwick, 4 LAT 27 (May/June 1987).

179. *Illinois State Bar Association Position Paper on Use of Attorney Assistants in Real Estate Transactions* (May 16, 1984).

180. *The Immigration Paralegal* by J. Mason, 8 LAT 76 (Nov./Dec. 1990).

181. *Impact of ABA Associate Membership,* 15 F&F 24 (NALA, Fall 1988).

182. *In California, It's Better to Stay Put Than to Switch: A Paralegal's Past Forces New Boss to Drop Cases* by B. Motamedi, 7 LAT 37 (May/June 1990).

183. *Income Up in Legal and Paralegal Fields,* 26 LOEM 489 (1986).

184. *Independent Paralegals: Entrepreneurs or Imposters?* by B. Motamedi, 7 Legal Professional 16 (renamed LAT) (Mar./Apr. 1990).

185. *The Independent Paralegal's Handbook: How to Provide Legal Services Without Going to Jail* by R. Warner (Nolo Press, 1991).

186. *The Information Resource Manager: A New Career for Legal Assistants?* by C. Griffith, 5 LAT 52 (Mar./Apr. 1988).

187. *Inmate Involvement in Prison Legal Services* by W. Statsky (ABA Resource Center on Correctional Law and Legal Services, 1974).

188. *Innovative Training Techniques* by D. Patrick, 8 LAT 31 (Jan./Feb. 1991).

189. *In Praise of the CLA* [Certified Legal Assistant] by Villines, 18 F&F 28 (July 1991).

190. *The Institute of Legal Executives* by G. Schrader, 4 JPE&P 19 (Oct. 1987) (England).

191. *Intellectual Property: Trademarks, Patents, Copyrights* by J. Cone, 5 LAT 26 (Jan./Feb. 1988).

192. *Interviewing: The Employer Perspective* by C. Kauffman, 7 The LAMA Manager 11 (LAMA, Winter 1991).

193. *Interviews and Statements* by K. Andrews, 13 NPR 14 (NFPA, Spring 1989) (interviewing and investigation).

194. *An Interview with Clark Durant* by B. Albert, 12 NPR 6 (NFPA, Winter 1988) (deregulation of the legal profession).

195. *Introducing Student [Paralegal] Associations* by C. Cattie, 15 NPR 10 (NFPA, Spring 1991).

196. *Investigation Techniques: Locating People* by S. Peterson, 13 NPR 14 (NFPA, Winter 1989).

197. *Issues in Paralegalism: Education, Certification, Licensing, Unauthorized Practice* by Haskell, 15 Georgia Law Review 631 (1981).

198. *Is There Life After the Law Firm?* by C. Estrin, 8 LAT 65 (May/June 1991).

199. *Is There Room for a Paralegal on L.A. Law?* by Hangley, 12 NPR 7 (NFPA, Spring 1988).

200. *It's Not Easy Being Second Chair: A Basic Approach to Trial Assistance* by R. Sova, 5 LAT 45 (Jan./Feb. 1988).

201. *Job-Hunting: How to Bag the Big One* by F. Grones, 5 LAT 48 (Sept./Oct. 1987).

202. *Job Satisfaction: Mental and Environmental Improvements* by Y. Garman, 6 LAMA Manager 14 (LAMA, Fall 1990). Reprinted in 17 F&F 10 (Nov. 1990).

203. *Journal of Paralegal Education and Practice* (AAfPE, P.O. Box 40244, Overland Park, KS, 66204).

204. *Judging Credentials: Nonlawyer Judges and the Politics of Professionalism* by D. Provine (Univ. of Chicago Press, 1986).

205. *Kentucky Supreme Court Rule 3.700* (Provisions Relating to Paralegals, 1979).

206. *Labor Department Groups Paralegals with "Crafts, Sales, Secretarial," Attempts to Avoid Aptitude Testing* by M. Dick, 13 NPR 9 (NFPA, Fall 1988).

207. *Landmark Ethics Case Takes Toll on Paralegal's Career, Family* by B. Motamedi, 7 LAT 39 (May/June 1990).

208. *Law Clerks and the Unauthorized Practice of Law,* 46 Chicago-Kent Law Review 214 (1969).

209. *Law Firm Diversification and Affiliation Between Lawyers and Nonlaywer Professionals* by D. Pitofsky, 3 Georgetown Journal of Legal Ethics 885 (1990).

210. *Law Office Management: Leveraging with Legal Assistants* by E. Clark, 25 Arizona Attorney 36 (Oct. 1989).

211. *Law Office Staff Manual* by B. Rolston (ABA, 1982).

212. *Law School: Legal Education in America from the 1850s to the 1980s* by R. Stevens (Univ. of North Carolina Press, 1983).

213. *The Lawyer from Antiquity to Modern Times* by R. Pound (West, 1953).

214. *Lawyers Aiding Nonlawyers in the Unlawful Practice of Law,* Oregon State Bar Bulletin, 37 (Feb./Mar. 1990).

215. *Lawyers, Clients Gain from Paralegals' Legal Expertise,* Kansas City Business Journal (Aug. 21, 1989).

216. *Lawyer's Professional Obligations Concerning Paralegals* by Conn. Bar Ass'n Inter-Committee Group to Study the Role of Paralegals, 59 Conn. Bar Journal 425 (1985).

217. *The Lay Advocate* by Sparer, 43 University of Detroit Law Journal 493 (1966).

218. *Layman's Assistance to Party in Divorce Proceeding as Unauthorized Practice of Law,* 12 American Law Reports, 4th 656 (1982).

219. *Lay Practice Before Administrative Tribunals: Clarification Needed* by Pollack, 66 Michigan Bar Journal 675 (1987).

220. *The Legal Assistant & Preparing Deposition Summaries,* 15 F&F S1 (NALA, Jan. 1989).

221. *Legal Assistant as Law Librarian* by J. Lewek, 17 F&F 28 (NALA, Mar. 1991).

222. *The Legal Assistant as Librarian* by N. Wendt, 6 LAT 19 (Sept./Oct. 1988).

223. *Legal Assistant as the Office Manager* by C. Amira, 11 F&F 25 (NALA, Jan./Feb. 1985).

224. *Legal Assistant at the Computer Forefront* by M. George, 5 LAT 49 (Nov./Dec. 1987).

225. *Legal Assistant Charges as Recoverable Attorney Fees: An Arizona Case,* 27 LOEM 453 (1986–87).

226. *Legal Assistant Education* by D. Dye, 38 Journal of the Missouri Bar 111 (Mar. 1982).

227. *Legal Assistant Hiring Techniques* by M. Coyne, 6 LAMA Manager 10 (LAMA, Summer 1990).

228. *The Legal Assistant in Corporations* by D. Templeton, 5 LAT 35 (July/Aug. 1988).

229. *A Legal Assistant Is Elected Probate Judge* by T. Howard, 5 LAT 32 (Mar./Apr. 1988).

230. *Legal Assistant Manager Discusses Hiring and Firing* by C. Gibson, 11 NPR 22 (NFPA, Spring 1987).

231. *Legal Assistant Manager Improves Bottom Line (Deborah Wahl)* by T. Howard, 8 LAT 34 (Jan./Feb. 1991).

232. *Legal Assistant Managers Enhance Productivity* by P. Curtis, 15 NPR 28 (NFPA, Summer 1990).

233. *A Legal Assistant of Note* by H. Kaufman, 6 LAT 56 (May/June 1989) (copyright paralegal).

234. *The Legal Assistant Profession: National Utilization and Compensation Survey Report* (NALA, 1991).

235. *A Legal Assistant Program Evaluation Design* by J. Snell & D. Green, 4 JPE&P 53 (Oct. 1987).

236. *Legal Assistant Programs: A Guide to Effective Program Implementation and Maintenance* (ABA, 1978).

237. *Legal Assistants* (NY, Practicing Law Institute) (annual).

238. *Legal Assistants: A Case of Uncertain Identity* by D. Parker, 7 Legal Professional 10 (renamed LAT) (Sept./Oct. 1989).

239. *Legal Assistants: A Growing Role in the Practice of Law in Alabama* by K. Rasmussen, 52 The Alabama Lawyer 214 (July 1991).

240. *Legal Assistants as Law Office Managers* by Kreipe, 59 The Journal of the Kansas Bar Ass'n 19 (July 1990).

241. *Legal Assistants Can Increase Your Profits* by P. Ulrich, 69 ABA Journal 1634 (1983).

242. *Legal Assistants Division Proposes Voluntary Certification Program,* 49 Texas Bar Journal 886 (1986).

243. *Legal Assistants: Even a Small Firm Can Use Them* by Simpson, 15 Legal Economics 20 (ABA, Apr. 1989).

244. *Legal Assistants Going Freelance* by L. Jevahirian, 17 F&F 22 (NALA, Mar. 1991).

245. *The Legal Assistant's Handbook,* 2d ed. by T. Brunner et al. (Bureau of National Affairs, 1988).

246. *Legal Assistants Increase Productivity* by M. Douglass, 45 The Alabama Lawyer 334 (Nov. 1984).

247. *Legal Assistants in Northern Michigan* by C. Andary, 68 Michigan Bar Journal 398 (May 1989).

248. *Legal Assistants in Probate Administration* by M. Mulligan & S. Grabert, 30 The St. Louis Bar Journal 28 (Summer, 1983).

249. *Legal Assistants in Public Law: Their Role in Attorney Generals' Offices* by N. Helmich & R. Larson, 5 LAU 109 (ABA, 1986).

250. *Legal Assistants in the Courtroom* by Hogan, 18 F&F 24 (July 1991).

251. *Legal Assistants: Measuring Profitability* by Green, 14 Legal Economics 26 (ABA, Mar. 1988). *See also* 14 F&F 10 (NALA, Apr. 1988).

252. *Legal Assistants of New Mexico: Statement of Professional Standards* (Dec. 1989).

253. *Legal Assistants: Sample Job Descriptions,* 12 F&F 21 (NALA, Apr. 1986).

254. *Legal Assistants Share the Spotlight at Historic Minneapolis Firm* by T. Howard, 4 LAT 16 (Mar./Apr. 1987).

255. *Legal Assistants Supervising Lawyers* by T. Howard, 4 LAT 28 (July/Aug. 1987).

256. *Legal Assistant's Time to Be Included in Award of Reasonable Attorney Fees in Florida,* 13 F&F 24 (NALA, Aug. 1986).

257. *Legal Assistants Will Increase Your Income* by H. Draper, 62 Michigan Bar Journal 1083 (Dec. 1983).

258. *Legal Assistants Will Increase Your Income* by P. Ulrich, 69 ABA Journal 1634 (Nov. 1983).

259. *Legal Assistant Time in Attorney Fee Awards* by K. Judd, 14 F&F 10 (NALA, June 1988).

260. *Legal Assistant Today* (James Publishing Co., 3520 Cadillac Ave., Suite E, Costa Mesa, CA 92626).

261. *Legal Assistant Utilization in Connecticut Law Firms* by S. Endleman, 55 Connecticut Bar Journal 324 (Aug. 1981).

262. *Legal Assistant Wise* by J. Gish (Professional Publishing Group, 1990).

263. *The Legal Assistant: Your Profit Center* by A. Callum, 69 Michigan Bar Journal 558 (1990).

264. *Legal Investigation & Informal Discovery* by K. Andrews, 7 LAT 36 (July/Aug. 1990).

265. *Legal Malpractice: Prevention through Automation* by H. Snyder, 7 LAT 34 (May/June 1990).

266. *Legal Paraprofessionals and Unauthorized Practice*, Note, 8 Harvard Civil Rights–Civil Liberties Law Review 104 (1973).

267. *Legal Skills Training for the Non-Lawyer Advocate in the Public Sector* by R. Hoffman, 2 LAT 27 (Fall 1984).

268. *Legal Technician: Friend of the People* by S. Braverman, 15 NPR 28 (NFPA, Fall 1990).

269. *Legal Technician: Friend or Foe?* by S. Lewis, 14 NPR 22 (NFPA, Spring 1990).

270. *The Leveraged Legal Assistant* by L. Werthheim & R. Berkow, 5 LAT 22 (Nov./Dec. 1987) (profitability).

271. *Life in a Corporate Law Department* by E. McCann, 6 LAMA Manager 4 (LAMA, Spring 1990).

272. *The Limited Practice Rule: Its Track Record after Four Years* by Fuller, 40 Washington State Bar News 15 (Oct. 1986).

273. *The Litigation Manager* by C. Kaufman, 7 Legal Professional 551 (renamed LAT) (July/Aug./Oct. 1989).

274. *The Litigation Paralegal* by J. McCord (West, 1988).

275. *Long-Term Legal Assistant Job Enrichment* by P. Ulrich, 24 LOEM 366 (1983). *See also* 4 LAU 37 (ABA 1984).

276. *Look Before You Leap into Law School* by C. Bruno, 7 Legal Professional 22 (renamed LAT) (Sept./Oct. 1989).

277. *Looking for a Job Is a Job* by K. Allen, 15 NPR 22 (NFPA, Spring 1991).

278. *Make the Most of Legal Assistants in Tax Practice* by F. Berall, 2 Practical Tax Lawyer 59 (Winter 1988).

279. *Management and Motivation Can Improve Your Legal Assistant Program* by P. Ulrich, 3 LAT 31 (Spring 1986).

280. *Management of Legal Assistants: The Ethical Obligations of the Attorney,* 26 Arizona Attorney, 27 (Jan. 1989).

281. *Managing Paralegals as a Human Resource* by M. George, 4 LAT 26 (Jan./Feb. 1987).

282. *Managing Temporary Legal Aids* by L. Hill, National Law Journal p. 15 (Aug. 15, 1988).

283. *Manual for Legal Assistants,* 2d ed. by NALA (West, 1992).

284. *Manual for the Lawyer's Assistant,* 2d ed. by NALS (West, 1988).

285. *Marching to a Different Drummer: Paralegal Work in the Military* by D. Richards, 2 Calif. Paralegal Magazine 8 (Oct./Dec. 1990).

286. *Mediation and the Legal Assistant* by W. Evarts, 2 LAT 29 (Fall 1984).

287. *Minnesota Parental Leave Law Extends Coverage to Law Firms* by M. Jacobs, 13 NPR 25 (NFPA, Summer 1988).

288. *Missouri Guidelines for Practicing with Paralegals* (Missouri Bar Ass'n, 1987).

289. *Missouri v. Jenkins,* 491 U.S. 274, 109 S.Ct. 2463, 105 L.Ed.2d 229 (1989) (paralegal fees).

290. *Model Guidelines for the Utilization of Legal Assistant Services* (ABA, Standing Committee on Legal Assistants, Mar. 1, 1991) (tentative draft).

291. *Model Standards and Guidelines for Utilization of Legal Assistants Annotated,* 17 F&F 48 (NALA, Fall 1990).

292. *Modern Legal Ethics* by C. Wolfram (West, 1986).

293. *More Firms Use Paralegal Managers* by L. Jevahirian, 13 National Law Journal 23 (Feb. 25, 1991).

294. *Mortgage Foreclosure Litigation: Avoiding the Pitfalls* by R. Hubbell, 16 F&F 10 (NALA, Nov. 1989).

295. *Motivation: The Manager's Approach* by M. Seeley, LAMA Newsletter 5 (LAMA, Winter 1989).

296. *NALA and Arizona Affiliates File Brief on Work Product,* 17 F&F 18 (NALA, Jan. 1991) (attorney-client privilege and paralegal work product).

297. *NALA and NFPA State Positions on Issues,* 12 NPR 20 (NFPA, Fall 1987).

298. *NALA Model Standards and Guidelines* by K. Sanders-West, 2 LAT 9 (Summer 1985).

299. *National Paralegal Reporter* (magazine) (NFPR, 5700 Old Orchard Rd., Skokie, IL, 60077, 708-966-6066).

300. *Nature of Legal Services or Law-Related Services Which May Be Performed for Others by Disbarred or Suspended Attorney,* 87 American Law Reports 3rd 279 (1978).

301. *New Career Opportunities in the Paralegal Profession* by R. Berkey (Arco, 1983).

302. *New Mexico Rules Governing the Practice of Law, Rule 20-102 (A)* (1989) (defining legal assistant).

303. *The New Model Rules: How Will They Apply to the Legal Assistant?* by R. Cleary, 10 F&F 9 (NALA, Jan./Feb. 1984).

304. *New Responsibilities Being Given to Paralegals* by C. Milano, 8 LAT 27 (Nov./Dec. 1990).

305. *NFPA Affirms Self-Direction for Paralegal Profession* by R. Major, 12 NPR 1 (NFPA, Summer 1987).

306. *NFPA Delegates Define Limited Licensure* by A. Retz, 13 NPR 6 (NFPA, Summer 1988).

307. *Nine Factors to Consider in Managing Case Documents* by S. Mohney, 8 LAT 91 (Mar./Apr. 1991).

308. *1990 Index of NALA Files of State Bar Activity,* 17 F&F 26 (NALA, Fall 1990) (paralegal ethics).

309. *The Nixon, Hargrave Environmental Team Walks a Fine Line Between Legal and Technical Advice* by J. Bassett, 7 Legal Professional 26 (renamed LAT) (Jan./Feb. 1990).

310. *The Nonlawyer Partner: Moderate Proposals Deserve a Chance* by S. Gilbert & L. Lempert, 2 Georgetown Journal of Legal Ethics 383 (1988).

311. *Nonlawyer Practice before Federal Administrative Agencies Should Be Discouraged* by Heiserman, 37 Administrative Law Review 375 (1985).

312. *Nonlawyer Practice before Federal Administrative Agencies Should Be Encouraged* by Rose, 37 Administrative Law Review 363 (1985).

313. *Nonlawyers in the Business of Law* by R. Andrews, 40 Hastings Law Journal 577 (1989).

314. *Nontraditional Paralegal Careers* by M. Rattermann, 8 LAT 60 (Jan./Feb. 1991).

315. *Notice of Public Hearings: Texas Voluntary Certification of Legal Assistants,* 48 Texas Bar Journal 1358 (1985).

316. *Novel Ways Paralegals Are Using Computers* by C. Milano, 8 LAT 22 (Mar./Apr. 1991).

317. *Nurses Give Medical Litigation a Booster Shot* by T. Howard, 7 Legal Professional 41 (renamed LAT) (July/Aug./Oct. 1989).

318. *N.Y. Court Questions Use of Paralegal to Screen Documents,* 12 NPR 8 (NFPA, Spring 1988).

319. *Obtaining ABA Approval: A Reference Manual for Legal Assistant Educators* (ABA, 1989).

320. *Occupational Regulation: Issues of Particular Importance to the Paralegal Profession* by R. McManus, 10 NPR 8 (NFPA, Aug. 1986).

321. *Office Politics* by A. Stern, 7 LAT 61 (May/June 1990).

322. *$100,000 a Year for Paralegals?* by P. Marcotte, 73 ABA Journal 19 (Oct. 1987).

323. *The Online Legal Assistant: Legal Databases* by C. Griffith, 4 LAT 39 (Mar./Apr. 1987).

324. *Opportunities in Paralegal Careers* by A. Fins (National Textbook Co., 1979).

325. *Order in the Court: Trial Management and Assistance* by C. Smith, 14 NPR 6 (NFPA, Spring 1990).

326. *Oregon State Bar Certifies Legal Assistants,* 17 LOEM 118 (Sept. 1976).

327. *Organizing and Digesting Depositions* by B. Piatz, 7 LAT 45 (July/Aug. 1990).

328. *Organizing, Developing and Managing a Legal Assistant Program* by P. Ulrich, 22 LOEM 197 (1981). Reprinted in 1981 LAU, 103 (ABA).

329. *Organizing Reorganization: The Legal Assistants Role in Initiating a Chapter 11 Case* by K. Morzak, 5 LAT 33 (Jan./Feb. 1988).

330. *Overcoming the Fear of Legal Writing* by S. McInnis, 17 F&F 38 (NALA, Jan. 1991).

331. *Overcrowding Plagues Field* by G. Sea, Houston Chronicle, pp. 1L & 4L (Oct. 2, 1988).

332. *Parajudges and the Administration of Justice* by Clark, 24 Vanderbilt Law Review 1167 (1971).

333. *Paralegal Advisory Boards Influence Education* by B. King, 15 NPR 24 (NFPA, Summer 1990).

334. *Paralegal Advocacy before Administrative Agencies* by W. Statsky, 4 University of Toledo Law University Review 439 (1973).

335. *The Paralegal and the Principle of Confidentiality* by G. Davis, 3 Journal of Paralegal Education 23 (Oct. 1986).

336. *The Paralegal: An Effective Part of the Legal Service Team* by J. Harwell, 23 Tennessee Bar Journal 37 (July/Aug. 1987).

337. *The Paralegal: A New Career* by R. Deming (Elsevier/Nelson Books, 1980).

338. *Paralegal: An Insider's Guide to the Fastest-Growing Occupation in the 1990s* by B. Bernardo (Peterson's Guides, 1990).

339. *The Paralegal Boom,* by K. Liebler, 12 Pennsylvania Lawyer 12 (Apr. 1990).

340. *Paralegal Burnout: Challenging Work Wanted* by Frank, 70 ABA Journal 30 (Dec. 1984).

341. *Paralegal Career Advancement* by J. Reinard, 6 JPE&P 1 (1989).

342. *Paralegal Careers* by W. Fry & R. Hoopes (Enslow Publishers, 1986).

343. *Paralegal Degree Program Offers Prisoners Hope,* New York Times 40 (Dec. 1, 1985).

344. *Paralegal Education: Advice from the Experts* by J. Bassett, 8 LAT 21 (Jan./Feb. 1991).

345. *Paralegal Education in Prison* by A. Wolk, 4 LAT 49 (Jan./Feb. 1987).

346. *Paralegal Education in the United States* by T. Cannon, 15 F&F 42 (NALA, May 1989).

347. *Paralegal Education: Who Will Control the Future of the Profession?* by B. Albert, 6 LAT 36 (Jan./Feb. 1989).

348. *Paralegal Educators Identify Trends* by T. Cannon, 12 NPR 28 (NFPA, Spring 1988).

349. *Paralegal Employment Opportunities in State Government* by M. Baker & T. Eimmermann, 6 JPE&P 9 (1989).

350. *The Paralegal Factor* by B. Palermo, 9 Calif. Lawyer 47 (June 1989) (paralegal billing).

351. *Paralegal Growth Paralleled 1980s Law-Firm Expansion* by M. Goldberg, 26 Trial 97 (May 1990).

352. *The Paralegal: Key Link on the Team* by J. Harwell, Tennessee Bar Journal (July/Aug. 1987).

353. *The Paralegal in Army Legal Practice* by R. Black, Army Lawyer 70 (Nov. 1990).

354. *The Paralegal in Practice* by A. Clinton, 23 The Arkansas Lawyer 22 (Jan. 1989).

355. *A Paralegal in the Courthouse: An Answer to Crowded Dockets?* by T. Howard, 3 LAT 51 (Summer 1986).

356. *The Paralegal Job-Hunting Handbook* (National Capital Area Paralegal Ass'n, 1982, 1985).

357. *Paralegal Litigation Handbook* by C. Bruno (Institute for Business Planning, 1980).

358. *Paralegal Malpractice: New Profession, New Responsibility* by M. Moon, 18 Trial 40 (Jan. 1982) *See also* 6 NPR 1.

359. *Paralegal Medical Records Review* by K. Appleby & J. Tarver (James, 1989).

360. *Paralegal Opportunities in Environmental Law* by A. Parisi, 8 LAT 83 (Jan./Feb. 1991).

361. *Paralegal Paradox: Job Satisfaction* by J. Whalen, 12 F&F 17 (NALA, June 1986).

362. *Paralegal Parallax: Are Legal Technicians Parasites? Or Are Lawyers Just Paranoid?* by D. Olin, 10 Calif. Lawyer 20 (Nov. 1990).

363. *Paralegal Personnel for Attorneys General's Offices* (National Ass'n of Attorneys General, May 1976).

364. *Paralegal Placement Executive Speaks Out* by J. Hosea, 14 NPR 14 (NFPA, Spring 1990).

365. *Paralegal Practice and Procedure*, 2d ed. by D. Larbalestrier (Prentice Hall, 1986).

366. *Paralegal Pride: Is There Such a Thing?* by J. Mandla, 12 NPR 12 (NFPA, Winter 1988).

367. *The Paralegal Profession* by N. Shayne (Oceana, 1977).

368. *The Paralegal Profession* by Brown, 19 Howard Law Journal 117 (1976).

369. *Paralegal Profitability Analysis* by T. Hemnes, 25 LOEM 100 (1984).

370. *Paralegal Profitability Enhancement* by L. Leraul, 27 LOEM 448 (1987).

371. *Paralegal Programs: An Educational Alternative for Law Librarians* by C. Harris, 77 Law Library Journal 171 (1984–85).

372. *Paralegal Regulation and the New Professionalism* by E. Wheat, 3 Journal of Paralegal Education 1 (Oct. 1986).

373. *Paralegal Representation of Persons before State Administrative Agencies* by T. Aaron, 10 NPR 4 (NFPA, Oct. 1985).

374. *Paralegals' Acceptance and Utilization Increasing in Indy's Legal Community* by D. Brandt, 1 The Indiana Lawyer 1 (No. 5, June 20–July 3, 1990).

375. *Paralegal Salary and Job Function Survey of 1980—Arizona* by B. Childers & M. Jennings, 21 LOEM 506 (1981).

376. *Paralegals and Administrative Assistants for Prosecutors* by J. Stein & B. Hoff (National District Attorneys Ass'n, 1974).

377. *Paralegals and Sublegals: Aids to the Legal Profession* by Holme, 46 Denver Law Journal 392 (1969).

378. *Paralegals and the Imputed Disqualification Rule* by M. Schairer, 7 JPE&P 1 (1990).

379. *Paralegals Are Invaluable Pro Bono Resource* by W. Dean, 15 NPR 10 (NFPA, Winter 1991).

380. *Paralegals: A. Resource for Defenders and Correctional Services* by J. Stein (U.S. Gov't Printing Office, No. 027-000-00399-1) (Dec. 1976).

381. *Paralegals Average $14,000 to Start, Bring Profits to Firm* by Reskin, 70 ABA Journal 52 (Dec. 1984).

382. *Paralegals Can Be More Profitable than Associates* by A. Jones, 16 The Montana Lawyer 7 (Dec. 1990).

383. *Paralegal Serves as Bailiff of Probate Court* by C. Hunt, 10 NPR 18 (NFPA, Spring 1986).

384. *Paralegal Services and Awards of Attorneys' Fees* by Stahl & Smith, Arizona Bar Journal 21 (Oct./Nov. 1984).

385. *Paralegals: Firms Respond to Their Changing Role* by L. Myrick, 8 Of Counsel 3 (Apr. 3, 1989) (corporate paralegals).

386. *Paralegal's Guide to Dallas/Fort Worth Law-Related Careers* (Scrivener Publications, 1989).

387. *Paralegal's Guide to Manhattan Law Firms* by G. Pirozzi (West Heath Press, 1988).

388. *The Paralegal's Guide to U.S. Government Jobs: How to Land a Job in 70 Law-Related Careers*, 3rd ed. by J. Harris (Federal Reports, 1988).

389. *Paralegals in Australia* by J. Johnson, 15 NPR 8 (NFPA, Spring 1991).

390. *Paralegals in the Bush* by Conn & Hippler, 3 UCLA-Alaska Law Review 85 (1973).

391. *Paralegals in the Corporate Setting* by J. Campbell, 30 The St. Louis Bar Journal 22 (Summer, 1983).

392. *Paralegals in the Federal Government* by C. Perko, 4 LAU 75 (ABA 1984).

393. *Paralegals Move Up to Management* by R. Granat & D. Saewitz, National Law Journal p. 19 (Jan. 30, 1989).

394. *Paralegals Needed in Pro Bono Projects* by I. Woody, 15 NPR 12 (NFPA, Fall 1990).

395. *Paralegals: Out of the Shadows and into the Light* by D. Vitucci, Report 22 (Cincinnati Bar Ass'n, Feb. 1991).

396. *A Paralegal Speaks on Professional Issues* by J. Hughbanks, 2 Probate and Property 33 (May/June 1988).

397. *Paralegal Splitting Fees* by J. Unrath, 12 NPR 12 (NFPA, Winter 1988).

398. *Paralegals: Progress and Prospects of a Satellite Occupation* by Q. Johnstone & M. Wenglinsky (Greenwood Press, 1985).

399. *A Paralegal's Role in Insurance Defense Litigation* by S. Bullock, 17 F&F 60 (NALA, May 1990).

400. *Paralegals Seen Taking Jobs from Associates* by Winter, 68 ABA Journal 527 (1982).

401. *Paralegals: Should Legal Technicians Be Allowed to Practice Independently?* by D. Chalfie, 77 ABA Journal 40 (Mar. 1991).

402. *Paralegals: The Making of a Profession* by C. Gilsinan & S. Pope, 30 The St. Louis Bar Journal 6 (Summer, 1983).

403. *Paralegals: The National and State Outlook* by R. Beard, 18 Arkansas Lawyer 189 (Oct. 1984).

404. *Paralegal Survey Reveals Rising Salaries*, 27 Arizona Attorney 9 (Nov. 1990).

405. *Paralegals Use Their Heads and Hearts in Pro Bono Programs* by D. Barr, 15 NPR 4 (NFPA, Fall 1990).

406. *Paralegals Volunteer Pro Bono to Alternative Dispute Resolution Program* by G. Fitleberg, 15 NPR 10 (NFPA, Fall 1990).

407. *Paralegal Trial Handbook* by B. Hutson (James, 1991).

408. *Paralegal: Wills, Trusts and Estates* by P. Carter (D&E Publishers, 1982) (Florida).

409. *Paraprofessionals: Expanding the Legal Service Delivery Team* by W. Statsky, 24 Journal of Legal Education 397 (1972).

410. *Participation of a Legal Assistant in a Commercial Real Estate Transaction* by J. Kauffold, 16 F&F 14 (NALA, Nov. 1989).

411. *Partners in Performance: The Corporate Legal Assistant and the Service Company* by H. Rosenberg, 5 LAT 38 (July/Aug. 1988).

412. *Patricia Coleman of Chicago Creates Her Niche in Taxes, Trusts and ERISA* by T. Howard, 3 LAT 40 (Winter 1986).

413. *Perry Mason They're Not: But "Legal Technicians" Are Cutting into the Establishment's Market* by M. Shao, Business Week, p. 83 (Nov. 20, 1989) (independent paralegals).

414. *Personnel Management Techniques for the First-Time Supervisor* by A. Guinn, 8 LAT 56 (Mar./Apr. 1991).

415. *Policing the Professional Monopoly: A Constitutional and Empirical Analysis of Unauthorized Practice Prohibitions* by D. Rhode, 34 Stanford Law Review 1 (1981).

416. *Polish Your People Skills to Specialize in Family Law* by R. Bilz, 6 LAT 47 (Jan./Feb. 1989).

417. *Position Yourself for Success* by A. Wagner, 7 Legal Professional 16 (renamed LAT) (July/Aug./Oct. 1989).

418. *The Positive Side of Associate Membership* by D. Prehm, 10 NPR 1 (NFPA, Spring 1986).

419. *Practical Considerations in Establishing an Independent Practice* by D. Secol, 16 F&F 18 (NALA, Sept. 1989).

420. *Practice before Administrative Agencies and the Unauthorized Practice of Law* by Vom Baur, 15 Federal Bar Journal 103 (1955).

421. *Practice by Non-Lawyers before the National Labor Relations Board* by Gall, 15 Federal Bar Journal 222 (1955).

422. *Practice by Non-Lawyers before the United States Patent Office* by Bailey, 15 Federal Bar Journal 211 (1955).

423. *Practice with a Paralegal: Making an Educated Choice* by C. Dietrich, 13 Legal Economics 51 (ABA, Oct. 1987).

424. *Practicing with Paralegals* (Missouri Bar Legal Assistants Committee, 1989).

425. *Preparing for the First-Time Teaching Experience* by C. McKernan & A. Stover, 15 NPR 6 (NFPA, Summer 1990).

426. *Preparing for the Job Interview* by J. Penrose, 7 Legal Professional 48 (renamed LAT) (Nov./Dec. 1989).

427. *Preparing for Trial* by C. Wilson, 8 LAT 45 (Sept./Oct. 1990).

428. *Pretrial Preparation Procedures* by M. Farrington, 7 LAT 60 (July/Aug. 1990).

429. *Preventive Law and the Paralegal* by L. Brown, 24 Vanderbilt Law Review 1181 (1971).

430. *The Price of Success* by P. Zavalney, 6 Texas Lawyer 10 (Jan. 21, 1991).

431. *Prisoner Access to Justice and Paralegals* by B. Kempinen, 14 New England Journal on Crim. & Civil Confinement 67 (Winter 1988).

432. *Private Investigator* by T. McGowan, 2 LAT 24 (Fall 1984).

433. *Pro Bono Is for Legal Assistants, Too* by R. Yegge & W. Moore, 15 NPR 8 (NFPA, Fall 1990). Reprinted in 17 F&F 12 (NALA, July 1990).

434. *Pro Bono Opportunities for Nonlawyers,* 17 F&F 38 (NALA, July 1990).

435. *Pro Bono Program* by L. Olmstead, 17 F&F 30 (NALA, July 1990).

436. *Pro Bono Publico: How Paralegal Associations Can Contribute,* 12 NPR 11 (NFPA, Fall 1987).

437. *The Professionalization of the Legal Assistant* by D. Green et al., 7 JPE&P 35 (1990).

438. *Professional Negligence, Paralegals and Modern Legal Ethics between the Bookends* by H. Cohen, 11 The Journal of the Legal Profession 143 (1986).

439. *Professional Teamwork between Attorney and Secretary* by Ralston, 14 Legal Economics 25 (ABA, Sept. 1988).

440. *Profiles of Highly Successful Paralegals* by K. Garrett, 5 LAU 95 (ABA, 1986).

441. *Profitability Formulas and Paralegal/Associate Comparisons* by J. Tate, 15 NPR 18 (NFPA, Spring 1991).

442. *Progressive Paralegal Planning* by C. Acree, 29 The Colorado Lawyer 725 (1991).

443. *The Proper Scope of Nonlawyer Representation in State Administrative Proceedings* by G. Stevens, 43 Vanderbilt Law Review 245 (1990).

444. *Proposed Guidelines for the Utilization of Legal Assistants,* 15 The Colorado Lawyer 183 (1986).

445. *Rate Your Resume* by R. Nesbit, 16 F&F 43 (NALA, July 1989).

446. *The Real Estate Paralegal* by D. Johnson, 8 LAT 73 (Mar./Apr. 1991).

447. *Recognition and Opportunity: The Genesis for a Growing Profession* by S. Keaton, 10 F&F 13 (NALA, May/June 1984) (Texas Legal Assistants Division).

448. *Reflections on the Law Firm Environment* by C. Gorden, 13 NPR 7 (NFPA, Fall 1988).

449. *Registering Legal Assistants* by J. Noll & K. Buss, 5 Bar Bulletin, Issue 7 (Seattle-King County Bar Ass'n, Mar. 1987).

450. *Regulation: A New Forecast on a Timeworn Question* by S. Kaiser, NPR 14 (NFPA, Winter 1990).

451. *Regulation: The Sleeping Giant Awakens* by Murry, 4 LAT 16 (Sept./Oct. 1986).

452. *Removing the Veil of Mystery From the CLA Exam* [Certified Legal Assistant] by Dunn, 18 F&F 38 (July 1991).

453. *The Right Stuff* by T. Howard, 7 Legal Professional 36 (renamed LAT) (July/Aug./Oct. 1989) (upward mobility).

454. *Report from the Committee of Expansion of Professional Responsibilities* by Y. Spiegel, 10 NPR 4 (NFPA, Spring 1986).

455. *Report of the Connecticut Bar Association Special Inter-Committee Group to Study the Role of Paralegals* (12/11/85).

456. *Report of the State Bar of California Commission on Legal Technicians* (State Bar of Calif., July 1990).

457. *Representation of Clients before Administrative Agencies: Authorized or Unauthorized Practice of Law?* 15 Valparaiso University Law Review 567 (1981).

458. *Resumes for Paralegals and Other People with Legal Training* by R. Berkey (Arco, 1984).

459. *Revitalization of the Legal Profession through Paralegalism,* 30 Baylor Law Review 841 (1978).

460. *The Rhode Island Paralegal Association Hosts Conference,* 33 Rhode Island Bar Journal 43 (June/July, 1985).

461. *Rhode Island Supreme Court Provisional Order No. 18* (1983) (covering legal assistants).

462. *A Risky Stand-in? Paralegals at Realty Closings* by Silas, 69 ABA Journal 1812 (Dec. 1982).

463. *The RMLAA [Rocky Mountain Legal Assistants Association] Employment and Salary Survey: A 1990 Paralegal Profile* by B. Lilly, 19 The Colorado Lawyer 2213 (Nov. 1990).

464. *The Role of Accreditation and the Public Interest* by C. Chambers, 11 NPR 15 (NFPA, Spring 1987).

465. *The Role of Paralegals in Inmate Litigation* by F. Devine, 5 JPE&P 1 (Oct. 1988).

466. *The Role of Paralegals in Real Estate Transactions,* 68 Illinois Bar Journal 391 (Feb. 1980).

467. *The Role of the Legal Assistant [Paralegal] in Iowa* by the Iowa State Bar Ass'n (1979).

468. *The Role of the Legal Assistant in Real Estate/ Franchise Transactions* by B. Sacks, 16 F&F 36 (NALA, Nov. 1989).

469. *The Role of the Paralegal in the Civil Commitment Process* by R. Lockwood, 10 Capital University Law Review 721 (Summer 1981).

470. *The Role of the Paralegal in Corporate Acquisition* by S. Decker, 11 NPR 8 (NFPA, 1987).

471. *Running with Hares and Chasing with the Hounds: The Emerging Dilemma of Paralegal*

*Mobility* by R. Marquardt, 2 Journal of Legal Education 57 (Oct. 1984).

472. *Salaried Personnel: Are They Really Exempt from Minimum Wage and Overtime Requirements?* by P. Stewart, 9 Legal Management 11 (ALA, Jan./Feb. 1990).

473. *Salary Survey Results* by C. Milano, 8 LAT 27 (May/June 1991).

474. *The Salary Wars: Paralegals Could Come Out the Winners* by R. McCroskey, 4 LAT 37 (May/June 1987).

475. *Sale of Books or Forms. . .As Unauthorized Practice of Law,* 71 American Law Reports 3rd 1000 (1976).

476. *School Trains Jail-House Lawyers* by D. Horine, p. 20. The Los Angeles Daily Journal (Mar. 26, 1991).

477. *Searching for a Job? Here Are Some Helpful Hints* by M. Vaneecke, 13 F&F 20 (NALA, Apr. 1987).

478. *Secretary to Paralegal: A Career Manual and Guide* by L. Prendergast (Institute for Business Planning, 1984).

479. *Self-Help for the "Frustrated" Legal Assistant* by L. Fiegener, 15 F&F 20 (NALA, May 1989).

480. *Senior Legal Assistants: How to Keep Them* by M. Coyne, 3 LAMA Manager 7 (LAMA, Summer 1989).

481. *"Senior Paralegal" Is More Than Just a Title* by B. Grajski, 125 New Jersey Law Journal 14 (Apr. 19, 1990).

482. *Senior Paralegals Counsel Newcomers: Computer Litigation Support Can Help* by D. Bernhard, 9 Legal Management 48 (ALA, Mar./Apr. 1990).

483. *$etting Compensation* by M. Reger & L. Doll, 14 NPR 23 (NFPA, Summer 1989).

484. *SFALA Job Hunt Skills: Career Guide* (San Francisco Ass'n of Legal Assistants).

485. *A Short Course in Human Relations I for Legal Assistants* by L. Barth, 17 F&F 52 (NALA, May 1990).

486. *Should Lawyers Compete with Paralegals?* by E. Tronsrue, 12 NPR 4 (NFPA, Fall 1987).

487. *Should Paralegals Have More Responsibility?* by D. Austern, 23 Trial 19 (May 1987).

488. *Should Paralegals Prepare Wills?* 24 Maryland Bar Journal 38 (Jan./Feb. 1991).

489. *Should the ABA Appeal Process Be the Only Game in Town?* by M. Pener, 11 NPR 9 (NFPA, Spring 1987).

490. *Should the ABA or Anyone Else Be Involved in Approving or Accrediting Paralegal Training Programs?,* 1 LAT 14 (Spring 1984).

491. *Show and Tell: The Legal Assistant as Demonstrative Exhibit Specialist* by D. Filter, 5 LAT 26 (Sept./Oct. 1987).

492. *Six Legal Assistant Service Firms: How They Use Technology Creatively* by M. George, 6 LAT 37 (Nov./Dec. 1988).

493. *Slugging It Out for Justice* by J. Murry, 1 LAT 20 (Summer 1984) (Rosemary Furman and the Florida Bar).

494. *Statement to State Bar of California,* 17 F&F 18 (NALA, Fall 1990) (limited licensing).

495. *Strategies for Developing a Successful Computerized Conflict of Interest Management System* by S. Craig, 4 LAT 45 (May/June 1987).

496. *Strategies for Organizing Everyday Cases* by S. Mohney, 8 LAT 86 (Mar./Apr. 1991).

497. *Strategies for Paralegal Career Development* by T. Coyne, NPR 20 (NFPA, Winter 1990).

498. *Strategies for Working with Challenging People* by T. Howard, 8 LAT 54 (Sept./Oct. 1990).

499. *Stress Busters* by T. Howard, 6 LAT 16 (Mar./Apr. 1989).

500. *Success and Survival in a Law Firm* by B. Morgan, 7 LAT 65 (July/Aug. 1990).

501. *Successful Interviewing* by R. Berkey, 5 LAT 64 (Sept./Oct. 1987).

502. *Survey of Legal Assistants Shows Field Increasing in Numbers,* 31 LOEM 94 (1990).

503. *Survey on Law Office Compensation of Legal Assistants/Administrative Support Staff* (Michigan, Institute on Law Office Management; Institute on Continuing Legal Education).

504. *Survey Results of Non-Traditional Paralegal Responsibilities* by P. Ruse & J. Whelan, NPR 18 (NFPA, Winter 1990).

505. *Survey Results of Paralegal Instructors* by J. Hosea, 15 NPR 8 (NFPA, Summer 1990) (paralegals as teachers).

506. *Survival Kit for a New Paralegal* by M. Rosetti, 1 LAT 24 (Winter 1984).

507. *Surviving a Large Document Case,* 15 F&F 24 (NALA, Aug. 1988).

508. *Sweet-Talking Clients and Intransigent Bureaucrats: Immigration Paralegals Know Them All* by M. Myers & K. Raman, 15 NPR 4 (NFPA, Winter 1991).

509. *Systematic Trial Preparation* by B. Kidder, 8 LAT 103 (May/June 1991).

510. *A System for Managing Small to Medium-Sized Cases* by D. Bruegl, 8 LAT 71(Sept./Oct. 1990).

511. *Systemization and the Legal Assistant in the Law Office* by Endacott, 54 Nebraska Law Review 46 (1975).

512. *Teaching Corrections Law to Corrections Personnel* by W. Statsky, 37 Federal Probation 42 (June 1973).

513. *The Team Approach to Practice Development: Substantive and Procedural Guidelines for Law Office Staff* (Professional Education Systems, 1989).

514. *The Teaming of Legal Assistants and Librarians* by M. Wallace, 6 LAT 30 (May/June 1989).

515. *Team Teaching: The Role of Paralegals in Teaching Practical Skills* by S. DiLullo, 7 Legal Professional 45 (renamed LAT) (Jan./Feb. 1990).

516. *Technician, Attorney & Manager* by R. Granat, 7 Legal Professional 53 (renamed LAT) (Mar./Apr. 1990).

517. *Techniques for Supervising Paralegals* by W. Statsky, 22 The Practical Lawyer 81 (No. 4, 1976). (Reprinted in Law Office Management Manual No. 5, p. 27 (ABA-ALI, 1984).

518. *Television Commercial Portrays Paralegal in a Negative Light* by B. Schultz, 13 NPR 7 (NFPA, Winter 1989).

519. *Temporary Employment* by C. Toncray, 15 NPR 9 (NFPA, Winter 1991).

520. *Ten Tips for Effectively Assisting at Trial* by D. Patrick, 8 LAT 22 (Sept./Oct. 1990).

521. *Ten Ways to Make Paralegals More Profitable* by E. Wesemann, 134 Pittsburgh Legal Journal 20 (Apr. 1986).

522. *Texas Certification,* 10 NPR 6 (NFPA, Spring 1986).

523. *The Texas Division Rides Again, but Which Way?* by J. Murry, 3 LAT 42 (Summer 1986) (certification).

524. *Texas Opts for NALA CLA by Default* by J. Browning, 15 F&F 27 (NALA, Fall 1988).

525. *Time Management* by J. Hosea, NPR 2 (NFPA, Winter 1990).

526. *Tips and Traps for the New Paralegal* by A. Wagner, 8 LAT 78 (Mar./Apr. 1991).

527. *Tips on Hiring and Training Paralegals* by C. Tupis, 7 LAT 53 (July/Aug. 1990).

528. *To Be or Not to Be* by D. Villines, 17 F&F 12 (NALA, Mar. 1991) (freelance legal assistants).

529. *Tools for the Successful Paralegal Job Search* by E. Moorer, 6 LAT 20 (Jan./Feb. 1989).

530. *Tort Liability of Legal Paraprofessionals and Lawyers Who Utilize Their Services* by Wade, 24 Vanderbilt Law Review 1133 (1971).

531. *Training Paralegals In-House* by C. Bruno, 27 LOEM 184 (1986–87).

532. *Training the Legal Assistant for Litigation Practice in a Large Law Firm* by J. Goodman, 57 New York State Bar Journal 34 (Apr. 1985).

533. *The Training of Community Judges* by W. Statsky, 4 Columbia Human Rights Law Review 401 (1972).

534. *Turnabout: The Male Perspective of the Paralegal Profession* by D. Sesit, 4 LAT 21 (Nov./Dec. 1986).

535. *Twalla DuPriest: Bankruptcy Trustee [and Paralegal]* by J. Basset, 7 Legal Professional 73 (renamed LAT) (Sept./Oct. 1989).

536. *Unauthorized Practice and Legal Assistants* by Whidden, 13 The Journal of the Legal Profession 327 (1988).

537. *Unauthorized Practice and Pro Se Divorce: An Empirical Analysis,* 86 Yale Law Journal 104 (1976).

538. *The Unauthorized Practice of Law and the Legal Assistant* by D. Orlik, 2 Journal of Legal Education 120 (Apr. 1985).

539. *Unauthorized Practice of Law by Insurance Claims Adjusters* by Jordan, 10 The Journal of the Legal Profession 171 (1985).

540. *The Unauthorized Practice of Law: Do Good Fences Really Make Good Neighbors?* by Christensen, 1980 American Bar Foundation Research Journal 159.

541. *Unionization: Raising the Issue* by S. Peeples, 6 NPR 4 (NFPA, Summer 1982).

542. *Use of Lay Representatives,* 58 Michigan Law Review 456 (1960).

543. *The Use of Legal and Technical Assistants by Administrative Law Judges in Administrative Proceedings* by Mathias, 1 The Administrative Law Journal 107 (1987).

544. *Use of Legal Assistants in a Plaintiff's Trial Practice* by T. Boyer & T. Arington, 5 F&F 10 (NALA, Apr. 1988).

545. *The Use of Legal Assistants in a Small Office* by V. Nicholas & J. Kirk, Arizona Bar Journal 36 (Oct. 1978).

546. *The Use of Paralegal Assistants in Divorce Practice* by P. Grove & M. Binter, 4 American Journal of Family Law 41 (Spring 1990).

547. *Use of Paralegals in Probate Administration* by D. Kennedy, 32 Res Gestae 501 (Apr. 1989).

548. *Use of Paralegals Makes Good Economic Sense,* 69 ABA Journal 1626 (1983).

549. *Using Computers in Litigation Support* by M. Moses, 8 LAT 38 (Nov./Dec. 1990).

550. *Using Legal Assistants in Estate Planning* by G. Cohen, 30 The Practical Lawyer 73 (Oct. 1984).

551. *Using Paralegals in Pre-Trial Litigation* by L. Zimet, 14 Legal Economics 63 (ABA, Mar. 1988).

552. *Using Paralegals in Small and Mid-Sized Law Firms* by D. Howard, 5 JPE&P 67 (Oct. 1988).

553. *Utilization of Legal Assistants* by Y. Garman, 17 F&F 32 (NALA, July 1990). [*See also* 6 LAMA Manager 10 (Winter 1990)].

554. *Utilization of Legal Assistants in the Private Law Firm* by Klessing, 58 Wisconsin Bar Bulletin 33 (1985).

555. *Validity of Will Drawn by Layman Who, in So Doing, Violated Criminal Statute Forbidding Such Activities by One Other Than Licensed Attorneys,* 18 American Law Reports, 2d 918 (1951).

556. *Vertical Expansion of the Legal Service Team* by Smith, 56 ABA Journal 664 (July 1970).

557. *View [of Paralegals] from the Bench,* 17 F&F 36 (NALA, July 1990).

558. *Wage and Hour Law Applications for Paralegals* by J. Jeffries, 7 Legal Administrator 10 (ALA, Mar./Apr. 1988).

559. *Walt Disney World Company's Legal Assistants: Their Role in the Show* by Miquel, 16 F&F 29 (NALA, Jan. 1990).

560. *Washington's Paralegals: An '80s Takeoff Becomes a '90s Institution* by M. Marklein, The Washington Lawyer 26 (Jan./Feb. 1990).

561. *The Weekend Retreat: A New Benefit for Paralegals* by C. Estrin, 6 LAT 26 (Mar./Apr. 1989).

562. *What Activities of Stock or Securities Broker Constitute Unauthorized Practice of Law,* 34 American Law Reports 3d 1305 (1970).

563. *What Are You Worth?* by S. Yost, 7 Legal Professional 33 (renamed LAT) (Sept./Oct. 1989).

564. *Whatever Happened to Paralegal Paradise?* by Boardman, Texas Lawyer (Jan. 7, 1991).

565. *What Is LAMA? The Legal Assistant Management Association* by J. Murry, 4 LAT 13 (May/June 1987).

566. *What Is the Profit from Associates and Paralegals?* 62 Wisconsin Lawyer 6 (Apr. 1989).

567. *What to Consider When Drafting Simple Wills* by C. Carter, 8 LAT 63 (Mar./Apr. 1991).

568. *What Your Law Office Management Professor Never Told You* by C. Elwell, 5 LAT 66 (Nov./Dec. 1987).

569. *When Is a Paralegal Really a Paralegal?* by R. Lais, 32 Orange County Lawyer 6 (May 1990).

570. *When to Hire a Lawyer; When to Hire a Legal Assistant* by L. Dmytryk, 6 LAT 32 (Sept./Oct. 1988).

571. *Who Gets the Best Jobs?* by C. Milano, 8 LAT 39 (Sept./Oct. 1990).

572. *Winds of Change in the Paralegal Profession* by F. Setterberg, 7 Calif. Lawyer 26 (Jan. 1987).

573. *Witnesses: Who, Where, When, Why, How* by V. Nichols, 14 F&F 52 (NALA, Oct./Nov. 1987) (investigation).

574. *Working Effectively with Legal Assistants* by A. Olson, 62 Wisconsin Lawyer 25 (Nov. 1989).

575. *Working with Legal Assistants,* Ulrich & Mucklestone, eds. (ABA, 1980, 1981).

576. *Working with Legal Assistants: Professional Responsibility* by Ulrich & Clarke, 67 ABA Journal 992 (1981).

577. *Write a Letter: Letter Writing in a Law Office* by R. Bilz, 7 Legal Professional 44 (renamed LAT) (Nov./Dec. 1989).

578. *You're the Best: Esteem Building for Paralegals* by R. Roepp, 3 LAT 14 (Summer 1986).

579. *Your Secretary: Paralegal in Disguise* by Sternin, 88 Case & Comment 12 (July/Aug. 1983).

# APPENDIX

# B

# Paralegal Associations and Related Organizations

 **PARALEGAL ASSOCIATIONS (NATIONAL)**

(Membership statistics, where known, are presented in brackets.)

National Association of Legal
  Assistants [15,000]
1601 S. Main St., Suite 300
Tulsa, OK 74119
918-587-6828

National Federation of Paralegal
  Associations [17,500]
P.O. Box 33108

Kansas City, MO 64114
816-941-4000

(NALA and NFPA have numerous affiliated local paralegal associations. NALA affiliates are indicated by one asterisk (*) below; NFPA affiliates are indicated by two asterisks below (**). The addresses of these local associations change frequently. If the address given below turns out to be unproductive, contact the national office of NALA or NFPA for a more current address. Local associations without an asterisk are unaffiliated at this time.)

 **PARALEGAL ASSOCIATIONS (STATE)**

### ALABAMA

Alabama Association of Legal
  Assistants (*) [215]
P.O. Box 55921
Birmingham, AL 35255

Huntsville Association of
  Paralegals
P.O. Box 244
Huntsville, AL 35804-0244

Mobile Association of Legal
  Assistants [75]
P.O. Box 1988
Mobile, AL 36633

### ALASKA

Alaska Association of Legal
  Assistants (**) [130]
P.O. Box 101956
Anchorage, AK 99510-1956

Fairbanks Association of Legal
  Assistants (*)
P.O. Box 73503
Fairbanks, AK 99707

Juneau Legal Assistants Association
  (**) [20]
P.O. Box 22336
Juneau, AK 99802

### ARIZONA

Arizona Association of Professional
  Paralegals (**) [50]
P.O. Box 25111
Phoenix, AZ 85002

Arizona Paralegal Association (*)
P.O. Box 392
Phoenix, AZ 85001
602-258-0121

Legal Assistants of Metropolitan
  Phoenix (*)

P.O. Box 13005
Phoenix, AZ 85002

Southeast Valley Association of
  Legal Assistants (*)
% Sandy Slater
1707 N. Temple
Mesa, AZ 85203

Tucson Association of Legal
  Assistants (*)
P.O. Box 257
Tucson, AZ 85702-0257

### ARKANSAS

Arkansas Association of Legal
  Assistants (*)
P.O. Box 2162
Little Rock, AR 72203-2162

### CALIFORNIA

California Alliance of Paralegal
  Associations [4000]

P.O. Box 2234
San Francisco, CA 94126
415-576-3000

California Association of Freelance
   Paralegals [94]
P.O. Box 3267
Berkeley, CA 94703-0267
213-251-3826

Central Coast Legal Assistant
   Association (**) [70]
P.O. Box 93
San Luis Obispo, CA 93406

Central Valley Paralegal
   Association
P.O. Box 4086
Modesto, CA 95352

East Bay Association of Paralegals
   [200]
P.O. Box 29082
Oakland, CA 94604

Inland Counties Paralegal
   Association
P.O. Box 292
Riverside, CA 92502-0292

Kern County Paralegal Association
   [63]
P.O. Box 2673
Bakersfield, CA 93303

Legal Assistants Association of
   Santa Barbara (*)
P.O. Box 2695
Santa Barbara, CA 93120
805-965-7319

Los Angeles Paralegal Association
   (**) [1150]
P.O. Box 241928
Los Angeles, CA 90024
213-251-3755

Marin Association of Legal
   Assistants
P.O. Box 13051
San Rafael, CA 94913-3051
415-456-6020

Orange County Paralegal
   Association (**) [490]
P.O. Box 8512
Newport Beach, CA 92658-8512
714-744-7747

Paralegal Association of Santa
   Clara County (*)

P.O. Box 26736
San Jose, CA 95159

Redwood Empire Association of
   Legal Assistants
1275 4th St. Box 226
Santa Rosa, CA 95404

Sacramento Association of Legal
   Assistants (**) [271]
P.O. Box 453
Sacramento, CA 95812-0453

San Diego Association of Legal
   Assistants (**) [450]
P.O. Box 87449
San Diego, CA 92138-7449
619-491-1994

San Francisco Association of Legal
   Assistants (**) [975]
P.O. Box 26668
San Francisco, CA 94126-6668
415-777-2390

San Joaquin Association of Legal
   Assistants
P.O. Box 1306
Fresno, CA 93715

Sequoia Paralegal Association
P.O. Box 3884
Visalia, CA 93278-3884

Ventura County Association of
   Legal Assistants (*)
P.O. Box 24229
Ventura, CA 93002

## COLORADO

Association of Legal Assistants of
   Colorado (*) [106]
% Alma Rodrigues
4150 Novia Dr.
Colorado Springs, CO 80911

Rocky Mountain Legal Assistants
   Association (**) [440]
P.O. Box 304
Denver, CO 80201
303-369-1606

## CONNECTICUT

Central Connecticut Association of
   Legal Assistants (**) [290]
P.O. Box 230594
Hartford, CT 06123-0594

Connecticut Association of
   Paralegals, Fairfield County (**)
   [135]
P.O. Box 134
Bridgeport, CT 06601

Connecticut Association of
   Paralegals, New Haven (**)
   [100]
P.O. Box 862
New Haven, CT 06504-0862

Legal Assistants of Southeastern
   Connecticut (**) [55]
P.O. Box 409
New London, CT 06320

## DELAWARE

Delaware Paralegal Association
   (**) [295]
P.O. Box 1362
Wilmington, DE 19899

## DISTRICT OF COLUMBIA

National Capital Area Paralegal
   Association (**) [620]
1155 Connecticut Ave. N.W.
Wash. D.C. 20036-4306
202-659-0243

## FLORIDA

Broward County Paralegal
   Association
% Leigh Williams
Ruden, Barnett, McClosky
P.O. Box 1900
Ft. Lauderdale, FL 33302

Dade Association of Legal
   Assistants (*)
% Maxine Stone
14027 S.W. 84th St.
Miami, FL 33183

Florida Legal Assistants (*)
% Nancy Martin
P.O. Box 503
Bradenton, FL 34206

Jacksonville Legal Assistants (*)
P.O. Box 52264
Jacksonville, FL 32201

Orlando Legal Assistants (*)
% Roxane MacGillivray
Akerman, Senterfitt & Eidson

P.O. Box 231
Orlando, FL 32802

Pensacola Legal Assistants (*)
% Deborah Johnson
Levin, Middlebrooks & Mabie
226 S. Palafox St.
Pensacola, FL 32581

Volusia Association of Legal
  Assistants (*)
P.O. Box 15075
Daytona Beach, FL 32115-5075

## GEORGIA

Georgia Association of Legal
  Assistants (**) [820]
P.O. Box 1802
Atlanta, GA 30301

Southeastern Association of Legal
  Assistants of Georgia (*)
% Debra Sutlive
2215 Bacon Park Drive
Savannah, GA 31406

South Georgia Association of Legal
  Assistants (*)
% Martha Tanner
L. Andrew Smith, P.C.
P.O. Box 1026
Valdosta, GA 31603-1026

## HAWAII

Hawaii Association of Legal
  Assistants (**) [150]
P.O. Box 674
Honolulu, HI 96809

## IDAHO

Idaho Association of Legal
  Assistants (*) [54]
P.O. Box 1254
Boise, ID 83701

## ILLINOIS

Central Illinois Paralegal
  Association (*)
% Debra Monke
GTE North Inc.
1312 E. Empire St.
Bloomington, IL 61701

Illinois Paralegal Association (**)
  [1059]

P.O. Box 8089
Bartlett, IL 60103-8089
708-837-8088

Independent Contractors
  Association of Illinois
6400 Woodward Ave.
Downers Grove, IL 60516

Peoria Paralegal Association
% Sharon Moke
1308 Autumn Lane
Peoria, IL 60604

## INDIANA

Indiana Legal Assistants (*)
% Dorothy French
14669 Old State Rd.
Evansville, IN 47711

Indiana Paralegal Association (**)
  [300]
P.O. Box 44518, Federal Station
Indianapolis, IN 46204

Michiana Paralegal Association
  (**) [40]
P.O. Box 11458
South Bend, IN 46634

## IOWA

Iowa Association of Legal
  Assistants [400]
P.O. Box 335
Des Moines, IA 50302-0337

Paralegals of Iowa, Ltd.
P.O. Box 1943
Cedar Rapids, IA 52406

## KANSAS

Kansas Association of Legal
  Assistants (*) [138]
% Jimmie Sue Marsh
Foulston & Siefkin
700 Fourth Financial Center
Wichita, KS 67202

Kansas City Association of Legal
  Assistants (**)
P.O. Box 13223
Kansas City, MO 64199
913-381-4458

Kansas Legal Assistants Society
  (**) [190]
P.O. Box 1657
Topeka, KS 66601

## KENTUCKY

Kentucky Paralegal Association
  [232]
P.O. Box 2675
Louisville, KY 40201-2657

Lexington Paralegal Association
  (**) [80]
P.O. Box 574
Lexington, KY 40586

Louisville Association of Paralegals
  (**) [182]
P.O. Box 962
Louisville, KY 40201

## LOUISIANA

Baton Rouge Paralegal Association
P.O. Box 306
Baton Rouge, LA 70821

Lafayette Paralegal Association
P.O. Box 2775
Lafayette, LA 70502

Louisiana State Paralegal
  Association [200]
P.O. Box 56
Baton Rouge, LA 70821-0056

New Orleans Paralegal Association
  (**) [190]
P.O. Box 30604
New Orleans, LA 70190

Northwest Louisiana Paralegal
  Association (*)
P.O. Box 1913
Shreveport, LA 71166-1913

Southwest Louisiana Association of
  Paralegals
P.O. Box 1143
Lake Charles, LA 70602-1143

## MAINE

Maine Association of Paralegals (*)
P.O. Box 7554
Portland, ME 04112

## MARYLAND

Baltimore Association of Legal
  Assistants (**) [140]
P.O. Box 13244
Baltimore, MD 21203
301-576-BALA

## MASSACHUSETTS

Berkshire Association for
   Paralegals and Legal Secretaries
% Nancy Schaffer
Stein, Donahue & Zuckerman
54 Wendell Ave.
Pittsfield, MA 01201

Central Massachusetts Paralegal
   Association (**) [80]
P.O. Box 444
Worcester, MA 01614

Massachusetts Paralegal
   Association (**) [440]
P.O. Box 423
Boston, MA 02102
617-642-8338

Western Massachusetts Paralegal
   Association (**) [50]
P.O. Box 30005
Springfield, MA 01102-0005

## MICHIGAN

Legal Assistants Association of
   Michigan (*)
% Cora Webb
Woll, Crowley, Berman
315 S. Woodward
Royal Oak, MI 48067

Legal Assistant Section [400]
State Bar of Michigan
440 E. Congress, 4th Fl.
Detroit, MI 48226

Legal Assistants Section
State Bar of Michigan
306 Townsend St.
Lansing, MI 48933-2083
517-372-9030

## MINNESOTA

Minnesota Association of Legal
   Assistants (**) [1138]
2626 E. 82nd St. #201
Minneapolis, MN 55425

Minnesota Paralegal Association
   (*)
% Tracy Blanshan
Kennedy Law Office
724 SW First Ave.
Rochester, MN 55902

## MISSISSIPPI

Gulf Coast Paralegal Association
942 Beach Drive
Gulfport, MS 39507

Mississippi Association of Legal
   Assistants (*)
P.O. Box 996
600 Heritage Bldg.
Jackson, MS 39205

Paralegal Association of Mississippi
P.O. Box 22887
Jackson, MS 39205

## MISSOURI

Gateway Paralegal Association
P.O. Box 50233
St. Louis, MO 63105

Kansas City Association of Legal
   Assistants (**) [470]
P.O. Box 13223
Kansas City, MO 64199
913-381-4458

Southwest Missouri Paralegal
   Association [80]
2148 South Oak Grove
Springfield, MO 65804-2708

St. Louis Association of Legal
   Assistants (*) [434]
P.O. Box 9690
St. Louis, MO 63122

## MONTANA

Big Sky Paralegal Association
P.O. Box 2753
Great Falls, MT 59403

Montana Paralegal Association
P.O. Box 693
Billings, MT 59101

## NEBRASKA

Nebraska Association of Legal
   Assistants (*)
P.O. Box 24943
Omaha, NE 68124

## NEVADA

Clark County Organization of
   Legal Assistants (*)
% Angel A. Price

3800 S. Nellis #235
Las Vegas, NV 89121

Sierra Nevada Association of
   Paralegals (*)
P.O. Box 40638
Reno, NV 89504

## NEW HAMPSHIRE

Paralegal Association of New
   Hampshire (*)
% Frances Dupre
Wiggin & Nourie
P.O. Box 808
Manchester, NH 03105

## NEW JERSEY

Central Jersey Paralegal
   Association
P.O. Box 7015
Freehold, NJ 07728

Legal Assistants Association of
   New Jersey (*) [260]
P.O. Box 142
Caldwell, NJ 07006

South Jersey Paralegal Association
   (**) [160]
P.O. Box 355
Haddonfield, NJ 08033

## NEW MEXICO

Legal Assistants of New Mexico
   (**) [200]
P.O. Box 1113
Albuquerque, NM 87103-1113
505-260-7104

## NEW YORK

Adirondack Paralegal Association
% Maureen Provost
Bartlett, Pontiff, Stewart
One Washington Street
Box 2168
Glen Falls, NY 12801

Legal Professionals of Dutchess
   County
51 Maloney Rd.
Wappingers Falls, NY 12590

Long Island Paralegal Association
   (**) [130]

P.O. Box 31
Deer Park, NY 11729

Manhattan Paralegal Association
[515]
200 Park Ave., Suite 303 East
New York, NY 10166
212-986-2304

Paralegal Association of Rochester
(**) [170]
P.O. Box 40567
Rochester, NY 14604

Southern Tier Association of
Paralegals (**) [45]
P.O. Box 2555
Binghamton, NY 13902

Western New York Paralegal
Association (**) [275]
P.O. Box 207
Buffalo, NY 14202
716-862-6132

West/Roc Paralegal Association
[130]
Box 101
95 Mamaroneck Ave.
White Plains, NY 10601

## NORTH CAROLINA

Cumberland County Paralegal
Association
P.O. Box 1358
Fayetteville, NC 28302

Metrolina Paralegal Association
P.O. Box 36260
Charlotte, NC 28236

North Carolina Paralegal
Association (*)
% T. William Tewes
Fuller & Corbett
P.O. Box 1121
Goldsboro, NC 27533-1121

Professional Legal Assistants
P.O. Box 31951
Raleigh, NC 27622
919-821-7762

Raleigh Wake Paralegal
Association
P.O. Box 1427
Raleigh, NC 27602

Triad Paralegal Association
Drawer U
Greensboro, NC 27402

## NORTH DAKOTA

Red River Valley Legal Assistants
(*)
P.O. Box 1954
Fargo, ND 58106

Western Dakota Association of
Legal Assistants (*)
P.O. Box 7304
Bismarck, ND 58502

## OHIO

Cincinnati Paralegal Association
(**) [380]
P.O. Box 1515
Cincinnati, OH 45201
513-244-1266

Cleveland Association of Paralegals
(**) [480]
P.O. Box 14247
Cleveland, OH 44114

Greater Dayton Paralegal
Association (**) [160]
P.O. Box 515, Mid City Station
Dayton, OH 45402

Legal Assistants of Central Ohio
(**) [270]
P.O. Box 15182
Columbus, OH 43215-0812
614-224-9700

Northeastern Ohio Paralegal
Association
P.O. Box 9236
Akron, OH 44305

Toledo Association of Legal
Assistants (*) [176]
P.O. Box 1322
Toledo, OH 43603

## OKLAHOMA

Oklahoma Paralegal Association
(*)
P.O. Box 18476
Oklahoma City, OK 73154

Tulsa Association of Legal
Assistants (*)
P.O. Box 1484
Tulsa, OK 74101

## OREGON

Oregon Legal Assistants
Association (**) [340]

P.O. Box 8523
Portland, OR 97207

Pacific Northwest Legal Assistants
(*)
P.O. Box 1835
Eugene, OR 97440

## PENNSYLVANIA

Berks County Paralegal Association
544 Court St.
Reading, PA 19601
215-375-4591

Central Pennsylvania Paralegal
Association (**) [70]
P.O. Box 11814
Harrisburg, PA 17108

Keystone Legal Assistant
Association (*)
% Catrine Nuss
3021 Guineveer Drive, Apt. B4
Harrisburg, PA 17110

Lancaster Area Paralegal
Association
% Rosemary Merwin
Gibble, Kraybill & Hess
41 East Orange St.
Lancaster, PA 17602

Paralegal Association of
Northwestern Pennsylvania (**)
[40]
P.O. Box 1504
Erie, PA 16507

Philadelphia Association of
Paralegals (**) [775]
1411 Walnut St., Suite 200
Philadelphia, PA 19102
215-564-0525

Pittsburgh Paralegal Association
(**) [400]
P.O. Box 2845
Pittsburgh, PA 15230

Wilkes-Barre Area Group
% Tom Albrechta
6 East Green St.
West Hazelton, PA 18201

## RHODE ISLAND

Rhode Island Paralegal Association
(**) [200]
P.O. Box 1003
Providence, RI 02901

## SOUTH CAROLINA

Charleston Association of Legal
   Assistants
P.O. Box 1511
Charleston, SC 29402

Columbia Association of Legal
   Assistants (**)
P.O. Box 11634
Columbia, SC 29211-1634

Greenville Association of Legal
   Assistants (*)
P.O. Box 10491 F.S.
Greenville, SC 29603

Paralegal Association of the Pee
   Dee [31]
P.O. Box 5592
Florence, SC 29502-5592

## SOUTH DAKOTA

South Dakota Legal Assistants
   Association (*) [61]
% Louise Peterson
May, Johnson, Doyle
P.O. Box 1443
Sioux Falls, SD 57101-1443

## TENNESSEE

Memphis Paralegal Association
   (**) [105]
P.O. Box 3646
Memphis, TN 38173-0646

Middle Tennessee Paralegal
   Association (**) [145]
P.O. Box 198006
Nashville, TN 37219

Southeast Tennessee Paralegal
   Association
% Calecta Veagles
P.O. Box 1252
Chattanooga, TN 37401

Tennessee Paralegal Association (*)
P.O. Box 11172
Chattanooga, TN 37401

## TEXAS

Alamo Area Professional Legal
   Assistants [245]
P.O. Box 524
San Antonio, TX 78292 ·

Capital Area Paralegal Association
   (*) [252]
% Chris Hemingson
Pope, Hopper, Roberts & Warren
111 Congress, Suite 1700
Austin, TX 78701

Dallas Association of Legal
   Assistants (**) [799]
P.O. Box 117885
Carrollton, TX 75011-7885

El Paso Association of Legal
   Assistants (*) [106]
P.O. Box 121
El Paso, TX 79941-0121

Fort Worth Paralegal Association
   [226]
P.O. Box 17021
Fort Worth, TX 76102

Houston Legal Assistants
   Association
P.O. Box 52266
Houston, TX 77052

Legal Assistant Division [2046]
State Bar of Texas
P.O. Box 12487
Austin, TX 78711
512-463-1383

Legal Assistants Association/
   Permian Basin (*)
P.O. Box 10683
Midland, TX 79702

Legal Assistants Professional
   Association (Brazos Valley)
P.O. Box 925
Madisonville, TX 79702

Northeast Texas Association of
   Legal Assistants (*) [29]
P.O. Box 2284
Longview, TX 75606

Nueces County Association of
   Legal Assistants (*)
% Joyce Hoffman
Edwards & Terry
P.O. Box 480
Corpus Christi, TX 78403

Southeast Texas Association of
   Legal Assistants (*) [130]
% Janie Boswell
8335 Homer
Beaumont, TX 77708

Texarkana Association of Legal
   Assistants (*) [40]
P.O. Box 6671
Texarkana, TX 75505

Texas Panhandle Association of
   Legal Assistants (*) [63]
% Lisa Clemens
Morgan, Culton
P.O. Box 189
Amarillo, TX 79105

Tyler Area Association of Legal
   Assistants [94]
P.O. Box 1178
Tyler, TX 75711-1178

West Texas Association of Legal
   Assistants (*) [44]
P.O. Box 1499
Lubbock, TX 79408

## UTAH

Legal Assistants Association of
   Utah (*)
P.O. Box 112001
Salt Lake City, UT 84147-2001
801-531-0331

## VERMONT

Vermont Paralegal Association [80]
% Trudy Seeley
Langrock, Sperry & Wool
P.O. Drawer 351
Middlebury, VT 05753

## VIRGINIA

American Academy of Legal
   Assistants
1022 Paul Avenue N.E.
Norton, VA 24273

Peninsula Legal Assistants (*)
% Diane Morrison
Jones, Blechman, Woltz & Kelly
P.O. Box 12888
Newport News, VA 23612

Richmond Association of Legal
   Assistants (*) [318]
% Vicki Roberts
McGuire, Woods, Battle & Boothe
One James Center
Richmond, VA 23219

Roanoke Valley Paralegal
   Association (**) [70]

P.O. Box 1505
Roanoke, VA 24001
703-224-8000

Tidewater Association of Legal
  Assistants (*)
% Claire Isley
Wilcox & Savage
1800 Sovran Center
Norfolk, VA 23510

VIRGIN ISLANDS

Virgin Islands Paralegals (*)
% Eloise Mack
P.O. Box 6276
St. Thomas, VI 00804

WASHINGTON

Washington State Paralegal
  Association (**) [453]
P.O. Box 232
Ardenvoir, WA 98811
509-784-9772

WEST VIRGINIA

Legal Assistants of West Virginia
  (*)
% Mary Hanson
Hunt & Wilson
P.O. Box 2506
Charleston, WV 25329-2506

WISCONSIN

Paralegal Association of Wisconsin
  (**) [380]
P.O. Box 92882
Milwaukee, WI 53202
414-272-7168

WYOMING

Legal Assistants of Wyoming (*)
% Nancy Hole
Brown & Drew
123 West First St.
Casper, WY 82601

# OTHER ORGANIZATIONS

Alberta Association of Legal
  Assistants
% Mackimme Mathews
700, 401 9th Ave. SW
P.O. Box 2010
Calgary, AB Canada T2P 2M2

American Association for Paralegal
  Education
10100 Santa Fe Dr., Suite 105
P.O. Box 40244
Overland Park, KS 66204
913-381-4458

American Association of Law
  Libraries
53 W. Jackson Blvd., Suite 940
Chicago, IL 60604
312-939-4764

American Association of Petroleum
  Landsmen
4100 Fossil Creek Blvd.
Fort Worth, TX 76137
817-847-7700

American Bar Association
750 N. Lake Shore Dr.
Chicago, IL 60611
312-988-5000
312-988-5618 (Standing
  Committee on Legal Assistants)
202-331-2200 (Wash. D.C. office)

American Paralegal Association
P.O. Box 35233
Los Angeles, CA 90035

American Society of Notaries
918 16th St., NW
Wash. D.C. 20006
202-955-6162

American Society of Questioned
  Document Examiners
1432 Esperson Bldg.
Houston, TX 77002
713-227-4451

Association of American Law
  Schools
1201 Connecticut Ave., NW
Wash. D.C. 20036
202-296-8851

Association of Federal Investigators
1612 K. ST., NW, Suite 506
Wash. D.C. 20006
202-466-7288

Association of Legal
  Administrators
175 E. Hawthorn Parkway
Vernon Hills, IL 60061-1428
312-816-1212

Association of Transportation
  Practitioners
1211 Connecticut Ave., NW
Wash. D.C. 20036
202-466-2080

Canadian Association of Legal
  Assistants
P.O. Box 967
Station "B"

Montreal, Quebec, Canada H3B
  3K5

Coalition for Paralegal and
  Consumer Rights
1714 Stockton St., Suite 400
San Francisco, CA 94133

Federal Criminal Investigators
  Association
P.O. Box 1256
Detroit, MI 48231
512-229-5610

HALT (Help Abolish Legal
  Tyranny)
1319 F. St. NW, Suite 300
Wash. D.C. 20004
202-347-9600

Independent Association of
  Questioned Document
  Examiners
403 W. Washington
Red Oak, IA 51566
712-623-9130

Institute of Law Clerks of Ontario
Suite 502, 425 University Avenue
Toronto, ON Canada M5G 1T6

Institute of Legal Executives
Kempston Manor
Kempston, Bedford England

International Association of Arson
  Investigators
5428 Del Maria Way

Louisville, KY 40291
502-491-7482

International Association of Auto
  Theft Investigators
255 S. Vernon
Dearborn, MI 48124
313-561-8583

Legal Assistant Management
  Association
Overland Park, KS 66204
913-381-4458

National Association for Law
  Placement
166 Conn. Avenue, Suite 450
Wash. D.C. 20009
202-667-1666

National Association of Document
  Examiners
20 Nassau St.
Princeton, NJ 08542
609-924-8193

National Association of Enrolled
  Agents
6000 Executive Blvd., Suite 205
Rockville, MD 20852
800-424-4339

National Association for
  Independent Paralegals

635 5th St. West
Sonoma, CA 95476
800-542-0034
800-332-4557

National Association of Law Firm
  Marketing Administrators
60 Revere Drive, #500
Northbrook, IL 60062
708-480-9641

National Association of Law
  Placement
1666 Connecticut Ave. NW
Wash. D.C. 20009
202-667-1666

National Association of Legal
  Secretaries
2250 East 73d St., Suite 550
Tulsa, OK 74136-6864
918-493-3540

National Association of
  Professional Process Servers
306 H. St. NE
Wash. D.C. 20002
202-547-5710

National Indian Paralegal
  Association
7524 Major Ave.
Brooklyn Park, MN 55443

National Legal Assistant
  Conference Center
2444 Wilshire Blvd., Suite 301
Santa Monica, CA 90403

National Notary Association
8236 Remmet Ave.
Canoga Park, CA 91304-7184
818-713-4000

National Organization of Social
  Security Claimants
  Representatives
19 E. Central Ave., 2nd Fl.
Pearl River, NY 10965
800-431-2804

National Paralegal Association
P.O. Box 406
Solebury, PA 18963
215-297-8333

National Resource Center for
  Consumers of Legal Services
1444 Eye St. NW
Wash. D.C. 20005
202-842-3503

National Shorthand Reporters
  Association
118 Park St., SE
Vienna, VA 22180
703-281-4677

# Associations of Attorneys

## STATE AND LOCAL BAR ASSOCIATIONS

### ALABAMA

Alabama State Bar
P.O. Box 671
Montgomery, AL 36104
205-269-1515

Birmingham Bar Association
109 N. 20th St., 2nd Fl.
Birmingham, AL 35203
205-251-8006

### ALASKA

Alaska Bar Association
P.O. Box 100279
Anchorage, AK 99501
907-272-7469

### ARIZONA

Maricopa County Bar Association
333 W. Roosevelt St.
Phoenix, AZ 85003
602-257-4200

State Bar of Arizona
363 N. 1st Ave.
Phoenix, AZ 85003
602-252-4804

### ARKANSAS

Arkansas Bar Association
400 W. Markham
Little Rock, AR 72201
501-375-4605

### CALIFORNIA

Alameda County Bar Association
405 14th St., Suite 208
Oakland, CA 94612
415-893-7160

Bar Association of San Francisco
685 Market St., #700
San Francisco, CA 94105
415-764-1600

Beverly Hills Bar Association
300 S. Beverly Dr., #201
Beverly Hills, CA 90212
213-553-6644

Lawyers Club of Los Angeles
700 S. Flower St.
Los Angeles, CA 90017
213-624-2525

Lawyers' Club of San Francisco
685 Market St., #750
San Francisco, CA 94105
415-882-9150

Los Angeles County Bar
   Association
617 S. Olive St.
Los Angeles, CA 90014
213-627-2727

Orange County Bar Association
601 Civic Center Dr. West
Santa Ana, CA 92701
714-541-6222

San Diego County Bar Association
1333 7th Ave.
San Diego, CA 92101
619-231-0781

Santa Clara County Bar
   Association
2001 Gateway Pl., #220 West
San Jose, CA 95110
408-453-3448`

State Bar of California
555 Franklin St.
San Francisco, CA 94102
415-561-8200

### COLORADO

Colorado Bar Association
1900 Grant St., #950
Denver, CO 80203-4309
303-860-1115

Denver Bar Association
1900 Grant St., Suite 950
Denver, CO 80201-4309
303-860-1115

### CONNECTICUT

Connecticut Bar Association
101 Corporate Pl.
Rocky Hill, CT 06067
203-721-0025

### DELAWARE

Delaware Bar Association
708 Market Street
Wilmington, DE 19899
302-658-5278

### DISTRICT OF COLUMBIA

Bar Association of the District of
   Columbia
1819 H. St. NW, 12th Fl.
Wash. D.C. 20006
202-293-6600

District of Columbia Bar
1707 L. St. NW, 6th Fl.

Wash. D.C. 20036
202-331-3883

## FLORIDA

Florida Bar
650 Apalachee Parkway
Tallahassee, FL 32399-2300
904-561-5600

Dade County Bar Association
111 N.W. First Ave.
Miami, FL 33128
305-371-2220

## GEORGIA

Atlanta Bar Association
100 Peachtree St. NW
Atlanta, GA 30303
404-521-0781

State Bar of Georgia
800 The Hurt Bldg.
Atlanta, GA 30303
404-527-8700

## HAWAII

Hawaii State Bar
1001 Bishop St., Suite 950
Honolulu, HI 96813
808-537-1868

## IDAHO

Idaho State Bar
P.O. Box 895
Boise, ID 83702
208-342-8958

## ILLINOIS

Chicago Bar Association
321 S. Plymouth Ct.
Chicago, IL 60603-1575
312-782-7348

Chicago Council of Lawyers
220 S. State St., Rm. 800
Chicago, IL 60604
312-427-0710

Illinois State Bar Association
424 S. Second St.
Springfield, IL 62701
217-525-1760
800-252-8908
312-726-8775 (Chicago)
800-442-ISBA

Illinois Trial Lawyers Association
110 W. Edwards St.
P.O. Box 5000
Springfield, IL 62705
217-798-0755
800-252-8501

## INDIANA

Indianapolis Bar Association
10 West Market St.
Indianapolis, IN 46204
317-632-8240

Indiana State Bar Association
230 E. Ohio St., 6th Fl.
Indianapolis, IN 46204
317-639-5465

## IOWA

Iowa State Bar Association
1101 Fleming Bldg.
Des Moines, IA 50309
515-243-3179

## KANSAS

Kansas Bar Association
1200 Harrison St.
Topeka, KS 66612
913-234-5696

## KENTUCKY

Kentucky Bar Association
West Main at Kentucky River
Frankfort, KY 40601
502-564-3795

Louisville Bar Association
707 W. Main St., #200
Louisville, KY 40202
502-583-5314

## LOUISIANA

Louisiana State Bar Association
601 St. Charles Ave.
New Orleans, LA 70130
504-566-1600

Louisiana Trial Lawyers
  Association
442 Europe St.
P.O. Drawer 4289
Baton Rouge, LA 70821
504-383-5554

## MAINE

Maine State Bar Association
124 State St.
P.O. Box 788
Augusta, ME 04330
207-622-7523

## MARYLAND

Bar Association of Baltimore City
111 N. Calvert St.
Baltimore, MD 21202
301-539-5936

Maryland State Bar Association
520 W. Fayette St.
Baltimore, MD 21201
301-685-7878

## MASSACHUSETTS

Boston Bar Association
16 Beacon St.
Boston, MA 02108
617-742-0615

Massachusetts Bar Association
20 West St.
Boston, MA 02111
617-542-3602

## MICHIGAN

Detroit Bar Association
2380 Penobscot Bldg.
Detroit, MI 48226
313-961-6120

Michigan Trial Lawyers
  Association
501 S. Capitol Ave., Suite 405
Lansing, MI 48933-2327
517-482-7740

Oakland County Bar Association
1200 N. Telegraph Rd., Suite 532
Pontiac, MI 48053
313-338-2100

State Bar of Michigan
306 Townsend St.
Lansing, MI 48933-2083
517-372-9030

## MINNESOTA

Hennepin County Bar Association
430 Marquette Ave., No. 402
Minneapolis, MN 55487
612-340-0022

Minnesota State Bar Association
430 Marquette Ave., Suite 403
Minneapolis, MN 55401
612-333-1183
800-292-4152

## MISSISSIPPI

Mississippi State Bar
643 N. State St.
Jackson, MS 39202
601-948-4471

## MISSOURI

Bar Association of Metropolitan
  Saint Louis
One Mercantile Center #3600
St. Louis, MO 63101
314-421-4134

Kansas City Metropolitan Bar
  Association
1125 Grand Ave.
Kansas City, MO 64106
816-474-4322

Missouri Bar
326 Monroe
Jefferson City, MO 65102
314-635-4128

## MONTANA

State Bar of Montana,
46 N. Last Chance Gulch
P.O. Box 577
Helena, MT 59624
406-442-7660

## NEBRASKA

Nebraska State Bar Association
635 S. 14th St.
Lincoln, NE 68508
402-475-7091

## NEVADA

State Bar of Nevada
295 Holcomb Ave., Suite 2
Reno, NV 89502-1085
702-382-0502

## NEW HAMPSHIRE

New Hampshire Bar Association
112 Pleasant Street
Concord, NH 03301
603-224-6942

## NEW JERSEY

Essex County Bar Association
5 Becker Farm Road
Roseland, NJ 07068
201-622-6207

New Jersey State Bar Association
1 Constitution Sq.
New Brunswick, NJ 08901-1500
201-249-5000

## NEW MEXICO

State Bar of New Mexico
121 Tijeras St. NE
Albuquerque, NM 87102
505-842-6132
800-876-6227

New Mexico Trial Lawyers'
  Association Foundation
P.O. Box 301
Albuquerque, NM 87103
505-243-6003

## NEW YORK

Association of the Bar of the City
  of New York
42 W. 44th St.
New York, NY 10036
212-382-6600

New York County Lawyers
  Association
14 Vesey St.
New York, NY 10007
212-267-6646

New York State Bar Association
1 Elk St.
Albany, NY 12207
518-463-3200

New York State Trial Lawyers
  Association
132 Nassau St.
New York, NY 10038
212-349-5890

## NORTH CAROLINA

North Carolina Bar Association
1312 Annapolis Dr.
Raleigh, NC 27611
919-828-0561

North Carolina State Bar
1312 Annapolis Dr.
Raleigh, NC 27611
919-828-0561

## NORTH DAKOTA

State Bar Association of North
  Dakota
515½ E. Broadway, Suite 101
Bismarck, ND 58501
701-255-1404
800-472-2685

## OHIO

Cincinnati Bar Association
35 E. 7th St., 8th Fl.
Cincinnati, OH 45202-2411
513-381-8213

Cleveland Bar Association
118 St. Clair Ave., NE
Cleveland, OH 44114-1523
216-696-3525

Columbus Bar Association
40 S. 3rd St., 6th Fl.
Columbus, OH 43215-5134
614-221-4112

Cuyahoga County Bar Association
1228 Euclid Ave., No. 370
Cleveland, OH 44115
216-621-5112

Ohio State Bar Association
33 W. 11th Ave.
Columbus, OH 43201
614-421-2121

## OKLAHOMA

Oklahoma Bar Association
1901 N. Lincoln
Oklahoma City, OK 73105
405-524-2365
800-522-8065

Oklahoma County Bar Association
119 W. Robinson #240
Oklahoma City, OK 73102
405-236-8421

Tulsa County Bar Association
1446 S. Boston
Tulsa, OK 74119-3613
918-584-5243

## OREGON

Multnomah Bar Association
711 SW Adler, Suite 311
Portland, OR 97205
503-222-3275

Oregon State Bar
5200 S.W. Meadows Rd.

P.O. Box 1689
Lake Oswego, OR 97035
503-620-0222

## PENNSYLVANIA

Allegheny County Bar Association
420 Grant Bldg.
Pittsburgh, PA 15219
412-261-6161

Pennsylvania Bar Association
100 South St.
P.O. Box 186
Harrisburg, PA 17108
717-238-6715

Philadelphia Bar Association
One Reading Bldg.
Philadelphia, PA 19107
215-238-6300

## PUERTO RICO

Puerto Rico Bar Association
P.O. Box 1900
San Juan, PR 00908
809-721-3358

Puerto Rican Bar Association
888 Grand Concourse, Suite 1-0
Bronx, NY 10451
212-292-8201

## RHODE ISLAND

Rhode Island Bar Association
91 Friendship St.
Providence, RI 02903
401-421-5740

## SOUTH CAROLINA

South Carolina Bar Association
950 Taylor St.
Columbia, SC 29202
803-799-6653

## SOUTH DAKOTA

State Bar of South Dakota
Pierre, SD 57501
605-224-7554

## TENNESSEE

Tennessee Bar Association
3622 Westend Ave.
Nashville, TN 37205
615-383-7421

## TEXAS

Dallas Bar Association
2101 Ross Ave.
Dallas, TX 75201
214-969-7066

Houston Bar Association
1001 Fannin, Suite 1300
Houston, TX 77002
713-759-1133

State Bar of Texas
1414 Colorado
Austin, TX 78711
512-463-1463

## UTAH

Utah Bar Association
645 S. 200 East
Salt Lake City, UT 84111
801-531-9077

## VERMONT

Vermont Bar Association
P.O. Box 100
Montpelier, VT 05602
802-223-2020
800-642-3153

## VIRGINIA

Virginia Bar Association
701 E. Franklin St., Suite 1515
Richmond, VA 23219
804-644-0041

Virginia State Bar
801 E. Main St., Suite 1000
Richmond, VA 23219
804-786-2061

## VIRGIN ISLANDS

Virgin Islands Bar Association
46 King St.
Christiansted, VI 00822
809-778-7497

## WASHINGTON

Seattle-King County Bar
900 4th Ave., #600
Seattle, WA 98164
206-624-9365

Washington State Bar Association
2001 6th Ave.
Seattle, WA 98121-2599
206-448-0441

## WEST VIRGINIA

West Virginia Bar Association
100 Capitol St.
Charleston, WV 25301
304-342-1474

West Virginia Sate Bar
E-400 State Capitol
Charleston, WV 25305
304-346-8414

West Virginia Trial Lawyers
   Association
P.O. Box 3968
Charleston, WV 25339
304-344-0692

## WISCONSIN

Milwaukee Bar Association
533 E. Wells St.
Milwaukee, WI 53202
414-274-6760

State Bar of Wisconsin
402. W. Wilson
Madison, WI 53703
608-257-3838
800-362-8906

## WYOMING

Wyoming State Bar
500 Randall Ave.
Cheyenne, WY 82001
307-632-9061

# OTHER ATTORNEY ASSOCIATIONS

American Academy of Hospitals
  Attorneys
American Hospital Association
840 N. Lake Shore Dr.
Chicago, IL 60611
312-280-6601

American Academy of Matrimonial
  Lawyers
20 N. Michigan Ave., Suite 540
Chicago, IL 60602
312-263-6477

American Association of Public
  Welfare Attorneys
810 1st St. NE, Suite 500
Wash. D.C. 20002
202-682-0100

American Bar Association
750 N Lake Shore Dr.
Chicago, IL 60611
312-988-5000
202-331-2200 (Wash. D.C. office)

American Blind Lawyers
  Association
1010 Vermont Ave., NW
Wash. D.C. 20005
202-393-3666
800-424-8666

American Board of Professional
  Liability Attorneys
175 E. Shore Rd.
Great Neck, NY 11023
516-487-1990

American Board of Trial Advocates
16633 Ventura Blvd., Suite 1015
Encino, CA 91436
818-501-3250

American College of Probate
  Counsel
2716 Ocean Park Blvd., Suite 1080
Santa Monica, CA 90405
213-450-2033

American College of Trial Lawyers
10886 Wilshire Blvd.
Los Angeles, CA 90024
213-879-0143

American Corporate Counsel
  Association
1225 Connecticut Ave., Suite 302

Wash. D.C. 20036
202-296-4522

American Immigration Lawyers
  Association
1000 16th St., NW, Suite 604
Wash. D.C. 20036
202-331-0046

Association of Defense Trial
  Attorneys
600 Jefferson Bank Bldg.
Peoria, IL 61602
309-676-0400

Association of Life Insurance
  Counsel
201 Park Ave. South
New York, NY 10003
212-679-1110

Association of Trial Lawyers of
  America
1050 31st St. NW
Wash. D.C. 20007
202-965-3500
800-424-2727

Black Entertainment & Sports
  Lawyers Association
111 Broadway
New York, NY 10006
212-587-0300

Decalogue Society of Lawyers
179 W. Washington St., Suite 350
Chicago, IL 60602
312-263-6493

Federal Bar Association
1815 H. St., Suite 408
Wash. D.C. 20006
202-638-0252

Federal Communications Bar
  Association
1150 Connecticut Ave., NW
Wash. D.C. 20036
202-833-2684

Federal Energy Bar Association
1900 M. St. NW, Suite 620
Wash. D.C. 20006
202-223-5625

Federation of Insurance &
  Corporate Counsel
15 Ridge Rd.

Marblehead, MA 01945
617-639-0698

Hispanic National Bar Association
100 W. Randolph
Chicago, IL 60601
312-814-3813

Incorporated Society of Irish/
  American Lawyers
15140 Farmington Rd.
Livonia, MI 48154
313-522-5900

Inter-American Bar Association
1889 F. St. NW, Suite LL-2
Wash. D.C. 20006
202-789-2747

International Academy of Trial
  Lawyers
210 S. 1st St., Suite 206
San Jose, CA 95113
408-275-6767

International Association of
  Defense Counsel
20 N. Wacker Dr., Suite 3100
Chicago, IL 60606
312-368-1494

International Federation of Women
  Lawyers
186 5th Ave.

New York, NY 10010
212-206-1666

International Legal Defense
  Counsel
111 S. 15th St., 24th Fl.
Philadelphia, PA 19102
215-977-9982

International Trade Commission
  Trial Lawyers Association
815 Connecticut Ave. NW
Wash. D.C. 20006
202-659-5070

Maritime Law Association of the
  United States
1 Battery Park Plaza
New York, NY 10004
212-422-7585

Mexican-American Legal Defense
  and Education Fund

1430 K. St. NW
Wash. D.C. 20005
202-628-4074

NAACP Legal Defense and
    Education Fund
1275 K. St. NW
Wash. D.C. 20005
202-682-1300

National Academy of Elder Law
    Attorneys
1730 E. River Rd., Suite 107
Tucson, AZ 85718

National American Indian Court
    Judges Association
1000 Connecticut Ave., NW
Wash. D.C. 20036
202-296-0685

National Association of Attorneys
    General
444 N. Capitol St. NW, Suite 403
Wash. D.C. 20001
202-628-0435

National Association of Black
    Women Attorneys
3711 Macomb St. NW
Wash. D.C. 20016
202-966-9693

National Association of Bond
    Attorneys
P.O. Box 397
Hinsdale, IL 60522
312-920-0160

National Association of College &
    University Attorneys
1 Dupont Circle, NW, Suite 620
Wash. D.C. 20036
202-833-8390

National Association of Counsel
    for Children
1205 Oneida St.
Denver, CO 80220
303-321-3963

National Association of County
    Civil Attorneys
440 1st St. NW
Wash. D.C. 20001
202-393-6226

National Association of Criminal
    Defense Lawyers
1110 Vermont Ave., Suite 1150
Wash. D.C. 20005
202-872-8688

National Association of Railroad
    Trial Counsel
88 Alma Real Dr., Suite 103A
Pacific Palisades, CA 90272
213-459-7659

National Association of Women
    Judges
300 Newport Ave.
Williamsburg, VA 23185
804-253-2000

National Association of Women
    Lawyers
750 N. Lake Shore Dr.
Chicago, IL 60611
312-988-6186

National Bar Association
1225 11th St., NW
Wash. D.C. 20001
202-842-3900

National Conference of Black
    Lawyers
126 W. 119th St.
New York, NY 10026
212-864-4000

National Conference of Women's
    Bar Associations
113 W. Franklin St.
Baltimore, MD 21201
504-835-6705

National District Attorneys
    Association
1033 N. Fairfax St., Suite 200

Alexandria, VA 22314
703-549-9222

National Gay Rights Advocates
540 Castro St.
San Francisco, CA 94114
415-863-3624

National Lawyers Guild
55 6th Ave.
New York, NY 10013
212-966-5000

National Legal Aid & Defender
    Association
1625 K. St., Suite 800
Wash. D.C. 20006
202-452-0620

National Women's Law Center
1616 P. St. NW
Wash. D.C. 20036
202-328-5160

Native American Rights Fund
1712 N. St. NW
Wash. D. C. 20036
202-785-4166

Puerto Rican Legal Defense &
    Education Fund
99 Hudson St., 24th Fl.
New York, NY 10013
212-219-3360

Sports Lawyers Association
P.O. Box 5684
Lakeland, FL 33807
813-646-5091

Transportation Lawyers
    Association
3310 Harrison
Topeka, KS 66611
913-266-7014

Volunteer Lawyers for the Arts
1285 Avenue of the Americas
New York, NY 10019
212-977-9270

# ■ MISCELLANEOUS

American Arbitration Association
140 W. 51st St.
New York, NY 10020
212-484-4100

American Prepaid Legal Services
    Institute
750 N. Lake Shore Dr.

Chicago, IL 60611
312-988-5751

Legal Services Corporation
400 Virginia Ave. SW
Wash. D.C. 20024
202-863-1820

National Clients Council
2617 Martha St.

Philadelphia, PA 19125
215-686-2913

National Conference of Bar
    Examiners
333 N. Michigan, Suite 1025
Chicago, IL 60601
312-641-0963

# Federal Government
# Organization Chart

The Government of the United States

THE CONSTITUTION

**LEGISLATIVE BRANCH**

**THE CONGRESS**

Senate    House

Architect of the Capitol
United States Botanic Garden
General Accounting Office
Government Printing Office
Library of Congress
Office of Technology Assessment
Congressional Budget Office
Copyright Royalty Tribunal
United States Tax Court

**EXECUTIVE BRANCH**

**THE PRESIDENT**

**Executive Office of the President**

White House Office
Office of Management and Budget
Council of Economic Advisers
National Security Council
Office of Policy Development
Office of National Drug Control Policy

National Critical Materials Council
Office of the U.S. Trade Representative
Council on Environmental Quality
Office of Science and Technology Policy
Office of Administration
National Space Council

**THE VICE PRESIDENT**

**JUDICIAL BRANCH**

**The Supreme Court of the United States**

United States Courts of Appeals
United States District Courts
United States Claims Court
United States Court of Appeals for the Federal Circuit
United States Court of International Trade
Territorial Courts
United States Court of Military Appeals
Veterans Appeals
United States Courts
Administrative Office of the United States Courts
Federal Judicial Center

DEPARTMENT OF AGRICULTURE
DEPARTMENT OF THE INTERIOR
DEPARTMENT OF COMMERCE
DEPARTMENT OF JUSTICE
DEPARTMENT OF DEFENSE
DEPARTMENT OF LABOR
DEPARTMENT OF EDUCATION
DEPARTMENT OF STATE
DEPARTMENT OF ENERGY
DEPARTMENT OF TRANSPORTATION
DEPARTMENT OF HEALTH AND HUMAN SERVICES
DEPARTMENT OF THE TREASURY
DEPARTMENT OF HOUSING AND URBAN DEVELOPMENT
DEPARTMENT OF VETERANS AFFAIRS

**INDEPENDENT ESTABLISHMENTS AND GOVERNMENT CORPORATIONS**

ACTION
Administrative Conference of the U.S.
African Development Foundation
Central Intelligence Agency
Commission on the Bicentennial of the United States Constitution
Commission on Civil Rights
Commodity Futures Trading Commission
Consumer Product Safety Commission
Defense Nuclear Facilities Safety Board
Environmental Protection Agency
Equal Employment Opportunity Commission
Export-Import Bank of the U.S.
Farm Credit Administration
Federal Communications Commission
Federal Deposit Insurance Corporation
Federal Election Commission

Federal Emergency Management Agency
Federal Housing Finance Board
Federal Labor Relations Authority
Federal Maritime Commission
Federal Mediation and Conciliation Service
Federal Mine Safety and Health Review Commission
Federal Reserve System, Board of Governors of the
Federal Retirement Thrift Investment Board
Federal Trade Commission
General Services Administration
Inter-American Foundation
Interstate Commerce Commission
Merit Systems Protection Board
National Aeronautics and Space Administration
National Archives and Records Administration

National Capital Planning Commission
National Credit Union Administration
National Foundation on the Arts and the Humanities
National Labor Relations Board
National Mediation Board
National Railroad Passenger Corporation (Amtrak)
National Science Foundation
National Transportation Safety Board
Nuclear Regulatory Commission
Occupational Safety and Health Review Commission
Office of Government Ethics
Office of Personnel Management
Office of Special Counsel
Oversight Board
Panama Canal Commission

Peace Corps
Pennsylvania Avenue Development Corporation
Pension Benefit Guaranty Corporation
Postal Rate Commission
Railroad Retirement Board
Resolution Trust Corporation
Securities and Exchange Commission
Selective Service System
Small Business Administration
Tennessee Valley Authority
U.S. Arms Control and Disarmament Agency
U.S. Information Agency
U.S. International Development Cooperation Agency
U.S. International Trade Commission
U.S. Postal Service

**Source:** United States Government Manual 1989-90.

# Survey of Nonlawyer Practice before Federal Administrative Agencies

**Standing Committee on Lawyers' Responsibility for Client Protection and the American Bar Association Center for Professional Responsibility**

*February, 1985*

## I. Background

The American Bar Association Standing Committee on Lawyers' Responsibility for Client Protection disseminated this survey to thirty-three (33) federal administrative agencies in late August, 1984. The survey was intended to provide background information on the experiences of agencies permitting non-lawyer practice (other than for purposes of self-representation). During September and October ninety-seven percent (97%) of the agencies responded either over the phone or by mail following initial contact with their Offices of General Counsel. The ABA Center for Professional Responsibility tabulated the results in October, 1984.

## II. Brief Analysis and Conclusions

We found that the overwhelming majority of agencies studied permit non-lawyer representation in both adversarial and nonadversarial proceedings.* However, most of them seem to encounter lay practice very infrequently (in less than 5% of adjudications), while only a few encounter lay practice as often as lawyer practice. Thus, although universally permitted, lay practice before federal agencies rarely occurs.

Few of the responding agencies comprehensively monitor or control the lay practice that does occur. Only about twenty percent (20%) require nonlawyers to register with the agency before permitting them to practice. Registration procedures may range from simply listing nonlawyers' names to more formalized certifying or licensing procedures which may include testing and character reviews. Proceedings in most of these agencies tend to require highly technical or specialized knowledge. Registration insures that lay representation meets an appropriate level of quality and competence. In at least one agency, registration insures that nonlawyer representatives will charge only nominal fees or no fees at all.

---

*A proceeding is adversarial if there is an opposing side in the controversy, whether or not the other side is represented. A proceeding is nonadversarial if only one side is appearing before the agency official.

**CHART I** Regulations Governing Nonlawyer Representation, Frequency, and Type of Practice

| Agency | Statute/ Regulation Permitting Appearance | Permits Nonlawyer Adversarial Representation | Permits Nonlawyer Nonadversarial Representation | Provisions Limiting or Governing Practice | Frequency of Nonlawyer Representation | Change in Frequency of Nonlawyer Rep. w/in Past 6 Years | Most Common Type(s) of Nonlawyer Representation |
|---|---|---|---|---|---|---|---|
| Bd. of Immigration Appeals: Immigration and Naturalization Serv. | 8 CFR § 292.1-3 | Yes | Yes | "Accredited representative"[1] working for "recognized organization"[2] may charge only nominal fees. "Reputable individual"[3] may not charge fees | No statistics available | No statistics available | One time only by family member/ friend; charitable, religious or social service organization |
| Civil Aeronautics Bd. | 14 CFR § 300.1-6 14 CFR § 302.11 | Yes | Yes | None | Fewer than 6 appearances per yr., less than 1% of appearances[4] | None | Economic consultants for corporations |
| Comptroller of the Currency | 12 CFR § 19.3 | Yes[5] | Yes | Nonlawyer may be required to file a power of attorney or show to the satisfaction of the Comptroller the possession of requisite qualifications | None | None | None |
| Consumer Product Safety Comm'n | 16 CFR § 1025.61 et seq. | Yes | Yes | Filing and approval of proof of qualifications. See 16 CFR § 1025.65 | Very infrequent, 2–5% of appearances | None | Non-fee by industry rep., consultant, or private service agency |

| Agency | Citation | | | None / Fees | Fewer than 3 appearances per yr., less than 1% of appearances | Decreased,[6] no statistics available | Economist/accountant providing assistance prior to appearance |
|---|---|---|---|---|---|---|---|
| Dep't of Agric., Agricultural Marketing Serv. | 7 CFR § 50.27 | Yes | Yes | None | Fewer than 3 appearances per yr., less than 1% of appearances | Decreased,[6] no statistics available | Economist/accountant providing assistance prior to appearance |
| Dep't of Commerce, Office of Secretary | Those of other agencies governing appearances before administrative bodies, e.g., MSPB, 5 CFR Part 1201 | Yes | Yes | Reasonable atty's fees for litigated matters set by agency; maximum atty's fees for settlement set at $75./hr.; government pays fees to winning atty | No statistics available | No statistics available | Non-fee by union reps. |
| Dep't of Commerce, Patent and Trademark Office | 35 U.S.C. §§ 31-33 | Yes | Yes | Only registered[7] practitioners permitted to practice | Less than 16% of appearances[8] | None | Repeated practice for a fee by registered agents |

[1] May become accredited by the Department of Immigration Appeals (D.I.A.) by submitting an application through a recognized organization for review of character and fitness and experience with and knowledge of immigration law. No formal testing requirement or licensing fee.

[2] Typically a religious, charitable or social service organization becomes recognized by submitting an application for approval to the D.I.A. assuring that it will charge only nominal fees and assess no representation charges.

[3] Typically a family member or friend submits declaration that he or she charges no fee, has a preexisting relationship with immigrant-applicant, and appears only on individual basis at request of immigrant-applicant.

[4] Although nonlawyer practice [is] not discouraged, complexity of agency proceedings tends to require specialized legal practice. Typical parties, large corporations or businesses, tend to hire lawyers.

[5] Permitted but lay representation rare because of complex proceedings and substantial rights or amounts of money involved.

[6] In agency's early history, economists provided a substantial amount of representation because of the economic nature of agency proceedings. As proceedings become more sophisticated, economists began aiding lawyers rather than assuming primary responsibility for legal representation. Representation by economists is now rare, and lawyers handle the bulk of representation.

[7] Nonlawyers become registered by passing a character and fitness review and an examination. Nonlawyers having served four years in the examining corps of the Patent and Trademark Office (P.T.O.) may waive the exam. See 57 CFR § 1.341.

[8] Nonlawyers comprise about 16% of registered practitioners, but not all registered practitioners appear before P.T.O., so that nonlawyers probably appear in less than 16% of patent applications filed with P.T.O.

**CHART I** Regulations Governing Nonlawyer Representation, Frequency, and Type of Practice—*Continued*

| Agency | Statute/Regulation Permitting Appearance | Permits Nonlawyer Adversarial Representation | Permits Nonlawyer Nonadversarial Representation | Provisions Limiting or Governing Practice | Frequency of Nonlawyer Representation | Change in Frequency of Nonlawyer Rep. w/in Past 6 Years | Most Common Type(s) of Nonlawyer Representation |
|---|---|---|---|---|---|---|---|
| Dep't of Health and Human Services, Food and Drug Admin. | 32 CFR §§ 12.40, 12.45 | Yes | Yes | None | No appearances in recent years | None | None |
| Dep't of Justice, Drug Enforcement Admin. | 21 CFR § 1316.50 | Yes | N/A, all proceedings adversarial | None | 2 to 3 appearances per yr., 5% of appearances[9] | None | One time only by officer/employee of small family-owned business |
| Dep't of Justice, Foreign Claims Settlement Comm'n | 45 CFR § 500.1-6 | No | No[10] | Lawyer's fees set by statute at 10% of claim award and deducted from award | N/A[11] | N/A[11] | Family member providing assistance prior to appearance |
| Dep't of Labor, Benefits Review Bd. | 20 CFR § 802.201(b) 20 CFR § 802.202 | Yes | N/A, all proceedings adversarial | Employer pays fee for successful claimant represented by lawyer; claimant pays fee when represented by nonlawyer; lawyer may acquire lien against award; nonlawyers may not.[12] Professional status is criterion for determining fees.[13] | 2–4% of appearances | None | Repeated practice for fee |
| Dep't of Labor, Employees Compensation Appeals Bd. | 20 CFR § 501.11 | Yes | N/A, all proceedings adversarial | All fees approved by board | Appear as frequently as lawyers | None | One time only by family member/friend; repeated practice for a fee |

| | | | | | | |
|---|---|---|---|---|---|---|
| Dep't of Labor, National Railroad Adjustment Bd. | 45 U.S.C. § 3153 | Yes | N/A | Only entities identified in 45 U.S.C. § 151 allowed to practice | Almost 100% of appearances | None | Industry employees |
| Dep't of Labor, Wage and Appeals Bd. | 20 CFR § 725.362(a) 20 CFR § 725.365 20 CFR § 725.366(b) | Yes | N/A | Fees must be reasonably commensurate with services performed;[14] attorney's fee deducted from award; employer pays fee for successful claimant represented by lawyer; claimant prep fee when represented by nonlawyer; lawyer may require lien against award, nonlawyers may not.[15] | 3% of appearances; as in 180 case/yr. | Decrease due to investigations by Office of Inspector General into unauthorized receipt of fees | One time only by family member or friend; repeated practice for fee; assistance prior to appearance |

[9] Appearances are by the employees or officers of small family-owned businesses, analogous to pro se appearances.

[10] The agency only allows "representation" by bar members. Family members may sometimes assist in preparation of claims or at oral hearings, typically where elderly parent has language barrier problems.

[11] No nonlawyer representation allowed.

[12] These policies may tend to discourage lay representation.

[13] Typically approved rates for nonlawyers are less than half of those attorneys receive.

[14] See 20 CFR § 725.366(b) (black lung) and 20 CFR § 702.132 (longshore).

[15] These policies may tend to discourage lay representation.

**CHART I** Regulations Governing Nonlawyer Representation, Frequency, and Type of Practice—*Continued*

| Agency | Statute/ Regulation Permitting Appearance | Permits Nonlawyer Adversarial Representation | Permits Nonlawyer Nonadversarial Representation | Provisions Limiting or Governing Practice | Frequency of Nonlawyer Representation | Change in Frequency of Nonlawyer Rep. w/in Past 6 Years | Most Common Type(s) of Nonlawyer Representation |
|---|---|---|---|---|---|---|---|
| Dep't of Transportation, Maritime Admin. | 46 CFR § 201.21 | Yes | Yes | Only registered nonlawyers permitted to practice | Very infrequent | None | |
| Federal Deposit Ins. Corp. | 12 CFR § 308.04 | Yes | Yes | Only qualified nonlawyers permitted to represent | 10 to 20 appearances per yr., 5% of appearances | 50% decrease | One time only by family member/friend; nonlawyer assistance prior to appearance |
| Federal Energy Regulatory Comm'n | 18 CFR § 385.2101 | Yes | Yes | None | 1 or 2 per yr. | None | Engineering firm assisting in technical nonadversarial proceeding |
| Federal Maritime Comm'n | 46 CFR § 502.30 | Yes | Yes | Only registered nonlawyers permitted to appear[16] | .5 to 1% of appearances | None | One time only by family member/friend; non-fee by industry rep., consultant or private service agency |
| Federal Mine Safety & Health Review Comm'n | 29 CFR § 2700.3(b) | Yes, at trial hearings before Administrative Law Judges (ALJ); at appellate reviews before commissioners | N/A | Nonlawyer may practice only if party, "representative of miners,"[17] or owner, partner, full time officer or employee of party-business entity; otherwise permitted to appear for limited purpose in special proceedings | 5–10% of appearances | None | Non-fee by industry rep., consultant or private service agency |

| | | | | | | | |
|---|---|---|---|---|---|---|---|
| General Accounting Office | 31 U.S.C. § 731-732; 4 CFR §§ 11 and 28; GAO Orders 2713.2, 2752.1, and 2777.1 | Yes, in adverse actions, grievance proceedings, and discrimination complaints | Yes | Nonlawyers not permitted fees; government pays fees to winning representatives[18] | Very infrequent | Not aware of any | Repeated practice for fee by certified public accountant or enrolled agent |
| Internal Revenue Serv. | 13 CFR Part 10; 31 U.S.C. § 330; Treasury Dept. Circular 230 | Yes | Yes | Noncertified public accountant and nonlawyer must become enrolled agent[19] to practice | As frequent as lawyer representation[20] | Increased, no statistics available | |
| Interstate Commerce Comm'n | 49 CFR § 1103 | Yes | Yes | Fee limitations;[21] only registered nonlawyer permitted to practice,[22] however, self-representation is allowed without registration | 1,600 nonlawyers now registered and account for 5% of appearances.[23] | Decreased,[24] no statistics available | Repeated practice for a fee |
| National Credit Union Admin. | 12 CFR § 747 | Yes | Yes | None | No statistics available | Decreased, no statistics available | Credit union representatives |

[16] Certificates of registration are issued on payment of $13.00 processing fee and completion of application form indicating sufficient educational qualifications and recommendations. There is no testing or formal licensing.

[17] See generally 30 CFR § 40.1(b).

[18] As provided in discrimination statutes, backpay act, and appeals authorized by law.

[19] Nonlawyers and noncertified public accountants become enrolled agents by 1) passing a character and fitness review, and 2) successful completion of special enrollment examination testing on federal taxation and related matters, or 3) former employment with the IRS, provided duties qualify the individual. Lawyers and certified public accountants may practice without enrollment.

[20] Includes representation by certified public accountants as well as enrolled agents.

[21] Practitioners may not overestimate the value of services, accept compensation from party other than client, make contingent fee arrangements or divide fees with laypersons. See 49 CFR § 1103.70.

[22] To become registered applicant must 1) meet educational and experience requirements, 2) undergo character and fitness review, 3) pass exam administered by the agency testing knowledge in the field of transportation, and 4) take an oath. See 49 CFR § 1103.3.

[23] Figure includes appearances in rulemaking as well as adjudicatory proceedings.

[24] Deregulation has reduced the caseload while proceedings have become more complex, creating a greater need for legal expertise.

**CHART I** Regulations Governing Nonlawyer Representation, Frequency, and Type of Practice—*Continued*

| Agency | Statute/ Regulation Permitting Appearance | Permits Nonlawyer Adversarial Representation | Permits Nonlawyer Nonadversarial Representation | Provisions Limiting or Governing Practice | Frequency of Nonlawyer Representation | Change in Frequency of Nonlawyer Rep. w/in Past 6 Years | Most Common Type(s) of Nonlawyer Representation |
|---|---|---|---|---|---|---|---|
| National Labor Relations Bd. | | Yes | Yes | None | Infrequent | None | |
| National Mediation Bd. | None, agency governed by 29 CFR § 1200 et seq. | N/A, all proceedings adversarial | Yes | None | 200 appearances per yr., appear twice as frequently as lawyers | Decreased, no statistics available | Union representatives |
| National Transportation Safety Bd. | 49 CFR § 821 49 CFR § 831 49 CFR § 845 | Yes | Yes | In adjudication lawyer representation encouraged; in investigation lawyer participation discouraged because technical expertise required; parties[25] participate in investigations | Very infrequent except at investigatory levels | None | Manufacturers at investigatory levels |
| Occupational Safety and Health Review Comm'n | 29 CFR § 2200.22 | Yes | N/A, all proceedings adversarial | Optional simplified procedures to encourage self-representation by small businesses | 20% of appearances[26] | 20% decrease[27] | Nonlegal employee representing employer; union representative |
| Small Business Admin. | 13 CFR § 121.11 13 CFR § 134.16 | Yes | N/A, all proceedings adversarial | None | Less than 1% of appearances[28] | None | |

| Social Security Admin. | 42 USC § 406(a) 29 CFR | Yes, tentatively as part of experiment; generally agency has no adversarial proceedings | Yes | Claimants advised of advantages of representation at hearing level;[29] fees set by agency;[30] attorneys' fees withheld from awards[31] | Appear in 13% of total hearings or in 25–30% of hearings with representation | None, although lawyer representation increased by 56% since 1978[32] | One time only by family member/friend; repeated practice for fee; non-fee rep. by legal services paralegal |
|---|---|---|---|---|---|---|---|
| U.S. Customs Serv. | None | Yes | Yes | None | 5 to 15% of caseload volume | None | Repeated practice for fee by licensed customs brokers and former customs officials |
| U.S. Environmental Protection Agency | 40 CFR § 124 40 CFR § 164.30 40 CFR § 22.10 | Yes | N/A | None | No appearances | None | None |

[25] "Parties" includes manufacturers, unions, operators and other regulatory agencies.

[26] Statistic includes pro se representation.

[27] Nonlawyer practice accounted in 1980 for 40% of the agency's caseload but decreased in 1982–83 to 20%. Decrease may result from increasing complexity in cases causing claimants to seek legal representation.

[28] Figure excludes pro se appearances in size and Standard Industrial Classification (SIC) Appeals. Approximately 50% of size and SIC appeals are conducted pro se by nonlawyers.

[29] When hearing request [is] filed, agency sends a letter to unrepresented claimant describing advantages of representation. Attached to letter is a list of organizations which may provide representation. The list includes lawyer referral services, legal aid groups, law schools, etc.

[30] The agency sets all fees based on criteria listed in 20 CFR § 404.1725(b), including extent and type of services, complexity of case, level of skill and competence required in performing services, time spent, results achieved, level at which representative became involved, and amount requested.

[31] When decision is entered in favor of a claimant represented by a lawyer in a Title II or Black Lung case, normally 25% of the benefits awarded are withheld. After agency has set the fee it forwards fee directly to the lawyer from the amount withheld. If attorney's fees exceed the amount withheld, the lawyer must seek the remainder from the claimant. If the attorney's fees are less than the amount withheld, the claimant receives the remainder. Nonlawyer representatives do not have this withholding benefit.

[32] In fiscal year 1978 lawyers appeared in 32% of hearings; nonlawyers in 12%. In fiscal year 1983 lawyers appeared in 50% of hearings; nonlawyers in 13%. Though the letter discussed in footnote 29 does not exclusively reference lawyers' services, this list may attribute to the increase in lawyer representation. Lawyers also have a high success rate before the agency as well as the advantage of award withholdings to secure fees in Title II and Black Lung cases (see footnote 31).

No agencies indicated that they would discipline nonlawyers differently from lawyers, although they clearly have an additional ability to pursue sanctions against lawyers through external disciplinary mechanisms. Only a few agencies indicated any special need for nonlawyer discipline. Most reported they had not encountered any problems with misconduct by nonlawyers or any inability of nonlawyers to meet appropriate ethical standards (though fewer than a third of the agencies studied have actually defined any specific ethical standards). Of those that voiced complaints about nonlawyers' skills in representation, most indicated that the problem they encounter most frequently is nonlawyers' lack of familiarity with procedural rules and tactics. The majority of responses suggest that nonlawyers do not pose any special practice problems, nor do they receive any special disciplinary consideration. Overall, the concern for nonlawyers' competence and ethical conduct seems limited, perhaps because nonlawyer practice is not widespread.

## III. Methodology

Throughout the survey our questions focused on lay representation (other than self-representation) occurring in adjudicatory proceedings. In question 1, in which we asked whether agencies permitted nonlawyer representation, we attempted to distinguish between adversarial and nonadversarial proceedings. Our distinction did not prove particularly informative because all agencies permitting nonlawyer practice (97%) allow such practice in both arenas.

Question 2 sought the methods by which agencies control or limit those practicing before them. The responses vary considerably from agency to agency. Questions 3 and 4 requested statistics concerning the frequency of nonlawyer practice. Many of the agencies indicated that statistics were unavailable. These responses also vary considerably. The results of questions 1 through 4 are tabulated in Chart I beginning on page 782.

# State Survey: Ethics Opinions, Rules, and Reports Involving Paralegals

The following ethics summary covers paralegals and other nonattorneys in each state. The purpose of the summary is to give an overview of the kinds of issues that have arisen. It is *not* meant to provide the current state of the law or the current ethics regulations of any particular state. Keep in mind that the rules governing paralegals are undergoing considerable change. See Section D of Chapter 5 on how to do legal research to determine the current ethics rules that apply to your state.

 Alabama

Under Rule 7.6 of the Rules of Professional Conduct, the title "Legal Assistant" is acceptable on a business card that also contains an attorney's or a law firm's name. The title of the nonattorney employee should be legibly and prominently displayed in close proximity to the employee's name. Cards that present an attorney's or law firm's name so prominently that they obscure the employee's nonattorney status are prohibited. An earlier ethics opinion preferred the title, "non-lawyer assistant," since "paralegal" could be a misleading title. *Alabama State Bar Opinion 86–04* (3/17/86). See also *Opinion 86–120* (12/2/86).

When a paralegal signs a letter to a nonattorney, the paralegal's name should be followed by one of these titles: "nonlawyer assistant," "nonlawyer paralegal," or "nonlawyer investigator." *Alabama State Bar Opinion 87–77* (6/16/87).

It is improper to include the name of a nonattorney assistant on the letterhead of law firm stationery. *Alabama State Bar Opinion 83–87* (5/23/83).

The business card of a legal secretary can list the fact that he or she has been certified by passing an examination of the National Association of Legal Secretaries. *Alabama State Bar Opinion 90–01* (1/17/90).

When a plaintiff's law firm hires an investigator who worked for a defense law firm, the plaintiff's law firm must withdraw from all cases in which the investigator previously worked, unless the defense law firm and its clients consent. Screening the investigator from such cases is not enough. *Alabama State Bar Opinion 89–41* (4/5/89). See also *Opinion 89–91* (8/7/89) on job switching by a secretary and the effectiveness of a Chinese Wall (screening) around her.

Paralegals may draft documents if supervised by an attorney, but they cannot make court appearances or give legal advice. *Alabama State Bar Opinion 86–120* (12/2/86).

An attorney engaged in collection work may not pay his lay employees on a commission basis. *Opinion of the General Counsel* (2/3/88, revised 2/14/90).

Nonattorney independent contractors who sell legal research services to attorneys are not engaged in the unauthorized practice of law. *Alabama State Bar Opinion 90–04* (1/18/90).

Other Alabama State Bar Opinions involving nonattorneys: *86–101* (10/30/86); *86–124* (12/15/86); *87–31* (5/20/87); *87–38* (3/6/87); *87–129* (12/31/87); *87–135* (10/30/87); *75–151* (2/4/88); *88–03* (2/4/88); *89–92* (9/25/89); *89–94* (10/5/89); *98–18* (2/21/90). See also *Birmingham Bar Ass'n Opinion 88–4* (7/8/88).

 ## Alaska

A suspended attorney may work as a paralegal, but only under the supervision of an attorney in good standing. He or she may not have a direct relationship with a client. *Alaska Bar Ass'n Ethics Opinion 84–6* (8/25/84).

Under the supervision or review of an attorney, a legal assistant can investigate claims and have contact with insurance agents regarding the settlement of claims in worker's compensation cases. *Alaska Bar Ass'n Ethics Opinion 73–1* (10/6/73).

Paralegal employees of attorneys may not conduct worker's compensation hearings. *Alaska Bar Ass'n Ethics Opinion 84–7* (8/25/84). Note: this Opinion was suspended 11/9/84 pending reconsideration.

 ## Arizona

The letterhead of an attorney or law firm can list nonattorney support personnel if their nonattorney status is made clear. *Ethics Opinion 90–03* (3/16/90). This overrules *Opinion 84–14* (10/5/84), which held to the contrary. (The latter opinion also said that separate letterhead for paralegals is not allowed).

A corporation consisting of independent contractor paralegals and a salaried attorney employee is impermissible. *Opinion 82–18* (12/1/82).

Other State Bar of Arizona Opinions involving nonattorneys: *86–7* (2/26/86); *87–13* (6/17/87).

 ## Arkansas

"The paralegal should never be placed in a position to decide what information takes priority over other information or to make decisions which affect the client." This function should never be delegated to a paralegal, even though "sometimes a fine line exists in the area of professional judgment." Paralegals need "specific guidelines," preferably in writing, in carrying out responsibilities. *The Paralegal in Practice* by A. Clinton, chairperson of the Paralegal Committee of the Arkansas Bar Ass'n, 23 Arkansas Lawyer 22 (January 1989).

# California

When a paralegal is authorized to represent a client before the Workers' Compensation Appeals Board, a law firm can use its paralegal to represent a client of the firm before this Board if the client consents and the firm supervises the paralegal. *State Bar of California Opinion 1988–103.*

A paralegal who switches jobs might cause the disqualification of his or her new employer to represent clients about whom the paralegal obtained confidential information while working at a prior (opposing) law firm. A rebuttable presumption exists that the paralegal shared this information with the new employer. The most likely way for the new employer to rebut this presumption, and hence to avoid the disqualification, is to show that when the paralegal was hired, a Chinese Wall was built around the paralegal with respect to any cases that are substantially related to cases the paralegal worked on while at the prior employment. *In re Complex Asbestos Litigation,* \_\_\_\_Cal.App.3d \_\_\_\_, 283 Cal. Rptr. 732 (Cal. Ct. App. 1991).

A nonattorney may use a business card if it is used for identification rather than for solicitation of business. *Los Angeles County Bar Ass'n Opinion 381.*

A law firm can pay a bonus to its paralegal as long as the bonus does not involve a sharing of legal fees. *Los Angeles County Bar Ass'n Opinion 457* (11/ 20/89).

A nonprofit legal services center for the elderly cannot advertise in a local newspaper the availability of "legal help" from "para-legal aides" trained by a local attorney. Legal help implies legal services. *San Diego Bar Ass'n, Opinion 1976–9* (7/1/76).

A business that provides paralegal services to the public should have attorney supervision except for some purely ministerial tasks. *San Diego Bar Ass'n, Opinion 1983–7.*

Other State Bar of California Opinion involving nonattorneys: *Opinion 1988–97.* Other Los Angeles County Bar Ass'n Opinions involving nonattorneys: *Opinion 391, Opinion 444.*

# Colorado

The names of support personnel can be printed on law firm letterhead, and these employees can have their own business cards as long as they reveal clearly that they are not attorneys. *Colorado Bar Ass'n, Formal Ethics Opinion 84* (4/90).

Paralegals must disclose their nonattorney status to everyone at the outset of any professional relationship. They should be given no task that requires the exercise of unsupervised legal judgment. They can write letters and sign correspondence on attorney letterhead as long as their nonattorney status is clear and the correspondence does not contain legal opinions or give legal advice. They can have their own business cards with the name of the law firm on them if their nonattorney status is made clear. The services performed by the paralegal must supplement, merge with, and become part of the attorney's work product. *Colorado Bar Ass'n, Guidelines for the Utilization of Legal Assistants* (1986).

A law firm can use a paralegal to represent clients at administrative proceedings when authorized by statute and when the practice of law is not involved. To ensure competent representation, the attorney must train and supervise the paralegal. *Colorado Bar Ass'n Opinion 79* (2/18/89).

An attorney may not participate with nonattorneys in preparing and marketing estate planning documents when the venture consists of the unauthorized practice of law. *Colorado Bar Ass'n Opinion 87* (7/14/90).

An attorney shall continually monitor and supervise the work of assistants to assure that the services they render are performed competently and efficiently. *Colorado Bar Ass'n Ethics Opinion 61* (10/23/82).

 ## Connecticut

The names of paralegals can be printed on law firm letterhead, and they may have their own business cards if their nonattorney status is made clear. *Ethics Committee Opinion 85–17* (11/20/85).

Paralegals can communicate the legal advice of attorneys if they refrain from interpreting or expanding on that advice. They can attend a real estate closing to distribute or receive documents or funds, but they may not attend as the sole representative of a client. They can attend a deposition but may not conduct one. They may not supervise the execution of a will, but they can act as witnesses to such execution. In contacts with clients, courts, and agencies, paralegals must disclose at the outset that they are not attorneys. Paralegals should not accept or reject cases or set fees if these tasks entail any discretion on their part. *Connecticut Bar Ass'n.*

 ## Delaware

A law firm cannot allow its paralegal to represent a client before the Industrial Accident Board on a worker's compensation case. *Delaware State Bar Ass'n Opinion 1985–3.*

A nonattorney law clerk cannot work on a case where the other side is represented by the clerk's former employer. The clerk must be screened from involvement in the case. *Delaware State Bar Ass'n Opinion 1986–1.*

## District of Columbia

Rule 5.4 of the Model Rules of Professional Conduct has been modified to permit a nonattorney to be a partner of a law firm. Hence the firm can share fees with nonattorneys under the guidelines of Rule 5.4. For example, a lobbyist or an economist could form a partnership with an attorney. The nonattorney must agree to abide by the Rules of Professional Conduct.

Nonattorneys can have a business card that prints the name of the law firm where they work as long as their nonattorney status is made clear. *D.C. Bar Ethics Opinion 19.* See also *Speaking of Ethics, Bar Report, p. 2* (February/March 1988).

Other ethical opinions involving nonattorneys: *172* (4/15/86); *176* (10/21/86); *182* (5/19/87); *201* (4/18/89); *203* (6/20/89).

Florida

An attorney can allow a nonattorney to conduct a real estate closing if certain conditions are met, e.g., an attorney is available (in person or by telephone) to answer legal questions, the nonattorney only performs ministerial acts, and the client consents to having the closing handled by a nonattorney. *Florida Bar Opinion 89–5* (11/89) (overruling *Opinion 73–43*).

It is ethically improper for lawyers to delegate to laypersons the handling of negotiations with adjusters on claims of clients of the lawyers. *Florida Ethics Opinion 74–35.* But the nonlawyer employee can transmit information from the attorney. "For example, the nonlawyer employee may call the adjuster and inform the adjuster that the attorney will settle the matter for X. If the adjuster comes back with a counteroffer, the nonlawyer employee must inform the attorney. The employee cannot be given a range in which to settle." *Ethically Speaking* 15, The Florida Bar News (9/15/91).

Paralegals can have their own business cards. They may also be listed on a law firm's letterhead, but a title indicating their nonattorney status should appear beneath their name. Attorneys should not hold their paralegals out as "certified" if they are not. *Florida Bar Opinion 86–4* (8/1/86).

When a nonattorney changes jobs to an opposing law firm, the old and new employer must admonish him or her not to reveal any confidences or secrets obtained during prior employment. *Florida Bar Opinion 86–5* (8/1/86).

Attorneys cannot authorize a nonattorney to sign their name on pleadings. *Florida Bar Opinion 87–11.*

An attorney can allow a supervised nonattorney to conduct an initial interview of a prospective client if his or her nonattorney status is disclosed to the client and only factual information is obtained. *Florida Bar Opinion 88–6.*

Other Florida Bar Opinions involving nonattorneys: *62–26* (12/15/86); *64–40* (5/1/87); *87–8* (7/1/87); *89–43; 88–15.*

An attorney was suspended for failing to supervise his nonattorney personnel. *Florida Bar v. Carter,* 502 So.2d 904 (FL, 1987).

Nonattorneys from the Health & Rehabilitative Services Department can no longer draft documents or represent the Department in court. *Florida Bar re Advisory Opinion HRS Nonlawyer Counselor,* Fla SupCt, No. 70,615 (5/25/89) Earlier opinion in the case: 518 So.2d 1270.

 Georgia

It is the unauthorized practice of law for a law firm to allow a nonattorney to conduct a real estate closing. *State Bar of Georgia Opinion 86–5* (5/12/89).

An attorney should not allow a paralegal to correspond with an adverse party (or the party's agents) on the attorney's letterhead if the letter discusses legal matters that suggest or assert claims. (Routine contacts with opposing counsel not involving the merits of the case are, however, permitted.) *Advisory Opinion 19* (7/18/75).

An attorney may delegate tasks to a paralegal which ordinarily comprise the practice of law, but only if the attorney has direct contact with the client and maintains "constant supervision" of the paralegal. The paralegal can render specialized advice on scientific or technical topics. The paralegal cannot negotiate with parties or opposing counsel on substantive issues. The paralegal's name may not appear on the letterhead or office door. The paralegal must not sign any pleadings, briefs, or other legal documents to be presented to a court. The paralegal can have a business card with the name of the firm on it if the word *paralegal* is clearly used to indicate nonattorney status. Unless previous contacts would justify the paralegal in believing that his or her nonattorney status is already known, the paralegal should begin oral communications, either face-to-face or on the telephone, with a clear statement that he or she is a paralegal employee of the law firm. *Advisory Opinion 21 (9/16/77)*.

Other State Bar Opinion involving nonattorneys: *82–2 (11/10/88)*.

 Hawaii

An attorney may list a paralegal on professional cards, letterhead, and professional notices or announcement cards as long as the employee is identified as a paralegal or a legal assistant. A paralegal can use business cards identifying himself or herself as an employee of the law firm. A paralegal can sign correspondence as a paralegal. *Hawaii Supreme Court Disciplinary Board, Formal Opinion 78–8–19. (6/28/84)*. See also *Opinion 78–8–19–Supp*.

 Idaho

An attorney must not share fees with nonattorneys. The attorney can request compensation for the work of a paralegal or other laymen acting under his or her supervision as long as the request specifies that laymen performed the work. *Formal Ethics Opinion 125*.

A law firm cannot list legal assistants on its letterhead. *Formal Opinion 109 (11/30/81)*.

Other Idaho State Bar Opinion involving nonattorneys: *117 (3/14/86)*.

 Illinois

Paralegal names can be printed on a firm's letterhead; the nonattorney status of the employee must be indicated. *Illinois State Bar Ass'n Opinion 87–1 (9/8/87)*.

An attorney can charge an hourly rate for paralegal work but not for "expenses" that includes an hourly rate for a salaried paralegal. *Illinois State Bar Ass'n Opinion 86–1 (7/7/86)*.

A paralegal cannot handle phone calls involving legal matters of her law firm while at a collection agency that is one of the clients of the law firm. The law firm would not be able to supervise the paralegal. *Illinois State Bar Ass'n Opinion 88–8 (3/15/89)*.

Sharing fees with a nonattorney via profit-sharing is proper provided the sharing is based on a percentage of overall firm profits and is not tied to fees in a particular case. *Illinois State Bar Ass'n Opinion 89–5 (7/17/89)*.

A paralegal can conduct a real estate closing without his or her attorney-supervisor present if no legal advice is given, if all the documents have been prepared in advance, if the attorney-supervisor is available by telephone to provide help, and if the other attorney consents. *Chicago Bar Ass'n (1983).*

Legal assistants can be listed on law firm letterhead or on the door as long as their nonattorney status is made clear. *Chicago Bar Ass'n Opinion 81–4.*

Disqualification of a law firm is not required simply because it hired a law office manager–secretary who had worked for opposing party at another law firm. *Kapco Mfg. Co., Inc. c. C&O Enterprises, Inc.,* 637 F. Supp. 1231 (N.D. Ill., 1985).

# Indiana

Paralegal names can be printed on a firm's letterhead if their nonattorney status is clear. The attorneys and nonattorneys must be distinguished clearly. *Indiana Bar Ass'n Legal Ethics Committee Opinion 9* (1985) (which overrules *Opinion 5*).

Paralegals may have a business card as long as their capacity is stated and the identity of their employing attorney is disclosed. *Indiana Bar Ass'n Legal Ethics Committee Opinion 8* (1984).

# Iowa

A legal assistant who has passed the CLA exam (Certified Legal Assistant) of the National Association of Legal Assistants may not sign law firm correspondence with the designation "CLA, Legal Assistant" or "Certified Legal Assistant," since the public might be misled about his or her nonattorney status. (A reader might think that CLA was a legal degree.) *Iowa State Bar Ass'n Opinion 88–5 (9/9/88)* and *Opinion 88–19 (6/8/89).* It is proper, however, to sign the letter with the titles "Legal Assistant" or "Paralegal." *Opinion 89–22 (12/8/89).*

Paralegals and other nonattorney employees may not be listed on the law firm letterhead. *Iowa State Bar Ass'n Opinion 87–18 (2/2/88).* The office of the county public defender may not list the names of nonattorney personnel on its letterhead. *Opinion 89–35 (12/14/89).*

A sign outside the door of a law firm may not list the name of nonattorney employees even if they are called legal assistants. *Iowa State Bar Ass'n Opinion 89–23 (12/26/88).*

In oral communications, a paralegal should disclose his or her nonattorney status at the outset of the conversation. *Iowa Code of Professional Responsibility, EC 3–6, subparagraph 5.*

A law firm can pay a paralegal a percentage of the total income it earns as long as the compensation relates to the firm's profits and not the receipt of specific legal fees. *Iowa State Bar Ass'n Opinion 90–9 (8/23/90).*

It would be the unauthorized practice of law for a paralegal to represent a client in Small Claims Court. *Iowa State Bar Ass'n Opinion 89–30 (12/8/89).*

Other Iowa State Bar Ass'n Opinions involving nonattorneys: *87–28 (5/16/88); 88–16 (2/17/89); 88–25 (6/8/89); 89–3 (9/6/89); 90–20 (8/23/90).*

# Kansas

An attorney cannot include the name of a legal assistant on its letterhead. *Kansas Bar Ass'n Ethics Advisory Committee Opinion 88–02* (7/15/88). See also *Opinion 82–38* (11/4/82).

A legal assistant can use a business card that prints the name of his or her law firm if the legal assistant is identified as such. *Kansas Bar Ass'n Ethics Advisory Committee, Opinion 85–4.* Overrules *Opinion 84–18.*

Clients must be fully informed that the legal assistant is not an attorney. An attorney shall not share legal fees with a legal assistant, meaning that no form of compensation must be tied to a particular fee. A legal assistant shall not be compensated for recommending an attorney. At the beginning of a professional contact, the legal assistant should disclose that he or she is not an attorney. A legal assistant can sign correspondence on law firm letterhead if the signature is followed by a designation that makes clear that he or she is not an attorney. If an attorney accepts a case in which the legal assistant has a conflict of interest, the attorney should exclude the legal assistant from participating in that case. The client must be told of this conflict. *Standards and Guidelines for the Utilization of Legal Assistants in Kansas* (Kansas Bar Ass'n Committee on Legal Assistants, 12/2/88).

# Kentucky

The letterhead of an attorney can include the name of a paralegal. An attorney's name can appear on the business card of a paralegal if the latter's non-attorney status is clear. An attorney shall not share, on a proportionate basis, legal fees with a paralegal. When dealing with a client, a paralegal must disclose at the outset that he or she is not an attorney. This disclosure must be made to anyone who may have reason to believe that the paralegal is an attorney or is associated with an attorney. *Kentucky Paralegal Code, Supreme Court Rule 3.700.*

Without client consent, it is unethical for an attorney to charge a client for paralegal services when the attorney's contract with the client calls for a statutory-set fee, a lump-sum fee, or a contingent fee. The attorney who charges an hourly rate *can* charge for paralegal services which may be separately stated. *Kentucky Bar Ass'n Opinion E–303* (5/85).

A suspended attorney may work in a law firm as a paralegal after the period of his suspension has expired, even if he has not been reinstated. *Kentucky Bar Ass'n Opinion E–336.*

A paralegal cannot appear in court on motion day or for the motion docket. *Kentucky Bar Ass'n Opinion E–266.*

A nonlawyer may not represent a corporation in a court other than the small claims court. *Kentucky Bar Ass'n Opinion E–345.*

A lay assistant cannot take (i.e., conduct) a deposition. *Kentucky Bar Ass'n Opinion E–341.*

#  Louisiana

An attorney can be disbarred for delegating too much to a paralegal and for failing to supervise the paralegal. *Louisiana State Bar v. Edwins,* 540 So.2d

294 (LA 1989). See also *Louisiana State Bar v. Lindsay, 553 So.2d 807* (LA 1989) (an attorney charged with professional misconduct tries to shift the blame to his paralegal).

 ## Maine

The names of paralegals can be printed on a firm's letterhead as long as this is not misleading. *Maine Professional Ethics Comm'n Opinion 34* (1/17/83).

An attorney cannot form a partnership or professional corporation with a nonattorney to provide legal and nonlegal services to clients. *Maine Professional Ethics Comm'n Opinion 79* (5/6/87).

Other Opinions of the Maine Professional Ethics Comm'n involving non-attorneys: *69* (3/17/86); *99* (9/6/89); *102* (2/2/90).

 ## Maryland

Legal assistants can have business cards as long as their legal assistant status is designated. *Maryland Bar Ass'n Ethics Opinion 77–28* (10/18/76).

An attorney can list the names of paralegals on office letterhead or on the office door as long as their nonattorney status is designated. *Maryland Bar Ass'n Ethics Opinion 81–69* (5/29/81).

A nonattorney once worked for attorney #A. She now works for attorney #B. These attorneys are opponents on a case in litigation. This case was under-way when the nonattorney worked for attorney #A. If effective screening (i.e., a Chinese Wall) is used to insulate the nonattorney from the case, attorney #B does not have to withdraw from the litigation. *Maryland Bar Ass'n Ethics Docket 90–17* (1990).

An attorney can hire a freelance paralegal as long as he or she is supervised at all times by the attorney. *Maryland Bar Ass'n Opinion 86–83* (7/23/86).

An attorney cannot divide a fee with a nonattorney. *Maryland Bar Ass'n Opinion 86–59* (2/12/86). A legal assistant cannot be paid a percentage of the recovery in a case on which the assistant works. *Maryland Bar Ass'n Opinion 84–103* (1984).

An attorney can rent office space to a nonattorney as long as confidentiality of the attorney's clients is not compromised. *Maryland Bar Ass'n Opinion 89–45* (6/12/89).

Other Maryland Bar Ass'n Opinions involving nonattorneys: *84–6* (7/20/76); *86–45* (9/11/86); *86–57* (2/12/86); *86–69* (7/15/86); *86–45* (9/11/86); *88–56* (3/13/88); *89–18* (3/23/89); *89–64* (8/11/89); *90–26* (2/21/90).

 ## Massachusetts

Paralegal names can be printed on a firm's letterhead if their nonattorney status is clear. *Massachusetts Bar Ass'n Ethics Opinion 83–10* (11/29/83).

A paralegal can sign his or her name on law firm letterhead. *Massachusetts Bar Ass'n Ethics Opinion 73–2.*

A law firm cannot pay its office administrator, a nonattorney, a percentage of the firm's profits in addition to his fixed salary. *Massachusetts Bar Opinion 84–2* (1984).

##  Michigan

It is not possible for an attorney to give quality supervision to twenty-four paralegals located at six separate sites in the state. *State Bar of Michigan Opinion R–1* (12/16/88).

When nonattorney employees with access to the files move to another law firm, a Chinese Wall may have to be erected around them to prevent the imputed disqualification of the new firm. *State Bar of Michigan Formal Opinion R–4* (9/22/89).

Business cards and law firm letterhead can list the name of nonattorney employees with titles such as *legal assistant* or *paralegal*. The public must not be confused as to their nonattorney status. *State Bar of Michigan Informal Opinion RI–34* (12/15/89).

A paralegal works for a legal service organization that represents a plaintiff in a case against a potential defendant, who is the paralegal's fiance. The organization is not disqualified if the paralegal is screened from the case and the client (the plaintiff) is made aware of this relationship and consents. *State Bar of Michigan Informal Opinion CI–1168* (12/10/86).

Other State Bar of Michigan Informal Opinions involving nonattorneys: *CI–1155* (7/25/86); *CI–1203* (8/5/88); *R–6* (12/15/89); *RI–36* (11/20/89); *RI–55* (8/1/90).

## Minnesota

Paralegal names can be printed on a firm's letterhead, on professional cards, on professional announcement cards, office signs, telephone directory listings, law lists, and legal directory listings, if their nonattorney status is clear. Paralegals, so identified, may sign correspondence on behalf of the law firm if acting under an attorney's direction. But they cannot be named on pleadings under any identification. *Minnesota Bar Ass'n Ethics Opinion 8* (6/26/74, amended 6/18/80). On letterheads, see also *Opinion 93* (6/7/84).

##  Mississippi

Paralegal names can be printed on a firm's letterhead if their nonattorney status is made clear. The paralegal should not be called a *paralegal associate*, since in common usage the term *associate* carries a connotation of being an attorney in the firm. *Mississippi Bar Ass'n Ethics Opinion 93* (6/7/84).

An attorney can pay a paralegal a bonus based on the number of her hours billed and collected in excess of a designated minimum. A nonattorney compensation or retirement plan can be based in whole or in part on a profit-sharing arrangement. *Mississippi State Bar Opinion 154* (9/12/88).

A disbarred or suspended attorney cannot work as a paralegal. *Mississippi State Bar Opinion 96* (6/7/84).

## Missouri

At the outset of any professional dealings for the attorney, the paralegal must disclose to clients, the public, or other attorneys that he or she is a paralegal. The name of a paralegal may appear on the letterhead of a law firm and on business cards. A paralegal can sign correspondence on law firm letterhead provided the signature is followed by a title that identifies him or her as a paralegal. Under the supervision of an attorney, a paralegal can handle real estate closings. An attorney cannot share legal fees with a paralegal, but a paralegal can be included in a compensation or retirement plan that is based in whole or part on a profit-sharing arrangement. A bonus cannot be tied to the existence or amount of any particular legal fee. A paralegal cannot participate in a stock ownership plan, since a paralegal cannot become a part-owner of a professional corporation. A paralegal cannot be compensated for recommending an attorney's services. A copy of these guidelines and the ethical rules governing attorneys shall be delivered to or discussed with the paralegal immediately upon employment. *Guidelines for Practicing with Paralegals*, Missouri Bar Ass'n (1987).

# Montana

An attorney must not split a fee with a nonattorney. *State Bar of Montana Opinion (1) (9/13/85)*.

# Nebraska

Paralegals can be listed on law firm letterhead if their nonattorney status is made clear. *Nebraska State Bar Ass'n Advisory Committee Opinion 88–2*.

Several attorneys who are not partners, associates, or otherwise affiliated with each other share office space and share nonattorney personnel. They represent clients who are opposite each other in cases. This is not improper if the clients are aware of and consent to the arrangement. Steps must be taken to ensure confidentiality—such as preventing common access to case files and preventing the nonattorneys from working for both sides on a case. *Nebraska State Bar Ass'n Advisory Committee Opinion 89–2*.

# New Hampshire

According to New Hampshire Supreme Court Rules: *Rule 1.* Paralegals must not give legal advice, but they can, with adequate attorney supervision, provide information concerning legal matters. *Rule 3.* A paralegal shall not be delegated any task that requires the exercise of professional legal judgment. *Rule 5.* An attorney shall not form a partnership with a paralegal if any part of the partnership consists of the practice of law. *Rule 6.* An attorney shall not share fees with a paralegal but can include the paralegal in a retirement plan based on a profit-sharing arrangement. *Rule 7.* A paralegal's name may not be included on the letterhead of an attorney. A paralegal can have a business card that prints the name of the law firm where he or she works, if the card indicates the paralegal's nonattorney capacity and the firm does not use the paralegal to solicit business for the firm improperly. *Rule 8.* When dealing with clients, attorneys, or the public, the paralegal must disclose at the outset that he or she is not an attorney.

A law firm cannot list legal assistants on its letterhead. *New Hampshire Bar Ass'n Ethics Opinion 1982–3/20 (3/17/83)*.

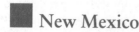

# New Jersey

New Jersey has added an additional subsection to Rule 5.3 of the Model Rules of Professional Conduct. The addition is (c)(3): Attorneys must make a "reasonable investigation of circumstances that would disclose past instances of conduct by the nonlawyer" that are "incompatible with the professional obligations of an attorney, which evidence a propensity for such conduct."

Attorneys cannot hire paralegals as independent contractors because of the difficulty of providing them with needed day-to-day supervision. The required "direct supervision" is not always provided when attorneys use such paralegals in areas where the attorneys have no expertise. And there is an increased danger of conflict-of-interest; independent paralegals might offer services to two opposing attorneys. Furthermore, an attorney using an independent paralegal for a single transaction would not interview him or her with the same care (for instance, regarding level of training and experience) as during a regular interview for full-time traditional employment. *New Jersey Unauthorized Practice of Law Committee Opinion 24* (11/15/90). Modified in 607 A.2d 962.

A paralegal can have a business card as long as the name of the employing law firm is also printed on it. *New Jersey Advisory Committee on Professional Ethics Opinion 647* (1990).

Nonattorney employees of the county welfare agency may represent litigants before the Office of Administrative Law. *New Jersey Advisory Committee on Professional Ethics Opinion 580* (2/27/86).

Paralegals can sign law firm correspondence concerning routine tasks such as gathering factual information and documents. They should not sign correspondence to clients, adverse attorneys, or tribunals. Minor exceptions are allowed such as "a purely routine request to a court clerk for a docket sheet." *New Jersey Advisory Committee on Professional Ethics Opinion 611* (2/23/88).

A law firm litigating tobacco cases can hire a nonattorney who had been involved in tobacco litigation at another firm, if the nonattorney had no substantial responsibility in the tobacco litigation at the other firm, obtained no confidential information concerning the litigation, and is screened from such litigation at the present firm. *New Jersey Advisory Committee on Professional Ethics Opinion 633* (11/2/89).

A law firm currently in litigation cannot hire a paralegal who formerly worked for the opposing attorney's law firm. There is an irrebuttable presumption that confidences gained in a prior employment have been revealed to the new employer. The disqualification of the law firm where the paralegal now works is automatic. *New Jersey Advisory Committee on Professional Ethics Opinion 546* (1984).

Other New Jersey Advisory Committee on Professional Ethics Opinions involving nonattorneys: *296* (2/6/75); *296 Supplement* (2/12/76); *598* (3/26/87); *631* (10/12/89).

An attorney cannot share fees with an investigator–paralegal. *Infante v. Gottesman,* 233 N.J. Super 310, 558 A.2d 1338 (1989).

# New Mexico

A paralegal shall disclose to all persons with whom he or she communicates—at the beginning of any dealings with them—that the paralegal is not an attorney. The word *associate* should not be used when referring to a paralegal since it might be interpreted as an attorney–associate. An attorney shall not share fees with a paralegal. The compensation of a paralegal shall not include a percentage of profits or fees received from clients referred to the attorney by the paralegal. A paralegal's name cannot be printed on the letterhead of an attorney. A paralegal can have a business card that prints the name of the law firm as long as his or her nonattorney status is made clear. A paralegal can sign correspondence on attorney letterhead as long as his or her nonattorney status is disclosed by a title such as *legal assistant* or *paralegal*. "In addition, a lawyer should explain to the legal assistant that the legal assistant has a duty to inform the lawyer of any assignment which the assistant regards as beyond his capability." *New Mexico Rules Governing the Practice of Law* (Judicial Pamphlet 16).

Attorneys must tell clients how much services to be rendered by office nonattorneys will cost. *Advisory Opinions Committee of the State Bar of New Mexico 1990–4.*

Another opinion of the Advisory Opinions Committee of the State Bar of New Mexico involving nonattorneys: *Opinion 1983–3.*

An attorney was suspended for failing to supervise a paralegal; the attorney failed to ensure that the conduct of the paralegal complied with the ethical obligations of the attorney. *In the Matter of Martinez,* 754 P.2d 842 (N.M. 1988).

# New York

An attorney cannot form a partnership with, or share legal fees with, a paralegal. An attorney's name can be printed on the business card of a paralegal as long as the latter's legal assistant status is clearly indicated. When dealing with a client, the paralegal must disclose at the outset that he or she is not an attorney. The same is true when dealing with a court, an agency, or the public if there is any reason for believing he or she is an attorney or associated with an attorney. *Guidelines for Utilization of Legal Assistants by Attorneys* (N.Y. State Bar Assn., 1976).

A paralegal cannot conduct a deposition or supervise the execution of a will. *New York State Bar Ass'n Ethics Opinions 304, 343.*

An attorney can give recognition to a nonattorney for work performed in the preparation of a brief as long as his or her nonattorney status is clear. *New York State Bar Ass'n Ethics Opinion 299.*

Paralegal names can be printed on a firm's letterhead if their nonattorney status is clear. *New York State Bar Ass'n Ethics Opinion 500 (12/6/78) (52–78).*

An attorney cannot allow a nonattorney to engage in settlement negotiations or to appear at a pretrial conference. *Committee of Professional Ethics of the Bar Ass'n of Nassau County Opinion 86–40 (9/12/89).*

A nonattorney can attend a real estate closing to perform ministerial functions involving mere formalities. His or her nonattorney status must be disclosed at the closing. *Committee of Professional Ethics of the Bar Ass'n of Nassau County Opinion 86–43* (10/21/86); reaffirmed in *Opinion 90–13* (3/18/90).

An attorney cannot divide a fee with a paralegal who brings clients to the attorney. *Committee of Professional Ethics of the Bar Ass'n of Nassau County Opinion 37–87* (10/1/87).

Nonattorneys cannot be referred to as *associates* of an attorney. *Committee of Professional Ethics of the Bar Ass'n of Nassau County 88–34 (9/29/88).*

An attorney may not represent a defendant in a criminal case when the complainant in the case is an investigator whom the attorney used in an unrelated case. There would be an appearance of impropriety in such a representation. *Committee of Professional Ethics of the Bar Ass'n of Nassau County 89–1 (1/18/89).*

An attorney cannot form a partnership with a nonattorney to practice law. *Committee on Professional Ethics of the Ass'n of the Bar of the City of New York Opinion 1987–1 (2/23/87).*

Paralegals can be listed on the letterhead of a law firm and on a business card that prints the name of the law firm (without printing the name of the supervising attorney) as long as their nonattorney status is indicated. *Committee on Professional Ethics of the New York County Lawyers' Ass'n Opinion 673 (12/23/89).*

## North Carolina

When acting on behalf of an attorney, a paralegal should disclose at the outset to clients, courts, attorneys, or the public that he or she is not an attorney. If an attorney accepts a matter in which a paralegal may have a conflict of interest, the attorney should exclude the paralegal from participating in any services performed in connection with that matter. The client should be told of this conflict. When using independent paralegals, the attorney must use special care to ensure that they are performing competently and ethically. An attorney shall not share fees with a paralegal. The compensation of a paralegal shall not include a percentage of the fees received by the attorney. A paralegal shall receive no compensation for referring matters to the attorney. The letterhead of an attorney shall not include the names of paralegals, but the latter may have business cards that print the name of their employer provided the paralegal's nonattorney capacity is clearly indicated. A paralegal can sign correspondence on an attorney's letterhead as long as his or her title, such as *paralegal* clearly indicates his or her nonattorney status. North Carolina Paralegal Committee, *Proposed Guidelines for Use of Non-Attorneys in Rendering Legal Services.*

Paralegals can negotiate with the claims adjuster of an insurance company of an opposing party as long as they do not exercise independent legal judgment and are supervised by an attorney. *Ethics Committee of the North Carolina State Bar Ass'n Opinion 70 (7/13/89).*

An attorney is not disqualified from representing a defendant even though his paralegal once worked for the attorney who now represents the plaintiff in the same case *if* the paralegal is screened from the case at his or her current office. *Ethics Committee of the North Carolina State Bar Ass'n Opinion 74 (7/13/89).*

## Ohio

A legal assistant can sign law firm correspondence on law firm stationery as long as his or her nonattorney status is clearly indicated. *Board of Commissioners on Grievances and Discipline Opinion 89–11 (4/14/89).*

Nonattorneys cannot be listed on law firm letterhead. They can, however, have business cards as long as their nonattorney status is made clear. *Board of Commissioners on Grievances and Discipline Opinion 89–16 (6/16/89).*

Law firm letterhead *can* print the names and titles of nonattorney employees as long as their nonattorney status is indicated and they are listed separately from the attorneys. *Professional Ethics Committee of the Columbus Bar Ass'n Opinion (6)* (11/71/88).

Law firm letterhead *can* print the names and titles of nonattorney employees, and the latter can also have their own business cards as long as their nonattorney status is made clear. *Professional Ethics Committee of the Cleveland Bar Ass'n Opinion 89–1* (2/25/89).

# Oregon

Nonattorneys in an estate-planning service are engaged in the unauthorized practice of law when they give legal advice to clients in connection with the service, even if an attorney reviews and executes the documents involved. *Legal Ethics Committee of the Oregon State Bar Opinion 523* (3/89).

Nonattorney employees can have their own business cards which contain the name of their employer–attorney. *Legal Ethics Committee of the Oregon State Bar Opinion 295* (7/75).

A paralegal can write and sign letters on attorney letterhead. *Legal Ethics Committee of the Oregon State Bar Opinion 349* (6/77).

A paralegal cannot take depositions. *Legal Ethics Committee of the Oregon State Bar Opinion 449* (6/77).

Other relevant opinions of the Legal Ethics Committee of the Oregon State Bar: *Opinion 208* (6/6/72); *Opinion 435.*

# Pennsylvania

Paralegals can sign letters on attorney letterhead if their nonattorney status is indicated. A supervised paralegal can correspond with the attorney for the opponent. *Committee on Legal Ethics and Professional Responsibility of the Pennsylvania Bar Ass'n Opinion 80–46.*

An attorney's letterhead can print the name of paralegals or other nonattorneys if their nonattorney status is indicated. *Committee on Legal Ethics and Professional Responsibility of the Pennsylvania Bar Ass'n Opinion 85–145* (11/14/85).

A paralegal can have a business card with the title of *legal assistant* and listing the name of the law firm. *Committee on Legal Ethics and Professional Responsibility of the Pennsylvania Bar Ass'n Opinion 80–15.*

A law student who has not taken and passed the bar examination is a paralegal and cannot practice law. *Committee on Legal Ethics and Professional Responsibility of the Pennsylvania Bar Ass'n Opinion 86–97* (5/27/87).

An attorney cannot hire an independent paralegal to do accident investigations if the paralegal is not a licensed private detective. *Committee on Legal Ethics and Professional Responsibility of the Pennsylvania Bar Ass'n Opinion 87–31* (6/87).

An attorney cannot allow a paralegal to conduct a deposition even if the attorney prepares the questions to be asked. *Committee on Legal Ethics and Professional Responsibility of the Pennsylvania Bar Ass'n Opinion 87–127* (12/87).

Other opinions of the Committee on Legal Ethics and Professional Responsibility of the Pennsylvania Bar Ass'n involving nonattorneys: *87–102* (1/88); *89–145.*

It is not unethical for an attorney to employ as a paralegal an attorney who is not permitted to practice law in Pennsylvania (because of suspension and later disbarment). Furthermore, the attorney may permit this paralegal to have client contact. *In re Anonymous No. 27 D.B. 89* (January 16, 1990).

A nonattorney cannot sign papers to be filed with the court, ask questions at a deposition, or handle court appearances. *Professional Responsibility for Nonlawyers, Professional Responsibility of the Philadelphia Bar Ass'n* (1989).

A paralegal can use a business card bearing the name of the law firm, provided his or her nonattorney status is clearly designated. *Professional Guidance Committee of the Philadelphia Bar Ass'n Opinion 74–1* (1974).

Law firm letterhead can include the names of paralegals as long as their nonattorney status is made clear. *Professional Guidance Committee of the Philadelphia Bar Ass'n Opinion 87–18* (6/25/87).

A professional corporation that practices law cannot have a nonattorney as a corporate officer. *Professional Guidance Committee of the Philadelphia Bar Ass'n Opinion 86–76* (6/19/86).

An attorney can accept referrals from a bilingual paralegal even though the paralegal charges the client for translation and investigation services. *Professional Guidance Committee of the Philadelphia Bar Ass'n Opinion 88–15* (6/27/88).

Disqualification of a law firm can be avoided if adequate screening devices requiring a nonattorney employee to maintain confidences gained in a prior job are in place. *Professional Guidance Committee of the Philadelphia Bar Ass'n Opinion 80–77; 80–119.*

Other opinions of the Professional Guidance Committee of the Philadelphia Bar Ass'n involving nonattorneys: *81–44* (undated); *86–162* (12/18/86); *87–3* (5/8/87); *87–6* (5/5/87); *87–21* (9/8/87); *89–5* (3/89); *90–5* (6/90).

## Rhode Island

In contacts with clients, courts, agencies, attorneys, or the public, paralegals must disclose at the outset that they are not attorneys. They can assist at a real estate closing. They can sign correspondence as long as their nonattorney status is made clear and the letter does not give legal advice or substantive instructions to a client. They can use a business card with the name of the law firm on it if their nonattorney status is disclosed. An attorney shall not form a partnership with a paralegal if any part of the partnership involves the practice of law. A paralegal cannot share legal fees or be compensated for referring matters to an attorney. An attorney cannot hire a suspended or disbarred attorney as a paralegal (or an attorney who has resigned because of a breach of ethics). *Rhode Island Supreme Court Provisional Order No. 18* (2/1/83), Revised 10/31/90.

Other opinions of the Ethics Advisory Panel of the Rhode Island Supreme Court involving nonattorneys: *88–4* (4/15/88); *87–3* (1/8/88); *88–7* (5/13/88).

# South Carolina

If a legal assistant has contact with a client, the latter must understand that the legal assistant is not an attorney. This should be disclosed at the beginning of any dealings with the client. It should be disclosed to others if they have any reason to believe the legal assistant is an attorney or is associated with an attorney. An attorney shall not share, on a proportionate basis, legal fees with a legal assistant. The letterhead of an attorney may not include the name of a nonattorney. A legal assistant can sign correspondence on attorney letterhead and can have a business card with the name of his or her law firm printed on it as long as the legal assistant's capacity is clearly indicated. *Guidelines for the Utilization by Lawyers of the Services of Legal Assistants by the South Carolina Bar* (12/11/81).

Nonattorney employees can have their own business cards as long as the title *legal assistant* is used on the card. The name of the law firm can also be printed on the card but only if the legal assistant performs significant duties outside the law office. *Ethics Advisory Committee of the South Carolina Bar Opinion 88–6.*

An attorney can hire a legal assistant with a criminal record for vehicular manslaughter but cannot hire a legal assistant who is a lawyer who has been disciplined. *Ethics Advisory Committee of the South Carolina Bar Opinion 87–6.*

An attorney can hire nonattorneys to fill in preprinted real estate forms and do title searches as long as they are supervised by the attorney and the attorney maintains direct contact with clients. *Ethics Advisory Committee of the South Carolina Bar Opinion 88–2.*

Other opinions of the Ethics Advisory Committee of the South Carolina Bar involving nonattorneys: *86–5; 88–14; 88–18.*

# South Dakota

A law firm can list paralegals on their letterhead (graduates of law school who have not yet passed the bar exam). *Ethics Committee of the State Bar of South Dakota Opinion 90–10* (9/22/90).

# Tennessee

If appropriate screening devices are in place, and Client "A" consents, an entire law firm need not be disqualified from representing that client simply because a "tainted" attorney in the firm once worked at another firm that represented client "B" in a case adverse to client "A." Furthermore, "the disqualification rules and screening procedures are applicable to lawyer, law clerk, paralegal, and legal secretary." *Board of Professional Responsibility of the Supreme Court of Tennessee, Formal Ethics Opinion 89–F–118* (3/10/89). Note: this Opinion may overrule Opinion 87–F–110, which disqualified a law firm because of a tainted paralegal who switched jobs, even though screening mechanisms were in place.

# Texas

The client must understand that the legal assistant is not an attorney. An attorney must not share legal fees with a paralegal, and shall not give the latter any compensation for referring business to the attorney. The nonattorney status of the legal assistant must be specifically disclosed at the outset to clients, courts, agencies, etc. Disclosure may be made in any way that avoids confusion. A legal assistant can use a business card containing the name and address of the employing attorney or firm. The card must designate the legal assistant's status. *General Guidelines for the Utilization of the Services of Legal Assistants by Attorneys* (State Bar of Texas, 1981).

Law firm letterhead can print the name of legal assistants and can indicate that they have been certified (with a notation that they are legal assistants and are not licensed to practice law). *Professional Ethics Committee of the State Bar of Texas Opinion 436* (6/20/86), which overrules Opinion 390.

A legal assistant can write a letter on the law firm's letterhead as long as he or she signs as a legal assistant. The letter should not contain legal advice, judgment, strategy, or settlement negotiations. Such letters should be signed by an attorney. *Professional Ethics Committee of the State Bar of Texas Opinion 381* (3/75).

A legal assistant may have a business card with the law firm's name appearing on it provided the status of the legal assistant is clearly disclosed. *Professional Ethics Committee of the State Bar of Texas Opinion 403* (1982).

The name of an employee can be printed on an outdoor sign of a law firm as long as the nonattorney status of the employee is clear on the sign. *Professional Ethics Committee of the State Bar of Texas Opinion 437* (6/20/86).

Other opinions of the Professional Ethics Committee of the State Bar of Texas involving nonattorneys: *438* (3/16/87); *458* (3/11/88).

When an attorney fails to supervise his paralegal, the attorney is responsible for the malpractice of the paralegal, such as the theft of client funds by the paralegal. "In the future, you should establish greater controls over your paralegals," wrote the *Legal Ethics Committee of the Dallas Bar Ass'n, Opinion 1989–5.*

# Vermont

A law firm cannot continue to represent a defendant in a civil case after hiring a nonattorney employee who had previously performed extensive work on the same case while employed by the law firm representing the plaintiff. *Committee on Professional Responsibility of the Vermont Bar Ass'n Ethics Opinion 85–8* (1985).

In a conversation with a nonattorney employee, if a prospective client threatens to kill someone, the employee who believes the threat can warn the potential victim. *Committee on Professional Responsibility of the Vermont Bar Ass'n Opinion 86–3.*

An attorney represents a client in a real estate transaction where the opposing party is the spouse of a paralegal who works for that attorney. The attorney is not disqualified from the case if the client is told about the paralegal's relationship to the spouse and if the paralegal does not work on the case. *Committee on Professional Responsibility of the Vermont Bar Ass'n 87–15.*

A paralegal works for an attorney who represents the plaintiff in a case. The paralegal also works in a court diversion program that processed the brother of the defendant in this case. What this brother did or didn't do is relevant to the case between the plaintiff and defendant. The attorney can still represent this plaintiff, but the paralegal should be screened from the case and must not tell the attorney any secrets he learned in the diversion program. *Committee on Professional Responsibility of the Vermont Bar Ass'n 89–4.*

Other Vermont Bar Ass'n opinions involving nonattorneys: *78–2; 85–9.*

# ■ Virginia

A paralegal shall not communicate with clients, outside attorneys, or the public without disclosing his or her nonattorney status. *Code of Professional Responsibility, DR 3–104(E).*

A "real estate paralegal company" can provide assistance to an attorney in closing real estate loans that have been referred to this company by the closing attorney. This is not the unauthorized practice of law as long as designated procedures are followed. *Unauthorized Practice of Law Opinion 147* (June 1991).

An attorney is not required to withdraw from a case as long as a nonattorney employee does not disclose confidential information learned while she worked for an opposing attorney. *Standing Committee on Legal Ethics of the Virginia State Bar Opinion 745* (1985).

A law firm can print the names of nonattorney employees on its letterhead as long as their nonattorney status is made clear. These employees can participate in a profit-sharing plan of the firm as part of a compensation or retirement program. *Standing Committee on Legal Ethics of the Virginia State Bar Opinion 762* (1/29/86).

An attorney must not split fees with nonattorneys, but nonattorneys can be paid a bonus based on profit sharing. *Standing Committee on Legal Ethics of the Virginia State Bar Opinion 806* (6/25/86).

A law firm engaged in collection work can pay its nonattorney employee a percentage of profits from the collections received, plus a salary. *Standing Committee on Legal Ethics of the Virginia State Bar Opinion 885* (3/11/87).

An attorney represents a client in a case in which the attorney's former nonattorney employee will testify against this client. The attorney is not disqualified from representing this client as long as the client is informed of this situation and still wants the attorney to represent him. *Standing Committee on Legal Ethics of the Virginia State Bar Opinion 891* (4/1/87).

It is unethical for a nonattorney employee of a law firm to contact prospective collections clients to suggest that they hire the law firm for their collections work. *Standing Committee on Legal Ethics of the Virginia State Bar Opinion 1290* (10/25/89).

Other opinions of the Standing Committee on Legal Ethics of the Virginia State Bar involving nonattorneys: *823* (9/19/86); *875* (1/30/87); *909* (4/1/87); *946* (6/25/87); *970* (9/30/87); *1003* (11/24/87); *1054* (3/29/88); *1077* (5/23/88); *1258* (7/25/89); *1276* (10/3/89); *1288* (10/19/89).

# ■ Virgin Islands

An attorney who has been suspended from practice before a federal court of appeals can work on a federal case as a paralegal if supervised by an attorney in good standing and if there is no contact with clients. *In re Mitchell,* 901 F.2d 1179, 1190 (3rd Cir. 1990).

Washington

A disbarred attorney cannot be employed as a paralegal. *Washington State Bar Ass'n Opinion 184* (1990).

 West Virginia

Anything delegated to a nonattorney must lose its separate identity and be merged in the service of the lawyer. When communicating with persons outside the office, a paralegal "must disclose his status as such." Nonattorneys can sign letters on law firm stationery as long as their nonattorney status is clearly indicated. *Legal Ethics Inquiry No. 76–7* (3 W.Va. State Bar Journal, Spring 1977).

 Wisconsin

Law firm letterhead can include the names of paralegals as long as their nonattorney status is made clear. *Wisconsin Bar Ass'n Ethics Opinion E–85–6* (10/85).

The office of the district attorney and the office of a circuit judge can share the services of a paralegal as long as the paralegal is supervised so as to maintain the confidentiality of each office. *Committee on Professional Ethics of the State Bar of Wisconsin Opinion E–86–13* (9/24/86).

A paralegal can have a business card containing the law firm's name but cannot be listed on the law firm's letterhead. *Committee on Professional Ethics of the State Bar of Wisconsin Opinion E–75–22.* (Note: Opinion E–85–6 changes the letterhead ruling of E–75–22.)

A paralegal *can* be listed on law firm letterhead. *Committee on Professional Ethics of the State Bar of Wisconsin Opinion E–85–6.*

A paralegal who is a licensed real estate broker cannot appear at a real estate closing. "If a paralegal from the attorney's office appears at the closing, it will *seem* that he is there in a legal capacity." *Committee on Professional Ethics of the State Bar of Wisconsin Opinion E–80–2.*

A law firm can hire a litigation paralegal who will also provide court-reporting services to other attorneys. *Committee on Professional Ethics of the State Bar of Wisconsin Opinion E–86–19* (12/12/86).

 Wyoming

A "lawyer who approaches a represented third party without going through counsel should be severely punished. And this is so though the lawyer uses a law representative or paralegal to do his dirty work." *Brooks v. Zebre,* 792 P.2d 196, 220 (WY 1990).

A suspended attorney shall not participate in the practice of law as an attorney or paralegal. *Medicino v. Whitchurch,* 565 P.2d 460, 478 (WY 1977).

# Paralegal Business Cards

Most paralegals have their own business card. As indicated in Chapter 5 and in Appendix F, it is ethical for an attorney to allow a paralegal employee to have a business card which also prints the name of the employer. Here are several examples of such cards in use today:

# Federal Job Information

■ Office of Personnel Management Federal Job Information Centers

Contact the Federal Job Information Center which is nearest the location where you would like to work for information on the job opportunities in that area and the forms needed to apply.

**ALABAMA**
Huntsville:
Building 600, Suite 341
3322 Memorial Pkwy., South
35801-5311
(205) 544-5802

**ALASKA**
Anchorage:
222 W. 7th Ave., #22,
99513-7572
(907) 271-5821

**ARIZONA**
Phoenix:
Century Plaza Bldg., Rm. 1415
3225 N. Central Ave., 85012
(602) 640-5800

**ARKANSAS**
(See Oklahoma Listing)

**CALIFORNIA**
Los Angeles:
9650 Flair Drive
Ste. 100A
El Monte, 91731
(818) 575-6510

Sacramento:
4695 Watt Ave., North Entrance
95660-5592
(916) 551-1464

San Diego:
Federal Bldg., Room 4-S-9
880 Front St., 92188
(619) 557-6165

San Francisco:
P.O. Box 7405, 94120
(Located at 211 Main St.,
2nd Floor, Room 235)
(415) 974-5627

**COLORADO**
Denver:
P.O. Box 25167, 80225
(303) 969-7050
(Located at 12345 W. Alameda
Pkwy., Lakewood)

*For Job Information (24 hours a day) in the following States, dial:*
Montana: (303) 969-7052
Utah: (303) 969-7053
Wyoming: (303) 969-7054
*For forms and local supplements, dial:* (303) 969-7055

**CONNECTICUT**
Hartford:
Federal Bldg., Room 613
450 Main St., 06103
(203) 240-3096 or 3263

**DELAWARE**
(See Philadelphia Listing)

**DISTRICT OF COLUMBIA**
Metro Area:
1900 E St., N.W., Room 1416,
20415
(202) 606-2700

**FLORIDA**
Orlando:
Commodore Bldg., Suite 150
3444 McCrory Pl., 32803-3701
(407) 648-6148

**GEORGIA**
Atlanta:
Richard B. Russell Federal Bldg.,
Room 940A, 75 Spring St., S.W.,
30303
(404) 331-4315

**HAWAII**
Honolulu (and other Hawaiian
Islands and Overseas):
Federal Bldg., Room 5316
300 Ala Moana Blvd., 96850
(808) 541-2791
Overseas Jobs—(808) 541-2784

**IDAHO**
(See Washington Listing)

**ILLINOIS**
Chicago:
175 W. Jackson Blvd., Room 530
60604
(312) 353-6192
(For Madison & St. Clair Counties,
see St. Louis, MO listing)

**INDIANA**
Indianapolis:
Minton-Capehart Federal Bldg.,
575 N. Pennsylvania St., 46204
(317) 226-7161

(For Clark, Dearborn, & Floyd Counties, see Ohio listing)

## IOWA
(816) 426-7757
(For Scott County see Illinois listing; for Pottawattamie County, See Kansas listing)

## KANSAS
Wichita:
One-Twenty Bldg., Room 101
120 S. Market St., 67202
(316) 269-6794
(For Johnson, Leavenworth, and Wyandotte Counties, dial (816) 426-5702)

## KENTUCKY
(See Ohio listing: for Henderson County, see Indiana listing)

## LOUISIANA
New Orleans:
1515 Poydras St., Suite 680, 70112
(504) 589-2764

## MAINE
(See New Hampshire Listing)

## MARYLAND
Baltimore:
Garmatz Federal Building
101 W. Lombard Street, 21201
(301) 962-3822

## MASSACHUSETTS
Boston:
Thos. P. O'Neill, Jr. Federal Bldg.
10 Causeway St., 02222-1031
(617) 565-5900

## MICHIGAN
Detroit:
477 Michigan Ave., Rm. 565, 48225
(313) 226-6950

## MINNESOTA
Twin Cities:
Federal Building, Room 501
Ft. Snelling, Twin Cities, 55111
(612) 725-3430

## MISSISSIPPI
(See Alabama Listing)

## MISSOURI
Kansas City:
Federal Building, Rm. 134
601 E. 12th Street, 64106
(816) 426-5702

(For Counties west of and including Mercer, Grundy, Livingston, Carroll, Saline, Pettis, Benton, Hickory, Dallas, Webster, Douglas, and Ozark)

St. Louis:
400 Old Post Office Bldg.
815 Olive St., 63101
(314) 539-2285
(For all other Missouri counties not listed under Kansas City above)

## MONTANA
(See Colorado Listing)

## NEBRASKA
(See Kansas Listing)

## NEVADA
(See Sacramento, CA Listing)

## NEW HAMPSHIRE
Portsmouth:
Thomas J. McIntyre Federal Bldg.
Room 104
80 Daniel Street, 03801-3879
(603) 431-7115

## NEW JERSEY
Newark:
Peter W. Rodino, Jr., Federal Bldg.
970 Broad Street, 07102
(201) 645-3673
*In Camden, dial (215) 597-7440*

## NEW MEXICO
Albuquerque:
Federal Building
421 Gold Avenue, S.W., 87102
(505) 766-5583

## NEW YORK
New York City:
Jacob K. Javits Federal Bldg.
26 Federal Plaza, 10278
(212) 264-0440, 0441, or 0442

Syracuse:
James M. Hanley Federal Building
100 S. Clinton Street, 13260
(315) 423-5660

## NORTH CAROLINA
Raleigh:
P.O. Box 25069
4505 Falls of the Neuse Rd.
Suite 450, 27611-5069
(919) 856-4361

## NORTH DAKOTA
(See Minnesota Listing)

## OHIO
Dayton:
Federal Building, Rm. 506
200 W. 2nd Street, 45402
(513) 225-2720
(For Van Wort, Auglaize, Hardin, Marion, Crawford, Richland, Ashland, Wayne, Stark, Carroll, Columbiana counties and all counties north of these see Michigan listing)

## OKLAHOMA
Oklahoma City:
(Mail or phone only)
200 N.W. Fifth St., 2nd Floor, 73102
(405) 231-4948
TDD-(405) 231-4614
For Forms, dial (405) 231-5208

## OREGON
Portland:
Federal Bldg., Room 376
1220 S.W. Third Ave., 97204
(503) 326-3141

## PENNSYLVANIA
Harrisburg:
Federal Bldg., Room 168
P.O. Box 761, 17108
(717) 782-4494

Philadelphia:
Wm. J. Green, Jr., Federal Bldg.
600 Arch Street, 19106
(215) 597-7440

Pittsburgh:
Federal Building
1000 Liberty Ave., Rm. 119, 15222
(412) 644-2755

## PUERTO RICO
San Juan:
Federico Degetau Federal Building
Carlos E. Chardon Street
Hato Rey, P. R. 00918
(809) 766-5242

## RHODE ISLAND
Providence:
Pastore Federal Bldg.
Room 310, Kennedy Plaza, 02903
(401) 528-5251

## SOUTH CAROLINA
(See Raleigh, NC Listing)

## SOUTH DAKOTA
(See Minnesota Listing)

**TENNESSEE**
Memphis:
200 Jefferson Avenue
Suite 1312, 38103-2335
(901) 521-3958

**TEXAS**
Dallas:
(Mail or phone only)
1100 Commerce St., Rm. 6B12,
75242
(214) 767-8035

San Antonio:
8610 Broadway, Rm. 305, 78217
(512) 229-6611 or 6600

**UTAH**
(See Colorado Listing)

**VERMONT**
(See New Hampshire Listing)

**VIRGINIA**
Norfolk:
Federal Building, Room 500
200 Granby St., 23510-1886
(804) 441-3355

**WASHINGTON**
Seattle:
Federal Building
915 Second Ave., 98174
(206) 442-4365

**WEST VIRGINIA**
Phone only:
(513) 225-2866

**WISCONSIN**
For Dane, Grant, Green, Iowa,
Lafayette, Rock, Jefferson,
Walworth, Milwaukee, Waukesha,
Racine, and Kenosha counties call
(312) 353-6189

(For all other Wisconsin counties
not listed above see Minnesota
listing)

**WYOMING**
(See Colorado Listing)

# How to Start a Freelance Paralegal Business

by Linda Harrington

The best way to get into business is to do it, not talk forever about it. In fact, you may be doing it before you know that you are actually running a business.

The conservative approach to getting into freelance business it to take work on the side while you maintain a salaried position. When your side business interferes with your job, then you must decide whether or not the business is enticing enough to promote. If it is not, give up the business, keep the salaried job, and be thankful to have learned a lesson in an undramatic way about running a business.

If the business is satisfying and if you enjoy it, the time has come to devote more time and energy to it. Therefore, you will be resigning your salaried job to tackle a business.

Perhaps you have impressed your current employer enough so that he, she, or it will be your client after you resign.

## Preliminary Considerations in Getting Started

What is your area of expertise? Is it likely to generate some cash for you if you go freelance? One of the areas to avoid is claimants' personal injury work where it's contingent, that is, the attorney will get a fee contingent upon success in court. It's been my experience that attorneys will pay you when they get paid on a case. So, if you're working for an attorney who will pay you when that attorney gets paid and that attorney loses the case, then it's likely you won't get paid.

I work in probate. Everyone knows that death and taxes are inevitable. That being the case, I find it a very lucrative and interesting area.

An extremely important aspect of being a freelance paralegal is having a network. A network can be one of two kinds: first, a network of prior employers who respect your skills a lot and will use you when you go freelance; second, the network of your peers that's developed through paralegal associations and contacts. Both are equally important; one does not substitute for the other. I found that my activities in the local association have been extremely rewarding. They have given me leadership opportunities, the ability to learn current law from the people who work in large law firms, and a chance to meet friends who have the same kind of responsibilities I do. For the most part, my job leads have come from people I worked for before I became a freelancer.

The other part of the network to explore is the school system. The local paralegal programs can assist you a great deal in establishing a freelance business. For one thing you can teach there, and that provides some of the income you need when you're first starting a business. (The income does come slowly in a new business.) Second, if you're teaching, you're meeting people who will one day be your peers—and that's expanding your professional network. Third, many paralegal programs have work-study experiences available for the students. The students are placed in offices where they get on-the-job training. I have lots of them come to my office. That keeps my overhead down. I give the student on-the-job training in all aspects of probate and death taxes, and in return, I have people to staff my office. It benefits the school, my office, and the students as well. So there are resources, lots of resources, available from the local schools.

A high level of expertise is something that I would like to stress. I have seen a lot of people come out of paralegal training programs and not get their dream job. They then decide that they're going to open freelance business operations, knowing not too much about the practical reality of dealing with attorneys, not to mention the practical reality of working as a paralegal. *I would think that you'd need about four or five years' experience in your field before attempting to go freelance.* The first reason, of course, is that you want to have strength in your practice area and be able to handle some of the problems that you will later encounter as a freelance paralegal.

The second reason is that you have to know about attorneys. You have to know about their personalities, you have to be able to manage the problems that they often present. I tell all my students that attorneys now have to pass "arrogance" before they are allowed to take the Bar exam, and you have to learn how to deal with this attitude in as cheerful a manner as you possibly can. Dealing with attorneys is just as important an area of expertise to develop as any other aspect of expertise in a practice field. If you're going to go freelance, you have to handle the situation of hundreds of attorneys calling you up, each one considering himself or herself the most important person in the world. You have to deal with that reality.

The most important things I had to learn were to keep a sense of humor and to remember to be compulsive. Some people say that I'm a workaholic; I prefer to state that I work hard. I work very, very hard. The things that most people think are available in freelance work are independence and free time. The reality is that they don't always exist. If your office does not get the work done, the buck stops with you. You can't blame your staff. The final responsibility rests on your shoulders. If everybody else leaves and the computer breaks down, you must still perform. If you don't get it done, you face the possibility of jeopardizing your entire business operation.

## Other Practical Suggestions

*Step 1.*   Have business cards printed. The cards should state your name, specialty area, and telephone number.

Have an answering service. A business answering service provides a real, live voice to a caller, not a recording. It is reassuring to a potential customer to hear "a live one" on the line. Limit the service to the hours 9–5 to keep the cost of the service down.

Have "call waiting" installed by the phone company. This feature enables one line to handle several calls at once by a mere flick of a button.

Have "call forward" installed by the phone company. This feature enables you to have incoming calls automatically forwarded to the telephone number of your choice. If you are waiting for an important call but have a visit to make, you can have your call forwarded to your destination automatically.

*Step 2.* Systematize your operation immediately. The systems you will need are:

1. Calendar system
2. Timekeeping system
3. Billing system
4. Filing system for both open and closed matters
5. Procedural manual for your specialty area

A *calendar system* should include: a master calendar that is easily spotted among clutter; a pocket calendar, which you must carry at all times; and some sort of statute-of-limitations reminder system. Many companies offer calendar systems at relatively low cost. Two are: Safeguard Business Systems and Lawfax System.

A *timekeeping system* should include: a master time record repository (separate from the case file), time slips, and decision-making on your part concerning standard charges for services and costs. It is easiest to assign a set charge for a particular service, subject to increases for complications or quirks. For example, typical time charges will be incurred for telephone calls. Assign a minimum charge for each call. Each duty should have a minimum charge assigned to it. In this way, your billing will reflect all applicable charges for the particular service involved in the transaction as well as your research, investigation, and other "write up" expenses. Costs such as photocopies should also reflect the time involved to perform the service. Therefore, standard mark-up for costs is advisable. Naturally, these are matters that are internal to the business. Therefore, establish your standards and then keep your mouth shut.

A *billing system* should include a retainer, which is received when the case work comes in, and a statement for services submitted at an advantageous time and in a personal manner which makes it clear that a bill is an important document to the sender. Set up a system for billing that is realistic. If your clients are most likely to pay on the 30th of the month, send your bills on the 25th. If your clients will not pay the bill until the receipts from the case are received, bill at the end of the work. Billing is as much psychology as anything else. Figure out when the client will want to pay and bill at that time.

A *filing system* for open cases will include: a repository for case documents, an identification system for file labels, a spot for the files to be stored; and a case matter sheet that generally describes the client, the case, and the work to be done, as well as the billing arrangements between you and the client. Casework can be stored in file folders, in binders, in boxes, and a number of other places. Make sure that all cases are stored in the same fashion and that the case files are easily located.

Closed cases should be stored and retained. A closed file system should be a numerical system. For this type of system, you need: file folders, a rolodex to store the case name and closed file number (retained in alphabetical order by case), and a central register to show the numbers used for previously closed files, so that the number chosen for a closed file will not have been used previously.

A *procedural manual* will contain: standard correspondence sent for the particular areas of law you specialize in, standard (completed) court forms used in your field, instructions to others concerning processing the documents. A procedural manual can also contain information concerning special and standard requirements of area courts, if your work involves preparing and filing court papers. The latter will help you avoid procedural errors and will save time, if it is updated regularly.

*Step 3.*   Fix your goals, make a budget, and prepare to stick to them.

*Fixing a goal* involves knowing why you want to run a business. There are many reasons to want to be in business for yourself. Some are: ego gratification—now you are going to get recognition for how great you've always known you are; free time—now you can set your own hours and go to the beach whenever you want; money—now you are going to get a piece of the action and get rich.

Caution: be prepared for reality. None of your original goals will be unchanged if you are still in business one year later. Most of the people you work for will never be impressed by your brilliance—you said you could do the work, you did do the work, so what's the big deal? If you are successful, the last thing you will have is free time. Even in the beginning, your clients will want to see you or talk to you when *they* want to do so, not when you want them to. Most attorneys feel that if you only knew that they wanted to talk to you, you would jump to attention at four in the morning and be grateful for the phone call. All the money you earn will be hard earned. When you finally do earn money, some of it will go to your staff, some to your landlord, some to the IRS, and some to you.

To keep your wits about you, you must budget and you must set limits. How much of what you want do you have to receive in order to stick with it? If you want ego gratification, how many clients have to tell you you are great to make the business worthwhile? If you want free time, how much free time do you have to have to make the business worthwhile? If you want money, how much profit must you make to make the business worthwhile? The "how much" is your minimum. Obviously, the sky is the limit.

If you do not get your minimum, are you willing to quit? If not, do not go into business.

You can generally figure out how you are doing by using the following calculation: Monthly gross × 12 = Year's gross. Do not count on new business to get you by. Count on the status quo as far as income is concerned to figure out how much money you will make by December 31 and budget accordingly. If you need income from the business to pay your personal bills, how much do you need monthly? Does this leave any money to run the business? Of the money that is left, how much will be required for telephone, answering service, supplies, and other fixed expenses? Now how much is left? Use the rest for expansion of your business (equipment purchases, rent, personnel, etc.).

*Step 4.*   Develop realistic employee relationships.

If you have done everything you can do to avoid hiring your first employee and that is not enough to keep pace with your work or to allow you the time off you desire, then it is time to hire help.

*Accept what you are.* You are the owner of a very small business and cannot offer big-firm benefits, bonuses, or vacations to your prospective employee.

Also, you are a person who wishes to protect your business position, so you do not want to hand your business over to a potential competitor. Last, you are a person who has certain expectations concerning job performance, productivity, and attendance. You have developed your own ideas about what constitutes a good job in your field.

*Do not hire a friend.* Being someone's boss does not improve a friendship when you also own the business.

*Hire someone trainable.* A trainable person is likely to be a recent graduate from a paralegal school. The fact that an applicant has sought education in the field and completed some or all of it is a strong indication that the person has an interest in the field and a desire for practical experience.

*Do not hire someone just like you.* You are the person who decided to start up the business, who worked (slaved?) to get it going, who knows everything, and who does not want to work so hard now. If you hire someone just like you, you will have two people not wanting to work so hard (you and your employee) *or* one who wants to start a business and has access to all your clients.

*Establish a trial employment first.* Whether you're hiring a work-study student at minimum wage from a local paralegal program or hiring an experienced person from some other source, set a review period or termination period for the relationship. Tell your employee what that period is and stick to it.

*Be realistic about your employee.* Because you are a small business, you cannot compete with larger firms that will offer your employee a better deal after the employee has experience and training. Therefore, accept the fact that the employee will probably move on. Tell the employee that you accept this fact and will help the person find a better position after the training has been completed (one to two years, usually). This will motivate the employee to learn as much as possible and to do a good job. This will also avoid you taking personally the job move, which any sensible employee will consider after becoming competent on the job.

*Be sure you understand the tax and insurance requirements for your employee.* You must have an employer I.D. number, you must withhold taxes and social security and state disability insurance, you must file quarterly reports with the taxing authorities and provide your employee with a W-2 at year end, you must have Worker's Compensation Insurance, and you must contribute as the employer into the unemployment fund and to Social Security. Each employee's salary is hardly your total cost in keeping that employee.

*Have your employee work on your premises.* This is mandatory during the training period, at bare minimum, so that you can become familiar with the employee's work habits and control work production.

*Review the employee's time slips.* The time slip review will educate you concerning how long a particular job takes the employee to perform, how many hours during the day the employee devotes to office matters, and how the cases are progressing.

*Fire the hopeless.* When you know that an employee is not going to work out, do not wait for the realization to come to the employee. It never will. Call the person in to your office, look the person in the eyes, and tell the person how wonderful he or she is and how many fantastic qualities he or she has and how unfortunate it is that the job is so miserable for such a terrific individual and that the job just isn't good enough for such a talented person. *Or* call the person in and tell him or her that the employment is not working out and that you wish to ask for his or her resignation, to avoid the stigma to the employee of being fired. *Or* call the person in and tell him or her that you can no longer tolerate his or her presence and that he or she is fired. In whatever way you can do it, be sure that it gets done as soon as you have given up hope for improvement. That's your money that your employee is taking home every two weeks. Nothing rankles so much as feeling that you are paying for a mistake again and again.

*Reward the hearty.* Go out to lunch for a chat and pay the bill. Send the employee home early or give him or her a surprise day off after a hard week. Leave town yourself and let him or her have the office to himself or herself. Give bonuses when a difficult case is completed. Give a raise of one-day off a week. Compliment the employee for work well done.

*Accept criticism.* Your employee will probably be compelled to express criticism of the systems in your office or, perhaps, your own style. So what? This is how good ideas get born. Think about the recommendations and, if they are good ones, change your office systems.

## ■ Conclusion

The worst way to get into business is to assume that there is no way you can fail (90% of all new businesses do fail, the Small Business Administration says), to buy the most expensive equipment, rent the most costly office space, get the most sophisticated telephone system, and generally count on the birds in the bushes before they land in your hand. Hope that you are able to start building your business slowly so that you will have time to learn about building and problem solving. Give it a good try. If it works out and if you like it, keep going. If it works out and you do not like it, or if it does not work out, then give it up and congratulate yourself on having given it a good try-out.

# "Legal Assistant Day"

In many states, governors and mayors have issued proclamations that set aside a particular day or week to honor paralegals. Here are two examples:

State of Louisiana

**Buddy Roemer**
Governor

**Proclamation**

WHEREAS, the paralegal profession is a new and growing field; and

WHEREAS, paralegals provide an invaluable service to the legal profession as well as to the general public which utilizes legal services; and

WHEREAS, the legal community in this state includes many qualified paralegals who are able to reduce the workloads of their employers and employers' clients; and

WHEREAS, Louisiana citizens should become aware of the field of paralegalism and encourage the use of the services of paralegals.

NOW, THEREFORE, I, BUDDY ROEMER, Governor of the State of Louisiana, do hereby proclaim the week of September 9 through 15, 1990, as

**PARALEGAL WEEK**

in the State of Louisiana.

In Witness Whereof, I have hereunto set my hand officially and caused to be affixed the Great Seal of the State of Louisiana, at the Capitol, in the City of Baton Rouge, on this the 9th day of September A.D. 1990

Attest By
Secretary of State

Governor of Louisiana

# State of Iowa

## Executive Department

IN THE NAME AND BY THE AUTHORITY OF THE STATE OF IOWA

## Proclamation

**Whereas,** the legal assistant profession is an expanding element of the legal community, striving to assist in the delivery of quality and affordable legal services to all citizens; and

**Whereas,** legal assistants are presently employed with private law firms, corporate legal departments, real estate, banks, insurance, government and public agencies and legal clinics throughout the state of Iowa; and

**Whereas,** the Legal Assistants Association encourages and provides continuing legal education opportunities for their members by offering workshops, seminars and a monthly newsletter; and

**Whereas,** there should be a day set aside for the recognition of the legal assistant and to acknowledge the services that they provide to the legal community and the people of the state of Iowa:

**Now, Therefore, I,** Robert D. Ray, Governor of the State of Iowa, do hereby proclaim August 25, 1982, as

## Legal Assistant Day

in Iowa and encourage all Iowans to join in this observance.

**In Testimony Whereof,** I have hereunto subscribed my name and caused the Great Seal of the State of Iowa to be affixed. Done at Des Moines this 25th day of August in the year of our Lord one thousand nine hundred eighty-two.

Attest

Deputy Secretary

*Robert D. Ray*
Governor

# News Stories, War Stories, and Parting Shots

## ■ Legal Assistant Elected Probate Judge

In November of 1987, Arlene G. Keegan, a legal assistant, was elected Probate Judge in the town of Litchfield, Connecticut. A law degree is not required to be a Probate Judge in Connecticut. Judge Keegan handles a wide variety of cases. In one case, for example, family members argued that their mother was incompetent when she prepared her will. "It was a tough decision, because I had to get in the middle of a situation with family members pulling against a close friend of the decedent." "I get to deal with a lot of people, and I find people totally intriguing." Howard, *A Legal Assistant Is Elected Probate Judge,* 5 Legal Assistant Today 32 (March/April 1988).

Former Legal Assistant, now Probate Judge Arlene Keegan, at the courthouse in Litchfield, Connecticut

## ■ Paralegal Appointed Chairman of Bar Association Committee

The Colorado Bar Association has appointed Joanna Hughbanks "to serve as chairman of the Legal Assistants Committee of the Colorado Bar Association." Ms. Hughbanks is an independent paralegal in Denver. She is believed to be the first nonattorney to chair a standing committee of a bar association. Letter from Christopher R. Brauchi, President of the Colorado Bar Association, to Joanna Hughbanks, 6/27/89.

## Paralegal Appointed Bankruptcy Trustee

A Fort Worth paralegal, Twalla Dupriest, has been appointed by the Bankruptcy Court as trustee for the estate of T. Cullen Davis, who was one of the wealthiest men in the United States. Twalla will be responsible for gathering all of the assets of Davis for the purpose of repaying creditors, and will preside at the meetings of creditors. *Paralegal Appointed Trustee to Cullen Davis Estate,* Newsletter, Dallas Ass'n of Legal Assistants, (Sept. 1987).

## Freelance Paralegal Named Pro Bono Paralegal of the Year

A freelance paralegal, Jim Carrao of Dallas, has been named Pro Bono Paralegal of the Year by the Dallas Bar Association and Legal Services of North Texas, Inc. for donating 176 hours of his time to help provide legal services to the poor. Parchman, *Communiqué,* AAPLA Advocate 17 (Alamo Area Professional Legal Assistants, Inc. July/August 1991).

## Paralegal Runs for the Legislature

Rosemary Mulligan, an Illinois paralegal, ran for a seat in the Illinois House of Representatives in 1990 against an incumbent. The election was held in a district in a suburb of Chicago. The vote was so close that it was declared a tie. By law, such elections are decided by lottery—a toss of the coin. Although the paralegal won the toss, a court later declared her opponent the victor after reviewing some disputed ballots. *Toss of Coin to Decide Race in Illinois,* A12 (New York Times, 7/18/90).

## Paralegal Sued for Civil Rights Violations

A Kentucky paralegal was sued, along with a prosecutor, for civil rights violations. In the complaint, an automobile dealership alleged that the prosecutor and paralegal fraudulently conspired to obtain the business records of the plaintiff. The paralegal allegedly caused invalid and unenforceable subpoena duces tecum to be issued in order to illegally obtain the records of the dealership. Hectus, *Paralegal Sued for Civil Rights Violations,* One Voice (Kentucky Paralegal Ass'n, March/April 1991).

##  Paralegal Charged with Insider Trading

A twenty-four old paralegal has been charged with insider trading by the Securities and Exchange Commission. The complaint against the paralegal alleged that she had access to confidential information pertaining to the proposed merger of a client of the firm where she worked. She "tipped" her friends by giving them confidential information. The friends then used this information to earn $823,471 in the purchase of 65,020 shares. A civil complaint seeks damages of $3.29 million. The paralegal has been fired by the law firm. *SEC v. Hurton,* Civ. #89–1070, DC Mass. (5/16/89); *Federal Securities and Corporate Developments,* 21 Securities & Law Report (5/21/89).

##  A $90,000,000 Mistake!

Several years ago, a paralegal for Prudential inadvertently left off the last three zeros on a mortgage used to secure a $92,885,000 loan made by Prudential to a company that is now bankrupt. As a result of the mistake, Prudential was left with only a $92,885 lien. Litigation is pending before the U.S. Bankruptcy Court in New York City. Prudential's attorneys are trying to convince the Court that Prudential should not be held to the mistake. 17 *At Issue* (San Francisco Legal Assistants Ass'n, Dec. 1990).

##  Paralegal Convicted

Mershan Shaddy was an independent paralegal in San Diego. He charged clients $180 to handle uncontested divorces, plus $50 if property had to be divided, and $30 for each child. He was arrested after an undercover investigator posed as a divorce client and secretly recorded him giving legal advice in violation of the California law against the unauthorized practice of law. He was convicted and sentenced to forty-five days in jail. *Paralegal's Role in Legal System Stirs a Debate,* San Diego Union B-1 (March 29, 1990).

##  Law Firm Sues Its Former Paralegal

Richard Trotter once worked as a paralegal for a Denver law firm. He wrote a book called *A Toothless Paper Tiger* about his experiences at the law firm. The book alleges that the firm improperly authorized him and other paralegals at the firm to perform the work of attorneys. The law firm has sought an injunction to prevent the release of the book. Hicks, *Law Firm Fights Book by Former Employee,* National Law Journal 39 (Aug. 6, 1990).

## Law Firm Settles Suit Brought by Paralegals

A class action was brought by paralegals and clerical workers who claimed that the Oakland firm where they worked failed to pay them overtime compensation. The case was eventually settled for $170,000 which was distributed among the paralegals and clerical workers. Ziegler, *Firm Settles Suit on Overtime for Paralegals*, San Francisco Banner Daily Journal (1/25/89).

## ■ "Will the Legal Assistant Please Tell the Court the Facts of the Case?"

At a paralegal association meeting in Houston, Judge Lynn Hughes, a federal District Court judge, recently drew a "big laugh" concerning an incident in her courtroom. During a hearing, she watched a "Big Gun" senior partner constantly turn to his associate for information on the facts of the case. This associate, in turn, would ask his legal assistant for this information. Finally, Judge Hughes asked the legal assistant to stand up and tell the court the facts of the case! *National News . . . Houston Legal Assistants Association*, 21 Outlook 5 (Illinois Paralegal Ass'n, Spring 1991).

## ■ "Then You Should Have Used a Paralegal!"

At oral argument before the United States Supreme Court in a case on paralegal fees, an attorney was interrupted by Justice Thurgood Marshall during the attorney's description of the custom of billing in New Orleans. In the following fascinating excerpt from the transcript of the oral argument, a clearly irritated Justice Marshall suggested that the attorney was unprepared because he did not have a paralegal working with him on the case:

JUSTICE MARSHALL: Is all that in the record?
ATTORNEY: I'm sorry. . . .
JUSTICE MARSHALL: Is that in the record?
ATTORNEY: I'm not. . . .
JUSTICE MARSHALL: What you've just said, that the custom of billing and all in New Orleans, is that in the record?
ATTORNEY: I think it is Justice Marshall.
JUSTICE MARSHALL: You think? Didn't you try the case?
ATTORNEY: I tried the case, but whether or not that particular item is in the record, it is certainly in the briefs, but. . . .
JUSTICE MARSHALL: Then you should have used a paralegal!

*Official Transcript Proceedings Before The Supreme Court of the United States, Arthur J. Blanchard, petitioner V. James Bergerson, et al.*, Case 87–1485, page 25 (11/28/88).

## ■ The Perfect Recipe

"To one paralegal, add a pound of variety, eight ounces of flexibility, four ounces of creativity, and a healthy sense of humor. The result? One cost-effective, efficient litigation paralegal." Vore, *A Litigation Recipe,* On Point (Nat'l Capital Area Paralegal Ass'n, Nov. 1990).

## ■ Paralegal Trapped

A paralegal, on his way to an assignment on another floor, became trapped in an elevator just after getting on. Fellow employees gathered around the elevator door. The time-conscious paralegal called out from inside the elevator, "Is this billable or nonbillable time?" *A Lighter Note,* MALA Advance 15 (Summer 1989).

 ## Suspense Novel about a Paralegal by a Paralegal

E. P. Dalton has published *Housebreaker,* a novel by David Linzee, who has worked as a litigation paralegal. It is about Megan Lofting. "Megan used to be a probate paralegal at a Connecticut law firm. She used to try hard never to do something wrong. But then she was unjustly fired. Now a big-time criminal is offering her a chance to make a fortune, and to strike back at the client who got her fired, and the lawyer—once her lover—who let it happen." *The First Suspense Novel Ever About a Paralegal . . . by a Former Paralegal,* 4 Viewpoint 10 (Massachusetts Paralegal Association, July/August 1987).

 ## The Cost of What?

Recently, a paralegal was given an unusual assignment by her supervising attorney. She was asked to determine how much it would cost to purchase a penguin! *How Much Does a Penguin Cost?* SJPA Reporter, p. 3 (South Jersey Paralegal Ass'n, Sept. 1990).

 ## Paralegal Watches Exorcism

Kevin McKinley is a paralegal at a West Palm Beach law firm that represented a defendant in a murder case. While working on the case, Kevin found an urn in the room of the defendant where the latter allegedly practiced voodoo and black magic. The family of the defendant was concerned that if the urn was opened in the courtroom, the spirit within it would harm those attending the trial. Hence an exorcism was performed to remove the defendant's control over this spirit. Kevin's assignment was to be a witness at this exorcism. *Columbus Dispatch* (January 6, 1991).

 ## The Paralegal Floral Strategy

A litigation legal assistant was given the task of serving a subpoena on a defendant who was unlikely to open the door. She came up with a creative approach. On her way to the defendant's house, she stopped at a flower shop and picked up a plant. Upon her arrival, she rang the doorbell. The defendant looked out, saw a person with flowers, opened the door, and was presented with a plant . . . and a subpoena! Anderson, *In the Line of Duty,* MALA Advance 17 (Minnesota Ass'n of Legal Assistants, Spring 1991).

## ■ I Don't Believe He Said That

- ■ "I told him that I'm a paralegal. He thinks I am a lawyer who jumps out of planes"—in parachutes. *Compendium* (Orange County Paralegal Ass'n, Oct. 1990).

- ■ When asked what to do for your secretary when she needs recognition but doesn't deserve a raise, the attorney answered, "Make her a paralegal!" *The Question of Paralegals,* 20 The Legal Investigator 35 (2/91).

- ■ At a cocktail party, Therese Carey was introduced to a middle-aged businessman. He asked her what she did for a living. Answering that she was a legal assistant, Therese enthusiastically explained her duties. After her response, the man turned to her and earnestly said, "Say, you know, with your background, have you ever considered becoming a paralegal?" Burdett, *Rodney Dangerfield: You're Not Alone,* Newsletter 2, Rhode Island Paralegal Ass'n (Jan. 1987).

## ■ Bumper Sticker Award

The Alaska Association of Legal Assistants had a bumper sticker contest. The top three winners were as follows:

"Paralegals Know Their Motions"
"Paralegals Get on Your Case"
"Paralegals Know Briefs"

Paralegals in Tennessee also have a bumper sticker:

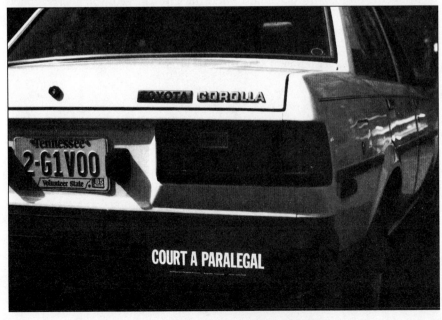

## "What It Is That I Do"

A. Pergola, Newsletter, Rocky Mountain Legal Assistants Association (June 1980)

## The World of Attorneys

- "I served with General Washington in the legislature of Virginia before the revolution, and during it, with Dr. Franklin in Congress. . . . If the present Congress errs in too much talking, how could it do otherwise in a body to which the people send 150 lawyers, whose trade it is to question everything, yield nothing & talk by the hour?" *Autobiography 1743–1790*, Thomas Jefferson.

- If a man were to give another man an orange, he would say, simply, "Have an orange." But if the transaction were entrusted to an attorney, he would say: "I hereby give, grant, bargain and sell to you, all my right, title and interest in, of, and to said orange, together with all its rind, skin, juice, pulp, and pips, and all rights and advantages therein, with full power to bite, cut, and otherwise eat of the same, or give the same away, with or without the rind, skin, juice, pulp, and pips, anything hereinbefore or hereinafter, or in any other deed or deeds, instrument or instruments, of whatever kind or nature whatsoever to the contrary in any wise notwithstanding." Hirsch, *Pittsburgh Legal Journal.*

■ A document recently filed in the United States Bankruptcy Court in Tennessee contained the following language: "Debtors hereby amend the Amendment to Second Amended and Restated Disclosure Statement, Third Amended and Restated Plan of Reorganization, and Amendment to Third Amended and Restated Plan of Organization as follows. Wherever the name 'Mortgage Company' appears in the Amendment to Second Amended and Restated Disclosure Statement, Third Amended and Restated Plan of Reorganization and Amendment to Third Amended and Restated Plan of Organization, the name 'Bank' shall be inserted in lieu thereof." *The Reporter,* 15 (Delaware Paralegal Association, May/June 1991).

■ Question: How many lawyers does it take to change a light bulb? Answer: Three senior partners to contemplate the history of light; two junior partners to check for conflicts of interest; ten associates to do the research on the anti-trust implications of using a particular brand, on the cost-benefits of electric lighting versus candle light, on the health aspects of incandescent versus fluorescent bulb lighting, on the electric components that make light bulbs work, etc. And, of course, a paralegal to screw the bulb into the socket! *On the Lighter Side,* Par·Spectives 5, Paralegal Association of Rochester (May 1990).

## Murphy's Law for Paralegals

1. The day you wear comfortable, ugly old shoes is the day you are called into the managing partner's office or have to meet with an important client.

2. The day you wear attractive, stylish pumps that pinch your toes, bite your instep and chafe your heels is the day that you have to serve papers at Nick Tahou's and the Eastern School of Music—before 11 A.M. or after 2 P.M.

3. The night when you have a date, theatre tickets, or fifteen dinner guests due at 7:30 is the night you have to stay late.

4. The day your car is in the garage and you carpooled is the day that you receive a 15-hour project that has to be done before you go home.

5. Your mother, your husband, your boyfriend or your bookie always calls when the boss is standing in your office.

6. Clients that work near you never have to sign anything. The number of documents that need to be signed by a client increases in proportion to the number of miles between their home or office and your office.

7. Whatever you lost is what everyone must have immediately.

8. Whatever can't be found was last in the possession of a paralegal.

9. Whatever needs to be hand delivered or picked up is always beyond the messenger's responsibility.

10. The day you have liverwurst and onion for lunch is the day that you have to attend an unscheduled meeting with an important client or another attorney.

11. The volume of Carmody-Wait 2nd that you require to prepare a motion is always missing from the library.

12. Nobody ever asks you about subjects with which you are familiar. If you are an expert on the mating habits of mosquitoes, you will be asked to digest a deposition or prepare research about the malfunction of the farabus and ullie pin connection in Yugoslavian lawnmowers.

Ciaccia, *Murphy's Laws for Paralegals,* 9 Newsletter 12 (Dallas Ass'n of Legal Assistants, Sept. 1985).

# ■ Glossary

**AAfPE**   American Association for Paralegal Education.

**ABA**   American Bar Association.

**Abstracts**   *See* Digests.

**Accounts Receivable**   A list of who owes money to the office, how much, how long the debt has been due, etc.

**Accreditation**   The process by which an organization evaluates and recognizes a program of study (or an institution) as meeting specified qualifications or standards.

**Acquit**   To find not guilty.

**Act**   *See* Statute.

**Ad Damnum**   The amount of damages claimed in the complaint.

**Adjudication**   The process by which a court resolves a legal dispute through litigation. The verb is *adjudicate*.

**Administrative Agency**   A unit of government whose primary mission is to carry out or administer the statutes of the legislature and the executive orders of the chief of the executive branch.

**Administrative Code**   A collection of administrative regulations organized by subject matter.

**Administrative Decision**   A resolution of a controversy involving application of the regulations of an administrative agency or its governing statutes and executive orders. Also called a *ruling*.

**Administrative Hearing**   A proceeding at an administrative agency presided over by a hearing officer (e.g., an Administrative Law Judge) to resolve a controversy.

**Administrative Law Judge**   A hearing officer who presides over a hearing at an administrative agency.

**Administrative Procedure Act**   The statute that governs aspects of procedure before administrative agencies.

**Administrative Regulation**   A law of an administrative agency designed to explain or carry out the statutes and executive orders that govern the agency. Also called a *rule*.

**Admiralty Law**   An area of the law that covers accidents and injuries on navigable waters. Also called *maritime law*.

**Admissible Evidence**   Evidence that a judge will allow a jury to consider.

**Admission**   An out-of-court statement made by a party to the litigation that is inconsistent with a position the party is taking in the litigation. (An exception to the hearsay rule.)

**Admonition**   A nonpublic declaration that the attorney's conduct was improper. This does not affect his or her right to practice. Also called a private reprimand.

**ADR**   Alternative dispute resolution.

**Advance Sheet**   A pamphlet that comes out before (in advance of) a later volume.

**Adversarial Hearing**   A proceeding in which both parties to a controversy appear before a judge.

**Adversarial Memorandum**   *See* External Memorandum, Memorandum of Law.

**Adversarial System**   Justice and truth have a greater chance of emerging when parties to a controversy appear before a neutral judge and jury to argue their conflicting positions.

**Adverse Interests**   Opposing purposes or claims.

**Adverse Judgment**   A judgment or decision against you.

**Advice**   *See* Professional Judgment.

**Advocacy**   An attempt to influence actions of others.

**Affiant**   *See* Affidavit.

**Affidavit**   A written statement of fact in which a person (called the affiant) swears that the statement is true.

**Affiliate Member**   *See* Associate Member.

**Affirmation of Professional Responsibility**   A statement of the ethical guidelines of the National Federation of Paralegal Associations.

**Affirmative Defense**   A defense that is based on new factual allegations by the defendant not contained in the plaintiff's allegations.

**Agency Practitioner**   An individual authorized to practice before an administrative agency. This individual often does not have to be an attorney.

**Aging Report**   A listing of accounts receivable indicating the time outstanding on each account.

**ALA**   Association of Legal Administrators.

**Allegation**   A claimed fact.

**Ambulance Chasing**   Aggressively going to individuals with potentially good claims as plaintiffs (e.g., personal-injury victims) to encourage them to hire a particular attorney. If the attorney uses someone else to do the soliciting, the latter is called a *runner*. If this other person uses deception or fraud in the solicitation, he or she is sometimes called a *capper*.

**Amicus Curiae Brief**  A friend-of-the-court brief. An appellate brief submitted by someone who is not a party to the litigation.

**Analogous**  Sufficiently similar in the facts and law being applied. Also referred to as *on point*.

**Annotate**  To provide notes or commentary. A text is annotated if such notes and commentary are provided along with the text.

**Annotated Bibliography**  A bibliography that briefly states why you included each entry in the bibliography.

**Annotated Code/Annotated Statutes**  A collection of statutes organized by subject matter, along with notes and commentary.

**Annotation**  The notes and commentary that follow opinions printed in A.L.R., A.L.R.2d, etc.

**Answer**  The pleading that responds to or answers the allegations of the complaint.

**Antitrust Law**  The law governing unlawful restraints of trade, price fixing, and monopolies.

**APA**  *See* Administrative Procedure Act.

**Appeal as a Matter of Right**  The appeal of a case that an appellate court must hear; it has no discretion on whether to take the appeal.

**Appearance**  Going to court to act on behalf of a party to the litigation. The first time this is done, the attorney files a *notice of appearance*.

**Appellant**  The party bringing an appeal because of dissatisfaction with something the lower tribunal did.

**Appellate Brief**  A document submitted to an appellate court containing arguments on whether a lower court made errors of law.

**Appellate Jurisdiction**  The power of a court to hear an appeal of a case from a lower tribunal to determine whether it made any errors of law.

**Appellee**  The party against whom an appeal is brought. Also called the *respondent*.

**Appendixes**  Additions to a volume or document printed after the body of the text.

**Apprentice**  A person in training for an occupation under the supervision of a full member of that occupation.

**Approval**  The recognition that comes from accreditation, certification, licensure, or registration. The ABA uses *approval* as a substitute for the word *accreditation*.

**Approval Commission**  A group of individuals who investigate whether a paralegal school meets the criteria for approval established by the ABA.

**Arbitration**  In lieu of litigation, both sides agree to allow a neutral third party to resolve their dispute.

**Arraignment**  A court proceeding in which the defendant is formally charged with a crime and enters a plea.

**Arrest**  To take someone into custody in order to bring him or her before the proper authorities.

**Assertive**  Confident, prepared, and tactfully demonstrative about one's accomplishments and needs.

**Assigned Counsel**  An attorney appointed by the court and paid with government funds to represent an individual who cannot afford to hire an attorney.

**Associate**  An attorney employee of a law firm who hopes eventually to become a partner.

**Associated**  Pertaining to an attorney who is an associate in a law firm.

**Associate Member**  A nonattorney who is allowed to become part of—but not a full member of—a bar association. Sometimes called *affiliate member*.

**Attestation Clause**  A clause stating that a person saw a witness sign a document.

**Attorney Attestation**  A signed statement by an attorney that a paralegal applying for membership in a paralegal association meets designated criteria of the association, e.g., is employed as a paralegal.

**Attorney–Client Privilege**  A client and an attorney can refuse to disclose communications between them whose purpose was to facilitate the provision of legal services for the client.

**Attorney General**  The chief attorney for the government. *See also* Opinion of the Attorney General.

**Attorney of Record**  The attorney who has filed a notice of appearance. *See also* Appearance.

**Attorney Work Product**  *See* Work-Product Rule.

**Authentication**  Evidence that a writing or other physical item is genuine and is what it purports to be.

**Authority**  Anything that a court could rely on in reaching its decision.

**Authorized Practice of Law**  Services that constitute the practice of law which a nonattorney has authorization to provide. *See also* Practice of Law, Professional Judgment.

**Automatic Pagination**  A feature that enables a word processor to number the pages of the printed page automatically.

**Background Research**  Checking secondary sources to give you a general understanding of an area of law that is new to you.

**Backup**  To copy information.

**Bail**  Property or a sum of money deposited with the court to ensure that the defendant will reappear in court at designated times.

**Bailiff**    A court employee who keeps order in the courtroom and renders general administrative assistance to the judge.

**Bar**    Prevent or stop.

**Bar Coding**    A series of lines of different widths that can be read by a scanner.

**Barratry**    Stirring up quarrels or litigation; illegal solicitation of clients.

**Barrister**    A lawyer in England who represents clients in the higher courts.

**Bar Treaties**    Agreements between attorneys and other occupations on what law-related activities of these other occupations do and do not constitute the unauthorized practice of law.

**Baud Rate**    A unit of measurement used to indicate the speed of transmission over a modem.

**Below**    (1) The lower tribunal that heard the case before it was appealed. (2) Later in the document.

**Best Evidence Rule**    To prove the contents of a private writing, the original writing should be produced unless it is unavailable.

**Beyond a Reasonable Doubt**    There is no reasonable doubt that every one of the elements of the crime has been established.

**Bias**    Unfairly leaning in favor of or against someone; the potential for unfairness because of prior knowledge or involvement, leading to possible preconceptions and a lack of open-mindedness.

**Bicameral**    Having two houses in the legislature. If there is only one house, it is *unicameral*.

**Bill**    A proposed statute.

**Billable Tasks**    Those tasks requiring time that can be charged to a client.

**Billing Memorandum**    A draft bill which states disbursements, time expended, and billing rates of those working on the matter.

**Blended Hourly Rate**    A rate is set depending on the mix of partners and associates working on the case.

**Blind Ad**    A want ad that does not print the name and address of the prospective employer. The contact is made through a third party, e.g., the newspaper.

**Block**    A group of characters, e.g., a word, a sentence, a paragraph. Block movement is a feature of a word processor that allows the user to define a block of text and then do something with that block, e.g., move it, delete it.

**Board of Appeals**    The unit within an administrative agency to which a party can appeal a decision of the agency.

**Boilerplate**    Standard language that is commonly used in a certain kind of document.

**Boldface**    Heavier or darker than normal type.

**Bond**    A sum of money deposited in court to ensure compliance with a requirement.

**Brief**    *See* Appellate Brief, Brief of a Case, Trial Brief.

**Brief of a Case**    A set of notes on the essential parts of a court opinion, e.g., facts, issues, holding, reasoning.

**"Bugs"**    Manufacturing or design errors that exist in products such as computer hardware or software.

**Bulletin Board**    An inexpensive, relatively small, user-run version of a commercial information service.

**Bundled/Unbundled**    An hourly rate is *bundled* if overhead is included in this rate. It is *unbundled* if the various charges are broken out separately.

**Burden of Proof**    The responsibility of proving a fact at trial.

**Business Entry**    An out-of-court statement found in business records made in the regular course of business by someone whose duty is to make such entries. (An exception to the hearsay rule.)

**Byte**    The storage equivalent of one letter, one punctuation mark, or one blank space typed into the computer.

**CALR**    Computer-Assisted Legal Research.

**Capital Partner**    *See* Income Partner.

**Capper**    *See* Ambulance Chasing.

**Caption of Appellate Brief**    The front of an appellate brief that prints the name of the parties, the name of the court, the docket number, and the kind of appellate brief it is.

**Caption of Complaint**    The top of a complaint that identifies the names of the parties, the court in which the action is brought, the number assigned by the court, etc.

**Caption of Opinion**    The title of an opinion (usually consisting of the names of the parties), the name of the court that wrote it, the docket number, the date of decision—all printed just before the opinion begins.

**Career Ladder**    A formal promotion structure within a company or office.

**CARTWHEEL**    A technique designed to help you think of a large variety of words and phrases to check in the index and table of contents of a law book.

**Case**    (1) A legal matter in dispute or potential dispute. (2) The written decision of a court. *See also* Opinion.

**Casebook**    A law-school textbook containing numerous edited court opinions.

**Case Clerk**    An assistant to a paralegal; an entry-level paralegal.

**Case Manager** An experienced legal assistant who can coordinate or direct legal assistant activities on a major case or transaction.

**Case Note** A summary of and commentary on a court opinion in a law review.

**Cause of Action** A legally acceptable reason for suing.

**CD-ROM** Computer disk read-only memory. An optical information-storage system.

**Cell** A storage location within a spreadsheet, used to store a single piece of information that is relevant to the spreadsheet.

**Censure** A formal disapproval or declaration of blame. *See also* Reprimand.

**Certificated** Having met the qualifications for certification from a school or training program.

**Certification** The process by which a nongovernmental organization grants recognition to an individual who has met qualifications specified by that organization. *See also* Specialty Certification.

**Certified** Having complied with or met the qualifications for certification.

**Certified Legal Assistant (CLA)** The title bestowed by the National Association of Legal Assistants on a paralegal who has passed the CLA exam and has met other criteria of NALA. *See also* Specialty Certification.

**Certified PLS** A Certified Professional Legal Secretary. This status is achieved after passing an examination and meeting other requirements of NALS, the National Association of Legal Secretaries.

**CFLA** Certified Florida Legal Assistant. To earn this title, a paralegal must first pass the CLA (Certified Legal Assistant) exam of NALA, and then pass a special exam on Florida law.

**Challenge for Cause** A request to exclude someone from a jury for a specified reason.

**Character** A letter, number, or symbol. Character enhancement includes underlining, boldfacing, subscripting, and superscripting.

**Chargeable Hour Schedule** A report that summarizes hours invested by attorneys and paralegals, usually on a monthly basis.

**Charge to Jury** Instructions to the jury on how to go about determining the facts and reaching its verdict.

**Charter** The fundamental law of a municipality or other local unit of government authorizing it to perform designated governmental functions.

**Chinese Wall** Steps taken to prevent a tainted employee (attorney, paralegal, or secretary) from having any contact with the case of a particular client in the office. The employee is tainted because he or she has a conflict of interest with that client. A Chinese wall is also called an *ethical wall.* A tainted employee is also called a *contaminated employee.* Once the Chinese wall is set up around the tainted employee, the latter is referred to as a *quarantined employee.*

**Circumstantial Evidence** Evidence of one fact from which another fact can be inferred.

**Citation** A reference to any written material. It is the "address" where the material can be found in the library. Also called a *cite.*

**Citator** A book containing lists of citations that can help you assess the current validity of an item and can give you leads to additional laws.

**Cite** (1) A citation. (2) To give the volume and page number, name of the book, etc. where written material can be found in a library.

**Cite Checking** Reading every cite in a document to determine whether the format of the cite conforms to the citation rules being used (e.g., the Bluebook rules), whether the quotations in the cite are accurate, etc.

**Cited Material** The case, statute, regulation, or other document that you are shepardizing.

**Citing Material** The case, article, or annotation that mentions whatever you are shepardizing, i.e., that mentions the cited material.

**Civil Dispute** One private party suing another, or a private party suing the government, or the government suing a private party for a matter other than the commission of a crime.

**CLA** *See* Certified Legal Assistant.

**Claims-Made Policy** Insurance that covers only claims actually filed (i.e., made) during the period in which the policy is in effect.

**CLAS** Certified Legal Assistant Specialist (an advanced certification status of NALA).

**CLE** Continuing Legal Education. Undertaken after an individual has received his or her primary education or training in a law-related occupation.

**Clergy-Penitent Privilege** A member of the clergy and a penitent can refuse to disclose communications between them that relate to spiritual counseling or consultation.

**Closed-Ended Question** A relatively narrow question (e.g., how old are you?) that discourages the interviewee from rambling. Also called a *directed question.*

**Closing** The event during which steps are taken to finalize the transfer of an interest in property.

**Code** A set of rules, organized by subject matter.

**Codefendant**   More than one defendant being sued in a civil case (or prosecuted in a criminal case) in the same litigation.

**Code of Ethics and Professional Responsibility**   A statement of the ethical guidelines of the National Association of Legal Assistants.

**Codified Cite**   The citation to a statute that has been printed in a code and, therefore, has been organized by subject matter. *See also* Session Law Cite.

**Codify**   To arrange material by subject matter.

**Command**   An instruction typed into a computer.

**Commingling**   Mixing general law firms funds with client funds in a single account.

**Common Law**   Judge-made law in the absence of controlling statutory law or other higher law. *See also* Enacted Law.

**Common Representation**   *See* Multiple Representation.

**Communications**   A program that allows computers to communicate with each other, usually through telephone lines. *See also* Modem.

**Compatible**   (1) Information generated on an IBM computer that can also be used by another computer. (2) A program designed for an IBM computer that can also be run by other computers.

**Competence, Attorney**   Having the knowledge and skill that is reasonably necessary to represent a particular client.

**Competent (evidence)**   Capable of giving testimony because the person understands the obligation to tell the truth, has the ability to communicate, and has knowledge of the topic of his or her testimony.

**Complaint**   The pleading filed by the plaintiff that tries to state a claim or cause of action against the defendant.

**Concurrent Jurisdiction**   The power of a court to hear a particular kind of case, along with other courts that could also hear it.

**Concurring Opinion**   An opinion written by less than a majority of the judges on the court that agrees with the *result* reached by the majority but not with all of its reasoning.

**Conference Committee**   A committee made up of members of both houses of the legislature which meets to try to resolve differences in the versions of a bill that each house passed.

**Confidential**   That which should not be revealed; pertaining to information that others do not have a right to receive.

**Conflict of Interest**   Divided loyalty that actually or potentially places one of the participants to whom undi-vided loyalty is owed at a disadvantage. *See also* Divided Loyalty.

**Conflicts Check**   A check of the client files of a law firm to help determine whether a conflict of interest might exist between a prospective client and current or past clients. The person performing this check is often called a *conflicts specialist*.

**Conflicts of Law**   An area of the law that determines what law applies when a choice must be made between the laws of different, coequal legal systems, e.g., two states.

**Confrontation**   The right to face your accuser.

**Connectors**   Characters, words, or symbols used to show the relationship between the words and phrases in a query.

**Constitution**   The fundamental law that creates the branches of government and that identifies basic rights and obligations.

**Contaminated Paralegal**   *See* Chinese Wall.

**Contest**   To challenge.

**Contingent Fee**   A fee that is dependent on the outcome of the case.

**Contract Attorney**   *See* Project Attorney.

**Contract Paralegal**   A self-employed paralegal who often works for several different attorneys on a freelance basis. *See also* Freelance Paralegal.

**Control Character**   A coded character that does not print but is part of the command sequence in a word processor.

**Coordinates**   In a spreadsheet program, the column letter and row number that define the location of a specific cell.

**Corporate Counsel**   The chief attorney of a corporation. Also called the *general counsel*.

**Corporate Legal Department**   The law office within a corporation containing salaried attorneys (in-house attorneys) who advise and represent the corporation.

**Counterclaim**   A claim or cause of action against the plaintiff stated in the defendant's answer.

**Court of First Instance**   A trial court; a court with original jurisdiction.

**Credentialization**   A form of official recognition based on one's training or employment status.

**Credible**   Believable.

**Criminal Dispute**   A suit brought by the government for the alleged commission of a crime.

**Cross-claim**  Usually, a claim by one codefendant against another.

**Cross-examination**  Questioning the witness called by the other side after direct examination.

**Cumulative**  That which repeats earlier material and consolidates it with new material. A cumulative supplement contains new supplemental material and repeats earlier supplemental material.

**Cured**  Corrected.

**Cursor**  The marker on the display screen indicating where the next character can be displayed.

**Daisy Wheel Printer**  A printer which uses a device resembling a flower that contains the alphabet and other characters on spokes.

**Damages**  An award of money paid by the wrongdoer to compensate the person who has been harmed.

**Data**  Information that can be used by a computer.

**Database**  A program used to store and organize information; a grouping of independent files into one integrated whole that can be accessed through one central point.

**Data Manager**  A data management software package that consolidates data files into an integrated whole, allowing access to more than one data file at a time.

**Data Redundancy**  The repetition of the same data in several different files.

**Decision**  *See* Administrative Decision, Opinion.

**Declaration against Interest**  An out-of-court statement made by a nonparty to the litigation that is against the interest of that nonparty. (An exception to the hearsay rule.)

**Declaration of Bodily Feelings**  An out-of-court statement or utterance made spontaneously about the person's present bodily condition. (An exception to the hearsay rule.)

**Declaration of Mental State of Mind**  An out-of-court statement made about the person's present state of mind. (An exception to the hearsay rule.)

**Declaration of Present Sense Impression**  An out-of-court statement that describes an event while it is being observed by the person making the statement. (An exception to the hearsay rule.)

**Declaratory Judgment**  A court decision establishing the rights and obligations of the parties but not ordering them to do or to refrain from doing anything.

**Dedicated Word Processor**  A system that can perform only word processing tasks.

**Deep Pocket**  Slang for the person or organization with enough money or other assets to be able to pay a judgment.

**Default Judgment**  A judgment for the plaintiff because the defendant failed to appear or to file an answer before the deadline.

**Default Setting**  A value used by the word processor when it is not instructed to use any other value.

**Defense**  An allegation of fact or the presentation of a legal theory that is offered to offset or defeat a claim or demand.

**"Delegatitis"**  An inordinate fear of delegating tasks to others.

**Deletion**  A feature of a word processor that allows you to remove a character, word, sentence, or larger block of text from the existing text.

**Demurrer**  Even if the plaintiff proved all the facts stated in the complaint, a cause of action would not be established.

**Denturist**  A nondentist who produces and dispenses removable dentures directly to the public.

**Deponent**  *See* Deposition.

**Deposition**  A pretrial discovery device consisting of a question-and-answer session involving a party or witness designed to assist the other party prepare for trial. The person who is questioned is called the *deponent*.

**Depository Library**  A library that receives free government publications to which it must admit the general public.

**Depo Summarizer**  An employee whose main job is digesting discovery documents.

**Dictum**  A statement made by a court that was not necessary to resolve the specific legal issues before the court. The plural of dictum is dicta.

**Digest by Person**  A summary of the information in a document pertaining to a certain individual.

**Digest by Subject**  A summary of the information in a document pertaining to a certain topic or subject.

**Digesting**  Summarizing discovery documents. *See also* Depo Summarizer.

**Digests**  (1) Volumes that contain summaries of court opinions. These summaries are sometimes called *abstracts* or *squibs*. (2) Volumes that contain summaries of annotations in A.L.R., A.L.R.2d, etc.

**Directed Question**  *See* Closed-Ended Question.

**Directed Verdict**  An order by the court that the jury reach a verdict for the party making the motion for a directed verdict.

**Direct Evidence**  Evidence that tends to establish a fact (or to disprove a fact) without the need for an inference.

**Direct Examination**  The first questioning of a witness you have called.

**Disbarment**  The temporary or permanent termination of the right to practice law.

**Disbursements**  Out-of-pocket expenses.

**Disciplinary Rule (DR)**  *See* Model Code of Professional Responsibility.

**Discount Adjustment**  A write down (decrease) in the bill.

**Discoverable**  Obtainable through one of the devices of pretrial discovery, e.g., interrogatories.

**Discovery**  Pretrial devices designed to assist a party prepare for trial. *See* Deposition, Interrogatories.

**Disinterested**  Not working for one side or the other in a controversy or other legal matter; not deriving benefit if one of the sides prevails.

**Disk Drive**  Hardware used to store and retrieve programs and information to and from diskettes.

**Diskette**  A flat piece of plastic on which information can be placed or removed by the computer.

**Dismissal without Prejudice**  A dismissal based on procedural, not substantive, grounds. The party can try to bring the case again.

**Disqualification**  *See* Vicarious Disqualification.

**Dissenting Opinion**  An opinion that disagrees with the result and the reasoning used by the majority.

**District Court**  *See* United States District Court.

**Diversity of Citizenship**  The parties to the litigation are from different states, and the amount in controversy exceeds the amount specified by federal statute.

**Divided Loyalty**  The responsibility of protecting the interest of parties who are competitors or are otherwise at odds with each other. *See also* Conflict of Interest.

**Docket Number**  The number assigned to a case by the court.

**Doctor-Patient Privilege**  A doctor and a patient can refuse to disclose any confidential (private) communications between them that relate to medical care.

**Document Clerk**  An individual whose main responsibility is to organize, file, code, or digest litigation or other client documents.

**Documentation**  The manual on operating a computer; the accompanying documents.

**Dot Matrix Printer**  A printer which uses tiny pins that press against or punch a ribbon to create a pattern of dots.

**Double Density**  The disk drive can store information on the diskette in condensed mode.

**Downtime**  The period during which the computer is unavailable because of technical difficulties.

**DR**  Disciplinary Rule. *See* Model Code of Professional Responsibility.

**Draft**  Write.

**Draft Bill**  *See* Billing Memorandum.

**Draw**  A partner's advance against profits.

**Dual Sided**  The disk drive is capable of writing on both sides of the diskette.

**DWI**  Descriptive Word Index, an index to the digests of West.

**Dying Declaration**  An out-of-court statement concerning the causes or circumstances of death made by a person whose death is imminent. (An exception to the hearsay rule.)

**EC**  Ethical Consideration. *See* Model Code of Professional Responsibility.

**Editing**  In word processing, the act of changing or amending text.

**EEOC**  Equal Employment Opportunity Commission, a federal agency that investigates job discrimination.

**Element**  A portion of a rule which is a precondition of the applicability of the entire rule. The *element in contention* is the element of the rule about which the parties cannot agree. The disagreement may be over the meaning of the element or how it applies to a given set of facts.

**Enacted Law**  Law written by the legislature (statutes), by the people (constitutions), and by an administrative agency (regulations). Law that is not the product of adjudication. *See* Adjudication.

**En Banc**  By the entire court.

**Enrolled Agent**  An individual authorized to represent taxpayers at all administrative proceedings within the Internal Revenue Service—this person does not have to be an attorney.

**Enrollment**  *See* Registration.

**Entry-Level Certification**  Certification of individuals who have just begun their careers.

**Equity Partner**  A full owner of a law firm. *See also* Income Partner.

**Estate**  All the property left by a decedent from which his or her debts can be paid.

**Et al.**  And others.

**Ethical Wall**  *See* Chinese Wall.

**Ethical Consideration** (EC)  *See* Model Code of Professional Responsibility.

**Ethics**  Rules embodying standards of behavior to which members of an organization are expected to conform.

**Et Seq.**  And following.

**Evidence**  That which is offered to help establish or disprove a factual position. A separate determination must be made on whether a particular item of evidence is relevant or irrelevant, admissible or inadmissible, etc.

**Exclusive Jurisdiction**  The power of a court to hear a particular kind of case, to the exclusion of other courts.

**Execution**  Carrying out or enforcing a judgment.

**Executive Branch**  The branch of government that carries out, executes, or administers the law.

**Executive Department Agency**  An administrative agency that exists within the executive branch of government, often at the cabinet level.

**Executive Order**  A law passed by the chief executive pursuant to a specific statutory authority or to the executive's inherent authority.

**Exempt Employee**  An employee who is not entitled to overtime compensation under the Fair Labor Standards Act because the employee is a professional, administrative, or executive employee. Paralegals are nonexempt, except for paralegal managers.

**Exhausting Administrative Remedies**  Pursuing all available methods of resolving a dispute within the administrative agency before asking a court to review what the agency did.

**Exhibit**  An item of physical or tangible evidence offered in court for inspection.

**Ex Parte Hearing**  A hearing at which only one party is present. A court order issued at such a hearing is an *ex parte order.*

**External/Adversary Memorandum of Law**  A memorandum written primarily for individuals outside of the office to convince them to take a certain course of action. *See also* Memorandum of Law.

**Fact Particularization**  A technique designed to help you list numerous factual questions in order to obtain a comprehensive picture of all the facts that are relevant to a legal matter.

**Fact Pleading**  A statement of every ultimate (i.e., essential) fact in the complaint.

**Facts & Findings**  A periodical of the National Association of Legal Assistants.

**Fair Labor Standards Act**  The federal statute that regulates conditions of employment such as when overtime compensation must be paid. *See also* Exempt Employee.

**Federalism**  The coexistence of, and the interrelationships among, the state governments and the federal government, particularly with respect to the powers of each of these levels of government.

**Federal Question**  A legal question that arises from the application of the United States Constitution, a statute of Congress, or a federal administrative regulation.

**Fee-Generating Case**  The case of a client who can pay a fee out of the damages awarded or from his or her independent resources.

**Fee Splitting**  A single client bill covering the fee of two or more attorneys who are not in the same firm.

**Felony**  A crime punishable by a sentence of one year or more.

**Field**  A subdivision of a record that holds a meaningful item of data, e.g., an employee number.

**Field Search**  In WESTLAW, a search that is limited to a certain part of cases in its databases.

**File**  A group of related data records, e.g., employee records.

**Filed**  Formally presented to a court.

**First Instance, Court of**  A trial court; a court with original jurisdiction.

**Fixed Fee**  A flat fee for services. A set amount paid regardless of the outcome of the case or the amount of time needed to complete it.

**Floppy Disk**  A disk drive that can use diskettes.

**Format**  In word processing, the layout of the page, e.g., the number of lines and margin settings.

**Formbook**  A manual that contains forms, checklists, practice techniques, etc. Also called a *practice manual* or *handbook.*

**Formula**  A mathematical expression that is used in a spreadsheet.

**Forum**  The court where the case is to be tried.

**Forwarding Fee**  *See* Referral Fee.

**FRCP**  Federal Rules of Civil Procedure.

**Freedom of Information Act**  A statute that gives citizens access to certain information in the possession of the government.

**Freelance Paralegal** A self-employed paralegal who works for several different attorneys, or a self-employed paralegal who works directly for the public. Also referred to as an *independent paralegal.*

**Friendly Divorce** A divorce proceeding in which the parties have no significant disputes between them.

**Full-Text Search** A search through all of the information in a database.

**Functional Resume** A resume that clusters skills and talents together regardless of when they were developed.

**General Counsel** The chief attorney in a corporate law department.

**General Jurisdiction** The power of the court (within its geographic boundaries) to hear any kind of case, with certain exceptions.

**General Practitioner** An attorney who handles any kind of case.

**General Schedule (GS)** The pay-scale system used in the federal government.

**Geographic Jurisdiction** The area of the state or country over which a court has power to render decisions.

**Global** In word processing, an instruction that will be carried out throughout the document.

**Go Bare** To engage in an occupation or profession without malpractice insurance.

**GOD** The "Great Overtime Debate." *See* Exempt Employee.

**Grand Jury** A special jury whose duty is to hear evidence of felonies presented by the prosecutor to determine whether there is sufficient evidence to return an indictment against the defendant and cause him or her to stand trial on the charges.

**Grounds** Reasons.

**Group Legal Services** A form of legal insurance in which members of a group pay a set amount on a regular basis, for which they receive designated legal services. Also called *prepaid legal services.*

**GS** *See* General Schedule.

**Guideline** Suggested conduct that will help an applicant obtain accreditation, certification, licensure, registration, or approval.

**HALT** Help Abolish Legal Tyranny, an organization that seeks to reform the legal profession, primarily by eliminating the monopoly of attorneys over the practice of law.

**Handbook** *See* Formbook.

**Harassment** *See* Hostile Environment, Quid Pro Quo Harassment.

**Hard Disk** A disk drive that cannot be removed without taking the hardware apart.

**Hardware** The computer and its physical parts.

**Header** In word processing, a piece of text that is stored separately from the text and printed at the top of each page.

**Heading** The beginning of a memorandum that lists who the memo is for, who wrote it, what it is about, etc.

**Headnote** A small-paragraph summary of a portion of a court opinion, written by a private publisher.

**Hearing Examiner** One who presides over an administrative hearing.

**Hearing Memorandum** A memorandum of law submitted to a hearing officer.

**Hearsay** Testimony in court, or written evidence, of a statement made out of court when the statement is offered to show the truth of matters asserted therein, and thus resting for its value on the credibility of the out-of-court asserter.

**Historical Note** Information on the legislative history of a statute printed after the text of the statute.

**Holding** A court's answer to one of the legal issues in the case. Also called a *ruling.*

**Hornbook** A treatise that summarizes an area of the law.

**Hostile Environment Harassment** Pervasive unwelcome sexual conduct or sex-based ridicule which unreasonably interferes with an individual's job performance or creates an intimidating, hostile, or offensive working environment.

**Hourly Plus Fixed Fee** A specified hourly rate is used until the nature and scope of the problem are defined; a fixed fee is used thereafter.

**Hypothetical Question** A question in which the interviewee is asked to respond to a set of facts provided by the interviewer.

**Id.** Same citation as immediately above.

**Impaired Attorney** An attorney with a drug or alcohol problem.

**Impaneled** Selected, sworn in, and seated.

**Impeach** To challenge; to attack the credibility of.

**Imputed Disqualification** *See* Vicarious Disqualification.

**Income Partner** A special category of partner who does not own the firm in the sense of a full equity or capital partner. Also called a *permanent associate* and a *non-equity partner.*

**Incremental Spacing**   In word processing, a method by which the printer inserts spaces between words and letters to produce margins that are justified. Also called *microspacing.*

**Independent Contractor**   One who operates his or her own business and contracts to do work for others who do not control the details of how that work is performed.

**Independent Paralegal**   *See* Freelance Paralegal.

**Independent Regulatory Agency**   An administrative agency (often existing outside of the executive department) created to regulate an aspect of society.

**Indexing**   Identifying the page numbers on which certain topics appear in a document.

**Indictment**   A formal document issued by a grand jury accusing the defendant of a crime. *See also* Grand Jury.

**Indigent**   Poor, unable to pay for needed services.

**Inferior Court**   A lower court.

**Information**   A document accusing the defendant of a crime (used in states without a grand jury).

**Informational Interview**   An interview in which you find out about a particular kind of employment. It is *not* a job interview.

**Information and Belief**   To the best of my knowledge; good faith understanding.

**Infra**   Below, mentioned or referred to later in the document.

**In-house Attorney**   An attorney who is an employee of a business corporation. *See* Corporate Legal Department.

**Initial Appearance**   A court appearance during which the accused is told of the charges, a decision on bail is made, and arrangements for the next court proceeding are specified.

**In Issue**   In dispute or question.

**Ink Jet Printer**   A printer that uses a stream of ink sprayed on paper to produce the print.

**In Personam Jurisdiction**   *See* Personal Jurisdiction.

**In Re**   In the matter of.

**Insertion**   In word processing, a feature by which a character, word, sentence, or larger block of text is added to the existing text.

**Instrument**   A formal document that gives expression to a legal act or agreement, e.g., a mortgage.

**Intake Memo**   A memorandum that summarizes the facts given by a client upon becoming a client of the office.

**Integrated Bar Association**   A state bar association to which an attorney must belong in order to practice law in the state. Also called a *mandatory* or *unified bar association.*

**Integrated Package**   A software program that enables the user to use more than one kind of program simultaneously, e.g., word processing, database management, spreadsheet.

**Intellectual Property Law**   The law governing patents, copyrights, trademarks, and trade names.

**Interim Suspension**   A temporary suspension, pending the imposition of final discipline.

**Interlocutory Appeal**   An appeal of a trial court ruling before the trial court reaches its final judgment.

**Intermediate Appellate Court**   A court with appellate jurisdiction to which parties can appeal before they appeal to the highest court in the judicial system.

**Internal/Interoffice Memorandum of Law**   A memorandum written for members of one's own office. *See also* Memorandum of Law.

**Interrogatories**   A pretrial discovery device consisting of written questions sent by one party to another to assist the sender of the questions to prepare for trial.

**Interstate Compact**   An agreement between two or more states governing a problem of mutual concern.

**Intra-agency Appeal**   An appeal within an administrative agency, before the case is appealed to a court.

**Jailhouse Lawyer**   A paralegal in prison, usually self-taught, who has a limited right to practice law and to give legal advice to fellow inmates if the prison does not provide adequate alternatives for legal services. Also known as a *writ writer.*

**Jargon**   Technical language; language that does not have an everyday meaning.

**Job Bank**   A service that lists available jobs, usually available only to members of an organization.

**Joint and Several Liability**   Legally responsible together and individually.

**Judgment**   The decision of the court on the controversy before it.

**Judgment Creditor**   The party to whom damages must be paid.

**Judgment Debtor**   The party who must pay damages.

**Judgment nov**   A judgment of the court that is opposite or contrary to the verdict reached by the jury.

**Judgment on the Merits** A decision on the substance of the claims raised.

**Judicare** A system of paying private attorneys to provide legal services to the poor on a case-by-case basis.

**Judicial Branch** The branch of government with primary responsibility for interpreting laws and resolving disputes that arise under them.

**Jurisdiction** The power of a court. *See also* Geographic Jurisdiction, Subject-Matter Jurisdiction.

**Justification** In word processing, a feature for making lines of text even at the margins.

**K** A measure of capacity in a computer system.

**Kardex** A file in which the library records the volume numbers and dates of incoming publications that are part of subscriptions.

**Key Fact** A critical fact; a fact that was essential to the holding of the court.

**Key-Word Search** A search through a list of specified words that function like an index to a database.

**Label** Information used for describing some aspect of a spreadsheet.

**LAMA** Legal Assistants Management Association.

**Landmen** Paralegals who work in the area of oil and gas law. Also called *land technicians.*

**Language** A program that allows a computer to understand commands and to carry them out.

**Laptop** A portable computer, often powered by a rechargeable battery.

**Laser Printer** A printer that uses a laser beam of light to reproduce images.

**Lateral Hire** An attorney, paralegal, or secretary who has been hired from another law office.

**Law Clerk** An employee of an attorney who is in law school studying to become an attorney or who has graduated from law school and is waiting to pass the bar examination. In Ontario, Canada, a law clerk is a trained professional doing independent legal work, which may include managerial duties, under the direction and guidance of a lawyer, and whose function is to relieve a lawyer of routine and administrative matters and to assist a lawyer in the more complex ones.

**Law Directory** A list of attorneys.

**Law Review** A legal periodical published by a law school. Sometimes called a *law journal.*

**Lay Opinion Evidence** The opinion of someone who is not an expert.

**Leading Question** A question that suggests an answer within the question.

**Legal Administrator** An individual, usually a nonattorney, with broad management responsibility for a law office.

**Legal Advice** *See* Professional Judgment.

**Legal Analysis** The process of connecting a rule of law to a set of facts in order to determine how that rule might apply to a particular situation. The goal of the process is to solve a legal dispute or to prevent one from arising.

**Legal Assistant** *See* Paralegal.

**Legal Assistant Clerk** A person who assists a legal assistant in clerical tasks such as document numbering, alphabetizing, filing, and any other project that does not require substantive knowledge of litigation or of a particular transaction. *See also* Document Clerk.

**Legal Assistant Division** A few state bar associations, e.g., Texas, have established special divisions which paralegals can join as associate members.

**Legal Assistant Manager** A person responsible for recruiting, interviewing, and hiring legal assistants who spends little or no time working on client cases as a legal assistant. He or she may also be substantially involved in other matters pertaining to legal assistants, e.g., training, monitoring work assignments, designing budgets, and overseeing the billing of paralegal time. Also known as a *paralegal manager.*

**Legal Bias** *See* Bias.

**Legal Executive** A trained and certified employee of a solicitor in England; the equivalent of an American paralegal but with more training and credentials.

**Legal Insurance** *See* Group Legal Services.

**Legal Issue** A question of law; a question of what the law is, or what the law means, or how the law applies to a set of facts. If the dispute is over the truth or falsity of the facts, it is referred to as a *question of fact* or a *factual dispute.*

**Legalman** A nonattorney in the Navy who assists attorneys in the practice of law.

**Legal Technician** A self-employed paralegal who works for several different attorneys, or a self-employed paralegal who works directly for the public. Sometimes called an *independent paralegal* or a *freelance paralegal.*

**Legislation** (1) The process of making statutory law. (2) A statute.

**Legislative Branch** The branch of government with primary responsibility for making or enacting the law.

**Legislative History** All of the events that occur in the legislature before a bill is enacted into a statute.

**Letterhead**   The top part of stationery, which identifies the name and address of the office (often with the names of selected employees).

**Leverage**   The ability to make a profit from the income-generating work of others.

**LEXIS**   The legal research computer service of Mead Data Co.

**Liable**   Legally responsible.

**Licensed Independent Paralegal**   A paralegal who holds a limited license. *See* Limited Licensure.

**Licensure**   The process by which an agency of government grants permission to persons meeting specified qualifications to engage in an occupation and to use a particular title.

**Limited Jurisdiction**   The power of a court to hear only certain kinds of cases. Also called *special jurisdiction*.

**Limited Licensure**   The process by which an agency of government grants permission to persons meeting specified qualifications to engage in designated activities that are now customarily (although not always exclusively) performed by another license holder, i.e., that are part of someone else's monopoly.

**Limited Practice Officer**   A nonattorney in Washington state who has the authority to select and prepare designated legal documents pertaining to real estate closings.

**Litigation**   The formal process of resolving legal controversies through special tribunals established for this purpose. The major tribunal is a court.

**Load**   To move a program or information from a disk drive into the computer.

**Lodestar**   A mathematical formula based on a multiplier which relies on hourly rates and other factors.

**Loose-leaf Service**   A three-ring (or post) binder containing pages that can be easily inserted or taken out. The service covers current information on a broad or narrow topic.

**Magistrate**   A judicial officer having some but not all the powers of a judge.

**Majority Opinion**   The opinion whose result and reasoning is supported by at least half plus one of the judges on the court.

**Malpractice**   Serious wrongful conduct committed by an individual, usually a member of a profession.

**Mandate**   The order of the court.

**Mandatory Authority**   Whatever a court must rely on in reaching its decision.

**Mandatory Bar Association**   *See* Integrated Bar Association.

**Marital Communications**   A husband and a wife can refuse to disclose communications between them during the marriage.

**Maritime Law**   *See* Admiralty Law.

**Market Rate**   The prevailing rate in the area.

**Martindale–Hubbell**   A national directory of attorneys.

**Med-arb**   In lieu of litigation, the parties to a dispute try arbitration after mediation is unsuccessful.

**Mediation**   In lieu of litigation, a neutral third party (the mediator) tries to encourage the parties to a dispute to reach a compromise.

**Memorandum of Law**   A memorandum is simply a note, a comment, or a report. A legal memorandum is a written explanation of what the law is and how it might apply to a fact situation.

**Memorandum Opinion**   A court opinion that does not name the judge who wrote the opinion.

**Memory**   The area inside the computer that contains programs, and data which the programs help generate.

**Menu**   In word processing and other programs, a list of commands or prompts on the display screen.

**Merge Printing**   In word processing and other programs, a feature that allows a user to combine whole files and to place data from one file into specified locations in another.

**Microcomputer**   A computer small enough to fit on a desk.

**Microfiche**   *See* Microform.

**Microform**   Images or photographs that have been reduced in size. Microforms can be *microfilms* that store materials on film reels or cassettes, or *microfiche* and *ultrafiche* that store materials on single sheets of film..

**Minimum-Fee Schedule**   A published list of fees recommended by a bar association.

**Misdemeanor**   A crime punishable by a sentence of less than a year.

**Model Code of Professional Responsibility**   An earlier edition of the ethical rules governing attorneys recommended by the American Bar Association. The Model Code consisted of Ethical Considerations (ECs), which represented the objectives toward which each attorney should strive, and Disciplinary Rules (DRs), which were mandatory statements of the minimum conduct below which no attorney could fall without being subject to discipline.

**Model Rules of Professional Conduct**   The current set of ethical rules governing attorneys recommended by the American Bar Association. These rules revised the ABA's earlier rules found in the Model Code of Professional Responsibility.

**Model Standards and Guidelines for Utilization of Legal Assistants** A statement of ethical and related guidelines of the National Association of Legal Assistants.

**Modem** A device that allows one computer to send and receive information using regular telephone lines.

**Monitor** A display screen; a TV-like device used to display what is typed at the keyboard and the response of the computer.

**Monitoring Legislation** Finding out current information on the status of a proposed statute in the legislature.

**Mouse** A clicking device used as a partial substitute for typing commands into a computer.

**Movant** The party who formally requests a court to do something.

**Multiple Representation** Representing more than one side in a legal matter or controversy. Also called *common representation*.

**Multitasking** Having the capacity to run several large programs simultaneously.

**NALA** National Association of Legal Assistants.

**NALS** National Association of Legal Secretaries. *See also* Certified PLS.

**National Paralegal Reporter** A periodical of the National Federation of Paralegal Associations.

**Neighborhood Legal Service Office** A law office that serves the legal needs of the poor, often publicly funded.

**Network** Several computers connected together to share printers or hard disk drives.

**Networking** Establishing contacts with a relatively large number of people who might be helpful to you later. Similarly, you become such a contact for others.

**NFPA** National Federation of Paralegal Associations.

**NJC** Neighborhood Justice Center.

**Nolle Prosequi** A statement by the prosecutor that he or she is unwilling to prosecute the case.

**Nominative Reporter** A reporter volume that is identified by the name of the person responsible for compiling and printing the opinions in the volume.

**Nonadversarial Proceeding** Only one party appears in the proceeding, or both parties appear but they have no real controversy between them.

**Nonbillable task** A task for which an office cannot bill a client.

**Nonequity Partner** *See* Income Partner.

**Nonexempt Employee** *See* Exempt Employee.

**Nonrebuttable Presumption** *See* Presumption.

**Notary Public** A person who witnesses (i.e., attests to the authenticity of) signatures, administers oaths, and performs related tasks. In Europe, a notary often has more extensive authority.

**Notes of Decisions** Summaries of court opinions that have interpreted a statute. The notes are printed after the statute in annotated codes.

**Notice Pleading** A short and plain statement of the claim showing that the pleader is entitled to relief.

**Notice of Appearance** *See* Appearance.

**Oath** A sworn statement that what you say is true.

**Occurrence Policy** Malpractice insurance that covers all occurrences (e.g., a negligent error or omission) during the period the policy is in effect, even if the claim is not actually filed until after the policy expires.

**Of Counsel** An attorney with a special status in the firm, e.g., a semiretired partner.

**Office Sharing** Attorneys with their own independent practices who share the use and cost of administration such as rent, copy machine, etc.

**Official Reporter** A reporter that is published under the authority of the government, often printed by the government itself. An unofficial reporter is printed by a private or commercial publisher without specific authority from the government.

**OJT** On-the-job training.

**On All Fours** The facts are exactly the same, or almost the same.

**Online** Within the control of, or coming from, a central computer; in communication with a computer; through equipment under the control of a central processing unit.

**On Point** *See* Analogous.

**Open-Ended Question** A relatively broad question or request (e.g., "tell me about yourself") that forces the interviewee to organize his or her thoughts and to exert a relatively large measure of control over the kind and quantity of information provided.

**Operating System** A program that controls the overall operation of the computer, allowing it to do anything.

**Opinion** A court's written explanation of how and why it applied the law to the specific facts before it to reach its decision. Also called a *case*. Opinions are printed in volumes called *reporters*.

**Opinion Letter** A letter to a client explaining the application of the law and advising the client what to do.

**Opinion of the Attorney General**   Formal legal advice given by the attorney general to government officials.

**Ordinance**   A law passed by the local legislative branch of government (e.g., city council).

**Original Jurisdiction**   The power of a court to hear a particular kind of case initially. A trial court has original jurisdiction.

**Outstanding**   Still unresolved; still unpaid.

**Overhead**   The operating expenses of a business, e.g., cost of office space, furniture, equipment, insurance, clerical staff.

**Padding**   Adding something without justification.

**Paralegal**   A person with legal skills who works under the supervision of an attorney or who is otherwise authorized to use those skills; this person performs tasks that do not require all the skills of an attorney and that most secretaries are not trained to perform. Synonymous with *legal assistant*.

**Paralegal Manager**   *See* Legal Assistant Manager.

**Paralegal Specialist**   A job classification in the federal government.

**Parallel Cite**   An additional citation where you can find the same written material in the library.

**Paraphrase**   To rephrase something in your own words.

**Parol Evidence Rule**   Oral evidence cannot be introduced to alter or contradict the contents of a written document if the parties intended the written document to be a complete statement of the agreement.

**Partner, Full**   An attorney who contributes the capital to create the firm and to expand it, who shares the profits and losses of the firm, who controls the management of the firm, and who decides whether the firm will go out of existence.

**Partnership**   A group of individuals who practice law jointly and who share in the profits and losses of the venture.

**People**   The state or government.

**Percentage Fee**   The fee is a percentage of the amount involved in the transaction or award.

**Per Curiam**   By the court. A court opinion that does not name the particular judge who wrote the opinion.

**Peremptory Challenge**   A request that someone be excluded from a jury without any reasons stated for this request.

**Personal Jurisdiction**   The court's power over a particular person. Also called *in personam jurisdiction*.

**Personal Liability**   Being responsible because of what you wrongfully did or wrongfully failed to do. *See also* Vicarious Liability.

**Personal Recognizance**   The release of a defendant charged with a crime after a personal promise to return to court at a designated time. No bail is deposited.

**Persuasive Authority**   Whatever a court relies on in reaching its decision when it is not required to do so.

**Petition**   (1) A formal request or motion. (2) A complaint.

**Physical Evidence**   That which can be seen or touched. Also called *tangible evidence*.

**Physician Assistant**   An individual who is qualified by academic and clinical training to provide patient care services under the supervision and responsibility of a doctor of medicine or osteopathy.

**PI Cases**   Personal injury (tort) cases.

**Plaintiff**   The party initiating the lawsuit.

**Plea Bargaining**   An attempt to avoid a criminal trial by negotiating a plea, e.g., the defendant agrees to plead guilty to a lesser charge than initially brought.

**Plead**   To deliver a formal statement or response.

**Pleading**   A paper or document filed in court stating the position of one of the parties on the cause(s) of action or on the defense(s).

**PL Number**   Public Law number.

**Plotter**   A device that will hold a pen to a piece of paper and draw lines as instructed by commands you enter into the computer.

**PLS**   Professional Legal Secretary. *See also* Certified PLS.

**Pocket Part**   An insert that fits into a small pocket built into the inside back cover of a bound volume.

**Point Heading**   A party's conclusion to an argument it is making in an appellate brief.

**Points and Authorities Memorandum**   A memorandum of law submitted to a judge or hearing officer. Sometimes called a *trial memorandum*.

**Poll**   To question jurors individually in open court as to whether each agrees with the verdict announced by the foreman.

**Popular Name**   A statute that is identified by the name of a person, place, or topic rather than simply by a title and section number.

**Practical Manual**   *See* Formbook.

**Practice Analysis Report**   A report that analyzes where the firm is investing its time, where its income and profit are coming from, the amount of disbursements, etc.

**Practice of Law**   Engaging in any of the following activities on behalf of another: representation in court, representation in an agency proceeding, preparation of legal documents, or providing legal advice.

**Praecipe** A formal request to the court (usually through the clerk) that something be done.

**Prayer for Relief** The request for damages or other form of relief.

**Pre-evaluation Memo** A memorandum sent to a supervisor before a formal evaluation in which the employee lists the following information (since the last formal evaluation): major projects, functions on those projects, names of co-workers on the projects, evidence of initiative, quotations on the quality of work, etc.

**Preliminary Hearing** A hearing during which the state is required to produce sufficient evidence to establish that there is probable cause to believe the defendant committed the crimes charged.

**Premium Adjustment** A write up (increase) of a bill.

**Prepaid Legal Services** *See* Group Legal Services.

**Preponderance of the Evidence** It is more likely than not that the fact is as alleged.

**Presumption** An assumption that a certain fact is true. It is rebuttable if the court will consider evidence that it is false, and nonrebuttable if no such contrary evidence will be considered.

**Pretrial Conference** A meeting between the judge (or magistrate) and the attorneys to prepare the case for trial, and perhaps to make one last effort to settle the case.

**Prima Facie** On the face of it; that which would be legally sufficient, if believed, to support a verdict.

**Primary Authority** Any *law* that a court could rely on in reaching its decision.

**Print Formatting** The function of a word processor that communicates with the printer to tell it how to print the text on paper.

**Print Review** In word processing, a feature that enables you to view a general representation on the screen of how the document will look when printed.

**Private Law** *See* Statute.

**Private Law Firm** A law firm that generates its income from the fees of individual clients.

**Private Reprimand** *See* Admonition.

**Private Sector** An office where the funds come from client fees or the corporate treasury.

**Private Statute** *See* Statute.

**Privilege** A special benefit, right, or protection. In the law of evidence, a privilege is the right to refuse to testify or to prevent someone else from testifying.

**Privilege against Self-Incrimination** Persons cannot be compelled to testify in a criminal proceeding or to answer incriminating questions that directly or indirectly connect themselves to the commission of a crime.

**Probable Cause** A reasonable basis to believe that the defendant is guilty of the crime(s) charged.

**Probation** Supervised punishment in the community in lieu of incarceration. In the field of ethics, probation means: to allow an attorney to continue to practice, but under specified conditions, e.g., submit to periodic audits, make restitution to a client.

**Pro Bono Work** Services that one volunteers to provide another at no charge.

**Procedural Due Process** Procedural protections that are required before the government can take away or refuse to grant liberty or a public benefit.

**Procedural Law** The rules that govern the mechanics of resolving a dispute in court or in an administrative agency, e.g., a rule on the time a party has to respond to a complaint.

**Professional Corporation** The organization of a law practice as a corporation.

**Professional Judgment** Relating or applying the general body and philosophy of law to a specific legal problem. When communicated to a client, the result is known as *legal advice.*

**Project Attorney** An attorney who works either part-time or full time over a relatively short period. Also referred to as a *contract attorney.*

**Prosecution** (1) Bringing a criminal case. (2) The attorney representing the government in a criminal case. (3) Going through the steps to litigate a civil case.

**Prosecutor** The attorney representing the government in a criminal case.

**Public Benefits** Government benefits.

**Public Censure.** *See* Reprimand.

**Public Defender** An attorney who is paid by the government to represent low-income people charged with crimes.

**Public Domain** Available for use without permission or cost; not protected by copyright.

**Public Law** *See* Statute.

**Public Sector** An office where the funds come from charity or the government.

**Public Statute** *See* Statute.

**Quarantined Paralegal** *See* Chinese Wall.

**Quasi-adjudication** An administrative decision of an administrative agency which has characteristics of a court opinion.

**Quasi-independent Agency** An administrative agency that has characteristics of an executive department agency and of an independent regulatory agency.

**Quasi-judicial** Like or similar to a court.

**Quasi-legislation** A regulation of an administrative agency that has characteristics of the legislation (statutes) of a legislature.

**Query** A question that asks a computer to find something in its database.

**Question of Law/Question of Fact** *See* Legal Issue.

**Quid Pro Quo Harassment** Using submission to or rejection of unwelcome sexual conduct as the basis for making employment decisions affecting an individual.

**Rainmaker** A person who brings fee-generating cases into the office.

**RE** Concerning

**Reasonable Fee** A fee that is not excessive in light of the amount of time and labor involved, the complexity of the case, the experience and reputation of the attorney, the customary fee charged in the locality for the same kind of case, etc.

**Rebuttable Presumption** *See* Presumption.

**Record** (1) The official collection of all the trial pleadings, exhibits, orders, and word-for-word testimony that took place during the trial. (2) A collection of data fields that constitute a single unit, e.g., employee record.

**Redirect Examination** Questioning your own witness (i.e., one you called) after cross-examination by the other side of that witness.

**Referral Fee** A fee received by an attorney from another attorney to whom the first attorney referred a client. Also called a *forwarding fee*.

**Regional Digest** A digest that summarizes court opinions that are printed in full in its corresponding regional reporter.

**Regional Reporter** A reporter that contains state-court opinions of states within a region of the country.

**Registered Agent** An individual authorized to practice before the United States Patent Office. He or she does not have to be an attorney.

**Registration** The process by which individuals or institutions list their names on a roster kept by an agency of government or by a nongovernmental organization. The agency or organization will often establish qualifications for the right to register, and determine whether applicants meet these qualifications. Also called *enrollment*.

**Regulation** Any governmental or nongovernmental method of controlling conduct. *See also* Administrative Regulation.

**Relevance** That which reasonably has a bearing on something; that which tends to help establish a fact as true or as false, as present or as missing. Evidence is relevant when it reasonably tends to make the existence of a fact more probable or less probable than it would be without that evidence.

**Remand** Send the case back to a lower tribunal with instructions from the appellate court.

**Reply Brief** An appellate brief of the appellant that responds to the appellate brief of the appellee.

**Reporters** Volumes containing the full text of court opinions. *See also* Official Reporter.

**Reprimand** A public declaration that an attorney's conduct was improper. This does not affect his or her right to practice. Also called a *censure* and a *public censure*.

**Request for Admissions** A pretrial discovery device consisting of a series of written factual statements that a party is asked to affirm or deny.

**Res Gestae Exceptions** Exceptions to the hearsay rule that consist of statements or utterances closely connected to or concurrent with an occurrence.

**Res Judicata** A judgment on the merits will prevent the same parties from relitigating the same cause of action on the same facts.

**Respondeat Superior** Let the superior answer. An employer is responsible for the wrongs committed by an employee within the scope of employment.

**Respondent** *See* Appellee.

**Restatements** A series of volumes that attempt to formulate existing law in a given area.

**Retainer** (1) The contract of employment between attorney and client. (2) An amount of money paid by a client to make certain that an attorney will be available to work for him or her. (3) The amount of money or other assets paid by the client as a form of deposit or advance payment against future fees and costs.

**Review** To examine in order to determine whether any errors of law were made. *See also* Appellate Jurisdiction.

**Right Justified** In word processing, an even right side margin.

**Root Expander (!)** The exclamation mark stands for one or more characters or letters added to the root of a word.

**Rule** *See* Administrative Regulation, Rules of Court.

**Rule-Making Function** Writing administrative regulations.

**Rule of Three** Gross revenue generated through paralegal billing should equal three times a paralegal's salary.

**Rules of Court** Rules of procedure that govern the conduct of litigation before a particular court.

**Ruling** *See* Administrative Decision, Holding.

**Run** To cause a program to (1) be loaded into the computer from a disk drive and (2) begin to perform its task.

**Runner** *See* Ambulance Chasing.

**Sanction** (1) A penalty or punishment imposed for unacceptable conduct. (2) To authorize or give approval.

**Satisfy** To comply with a legal obligation.

**Save** To cause a program or data that is in the computer memory to be moved or stored on a diskette or hard drive.

**Scanner** A machine that allows a user to enter text and graphics without traditional typing.

**Scope Note** The summary of coverage of a topic within a West digest.

**Screen Formatting** In word processing and other programs, a feature that controls how the text will appear on the screen.

**Scrolling** In word processing and other programs, moving a line of text onto or off the screen.

**Search and Find** In word processing and other programs, a routine that searches for and places the cursor at a specified string of characters.

**Search and Replace** In word processing and other programs, a routine that searches for a specified string of characters and replaces it with another string.

**Search Criteria/Query** A computer research question; what you ask the computer in order to find something in a database.

**Secondary Authority** Any *nonlaw* that a court could rely on in reaching its decision.

**Second Chair** A seat at the counsel's table in the courtroom used by an assistant to the trial attorney during the trial.

**Second-Tiered Attorney** *See* Staff Attorney.

**Section (§)** A portion of a statute, regulation, or book.

**Segment Search** In LEXIS, a search that is limited to a certain part of cases in its databases.

**Self-Regulation** A process by which members of an occupation or profession establish and administer the rules to become a member and when members

experienced legal assistant other legal assistant specialty in a

**Series** A set of books with its own internal volume-numbering system. When a new series in the set begins, the volume number starts again with 1.

**Service Company** A business that sells particular services, usually to other businesses.

**Service of Process** The delivery of a formal notice to a defendant ordering him or her to appear in court to answer the allegations of the plaintiff.

**Session Law Cite** The citation to a statute that has not yet been printed in a code and therefore is organized chronologically. *See also* Codified Cite.

**Settlement Work-up** A summary of the major facts in the case presented in a manner designed to encourage the other side (or its insurance company) to settle the case.

**Sexual Harassment** *See* Hostile Environment, Quid Pro Quo Harassment.

**Shepardizing** Using the volumes of *Shepards' Citations* in order to obtain the data available in these volumes, e.g., whether a case has been appealed, whether a statute has been repealed.

**Slip Law** A single act passed by the legislature and printed separately, often in a small pamphlet. It is the first official publication of the act.

**Slip Opinion** A single court opinion, which for many courts is the first printing of the case.

**Software** Computer programs for performing tasks such as word processing and database management.

**Sole Practice** A single attorney owns and manages the law firm.

**Solicitor** (1) A lawyer in England who handles day-to-day legal problems of clients with only limited rights to represent clients in certain lower courts. *See also* Barrister. (2) In the United States, some high government attorneys are called solicitors, e.g., the Solicitor-General of the United States who argues cases before the United States Supreme Court for the federal government.

**Special Edition State Reporter** A reporter that prints the court opinions of one state, which are also printed within the regional reporter that covers that state.

**Special Interest Group** An organization that serves a particular group of people, e.g., a union.

**Special Jurisdiction** *See* Limited Jurisdiction.

**Specialty Certification** Official recognition of competency in a particular area of law. The National Association of Legal Assistants, for example, has a specialty certification program to recognize a person as a Certified Legal Assistant Specialist (CLAS). A paralegal must first become a Certified Legal Assistant (CLA), and then pass one of NALA's specialty exams. *See also* Certified Legal Assistant.

**Spelling Checker** A computer software program that checks the spelling of words entered through a word processing program.

**Spontaneous Declaration** An out-of-court statement or utterance made spontaneously during or immediately after an exciting event by an observer. (An exception to the hearsay rule.)

**Spreadsheet** A ledger or table used for financial calculations and for the recording of transactions.

**Squibs** *See* Digests.

**Staff Attorney** A full-time attorney who has no expectation of becoming a full partner. Sometimes called a *second-tiered* attorney.

**Staffing Agency** An employment agency providing part-time employees for businesses. Often the business pays the agency, which in turn pays the employee.

**Standard Form** A preprinted form used frequently for various kinds of transactions or proceedings.

**Standard of Proof** A statement of how convincing a version of a fact must be before the trier of facts can accept it as true.

**Star-Paging** A notation (e.g., an asterisk or star) next to text within a page of an unofficial reporter which indicates where the same text is found in an official reporter. *See also* Official Reporter.

**State Question** A legal question that arises from the application of the state constitution, a state statute, or a state administrative regulation.

**Stating a Cause of Action** Including in the complaint those facts which, if proved at trial, would entitle the plaintiff to win.

**Status Line** In word processing and other programs, a message line above or below the text area on a display screen that gives format and system information.

**Statute** A law passed by the legislature declaring, commanding, or prohibiting something. The statute is contained in a document called an *act*. If the statute applies to the general public or to a segment of the public, it is called a *public law* or *public statute*. If the statute applies to specifically named individuals or to groups—and has little or no permanence or general interest—it is called a *private law* or *private statute*.

**Statute in Derogation of the Common Law** A statute that changes the common law. *See* Common Law.

**Statute of Limitations** The period within which the lawsuit must be commenced or it can never be brought.

**Statutory Code** A collection of statutes organized by subject matter.

**Stay** To delay the enforcement or the execution of a judgment.

**Stipulated** Agreed to.

**Subject-Matter Jurisdiction** The power of the court to resolve a particular category of dispute.

**Subscript** In word processing and other programs, a character that prints below the usual text baseline.

**Subscription** The signature of the attorney who prepared the complaint.

**Substantive Law** The nonprocedural rules that govern rights and duties.

**Summary** Quick, expedited, without going through a full adversarial hearing.

**Summary Judgment, Motion for** A request by a party that a decision be reached on the basis of the pleadings alone, without going through an entire trial, because there is no dispute on any material facts.

**Summons** A formal notice from the court ordering the defendant to appear.

**Superior Court** Usually a trial court.

**Superscript** In word processing and other programs, a character that prints above the usual text baseline.

**Superseded** Outdated and replaced.

**Supervising Legal Assistant** Someone who spends about fifty percent of his or her time supervising other legal assistants and about fifty percent on client cases as a legal assistant.

**Supplemented** Added to.

**Supra** Above, mentioned or referred to earlier in the document.

**Supremacy Clause** The clause in the United States Constitution that gives the federal government supremacy over state and local governments in regulating designated areas.

**Supreme Court** The highest court in a judicial system. (In New York, however, the supreme court is a trial court.)

**Surrogate Courts** A special court with subject-matter jurisdiction over wills, probate, guardianships, etc.

**Suspension** The removal of an attorney from the practice of law for a specified minimum period, after which the attorney can apply for reinstatement.

**Sustain** To affirm the validity of.

**"Swoose" Syndrome** Being recognized as part of the clerical staff in some respects and as part of the professional staff in others.

**Syllabus** (1) A one-paragraph summary of an enti[re] court opinion, usually written by a p[ublisher] rather than by the court. ( )

syllabus refers to the headnotes of an opinion that summarize a portion of the opinion.

**System** An organized method of performing a recurring task.

**Table of Authorities** A list of the authorities a party is citing in a document, e.g., cases, statutes, law review articles.

**Table of Cases** A list of all the cases printed or referred to in the volume, and where they are found in the volume.

**Table of Statutes** A list of all the statutes printed or referred to in the volume, and where they are found in the volume.

**Tainted Paralegal** *See* Chinese Wall.

**Tangible Evidence** *See* Physical Evidence.

**Template** A set of formulas created to perform a designated task.

**Testimonial Evidence** That which someone says.

**Text Buffer** In word processing and other programs, an area set aside in memory to hold text temporarily.

**Text Editing** In word processing and other programs, the function that enables the user to enter and edit text.

**Text File** In word processing and other programs, a file that contains text, as opposed to a program.

**Third-Party Complaint** A complaint filed by the defendant against a third party.

**Tickler** A reminder system that helps office staff remember important deadlines.

**Title Page** A page at the beginning of a book that lists the name of the book, the author(s), publisher, etc. On this page, or on the next page, the latest copyright date of the book is printed.

**Topic and Key Number** The system used by West Publishing Company to organize the millions of small-paragraph summaries of court opinions in its digests.

**Tort** A private wrong or injury other than a breach of contract or the commission of a crime, although some breaches of contract and crimes can also constitute torts.

**Transcribed** Copied or written out word for word.

**Transcript** A word-for-word account.

**Treatise, Legal** A book written by a private individual (or by a public official writing as a private citizen) that provides an overview, summary, or commentary of a legal topic.

**Treaty** An international agreement between two or more countries.

**Trial Book** *See* Trial Brief.

**Trial Brief** An attorney's set of notes on how to conduct a trial, often placed in a *trial notebook*. Sometimes called a *trial manual* or *trial book*.

**Trial de Novo** A totally new fact-finding hearing.

**Trial Manual** *See* Trial Brief.

**Trial Memorandum** *See* Points and Authorities Memorandum.

**Trial Notebook** A collection of documents, arguments, and strategies that an attorney plans to use during a trial. Sometimes referred to as the *trial brief*. (It can mean the notebook in which the trial brief is placed.)

**Ultrafiche** *See* Microform.

**Unauthorized Practice of Law** Services that constitute the practice of law, which a nonattorney has no authorization to provide. *See also* Practice of Law, Professional Judgment.

**Unbundled** *See* Bundled.

**Uncodified** Organized chronologically rather than by subject matter.

**Unicameral** *See* Bicameral.

**Unified Bar Association** *See* Integrated Bar Association.

**Uniform State Law** A proposed statute presented to all the state legislatures by the National Conference of Commissioners on Uniform State Laws.

**United States Court of Appeals** The main federal appellate court just below the United States Supreme Court.

**United States District Court** The main federal trial court.

**United States Supreme Court** The highest court in the federal judicial system.

**Universal Character** (*) The asterisk stands for any character or letter in a query.

**Unofficial Reporter** *See* Official Reporter.

**User Group** Individuals using the same computer product who meet to discuss their experiences with it.

**Validation Research** Using citators and other sources to check the current validity of every authority you intend to rely on in your document.

**Value** A single piece of numeric information used in the calculations of a spreadsheet.

**Value Billing** The amount to be paid is based on the complexity of the legal problem, the expertise required of the attorney, and the number of hours devoted to the matter.

**Valuing the Bill** Determining whether there should be a write up or a write down of the bill.

**Venue**   The place of the trial.

**Verdict**   The final conclusion of the jury.

**Verification**   An affidavit stating that a party has read the complaint and swears that it is true to the best of his or her knowledge.

**Veto**   A rejection by the chief executive of a bill passed by the legislature.

**Vicarious Disqualification**   A law firm cannot continue to represent a client or cannot accept a new client because it has hired someone (attorney, paralegal, or secretary) who has a conflict of interest with that client.

**Vicarious Liability**   Being responsible because of what someone else has wrongfully done or wrongfully failed to do. *See also* Personal Liability.

**Virtual Representation**   In word processing and other programs, an approach to screen formatting that enables the user to see on the screen exactly how the printed output will look.

**Voir Dire**   The oral examination of prospective jurors for purposes of selecting a jury.

**Wage and Hour Division**   The unit within the U.S. Department of Labor that administers the Fair Labor Standards Act, which governs overtime compensation and related matters. *See also* Exempt Employee, Fair Labor Standards Act.

**Waiver**   The loss of a right or privilege because of an explicit rejection of it or because of a failure to claim it at the appropriate time.

**Warrant**   An order from a judicial officer authorizing an act, e.g., the arrest of an individual, the search of property.

**WESTLAW**   The legal research computer service of West Publishing Co.

**Window**   In a spreadsheet program, the portion of a worksheet that can be seen on the computer display screen.

**Word Processor**   A computerized system of entering, editing, storing, retrieving, etc. data.

**Word Wrap**   A word is automatically moved to the next line if it goes past the right margin.

**Work-Product Rule**   Notes, working papers, memoranda, or similar documents and tangible things prepared by the attorney in anticipation of litigation are not discoverable. *See also* Discoverable.

**Write Down**   Deduct an amount from the bill.

**Write Up**   Add an amount to the bill.

**Writ of Certiorari**   An order by an appellate court requiring a lower court to certify the record of a lower court proceeding and to send it up to the appellate court which has decided to accept the appeal.

**Writ Writer**   *See* Jailhouse Lawyer.

**WYSIWYG**   What You See (on the screen) Is What You Get (when the screen is printed).

# ■ Index

## ■ A

AAfPE, 238, 747
AALS. *See* American Association of
    Law Libraries
ABA. *See* American Bar Association
Abbreviations, 12, 530, 542, 566
Ability, 108, 120, 244, 246
Abraham Lincoln, 44, 690
Abstracters, 172, 306
Abstracts (Digests), 497
Abstracts, Prepare, 95, 472
Acceptance of Cases, 314
Access to Records, 410
Access to the Courts, 218, 221
Accident Report, 410
Accomplishments, Work, 193
Accountant, 36, 45, 100, 135, 172,
    212, 223, 239, 264, 298
Accountant, Fiduciary, 172
Accounting, 111, 109, 112, 182,
    277, 641
Accounts, Bank, 277
Accounts Payable Clerk, 690
Accounts Receivable, 702, 705,
    831
Accounts Receivable Clerk, 690
Accreditation, 210, 237, 244, 747,
    831
Accusation, 266
Accuser, 729
Acquit, 452, 831
Act, 329, 486, 533, 850
Acts and Resolves, 486
Actuarial Associate, 172
Ad Damnum, 438, 831
Adirondack, 768
Adjourn, 445
Adjudication, 223, 328, 336, 831.
    *See also* Quasi Adjudication
Adjusters. *See* Claims Adjuster
Administration of Estate, 112
Administrative Advocacy, 719
Administrative Agency, 81, 97,
    222, 249, 327, 331, 334, 409,
    435, 452, 502, 550, 592, 600,
    602, 719, 747, 831
Administrative Aide, 83
Administrative Assistant, 88
Administrative Benefits, 96
Administrative Clerk, 116
Administrative Code, 2, 486, 831
Administrative Decision, 329, 337,

452, 454, 456, 488, 506, 603,
    831
Administrative Employee, 253
Administrative Hearing, 101, 122,
    310, 453, 831
Administrative Law, 101, 246, 602
Administrative Law Judge, 122,
    123, 173, 453, 831
Administrative Opinion, 329
Administrative Paralegal, 60
Administrative Procedure Act, 222,
    225
Administrative Regulation, 329,
    346, 358, 456, 486, 488, 496,
    502, 506, 516, 602, 603, 831
Administrative Reports, 702
Administrative Representation,
    226, 310, 394
Administrative Rule or Ruling, 329
Administrative Supervisor, 118
Administrative Technician, 94
Administrator. *See* Legal
    Administrator
Admiralty Law, 101, 120, 831
Admissible Evidence, 421, 444,
    831
Admission, 425, 831
Admissions, Request for, 119, 404,
    441, 470
Admonition, 268, 831
ADR, 458, 831
Ads, 108, 135, 136, 137
Advance Payment, 701
Advance Sheet (Reporter), 140,
    486, 555, 831
Advance Sheet (Shepard's), 487,
    495, 563, 831
Advanced Professional
    Competency, 251
Advancement, 178
Adversarial, 189, 213, 222, 277,
    395
Adversarial System, 831
Adversary, 287
Adversary Hearing, 441
Adversary Memorandum of Law,
    620, 840
Adverse Interests, 113, 286, 831
Adverse Judgment, 440, 831
Advertisements, Attorney, 59, 235,
    239, 296, 303, 305, 320
Advertising Law, 102
Advice, Legal, 32, 114, 229, 264,

295, 298, 304, 306, 307, 316,
    329, 394
Advice, Nonlegal, 309
Advisement, 445
Advisor, Patent, 82
Advocacy, 128, 129, 141, 146,
    190, 214, 222, 276, 393, 719,
    747, 831
Advocate, 50, 96, 121, 126, 286
AFDC, 96, 98
Affiant, 438
Affidavit, 86, 113, 127, 217, 233,
    273, 438, 459, 831
Affiliate Member of Bar
    Association, 240
Affiliation, 52, 242
Affirm, 357, 448, 449
Affirmation of Professional
    Responsibility, 248, 281, 313,
    831
Affirmative Defense, 439, 831
Aged Accounts Receivable, 702,
    706, 708
Agency. *See* Administrative Agency
Agency Appeal, 125, 454
Agency Hearing, 454, 792
Agency Representation, 97, 128,
    210, 220, 222, 781, 792
Agents, 125, 172, 212, 222, 223,
    236, 259
Aggressive, 147, 189, 743
Aging Report, 702, 831
Aide, 26, 47, 48, 83, 91, 93, 136
AIDS, 117, 122
Akron, 769
ALA, 25
Alabama, 60, 84, 266, 494, 502,
    535, 613, 747, 765, 773, 791,
    812
Alameda County, 773
Alamo, 770, 824
Alaska, 60, 84, 92, 179, 266, 494,
    500, 502, 535, 613, 699, 747,
    765, 773, 792, 812, 828
Albany, 775
Alberta, 771
Albuquerque, 73, 768, 775, 813
Alcohol, 279
Alias, 409
ALJ, 122, 123, 453
Allegation, 437, 439
Allegheny, 776
Allen County, 216

Alphabetical Filing, 710
ALR. *See* American Law Reports
ALR2d Later Case Service, 560
ALR Blue Book, 490, 560
Alternate, 442
Alternative Careers, 747
Alternative Dispute Resolution, 458
Altman and Weil, 34
Am.Jur.2d. *See* American Jurisprudence
Amarillo, 770
Ambiguity, 14, 479, 594, 601
Ambulance Chasing, 126, 295, 831
Amendment, Constitutional, 212, 296
Amendments, 111, 339, 536, 572, 598, 601
America, Colonial, 44
American Association of Law Libraries, 485
American Bar Association, 25, 28, 46, 51, 53, 210, 223, 230, 237, 241, 248, 251, 254, 266, 293, 298, 312, 315, 700, 747, 771
American Bar Association Committee on Legal Assistants, 46, 237, 241
American Dental Association, 47
American Digest System, 257, 487, 498, 501, 554, 555, 557
American Indians, 778
American Jurisprudence 2d, 487, 504, 508, 515, 522, 538, 550, 582, 596
American Law Institute, 508, 523, 538
American Law Reports, 487, 515, 538, 550, 557, 585, 587
American Legal System, 246
American Samoa, 84
Americans, Native, 126
Amicus Curiae, 491, 627, 832
Analogies, 356, 373
Analogous, 518, 832
Analysis, 2, 85, 93, 102, 111, 267, 345, 349, 368, 406, 623
Analyst, 36, 82, 83, 88, 115, 172, 173, 690
Analytic Ability, 108, 120, 148, 186, 246
Analytical Research, 88
Anchorage, 60, 699, 765, 773, 812
AND Connector, 666, 669
AND NOT Connector, 669

Anger, 722, 725, 747
Annotate, 487, 832
Annotated Bibliography, 151, 608, 832
Annotated Code, 490
Annotated Reporter, 487, 558
Annotation, 487, 538, 550, 557, 567, 570, 588, 595, 602, 832
Annotation History Table, 561
Annuity, 109
Answer, 167, 349, 439, 454, 463, 832
Answer, Examination, 349
Answering Court Calls, 216
Answering Service, 816
Answers to Interrogatories, Drafting, 464, 466
Antitrust Law, 102, 133, 212, 237, 239, 270, 272, 658, 747, 832
Anxiety, 107
APA, 222
Apartments, 117, 119
Appeal, 114, 331, 355, 376, 447, 454, 457, 472, 722, 729, 744
Appeal, Agency, 125
Appeal as a Matter of Right, 449, 832
Appeal, Issues on, 448
Appeal, Notice of, 119, 447, 456, 458
Appeals Board, 226
Appeals Record, 96
Appearance, 729, 832
Appearance, Court, 114, 215, 298, 309
Appearance, Initial, 450, 457
Appearance, Notice of, 278, 436
Appearance of Impropriety, 297, 316, 804
Appellant, 355, 448, 456, 458, 832
Appellate Brief, 47, 111, 113, 117, 121, 305, 332, 353, 448, 456, 458, 473, 491, 539, 607, 627, 803, 832
Appellate Courts, 333
Appellate Jurisdiction, 331, 447, 832
Appellee, 355, 448, 456, 832
Appendix, 96, 544, 624, 631, 832
Appointment of Representative, 224
Appraisers, 113
Appreciation, 124
Apprentice, 832
Approval, ABA, 210, 237, 238, 244, 315, 832

Arbitration, 106, 117, 173, 459, 778, 832
Architects, 47
Archives, State, 127
Argument, 345, 448, 629, 631
Argument, Closing, 129, 445
Argumentative, 213
Arizona, 28, 60, 84, 192, 247, 250, 266, 296, 321, 494, 502, 535, 613, 640, 747, 765, 773, 792, 811, 812
Arkansas, 85, 494, 502, 535, 613, 747, 765, 773, 792, 812
Army, 747
Arraignment, 451, 457, 832
Arrest, 108, 450, 457, 832
Arrogance, 816
Arson, 771
Articles of Incorporation, 106, 151, 167
Asbestos Litigation, 126, 292, 793
Assembly, 236, 337
Assertiveness, 120, 189, 747, 832
Assets, 104, 113, 125
Assets and Liabilities, 111, 398
Assigned Counsel, 450, 832
Assignments, Paralegal, 3, 16, 186, 300, 311, 402, 622
Assistance of Counsel, 268
Assistant. *See* Legal Assistant; Paralegal
Associate, 40, 172, 242, 302, 688, 694, 747, 801, 803, 832
Associate General Counsel, 689
Associate Membership in Bar Association, 25, 133, 194, 240, 747, 832
Associated, 302, 832
Association, Bar, 18, 25, 27, 46, 229. *See also* American Bar Association
Association of Legal Administrators, 25, 691, 747, 771
Association of Legal Secretaries, National, 199, 772
Associations, Paralegal, 18, 25, 47, 52, 132, 158, 176, 198, 201, 204, 252, 317, 765
Assumption, 446
Atlanta, 67, 81, 87, 101, 767, 774, 812
Atlantic Digest, 490, 499, 501
Atlantic Reporter, 490, 501, 512
Attachment, 105
Attention to Detail, 113, 114, 126, 136

Attestation, 243, 427, 832
Attitude, 192, 197, 747
Attorney, 31, 40, 108, 279, 302, 685, 816, 829
Attorney Advertising, 59, 235, 239, 303, 305, 320
Attorney as Paralegal, 31
Attorney Assistant, 26, 229, 301
Attorney Associations, 773. *See also* American Bar Association
Attorney Attestation, 243, 832
Attorney Attitudes and Traits, 52, 145, 188, 202, 203, 213, 816, 828
Attorney Client Privilege, 280, 426, 466, 747, 832
Attorney Competence. *See* Competence
Attorney Competition, 210, 212, 230
Attorney Directories, 135, 139, 152
Attorney Ethics, 263, 791
Attorney Fees, 33, 38, 44, 99, 146, 270, 383, 747
Attorney General, 59, 87, 98, 355, 747, 778, 832
Attorney General, Opinion of the, 329, 489
Attorney, Hispanic, 265
Attorney Malpractice. *See* Legal Malpractice
Attorney of Record, 437, 584, 832
Attorney, Power of, 111, 122
Attorney Profits, 686
Attorney Regulation, 265
Attorney Supervision, 31, 81. *See also* Supervision
Attorney, Unemployed, 31, 58, 135
Attorney Work Product, 280, 466, 793
Attorney Wrongdoing, 265, 274
Attorneys Competing with Paralegals, 40, 57
Audit, 95, 130, 703
Augusta, 89, 774
Austin, 78, 94, 770, 776
Australia, 747
Authentication, 427, 832
Authority, 111, 346, 355, 472, 517, 629, 726, 832
Authorization, 213, 722, 726, 734
Authorized Practice of Law, 31, 210, 213, 245, 297, 832
Auto-Cite, 496, 515, 559, 562, 586
Automatic Pagination, 653, 832

Automation, 691, 694, 712, 713
Autonomy, 101, 189
Autopsy, 104
Auxiliary Personnel, 47

### ■ B

Background Legal Research, 549, 588, 832
Background Research for Employment, 145, 155, 166, 169, 181
Background Research in Labor Law, 117
Backup, 644, 681, 832
Bail, 108, 450, 457, 832
Bailiff, 442, 833
Bakersfield, 766
Baltimore, 69, 89, 133, 274, 767, 774, 813
Banc, En, 449
Bangor, 69
Bank Accounts, 277
Bank Associate, 172
Banking, 34, 48, 58, 97, 103, 109, 146, 172, 212, 747
Bankruptcy, 27, 96, 103, 122, 126, 139, 230, 235, 246, 366, 747, 824
Bankruptcy Digest, 499
Bankruptcy Reporter, 492
Bankruptcy Trustee, 824
Bar, 448, 833
Bar Association, 18, 25, 27, 28, 46, 133, 210, 223, 229, 230, 236, 237, 241, 251, 265, 266, 293, 298, 312, 315, 337, 505, 600, 747, 773, 823
Bar Association, Associate Membership in, 194, 240
Bar Association, Kinds of, 265
Bar Coding, 714, 833
Bar Journal, 141, 505
Bar Treaties, 212, 833
Bare, Go, 257
Bargaining, 403, 451, 722, 727
Barratry, 295, 833
Barrister, 49, 833
Bates Stamping, 119
Bates v. Arizona, 296, 321
Baton Rouge, 89, 102, 116, 767, 774
Battery, 255, 270
Baud Rate, 679, 833
Beaumont, 770
Below, 448, 456, 833

Bench Conference, 443
Benefits. *See* Employee Benefits; Fringe Benefits
Berkeley, 766
Berks County, 769
Berkshire, 768
Best Evidence Rule, 427, 833
Beverly Hills, 773
Beyond Reasonable Doubt, 452, 833
Bias, 212, 442, 729
Bibliography, 85, 110, 119, 143, 151, 747
Bicameral, 337, 833
Bilingual Paralegal, 806
Bill, 236, 337, 339, 490, 833
Bill, Law Firm, 256, 703
Billable Hour Quotas, 159, 176, 198
Billable Hours, 30, 38, 41, 157, 159, 176, 191, 198, 273, 311, 658, 693, 694, 698, 699, 702, 747, 827, 833
Billing, 42, 641, 656, 657, 691, 700, 768, 826
Billing Assistant, 690
Billing Attorney, 701
Billing, Double, 273
Billing Memorandum, 701, 833
Billing Methods, 701
Billing Review, 695
Billing System, 817
Bills, 536, 598, 599
Binghamton, 769
Birmingham, 60, 765, 773, 792
Bismarck, 93, 769, 775
Black Attorneys, 777, 778
Black's Law Dictionary, 504, 522, 550
Blame, 181
Blended Hourly Rate, 701, 833
Blind Ad, 136, 833
Blind Attorneys, 777
Block (Work Processing), 653, 833
Bloomington, 767
Blue and White Book, 527
Bluebook, 117, 490, 524, 539, 540, 834
Blue Book of Annotations, 560
Blue Sky, 107, 108
BNA. *See* Bureau of National Affairs
Board of Appeals, 226, 456, 833
Board of Directors, 107, 124, 689. *See also* Professional Corporation

Body Language, 155
Body of Complaint, 469
Body of Memorandum, 367
Boilerplate, 467, 833
Boise, 87, 767, 774
Boldface, 653, 833
Bond Attorneys, 778
Bonds, 121, 124, 447, 450, 833
Bonus, 34, 158, 191, 194, 272, 793, 801, 809, 818
Book Review, 580, 583, 578
Book, Trial, 353, 470
Bookkeeping, 45, 112, 126, 277, 677, 690
Books, Law, 220, 477
Books, Self-Help, 211
Boredom, 4, 105, 107, 124, 179
Boston, 69, 81, 90, 136, 274, 768, 774, 813
Bound Over, 451
Bounds v. Smith, 221
Bradenton, 766
Branch Office, 59, 100, 116
Branches of Government, 600, 601
Breach of Contract, 106, 255
Bridgeport, 766
Brief. See Appellate Brief; Trial Brief
Brief of a Case, 353, 833
Briefcase, 155
Broad-Based Licensing, 228
Broker, 113, 123, 125, 213, 228, 810
Bronx, 776
Broward County, 766
Brownfield, 811
Brussels, 642
Budget, 121, 144, 162, 672, 691, 706, 708, 818
Bufetes, 50
Buffalo, 73, 769
"Bugs", 202, 655, 833
Bulletin, 491, 492, 603
Bulletin Board, 680, 833
Bundled, 701, 833
Burden of Proof, 443, 833
Bureau of Labor, 37
Bureau of National Affairs, 492, 506, 576, 585
Bureaucracy, 110
Burger, Warren, 23, 38
Burnout, 747
Business, 58, 97
Business Card of Paralegal, 159, 194, 302, 305, 791, 794, 796, 797, 798, 799, 800, 801, 802,
803, 804, 805, 806, 807, 808, 811
Business Entry, 425, 833
Business Law, 232, 247
Business Planning, 692
Business Records, 124
Business Transaction with Client, 284
BUT NOT Connector, 667
Bylaws, 107, 151, 167, 240, 241
Byte, 646, 833


■ C

Calculations, 672
Calendar Attorney, 695
Calendar Control, 111, 114, 124, 126, 464, 657, 817
Calendar, Court, 85, 355, 448, 505
Calgary, 771
California, 46, 60, 85, 110, 112, 113, 119, 121, 122, 150, 181, 184, 198, 202, 203, 219, 221, 226, 230, 240, 241, 247, 248, 266, 282, 291, 292, 308, 317, 353, 493, 494, 502, 535, 554, 583, 614, 747, 765, 773, 793, 811, 812, 825
California Digest, 555
California Reporter, 354, 491, 493
Call Number, 552
CALR. See Computer Assisted Legal Research
Camden, 813
Canada, 50, 581, 748, 771, 843
Canons, 266, 314
Capital Area, 770. See also Austin; District of Columbia
Capital Budget Committee, 687
Capital Partner, 688
Capper, 296, 833
Caption (Appellate Brief), 628, 833
Caption (Complaint), 466, 833
Caption (Opinion), 527, 552
Card Catalog, 552, 577
Card. See Business Card
Career, 49, 156, 748
Career Change, 149
Career Development File, 191
Career Ladders, 29, 35, 156, 159, 176, 178, 203, 688, 833
Career Objective, 142, 147
Carrollton, 770
Carson City, 91
CARTWHEEL, 544, 833

Case, 314, 329, 353, 445, 446, 491, 833
Case Advocate, 96
Case Analysis, 93, 353
Case Clerk, 26, 204, 688, 833
Case Files, 86, 254
Case Finder, 504
Case Law, 491, 587
Case Manager, 30, 35, 203, 834
Case Note, 567, 578, 834
Casebook, 495, 833
Caseload, 123, 129
Caseworker, 720
Cash Flow, 691, 705, 706
Cash Receipts, 702
Casinos, 92
Casper, 771
Categories of Law, 329, 485
Cause, Challenge for, 442
Cause of Action, 349, 437, 445, 469, 834
Cause, Probable, 451, 457
CCH. See Commerce Clearing House
CD-ROM, 495, 579, 581, 587, 834
Cedar Rapids, 767
Cell, 672, 673, 834
Censure, 268, 834, 848
Central Coast, 766
Central Valley, 766
Century City, 60, 110
Century Digest, 495, 498, 555, 557
Certificated, 210, 834
Certification, 52, 84, 199, 210, 216, 228, 243, 247, 251, 748, 834
Certification Examination, 199
Certification, Specialty, 247
Certification, Voluntary, 244, 251
Certified, 210, 795, 808, 834
Certified Closing Officer, 27, 233
Certified Domestic Violence Officer, 214
Certified Florida Legal Assistant, 250
Certified Legal Assistant, 26, 245, 250, 303, 305, 315, 699, 797, 811, 834
Certified Legal Assistant Specialist, 248
Certified Mail, 709
Certified PLS, 199, 834
Certified Public Accountant, 223
Certifying Board, 244
Certiorari, Writ of, 449

CFLA, 250, 834
CFR Index and Finding Aids, 596, 603
CFR Parts Affected, 574, 604
CFR. See Code of Federal Regulations
Chain of Command, 411, 722, 725
Chain of Title, 123
Challenge, 23, 53, 126, 134, 180
Challenge for Cause, 442, 834
Challenge, Peremptory, 442
Change, 182
Change, Career, 149
Changing Jobs, 748, 793, 795, 799, 802, 804, 807, 808
Chapter 11 Bankruptcy, 126
Character (Word Processing), 653, 834
Character, Moral, 233
Characteristics of Attorneys. See Attorney Attitudes and Traits
Charge to Jury, 349, 446, 455, 458, 834
Chargeable Hour Schedule, 706, 707, 834
Charity, 123
Charlatan, 211
Charleston, 77, 81, 95, 770, 771, 776
Charlotte, 75, 769
Charter, 329, 349, 489, 532, 604, 834
Chattanooga, 770
Check. See Conflicts Check; Cite Checking
Checklists, 10, 17, 156, 197, 202, 245, 311, 368, 380, 482, 503, 551, 562
Cheyenne, 96, 776
Chicago, 67, 81, 309, 712, 748, 767, 774, 797, 824
Chicago Manual of Legal Citation, 539
Chief Executive, 336, 337
Chief Justice, 23, 38
Child Advocate, 96
Child Custody, 110, 113
Child Support Enforcement, 85
Chinese Wall, 288, 791, 793, 799, 800, 834
Choice of Venue, 437
Christiansted, 776
Chronological Resume, 144, 147
Chronological Sequence, 740
Cincinnati, 24, 75, 748, 769, 775
Circuit Court, 331

Circuit, Federal, 332
Circumlocution, 631
Circumstantial Evidence, 421, 834
Citation, 117, 355, 472, 496, 510, 524, 539, 658, 834
Citation of Administrative Regulations, 534
Citation of Cases, 525
Citation of Legislative History, 536
Citation of Secondary Authority, 537
Citation of Statutes, 532
Citations List, 660
Citator, 496, 510, 834
Cite. See Citation
Cite Checking, 30, 42, 85, 102, 111, 117, 119, 473, 539, 541, 748, 834
Cited Material, 510, 565, 834
CiteRite, 541
Cities, 34
Citing Material, 510, 559, 565, 834
City Council, 328, 337, 358
City Court, 331
City Government, 83, 327, 604
Civil Aeronautics Board, 782
Civil Case, 219, 247, 256, 298, 435, 446, 454, 834
Civil Commitment, 748
Civil Procedure, 93, 116
Civil Rights, 42, 81, 82, 104, 117, 201, 824
Civil Servant, 722
Civil Service, 34, 48, 83, 84
CJS. See Corpus Juris Secundum
CLA. See Certified Legal Assistant
Claim, 105, 114, 121, 129, 258, 438, 439
Claim Adjusting, 126, 212, 239, 795, 804
Claims Coordinator, 173
Claims Court Digest, 499
Claims Court. See Small Claims Court; United States Claims Court
Claims Examiner, 83, 173
Claims Made Policy, 259, 834
Clark County, 768, 813
CLAS, 244, 248, 834, 849
Class Action, 119, 695, 825
Classifications, Job, 83, 84
Classified Pages, 135
CLE. See Continuing Legal Education
Clear and Convincing, 446

Clergy and Penitent Privilege, 426, 834
Circumstantial Evidence, 421, 834
Clerical Position, 30, 31, 41, 42, 45, 85, 86, 95, 137, 148, 194, 825
Clerical Skills, 686
Clerk, 26, 30, 35, 82, 86, 116, 121, 138, 172, 203, 204, 217, 306, 436, 444, 690
Clerk, Law (America), 30, 57, 87, 215, 280
Clerk, Law (Canada), 50
Cleveland, 75, 129, 199, 769, 775, 805
CLI. See Current Law Index
Client Accounts, 276
Client and Attorney Privilege. See Attorney Client Privilege
Client Bill, 703
Client Confidence, 314, 379, 383
Client Consent, 280, 286, 302
Client Contact, 126, 129, 157, 159, 176, 187, 269, 806, 809
Client Counseling, 298
Client Crime, 275
Client Desires and Expectations, 376, 391
Client Fees. See Attorney Fees; Paralegal Fees
Client Funds, 268, 276
Client Guarantees, 396
Client Interview, Initial, 365
Client Ledger, 697
Client List, 292
Clinic, Legal, 59
Closed Cases, 128, 254, 696, 712, 817
Closed Ended Assignment, 402
Closed Ended Questions, 153, 389, 834
Closing, 27, 36, 103, 107, 112, 121, 123, 230, 233, 316, 322, 834
Closing Argument, 129, 445
Code, 2, 210, 298, 490, 496, 834
Code of Ethics, 281, 314, 835
Code of Federal Regulations, 496, 502, 503, 512, 516, 534, 536, 559, 574, 603, 604
Code of Professional Conduct, 231, 254, 266, 314
Code Violations, 119
Code Words (Computers), 655
Codefendant, 109, 437, 439, 835
Codification, 597
Codified, 496, 571, 835

Codify, 496, 835
Collection, Data, 106, 110
Collection, Judgment, 416
Collection Work, 89, 103, 105, 691, 706, 748, 792, 796, 809
Collections Committee, 687
Collections Manager, 690
Colonial America, 44
Color Coded Files, 711
Colorado, 34, 63, 85, 109, 110, 247, 494, 502, 535, 614, 748, 766, 773, 793, 812, 823
Columbia, 78, 94, 748, 770, 776
Columbus, 76, 240, 748, 769, 775, 805, 811
Command, 644, 835
Commerce Clearing House, 492, 576, 585
Commercial Databases, 680
Commercial Law, 103, 105, 233, 247, 748
Commercial Real Estate, 117, 124
Commingling, 276, 835
Commitment, 186
Committee on Legal Assistants. See American Bar Association
Committee Report, 339, 515, 536, 550
Common Law, 358, 587, 835
Common Pleas, 331
Common Representation, 285, 845
Common Sense, 374, 722, 726
Commonwealth, 530
Communication, 108, 112, 126, 127, 148, 180, 212, 214, 245, 377, 748, 835
Communication, Client, 269
Communication, Nonverbal, 391
Communication with Judges, 218
Communication with Opponent, 294
Communications Law, 105, 777
Communications, Privileged, 281, 312, 314, 326
Communications Software, 651, 679
Community Courts, 748
Community Law Specialist, 96
Community Legal Education, 254
Compatible, 649, 835
Compensation. See Paralegal Salary; Unemployment Compensation
Competence, 4, 173, 184, 244, 248, 251, 267, 268, 311, 314, 835

Competence of Witnesses, 422, 443
Competencies, 748
Competition, 57, 116, 162, 164, 176, 189, 212, 230, 239
Complaint, 18, 102, 151, 167, 349, 409, 437, 440, 449, 454, 465, 466, 468, 835
Complaint Analyst, 88
Complaints Against Attorneys, 269
Complexity, 231, 268, 270
Compliance, 95, 102, 109, 110, 129, 447
Compliance Officer, 172
Compliance Specialist, 115
Compromise, 190, 340, 451, 722, 727
Comptroller, 690, 782
Computer, 36, 63, 99, 108, 112, 114, 117, 118, 119, 125, 159, 194, 290, 460, 480, 541, 585, 639, 643, 646, 671, 697, 699, 748, 816
Computer Assisted Legal Research, 480, 585, 658, 835
Computer Based Records Management, 712
Computer Conflicts Clerk. See Conflicts Check
Computer Consultant, 641, 690
Computer Timekeeping, 699
Conclusion of Law, 469
Concord, 72, 91, 775
Concurrent Jurisdiction, 331, 835
Concurring Opinion, 357, 449, 835
Condemnation, 124
Condominium, 123
Cone of Silence, 289
Conference, Bench, 443
Conference Committee, 339, 835
Conference, Pretrial, 216, 441
Confidence, 120, 187, 189, 379, 383, 806
Confidentiality, 113, 134, 150, 167, 245, 279, 289, 293, 312, 314, 316, 381, 385, 411, 686, 748, 799, 801, 808, 809, 810, 825, 835
Conflict of Interest, 112, 193, 237, 241, 249, 278, 283, 686, 691, 714, 748, 798, 802, 804, 807, 835
Conflict-of-Interest Coordinator, 27
Conflicts Check, 290, 292, 640, 641, 642, 696, 714, 835

Conflicts Index, 290
Conflicts of Law, 520, 835
Conflicts Specialist, 112, 835
Confrontation, 181, 183, 189, 729, 835
Congress, 46, 110, 222, 225, 327, 496, 504, 515, 536, 829
Congressional Record, 496, 536, 537, 599
Connecticut, 64, 86, 240, 309, 494, 501, 526, 530, 535, 614, 748, 766, 773, 794, 812, 823, 827
Connectors, 664, 835
Consent, 280, 286, 809
Conservatism, Attorney, 145
Conservative Dress, 155
Conservatorship, 232
Consistency, 463
Consolidated Litigation, 530
Constitution, 49, 212, 225, 268, 329, 347, 358, 488, 517, 532, 594, 600, 730, 835. See also United States Constitution
Construction Law, 105
Consultant, 172
Consulting Firms, 58, 99
Consumer Product Safety Commission, 782
Consumers, 87, 98, 102, 108, 230, 232
Contaminated Employee, 289, 835
Contempt, 473
Contention, Element in, 349, 350
Contest, 440, 441, 835
Contingency, 285
Contingent Fee, 270, 696, 701, 798, 835
Continuance, 215
Continuing Legal Education, 51, 132, 159, 195, 198, 231, 644, 748, 836
Contract Attorney, 40, 689, 835
Contract Forms, 106
Contract Negotiation, 117
Contract Paralegal, 27, 99, 835
Contract Specialist, 82
Contractor. See Independent Contractor
Contracts, 106, 110, 114, 115, 122, 123, 198, 213, 246, 255, 285
Contracts Monitor, 91
Control Character, 653, 835
Conversion, 255
Conviction, 268, 271, 452
Cooperation, 187

Coordinates (Computer), 673, 835
Coordination, 30, 89, 104, 121, 127, 693
Coordinator, Claims, 173
Coordinator, Information, 63
Coordinator, Paralegal, 30, 60, 63, 97
Coordinator, Referral, 172
Coordinator, Transaction, 65
Copying, 700, 707, 709
Copyright, 82, 110, 115, 534, 748
Copyroom Clerk, 690
Corporate Counsel, 59, 97, 146, 168, 329, 777, 835
Corporate Law, 34, 45, 58, 97, 106, 109, 125, 139, 143, 146, 232, 246, 247, 272, 290, 329, 640, 720, 748, 798
Corporate Legal Department, 689, 835
Corporate Manager, 173
Corporate Paralegal, 27, 38, 136
Corporate Specialist, 172
Corpus Christi, 770
Corpus Juris Secundum, 496, 504, 522, 538, 550, 582, 596
Correspondence, 42, 92, 113, 157, 304, 305, 316, 793, 798, 800, 804, 805, 806, 807, 808
Corroboration, 413
Costa Mesa, 60
Costs, 38, 41, 42, 158, 232, 691
Council, City, 328, 337, 358
Council of Government, 337, 600
Counsel, 688. See also Attorney; Corporate Counsel; General Counsel
Counsel, Assigned, 450
Counsel, Assistance of, 268
Counsel's Table, 119, 159, 310
Counseling, 298, 691
Counselor, Municipal, 93
Counterclaim, 439, 835
Countries, Foreign, 31, 49, 107, 115
Counts in Complaint, 469
County Clerk, 104
County Commission, 328
County Court, 121, 331
County Government, 83
Court Administrator, 172
Court Appearance, 114, 214, 298, 309, 798, 806
Court Calendar, 85, 448, 505
Court Calls, Answering, 216
Court Clerk, 83, 86, 116, 172, 217,

306, 436, 444, 531
Court Docket, 119, 416
Court Filing, 127, 129, 189
Court Holding, 358
Court Interpreter, 748
Court Martial, 120
Court of Appeals, 332, 335, 355
Court of Common Pleas, 331
Court of First Instance, 331, 835, 840
Court of Inquiry, 120
Court of International Trade, 332
Court of Military Appeals, 492
Court Opinion, 306, 329, 346, 448
Court Opinion as Mandatory Authority, 518
Court Opinion as Persuasive Authority, 520
Court Paralegal, 116
Court Reporter, 121, 810
Court, Representation in, 210, 214, 220, 230, 309
Court Rules. See Rules of Court
Court Ruling, 356, 358
Court Supervision, 265
Court Witness, Paralegal as, 119
Courts, 84, 97, 103, 105, 107, 116, 121, 126, 127, 212, 214, 215, 218, 226, 247, 265, 270, 309, 328, 330, 331, 332, 333, 335, 355, 416, 441, 455, 458, 467, 485, 491, 499, 748
Cover Letter, 142, 149
CPA. See Certified Public Accountant
Creativity, 147, 162, 163, 183
Credentials, 32, 53, 96, 228, 835
Credibility, 404, 416, 422, 443, 835
Credit Bureau, 409, 417
Credit Manager, 690
Credit Union, 787
Creditor, 104, 416, 473
Crime by Attorney, 274
Crime by Client, 275
Criminal Case, 354, 804, 825, 827, 837
Criminal Investigators, 771
Criminal Law, 90, 108, 123, 219, 246, 247, 255, 256, 267, 271, 435, 449, 457, 640, 748
Criminal Law Paralegals, 58, 98
Criminal Record, 807
Criticism, 189, 820
Cross Claim, 439, 836
Cross Examination, 128, 214, 443,

455, 458, 466, 471, 472, 729, 738, 741, 836
Cross Index, 460, 472
Cuba, 50
Cumberland County, 769
Cumulated, Cumulative, 497, 578, 836
Cure, 447, 838
Current Law Index, 505, 550, 578, 579, 588, 595
Curriculum. See Paralegal Education; Paralegal School
Cursor, 653, 836
Custody, 110, 219, 457
Customs, 172, 789
Cuyahoga, 775

■ D

Dade County, 766
Daily Journal, 16
Daily Law Journal, 505
Daily Time Sheet, 694, 697
Daisy Wheel Printer, 650, 836
Dakota, Western, 193. See also North Dakota; South Dakota
Dallas, 78, 81, 126, 180, 308, 460, 748, 770, 776, 808, 813, 814, 824, 830
Damage Calculation, 676
Damages, 217, 257, 328, 436, 438, 447, 465, 470, 471, 622, 701 836
Data, 42, 102, 106, 110, 393, 459, 644, 836
Data Manager, 656, 836
Data Processing, 61, 690
Data Redundancy, 656, 836
Data Retrieval, 459, 656
Database, 108, 112, 313, 585, 641, 656, 677, 836
Database Management, 194, 651, 656
Dayton, 769, 813
Daytona Beach, 767
De Novo, Trial, 458
Deadlines, 102, 108, 126, 176, 180, 197, 267, 300, 470
Debt Instruments, 124
Debtor, 104, 416, 473
Decedents, 111, 437
Deceit, 226
Decennial Digest, 257, 497, 499, 554, 555, 557
Deception, 277, 296

Decision. *See* Administrative Decision

Declaration Against Interest, 425, 836

Declaration, Dying, 425

Declaration of Bodily Feelings, 836

Declaration of Mental State of Mind, 836

Declaration of Present Sense Impression, 836

Declaration, Spontaneous, 425

Declaratory Judgment, 447, 836

Dedicated Word Processor, 652, 836

Dedication, 152

Deeds, 123, 233

Deep Pocket, 256, 836

Deer Park, 769

Defamation, 126

Default Judgment, 116, 216, 439, 470, 836

Default Setting, 653, 836

Defendant Plaintiff Tables, 556

Defender Services, 83, 96

Defense, 349, 439, 836

Defense Attorney, 108

Defense Exhibits, 120

Definitions, 10, 28, 351, 594, 748

Degree, 30, 137, 246, 253, 305, 315

Delaware, 64, 86, 108, 123, 494, 501, 535, 766, 773, 794, 812

Delay, Unwarranted, 269

Delegation, 28, 40, 43, 45, 49, 176, 179, 197, 227, 229, 254, 298, 310, 314, 316, 689, 692, 748, 795, 801, 810

Delegatitis, 310, 836

Demonstrative Evidence Specialist, 173

Demurrer, 438, 836

Dental Occupations, 36, 47

Denturist, 47, 836

Denver, 63, 81, 85, 766, 773, 812

Department of Agriculture, 783

Department of Commerce, 783

Department of Justice, 46, 82, 130, 239, 784

Department of Labor, 253, 254, 784

Department of Social Services, 214

Department of Transportation, 786

Dependability, 186

Depo Summarizer, 26, 460, 836

Deponent, 441, 836

Deposed, 441

Deposition, 42, 84, 102, 119, 309, 349, 404, 409, 428, 441, 454, 748, 794, 798, 803, 805, 806, 836

Deposition Index, 461

Deposition Testimony, Summarize, 471

Depositions, Digesting, 120, 254, 309

Depository Library, 482, 836

Deputy General Counsel, 689

Deregulation, 748

Derogation, 358

Des Moines, 88, 767, 774

Descriptive Word Index, 556, 839

Desktop Computer, 645

Desktop Publishing, 641

Detail, Attention to, 108, 110, 113, 114, 126, 136, 379, 381

Detainer, 219

Detectives, 298

Detention, 219

Detroit, 70, 768, 774, 813

Development File, Career, 191

DIALOG, 585, 587

Diary, 16, 191

Dicta, Dictum, 357

Dictionary. *See* Legal Dictionary

Dictum, 520, 836

Digest (Martindale-Hubbell), 506

Digest by Person, 462, 464, 836

Digest by Subject Matter, 462, 836

Digest Search (Computer), 671

Digesting, 85, 99, 102, 112, 119, 167, 254, 460, 463, 748, 836

Digests (Lawyers Co-op), 553

Digest (West), 257, 355, 490, 602, 497, 503, 553, 588, 836

Dignity, 389

Diploma, 247

Direct Evidence, 421, 837

Direct Examination, 128, 443, 455, 458, 471, 472, 738, 739, 837

Direct Supervisor, 299

Directed Questions, 390

Directed Verdict, 445, 836

Director of Administration, 70

Director of Legal Assistant Services, 30

Directories, Attorney, 135, 139, 152, 305

Directors. *See* Board of Directors

Directory of Corporate Counsel, 168

Directory of Legal Employers, 135, 139

Disability, 125

Disbarment, 222, 268, 299, 806, 837

Disbarred Attorney, 31, 302, 748, 798, 800, 806, 810

Disbursement, 124, 696, 700, 837

Disc, 495

Discharge, Wrongful, 116

Disciplinary Body, 112, 265, 266, 299, 300

Disciplinary Rule, 266, 844

Discipline, 227, 268, 297, 691

Disclaimer, 258

Disclosure, 279, 281, 302, 316, 800, 803

Discount Adjustment, 702, 837

Discoverable, 280, 837

Discovery, 99, 102, 109, 113, 118, 119, 167, 404, 441, 454, 748, 837

Discovery Documents, Digesting, 463

Discretion, 82, 253, 254, 311, 449, 456, 722, 726

Discretionary Statute, 595

Discrimination, 104, 117, 142, 152

Dishonesty, 226

Disinterested, 295, 414, 837

Disk Drive, 645, 649, 837

Diskette, 645, 646, 837

Dismiss, Motion to, 438

Dismissal, 216, 447, 837

Dispute Resolution, 336, 458

Disputes, 345, 435, 452

Disqualification, 193, 288, 291, 797, 800, 802, 804, 806, 807, 808, 809

Dissenting Opinion, 357, 449, 837

District Attorney, 98, 355, 810

District Court, 331, 335, 441, 455, 458, 467

District of Columbia, 64, 86, 119, 124, 130, 240, 241, 264, 272, 332, 494, 501, 535, 614, 642, 748, 766, 773, 794, 812

Diversion, 108, 109, 117, 180, 808

Diversity of Citizenship, 437, 837

Divided Loyalty, 283, 837

Division, Legal Assistant, 250

Divorce, 98, 110, 113, 122, 216, 219, 235, 271, 286, 298, 368, 376, 748, 825

Docket, 89, 119, 355, 416, 448, 528, 531, 621, 837

Docket Clerk, 84

Docket Systems, 691

Doctors, 47, 257, 426, 734, 837
Document Clerk, 26, 204, 690, 837, 843
Document Control, 99, 247, 459, 658
Document Examiners, 771
Document Preparation, 106, 109, 116
Document Production, 42
Documentary Evidence, 735
Documentation, 392, 644, 837
Do-It-Yourself Divorce, 298
Domestic Relations Law, 96, 113
Domestic Violence Officer, Certified, 214
DOS, 647
Dot Matrix Printer, 650, 837
Double Billing, 273
Double Density, 649, 837
Douglas, Justice, 218
Dover, 86
Down Time, 681
Downers Grove, 767
Downtime, 837
DR, 266, 844
Draft, 837
Draft Bill, 701
Drafting, 748, 795. *See also* Legal Writing; Writing
Draw (Partner), 688, 837
Drudgery, 44
Drug Enforcement, 784
Drugs, 279
DS DD, 649
Dual Sided, 649, 837
Due Dates, 16, 191, 311, 464
Due Process of Law, 221, 728
Dues, 158, 240, 242
Duties. *See* Paralegal Functions
DWI. *See* Descriptive Work Index
Dying Declaration, 425, 837

■ E

East Bay, 766
EC, 266, 844
Economic Advice, 309
Economic Self-Interest, 213, 237
Economics, 37, 48, 91, 94, 100, 102, 119, 122, 222, 310, 794
Editing, 88, 111, 173, 254, 653, 713, 837
Edition, 509, 537
Education. *See* Continuing Legal Education; Paralegal

Education
EEOC, 201, 837
Efficiency, 43, 45, 232, 310
Ego, 19, 124, 181, 183, 818
El Paso, 79, 770
Elder Law, 778
Elderly, 123
Election, 122, 823
Electronic Calendar, 643
Elements, 11, 346, 347, 349, 446, 466, 623, 837
Element in Contention, 350, 837
Eligibility, 249, 389
E-Mail, 643
Embezzlement, 255
Emergencies, 45
Eminent Domain, 124
Empathy, 245, 388
Employee Benefits Law, 109
Employee Benefits Manager, 690
Employee Benefits Specialist, 172
Employees, 686, 818
Employment Agency, 138
Employment, Background Research for, 145, 155, 166, 169, 181
Employment Contract, 700
Employment Discrimination, 142
Employment, Finding, 130
Employment Interview, 151
Employment Law, 96, 116, 748
Employment Realities, 175
Employment References, 145
Employment Statistics, 37
Employment Transfer, 290
En Banc, 449, 837
Enacted into Positive Law, 533
Enacted Law, 358, 517, 837
Encodation, 119
Encumbrance, 127
Encyclopedia. *See* Legal Encyclopedia
End Tabs, 472
Energy Law, 777
Energy Regulatory Commission, Federal, 122
Enforcement, 81, 105, 108, 264, 447, 473
Enforcement, Child Support, 85
Enforcement Inspector, 172
Engineering, 105, 124, 239
England, 49, 245, 642, 748, 771, 849
Enrolled Agent, 126, 172, 259, 223, 772, 837
Enrollment, 210, 222, 848
Entertainment Law, 110, 748, 777

Enthusiasm, 124, 149, 156, 192
Entry Level Certification, 837
Entry Level Paralegal, 29, 34, 130, 136, 180, 244, 251
Environmental Law, 83, 110, 748
Environmental Protection, 98, 789
Environmental Specialist, 173
Equal Employment Opportunity, 82, 104, 172, 201
Equipment, 694
Equipment Manager, 690
Equity Partner, 688, 837
Erie, 769
ERISA, 109, 126, 748
Error, Prejudicial, 447
Error, Procedural, 447
Errors and Omissions, 233, 257
Errors Below, 448
Errors of Law, 332, 448
Escrow, 107, 123, 125
Estate Administration, 112, 172
Estate Planning, 794, 805
Estates, 36, 83, 111, 125, 267, 232, 246, 247, 309, 331, 437, 748, 837
Estates and Trusts, 97, 642
Et al, 530, 838
Et seq, 573, 838
Ethical Competence, 267
Ethical Consideration (EC), 266, 838
Ethical Hearing, 267, 300
Ethical Liability, 298
Ethical Rules, 267, 311
Ethical Wall, 289, 838
Ethics, 112, 210, 226, 245, 263, 281, 298, 314, 748, 791, 838
Evaluation of Paralegal, 19, 35, 157, 159, 162, 165, 184, 185, 191, 197, 269, 300, 311, 382, 748
Evansville, 767
Evening Paralegals, 74
Evidence, 247, 277, 280, 404, 409, 411, 413, 415, 421, 423, 427, 441, 442, 444, 446, 455, 457, 730, 838
Evidence Specialist, 173
Evidence Technician, 173
Examination and Testing, 49, 210, 223, 228, 231, 245, 248, 748
Examination, Cross, 128, 443, 455, 458, 466, 471, 472
Examination, Direct, 128, 443, 455, 458, 471, 472
Examiner, 82, 95, 172, 173, 453

Excitement, 107, 110, 124, 192

Exclusive Jurisdiction, 331, 838

Excuse, 443

Execution of Judgment, 105, 447, 473, 838

Execution of Will, 309, 794, 803

Executive Assistant, 83

Executive Branch, 327, 334, 336, 337, 601, 838

Executive Department Agencies, 336, 838

Executive Director, 70

Executive Employee, 253

Executive, Legal, 49, 245

Executive Order, 329, 334, 456, 489, 502, 602, 838

Executive Secretary, 96

Exempt Employee, 94, 253, 838

Exhaust Administrative Remedies, 456, 744, 838

Exhibits, 91, 94, 102, 113, 117, 119, 120, 353, 444, 448, 470, 508, 838

Ex Parte Hearing, 441, 838

Expectations, 181, 397

Expenses, 285, 672, 690

Expenses of Litigation, 285

Experience, 28, 31, 34, 36, 57, 84, 85, 99, 108, 139, 143, 161, 162, 170, 268, 315

Expert Witness, 102, 113, 119, 423, 444, 584, 659, 664

Expertise, 106, 124, 173, 244, 308, 315

External Memorandum of Law, 620, 621, 838

Eyewitness, 413


■ F

F.2d. See Federal Reporter

Facilities Management, 691

Fact Analysis, 85, 406

Fact Comparison, 518

Fact Findings, 453

Fact Gathering, 42, 119, 186, 366

Fact Issue, 438, 441

Fact Particularization, 370, 734, 838

Fact Pleading, 469, 838

Fact Versions, 370, 406

Facts and Findings, 132

Facts, Key, 357, 359

Factual Detail, 379, 381

Factual Dispute, 843

Factual Gaps, 360

Factual Research, 30, 112, 117

Failure to Disclose, 277

Failure to State a Cause of Action, 438

Fair Hearing, 128, 394

Fair Labor Standards Act, 195, 252, 838, 852

Fairbanks, 765

Fairness, 740

False Evidence, 277

False Notarization, 278

Family Law, 110, 113, 230, 271, 748

Family Services, 92

Fargo, 769

Farms, 90

Fax Machine, 281, 640

Fayetteville, 769

Federal Agencies, 222, 327, 334, 781

Federal Cases, 500

Federal Circuit, 332

Federal Communication Commission, 105

Federal Court, 330, 491

Federal Court Rules, 605

Federal Deposit Insurance Corporation, 786

Federal Digest, 498

Federal Energy Regulatory Commission, 122

Federal Government, 327, 748, 780

Federal Government Paralegals, 58, 81

Federal Practice Digest, 498, 499, 554, 605

Federal Question, 330, 838

Federal Register, 502, 516, 534, 536, 574, 603, 604

Federal Regulations, 502, 516

Federal Reporter, 492, 501, 502, 509, 511, 525, 529, 554, 565

Federal Rules Decisions, 492, 502

Federal Rules of Appellate Procedure, 247, 534

Federal Rules of Civil Procedure, 247, 281, 439, 534

Federal Rules of Criminal Procedure, 247, 534

Federal Rules of Evidence, 247, 534

Federal Statute, 512, 532, 598

Federal Supplement, 492, 501, 503, 511, 525, 529, 555

Federal Tort Claims, 121

Federal Trade Commission, 102, 108

Federalism, 327, 838

Federation of Paralegal Associations. See NFPA

Fee Generating, 40, 838

Fee Income, 690

Fee Recoverability, 41

Fee Schedules, Minimum, 237, 239, 270

Fee Shifting, 748

Fee Splitting, 271, 748, 838

Feedback, 14, 18, 151, 192, 382

Fees, 40, 117, 223, 270, 271, 272, 273, 696, 701, 797

Fees, Attorney, 33, 38, 44, 59, 99, 146, 270, 273

Fees, Filing, 115, 285

Fees, Paralegal, 33, 38, 273

Felony, 450, 838

Fiche Reader, 507

Fiduciary, 111, 172, 227

Fiduciary Specialists, 45

Field, 656, 838

Field Investigation, 108, 366

Field Search, 671, 838

File, 646, 656, 838

File Maintenance, 86, 113, 117, 124

File Manager, 107, 690

File Monitoring, 118

File Room Clerk, 690

File System, 712

File Worksheet, 694

Filed, 438, 838

Filing, 86, 105, 119, 127, 129, 180, 707

Filing Fees, 115, 285

Filing Forms, 212

Filing Motions, 216

Filing System, 460, 710, 817

Finance Committee, 687

Finance Companies, 146

Finance Law, Municipal, 121

Financial Advice, 309

Financial Affidavits, 113

Financial Analyst, 172

Financial Calculations, 676

Financial Data, 42, 107

Financial Manager, 690

Financial Planning, 691

Financial Research, 107

Financing, 123

Find Command (Computer), 672

Finding Aids, 596, 603

Finding Employment, 130
Findings of Fact, 453
Fingerprint Technician, 173
Fingerprints, 409
Finland, 50
Firing, 748, 819
First Amendment, 296
First Instance, Court of, 331
Fishing Exhibition, 396
Fitness to Practice Law, 297
Fixed Fee, 40, 696, 701, 838
Flat Fee, 701
Flex Time, 191
Flexibility, 125, 144, 152, 153, 374, 401, 481, 736
FLITE, 121
Floor Debate, 339
Floppy Disk, 645, 838
Floppy Drives, 649
Florence, 770
Florida, 66, 86, 109, 136, 211, 225, 240, 247, 250, 266, 494, 502, 504, 535, 583, 614, 640, 748, 766, 774, 795, 812, 827, 836
Florida Legal Assistant, Certified, 250
FOIA, 83, 411, 412
Follow-Up Letter, 159, 170
Food & Drug Administration, 102
Food Industry, 116
Footnotes, 523, 543
Foreclosure, 104, 122, 124, 748
Foreign Countries, 31, 49, 107, 115
Foreign Law, 506, 581
Form Drafting, 111. See also Legal Writing; Writing
Formal Advocacy, 128, 129, 222, 393, 719, 728
Formal Hearing, 254
Format (Computer), 653
Format, 838
Formbook, 467, 503, 515, 522, 550, 583, 619, 838
Forms, 211, 212, 807
Forms Practitioner, 27
Forms Preparation, 87
Forms, Standard, 119, 202, 214, 466, 467
Formula (Computer), 673
Forum, 437, 838
Forward, 542
Forwarding Fee, 271
Foundation for Evidence, 735
Fours, On All, 359

Franchise, 748
Frankfort, 88, 774
Fraud, 211, 273, 274, 275, 296
Fraud, Consumer, 108
Fraud on Resumes, 142
FRCP, 439, 838
Freedom of Information Act, 603, 838
Freehold, 768
Freelance Paralegals, 27, 58, 99, 172, 228, 259, 292, 312, 320, 799, 802, 815, 824, 839, 843
Fresno, 766
Friend of the Court, 627
Friendly Divorce, 286, 839
Friendly Witness, 414
Fringe Benefits, 36, 42, 158, 176, 191, 800
Frivolous Legal Position, 276
Frustration, 23, 105, 134, 153, 179, 181, 202, 381, 480
F. Supp. See Federal Supplement
Ft. Lauderdale, 66, 766
Ft. Worth, 79, 748, 770
FTC, 247
Full Faith and Credit, 520
Full Text Search, 657, 839
Functional Resume, 148, 839
Functions, 748
Furman, Rosemary, 211, 229, 748

## G

Gainesville, 211
Galveston, 98
Garnishment, 105
Gas and Oil, 122, 248
Gay Rights, 778
GED, 98
General Accounting Office, 787
General Counsel, 81, 97, 689, 837, 839
General Digest, 257, 498, 499, 503, 554, 555, 557
General Expenses, 694
General Jurisdiction, 328, 330, 839
General Ledger Accounting, 691
General Partner, 290
General Practitioner, 686, 839
General Resume, 166
General Schedule (GS), 81, 839
Generalist Paralegal, 96
Geographic Jurisdiction, 839
Georgia, 67, 86, 101, 213, 253, 266, 494, 500, 502, 535, 614, 767, 774, 795, 812

Germany, 50
Gift Tax, 125
Gifts from Client, 285
Global, 839
Glossary, 485, 544, 833
Go Bare, 257, 839
Goals, 4, 153, 188, 723, 818
GOD, 253, 839
Goldsboro, 769
Good Faith, 276
Government Agency Paralegal, 28
Government Benefits, 123
Government, City, 327
Government Contracts, 114
Government, Federal, 327
Government Grant, 97
Government Paralegals, 34, 45, 58, 59, 81, 83, 84, 101, 104, 748, 811
Government Regulation, 210, 228
Government, State, 327
Governor, 83, 337
GPA, 143
Grace Commission, 46
Grades, 143, 153
Grammar, 7, 112, 145, 149, 167, 187, 245, 428
Grammatical Connector, 667
Grand Jury, 451, 457, 839
Grand Rapids, 70
Grandfather Clause, 231
Great Falls, 768
Greensboro, 75, 769
Greenville, 78, 212, 770
Grievance Commission, 265, 267
Gross Profit, 39
Gross Revenue, 694
Ground, 368, 405, 443, 839
Group Interview, 152
Group Legal Services, 98, 839
GS. See General Schedule
Guam, 87, 332
Guarantee, 258, 396
Guardianship, 122, 232
Guidelines, 46, 210, 315, 839
Guilt, 271, 452
Gulfport, 768

## H

Haddonfield, 768
HALT, 232, 771, 839
Handbook, 503, 550, 583, 839
Handicapped People, 123
Harassment, 116, 199, 276, 839
Hard Disk, 645, 839

Hardware, 644, 649, 839

Harrisburg, 93, 769, 776, 813

Hartford, 64, 86, 766, 812

Hawaii, 30, 67, 87, 126, 253, 362, 494, 502, 535, 614, 767, 774, 796, 812

Header, 653, 839

Heading (Memo), 367, 620, 839

Headnote, 355, 495, 503, 554, 556, 567, 588, 671, 839

Health and Human Services, 784

Health Inspector, 172

Health Insurance, 109, 158

Health Law, 96, 98

Hearing, 88, 118, 122, 128, 236, 254, 267, 300, 339, 394, 441, 450, 457, 729, 732, 839

Hearing, Administrative, 101, 122, 310, 453, 454

Hearing Assistant, 93

Hearing Memorandum, 620, 839

Hearing Officer, 82, 453

Hearing Preparation, 84, 111

Hearing Representation, 97, 98, 128

Hearing Strategy, 128

Hearing Transcript, 129, 641

Hearsay, 413, 423, 443, 466, 737, 839

Helena, 91, 775

Hennepin County, 774

High School, 164, 247

Highest Court, 265

Hispanic Attorneys, 265, 777

Historical Note, 590, 839

History, 748. See also Legislative History

Hobbies, 144, 163

Holding, 356, 357, 358, 839

Hollywood, 811

Homemaker, 144, 163

Honesty, 297

Honolulu, 87, 767, 774, 812

Hornbook, 504, 515, 550, 583, 839

Hospital Records, 734

Hospitals, 97, 734, 777

Hostile Environment, 199, 839

Hostile Witness, 414

Hostility, 722, 725, 743

Hour Division, Wage and, 253, 254

Hourly Fee, 696

Hourly Plus Fixed Fee, 701, 839

Hourly Rate, 39, 157, 701, 796, 798

Hourly Time and Rate Chart, 697, 698

House of Representatives, 337, 536, 537, 599, 824

Housing, 96, 109, 123, 232

Houston, 38, 79, 98, 700, 748, 770, 776, 826

How-To-Do-It Manual, 17

HR, 339

Human Relations, 178, 183, 245, 377, 692

Human Resource Management, 67, 691

Human Rights, 104, 117

Huntington, 81

Huntsville, 765, 812

Hybrid Titles, 27

Hypothetical, 14, 839


■ I

IBM, 641, 649, 713

ICC, 223

Id, 839

Idaho, 87, 266, 494, 500, 502, 535, 614, 748, 767, 774, 796, 812

Identification, Issue, 128

Identification, Role, 387

Illegal Practice of Law, 211

Illegal Questions, 152, 154

Illinois, 25, 67, 88, 215, 229, 233, 234, 240, 309, 493, 494, 500, 501, 535, 583, 614, 712, 748, 765, 767, 774, 796, 812, 824

Illinois Decisions, 493

ILP. See Index to Legal Periodicals

Imagination, 82, 108, 163, 401

Immigration, 96, 114, 136, 232, 240, 334, 748, 777, 782

Impaired Attorney, 279, 839

Impanel, 451, 839

Impeach, 120, 404, 452, 839

Implied Legal Advice, 307

Impropriety, Appearance of, 297, 316

Imputed Disqualification, 288, 291

In House Attorney, 842

In Issue, 441, 842

In Personam Jurisdiction, 328, 438, 846

In Re, 531, 842

In House Paralegal, 259

In House Training, 249, 315

In Person Solicitation, 295

Inadvertent Disclosure, 281

Income, 52, 688, 818

Income Statement, 708

Incoming Mail, 707

Incompetence, 234, 267

Incompetent, Mentally, 331

Incorporation, 100, 106, 118, 151, 167

Incremental Spacing, 653, 840

Indemnity Insurance, Professional, 259

Independence, 105, 120, 126, 144, 163, 186

Independent Contractor, 27, 748, 767, 792, 802, 840

Independent Judgment, 82, 253, 254, 272, 286, 316, 804

Independent Paralegal, 27, 28, 58, 99, 130, 172, 179, 228, 230, 259, 292, 312, 320, 748, 772, 804, 805, 815, 840, 843

Independent Regulatory Agencies, 336, 840

Index, 290, 460, 461, 472, 544, 654, 711

Index Medicus, 581

Index to Annotations, 550, 559, 588, 599, 604, 605

Index to Legal Periodicals, 505, 550, 578, 588, 595

Indexing, 84, 105, 111, 113, 118, 119, 167, 459, 657, 840

Indian Reservations, 126, 215

Indiana, 68, 88, 109, 180, 216, 494, 500, 501, 535, 614, 748, 767, 774, 797, 812

Indianapolis, 68, 88, 109, 767, 774, 812

Indians, 772

Indictment, 355, 451, 457, 840

Indigent, 97, 122, 214, 450, 840

Industrial Accident Commission, 226

Infected Employee, 289

Inferior Court, 331, 840

Informal Advocacy, 128, 129, 393, 719, 721, 732

Informal Hearing, 254

Information, 355, 451, 457, 840

Information and Belief, 438, 469, 840

Information Coordinator, 63

Information Services, 691

Information Storage and Retrieval, 691

Informational Interview, 133, 840

Infra, 541, 840
Infringement, 115
Inheritance, 416
Initial Appearance, 450, 457, 840
Initial Client Interview, 365
Initiative, 124, 132, 144, 151, 155, 162, 185, 187, 192, 270, 393
Injunction, 113
Injury, Personal, 102, 126, 296, 465
Ink Jet Printer, 650, 840
Inland County, 766
Inmates. *See* Prison; Jailhouse Lawyer
Innovation, 249
Insertion, 840
Insider Trading, 274, 825
Insta-Cite, 496, 585, 661
Institute of Legal Executives, 245
Instructions from Supervisor, 15, 197, 368, 463, 466
Instructions Notebook, 16
Instructions to Jury, 349, 446, 455, 458, 471
Instructions to Secretaries, 199
Instrument, 82, 619, 840
Instruments, Debt, 124
Insurance, 109, 111, 112, 129, 158, 176, 255, 257, 290, 429, 642, 819
Insurance Agents, 792
Insurance Certificate, 124
Insurance Claims Adjusters, 748
Insurance Companies, 34, 58, 97, 258, 290, 804
Insurance Defense Litigation, 748
Insurance, Errors and Omissions, 233
Insurance Law, 115
Insurance, Prepaid Legal, 235
Insurance, Professional Indemnity, 259
Insurance, Title, 123, 213
Insured, 259
Intake Memorandum, 151, 167, 366, 466, 840
Integrated Bar Association, 265, 842
Integrated Package, 680, 840
Integrity, 142, 274, 314, 316, 416
Intellectual Property, 110, 115, 232, 748, 840
Intelligence, 144, 163
Intent, 601
Intentional Tort, 255
Interest Groups, 58

Interim Suspension, 268, 840
Interlocutory Appeal, 454, 457, 840
Intermediate Appeals Court, 333, 519, 840
Internal Memorandum of Law, 620, 840
Internal Revenue, 83, 124, 223, 225, 787
Internal Revenue Code, 534
International Law, 27, 103, 116, 329, 332, 506, 581, 606
Internship, 143, 164, 748
Interoffice Memorandum, 429, 620, 621, 624, 842
Interpretation of Law, 90
Interrogatories, 42, 85, 93, 102, 112, 119, 151, 167, 404, 409, 428, 441, 454, 464, 466, 748, 840
Interstate Commerce Commission, 223, 225, 787
Interstate Compact, 504, 840
Interview, Job, 151, 153, 169, 311
Interviewing, 42, 84, 95, 101, 109, 119, 127, 129, 151, 220, 221, 245, 254, 316, 349, 365, 402, 411, 795
Intra Agency Appeal, 454, 840
Introduce Evidence, 442, 741
Inventions, 115
Inventory, 124, 691
Investigation, 27, 42, 45, 82, 83, 84, 91, 93, 101, 108, 116, 118, 127, 128, 172, 186, 221, 272, 298, 316, 349, 365, 393, 401, 466, 623, 734, 748, 806
Investigator, 771, 791
Investigator Paralegal, 802
Investigator's License, 420
Investment Analysis, 111
Invoice, 702
Iowa, 88, 247, 302, 303, 305, 494, 501, 535, 748, 767, 774, 797, 813, 822
Irish Attorneys, 777
Irrebuttable Presumption, 802
Irrelevant, 466
IRS, 124, 223
Issue, 121, 222, 350, 357, 441, 732, 843
Issue Control, 736
Issue Identification, 128, 349
Issue Statement, 350
Issues on Appeal, 448
Italics, 530, 537

■ **J**

Jackson, 71, 90, 768, 775
Jacksonville, 109, 211, 640
Jail. *See* Prison
Jailhouse Lawyer, 28, 49, 218, 749, 840
Japan, 50, 116
Jargon, 382, 394, 840
Jefferson City, 90, 775
Jenkins, Missouri v., 42
Job Bank, 132, 840
Job Classifications, 84
Job Definitions, 28, 749
Job Discrimination, 142
Job Functions. *See* Paralegal Functions
Job Hunting, 749
Job Hunting Notebook, 160
Job Interview, 133, 151, 153, 169, 311, 749
Job Market, 57, 132
Job Realities, 175
Job Satisfaction, 121, 124, 176, 180, 749
Job Search, 130, 283
Job Switching, 120, 362
Job Title, 26, 381
Johnson v. Avery, 218
Joint and Several Liability, 436, 840
Jones Act, 101
Journal, Bar, 141
Judges, 83, 218, 444, 448, 453, 459, 749
Judge Advocate, 121
Judge Search (Computer), 671
Judgment, 105, 116, 216, 246, 253, 256, 311, 439, 440, 441, 447, 455, 458, 470, 473, 840
Judgment Collection, 416
Judgment Creditor, 416, 473, 840
Judgment Debtor, 416, 473, 840
Judgment, Independent, 82, 253, 254, 272, 286, 316
Judgment nov, 447, 840
Judgment on the Merits, 447, 841
Judgment, Professional, 32, 202, 286, 306, 314
Judicare, 97, 841
Judicial Administration, 116
Judicial Branch, 265, 327, 601, 841
Judicial History, 355, 358
Judicial Systems, 519
Judiciary, 226

Juneau, 84, 765
Junior Legal Assistant, 26
Junior Partner, 688
Jurisdiction, 127, 307, 328, 330, 331, 438, 447, 467, 841
Jurisprudence, 504
Jury, 119, 212, 438, 451, 452, 457
Jury, Charge to, 349, 446
Jury, Grand, 451, 457
Jury Instructions, 349, 446, 471, 836
Jury Panel, 442
Justice, 314
Justice of the Peace, 122, 214, 331
Justification (Margins), 653, 841
Juvenile Court, 331

■ **K**

K, 646, 841
Kansas, 88, 247, 493, 494, 502, 535, 564, 571, 614, 749, 767, 774, 798, 813
Kansas City, 42, 71, 81, 749, 767, 768, 775, 813
Kardex, 504, 553, 564, 841
Kentucky, 68, 88, 215, 266, 296, 494, 502, 535, 583, 614, 749, 767, 774, 798, 813, 824
Kern County, 766
Key Facts, 357, 359, 518, 841
Key Topic and Number, 355, 497, 503, 554, 556, 588
Key Word Search, 656, 841
Keystone, 769
KF Call Number, 552, 583
Kinds of Law, 329, 551
Kinds of Law Books, 486
King County, 776
Kits, 298

■ **L**

Label (Computer), 673, 841
Labor Department, 37, 109, 253, 254
Labor Law, 116
Labor Relations, 82, 332
Ladder, Career, 29, 35, 156, 159, 176, 178, 203
Lafayette, 767
Lake Charles, 767
Lake Oswego, 775
L.A. Law, 3, 33

LAMA, 25, 29, 34, 53, 190, 203, 747, 749, 772
Lancaster, 769
Land Law Examiner, 82
Land Technician, 122, 843
Land Titles, 94
Land Use, 111
Landlord and Tenant, 96, 117, 123, 214, 230, 248
Landmen, 122, 841
Language, 646, 841
Lansing, 90, 768, 774
Laptop, 646, 841
Las Vegas, 72, 768
Laser Printer, 651, 841
Later Case Service, 560
Lateral Hire, 290, 688, 841
Law Assistant, 26
Law Books, 220, 486, 541
Law Clerk, 30, 50, 87, 215, 688, 749, 771, 841
Law Degree, 30
Law Department, 139, 146, 689
Law Directory, 139, 146, 152, 168, 305, 841
Law Firm, 34, 52, 58, 59, 139, 506
Law Firm as a Corporation, 272
Law Firm Bill, 256
Law Firm Committees and Departments, 686
Law Firm Disqualification, 288
Law Firm Newsletter, 146
Law Firm Stationery, 303
Law Journal, 505, 550, 578, 843
Law Librarian, 58, 100, 111, 117, 172, 690, 749
Law Library, 2, 27, 45, 86, 125, 128, 146, 197, 221, 246, 267, 312, 477, 482, 552, 577, 598, 687, 691, 694, 749, 771
Law Library Assistant, 86, 136, 690
Law List, 305
Law Office Administration, 52, 58, 118, 685
Law Office Administrator. *See* Legal Administrator
Law Placement, National Association of, 135, 139
Law Professors, 584
Law Review, 505, 524, 550, 578, 841
Law Review Articles, 537
Law Review Comments, 537
Law Review Notes, 537

Law Revision Commission, 337, 598
Law School, 23, 40, 53, 90, 135, 158, 168, 203, 268, 749, 807
Law Student, 218, 220, 805
Law-Related Activities, 212, 315
Lawyer. *See* Attorney
Lawyer's Assistant, 26, 301
Lawyer's Co-op, 487, 514, 532, 558
Lawyer's Edition, 491, 498, 501, 516, 529, 561
Lay Advocacy, 214
Lay Opinion Evidence, 423, 841
Lay Practice, 223
Lay Representation, 394
Leading Question, 395, 407, 841
Learning, 1
Leases, 104, 117, 122, 127, 691
L.Ed. *See* Lawyer's Edition
Ledger Cards, 697
Legal Administrator, 52, 60, 131, 133, 142, 157, 169, 172, 687, 690, 691, 841
Legal Advice, 32, 114, 210, 229, 264, 270, 295, 298, 304, 306, 316, 329, 394, 749, 794, 796, 801, 806, 808, 847
Legal Advice, Implied, 307
Legal Aid, 34, 58, 83, 96, 117, 123, 249, 778
Legal Aide, 91, 93
Legal Analysis, 2, 83, 93, 267, 345, 368, 841
Legal Argument, 345
Legal Assistant, 26, 203, 301, 841. *See also* Paralegal
Legal Assistant Associate, 242
Legal Assistant Clerk, 30, 35, 203, 841
Legal Assistant Committee. *See* American Bar Association
Legal Assistant Day, 821
Legal Assistant Division, 240, 250, 841
Legal Assistant Manager, 30, 35, 203, 692, 841
Legal Assistants Management Association. *See* LAMA
Legal Authority, 355
Legal Bias, 729, 736, 742, 841
Legal Bibliography. *See* Bibliography
Legal Clerk, 82, 121
Legal Clinic, 59

Legal Degree, 797
Legal Dictionary, 504, 522, 550
Legal Directory, West's, 139, 141, 146
Legal Dispute, 345
Legal Education, 1, 51, 165, 254, 479. *See also* Continuing Legal Education; Paralegal Education
Legal Encyclopedia, 487, 496, 504, 522, 538, 550, 582, 596
Legal Ethics, 313
Legal Examiner, 95
Legal Executive, 49, 245, 749, 771, 841
Legal Experience, 143, 161
Legal Insurance, 98, 235
Legal Interviewing. *See* Interviewing
Legal Investigation. *See* Investigation
Legal Issue, 121, 222, 350, 357, 622, 630, 841
Legal Judgment, 314, 316, 808
Legal Malpractice, 123, 255, 257, 268, 274, 280, 290, 310, 480, 749, 808, 844
Legal Memorandum. *See* Memorandum
Legal Newspaper, 135, 169, 505, 522
Legal Opinion, 124, 316
Legal Paraprofessional, 26
Legal Periodical, 505, 522, 550, 570, 578, 588, 595
Legal Profession, 213, 218, 315
Legal Research, 9, 17, 84, 101, 118, 119, 167, 246, 267, 312, 366, 467, 472, 477, 734, 749, 792
Legal Resource Index, 505, 550, 578, 581, 588, 595
Legal Secretaries, National Association of, 199
Legal Secretary, 18, 27, 31, 38, 57, 87, 111, 133, 134, 137, 157, 159, 169, 197, 198, 199, 211, 244, 259, 280, 298, 299, 308, 311, 362, 686, 747, 772, 791, 836. *See also* Secretary
Legal Service Assistant, 26
Legal Service Office, 34, 58, 83, 96, 117, 123, 128, 170, 214, 235, 389
Legal Support Personnel, 97

Legal System, 126, 246, 327
Legal Technician, 26, 27, 28, 58, 82, 90, 99, 228, 230, 259, 841
Legal Thesaurus, 504, 505
Legal Treatise, 405, 504, 515, 522, 537, 550, 583, 589, 595, 851
Legal Typist, 27
Legal Writing, 619, 749. *See also* Writing
Legalman, 120, 841
LegalTrac, 581
Legislation, 85, 111, 180, 506, 590, 841
Legislation, Monitoring, 92, 96, 98, 118, 235
Legislation, Quasi, 336
Legislative Advocate, 96
Legislative Aide, 136
Legislative Assistant, 137, 172
Legislative Branch, 265, 327, 601, 841
Legislative Committee, 236, 339
Legislative Hearing, 118, 236, 339, 537, 599
Legislative History, 85, 118, 337, 346, 473, 496, 513, 536, 596, 841
Legislative Intent, 597
Legislative Service, 597
Legislature, 81, 137, 225, 233, 235, 265, 334, 337, 339, 358, 542
Lender, 103, 123
Letter, Cover, 142, 149
Letter, Follow-Up, 159
Letterhead, 159, 194, 303, 321, 323, 792, 793, 795, 796, 798, 799, 801, 803, 804, 805, 806, 807, 808, 809, 810, 842
Letters, 202, 305, 619, 628
Leverage, 38, 749, 842
Lexington, 68, 767
LEXIS, 139, 313, 488, 506, 528, 541, 559, 570, 579, 581, 585, 656, 658, 659, 665, 679, 842
LEXIS Queries, 668
Lexsee, 672
Lexstat, 672
Liabilities and Assets, 111, 398
Liability, 126, 140, 232, 255, 258, 298, 313, 429, 436, 449, 622
Liable, 436, 842
Liaison, 108, 114
Library. *See* Law Library
Library of Congress, 552, 598

License, Investigator's, 420
License, Paralegal, 228, 310, 420
License, Specialty, 210, 230
Licensed Independent Paralegal, 230, 842
Licensed Practice Officer, 233
Licensing, 96, 228, 244, 749. *See also* Limited License
Licensing, Broad-Based, 228
Licensure, 210, 228, 842
Liens, 123, 248, 416
Life Experiences, 162
Life Insurance, 109, 112, 158, 777
Life Insurance Agents, 212
Limited Jurisdiction, 328, 842
Limited License, 27, 53, 99, 210, 228, 229, 259, 842
Limited Partnership, 247
Limited Practice Officer, 27, 842
Lincoln, Abraham, 44
Lincoln, NE, 91, 775
List of Sections Affected, 604, 607
Lists, 348
Litigation, 118, 120, 122, 138, 232, 246, 247, 285, 425, 435, 454, 457, 460, 642, 749, 842
Litigation, Asbestos, 126, 292
Litigation Assistant, 27
Litigation Coordinator, 69
Litigation Costs, 42
Litigation Manager, 61
Litigation Paralegal, 102, 118, 180, 810, 827
Litigation Support, 641, 691
Litigation Tasks, 118, 459
Little Rock, 85, 765, 773
Load, 644, 647, 842
Loan Administrator, 172
Loan Department, 103
Loans, 123
Lobbying, 98, 118, 172, 600, 794
Local Bar Associations, 265, 773
Local Government, 327
Local Government Paralegals, 58
Local Law, 604
Lodestar, 701, 842
London, 642
Long Island, 768
Longview, 770
Loose-Leaf Service, 111, 117, 125, 137, 506, 522, 528, 576, 589, 595, 603, 842
Los Angeles, 61, 119, 150, 184, 292, 766, 771, 773, 793, 812
Louisiana, 69, 89, 102, 116, 240,

247, 266, 494, 502, 535, 614,
    767, 774, 798, 813, 821, 826
Louisville, 68, 767, 774
Loyalty, 144, 283, 286, 315
LPO, 233
LRI. *See* Legal Resource Index
LSA. *See* List of Sections Affected
Lubbock, 770
Luck, 170
Lump Sum Fee, 798
Lying, 142

# ▪ M

Madison, 96, 776
Madisonville, 770
Magistrate, 122, 441, 842
Magistrate Court, 214
Mail, 111, 707, 709
Mail Clerks, 690
Maine, 69, 89, 126, 196, 494, 501,
    535, 614, 749, 767, 774, 799,
    811, 813
Maintenance, File, 86, 113, 117
Majority Opinion, 357, 448, 842
Majority Rule, 521
Male Paralegal, 749
Mall, Shopping, 117
Malpractice. *See* Legal Malpractice
Malpractice, Medical, 120, 126,
    138, 459
Management and Managers, 5, 30,
    35, 41, 45, 46, 52, 53, 66, 67,
    106, 107, 115, 118, 173, 203,
    253, 685, 713, 749
Management Committee, 146, 156
Manager, Legal Assistant, 30, 35,
    60, 94, 118, 203
Managing Clerk, 138
Managing Partner, 156, 689
Manchester, 72, 768
Mandate, 449, 842
Mandatory Authority, 517, 549,
    842
Mandatory Bar Association, 265,
    842
Mandatory Statute, 595
Manhattan, 108, 116, 275, 769
Manual, 10, 17, 159, 177, 191,
    202, 311, 353, 522
Manufacturers, 97
Mariana Islands, 334
Marin, 766
Marital Communications, 426, 842
Marital Status, 142, 152, 154
Maritime Law, 101, 777, 786

Market Rate, 41, 43, 273, 842
Marketing, 115, 172, 692, 772
Marketing Director, 690
Marketplace, 33, 249
Maroon Book, 539
Marriage Records, 118
Martindale Hubbell, 139, 140,
    146, 152, 168, 506, 551, 585,
    695, 842
Maryland, 69, 89, 133, 214, 274,
    494, 501, 531, 535, 583, 614,
    642, 749, 767, 774, 799, 811,
    813
Massachusetts, 44, 69, 90, 136,
    240, 274, 494, 501, 531, 535,
    566, 568, 614, 768, 774, 799,
    813
Master Ledger Card, 697, 698
Math, 162
Matrimonial Attorneys, 777
Matthew Bender, 576
Maturity, 144
Mayor, 83
Mead Data Central, 587, 658
Med Arb, 459, 842
Media Advertising, 296
Media Portrayal of Law, 3
Media Portrayal of Paralegals, 33,
    211, 749
Mediation, 82, 173, 459, 749, 788,
    842
Medical Care, 123
Medical Examination, 404
Medical Insurance, 158
Medical Literature, 126
Medical Malpractice, 120, 126,
    138, 459, 749
Medical Occupations, 36, 47
Medical Practitioner, 465
Medical Profession, 32, 47
Medical Records, 118, 119, 126,
    129, 749
Medicare, 125, 127
MEDLINE, 581, 587
Megabyte, 64
Megafirm, 179
Membership in Bar Association,
    Associate, 25, 194, 241
Memorandum, 85, 110, 113, 119,
    122, 150, 167, 347, 453, 620,
    624, 842
Memorandum, Intake, 151, 167,
    366, 466
Memorandum Opinion, 355, 842
Memorandum, Pre-Evaluation, 187
Memorandum, Trial, 470

Memory, 13, 647, 649, 842
Memphis, 770, 814
Menial Tasks, 180, 253
Mental Condition of Attorney, 278
Mental Health, 97, 101
Mental State of Mind, 426
Mentally Incompetent, 331
Menu, 842
Merge Printing, 654, 842
Merged Work Product, 309, 316
Merger, 107, 110, 290
Merit System, 90
Merits, Judgment on, 447
Mesa, 765
Messengers, 29, 690
Metrolina, 769
Mexican Americans, 98, 777
Miami, 66, 774
Michigan, 70, 90, 228, 240, 266,
    304, 494, 501, 504, 535, 583,
    614, 749, 768, 774, 800, 813
Microcomputer, 647, 842
Microfiche, 842
Microfilm, 507, 581, 842
Microform, 506, 842
Microsoft Word, 641
Microspacing, 842
Middle Appeals, 355, 519
Middle Class, 59, 220, 235
Middlebury, 770
Midland, 770, 811
Military Appeals, Court of, 492
Military Justice Digest, 499
Military Justice Reporter, 492
Military Law, 120, 749
Milwaukee, 81, 771, 776, 814
Mine Safety, 786
Mini-Lawyers, 231
Minimum Fee Schedules, 237, 239,
    270, 842
Ministerial Tasks, 793, 795, 803
Minneapolis, 71, 642, 768, 774,
    813
Minnesota, 71, 90, 132, 200, 494,
    501, 514, 528, 535, 614, 642,
    749, 768, 774, 800, 813, 827
Minority Attorneys, 139
Minutes, Taking, 123
Misconduct, Reporting
    Professional, 297
Misdemeanor, 450, 842
Misrepresentation, 264, 275, 301
Missing Persons, 416
Mississippi, 71, 90, 120, 126, 266,
    494, 502, 535, 615, 768, 775,
    800, 813

Missouri, 42, 71, 90, 240, 266, 282, 494, 502, 535, 615, 749, 768, 775, 800, 813
Missouri v. Jenkins, 42
Mistakes, 18, 197, 256, 269, 311, 825
Mitigation, 299, 301
Mobile, 765
Model Code of Professional Responsibility, 266, 298, 312, 842
Model Penal Code, 247
Model Rule 5.3, 294, 299, 312
Model Rules of Professional Conduct, 266, 298, 842
Model Standards and Guidelines, 315, 843
Models, 17, 463
Modem, 541, 651, 679, 843
Modern Federal Practice Digest, 498, 499
Modesto, 766
Monitor (Computer), 647, 650, 843
Monitor, Contracts, 91
Monitor Documents, 124
Monitoring, 30, 92, 96, 98, 101, 107, 109, 110, 111, 115, 118, 127, 129, 235, 311, 316, 472, 693, 794
Monitoring Legislation, 92, 96, 235, 599, 843
Monopoly, 48, 210, 213, 237, 749
Montana, 91, 266, 494, 502, 535, 615, 768, 775, 801, 812, 813
Montgomery, 84, 773
Montpelier, 95, 776
Montreal, 771
Moral Character, 233
Moral Judgment, 126
Morristown, 72
Mortgage, 36, 103, 123, 124, 233, 749
Motion for Directed Verdict, 445
Motion for New Trial, 447
Motion for Summary Judgment, 441
Motion Pictures, 110
Motion to Dismiss, 438
Motions, 113, 120, 167, 215, 217, 439, 455
Motions, Filing, 216
Motivation, 110, 114, 124, 147, 192, 207, 691, 749
Mouse, 647, 843
Movant, 439, 843

Move, 439
Move into Evidence, 444
Multi-Party Litigation, 120
Multiple Representation, 285, 843
Multitasking, 647, 843
Multnomah, 775
Municipal Counselor, 93
Municipal Court, 333
Municipal Finance Law, 121
Municipality, 329
Murphy's Law, 830
Music, 110

# ■ N

NAACP, 778
NALA, 24, 28, 34, 42, 47, 52, 132, 190, 199, 231, 236, 238, 241, 243, 250, 252, 281, 305, 313, 747, 749, 765, 797, 836, 837, 843, 849
NALS, 199, 772, 791
Nashville, 78, 94, 770, 776
Nassau County, 803
National Association of Law Placement, 135, 139
National Association of Legal Assistants. See NALA
National Association of Legal Secretaries, 199, 772, 791
National Bar Associations, 265
National Capital Area, 766. See also District of Columbia
National Digest, 498
National Federation of Paralegal Associations. See NFPA
National Labor Relations Board, 117, 332, 526, 749, 788
National Law Journal, 135
National Legal Aid & Defender Association, 83, 96, 99
National Paralegal Reporter, 132, 843
National Reporter Blue Book, 527
National Reporter System, 493, 494, 569
Native Americans, 126, 778
Natural Resources, 87
Naturalization, 334, 782. See also Immigration
Navy, 120
Nebraska, 72, 91, 266, 494, 501, 535, 615, 768, 775, 801, 813
Neglect, 267, 269
Negligence, 126, 255, 268, 358, 468, 749

Negotiation, 105, 108, 113, 117, 173, 183, 190, 217, 254, 271, 309, 366, 393, 403, 727, 749, 795, 803, 804, 808
Neighborhood Justice Center, 459
Neighborhood Legal Service Office, 843
Network (Computer), 641, 649, 651, 843
Networking, 135, 204, 816, 845
Neutral Witness, 408, 414
Nevada, 72, 91, 266, 494, 502, 535, 615, 768, 775, 813
New Business Sheet, 694
New File Worksheet, 695
New Hampshire, 72, 91, 266, 494, 501, 513, 536, 749, 768, 775, 801, 813
New Haven, 766
New Jersey, 72, 92, 110, 240, 494, 500, 501, 525, 529, 536, 615, 749, 768, 775, 802, 813
New London, 766
New Matter Worksheet, 694
New Mexico, 73, 92, 240, 247, 266, 269, 273, 295, 494, 502, 536, 615, 749, 768, 775, 802, 813
New Occupations, 48
New Orleans, 69, 767, 774, 813, 826
New Trial, Motion for, 447
New York, 38, 73, 81, 92, 108, 116, 124, 235, 275, 331, 455, 458, 493, 494, 500, 501, 536, 583, 615, 749, 768, 775, 803, 813
New York Supplement, 493, 507
Newark, 72, 813
Newport Beach, 62, 766
Newport News, 770
Newsletter, Law Firm, 146
Newsletter, Paralegal, 51, 132, 151, 168, 193
Newspaper Ads, 135
Newspaper. See Legal Newspaper
NEXIS, 587
NFPA, 24, 29, 47, 52, 132, 232, 236, 238, 241, 243, 248, 252, 281, 313, 747, 749, 765
NLRB. See National Labor Relations Board
Nolle Prosequi, 451, 843
Nominative Reporter, 531, 843
Nonadversarial, 222, 843
Nonassertive, 189

Nonattorney Assistant, 301
Nonattorney, Partnership with, 227, 272
Nonauthority, 517
Nonbillable, 41, 191, 698, 702, 827, 843
Nonequity Partner, 688, 843
Nonexempt Employee, 253
Nonlawyers, 791
Nonlegal Advice, 309
Nonlegal Education, 164
Nonlegal Experience, 161
Nonprofessional, 195, 253
Nonprofit Corporation, 106, 123, 126
Nonrebuttable Presumption, 446
Nonverbal Communication, 391
Norfolk, 770, 814
North Carolina, 75, 92, 215, 229, 266, 494, 502, 536, 615, 749, 769, 775, 804, 813
North Dakota, 92, 120, 193, 214, 240, 266, 494, 501, 536, 615, 769, 775, 813
North Eastern Reporter, 501, 512
North Western Digest, 501, 507
North Western Reporter, 501
Notaries, 50, 274, 771, 772, 843
Notarization, 87, 103, 112, 257, 278
Note Taking, 11, 85, 119, 128, 381, 386, 472
Notebook, Instructions, 16
Notebook, Job Hunting, 160
Notebook, Trial, 102, 113, 119, 353, 461, 470
Notes of Decision, 588, 591, 602, 843
Notice, 113, 121, 729
Notice of Appeal, 119, 447, 456, 458
Notice of Appearance, 278, 436, 843
Notice Pleading, 469, 843
Notwithstanding the Verdict, 447
NOV, 447
Numerical Connector, 667, 669
Numerical Filing, 710
Nurse, 36, 47, 49, 138, 203, 228, 233, 749

■ O

Oakland, 62, 766, 773, 825
Oath, 441, 739, 843
Objections, 101, 443, 472, 744

Objective, Career, 142, 147
Objectivity, 388, 620, 723
Occupancy Expenses, 694
Occupational Outlook, 37
Occupational Regulation, 210, 228
Occupational Safety, 116, 172, 788
Occupations, Medical, 36, 47
Occupations, New, 48
Occurrence Policy, 258, 843
Of Counsel, 688, 843
Office Administration, Law, 118, 685
Office Clerk, 280
Office Directory, 176, 305
Office Environment, 182, 199
Office Management, 124, 685
Office Manager, 45, 53, 685, 687, 690
Office Manual, 191, 311
Office of Personnel Management, 81, 83
Office Politics, 176, 183, 190, 749
Office Procedures, 311
Office Sharing, 686, 843
Office Space, 157, 159, 693
Office Supplies, 694
Office Systems, 146, 197, 201, 270, 311
Office Training, 159. See also Paralegal Education
Official Cite, 354
Official Definitions, 29
Official Reporter, 491, 528, 843
Ohio, 24, 75, 93, 105, 117, 192, 199, 240, 494, 501, 536, 571, 583, 615, 643, 749, 769, 775, 804, 811, 813
Oil and Gas, 122, 248
OJT. See On-the-Job Training
Oklahoma, 76, 93, 247, 266, 274, 303, 494, 502, 536, 615, 765, 769, 775, 811, 813
Olympia, 95
Omaha, 72, 768
Omissions and Errors, 233, 257
On All Fours, 359, 843
On Point, 518, 843
On-the-Job Training, 15, 45, 52, 816
On the Merits, 447
Online, 487, 585, 658, 713, 843
Online Tutorial, 644
Ontario, 50, 771, 843
Open Ended Assignment, 402
Open Ended Question, 153, 389, 843

Opening Statement, 128, 442, 455, 457, 471
Operating System, 647, 843
Opinion, 124, 306, 316, 329, 346, 353, 355, 357, 358, 448, 449, 488, 491, 587, 730, 843. See also Case
Opinion, Briefing an, 353
Opinion, Ethics, 226
Opinion Evidence, 423, 737
Opinion, Expert, 119
Opinion Letter, 619, 843
Opinion of the Attorney General, 329, 489, 526, 844
Opinions, Application of, 358
OR Connector, 666, 669
Oral Argument, 448
Oral Communication, 127, 212, 214, 796, 797
Orange County, 317, 749, 766, 773
Order, Executive, 329, 334, 456
Orders, Protective, 122
Orders, Temporary, 113
Ordinance, 329, 331, 349, 358, 489, 604, 844
Oregon, 30, 43, 76, 93, 114, 178, 249, 266, 308, 494, 502, 536, 615, 749, 769, 775, 805, 813
Organization, 106, 113, 623
Organization Skills, 112, 125, 126, 148, 186, 331
Orientation, 691, Program, 692
Original Jurisdiction, 844
Original Writing, 427
Orlando, 66, 766, 812
Out of Pocket Costs, 701
Outreach Services, 254
Outstanding, 844
Overhead, 38, 40, 42, 139, 694, 844
Overrule, 443, 447, 519
Overtime, 103, 158, 176, 194, 252, 749, 825
Overutilization, 180

■ P

Pacific Digest, 499, 502, 507, 554
Pacific Reporter, 499, 502, 507, 512, 554
Padding Time Sheets, 273, 318, 844
Pages (Messengers), 690
Palo Alto, 62

Panel, Judges, 448
Panel, Jury, 442
Paperwork, 129
Paragraph Connector, 667
Parajudge, 122, 749
Paralegal, 26, 844. *See also*
    Freelance Paralegal;
    Independent Paralegal; Legal
    Assistant
Paralegal Administrator, 30, 53
Paralegal as Court Witness, 119
Paralegal Assignments, 133, 186,
    300, 311, 693
Paralegal Associate, 302, 800
Paralegal Associations, 18, 25, 47,
    52, 132, 158, 176, 190, 198,
    201, 204, 252, 317, 765
Paralegal-Attorney Relationship,
    134
Paralegal Bibliography, 747
Paralegal Billing, 38, 42, 702
Paralegal Business Card. *See*
    Business Card
Paralegal Certificate, 51, 84
Paralegal Compensation, 796, 798,
    800, 803, 804, 806, 808. *See
    also* Paralegal Salary
Paralegal Competence, 268
Paralegal Competing with
    Attorney, 40, 57
Paralegal Coordinator, 30, 60, 97,
    156
Paralegal Curriculum, 92. *See also*
    Paralegal Education
Paralegal Day, 821
Paralegal Definitions, 28
Paralegal Education, 51, 132, 143,
    158, 165, 191, 195, 197, 210,
    237, 315, 749
Paralegal, Entry Level, 29, 34, 130,
    136, 180, 251
Paralegal Ethics, 263, 298, 791
Paralegal Evaluations, 35, 157,
    184, 269, 300, 311, 693
Paralegal, Evening, 74
Paralegal Expenses, 694
Paralegal Experience, 57, 99, 108,
    139, 143, 170
Paralegal Fees, 33, 38, 179, 223,
    273, 749, 796
Paralegal Functions, 82, 84, 100,
    254, 459
Paralegal Generalist, 96
Paralegal, Government, 34, 45, 58,
    59, 81, 104
Paralegal History, 36, 44

Paralegal in the Media, 33, 211
Paralegal Job Satisfaction, 176
Paralegal License, 228, 230, 310,
    420
Paralegal Malpractice, 749
Paralegal Manager, 60, 94, 118,
    642, 692, 844
Paralegal Membership in Bar
    Associations, 25
Paralegal Mistakes, 197
Paralegal Newsletter, 51, 132, 151,
    168, 193
Paralegal Politics, 51
Paralegal Rate, 39, 41
Paralegal Profit, 38
Paralegal Recruitment, 66, 69, 100,
    693
Paralegal Regulation, 54, 210, 263
Paralegal Roles, 84, 100, 146, 254,
    459
Paralegal Salary, 34, 39, 42, 59, 84,
    123, 145, 155, 158, 176, 179,
    189, 190, 194, 198, 253, 272,
    748
Paralegal School, 51, 143, 236,
    237, 244
Paralegal/Secretary, 686
Paralegal Signature, 104, 264, 274,
    304
Paralegal Skills, 156, 197, 231, 244
Paralegal Specialist, 59, 81, 86,
    100, 306, 844
Paralegal Status, 301, 316, 791,
    808
Paralegal, Successful, 192
Paralegal Supervisor, 58, 61, 97,
    172, 300, 688
Paralegal Teacher, 58, 100, 172
Paralegal Technician, 92
Paralegal, Temporary, 179, 292,
    312
Paralegal Time, 42, 38, 703
Paralegal Titles, 301, 791, 796
Paralegal Trainee, 92
Paralegal Training Coordinator, 63
Paralegal Training. *See* Paralegal
    Education
Paralegal Wrongdoing, 265
Parallel Cite, 496, 510, 526, 540,
    566, 569, 844
Parallel Table of Authorities and
    Rules, 604
Paramedic, 33, 47
Paraphrase, 463, 521, 844
Paraprofessional, 26, 48, 93, 221,
    244, 299, 304

Parol Evidence Rule, 427, 844
Parole, 48, 173, 219
Part Time Employment, 40, 139,
    179, 312, 802
Particularization. *See* Fact
    Particularization
Partners and Partnership, 40, 156,
    247, 264, 290, 299, 686, 687,
    694, 794, 799, 801, 803, 844
Partnership with Nonattorney,
    227, 272
Patent Advisor, 82
Patent Law, 749
Patents, 115, 122, 222, 225, 246,
    332, 783
Patients, 257
Payroll Specialist, 690
PC. *See* Professional Corporation
Pee Dee, 770
Penal Code, Model, 247
Pendaflex, 712
Peninsula, 770
Pennsylvania, 24, 49, 76, 93, 110,
    240, 282, 302, 494, 501, 536,
    583, 615, 749, 769, 776, 772,
    805, 813
Pensacola, 767
Pension Specialist, 172
Pensions, 107, 109, 138, 691
People, 844
Peoria, 767
Per Curiam, 355, 844
Percentage Fee, 40, 701, 844
Peremptory Challenge, 442, 844
Performance Bonus, 191
Performance Evaluation, 185, 691
Periodicals. *See* Legal Periodical
Perjury, 278
Permanent ALR Digest, 559
Permanent Associate, 688, 842
Perseverance, 122
Personal Appearance, 381, 211
Personal Injury, 27, 126, 296, 686,
    701
Personal Jurisdiction, 328, 438,
    844
Personal Liability, 255, 844
Personal Property, 105, 233
Personal Recognizance, 450, 844
Personality Conflict, 181
Personality Traits, 144
Personnel Department, 83, 84
Personnel File, 191, 693
Personnel Manager, 66, 690
Personnel Manual, 177
Personnel Problems, 146

Persuasive Authority, 517, 521, 549, 844
Petition, 111, 113, 226, 449, 844
Petroleum Landsmen, 771
PH. *See* Prentice Hall
Philadelphia, 76, 81, 110, 282, 302, 642, 769, 776, 806, 812, 813
Phoenix, 60, 84, 765, 773, 812
Photocopying, 193, 194, 699, 817
Photograph, 372, 402, 409, 441
Phrase Searching, 668, 669
Physical Evidence, 411, 415, 441, 844
Physical Examination, 129
Physician Assistant, 32, 47, 844
PI Cases, 126, 844
Pierre, 94, 776
Pirated Software, 275
Pittsburgh, 77, 179, 749, 769, 776, 813
Pittsfield, 768
PL Number, 844
Placement, 135, 139, 172, 772
Plagiarism, 521
Plaintiff, 844
Plaintiff Defendant Tables, 556
Plan Administrator, 106, 109
Plea Bargaining, 451, 844
Plead, 451, 844
Pleading, 112, 113, 116, 119, 122, 151, 215, 305, 409, 437, 449, 454, 465, 469, 619, 796, 800, 844
Pleading, Fact, 469
Pleading, Notice, 469
Pleas, Court of Common, 331
Plotter, 677, 844
PLS, 199, 244, 844
Pocket Part, 497, 508, 543, 561, 596, 844
Point Heading, 629, 844
Points and Authorities Memorandum, 620, 844
Police, 108, 118, 410
Policy, Claims Made, 259
Policy Manual, 159
Policy, Occurrence, 258
Politician, 83, 169, 173
Politics, Office, 176, 183
Politics, Paralegal, 51, 59
Poll, 452, 844
Pollution, 110
Polygraph Examiner, 173
Pontiac, 774

Poor People, 97, 99, 117, 122, 220, 234
Popular Name, 532, 595, 844
Portland (Oregon), 76, 769, 775, 813
Portland (Maine), 69, 767
Portsmouth, 813
Positive Law, 533
Postponement, 128, 736
Poverty, 218
Power of Attorney, 111, 122
Practical Nurse, 49
Practice Analysis Report, 704, 844
Practice Book, 155, 522
Practice Law, Fitness to, 297
Practice Management Committee, 692, 693
Practice Manual, 10, 503, 550, 583, 840
Practice of Law, 32, 48, 146, 210, 213, 239, 245, 277, 290, 306, 313, 685, 749, 795, 801, 805, 825, 846
Practice Officer, Licensed, 233
Practice, Unauthorized, 27, 31, 302
Practitioner, Forms, 27
Practitioner, Medical, 465
Practitioner, Sole, 293, 305
Practitioners, 222
Praecipe, 436, 845
Prayer for Relief, 470, 845
Pre Evaluation Memorandum, 187, 845
Precedent, 356, 722
Preface, 542
Prehearing Conference, 733
Prejudice, Dismissal without, 447
Prejudicial Error, 447
Preliminary Hearing, 450, 457, 845
Premium Adjustment, 845
Prentice Hall, 506, 576
Prepaid Legal Services, 235, 778, 845
Preponderance of Evidence, 446, 845
Preprinted Forms, 807
President, 337
Pressure, 108, 126, 153, 162, 176, 180, 182, 186, 274, 311, 693
Presumption, 446, 802, 845
Pretrial Proceedings, 216, 441, 454, 457, 459, 847
Preventive Law, 749
Prima Facie, 219, 445, 845
Primary Authority, 517, 549, 551,

583, 607, 845
Print Formatting, 845
Print Preview, 653, 845
Printed Forms, 214
Printer, 650
Printout, 659
Priorities, 16, 182, 311, 403, 723
Prison and Prisoners, 28, 49, 97, 212, 219, 220, 256, 749
Privacy, 176
Private Detective, 805
Private Law, 329, 850
Private Law Firm, 34, 59, 685, 845
Private Reprimand, 268
Private Sector, 123, 845
Private Statute, 329, 850
Privilege, 280, 466, 749, 845
Privilege against Self Incrimination, 426, 845
Privileged Communication, 281, 314
Pro Bono, 122, 198, 235, 749, 824, 845
Probable Cause, 451, 457, 845
Probate, 105, 111, 217, 246, 247, 267, 331, 416, 749, 815, 823
Probate Counsel, 777
Probation, 48, 173, 268, 845
Procedural Due Process, 728, 845
Procedural Error, 447
Procedural Law, 2, 315, 439, 845
Procedural Tasks, 29
Procedures Manual, 202, 691, 693, 707, 817
Process Server, 772. *See also* Service of Process
Proclamations, 821
Procunier v. Martinez, 221
Product Liability, 126, 140
Production of Documents, 42, 108, 114
Production, Request for, 119, 464, 470
Productivity, 191, 749
Profession, Professional, 167, 185, 193, 198, 213, 218, 253, 315, 749
Professional Conduct, 231, 266
Professional Corporation, 689, 799, 801, 806, 845
Professional Development, 314, 693
Professional Employee, 253
Professional Indemnity Insurance, 259

Professional Judgment, 32, 202, 286, 306, 314, 316, 792, 801, 845

Professional Legal Assistants, 769

Professional Legal Secretary, 199, 244

Professional Misconduct, Reporting, 297

Professional Responsibility, 112, 226, 248, 254, 266, 298, 312, 313, 314, 642, 791

Professional Staff, 194

Professional Standards, 244

Professionalism, 186, 188, 230, 283

Profit, 38, 39, 41, 52, 119, 129, 176, 179, 237, 272, 686, 688, 702, 749, 797, 799

Profit Sharing, 796, 800, 809

Project Assistant, 26

Project Attorney, 40, 689, 845

Promissory Notes, 233

Promotion, 162, 203

Pronoun Reference, 636

Proof, Burden of, 443

Proof, Standard of, 446, 452

Proofreading, 88, 94, 112, 120, 136, 145, 150, 654, 690

Prosecution, 27, 58, 90, 108, 211, 307, 449, 845

Prosecutor, 98, 452, 845

Protection, Consumer, 87, 98

Protection of Public, 213, 229

Protective Order, 122, 214

Providence, 77, 79, 769, 776, 813

Provisos, 348

Public Benefits, 123, 232, 845

Public Censure, 268, 848

Public Defender, 99, 108, 123, 221, 797, 845

Public Domain, 680, 845

Public Entitlement Paralegal, 97

Public Housing, 123

Public Interest, 314

Public Interest Groups, 600

Public Law, 87, 329, 515, 533, 590, 598, 850

Public Paralegal, 27

Public Protection, 213, 229

Public Safety, 92

Public Sector, 123, 749, 845

Public Statute, 329, 850

Public Utilities, 82, 336

Publisher, Legal, 172

Publisher's Page, 541

Puerto Rico, 332, 536, 776, 778, 813

Punctuality, 162

Punishment, 263

Purchasing, 691

Purchasing Clerks, 690

## ■ Q

Qualifications, 84, 149, 210, 222, 228, 315

Qualify a Witness, 444

Quarantined Employee, 289, 836

Quasi Adjudication, 336, 845

Quasi Independent Agency, 336, 846

Quasi Judicial, 95, 125, 435, 720, 846

Quasi Legislation, 336, 846

Query, 658, 660, 846, 849

Query, Search, 313

Question of Fact, 438, 441, 843

Question of Law, 438, 441

Questionnaire, 119, 381

Questions Presented, 630

Quick Cite, 585

Quick Index, 550, 559, 588

Quid Pro Quo Harassment, 199, 846

Quitting, 274

Quota on Billable Hours, 159, 176, 198

Quotations, 117, 491, 521, 531, 540

## ■ R

Race Discrimination, 104, 117, 176

Racine, 814

Radio, 105

Railroads, 82, 778

Rainmaker, 846

Raleigh, 75, 92, 769, 775, 813

Rate, Billing, 30, 38

Rate, Hourly, 39, 157

Rate, Market, 43

Ratification, 300

RE, 367, 621, 846

Reader's Guide, 587

Reading, 15, 769

Reagan, Ronald, 130

Real Estate, 36, 38, 74, 90, 108, 122, 123, 124, 125, 135, 172, 230, 232, 233, 246, 248, 749, 808, 809

Real Estate Agent, 212, 213, 236

Real Estate Closing, 309, 316, 322, 795, 796, 801, 803, 806, 810

Real Estate Forms, 807

Reasonable Doubt, Beyond, 452

Reasonable Efforts, 299, 301

Reasonable Fee, 270, 273, 846

Reasoning, 357

Rebuttable Presumption, 446, 793

Receptionist, 690

Recognition, 162

Recognizance, Personal, 450

Recommendation, 161, 162

Reconciliation, 271

Record, 111, 128, 332, 443, 448, 508, 656, 817, 846

Record, Attorney of, 437

Record Keeping, 170, 171, 386

Records, Access to, 410

Records Committee, 687

Records Management, 691

Records Manager, 690

Records, Medical, 118, 119, 126, 129

Records, Police, 118

Records Research, 119

Records, Time, 119, 273

Recoverability, Fee, 41

Recruiter, 173, 690

Recruitment, 41, 53, 66, 69, 100, 137, 691

Recruitment Committee, 687

Red River Valley, 120, 769

Redevelopment Projects, 123

Redirect Examination, 128, 443, 738, 846

Reduction of Verdict, 447

Redwood Empire, 766

Referee, 453

References, 145, 170, 204

Referral Coordinator, 172

Referral Fee, 271, 272, 846

Referrals, 114, 127, 806

Regional Digest, 499, 508, 556, 846

Regional Reporter, 499, 846

Registered Agent, 222, 846

Registration, 115, 210, 222, 225, 232, 265, 749, 846

Registry of Deeds, 105

Regulation, 749, 846. *See also* Administrative Regulation

Regulation of Attorneys, 265

Regulation of Paralegals, 53, 209
Regulation, Self, 243, 249, 265
Regulatory Agency, 336, 603
Rehearing, 449
Relevance, 128, 368, 393, 421, 452, 730, 737, 740, 846
Relief, 438, 470
Remand, 357, 449, 846
Remedies, 248
Remedies, Exhaust Administrative, 456
Reno, 72, 768, 775
Rent, 117
Rent a Judge, 459
Reorganization, 104
Repetition, 105
Replies to Interrogatories, 464
Reply Brief, 627, 846
Reporter, Annotated, 487
Reporters, 2, 140, 354, 448, 491, 509, 531, 845, 846
Reporting Professional Misconduct, 297
Reports, 491, 702
Representation, 730
Representation at Agencies, 97, 128, 210, 220, 222, 226, 310, 394
Representation, Competent, 267
Representation in Court, 210, 214, 220, 230, 309
Representatives, 222
Reprimand, 268, 299, 846
Reprographics, 691
Reputation, 181, 270
Request for Admissions, 119, 404, 441, 470, 846
Request for Production, 119, 464, 470
Res Gestae, 426, 846
Res Judicata, 448, 846
Research, 9, 17, 30, 84, 88, 101, 107, 112, 116, 117, 118, 119, 148, 167, 246, 267, 312, 316, 366, 467, 472, 549
Research Assistant, 83, 87, 136
Research for Employment, 145, 155, 166, 169, 181
Reservation Clerks, 690
Reservations, Indian, 214
Respect, 176
Respondeat Superior, 256, 846
Respondent, 355, 448, 627, 834
Responsibilities, Paralegal, 84, 100, 254, 459
Rest, 445

Restatements, 508, 523, 538, 606, 846
Restraining Order, 362
Resume, 131, 132, 141, 144, 146, 147, 166, 193, 375, 749
Retailer, 97
Retainer, 270, 436, 696, 700, 846
Retirement, 82, 109, 272, 800, 801
Retreats, 159, 749
Revenue, 38, 694
Reverse, 449
Review, 311, 331, 332, 449, 458, 846
Revocation Hearings, 88
Rhode Island, 77, 94, 199, 494, 501, 513, 536, 615, 749, 769, 776, 806, 813, 828
Richmond, 95, 770, 776
Right Justified, 654, 846
Risk Manager, 690
Riverside, 62, 766
Roanoke, 770
Rochester, 74, 768, 769, 830
Rocky Hill, 773
Rocky Mountain, 109, 766, 829
Role Playing, 151, 152
Roles, Paralegal, 84, 100, 459
Ronald Reagan, 130
Root Expander (!), 661, 663, 846
Roseland, 72, 775
Rosemary Furman, 211, 229
Routine Letters, 305
Routine Matters, 795
Routine Tasks, 43, 85, 103, 153, 253, 305, 795, 802
Royal Oak, 768
Rule Making, 105, 336, 846
Rule of Three, 38, 846
Rule on Witnesses, 442
Rules, Ethical, 267, 311
Rules of Court, 329, 489, 509, 605, 847
Ruling, 329, 453, 454, 457, 841
"Run," 645, 648, 847
Runner, 296, 833
Russia, 50

■ S

S.Ct. See Supreme Court Reporter
Sacramento, 45, 62, 85, 112, 113, 122, 181, 198, 308, 766, 812
Safekeeping Property, 276
Safety, Occupational, 116, 172
Salary. See Paralegal Salary
Salem, 93

Sales Representative, 172
Salt Lake City, 80, 94, 770, 776
Samoa, American, 84
San Antonio, 80, 770, 814
San Diego, 62, 766, 773, 793, 812, 825
San Francisco, 63, 81, 184, 240, 241, 282, 291, 749, 766, 773, 812, 825
San Joaquin, 203, 766
San Jose, 63, 766, 773
San Juan, 813
San Luis Obispo, 766
San Rafael, 766
Sanction, 263, 847
Santa Ana, 773
Santa Barbara, 766
Santa Clara, 766, 773
Santa Fe, 92
Santa Monica, 63
Santa Rosa, 766
SAT, 98
Satisfaction, Job, 121, 124, 176, 180
Satisfaction of Judgment, 256
Satisfy, 449, 847
Savannah, 767
Save, 648, 847
Scanner, 656, 714, 847
Scheduling, 84, 90, 111, 464, 657, 693
School, High, 164, 247. See also Law School; Paralegal School
Scientific, 222, 309, 795
Scope Note, 556, 847
Scope of Employment, 255
Screen Cases, 108
Screen Formatting, 847
Screen Preview, 653
Screening, 112, 113, 152, 289, 293, 791, 794, 799, 802, 804, 806, 807
Scrivener, 27, 50
Scrolling, 653, 847
Search and Find, 847
Search and Replace, 653, 847
Search Criteria, 657, 847
Search, Job, 130, 283
Search Query, 313, 658
Search Warrants, 109
Seattle, 80, 81, 217, 749, 771, 776, 814
SEC, 247, 274, 336, 337, 416
Second Chair, 310, 847
Second Tier Attorney, 40, 688, 847
Secondary Authority, 346, 517,

521, 537, 549, 607, 847
Secretary, 41, 42, 93, 176, 194, 199, 211, 244, 686, 690, 749, 828. *See also* Legal Secretary
Secretary of State, 104, 416
Secrets, 279, 316
Section (§), 847
Securities, 107, 125, 274, 336, 416
Securities Analyst, 36, 173
Securities and Exchange Commission, 102, 107, 274, 337, 720, 825
Security Agreements, 104
Segment Search, 847
Segments (LEXIS), 671
Self Assertiveness, 184
Self Employed, 27, 99
Self Evaluation, 155, 177, 184
Self Help Books, 211
Self Incrimination, 426
Self Interest, 237, 249
Self Promotion, 184
Self Regulation, 243, 249, 265, 847
Seminar, 19, 165, 193, 196, 246, 269, 311, 316, 405, 693
Senate, 329, 337, 536, 537, 599
Senior Associate, 688
Senior Attorney, 689
Senior Citizen Paralegal, 97
Senior Compliance Analyst, 115
Senior Legal Assistant, 26, 30, 35, 203, 847
Senior Paralegal, 61, 65, 688, 750
Senior Partner, 688
Sensitivity, 199, 389
Sentence, 450
Sentence Connector, 667
Sentence Structure, 635
Sequoia, 766
Series, 509, 847
Service Companies, 58, 99, 750, 847
Service of Process, 85, 90, 105, 113, 116, 119, 129, 438, 454, 827, 847
Session Law, 486, 509, 510, 533, 534, 570, 571, 596, 847
Settlement, 93, 105, 108, 113, 121, 123, 124, 309, 366, 403, 455, 792, 795, 803, 808
Settlement Work Up, 428, 847
Several Liability, 436
Sex Discrimination, 104, 117, 152, 841
Sex Harassment, 116, 199, 847
Sexism, 176, 178, 637

Shareholders, 107, 694
Sharing Fees, 796, 801
Sharing Offices, 801
Shepardize, 119, 355, 496, 509, 563, 607, 836, 847
Shepardizing a Case, 566, 569
Shepardizing a Regulation, 574
Shepardizing a Statute, 570
Shepard's, 488, 496, 509, 527, 540, 588
Shepard's Abbreviations, 542, 543
Shepard's Code of Federal Regulations Citations, 512, 574
Shepard's Federal Citations, 511, 566
Shepard's in WESTLAW, 663
Shepard's Online, 585
Shepard's PreView, 585, 662
Shepard's United States Citations, 511, 573, 605
Sheriff, 473
Shopping Mall, 117, 123
Shorthand, 13, 772
Shreveport, 116, 767
Sierra Nevada, 768
Sign Correspondence, 316
Signature, 104, 217, 264, 274, 304, 305, 470, 795, 796, 799, 802, 803, 805, 808
Signatures, Notarizing, 257
Sioux Falls, 770
Skills, 2, 30, 148, 165, 186, 197, 231, 244, 256, 267
Skills, Clerical, 148
Skills, Communication, 108, 112, 126, 148, 377
Skills, Management, 118
Skills, Organization, 112, 120, 125, 126, 148, 186
Skills, Research, 148
Skills, Typing, 137
Skills, Writing, 108, 126. *See also* Writing
Skokie, 765
Slander, 256
Slip Decision, 513
Slip Law, 490, 510, 847
Slip Opinion, 513, 847
Small Business Administration, 788
Small Claims Court, 214, 309, 328, 797, 798
Social Functions, 159
Social Security, 97, 98, 109, 111, 125, 127, 218, 222, 225, 308, 789

Social Services, Department of, 214
Social Services Representative, 82
Social Workers, 48, 214, 239, 720
Software, 117, 188, 290, 541, 649, 651, 847
Software, Pirated, 275
Sole Practice, 293, 305, 686, 847
Solebury, 772
Solicitation, 295, 793, 801
Solicitor, 49, 847
Sonoma, 772
South Bend, 767
South Carolina, 77, 94, 266, 494, 502, 536, 615, 750, 770, 776, 807, 813
South Dakota, 94, 266, 494, 501, 536, 615, 750, 770, 776, 807, 813
South Eastern Digest, 499, 502, 513
South Eastern Reporter, 502, 512, 513
Southern Reporter, 502, 513
Southern Tier, 769
South Western Reporter, 512, 513
Soviet Union, 50
Spacing, 653
Spanish Language, 98
Special Counsel, 688
Special Edition State Reporter, 493, 847
Special Interest Group, 58, 98, 551, 584, 847
Special Jurisdiction, 127, 328
Special Project, 693
Specialist, Compliance, 115
Specialist, Conflicts, 112
Specialist, Contract, 82
Specialist, Fiduciary, 45
Specialist, Litigation, 180
Specialist, Paralegal, 26, 59, 81, 86, 306
Specialist, Social Security, 97
Specialist, Tax, 45
Specialization, 48, 106, 308, 686, 836
Specialties, Paralegal, 100, 114, 179
Specialty Certification, 247, 248, 847
Specialty License, 210, 230
Specialty, Litigation, 179
Specialty Practice of Law, 146
Specificity, 469
Speed Reading, 15
Spell Checker, 652, 848

Spelling, 7, 145, 149, 167, 245, 428
Sperry v. Florida, 225
Splitting Fees, 271, 750, 798, 803, 806, 807, 809
Spontaneous Declaration, 425, 848
Sports Law, 777, 778
Spreadsheets, 651, 672, 848
Springfield, 88, 768, 774
Squibs, 497
SSI, 98, 125
St. Louis, 71, 240, 750, 768, 775, 813
St. Paul, 71, 90, 258, 291, 813
St. Thomas, 771, 776
Stability, 182
Staff Attorney, 40, 688, 689, 848
Staff, Clerical, 31, 45, 86, 95, 194
Staff Meetings, 157, 177, 693
Staff, Professional, 194
Staff Training, 118
Staffing, 693
Staffing Agency, 139, 168, 848
Stamford, 64
Stamping, 119, 709
Standard & Poors, 146
Standard Forms, 119, 202, 466, 467, 848
Standard of Proof, 446, 452, 848
Standardized Letters, 202
Standards, 176, 229, 231, 244, 252, 263, 314, 315
Standing Committee on Legal Assistants, 25, 46
Star Paging, 491, 848
Stat. See Statutes at Large
State Agencies, 224, 225, 327
State Archives, 127
State Bar Association, 25, 265, 773
State Court, 265, 330, 331, 493, 519, 605
State Government, 327
State Government Paralegals, 58, 83, 84
State Legislature, 339
State Question, 330, 848
State's Attorney, 109
State Statutes, 597
Statement for Professional Services, 703
Statement of Facts, 622
Statement of Jurisdiction, 628
Statement of Principles, 212, 239
Statement of the Case, 630
Statement, Witness, 427

Stating a Cause of Action, 437, 848
Stationery, 159, 303, 321, 323, 804
Statistical Research, 116, 316
Statistics, 37, 42, 86, 102, 105, 108, 110, 119, 122, 222, 409
Status, Disclosure of, 301, 302, 316
Status Line, 653, 848
Status, Paralegal, 301, 316
Statute, 329, 334, 349, 358, 488, 590, 848
Statute, Annotated, 490
Statute in Derogation of Common Law, 848
Statute of Limitations, 104, 256, 438, 464, 657, 848
Statute, Private, 329
Statute, Public, 329
Statutes at Large, 513, 516, 533, 571, 590, 596
Statutory Code, 2, 510, 513, 848
Statutory Fee, 798
Statutory History Table, 542
Stay, 447, 848
Stenographer, 280
Stipulation, 113, 216, 441, 848
Stock, 107, 274
Stock Ownership, 801
Stockholders (Practice of Law), 689
Storage, 714
Strategic Planning, 691
Strategy, 159, 183, 194, 197, 204, 470, 736
Stress, 112, 126, 750
Strict Liability, 126
Strike, 443
Student. See Paralegal School
Studying, 1
Sub Professional, 218
Subject and Author Index, 578
Subject Index, 580
Subject Matter, Digest by, 462
Subject Matter Jurisdiction, 328, 628, 848
Subpoena, 129, 824, 827
Subscript, 654, 848
Subscription, 470, 504, 848
Subsidiary, 290
Substantive Law, 2, 246, 315, 439, 848
Substantive Work, 29
Summarizer, Depo, 26, 460
Summarizing, 85, 103, 111, 119, 120, 126, 127, 309, 471
Summary, 441, 456, 848

Summary Judgment, 102, 441, 848
Summons, 113, 438, 454, 848
Superior Court, 331, 848
Supermarket, 117
Superscript, 654, 848
Superseded, 848
Superseded Annotation, 561
Supervising Attorney, 692
Supervising Legal Assistant, 30, 35, 203, 848
Supervision, 15, 28, 42, 46, 81, 85, 95, 112, 117, 121, 124, 125, 144, 157, 159, 186, 196, 217, 227, 232, 253, 256, 292, 293, 300, 308, 310, 314, 690, 750, 792, 795, 796, 800, 801, 802, 803, 808, 810
Supervision, Court, 265
Supervisor, 27, 58, 61, 97, 118, 161, 172, 196, 299, 368, 463, 466
Supplemental Decisions, 560
Supplemental Security Income, 125
Supplemented, 848
Supplemented Annotation, 561
Supplements, 504, 532, 573
Support, Enforcement of, 108
Support, Litigation, 72, 120
Support Staff, 134, 689, 694, 750
Suppress, 357
Supra, 541, 848
Supremacy Clause, 225, 848
Supreme Court, 42, 212, 214, 218, 237, 247, 265, 270, 331, 332, 355, 485, 848. See also United States Supreme Court
Supreme Court Reporter, 491, 501, 511, 514, 529, 555
Surrogate Court, 331, 416, 848
Surveys, 34, 45, 190, 639, 690, 694
Suspended Attorney, 31, 302, 792, 795, 798, 800, 803, 806, 809, 810
Suspension, 268, 299, 848
Sustain, 443, 848
Sweatshops, 179
Switching Jobs, 362
Switching Sides, 287
Swoose Syndrome, 194, 848
Syllabus (Reporter), 355, 848
Syllabus (Shepard's), 567, 848
Syndication, Real Estate, 108, 125
Synopsis Search (Computer), 671
Syracuse, 75
Systems, 4, 52, 146, 197, 201, 270,

311, 327, 460, 750, 849
Systems Analyst, 172
Systems Management, 691


■ T

Table of Authorities, 111, 540,
    629, 849
Table of Cases, 495, 528, 531, 542,
    556, 578, 580, 849
Table of Contents, 111, 464, 470,
    544, 556, 629
Table of Courts and Circuits, 560
Table of Jurisdictions Represented,
    560
Table of Key Numbers, 557
Table of Laws, Rules, and
    Regulations, 339, 589, 599
Table of Statutes, 542, 578, 580,
    583, 849
Table of Statutes Construed, 495
Tables of Laws, Rules, and
    Regulations, 604, 605
Tables Volume, 596, 573
Tacoma-Pierce County, 218
Tainted Employee, 283, 288
Tallahassee, 86, 774
Tampa, 66
Tangible Evidence, 411, 415, 441,
    846
Tasks, Clerical, 30, 41, 42
Tasks, Litigation, 459
Tasks, Routine, 43, 85, 103, 153,
    180
Tasks. See Paralegal Functions
Tax, 45, 82, 104, 110, 111, 124,
    125, 230, 332, 581, 691, 750,
    815
Teacher Aides, 47
Teaching, 164, 166, 750
Team Members, 202, 750
Technical Advice, 309, 795
Technician, 94, 122, 173
Technician, Legal, 26, 27, 28, 58,
    82, 90, 92, 99, 228, 230, 259
Technology, 48
Telecommunications, 691
Telephone Directory, 305, 800
Television, 105, 297
Template, 677, 849
Temporary Attorney, 689
Temporary Disbarment, 268
Temporary Employment, 802
Temporary Orders, 113, 362

Temporary Paralegal, 108, 138,
    197, 292, 750
Tenant and Landlord, 96, 117,
    123, 214, 230, 248
Tennessee, 78, 94, 213, 494, 502,
    536, 615, 750, 770, 776, 807,
    813, 828
Tension, 153, 180
Termination, 104, 139, 691, 819
Terminology, 32, 643
Test Cases, 98
Testimonial Evidence, 411, 413,
    441, 849
Testing and Examination, 49, 210,
    223, 228, 231, 245, 248
Texarkana, 770
Texas, 38, 78, 94, 98, 126, 180, 194,
    240, 247, 250, 266, 282, 295,
    308, 460, 494, 502, 536, 583,
    616, 692, 700, 750, 770, 776,
    808, 811, 813, 824, 830, 843
Text Buffer, 654, 849
Text Editing, 654, 849
Text File, 654, 849
Theft, 231, 273, 772, 808
Thesaurus, Legal, 504, 505
Third Party Complaint, 440, 849
Thoroughness, 396
Tickler System, 86, 107, 111, 117,
    124, 127, 129, 300, 464, 641,
    656, 849
Tidewater, 771
Tiers of Partners, 688
Time and Billing Assistant, 690
Time Charge, 817
Time Entry, 696
Time Management, 5, 750
Time Pressures, 162
Time Records, 119, 273, 693
Time Sheets, 273, 318, 693
Time Slips, 817, 819
Time Ticket, 697, 698
Timekeeping, 656, 657, 690, 699,
    700, 817
Timely, 447
Title Abstractor, 172
Title Company, 123
Title Examiner, 172
Title Insurance, 123, 213
Title, Job, 26, 301, 381, 800
Title, Land, 94, 124, 248
Title Page, 541, 849
Title Search (Computer), 671
Title Search, 122, 807
Title VII, 201

Tokyo, 116
Toledo, 76, 192, 769
Topeka, 88, 767, 774
Topic and Key Number, 355, 849
Topic Search (Computer), 671
Tort Law, 121, 126, 247, 255, 643,
    750, 849
Total Client Service Library, 514
Trace a Key Topic and Number,
    556
Trade, 116
Trademark Specialist, 172
Trademarks, 100, 110, 115, 246,
    332, 750, 783
Traffic Court, 84
Trainee, Paralegal, 92
Training, 18, 31, 40, 45, 51, 52,
    118, 143, 159, 161, 164, 191,
    195, 197, 210, 249, 315, 691
Transaction Coordinator, 65
Transcribed, 599, 849
Transcript, 88, 101, 114, 129, 309,
    332, 339, 441, 443, 448, 461,
    472, 508, 849
Transfer Tables, 596
Translation, 806
Transportation Law, 778
Transportation Practitioners, 771
Transportation Safety, 788
Travel, 157, 159
Treasury Department, 124, 126,
    223
Treaties, 329, 489, 606, 849
Treaties, Bar, 212
Treatise. See Legal Treatise
Trenton, 92
Triad Association, 769
Trial, 84, 88, 212, 331, 332, 366,
    403, 438, 443, 472, 485
Trial Assistance, 102, 750
Trial Attorney, 120, 240, 265
Trial Book, 353, 470
Trial Brief, 353, 470, 627, 849
Trial De Novo, 458, 849
Trial Exhibit, 91, 102, 113, 119
Trial Judge, 444, 448
Trial Manual, 353, 627
Trial Memorandum, 470, 620,
    627, 846
Trial Notebook, 102, 113, 119,
    353, 461, 470, 627, 849
Trial Rulings, 454, 457
Tribal Court, 97, 126, 215
Trust Accountants, 135
Trust Administrator, 172

Trust Associate, 172
Trust Department, 97, 103, 212
Trust Officer, 172
Trustee in Bankruptcy, 103
Trusts, 111, 247
Trustworthiness, 297
Tucson, 640, 765, 811
Tuition, 158
Tulsa, 76, 274, 765, 769, 775
Turnover, 40, 157, 159, 178
TV, 296
Tweener, 194
Tyler, 770
Typesetting, 145, 525
Typewriters, 44
Typing, 15, 98, 137, 159, 193, 194, 230, 473, 652
Typing Services, 298
Typist, Legal, 27


# ▪ U

U.S. See United States
UCC, 100, 103, 119, 124, 233, 247, 416
Ultimate Fact, 469
Ultrafiche, 507, 844
Unauthorized Practice, 27, 31, 210, 213, 245, 270, 297, 302, 306, 313, 750, 792, 809, 825, 849
Unbundled, 701, 833
Uncodified, 496, 513, 849
Unconstitutional, 517
Uncontested Divorce, 216
Underutilization, 179
Undivided Loyalty, 286
Undue Influence, 296
Unemployed Attorneys, 31, 58, 135
Unemployment Compensation, 83, 98, 453
Unethical Behavior, 112, 264, 266, 267, 297
Unfair, 447
Unicameral, 337, 835
Unified Bar Association, 265, 842
Uniform Commercial Code. See UCC
Uniform State Law, 339, 849
Uniform System of Citation, 490, 496, 524, 539
Union List of Legislative Histories, 598
Unions, 98, 110, 117, 750
United States Citations (Cases), 570

United States Claims Court, 332, 499
United States Code, 512, 514, 515, 532, 559, 565, 571, 588, 595, 598, 603
United States Code Annotated, 512, 514, 515, 532, 559, 571, 588, 595, 603
United States Code Congressional and Administrative News, 515, 533, 550, 598
United States Code Service, 512, 514, 516, 532, 559, 571, 588, 595, 598, 603
United States Constitution, 225, 268, 518, 600. See also Constitution
United States Court of Appeal, 332, 335, 498, 501, 502, 529, 554, 849
United States Department of Justice, 46
United States District Court, 332, 335, 441, 455, 458, 467, 498, 501, 502, 529, 849
United States Law Week, 492, 516
United States Patent Office, 222, 225
United States Reports, 491, 501, 516, 529
United States Statutes at Large, 516, 533
United States Supreme Court, 42, 212, 214, 218, 237, 247, 270, 332, 491, 498, 499, 500, 511, 525, 529, 561, 826, 849
United States Supreme Court Digest, 602
Universal Character (*), 661, 662, 849
Universities, 97, 778
Unofficial Cite, 354
Unofficial Reporter, 491, 528
Unreasonable Fees, 270
Unwarranted Delay, 269
Updating, 659
URESA, 108
US. See United States Reports
USC. See United States Code
USCA. See United States Code Annotated
USCCAN. See United States Code Congressional and Administrative News
USCS. See United States Code Service

User Group, 644, 849
USLW. See United States Law Week
Utah, 80, 94, 213, 266, 494, 502, 536, 770, 776, 812, 813
Utilities, Public, 82, 336
Utilization, 179


# ▪ V

Valdosta, 767
Validation Research, 541, 549, 567, 606, 659, 849
Valuation, 104, 111
Value (Computer), 673
Value Billing, 701, 702, 849
Variety, 177, 197
Ventura, 766
Venue, 437, 467, 850
VERALEX, 487, 586
Verbosity, 635
Verdict, 445, 446, 447, 455, 458, 850
Verification, 105, 217, 372, 381, 404, 470, 850
Vermont, 95, 494, 501, 536, 616, 770, 776, 808, 813
Vessels, 101
Veterans, 97, 219
Veto, 340, 850
Vicarious Disqualification, 288, 850
Vicarious Liability, 255, 850
Virgin Islands, 332, 771, 809
Virginia, 80, 95, 239, 266, 494, 502, 536, 616, 642, 770, 776, 809, 813, 829
Virtual Representation, 654, 850
Visalia, 766
Vital Statistics, 409
Vocational Training, 164
Voir Dire, 119, 442, 455, 457, 471, 850
Voluntary Bar Association, 265
Voluntary Certification, 244, 251
Volunteer Activity, 117, 161, 170, 192, 292
Volusia, 767


# ▪ W

Wage and Appeals Board, 785
Wage and Hour Office, 82, 253, 254, 850

Waiver, 123, 125, 281, 282, 411, 449, 734, 744, 850
Wall. *See* Chinese Wall
Wang, 641
Want Ads, 108, 137
Wappingers Falls, 768
Warrant, 109, 450, 850
Wash. D.C. *See* District of Columbia
Washington, 80, 95, 117, 217, 233, 243, 266, 494, 502, 536, 616, 750, 771, 776, 810, 813, 844
Water Court, 127
Water Law, 27, 110, 127
Waterbury, 64
Weight of Evidence, 423
Welfare, 27, 98, 123, 127, 129, 394, 730, 802
West Palm Beach, 136, 827
West Publishing Company, 355, 492, 553, 658
West Reporters, 494
West Virginia, 81, 95, 240, 266, 309, 494, 502, 536, 771, 776, 810, 813
West's Legal Directory, 139, 141, 146, 585
WESTcheck, 541
Western Dakota, 193
WESTLAW, 118, 135, 139, 313, 488, 517, 528, 541, 570, 579, 581, 585, 656, 658, 679, 840, 850
WESTLAW Queries, 664
White Book. *See* Blue and White Book
White Collar Exemption, 253
White House, 130
White Plains, 769

Wichita, 767, 813
Wilkes-Barre, 77, 769
Wills, 97, 111, 230, 247, 259, 285, 309, 316, 750
Wilmington, 64, 766, 773
WILSONDISC, 587
WILSONLINE, 579, 587
Window, 647, 673, 850
Winston-Salem, 75
Wisconsin, 81, 96, 240, 266, 494, 501, 525, 536, 616, 750, 771, 776, 810, 813
Withdrawal, 278, 293, 791
Witness Fees, 700
Witnesses, 86, 94, 102, 104, 111, 113, 119, 128, 245, 316, 353, 408, 414, 422, 427, 442, 443, 444, 470, 734, 750
Witnesses, Interviewing, 42, 109, 411
Women, Abused, 122
Women Attorneys, 139, 777
Women in the Law, 200
Woodbridge, 72
Worcester, 70, 768
Word Index to Annotations, 559
Word Processing, 137, 157, 176, 194, 525, 640, 651, 652, 686, 690, 850
Word Wrap, 652, 654, 850
WordPerfect, 641, 648
Words and Phrases, 10, 504, 588
Work Accomplishments, 193
Work Environment, 159
Work Experience, 143
Work in Progress, 704
Work, Part Time, 40, 139, 179, 312
Work Product, 185, 256, 280, 316, 466, 750, 850

Work Summary, 705
Work Up, Settlement, 428
Worker's Compensation, 27, 83, 89, 109, 126, 129, 219, 226, 691, 792, 793
Working Conditions, 198
Workload, 52, 185, 693
Workshop, 132, 316
Writ of Certiorari, 449, 850
Writ Writer, 219, 850
Write Down, 702, 850
Write Up, 702, 817, 850
Writing, 7, 9, 42, 84, 85, 88, 91, 94, 101, 109, 110, 111, 113, 118, 120, 121, 129, 189, 210, 247, 309, 316, 349, 439, 464, 465, 466, 652
Writing a Resume, 142, 166
Writing Guidelines, 631
Writing Samples, 150, 155, 160, 164, 167, 170, 283
Writing Skills, 108, 110, 126
Written Evidence, 415
Wrongdoing, 255, 265
Wrongful Conduct, 257
Wrongful Death, 126
Wrongful Discharge, 104
Wyoming, 96, 266, 494, 502, 536, 616, 771, 776, 810, 812, 813
WYSIWYG, 654, 850

# ■ Y

Yellow Pages, 138, 296

# ■ Z

Zoning, 123

## PRODUCTION CREDITS

**Text Design:** Roslyn Stendahl, Dapper Design
**Copyediting:** Sarah Entenmann
**Composition:** Parkwood Composition
**Illustrations:** Randy Miyake
**Cover:** Roslyn Stendahl, Dapper Design

## PHOTO CREDITS

**219** Anne Dowie; **232** Susan Spann Photography; **330 (top) Wyoming Department of Commerce; 330** (bottom) Courtesy of Hellmuth, Obata & Kassabaum; **444** James L. Shaffer; **471** Courtesy of Bindertek, Sausalito, California; **578** Information Access Company; **584** (bottom) Reprinted with permission of Mead Data Central, Inc., provider of the LEXIS®/ NEXIS® services. LEXIS® and NEXIS® are registered trademarks for information products and services of Mead Data Central, Inc.; **643** (top) Courtesy of International Business Machines Corporation; **643** (bottom) Photo by Walter Urei; **644** Courtesy of 3M, Inc.; **646** (top) Courtesy of International Business Machines Corporation; **646** (bottom) Courtesy of International Business Machines Corporation; **649** Courtesy of International Business Machines Corporation; **712** Courtesy of White Storage & Retrieval Systems, Inc.

# Paralegal Associations: Local

1. Determine how many paralegal associations exist in your state (or in any state where you hope to work). See Appendix B.

2. Photocopy the following form, fill out one form for each association you identify in step one, and mail the form to each association.

Date: _____

Dear Paralegal Association:

I am a student at the following paralegal school:

_____

Would you be kind enough to answer the following questions:

1. Can paralegal students be members of your association? If so, what are the dues for students?

2. Does your association have a mentor program where an experienced paralegal member provides guidance or advice to new members?

3. Do you have a student rate for subscriptions to your newsletter?

4. Does your association have a job bank service? If so, can student members take advantage of this service?

5. Would your association consider conducting a "Career Day" in which experienced paralegal members of your association describe work in different employment settings in the state?

Any other information you can send me about the association would be greatly appreciated.

I hope to hear from you.

Sincerely,

_____

My Address: _____

_____

_____

Source: Statsky, *Introduction to Paralegalism* (West)

# Paralegal Associations: National

Please send me information about the Federation.

My Name and Address:

Clip this form and mail to:

_____

Nat'l Federation of Paralegal
Associations
P.O. Box 33108
Kansas City, MO 64114

_____

_____

Statsky, *Introduction to Paralegalism* (West)

---

Please send me information about NALA.

My Name and Address:

Clip this form and mail to:

_____

Nat'l Association of
Legal Assistants
1601 South Main St., Suite 300
Tulsa, OK 74119

_____

_____

Statsky, *Introduction to Paralegalism* (West)

---

Please send me information about PLA

My Name and Address:

Clip this form and mail to:

_____

Professional Legal
Assistants, Inc.
P.O. Box 31951
Raleigh, NC 27622

_____

_____

Statsky, *Introduction to Paralegalism* (West)